D1090877

APPELLATE COURTS

STRUCTURES, FUNCTIONS, PROCESSES, AND PERSONNEL

Second Edition

Daniel J. Meador
James Monroe Professor of Law Emeritus
University of Virginia

Thomas E. Baker
Professor of Law
Florida International University

Joan E. Steinman
Distinguished Professor of Law
Chicago-Kent College of Law

 LexisNexis®

Library of Congress Cataloging-in-Publication Data

Meador, Daniel John.
    Appellate courts : structures, functions, processes, and personnel / Daniel J.
Meador, Thomas E. Baker, Joan E. Steinman.—2nd ed.
      p. cm.
    Includes bibliographical references and index.
    ISBN 0-8205-7015-X (hardbound : alk. paper)
    1. Appellate courts—United States. 2. Appellate procedure—United States.
I. Baker, Thomas E., 1953-. II. Steinman, Joan E. III. Title.
    KF8750.M43 2006
    347.73'24—dc22

                                               2006010866

This publication is designed to provide accurate and authoritative information in
regard to the subject matter covered. It is sold with the understanding that the
publisher is not engaged in rendering legal,accounting, or other professional
services. If legal advice or other expert assistance is required, the services
of a competent professional should be sought.

LexisNexis and the Knowledge Burst logo are trademarks of Reed Elsevier Properties Inc,
used under license. Matthew Bender is a registered trademark of Matthew Bender
Properties Inc. Copyright © 2006 Matthew Bender & Company, Inc., a member
of the LexisNexis Group.All Rights Reserved.

No copyright is claimed in the text of statutes, regulations, and excerpts from court
opinions quoted within this work. Permission to copy material exceeding fair
use, 17 U.S.C. § 107, may be licensed for a fee of 10¢ per page per copy
from the Copyright Clearance Center, 222 Rosewood Drive, Danvers,
Mass. 01923, telephone (978) 750-8400.

Editorial Offices
744 Broad Street, Newark, NJ 07102 (973) 820-2000
201 Mission St., San Francisco, CA 94105-1831 (415) 908-3200
701 East Water Street, Charlottesville, VA 22902-7587 (434) 972-7600
www.lexis.com

(Pub. 3043)

DEDICATIONS

To the memory of Maurice Rosenberg
Great wit, boon companion, proceduralist par excellence

- D.J.M.

To Jane Marie, with love and appreciation

- T.E.B.

To My late father Jack, My mother Ruth, Jenny & Amanda, and
Adrien

- J.E.S.

PREFACE

This is the second edition of this casebook first published in 1994, co-authored by Professors Daniel J. Meador, Maurice Rosenberg, and Paul D. Carrington, some of the few academicians who had long devoted scholarly attention to the appellate courts. In the preparation of this new edition, Professor Meador has been joined by Professor Thomas E. Baker of the Florida International University College of Law and Professor Joan E. Steinman of the Chicago-Kent College of Law, scholars who likewise have long labored in the appellate vineyard. They have carried forward the basic themes and organization of the first edition, with some modifications and with substantial updating to include new material. Reasons for producing the first edition for use in American law schools still obtain and justify this new edition.

Although appeals constitute a relatively small portion of American judicial business, appellate courts are profoundly significant institutions whose role in law and government is far greater than such statistics might suggest. The opinions of appellate courts — the written explanations of the reasons for appellate decisions — collectively form the body of the common law. Despite the growth in statutory law and the advent of the administrative state over the last century, case law still looms large in American jurisprudence. Indeed, many important fields — not the least of them constitutional law — continue to be dominated by decisional law. Even in those areas blanketed by legislative and administrative enactments, case law plays a significant role. All of this law, in state and federal spheres, is generated by appellate courts in the course of deciding appeals. In other words, appellate courts are major sources of law in the United States.

To understand this body of law it is helpful, even essential, to understand how these tribunals function and the nature and limits of their authority. Thus, the material in this course should be part of the learning of all well-educated lawyers, whatever professional paths they may take. Case law must be dealt with in every line of legal work. Moreover, if lawyers are to be faithful to their ethical and professional obligations to improve the administration of justice, they need to be aware of the problems facing appellate courts and judges today so that they can contribute to solutions that will preserve appellate forums as the authoritative adjudicators of cases and controversies and as prominent enunciators of legal doctrine.

More immediately, law students must read and analyze appellate opinions in most of their courses; these writings pervade the study of law. Student comprehension of the opinions they read will be facilitated by a grasp of the structure, jurisdiction, procedure, internal processes, and personnel of the tribunals from which these opinions emanate. Judge Jerome Frank said that studying law only by reading appellate opinions is like studying horticulture by examining cut flowers.* This course examines the plants that produce those flowers.

With the exception of the Supreme Court of the United States, appellate courts are relatively low visibility institutions. They operate without flesh-and-blood witnesses, without the drama of the trial, and usually without the glare of publicity. Their judges appear on the bench infrequently and are therefore little known to the public. Apart from a few celebrated cases, appellate proceedings receive little attention from the press. Movies, television programs, and novels typically feature the more familiar drama of the trial. Even many lawyers are largely uninformed about the workings of appellate courts and about much that appears in this book. Unless the law school curriculum incorporates a study of these topics, graduates — except for the few who serve as law clerks to appellate judges — will continue to join the ranks of the poorly informed, and the profession will be the poorer for it.

Trial courts, in a sense, function in the shadow of appellate courts. Appellate opinions govern what a trial judge does, even if no appeal is taken in a particular case. If a trial judge departs from the appellate court's precedential enunciations of the law, the losing litigant may take the case up to the appellate court where the judgment may be reversed, a fate no trial judge relishes. Trial lawyers, too, must be ever mindful of appellate functions. They must be attentive to building a record through the presentation of evidence and the obtaining of rulings from the trial judge, always with an eye toward a possible appeal, either by themselves or by their opponents. At every step of trial court proceedings the advocates' conduct is heavily influenced by an awareness of what the appellate court can and may do. Thus, the appellate courts' authority and influence are felt by both judges and lawyers throughout the trial process at the base of the system.

Appellate courts have been affected to a much greater extent than trial courts by the litigation explosion that began in the late twentieth century. Nationwide, appellate dockets have grown several times more than trial dockets over the last four decades. In the federal system the impact has been far larger; appellate caseloads there have increased ten-fold since 1960, while trial court caseloads have increased only three-fold. In short, in both absolute numbers and percentages, appeals are being taken in many more cases now than formerly. Appellate courts thus loom larger on the American judicial scene than ever before, and lawyers involved in litigation are much more likely to become involved in appellate work than they would have been a few decades ago. It is therefore especially important for lawyers to understand the dramatic changes in the workings of those courts that have resulted from the pressures of docket growth — the so-called "crisis of volume."

Apart from their case-deciding functions (involving both error-correcting and lawmaking), appellate courts perform important roles in the governance and operations of the judiciary through their supervisory and rule making powers. This is especially true of the court of last resort, the court at the apex of a judicial system. Such courts are considered to have a measure of inherent authority to supervise courts below them in the judicial hierarchy. Typically, they also have authority to make rules for the conduct of proceedings in the lower courts, thus governing the in-court actions of lawyers, parties, and judges. In other words, in addition to its purely judicial role, a court of last resort exercises important legislative and administrative powers in our governmental scheme.

For all of the foregoing reasons a study of these legal institutions should be an integral part of every law student's professional education. Yet, paradoxically, at the very time that the subject has grown in importance, its place in the law school curriculum has shrunk. Indeed, the subject has disappeared from many schools. For a time, required first-year courses in civil procedure included a segment on appellate jurisdiction and perhaps some snippets about appellate procedure. Some civil procedure casebooks still have chapters dealing with those matters. Because of coverage pressure from other aspects of that subject and the reduction in the number of hours allotted to the course in some schools, however, the appellate material is rarely taught. Likewise, courses on federal courts long included material on appellate jurisdiction, but the press of new developments regarding other facets of the course has led many instructors to omit it entirely. The upshot of these curricular developments is that law students graduate with knowledge of trial court jurisdiction and procedure from their first-year courses (and perhaps additional exposure in upper-class electives) and in trial advocacy courses, but with an almost total lack of education concerning the appellate courts. The typical moot court competition does involve brief writing and oral argument set in a hypothetical appellate court, but most such programs do not involve serious instruction about the functioning of appellate courts.

The course for which this book is designed is intended to fill that void and place appellate courts in their rightful place in the law school curriculum. This book is unique in that it involves a study of appellate courts and the appellate process in all of their varied aspects. It deals with far more than the jurisdiction and procedure of appellate courts, although those important subjects are treated extensively. A substantial part of the book is concerned with the structure, organization, internal processes, and personnel throughout the American appellate realm. No other casebook promises this much depth and breadth of coverage of appellate courts. A student should emerge from this course with a thorough understanding of the appellate world and thus with a much better understanding of the contemporary American legal order.

Chapter 1 presents an overview of appellate courts and their work. It sketches the basic roles of these courts, the nature and volume of their business, and some assumptions and concepts underlying their work.

Chapters 2, 3, and 4 present traditional material on appellate jurisdiction and procedure, although in a fresh way. Important questions explored here concern access to an appellate forum — when and how a case can be brought to such a forum — and the scope of the court's authority when a case is properly before it. The dual roles of American appellate courts are examined: the role of correcting trial court errors and the role of generating law.

The book then shifts in Chapter 5 to a major theme of this course: the impact on appellate courts of the dramatic rise in the volume of appeals over the last third of the twentieth century. High volume has become the dominant reality of American appellate life, and this book examines at length the responses of legislators and judges to that challenge. Chapter 6 deals with structural responses, alterations in the architecture of judicial systems at the appellate level to enable appellate courts to absorb the increased caseloads. Chapter 7 then addresses the next line of response to volume: enlarging the number and types of judicial personnel involved in the decisional process. Chapter 8 focuses on the most recent response to the perceived crisis of volume: basic modifications in the traditional ways in which appellate courts consider and decide appeals. The collective impact of all these responses on collegiality among judges and how judges have had to come to rely on staff are examined in Chapter 9, and their impact on the work of appellate advocates is addressed in Chapter 10. Chapter 11 presents information and concerns about the appellate judges themselves, the key actors in the system — including who they are and how they come to the bench.

Chapter 12 focuses on the Supreme Court of the United States and the exercise of its distinctive discretionary jurisdiction through the writ of certiorari. Chapter 13 examines the appellate courts in England and Germany, providing comparative insights from our parent legal system in the Anglo-American legal world and from a representative civil law system. In studying those appellate arrangements and the judges who function in them, students are invited to think more critically about familiar features of American appellate courts and their procedures.

The book concludes in Chapter 14 by imagining the alternative futures of the appellate courts, the various ideas still "on the drawing board" for redesigning appellate structures so as to provide solutions to current and impending problems. Students are encouraged to think creatively about the future of the appellate judiciary and about means for maintaining an effective legal order amidst the ever-changing circumstances of our time.

Editorial Note

This casebook is primarily a teaching book, not a research book. For the sake of readability, in the extracts from the law review articles and judicial opinions, footnotes and citations of authorities are omitted without ellipses, but ellipses are inserted when text is omitted. Footnotes have been numbered consecutively throughout each chapter. Footnotes in excerpts from articles, books, and judicial opinions have been renumbered accordingly, but the original footnote number is shown in brackets at the begining of each note. An attempt have been made to harmonize the original headings, styles, and fonts of the excerpts to fit into the format of the casebook.

ACKNOWLEDGEMENTS

Professor Meador expresses appreciation to Kathy Zentgraf, Ginger Bauer, Wistar Murray and Mary Ketcham for their assistance in revising and preparing segments of this material for publication. Important updating information from England was furnished by Roger Venne, Registrar of Criminal Appeals, Royal Courts of Justice; Alistair Shaw of the Department for Constitutional Affairs in London; and D.A. Thomas of Trinity Hall, Cambridge. From Germany, updating information was provided by Harald Reichenbach, David Hawkes, and Christian Meyer-Seitz of the Federal Ministry of Justice in Berlin. Irene Williams assisted in collecting the information from England and Germany. Continuing appreciation is due to all of those who assisted in developing the first edition of this book; their efforts remain evident here.

Professor Baker is grateful for the secretarial assistance of Maria Madriz and the reference librarianship of Janet Reinke. He also appreciates the able research assistance of: Paige Boiko, Daniel Cervantes, Denise Kalland, Cristina Lombillo Bencomo, Jeremy Scott, Cristina Suarez, and Marieke Tieges. He thanks Dean Leonard P. Strickman and Associate Deans Scott F. Norberg and Ediberto Roman, at the FIU College of Law for their professional support and personal encouragement.

Professor Steinman thanks Vincent Rivera for administrative and secretarial assistance extraordinaire, Thomas Gaylord of the Chicago-Kent library and students Adrienne Goss, Lisa Mitchell, and Zhiyuan "Mike" Xu, for enormously helpful research assistance, and Dean Harold Krent for his support of this project.

SUMMARY TABLE OF CONTENTS

TABLE OF CONTENTS

TABLE OF SECONDARY AUTHORITIES

FEDERAL-STATE COURT SYSTEM *

The Federal Courts

The State Courts

THE SUPREME COURT OF THE UNITED STATES

Created by the Constitution, Article III: nine justices, appointed for life by the President, with the "advice and consent" of the Senate. Interprets and applies the Constitution and all federal statutes, after decision by federal courts of appeals and state supreme courts.

Discretionary Review

Discretionary Review

Discretionary Review

U.S COURTS OF APPEALS

11 Circuits and D.C. | The Federal Circuit (i.e. Patents, Customs, Taxes . . .)

US CT. of FED. CLAIMS

U.S. COURT OF INTERNATIONAL TRADE

ADMINISTRATIVE AGENCIES

Merit Systems Protection Board, Boards of Contract Appeals, Int'l Trade Commission, Patent and Trademark Boards, certain decisions of the secretaries of Commerce and Agriculture.

FEDERAL AGENCIES

Interstate Commerce Commission, Tax Court, Securities and Exchange Commission, National Labor Relations Board, Federal Trade Commission, etc.

ADMINISTRATIVE LAW JUDGES

Civil service position. Conduct hearings and submit reports and recommendations to administrative boards or agencies.

U.S. DISTRICT COURTS

Ninety-four districts. Each district has from two to twenty-eight judges (Southern District of New York). Jurisdiction: claims under federal law; civil claims between citizens of different states, if over a fixed amount. Trials with or without jury.

U.S. MAGISTRATE JUDGES

Conduct preliminary hearings, set bail, assist district judges in complex cases.

BANKRUPTCY JUDGES

Preside over bankruptcy cases.

STATE COURTS OF LAST RESORT

(Texas and Oklahoma have two)

MANDATORY REVIEW

LARGELY DISCRETIONARY REVIEW

INTERMEDIATE COURTS OF APPEAL (IACs)

in 39 states

LARGELY MANDATORY REVIEW

STATE SUPERIOR COURTS

All cases, criminal and civil, trials with or without jury. One in each county or similar geographic area. Jurisdiction: state constitution; statutes, common law; also federal Constitution (including most of Bill of Rights) and statutes. Limited by the supremacy, commerce, full faith and credit, and equal protection and due process clauses of the Fourteenth Amendment.

STATE/LOCAL AGENCIES

Industrial accidents, zoning boards, licensing boards etc.

SPECIALIZED COURTS

Probate (wills), domestic relations, juvenile.

DISTRICT COURTS

Small towns, a justice of the peace; large urban centers, a municipal or district court. Jurisdiction: petty crimes, traffic offenses, small claims. No jury.

*From ON APPEAL: Courts, Lawyering, and Judging by Frank M. Coffin. Copyright (c) 1994 by W. W. Norton & Company, Inc. Used by permission of W. W. Norton & Company, Inc.

Chapter 1

APPEALS AND APPELLATE COURTS: BACKGROUND AND GENERAL CONSIDERATIONS

I. COURTS AND JUDGES: TRIAL AND APPELLATE

The idea of two kinds of judicial tribunals — trial and appellate — was inherited from English colonial arrangements. Courts sat in the North American colonies to decide cases in the first instance. The Privy Council, sitting in London, exercised power to review decisions of the colonial courts. Thus, having a higher forum to which a case already decided by one court could be taken for review was familiar to the colonists. The Federal Constitution in 1787 contemplated a multi-tiered judiciary with the Supreme Court as a reviewing forum of that sort. Such multi-tiered judicial systems became established in all states. That basic structure has continued, with some evolution, through two centuries of massive growth in territory, population, and volume of cases.

Appellate courts today are reviewing courts. With rare exceptions, litigation is never initiated there. Instead, appellate courts scrutinize proceedings and decisions that have taken place either in a lower court or in an administrative agency. Trial courts — also known as courts of first instance or in early English terminology, *nisi prius* — are the forums in which judicial proceedings are begun. Trials involve the adversary presentation of evidence; by this means contested facts are fought out and resolved. In American practice, an appellate court does not receive evidence; it disposes of an appeal solely on the basis of the record made in a lower court or in an administrative agency.

Trial and appellate settings differ, as do the circumstances under which trial and appellate judges work. A trial judge presides over proceedings in a courtroom typically occupied by numerous members of the public. Sitting alone, the trial judge makes decisions without collaboration with fellow judges. An appellate judge, however, always decides cases as part of a group, with two or more judicial colleagues. Much of appellate judges' work is out of sight in a conference room, library, or judges' chambers. A trial courtroom is a busy working arena much of the time, whereas appellate courtrooms are the infrequently used sites of formal argument. From the public perspective, trial judges are highly visible; appellate judges are relatively invisible.

Both types of judges are essential in the administration of justice under law. A case can be made that the trial judge is the single most important judicial figure in our legal system, the judicial officer most known to the public. All persons who get involved in court proceedings as litigants, witnesses, or jurors come in contact with the trial judge. Those persons' impressions of the legal system and their sense of justice or injustice will be affected greatly by their

1

perceptions of that judge. A trial judge's powers are large, involving control of the proceedings in all respects, much of which is not reviewable by an appellate court. The trial judge has been called "the parish priest of our legal order."[1]

If that is so, the appellate judges are the bishops. One writer has called them the "cardinals."[2] To invoke another analogy, if the trial judges are the front-line troops of the legal order, the appellate judges are the battalion commanders. They are much fewer in number, and they exercise control over the trial judges; but they are not in direct contact with the citizenry. Litigants, witnesses, and jurors never see appellate judges, nor do other members of the public, unless out of curiosity they attend oral argument sessions, which they rarely do. Those who sit on the appellate courts are the unknown judges, the behind-the-scenes judges. Yet their role in the legal order as a whole is large indeed.

In an appellate court, function combines with symbolism. Through its collegial, deliberative decisions, accompanied by reasoned explanations, an appellate court serves as a major symbol of government under law. It is the ultimate forum to which citizens can take their grievances and get individualized, principled, and fair consideration by high officials themselves. Appellate courts, in this respect, stand in sharp contrast to governmental bureaucracy which mass processes matters in an impersonal and anonymous style. They contrast also with political officials and agencies whose decisions may be influenced by partisan concerns or ideological programs. Citizens, executive officials, and trial judges all are subject ultimately to the judgment of the appellate courts, which themselves sit under law and act through a legal process. Thus, appellate courts not only enforce the rule of law; they also symbolize it.

Each of the fifty states (as well as the District of Columbia and the Commonwealth of Puerto Rico) maintains one or more appellate courts as part of its own independent judicial system, structured like a pyramid. Trial courts form its broad base, and the state supreme court is at the apex. In more than two-thirds of the states there is also a middle tier, the intermediate appellate courts. The federal judicial system is similarly structured, with the district courts at the base, the courts of appeals at the intermediate level, and the Supreme Court at the top.

The focus of this study is on the intermediate and top tiers — the two appellate levels — in these state and federal judicial systems. Although there are some distinctively federal problems (and these will be addressed), we do not concentrate on these to the neglect of the state courts. After all, the state courts are the front-line adjudicators in this country, and the amount of appellate work they perform is vastly greater than that done by the federal courts. In the year ending in 2004, the federal appellate courts terminated 58,217 appeals. By contrast, in 2002 (the latest year for which statistics are available), the state appellate courts disposed of 293,960 cases, a figure which understates the actual total, as not all states reported complete data. However, the jurisdictional and procedural concepts, internal processes, and

---

[1] Harry Jones, *The Trial Judge — Role Analysis and Profile, in* THE COURTS, THE PUBLIC, AND THE LAW EXPLOSION 124, 125 (H. Jones ed., 1965).

[2] DONALD JACKSON, JUDGES 304 (1974).

modes of judicial behavior common to appellate courts in all American judicial systems outnumber their differences, and those common features are the principal subjects of this study.

The role of appellate courts in the legal order far exceeds the relatively small percentage of all litigation that is pursued through appeal. Consider, for example, that a representative sample of 100 civil cases initiated in the federal trial courts produced:

> 44 settlements without court action
>
> 35 dispositions before pretrial
>
> 14 dispositions after pretrial but without trial
>
> 4 dispositions after bench trials
>
> 3 dispositions after jury trials
>
> 0.3 trials lasting more than 10 days
>
> 10 appellate filings
>
> 5 appellate submissions
>
> 1 reversal on appeal
>
> 0.8 certiorari petitions
>
> 0.06 dispositions by Supreme Court[3]

The statistics concerning appeals in civil cases in state trial courts of general jurisdiction are similar to those shown above for federal cases. In criminal cases the proportion of final convictions that is appealed is much greater than the percentage of appeals from final judgments in civil cases. But, overall, appeals form a relatively small part of the totality of judicial business.

Likewise, appellate judges constitute a relatively small proportion of all judicial personnel. In the federal system, there are 188 appellate judges, but there are 632 district judges, 352 bankruptcy judges, and 496 full-time magistrate judges, making a total of 1,480 trial level judges. Thus there are approximately eight trial judges for every appellate judge. In the courts of the fifty states there are approximately 1,343 appellate judges. At the state trial level there are approximately 11,230 judges on trial courts of general jurisdiction, and 17,980 judges on courts of limited and special jurisdiction, making a total of 29,210 trial level judges in the fifty states — producing a ratio of one appellate judge to approximately 22 trial judges.

APPELLATE COURT PERFORMANCE STANDARDS COMMISSION, COURT PERFORMANCE STANDARDS AND MEASURES
(National Center For State Courts 1999)

Standard 2.1   Quality of the Judicial Process

Appellate court systems should ensure adequate consideration of each case and decisions based on legally relevant factors, thereby affording every litigant the full benefit of the judicial process.

---

[3]PAUL CARRINGTON & BARBARA BABCOCK, CIVIL PROCEDURE: CASES AND COMMENTS ON THE PROCESS OF ADJUDICATION 355-56 (3d ed. 1983).

Commentary

Appellate court systems should provide the ultimate assurance that the judicial branch fulfills its role in our constitutional scheme of government by ensuring that due process and equal protection of the law, as guaranteed by the federal and state constitutions, have been fully and fairly applied throughout the judicial process. The rendering of justice demands that these fundamental principles be observed, protected, and applied by giving every case sufficient attention and deciding cases solely on legally relevant factors. Quality of the judicial process depends on these principles and the perception that the reviewing court has considered the issues on appeal fairly.

The integrity of appellate court systems rests on their ability to fashion procedures and make decisions that afford each litigant access to justice. Constitutional principles of equal protection and due process should be guideposts for an appellate court system's procedures and decisions. Toward this end, court procedures that are designed with these principles in mind should be fairly and consistently applied in all cases.

It is expected that an appellate court system's rules and procedures will be available and open to the public. In contrast, the decision-making process is, for the most part, a cloistered, deliberative undertaking that by its very nature is not conducive to being open to public view. Nonetheless, decision making should be conducted in accordance with constitutionally guaranteed principles of fairness and justice. Appellate court decisions should be based solely on legally relevant factors fairly applied and devoid of extraneous considerations or influences.

Finally, each case should be given the necessary time based on its particular facts and legal complexities to render just decisions, although each case need not be allotted a standard amount of time for review. Quality of the appellate judicial process is not measured by the amount of time devoted to each case, but rather that each case is managed — from beginning to end — in a manner consistent with the principles of fairness and justice.

II. FUNCTIONS AND PURPOSES OF APPEALS AND APPELLATE COURTS

The material in this section suggests reasons why appeals are provided in a judicial system and the purposes to be served by appeals. You should attempt to identify these various reasons and purposes and, at the conclusion of the section, undertake to evaluate the merits of each. In addition, consider whether there are any other policy justifications for a system of appeals.

Daniel J. Meador, Appellate Courts: Staff and Process in the Crisis of Volume 1-3(1974)[4]

When we speak of appeals, by definition we refer to a phase of litigation which takes place normally after a case has already been brought to conclusion in one court. Even in an interlocutory appeal, the case has been litigated

---

[4] Copyright © 1974 by the National Center for State Courts. All Rights Reserved. Reprinted with permission.

to some interim juncture in a court of first instance. The concept of an appeal is that another forum will thereafter scrutinize the case; it will subject the first court's action to a second look, examining not a raw controversy in the course of being presented, but rather a controversy as already packaged and decided in a trial court proceeding. The packaging and deciding may have put the dispute between the parties in a different posture; issues which were the subject of lively contest as the case unfolded may have disappeared or been recast; new issues may have been born. An appeal presupposes that at least one of the parties is dissatisfied with the trial court result and wishes to continue to litigate issues which arguably survive. The maintenance of an appellate system rests on society's view that it is undesirable for the resolution of at least some controversies to be the final responsibility of a single tribunal.

In the common law courts the ancestor of what we now call appellate review — the writ of error — centered exclusively on the correcting of error committed by the trial judge. Other purposes and functions were incidental. In this century, with more fully developed legal systems and more sophisticated perception of their workings, we see appellate courts serving several purposes. Though their relative importance may be assessed differently, these are:

1. To correct error in the trial proceedings and to insure justice under law to the litigants. This is the historic basis for the intervention of an upper court. Though still central to the mission of an appellate system, it is no longer viewed as the sole or even (in the eyes of some) as the primary purpose.

2. To enunciate and harmonize the decisional law of the jurisdiction. This is the "law making" role of courts in the common law tradition. A recognition of this as a purpose of appellate review is a product of modern legal realism. Under the earlier view of courts as simply finding and declaring the law, this would have been perceived as merely a by-product or an incidental feature of appellate adjudication. Yet in fact this role was no less important then than now; the corpus of the common law resulted largely from appellate adjudication. Some now think of this law-enunciating function as a more important justification for appeals than the error correcting purpose. The complexity of society apparently requires more law-giving and law-clarifying than legislation alone can provide.

Broadly viewed, these dual purposes may subsume all the roles and functions of appellate courts. But a more definitive statement would add the following:

3. To supervise the trial courts throughout the jurisdiction. Although much of this role is performed through the case-deciding process, either by error correcting or law development decisions, there may also be rule making by the appellate courts for the governance of trial proceedings, and there may be appellate court managerial authority going outside of the case-deciding type of control. It is important that the multiple trial courts in a judicial system abide by the same standards in the administration of justice. Only the existence of some common, higher authority can insure such uniformity.

In serving these purposes appellate courts also provide for the litigants and the public two reassuring functions. One is a degree of detachment, perspective, and opportunity for reflection by a group of judges, beyond that which a single trial judge can provide, thereby enhancing the likelihood of a sound resolution. In addition, an appeal spreads responsibility, thereby making difficult or sensitive decisions more livable for the decision makers and the mistakes more tolerable for all concerned.

These are the purposes and functions of an appellate system taken as a whole. Where there is a single appellate court . . . that court carries the total appellate responsibility. The idea of sharing the responsibility between two different levels of appellate courts is relatively new. Where intermediate appellate courts have been created . . . appeals are typically authorized to be taken from the trial courts directly to those courts as a matter of right. From there application for further review may be made in the highest court, which selects in its discretion the cases it wishes to hear and decide.

The intermediate court is usually viewed as having primary — and perhaps exclusive — responsibility for fulfilling the error-correcting and justice-doing purpose. The highest court is viewed as serving primarily the law development and supervisory purposes, often referred to as institutional review. This allocation of responsibility in a bi-level appellate system is not always airtight or tidy. Intermediate courts cannot completely ignore doctrinal development, and supreme courts are not oblivious to errors and injustices affecting only the parties. Yet the concept of differing roles does influence in large measure the decision-making atmosphere in two types of appellate courts.

MARTIN M. SHAPIRO, COURTS: A COMPARATIVE AND POLITICAL ANALYSIS 49-53 (1981)[5]

The Uses of Appeal

[O]ne of the principal virtues of a trial is that it provides an official termination to conflict, relieving the disputants of the necessity of further reciprocal assertions or retributions. But too much finality may be disturbing to the losing [party]. One of the functions of a "right of appeal" may be to provide a psychological outlet and a social cover for the loser at trial. For appeal allows the loser to continue to assert his rightness in the abstract without attacking the legitimacy of the legal system or refusing to obey the trial court. Indeed the loser's displeasure is funneled into a further assertion of the legitimacy of the legal system. Appealing to a higher court entails the acknowledgment of its legitimacy.

. . . [T]he principal problem of the triadic form of conflict resolution was keeping the loser from perceiving the final situation as "two against one." Appeals mechanisms are devices for telling the loser that if he believes that it did turn out two against one, he may try another triadic figure. Perhaps just as important, the availability of appeal allows the loser to accept his loss without having to acknowledge it publicly. The purpose of a trial is to effect a termination of conflict. But too abrupt a termination may be counterproductive of true conflict resolution. Appeal, whether actually exercised, threatened, or

---

[5] Copyright © 1981 by the UNIVERSITY OF CHICAGO PRESS Reprinted with permission.

only held in reserve, avoids adding insult to injury. The loser can leave the courtroom with his head high talking of appeal and then accept his loss, slowly, privately, and passively by failing to make an appeal. We often see appeal principally as a mode of ensuring against the venality, prejudice, and/or ignorance of trial court judges and of soothing the ruffled feelings of the loser. Appeal does indeed serve these functions, but it does so by the imposition of hierarchical controls on trial court behavior. A great deal of interest to political scientists lurks in that hierarchical element.

. . . [I]n a predominant share of the governing systems that have existed in the world, judging is either a facet of administration, or is closely aligned with it. . . . A "right" of appeal is a mechanism providing an independent flow of information to the top on the field performance of administrative subordinates.

It is not only an independent flow, but one highly complementary to the normal administrative reporting. Such reporting usually takes the form of summarization. . . . And not unnaturally, what tend to get lost most easily are those instances in which the subordinate has done badly. The superior never sees the full details of any specific things his subordinates have done. The summaries he sees tend to emphasize his subordinates' successes and leave out the failures. ("Last year this office handled over three thousand claims of which 91 percent were settled within forty-eight hours.")

The appeals process cuts across this summarization because the unit of appeal is a single case, in all its details, rather than a summary of overall performance. It is not a single instance chosen by an administrator to illustrate his success, but an instance chosen by a consumer of administration who feels that the administrator has failed. Finally, not only is the appeals case a detailed sample of administrative work product, but it is a partially random sample. The distribution of cases appealed is not determined by either the goals of the administrative subordinate or his superior but by the nonadministrative motivations of individual litigants. . . .

Thus, on the one hand, while appeal is a partially random sample, it is one loaded toward administrative failure. . . . On the other hand, the administrative superior may impose some patterning by making it known what kinds of appeal are most likely to be successful. . . . English appeals courts at one time said they would listen to appeals on questions of law but not of fact. Thus they got to see cases in which trial courts had made mistakes of law, but not those where the court had done bad fact-finding. . . . [A] Chinese local magistrate who did not wish his superiors to know about his performance in a particular dispute could pressure the parties to settle by mediation. A mediated settlement could not be appealed.

At the opposite extreme, it is possible to run an appeals system that takes 100 percent or at least a very full sample. In Tokagawa, Japan, every opinion of a trial court was prepared as only a draft of an opinion by the higher authorities. Each draft went forward and came into legal force only after the higher authorities had approved it. In this system, then, all cases are appealed. Most American states provide one appeal in criminal cases as a matter of right. The common practice of the defense bar in many of those states is routinely to file an appeal for every losing defendant. Some states have mandatory first appeals for all cases in which the punishment is severe. These state systems approach 100 percent appeal. Whenever a central government seems to be attempting 100 percent sampling, however, the reality will usually turn out to be otherwise. Thus in states where a first appeal is routine, the intermediate appellate court that hears such appeals will usually deny 90 percent of them in one-line orders that show that they were given only a cursory glance. The appellate court will decide the other 10 percent. And of those only a very few will move on to a further appeal to the state supreme court.

Of course, where there is a separate judicial hierarchy, appeal is typically the central mode of supervision by higher courts over lower, and reversal on appeal a central form of administrative sanction. In such instances the need for multiple channels of information and control leads the top to demand other institutions in addition to appeal, such as judicial conferences, centralized personnel systems, and administrative reporting, to increase their control over their subordinates.

The insistence, so frequently encountered, that the chain of appeal eventually arrive at the chief, the king, or the capital, instead of stopping at some intermediate level, is difficult to explain except in terms of centralized political control. If the only function of appeal were to ensure against corruptness or arbitrariness on the part of the trial judge, then appeal to anyone even a single step higher in the scale of authority would be sufficient. In the American states we have just discussed, for instance, appeals could all stop at intermediate appellate courts. Why should any go on to a state supreme court? Its justices are really no more capable of righting the injustices done to the loser in the trial court than are the appeals court judges who first heard the appeal. The top insists on being the ultimate level of appeal because it serves its purposes, not those of a losing disputant.

Of course, just as one of the functions of any appeal may be to reduce the psychic shock to losers, so the right to "take the case all the way to the Supreme Court" provides even greater catharsis for the loser whether he employs it only rhetorically or actually does it. Yet even at this personal level, and quite apart from the question of hierarchical control, the top is likely to see advantages in preserving a right of ultimate appeal. . . . [T]he extension of judicial services outward and downward is a device for wedding the countryside to the regime. So the preservation of appeal to the chief-king-emperor-capital is a device for keeping the strings of legitimacy tied directly between the ruled and the person of the ruler or the highest institutions of government. In the imperial Chinese legal system . . . cases involving capital punishment were automatically appealed from local courts through intermediate appeals courts and ultimately to the emperor himself. The accused was shipped along with his appeal up the appeals ladder. When the death sentence was ultimately commuted, the commutation was ceremonially delivered to the prisoner in the capital and depicted as the personal mercy of the emperor. When the death penalty was confirmed, the prisoner was shipped back down the appeals ladder. He was dispatched on the local execution ground of the trial court that had convicted him initially. No clearer declaration of the political purposes of appeal could be made.

Conversely, the ability to reach down occasionally into the most particular affairs of the countryside provides an important means of reminding the rank and file that the rulers are everywhere, that no one may use his insignificance or his embeddedness in the mass to hide from central authority. Thus the personal ruler, be he Zulu war chief or medieval monarch, rarely totally gives up his personal participation in appeals. Nor do modern central governments often provide that there be only a single appeal from trial court to regional appeals court without any opportunity to go on to a central appeals court.

Thus appellate institutions are more fundamentally related to the political purposes of central regimes than to the doing of individual justice. That this is true is evidenced by the nearly universal existence of appellate mechanisms in politically developed societies, even those whose governments place little or no value on individual rights. . . .

Even if judges did nothing but conflict resolution, appeal would be an important political mechanism both for increasing the level of central control over administrative subordinates and for ensuring the authority and legitimacy of rulers. When we enter the realms of social control and lawmaking, the multiple functions of appeal are even more apparent. When trial courts or first-instance judging by administrators is used as a mode of social control, appeal is a mechanism for central coordination of local control. The "questions of law" passed on to the appeals courts are in reality requests for uniform rules of social conduct and indicators of what range of case-by-case deviation from those rules is permissible by first-line controllers.

John Leubsdorf, *Constitutional Civil Procedure*, 63 TEX. L. REV. 579, 628-31 (1984)[6]

That the Supreme Court has never recognized a right to appeal in the civil context is [a] strange gap in our constitutional law. It is difficult to imagine a civilized system of justice without appeals. Indeed, many societies go further than ours in permitting appeals, and some confer a constitutional right to appeal.

It makes sense to include some right to an appeal in a constitution, because appellate review is essential to the consistent and accurate application of the law. Partly for this reason, H. M. Hart argued that, despite the Constitution's proviso that Congress may regulate the Supreme Court's appellate jurisdiction, to allow Congress to exclude constitutional issues entirely from Supreme Court review would "destroy the Constitution." It would menace the rule of law to leave even nonconstitutional issues to the diverse decisions of a state's trial courts without any review of those courts' decisions. In such a system, an arbitrary judge could rule on the law or facts as he pleased without any means of correction.

III. HISTORICAL BACKGROUND AND THE NON-INEVITABILITY OF APPEALS

Bear in mind questions as to why we have appeals and as to the value of appeals as you study the materials in this section. Appeals have not always

---

[6] Copyright © 1984 by the TEXAS LAW REVIEW. All Rights Reserved. Reprinted with permission.

been provided for in a comprehensive way in the United States. Indeed, the U.S. Supreme Court has never held that the Constitution requires an appeal. *See, e.g., Griffin v. Illinois*, 351 U.S. 12, 18 (1955). In light of these circumstances, consider why our appellate structure and process are designed as they are today.

ROBERT L. STERN, APPELLATE PRACTICE IN THE UNITED STATES 3-4 (2d ed. 1989)[7]

Appellate practice in the United States did not of course begin in 1789 with the adoption of the Constitution. Prior to the Declaration of Independence each colony had a judicial system. The highest appellate tribunal, however, was not a colonial supreme court but the Privy Council in London. The colonies, or some of them, had their own councils, but, following the British model, these often were composed of the King's (or governor's) advisers and not of judges or even lawyers. Appeals from trial courts often called merely for new trials by other trial judges in superior trial courts, not by true courts of appeal. . . .

Between 1776 and 1789 most of the independent states created their own appellate structures . . . And Congress acting under the Articles of Confederation established a United States Court of Appeals to hear appeals from the state courts in cases of capture of vessels at sea, so that a uniform body of law would govern that then important subject.

These appellate tribunals antedating the Constitution drew on the British practice as a source of their appellate procedures. Lawyers were familiar with writs of error in actions at law and appeals in chancery. Appeal by writ of error, directing that the record be sent to an appellate court to be examined for error, historically was a new proceeding rather than continuation of a case begun in a lower court. A petition for allowance of the writ and a formal order of a judge granting the petition were accompanied by an assignment of errors and a citation notifying the other parties that the case was to come before the appellate court. The bill of exceptions combined a statement of the exceptions or errors with the pertinent portions of the record as submitted to and approved or "settled" by the trial court. Since this was before the days of typewriters and shorthand reporting, the testimony was summarized or abstracted on the basis of the notes or memories of counsel and the trial judge. In contrast to the action at law, the appeal in equity was not regarded as a new proceeding but as a removal to a higher court for retrial on the old record below and evidence taken de novo if necessary.

These procedures survived for many years in the state and federal courts. They did not disappear in the United States Supreme Court until 1954. And some remnants, or at least the terminology, still exist in a few of the states.

NOTES

1. The word "appeal" has had various meanings throughout Anglo-American legal history. *See* WILLIAM BLACKSTONE, 3 COMMENTARIESS *402-11. In the early

---

[7] Copyright © 1989 by Bureau of National Affairs. All Rights Reserved. Reprinted with permission.

days of the common law it referred to a charge by one person against another of a wrongful or felonious act; it had nothing to do with the concept of review by one tribunal of action taken by another. *See* Arthur Allen Leff, *The Leff Dictionary of Law: A Fragment*, 94 YALE L.J. 1855, 2039-40 (1985).

2. At times "appeal" has been used to refer to the transfer or removal of a case for trial from one court to another. In this sense, the removal procedure provided for in the federal district courts by 28 U.S.C. § 1441 was thought of as an appeal, although it is not so considered today.

3. The word "appeal" was not used in the English common-law courts or in American law courts prior to the merger of law and equity. As explained in the Stern excerpt above, a review proceeding in the law courts, analogous to the modern appeal, was carried out by a writ of error. In effect, the writ put the trial judge's actions on trial, based on the record made in the lower court. The influence of that procedure can still be seen in the general rule that points not raised and passed upon below cannot be raised on appeal.

4. The modern use of "appeal" comes from equity practice. In the English Court of Chancery the decision of a vice-chancellor could be appealed to the chancellor and the case heard de novo. That is, the reviewing judge could receive evidence and make determinations of fact as though no proceeding had taken place previously.

5. The concept of appeal de novo still obtains in some American courts. The term is most often used in contrast to "review on the record," a review based solely on the evidence taken in the trial court. In some states decisions of trial courts of limited jurisdiction can be appealed de novo to the trial courts of general jurisdiction. In such circumstances the lower court is often spoken of as a "court not of record."

6. De novo is used in a second sense. A "de novo review of the record" means that although the reviewing court confines itself to the record made below it decides the issues for itself without regard to the decision in the lower court.

7. These distinctions are further explained in the following piece.

Martin M. Shapiro, Courts: A Comparative and Political Analysis 37-41 (1981)[8]

. . . It is often said that appellate courts are to hear questions of law but not questions of fact, which are to be left to the trial court. A similar practice obtains in many other common law jurisdictions. However, side by side with this appellate division of fact and law, we find many other legal systems that use or have used trial de novo as the standard mode of appeal. Where appeal is by trial de novo, the appellate court simply hears the whole case all over again. Trial de novo is found in most nonliterate societies, no doubt in large part because of the difficulty of preserving trial court findings of fact to serve as a basis for appellate decision.

---

[8] Copyright © 1981 by the UNIVERSITY OF CHICAGO PRESS. Reprinted with permission.

One of the principal differences in the development of the English common law courts . . . and the Roman law courts of Western Europe . . . lies in the realm of appellate fact-finding. The basic instrument of appeal developed in England was the writ of error. Issued by an appellate court, it ordered that the "record" of the trial court be sent to it to be examined for error. In English trials the evidence was almost entirely oral or lay in the personal knowledge of the jurors. For jurors were originally summoned not to hear the facts but because they themselves knew the facts. Thus the written record of an English trial court would contain almost no factual material. It would be limited largely to the legal claims of the two parties and the findings of law made by the court. It might contain the conclusions of fact made by the court, but not the evidence on which these were based. At least until the eighteenth century, English trial courts rarely issued long written opinions. Indeed Anglo-American trial courts still feel no particular compulsion to do so and frequently do not. Thus the record on appeal often consisted of very cryptic entries of what legal claim had been made, which parties won and what remedy had been given. An English appeals court had little choice but to confine itself to spotting errors of law in the record. It could not have spotted errors of fact even if it wanted to, since it had none of the evidence before it.

Romanist procedures, on the other hand, emphasized the compilation by lower-level judges of a complete written record and analysis of all the evidence. There rarely was a trial in the English sense of everyone appearing at one time in a court room, telling their stories, and immediately receiving a verdict. Instead, a case proceeded by the gradual accumulation of papers in successive waves. The stack of papers literally became the case. If there was an appeal from the decision of the trial court, the whole file went up to the appeals court. The appellate court in effect decided the whole case all over again.

A number of causes for these differences in scope of appeal may be suggested. The introduction of the jury in England . . . is no doubt crucial. An appellate court cannot review what went on in the minds of the jurors. And, unlike professional judges, jurors cannot be expected to submit written records of their fact-finding.

The English preference for verbal [oral] presentation of evidence preceded the introduction of the jury, however, and so is probably an independent cause of the difference. It is, of course, impossible for an appellate court to review verbal evidence unless it holds the whole trial all over again. Modern Anglo-American courts may have a transcript of the oral evidence. Nevertheless, where oral evidence is the rule, an appellate court feels less capable of making factual judgments than the trial court which actually heard and saw the witnesses. Romanist procedures used a system of written questions and answers exchanged between the two parties as the mode of gathering evidence. Low-level judicial officers then shaped up the file of these questions and answers and supporting documents and presented them to the trial court judge. Exactly the same file could be presented to an appellate court. So Romanist appellate judges did not feel they were any further from the parties, the witnesses and the evidence than the trial court they were reviewing.

Also, . . . appeal is essentially a device for exercising centralized supervision over local judicial officers. The Continental pattern was one of scattered trial courts supervised by more centralized appellate bodies. Appeal by trial de novo greatly strengthens the supervisory powers of the centralized appellate courts over their scattered subordinates. Dawson argues that the appeals mechanism was one of the principal devices used by Continental regimes to impose a uniform and centralized Roman law on local courts in place of the localized, customary law they had been employing in the medieval period. . . . [T]he English centralized the trial courts themselves and so had less need of a strong appellate mechanism to enforce the will of the central government on the trial judges.

Finally, although it is not clear whether we are dealing here with a cause or an effect, the English system of appeal requires far less governmental resources than the Romanist one. The Continental system, with its emphasis on a complete written record, requires a huge number of judicial officials to collect, correlate and analyze the huge pile of papers that become the case. A system of appeal that involves reexamining the whole file requires an enormous number of appellate judicial man hours. It took hours for a French appellate judge to read his "records"; minutes for an English judge. The limited appeal constituted by the writ of error is part of an overall English pattern of attempting to run a government cheaply and with as few government personnel as possible. Trial de novo on appeal is part of a Continental pattern that tolerated and even encouraged the growth of large governmental bureaucracies, judicial and otherwise.

The differing consequences of limiting appeal to questions of law and employing trial de novo are important to the balance of power between trial and appellate courts. Trial de novo, of course, gives an appellate court far more general supervisory power. It sees the whole rather than only a small part of what the trial court has been doing. Moreover, where appeal is by trial de novo, the appellate court issues a final order binding on the parties. Where appeal is on questions of law only, the procedure is different. After the appeals court makes a binding declaration of law, it sends the case back to the trial court for retrial or a new decision consonant with the legal rule announced by the appeals court. Thus the trial court still has the final say. Given the complex interaction of law and fact, in many instances a trial court again can find in favor of the same party who won the first trial. The trial court can always argue that a proper analysis of the facts shows that, even under the new rule of law announced by the appeals court, the party who won the first time is legally right and the winning appellant legally wrong. Of course such a decision may result in another appeal. It is not unheard of in the United States to have three or four rounds of this sort. . . .

In their nineteenth-century judicial reforms, the English recognized the weaknesses of the writ of error as a form of appellate procedure and sought to introduce trial de novo on appeal. The reforms were subsequently greatly whittled back but still remain in part. . . . The most important impact of the writ of error has been in the United States, which has strongly preserved the English tradition. American appellate courts have often greatly expanded the concept of "the record" so as to allow themselves to see more of what went on at trial. In theory at least, however, they still limit themselves largely to questions of law, leaving questions of fact to the trial court. And . . . while often breached in practice, this theoretical limitation still has important consequences.

In advanced societies, trial de novo frequently does not take the form of a complete rehearing of oral testimony, but instead involves appellate court review of the trial court record and then its own independent findings of fact. In the United States, trial de novo is usually a device for bringing cases from minor courts of incomplete jurisdiction and incomplete judicial status into higher courts of general jurisdiction and completely judicialized procedures. . . .

Trial de novo would therefore appear to be something more than a necessity forced on preliterate societies.

NOTES

1. The difference today between the appellate treatment of facts in the United States and such treatment in the continental civil law systems can be seen in Chapter 13, Section II, describing the German appellate courts.

2. In this book the term "appeal" is used in its contemporary American sense as referring to a proceeding in a court — designated as an appellate court — to review the record made and decision rendered in a lower court or an administrative agency.

3. In the historical extract that follows, the phrase "appellate-review court" makes clear that the court is engaged in reviewing lower court decisions on the record in the modern sense of an appeal.

WILFRED RITZ, REWRITING THE HISTORY OF THE JUDICIARY ACT OF 1789: EXPOSING MYTHS, CHALLENGING PREMISES, AND USING NEW EVIDENCE 35, 5-6, 36-8, 44-9 (1990)[9]

Obviously, the delegates to the Constitutional Convention of 1787 and the members of the First Congress were familiar with the structure of their own state judiciary systems. The national system was developed in light of that knowledge. But contrary to what may be generally thought, the national judiciary was not modeled on the then-existing judicial systems of the states, or of England, but represents a new departure from established systems. This departure in the national system is not so much a radical or sharp break with the past, but rather the assumption of a leadership role. At the time the process of organizing the state judicial systems was in a state of flux. In organizing the national system, the men of the period used what must have been considered the "best ideas" of the period. Inasmuch as these ideas were good ones, especially for a rapidly growing and expanding nation, the national system became the model upon which the state judiciaries were based. The consequences of some of the novel provisions used for the national system could only then be dimly perceived, if perceived at all.

The principal characteristic of the modern judicial system is its hierarchical structure. It is vertically structured, with a number of coequal courts at each vertical level, the number of such courts at each level decreasing sharply as the vertical structure is ascended. At the apex is one supreme, appellate-review court.

---

[9] Copyright © 1990 by the UNIVERSITY OF OKLAHOMA PRESS. Reprinted with permission.

Today this hierarchical structure is so taken for granted that it seems almost impossible to have any other structure.

. . .

However, it must be emphasized that the state judiciaries that existed at the end of the eighteenth century were not organized in this fashion, and that part of the controversy surrounding Article III arose on this historical fact. Consequently, it is desirable to say a few things about the then-existing state judiciaries. Only in this way can one appreciate the nature of the achievement of the First Congress. . . .

If one examines closely the then-existing state judiciaries, they might be described in the following way: Most states had a corps of judges who sometimes went singly into the field to try cases, and who at other times assembled together in the capital to try cases and consider "appeals." In other words, even when there existed the formality of designation that distinguished "inferior" courts from "superior" courts, there was no distinction in judicial personnel. The same group of judges sat at different times in the different "courts." Furthermore, the "superior" or "supreme" courts were all "trial" courts as well as "appellate" courts, and the "review" of an inferior court by a superior court was commonly a retrial, with a new jury. Finally, the courts of last resort were commonly a branch of the legislature, or a body amalgamating judges, legislators, and members of the executive. Distinctness and hierarchy did not characterize the court structures, and "superior" usually meant only that a reviewing court had more judges sitting on it. . . .

. . .

The present-day national judicial system illustrates the vertical hierarchical judicial structure to which judicial organization has tended. One supreme court at the top; thirteen courts of appeal at the next level; district courts at a still lower level, these being the principal trial courts; and below them a large number of magistrates, representing the lowest trial level. Being a federal system, the Supreme Court of the United States also sits as the one supreme court reviewing the fifty state judicial systems, each of which is again organized in a hierarchical structure.

In 1787-89 the highest judicial court in eleven of the thirteen states had all four of the following characteristics:

1. The highest judicial court was first and most importantly a trial court. While it might have some functions in the nature of appellate review, they were of secondary significance.

2. The appellate-review function was performed by some part of the legislature, or the executive, or by some combination of legislative, executive, and judicial officials. The ultimate reviewing authority of judicial proceedings was not vested exclusively in the judiciary in any state.

3. Every judge was a trial judge, and he participated along with others in reviewing his own actions as a trial judge, and might or might not have a vote in this review.

4. Judges did not write opinions and so there were no opinions to publish.

The other two states are Maryland and Virginia. As early as 1776 Maryland had provided on paper for a "modern" appellate-review court, but did not have such a court; it was not until three-quarters of a century later that Maryland actually established a true appellate-review court. As a result of legislation adopted in 1788, Virginia was in the process of establishing a true appellate-review court.

The modern appellate-review court has four characteristics distinguishing it from all the American courts of the late eighteenth century. These characteristics relate to the structure of the court and its place in the whole judicial system. As a part of the modern court's function, certain distinctive law-reporting characteristics have developed. These four characteristics are as follows:

1. The principal function of the court is to review lower-court proceedings, and only incidentally, if at all, to function as a trial court;

2. The court is completely separated from the executive and legislative branches, and its members are all judicial officers;

3. The court and all of its permanent members are separate and distinct from the trial courts and lower appellate courts, which lower courts have their own permanent members;

4. The judges write opinions for publication. These opinions are published:

   a. verbatim;

   b. on a regular basis, continually and timely; and

   c. with some "official" sanction.

. . .

The date 1789 is as satisfactory as any for dating the beginning of the development of the American appellate-review court. It is the year in which the first "true" American law report was published and the year the national judicial system was established. Both of these events had large significance in the development of the modern American appellate-review court.

. . .

The Relationship Between the Development of Appellate-Review Courts and Modern Law Reporting

The modern system of law reporting could not develop until judges wrote opinions and made them available for publication on a timely and regular basis. At the same time, there was no incentive for judges to craft judicial opinions until a system developed whereby the opinions would be published.

The two developments are interdependent. We could not have the one without the other. The mainstay of early law reporting was the reporting of trial decisions, with some reporting of appeals when such took place. But with the development of the appellate-review court, law reporting became increasingly identified with the reporting of the opinions of these courts. There is still some reporting of trial court decisions, particularly of the United States district courts, but both the heart and the bulk of law reporting today is the reporting of the "law" being made by the appellate-review tribunals.

NOTES

1. Except for Vermont and Tennessee (the first two states admitted after the original thirteen), the states admitted in the decades following the formation of the Union all provided in their constitutions for supreme courts and separate trial courts. With some variations, the wording in those state constitutions was modeled on Art. III, § 1 of the Federal Constitution: "The judicial Power of the United States, shall be vested in one supreme Court, and in such inferior Courts as the Congress may from time to time ordain and establish." The following are typical:

Kentucky, Const. of 1792, Art. V:

> The judicial power of this commonwealth, both as to matters of law and equity, shall be vested in one supreme court, which shall be styled the court of appeals, and in such inferior courts as the legislature may, from time to time ordain and establish. . . . The Supreme Court shall have original and final jurisdiction in all cases respecting the titles to land. . . . In all other cases the Supreme Court shall have appellate jurisdiction only, with such exceptions and under such regulations as the legislature shall make . . .

Alabama, Const. of 1819, Art. V, §§ 1-2:

> The judicial power of this State shall be vested in one supreme court, . . . and such inferior courts of law and equity . . . as the general assembly may, from time to time, direct, ordain and establish. . . .
>
> The supreme court, except in cases otherwise directed by this constitution, shall have appellate jurisdiction only. . . .

For the judicial articles in the constitutions of all states admitted in the next half century, see BENJAMIN POORE, THE FEDERAL AND STATE CONSTITUTIONS, COLONIAL CHARTERS, AND OTHER ORGANIC LAWS OF THE UNITED STATES (2d ed. 1878).

2. What are the advantages and disadvantages of a judge's serving in both trial and appellate capacities, as was the practice earlier in American history? Is it preferable to have clearly differentiated trial and appellate forums, as is now the general American pattern?

3. In some appellate systems today (for example, the federal), trial judges are designated from time to time to sit temporarily with the appellate court. Is this practice desirable?

4. The following article explains that in the newly created federal judicial system many types of cases could not be subjected to appellate review. As shown in Section B of this chapter, today a comprehensive system of appellate review exists; there is a widespread view that every losing litigant should have the opportunity to take one appeal as a matter of right. What happened over the last 200 years to bring about this change?

David E. Engdahl, *What's in a Name? The Constitutionality of Multiple "Supreme" Courts,* 66 Ind. L. J. 457, 463-4, 473, 493-501 (1991)[10]

The Pyramidic Model

James Wilson wrote in his Lectures on Law two hundred years ago:

> According to the rules of judicial architecture, a system of courts should resemble a pyramid . . . [I]ts summit should be a single point . . . [O]ne supreme tribunal should superintend and govern all others . . . [Otherwise] different courts might adopt different and even contradictory rules of decision, and the distractions, springing from these different and contradictory rules, would be without remedy and without end.

Wilson was one of the ablest of his generation, and an original Justice of the United States Supreme Court. He had been prominent at the Constitutional Convention, and served on its Committee of Detail. He wrote his Lectures within five years after the Constitution was drafted, and during his judicial tenure. Particularly given the "plain words" of article III, therefore, it does seem reasonable to believe that the institution Wilson had helped devise conformed to the model that he described.

Nonetheless, such belief is in error. In fact, Wilson found the federal judiciary of his time so out of conformity with his ideal that elsewhere in his Lectures he called it a "very uncommon establishment." His advocacy of the pyramidic model, far from reflecting what then was in place, constituted an argument for fundamental change!

. . .

The most striking characteristic of the Judiciary Act of 1789 (the "Judiciary Act") is that it dispersed not only first instance but also final competence, ignoring the so-called "rules of judicial architecture" expounded in James Wilson's lectures. Instead of erecting a judicial pyramid, the First Congress effectuated the Convention's June 5 compromise by ensuring that decisions of "inferior" national tribunals would be "final . . . in many cases."

Recognizing the disruptive potential of inconsistent state court dispositions of cases within the scope of article III subject matter jurisdiction, Congress made it possible for all such cases to be determined in some federal court. What the Judiciary Act contemplated, however, was determination not by any single one, but rather by one or another of the federal courts: the First Congress declined to establish any mechanism to ensure that decisions of the several federal tribunals would be consistent or uniform. It gave highest priority, instead, to curtailing the risk of "vexatious appeals," by severely limiting the availability of Supreme Court review.

The attitude that apparently prevailed toward appellate review within the federal court structure was best articulated by Oliver Ellsworth, principal draftsman of the Judiciary Act, five years later and after he had become Chief

---

[10] Copyright © 1991 by David E. Engdahl. All Right Reserved. Reprinted with permission.

Justice. Ellsworth observed: "[S]urely, it cannot be deemed a denial of justice, that a man shall not be permitted to try his cause two or three times over. If he has one opportunity for the trial of all the parts of his case, justice is satisfied"; and, continued Ellsworth, even if no appellate review of federal court decisions had been provided (even as to purported errors of law), "no denial of justice could be imputed to our government."[11] . . .

At that time it was routine, even with juries involved, for trial courts to sit with more than one judge. The Judiciary Act departed from this tradition by providing that the district courts (to which it gave very limited jurisdiction) should be staffed by single judges sitting alone. The resulting risk of idiosyncratic rulings was moderated, as to most district court decisions, by authorizing review in one of the multi-judge circuit courts. However, [except for writs of error from Kentucky,] no direct Supreme Court review of cases commenced in district courts was provided. And further, of those district court matters reviewable even by circuit courts, none but admiralty and maritime matters could proceed thence to the Supreme Court.

In other words, excepting those within the admiralty and maritime jurisdiction, for every case commenced in a federal district court either that court or a circuit court was the end of the road.

Even as to the circuit courts, which were the principal federal trial tribunals, review by the Supreme Court was not generally allowed. [However, the Supreme Court was authorized to review by writ of error final judgments of state courts against any party's reliance on a federal constitutional, statutory, or treaty provision.] No Supreme Court review was available for any criminal case. The only non-criminal circuit court decisions eligible for Supreme Court review were those made in: (1) admiralty and maritime cases reviewed by a circuit court on "appeal" from a district court; (2) cases removed from a state court to a circuit court for trial; and (3) cases originally commenced in a circuit court.

Where the Judiciary Act did not totally preclude review (for example, in civil cases originating in circuit courts), it still interposed a substantial impediment: The Supreme Court could review no circuit court judgment unless more than $2,000 was at stake. [There was no amount in controversy prerequisite to Supreme Court review of state court judgments.] In stark contrast, circuit courts could review district court judgments so long as more than $300 in admiralty and maritime causes, or $50 in other civil actions, was in controversy.

Because "amount in controversy" limitations long had been applicable to certain courts in England, and were accepted features of the judicial establishments of American states, this requisite might be thought worthy of little remark. However, $2,000 was a great deal of money in those days: Few persons could earn that much money in a year.[12] This extraordinarily high

---

[11] [182] *Wiscart v. Dauchy,* 3 U.S. (3 Dall.) 321, 329 (1796).

[12] [201] District judges could not. Critics considered the $2,000 salary proposed for the new federal judgeships in 1801 an extravagant sum. At that time judges in some states were paid only $500 per year. Supreme Court Associate Justices were paid $3,500 per year. The Attorney General's salary was only $1,500 per year, although he might supplement this with fees from private practice; a successful lawyer in full-time private practice might earn as much as $4,000 per year.

amount in controversy requisite was deliberately calculated to curtail substantially the Supreme Court's appellate role.

. . .

Whether by "Bill of Rights" provision or statute, however, the very large amount in controversy prerequisite to review of decisions made by other federal courts was not designed to lighten the Supreme Court's work load or to free its docket of inconsequential concerns. Rather, it was calculated to guarantee litigants with modest resources, or where modest amounts were at stake, final and unappealable ends to their ordeals of litigation in tribunals reasonably proximate to their homes.

Statistics from the earliest period demonstrate a consequence of the First Congress' rejection of the pyramidic judiciary model: Most federal court litigation began, and almost all of it ended, in the circuit courts. Of 3,111 cases decided in circuit courts between 1790 and 1797, only twenty went on to the Supreme Court. Fifteen of these were in admiralty, where satisfaction of the $2,000 amount in controversy requirement could seldom present a practical problem. Even including cases on writ of error to state courts, Professor Goebel's careful search could find only 79 appellate cases disposed of by the Supreme Court prior to 1801. In contrast, by 1801 approximately 10,000 cases had been decided by the circuit and district courts combined, approximately 6,800 of them by circuit courts. Even allowing for litigant discretion not to seek Supreme Court review in cases where it might have been had, these statistics confirm that the Judiciary Act did not establish a pyramidic scheme.

. . .

Indeed, the Justices rarely would meet together.[13] To sit as the "supreme" court on original matters or to consider eligible writs of error was distinctly their secondary task.[14] Most of their time and energy would be used traveling and sitting at the twenty-two circuit court sessions each year, where they sat as trial judges and to review some district court proceedings.

Even the number of Justices was determined with reference to their principal function of staffing the circuit system: The number was set at six to provide two Justices for each of the three circuits originally prescribed. Had it been conceived that the Supreme Court should "superintend and govern all others" in order to prevent the "distractions" resulting from "different and even contradictory rules of decision," as James Wilson counseled, it would have been strange to compose it of an even number, manifestly inviting ties. Moreover, had it been conceived that this Court should serve as authoritative oracle on recurring issues, rather than simply as one of several arbiters of particular

---

[13] [217] . . . Among the earliest Justices only James Iredell chose to move his family and home to the seat of the national government; the others kept their several residences dispersed as they had been prior to their respective appointments, reinforcing the image of the Supreme Court as merely an occasional tribunal called together briefly for its semi-annual terms.

[14] [218] Even when they sat as a body on a case, the Justices ordinarily delivered separate opinions seriatim . . . more like an occasional congregation of judges than an integrated tribunal of ultimate resort. In substance, the Supreme Court originally resembled more closely the English Court of Exchequer Chamber . . . than the apex of a pyramided judiciary.

disputes, some means surely would have been provided to inform other courts and members of the legal profession of its rulings; but none was.[15]

NOTES

1. Although, as pointed out by Professor Ritz, Article III of the Federal Constitution pioneered in establishing a Supreme Court as an appellate review court, the preceding article shows that the 1st Congress, in the Judiciary Act of 1789, did not fully implement that concept but rather established a system in which the line between trial and appellate functions was much less sharp than it is today. The same judges often performed both first-instance and review functions. It was only over a long period of time that the work of reviewing courts became more clearly differentiated from that of courts of first instance.

2. In *Martin v. Hunter's Lessee*, 14 U.S. (1 Wheat) 304, 347-48 (1816), Justice Joseph Story explained the founders' motive in authorizing U.S. Supreme Court jurisdiction over state court decisions:

> That motive is the importance, and even necessity of *uniformity* of decisions throughout the whole United States, upon all subjects within the purview of the constitution. Judges of equal learning and integrity, in different states, might differently interpret a statute, or a treaty of the United States, or even the constitution itself: If there were no revising authority to control these jarring and discordant judgments, and harmonize them into uniformity, the laws, the treaties, and the constitution of the United States would be different in different states, and might, perhaps, never have precisely the same construction, obligation, or efficacy, in any two states. The public mischiefs that would attend such a state of things would be truly deplorable; and it cannot be believed that they could have escaped the enlightened convention which formed the constitution.

Given this concern over the importance of nationwide uniformity in federal law, why do you suppose that the Judiciary Act of 1789 made circuit court decisions in many cases unreviewable by the Supreme Court? Was it because the judges sitting on the circuit courts were the same judges who served on the Supreme Court? Or was it because state judges were viewed differently from federal judges? Why would conflicting decisions between circuits on federal questions be more tolerable than conflicting state court decisions on the same federal questions?

3. Many appellate courts today continue to be vested with some measure of original, trial-type jurisdiction. The Supreme Court of the United States, for example, pursuant to Article III of the Federal Constitution, has original jurisdiction over suits to which a state is a party and over actions involving ambassadors and other public ministers and consuls.

State constitutions or statutes give state supreme courts authority over a variety of original proceedings. Examples include disbarment proceedings against lawyers, habeas corpus proceedings, and actions to impeach lower executive officials. *See, e.g., State ex rel. Mullis v. Mathews*, 66 So.2d 105 (Ala. 1953) (impeachment trial of county sheriff).

---

[15] [222] The Justices sitting on their respective circuits might remember any collective discussions on questions which later recurred, but lawyers and other judges had no reliable way of learning what might have been decided by the Justices as a group as no provision was made for reporting decisions.

4. Often an appellate court exercising original trial jurisdiction will appoint a special master to take the testimony of witnesses and make recommended findings of fact, thus relieving the appellate forum of the chore of having its several judges sit through days or weeks of an evidentiary hearing. *See, e.g., South Carolina v. Baker*, 485 U.S. 505 (1988).

5. Original jurisdiction in an appellate court is frowned upon by late twentieth-century judicial architects. The view has evolved that it is preferable as a matter of efficient judicial administration for a reviewing court to confine itself to the reviewing function, leaving all proceedings of first instance to the trial courts. It is the routine business of trial courts to summon witnesses, to take testimony, and to make factual determinations, whereas appellate courts are not designed primarily for those purposes. This is the view taken in AMERICAN BAR ASSOCIATION, STANDARDS RELATING TO APPELLATE COURTS § 3.00 (1994) and in AMERICAN BAR ASSOCIATION, STANDARDS RELATING TO COURT ORGANIZATION, § 1.12 (1990). This course is not concerned with the work of appellate courts in original proceedings but deals entirely with their primary mission, which is to review decisions made by other tribunals.

6. In contrast to views about the value of appeals in Western legal systems, compare the absence of appeals in the Islamic system, as described below.

MARTIN M. SHAPIRO, COURTS: A COMPARATIVE AND POLITICAL ANALYSIS 201-03 (1981)[16]
Islamic Legal Culture and Appeal

. . . In Western legal systems this uniformity [of law] is typically achieved through the announcement of general legal definitions, concepts, and doctrines by the highest courts. These pronouncements then provide guidance for future decisions of lower courts. The legal environment of the *kadi* [Islamic judge] was far different from that in the West, however. He worked in a world of highly particularized legal rules rather than general legal concepts. His job was to find which hundreds of very, very specific and detailed rules most closely fitted the particular facts before him. . . . [These rules were fixed and frozen by the tenth century and consequently] no legal authority beyond the immediate case could attach to the pronouncements of any legal tribunal.

In such a system appeals courts would be robbed of many of their major functions. They could not announce uniform legal rules or doctrines. Only the words of the Prophet or the consensus of the community of the faithful can do that. In other words, in a legal culture that rejects all lawmaking, there can hardly be appellate lawmaking. Indeed, appellate courts could not do any of the kinds of doctrinal pronouncement in which Western appeals courts engage. For the legal culture rejects generalization, broad conceptualizing, and any sort of direct reinterpretation of the basic law. The Hanbali tradition is the extreme statement of rejection of broad reasoning upon the words of the Prophet, but that rejection runs deeply through all of Islam. In a legal culture that rejects generalized legal reasoning, even the most "hard cases" come down to a rather arbitrary choice among a number of highly concrete and

---

[16] Copyright © 1981 by the UNIVERSITY OF CHICAGO PRESS. Reprinted with permission.

particularized rules. There can be little or no attempt even to rationalize this choice. Thus there would appear to be no reason why a second choice by an appellate court would be any better than the initial one made by the trial *kadi*.

Not only would Islam rob appellate courts of the power of legal generalization and rationalization, which is one of their principal legal tasks in the West, but it would rob them of their ultimate weapon in the struggle for institutional legitimacy. In the West it appears obviously intolerable that, given two trial courts applying the same statute, one should say it means one thing and the other that it means the opposite. Because appeal is the major insurance against this nonuniformity, it is almost impossible for Westerners to accept the abolition of appellate courts, no matter how much they are opposed to the policies being pursued by those courts at any given time.

In Islam, however, no overwhelming compulsion towards uniformity of law exists. . . . Thus appellate courts are not essential to counter the terrible vice of nonuniform law because legal nonuniformity is not considered a terrible vice.

IV.   THE CRISIS OF VOLUME: A PRELIMINARY NOTE

Under the best of circumstances, American appellate courts face challenging tasks in correcting trial court errors and enunciating the law of the jurisdiction, but the performance of these functions in a timely and sound manner has been made unusually difficult by the onset of what has been characterized as the "crisis of volume." This extraordinary rise in the number of appellate filings, beginning in the late 1960s and continuing through the last third of the twentieth century, has placed unusual pressures on the appellate courts, especially those to which appeals are taken as a matter of right directly from the trial courts. Many such courts live under the constant threat of engulfment and the build-up of unacceptable backlogs. That threat in turn threatens the quality and effectiveness of appellate justice.

Chapters 6 through 9, *infra*, focus on the impact of this crisis of volume and the alterations it has produced in appellate court structures, personnel, and processes. The dimensions of the volume-rooted crisis are developed in detail in Chapter 5, *infra*, but we introduce the phenomenon here because it so influences the work of appellate courts that readers need to have it clearly in mind from the outset. The following excerpt describes the "crisis" as it was perceived in the mid-1970s. Chapter 5 brings the picture up-to-date; it remains one of high and growing volume.

Paul D. Carrington, Daniel J. Meador, & Maurice Rosenberg, Justice on Appeal 4-7 (1976)[17]
Increases in Workload: The Threat to Function

The performance of both appellate functions [error correcting and law declaring] is now threatened in most American appellate systems by a torrent of appellate business which threatens to engulf existing procedures and institutions. In the federal courts, appellate filings increased 300% (four-fold) from 1961 to 1974. In

---

[17] Copyright © 1976 by West. Reprinted with permission.

California, there was an increase from 3872 in 1964 to 9186 in 1973 . . . Similar increases have been experienced in almost every populous state for which figures are available. [In the federal system and that of many states, growth in appeals continued unrelentingly through the remainder of the 20th century and into the 21st.]

Causation is a complex question. Clearly, much of the increase is explained by the increased availability of legal services to persons convicted of crime, which has produced vast increases in the number of criminal appeals in all systems. There is also some increase attributable to specific substantive developments which have made the courts more hospitable to the assertion of certain kinds of claims; especially in the federal system, but also elsewhere, this kind of growth is most notable in the field of civil rights. In addition, in some classes of cases, there seems to be an increase in the number of appellate filings relative to the number of trial filings . . . Some litigants are less prone to settle or to accept results of trials and more prone to persist in their contentions. In theory, this phenomenon might be attributable to altered social attitudes toward courts and litigation, or perhaps to decreased relative costs, tangible or intangible, in litigating persistently. There is little reason to doubt that there has been some change in social attitudes toward litigation. The society seems to be experiencing a tide of rising expectations or demands which has extended over a period of about two decades. The result is that courts are being asked to resolve not only more numerous, but ever more intricate and ramified disputes involving ever increasing numbers of citizens.

However caused, the great shifts in the practice of lodging appeals . . . has altered the mix and nature of the work. On the one hand, the tremendous increase in the number of criminal appeals does not represent a corresponding increase in the amount of work required of the courts. Criminal appeals tend to be easier to decide, presenting evidence that is less complex, and legal issues which are familiar and less frequently of a type to invoke the "institutional" as distinguished from the "correcting" function of the appellate courts.

On the other hand, there has been a discernible increase in the number of appeals which are exceedingly demanding of the time and talents of appellate judges. Environmental litigation, for example, has a propensity to absorb judicial energy far in excess of the average case. A growing breed of appeals is not of the classic, bipolar mold, with A suing B for damages, divorce, or disseisin, but is polycentric, affecting rights of large groups of people, with many possible outcomes, and requiring assimilation of complex data. In contrast to the criminal appeals, this bulk of new cases creates a workload which is understated by the mere numbers involved.

These heavy increases in workload threaten the ability of the appellate courts to perform their functions. Adequate performance of the correcting function requires personal involvement and attention to detail by the judges which cannot be provided by judges whose attentions and energies are divided among too many cases. In many different ways, a wasting process is set in motion. The process can for the moment be termed a trend toward bureaucratization. Changes which are characteristic of any shift from individually crafted works to mass production methods can be seen to be occurring in appellate processes and institutions. Projected to their conceivable extremes, these changes would leave an appellate process which gives little or no assurance to individual litigants that the appeal has served the correcting function. At the same time, the institutional function is also jeopardized. It is threatened by the rising complexity and political significance of many appellate cases. It is threatened by haste. It is threatened by the growing unconnectedness of lower court judges and administrative agencies who are by degrees cut loose from the increasingly remote and erratic controls of the tribunals which are expected to perform the institutional function. Sheer numbers, both of cases and judges, can ultimately block the channels or lines of command. This leads in the direction of a disintegration of law and its authority . . .

NOTES

1. The following table shows the reversal rates — *i.e.*, the percentage of appeals in which the judgment below is reversed — in cases on appeal in the federal courts of appeals in the years indicated. Notice how in general the reversals declined over the years. Is there some relationship between that development and the rise in the volume of appeals during those years? The second table shows reversal rates in some states.[18] Given the small hope of success on appeal, why do you suppose that litigants continue to appeal in record numbers?

U.S. Courts of Appeals — National Average

Nature of Proceeding	1986	1987	1988	1989	1990
ALL APPEALS	15.5%	13.5%	14.2%	13.8%	12.4%
Criminal	8.8	7.9	8.5	9.3	8.0
U.S. prisoner petitions	12.3	7.6	7.6	5.9	5.6
Other U.S. civil	21.4	22.1	21.6	20.3	17.9
Private prisoner petitions	13.1	9.6	10.2	10.4	9.8
Other private civil	18.7	16.0	17.4	16.4	15.6
Bankruptcy	31.9	17.7	15.7	20.8	18.4
Administrative appeals	11.5	9.6	14.2	14.1	15.1

State Intermediate Courts

State	Reversal Percentage (1990)
Arkansas	9.0%
California	11.6
Connecticut	24.2
Hawaii	28.0
Illinois†	18.6
Iowa	13.7
Kansas	24.0
Maryland	17.3
Missouri	20.0
New Jersey†	18.3
New Mexico	27.8
North Carolina	24.8
Pennsylvania†	15.0
Texas	13.3
Virginia	21.2
Wisconsin	30.3

† Statistics are for the 1989 fiscal or court year.

[18] These two tables are taken from RUGGERO ALDISERT, WINNING ON APPEAL 10-11 (1992).

2. The major impact of growth has been at the intermediate appellate level where the volume is greater than in the top court and where appeals come as a matter of right, with an obligation on the court to decide them. By contrast, in most instances courts of last resort can control their dockets by denying review as a matter of discretion. The decline in the number of cases being decided on the merits by state supreme courts and the rise of petitions for review from 1870 to 1970 are described in Robert Kagan, Bliss Cartwright, Lawrence Friedman, & Stanton Wheeler, *The Evolution of State Supreme Courts*, 76 MICH. L. REV. 961 (1978). The shift from commercial to noncommercial cases in the work of state supreme courts during that period is analyzed in Robert Kagan, Bliss Cartwright, Lawrence Friedman, & Stanton Wheeler, *The Business of State Supreme Courts, 1870-1970*, 30 STAN L. REV. 121 (1977).

V. TRADITIONAL PROCESS AND CONTINUING IMPERATIVES

Until the onset of the "crisis of volume" in the late 1960s, appeals taken as a matter of right to appellate courts in the United States were litigated through what has come to be called the traditional process: briefs for the opposing parties were filed by their lawyers, and the lawyers appeared in person before the judges to present oral argument; the judges conferred on each case, and one of them announced the court's decision in a fully explanatory opinion, which was published in a bound reporter. The extraordinary growth of appeals caused courts to modify that process in novel ways that will be examined hereafter. Those developments set off rising concerns among many lawyers and judges that the appellate process was being compromised and appellate courts were being undesirably transformed. In response to those concerns, in an effort to buttress appellate courts against pressures from the rising tide of appeals, the authors whose writings are excerpted below formulated some "imperatives," observance of which would ensure the preservation of appropriate appellate process and the appellate system, in the face of the crisis of volume. As you proceed through this course, consider whether these imperatives are a *sine qua non* in the appellate world of the 21st century.

Paul D. Carrington, Daniel J. Meador, & Maurice Rosenberg, Justice on Appeal 7-12 (1976)[19]

The Imperatives of Appellate Justice

[The following is a statement of] the characteristics which it is most essential to preserve if the dual functions [of appellate courts] are to be maintained. Some may emanate from a constitutional source. True, the constitutional status of the right to appeal is itself without express support; yet, within many, if not all, the imperatives we shall identify we discern elements of the constitutional concept of due process of law. Whether constitutional or not, they are so linked to the functions of appeal that a failure to observe them will have the effect of robbing appellate litigation of much of its purpose.

---

19 Copyright © 1976 by West. Reprinted with permission.

Despite their importance, we do not present this list of imperatives as rules engraved in stone. The essential qualities of the appeal could be described in different terms. The list might be supplemented in several ways. Some pertain chiefly to the correcting function, some chiefly to the institutional function. The latter, especially, are goals or ideals which can never be fully attained. We present our list of these essential characteristics with all appropriate humility. Such noted thinkers as Karl Llewellyn[20] and Roscoe Pound[21], long ago uttered every pertinent observation we could now advance.[22] Still, the reader is entitled to know what aspects of the matter we think are vital. . . .

1. *Process Imperatives.*

To do appellate justice the courts must be in the charge of judges whose qualities of mind and person, working habits, attitudes and relationships meet uncompromised standards. Adherence to these standards will assure, as nearly as anything can, that the "process imperatives" are vindicated, thereby advancing both the reality and the appearance of appellate justice. The imperatives we speak of are those which assure that an appeal of right is taken to judges who

— are impartial;
— are multi-partite;
— are identifiable, not anonymous, and not mere auxiliaries;
— think individually, but
— act collegially;
— respect the interest of adversaries in being heard, but
— inform themselves fully on the material issues, evidence, and law on which decisions are to be made; and
— announce their reasons for decisions.

The link between most of these imperatives and the functions is self-evident. Indeed, the first two require no discussion here.

The identifiability of appellate judges is perhaps a less familiar ingredient of the quality of justice. Most systems presently safeguard it, but recently developing practices call it into question. We believe it is a necessary assurance of integrity to the process and a bond of faith to defeated litigants, that named judges take personal responsibility for the appellate court's decision. It is not an adequate assurance of correctness if the decision is handed down by a faceless institution. If too many persons are responsible, none are. Moreover, it is an important source of institutional coherence that the judges be known, for this increases the pressure to be consistent and gives lawyers a better opportunity to predict outcomes.

---

[20] [20] See generally his THE COMMON LAW TRADITION — DECIDING APPEALS (1960). Our imperatives bear a partial resemblance to Llewellyn's list of sources of "steadiness." *Id.* at 11-15.

[21] [21] . . . Our imperatives also bear a partial resemblance to some of Pound's *Causes of Popular Dissatisfaction with the Administration of Justice,* 40 Amer. L. Rev. 729 (1906). As others have noted, the dissatisfactions described were more those of Pound himself than of any visible populace.

[22] [22] We do not mean to disparage the efforts of contemporary theorists, from whom we have also learned. E.g., Robert Summers, *Evaluating the Improving Legal Processes — A Plea for "Process Values,"* 60 Cornell L. Rev. 1 (1974).

The imperatives of judicial individuality and collegiality are corollaries to identifiability. There is some tension between these two, but the reconciliation lies in the distinction between deliberating about a case and deciding it. If each judge is effectively to apply a personal imprimatur to the decision, he must have at least the opportunity, and must present the appearance, of doing individual thinking and evaluating. Yet the functions of the appeal are adequately served only if the decision is a joint decision based on shared thinking. It is both a source of institutional coherence and an assurance of correctness that the appellate decision be the result of a collaborative effort. Traditional appellate process in America has assured both imperatives by providing for group deliberation based on independent preparation. A failure to observe either of these twin imperatives is a serious omission. If the judges do not think for themselves, they cannot be fully responsible for the results; and if they do not act together, their decision may be properly viewed simply as an official event, not as a rational process.

The imperatives of hearing the adversaries and becoming fully informed can also be viewed as a pair. The reasons for the adversary tradition require no lengthy elaboration here. Adversarial presentation contributes significantly to the quality of the courts' performance of the institutional function, and is essential to the correcting function. It provides the loser with a measure of satisfaction that is crucial to the success of the legal process as a substitution for disorderly means of dispute resolution. The imperative of full information may serve the correcting function in assuring that serious error is not uncorrected merely because the error goes unnoted by counsel. It is also vital to the institutional function of declaring and harmonizing trial court decisions, a function which importantly affects persons other than the parties. To the extent that this function is being performed by any appellate court, it is the duty of that court to be fully informed as to any information bearing on the law or policy which provides the basis for decision, and to make no decision that is not required by the dispute before it.

The obligation to give reasons is vital to both functions. When reasons are announced and can be weighed, the public can have assurance that the correcting process is working. Announcing reasons can also provide public understanding of how the numerous decisions of the system are integrated. In a busy court, the reasons are an essential demonstration that the court did in fact fix its mind on the case at hand. An unreasoned decision has very little claim to acceptance by the defeated party, and is difficult or impossible to accept as an act reflecting systematic application of legal principles. Moreover, the necessity of stating reasons not infrequently changes the results by forcing the judges to come to grips with nettlesome facts or issues which their normal instincts would otherwise cause them to avoid.

Taken together, these imperatives require a process which can perhaps be succinctly described as visibly rational. Their importance can be emphasized by considering the futility of a process which fails to observe them. If the judges do not perform by a process which is visibly rational, they may as well abandon the enterprise and leave the litigants as they are found after trial courts and administrative agencies have made their decisions. The burden and expense of the appeal are not justified if these imperatives are not observed.

2. *Systemic Imperatives.*

A second set of imperatives pertains less to the way in which the judges make their decisions and more to the way in which the judicial system functions. If the purposes of an appeal are to be achieved, the system must provide

— uniform and coherent enunciation and application of the law;
— decisions that are expeditious, involving as few steps as possible;
— working conditions for judges which attract lawyers of high quality, who command professional respect; and
— working conditions for judges which will foster their humane concern for individual litigants.

These imperatives are ideals, in a sense, which can never be fully or totally secured. What is imperative is the need to maintain the pursuit of these goals. For example, uniformity of decisions is not attainable. Perfection would require that all legal decisions be made by one ageless being who forgot nothing and never changed his or her mind, whatever the influences of advocacy or external reality. We would not want that much perfection if we could attain it. Indeed, it would conflict with other imperatives which assume some human interaction. What is nevertheless important is the striving for uniformity. A legal system which tolerates needless disuniformity and incoherence is not keeping faith with those who are subject to its dominion, for it has forsaken its commitment to even-handed decision-making.

Without attempting a full elaboration of these systemic imperatives, we pause to emphasize the pervasive importance we assign to judicial working conditions. If the office of appellate judge is so organized that the person occupying it is discouraged and hindered by haste and competing demands from facing litigants individually, one at a time, as fellow beings, the other imperatives are also lost. Few individuals who are capable of performing the appellate functions will be willing to serve, and those who do will soon despair and grow in cynicism. Although the appellate process is steeped in tradition, its integrity and idealism are in fact quite fragile. It is an easy thing for judges who are too busy or too uncaring to disregard the values of the system. It is the responsibility of legislators and others overseeing our judicial institutions to maintain them in a manner which will reinforce the best professional instincts of the judges and dissuade them from an easy lapse into practices which discard the imperatives and impair the functions of appellate justice.

One could quite properly add to this list the requirement that the judges be persons of attainment and integrity. In omitting the personal qualities of the judges from our list, we do not mean to suggest that these are less important. Quite the contrary. We heartily subscribe to the principle of merit selection of appellate judges. But the meaning of merit and the processes by which merit might be identified are subjects for another book . . . [Those subjects are treated in Chapter 11, *infra.*]

NOTES

1. These imperatives will be revisited in the course ahead as we evaluate the changes in the appellate world that are studied in Chapters 6, 7, 8, and 9. Students therefore should get them firmly in mind at this point. The question

to be considered in connection with each change made in response to the growth in appeals is whether the change is compatible with the imperatives or whether the imperatives themselves need modification in light of contemporary circumstances.

2. Procedure in every appellate court is governed by rules promulgated by the court or by a combination of court-promulgated rules and statutes. For an illustration of such rules, *see* the Federal Rules of Appellate Procedure, issued by the Supreme Court to govern procedure in the U. S. courts of appeals. Rules such as those govern the actions of parties and counsel. In addition to those rules, courts in recent decades have begun to publish "internal operating procedures," describing the various ways in which the judges and their staffs process appeals, ways that differ from the traditional process, as will be examined in Chapter 8.

VI. A WORD TO LAW STUDENTS: THIS COURSE AND "REAL WORLD" CONCERNS

ROBERT L. STERN, APPELLATE PRACTICE IN THE UNITED STATES 1 (2D ED. 1989)[23]

The Relationship Between Appellate Court Administration and Appellate Practice

What lawyers must and should do in appellate courts can best be understood if they know how and why those courts function as they do. Thus, the differences between an ordinary brief and a petition for review or certiorari become intelligible in the light of the reasons for a two-court appellate structure and of the workload confronting the highest court. The way in which a record or appendix must be prepared for an appellate court, the number of copies required, and the time when it must be filed reflect the use the judges will make of it. How a brief should be written depends on what function it serves, and on how much and what the judges, staff attorneys, or law clerks reading it know about the record as well as the law. How a case should be argued, and even whether it will be argued, depends upon the extent to which the judges, or some of them, have read the briefs or record prior to the argument (and how much time they can devote to such reading), the time allowed for arguing, and the proclivity of the judges to question counsel at length. All of this may depend to a large extent on the size of the court's workload.

Knowledge of the structure of the appellate courts in a jurisdiction and, to some extent, of the courts' internal workings will accordingly provide a useful prologue to the treatment of procedural problems and requirements.

NOTES

1. The late 20th century growth in appellate litigation has focused attention on appellate courts as never before. Not surprisingly, those most concerned with this development have been the judges of those courts, the individuals who must bear the brunt of the ever-rising tide of appeals. Appellate judges

---

23 Copyright © 1989 by Bureau of National Affairs. All Rights Reserved. Reprinted with permission.

have become more aware than ever of the importance of good advocacy on the part of lawyers appearing before them. These judges are under constant pressure to decide appeals expeditiously, avoiding unacceptable backlogs, and they want as much help as possible from the parties' lawyers. A belief has developed, now widespread among appellate judges, that the quality of work being done by appellate lawyers is not what it should be. The lawyers' shortcomings have in turn been blamed to a large extent on American law schools.

These concerns led the Appellate Judges Conference of the American Bar Association (the nationwide organization of state and federal appellate judges) to appoint a special committee to study the matter and prepare a report. The committee's report was adopted by the Conference in 1985. *See Appellate Litigation Skills Training: The Role of the Law Schools*, 54 U. CIN. L. REV. 129 (1985). That report correctly pointed out that law schools generally do not provide substantial training in the procedure and skills involved in appellate practice. Such lack of training stands in contrast to the significant training opportunities in trial practice provided to most law students. The report recommended that the law schools do much more on appellate practice, and it set forth specific steps to be taken to that end.

Going beyond skills training, the report echoed what is said in the Preface to this book:

Looking first at the appellate court as an institution, it would be a reasonable assumption that because the textual substance of most law school courses is made up of appellate court opinions, an examination of appellate courts — their history, structure, function, jurisdiction, and operating procedures — would occupy an important place in the law school curriculum. The reality is, however, completely to the contrary. Other than the attention given to the United States Supreme Court in federal jurisdiction and in the judicial review portion of the typical constitutional law course, the appellate court as an institution and its relationship to the trial court is almost completely ignored in the normal law school curriculum. This is unfortunate because a lawyer cannot be a competent litigator unless he possesses this basic knowledge about the appellate court and understands its relationship to successful litigation at both the trial and appellate level[s]. Fundamental questions such as the functions of the appellate court (error correction and law development), the goal of the appellate judge (to do justice between the parties in accordance with law), and the difference in functions between an intermediate appellate court and a supreme court are ignored in the education of most law students. Similarly overlooked except in a few civil procedure casebooks are issues concerning the jurisdiction of appellate courts and the difference between the right to appeal and discretionary review.

2. The competent appellate litigator must be cognizant of the "crisis of volume" that has been caused by the dramatic increase in the number of appeals in both federal and state appellate courts in the past 40 years. The impact upon appellate practice and procedure has been so great that there is little relationship between the appellate process in the early 21st century and that of only a few decades ago. Any sound program in appellate courts must

introduce students to these dramatic changes, their effect on appellate practice today, and the effect they are likely to have in the future.

This course should do much to overcome the deficiencies in legal education decried by the ABA report. However, it does not purport to do all that is recommended in the area of skills training. The next three chapters do address some intensely practical (as well as theoretically significant) doctrines and procedures, understanding of which is crucial to effective and competent appellate lawyering. Moreover, in Chapter 10 we explore practical implications of the crisis of volume on the work of appellate advocates. But the primary concerns of this course are not with skills training of the sort envisioned in the ABA report. This is not to say that those matters are unimportant or that they should not be dealt with in the law schools through appropriate courses and clinical programs. It is only to say that they do not form a primary theme of this course.

This course is a study of American appellate courts as key institutions of government and as major elements in our judicial systems. The theory of the course is that an awareness of these courts' structures, functions, processes, and personnel is as essential to appellate advocacy as is knowledge of such "real world" matters as how to file a notice of appeal, how to prepare the record, how to write a brief, and so on. The course is premised on the belief that training in such skills without a thorough understanding of the material embraced here would not likely produce a first-rate appellate advocate and would certainly not produce the kind of enlightened citizen-lawyer who can contribute constructively to the never-ending task of maintaining an effective judiciary in ever-changing times.

Chapter 2

APPELLATE REVIEW: WHEN, HOW, WHERE, FOR WHOM, AND FOR WHAT ISSUES

As institutions of governance in the American legal order, appellate courts perform two functions, often simultaneously. As pointed out earlier, they review lower court decisions to correct harmful errors, and they articulate and generate substantive legal rules. This latter, lawmaking role, often referred to as "institutional review," is the result of the common-law style of adjudication, combined with the doctrine of *stare decisis*. Chapter IV explores some aspects of that significant appellate function. A large part of appellate work, however, contributes little or nothing to legal doctrine. In that aspect of their work the appellate courts are simply keeping the trial courts in line, ensuring that the various trial forums in their domain are correctly applying procedural rules and substantive doctrine. If less glamorous and intellectually exciting than shaping the *corpus juris*, this error-correcting function is no less important to the sound administration of justice.

Whether it is to engage in error-correcting or lawmaking or both, an appellate court can be activated only pursuant to a rather elaborate array of rules deriving from statutes, court-made doctrines, written rules of procedure, or some combination of these. This technically intricate body of law governs access to the appellate courts, determining when, how, where, by whom, and as to what issues, appellate authority can be invoked. It also determines the relationship between trial and appellate courts, defining the circumstances under which and the extent to which the latter may interfere with the actions of the former. Lawyers must understand the rules that govern this process in order to know the circumstances under which they, on behalf of their clients, can pursue litigation at the appellate level to try to obtain redress from adverse trial court actions. Appellate judges must know these rules in order to function within the limits of their lawful authority. This chapter surveys these rules.

As a preliminary matter, however, it is worthwhile for you to recognize that there exist post-trial attacks on judgments that do not fall under the rubric of appeals. Read Federal Rules of Civil Procedure 50, 59, and 60 to see what each of them permits a litigant to do. Each of these mechanisms has an analogue in state court systems. They allow litigants to seek judgment as a matter of law (which in many state systems is called a motion notwithstanding the verdict, in Latin a judgment "non obstante verdicto" or "jnov"), or a new trial, or relief from the judgment for a variety of reasons. They are not appeals. They contemplate motions that are directed to the trial judge, and are made available to avoid appeals when the trial judge recognizes that errors were made that entitle the losing party to judgment in its favor or at least to a new trial. An additional procedure for attacking a judgment is a "collateral attack." The circumstances in which collateral attacks are available are quite limited. They generally are available only for violations of constitutional rights that a litigant had no opportunity to raise in the earlier proceeding. You may recall from your Civil Procedure course that a defendant who altogether fails to appear and who suffers a default judgment may collaterally attack the judgment for lack of personal jurisdiction (for example, when an effort is made to enforce the judgment). This too is a post-trial attack on a judgment through a means other than an appeal.

A second preliminary matter is this: To have any chance of succeeding on an appeal, a trial attorney ordinarily will have had to properly preserve the error he asserts on appeal. There are a few kinds of matters that an appellate court will entertain even if no objection was raised in the trial court; some it will even raise *sua sponte* (on its own motion). Appellate courts have a duty to raise issues of their own subject-matter jurisdiction and that of the lower court, and "plain error" is an exception to the requirement that an error have been raised and properly preserved below. On occasion, courts may make other exceptions, but, in general, attorneys must raise an issue in the trial court, and sometimes take specific steps indicated in common law and in codified rules such as the applicable rules of civil procedure and of evidence, to make that issue eligible for consideration by the appeals court. Examples of such codified rules are Federal Rule of Evidence 103 (concerning rulings on evidence), and Federal Rule of Civil Procedure 51 (concerning the preservation of claims of error as to jury instructions); of course, state courts have their own sets of rules. When an attorney has properly preserved error in the trial court, the attorney handling the appeal has to take care not to waive error in the appeals process. But more on this in Chapter 3. Unless indicated otherwise in the remainder of this book, we have assumed that errors have been properly preserved.

I. CONSTITUTIONAL AND STATUTORY BASES OF APPELLATE JURISDICTION

In any court system, federal or state, appellate courts can exist only if the system's constitution directly creates them and establishes their jurisdiction or if the system's constitution permits or requires the legislature to create appellate courts and to determine their jurisdiction. To some extent the "rules" determining when, how, where, by whom and as to what issues appellate power may be brought into play are regarded as matters of appellate jurisdiction. To the extent these matters ultimately are up to the legislature to control, they can be altered to meet the changing needs of a judicial system.

As one example — an example that has been replicated to varying degrees by the states — let us consider how the federal court system operates. Read Article III, Sections 1 and 2 of the Constitution, and 28 U.S.C. §§ 1291 and 1292, which are the primary statutes in which Congress created and conferred appellate jurisdiction upon intermediate federal courts. Scholars have long debated questions such as whether Congress was required to create these lower federal courts and, if so, what kinds of cases those courts had to be empowered to entertain. Related questions persist as to whether there are any limits on the power of Congress to abolish federal appellate courts or federal district courts, or more realistically, to curtail their jurisdiction in particular ways.

The view that Congress has broad authority to limit the jurisdiction of the federal courts drew early support from the case of *Sheldon v. Sill*, 49 U.S.

(8 How.) 441 (1850). It posed the question whether Congress could restrict diversity jurisdiction by denying such jurisdiction when a debt had been assigned and a suit upon the debt could not properly have been brought to federal court absent the assignment. Upholding the jurisdiction-restricting statute, the Court declared that

> if the Constitution had ordained and established the inferior courts, and distributed to them their respective powers, they could not be restricted or divested by Congress. But as it has made no such distribution, one of two consequences must result, — either that each inferior court created by Congress must exercise all the judicial powers not given to the Supreme Court, or that Congress, having the power to establish the courts, must define their respective jurisdictions. The first of these inferences has never been asserted, and could not be defended with any show of reason, and if not, the latter would seem to follow as a necessary consequence. And it would seem to follow, also, that, having a right to prescribe, Congress may withhold from any court of its creation jurisdiction of any of the enumerated controversies. Courts created by statute can have no jurisdiction but such as the statute confers.

Shortly thereafter, in *Ex parte McCardle*, 74 U.S. (7 Wall.) 506 (1869), the Court upheld a congressional statute that expressly repealed the portion of a federal statute that had conferred on the Supreme Court authority to hear appeals from federal circuit courts in actions for writs of habeas corpus.

The Court has upheld restrictions on federal jurisdiction in more recent cases as well, including one in which Congress had provided that government price controls could be challenged only by filing a protest with a designated Administrator, with appeals to a three-judge Emergency Court of Appeals. No federal court other than the Supreme Court had authority to determine the validity of a price control regulation or to grant relief. *Lockerty v. Phillips*, 319 U.S. 182 (1943). Although the Court has on a number of occasions construed statutes so that they did not foreclose all judicial review, and although scholars have offered a variety of theories that would limit Congress's authority to restrict the jurisdiction of the federal courts, the parameters of Congress's power remain unclear.

You may have the opportunity to further explore these issues elsewhere in the law school curriculum, particularly in a Federal Courts or Constitutional Law course. These issues are introduced here because they are relevant to our course in a number of respects. First, since, as a matter of congressional statute, the federal appellate courts can hear only cases that come up from the federal district courts, any restrictions on the subject-matter jurisdiction of the district courts have implications for the jurisdiction of the federal appellate courts. Second, as subordinate federal courts themselves, federal courts of appeals are courts whose jurisdiction Congress can control. Although the Congressional statutes that currently govern the jurisdiction of federal appellate courts are broad in scope, it is important for you to realize that Congress has the authority to restrict that jurisdiction, subject to few and ill-defined constitutional limitations. As recently as 2004, a measure was proposed in Congress that would have barred federal courts, including the Supreme Court, from hearing cases concerning the Defense of Marriage Act. Awareness of this Congressional power is a necessary backdrop for the occasions when we will discuss potential reforms to the federal appellate system that would entail re-structuring it. Most immediately, because a number of the aspects of the federal appeals courts' operations are deemed to be matters of jurisdiction, you should understand the degree to which the decisions on these matters are legislatively controlled.

Similar generalizations could be made about state judicial systems, although the details of their architecture, what is compelled by state constitutions, what is left to state legislatures to decide, and what aspects of the functioning of state appellate courts are deemed to be jurisdictional, vary among the states.

II. MOOTNESS AS A LIMIT ON APPEALABILITY

Article III's "case or controversy" requirement imposes constraints on the matters that federal courts can hear. Some of these requirements bear only on what can be heard by the district courts. For example, the requirement that a dispute be "ripe" for adjudication has no application at the appellate level, where the appropriate question instead is appealability. *See United States v. Jose*, 519 U.S. 54, 57 (1996) (per curiam) (noting that "[f]inality, not ripeness, is the doctrine governing appeals from district court to court of appeals"). Of course, appellate courts may be asked to review whether plaintiffs had standing to sue, whether a dispute was ripe, and whether hearing a case violates the prohibition against hearing nonjusticiable "political questions," but all those are issues that arise at the district court level. Other Article III issues may arise, or can arise, only in the courts of appeals. Section V of this chapter will consider standing to appeal or to be a proper appellee. Now, we touch upon the mootness doctrine (also an aspect of justiciability) which applies to the district courts but also to courts higher in the judicial hierarchy, where the issue will arise for the first time if a case arguably becomes moot while on appeal. Mootness relates to the timing of review in the sense that, in order to obtain an appellate decision, one must take and complete the appeal while the issues remain alive and the parties continue to have a legally cognizable interest in the outcome. If no party argues that a case has become moot, the appellate court must raise the issue itself, and if the court holds that a case has become moot — even while on appeal — the appellate court must dismiss the appeal without deciding the issues it raised. The court also may vacate the judgment and the decisions that were entered by the lower court or courts.

LEWIS v. CONTINENTAL BANK CORPORATION
494 U.S. 472 (1990)

JUSTICE SCALIA delivered the opinion of the Court.

. . .

Under Article III of the Constitution, federal courts may adjudicate only actual, ongoing cases or controversies. To invoke the jurisdiction of a federal court, a litigant must have suffered, or be threatened with, an actual injury traceable to the defendant and likely to be redressed by a favorable judicial decision. Article III denies federal courts the power "to decide questions that cannot affect the rights of litigants in the case before them," and confines them to resolving "'real and substantial controvers[ies] admitting of specific relief through a decree of a conclusive character, as distinguished from an opinion advising what the law would be upon a hypothetical state of facts.'" This case-or-controversy requirement subsists through all stages of federal judicial proceedings, trial and appellate. To sustain our jurisdiction in the present case, it is not enough that a dispute was very much alive when suit was filed, or when review was obtained in the Court of Appeals. The parties must continue to have a "'personal stake in the outcome'" of the lawsuit.

PRINCETON UNIVERSITY v. SCHMID
455 U.S. 100 (1982)

PER CURIAM

Appellee Schmid was arrested and charged with criminal trespass while distributing political materials on the campus of Princeton University. Schmid was not a student at Princeton University. Under University regulations then in effect, members of the public who wished to distribute materials on the campus were required to receive permission from University officials. Appellee was tried in Princeton Borough Municipal Court and . . . the trial judge issued an opinion convicting appellee and fining him $15 plus $10 costs. A *de novo* trial in the New Jersey Superior Court, Law Division, also resulted in conviction and the same fine was imposed. While appeal was pending to the Superior Court, Appellate Division, the case was certified for review by the New Jersey Supreme Court. That court invited the University to intervene and participate as a party, which it did.

The New Jersey Supreme Court reversed the judgment of conviction, holding that appellee's rights of speech and assembly under the New Jersey Constitution had been violated. The University filed a notice of appeal. . . . Its claim is that the judgment below deprives it of its rights under the First, Fifth, and Fourteenth Amendments of the United States Constitution. The State of New Jersey . . . joined in [the jurisdictional statement] of the University. We . . . now dismiss the appeal for want of jurisdiction.

. . .

The State of New Jersey has filed a brief in this Court asking us to review and decide the issues presented, but stating that it "deems it neither necessary nor appropriate to express an opinion on the merits of the respective positions of the private parties to this action." Had the University not been a party to this case in the New Jersey Supreme Court and had the State filed a jurisdictional statement urging reversal, the existence of a case or controversy — and of jurisdiction in this Court — could not be doubted. However, if the State were the sole appellant and its jurisdictional statement simply asked for review and declined to take a position on the merits, we would have dismissed the appeal for want of a case or controversy. We do not sit to decide hypothetical issues or to give advisory opinions about issues as to which there are not adverse parties before us. . . .

Princeton defends its own standing and our jurisdiction on the grounds that it was a party to the case in the New Jersey Supreme Court, that it is bound by the judgment of that court with respect to the validity of its regulations, and that no other forum is available in which to challenge the judgment on federal constitutional grounds. We have determined, however, that we lack jurisdiction with respect to Princeton. The New Jersey Supreme Court noted that while the case was pending on appeal, the University substantially amended its regulations governing solicitation, distribution of literature, and similar activities on University property by those not affiliated with the University. The opinion below rested on the absence of a reasonable regulatory scheme governing expressional activity on University property, but the regulation at issue is no longer in force. Furthermore, the lower court's opinion was careful not to pass on the validity of the revised regulation under either the Federal or the State Constitution. Thus the issue of the validity of the old regulation is moot, for this case has "lost its character as a present, live controversy of the kind that must exist if we are to avoid advisory opinions on abstract questions of law."

Princeton does not claim standing on the ground that a private party may intervene and challenge the reversal of a criminal conviction of another party. Its alleged standing in this Court rests on its claim that the judgment below would be res judicata against it and that it has thus finally been deprived of the authority to enforce the regulation as it stood prior to amendment. Since the judgment, however, does not prevent it from having the validity of its new regulation ruled upon in another enforcement action, the University is without standing to invoke our jurisdiction. Accordingly, we dismiss the appeal.

So ordered.

JUSTICE BRENAN took no part in the consideration or decision of this case.

NOTES

1. *Schmid* is somewhat unusual in that it was a three-cornered dispute. Had the State sought to challenge the adverse decision of the New Jersey Supreme Court, could it have done so, or was its dispute with the criminal defendant also moot as a result of the University having abrogated the regulations in question in the litigation?

2. Some Justices of the Supreme Court and some commentators have questioned whether mootness doctrine truly is compelled by Article III. *See, e.g.*, *Honig v. Doe*, 484 U.S. 305, 329 (1988) (Rehnquist, J., concurring). And Chief Justice Rehnquist proposed that the Court decide cases that become moot after the grant of certiorari in order to avoid wasting Court resources and to fully utilize the opportunity to bind all other U.S. courts by its decisions. *Id* at 329-32. Justice Scalia, by contrast, does not see how the Court can ignore the impediment of mootness for purposes of its own appellate review without affecting the principles that govern lower federal courts in their assertions and retentions of jurisdiction. *Id* at 341-42. (Scalia, J., dissenting). Do you think a principled distinction can be made between the limitations that mootness doctrine imposes on the intermediate federal appellate courts and those it imposes on the Supreme Court?

3. State courts also have justiciability doctrines, including mootness doctrines, although state courts are not bound by Article III. As a result, they too

may face situations in which cases have become moot while on appeal, and have to dismiss those cases. For example, in *Liner v. Jafco, Inc.,* 375 U.S. 301 (1964), a Tennessee court enjoined labor picketing at a construction site. While the state court appeal of that injunction was pending, the construction project was completed, and the state appellate court found the appeal moot. An interesting wrinkle here was that the United States Supreme Court found the case justiciable under federal standards because of the financial consequences of the injunction. The Court reversed, holding that the injunction had been improperly issued. In a subsequent case, *Village of Arlington Heights v. Metropolitan Housing Development Corp.,* 429 U.S. 252 (1977), the Court held that a state court is not required to decide a federal issue if the dispute in which it is embedded does not satisfy the state court's justiciability rules. *See* William A. Fletcher, *The "Case or Controversy" Requirement in State Court Adjudication of Federal Questions,* 78 CAL. L. REV. 263 (1990) (arguing that this was "the wrong answer"). Fletcher notes, however, that state courts rarely employ a more stringent "case or controversy" requirement than the federal courts, so they rarely decline, on justiciability grounds, to decide a dispute that federal courts could have decided.

4. The mootness doctrine has particular complexity in the context of class actions. The *Geraghty* case that follows both describes a number of the Supreme Court's decisions in this area of law and illustrates the unusual manner in which the Court interprets and applies the concept of "personal stake" in class actions.

UNITED STATES PAROLE COMMISSION v. GERAGHTY
445 U.S. 388 (1980)

MR. JUSTICE BLACKMUN delivered the opinion of the Court.

This case raises the question whether a trial court's denial of a motion for certification of a class may be reviewed on appeal after the named plaintiff's personal claim has become "moot." . . .

[Respondent Geraghty commenced a civil suit, as a class action, challenging parole release guidelines as inconsistent with the statute under which they were purportedly issued and with the Constitution. He sought certification of a class of "all federal prisoners who are or will become eligible for release on parole." The district court eventually denied the request for class certification and granted summary judgment to the Parole Commission on all Geraghty's claims. Geraghty appealed both individually and on behalf of the class he had proposed. Before any brief was filed in the court of appeals, Geraghty was released from prison. The Parole Commission then moved to dismiss the appeal as moot.]

II

. . . [M]ootness has two aspects: "when the issues presented are no longer 'live' or the parties lack a legally cognizable interest in the outcome." *Powell v. McCormack,* 395 U.S. 486, 489 (1969).

It is clear that the controversy over the validity of the Parole Release Guidelines is still a "live" one between petitioners and at least some members of the class respondent seeks to represent. This is demonstrated by the fact that prisoners currently affected by the guidelines have moved to be substituted, or to intervene, as "named" respondents in this Court. We therefore are concerned here with the second aspect of mootness, that is, the parties' interest in the litigation. The Court has referred to this concept as the "personal stake" requirement.

The personal-stake requirement relates to the first purpose of the case-or-controversy doctrine — limiting judicial power to disputes capable of judicial resolution. . . .

The "personal stake" aspect of mootness doctrine also serves primarily the purpose of assuring that federal courts are presented with disputes they are capable of resolving. One commentator has defined mootness as "the doctrine of standing set in a time frame: The requisite personal interest that must exist at the commencement of the litigation (standing) must continue throughout its existence (mootness)." [Henry Paul] Monaghan, *Constitutional Adjudication: The Who and When*, 82 YALE L. J. 1363, 1384 (1973).

III

On several occasions the Court has considered the application of the "personal stake" requirement in the class-action context. In *Sosna v. Iowa*, 419 U.S. 393 (1975), it held that mootness of the named plaintiff's individual claim *after* a class has been duly certified does not render the action moot. It reasoned that "even though appellees . . . might not again enforce the Iowa durational residency requirement against [the class representative], it is clear that they will enforce it against those persons in the class that appellant sought to represent and that the District Court certified."

. . . When the claim on the merits is "capable of repetition, yet evading review," the named plaintiff may litigate the class certification issue despite loss of his personal stake in the outcome of the litigation. *E.g., Gerstein v. Pugh*, 420 U.S. 103, 110, n. 11 (1975). . . . Since the litigant faces some likelihood of becoming involved in the same controversy in the future, vigorous advocacy can be expected to continue.

In two different contexts the Court has stated that the proposed class representative who proceeds to a judgment on the merits may appeal *denial* of class certification. . . . And today, the Court holds that named plaintiffs whose claims are satisfied through entry of judgment over their objections may appeal the denial of a class certification ruling. *Deposit Guaranty Nat. Bank* v. *Roper*, [445 U.S. 326 (1980)].

Gerstein, McDonald, and *Roper* are all examples of cases found not to be moot, despite the loss of a "personal stake" in the merits of the litigation by the proposed class representative. . . . [A]fter judgment had been entered in their favor, the named plaintiffs in *McDonald* had no continuing narrow personal stake in the outcome of the class claims. And in *Roper* the Court points out that an individual controversy is rendered moot, in the strict Art. III sense, by payment and satisfaction of a final judgment.

These cases demonstrate the flexible character of the Art. III mootness doctrine. . . .

IV

. . . Geraghty's "personal stake" in the outcome of the litigation is, in a practical sense, no different from that of the putative class representatives in *Roper*. Further, the opinion in *Roper* indicates that the approach to take in applying Art. III is issue by issue. . . . We can assume that a district court's final judgment fully satisfying named plaintiffs' private substantive claims would preclude their appeal on that aspect of the final judgment; however, it does not follow that this circumstance would terminate the named plaintiffs' right to take an appeal on the issue of class certification." *Ante*, at 333. . . .

Similarly, the fact that a named plaintiff's substantive claims are mooted due to an occurrence other than a judgment on the merits does not mean that all the other issues in the case are mooted. A plaintiff who brings a class action presents two separate issues for judicial resolution. One is the claim on the merits; the other is the claim that he is entitled to represent a class. "The denial of class certification stands as an adjudication of one of the issues litigated," *Roper, ante*, at 336. We think that in determining whether the plaintiff may continue to press the class certification claim, after the claim on the merits "expires," we must look to the nature of the "personal stake" in the class certification claim. Determining Art. III's "uncertain and shifting contours," see *Flast v. Cohen*, 392 U.S. at 97, with respect to nontraditional forms of litigation, such as the class action, requires reference to the purposes of the case-or-controversy requirement.

Application of the personal-stake requirement to a procedural claim, such as the right to represent a class, is not automatic or readily resolved. A "legally cognizable interest" . . . in the traditional sense rarely ever exists with respect to the class certification claim. . . . Although the named representative receives certain benefits from the class nature of the action, some of which are regarded as desirable and others as less so, these benefits generally are by-products of the class-action device. In order to achieve the primary benefits of class suits, the Federal Rules of Civil Procedure give the proposed class representative the right to have a class certified if the requirements of the Rules are met. This "right" is more analogous to the private attorney general concept than to the type of interest traditionally thought to satisfy the "personal stake" requirement. See *Roper, ante*, at 338.

As noted above, the purpose of the "personal stake" requirement is to assure that the case is in a form capable of judicial resolution. The imperatives of a dispute capable of judicial resolution are sharply presented issues in a concrete factual setting and self-interested parties vigorously advocating opposing positions. . . . We conclude that these elements can exist with respect to the class certification issue notwithstanding the fact that the named plaintiff's claim on the merits has expired. The question whether class certification is appropriate remains as a concrete, sharply presented issue. In *Sosna* v. *Iowa* it was recognized that a named plaintiff whose claim on the merits expires *after* class certification may still adequately represent the class. Implicit in that decision was the determination that vigorous advocacy can be assured through means other than the traditional requirement of a "personal stake in the outcome." Respondent here continues vigorously to advocate his right to have a class certified.

We therefore hold that an action brought on behalf of a class does not become moot upon expiration of the named plaintiff's substantive claim, even though class certification has been denied. The proposed representative retains a "personal stake" in obtaining class certification sufficient to assure that Art. III values are not undermined. If the appeal results in reversal of the class certification denial, and a class subsequently is properly certified, the merits of the class claim then may be adjudicated pursuant to the holding in *Sosna*.

Our holding is limited to the appeal of the denial of the class certification motion. A named plaintiff whose claim expires may not continue to press the appeal on the merits until a class has been properly certified. See *Roper, ante*, at 336-337. If, on appeal, it is determined that class certification properly was denied, the claim on the merits must be dismissed as moot.

Our conclusion that the controversy here is not moot does not automatically establish that the named plaintiff is entitled to continue litigating the interests of the class. "[It] does shift the focus of examination from the elements of justiciability to the ability of the named representative to 'fairly and adequately protect the interests of the class.' Rule 23 (a)." . . . We hold only that a case or controversy still exists. The question of who is to represent the class is a separate issue.

We need not decide here whether Geraghty is a proper representative for the purpose of representing the class on the merits. No class as yet has been certified. Upon remand, the District Court can determine whether Geraghty may continue to press the class claims or whether another representative would be appropriate. We decide only that Geraghty was a proper representative for the purpose of appealing the ruling denying certification of the class that he initially defined. Thus, it was not improper for the Court of Appeals to consider whether the District Court should have granted class certification. . . .

NOTES

1. *Geraghty* illustrates how mootness doctrine operates differently in the class action context than it does in suits by individuals solely on their own behalf. Is the Court's reasoning persuasive? Is the outcome desirable? Is your view influenced by knowing that although class members may intervene to appeal a denial of class certification, class members may have been given no notice of the action purportedly brought on their behalf, no notice that class certification was denied, and no notice of the mootness of the representative party's claim?

2. A very different situation is presented when, after commencement of a class action, an event occurs that prevents relief from being granted to any of the named representatives and any member of the proposed class. Then, the entire action will be dismissed as moot.

U. S. BANCORP MORTGAGE COMPANY v. BONNER MALL PARTNERSHIP
513 U.S. 18 (1994)

SCALIA, J., delivered the opinion for a unanimous Court.

The question in this case is whether appellate courts in the federal system should vacate civil judgments of subordinate courts in cases that are settled after appeal is filed or certiorari sought. [Bancorp held a mortgage on property owned by the Bonner Mall Partnership. After the bank sought to foreclose on the property, the Partnership declared bankruptcy, and the Court granted certiorari and received briefing on the merits of their dispute, the parties stipulated to a consensual plan of reorganization which, they agreed, constituted a settlement that mooted the case. Bancorp, however, asked the Court to exercise its statutory power to vacate the judgment of the Court of Appeals. Bonner opposed the motion.]

II

Respondent questions our power to entertain petitioner's motion to vacate, suggesting that the limitations on the judicial power conferred by Article III, see U.S. Const., Art. III, § 1, "may, at least in some cases, *prohibit* an act of vacatur when no live dispute exists due to a settlement that has rendered a case moot."

The statute that supplies the power of vacatur provides:

> "The Supreme Court or any other court of appellate jurisdiction may affirm, modify, vacate, set aside or reverse any judgment, decree, or order of a court lawfully brought before it for review, and may remand the cause and direct the entry of such appropriate judgment, decree, or order, or require such further proceedings to be had as may be just under the circumstances." 28 U.S.C. § 2106.

Of course, no statute could authorize a federal court to decide the merits of a legal question not posed in an Article III case or controversy. For that purpose, a case must exist at all the stages of appellate review. But reason and authority refute the quite different notion that a federal appellate court may not take any action with regard to a piece of litigation once it has been determined that the requirements of Article III no longer are (or indeed never were) met. That proposition is contradicted whenever an appellate court holds that a district court lacked Article III jurisdiction in the first instance, vacates the decision, and remands with directions to dismiss. In cases that become moot while awaiting review, respondent's logic would hold the Court powerless to award costs, or even to enter an order of dismissal.

Article III does not prescribe such paralysis. "If a judgment has become moot [while awaiting review], this Court may not consider its merits, but may make such disposition of the whole case as justice may require." *Walling v. James V. Reuter, Inc.*, 321 U.S. 671, 677 (1944). As with other matters of judicial administration and practice "reasonably ancillary to the primary, dispute-deciding function" of the federal courts, *Chandler v. Judicial Council of Tenth Circuit*, 398 U.S. 74, 111 (1970) (Harlan, J., concurring in denial of writ), Congress may authorize us to enter orders necessary and appropriate to the final disposition of a suit that is before us for review.

III

The leading case on vacatur is *United States v. Munsingwear, Inc.*, 340 U.S. 36 (1950), in which the United States sought injunctive and monetary relief for violation of a price control regulation. The damages claim was held in abeyance pending a decision on the injunction. The District Court held that the respondent's prices complied with the regulations and dismissed the complaint. While the United States' appeal was pending, the commodity at issue was decontrolled; at the respondent's request, the case was dismissed as moot, a disposition in which the United States acquiesced. The respondent then obtained dismissal of the damages action on the ground of res judicata, and we took the case to review that ruling. The United States protested the unfairness of according preclusive effect to a decision that it had tried to appeal but could not. We saw no such unfairness, reasoning that the United States should have asked the Court of Appeals to vacate the District Court's decision before the appeal was dismissed. We stated that "the established practice of the Court in dealing with a civil case from a court in the federal system which has become moot while on its way here or pending our decision on the merits is to reverse or vacate the judgment below and remand with a direction to dismiss." *Id.* at 39. We explained that vacatur "clears the path for future relitigation of the issues between the parties and eliminates a judgment, review of which was prevented through happenstance." *Id.* at 40. Finding that the United States had "slept on its rights," *id.* at 41, we affirmed.

The parties in the present case agree that vacatur must be decreed for those judgments whose review is, in the words of *Munsingwear*, "prevented through happenstance" — that is to say, where a controversy presented for review has "become moot due to circumstances unattributable to any of the parties." *Karcher v. May*, 484 U.S. 72, 82, 83 (1987). They also agree that vacatur must be granted where mootness results from the unilateral action of the party who prevailed in the lower court. The contested question is whether courts should vacate where mootness results from a settlement. . . .

The principles that have always been implicit in our treatment of moot cases counsel against extending *Munsingwear* to settlement. From the beginning we have disposed of moot cases in the manner "'most consonant to justice' . . . in view of the nature and character of the conditions which have caused the case to become moot." *United States v. Hamburg-Amerikanische Packetfahrt-Actien Gesellschaft*, 239 U.S. 466, 477-478 (1916). The principal condition to which we have looked is whether the party seeking relief from the judgment below caused the mootness by voluntary action.

The reference to "happenstance" in *Munsingwear* must be understood as an allusion to this equitable tradition of vacatur. A party who seeks review of the merits of an adverse ruling, but is frustrated by the vagaries of circumstance, ought not in fairness be forced to acquiesce in the judgment. The same is true when mootness results from unilateral action of the party who prevailed below. Where mootness results from settlement, however, the losing party has voluntarily forfeited his legal remedy by the ordinary processes of appeal or certiorari, thereby surrendering his claim to the equitable remedy of vacatur. The judgment is not unreviewable, but simply unreviewed by his own choice. . . .

In these respects the case stands no differently than it would if jurisdiction were lacking because the losing party failed to appeal at all. . . .

It is true, of course, that caused the mootness. Petitioner argues that vacatur is therefore fair to respondent, and seeks to distinguish our prior cases on that ground. But that misconceives the emphasis on fault in our decisions. That the parties are jointly responsible for settling may in some sense put them on even footing, but petitioner's case needs more than that. Respondent won below. It is petitioner's burden, as the party seeking relief from the status quo of the appellate judgment, to demonstrate not merely equivalent responsibility for the mootness, but equitable entitlement to the extraordinary remedy of vacatur. Petitioner's voluntary forfeiture of review constitutes a failure of equity that makes the burden decisive, whatever respondent's share in the mooting of the case might have been.

As always when federal courts contemplate equitable relief, our holding must also take account of the public interest. "Judicial precedents are presumptively correct and valuable to the legal community as a whole. They are not merely the property of private litigants and should stand unless a court concludes that the public interest would be served by a vacatur." *Izumi Seimitsu Kogyo Kabushiki Kaisha v. U.S. Philips Corp.*, 510 U.S. 27, 40 (1993) (STEVENS, J., dissenting). Congress has prescribed a primary route, by appeal as of right and certiorari, through which parties may seek relief from the legal consequences of judicial judgments. To allow a party who steps off the statutory path to employ the secondary remedy of vacatur as a refined form of collateral attack on the judgment would — quite apart from any considerations of fairness to the parties — disturb the orderly operation of the federal judicial system. *Munsingwear* establishes that the public interest is best served by granting relief when the demands of "orderly procedure," 340 U.S. at 41, cannot be honored; we think conversely that the public interest requires those demands to be honored when they can.

Petitioner advances two arguments meant to justify vacatur on systemic grounds. The first is that appellate judgments in cases that we have consented to review by writ of certiorari are reversed more often than they are affirmed, are therefore suspect, and should be vacated as a sort of prophylactic against legal error. It seems to us inappropriate, however, to vacate mooted cases, in which we have no constitutional power to decide the merits, on the basis of assumptions about the merits. Second, petitioner suggests that "vacating a moot decision, and thereby leaving an issue . . . temporarily unresolved in a Circuit, can facilitate the ultimate resolution of the issue by encouraging its continued examination and debate." We have found, however, that debate *among* the courts of appeal sufficiently illuminates the questions that come before us for review. The value of additional intracircuit debate seems to us far outweighed by the benefits that flow to litigants and the public from the resolution of legal questions.

A final policy justification urged by petitioner is the facilitation of settlement, with the resulting economies for the federal courts. But while the availability of vacatur may facilitate settlement after the judgment under review has been rendered and certiorari granted (or appeal filed), it may *deter* settlement at an earlier stage. *Some* litigants, at least, may think it worthwhile to roll the dice rather than settle in the district court, or in the court of appeals, if, but only if, an unfavorable outcome can be washed away by a settlement-related vacatur. And the judicial economies achieved by settlement at the district-court level are ordinarily much more extensive than those achieved by settlement on appeal. We find it quite impossible to assess the effect of our holding, either way, upon the frequency or systemic value of settlement.

Although the case before us involves only a motion to vacate, by reason of settlement, the judgment of a court of appeals (with, of course, the consequential vacation of the underlying judgment of the district court), it is appropriate to discuss the relevance of our holding to motions at the court of appeals level for vacatur of district-court judgments. Some opinions have suggested that vacatur motions at that level should be more freely granted, since district-court judgments are subject to review as of right. Obviously, this factor does not affect the primary basis for our denying vacatur. Whether the appellate court's seizure of the case is the consequence of an appellant's right or of a petitioner's good luck has no bearing upon the lack of equity of a litigant who has voluntarily abandoned review. If the point of the proposed distinction is that district-court judgments, being subject to review as of right, are more likely to be overturned and hence presumptively less valid: We again assert the inappropriateness of disposing of cases, whose merits are beyond judicial power to consider, on the basis of judicial estimates regarding their merits. Moreover, as petitioner's own argument described two paragraphs above points out, the reversal rate for cases in which this Court grants certiorari (a precondition for our vacatur) is over 50% — more than double the reversal rate for appeals to the courts of appeals. *See* [Jill E.] Fisch, *Rewriting History: The Propriety of Eradicating Prior Decisional Law Through Settlement and Vacatur*, 76 CORNELL L. REV. 589, 595, n. 25 (1991) (citing studies).

We hold that mootness by reason of settlement does not justify vacatur of a judgment under review. This is not to say that vacatur can never be granted when mootness is produced in that fashion. . . . [T]he determination is an equitable one, and exceptional circumstances may conceivably counsel in favor of such a course. It should be clear from our discussion, however, that those exceptional circumstances do not include the mere fact that the settlement agreement provides for vacatur — which neither diminishes the voluntariness of the abandonment of review nor alters any of the policy considerations we have discussed. Of course even in the absence of, or before considering the existence of, extraordinary circumstances, a court of appeals presented with a request for vacatur of a district-court judgment may remand the case with instructions that the district court consider the request, which it may do pursuant to Federal Rule of Civil Procedure 60(b).

Petitioner's motion to vacate the judgment of the Court of Appeals for the Ninth Circuit is denied. The case is dismissed as moot. . . .

NOTES

1. Why does an appeals court have power to do anything, including vacate a lower court's judgment, when a case has become moot?

2. Should an appeals court order a lower court's judgment to be vacated when a case becomes moot because:

a. The appellant unilaterally rendered the case moot? *See Kerkhof v. MCI Worldcom, Inc.*, 282 F.3d 44 (1st Cir. 2002) (vacating the judgment in favor of an employee who sought the vesting of stock options and shares pursuant to a profit-sharing plan, where WorldCom mooted the issue by vesting the shares for a reason, grounded in the plan, that the parties had not previously noticed, and vacating the judgment would preserve a complex legal issue for the future).

b. "Happenstance" renders the case moot? *See Soliman v. United States ex rel. INS*, 296 F.3d 1237 (11th Cir. 2002) (vacating the denial of a petition for habeas corpus relief in which an alien challenged his indefinite detention and his force-feeding during hunger strikes, where the alien had been returned to his native country and no longer was being detained or force-fed, observing that a party who seeks review that is frustrated by happenstance should not be forced to acquiesce in the judgment).

c. Settlement renders the case moot? *See Microsoft Corp. v. Bristol Technology, Inc.*, 250 F.3d 152 (2d Cir. 2001) (vacating the judgment ordering a punitive damages award in favor of a software licensee who sued on an unfair trade practices claim, where the parties settled, reasoning that, although settlement itself did not warrant vacatur, exceptional circumstances justified the vacatur because it was unclear (a) whether the district court had the power to reach the punitive damages issue since the parties had failed to request jury instructions on that issue, (b) whether the judge's imposition of punitive damages violated the defendant's Seventh Amendment right to jury trial, and for other reasons).

3. *Bancorp* is often followed and cited by state appellate courts. *See, e.g., Young's Realty, Inc. v. Brabham*, 896 So.2d 581 (Ala. Civ. App. 2004); *In re Candace H.*, 259 Conn. 523 (2002) (both vacating lower court decisions, following *Bancorp*).

4. Note that on the criminal side a correlate doctrine, accepted by some courts, is that of abatement ab initio, pursuant to which appellate courts will vacate a judgment of conviction and remand with instructions to dismiss the complaint or indictment when a defendant dies while his case is on direct review. *See, e.g., Commonwealth v. De La Zerda*, 619 N.E.2d 617 (Mass. 1993); *see generally*, Rosanno Cavallaro, *Better Off Dead: Abatement, Innocence, and the Evolving Right of Appeal*, 73 U. COLO. L. REV. 943 (2002).

III. TIMING AND METHODS OF SEEKING REVIEW

The cases in the following sections demonstrate the review scheme in the federal courts. The purpose here is to acquire experience and judgment in the use of the doctrines that govern when how, where, by whom, and as to what issues, federal appellate power may be brought into play. The broad question posed in this section is the extent to which it is possible, given the limits on access, for the appellate courts to monitor the conduct of pretrial business in the trial courts. This section focuses on the federal practice so that attention can be devoted to a single set of statutes and rules governing the appellate role. However, a similar examination of the interplay of appellate authority and trial court procedure could be made in any state. The patterns would vary from one state to another, and between state and federal arrangements, but the basic questions and tensions revealed in this section would be essentially the same.

Most procedural rules, whether promulgated by courts pursuant to rule-making powers or by legislative bodies, are designed to leave substantial discretion in the trial court. One reason is that long experience has taught that rigid procedural rules are mischievous in their substantive consequences, many of which are not foreseeable by the drafters of procedural rules. Thus, the plastic doctrines of access applied here are not atypical of procedural law in their indeterminacy.

Issues of mootness aside, when is a particular order or action of a trial judge subject to review in the appellate court? This question is often spoken of as one of "appealability," as distinguished from "reviewability." The latter term refers to whether a trial judge's action can be scrutinized by an appellate court at any time. The question of appealability assumes that the trial judge's action is reviewable at some point; the question is whether it can be reviewed immediately or whether review must await final resolution of the entire case in the trial court.

Two extreme positions could be taken. The rule makers (usually the legislature) could say that no action of the trial judge can be reviewed in the appellate court until the entire case has been finally adjudicated by the trial court. At the other end of the spectrum, the rule makers could provide that any and every ruling or action of the trial judge can be immediately appealed. No American jurisdiction has adopted either of these extreme positions. Some jurisdictions lean more toward the "finality" end of the spectrum, while others incline toward the other end, allowing more "interlocutory" appeals (meaning appeals from trial court orders that are not final dispositions of the whole case). For a classic discussion of this problem, see Carleton M. Crick, *The Final Judgment as a Basis for Appeal*, 41 YALE L.J. 539 (1932).

We begin with a look at the finality doctrine, the basic starting point for appealability in the federal courts and, in varying degrees, in the states. Generally speaking, in every jurisdiction a case is appealable when the trial court proceeding has reached final judgment. A major question here is when the trial court proceeding is "final" for appeal purposes.

Special attention should be paid to the tension between the reasons supporting the finality doctrine and the considerations that press toward allowing interlocutory appeals. Accommodating these conflicting pressures involves an important policy decision by those charged with determining the jurisdiction of the appellate courts, which in turn determines the relationship between, and the respective powers of, the courts of first instance and those at the review level. This policy question should be kept in mind in examining the finality doctrine and the exceptions that have been made to it.

Consideration of this material necessarily involves an understanding of the appropriate procedure through which a case can be taken to the appellate court.

A. The Finality Doctrine and its Permutations

1. Traditional Finality Requirements

The finality doctrine rests on the widely-accepted proposition that cases should not go to the appellate courts in fragments, prematurely, or repetitively, since the final decision may render unnecessary an appeal of some particular ruling made along the way. Nevertheless, whereas the finality requirement is designed to prevent the time-wasting interruption caused by piecemeal and possibly needless review of an interlocutory ruling in a case, there are situations in which early review would lead to a quick and efficient termination. Thus, the goal has been to identify those trial rulings that should be eligible for an immediate appeal rather than have their appeal postponed until a final judgment disposes of the entire dispute.

The final judgment rule is the basic principle of federal appealability. It is established by 28 U.S.C. § 1291:

> The courts of appeals . . . shall have jurisdiction of appeals from all final decisions of the district courts of the United States, . . . except where a direct review may be had in the Supreme Court. . . .

Similar provisions exist in state law, subject to exceptions that vary in their breadth for interlocutory orders, to be explored later.

In reading the materials that follow, consider whether the appropriate balance has been struck between the considerations underlying the finality rule and the interests served by interlocutory appeals. Consider also whether the criteria for appealability should be explicitly enumerated by statute or rule or left to the discretion of the trial or appellate courts on a case by case basis.

The first question to be considered is what is meant by "final" for purposes of appeal.

SWARTHOUT v. GENTRY
167 P.2d 501 (Cal. Dist. Ct. App. 1946)

MARKS, JUSTICE.

This is a motion to dismiss an appeal from a judgment which defendant maintains is final and which plaintiff argues is only interlocutory and therefore not appealable. The appeal is also submitted on the merits but if the motion is granted there will be no occasion to consider the merits of the cause.

Plaintiff brought this action, alleging that he and defendant were partners in the cattle business; that the assets of the partnership consisted of personal property; that he and defendant owned real property as tenants in common. He sought a dissolution of the partnership and a partition of the real property. Defendant denied that any real property was owned by the parties as tenants in common. He alleged the real and personal property belonged to the partnership and sought its dissolution. . . .

The trial court found that a division of the partnership real property between the two partners would be the most fair, just and equitable method for its disposition . . . and that the partnership properties could not be sold and the sale price divided "without serious prejudice and loss to the partners." . . .

In the judgment three referees were appointed to partition the property. . . .

The question of whether a judgment is final or merely interlocutory has been a close and troublesome one and numerous appeals have been taken out of an abundance of caution, because of that uncertainty, to protect the rights of an appellant against a possible holding that a judgment although termed interlocutory was in fact final, . . . which may be the reason for the appeal before us.

The rule in effect now is stated . . . as follows: "The general rule is that where a decree is made fixing the liability and rights of the parties which refers the case to a master or subordinate tribunal for a judicial purpose, such, for instance, as the statement of an account, upon which a further decree is to be entered, the decree is not final."

This rule was further amplified . . . as follows:

> The general test for determining whether the judgment is final is "that where no issue is left for future consideration except the fact of compliance or noncompliance with the terms of the first decree, that decree is final, but where anything further in the nature of judicial action on the part of the court is essential to a final determination of the rights of the parties, the decree is interlocutory. . . ."

It clearly appears . . . that much remains of a judicial nature to be finally settled by the trial court.

The referees may report on easements and rights of way that are necessary or convenient for use by one party over property of the other. Of course such a report could only amount to a recommendation with final decision resting in the court. This is clearly a judicial matter reserved for future determination.

The referees are required to report any inequality in value in the properties awarded to the partners and to recommend the amount to be paid by one to the other. The trial court would have to make an award of such amount in a final judgment. . . .

Finally the right is given to either party to move "to confirm, change, modify or set aside such report" with the further power reserved to the court to "appoint new referees" presumably so the entire proceeding may be repeated if the partition made by the first referees does not meet the approval of the court.

Clearly much is left to future judicial determination by the trial court. The judgment before us is an interlocutory, not a final judgment from which an appeal may be taken. . . .

The appeal is dismissed.

NOTES

1. A modern illustration of the point is *Henrietta D. v. Giulani*, 246 F.3d 176 (2d Cir. 2001). The district court entered judgment for New York City residents with AIDS or HIV-related illnesses who sued as a class alleging violations of the Americans with Disabilities Act and other federal, state, and city laws, through defendants' failure to provide meaningful access to public assistance programs. The court however left the terms of an injunction for later determination by a magistrate judge. Defendants appealed, and the court of appeals held that the determination below was not "final"; an award of declaratory relief is final only when no other remedial issues remain unresolved. If any injunction at all was entered here, it was far too lacking in detail and specificity to be regarded as granting any part of the ultimate coercive relief plaintiffs sought; thus it did not constitute an injunction within the meaning of the federal statute allowing immediate appeal of an injunction. Moreover, neither the court's broad pronouncement that judgment was entered, nor its directive to close the case, rendered the judgment final.

2. If the court had held the order in *Swarthout* to be appealable and reviewed it on the merits, how might that have shortened the litigation and thus saved time and expense at the trial level? How might that have caused unnecessary appeals? How might it have resulted in a second appeal?

Considering your answers to these questions, do you think that the court's decision holding this order nonappealable was sound? More generally, what purposes are served by insisting on finality as a prerequisite to appeal?

3. Should a judgment directing immediate delivery of physical property be immediately appealable if the trial court also has ordered an accounting that has not yet taken place? In *Forgay v. Conrad*, 47 U.S. (6 How.) 201 (1848), the Supreme Court said "yes." Are there good policy reasons for this result?

4. Issues of finality arise in cases seeking money damages as well as in cases for equitable relief. Where a judgment on liability is entered, but damages have yet to be determined, the judgment is not final. *Guarantee Co. v. Mechanics Sav. Bank & Trust Co.*, 173 U.S. 582 (1899); *Caradelis v. Refineria Panama, S. A.*, 385 F.2d 589, 591 (5th Cir. 1967). Was the Supreme Court being consistent in holding that a district court order is final even though the recoverability and amount of attorneys' fees to be awarded in the litigation have yet to be determined? *See Budinich v. Becton Dickinson & Co.*, 486 U.S. 196 (1988).

HOBERMAN v. LAKE OF ISLES
87 A.2d 137 (Conn. 1952)

INGLIS, ASSOCIATE JUSTICE.

This action was brought to foreclose a mortgage. The answer denied the execution of the mortgage and alleged that the loan purporting to be secured had not been made. Judgment was entered for the defendants. Thereafter the plaintiff filed his motion for a new trial [which was granted]. . . . From that order this appeal has been taken. The only questions raised or argued on the appeal related to the propriety of the order. The appeal, however, necessarily raises another and more fundamental question, namely, whether the order is one from which an appeal lies.

Section 8003 of the General Statutes authorizes an appeal only from a final judgment or from a decision granting a motion to set aside a verdict. The jurisdiction of this court is therefore limited to appeals which are within either of those two categories. Since it is a matter of jurisdiction, this court may and should upon its own motion reject any purported appeal which is not within the statute even though the question has not been raised by a motion to erase. . . .

The present appeal is clearly not one from a decision granting a motion to set aside a verdict. The sole question, therefore, is whether the order granting the motion for a new trial is a final judgment under the statute. In determining whether a decision of a trial court is a final judgment, . . . "The test lies, not in the nature of the judgment, but in its effect as concluding the rights of some or all of the parties. If such rights are concluded, so that further proceedings after the entry of the order or decree of the court cannot affect them, then the judgment is a final judgment from which an appeal lies." . . . [However,] "[t]here are many rulings in the course of an action by which rights are determined which are interlocutory in their nature and reviewable only upon an appeal taken from a judgment later rendered."

Proceedings upon a motion to open a judgment and for a new trial are interlocutory. The rule requires such a motion to be filed within six days after the rendition of the judgment. It contemplates that action on the motion shall be taken while the court has power to modify its judgment, that is, during the term in which the judgment is rendered or while the court has the power by virtue of the fact that the motion is pending. . . . The granting of the motion does not determine any of the substantive rights of the parties. . . . It determines merely that the parties must retry the issues in order to obtain a final adjudication of those rights. After the retrial is had and judgment is entered, on appeal from that judgment the granting of the motion for a new trial may be assigned as error. . . .

The order for a new trial from which this appeal was taken was purely interlocutory. It was entered at a time when the trial court still had control over and power to modify the judgment which it had rendered. The order did not finally conclude any of the rights of the parties which were in litigation. It, therefore, is not a final judgment from which an appeal lies. This court is without jurisdiction and the appeal must be dismissed. . . .

NOTES

1. Consider in connection with *Hoberman* the questions posed above about the *Swarthout* case.

2. For an example of the problems determining finality in a state system, *see* Elaine A. Carlson & Karlene S. Dunn, *Navigating Procedural Minefields: Nuances in Determining Finality of Judgments, Plenary Power, and Appealability*, 41 S. TEX. L. REV. 953 (2000) (concerning the Texas system).

QUACKENBUSH v. ALLSTATE INSURANCE COMPANY
517 U.S. 706 (1996)

JUSTICE O'CONNOR delivered the opinion of the Court.

In this case, we consider whether an abstention-based remand order is appealable as a final order under 28 U.S.C. § 1291. . . .

Petitioner, the Insurance Commissioner for the State of California, was appointed trustee over the assets of the Mission Insurance Company and its affiliates (Mission companies) in 1987, after those companies were ordered into liquidation by a California court. In an effort to gather the assets of the defunct Mission companies, the Commissioner filed the instant action against respondent Allstate Insurance Company in state court, seeking contract and tort damages for Allstate's alleged breach of certain reinsurance agreements, as well as a general declaration of Allstate's obligations under those agreements.

Allstate removed the action to federal court on diversity grounds and filed a motion to compel arbitration under the Federal Arbitration Act, 9 U.S.C. § 1 *et seq.* (1988 ed. and Supp. V). The Commissioner sought remand to state court, arguing that the District Court should abstain from hearing the case under *Burford* [v. *Sun Oil Co.*, 319 U.S. 315 (1943)], because its resolution might interfere with California's regulation of the Mission insolvency. Specifically, the Commissioner indicated that Allstate would be asserting its right to set off its own contract claims against the Commissioner's recovery under the contract, that the viability of these setoff claims was a hotly disputed question of state law, and that this question was currently pending before the state courts in another case arising out of the Mission insolvency.

The District Court observed that "California has an overriding interest in regulating insurance insolvencies and liquidations in a uniform and orderly manner," and that in this case "this important state interest could be undermined by inconsistent rulings from the federal and state courts." Based on these observations, and its determination that the setoff question should be resolved in state court, the District Court concluded this case was an appropriate one for the exercise of *Burford* abstention. The District Court did not stay its hand pending the California courts' resolution of the setoff issue, but instead remanded the entire case to state court. . . .

After determining that appellate review of the District Court's remand order was not barred by 28 U.S.C. § 1447(d) and that the remand order was appealable under 28 U.S.C. § 1291 as a final collateral order, see 47 F.3d at 353-354 (citing *Moses H. Cone Memorial Hospital* v. *Mercury Constr. Corp.*, 460 U.S. 1 (1983)), the Court of Appeals for the Ninth Circuit vacated the District Court's decision and ordered the case sent to arbitration. The Ninth Circuit . . . held that abstention was inappropriate in this case. . . . 47 F.3d at 354-356. . . .

II

We first consider whether the Court of Appeals had jurisdiction to hear Allstate's appeal under 28 U.S.C. § 1291, which confers jurisdiction over appeals from "final decisions" of the district courts, and 28 U.S.C. § 1447(d), which provides that "an order remanding a case to the State court from which it was removed is not reviewable on appeal or otherwise."

We agree with the Ninth Circuit and the parties that § 1447(d) interposes no bar to appellate review of the remand order at issue in this case. . . . The District Court's abstention based remand order does not fall into either category of remand order described in § 1447(c), as it is not based on lack of subject matter jurisdiction or defects in removal procedure.

Finding no affirmative bar to appellate review of the District Court's remand order, we must determine whether that review may be obtained by appeal under § 1291. The general rule is that "a party is entitled to a single appeal, to be deferred until final judgment has been entered, in which claims of district court error at any stage of the litigation may be ventilated." *Digital Equipment Corp.* v. *Desktop Direct, Inc.*, 511 U.S. 863 (1994) (citations omitted). Accordingly, we have held that a decision is ordinarily considered final and appealable under § 1291 only if it "ends the litigation on the merits and leaves nothing for the court to do but execute the judgment." *Catlin* v. *United States*, 324 U.S. 229, 233 (1945). . . .

The application of these principles to the appealability of the remand order before us is controlled by our decision in *Moses H. Cone Memorial Hospital* v. *Mercury Constr. Corp., supra.* The District Court in that case entered an order under *Colorado River Water Conservation Dist.* v. *United States*, 424 U.S. 800 (1976), staying a federal diversity suit pending the completion of a declaratory judgment action that had been filed in state court. The Court of Appeals held that this stay order was appealable under § 1291, and we affirmed that determination on two independent grounds.

We first concluded that the abstention-based stay order was appealable as a "final decision" under § 1291 because it put the litigants "'effectively out of court,'" 460 U.S. at 11, n. 11, and because its effect was "precisely to surrender jurisdiction of a federal suit to a state court," 460 U.S. at 11, n. 11. These standards do not reflect our oft-repeated definition of finality, but in *Moses H. Cone* we found their application to be compelled by precedent. . . .

The District Court's order remanding on grounds of *Burford* abstention is in all relevant respects indistinguishable from the stay order we found to be appealable in *Moses H. Cone.* No less than an order staying a federal-court action pending adjudication of the dispute in state court, it puts the litigants in this case "'effectively out of court,'" *Moses H. Cone, supra,* at 11, n. 11, and its effect is "precisely to surrender jurisdiction of a federal suit to a state court," 460 U.S. at 11, n. 11. Indeed, the remand order is clearly more "final" than a stay order in this sense. When a district court remands a case to a state court, the district court disassociates itself from the case entirely, retaining nothing of the matter on the federal court's docket. . . .

We have previously stated that "an order remanding a removed action does not represent a final judgment reviewable by appeal." *Thermtron Products, Inc.* v. *Hermansdorfer*, 423 U.S. at 352-353. Petitioner asks that we adhere to that statement and hold that appellate review of the District Court's remand order can only be obtained through a petition for writ of mandamus. To the extent *Thermtron* would require us to ignore the implications of our later holding in *Moses H. Cone*, however, we disavow it. *Thermtron's* determination that remand orders are not reviewable "final judgments" doubtless was necessary to the resolution of that case, see 423 U.S. at 352 (posing the question whether mandamus was the appropriate vehicle), but our principal concern in *Thermtron* was the interpretation of the bar to appellate review embodied in 28 U.S.C. § 1447(d), and our statement concerning the appropriate procedural vehicle for reviewing a district court's remand order was peripheral to that concern. . . .

Admittedly, remand orders like the one entered in this case do not meet the traditional definition of finality — they do not "end the litigation on the merits and leav[e] nothing for the court to do but execute the judgment,"*Catlin*, 324 U.S. at 233. But because the District Court's remand order is functionally indistinguishable from the stay order we found appealable in *Moses H. Cone*, we conclude that it is appealable. . . .

[The Court then held that abstention was appropriate.]

NOTES

1. Considering the *Swarthout, Hoberman,* and *Quackenbush* opinions, can you formulate a statement as to when, in general, a trial court proceeding becomes "final" for purposes of appeal?

2. If a plaintiff dismisses some claims without prejudice, and the trial court then enters an order disposing of the remaining claims, the losing party has a final, appealable, judgment. *E.g., Schoenfeld v. Babbitt*, 168 F.3d 1257 (11th Cir. 1999). A question that has split the courts is whether and in what circumstances a voluntary dismissal without prejudice of all claims that remain *after* entry of an order disposing of some, but not all, claims renders the order permitting voluntary dismissal final and appealable. Litigation of the claims that have been voluntarily dismissed may not be over, and among the issues just under the surface is whether litigants should be permitted to obtain early appellate review by voluntarily dismissing their unresolved claims. *Compare Black Horse Lane Assoc. v. Dow Chemical Corp.*, 228 F.3d 275 (3d Cir. 2000) (holding that counterclaim's dismissal without prejudice for lack of ripeness did not deprive appeals court of jurisdiction over plaintiff's appeal from grant of summary judgment to defendant on plaintiff's claims) *with Chappelle v. Beacon Communications Corp.*, 84 F.3d 652 (2d Cir. 1996) (dismissing appeal for lack of a final judgment where plaintiff, having had some of her claims dismissed on the merits or for lack of subject-matter jurisdiction, voluntarily dismissed her remaining claims in order to pursue a single action in state court). *Contrast Erie County Retirees Ass'n v. County of Erie*, 220 F.3d 193 (3d Cir. 2000) (holding grant of partial summary judgment to be final and immediately appealable where appellants withdrew their other federal law claims *with* prejudice and district court dismissed appellants' state law claims without prejudice, in the exercise of its discretion not to hear those claims under its supplemental jurisdiction). *See* Rebecca A. Cochran, *Gaining Appellate Review by "Manufacturing" a Final Judgment Through Voluntary Dismissal of Peripheral Claims*, 48 MERCER L. REV. 979 (1997).

3. A similar phenomenon is the "consent judgment," which a few federal appeals courts have endorsed when a stipulation among the parties makes

clear the intent to appeal the judgment or reserves the right to appeal. In *Keefe v. Prudential Property & Casualty Insurance Co.*, 203 F.3d 218 (3d Cir. 2000), for example, the parties stipulated to entry of judgment for plaintiff for $1, subject to plaintiff's right to appeal the district court's determination of a question of law in its ruling upon a motion for summary judgment, which left disputed questions of fact to be tried. The parties agreed between themselves on varying amounts the plaintiff would receive from defendant if plaintiff lost the appeal, if the court of appeals declined to decide the issue, and if plaintiff won the appeal. The court of appeals held that the "consent judgment" was final and appealable, and that the case was not mooted by the "settlement," since the parties continued to be adverse on the legal issue put to the court of appeals.

4. When a case does go to final judgment, orders entered along the way — rulings on motions directed to the pleadings, discovery issues, on proposed jury instructions, post-trial motions, for example — "merge into the judgment," and are reviewable upon appeal from the final judgment. The courts are split upon whether interlocutory orders may be reviewed on appeal from a dismissal for failure to prosecute. Most hold that interlocutory orders do not merge into the judgment based on such a dismissal, and are not reviewable on appeal of the judgment. They regard the only reviewable issue as whether the dismissal was valid, and the fact that earlier rulings may have been erroneous as irrelevant. *See, e.g., John's Insulation, Inc. v. L. Addison & Assocs.*, 156 F.3d 101 (1st Cir. 1998); *DuBose v. State of Minnesota*, 893 F.2d 169 (8th Cir. 1990); *Richardson v. Lane*, 6 Haw. App. 614 (1987). The Court of Appeals for the Second Circuit, by contrast, has held interlocutory orders entered in cases later dismissed for failure to prosecute to be reviewable. *See Allied Freight, Inc. v. Pan American World Airways, Inc.*, 393 F.2d 441 (2d Cir. 1968); *see also* Koonce v. Union Elec. Co., 831 S.W.2d 702 (Mo. App. 1992) (hearing appeal of interlocutory orders after dismissal for failure to prosecute). What reasons can you see for each viewpoint?

5. Compare a dismissal "without prejudice" on grounds such as lack of subject-matter jurisdiction. Should a sanction order entered in the case be appealable after the dismissal? *American National Bank & Trust Co. of Chicago v. Equitable Life Assurance Society of the United States*, 406 F.3d 867 (7th Cir. 2005), held yes: the district court was finished with the action, which had an incurable jurisdictional defect; defendant, while not aggrieved by the dismissal of the suit, was aggrieved by the sanction; and the propriety of the sanction entered by the federal court would not be in issue in any subsequent proceeding over which a court did have jurisdiction.

2. Partial Final Judgment under Rule 54(b) and State Law Counterparts

Federal Rules of Civil Procedure

Rule 54

. . . .

(b) Judgment Upon Multiple Claims or Involving Multiple Parties. When more than one claim for relief is presented in an action, whether as a claim, counterclaim, cross-claim, or third-party claim, or when multiple parties are

involved, the court may direct the entry of a final judgment as to one or more but fewer than all of the claims or parties only upon an express determination that there is no just reason for delay and upon an express direction for the entry of judgment. In the absence of such determination and direction, any order or other form of decision, however designated, which adjudicates fewer than all the claims or the rights and liabilities of fewer than all the parties shall not terminate the action as to any of the claims or parties, and the order or other form of decision is subject to revision at any time before the entry of judgment adjudicating all the claims and the rights and liabilities of all the parties.

In applying this Rule, logically the first question to address is whether an action presents more than one claim. How do courts make that determination?

SEARS, ROEBUCK & CO. v. MACKEY
351 U.S. 427 (1956)

MR. JUSTICE BURTON delivered the opinion of the Court.

This action, presenting multiple claims for relief, was brought by Mackey and another in the United States District Court for the Northern District of Illinois, Eastern Division, in 1953. The court expressly directed that judgment be entered for the defendant, Sears, Roebuck & Co., on two, but less than all, of the claims presented. It also expressly determined that there was no just reason for delay in making the entry. After Mackey's notice of appeal from that judgment to the Court of Appeals for the Seventh Circuit, Sears, Roebuck & Co. moved to dismiss the appeal for lack of appellate jurisdiction. The Court of Appeals upheld its jurisdiction and denied the motion, relying upon 28 U.S.C. § 1291 and Rule 54(b) of the Federal Rules of Civil Procedure. Because of the importance of the issue in determining appellate jurisdiction and because of a conflict of judicial views on the subject, we granted certiorari. For the reasons hereafter stated, we sustain the Court of Appeals and its appellate jurisdiction.

Although we are here concerned with the present appealability of the judgment of the District court and not with its merits, we must examine the claims stated in the complaint so as to consider adequately the issue of appealability.

The complaint contains six counts. We disregard the fifth because it has been abandoned and the sixth because it duplicates others. The claims stated in Counts I and II are material and have been dismissed without leave to amend. The claim contained in Count III and that in amended Count IV are at issue on the answers filed by Sears, Roebuck & Co. The appeal before us is from a judgment striking out Counts I and II without disturbing Counts III and IV, and the question presented is whether such a judgment is presently appealable when the District Court, pursuant to amended Rule 54(b), has made "an express determination that there is no just reason for delay" and has given "an express direction for the entry of judgment."

In Count I, Mackey, a citizen of Illinois, and Time Saver Tools, Inc., an Illinois corporation owned by Mackey, are the original plaintiffs and the respondents here. Sears, Roebuck & Co., a New York corporation doing business in Illinois, is the original defendant and the petitioner here. Mackey charges Sears with conduct violating the Sherman Antitrust Act in a manner prejudicial to three of Mackey's commercial ventures causing him $190,000 damages for which he seeks $570,000 as treble damages. His first charge is unlawful destruction by Sears, since 1949, of the market for nursery lamps manufactured by General Metalcraft Company, a corporation wholly owned by Mackey. Mackey claims that this caused him a loss of $150,000. His second charge is unlawful interference by Sears, in 1952, with Mackey's contract to sell, on commission, certain tools and other products of the Vascoloy-Ramet Corporation, causing Mackey to lose $15,000. His third charge is unlawful destruction by Sears, in 1952, of the market for a new type of carbide-tipped lathe bit and for other articles manufactured by Time Saver Tools, Inc., resulting in a loss to Mackey of $25,000. Mackey combines such charges with allegations that Sears has used its great size to monopolize commerce and restrain competition in these fields. He asks for damages and equitable relief.

In Count II, Mackey claims federal jurisdiction by virtue of diversity of citizenship. He incorporates the allegations of Count I as to the Metalcraft transactions and asks for $250,000 damages for Sears' wilful destruction of the business of Metalcraft, plus $50,000 for Mackey's loss on obligations guaranteed by him.

In Count III, Mackey seeks $75,000 in a common-law proceeding against Sears for unlawfully inducing a breach of his Vascoloy commission contract.

In Count IV, Time Saver seeks $200,000 in a common-law proceeding against Sears for unlawfully destroying Time Saver's business by unfair competition and patent infringement.

The jurisdiction of the Court of Appeals to entertain Mackey's appeal from the District Court's judgment depends upon 28 U.S.C. § 1291, which provides that "The courts of appeals shall have jurisdiction of appeals from *all final decisions* of the district courts of the United States. . . ." (emphasis supplied).

If Mackey's complaint had contained only Count I, there is no doubt that a judgment striking out that count and thus dismissing, in its entirety, the claim there stated would be both a final and an appealable decision within the meaning of § 1291. Similarly, if his complaint had contained Counts I, II, III, and IV, there is no doubt that a judgment striking out all four would be a final and appealable decision under § 1291. The controversy before us arises solely because, in this multiple claims action, the District Court has dismissed the claims stated in Counts I and II, but has left unadjudicated those stated in Counts III and IV.

Before the adoption of the Federal Rules of Civil Procedure in 1938, such a situation was generally regarded as leaving the appellate court without jurisdiction of an attempted appeal. It was thought that, although the judgment was a final decision on the respective claims in Counts I and II, it obviously was not a final decision of the whole case, and there was no authority for treating anything less than the whole case as a judicial unit for purposes of appeal. This construction of the judicial unit was developed from the common law which had dealt with litigation generally less complicated than much of that of today.

With the Federal Rules of Civil Procedure, there came an increased opportunity for the liberal joinder of claims in multiple claims actions. This, in turn, demonstrated a need for relaxing the restrictions upon what should be treated as a judicial unit for purposes of appellate jurisdiction. Sound judicial administration did not require relaxation of the standard of finality in the disposition of the individual adjudicated claims for the purpose of their appealability. It did, however, demonstrate that, at least in multiple claims actions, some final decisions, on less than all of the claims, should be appealable without waiting for a final decision on *all* of the claims. Largely to meet this need, in 1938, Rule 54(b) was promulgated in its original form through joint action of Congress and this Court.

. . . [The court here quoted the present version of Rule 54(b).]

In this form, it does not relax the finality required of each decision, as an individual claim, to render it appealable, but it does provide a practical means of permitting an appeal to be taken from one or more final decisions on individual claims, in multiple claims actions, without waiting for final decisions to be rendered on *all* the claims in the case. The amended rule does not apply to a single claim action nor to a multiple claims action in which all of the claims have been finally decided. It is limited expressly to multiple claims actions in which "one or more but less than all" of the multiple claims have been finally decided and are found otherwise to be ready for appeal.

To meet the demonstrated need for flexibility, the District Court is used as a "dispatcher." It is permitted to determine, in the first instance, the appropriate *time when each "final decision"* upon "one or more but less than all" of the claims in a multiple claims action is ready for appeal. This arrangement already has lent welcome certainty to the appellate procedure. Its "negative effect" has met with uniform approval. The effect so referred to is the rule's specific requirement that for "one or more but less than all" multiple claims to become appealable, the District Court must make both "an express determination that there is no just reason for delay" and "an express direction for the entry of judgment." A party adversely affected by a final decision thus knows that his time for appeal will *not* run against him until this certification has been made.

In the instant case, the District Court made this certification, but Sears, Roebuck & Co. nevertheless moved to dismiss the appeal for lack of appellate jurisdiction under § 1291. The grounds for such a motion ordinarily might be (1) that the judgment of the District Court was not a decision upon a "claim for relief," (2) that the decision was not a "final decision" in the sense of an ultimate disposition of an individual claim entered in the course of a multiple claims action, or (3) that the District Court abused its discretion in certifying the order.

In the case before us, there is no doubt that each of the claims dismissed is a "claim for relief" within the meaning of Rule 54(b), or that their dismissal constitutes a "final decision" on individual claims. Also, it cannot well be argued that the claims stated in Counts I and II are so inherently inseparable from, or closely related to, those stated in Counts III and IV that the District Court has abused its discretion in certifying that there exists no just reason for delay. They certainly *can* be decided independently of each other.

Petitioner contends that amended Rule 54(b) attempts to make an unauthorized extension of § 1291. We disagree. . . . The District Court *cannot*, in the exercise of its discretion, treat as "final" that which is not "final" within the meaning of § 1291. But the District Court *may*, by the exercise of its discretion in the interest of sound judicial administration, release for appeal final decisions upon one or more, but less than all, claims in multiple claims actions. The timing of such a release is, with good reason, vested by the rule primarily in the discretion of the District Court as the one most likely to be familiar with the case and with any justifiable reasons for delay. With equally good reason, any abuse of that discretion remains reviewable by the Court of Appeals.

Rule 54(b), in its original form, thus may be said to have modified the single judicial unit practice which had been developed by court decisions. The validity of that rule is no longer questioned. . . .

Rule 54(b), in its amended form, is a comparable exercise of the rulemaking authority of this Court. It does not supersede any statute controlling appellate jurisdiction. It scrupulously recognizes the statutory requirement of a "final decision" under § 1291 as a basic requirement for an appeal to the Court of Appeals. It merely administers that requirement in a practical manner in multiple claims actions and does so by rule instead of by judicial decision. By its negative effect, it operates to restrict in a valid manner the number of appeals in multiple claims actions.

We reach a like conclusion as to the validity of the amended rule where the District Court acts affirmatively and thus assists in properly timing the release of final decisions in multiple claims actions. The amended rule adapts the single judicial unit theory so that it better meets the current needs of judicial administration. . . .

Accordingly, the appellate jurisdiction of the Court of Appeals is sustained, and its judgment denying the motion to dismiss the appeal for lack of appellate jurisdiction is *affirmed*.

NOTES

1. Why is Rule 54(b) desirable? What purposes are served by having the district court decide whether to direct the entry of final judgment and certify that there is no just reason to delay the appeal? *See Dickinson v. Petroleum Conversion Corp.*, 338 U.S. 507 (1950): "The liberalization of our practice to allow more issues and parties to be joined in one action and to expand the privilege of intervention by those not originally parties has increased the danger of hardship and denial of justice through delay if each issue must await the determination of all issues as to all parties before a final judgment can be had."

2. Compare *Cold Metal Process Co. v. United Engineering & Foundry Co.*, 351 U.S. 445 (1956), where the Court held that the defendant could appeal from an adverse judgment on plaintiff's claim although defendant's counterclaims arose in part out of the same transaction as plaintiff's claim and remained undecided. The court there explained that under Rule 54(b), in its original form, the test of appealability was whether the adjudicated claims were separate from, and independent of, the unadjudicated claims. However, that test led to uncertainty, that (the Court said) the amended rule overcame. "[U]nder its terms we need not decide whether United's counterclaim is

compulsory or permissive. The amended rule . . . treats counterclaims, whether compulsory or permissive, like other multiple claims. . . . Therefore, under the amended rule, the relationship of the adjudicated claims to the unadjudicated claims is one of the factors which the District Court can consider in the exercise of its discretion. If the District Court certifies a final order on a claim which arises out of the same transaction and occurrence as pending claims, and the Court of Appeals is satisfied that there has been no abuse of discretion, the order is appealable. . . . The amended rule meets the needs and problems of modern judicial administration by adjusting the unit for appeal to fit multiple claims actions, while retaining a right of judicial review over the discretion exercised by the District Court in determining when there is no just reason for delay. This does not impair the statutory concept of finality embraced in § 1291, and . . . is within the rulemaking power of this Court."

3. Note that multiple counts in the complaint do not necessarily mean that there are multiple claims for purposes of Rule 54(b). A single claim, for example, could be stated in four counts. How did the Court in *Sears, Roebuck* and *Cold Metal* determine that the cases contained more than one claim?

4. A sues B to recover damages for personal injuries resulting from A's use of B's product. Count 1 of the complaint alleges negligent manufacture by B. Count 2 alleges B's breach of warranty. The trial court holds that under the governing substantive law A has no right of recovery under a breach of warranty theory; thus, the court dismisses Count 2. Assuming that the trial judge makes the determination required by Rule 54(b), does the appellate court have jurisdiction over A's appeal from the dismissal of Count 2? *See* 10 CHARLES A. WRIGHT, ARTHUR R. MILLER AND MARY KAY KANE, FEDERAL PRACTICE AND PROCEDURE § 2657 (1998 & Supp. 2005). Does it matter whether the two legal theories constitute two claims for pleading purposes? for purposes of res judicata? What considerations should influence whether plaintiff asserts more than one claim for relief for purposes of Rule 54(b)?

5. In thinking about the scope of a single claim, consider *In re Collins*, 233 F.3d 809 (3d Cir. 2000). Plaintiffs seeking to recover for personal injuries resulting from asbestos exposure sought a writ of mandamus directing the Judicial Panel on Multidistrict Litigation to remand punitive damages claims for trial with compensatory damages claims, rather than allow the pretrial transferee court to separate the punitive damages claims for later trial. 28 U.S.C. § 1407(a) provides in pertinent part that "the panel may separate any claim . . . and remand any of such claims before the remainder of the action is remanded." Plaintiff argued that requests for punitive damages are not separate claims. The Third Circuit, relying on statutory language, legislative history, the commonness of trials devoted solely to punitive damages, principles governing mandamus, and public policy, denied the writ.

If plaintiffs sued for compensatory and punitive damages and the court finally resolved the liability and compensatory damages issues in favor of plaintiff before resolving the punitive damages issues, would it be appropriate for the court to provide a Rule 54(b) certification allowing immediate appeal of the former? Are there two separate claims within the meaning of Rule 54(b)?

6. Also note that the disposition of a defense is not the equivalent of disposition of a claim. *Reiter v. Cooper*, 507 U.S. 258 (1993) ("A defense cannot possibly be adjudicated separately from the plaintiff's claim to which it applies. . . .").

7. A and B, riding together in an automobile, had a collision with an automobile driven by C. A and B join as plaintiffs and sue C to recover damages for their injuries arising out of the collision. The trial court enters summary judgment for C against A on the ground that A released his claim against C. Assuming the trial judge makes the determination required by Rule 54(b), does the appellate court have jurisdiction over A's appeal from this adverse judgment?

8. Some circuits have taken the position that a party who seeks to create finality by dismissing unresolved claims without prejudice must file for Rule 54(b) certification. This permits the trial court to independently determine whether an appeal is warranted. The Fifth Circuit has opined that this bright-line rule provides greater predictability and is more efficient than the approach — sometimes taken by the Seventh and Ninth Circuits — of finding jurisdiction over an appeal after the voluntary dismissal of unresolved claims so long as, in the view of the appeals court, the parties are not seeking to manipulate the appellate system. *See Swope v. Columbian Chemicals Co.*, 281 F.3d 185 (5th Cir. 2002).

9. Assuming separate claims and a final judgment as to one or more but fewer than all claims or parties, the next issue under Rule 54(b) and state law counterparts is whether there is just reason to delay appeal.

CURTISS-WRIGHT CORP. v. GENERAL ELECTRIC CO.
446 U.S. 1 (1980)

BURGER, C. J., delivered the opinion for a unanimous Court.

I

From 1968 to 1972, respondent General Electric Co. entered into a series of 21 contracts with petitioner Curtiss-Wright Corp. for the manufacture of components designed for use in nuclear powered naval vessels. These contracts had a total value of $215 million.

In 1976, Curtiss-Wright brought a diversity action in the United States District Court for the District of New Jersey, seeking damages and reformation with regard to the 21 contracts. The complaint asserted claims based on alleged fraud, misrepresentation, and breach of contract by General Electric. It also sought $19 million from General Electric on the outstanding balance due on the contracts already performed.

General Electric counterclaimed for $1.9 million in costs allegedly incurred as the result of "extraordinary efforts" provided to Curtiss-Wright during performance of the contracts which enabled Curtiss-Wright to avoid a contract default. General Electric also sought, by way of counterclaim, to recover $52 million by which Curtiss-Wright was allegedly unjustly enriched as a result of these "extraordinary efforts."

The facts underlying most of these claims and counterclaims are in dispute. As to Curtiss-Wright's claims for the $19 million balance due, however, the sole dispute concerns the application of a release clause contained in each of the 21 agreements, which states that "Seller . . . [agrees] as a condition precedent to final payment, that the Buyer and the Government . . . are released from all liabilities, obligations and claims arising under or by virtue of this order." When Curtiss-Wright moved for summary judgment on the balance due, General Electric contended that so long as Curtiss-Wright's other claims remained pending, this provision constituted a bar to recovery of the undisputed balance.

The District Court rejected this contention and granted summary judgment for Curtiss-Wright on this otherwise undisputed claim. Applying New York law by which the parties had agreed to be bound, the District Court held that Curtiss-Wright was entitled to payment of the balance due notwithstanding the release clause. The court also ruled that Curtiss-Wright was entitled to prejudgment interest at the New York statutory rate of 6% per annum.

Curtiss-Wright then moved for a certification of the District Court's orders as final judgments under Federal Rule of Civil Procedure 54 (b). . . . The court expressly directed entry of final judgment for Curtiss-Wright and made the determination that there was "no just reason for delay" pursuant to Rule 54 (b).

The District Court . . . acknowledged that Rule 54 (b) certification . . . should be reserved for the infrequent harsh case because of the overload in appellate courts which would otherwise result from appeals of an interlocutory nature. The essential inquiry was stated to be "whether, after balancing the competing factors, finality of judgment should be ordered to advance the interests of sound judicial administration and justice to the litigants."

The District Court then went on to identify the relevant factors in the case before it. It found that certification would not result in unnecessary appellate review; that the claims finally adjudicated were separate, distinct, and independent of any of the other claims or counterclaims involved; that review of these adjudicated claims would not be mooted by any future developments in the case; and that the nature of the claims was such that no appellate court would have to decide the same issues more than once even if there were subsequent appeals.

Turning to considerations of justice to the litigants, the District Court found that Curtiss-Wright would suffer severe daily financial loss from nonpayment of the $ 19 million judgment because current interest rates were higher than the statutory prejudgment rate, a situation compounded by the large amount of money involved. The court observed that the complex nature of the remaining claims could, without certification, mean a delay that "would span many months, if not years."

The court found that solvency of the parties was not a significant factor, since each appeared to be financially sound. Although the presence of General Electric's counterclaims and the consequent possibility of a setoff recovery were factors which weighed against certification, the court, in balancing these factors, determined that they were outweighed by the other factors in the case. Accordingly, it granted Rule 54 (b) certification. It also granted General Electric's motion for a stay without bond pending appeal.

A divided panel of the United States Court of Appeals for the Third Circuit held that the case was controlled by its decision in *Allis-Chalmers Corp.* v. *Philadelphia Electric Co.*, 521 F.2d 360 (1975), where the court had stated:

"In the absence of unusual or harsh circumstances, we believe that the presence of a counterclaim, which could result in a set-off against any amounts due and owing to the plaintiff, weighs heavily against the grant of 54 (b) certification." *Id.* at 366 (footnote omitted). In *Allis-Chalmers*, the Court defined unusual or harsh circumstances as those factors "involving considerations of solvency, economic duress, etc." *Id.* at 366, n. 14.

In the Third Circuit's view, the question was which of the parties should have the benefit of the amount of the balance due pending final resolution of the litigation . . . . The Court of Appeals acknowledged that Curtiss-Wright's inability to have use of the money from the judgment might seem harsh, but noted that the same could be said for General Electric if it were forced to pay Curtiss-Wright now but later prevailed on its counterclaims.

The Court of Appeals concluded that the District Court had abused its discretion by granting Rule 54 (b) certification in this situation and dismissed the case for want of an appealable order. . . . We reverse.

II

Nearly a quarter of a century ago, in *Sears, Roebuck & Co.* v. *Mackey*, 351 U.S. 427 (1956), this Court outlined the steps to be followed in making determinations under Rule 54 (b). A district court must first determine that it is dealing with a "final judgment." It must be a "judgment" in the sense that it is a decision upon a cognizable claim for relief, and it must be "final" in the sense that it is "an ultimate disposition of an individual claim entered in the course of a multiple claims action." 351 U.S. at 436.

Once having found finality, the district court must go on to determine whether there is any just reason for delay. Not all final judgments on individual claims should be immediately appealable, even if they are in some sense separable from the remaining unresolved claims. The function of the district court under the Rule is to act as a "dispatcher." *Id.* at 435. It is left to the sound judicial discretion of the district court to determine the "appropriate time" when each final decision in a multiple claims action is ready for appeal. *Ibid.* This discretion is to be exercised "in the interest of sound judicial administration." *Id.* at 437.

Thus, in deciding whether there are no just reasons to delay the appeal of individual final judgments in a setting such as this, a district court must take into account judicial administrative interests as well as the equities involved. Consideration of the former is necessary to assure that application of the Rule effectively "preserves the historic federal policy against piecemeal appeals." *Id.* at 438. It was therefore proper for the District Judge here to consider such factors as whether the claims under review were separable from the others remaining to be adjudicated and whether the nature of the claims already determined was such that no appellate court would have to decide the same issues more than once even if there were subsequent appeals.[1]

Here the District Judge saw no sound reason to delay appellate resolution of the undisputed claims already adjudicated. The contrary conclusion of the Court of Appeals was strongly influenced by the existence of nonfrivolous counterclaims. The mere presence of such claims, however, does not render a Rule 54 (b) certification inappropriate. If it did, Rule 54 (b) would lose much of its utility. In *Cold Metal Process Co.* v. *United Engineering & Foundry Co.*, 351 U.S. 445 (1956), this Court explained that counterclaims, whether compulsory or permissive, present no special problems for Rule 54 (b) determinations; counterclaims are not to be evaluated differently from other claims. 351 U.S. at 452. Like other claims, their significance for Rule 54 (b) purposes turns on their interrelationship with the claims on which certification is sought. Here, the District Judge determined that General Electric's counterclaims were severable from the claims which had been determined in terms of both the factual and the legal issues involved. The Court of Appeals did not conclude otherwise.

What the Court of Appeals found objectionable about the District Judge's exercise of discretion was the assessment of the equities involved. The Court of Appeals concluded that the possibility of a setoff required that the status quo be maintained unless petitioner could show harsh or unusual circumstances; it held that such a showing had not been made in the District Court.

This holding reflects a misinterpretation of the standard of review for Rule 54 (b) certifications and a misperception of the appellate function in such cases. The Court of Appeals relied on a statement of the Advisory Committee on the Rules of Civil Procedure, and its error derives from reading a description in the commentary as a standard of construction. When Rule 54 (b) was amended in 1946, the Notes of the Advisory Committee which accompanied the suggested amendment indicated that the entire lawsuit was generally the appropriate unit for appellate review, "and that this rule needed only the exercise of a discretionary power to afford a remedy in the infrequent harsh case to provide a simple, definite, workable rule." 5 F.R.D. 433, 473 (1946). However accurate it may be as a description of cases qualifying for Rule 54 (b) treatment, the phrase "infrequent harsh case" in isolation is neither workable nor entirely reliable as a benchmark for appellate review. There is no indication it was ever intended by the drafters to function as such.

In *Sears*, the Court stated that the decision to certify was with good reason left to the sound judicial discretion of the district court. At the same time, the Court noted that "[with] equally good reason, any *abuse* of that discretion remains reviewable by the Court of Appeals." 351 U.S. at 437 (emphasis added). The Court indicated that the standard against which a district court's

---

1 [1] We do not suggest that the presence of one of these factors would necessarily mean that Rule 54 (b) certification would be improper. It would, however, require the district court to find a sufficiently important reason for nonetheless granting certification. For example, if the district court concluded that there was a possibility that an appellate court would have to face the same issues on a subsequent appeal, this might perhaps be offset by a finding that an appellate resolution of the certified claims would facilitate a settlement of the remainder of the claims. See Cold Metal Process Co. v. United Engineering & Foundry Co., 351 U.S. 445, 450, n. 5 (1956).

exercise of discretion is to be judged is the "interest of sound judicial administration." *Ibid.* Admittedly this presents issues not always easily resolved, but
the proper role of the court of appeals is not to reweigh the equities or reassess
the facts but to make sure that the conclusions derived from those weighings
and assessments are juridically sound and supported by the record.

There are thus two aspects to the proper function of a reviewing court in
Rule 54 (b) cases. The court of appeals must, of course, scrutinize the district
court's evaluation of such factors as the interrelationship of the claims so as to
prevent piecemeal appeals in cases which should be reviewed only as single
units. But once such juridical concerns have been met, the discretionary
judgment of the district court should be given substantial deference, for that
court is "the one most likely to be familiar with the case and with any justifiable reasons for delay." *Sears, supra*, at 437. The reviewing court should disturb the trial court's assessment of the equities only if it can say that the
judge's conclusion was clearly unreasonable.

Plainly, sound judicial administration does not require that Rule 54 (b)
requests be granted routinely. That is implicit in commending them to the sound
discretion of a district court. Because this discretion "is, with good reason, vested
by the rule primarily" in the district courts, *Sears, supra*, at 437, and because the
number of possible situations is large, we are reluctant either to fix or sanction
narrow guidelines for the district courts to follow. We are satisfied, however, that
on the record here the District Court's assessment of the equities was reasonable.

One of the equities which the District Judge considered was the difference
between the statutory and market rates of interest. Respondent correctly
points out that adjustment of the statutory prejudgment interest rate is a matter within the province of the legislature, but that fact does not make the existing differential irrelevant for Rule 54 (b) purposes. If the judgment is
otherwise certifiable, the fact that a litigant who has successfully reduced his
claim to judgment stands to lose money because of the difference in interest
rates is surely not a "just reason for delay."

The difference between the prejudgment and market interest rates was not
the only factor considered by the District Court. The court also noted that the
debts in issue were liquidated and large, and that absent Rule 54 (b) certification they would not be paid for "many months, if not years" because the rest of
the litigation could be expected to continue for that period of time. The District
Judge had noted earlier in his opinion on the merits of the release clause issue
that respondent General Electric contested neither the amount of the debt nor
the fact that it must eventually be paid. The only contest was over the effect of
the release clause on the timing of the payment, an isolated and strictly legal
issue on which summary judgment had been entered against respondent.

The question before the District Court thus came down to which of the parties should get the benefit of the difference between the prejudgment and market rates of interest on debts admittedly owing and adjudged to be due while
unrelated claims were litigated. The central factor weighing in favor of General
Electric was that its pending counterclaims created the possibility of a setoff
against the amount it owed petitioner. This possibility was surely not an
insignificant factor, especially since the counterclaims had survived a motion to
dismiss for failure to state a claim. But the District Court took this into account
when it determined that both litigants appeared to be in financially sound

condition, and that Curtiss-Wright would be able to satisfy a judgment on the counterclaims should any be entered. . . .

Nor is General Electric's solvency a dispositive factor; if its financial position were such that a delay in entry of judgment on Curtiss-Wright's claims would impair Curtiss-Wright's ability to collect on the judgment, that would weigh in favor of certification. But the fact that General Electric is capable of paying either now or later is not a "just reason for delay." At most, . . . the fact that neither party is or will become insolvent renders that factor neutral in a proper weighing of the equities involved.

The question in cases such as this is likely to be close, but the task of weighing and balancing the contending factors is peculiarly one for the trial judge, who can explore all the facets of a case. As we have noted, that assessment merits substantial deference on review. Here, the District Court's assessment of the equities between the parties was based on an intimate knowledge of the case and is a reasonable one. The District Court having found no other reason justifying delay, we conclude that it did not abuse its discretion in granting petitioner's motion for certification under Rule 54 (b).[2]

NOTES

1. The district court's determination that there is no just reason for delay is reviewed deferentially, for abuse of discretion. It is in the interest of appeals courts that trial courts not be unduly generous in making Rule 54(b) certifications because of the direct impact upon the appellate courts' dockets. If the district court fails to provide reasons for its certification, and the reasons are not apparent, the court of appeals may find an abuse of discretion and refuse to hear the appeal. *See, e.g., Waldorf v. Shuta*, 142 F.3d 601, 610-11 (3d Cir. 1998); *Brandt v. Bassett (In re Se. Banking Corp.)*, 69 F.3d 1539 (11th Cir. 1995) (noting that if district court does not explain the certification, any deference the court of appeals otherwise might give will be withheld). The district court's determination that it has made a final judgment as to fewer than all of the claims (a determination that entails both a determination of finality and a determination that what has been decided is not the same claim as that which remains to be decided) may be reviewed *de novo. See, e.g., Info. Res., Inc. v. Dun & Bradstreet Corp.*, 294 F.3d 447 (2d Cir. 2002); *Ginett v. Computer Task Group Inc.*, 962 F.2d 1085 (2d Cir. 1992). Other courts appear to look for an abuse of discretion.

2. A number of the states have rules that are counterparts of Federal Rule 54(b), so the issues that you have been examining arise in many state court systems as well. Among the states with similar rules are Alaska, Arizona, Illinois, Louisiana, Maine, Maryland, Minnesota, Missouri, Montana, New Mexico, North Carolina, North Dakota, Utah, West Virginia, and Wyoming. States with such rules often are guided by federal court decisions in interpreting their version of Rule 54(b). *See* Diane M. Allen, Annotation, *Modern*

---

2 [2] . . . Under this Rule [Federal Rule of Civil Procedure 62 (h)], we assume it would be within the power of the District Court to protect all parties by having the losing party deposit the amount of the judgment with the court, directing the Clerk to purchase high yield government obligations and to hold them pending the outcome of the case. In this way, valid considerations of economic duress and solvency, which do not affect the juridical considerations involved in a Rule 54 (b) determination, can be provided for without preventing Rule 54 (b) certification. . . .

Status of State Court Rules Governing Entry of Judgment on Multiple Claims,
80 A.L.R.4th 707 (1990).

3. The Collateral Order Doctrine

a. Generally

One of the consequences of the courts' effort to adjust to the statutory
requirement of finality was the development of the collateral order doctrine,
discussed in the following excerpt and involved in the following cases.

Maurice Rosenberg, *Solving the Federal Finality-Appealability Problem,* 47 LAW AND CONTEMPORARY PROBLEMS 171, 172 (1984)[3]

The existing federal finality-appealability situation is an unacceptable
morass. The problem is not merely that the law of appealability is a hodge-
podge, a kind of crazy quilt of legislation and judicial decisions. Crazy quilts
can be useful and there are occasions when inelegance in the legal system
works, but this is definitely not one of those occasions. Entirely too much of the
appellate courts' energy is absorbed in deciding whether they are entitled
under the finality principle and its exceptions to hear cases brought before
them — and in explaining why or why not. These explanations add to the complexity of the problem, but do nothing to dispel the confusion.

Many unkind remarks have been made about the maze of intricately unconnected legislative and judicial prescriptions governing federal appealability today.
One of the most blameworthy features of the legislation appears in the first sentence of the finality requirement, Section 1291 of the Judicial Code. It causes difficulties from that point on. Section 1291 declares: "The courts of appeals . . . shall
have jurisdiction of appeals from final decisions of the district courts. . . ." By negative implication, there is no "jurisdiction" in the court of appeals if the decision
is not final. Why make finality a predicate for jurisdiction? Presumably doing so
underlines the fact that Congress intends the finality requirement to be a serious
and unyielding prerequisite and one that not even the appellate courts themselves may set aside. The apparent analogy is to subject matter competence based
upon diversity of citizenship or amount in controversy. The analogy is misconceived. Diversity of citizenship is properly and necessarily prerequisite to federal
court jurisdiction in non-federal-question cases because Article 3 of the United
States Constitution so provides. Amount-in-controversy restrictions on the competence of major courts are sensible legislative means of protecting those courts
from inundation by small-claims suits. An important point about both the diversity and amount requirements is that they condition the courts' competence to
hear the action on attributes of the case itself, not on incidental procedural circumstances such as whether more remains to be done before the action is at an
end. Making the power of the appellate courts to proceed depend on finality
causes the courts to try to satisfy the requirement by inventing artificial forms of
finality. These strained interpretations, resulting in quasi-finality, are major

---

[3] Copyright © 1984 by Duke University School of Law and Gloria Rosenberg. Reprinted with
permission.

contributors to the morass. Any worthwhile reform of the federal finality-appealability rules should eliminate the "jurisdiction" language of Section 1291. Jurisdiction terminology should also be dropped from the other sections governing appealability, including the time-for-appeal provisions of Section 1297.

COHEN v. BENEFICIAL INDUSTRIAL LOAN CORPORATION
337 U.S. 541 (1949)

[Petitioner, representing a deceased shareholder of Beneficial, filed a shareholder's derivative suit in federal court in New Jersey, under diversity jurisdiction, claiming that managers and directors of Beneficial who were named as defendants had enriched themselves at the corporation's expense, in violation of their fiduciary duties. Beneficial moved to require petitioner to post a $125,000 bond, pursuant to a state statute that required the posting of such a bond in some derivative suits to cover defendants' costs, including attorneys' fees, if defendants prevailed in the litigation. The district court held that the state law did not apply to suits in federal court, and defendants appealed. Before reaching the merits, the Court addressed the appealability of the district court's decision.]

MR. JUSTICE JACKSON delivered the opinion of the Court.

At the threshold we are met with the question whether the District Court's order refusing to apply the statute was an appealable one. Title 28 U.S.C. § 1291 provides, as did its predecessors, for appeal only "from all final decisions of the district courts," except when direct appeal to this Court is provided. Section 1292 allows appeals also from certain interlocutory orders, decrees and judgments, not material to this case except as they indicate the purpose to allow appeals from orders other than final judgments when they have a final and irreparable effect on the rights of the parties. It is obvious that, if Congress had allowed appeals only from those final judgments which terminate an action, this order would not be appealable.

The effect of the statute is to disallow appeal from any decision which is tentative, informal or incomplete. Appeal gives the upper court a power of review, not one of intervention. So long as the matter remains open, unfinished or inconclusive, there may be no intrusion by appeal. But the District Court's action upon this application was concluded and closed and its decision final in that sense before the appeal was taken.

Nor does the statute permit appeals, even from fully consummated decisions, where they are but steps towards final judgment in which they will merge. The purpose is to combine in one review all stages of the proceeding that effectively may be reviewed and corrected if and when final judgment results. But this order of the District Court did not make any step toward final disposition of the merits of the case and will not be merged in final judgment. When that time comes, it will be too late effectively to review the present order, and the rights conferred by the statute, if it is applicable, will have been lost, probably irreparably. We conclude that the matters embraced in the decision appealed from are not of such an interlocutory nature as to affect, or to be affected by, decision of the merits of this case.

This decision appears to fall in that small class which finally determine claims of right separable from, and collateral to, rights asserted in the action, too important to be denied review and too independent of the cause itself to require that appellate consideration be deferred until the whole case is adjudicated. The Court has long given this provision of the statute this practical rather than a technical construction.

We hold this order appealable because it is a final disposition of a claimed right which is not an ingredient of the cause of action and does not require consideration with it. But we do not mean that every order fixing security is subject to appeal. Here it is the right to security that presents a serious and unsettled question. If the right were admitted or clear and the order involved only an exercise of discretion as to the amount of security, a matter the statute makes subject to reconsideration from time to time, appealability would present a different question. . . .

DIGITAL EQUIPMENT CORPORATION v. DESKTOP DIRECT, INC.
511 U.S. 863 (1994)

[Desktop Direct sued Digital Equipment for unlawful use of the "Desktop Direct" name. Soon after the filing of the complaint, the parties reached a settlement pursuant to which Digital agreed to pay Desktop for the right to use the "Desktop Direct" trade name and trademark, in exchange for dismissal of the trademark infringement suit. Desktop then filed a notice of dismissal in the district court. Several months later, however, Desktop moved to vacate the dismissal and rescind the settlement agreement on the ground that Digital had misrepresented material facts during the settlement negotiations. The district court granted this motion. Digital then appealed. The Court of Appeals for the Tenth Circuit dismissed Digital's appeal for lack of appellate jurisdiction, holding that the District Court order was not immediately appealable under the collateral order doctrine.]

JUSTICE SOUTER delivered the opinion of the Court.

. . . Applying the three-pronged test for determining when "collateral order" appeal is allowed, the Court of Appeals concluded that any benefits claimed under the settlement agreement were insufficiently "important" to warrant the immediate appeal as of right. Although Digital claimed . . . a "right not to go to trial," the court reasoned that any such privately negotiated right as Digital sought to vindicate was different in kind from an immunity rooted in an explicit constitutional or statutory provision or "compelling public policy rationale," the denial of which has been held to be immediately appealable. . . .

II

A

The collateral order doctrine is best understood not as an exception to the "final decision" rule laid down by Congress in § 1291, but as a "practical construction" of it, *Cohen, supra,* at 546. We have repeatedly held that the statute entitles a party to appeal not only from a district court decision that "ends the litigation on the merits and leaves nothing more for the court to do but execute the judgment," *Catlin* v. *United States*, 324 U.S. 229, 233 (1945), but also from a narrow class of decisions that . . . must, in the interest of "achieving a healthy legal system," . . . be treated as "final.". . .

But we have also repeatedly stressed that the "narrow" exception should . . . never be allowed to swallow the general rule, that a party is entitled to a single appeal, to be deferred until final judgment has been entered, in which claims of district court error at any stage of the litigation may be ventilated. We have accordingly described the conditions for collateral order appeal as stringent, see, *e. g., Midland Asphalt Corp.* v. *United States*, 489 U.S. 794, 799 (1989), and have warned that the issue of appealability under § 1291 is to be determined for the entire category to which a claim belongs, without regard to the chance that the litigation at hand might be speeded, or a "particular injustice" averted, *Van Cauwenberghe* v. *Biard*, 486 U.S. 517, 529 (1988), by a prompt appellate court decision.

B

Here, the Court of Appeals accepted Digital's claim that the order vacating dismissal (and so rescinding the settlement agreement) was the "final word on the subject addressed," and held the second *Cohen* condition, separability, to be satisfied, as well. Neither conclusion is beyond question, but each is best left untouched here . . . because the failure to meet the . . . condition . . . that the decision on an "important" question be "effectively unreviewable" upon final judgment, would in itself suffice to foreclose immediate appeal under § 1291. . . . [W]e conclude, despite Digital's position that it holds a "right not to stand trial" requiring protection by way of immediate appeal, that rights under private settlement agreements can be adequately vindicated on appeal from final judgment.

C

The roots of Digital's argument . . . are readily traced to *Abney* v. *United States*, 431 U.S. 651(1977), where we held that § 1291 entitles a criminal defendant to appeal an adverse ruling on a double jeopardy claim, without waiting for the conclusion of his trial. After holding the second *Cohen* requirement satisfied by the distinction between the former jeopardy claim and the question of guilt to be resolved at trial, we emphasized that the Fifth Amendment not only secures the right to be free from multiple punishments, but by its very terms embodies the broader principle . . . that it is intolerable for "'the State, with all its resources . . . to make repeated attempts to convict an individual [defendant], thereby subjecting him to embarrassment, expense and ordeal and compelling him to live in a continuing state of anxiety and insecurity.'" 431 U.S. at 661-662 (quoting *Green* v. *United States*, 355 U.S. 184, 187-188 (1957)). We found that immediate appeal was the only way to give "full protection" to this constitutional right "not to face trial at all."

Abney's rationale was applied in *Nixon* v. *Fitzgerald*, 457 U.S. 731, 742 (1982), where we held to be similarly appealable an order denying the petitioner absolute immunity from suit for civil damages arising from actions taken while petitioner was President of the United States. Seeing this immunity as a "functionally mandated incident of the President's unique office, rooted in the . . . separation of powers and supported by our history," we stressed that it served "compelling public ends," and would be irretrievably lost if the former President were not allowed an immediate appeal to vindicate this right to be free from the rigors of trial.

Next, in *Mitchell* v. *Forsyth*, 472 U.S. 511 (1985), we held that similar considerations supported appeal under § 1291 from decisions denying government officials qualified immunity from damages suits. An "essential attribute," of this freedom from suit for past conduct not violative of clearly established law, we explained, is the "entitlement not to stand trial or face the other burdens of litigation," one which would be "effectively lost if a case [were] erroneously permitted to go to trial". Echoing the reasoning of *Nixon* v. *Fitzgerald, supra* (and *Harlow* v. *Fitzgerald*, 457 U.S. 800 (1982)), we explained that requiring an official with a colorable immunity claim to defend a suit for damages would be "peculiarly disruptive of effective government," and would work the very "distraction . . . from . . . duty, inhibition of discretionary action, and deterrence of able people from public service" that qualified immunity was meant to avoid. See also *Puerto Rico Aqueduct and Sewer Authority* v. *Metcalf & Eddy, Inc.*, 506 U.S. 139, 147 (1993) (State's Eleventh Amendment immunity from suit in federal court may be vindicated by immediate appeal under § 1291).

D

Digital puts this case on all fours with *Mitchell*. It maintains that it obtained . . . under the settlement agreement . . . not only a broad defense to liability but the "right not to stand trial". . . . Digital's argument . . . does not hold up. . . . Digital's larger contention, that a party's ability to characterize a district court's decision as denying an irreparable "right not to stand trial" altogether is sufficient as well as necessary for a collateral order appeal, is neither an accurate distillation of our case law nor an appealing prospect for adding to it.

. . . [O]ur cases have been at least as emphatic in recognizing that the jurisdiction of the courts of appeals should not, and cannot, depend on a party's agility in so characterizing the right asserted. This must be so because the strong bias of § 1291 against piecemeal appeals almost never operates without some cost. . . . Thus, erroneous evidentiary rulings, grants or denials of attorney disqualification, and restrictions on the rights of intervening parties, may burden litigants in ways that are only imperfectly reparable by appellate reversal of a final district court judgment; and other errors, real enough, will not seem serious enough to warrant reversal at all, when reviewed after a long trial on the merits. In still other cases, see *Coopers & Lybrand* v. *Livesay*, 437 U.S. 463 (1978), an erroneous district court decision will, as a practical matter, sound the "death knell" for many plaintiffs' claims that might have gone forward if prompt error correction had been an option. But if immediate appellate review were available every such time, Congress's final decision rule would end up a pretty puny one, and so the mere identification of some interest that would be "irretrievably lost" has never sufficed to meet the third *Cohen* requirement.

Nor does limiting the focus to whether the interest asserted may be called a "right not to stand trial" offer much protection against the urge to push the

§ 1291 limits. . . . [V]irtually every right that could be enforced appropriately by pretrial dismissal might loosely be described as conferring a "right not to stand trial." Allowing immediate appeals to vindicate every such right would move §1291 aside for claims that the district court lacks personal jurisdiction, that the statute of limitations has run, that the movant has been denied his Sixth Amendment right to a speedy trial, that an action is barred on claim preclusion principles, that no material fact is in dispute and the moving party is entitled to judgment as a matter of law, or merely that the complaint fails to state a claim. Such motions can be made in virtually every case . . . ; the damage to the efficient and congressionally mandated allocation of judicial responsibility would be done, and any improper purpose the appellant might have had in saddling its opponent with cost and delay would be accomplished. Thus, . . . we have held that § 1291 requires courts of appeals to view claims of a "right not to be tried" with skepticism, if not a jaundiced eye. . . .

E

. . . The . . . fundamental response, however, to the claim that an agreement's provision for immunity from trial can distinguish it from other arguable rights to be trial free is simply that such a right by agreement does not rise to the level of importance needed for recognition under § 1291. . . . In disparaging any distinction between an order denying a claim grounded on an explicit constitutional guarantee of immunity from trial and an order at odds with an equally explicit right by private agreement of the parties, Digital stresses that the relative "importance" of these rights . . . is a rogue factor. No decision of this Court, Digital maintains, has held an order unappealable as "unimportant" when it has otherwise met the three *Cohen* requirements, and whether a decided issue is thought "important," it says, should have no bearing on whether it is "final" under § 1291.

If . . . "importance" were truly aberrational, we would not find it featured so prominently in the *Cohen* opinion itself . . . . To be sure, Digital may validly question whether "importance" is a factor "beyond" the three *Cohen* conditions or whether it is best considered, as we have sometimes suggested it should be, in connection with the second, "separability," requirement, but neither enquiry could lead to the conclusion that "importance" is itself unimportant. To the contrary, the third *Cohen* question, whether a right is "adequately vindicable" or "effectively reviewable," simply cannot be answered without a judgment about the value of the interests that would be lost through rigorous application of a final judgment requirement.

While there is no need to decide here that a privately conferred right could never supply the basis of a collateral order appeal, there are surely sound reasons for treating such rights differently from those originating in the Constitution or statutes. When a policy is embodied in a constitutional or statutory provision entitling a party to immunity from suit (a rare form of protection), there is little room for the judiciary to gainsay its "importance." Including a provision in a private contract, by contrast, is barely a prima facie indication that the right secured is "important" to the benefitted party (contracts being replete with boilerplate), let alone that its value exceeds that of other rights not embodied in agreements (*e. g.*, the right to be free from a second suit based on a claim that has already been litigated), or that it qualifies as "important" in *Cohen's* sense, as being weightier than the societal interests advanced by the ordinary operation of final judgment principles. Where statutory and constitutional rights are concerned, "irretrievable los[s]" can hardly be trivial, and the collateral order doctrine might therefore be understood as reflecting the familiar principle of statutory construction that, when possible, courts should construe statutes (here § 1291) to foster harmony with other statutory and constitutional law. But it is one thing to say that the policy of § 1291 to avoid piecemeal litigation should be reconciled with policies embodied in other statutes or the Constitution, and quite another to suggest that this public policy may be trumped routinely by the expectations or clever drafting of private parties.**4**

Nor are we swayed by Digital's last-ditch effort to come within *Cohen's* sense of "importance" by trying to show that settlement-agreement "immunities" merit first-class treatment for purposes of collateral order appeal, because they advance the public policy favoring voluntary resolution of disputes. It defies common sense to maintain that parties' readiness to settle will be significantly dampened (or the corresponding public interest impaired) by a rule that a district court's decision to let allegedly barred litigation go forward may be challenged as a matter of right only on appeal from a judgment for the plaintiff's favor.

III

A

Even, finally, if the term "importance" were to be exorcised from the *Cohen* analysis altogether, Digital's rights would remain "adequately vindicable" or "effectively reviewable" on final judgment to an extent that other immunities, like the right to be free from a second trial on a criminal charge, are not. As noted already, experience suggests that freedom from trial is rarely the *sine qua non* (or "the essence,") of a negotiated settlement agreement. Avoiding the burden of a trial is no doubt a welcome incident of out-of-court dispute resolution (just as it is for parties who prevail on pretrial motions), but in the run-of-the-mill cases this boon will rarely compare with the "'embarrassment'" and "'anxiety'" averted by a successful double jeopardy claimant, or the "'distraction from . . . duty,'" *Mitchell*, avoided by qualified immunity. Judged within the four corners of the settlement agreement, avoiding trial probably pales in comparison with the benefit of limiting exposure to liability (an interest that

---

4 [7] This is not to say that rights originating in a private agreement may never be important enough to warrant immediate appeal. To the contrary, Congress only recently enacted a statute, 102 Stat. 4671, see 9 U.S.C. § 16 (1988 ed., Supp. IV), essentially providing for immediate appeal when a district court rejects a party's assertion that, under the Arbitration Act, a case belongs before a commercial arbitrator and not in court, a measure predicted to have a "sweeping impact," 15B C. Wright, A. Miller, & E. Cooper, Federal Practice and Procedure § 3914.17, p. 11 (1992); see generally *id.* at 7-38. That courts must give full effect to this express congressional judgment that particular policies require that private rights be vindicable immediately, however, by no means suggests that they should now be more ready to make similar judgments for themselves. Congress has expressed no parallel sentiment, to the effect that settlement-agreement rights are, as a matter of federal policy, similarly "too important" to be denied immediate review.

is fully vindicable on appeal from final judgment). In the rare case where a party had a special reason, apart from the generic desire to triumph early, for having bargained for an immunity from trial, *e.g.*, an unusual interest in preventing disclosure of particular information, it may seek protection from the district court.

The case for adequate vindication without immediate appeal is strengthened, moreover, by recognizing that a settling party has a source of recompense unknown to trial immunity claimants dependent on public law alone. The essence of Digital's claim here is that Desktop, for valuable consideration, promised not to sue, and we have been given no reason to doubt that Utah law provides for the enforcement of that promise . . . through an action for breach of contract. . . .

B

In preserving the strict limitations on review as of right under § 1291, our holding should cause no dismay, for the law is not without its safety valve to deal with cases where the contest over a settlement's enforceability raises serious legal questions taking the case out of the ordinary run. While Digital's insistence that the District Court applied a fundamentally wrong legal standard in vacating the dismissal order here may not be considered in deciding appealability under § 1291, it plainly is relevant to the availability of the discretionary interlocutory appeal from particular district court orders "involving a controlling question of law as to which there is substantial ground for difference of opinion," provided for in § 1292(b) of Title 28. Indeed, because we suppose that a defendant's claimed entitlement to a privately negotiated "immunity from suit" could in some instances raise "a controlling question of law . . . [which] . . . may materially advance the ultimate termination of the litigation," the discretionary appeal provision (allowing courts to consider the merits of individual claims) would seem a better vehicle for vindicating serious contractual interpretation claims than the blunt, categorical instrument of § 1291 collateral order appeal.[5]

IV

. . . [D]enying effect to the sort of (asserted) contractual right at issue here is far removed from those immediately appealable decisions involving rights more deeply rooted in public policy, and the rights Digital asserts may, in the main, be vindicated through means less disruptive to the orderly administration of justice than immediate, mandatory appeal. We accordingly hold that a refusal to enforce a settlement agreement claimed to shelter a party from suit altogether does not supply the basis for immediate appeal under § 1291.

---

[5] [9] We recognize that § 1292 is not a panacea, both because it depends to a degree on the indulgence of the court from which review is sought and because the discretion to decline to hear an appeal is broad, see, *e.g., Coopers & Lybrand*, 437 U.S. at 475 (serious docket congestion may be adequate reason to support denial of certified appeal). On the other hand, we find nothing in the text or purposes of either statute to justify the concern, expressed here by Digital, that a party's request to appeal under § 1292(b) might operate, practically or legally, to prejudice its claimed right to immediate appeal under § 1291.

NOTES

1. The Court sometimes referred to the collateral order doctrine as an exception to the final decision rule, but more recently has characterized it as an interpretation of the rule. Would it be illegitimate for the Court to make exceptions, but permissible for it to interpret the final decision rule to allow for immediate appeals in the circumstances described in the collateral order doctrine?

2. What are the functions of the various components of the collateral order doctrine? Why should it be necessary for the disputed issue to have been conclusively determined? to be so important that it should not evade review? to be completely separate from the merits? to be effectively unreviewable after final judgment? Should the elements of the doctrine be altered?

3. In *Eisen v. Carlisle & Jacquelin*, 417 U.S. 156, 171-72 (1974), the Court upheld an immediate appeal from an order imposing on defendants 90% of the cost of giving notice of the action to class members. It found that the decision was "a final disposition of a claimed right [of defendants not to be required to pay the cost of notice to the class] which is not an ingredient of the cause of action and does not require consideration with it." Why would the Court also have believed that the issue was important and that defendant's rights could not be adequately vindicated after final judgment?

4. In *Cohen*, if the district court had granted the motion to require plaintiffs to post a bond, would that order have been immediately appealable?

b. Monitoring Trial Court Jurisdiction

(orders governing forum selection by stay, dismissal, or remand)

VAN CAUWENBERGHE v. BIARD
486 U.S. 517 (1988)

JUSTICE MARSHALL delivered the opinion of the Court.

This case requires us to determine whether two types of orders by a district court are immediately appealable under 28 U.S.C. § 1291: first, an order denying a motion to dismiss based on an extradited person's claim that he is immune from civil service of process; and second, an order denying a motion to dismiss on the ground of *forum non conveniens*.

This case arises from a dispute over a loan. Petitioner, a real estate broker in Brussels, encouraged respondent, also a Brussels resident, to meet with one Alan Blair in the United States to discuss a real estate investment. Blair is a resident of Los Angeles. Following a business trip to Atlanta, respondent traveled to Los Angeles where he met petitioner, Blair, and others to talk about the investment. Blair described a real estate partnership . . . which was renovating a townhouse complex outside Kansas City known as Concorde Bridge Townhouses. At petitioner's urging, respondent agreed to lend the partnership $1,000,000 for three years at 20% per annum interest, secured by a mortgage on the Concorde Bridge complex. At the time, the partnership did not have title to the Concorde Bridge complex, but it held a contract to purchase the complex and had made a substantial deposit.

The partnership, after making some scheduled payments, eventually defaulted on its promissory note to respondent. The mortgage proved worthless because the partnership had not acquired title to the Concorde Bridge complex. Respondent retained American counsel, claiming that he had been misled into believing that the partnership held title to the Concorde Bridge Townhouses at the time of the loan. Soon thereafter, United States prosecutors became involved in the controversy. In October 1984, petitioner, Blair, and another American were indicted in the Central District of California on charges of wire fraud and causing the interstate transportation of a victim of fraud. The indictment charged that the three defendants had fraudulently induced respondent to lend them $1,000,000 by falsely representing that they owned the Concorde Bridge complex through the real estate partnership.

While on a trip to Geneva, petitioner was arrested pursuant to a request from the United States Department of Justice under the applicable extradition treaty with Switzerland. Petitioner was extradited and delivered to Los Angeles by United States Marshals after legal proceedings in Swiss courts. Following a jury trial, petitioner was found guilty on one count of wire fraud and one count of causing the interstate transportation of a victim of fraud. . . .

On November 12, 1985, one week before petitioner's criminal trial commenced, respondent filed a civil suit against petitioner, Blair, and others in the District Court for the Central District of California. The complaint asserted a civil RICO claim, a common-law claim of fraud, and other pendent state-law claims arising out of the defaulted loan. On February 5, 1986, about two weeks after his sentencing, petitioner was served with the summons and complaint as he was arriving at the office of his probation officer to keep a scheduled appointment. Petitioner moves to dismiss the suit on two separate grounds. First, he argued that because his presence in the United States was a result of extradition he was immune from civil process. Second, petitioner argued that the complaint should be dismissed on the ground of *forum non conveniens*. The District Court summarily denied both motions. The Court of Appeals dismissed petitioner's appeal for lack of jurisdiction in a one-line order, citing this Court's decision in *Cohen v. Beneficial Industrial Loan Corp.*, 337 U.S. 541 (1949), and *Mitchell v. Forsyth*, 472 U.S. 511 (1985). We granted certiorari and we now affirm.

The Courts of Appeals have jurisdiction under 28 U.S.C. § 1291 of appeals "from all final decisions of the district courts . . . except where a direct review may be had in the Supreme Court." A party generally may not take an appeal under § 1291 until there has been a decision by the District Court that "ends the litigation on the merits and leaves nothing for the court to do but execute the judgment." *Catlin v. United States*, 324 U.S. 229, 233 (1945). In *Cohen v. Beneficial Industrial Loan Corp.*, *supra*, however, we recognized a "small class" of decisions that are immediately appealable under § 1291 even though the decision has not terminated the proceedings in the district court. 337 U.S. at 546. The Court stated that a decision is final and appealable for purposes of § 1291 if it "finally determine[s] the claims of right separable from, and collateral to, rights asserted in the action, too important to be denied review and too independent of the cause itself to require that appellate consideration be deferred until the whole case is adjudicated." *Ibid.* The Court refined the "collateral order" doctrine of *Cohen* in *Coopers & Lybrand v. Livesay*, 437 U.S. 463

(1978). In *Coopers & Lybrand*, the Court held that to come within the collateral order doctrine of *Cohen*, the order must satisfy each of three conditions: it must (1) "conclusively determine the disputed question," (2) "resolve an important issue completely separate from the merits of the action," and (3) "be effectively unreviewable on appeal from a final judgment." 437 U.S. at 468.

As petitioner acknowledges, the order of the District Court denying petitioner's motion to dismiss on grounds of immunity from civil process or *forum non conveniens* did not end the litigation on the merits. Therefore, the order is appealable as to either ground only if the three requirements set out in *Coopers & Lybrand* are met.

In asserting the appealability of his claim of immunity from civil process, petitioner principally relies on this Court's decision in *Mitchell & Forsyth*, *supra*. The Court held in *Mitchell* that the denial of a claim of qualified immunity by the Attorney General was immediately appealable under the collateral order doctrine. The crucial issue in *Mitchell* was whether the order was effectively unreviewable on appeal from final judgment. *See Id.* at 525. In holding that such an order was effectively unreviewable, the Court reasoned that an "essential attribute" of qualified immunity is "an entitlement not to stand trial under certain circumstances," and thus is "an *immunity from suit* rather than a mere defense to liability." *Id.* at 526. As with absolute immunity, the Court concluded, "[the entitlement] is effectively lost if a case is erroneously permitted to go to trial." *Id.* at 526.

Petitioner argues that under *United States v. Rauscher*, 119 U.S. 407 (1886), as well as under federal extradition statutes and the extradition treaty between the United States and Switzerland, he is immune from civil service of process while his presence in the United States is compelled by extradition for criminal charges. Petitioner further contends that his immunity under *Rauscher*, like the immunity in *Mitchell*, entails the right not to stand trial, which cannot be effectively vindicated on appeal from final judgment. In *Rauscher*, the Court stated the general "principle of specialty" in federal extradition law:

> [A] person who has been brought within the jurisdiction of the court by virtue of proceedings under an extradition treaty, can only be tried for one of the offenses described in that treaty, and for the offence with which he is charged in the proceedings for his extradition, until a reasonable time and opportunity have been given him, after his release or trial upon such charge, to return to the country from whose asylum he had been forcibly taken under those proceedings. 119 U.S. at 430.

Petitioner argues that the principle of specialty requires not merely that an extradited person be immune from criminal prosecutions other than the offenses for which he was extradited, but that he be generally "free from any judicial interference," including civil suit. Brief for Petitioner 18.

The issue on which we granted certiorari, however, and on which the Court of Appeals based its decision, is not whether petitioner's underlying claim of immunity is meritorious, but whether the denial of petitioner's motion to dismiss on grounds of immunity from service of process is immediately appealable. For purposes of determining appealability, therefore, we will assume, but do not decide, that petitioner has presented a substantial claim of immunity from civil service of process that warrants appellate consideration. Making this assumption, we conclude that petitioner's claim of immunity from service is effectively reviewable on appeal from final judgment, and thus is not an immediately appealable collateral order under *Cohen* and *Coopers & Lybrand.*

The critical question, following *Mitchell,* is whether "the essence" of the claimed right is a right not to stand trial. . . .

We . . . conclude that a right not to stand trial in a civil suit is not an essential aspect of a claim of immunity under the principle of specialty.

Given that the principle of specialty provides no independent support for petitioner's claim that he has a right not to stand trial, the question becomes whether such a right is entailed in the mere assertion that the district court lacks personal jurisdiction because of immunity from service of process. In the context of due process restrictions on the exercise of personal jurisdiction, this Court has recognized that the individual interest protected is in "not being subject to the binding judgments of a forum with which [the defendant] has established no meaningful 'contacts, ties or relations.'" *Burger King v. Rudzewicz.* Similarly, we believe petitioner's challenge to the District Court's exercise of personal jurisdiction because he is immune from civil process should be characterized as the right not to be subject to a binding judgment of the court. Because the right not to be subject to a binding judgment may be effectively vindicated following final judgment, we have held that the denial of claim of lack of jurisdiction is not an immediately appealable collateral order. *See Catlin v. United States,* 324 U.S. at 236. The Court of Appeals was therefore correct to conclude that the District Court's denial of petitioner's motion to dismiss on the ground of immunity from civil process is not immediately appealable.

Petitioner also argues that the District Court's order denying the motion to dismiss on the ground of *forum non conveniens* falls within the collateral order doctrine of *Cohen* and thus is immediately appealable under § 1291. We conclude, however, as have the majority of the Courts of Appeals that have considered the issue, that the question of the convenience of the forum is not "completely separate from the merits of the action," *Coopers & Lybrand,* 437 U.S. at 468 . . . and thus not immediately appealable as of right.

The requirement that the order be completely separate from the merits is "a distillation of the principle that there should not be piecemeal review of 'steps towards final judgment in which they will merge.'" *Moses H. Cone Mem. Hosp. v. Mercury Constr. Corp.,* 460 U.S. 1, 12, n.13 (1983), quoting *Cohen,* 337 U.S. at 546. Allowing appeals from interlocutory orders that involve considerations enmeshed in the merits of the dispute would waste judicial resources by requiring repetitive appellate review of substantive questions in the case. In *Gulf Oil Corp. v. Gilbert,* 330 U.S. 501, 508 (1947), the Court described various "[i]mportant considerations" for district courts to balance in deciding whether a particular forum is so inconvenient for the defendant as to warrant dismissal. We believe these considerations make clear that in assessing a *forum non conveniens* motion, the district court generally becomes entangled in the merits of the underlying dispute.

The Court in *Gulf Oil* stated that district courts must look into "the relative ease of access to sources of proof; availability of compulsory process for attendance of unwilling . . . witnesses; possibility of view of premises, if view would be appropriate to the action; and all other practical problems that make trial of a case easy, expeditious and inexpensive." *Ibid.* . . . To evaluate these factors, the court must consider the locus of the alleged culpable conduct, often a disputed issue, and the connection of that conduct to the plaintiff's chosen forum.

. . . As we previously have recognized, the district court is accorded substantial flexibility in evaluating a *forum non conveniens* motion, *id.* at 249, and "[e]ach case turns on its facts." *Williams v.Green Bay & Western R. Co.,* 326 U.S. 549, 557 (1946). It is thus undoubtedly true that in certain cases, the *forum non conveniens* determination will not require significant inquiry into the facts and legal issues presented by a case, and an immediate appeal might result in substantial savings of time and expense for both the litigants and the courts. In fashioning a rule of appealability under § 1291, however, we look to categories of cases, not to particular injustices. We believe that in the main, the issues that arise in *forum non conveniens* determinations will substantially overlap factual and legal issues of the underlying dispute, making such determinations unsuited for immediate appeal as of right under § 1291.

Our conclusion that the denial of a motion to dismiss on the ground of *forum non conveniens* is not appealable under § 1291 is fortified by the availability of interlocutory review pursuant to 28 U.S.C. § 1292(b). Under § 1292(b), a district court may certify a nonfinal order for interlocutory review when the order "involves a controlling question of law as to which there is substantial ground for difference of opinion and . . . an immediate appeal from the order may materially advance the ultimate termination of the litigation." A court of appeals may then, in its discretion, determine whether the order warrants prompt review. Section 1292(b) therefore provides an avenue for review of *forum non conveniens* determinations in appropriate cases.

We hold that neither an order denying a motion to dismiss on grounds that an extradited person is immune from civil process, nor an order denying a motion to dismiss on the ground of *forum non conveniens*, is a collateral order subject to appeal as a final judgment under 28 U.S.C. § 1291. The Court of Appeals therefore lacked jurisdiction to consider petitioner's appeal. Accordingly, the judgment of the Court of Appeals is affirmed.

LAURO LINES S.R.L. v. CHASSER
490 U.S. 495 (1989)

JUSTICE BRENNAN delivered the opinion of the Court.

We granted certiorari to consider whether an interlocutory order of a United States District Court denying a defendant's motion to dismiss a damages action on the basis of a contractual forum-selection clause is immediately appealable under 28 U. S. C. § 1291 as a collateral final order. We hold that it is not.

I

The individual respondents were, or represent the estates of persons who were, passengers aboard the cruise ship Achille Lauro when it was hijacked by terrorists in the Mediterranean in October 1985. Petitioner Lauro Lines s.r.l., an Italian company, owns the Achille Lauro. Respondents filed suits against Lauro Lines in the District Court for the Southern District of New York to recover damages for injuries sustained as a result of the hijacking and for the wrongful death of passenger Leon Klinghoffer. Lauro Lines moved before trial to dismiss the actions, citing the forum-selection clause printed on each passenger ticket. This clause purported to obligate the passenger to institute any suit arising in connection with the contract in Naples, Italy, and to renounce the right to sue elsewhere.

The District Court denied petitioner's motions to dismiss, holding that the ticket as a whole did not give reasonable notice to passengers that they were waiving the opportunity to sue in a domestic forum. Without moving for certification for immediate appeal pursuant to 28 U.S.C. § 1292(b), Lauro Lines sought to appeal the District Court's orders. The Court of Appeals for the Second Circuit dismissed petitioner's appeal on the ground that the District Court's orders denying petitioner's motions to dismiss were interlocutory and not appealable under § 1291. The court held that the orders did not fall within the exception to the rule of nonappealability carved out for collateral final orders in *Cohen v. Beneficial Industrial Loan Corp.*, 337 U.S. 541 (1949). We granted certiorari to resolve a disagreement among the Courts of Appeals. We now affirm.

II

Title 28 U. S. C. § 1291 provides for appeal to the courts of appeals only from "final decisions of the district courts of the United States." For purposes of § 1291, a final judgment is generally regarded as "a decision by the district court that 'ends the litigation on the merits and leaves nothing for the court to do but execute the judgment.'" *Van Cauwenberghe v. Biard*, 486 U.S. 517, 521 (1988), quoting *Catlin v. United States*, 324 U.S. 229, 233 (1945). An order denying a motion to dismiss a civil action on the ground that a contractual forum-selection clause requires that such suit be brought in another jurisdiction is not a decision on the merits that ends the litigation. On the contrary, such an order "ensures that litigation will continue in the District Court." *Gulfstream Aerospace Corp. v. Mayacamas Corp.*, 485 U.S. 271, 275 (1988). Section 1291 thus permits an appeal only if an order denying a motion to dismiss based upon a forum-selection clause falls within the "narrow exception to the normal application of the final judgment rule [that] has come to be known as the collateral order doctrine." *Midland Asphalt Corp. v. United States*, 489 U.S. 794, 798 (1989). . . . For present purposes, we need not decide whether an order denying a dismissal motion based upon a contractual forum-selection clause conclusively determines a disputed issue, or whether it resolves an important issue that is independent of the merits of the action, for the District Court's orders fail to satisfy the third requirement of the collateral order test [that is, that the order be effectively unreviewable on appeal from a final judgment].

We recently reiterated the "general rule" that an order is "effectively unreviewable" only "where the order at issue involves 'an asserted right the legal and practical value of which would be destroyed if it were not vindicated before trial.'" *Midland Asphalt Corp., supra*, at 798, quoting *United States v. MacDonald*, 435 U.S. 850, 860 (1978). If it is eventually decided that the District Court erred in allowing trial in this case to take place in New York, petitioner will have been put to unnecessary trouble and expense, and the value of its contractual right to an Italian forum will have been diminished. It is always true, however, that "there is value . . . in triumphing before trial, rather than after it," *MacDonald, supra*, at 860, n.7, and this Court has declined to find the costs associated with unnecessary litigation to be enough to warrant allowing the immediate appeal of a pretrial order, see *Richardson-Merrell Inc., supra*, at 436 ("[T]he possibility that a ruling may be erroneous and may impose additional litigation expense is not sufficient to set aside the finality requirement imposed by Congress" in § 1291). Instead, we have insisted that the right asserted be one that is essentially destroyed if its vindication must be postponed until trial is completed.

We have thus held in cases involving criminal prosecutions that the deprivation of a right *not to be tried* is effectively unreviewable after final judgment and is immediately appealable. Similarly, in civil cases, we have held that the denial of a motion to dismiss based upon a claim of absolute immunity from suit is immediately appealable prior to final judgment, *Nixon v. Fitzgerald*, 457 U.S. 731, 742-743 (1982), "for the essence of absolute immunity is its possessor's entitlement not to have to answer for his conduct in a civil damages action," *Mitchell v. Forsyth*, 472 U.S. 511, 525 (1985). And claims of qualified immunity may be pursued by immediate appeal, because qualified immunity too "is an *immunity from suit*." *Id.* at 526 (emphasis in original).

On the other hand, we have declined to hold the collateral order doctrine applicable where a district court has denied a claim, not that the defendant has a right not to be sued at all, but that the suit against the defendant is not properly before the particular court because it lacks jurisdiction. In *Van Cauwenberghe v. Biard*, 486 U.S. 517 (1988), a civil defendant moved for dismissal on the ground that he had been immune from service of process because his presence in the United States had been compelled by extradition to face criminal charges. We noted that, after *Mitchell*, "[t]he critical question . . . is whether 'the essence' of the claimed right is a right not to stand trial," 486 U.S. at 524, and held that the immunity from service of process defendant asserted did not amount to an immunity from suit — even though service was essential to the trial court's jurisdiction over the defendant. *See also Catlin v. United States*, 324 U.S. at 236 (order denying motion to dismiss petition for condemnation of land not immediately appealable, "even when the motion is based upon jurisdictional grounds").

Lauro Lines argues here that its contractual forum selection clause provided it with a right to trial before a tribunal in Italy, and with a concomitant right not to be sued anywhere else. This "right not to be haled for trial before tribunals outside the agreed forum," petitioner claims, cannot effectively be vindicated by appeal after trial in an improper forum. Brief for Petitioner 38-39. There is no obviously correct way to characterize the right embodied in petitioner's forum-selection provision: "all litigants who have a meritorious pretrial claim for dismissal can reasonably claim a right not to stand trial." *Van Cauwenberghe, supra,* at 524. The right appears most like the right to be free from trial if it is characterized — as by petitioner — as a right not to be sued at all except in a Neapolitan forum. It appears less like a right not to be subjected to suit if characterized — as by the Court of Appeals — as "a right to have the binding adjudication of claims occur in a certain forum." 844 F. 2d, at 55. *Cf. Van Cauwenberghe, supra,* at 526-527. Even assuming that the former characterization is proper, however, petitioner is obviously not entitled under the forum-selection clause of its contract to avoid suit altogether, and an entitlement to avoid suit is different in kind from an entitlement to be sued only in a particular forum. Petitioner's claim that it may be sued only in Naples, while not perfectly secured by appeal after final judgment, is adequately vindicable at that stage — surely as effectively vindicable as a claim that the trial court lacked personal jurisdiction over the defendant — and hence does not fall within the third prong of the collateral order doctrine.

Petitioner argues that there is a strong federal policy favoring the enforcement of foreign forum-selection clauses, citing *The Bremen v. Zapata Off-Shore Co.,* 407 U.S. 1 (1972), and that "the essential concomitant of this strong federal policy . . . is the right of immediate appellate review of district court orders denying their enforcement." Brief for Petitioner 40-41. A policy favoring enforcement of forum selection clauses, however, would go to the merits of petitioner's claim that its ticket agreement requires that any suit be filed in Italy and that the agreement should be enforced by the federal courts. Immediate appealability of a prejudgment order denying enforcement, insofar as it depends upon satisfaction of the third prong of the collateral order test, turns on the precise contours of the right asserted, and not upon the likelihood of eventual success on the merits. The Court of Appeals properly dismissed petitioner's appeal, and its judgment is

Affirmed.

JUSTICE SCALIA, concurring.

I join the opinion of the Court and write separately only to make express what seems to me implicit in its analysis.

The reason we say that the right not to be sued elsewhere than in Naples is "adequately vindicable" by merely reversing any judgment obtained in violation of it is, quite simply, that the law does not deem the right *important enough* to be vindicated by, as it were, an injunction against its violation obtained through interlocutory appeal. The importance of the right asserted has always been a significant part of our collateral order doctrine. When first formulating that doctrine in *Cohen v. Beneficial Industrial Loan Corp.,* 337 U.S. 541 (1949), we said that it permits interlocutory appeal of final determinations of claims that are not only "separable from, and collateral to, rights asserted in the action," but also, we immediately added, *"too important* to be denied review." *Id.* at 546 (emphasis added). Our later cases have retained that significant requirement. For example, in *Abney v. United States,* 431 U.S. 651 (1977), we said that in order to qualify for immediate appeal the order must involve "an *important* right which would be 'lost, probably irreparably,' if review had to await final judgment." *Id.* at 658 (emphasis added), quoting *Cohen, supra,* at 546. And in *Coopers & Lybrand v. Livesay,* 437 U.S. 463 (1978), we said that the order must "resolve an *important* issue completely separate from the merits of the action." *Id.* at 468 (emphasis added).

While it is true, therefore, that the "right not to be sued elsewhere than in Naples" is not fully vindicated — indeed, to be utterly frank, is positively destroyed — by permitting the trial to occur and reversing its outcome, that is vindication enough because the right is not sufficiently important to overcome the policies militating against interlocutory appeals. We have made that judgment when the right not to be tried in a particular court has been created through jurisdictional limitations established by Congress or by international treaty, see *Van Cauwenberghe, supra.* The same judgment applies — if anything, *a fortiori* — when the right has been created by private agreement.

MOSES H. CONE MEMORIAL HOSPITAL v. MERCURY CONSTRUCTION CORP.
460 U.S. 1 (1983)

[A dispute arose as to the amounts due under a construction contract for the performance of work at the Moses H. Cone Hospital. After considerable negotiations, the hospital filed an action in the North Carolina state court seeking a declaratory judgment as to the amounts due and that the claims were not subject to arbitration. While that suit was pending, the defendant commenced this action in a federal district court seeking to compel arbitration of the claims under the Federal Arbitration Act. Jurisdiction was based on diversity of citizenship. On the hospital's motion, the district court stayed the action pending resolution of the state court suit on the ground that the two suits involved the identical issue of the arbitrability of the claims against the hospital. The plaintiff in the federal action (Mercury) sought review of the district court stay in the U.S. Court of Appeals for the Fourth Circuit by filing both a notice of appeal and a petition for mandamus. After a rehearing en banc, the court of appeals held that it had appellate jurisdiction under 28 U.S.C. Section 1291, and it reversed the stay order and remanded the case to the district court with instructions for entry of an order to arbitrate.]

JUSTICE BRENNAN delivered the opinion of the Court.

. . . Before we address the propriety of the District Judge's stay order, we must first decide whether that order was appealable to the Court of Appeals under 28 U.S.C. § 1291.

Mercury sought appellate review through two alternative routes — a notice of appeal under § 1291, and a petition for mandamus under the All Writs Act, 28 U.S.C. § 1651. Mercury expressly stated that its appeal was based only on § 1291, and not on 28 U.S.C. § 1292 (relating to interlocutory appeals). The Hospital contends that the order appealed from was not a "final decisio[n]" within § 1291. We disagree and hold that the stay order was final for purposes of appellate jurisdiction.

Idlewild Liquor Corp. v. Epstein, 370 U.S. 713 (1962), is instructive in this regard. There the plaintiff brought a federal suit challenging the constitutionality of a state statute. The District Judge . . . stayed the federal suit under the . . . abstention doctrine. We held that the District Court's action was final and therefore reviewable by the Court of Appeals . . . [because] "appellant was effectively out of court." . . .

Here . . . the District Court predicated its stay order on its conclusion that the federal and state actions involved "the identical issue of arbitrability of the claims of Mercury Construction Corp. against the Moses H. Cone Memorial Hospital." That issue of arbitrability was the only substantive issue present in the federal suit. Hence, a stay of the federal suit pending resolution of the state suit meant that there would be no further litigation in the federal forum; the state court's judgment on the issue would be res judicata. Thus, here, even more surely than in *Idlewild*, Mercury was "effectively out of court." Hence, as the Court of Appeals held, this stay order amounts to a dismissal of the suit.[6]

In any event, if the District Court order were not final for appealability purposes, it would nevertheless be appealable within the exception to the finality rule under *Cohen v. Beneficial Loan Corp.*, 337 U.S. 541 (1949). . . .

An order that amounts to a refusal to adjudicate the merits plainly presents an important issue separate from the merits. For the same reason, this order would be entirely unreviewable if not appealed now. Once the State court decided the issue of arbitrability the federal court would be bound to honor that determination as res judicata.

The Hospital contends nevertheless that the District Court's stay order did not . . . "conclusively determine the disputed question." But this is true only in the technical sense that every order short of a final decree is subject to reopening at the discretion of the district judge. In this case, however, there is no basis to suppose that the District Judge contemplated any reconsideration of his decision to defer to the parallel statecourt suit. He surely would not have made that decision in the first instance unless he had expected the state court to resolve all relevant issues adequately. It is not clear why the judge chose to stay the case rather than to dismiss it outright; for all that the record shows, there was no reason other than the form of the Hospital's motion. Whatever the reason, however, the practical effect of his order was entirely the same for present purposes, and the order was appealable. . . .

[The opinion then addressed the propriety of the district court's stay. The Court concluded that the court of appeals was correct in reversing the stay order and in ordering arbitration.]

Affirmed.

---

[6] [11] Of course . . . *Idlewild* does not disturb the usual rule that a stay is not ordinarily a final decision for purposes of § 1291, since most stays do not put the plaintiff "effectively out of court." . . .

JUSTICE REHNQUIST, with whom THE CHIEF JUSTICE and JUSTICE O'CONNOR join, dissenting.

In its zeal to provide arbitration for a party it thinks deserving, the Court has made an exception to established rules of procedure. The Court's attempt to cast the District Court's decision as a final judgment fails to do justice to the meaning of the word "final," to the Act of Congress that limits the jurisdiction of the courts of appeals, or to the district judges who administer the laws in the first instance.

If the District Court had not stayed the proceeding, but had set a trial date two months away, there would be no doubt that its order was interlocutory, subject to review only by mandamus or pursuant to 28 U.S.C. § 1292(b). This would be true even though § 4 of the Arbitration Act provides that "the court shall proceed summarily" to trial, because an order setting a trial date only guides the course of litigation, and does not, of its own force, dispose of it on the merits. Such an order is tentative; that is, it is subject to change at any time on the motion of a party or by the court, *sua sponte*.

The order the District Court actually entered is no more final. It delayed further proceedings until the completion of pending litigation in the state courts. This order was also tentative; it was subject to change on a showing that the state proceedings were being delayed, either by the Hospital or by the court, or that the state courts were not applying the federal Act, or that some other reason for a change had arisen. This order did not dispose of the case on the merits. If the state court had found that there was no agreement to arbitrate within the meaning of the United States Arbitration Act, the District Court would have been bound by that finding. But res judicata or collateral estoppel would apply if the state court reached a decision before the District Court in the absence of a stay. The likelihood that a state court of competent jurisdiction may enter a judgment that may determine some issue in a case does not render final a federal district court's decision to take a two-day recess, or to order additional briefing by the parties in five days or five months, or to take a case under advisement rather than render an immediate decision from the bench. Such a possibility did not magically change that character of the order the District Judge entered in this case.

Section 1291 of the Judicial Code is a congressional command to the federal courts of appeals not to interfere with the district courts' management of ongoing proceedings. Unless the high standards for a writ of mandamus can be met, or the district court certifies an interlocutory appeal pursuant to § 1292(b), Congress has directed that the district courts be permitted to conduct their cases as they see fit. The reason for this rule is simple:

> Since the right to a judgment from more than one court is a matter of grace and not a necessary ingredient of justice, Congress from the very beginning has, by forbidding piecemeal disposition on appeal of what for practical purposes is a single controversy, set itself against enfeebling judicial administration. Thereby is avoided the obstruction to just claims that would come from permitting the harassment and cost of a succession of separate appeals from the various rulings to which a litigation may give rise, from its initiation to entry of judgment. To be

effective, judicial administration must not be leaden-footed. Its momentum would be arrested by permitting separate reviews of the component elements in a unified cause. *Cobbledick v. United States*, 309 U.S. 323, 325 (1940) (Frankfurter, J., for a unanimous Court).

The Court's decision places an unwarranted limitation upon the power of district courts to control their own cases. The Court's opinion does not establish a broad exception to § 1291 but it does create uncertainty about when a district court order in a pending case can be appealed. This uncertainty gives litigants opportunities to disrupt or delay proceedings by taking colorable appeals from interlocutory orders, not only in cases nearly identical to this but also in cases which the ingenuity of counsel disappointed by a district court's ruling can analogize to this one. . . .

I am not as certain as is the Court that by staying this case the District Court resolved "an important issue." An issue should not be deemed "important" for these purposes simply because the court of appeals or this Court thinks the appellant should prevail. The issue here was whether the factual question — whether there was an agreement to arbitrate — should be adjudicated in a state or federal court. Unless there is some reason to believe that the state court will resolve this factual question wrongly, which the Court quite rightly disclaims, I do not see how this issue is more important than any other interlocutory order that may place a litigant at a procedural disadvantage.

For these reasons, I do not believe the District Court's order was appealable. . . .

NOTES

1. If the court had held that the district court's stay order was not "final" within the meaning of § 1291 and therefore not appealable, could the stay order have been reviewed on a petition for mandamus in the court of appeals? See the material on mandamus, later in this chapter.

2. *Quackenbush v. Allstate Insurance Co., supra*, p. 53, described *Moses Cone* this way:

> [T]he stay order at issue in *Moses H. Cone* was appealable under the collateral order doctrine. We determined that a stay order based on the *Colorado River* doctrine "presents an important issue separate from the merits" because it "amounts to a refusal to adjudicate" the case in federal court; that such orders could not be reviewed on appeal from a final judgment in the federal action because the district court would be bound, as a matter of res judicata, to honor the state court's judgment; and that unlike other stay orders, which might readily be reconsidered by the district court, abstention-based stay orders of this ilk are "conclusive" because they are the practical equivalent of an order dismissing the case.

517 U.S. at 713 (*quoting Moses Cone*, 460 U.S. at 12). As an alternative to holding the abstention-based remand in question in *Quackenbush* to be a "final decision," the Court also held that the remand was indistinguishable

from the stay order considered in *Moses H. Cone* in that it conclusively determined an issue separate from the merits, namely, whether the federal court
should decline to exercise its jurisdiction in the interest of comity and federalism. In addition, the rights asserted on appeal were, in its view, sufficiently
important to warrant an immediate appeal. And, like the stay order found
appealable in *Moses H. Cone*, the district court's remand order in
Quackenbush would not be subsumed in any other appealable order entered
by the district court.

3. In *Gulfstream Aerospace Corp. v. Mayacamas Corp.*, 485 U.S. 271 (1988),
the parties had accused one another of breach of contract in separate actions.
The Court held that a denial of a federal court stay in deference to the prior-
filed state court action could not be treated as a denial of an injunction pursuant to § 1292(a)(1). (In so holding, the Court overruled a line of cases
distinguishing stays of actions at law from stays of suits in equity.) It also held
that the denial was not immediately appealable under the collateral order
doctrine:

> [T]he order fails to meet the initial requirement of a conclusive deter-
> mination of the disputed question. A district court that denies a
> *Colorado River* motion does not "necessarily contemplate" that the
> decision will close the matter for all time. In denying such a motion,
> the district court may well have determined only that it should await
> further developments before concluding that the balance of factors to
> be considered under *Colorado River* warrants a dismissal or stay. The
> district court, for example, may wish to see whether the state-court
> proceeding becomes more comprehensive than the federal-court
> action or whether the former begins to proceed at a more rapid pace.
> Thus, whereas the granting of a *Colorado River* motion necessarily
> implies an expectation that the state court will resolve the dispute,
> the denial of such a motion may indicate nothing more than that the
> district court is not completely confident of the propriety of a stay or
> dismissal at that time. Indeed, given both the nature of the factors to
> be considered under *Colorado River* and the natural tendency of
> courts to attempt to eliminate matters that need not be decided from
> their dockets, a district court usually will expect to revisit and
> reassess an order denying a stay in light of events occurring in the
> normal course of litigation. Because an order denying a *Colorado
> River* motion is "inherently tentative" in this critical sense — because
> it is not "made with the expectation that it will be the final word on
> the subject addressed" — the order is not a conclusive determination
> within the meaning of the collateral-order doctrine and therefore is
> not appealable under § 1291.

4. A stay order ostensibly based on *Colorado River* abstention is not necessarily final and appealable. In *Michelson v. Citicorp National Services, Inc.*,
138 F.3d 508 (3d Cir. 1998), the court held such a stay not to be final and
appealable because Michelson was not a party to the state court case which,
like his suit, challenged the reasonableness of Citicorp's method of calculating
termination charges (although under different bodies of law), and res judicata
therefore would not preclude him from proceeding with his claim in federal

court once the state court action was resolved. Michelson therefore had to await the completion of the state court suit, although the stay of his action likely was erroneous.

5. Consider *Green Tree Financial Corp.-Alabama v. Randolph*, 531 U.S. 79 (2000). A mobile home financing agreement required Randolph to buy insurance protecting certain financial institutions from costs of re-possession resulting from any default by Randolph, and further provided that all disputes under the contract would be resolved by binding arbitration. Randolph sued the institutions, alleging that they violated the Truth in Lending Act (TILA) by certain failures to disclose and that they violated the Equal Credit Opportunity Act by requiring her to arbitrate her statutory causes of action. The District Court granted defendants' motion to compel arbitration and dismissed Randolph's claims with prejudice. The Eleventh Circuit held that it had jurisdiction to review the District Court's order under the Federal Arbitration Act (FAA), which allows appeals from "a final decision with respect to an arbitration . . . subject to this title." The Supreme Court affirmed that aspect of the decision below, agreeing that the decision was "final" within the meaning of the FAA, and therefore appealable. It reasoned that the term "final decision" has a well-developed and longstanding meaning as a decision that ends the litigation on the merits and leaves nothing more for the court to do but execute the judgment. Because the FAA did not suggest that the ordinary meaning of "final decision" should not apply, the Court accorded the term its well-established meaning. And because the district court's order disposed of the entire case on the merits and left no part of it pending before the court, the order was "final." The fact that, under the FAA, parties may bring a separate proceeding to enter judgment on an arbitration award, or to vacate or modify such an award, did not undermine the finality of the resolution of the distinct claims presented below. Nor did it matter that this proceeding involved both an arbitration request and other claims for relief, so long as all the claims had been dismissed, as they were here.

6. In the wake of *Green Tree*, the Second Circuit held that a dismissal of a case without prejudice to reopening upon issuance of the arbitrator's decision was a final decision, *Salim Oleochemicals v. M/V Shropshire*, 278 F.3d 90 (2d Cir. 2002), while the Sixth Circuit held that an order staying proceedings pending arbitration is not final and appealable even if the court closes the case, subject to reopening, *ATAC Corp. v. Arthur Treacher's Inc.*, 280 F.3d 1091 (6th Cir. 2002). The parties have to decide what to ask for. The plaintiff might prefer dismissal so that it could immediately appeal being sent or left to arbitration, or the plaintiff might prefer to get on with its claim, in some forum, rather than wait through an appeal, and therefore might seek an unappealable stay. The defendant might seek dismissal because it prefers delay and an appeal by plaintiff could delay the arbitration, or defendant might prefer a stay so as to forestall any immediate appeal and get the parties through a resolution of the claims in arbitration.

c. Discovery Orders

One might think that many discovery orders, particularly those compelling disclosure, would be immediately appealable under the collateral order doctrine: that such orders would finally determine issues separate from the merits and sufficiently important that they ought not evade review, and be effectively unreviewable after final judgment. In fact, courts hold discovery orders to be immediately appealable in relatively few instances. They may rationalize this result under any of the prongs of the *Cohen* test. Often, the perception that the discovery issue is not sufficiently important to warrant an interlocutory appeal, and the fear of a flood of discovery appeals, underlie the decisions rejecting appealability under the collateral order doctrine. Courts have looked to other vehicles that allow immediate appellate examination of trial court orders (to mandamus, and to § 1292(b) certification, for example) to accommodate the relatively few discovery orders that cry out for immediate review. Most often, they have relied upon the ability of a party to have itself held in contempt, and subjected to sanctions for the contempt, as a way of identifying which discovery orders are worthy of immediate appellate review. As you read the cases that follow, consider whether resort to contempt of court as a trigger for appellate review is appropriate and an adequate mechanism for affording interlocutory review of discovery orders.

UNITED STATES v. COLUMBIA BROADCASTING SYSTEM, INC.
666 F.2d 364 (9th Cir. 1982)

BOOCHEVER, CIRCUIT JUDGE:

This is a consolidated appeal by five nonparty witnesses who were subpoenaed to produce massive quantities of documents and deposition testimony for use in antitrust suits brought by the Justice Department. The issues are whether this court has jurisdiction to review the district court's order denying the nonparty witnesses' post-production motion for reimbursement of their substantial discovery costs, and, if so, whether the denial of reimbursement without stated reasons constituted an abuse of discretion.

We conclude that the order was final as to these nonparty witnesses, and thus appealable under 28 U.S.C. § 1291, by operation of the collateral order doctrine first articulated in *Cohen v. Beneficial Industrial Loan Corp.*, 337 U.S. 541 (1949). We further conclude that, in light of the district court's failure to articulate findings of fact or conclusions of law in support of its decision, the record before us affords an insufficient basis for determining whether the court properly exercised its discretion in denying the nonparties any reimbursement for their discovery costs. Accordingly, we reverse and remand.

Appellants are five producers of television programming (the "studios") who were subpoenaed as nonparty witnesses by CBS and ABC (the "networks") to produce extensive pretrial discovery material for use in antitrust suits brought against the networks by the Justice Department. The Government's nearly identical complaints against the networks principally challenged the manner in which the networks acquired prime-time programming from independent producers such as the studios.

The first three and one-half years of the litigation consisted primarily of dis-putes over jurisdiction, the legal sufficiency of the Government's case, and the Government's discovery demands on the networks. The district court eventu-ally ordered the Government to identify "with particularity" each of its claims and the evidence it intended to offer. The Government's "Identification of Evidence" indicated that it planned to challenge a wide range of the networks' dealings with program suppliers and talent, specifically putting in issue sev-eral hundred transactions spread over more than a twenty-year period.

In August and September 1978, the networks served subpoenas duces tecum and ad testificandum upon the nonparty studios and a number of their officers and employees who the Government had identified as witnesses. Consistent with the breadth of the Government's case, the networks' discovery demands were extensive. The subpoenas sought production of most of the material in the studios' control that pertained to production of television programming and theatrical films since 1960.

The studios moved to quash the subpoenas pursuant to FED. R. CIV. P. 45(b). In the motion, the studios expressly "reserved" the right to seek reimburse-ment of discovery costs if production was ordered. The studios subsequently filed memoranda in support of their motion to quash in which they specifically requested the networks to pay at least some discovery costs.

The district court ruled on the motion to quash on March 6, 1979, enforcing most of the subpoenas with limited modifications and setting a deadline for compliance. The order contained no mention of costs. The studios did not seek timely reconsideration or appellate review of the order, and, instead, immedi-ately began to comply with its dictates.

In order to comply with the networks' discovery demands, the studios hired and trained large staffs of lawyers, paralegals, accountants, and clerks to glean relevant material from their warehouse-sized depositories of archived documents. Thousands of boxes of documents were transported to offices spe-cially set aside and equipped by the studios for discovery purposes, where the documents were reviewed, organized, copied, and sent to the networks. The networks also subpoenaed numerous officers and employees of the studios. Seventeen of these individuals were eventually deposed over a period of more than eighty work days.

The studios filed five Status Reports during the eighteen months it took to complete document production. In these five reports, the studios kept the dis-trict court informed of the progress they were making in production, the type of services and facilities they were providing, and the costs they were incur-ring. The studios also reiterated to the district court and the networks their intention to seek reimbursement of costs.

On March 14, 1980, after having produced all the requested documentary material, the studios filed a motion seeking termination of discovery and reim-bursement for some or all of the approximately $2.3 million out-of-pocket costs they allegedly incurred in complying with the networks' discovery demands. By minute order dated March 27, 1980, the district court declared discovery complete and declined to award the studios any reimbursement. The order contained no findings of fact or conclusions of law pertaining to the denial of costs.

The studios filed a timely appeal from the March 27, 1980 minute order, arguing that the denial of any reimbursement constituted an abuse of discretion. On October 20, 1980, a motions panel of this court denied the networks' motion to dismiss for lack of appellate jurisdiction without prejudice to its renewal before the present merits panel. Final consent judgments were entered against CBS and ABC on July 31, 1980 and November 14, 1980, respectively.

The networks contend that the studios' motion for costs was untimely under FED. R. CIV. P. 45(b) because it was made a year after the district court ruled on the motion to quash and after compliance with the subpoenas was virtually complete. . . .

Under the networks' logic, in order to avoid having any right to eventual reimbursement foreclosed, a nonparty witness would have no alternative but to file a motion to quash and to demand advancement of costs as a *sine qua non* of production. . . . [A] witness willing to produce would be forced to suffer contempt and to interrupt discovery, thereby indefinitely delaying trial, solely to resolve the question of entitlement to costs.

Whatever merit the networks' argument may have in the abstract, it has none on the facts of this case. The studios expressly reserved the right to seek post-compliance reimbursement in their motion to quash. The district court's March 6, 1979 order pertaining to the motion to quash contained no mention of costs. We see no reason why the court's failure to address the studios' reservation of the right to seek reimbursement constitutes an implied or *sub silentio* denial of the reservation. The court's silence, coupled with the subsequent conduct of the parties and court, is more susceptible to being interpreted as tacit approval of the reservation of the studios' right to seek post-compliance reimbursement. . . .

Having determined that the motion for costs was timely and that the district court possessed authority to award post-compliance reimbursement, we now turn to whether the court's March 27, 1980 minute order denying costs was an appealable final order. . . .

As already noted, discovery orders are generally characterized as interlocutory and review may be sought only through the contempt process or by waiting for the entry of a final judgment in the underlying action. As Professor Moore notes: "Most orders . . . denying discovery do not finally dispose of the proceeding or of any independent off-shoot of it, and are, therefore, not appealable." 4 Moore's *Federal Practice* ¶26.83[3], at 26-585.

The studios contend that the subject order, denying post-production reimbursement of costs, should not be governed by the general finality rule. They argue that the order falls within the collateral order exception to the finality rule established in *Cohen v. Beneficial Industrial Loan Corp.*, 337 U.S. 541 (1949). The studios emphasize that they have no other way of obtaining meaningful review because: (1) the contempt procedure was unavailable once the subpoenaed material was produced because there was nothing they could then do to be held in contempt — i.e., it is impossible to disobey an order denying costs; and (2) as nonparties, they would be unable to test the costs issue by appeal from a final judgment in the underlying action. We address this issue by first examining the interests served by the final judgment rule.

The finality requirement is designed to balance the institutional interests of the courts in efficiency against the individual litigant's interest in obtaining prompt review. By preventing premature interference with discretionary trial court orders, the finality rule minimizes the disruption and delay of trial court functions and the strain on both the parties and judicial system caused by proliferation of appellate proceedings by piecemeal review of interlocutory orders. . . .

Consistent with these considerations, the Court has given the finality requirement a "practical rather than a technical construction," *Cohen*, 337 U.S. at 545, and has recognized certain exceptions to the rule. . . . The critical inquiry in determining whether a particular order is appealable under one of these exceptions to the finality rule is not only whether the order fits neatly within the exception, but, additionally, whether appeal would be consistent with the purposes of the rule. . . .

To come within *Cohen*'s collateral order doctrine "the order must conclusively determine the disputed question, resolve an important issue completely separate from the merits of the action, and be effectively unreviewable on appeal from a final judgment." *Coopers & Lybrand v. Livesay*, 437 U.S. 463, 468 (1978). Although most discovery orders do not meet the requirements of the collateral order doctrine, even as to nonparties, the subject order clearly falls within the narrow class of orders that does. First, the order denying costs was not, in the language of *Cohen*, "tentative, informal or incomplete," 337 U.S. at 546. The order left no issue as to costs, or as to any other matter affecting the studios' involvement in the action, "open, unfinished or inconclusive." *Id*. Second, the order resolved an issue "separable from, and collateral to, rights asserted in the action." *Id*. Because discovery against the studios was complete when costs were denied, appeal entailed no risk of delaying proceedings in the underlying action. The post-production denial of costs was "too independent of the cause itself to require that appellate consideration be deferred until the whole case is adjudicated." *Id*. at 546. Third, this is not a case of merely "deferring" review, for we see no way that the nonparty studios could have protected themselves by appeal from the consent judgments eventually entered against the networks.

Accordingly, we conclude that the subject order fits well within *Cohen*'s narrow exception to the finality rule, and does so consistent with the beneficial purposes of the rule. As we stated in *Premium Service Corp. v. Sperry & Hutchinson Co.*, 511 F.2d 225, 228 (9th Cir. 1975):

> Regardless of how its holding is restated, . . . the Court in *Cohen* applied common sense to the statutory language. Congress limited our jurisdiction to review of "final decisions" not in order to deny appeal arbitrarily to some parties on some issues, but to enable all stages of litigation to be reviewed in one proceeding. [citation omitted]. If the district court has said its last word on an issue, and if its decision is of

a nature that it will not be subject to review on the appeal from the final judgment of the main proceeding, then the courts will not suppose Congress to have precluded immediate appeal of that decision.

We emphasize that the studios were willing to proceed with discovery, regardless of whether they could eventually recover costs. To require that they disobey the discovery orders and incur contempt citations in order to preserve their claim to costs would be counter-productive, resulting in considerable delays in the trial process. This is in marked contrast to the more common context in which the right to discovery itself is contested. Appeal of such discovery orders, without deterrence of the contempt requirement, would result in lengthy delays of trial and multiplication of appeals. Here, however, the added efficiency of promptly proceeding with the trial more than offsets any increased burden incurred by entertaining the appeal of the order denying costs. We conclude, therefore, that the order denying costs has the requisite finality to be appealable. . . .

Reversed and remanded.

NOTES

1. Was there any means by which the studios could have obtained immediate appellate review of the order denying their motion to quash the subpoenas?

2. The court notes that the trial judge did not make findings of fact and state conclusions of law in denying the motion for costs. Rule 52(a) provides: "Findings of fact and conclusions of law are unnecessary on decisions of motions under Rules 12 or 56 or any other motion except as provided in subdivision (c) of this rule." Subdivision (c) deals only with judgments as a matter of law. Did the appellate court disregard this rule? Why is the case being remanded?

INTERNATIONAL BUSINESS MACHINES CORP. v. UNITED STATES
493 F.2d 112 (2d Cir. 1973)

OAKES, CIRCUIT JUDGE:

. . . On petition of the Government filed June 25, 1973, Chief Judge Edelstein, after a hearing, entered an opinion, findings and order imposing a contingent, coercive fine of $150,000 per day until IBM complies with his discovery order. This order directed IBM to produce for the Government certain documents which IBM had previously delivered to a third party, Control Data Corporation, in the course of discovery in a civil antitrust action in the United States District Court for the District of Minnesota. IBM's claim both in the prior appeal and in this one is that the documents were protected from discovery by the attorney-client and work-product privileges. The trial judge, however, had ruled that, for purposes of the Government's antitrust suit, IBM had waived its claims of privilege by delivering the documents to Control Data in the Minnesota suit. . . . [A]n order punishing one criminally for contempt is a final judgment and review may immediately be obtained. *Union Tool Co. v. Wilson*, 259 U.S. 107, 111 (1922). The procedure in relation to criminal contempt is prescribed by 18 U.S.C. §§ 401 and 402 and FED. R. CRIM. P. 42. Appeals from criminal contempt orders are governed by FED. R. CRIM. P. 37. *See generally* [Dan B.] Dobbs, *Contempt of Court: A Survey*, 56 Cornell L. Rev. 183, 235-45 (1971).

Generally speaking, however, an order of civil contempt is interlocutory and may not be challenged on an appeal until the entry of final judgment. *Fox v. Capital Co.*, 299 U.S. 105, 107 (1936) (supplementary proceedings; contempt for failure to disclose assets); *Doyle v. London Guarantee Co.*, 204 U.S. 599, 608 (1907).

Appellant IBM argues first that Judge Edelstein's contempt order, although styled as a "civil" order, is in reality a criminal contempt order and is hence appealable. This argument has three underlying premises: (1) vindication of a court's authority is a characteristic of criminal, not civil, contempt and such was the purpose of the order here; (2) if the order were civil, it could not be entered without consideration of "the character and magnitude of the harm threatened by continued contumacy," *United States v. UMW*, 330 U.S. 258, 303-304 (1947); and (3) the severity of the penalties imposed here, i.e., $150,000 per day for noncompliance, is so great that necessarily the contempt order is criminal.

None of these premises are correct. The hallmark of civil contempt is that the sanction imposed is only contingent and coercive. *Shillitani v. United States*, 384 U.S. 364, 370 (1966). . . . Civil contempt, moreover, has a remedial purpose — compelling obedience to an order of the court for the purpose of enforcing the other party's rights, or obtaining other relief for the opposing party. . . . The distinction between civil and criminal contempt is, in short, "usually based on the purpose for which the contempt sentence is meted out."

The district court did not leave in doubt the purpose which the contempt citation here was to serve. The order, dated August 1, 1973, makes it clear that the fine is for each day that IBM "fails to comply with Pretrial Order No. 5" and that IBM is "entitled to purge itself of this contempt at any time" by compliance with the discovery order. The order of July 10, 1973, requiring that the hearing proceed in respect to the possibility of contempt, clearly states that the hearing is to be "on the issue of a coercive fine. . . ." Thus the order was both coercive and contingent, indicating a civil rather than criminal contempt.

In regard to the amount of the coercive fine it was proper for the court to take into account the contemnor's resources and ability to pay. This it did, noting in the contempt order that its 1972 annual report showed earnings for that year in excess of $1,279,000,000 as against $1,078,000,000 in 1971 and that the stockholders' equity as of December 31, 1972, was reported at $7,565,000,000. While $150,000 a day is a substantial sum, in reference to IBM's financial resources and the consequent seriousness of the burden to IBM, the sum represents only 5 per cent of any given day's earnings. In any case, we fail to see how the magnitude of such a sum can turn a civil contempt into a criminal one, any more than the sending of an individual to jail turns a civil contempt into criminal contempt. . . . In neither case does the severity of the penalty change the nature of the contempt. . . . It is not as if there were any punitive aspect in this contingent fine. Indeed, this is a classic case of using the court's power to afford "full remedial relief," *McComb v. Jacksonville Paper Co.*, 336 U.S. 187, 193 (1949), so as to enforce the right of the opposing party — here the right to discover certain documents.

IBM also claims that language in *United States v. UMW, supra,* compels a finding of criminal contempt here. There the Court said that a court imposing a civil, coercive fine "must . . . consider the character and magnitude of the harm threatened by continued contumacy. . . ." 330 U.S. at 304. Several independent reasons militate against our concluding that the district court's failure explicitly to weigh this consideration turns what would otherwise be civil contempt into a criminal contempt. First, it must be noted that the Government in the July 16, 1973, hearing attempted to offer evidence of the harm to it by continued refusal by IBM to comply with the court's order. IBM objected to the introduction of that evidence, and the objection was sustained. Thus, even if IBM had a right to consideration by the court of the harm to the Government, it waived that right by objecting to the evidence of it. Second, there is no reason to believe that a contempt order which is styled civil by the judge imposing it, which has a clearly civil purpose and which was imposed only after consideration of questions relevant only to civil contempt, would become criminal by failure to find explicitly with reference to one of the civil considerations. In other words, were we to read the language in the *UMW* case to require an explicit finding as to harm in all coercive, civil contempt, we still would not treat a failure to make such a finding as converting the civil contempt to a criminal contempt, which is essentially what IBM would have us do here. Third, in any case, we do not so read the language in the *UMW* case. The so-called requirement — that a court consider the harm of continued contempt — first appeared in *United States v. UMW,* and there it was propounded without explanation or citation. No case is cited to us where a civil, coercive contempt was voided for failure to meet this "requirement," nor do civil, coercive contempts always involve such findings. . . . We read this language in *UMW* as requiring that the coercive fine be reasonably set in relation to the facts, that it not be arbitrary. Judge Edelstein's memorandum is evidence that his decision was reasoned and that he gave consideration to the various factors which led to this particular fine — the ability of IBM to meet these payments without undue hardship and the imposition of a fine stiff enough to bring about expeditious compliance. Indeed, unlike the violation of a labor injunction, it is impossible to determine what harm is being suffered here by failure to provide this material for discovery. It may be worthless, or, more likely in view of the Government's offer of proof, it may be relevant and worthwhile, but to expect a finding of the "character and magnitude of the harm" involved in withholding essentially unknown documents would be to expect miracles of the court — indeed, would involve a prejudgment of the case on the merits. Fourth, and finally, the court's failure to make such a finding at worst would only go to the amount of the coercive fine, not to the merits of the civil contempt itself. In light of IBM's often stated intention that it will comply with a definitive ruling on the Pretrial Order, rather than stand in contempt, no matter how nominal the fine, there would be little point in delaying the process by remanding for reconsideration of the amount of the fine.

IBM argues next that even if the contempt here were civil in nature, it would be appealable under a decision of this court, *New York Tel. Co. v. Communications Workers,* 445 F.2d 39 (2d Cir. 1971). . . . In *New York Tel. Co.,* however, the court specifically noted that, even though the union was adjudged in civil contempt, the main action in which the order had been issued had effectively been terminated, so that the civil contempt adjudication being appealed from was no longer interlocutory. The court said: ". . . we doubt that anything further remains of the main action unless the district court grants leave to replead. Accordingly, our intervention by way of appeal runs no risk of disrupting the orderly course of proceedings below." 445 F.2d at 45. *Fox v. Capital Co., supra*, and *Doyle v. London Guarantee Co., supra*, both involved orders to produce books and records in civil proceedings and resulted in civil contempts. These were held to be interlocutory only and not appealable. This continues to be the law in this circuit . . . as well as in other circuits.

The rule of *Fox v. Capital Co., supra*, and *Doyle v. London Guarantee Co., supra*, is not affected by the authorities cited to us and this is as it should be, because discovery orders at the pretrial stages of litigation are especially inappropriate for interlocutory appeals, as this court has recognized. *Weight Watchers of Philadelphia v. Weight Watchers Int'l, Inc.*, 455 F.2d 770, 773-774 (2nd Cir. 1972). IBM makes a very emotional and rather heartwarming appeal relating to the sanctity of the attorney-client privilege and of the attorney's work-product and how — absent appealability in a civil contempt proceeding — they would be subject to invasion in the district court.[7] This emotional appeal, however, must be recognized for what it is — an attempt to provide a right of appeal of all discovery orders, for the same legal arguments IBM makes here with respect to its perhaps unique factual situation apply equally to the run-of-the-mill objections to discovery orders. And, indeed, attorney-client privilege and work-product are among the more common grounds of objection. The considerations advanced by IBM for review as well as the considerations to the contrary were well considered by this court in a not dissimilar situation in *American Express Warehousing, Ltd. v. Transamerica Ins. Co., supra*. There too a judge had ordered production of documents which appellants claimed were work-product. This court stated:

> The rule of non-appealability is no different when a claim of attorney's work-product . . . is made. Counsel have not cited, nor have we been able to find, a single case where an assertion of work-product, either accepted or rejected by the district court, so colored the case as to cause an appellate court to assert jurisdiction in contravention of the normal rule against appealability of discovery orders. . . .

In short, the conclusion is and has been that, barring certain extraordinary circumstances, the possibility of abuse and injustice would actually be increased by opening wide the gates of review to discovery orders, than by leaving the determination to the wise discretion of experienced trial judges.

It is not as if we leave IBM without any possible remedy. . . . [I]t may comply with the order and later appeal any final judgment to have its documents

---

[7] [7] . . . It may be true, as said in argument, that . . . if the order cannot be reviewed until after final decree it may come too late to be of any benefit to the party aggrieved. But the power to punish for contempt is inherent in the authority of courts, and is necessary to the administration of justice and part of the inconvenience to which a citizen is subject in a community governed by law regulated by orderly judicial procedure. . . .

returned, or it may pay the fine and after final judgment or settlement appeal for the return of its money.

IBM also suggests an argument that because the Government has at various times before this court or in the Supreme Court specifically stated that the only way to obtain review of Pretrial Order No. 5 before the end of the case was for IBM or its representative to risk contempt, and thereby demonstrate its good faith and a solid basis of objections, the Government should be foreclosed from asserting nonappealability here. While we do not approve of the Government's attempt to mislead IBM, if that is what it was, appellate jurisdiction cannot be conferred on a court of appeals by consent, *Stratton v. St. Louis Southwestern Railway Co.*, 282 U.S. 10, 18 (1930), or by waiver, *United States v. Griffin*, 303 U.S. 226, 229 (1938). . . .

We dismiss the appeal and deny the petition for mandamus.

TIMBERS, CIRCUIT JUDGE (dissenting):

IBM has been ordered to pay to the United States a continuing fine in excess of $1,000,000 per week for alleged contempt.

Its alleged contempt is for having respectfully declined to produce for the government's inspection some 1200 documents which concededly are attorney-client communications. IBM's claim of privilege was rejected out of hand by the district court — without an opinion, without findings of fact, without any examination whatsoever of the documents in question. IBM's claim of privilege with respect to those documents has never been judicially reviewed, despite its repeated assurances of willingness to comply with an appellate determination of its claim of privilege. Indeed, the contempt adjudication below was sought by IBM itself for the express purpose of obtaining precisely that judicial review of its claim of privilege which the government on at least four occasions had advised the Supreme Court and our Court was the only way that IBM in good faith could obtain such review before the end of the case.

The narrow question presently before us is whether the district court's contempt adjudication was civil or criminal. All agree that if it was criminal, the contempt adjudication is appealable to our Court now, since it is a final judgment in a proceeding separate from the antitrust action. The majority, by adopting its own reading of *United States v. UMW*, 330 U.S. 258 (1947), would ignore the Supreme Court's requirement that a district court in imposing a civil, coercive fine "must . . . consider the character and magnitude of the harm threatened by continued contumacy. . . ." 330 U.S. at 304. In the instant case, the district court's contempt order was not based upon any such consideration whatsoever. The majority so concedes. But the majority also blinks at the district court's omission of this indispensable requirement for a civil contempt adjudication on the ground, among others, as the majority puts it, that the Supreme Court's "so-called requirement — that a court consider the harm of continued contempt — first appeared in *United States v. UMW*, and there it was propounded without explanation or citation." I think this is an exceedingly slender reed upon which to deny appellate review of a contempt order which imposes a continuing fine of a million dollars per week.

In light of the undisputed underlying facts which led to the district court order which is the basis for the contempt adjudication below, I would hold the contempt order to be criminal in nature and as such reviewable now by our Court. Since IBM has never waived its attorney-client privilege with respect to the documents in question, I would vacate the production order and remand the case to the district court with instructions to rule on the yet-to-be-ruled-on claim of privilege.

It is difficult to conceive of a more glaring instance of a wrong for which the law should provide a remedy — unless that first lesson that some of us learned under the New Haven elms is to be totally discarded. . . .

To me nothing could be clearer than the invalidity of the production order below. It should be vacated. . . .

The principles here involved transcend in importance even the rights of the parties to this litigation. I think we have not only the jurisdiction but a plain duty to correct the clearly erroneous action of the district court below.

From the refusal of the majority to do so, I respectfully but most emphatically dissent.

NOTES

1. Apparently because of uncertainty as to the appropriate route to the court of appeals, counsel for IBM had simultaneously taken an appeal and petitioned for mandamus. Does either the majority or the dissenting opinion focus adequately on the availability of mandamus? What about a writ of prohibition? If the material ordered to be produced is indeed immunized from disclosure by FED. R. CIV. P. 26(b)(1), hasn't the district court acted beyond its authority? A traditional use of the writ of prohibition by an appellate court has been to prohibit a trial court from acting beyond its powers.

2. While most courts refuse to allow an interlocutory appeal from orders compelling the production of documents that the producing party contends should be protected from disclosure by the attorney-client privilege, an increasing number of courts of appeal now are allowing appeals of such orders under the collateral order doctrine. *See United States v. Philip Morris Inc.*, 314 F.3d 612 (D.C. Cir. 2003) (holding order determining that memorandum providing advice about modification of the company's document retention policy in light of litigation against tobacco companies was not protected by attorney-client privilege, because privilege had been waived, to be appealable under collateral order doctrine notwithstanding alleged ability of party asserting privilege to obtain review through disobedience and citation for contempt; emphasizing the importance of interlocutory review of such rulings so as to promote full and frank communications between attorney and client); *In re Grand Jury Subpoena*, 274 F.3d 563 (1st Cir. 2001) (asserting jurisdiction over appeal from denial of motion to quash subpoena duces tecum over attorney-client privilege objection); *Kelly v. Ford Motor Co. (In re Ford Motor Co.)*, 110 F.3d 954 (3d Cir. 1997) (holding to be immediately appealable under collateral order doctrine an order compelling discovery of documents reflecting what Ford knew about the propensity of Bronco II's to roll over, when Ford acquired this knowledge, and how it responded to the knowledge, notwithstanding

objections based on attorney-client privilege and work product immunity, finding the harm from disclosure to outweigh the inefficiencies of immediate appeal).

3. In *Cunningham v. Hamilton County*, 527 U.S. 198 (1999), the Supreme Court faced the question whether an order imposing sanctions on an attorney pursuant to Federal Rule of Civil Procedure 37(a)(4) is a final decision. It held that such an order is not a final decision, even where the attorney no longer represented a party in the case. Plaintiff's counsel had not produced requested documents, gave incomplete responses to several interrogatories, and scheduled a deposition in violation of a magistrate judge's order. The attorney was sanctioned and immediately appealed. The Sixth Circuit dismissed the appeal. The Supreme Court affirmed, reasoning that:

> [A] Rule 37(a) sanctions order often will be inextricably intertwined with the merits of the action. An evaluation of the appropriateness of sanctions may require the reviewing court to inquire into the importance of the information sought or the adequacy or truthfulness of a response. Some of the sanctions in this case were based on the fact that petitioner provided partial responses and objections to some of the defendants' discovery requests. To evaluate whether those sanctions were appropriate, an appellate court would have to assess the completeness of petitioner's responses . . . Such an inquiry would differ only marginally from an inquiry into the merits and counsels against application of the collateral order doctrine. Perhaps not every discovery sanction will be inextricably intertwined with the merits, but we have consistently eschewed a case-by-case approach to deciding whether an order is sufficiently collateral.

> Even if the merits were completely divorced from the sanctions issue, the collateral order doctrine requires that the order be effectively unreviewable on appeal from a final judgment. . . . [W]e do not think that the appealability of a Rule 37 sanction imposed on an attorney should turn on the attorney's continued participation. Such a rule could not be easily administered. For example, it may be unclear precisely when representation terminates, and questions likely would arise over when the 30-day period for appeal would begin to run under Federal Rule of Appellate Procedure 4. The rule also could be subject to abuse if attorneys and clients strategically terminated their representation in order to trigger a right to appeal with a view to delaying the proceedings in the underlying case. While we recognize that our application of the final judgment rule in this setting may require nonparticipating attorneys to monitor the progress of the litigation after their work has ended, the efficiency interests served by limiting immediate appeals far outweigh any nominal monitoring costs borne by attorneys. For these reasons, an attorney's continued participation in a case does not affect whether a sanctions order is "final" for purposes of § 1291.

Does this decision impose an undue burden on attorneys? *See* Laura C. Baucus, Note: *How Long Should Bad Attorneys Have to Wait? The Immediate Appeal of Attorney Sanctions under the Collateral Order Doctrine*, 46 WAYNE L. REV. 289 (2000).

d. Immunities from Suit

In *Harlow v. Fitzgerald*, 457 U.S. 800 (1982), a suit based upon an allegedly illegal discharge from employment by the Department of the Air Force, the Supreme Court held that presidential aides who allegedly participated in a conspiracy to violate the plaintiff's constitutional and statutory rights were entitled to assert a qualified immunity from suit as an affirmative defense. The Court concluded that, under a standard that would permit government officials performing discretionary functions to defeat insubstantial claims without going to trial, such officials could seek dismissal or summary judgment. The critical questions would be whether the officials violated statutory or constitutional rights that were clearly established at the time of their alleged conduct and whether, at that time, the official knew or, as a reasonable person, should have known of the rights.

Against this backdrop, the question arose whether a denial of summary judgment to a government official who sought summary judgment based upon qualified immunity was immediately appealable under the collateral order doctrine.

MITCHELL v. FORSYTH
472 U.S. 511 (1985)

[The Court faced this question in the context of a suit against Attorney General Mitchell, whom Forsyth had sued for authorizing a warrantless wiretap for the purpose of gathering intelligence for national security purposes, in alleged violation of Fitzgerald's rights under the Fourth Amendment and under a federal statute. Forsyth never had been the target of electronic surveillance; he merely had participated in conversations that were overheard by the federal government during the course of electronic surveillance authorized against another individual.]

Justice White delivered the opinion of the Court.

. . .

Although 28 U. S. C. § 1291 vests the courts of appeals with jurisdiction over appeals only from "final decisions" of the district courts, "a decision 'final' within the meaning of § 1291 does not necessarily mean the last order possible to be made in a case." *Gillespie* v. *United States Steel Corp.*, 379 U.S. 148, 152 (1964). Thus, a decision of a district court is appealable if it falls within "that small class which finally determine claims of right separable from, and collateral to, rights asserted in the action, too important to be denied review and too independent of the cause itself to require that appellate consideration be deferred until the whole case is adjudicated." *Cohen v. Beneficial Industrial Loan Corp.*, 337 U.S. at 546.

A major characteristic of the denial or granting of a claim appealable under *Cohen*'s "collateral order" doctrine is that "unless it can be reviewed before [the proceedings terminate], it never can be reviewed at all." When a district court has denied a defendant's claim of right not to stand trial, on double jeopardy grounds, for example, we have consistently held the court's decision appealable, for such a right cannot be effectively vindicated after the trial has occurred. *Abney v. United States*, 431 U.S. 651 (1977). Thus, the denial of a substantial claim of absolute immunity is an order appealable before final judgment, for the essence of absolute immunity is its possessor's entitlement not to have to answer for his conduct in a civil damages action.

At the heart of the issue before us is the question whether qualified immunity shares this essential attribute of absolute immunity — whether qualified immunity is in fact an entitlement not to stand trial under certain circumstances. The conception animating the qualified immunity doctrine as set forth in *Harlow v. Fitzgerald*, 457 U.S. 800 (1982), is that "where an official's duties legitimately require action in which clearly established rights are not implicated, the public interest may be better served by action taken 'with independence and without fear of consequences.'" *Id.* at 819, quoting *Pierson v. Ray*, 386 U.S. 547, 554 (1967). . . . [T]he "consequences" with which we were concerned in *Harlow* are not limited to liability for money damages; they also include "the general costs of subjecting officials to the risks of trial — distraction of officials from their governmental duties, inhibition of discretionary action, and deterrence of able people from public service." *Harlow*, 457 U.S. at 816. Indeed, *Harlow* emphasizes that even such pretrial matters as discovery are to be avoided if possible, as "[inquiries] of this kind can be peculiarly disruptive of effective government." *Id.* at 817.

With these concerns in mind, the *Harlow* Court refashioned the qualified immunity doctrine in such a way as to "permit the resolution of many insubstantial claims on summary judgment" and to avoid "[subjecting] government officials either to the costs of trial or to the burdens of broad-reaching discovery" in cases where the legal norms the officials are alleged to have violated were not clearly established at the time. Unless the plaintiff's allegations state a claim of violation of clearly established law, a defendant pleading qualified immunity is entitled to dismissal before the commencement of discovery. Even if the plaintiff's complaint adequately alleges the commission of acts that violated clearly established law, the defendant is entitled to summary judgment if discovery fails to uncover evidence sufficient to create a genuine issue as to whether the defendant in fact committed those acts. *Harlow* thus recognized an entitlement not to stand trial or face the other burdens of litigation, conditioned on the resolution of the essentially legal question whether the conduct of which the plaintiff complains violated clearly established law. The entitlement is an *immunity from suit* rather than a mere defense to liability; and like an absolute immunity, it is effectively lost if a case is erroneously permitted to go to trial. Accordingly, the reasoning that underlies the immediate appealability of an order denying absolute immunity indicates to us that the denial of qualified immunity should be similarly appealable: in each case, the district court's decision is effectively unreviewable on appeal from a final judgment.

An appealable interlocutory decision must satisfy two additional criteria: it must "conclusively determine the disputed question," *Coopers & Lybrand v. Livesay*, 437 U.S. 463, 468 (1978), and that question must involve a "[claim] of right separable from, and collateral to, rights asserted in the action," *Cohen, supra*, at 546. The denial of a defendant's motion for dismissal or summary judgment on the ground of qualified immunity easily meets these requirements. Such a decision is "conclusive" in either of two respects. In some cases, it may represent the trial court's conclusion that even if the facts are as asserted by the defendant, the defendant's actions violated clearly established law and are therefore not within the scope of the qualified immunity. In such a case, there will be nothing in the subsequent course of the proceedings in the district court that can alter the court's conclusion that the defendant is not immune. Alternatively, the trial judge may rule only that if the facts are as asserted by the plaintiff, the defendant is not immune. At trial, the plaintiff may not succeed in proving his version of the facts, and the defendant may thus escape liability. Even so, the court's denial of summary judgment finally and conclusively determines the defendant's claim of right not to *stand trial* on the plaintiff's allegations, and because "[there] are simply no further steps that can be taken in the District Court to avoid the trial the defendant maintains is barred," it is apparent that "*Cohen*'s threshold requirement of a fully consummated decision is satisfied" in such a case. *Abney v. United States*, 431 U.S. at 659.

Similarly, it follows from the recognition that qualified immunity is in part an entitlement not to be forced to litigate the consequences of official conduct that a claim of immunity is conceptually distinct from the merits of the plaintiff's claim that his rights have been violated. An appellate court reviewing the denial of the defendant's claim of immunity need not consider the correctness of the plaintiff's version of the facts, nor even determine whether the plaintiff's allegations actually state a claim. All it need determine is a question of law: whether the legal norms allegedly violated by the defendant were clearly established at the time of the challenged actions or, in cases where the district court has denied summary judgment for the defendant on the ground that even under the defendant's version of the facts the defendant's conduct violated clearly established law, whether the law clearly proscribed the actions the defendant claims he took. To be sure, the resolution of these legal issues will entail consideration of the factual allegations that make up the plaintiff's claim for relief . . . [but] the Court has recognized that a question of immunity is separate from the merits of the underlying action for purposes of the *Cohen* test even though a reviewing court must consider the plaintiff's factual allegations in resolving the immunity issue.[8]

Accordingly, we hold that a district court's denial of a claim of qualified immunity, to the extent that it turns on an issue of law, is an appealable "final decision" within the meaning of 28 U.S.C. § 1291 notwithstanding the absence of a final judgment. . . .

Justice Powell took no part in the decision on this case.

Justice Rehnquist took no part in the consideration or decision of this case.

NOTES

1. Suppose that a police officer, sued for use of excessive force in violation of an arrested person's rights, is denied summary judgment because the record raises a genuine issue of material fact concerning the officer's

---

[8] [10] . . . [T]he legal determination that a given proposition of law was not clearly established at the time the defendant committed the alleged acts does not entail a determination of the "merits" of the plaintiff's claim that the defendant's actions were in fact unlawful.

involvement in plaintiff's beating. Should this ruling be immediately appealable? Is the reasoning of *Mitchell v. Forsyth* applicable, or can and should the questions posed be distinguished? See *Johnson v. Jones*, 515 U.S. 304 (1995), holding that a denial of summary judgment predicated on the existence of a genuine issue of material fact is not immediately appealable. The Court took the position that to view this case as falling within the *Cohen* doctrine would entail abandoning the separability requirement, given the overlap between the merits and the question that the defendant sought to appeal. The Court also emphasized the greater expertise of trial courts (than appellate courts) in determining whether a genuine issue of material fact has been presented, and the substantial time it would take an appellate court to review the decision below, in concluding that it would not be a wise use of appellate resources to permit interlocutory appeals of summary judgment denials that were based on the presence of genuine issues of material fact.

2. If a government officer has invoked the collateral order doctrine to appeal the denial of a motion to dismiss for failure to state a claim on which relief can be granted, based on the qualified immunity defense, may the officer, having lost on that first appeal, immediately appeal the denial of the motion for summary judgment predicated on qualified immunity? In *Behrens v. Pelletier*, 516 U.S. 299 (1996), the Supreme Court, over a dissent by Justices Breyer and Stevens, held that the officer could appeal the denial of his summary judgment motion to the extent that it turned on issues of law, despite his prior appeal and notwithstanding that other claims, as to which qualified immunity was not a defense, would require defendant to submit to discovery and to trial. How many times may an officer delay the progress of a suit in district court, taking interlocutory appeals from denials of motions for summary judgment based on slightly augmented records?

3. Does a defendant's right to immediately appeal the denial of a qualified immunity defense also apply in state court, if defendants are sued there? In *Johnson v. Fankell*, 520 U.S. 911 (1997), the Supreme Court said "no." Plaintiff had filed a 42 U.S.C. § 1983 damages action in Idaho state court, alleging that she was deprived of property without due process in violation of the Fourteenth Amendment by defendant officials' termination of her state employment. The trial court denied defendants' motion to dismiss based upon qualified immunity. The Idaho Supreme Court dismissed their appeal from that ruling, explaining that the denial was neither an appealable final order under Idaho Appellate Rule 11(a)(1) nor appealable as a matter of federal right under § 1983. The U.S. Supreme Court affirmed, holding that defendants in a state-court § 1983 action do not have a federal right to an interlocutory appeal from a denial of qualified immunity. It reasoned that Idaho courts have the right to construe the Idaho Rule as they see fit, and their Rule is not preempted by § 1983 to the extent that the state Rule does not allow an interlocutory appeal. Idaho is entitled to balance the competing interests in protecting state officials from over-enforcement of federal rights against its interests in postponing appeals until after final judgment. Moreover, the right to immediate appellate review of such a ruling in a federal case has its source in § 1291, not § 1983, and thus is a federal procedural right that does not apply in a state forum.

4. Some states have anti-SLAPP statutes that provide for the dismissal of suits aimed at deterring "strategic lawsuits against public participation," suits brought to deter and punish citizens for exercising their political and legal rights. In *Batzel v. Smith*, 333 F.3d 1018 (9th Cir. 2003), a woman filed suit against, among others, Tom Cremers, a website operator and listserv moderator whom she accused of posting defamatory email by a third-party that indicated that plaintiff had possession of artwork taken by the Nazis. Cremers moved to strike the complaint under California's anti-SLAPP statute, asserting that the suit was filed to interfere with his First Amendment rights, and the court denied the motion. Cremers appealed. The question was whether the appeals court had jurisdiction over this inter-locutory appeal. How would you predict that the court ruled? It held the denial immediately appealable under the collateral order doctrine, conclud-ing *inter alia* that the ruling resolved a question separate from the merits because denial of the motion was based on a finding that the claim might have merit, not on a conclusion that it would succeed, and because the intent of the anti-SLAPP statute was to protect speakers from trial itself, not merely from liability.

5. Although the cases cited in this book's discussion of the collateral order doctrine have largely been federal court decisions, the appellate courts in a great number of states have adopted some form of this doctrine as well. These include Arkansas, California, Colorado, Delaware, the District of Columbia, Florida, Georgia, Hawaii, Kansas, Maine, Maryland, Massachusetts, Minnesota, New Mexico, Pennsylvania, Tennessee, Texas, Vermont, West Virginia, and Wisconsin. *See* Virginia R. Dugan, *The Adoption of the Collateral Order Doctrine in New Mexico*: Carrillo v. Rostro, 24 N.M. L. REV. 389 (1994); William M. Lukens, *The Collateral Order Doctrine in California*, 15 HASTINGS L.J. 105 (1963).

e. *Rooker-Feldman* Cases

The *Rooker-Feldman* doctrine, named for the two cases that gave rise to it (*District of Columbia Court of Appeals v. Feldman*, 460 U.S. 462 (1983), and *Rooker v. Fidelity Trust Co.*, 263 U.S. 413 (1923)), provides that federal district courts lack subject-matter jurisdiction to review state court adjudications or to hear constitutional claims that are inextricably intertwined with state court decisions. The doctrine generally is regarded as deriving from the statutory con-ferral upon the U.S. Supreme Court of exclusive jurisdiction to review state court judgments. Even the Supreme Court's authority to review state court judgments is limited to particular kinds of cases, by statute and likely by the Constitution itself. *See* 28 U.S.C. § 1257 and U.S. CONST. art. III of the Constitution. The doctrine also has roots in policies of respect for state court decisions and favoring finality. As a doctrine that sets limits upon federal dis-trict courts' ability to function in an appellate capacity *vis a vis* state courts, the doctrine itself should be of interest to you as students of the appellate systems in this country. In that connection, it is worth your notice that the Supreme Court recently clarified that the doctrine applies only where the losing party in state court filed suit in federal court after the state proceedings ended, com-plaining of an injury caused by the state court judgment and seeking rejection of that judgment; the doctrine does not supplant or override preclusion doctrine (which may or may not provide a defense to the federal suit once the state court action has gone to judgment) or allow federal courts to stay or dismiss proceedings in deference to state court actions. Thus, a state court judgment did not deprive the federal court of jurisdiction over a case filed while the state court suit was pending. *Exxon Mobil Corp. v. Saudi Basic Industries Corp.*, 544 U.S. 280 (2005). It is appropriate to raise the *Rooker-Feldman* doctrine here because issues have arisen as to whether an order dismissing or refusing to dismiss on *Rooker-Feldman* grounds is an immediately appealable final order.

BRYANT v. SYLVESTER
57 F.3d 308 (3rd Cir. 1995)

LEWIS, Circuit Judge.

This case raises an issue of apparent first impression: whether an order denying the *Rooker-Feldman* defense is final as a collateral order. We conclude that an order denying the *Rooker-Feldman* defense is not final as a collateral order and is not immediately appealable under the collateral order doctrine. We will therefore dismiss this appeal for lack of appellate jurisdiction. . . .

[A Family Court judge approved the closing on particular dates of a Family Court-operated nursery that included an area for supervised visitation ordered by the Family Court. Plaintiffs, a non-custodial parent restricted to visitation in the Family Court-operated nursery and an organization whose purpose was to insure children's access to their non-custodial parents and extended family members, sued to enjoin the closing of the nursery on the designated days. The Pennsylvania Supreme Court denied plaintiffs' request for a preliminary injunction, without hearing. No appeal to the United States Supreme Court was taken. Later, the judge again authorized the closing of the nursery on a designated date. Plaintiffs filed a class action lawsuit in which they claimed that by closing the nursery the defendants violated their rights under the First and Fourteenth Amendments. Defendants moved to dismiss for lack of federal subject-matter jurisdiction and for failure to state a claim, contending, *inter alia*, that the *Rooker-Feldman* doctrine required dismissal of the complaint. The district court denied the defendants' motion to dismiss and ordered that discovery proceed. This appeal followed.]

A decision denying a motion to dismiss for lack of subject matter jurisdiction is considered to fall outside the Cohen exception to the final decision rule. Likewise, decisions denying assertions of res judicata are considered to be beyond the collateral order exception. *See Digital Equipment Corporation*, 114 S. Ct. at 1998. Because the *Rooker-Feldman* doctrine has a close affinity both with notions of subject matter jurisdiction and claim preclusion, we might be tempted to resolve the issue of the immediate appealability of *Rooker-Feldman* denials by way of analogy to these categories of claims. However, underlying the *Rooker-Feldman* doctrine are concerns rooted in federalism and comity, concerns not necessarily present within the concepts of claim preclusion and subject matter jurisdiction. Therefore, we will address the immediate appealability of the denial of a *Rooker-Feldman* defense with explicit reference to the issue of respect for state courts that underlies the *Rooker-Feldman* doctrine.

Because we conclude that the third requirement — that the order be "effectively unreviewable" on appeal from a final judgment — is not met in this case, we need not discuss the first and second prerequisites for the collateral order doctrine to determine the immediate appealability of a denial of a *Rooker-Feldman* defense. The Supreme Court has explained that, as a general rule, an order is "effectively unreviewable" only where "the order at issue involves 'an asserted right the legal and practical value of which would be destroyed if it were not vindicated before trial.'" *Lauro Lines S.R.L. v. Chasser*, 490 U.S. 495, 499-500 (1989).

The Court's most recent discussion of the collateral order doctrine appears in *Digital Equipment Corporation*, decided less than a year ago. . . . During the course of its analysis of this question, analysis which led to an affirmance of the Tenth Circuit's dismissal of Digital's appeal, the Court rejected Digital's argument that the identification of some interest or right that would be "irretrievably lost" per se satisfies the third *Cohen* requirement . . . The Court also rejected Digital Equipment's contention that a party's ability to characterize the right allegedly denied as a "right not to stand trial" is both sufficient and necessary for a finding that the order appealed from is a collateral order. This contention, the Court explained, "is neither an accurate distillation of our case law nor an appealing prospect for adding to it." The Court further explained that limiting the collateral order analysis to a focus upon whether the interest asserted could be called a "right not to stand trial" is inadequate to protect against "the urge to push the § 1291 limits."

In the wake of *Digital Equipment Corporation*, a party's ability to characterize a district court's decision as denying an irreparable "right not to stand trial" of itself will not suffice to entitle that party to an immediate appeal of the decision. Following *Digital Equipment Corporation*, the analysis required under the third prong of the *Cohen* test does not entail so much the characterization of the right denied as it does inquiry into the relative value or importance of the interests "that would be [forever] lost through rigorous application of a final judgment requirement." *Digital Equipment*, [511 U.S. 863, 878-79 (1994)].

The defendants contend that the interests in federalism and comity sought to be protected by *Rooker-Feldman* would be irreparably harmed by the very fact of federal judicial inquiry into the state court decision at issue. "Once a state adjudication is subjected to discovery, inquiry, review, trial, etc., the integrity of the decision, as protected from federal court review by *Rooker-Feldman* is gone forever." Defendants' Reply at 6. According to the defendants, *Rooker-Feldman* is the "equitable corollary to judicial immunity":

> It is the immunity state decisions enjoy from federal district court review. Akin to Eleventh Amendment, absolute, or qualified immunity, *Rooker-Feldman* is of no practical value after final judgment and appeal, i.e., after federal review of a state court adjudication takes place. Any benefit to state courts conferred by *Rooker-Feldman* "is for

the most part lost as litigation proceeds past motion practice." Quite simply, the very fact of a federal court inquiry, without immediate appeal, into a state court adjudication . . . renders *Rooker-Feldman* worthless. Defendants' Reply at 7-8.

We disagree with the defendants' contention that *Rooker-Feldman* is of no practical value if its ultimate vindication must await the entry of final judgment following district court review of the state court adjudication at issue. The *Rooker-Feldman* doctrine's value as a protector of state courts is not irreparably undermined by district court review of state court adjudications; so long as district court review of a state court adjudication is followed by the proper application of the doctrine at the court of appeals level, the interests that *Rooker-Feldman* seeks to further will be secured. To understand why this is so, one need only compare *Rooker-Feldman* to the types of claims already deemed to fall within the ambit of the collateral order doctrine.

The purpose of the classic immunities — Eleventh Amendment, absolute and qualified immunity — all considered to fall within the collateral order doctrine, is to prevent the holder of the immunity from being dragged into federal district court to answer to civil suits for damages. . . . The same simply cannot be said in the context of *Rooker-Feldman*.

One of the interests that the *Rooker-Feldman* doctrine seeks to promote is respect for state courts. To further this interest, the *Rooker-Feldman* doctrine precludes federal district court review of state court adjudications. Significantly, the protection that *Rooker-Feldman* affords attaches not to the state courts themselves, but rather to their adjudications. Unlike people, states ['] and state entities ['] — the direct recipients and beneficiaries of the classic immunities, for example — adjudications do not suffer irreparably by being haled into federal district court for review. Indeed, once a court of appeals rules that under *Rooker-Feldman*, the district court lacked subject matter jurisdiction to review the state court adjudication, it is, both as a practical as well as a legal matter, as if the state court adjudication had never been reviewed by a federal district court in the first place. So long as the state court adjudication's *Rooker-Feldman*-derived "immunity" is acknowledged and vindicated by the court of appeals following the entry of a final judgment, the interest in respecting state courts by holding their adjudications beyond federal district court scrutiny is adequately protected.[9]

By concluding that the denial of a *Rooker-Feldman* defense does not give rise to an immediately appealable collateral order, we do not gainsay the importance of the interests in federalism and comity that the *Rooker-Feldman* doctrine seeks to protect. We simply believe that these interests are not irreparably harmed through rigorous application of the final

---

9 [7] We say that the Rooker-Feldman interests are adequately vindicable on appeal from a final judgment because we recognize, as has the Supreme Court, that section 1291 never operates without some cost. Litigants are always burdened in ways that are "only imperfectly reparable by appellate reversal of a final district court judgment." *Digital Equipment*, [511 U.S. 863, 872 (1994)].

judgment rule. We note that in other contexts these same interests have been understood to be adequately vindicable on appeal following the entry of final judgment.

IV. Conclusion

Having concluded that an order denying the *Rooker-Feldman* defense is not immediately appealable under the collateral order rule, we will dismiss for lack of appellate jurisdiction the defendants' appeal from the district court's order denying their *Rooker-Feldman* defense.

NOTES

1. The Supreme Court granted certiorari in *Bryant*, vacated the judgment of the Third Circuit, and remanded for consideration of whether the case had become moot. *Sylvester v. Bryant*, 516 U.S. 1105 (1996). The Third Circuit's decision that a refusal to dismiss a case based upon the *Rooker-Feldman* defense is not immediately appealable under the collateral order doctrine became a nullity. But the issue has not gone away.

2. In *Fontana Empire Center, LLC v. City of Fontana*, 307 F.3d 987 (9th Cir. 2002), Fontana (FEC) challenged the foreclosure sale on land that it had acquired, the foreclosure having been based on a judgment obtained before FEC purchased the property. The district court ruled that FEC had stated some claims for relief and dismissed the remaining claims pursuant to *Rooker-Feldman*. FEC appealed, and defendants filed a motion to dismiss on the ground that the appellate court lacked jurisdiction. Recognizing that the appeal was from an interlocutory order and that there was no Rule 54(b) certification, the court held that it had jurisdiction under the collateral order doctrine to review the dismissal of claims pursuant to *Rooker-Feldman*. It reasoned that the attributes that the Supreme Court identified as making a *Burford* abstention appealable as a collateral order in *Quackenbush v. Allstate Ins. Co.*, 517 U.S. 706 (1996), also are present in a *Rooker-Feldman* dismissal because it too effectively deprives litigants of the opportunity to litigate in federal court. "If an appeal of the district court's dismissal must await final judgment, it may well be too late to remedy. . . . As a result of the dismissal, FEC filed a separate lawsuit in state court to obtain an adjudication of the dismissed claims. The state court's judgment in that case would bind the district court in any further proceedings, thus permanently denying FEC the right to adjudicate its claims in federal court. Thus, in the absence of a collateral-order interlocutory appeal, the district court's *Rooker-Feldman* dismissal would be 'the practical equivalent of an order dismissing the case.' *Quackenbush*, 517 U.S. at 713." Moreover, the district court conclusively determined the applicability of the *Rooker-Feldman* doctrine, thereby satisfying another *Cohen* element. And the *Rooker-Feldman* issue was separate from the merits of the action. Having found appellate jurisdiction, the court held that the *Rooker-Feldman* doctrine did not bar the district court from exercising jurisdiction over FEC's claims of deprivation of procedural due process, unlawful taking of property, to set aside the foreclosure sale, promissory estoppel, and for cancellation of deed or instrument, and remanded all claims to the district court.

B.   Exceptions to the Rule: Interlocutory Review

1.   Statutory Exceptions to Finality

a.   Categories Specified by Statute or Rule

Maurice Rosenberg, Solving the Federal Finality-Appealability Problem, 47 LAW AND CONTEMPORARY PROBLEMS 171, 173 (Summer, 1984)[10]

After laying down the basic requirement of finality, the Code enumerates exceptions and methods of appealing without satisfying the finality provision. Section 1292(a), entitled "Interlocutory Decisions," creates a group of per se exceptions mostly identified categorically in terms of the nature of the action involved.

The courts of appeals are given jurisdiction of interlocutory orders in [three] situations. Appellate review is in each a matter of right, without regard to the need for immediate appeal in the particular case. Under section 1292(a)(1) the appellate courts are authorized to review interlocutory orders granting, continuing, modifying, refusing, or dissolving injunctions, or refusing to dissolve or modify injunctions. The rationale is that such orders may bring about a "serious, perhaps irreparable consequence." A large body of case law has grown up around the issue of the appealability of orders staying proceedings. In some circuits, but not in others, orders granting or denying stays of arbitration are appealable as injunctions.

Interlocutory orders appointing receivers or refusing to wind up receiverships or to take certain steps in such proceedings are appealable under section 1292(a)(2). The purpose of the exception is similar to that for injunction orders — forestalling irreparable damage. However, futility rather than irreparability is the danger sought to be avoided in section 1292(a)(3) which provides for appeals from interlocutory "decrees" determining the rights and liabilities of parties in admiralty cases in which appeals from final decrees are permitted. This allows appeals after determination of liability but before a determination of damages to avoid the expense and delay of computing damages in cases in which it turns out the libelant has no right to recover. . . .

28 U.S.C. § 1292. Interlocutory Decisions

(a) . . . [T]he courts of appeals shall have jurisdiction of appeals from:

(1) Interlocutory orders of the district courts of the United States, . . . or of the judges thereof, granting, continuing, modifying, refusing or dissolving injunctions, or refusing to dissolve or modify injunctions, except where a direct review may be had in the Supreme Court;

(2) Interlocutory orders appointing receivers, or refusing orders to wind up receiverships or to take steps to accomplish the purposes thereof, such as directing sales or other disposals of property;

---

[10] Copyright © 1984 by Duke University School of Law and Gloria Rosenberg. Reprinted with permission.

(3) Interlocutory decrees of such district courts or the judges thereof determining the rights and liabilities of the parties to admiralty cases in which appeals from final decrees are allowed.

IN THE MATTER OF VUITTON ET FILS S.A.
606 F.2d 1 (2d Cir. 1979)

PER CURIAM.

This is a petition by Vuitton et Fils S.A. ("Vuitton") for a writ of mandamus directed to the United States District Court for the Southern District of New York, Charles L. Brieant, Jr., Judge, instructing the court to issue *ex parte* a temporary restraining order in an action entitled *Vuitton et Fils S.A. v. Dame Belt & Bag Co., Inc., and Morty Edelstein*, 79 Civ. 0262. In our judgment, we are justified in asserting mandamus jurisdiction in this peculiar case, and we direct the district judge to issue an appropriate *ex parte* order under FED. R. CIV. P. 65.

Vuitton is a French company, a *societé anonyme*, engaged in the sale and distribution of expensive leather goods, including a wide variety of luggage, handbags, wallets and jewelry cases, all under a trademark registered with the United States Patent Office in 1932. This trademark, a distinctive arrangement of initials and designs, has been extensively advertised over the years. Recently, Vuitton has had the misfortune of having to compete with New York area retailers who have been able to obtain counterfeit Vuitton merchandise from various sources and who sell that merchandise at prices considerably below those charged by Vuitton for the authentic items. This, of course, has not pleased Vuitton and, in response, it has commenced 84 actions nationwide and 53 actions in this Circuit charging trademark infringement and unfair competition. This present dispute originated in one of these actions.

On January 16, 1979, Vuitton filed a complaint in the district court seeking preliminary and permanent injunctions against the defendants, Dame Belt & Bag Co., Inc., and an individual named Morty Edelstein, and requesting damages. The gist of the complaint was that the defendants had infringed Vuitton's trademark and engaged in unfair competition by offering for sale luggage and handbags identical in appearance to those merchandised by Vuitton. Accompanying the complaint was an affidavit by Vuitton's attorney explaining why service of process had not been effected and requesting that an *ex parte* temporary restraining order be issued against the defendants under FED. R. CIV. P. 65(b). Vuitton explains its need for an *ex parte* order in the following terms:

> Vuitton's experience, based upon the 84 actions it has brought and the hundreds of other investigations it has made . . . has led to the conclusion that there exist various closely-knit distribution networks for counterfeit Vuitton products. In other words, there does not exist but one or two manufacturers of counterfeit merchandise, but rather many more, but a few of which have been identified to date.

Vuitton's experience in several of the earliest filed cases also taught it that once one member of this community of counterfeiters learned that he had been identified by Vuitton and was about to be enjoined from continuing his illegal enterprise, he would immediately transfer his inventory to another counterfeit seller, whose identity would be unknown to Vuitton. . . .

The now too familiar refrain from a "caught counterfeiter" is "I bought only a few pieces from a man I never saw before and whom I have never seen again. All my business was in cash. I do not know how to locate the man from whom I bought and I cannot remember the identity of the persons to whom I sold.". . .

If after Vuitton has identified a counterfeiter with an inventory of fake merchandise, that counterfeiter is permitted to dispose of that merchandise with relative impunity after he learns of the imminence of litigation but *before* he is enjoined from doing so, Vuitton's trademark enforcement program will be stymied and the community of counterfeiters will be permitted to continue to play its "shell game" at great expense and damage to Vuitton.

A hearing on this application was held the next day, January 17, 1979, before Judge Brieant. Counsel for Vuitton explained: "All we seek this Court to do but for a few hours is to maintain the status quo, namely the defendants' inventory of counterfeit Vuitton merchandise." Vuitton also explained that, if notice of the pending litigation was required, "by the time this Court entered an order, most if not all of the merchandise would have been removed from the premises." Because Vuitton was capable of giving the defendants in this action notice, however, a matter readily conceded by Vuitton, the district court declined to grant the request. That decision is, of course, not appealable. The district court denied certification of the question presented by this case under 28 U.S.C. § 1292(b), and this petition followed. For the reasons that follow, we instruct the district court to grant an appropriate *ex parte* temporary restraining order pursuant to FED. R. CIV. P. 65(b), narrow enough and of brief enough duration to protect the interests of the defendants, the precise terms of which shall be determined by the district court.

Rule 65(b) provides in relevant part as follows:

> A temporary restraining order may be granted without written or oral notice to the adverse party or his attorney only if (1) it clearly appears from specific facts shown by affidavit or by the verified complaint that immediate and irreparable injury, loss, or damage will result to the applicant before the adverse party or his attorney can be heard in opposition, and (2) the applicant's attorney certifies to the court in writing the efforts, if any, which have been made to give the notice and the reasons supporting his claim that notice should not be required.

As explained by the Supreme Court in *Granny Goose Foods, Inc. v. Teamsters*, 415 U.S. 423, 438-39 (1974), "[the] stringent restrictions imposed . . . on the availability of *ex parte* temporary restraining orders reflect the fact that our entire jurisprudence runs counter to the notion of court action taken before reasonable notice and an opportunity to be heard has been granted [to] both sides of a dispute. *Ex parte* temporary restraining orders are no doubt necessary in certain circumstances, . . . but under federal law they should be restricted to serving their underlying purpose of preserving the status quo and preventing irreparable harm just so long as is necessary to hold a hearing, and no longer.". . .

[A]lthough this Court has "frowned upon temporary restraining orders issued without even telephoned notice," *Emery Air Freight Corp. v. Local Union 295*, [449 F.2d 586, 591 (2d Cir. 1971)], there are occasions when such orders are to be countenanced. In our judgment, this case is just such an occasion.

Assuming that all of the other requirements of Rule 65 are met, the rule by its very terms allows for the issuance of an *ex parte* temporary restraining order when (1) the failure to issue it would result in "immediate and irreparable injury, loss, or damage" and (2) the applicant sufficiently demonstrates the reason that notice "should not be required." In a trademark infringement case such as this, a substantial likelihood of confusion constitutes, in and of itself, irreparable injury sufficient to satisfy the requirements of Rule 65(b)(1). . . . Here, we believe that such a likelihood of product confusion exists. The allegedly counterfeit Vuitton merchandise is virtually identical to the genuine items. Indeed, the very purpose of the individuals marketing the cheaper items is to confuse the buying public into believing it is buying the true article.

We also believe that Vuitton has demonstrated sufficiently why notice should not be required in a case such as this one. If notice is required, that notice all too often appears to serve only to render fruitless further prosecution of the action. This is precisely contrary to the normal and intended role of "notice," and it is surely not what the authors of the rule either anticipated or intended.

Accordingly, we hold that, when a proper showing is made, such as was made in this case, and when the rule is otherwise complied with, a plaintiff is entitled to have issued an *ex parte* temporary restraining order. Such an order should be narrow in scope and brief in its duration. The petition is granted.

NOTES

1. Why was the denial of a temporary restraining order not appealable as the denial of an injunction under 28 U.S.C. § 1292(a)?

2. Did the availability of mandamus depend on the ground on which the district judge denied the temporary restraining order? What was that ground?

3. The grant or denial of injunctive orders traditionally has been within the equitable discretion of the trial judge. In reviewing the denial of a temporary restraining order in *Vuitton et Fils*, did the appellate court hold that the trial judge had abused this discretion? Precisely what did the appellate court hold?

AMERICAN MORTGAGE CORP. v. FIRST NATIONAL MORTGAGE CO.
345 F.2d 527 (7th Cir. 1965)

MERCER, DISTRICT JUDGE.

Plaintiff by its complaint alleged that First National Mortgage Company, alleged to be a corporation, through its agents, had obtained sums of money from plaintiff through false representations and fraud. The complaint prayed an attachment of bank accounts of First National at the three defendant banks. Attachment under the Illinois statute was ordered, *ex parte*, pursuant to the prayer of the complaint. Ill. Rev. Stat. 1963, c. 11, § 1 *et seq.*

Defendant, Leonard B. Stallman, entered his appearance in the cause, averring that First National was not a corporation, but was wholly owned by him. He moved to dismiss the attachment. On May 4, 1964, a memorandum order was entered by the trial judge finding that the attachment was providently issued, denying Stallman's motion to dismiss, directing pre-trial discovery and setting the cause for a pre-trial conference. This appeal was then taken by the defendants, Stallman, individually and doing business as First National Mortgage Company, and Joseph Stein.

Plaintiff filed a motion to dismiss the appeal upon the ground, inter *alia*, that there is no final judgment in the cause from which an appeal can be taken. On October 12, 1964, we ordered that motion be heard with the appeal on the merits.

After argument upon the motion and the appeal, and after due consideration of the record and the applicable authorities, we are convinced that the motion must be granted and the appeal dismissed.

The order sought to be appealed is not a final judgment to which appellate jurisdiction attaches under 28 U.S.C. § 1291, and the order is not of the type interlocutory orders for which interlocutory appeals are permitted. The principle that piecemeal appeals will not be entertained and that the appeals courts jealously guard their jurisdiction against the imposition of such attempted appeals is . . . well settled. . . .

Defendants argue that an attachment should be treated as a temporary injunction, and that an appeal is proper in this instance by analogy to the temporary injunction situation. They also suggest that an order denying dismissal of an attachment is appealable under the provisions of the Illinois attachment statute. Both arguments are completely specious. The distinction between attachments and injunctions has been so long recognized that we are convinced that Congress would have provided for interlocutory appeals in cases such as this had it deemed such appeals desirable. The argument based upon the Illinois statute is amply answered by the decision in *Smith v. Hodge*, 13 Ill. 2d 197, 199-200, which held that an interlocutory order in an attachment suit could not be appealed prior to a final decision on the merits of the case.

For the reasons stated the appeal is dismissed.

SWIFT & CO. PACKERS v. COMPANIA COLOMBIANA DEL CARIBE, S.A.
339 U.S. 684 (1950)

MR. JUSTICE FRANKFURTER delivered the opinion of the Court.

The question before us is the propriety of an order of the District Court for the Canal Zone vacating a foreign attachment of a vessel made in a libel *in personam*. We granted certiorari because important questions relating to the scope of admiralty jurisdiction and its exercise are in issue.

On March 7, 1948, the libel was filed against Compania Transmaritima Colombiana, S.A., a Colombian corporation, by Swift & Company Packers, a Nevada corporation, certain Cuban corporations and individuals, and a

Colombian citizen. They brought the libel as owners of rice shipped from Ecuador to Cuba. It was alleged that the cargo had been delivered in good order to the *M/V Cali*, owned and operated by Transmaritima, and that the vessel had sunk, or partially sunk, off the island of Grand Cayman with resulting nondelivery of the cargo. This was supplemented by allegations of negligence. Process was prayed with the further request that if the respondent could not be found its goods and chattels be attached, particularly a vessel known as the *Alacran*, or *Caribe*. This vessel was thereupon attached by the marshal. . . .

Attachment of the vessel was again prayed on what appears to have been either of two grounds: since Transmaritima and Del Caribe were really one and the same, it mattered not which was deemed to be the owner of the *Caribe*; since the transfer of the *Caribe* to Del Caribe was a fraudulent transfer to be set aside, the vessel was in reality Transmaritima's property and Del Caribe should be garnished. On the basis of the amended libel another attachment of the *Caribe* was made. . . .

On August 16, Del Caribe gave notice of a motion to dismiss the libel as to it and vacate the attachment. Various grounds were urged calling into question the jurisdiction of the court, the propriety of its exercise, and the adequacy of the allegations to state a claim in the libel. An accompanying affidavit set forth matters relating to the transfer.

On September 20, the District Court found that the nondelivery of the cargo was due to the beaching of the *Cali* in January, 1948; that Del Caribe had been organized in the latter part of February, 1948; and that Transmaritima had sold and transferred the *Caribe* to Del Caribe on February 25. From these facts the district judge concluded that there was no jurisdiction in admiralty to inquire into the relations between the two respondent companies or the sale of the *Caribe*. In any event, the court declined to exercise jurisdiction to look into the transfer since it had taken place between two foreign corporations and in a foreign country. Accordingly, the attachment was ordered to be vacated. While libellants submitted additional evidence upon a rehearing, the court adhered to its original views.

The Court of Appeals affirmed. . . .

There is a threshold question as to the jurisdiction of the court below to entertain the appeal. It is claimed that the order vacating the attachment was not a final order and therefore not reviewable.

We believe that the order comes squarely within the considerations of our recent decision in *Cohen v. Beneficial Indus. Loan Corp.*, 337 U.S. 541. The litigation arising out of the claim of the libellants has not run its entire course, but the order now here, like that in the Cohen case, "appears to fall in that small class which finally determine claims of right separable from, and collateral to, rights asserted in the action, too important to be denied review and too independent of the cause itself to require that appellate consideration be deferred until the whole case is adjudicated." 337 U.S. at 546. Appellate review of the order dissolving the attachment at a later date would be an empty rite after the vessel had been released and the restoration of the attachment only theoretically possible. *Cf. The Panaghia Kathariotisa*, 165 F.2d 430. Under these circumstances the provision for appeals only from final decisions in 28 U.S.C. § 1291 should not be construed so as to deny effective review of a claim fairly severable from the context of a larger litigious process. *See Cobbledick v. United States*, 309 U.S. 323, 328-29. The situation is quite different where an attachment is upheld pending determination of the principal claim. Such was *Cushing v. Laird*, 107 U.S. 69 (1882), which is urged on us. In such a situation the rights of all the parties can be adequately protected while the litigation on the main claim proceeds. . . .

Reversed and remanded.

MR. JUSTICE DOUGLAS took no part in the consideration or decision of this case.

NOTES

1. Whether and when seizures and attachments constitute immediately appealable injunctions continue to generate decisions in some tension with one another. For example, based on statutory language, Congressional intent, and the nature of an injunction as directed to a party, enforceable by contempt, and designed to accord some or all of the substantive relief sought, *In re Lorillard Tobacco Company*, 370 F.3d 982 (9th Cir. 2004), held that the denial of an ex parte seizure order sought by Lorillard to seize allegedly counterfeit cigarettes and other evidence of counterfeiting, pursuant to trademark law, was not an immediately appealable injunction, and that it also did not satisfy the requisites set down by the *Carson* case, discussed below, for an order having the practical effect of refusing an injunction. *Charlesbank Equity Fund II v. Blinds to Go, Inc.*, 370 F.3d 151 (1st Cir. 2004), held that an order denying a preliminary injunction to freeze company funds was immediately appealable, purporting to distinguish grants or denials of prejudgment attachments which, in the absence of special circumstances, federal appeals courts lack jurisdiction to review.

2. As the preceding cases reveal, federal district court grants or refusals of provisional remedies have been variously reviewed through each of the possible procedural routes to the courts of appeals:

- by appeal under § 1291, as a "collateral order";
- by appeal under § 1292(a), as an order granting or refusing a preliminary injunction;
- as a discretionary appeal, given the requisite certification, under § 1292(b); and
- by petition for mandamus in the appellate court.

Assuming that a provisional remedy is put before an appellate court through one of these procedural routes, the focus then becomes the appropriate standard of review, a subject dealt with in Chapter 3.

LIBERTY MUTUAL INSURANCE CO. v. WETZEL
424 U.S. 737 (1976)

MR. JUSTICE REHNQUIST delivered the opinion of the Court.

Respondents filed a complaint in the United States District Court for the Western District of Pennsylvania in which they asserted that petitioner's employee insurance benefits and maternity leave regulations discriminated against women in violation of Title VII of the Civil Rights Act of 1964, 78 Stat. 253, as amended by the Equal Employment Opportunity Act of 1972, 42 U.S.C. § 2000e *et seq.* (1970 ed. and Supp. IV). The District Court ruled in favor of respondents on the issue of petitioner's liability under that Act, and petitioner appealed to the Court of Appeals for the Third Circuit. That court held that it had jurisdiction of petitioner's appeal under 28 U.S.C. § 1291, and proceeded to affirm on the merits the judgment of the District Court. We granted certiorari and heard argument on the merits. Though neither party has questioned the jurisdiction of the Court of Appeals to entertain the appeal, we are obligated to do so on our own motion if a question thereto exists. *Mansfield, Coldwater & Lake Michigan Ry. Co. v. Swan*, 111 U.S. 379 (1884). Because we conclude that the District Court's order was not appealable to the Court of Appeals, we vacate the judgment of the Court of Appeals with instructions to dismiss petitioner's appeal from the order of the District Court.

Respondents' complaint, after alleging jurisdiction and facts deemed pertinent to their claim, prayed for a judgment against petitioner embodying the following relief:

(a) requiring that defendant establish non-discriminatory hiring, payment, opportunity, and promotional plans and programs;

(b) enjoining the continuance by defendant of the illegal acts and practices alleged herein;

(c) requiring that defendant pay over to plaintiffs and to the members of the class the damages sustained by plaintiffs and the members of the class by reason of defendant's illegal acts and practices, including adjusted backpay, with interest, and an additional equal amount as liquidated damages, and exemplary damages;

(d) requiring that defendant pay to plaintiffs and to the members of the class the costs of this suit and a reasonable attorneys' fee, with interest; and

(e) such other and further relief as the Court deems appropriate.

After extensive discovery, respondents moved for partial summary judgment only as to the issue of liability. FED. R. CIV. P. 56(c). The District Court on January 9, 1974, finding no issues of material fact in dispute, entered an order to the effect that petitioner's pregnancy-related policies violated Title VII of the Civil Rights Act of 1964. It also ruled that Liberty Mutual's hiring and promotion policies violated Title VII. Petitioner thereafter filed a motion for reconsideration which was denied by the District Court. Its order of February 20, 1974, denying the motion for reconsideration, contains the following concluding language:

> In its Order the court stated it would enjoin the continuance of practices which the court found to be in violation of Title VII. The Plaintiffs were invited to submit the form of the injunction order and the Defendant has filed Notice of Appeal and asked for stay of any injunctive order. Under these circumstances the court will withhold the issuance of the injunctive order and amend the Order previously issued under the provisions of FED. R. CIV. P. 54(b), as follows:

And now this 20th day of February, 1974, it is directed that final judgment be entered in favor of Plaintiffs that Defendant's policy of requiring female employees to return to work within three months of delivery of a child or be terminated is in violation of the provisions of Title VII of the Civil Rights Act of 1964; that Defendant's policy of denying disability income protection plan benefits to female employees for disabilities related to pregnancies or childbirth are [sic] in violation of Title VII of the Civil Rights Act of 1964 and that it is expressly directed that Judgment be entered for the Plaintiffs upon these claims of Plaintiffs' Complaint; there being no just reason for delay.

It is obvious from the District Court's order that respondents, although having received a favorable ruling on the issue of petitioner's liability to them, received none of the relief which they expressly prayed for in the portion of their complaint set forth above. They requested an injunction, but did not get one; they requested damages, but were not awarded any; they requested attorneys' fees, but received none.

Counsel for respondents when questioned during oral argument in this Court suggested that at least the District Court's order of February 20 amounted to a declaratory judgment on the issue of liability pursuant to the provisions of 28 U.S.C. § 2201. Had respondents sought only a declaratory judgment, and no other form of relief, we would of course have a different case.

But even if we accept respondents' contention that the District Court's order was a declaratory judgment on the issue of liability, it nonetheless left unresolved respondents' requests for an injunction, for compensatory and exemplary damages, and for attorneys' fees. It finally disposed of none of respondents' prayers for relief.

The District Court and the Court of Appeals apparently took the view that because the District Court made the recital required by FED. R. CIV. P. 54(b) that final judgment be entered on the issue of liability, and that there was no just reason for delay, the orders thereby became appealable as a final decision pursuant to 28 U.S.C. § 1291. We cannot agree with this application of the Rule and statute in question.

Rule 54(b) "does not apply to a single claim action. . . . It is limited expressly to multiple claims actions in which 'one or more but less than all' of the multiple claims have been finally decided and are found otherwise to be ready for appeal." *Sears, Roebuck Co. v. Mackey*, 351 U.S. 427, 435 (1956). Here, however, respondents set forth but a single claim: that petitioner's employee insurance benefits and maternity leave regulations discriminated against its women employees in violation of Title VII of the Civil Rights Act of 1964. They prayed for several different types of relief in the event that they sustained the allegations of their complaint, *see* FED. R. CIV. P. 8(a)(3), but their complaint advanced a single legal theory which was applied to only one set of facts. Thus, despite the fact that the District Court undoubtedly made the findings required under the Rule, had it been applicable, those findings do not in a case such as this make the order appealable pursuant to 28 U.S.C. § 1291.

We turn to consider whether the District Court's order might have been appealed by petitioner to the Court of Appeals under any other theory. The order, viewed apart from its discussion of Rule 54(b), constitutes a grant of partial summary judgment limited to the issue of petitioner's liability. Such judgments are by their terms interlocutory, see FED. R. CIV. P. 56(c), and where assessment of damages or awarding of other relief remains to be resolved have never been considered to be "final" within the meaning of 28 U.S.C. § 1291. . . . Thus, the only possible authorization for an appeal from the District Court's order would be pursuant to the provisions of 28 U.S.C. § 1292.

If the District Court had granted injunctive relief but had not ruled on respondents' other requests for relief, this interlocutory order would have been appealable under § 1292(a)(1). But, as noted above, the court did not issue an injunction. It might be argued that the order of the District Court, insofar as it failed to include the injunctive relief requested by respondents, is an interlocutory order refusing an injunction within the meaning of § 1292(a)(1). But even if this would have allowed respondents to then obtain review in the Court of Appeals, there was no denial of any injunction sought by *petitioner* and it could not avail itself of that grant of jurisdiction.

Nor was this order appealable pursuant to 28 U.S.C. § 1292(b). Although the District Court's findings made with a view to satisfying Rule 54(b) might be viewed as substantial compliance with the certification requirement of that section, there is no showing in this record that petitioner made application to the Court of Appeals within the 10 days therein specified. And that court's holding that its jurisdiction was pursuant to § 1291 makes it clear that it thought itself obliged to consider on the merits petitioner's appeal.

There can be no assurance that had the other requirements of § 1292(b) been complied with, the Court of Appeals would have exercised its discretion to entertain the interlocutory appeal.

Were we to sustain the procedure followed here, we would condone a practice whereby a district court in virtually any case before it might render an interlocutory decision on the question of liability of the defendant, and the defendant would thereupon be permitted to appeal to the court of appeals without satisfying any of the requirements that Congress carefully set forth.

We believe that Congress, in enacting present §§ 1291 and 1292 of Title 28, has been well aware of the dangers of an overly rigid insistence upon a "final decision" for appeal in every case, and has in those sections made ample provision for appeal of orders which are not "final" so as to alleviate any possible hardship. We would twist the fabric of the statute more than it will bear if we were to agree that the District Court's order of February 20, 1974, was appealable to the Court of Appeals.

The judgment of the Court of Appeals is therefore vacated, and the case is remanded with instructions to dismiss the petitioner's appeal.

MR. JUSTICE BLACKMUN took no part in the consideration or decision of this case.

SWITZERLAND CHEESE ASSOCIATION v. E. HORNE'S MARKET, INC.
385 U.S. 23 (1966)

MR. JUSTICE DOUGLAS delivered the opinion of the Court.

Petitioners brought this suit for trademark infringement and unfair competition under the trademark laws. 60 Stat. 427, 15 U.S.C. § 1051 *et seq.* They sought a preliminary injunction during the pendency of the action, a permanent injunction, and damages. After issue was joined, petitioners moved for a summary judgment granting a permanent injunction and awarding damages against respondent. The District Court could not say that there was "no genuine issue as to any material fact" within the meaning of Rule 56 of the FED. R. CIV. P. which governs summary judgments and accordingly denied the motion. Petitioners appealed, claiming that order to be an "interlocutory" one "refusing" an injunction within the meaning of § 1292(a)(1) of the Judicial Code, 28 U.S.C. § 1292(a)(1).

The Court of Appeals held that the order denying the motion for a summary judgment was not an "interlocutory" one within the meaning of § 1292 (a)(1) and dismissed the appeal for want of jurisdiction. 351 F.2d 552. We granted certiorari because of a conflict between that decision and those from the Second Circuit. *See, e.g., Federal Glass Co. v. Loshin,* 217 F.2d 936.

Unlike some state procedures, federal law expresses the policy against piecemeal appeals. *See Baltimore Contractors, Inc. v. Bodinger,* 348 U.S. 176.

Hence we approach this statute somewhat gingerly lest a floodgate be opened that brings into the exception many pretrial orders. It is earnestly argued, however, that, although this order denied a permanent injunction, it was nonetheless "interlocutory" within the meaning of § 1292(a)(1) because the motion for summary judgment did service for a motion for a preliminary injunction (*see Federal Glass Co. v. Loshin, supra,* at 938) and that therefore "interlocutory" must also include a denial of a permanent injunction.

We take the other view not because "interlocutory" or preliminary may not at times embrace denials of permanent injunctions, but for the reason that the denial of a motion for a summary judgment because of unresolved issues of fact does not settle or even tentatively decide anything about the merits of the claim. It is strictly a pretrial order that decides only one thing — that the case should go to trial. Orders that in no way touch on the merits of the claim but only relate to pretrial procedures are not in our view "interlocutory" within the meaning of § 1292(a)(1). We see no other way to protect the integrity of the congressional policy against piecemeal appeals.

Affirmed.

CARSON v. AMERICAN BRANDS, INC.
450 U.S. 79 (1981)

MR. JUSTICE BRENNAN delivered the opinion of the Court.

The question presented in this Title VII class action is whether an interlocutory order of the District Court denying a joint motion of the parties to enter a consent decree containing injunctive relief is an appealable order.

Petitioners, representing a class of present and former black seasonal employees and applicants for employment at the Richmond Leaf Department of the American Tobacco Co., brought this suit in the United States District Court for the Eastern District of Virginia under 42 U.S.C. § 1981 and title VII of the Civil Rights Act of 1964, 42 U.S.C. § 2000e *et seq.* Alleging that respondents had discriminated against them in hiring, promotion, transfer, and training opportunities, petitioners sought a declaratory judgment, preliminary and permanent injunctive relief, and money damages.

After extensive discovery had been conducted and the plaintiff class had been certified, the parties negotiated a settlement and jointly moved the District Court to approve and enter their proposed consent decree. *See* FED. R. CIV. P. 23(e). The decree would have required respondents to give hiring and seniority preferences to black employees and to fill one-third of all supervisory positions in the Richmond Leaf Department with qualified blacks.

While agreeing to the terms of the decree, respondents "expressly den[ied] any violation of . . . any . . . equal employment law, regulation, or order."

The District Court denied the motion to enter the proposed decree. 446 F. Supp. 780 (1977). Concluding that preferential treatment on the basis of race violated Title VII and the Constitution absent a showing of past or present discrimination, and that the facts submitted in support of the decree demonstrated no "vestiges of racial discrimination," *id.* at 790, the court held that the proposed decree illegally granted racial preferences to the petitioner class. It further declared that even if present or past discrimination had been shown, the decree would be illegal in that it would extend relief to *all* present and future black employees of the Richmond Leaf Department, not just to *actual* victims of the alleged discrimination. *Id.* at 789.

The United States Court of Appeals for the Fourth Circuit, sitting en banc, dismissed petitioners' appeal for want of jurisdiction. . . .

[W]e granted certiorari. . . . We hold that the order is appealable under 28 U.S.C. § 1292(a)(1), and accordingly reverse the Court of Appeals. . . .

Although the District Court's order declining to enter the proposed consent decree did not in terms "refus[e]" an "injunctio[n]," it nonetheless had the practical effect of doing so. *Cf. General Electric Co. v. Marvel Rare Metals Co.,* 287 U.S. 430, 433 (1932). This is because the proposed decree would have permanently enjoined respondents from discriminating against black employees at the Richmond Leaf Department, and would have directed changes in seniority and benefit systems, established hiring goals for qualified blacks in certain supervisory positions, and granted job-bidding preferences for seasonal employees. Indeed, prospective relief was at the very core of the disapproved settlement.

For an interlocutory order to be immediately appealable under § 1292(a)(1), however, a litigant must show more than that the order has the practical effect of refusing an injunction. Because § 1292(a)(1) was intended to carve out only a limited exception to the final-judgment rule, we have construed the statute narrowly to ensure that appeal as of right under § 1292(a)(1) will be available only in circumstances where an appeal will further the statutory purpose of "permit[ting] litigants to effectually challenge interlocutory orders of serious, perhaps irreparable, consequence." *Baltimore Contractors, Inc. v. Bodinger, supra*, at 181. Unless a litigant can show that an interlocutory order of the district court might have a "serious, perhaps irreparable, consequence," and that the order can be "effectually challenged" only by immediate appeal, the general congressional policy against piecemeal review will preclude interlocutory appeal.

In *Switzerland Cheese Assn., Inc. v. E. Horne's Market, Inc.*, 385 U.S. 23 (1966), for example, petitioners contended that the District Court's denial of their motion for summary judgment was appealable under § 1292(a)(1) simply because its practical effect was to deny them the permanent injunction sought in their summary-judgment motion. Although the District Court order seemed to fit within the statutory language of § 1292(a)(1), petitioners' contention was rejected because they did not show that the order might cause them irreparable consequences if not immediately reviewed. The motion for summary judgment sought permanent and not preliminary injunctive relief and petitioners did not argue that a denial of summary judgment would cause them irreparable harm *pendente lite*. Since permanent injunctive relief might have been obtained after trial, the interlocutory order lacked the "serious, perhaps irreparable, consequence" that is a prerequisite to appealability under § 1292(a)(1).

Similarly, in *Gardner v. Westinghouse Broadcasting Co.*, 437 U.S. 478 (1978), petitioner in a Title VII sex discrimination suit sought a permanent injunction against her prospective employer on behalf of herself and her putative class. After the District Court denied petitioner's motion for class certification, petitioner filed an appeal under § 1292(a)(1). She contended that since her complaint had requested injunctive relief, the court's order denying class certification had the effect of limiting the breadth of the available relief, and therefore of "refus[ing] a substantial portion of the injunctive relief requested in the complaint." 437 U.S. at 480.

As in *Switzerland Cheese*, petitioner in *Gardner* had not filed a motion for a preliminary injunction and had not alleged that a denial of her motion would cause irreparable harm. The District Court order thus had "no direct or irreparable impact on the merits of the controversy." 437 U.S. at 482.

Because the denial of class certification was conditional, Fed. Rule Civ. Proc. 23(c)(1), and because it could be effectively reviewed on appeal from final judgment, petitioner could still obtain the full permanent injunctive relief she requested and a delayed review of the District Court order would therefore cause no serious or irreparable harm. . . .

In the instant case, unless the District Court order denying the motion to enter the consent decree is immediately appealable, petitioners will lose their opportunity to "effectually challenge" an interlocutory order that denies them injunctive relief and that plainly has a "serious, perhaps irreparable, consequence." First, petitioners might lose their opportunity to settle their case on the negotiated terms. As *United States v. Armour & Co.*, 402 U.S. 673, 681 (1971), stated:

> Consent decrees are entered into by parties to a case after careful negotiation has produced agreement on their precise terms. The parties waive their right to litigate the issues involved in the case and thus save themselves the time, expense, and inevitable risk of litigation. Naturally, the agreement reached normally embodies a

compromise; in exchange for the saving of cost and elimination of risk, the parties each give up something they might have won had they proceeded with the litigation.

Settlement agreements may thus be predicated on an express or implied condition that the parties would, by their agreement, be able to avoid the costs and uncertainties of litigation. In this case, that condition of settlement has been radically affected by the District Court. By refusing to enter the proposed consent decree, the District Court effectively ordered the parties to proceed to trial and to have their respective rights and liabilities established within limits laid down by that court. Because a party to a pending settlement might be legally justified in withdrawing its consent to the agreement once trial is held and final judgment entered, the District Court's order might thus have the "serious, perhaps irreparable, consequence" of denying the parties their right to compromise their dispute on mutually agreeable terms.

There is a second "serious, perhaps irreparable, consequence" of the District Court order that justifies our conclusion that the order is immediately appealable under § 1292(a)(1). In seeking entry of the proposed consent decree, petitioners sought an immediate restructuring of respondents' transfer and promotional policies. They asserted in their complaint that they would suffer irreparable injury unless they obtained that injunctive relief at the earliest opportunity. Because petitioners cannot obtain that relief until the proposed consent decree is entered, any further delay in reviewing the propriety of the District Court's refusal to enter the decree might cause them serious or irreparable harm.

In sum, in refusing to approve the parties' negotiated consent decree, the District Court denied petitioners the opportunity to compromise their claim and to obtain the injunctive benefits of the settlement agreement they negotiated. These constitute "serious, perhaps irreparable, consequences" that petitioners can "effectually challenge" only by an immediate appeal. It follows that the order is an order "refusing" an "injunctio[n]" and is therefore appealable under § 1292(a)(1).

Reversed.

NOTES

1. Did the *Carson* Court correctly interpret the *Switzerland Cheese* case?

2. Section 1292(a)(1) does not by its terms require that a denial of a preliminary injunction cause irreparable harm in order for it to be appealable. What is the justification for the Court's reading that requirement into the statute? Does this requirement confuse the merits of the district court's action with the appealability of that action?

3. How broad is the scope of review available to a court of appeals hearing an appeal under § 1292(a)(1)? May it also consider issues that but for the § 1292(a)(1) appeal would not be reviewable until after final judgment? The court may hold itself entitled to consider other such issues under the doctrine of pendent appellate jurisdiction, discussed below. *See, e.g., Gen. Elec. Co. v. Deutz AG*, 270 F.3d 144 (3d Cir. 2001) (holding that appeals court had jurisdiction over

appeal from ruling that district court had personal jurisdiction over defendant); *Gates v. Cook*, 234 F.3d 221 (5th Cir. 2000) (holding that appeals court had jurisdiction over appeal from ruling denying a motion to substitute counsel).

4. State systems vary widely from some that purport to permit appeals only from final judgments (*see* WIS. STAT. ANN. §808.03 (2005)), to some (such as California) that largely follow the federal model, to others that are still more liberal in permitting interlocutory appeals. New York permits appeals from most interlocutory orders to the intermediate appellate courts. In JACK B. WEINSTEIN, HAROLD L. KORN & ARTHUR R. MILLER, NEW YORK CIVIL PRACTICE 5701.03, it is noted that CPLR 5701, which allows parties to "obtain immediate review as of right from almost any order made during the course of an action . . . represents an extreme position among American jurisdictions. . . ."

New York Civil Practice Law and Rules

§ 5701 Appeals to appellate division from supreme and county courts

(a) Appeals as of right. An appeal may be taken to the appellate division as of right in an action, originating in the supreme court or a county court:

1. from any final or interlocutory judgment except one entered subsequent to an order of the appellate division which disposes of all the issues in the action; or

2. from an order not specified in subdivision (b), where the motion it decided was made upon notice and it:

   (i)   grants, refuses, continues or modifies a provisional remedy; or

   (ii)   settles, grants or refuses an application to resettle a transcript or statement on appeal; or

   (iii) grants or refuses a new trial; except where specific questions of fact arising upon the issues in an action triable by the court have been tried by a jury, pursuant to an order for that purpose, and the order grants or refuses a new trial upon the merits; or

   (iv) involves some part of the merits; or

   (v)   affects a substantial right; or

   (vi) in effect determines the action and prevents a judgment from which an appeal might be taken; or

   (vii) determines a statutory provision of the state to be unconstitutional, and the determination appears from the reasons given for the decision or is necessarily implied in the decision; or . . .

3. from an order, where the motion it decided was made upon notice, refusing to vacate or modify a prior order, if the prior order would have been appealable as of right under paragraph two had it decided a motion made upon notice.

(b) Orders not appealable as of right. An order is not appealable to the appellate division as of right where it:

1. is made in a proceeding against a body or officer pursuant to article 78; or

2. requires or refuses to require a more definite statement in a pleading; or

3. orders or refuses to order that scandalous or prejudicial matter be stricken from a pleading.

5. One can argue that such receptivity to appeal reflects a lack of confidence in the trial judges of the state. If there were a high level of confidence that most trial judges would rule correctly most of the time on the great majority of questions, there would be little point in permitting litigants to promptly bring such a large number of rulings to the appellate courts.

Viewed this way, Virginia can be seen as a state in which confidence in the trial judges is quite high. There, with few exceptions, appeals are subject to the discretion of the supreme court and of the court of appeals. Litigants seeking review in either of those courts, even from a final judgment, must petition for leave to appeal. In effect, a presumption of correctness is applied to trial judges' actions in both civil and criminal cases, and the appellate court has to be shown, case by case, that a particular ruling or judgment is probably erroneous before full review will be accorded. *See* VA. CODE §§ 8.01-670, 17.1-405. The same jurisdictional arrangement prevails in West Virginia. *See* W. VA. CONST. art. VIII, § 4.

Because the variances among states are so great, meaningful generalizations could not be drawn from a small sampling of cases. But when in practice, a lawyer will have to learn the details of the state system in which he or she is working.

b. Case-by-Case Discretionary Review

28 U.S.C. § 1292

. . . .

(b) When a district judge, in making in a civil action an order not otherwise appealable under this section, shall be of the opinion that such order involves a controlling question of law as to which there is substantial ground for difference of opinion and that an immediate appeal from the order may materially advance the ultimate termination of the litigation, he shall so state in writing in such order. The Court of Appeals which would have jurisdiction of an appeal of such action may thereupon, in its discretion, permit an appeal to be taken from such order, if application is made to it within ten days after the entry of the order: *Provided, however,* That application for an appeal hereunder shall not stay proceedings in the district court unless the district judge or the Court of Appeals or a judge thereof shall so order.

WEST TENNESSEE CHAPTER OF ASSOCIATED BUILDERS AND CONTRACTORS, INC. v. CITY OF MEMPHIS
293 F.3d 345 (6th Cir. 2002)

RALPH B. GUY, JR., Circuit Judge.

Defendant, City of Memphis (City), applies for permission to appeal from the district court's order holding that postenactment evidence cannot be presented by the City to demonstrate a compelling need for awarding construction contracts based on racial preferences. Plaintiffs, West Tennessee Chapter of Associated Builders and Contractors, Inc., and Zellner Construction Company, Inc., argue that the City's application is not timely and that the statutory requirements for interlocutory review have not been met under 28 U.S.C. § 1292(b). . . . [W]e find interlocutory review is not appropriate under § 1292(b) and deny the application.

I.

Plaintiffs brought this action on January 4, 1999, challenging the use of minority preferences by the City in awarding construction contracts under the City's Minority & Women Business Enterprise Procurement Program (MWBE program). Plaintiffs alleged in relevant part that the MWBE program violated the Fourteenth Amendment.

The City adopted the MWBE program in 1996 as a remedy for past discrimination and to prevent future discrimination. At the time of enactment, the City relied on a disparity study covering the period from 1988 to 1992. Based on that study, the City concluded that it was an active and passive participant in discrimination.

In response to this litigation, the City proposed to commission a new study that would cover the period from 1993 to 1998. The City wishes to use this postenactment study as evidence to demonstrate a compelling governmental interest. The district court ruled on June 9, 1999, that the City could not introduce the postenactment study as evidence of a compelling governmental interest. . . .

[T]he district court certified an interlocutory appeal on December 20, 2000. It is undisputed that the parties did not receive notice of entry of the order until after the expiration of the 10-day period for filing an application for interlocutory appeal to this court. On January 9, 2001, the district court *sua sponte* entered an order granting the City an additional 30 days to file the interlocutory appeal. On May 1, 2001, this court denied the application for interlocutory appeal finding that the district court could not extend the 10-day period under 28 U.S.C. § 1292(b).

On May 17, 2001, the City filed a motion asking the district court to vacate and reenter its certification order. On July 5, 2001, the district court vacated its December 20, 2000 order. After considering anew whether certification would achieve the ends of § 1292(b), the district court reentered its certification order. On July 12, 2001, the City filed an application for permission to appeal.

II.

. . . [The court found that it had jurisdiction to consider the City's application for permission to appeal.]

B. Requirements for Interlocutory Appeal

This court in its discretion may permit an appeal to be taken from an order certified for interlocutory appeal if (1) the order involves a controlling question of law, (2) a substantial ground for difference of opinion exists regarding the correctness of the decision, and (3) an immediate appeal may materially advance the ultimate termination of the litigation. 28 U.S.C. § 1292(b). Review under § 1292(b) is granted sparingly and only in exceptional cases. *Kraus v. Bd. of County Rd. Comm'rs*, 364 F.2d 919, 922 (6th Cir. 1966).

The City argues that a substantial ground for difference of opinion exists. Some circuits permit postenactment evidence to supplement preenactment evidence. *See Engineering Contrs. Ass'n v. Metropolitan Dade County*, 122 F.3d 895, 911-12 (11th Cir. 1997). The district court relied on these cases to find that there is substantial disagreement as to the proper role played by postenactment evidence. This issue, however, appears to have been resolved in this circuit. . . . Although [*Associated Gen. Contractors of Ohio, Inc. v. Drabik*, 214 F.3d 730 (6th Cir. 2000)] did not directly address the admissibility of postenactment evidence, it held that a governmental entity must have preenactment evidence sufficient to justify a racially conscious statute. It also indicates that this circuit would not favor using postenactment evidence to make that showing.

Even if we concluded that there is a substantial difference of opinion, the issue presented in this case is not a controlling legal issue. A legal issue is controlling if it could materially affect the outcome of the case. A legal question of the type envisioned in § 1292(b), however, generally does not include matters within the discretion of the trial court. A ruling on the admissibility of evidence is reviewed for abuse of discretion. An allegation of abuse of discretion on an evidentiary ruling does not create a legal issue under § 1292(b).

Finally, resolution of the City's challenge to the district court's evidentiary ruling may not materially advance the ultimate termination of the litigation. "When litigation will be conducted in substantially the same manner regardless of [the court's] decision, the appeal cannot be said to materially advance the ultimate termination of the litigation." *White*, 43 F.3d at 378-79. Under *Drabik,* the City must present preenactment evidence to show a compelling state interest. The City has preenactment evidence. Thus, the City will pursue its defense in substantially the same manner. If the City prevails with its preenactment evidence, the exclusion of postenactment evidence will be moot. If it does not prevail, the City can then appeal on the evidentiary ruling and any other issues that may arise below. The application for permission to appeal, therefore, is DENIED.

CLAY, Circuit Judge, dissenting.

Because I am convinced that the district court's order barring the use of post-enactment evidence presents a controlling question of law, I would grant the interlocutory appeal and submit the matter to a panel for resolution on the merits.

This Court has previously recognized that the "controlling" nature of a legal question does not depend on whether its resolution will immediately dispose of the litigation. "'Rather, all that must be shown in order for a question to be "controlling" is that resolution of the issue on appeal could materially affect the outcome of the litigation in the district court.'" *Rafoth v. Nat'l Union Fire*

Ins. Co. (In re Baker & Getty Fin. Servs., Inc.), 954 F.2d 1169, 1172 n.8 (6th Cir. 1992) (quoting *Arizona v. Ideal Basic Indus. (In re Cement Antitrust Litigation)*, 673 F.2d 1020, 1026 (9th Cir. 1981)). WRIGHT AND MILLER recommend taking a practical view of the "controlling question" requirement, explaining that a question is controlling "if interlocutory reversal might save time for the district court, and time and expense for the litigants." 16 CHARLES ALAN WRIGHT, ARTHUR R. MILLER & EDWARD H. COOPER, FEDERAL PRACTICE AND PROCEDURE § 3930, at 426 (2d ed. 1996).

Under our characterization in *In re Baker & Getty Financial Services,* and the characterization advanced by WRIGHT AND MILLER, resolution of the admissibility of post-enactment evidence presents a controlling question inasmuch as resolving the admissibility of post-enactment evidence would dictate the course and duration of discovery in this litigation, as well as the content of any dispositive motions or trial. For example, if this Court determined on an interlocutory basis that the City of Memphis may utilize post-enactment evidence, that ruling would fundamentally shape the nature of the case presented in the district court, and would therefore have a material impact on the outcome of the litigation. In addition, upholding Judge Donald's certification order would ultimately save the parties time and expense, by avoiding the need for additional discovery and court proceedings if our Court determined after final judgment that a decision to permit post-enactment evidence was not erroneous. I therefore respectfully dissent.

NOTES

1. Section 1292(b) was added to the United States Code in 1958 to "expedite the ultimate termination of litigation and thereby save unnecessary expense and delay." H.R. REP. NO. 85-1667, at 1 (1958). Although the final decision rule shares that goal, it seeks to achieve it by postponing appeals until after final judgment, while § 1292(b) recognizes that the goal sometimes can be better achieved by allowing immediate appeal of certain orders.

"In addition to the legislatively defined and the judicially created categories of cases and decisions that are per se appealable even though not final in fact, Congress has provided in § 1292(b) a means of reviewing on an ad hoc basis an interlocutory order in a civil case if the trial court makes an appropriate certification and the appellate court accepts the case. This certification procedure permits selective avoidance of the finality requirement on a case-by-case basis. It supposedly allows dealing in a flexible way with 'occasions which defy precise delineation or description in which as a practical matter orderly administration is frustrated by the necessity of a waste of precious judicial time while the case grinds through to a final judgment as the sole medium through which to test the correctness of some isolated identifiable point of fact, of law, of substance or procedure, upon which in a realistic way the whole case or defense will turn.'" Maurice Rosenberg, *Solving the Federal Finality-Appealability Problem*, 47 LAW & CONTEMP. PROBS. 171, 174 (1984).

2. Studies of the use of the rule have shown that it is utilized relatively infrequently. *See* Michael E. Solimine, *Revitalizing Interlocutory Appeals in the Federal Courts*, 58 GEO. WASH. L. REV. 1165, 1193 (1990). It was reported

in 1994 that trial courts made § 1292(b) certifications in only about 100 cases a year, and that courts of appeals allowed the appeals in only about half those cases. CHARLES A. WRIGHT, LAW OF FEDERAL COURTS, § 102, at 758 (5th ed. 1994). Although the Administrative Office of the U.S. Courts does not maintain statistics on § 1292(b) appeals, the federal appeals courts sometimes mention their own recent experience. For example, the public records of the Second Circuit for 1994 and 1995 revealed a total for the two years of 35 motions for leave to appeal under § 1292(b), of which only eight were granted. *Koehler v. Bank of Bermuda*, 101 F.3d 863, 866 (2d Cir. 1966). In July, 2000, the Seventh Circuit noted that, since the beginning of 1999, it had received 31 petitions for appeal under § 1292(b) and granted only six. *Ahrenholz v. Bd. of Trs. of the Univ. of Ill.*, 219 F.3d 674 (7th Cir. 2000). That infrequent use is attributable in part to the dual requirement that the district court despatch the case to the court of appeals and that the court of appeals accept the certification. As a practical matter, both decisions are in the discretion of the respective courts. The trial court's discretion arises from the statute's prerequisites for certification, which themselves are a second reason for the relatively infrequent use of § 1292(b).

3. Beginning perhaps with *Milbert v. Bison Labs.*, 260 F.2d 431, 433 (3d Cir. 1958), some of the courts of appeals have found in § 1292(b)'s legislative history a Congressional intent that the section "be sparingly applied . . . [and] used only in exceptional cases where an intermediate appeal may avoid protracted and expensive litigation." The Supreme Court agrees that § 1292(b) should be used only in "exceptional circumstances" (*see Caterpillar Inc. v. Lewis*, 519 U.S. 61 (1996) (noting that "Routine resort to § 1292(b) requests would hardly comport with Congress' design to reserve interlocutory review for 'exceptional' cases while generally retaining for the federal courts a firm final judgment rule.")), whatever that means, but not all courts or commentators agree that its use should be limited to large, complex, cases. *See, e.g.,* Note, *Interlocutory Appeals in the Federal Courts Under 28 U.S.C. § 1292(b)*, 88 HARV. L. REV. 607, 626-27 (1975) ("[B]ecause the Act is premised on a notion that there should be a case-by-case evaluation of efficiency, any universal standard restricting certification seems out of place.")

4. When does an order involve a controlling question of law as to which there is substantial ground for difference of opinion? And when will an immediate appeal materially advance the ultimate termination of the litigation? There are no clear and generally accepted answers to these questions. In *Ahrenholz v. Bd. of Trs. of the Univ. of Ill.*, 219 F.3d at 676-77, Judge Posner, for the court, opined that, "[Q]uestion of law" as used in § 1292(b) has reference to a question of the meaning of a statutory or constitutional provision, regulation, or common law doctrine . . . a "pure" question of law. . . . The idea was that if a case turned on a pure [or "abstract"] question of law, something the court of appeals could decide quickly and cleanly without having to study the record, the court should be enabled to do so without having to wait till the end of the case." Would this view eliminate § 1292(b) review of any and all "mixed questions" of law and fact? Is it unduly narrow?

5. In the *Van Cauwenberghe* case, *supra* p. 76, the Supreme Court suggested the possibility that the order denying defendant's motion to dismiss on the

ground of *forum non conveniens* might be appealed under § 1292(b). Would such an order come within the provisions of this section?

6. One scholar has proposed that rules be promulgated for "(1) mandatory appellate review of narrowly defined categories of orders addressing 'problem areas' and (2) certification review for categories of orders addressing 'problem areas' that cannot be narrowed sufficiently to prevent overburdening the circuit courts . . . [and] that Congress amend § 1292(b) to require circuit courts to accept review of orders certified under § 1292(b) unless certification constitutes an abuse of discretion." Timothy P. Glynn, *Discontent and Indiscretion: Discretionary Review of Interlocutory Orders*, 77 NOTRE DAME L. REV. 175, 259 (2001). Would that improve the system?

7. Before leaving § 1292(b), return to the issue posed in *City of Memphis* as to the timeliness of the appeal. The Sixth Circuit had this to say:

> Under 28 U.S.C. § 1292(b), an application for appeal must be made within 10 days after the entry of the district court's certification order. *See also* FED. R. APP. P. 5(a)(2) and (3). Failure to file an appeal within the 10-day period is a jurisdictional defect that deprives this court of the power to entertain an appeal. Neither the district court nor the court of appeals can extend the 10-day period. *Woods v. Baltimore & Ohio R.R. Co.*, 441 F.2d 407, 408 (6th Cir. 1971). *See also* FED. R. APP. P. 26(b)(1).

> The question presented here is whether the district court can restart the 10-day period by vacating its original certification order and then reentering the order. In *Baldwin County Welcome Center v. Brown*, 466 U.S. 147 (1984), the district court had recertified its original interlocutory order nine months after the original 10-day period had expired due to the appellant's failure to properly file its petition in the circuit court for leave to appeal. The majority reached the merits of the appeal without mentioning this procedural history. Justice Stevens (joined by Justices Brennan and Marshall) noted these facts, and stated that he was "persuaded by the view, supported by the commentators, that interlocutory appeals in these circumstances should be permitted, notwithstanding the fact that this view essentially renders the 10-day time limitation, if not a nullity, essentially within the discretion of a district court to extend at will." *Id.* at 162.

> In *Woods*, 441 F.2d at 408, we refused to allow the district court to vacate and, *without reconsideration*, reenter the certification order. The petitioner in *Woods* missed the original filing deadline through its own inadvertence. . . . We declined to decide, however, "whether, following expiration of the time period for the filing of an application for permission to appeal, the Court of Appeals could acquire jurisdiction upon the District Court's reconsideration of its prior order and the timely filing of an application after the entry of such order upon reconsideration." *Id.*

> Other circuits allow the district court to vacate and reenter a certification order to permit a timely appeal. The Fifth Circuit concluded that because the district court retains jurisdiction until

final judgment, it can reconsider an interlocutory order. The Fifth Circuit, therefore, permits recertification even if the petitioner through its own inadvertence failed to take advantage of the original certification as long as the district court finds that the previous justification for interlocutory appeal continues to exist. *Aparicio v. Swan Lake,* 643 F.2d 1109, 1112 (5th Cir. 1981). To hold otherwise would preclude an interlocutory appeal where the criteria under § 1292(b) are met, and both the district court and the court of appeals have concluded that an interlocutory appeal is appropriate. Id. [The Court then discussed cases from the Second and Third Circuits.]

In this case, as distinguished from the petitioner in *Woods,* the City did not miss the 10-day filing period through its own inadvertence. . . . The missed filing deadline and improper attempt to extend the filing period were the results of the actions of the district court and not the City. Any prejudice from the delay and briefing on the initial petition were caused by the district court. This should not preclude the district court from granting relief through reconsideration of the interlocutory order.

Also as distinguished from *Woods,* after vacating the original certification order, the district court reconsidered and specifically found that certification was still proper under § 1292(b). We agree with the other circuits that it is within the broad power of the district court to reconsider an interlocutory order, particularly to avoid an injustice to a party caused by the inadvertent acts of the district court. We find, therefore, that we have jurisdiction to consider the City's application for permission to appeal. . . .

W. Tenn. Chapter of Associated Builders & Contractors v. City of Memphis (In re City of Memphis), 293 F.3d at 348-50.

Does this make it too easy to circumvent § 1292(b)'s time limit on appealing?

8. Provisions similar to 28 U.S.C. § 1292(b) exist in some states. *See, e.g., Castle v. Sherburne Corp.,* 446 A.2d 350 (Vt. 1982). Compare New York Civil Practice Law and Rules, § 5701 Appeals to Appellate Division from Supreme and County Courts, which provides:

. . . .

(c) Appeals by permission. An appeal may be taken to the appellate division from any order which is not appealable as of right in an action originating in the supreme court or a county court by permission of the judge who made the order granted before application to a justice of the appellate division; or by permission of a justice of the appellate division in the department to which the appeal could be taken, upon refusal by the judge who made the order or upon direct application.

How does this statutory authorization for discretionary appeals differ from 28 U.S.C. § 1292(b)? Which is the preferable approach?

9. Consider the approach to appealability taken in the ABA standards, set out below.

ABA COMMISSION ON STANDARDS OF JUDICIAL ADMINISTRATION, STANDARDS RELATING TO APPELLATE COURTS (1994)[11]

3.12 Appealable Judgments and Orders.

(a) Final Judgment. Appellate review ordinarily should be available only upon the rendition of final judgment in the court from which appeal or application for review is taken.

(b) Interlocutory Review. Orders other than final judgments disposing of all claims ordinarily should be subject to immediate appellate review only at the discretion of the reviewing court where it determines that resolution of the questions of law on which the order is based will:

(i)   Materially advance the termination of the litigation or clarify further proceedings;

(ii) Protect a party from substantial and irreparable injury; or

(iii) Clarify an issue of general public importance in the administration of justice.

The essence of this ABA proposal was adopted by Wisconsin in Section 808.03 of the Wisconsin Statutes. WIS. STAT. ANN. § 808.03 (West Supp. 1992). Robert J. Martineau, *Defining Finality and Appealability by Court Rule: Right Problem, Wrong Solution*, 54 U. PITT. L. REV. 717 (1993), argues that such a provision well serves the purpose of the final judgment rule while providing desirable flexibility, and is preferable to vesting courts with rulemaking authority, as was done in the two federal statutes set out below.

Observers hold opposing viewpoints on the best way to determine which issues are afforded interlocutory appeal, however. *Compare* John C. Nagel, Note, *Replacing The Crazy Quilt of Interlocutory Appeals Jurisprudence With Discretionary Review*, 44 DUKE L.J. 200 (1994) (approving the ABA/Wisconsin approach) *with* Timothy P. Glynn, *Discontent and Indiscretion: Discretionary Review of Interlocutory Orders*, 77 NOTRE DAME L. REV. 175, 179-80 (2001)[12]:

> Discretionary review, however, is not the answer. First, the current regime is in far better shape than commonly appreciated. The existing exceptions to the final judgment rule, although narrow, are clear, coherent, and produce limited collateral litigation. In addition, discretionary review — whether generally or in category-based rules like Rule 23(f) — will not result in dramatic increases in the correction of errors that threaten to inflict irreparable harm nor

---

[11] Copyright © 1994 by the American Bar Association. Reprinted with permission.

[12] Copyright © 2001. Reprinted with permission of *Notre Dame Law Review,* University of Notre Dame. LEXISNEXIS bears responsibility for any errors which have occurred in reprinting or editing.

enhance significantly the development of legal standards in areas that have traditionally evaded appellate review. Furthermore, discretionary review is more problematic than its advocates foresee: it will impose substantial new burdens on circuit courts and litigants, and will grant to the circuit courts a new kind of power that threatens the integrity of the courts' error correction and lawmaking functions. On balance, any benefits of discretionary review are outweighed by the added burdens and dangers.

There is a superior approach to reform. . . . [R]ulemaking should be utilized to supplement the current exceptions with narrowly drawn categories of mandatory review. Properly targeted, these categories of review will enhance error correction, reduce irreparable harm, and promote needed development of the law to the extent practicable, while avoiding the pitfalls of discretion. . . . Specifically, rulemaking should be utilized to provide for mandatory review of interlocutory orders confronting "problem areas" - such as class certification and certain privilege issues - that have received insufficient appellate attention and in which errors are probable and often cause significant, irreparable harm. When these categories cannot be narrowed sufficiently to avoid overburdening the circuit courts, district court certification, rather than circuit court discretion, provides the most fair and effective mechanism for weeding out orders that are not worthy of immediate appellate attention.

10. In 1990, Congress amended the Rules Enabling Act, 28 U.S.C. § 2072, by adding a new subsection:

"(c) Such rules may define when a ruling of a district court is final for the purposes of appeal under section 1291 of this title."

This amendment was based on a recommendation of the Federal Courts Study Committee in its 1990 Report (Part II, pp. 95-96). Then, in the Federal Courts Administration Act of 1992, Congress added the following subsection to 28 U.S.C. § 1292:

"(e) The Supreme Court may prescribe rules, in accordance with Section 2072 of this title, to provide for an appeal of an interlocutory decision to the courts of appeals that is not otherwise provided for under subsection (a), (b), (c), or (d)."

The Court has not promulgated any Rules defining finality for purposes of § 1291. Under the authority of § 1292(e), the Supreme Court has now promulgated Rule 23(f) of the Federal Rules of Civil Procedure, which permits interlocutory appeal of orders granting or denying class action certification. Rule 23(f) is discussed in the case that follows.

PRADO-STEIMAN Ex Rel PRADO v. BUSH
221 F.3d 1266 (11th Cir. 2000)

[Developmentally disabled persons and an advocacy group for them sued several Florida officials to challenge Florida's administration of a program to provide Medicaid-related services. The district court granted plaintiffs' motion to certify a class defined as "All persons with developmental disabilities who are presently receiving Home and Community-Based Waiver Services or who are eligible to receive Home and Community-Based Waiver Services, or who would receive or be eligible for Home and Community-Based Waiver Services in the future," and the state petitioned for interlocutory review of the class certification order.]

MARCUS, CIRCUIT JUDGE:

. . .

II.

We start by discussing Federal Rule of Civil Procedure 23(f), which allows federal courts of appeals to hear an interlocutory appeal of a district court's order granting or denying class certification. The Rule, which became effective on December 1, 1998, reads as follows:

> A court of appeals may in its discretion permit an appeal from an order of a district court granting or denying class action certification under this rule if application is made to it within ten days after entry of the order. An appeal does not stay proceedings in the district court unless the district judge or the court of appeals so orders.

FED. R. CIV. P. 23(f). This case is the first published opinion in this circuit, and one of the first in the nation, to address the standards to be used when evaluating a Rule 23(f) petition. Thus far, only the First and Seventh Circuits have explored this question in detail. *See Waste Management Holdings, Inc. v. Mowbray,* 208 F.3d 288 (1st Cir.2000); *Blair v. Equifax Check Services, Inc.,* 181 F.3d 832 (7th Cir.1999). We therefore begin our discussion with background on Rule 23(f), and then set forth some guideposts for evaluating when we should permit a Rule 23(f) appeal.

A.

A good starting point is the Committee Note accompanying Rule 23(f), which articulates the drafters' view of how courts should resolve petitions for appeal under this new rule. The Note emphasizes that "the court of appeals is given unfettered discretion whether to permit the appeal, akin to the discretion exercised by the Supreme Court in acting on a petition for certiorari. . . . Permission to appeal may be granted or denied on the basis of any consideration that the court of appeals finds persuasive." The Note then observes that "permission [to appeal] is most likely to be granted when the certification decision turns on a novel or unsettled question of law, or when, as a practical matter, the decision on certification is likely dispositive of the litigation." According to the Note:

> Many suits with class-action allegations present familiar and almost routine issues that are no more worthy of immediate appeal than many other interlocutory rulings. Yet several concerns justify expansion of present opportunities to appeal. An order denying certification may confront the plaintiff with a situation in which the only sure path to appellate review is by proceeding to final judgment on the merits of an individual claim that, standing alone, is far smaller than

the costs of litigation. An order granting certification, on the other hand, may force a defendant to settle rather than incur the costs of defending a class action and run the risk of potentially ruinous liability.

As summarized by the First Circuit, Rule 23(f) serves two key purposes: first, to provide a "mechanism through which appellate courts, in the interests of fairness, can restore equilibrium when a doubtful class certification ruling would virtually compel a party to abandon a potentially meritorious claim or defense before trial"; and second, to "furnish[ ] an avenue, if the need is sufficiently acute, whereby the court of appeals can take earlier-than-usual cognizance of important, unsettled legal questions, thus contributing to both the orderly progress of complex litigation and the orderly development of the law." *Mowbray,* 208 F.3d at 293.

Based on these purposes, the Seventh Circuit in *Blair* outlined three categories of cases for which Rule 23(f) review may be appropriate. As summarized in *Mowbray:*

> First, an appeal ordinarily should be permitted when a denial of class status effectively ends the case (because, say, the named plaintiff's claim is not of a sufficient magnitude to warrant the costs of stand-alone litigation). Second, an appeal ordinarily should be permitted when the grant of class status raises the stakes of the litigation so substantially that the defendant likely will feel irresistible pressure to settle. Third, an appeal ordinarily should be permitted when it will lead to clarification of a fundamental issue of law.

The Seventh Circuit put additional gloss on these three broad categories. It explained that a petitioner who sought to invoke either of the first two categories also would have to "demonstrate that the district court's ruling on class certification is questionable — and must do this taking into account the discretion the district judge possesses in implementing Rule 23, and the correspondingly deferential standard of appellate review." *Blair,* 181 F.3d at 835. The court further observed that when reviewing petitions invoking the third and final category, it would focus on the importance of the issue to be resolved, more so than the likelihood of reversal. Finally, it noted that even when an application touts a supposedly fundamental issue of law, a showing that an end-of-case appeal promises to be an adequate remedy will weigh heavily against granting a Rule 23(f) application.

Recently, the First Circuit adopted *Blair*'s Rule 23(f) taxonomy as "structurally sound" with one notable caveat. *Mowbray,* 208 F.3d at 294. The *Mowbray* court worried, we think rightly, that the third *Blair* category might "encourage too many disappointed litigants to file fruitless Rule 23(f) applications" since "a creative lawyer almost always will be able to argue that deciding her case would clarify some 'fundamental' issue." The First Circuit then emphasized that "interlocutory appeals should be the exception, not the rule" because "many (if not most) class certification decisions turn on 'familiar and almost routine issues.'" (citing Comm. Note, FED. R. CIV. P. 23(f)). As a result, the *Mowbray* court concluded that "*Blair* 's third category should be restricted to those instances in which an appeal will permit the resolution of an unsettled legal issue that is important to the particular litigation as well as important in itself and likely to escape effective review if left hanging until the end of the case."

We find both the *Blair* and *Mowbray* opinions to be cogent explications of the Rule 23(f) inquiry. We think it important, however, to emphasize some additional considerations that may weigh against frequent interlocutory appellate review of class action certification decisions.

To begin with, there are too many class actions filed each year for federal appeals courts practicably to adjudicate class certification decisions on an interlocutory basis as a matter of course. As a statistical point of reference, we observe that according to the Federal Judicial Center, as of 1998 there were 1,742 active federal cases with class action activity. In 1994, there were only 816 such cases. A similar rise is reported for this Circuit; in 1998, according to the data, there were 221 active cases in this Circuit with class action activity, almost double the number of such cases, 114, during 1994. Given these numbers, and the large volume of ordinary final judgments that by law must be considered by the courts of appeals, routinely granting interlocutory appellate review of class certification decisions is simply not practicable.

There are also powerful case management concerns that caution against routinely granting appellate review in these circumstances. Class certification orders also are not final judgments impervious to lower court review and revision. On the contrary, Rule 23(c)(1) specifically empowers district courts to alter or amend class certification orders at *any* time prior to a decision on the merits. That power is critical, because the scope and contour of a class may change radically as discovery progresses and more information is gathered about the nature of the putative class members' claims. Indeed, Rule 23 contemplates that the class certification decision will be made prior to the close of discovery. FED. R. CIV. P. 23(c)(1) (class status should be resolved "as soon as practicable after the commencement of" the action); *see also Armstrong v. Martin Marietta Corp.*, 138 F.3d 1374, 1389 (11th Cir.1998) (en banc) (citing data showing that most class certification decisions are made in the early stages of the litigation). Rule 23(f) should not be a vehicle for courts of appeals to micro-manage complex class action litigation as it unfolds in the district court.

Moreover, interlocutory appellate review of a class certification decision may short-circuit the district court's ability — or at least willingness — to exercise its power to reconsider its certification decision. If a decision on class certification has been fully reviewed and affirmed on an interlocutory basis, both the parties and the district judge may feel constrained from revisiting the issue and thereby potentially triggering a new round of appellate proceedings with the inevitable delay and effort of such proceedings. This possibility is troubling, because class certification determinations are so fluid and fact-sensitive that district courts should be encouraged rather than discouraged from reassessing whether the prerequisites of Rule 23 exist and whether a class action is the most efficacious way to resolve the dispute. Quite simply, "we should err, if at all, on the side of allowing the district court an opportunity to fine-tune its class certification order rather than opening the door too widely to interlocutory appellate review." *Mowbray,* 208 F.3d at 294 (citing FED. R. CIV. P. 23(c)(1)).

Finally, authorizing interlocutory review simply on the basis of a so-called "fundamental" or "unsettled" question of law sets a difficult precedent. We share the First Circuit's concern over encouraging a flood of Rule 23(f) petitions claiming that such a question is in dispute. Given the stakes of class action litigation, and the vast number of persons affected, many routine issues have the potential to take on substantial proportions and assume an importance they otherwise might not. Moreover, given the highly particularized nature of class action determinations, and the lack of case law applying Rule 23 in many contexts, we imagine it relatively easy for a litigant to identify some question of law implicated by the class certification decision and in good faith characterize that question as novel or unsettled. To justify immediate and interlocutory appellate review, something more is necessary — something that creates a compelling need for resolution of the legal issue sooner rather than later.

Taking into account all of these considerations, the following guideposts may be utilized in determining whether to grant an interlocutory appeal under Rule 23(f).

First, and most important, the court should examine whether the district court's ruling is likely dispositive of the litigation by creating a "death knell" for either plaintiff or defendant. The prospect of irreparable harm from delaying appellate review of the class certification decision until after final judgment undoubtedly creates a compelling need for immediate review. Nevertheless, even ordinary class certification decisions by their very nature may radically reshape a lawsuit and significantly alter the risk-benefit calculation of the parties, leading to claims of irreparable harm. For that reason, the decision to grant interlocutory review based primarily on this factor generally should be limited to those cases where the district court's ruling, as a practical matter, effectively prevents the petitioner from pursuing the litigation. This might be the case where a denial of class status means that the stakes are too low for the named plaintiffs to continue the matter, or where the grant of class status raises the cost and stakes of the litigation so substantially that a rational defendant would feel irresistible pressure to settle. The size of the putative class and any record evidence regarding the financial resources of the parties are relevant to this inquiry. Also relevant, especially when a class has been certified in a mass tort case against a corporate defendant, is the existence and potential impact of related litigation against that defendant. The nature of the remedy sought in the case (and in damages cases, the amount of money potentially recoverable) is likewise relevant to this factor. For example, even a large class seeking declaratory or injunctive relief may create less pressure on a defendant than a class seeking compensatory and punitive damages so substantial that they threaten a defendant's solvency. We anticipate that the number of decisions truly warranting immediate review on this basis alone will be small.

Second, a court should consider whether the petitioner has shown a *substantial* weakness in the class certification decision, such that the decision likely constitutes an abuse of discretion. Ordinarily, the appropriateness of allowing a Rule 23(f) appeal should turn on more than the outcome of a preliminary debate about the merits of the district court's ruling. Interlocutory review may be appropriate when it promises to spare the parties and the district court the expense and burden of litigating the matter to final judgment only to have it inevitably reversed by this Court on an appeal after final judgment. Such a situation may exist, for example, when the district court expressly applies the incorrect Rule 23 standard or overlooks directly controlling precedent. In that situation, interlocutory review may be warranted even if none of the other factors supports granting the Rule 23(f) petition.[13] Typically, however, class certification decisions require the application of broad and flexible legal standards to unique and complex sets of facts that do not fit squarely within prior precedent. Due to the highly fact-sensitive nature of this inquiry, district courts are given wide latitude to decide whether and how to certify a class, and appellate scrutiny of such decisions is limited at any stage. Accordingly, merely demonstrating that the district court's ruling is questionable generally will be insufficient to support a Rule 23(f) petition in the absence of other factors supporting immediate review.[14]

Third, a court should consider whether the appeal will permit the resolution of an unsettled legal issue that is "important to the particular litigation as well as important in itself." *Mowbray,* 208 F.3d at 294. Such an issue might be one that is of moment yet is "likely to escape effective review if left hanging until the end of the case." *Id.* Alternatively, the issue might be one as to which an appellate ruling sooner rather than later will substantially assist the bench and bar, as may be the case when an issue is arising simultaneously in related actions involving the same or similarly-situated parties or is one that seems likely to arise repeatedly in the future. The fact that the lawsuit involves a governmental entity, or has a strong public interest component, may also lend the issue particular importance and urgency. Moreover, interlocutory review under Rule 23(f) seems more appropriate if the unsettled issue relates specifically to the requirements of Rule 23 or the mechanics of certifying a class, given that one of the primary justifications for Rule 23(f) was a concern over the perceived lack of a substantial body of case law addressing the Rule 23 standards. *See Blair,* 181 F.3d at 835. We reiterate, however, that a class certification decision which "turns on case-specific matters of fact and district court discretion," Comm. Note, FED. R. CIV. P. 23 — as most certification decisions indisputably do — generally will not be appropriate for interlocutory review.

---

13 [9] The more the alleged error arises out of a mistake of law (as opposed to an improper application of the law to the facts), the more the case may be susceptible to interlocutory review, simply because such an error is more readily reviewable by this Court and does not require us to base our determination on an evolving factual record that may already have become incomplete.

14 [10] We do not mean to suggest that this factor weighs in favor of a Rule 23(f) appeal only when the party seeking interlocutory review meets the extremely demanding test applied to mandamus petitions. Rather, this factor should be viewed as a sliding scale. The stronger the showing of an abuse of discretion, the more this factor weighs in favor of interlocutory review. We note, however, that every litigant seeking to appeal under Rule 23(f) necessarily believes that the district court has abused its discretion. Accordingly, simply alleging an abuse of discretion may not in and of itself justify an interlocutory appeal.

Fourth, a court should consider the nature and status of the litigation before the district court. Some cases plainly will be in a better pre-trial posture for interlocutory appellate review than others. As noted above, the propriety of granting or denying a class, as well as the proper scope of any class that has been granted, may change significantly as new facts are uncovered through discovery. Similarly, a limited or insufficient record may adversely affect the appellate court's ability to evaluate fully and fairly the class certification decision. Moreover, a district court's ruling on dispositive motions or a motion to add new class representatives, parties, or claims may significantly redefine the issues in the case and thereby affect the scope of or need for a class. Accordingly, the decision on a Rule 23(f) petition may take into account such considerations as the status of discovery, the pendency of relevant motions, and the length of time the matter already has been pending. In certain circumstances the court may also consider the current impact on the parties of rulings by the district court that, while not themselves subject to Rule 23(f) review, nevertheless are inextricably tied to the class certification decision.

Finally, a court should consider the likelihood that future events may make immediate appellate review more or less appropriate. Simply by way of example, settlement negotiations involving some or all of the parties affected by the decision, or the prospect of an imminent change in the financial status of a party (such as a bankruptcy filing) may caution against hearing an interlocutory appeal. Conversely, if the case is likely to be one of a series of related actions raising substantially the same issues and involving substantially the same parties, then early resolution of a dispute about the propriety of certifying a class may facilitate the disposition of future claims. Also significant is whether the district court itself has indicated that it views its class certification decision as conditional or subject to revision at a later stage in the case.

We do not create any bright-line rules or rigid categories for accepting or denying Rule 23(f) petitions today. Our authority to accept Rule 23(f) petitions is highly discretionary, and the foregoing list of factors is not intended to be exhaustive; there may well be special circumstances that lead us to grant or deny a Rule 23(f) petition even where some or all of the relevant factors point to a different result. Moreover, none of the foregoing factors is necessarily conclusive; ordinarily, each relevant factor should be balanced against the others, taking into account any unique facts and circumstances.

We reiterate, however, that interlocutory appeals are inherently "disruptive, time-consuming, and expensive," *Mowbray,* 208 F.3d at 294, and consequently are generally disfavored. Piecemeal appellate review has a deleterious effect on judicial administration. It increases the workload of the appellate courts, to the detriment of litigants and judges. It requires the appellate courts to consider issues that may be rendered moot if the appealing party ultimately prevails in or settles the case. It undermines the district court's ability to manage the action. And it creates opportunities for abuse by litigants seeking to delay resolution of a case by raising with the appellate court objections to the scope of an order that should have been raised first with the district court itself. Most of these concerns are, if anything, even more compelling in the class action context, especially given the district court's broad authority under Rule 23(c)(1) to monitor and if necessary reconsider its class certification decision as discovery unfolds and the action progresses to trial.

We will therefore use restraint in accepting Rule 23(f) petitions, and these interlocutory petitions will not be accepted as a matter of course.

B.

Turning to the particulars of this case, we acknowledge that this lawsuit may not raise the kind of issues that ordinarily might warrant granting a Rule 23(f) petition. First, we do not believe the grant of class status here raises the stakes of litigation so substantially that the Defendants likely will feel irresistible pressure to settle. The certified Plaintiff class, while large, is only seeking declaratory and injunctive relief (not money damages). . . . And while . . . injunctive and declaratory relief would exert a significant impact on . . . the state HCBW program, Defendants' interlocutory appeal does not concern the scope of this potential relief.

Second, . . . Defendants do not demonstrate any *substantial* weakness or profound error of law in the class certification decision . . . . [B]ecause both parties agree that some kind of HCBW class(es) should be certified in this case, the issues raised on appeal are not dispositive of the litigation. . . .

Defendants' objection that Plaintiffs have not as yet demonstrated that a named class representative possesses individual or associational standing to bring each of the class's subclaims is of greater moment. But although . . . at least one named representative must have standing to bring each class subclaim, this argument should have been raised squarely with the district court . . . Outside the Rule 23(f) context, issues of standing are normally not available for review on interlocutory appeal.

Extensive interlocutory review of Defendants' standing objection seems particularly inappropriate given the circumstances of this case. First, the factual record is not fully developed . . . Second, . . . at worst several new named representatives would have to be added . . . or several of the class subclaims . . . amended or dropped. Simply put, Defendants' standing argument does not end the case; and given . . . the ability of the district court to alter or amend the certified class at any point prior to a ruling on the merits, . . . such standing challenges are best raised initially with the district court. . . .

Other Rule 23(f) factors might also weigh against interlocutory review were this an ordinary case. We see no truly novel or fundamental issue of law raised by the class certification decision. . . . On the other hand, this lawsuit has tremendous importance to thousands of developmentally-disabled persons in the State of Florida, many of whom have a critical need for prompt delivery of the services and benefits they claim to have been denied by the State. There is also a broader . . . public interest in determining promptly the scope of the State's administrative and financial obligations under the Medicaid program with respect to such persons. Given these considerations, as well as the fact that we have not previously enunciated Rule 23(f) standards . . . , we proceed to address certain aspects of the class certification ruling — particularly with respect to the creation of subclasses and typicality review.

[In the remainder of its opinion, the court ultimately concluded that the certification of a single class was inappropriate.]

NOTES

1. Recall *United States Parole Commission v. Geraghty*, 445 U.S. 388 (1980), *supra* page 39, where the Court struggled with whether a trial court's denial of a motion for class certification could be reviewed on appeal after the named plaintiff's personal claim had become moot, and note that in *Coopers & Lybrand v. Livesay*, 437 U.S. 463 (1978), the Supreme Court held that orders denying class certification are not immediately appealable under the collateral order doctrine. The Court strongly implied in *Coopers & Lybrand* that orders granting class certification similarly were not immediately appealable under the collateral order doctrine. That left, as possible vehicles for appeal prior to final judgment, petitions for the extraordinary writ of mandamus, § 1292(b) certifications — both difficult to obtain — , and in rare circumstances, appeals permitted by virtue of the grant or denial of an injunction or as pendent to other immediately appealable interlocutory orders. Does this background suggest to you why Rule 23(f) was adopted?

2. The courts of appeals still are feeling their way in deciding which factors ought to influence their decisions whether to accept interlocutory appeals of grants or denials of class certification decisions. Do the factors referred to in *Prado-Steiman* seem appropriate, in light of the considerations that come into play in the other judge-made and statutory provisions for interlocutory appeals?

3. When a court of appeals accepts a Rule 23(f) appeal, questions may arise as to the scope of the issues the court may address. *See, e.g., Poulos v. Caesars World, Inc.*, 379 F.3d 654, 668-70 (9th Cir. 2004)) (refusing to address issues including personal jurisdiction and abstention, holding them not within pendent appellate jurisdiction to Rule 23(f) appeal); *Rivera v. Wyeth-Ayerst Laboratories*, 283 F.3d 315 (5th Cir. 2002) (holding that the court could, and indeed had to, address plaintiff's standing to sue as part of a Rule 23(f) appeal; having found that plaintiff lacked standing to sue, the court did not reach the propriety of the class certification). Where should appellate courts draw the line?

4. According to a recent study,

[F]rom December 1, 1993 through early September 2003, the Courts of Appeal[s] published 44 opinions stemming from 53 requests to entertain interlocutory appeals of class certification orders . . . [A]ll but two Circuits (the Tenth and D.C. Circuits) have invoked Rule 23(f) at least once. . . . Plaintiffs and defendants both enjoyed a roughly 80% success rate in persuading courts of appeal[s] to grant their Rule 23(f) petitions. But once the . . . petition was granted, defendants won 70 per cent of the time — perhaps because four out of every five appeals presented the question whether the district court abused its discretion in certifying a case for class treatment. . . . Yet . . . nine of the 35 orders certifying class actions were affirmed . . . [and] in four of the nine cases in which plaintiffs appealed the denial of class treatment, they obtained a reversal. Those plaintiffs were not confined to what some regard as "liberal" Circuits. . . . [T]he increased body of federal appellate class action precedent . . . has provided much needed direction to the federal district courts . . . and has spawned great consistency of outcome among those state courts that follow federal court guidance in the class action arena.

Brian Anderson & Patrick McLain, *A Progress Report on Rule 23(f): Five Years of Immediate Class Certification Appeals*, 19 LEGAL BACKGROUNDER #5 (March 19, 2004).

5. *See generally*, Christopher A. Kitchen, *Interlocutory Appeal of Class Action Certification Decisions under Federal Rule of Civil Procedure 23(f): A Proposal for a New Guideline*, 2004 COLUM. BUS. L. REV. 231 (surveying various circuits' guidelines, as well as making a modest proposal); Linda S. Mullenix, *Some Joy in Whoville: Rule 23(f), A Good Rulemaking*, 69 TENN. L. REV. 97 (2001); Michael E. Solimine & Christopher Oliver Hines, *Deciding to Decide: Class Action Certification and Interlocutory Review by the United States Courts of Appeals under Rule 23(f)*, 41 WM & MARY L. REV. 1531 (2000).

2. Extraordinary Writs

The All Writs Act, 28 U.S.C. § 1651, provides that "[t]he Supreme Court and all courts established by Act of Congress may issue all writs necessary or appropriate in aid of their respective jurisdictions and agreeable to the usages and principles of law." Writs of mandamus and prohibition are among the writs that the Act authorizes. While those writs technically are within the original jurisdiction of courts of appeals, the writs can be sought by litigants who seek review, before final judgment, of decisions by the district courts, and in that sense, operate in a manner that resembles interlocutory appeals.

THERMTRON PRODUCTS, INC. v. HERMANSDORFER
423 U.S. 336 (1976)

MR. JUSTICE WHITE delivered the opinion of the Court.

The questions in this case are whether a Federal District Judge may remand a properly removed diversity case for reasons not authorized by statute, and, if not, whether such remand order may be remedied by writ of mandamus.[15]

On April 9, 1973, two citizens and residents of Kentucky filed an action in a Kentucky state court against Thermtron Products, Inc., an Indiana corporation without office or place of business in Kentucky, and one Larry Dean Newhard, an employee of Thermtron and a citizen and resident of Indiana, seeking damages for injuries arising out of an automobile accident between plaintiffs' automobile and a vehicle driven by Newhard. Service on the defendants, who are petitioners here, was by substituted service on the Secretary of

---

15 [*] The authority to issue writs of mandamus is conferred on the courts of appeals by 28 U.S.C. § 1651(a): "The Supreme Court and all courts established by Act of Congress may issue all writs necessary or appropriate in aid of their respective jurisdictions and agreeable to the usages and principles of law. . . ."

State of the Commonwealth, pursuant to Kentucky law. Later that month, petitioners removed the cause to the United States District Court for the Eastern District of Kentucky pursuant to 28 U.S.C. §§ 1441 and 1446. The case was assigned a number, and the defendants filed their answer and later proceeded with discovery. On February 5, 1974, respondent judge issued an order in the case which recited that the action "was removed from the Pike Circuit Court, Pike County, Kentucky, on April 30, 1973, pursuant to the provisions of 28 U.S.C. § 1446," that his court had reviewed its entire civil docket and found "that there is no available time in which to try the above-styled action in the foreseeable future" and that an adjudication of the merits of the case would be expedited in the state court. The order then called upon the defendants to show cause "why the ends of justice do not require this matter [to] be remanded to the Pike Circuit Court. . . ." In response to the order, petitioners asserted that they believed they could not have a fair and impartial trial in the state courts, that the cause had been properly removed pursuant to the applicable statutes, that petitioners had a federal right to have the cause tried in the federal court, that respondent had no discretion to remand the case merely because of a crowded docket, and that there was no other legal ground for the remand.

On March 22, 1974, respondent filed a memorandum opinion and order remanding the case to the Pike Circuit Court. The opinion noted petitioners' contention that they had a "right" to remove the action by properly invoking 28 U.S.C. § 1441, and remarked that "[t]he court must concede that fact." That right, the opinion then stated, nevertheless had to be "balanced against the plaintiffs' right to a forum of their choice and their right to a speedy decision on the merits of their cause of action." Because of the District Court's crowded docket and because other cases had priority on available trial time, "plaintiffs' right of redress is being severely impaired," which "would not be the case if the cause had not been removed from the state courts." Remarking that the purpose of the removal statute was to prevent prejudice in local courts and being of the view that petitioners had made no showing of possible prejudice that might follow from remand, respondent then ordered the case remanded.

Petitioners then filed in the Court of Appeals for the Sixth Circuit their alternative petition for writ of mandamus or prohibition, requesting relief on the ground that the action had been properly removed and that respondent had no authority or discretion whatsoever to remand the case on the ground asserted by him. . . . [T]he Court of Appeals denied the petition. . . . We granted the petition for certiorari and now reverse. . . .

It is unquestioned in this case and conceded by petitioners that this section [28 U.S.C. § 1447(d)] prohibits review of all remand orders issued pursuant to § 1447(c) whether erroneous or not and whether review is sought by appeal or by extraordinary writ. This has been the established rule under § 1447(d)[16] and its predecessors stretching back to 1887. . . . If a trial judge purports to

---

[16] [*] 28 U.S.C. § 1477(d) provides: "(d) An order remanding a case to the State court from which it was removed is not reviewable on appeal or otherwise, except that an order remanding a case to the State court from which it was removed pursuant to section 1443 of this title shall be reviewable by appeal or otherwise." Section 1443 is the removal statute for civil cases.

remand a case on the ground that it was removed "improvidently and without jurisdiction," his order is not subject to challenge in the court of appeals by appeal, by mandamus, or otherwise.

The issue before us now is whether § 1447(d) also bars review where a case has been properly removed and the remand order is issued on grounds not authorized by § 1447(c). Here, respondent did not purport to proceed on the basis that this case had been removed "improvidently and without jurisdiction." Neither the propriety of the removal nor the jurisdiction of the court was questioned by respondent in the slightest. Section 1447(c) was not even mentioned. Instead, the District Court's order was based on grounds wholly different from those upon which § 1447(c) permits remand. The determining factor was the District Court's heavy docket, which respondent thought would unjustly delay plaintiffs in going to trial on the merits of their action. This consideration, however, is plainly irrelevant to whether the District Court would have had jurisdiction of the case had it been filed initially in that court, to the removability of a case from the state court under § 1441, and hence to the question whether this cause was removed "improvidently and without jurisdiction" within the meaning of the statute.

Removal of cases from state courts has been allowed since the first Judiciary Act, and the right to remove has never been dependent on the state of the federal court's docket. It is indeed unfortunate if the judicial manpower provided by Congress in any district is insufficient to try with reasonable promptness the cases properly filed in or removed to that court in accordance with the applicable statutes. But an otherwise properly removed action may no more be remanded because the district court considers itself too busy to try it than an action properly filed in the federal court in the first instance may be dismissed or referred to state courts for such reason. . . .

We agree with petitioners: the District Court exceeded its authority in remanding on grounds not permitted by the controlling statute.

. . . Section 1447(d) is not dispositive of the reviewability of remand orders in and of itself. That section and § 1447(c) must be construed together. . . . This means that only remand orders issued under § 1447(c) and invoking the grounds specified therein — that removal was improvident and without jurisdiction — are immune from review under § 1447(d). . . .

There is no doubt that in order to prevent delay in the trial of remanded cases by protracted litigation of jurisdictional issues . . . Congress immunized from all forms of appellate review any remand order issued on the grounds specified in § 1447(c), whether or not that order might be deemed erroneous by an appellate court. But we are not convinced that Congress ever intended to extend carte blanche authority to the district courts to revise the federal statutes governing removal by remanding cases on grounds that seem justifiable to them but which are not recognized by the controlling statute. That justice may move more slowly in some federal courts than in their state counterparts is not one of the considerations that Congress has permitted the district courts to recognize in passing on remand issues. Because the District Judge remanded a properly removed case on grounds that he had no authority to consider, he exceeded his statutorily defined power; and issuance of the writ of mandamus was not barred by § 1447(d). . . .

There remains the question whether absent the bar of § 1447(d) against appellate review, the writ of mandamus is an appropriate remedy to require the District Court to entertain the remanded action. The answer is in the affirmative.

A "traditional use of the writ in aid of appellate jurisdiction both at common law and in the federal courts has been to confine an inferior court to a lawful exercise of its prescribed jurisdiction or to compel it to exercise its authority when it is its duty to do so." *Roche v. Evaporated Milk Assn.*, 319 U.S. 21, 26 (1943). . . .

The judgment of the Court of Appeals is reversed and the case is remanded to that court for further proceedings consistent with this opinion.

Mr. Justice Stevens took no part in the consideration or decision of this case.

Mr. Justice Rehnquist, with whom The Chief Justice and Mr. Justice Stewart join, dissenting.

The Court begins its discussion in this case by asking the wrong questions, and compounds its error by arriving at the wrong answer to at least one of the questions thus posed. The principal, and in my view only, issue presented for review is whether the Court of Appeals was correct in concluding that it was without jurisdiction to review the order of remand entered by the District Court for the Eastern District of Kentucky. If no jurisdiction existed, it of course follows that there was no power in the Court of Appeals to examine the merits of petitioners' contentions that the order of remand exceeded respondent's authority, and that its order denying relief must be affirmed. As I think it plain that Congress, which has unquestioned authority to do so, *Sheldon v. Sill*, 8 How. 441 (1850), has expressly prohibited the review sought by petitioners, I dissent. . . .

Congress' purpose in barring review of all remand orders has always been very clear — to prevent the additional delay which a removing party may achieve by seeking appellate reconsideration of an order of remand. The removal jurisdiction extended by Congress works a significant interference in the conduct of litigation commenced in state court. While Congress felt that making available a federal forum in appropriate instances justifies some such interruption and delay, it obviously thought it equally important that when removal to a federal court is not warranted the case should be returned to the state court as expeditiously as possible. If this balanced concern is disregarded, federal removal provisions may become a device affording litigants a means of substantially delaying justice. . . .

I do not doubt that the district courts may occasionally err in making these decisions, and certainly Congress was not unaware of these probabilities. All decision-makers err from time to time, and judicial systems frequently provide some review to remedy some of those errors. But such review is certainly not compelled. Congress balanced the continued disruption and delay caused by further review against the minimal possible harm to the party attempting removal — who will still receive a trial on the merits before a state court which cannot be presumed to be unwilling or unable to afford substantial justice — and concluded that no review should be permitted in these cases. Congress has explicitly indicated its intent to achieve this result; indeed "[i]t is difficult to see what more could be done to make the action of [remand] final, for all the purposes of the removal, and not the subject of review." *Morey v. Lockhart*, 123 U.S. 56, 57 (1887). Yet the Court today holds that Congress did not mean what it so plainly said. . . .

NOTES

1. Could the district court's remand order have been appealed as a final decision under § 1291? If so, would that have rendered mandamus unavailable as a means of review?

2. P sues D in a federal district court. D moves to dismiss the action for want of jurisdiction, asserting that the case does not arise under federal law and that there is no diversity of citizenship. The district court denies the motion. Assume that D's motion is well taken and there is no federal jurisdiction. When and how can D obtain appellate review of the district court's denial of the motion? *See BancOhio Corp. v. Fox*, 516 F.2d 29 (6th Cir. 1975) (holding that mandamus is available to compel dismissal where subject-matter jurisdiction is plainly lacking).

3. After *Quackenbush*, supra p. 53, if a district court dismisses or remands state law claims in its discretion not to adjudicate claims within its supplemental jurisdiction, is the dismissal or remand immediately appealable? *Compare Gaming Corp. of Am. v. Dorsey & Whitney*, 88 F.3d 536 (8th Cir. 1996) (finding jurisdiction over appeal where federal claims had been dismissed) *with Kaufman v. Checkers Drive-In Rests., Inc.*, 122 F.3d 892 (11th Cir. 1997) (holding collateral order doctrine not to apply where federal claims remained pending).

4. The inconsistency in the ways in which the courts of appeals have dealt with remand orders are analyzed in Rhonda Wasserman, *Rethinking Review of Remands: Proposed Amendments to the Federal Removal Statute*, 43 EMORY L.J. 83 (1994), Michael E. Solimine, *Removal, Remands, and Reforming Federal Appellate Review*, 58 Mo. L. Rev. 287 (1993), and Joan Steinman, *Removal, Remand and Review in Pendent Claim and Pendent Party Cases*, 41 VAND. L. REV. 923 (1988).

SCHLAGENHAUF v. HOLDER
379 U.S. 104 (1964)

MR. JUSTICE GOLDBERG delivered the opinion of the Court.

This case involves the validity and construction of Rule 35(a) of the Federal Rules of Civil Procedure as applied to the examination of a defendant in a negligence action. Rule 35(a) provides:

> Physical and Mental Examination of Persons. (a) Order for examination. In an action in which the mental or physical condition of a

party is in controversy, the court in which the action is pending may order him to submit to a physical or mental examination by a physician. The order may be made only on motion for good cause shown and upon notice to the party to be examined and to all other parties and shall specify the time, place, manner, conditions, and scope of the examination and the person or persons by whom it is to be made.

An action based on diversity of citizenship was brought in the District Court seeking damages arising from personal injuries suffered by passengers of a bus which collided with the rear of a tractor-trailer. The named defendants were The Greyhound Corporation, owner of the bus; petitioner, Robert L. Schlagenhauf, the bus driver; Contract Carriers, Inc., owner of the tractor; Joseph L. McCorkhill, driver of the tractor; and National Lead Company, owner of the trailer. Answers were filed by each of the defendants denying negligence.

Greyhound then cross-claimed against Contract Carriers and National Lead for damage to Greyhound's bus, alleging that the collision was due solely to their negligence in that the tractor-trailer was driven at an unreasonably low speed, had not remained in its lane, and was not equipped with proper rear lights. Contract Carriers filed an answer to this cross-claim denying its negligence and asserting "[that] the negligence of the driver of the . . . bus [petitioner Schlagenhauf] proximately caused and contributed to . . . Greyhound's damages."

Pursuant to a pretrial order, Contract Carriers filed a letter — which the trial court treated as, and we consider to be, part of the answer — alleging that Schlagenhauf was "not mentally or physically capable" of driving a bus at the time of the accident.

Contract Carriers and National Lead then petitioned the District Court for an order directing petitioner Schlagenhauf to submit to both mental and physical examinations by one specialist in each of the following fields:

(1) Internal medicine;
(2) Ophthalmology;
(3) Neurology; and
(4) Psychiatry.

For the purpose of offering a choice to the District Court of one specialist in each field, the petition recommended two specialists in internal medicine, ophthalmology, and psychiatry, respectively, and three specialists in neurology — a total of nine physicians. The petition alleged that the mental and physical condition of Schlagenhauf was "in controversy" as it had been raised by Contract Carriers' answer to Greyhound's cross-claim. This was supported by a brief of legal authorities and an affidavit of Contract Carriers' attorney stating that Schlagenhauf had seen red lights 10 to 15 seconds before the accident, that another witness had seen the rear lights of the trailer from a distance of three-quarters to one-half mile, and that Schlagenhauf had been involved in a prior accident.

The certified record indicates that petitioner's attorneys filed in the District Court a brief in opposition to this petition asserting, among other things, that "the physical and mental condition of the defendant Robert L. Schlagenhauf is not 'in controversy' herein in the sense that these words are used in Rule 35 of the Federal Rules of Civil Procedure; [and] that good cause has not been shown for the multiple examinations prayed for by the cross-defendant. . . ."

While disposition of this petition was pending, National Lead filed its answer to Greyhound's cross-claim and itself "cross-claimed" against Greyhound and Schlagenhauf for damage to its trailer. The answer asserted generally that Schlagenhauf's negligence proximately caused the accident. The cross-claim additionally alleged that Greyhound and Schlagenhauf were negligent "[by] permitting said bus to be operated over and upon said public highway by the said defendant, Robert L. Schlagenhauf, when both the said Greyhound Corporation and said Robert L. Schlagenhauf knew that the eyes and vision of the said Robert L. Schlagenhauf was [sic] impaired and deficient."

The District Court, on the basis of the petition filed by Contract Carriers, and without any hearing, ordered Schlagenhauf to submit to nine examinations — one by each of the recommended specialists — despite the fact that the petition clearly requested a total of only four examinations.

Petitioner applied for a writ of mandamus in the Court of Appeals against the respondent, the District Court Judge, seeking to have set aside the order requiring his mental and physical examinations. The Court of Appeals denied mandamus, one judge dissenting, 321 F.2d 43.

We granted certiorari to review undecided questions concerning the validity and construction of Rule 35.

A threshold problem arises due to the fact that this case was in the Court of Appeals on a petition for a writ of mandamus. Although it is not disputed that we have jurisdiction to review the judgment of the Court of Appeals, 28 U.S.C. § 1254(1) (1958 ed.), respondent urges that the judgment below dismissing the writ be affirmed on the ground that mandamus was not an appropriate remedy.

"The traditional use of the writ in aid of appellate jurisdiction both at common law and in the federal courts has been to confine an inferior court to a lawful exercise of its prescribed jurisdiction. . . ." *Roche v. Evaporated Milk Assn.*, 319 U.S. 21, 26.

It is, of course, well settled, that the writ is not to be used as a substitute for appeal, *Ex parte Fahey*, 332 U.S. 258, 259-260, even though hardship may result from delay and perhaps unnecessary trial. . . . The writ is appropriately issued, however, when there is "usurpation of judicial power" or a clear abuse of discretion. . . .

Here petitioner's basic allegation was lack of power in a district court to order a mental and physical examination of a defendant. That this issue was substantial is underscored by the fact that the challenged order requiring examination of a defendant appears to be the first of its kind in any reported decision in the federal courts under Rule 35, and we have found only one such modern case in the state courts. The Court of Appeals recognized that it had the power to review on a petition for mandamus the basic, undecided question of whether a district court could order the mental or physical examination of a defendant. We agree that, under these unusual circumstances and in light of the authorities, the Court of Appeals had such power.

The petitioner, however, also alleged that, even if Rule 35 gives a district court power to order mental and physical examinations of a defendant in an appropriate case, the District Court here exceeded that power in ordering examinations when petitioner's mental and physical condition was not "in controversy" and no "good cause" was shown, both as expressly required by Rule 35. As we read its opinion, the Court of Appeals reached the "in controversy" issue and determined it adversely to petitioner. It did not, however, reach the issue of "good cause," apparently considering that it was not appropriate to do so on a petition for mandamus.

We recognize that in the ordinary situation where the sole issue presented is the district court's determination that "good cause" has been shown for an examination, mandamus is not an appropriate remedy, absent, of course, a clear abuse of discretion. . . . Here, however, the petition was properly before the court on a substantial allegation of usurpation of power in ordering any examination of a defendant, an issue of first impression that called for the construction and application of Rule 35 in a new context. The meaning of Rule 35's requirements of "in controversy" and "good cause" also raised issues of first impression. In our view, the Court of Appeals should have also, under these special circumstances, determined the "good cause" issue, so as to avoid piecemeal litigation and to settle new and important problems.

Thus we believe that the Court of Appeals had power to determine all of the issues presented by the petition for mandamus. Normally, wise judicial administration would counsel remand of the cause to the Court of Appeals to reconsider this issue of "good cause." However, in this instance the issue concerns the construction and application of the Federal Rules of Civil Procedure. It is thus appropriate for us to determine on the merits the issues presented and to formulate the necessary guidelines in this area. . . . As this Court stated in *Los Angeles Brush Corp. v. James*, 272 U.S. 701, 706: "[we] think it clear that where the subject concerns the enforcement of the . . . Rules which by law it is the duty of this Court to formulate and put in force . . . it may . . . deal directly with the District Court." . . .

This is not to say, however, that, following the setting of guidelines in this opinion, any future allegation that the District Court was in error in applying these guidelines to a particular case makes mandamus an appropriate remedy. The writ of mandamus is not to be used when "the most that could be claimed is that the district courts have erred in ruling on matters within their jurisdiction." *Parr v. United States*, 351 U.S. 513, 520. . . .

Accordingly, the judgment of the Court of Appeals is vacated and the case remanded to the District Court to reconsider the examination order in light of the guidelines herein formulated and for further proceedings in conformity with this opinion.

Vacated and remanded.

MR. JUSTICE HARLAN, dissenting.

In my view the Court's holding that mandamus lies in this case cannot be squared with the course of decisions to which the majority at the threshold pays lip service. As the Court recognizes, mandamus, like the other extraordinary writs, is available to correct only those decisions of inferior courts which involve a "usurpation of judicial power" or, what is tantamount thereto, "a clear abuse of discretion"; such a writ "is not to be used as a substitute for appeal."

Mandamus is found to be an appropriate remedy in this instance, however, because (1) petitioner's challenge was based on an asserted lack of power in the District Court to issue the examination order, and (2) that being so, the Court of Appeals had the right also to inquire into the application of the "in controversy" and "good cause" requirements of Rule 35(a), particularly since those issues, like the question of "power," were matters of "first impression" which in "these special circumstances" should be determined by the Court of Appeals "so as to avoid piecemeal litigation and to settle new and important problems."

For me this reasoning is unacceptable. Of course a court of appeals when confronted with a substantial challenge to the power of a district court to act in the premises may proceed to examine that question without awaiting its embodiment in a final judgment, as the Court of Appeals did here by issuing an order to show cause why a writ of mandamus should not issue. But once it is determined that the challenged power did exist, and that the district court acted within the limit of that power, an extraordinary writ should be denied. I know of no case which suggests that a court of appeals' right to consider such a question at an interlocutory stage of the litigation also draws to the court the right to consider other questions — here the "in controversy" and "good cause" issues — which otherwise would not be examinable upon a petition for an extraordinary writ. Indeed, were an extraordinary writ to issue following a determination that the district court lacked power, that would put an end to the litigation and these questions would never be reached. And, as the Court correctly states, the fact that "hardship may result from delay and perhaps unnecessary trial," is not a factor that makes for the issuance of such a writ.

Manifestly, today's procedural holding, when stripped of its sugar-coating, is born of the Court's belief that the petitioner should not be exposed to the rigors of these examinations before the proper "guidelines" have been established by this tribunal. Understandable as that point of view may be, it can only be indulged at the expense of making a deep inroad into the firmly established federal policy which, with narrow exceptions, permits appellate review only of the final judgments of district courts. To be sure the Court is at pains to warn that what is done today puts an end to future "interlocutory" review of Rule 35 questions. Nevertheless, I find it hard to escape the conclusion that this decision may open the door to the extraordinary writs being used to test any question of "first impression," if it can be geared to an alleged lack of "power" in the district court. As such, it seems to me out of keeping with the rule of "finality," with respect to which Congress, wisely I think, has been willing to make only cautious exceptions.

The Court of Appeals having correctly concluded, as this Court now holds and as I agree, that the District Court had power to order the physical and mental examinations of this petitioner, and since I believe that there was no clear abuse of discretion in its so acting, I think the lower court was quite right in denying mandamus, and I would affirm its judgment on that basis.

NOTES

1. The Supreme Court recently has reaffirmed the general principles concerning mandamus: that it is a drastic and extraordinary remedy, justified only by exceptional circumstances amounting to a judicial usurpation of power or a clear abuse of discretion, that the party seeking its issuance must have no other adequate means to attain the relief he desires, must show that his right to the writ is clear and indisputable, and even then, that the court must be satisfied, in the exercise of its discretion, that the writ is appropriate. *Cheney v. U.S. Dist. Court for the Dist. of Columbia*, 542 U.S. 367 (2004). But the Court added something new for certain situations. In *Cheney*, a public interest organization and an environmental group sued the National Energy Policy Development Group and its members, including Vice President Cheney, alleging that the Group was subject to the Federal Advisory Committee Act and had failed to comply with its procedural and disclosure requirements. The district court permitted discovery against the Vice President and other Executive Branch officials, who sought mandamus vacating the discovery orders. The Court of Appeals refused the writ. The Supreme Court held, among other things, that in deciding whether to issue the writ, the court of appeals had to consider whether the district court's orders constituted an unwarranted interference with the Executive Branch in the performance of its constitutional duties, without regard to whether defendants had asserted executive privilege.

2. Additional factors that courts commonly list as influencing whether a petition for writ of mandamus should be granted are whether the district court's order is erroneous as a matter of law, is an instance of an often repeated error or manifests persistent disregard of the federal rules, and raises new and important problems. Some of the factors can co-exist, while others (such as the last two mentioned above) generally are found in the alternative. *See, e.g., DeGeorge v. U.S. Dist. Court for the Cent. Dist. of Cal.*, 219 F.3d 930 (9th Cir. 2000).

3. The Supreme Court generally has been restrictive in dealing with petitions for writs of mandamus, but does sometimes grant them and affirm their grant (or reverse their denial) by courts of appeal. In *La Buy v. Howes Leather Co.*, 352 U.S. 249 (1957), the Court upheld the Seventh Circuit's issuance of mandamus in the exercise of its supervisory power over district courts within its jurisdiction, overturning an order referring a large antitrust case to a master for trial. Finding that this trial judge repeatedly had referred cases to masters and was abdicating the judicial function, the Court agreed that his latest referral was a clear abuse of discretion that justified the grant of mandamus. More recently, in *Mallard v. United States District Court for the S. Dist. of Iowa*, 490 U.S. 296 (1989), the Court overturned a court of appeals' refusal to use mandamus to prohibit a district judge from compelling an attorney to

represent an indigent defendant in a civil rights suit pursuant to a statute that conferred federal power "to request" that an attorney undertake such representation. The Court held that the statute did not authorize compelled representation, and hence that the lower court had acted beyond its jurisdiction.

By contrast, in *Will v. United States*, 389 U.S. 90 (1967), the government had sought a writ of mandamus to compel Judge Will, a federal district court judge, to vacate his order directing the government to respond to a bill of particulars through which the defendant in a criminal case sought to ascertain information concerning oral statements that the defendant had made and upon which the prosecution relied, or face dismissal of the indictment. After the Seventh Circuit granted the writ, the Supreme Court granted certiorari, on Judge Will's petition. It recited some history of its decisions concerning the writ, and then vacated the writ.

> The peremptory writ of mandamus has traditionally been used in the federal courts only "to confine an inferior court to a lawful exercise of its prescribed jurisdiction or to compel it to exercise its authority when it is its duty to do so." *Roche v. Evaporated Milk Assn.*, 319 U.S. 21, 26 (1943). While the courts have never confined themselves to an arbitrary and technical definition of "jurisdiction," it is clear that only exceptional circumstances amounting to a judicial "usurpation of power" will justify the invocation of this extraordinary remedy. *De Beers Consol. Mines, Ltd. v. United States*, 325 U.S. 212, 217 (1945). Thus the writ has been invoked where unwarranted judicial action threatened "to embarrass the executive arm of the Government in conducting foreign relations," *Ex parte Peru*, 318 U.S. 578, 588 (1943), where it was the only means of forestalling intrusion by the federal judiciary on a delicate area of federal-state relations, *Maryland v. Soper*, 270 U.S. 9 (1926), where it was necessary to confine a lower court to the terms of an appellate tribunal's mandate, *United States v. United States Dist. Court*, 334 U.S. 258 (1948), and where a district judge displayed a persistent disregard of the Rules of Civil Procedure promulgated by this Court, *La Buy v. Howes Leather Co.*, 352 U.S. 249 (1957); see *McCullough v. Cosgrave*, 309 U.S. 634 (1940); *Los Angeles Brush Mfg. Corp. v. James*, 272 U.S. 701, 706, 707 (1927) (dictum). And the party seeking mandamus has "the burden of showing that its right to issuance of the writ is 'clear and indisputable.'" *Bankers Life & Cas. Co. v. Holland*, 346 U.S. 379, 384 (1953); *see United States v. Duell*, 172 U.S. 576, 582 (1899).

Will, 389 U.S. at 95-96. Noting that the government did not argue that Judge Will lacked jurisdiction to order a response to the bill of particulars, the Court found no pattern of refusals on his part to comply with the rules governing criminal trials, and berated the Seventh Circuit for failing to furnish reasoned justification for its issuance of the writ, a serious flaw because of the writ's "corrective and didactic function." *Will,* 389 U.S. at 107. Finding nothing extraordinary about the case, it vacated the writ of mandamus.

Upholding Judge Will eleven years later in *Will v. Calvert Fire Insurance Co.*, 437 U.S. 655 (1978), the Court, this time over dissents, again reversed a Seventh Circuit grant of mandamus. This writ ordered Judge Will to proceed with a case that he had stayed in large part until completion of a substantially identical proceeding in state court that had been filed before the federal suit. The Supreme Court concluded that the issuance of the stay was within Judge Will's discretion and that, "Where a matter is committed to the discretion of a district court, it cannot be said that a litigant's right to a particular result is 'clear and indisputable'." *Calvert*, 437 U.S. at 666.

Are the cases in which the Court disapproved mandamus distinguishable from those in which it approved use of the writ? Judge Easterbrook of the Seventh Circuit has opined that, "*LaBuy* is defunct. Although the Court has not yet erected the tombstone, it has ordered flowers." *First Nat'l Bank v. Warren*, 796 F.2d 999, 1004 (7th Cir. 1986). Do you agree?

DAIRY QUEEN, INC. v. WOOD
369 U.S. 469 (1962)

[The District Court proceeding arose out of a controversy between petitioner and the respondent owners of the trademark "DAIRY QUEEN" with regard to a written licensing contract made by them in December 1949, under which petitioner agreed to pay some $150,000 for the exclusive right to use that trademark in certain portions of Pennsylvania. The terms of the contract provided for a small initial payment with the remaining payments to be made at the rate of 50% of all amounts received by petitioner on sales and franchises to deal with the trademark and, in order to make certain that the $150,000 payment would be completed within a specified period of time, further provided for minimum annual payments regardless of petitioner's receipts. In August 1960, the respondents wrote petitioner a letter in which they claimed that petitioner had committed "a material breach of that contract" by defaulting on the contract's payment provisions and notified petitioner of the termination of the contract and the cancellation of petitioner's right to use the trademark unless this claimed default was remedied immediately. When petitioner continued to deal with the trademark despite the notice of termination, the respondents brought an action based upon their view that a material breach of contract had occurred. The plaintiff sought an injunction and an accounting of profits.]

MR. JUSTICE BLACK delivered the opinion of the Court.

The District Court . . . granted a motion to strike petitioner's demand for a trial by jury in an action now pending before it on the alternative grounds that either the action was "purely equitable" or, if not purely equitable, whatever legal issues that were raised were "incidental" to equitable issues, and, in either case, no right to trial by jury existed. The petitioner then sought mandamus in the Court of Appeals for the Third Circuit to compel the district judge to vacate this order. When that court denied this request without opinion, we granted certiorari because the action of the Court of Appeals seemed inconsistent with protection already clearly recognized for the important constitutional right to trial by jury in our previous decisions.

At the outset, we may dispose of one of the grounds upon which the trial court acted in striking the demand for trial by jury — that based upon the view that the right to trial by jury may be lost as to legal issues where those issues are characterized as "incidental" to equitable issues — for our previous decisions make it plain that no such rule may be applied in the federal courts. . . .

The result of this procedure in those cases in which it was followed was that any issue common to both the legal and equitable claims was finally determined by the court and the party seeking trial by jury on the legal claim was deprived of that right as to these common issues. This procedure finally came before us in *Beacon Theaters, Inc. v. Westover*, 359 U.S. 500 (1959), a case which, like this one, arose from the denial of a petition for mandamus to compel a district judge to vacate his order striking a demand for trial by jury.

Our decision reversing that case not only emphasizes the responsibility of the Federal Courts of Appeals to grant mandamus where necessary to protect the constitutional right to trial by jury but also limits the issues open for determination here by defining the protection to which that right is entitled in cases involving both legal and equitable claims. The holding in *Beacon Theaters* was that where both legal and equitable issues are presented in a single case, "only under the most imperative circumstances, circumstances which in view of the flexible procedures of the Federal Rules we cannot now anticipate, can the right to a jury trial of legal issues be lost through prior determination of equitable claims." . . .

Reversed and remanded.

[MR. JUSTICE FRANKFURTER took no part in the decision of this case; MR. JUSTICE WHITE took no part in the consideration or decision of this case.]

NOTES

1. How is the issuance of mandamus in *Dairy Queen* "necessary or appropriate" in aid of the appellate court's jurisdiction?

2. Contrast the view expressed by Judge Easterbrook in *First National Bank v. Warren*, 796 F.2d 999, 1002-06 (7th Cir. 1986):

> [T]he Court did not say why mandamus, rather than an appeal from the final judgment, is the right way to protect the right to jury trial conferred by the seventh amendment. Surely the answer is not . . . that there is a constitutional right at stake. Much federal litigation involves constitutional rights, but the nature of the right does not dictate whether review comes in mid-course or at the end of the district court's proceedings. Jury trial is not the most essential of rights, either. The right to a jury trial and the right to indictment by a grand jury are the only two provisions of the Bill of Rights that the Supreme Court has not applied to the states as important components of ordered liberty. [*Warren*, 796 F.2d at 1002] . . .
>
> The consequence of the developments since *Will v. United States* is that we must separate the two strands of the rationale in . . . *Dairy Queen* [and other cases]. To the extent these cases stand for the proposition that appellate courts should issue "supervisory" mandamus to spare the parties the need to go through the trial and present a claim of error on appeal, they have been undermined. To the extent these cases stand for the proposition that mandamus will lie when the "party seeking issuance [has] no other adequate means to attain the

relief he desires" (*Allied*, 449 U.S. at 35), they are as sound now as they ever were — provided the right to the jury trial is "clear and indisputable." The use of mandamus gives the person claiming a right to a jury trial greater access to interlocutory review than does the "collateral order" doctrine under 28 U.S.C. § 1291. As we have emphasized, one of the requirements of the collateral order doctrine is the independence of the merits and the order presented on appeal; the question whether there should be a jury trial may not be independent of the merits. . . . *Dairy Queen* [and other cases], then, sometimes authorize the use of mandamus when the rebuff of a demand for a jury would not be appealable, but they do this only when a clear right to a jury could not be vindicated on appeal from the final judgment.

3. Suppose the trial judge had ordered the case to be tried by jury. Could the party opposing the jury demand have obtained review by mandamus?

ROBERT L. STERN, APPELLATE PRACTICE IN THE UNITED STATES 95-99 (2d ed., 1989)[17]

Historically, mandamus and prohibition were writs used to compel an inferior court or official to perform a nondiscretionary duty, or to confine a court to a lawful exercise of its prescribed jurisdiction. Mandamus was a prayer for an affirmative order; prohibition for a negative one. . . .

With respect to lower courts, the writs were used to compel compliance with mandatory requirements and were often described as a means of correcting jurisdictional error. Such errors often occur early in a litigation, as when a right to trial by jury is denied, when a court is exercising a jurisdiction committed by Congress to another court or to an administrative agency, or when one court exceeds its power in transferring a case to another. The writs in such circumstances were in substance means of reviewing otherwise unappealable interlocutory orders. Indeed, one of the prerequisites to issuance of a writ was a showing of unavailability of other means of obtaining relief, such as appeal through the usual channels. *Helstoski v. Meanor*, 442 U.S. 500 (1979). . . .

The federal courts, however, have not confined themselves to "an arbitrary and technical definition of 'jurisdiction'" (*Will v. United States*, 389 U.S. 90, 95 (1967); *Kerr v. United States District Court for the N. Dist. of Cal.*, 426 U.S. 394, 402 (1976)). Indeed, on occasion, the line between lack of jurisdiction and abuse of discretion became very faint. The Supreme Court, concerned that the writs might breach too widely the rule banning interlocutory appeals (*Will, supra* at 96; *Kerr, supra* at 403), has retreated in the direction of the original lack-of-power approach, pointing out in *Will v. United States*, 389 U.S. at 98 n.6:

> Courts faced with petitions for the peremptory writs must be careful lest they suffer themselves to be misled by labels such as "abuse of discretion" and "want of power" into interlocutory review of nonappealable orders on the mere ground that they may be erroneous. "Certainly Congress knew that some interlocutory orders might be erroneous when it chose to make them nonreviewable."

---

[17] Copyright ©1989 BNA Books. Reprinted with permission.

See also Will v. Calvert Fire Ins. Co., 437 U.S. 655, 665 n.7 (1978). The Court has reemphasized "that the writ will issue only in extraordinary circumstances" and

> that the party seeking issuance of the writ have no other adequate means to attain the relief he desires . . . and that he satisfy "the burden of showing that [his] right to issuance of the writ is 'clear and indisputable.'"

Subsequently reiterating these limitations, the Court held that mandamus may "rarely, if ever" be used to review "a trial judge's ordering of a new trial." *Allied Chem. Corp. v. Daiflon, Inc.*, 449 U.S. 33, 34-36 (1980).

The difficulty in determining where the Court will draw the line is demonstrated by the *Calvert Fire Insurance* case in which four Justices found that Judge Will's "decision to defer proceedings because of concurrent state court litigation" was a discretionary matter not subject to mandamus. 437 U.S. at 665. Four other Justices described his action as "depriving Calvert of a federal court determination of a legal issue within the exclusive jurisdiction of the federal courts," *id.* at 677, and the ninth Justice concurred with the first four on different grounds, *id.* at 667-668.

In sum, the writs are occasionally usable in the federal courts to review interlocutory orders in certain circumstances: when a lower court exceeds its power, when no other adequate remedy is available, and when the court thinks the matter is of substantial importance.

A few of the states, notably California, treat writs more hospitably as an accepted method of providing interlocutory review. In California, "the writ is ordinarily allowed whenever the question presented is either of great practical importance in a particular case," as when great hardship would result to the petitioner if he could not appeal until after the final judgment, or "of general importance as a matter of procedural law." In Missouri, where the statutes permit interlocutory appeals in only a few situations, the appellate courts grant writs when the result will be "attractive," which presumably means fair and just. Other states, such as Arizona, Pennsylvania, Tennessee, Vermont, and Washington, accomplish substantially the same result by abolishing the writs, at least in name, and establishing a new remedy for reviewing otherwise unappealable orders previously reviewable by a writ or under one of the more modern procedures permitting review of interlocutory orders. In Arizona, the new flexible remedy is called "special action"; in Washington, "discretionary review." Tennessee Rule 10 provides for filing an "application for extraordinary appeal" addressed to the discretion of the appellate court to be exercised

> (1) if the lower court has so far departed from the accepted and usual course of judicial proceedings as to require immediate review, or (2) if necessary for complete determination of the action on appeal as otherwise provided in these rules. The appellate court may issue whatever order is necessary to implement review under this rule.

In Vermont a complaint showing that no adequate remedy is otherwise available may be filed in the Supreme Court or with a justice thereof.

Pennsylvania Appellate Rules 1501-1502, 1511-1513 abolish the writs and also actions for declaratory judgment against government officials and substitute a petition for review of governmental action. The governmental agency (including a lower court) is the respondent unless it in fact has no interest in the proceeding, in which case the real parties in interest are to be named as respondents.

The Illinois Supreme Court has been utilizing its general "supervisory authority," ILL. CONST. art. VI, § 16, as a substitute for the writs, in order to review administrative and other orders which otherwise would not be appealable "whenever the court feels that a lower court has erred or abused its discretion and immediate correction is needed." The effect of such provisions is to eliminate the historical, often technical, restrictions on the use of particular writs, and either to leave the court with unfettered discretion to do what seems right, as in Arizona, or to substitute general standards which concentrate on the practical reasons why allowing review before termination of a case is reasonable in the circumstances, as in Washington Rule 2.3. . . .

Lawyers must, of course, study the case law in their own jurisdictions to determine to what extent mandamus and the other writs, or substitutes therefore, can be used to obtain appellate review of interlocutory orders. Most jurisdictions, however, are still likely to heed the Supreme Court's admonition in *Kerr v. United States District Court for the N. Dist. of Cal.*, 426 U.S. 394, 402-403 (1976), that

> mandamus actions . . . "have the unfortunate consequence of making the [district court] judge a litigant, obliged to obtain personal counsel or to leave his defense to one of the litigants [appearing] before him" in the underlying case (citing *Bankers Life & Cas. Co. v. Holland,* 346 U.S. at 384-85 (1953), quoting *Ex parte Fahey*, 332 U.S. 258, 260 (1947)). More importantly, particularly in an era of excessively crowded lower court dockets, it is in the interest of the fair and prompt administration of justice to discourage piecemeal litigation. It has been Congress' determination since the Judiciary Act of 1789 that as a general rule "appellate review should be postponed . . . until after final judgment has been rendered by the trial court." *Will v. United States, supra*, at 96; *Parr v. United States*, 351 U.S. 513, 520-21 (1956). A judicial readiness to issue the writ of mandamus in anything less than an extraordinary situation would run the real risk of defeating the very policies sought to be furthered by that judgment of Congress.

The unreasonableness of strict adherence to the finality statutes in many situations has induced some courts to stretch almost beyond recognition the meaning of the concept of jurisdiction which has been the traditional guideline to the issuance of extraordinary writs, just as the courts have done with such seemingly simple statutory words as "final judgment" or "final decision."

NOTES

1. A proposed comprehensive recasting of appellate jurisdiction in the federal courts of appeals is contained in *Federal Civil Appellate Jurisdiction: An Interlocutory Restatement*, 47 LAW AND CONTEMP. PROBS. 13 (1984). However, Congress has shown little inclination to rework federal appellate jurisdiction, other than to authorize the Supreme Court to deal with some aspects of the

subject through its rule-making power. More recently, at least one scholar has advocated greater use of mandamus in mass tort cases. *See* Melissa A. Waters, *Common Law Courts in an Age of Equity Procedure: Redefining Appellate Review for the Mass Tort Era*, 80 N.C. L. Rev. 527 (2002).

2. For recent law review writing on mandamus in a state court system, see generally Charles W. "Rocky" Rhodes, *Demystifying the Extraordinary Writ: Substantive and Procedural Requirements for the Issuance of Mandamus*, 29 St. Mary's L.J. 525 (1998) (concerning mandamus jurisprudence in Texas).

3. If a state has an open-ended discretionary appeals statute like that in New York, is there any need for extraordinary writs?

C.   Timing Issues under Governing Rules

In addition to the statutes requiring an immediately appealable order as the predicate for an appeal, the codified rules of the various court systems impose time limitations upon parties aggrieved by trial court decisions, controlling how long they have to take an appeal. These rules are not always simple to understand and apply. An example is Fed. R. App. P. 4. It provides in part:

Rule 4. Appeal as of Right — When Taken

(a) Appeal in a Civil Case.

(1) Time for Filing a Notice of Appeal.

(A) In a civil case, except as provided in Rules 4(a)(1)(B), 4(a)(4), and 4(c), the notice of appeal required by Rule 3 must be filed with the district clerk within 30 days after the judgment or order appealed from is entered.

(B) When the United States or its officer or agency is a party, the notice of appeal may be filed by any party within 60 days after the judgment or order appealed from is entered.

(C) . . .

(2) Filing Before Entry of Judgment. A notice of appeal filed after the court announces a decision or order — but before the entry of the judgment or order — is treated as filed on the date of and after the entry.

(3) Multiple Appeals. If one party timely files a notice of appeal, any other party may file a notice of appeal within 14 days after the date when the first notice was filed, or within the time otherwise prescribed by this Rule 4(a), whichever period ends later.

(4) Effect of a Motion on a Notice of Appeal.

(A) If a party timely files in the district court any of the following motions under the Federal Rules of Civil Procedure, the time to file an appeal runs for all parties from the entry of the order disposing of the last such remaining motion:

(i) for judgment under Rule 50(b);

(ii) to amend or make additional factual findings under Rule 52(b), whether or not granting the motion would alter the judgment;

(iii) for attorney's fees under Rule 54 if the district court extends the time to appeal under Rule 58;

(iv) to alter or amend the judgment under Rule 59;

(v) for a new trial under Rule 59; or

(vi) for relief under Rule 60 if the motion is filed no later than 10 days after the judgment is entered.

(B) (i) If a party files a notice of appeal after the court announces or enters a judgment — but before it disposes of any motion listed in Rule 4(a)(4)(A) — the notice becomes effective to appeal a judgment or order, in whole or in part, when the order disposing of the last such remaining motion is entered.

(ii) A party intending to challenge an order disposing of any motion listed in Rule 4(a)(4)(A), or a judgment altered or amended upon such a motion, must file a notice of appeal, or an amended notice of appeal — in compliance with Rule 3(c) — within the time prescribed by this Rule measured from the entry of the order disposing of the last such remaining motion. . . .

The Supreme Court has held the requirements of Rule 4(a) to be "jurisdictional," so that the courts of appeals do not have discretion to override them. *Browder v. Director, Dep't of Corrs.*, 434 U.S. 257, 264 (1978) ("This 30-day time limit is 'mandatory and jurisdictional.' The purpose of the rule is clear: It is 'to set a definite point of time when litigation should be at an end, unless within that time the prescribed application has been made; and if it has not been, to advise prospective appellees that they are freed of the appellant's demands. Any other construction of the statute would defeat its purpose.'") (quoting *Matton Steamboat Co. v. Murphy*, 319 U.S. 412, 415 (1943)). But the Rule itself has been modified to avoid waivers of appeals that would have occurred under prior versions when, for example, an appeal was filed prematurely. Harsh consequences of "jurisdictional" rules also may be mitigated by liberal interpretations that allow courts to conclude that parties have substantially complied with jurisdictional requirements. A description of some of the workings of Rule 4(a) follows.

STONE v. IMMIGRATION AND NATURALIZATION SERVICE
514 U.S. 386 (1995)

JUSTICE KENNEDY delivered the opinion of the Court.

. . . [The filing of a Rule 60(b) motion to relieve a party from a final judgment or order] (at least when made more than 10 days after judgment, an exception discussed below) . . . does not toll the running of the time for taking an appeal, see FED. RULE CIV. PROC. 60(b). . . , and the pendency of the motion before the district court does not affect the continuity of a prior-taken appeal. And last but not least, the pendency of an appeal does not affect the district court's power to grant Rule 60 relief. *See Standard Oil Co. of Cal.* v. *United States*, 429 U.S. 17, 18-19 (1976) *(per curiam).* A litigant faced with an unfavorable district court judgment must appeal that judgment within the time allotted by Federal Rule of Appellate Procedure 4, whether or not the litigant first files a Rule 60(b) motion (where the Rule 60 motion is filed more than 10 days following judgment). Either before or after filing his appeal, the litigant may also file a Rule 60(b) motion for relief with the district court. The denial of the motion is appealable as a separate final order, and if the original appeal is still pending it would seem that the court of appeals can consolidate the proceedings. . . .

[I]n 1991 the Rules of Appellate Procedure were amended to provide that Rule 60(b) motions filed within 10 days of a district court's judgment do toll the time for taking an appeal. *See* FED. RULE APP. PROC. 4(a)(4)(F). That amendment added Rule 60(b) motions filed within 10 days of judgment to a list of other post-trial motions that toll the running of the time for appeal, a list that includes Rule 59 motions to alter or amend a judgment. *See* FED. RULE APP. PROC. 4(a)(4)(C). A consideration of this provision of the appellate rules is quite revealing. The list of post-trial motions that toll the time for appeal is followed, and hence qualified, by the language . . . that provides in express terms that these motions also serve to divest the appellate court of jurisdiction where the motions are filed after appeal is taken.

The language of Rule 4 undermines the dissent's reliance on a presumption that appellate court jurisdiction once asserted is not divested by further proceedings at the trial or agency level. Indeed, the practice is most often to the contrary where appellate court review of district court judgments subject to post-trial motions is concerned. *See* FED. RULE APP. PROC. 4(a)(4) (specifying that the majority of postjudgment motions filed with the district court divest the appellate court of jurisdiction that had once existed). A district court judgment subject to one of these enumerated motions, typified by Rule 59, is reviewable only after, and in conjunction with, review of the denial of the post-trial motion, and just one appeal pends before the appellate court at any one time.

In short, the Rules of Appellate Procedure evince a consistent and coherent view of the finality and appealability of district court judgments subject to post-trial motions. The majority of post-trial motions, such as Rule 59, render the underlying judgment nonfinal both when filed before an appeal is taken (thus tolling the time for taking an appeal), and when filed after the notice of appeal (thus divesting the appellate court of jurisdiction). Other motions, such as Rule 60(b) motions filed more than 10 days after judgment, do not affect the finality of a district court's judgment, either when filed before the appeal (no tolling), or afterwards (appellate court jurisdiction not divested). Motions that do toll the time for taking appeal give rise to only one appeal in which all matters are reviewed; motions that do not toll the time for taking an appeal give rise to two separate appellate proceedings that can be consolidated.

NOTES

1. Some lower courts, mostly district courts, have held that a timely-filed notice of appeal divests a district court of jurisdiction to grant a Rule 60(b)

motion for relief from judgment that is filed more than 10 days after entry of judgment, although the district court may deny such a motion while an appeal is pending, viewing the contrary indication in *Stone* as non-binding dicta. This position was accepted by the Fifth Circuit court of appeals. *See Shepherd v. Int'l Paper Co.*, 372 F.3d 326 (5th Cir. 2004). Where that is the law, a litigant may have to obtain an indication from the district court that it would grant the Rule 60(b) motion and then ask the appeals court to remand the case so that the district court may do so.

2. Even when the Court has held a rule to be "jurisdictional," it may narrowly construe the unyielding requirements. *See, e.g.*, *Becker v. Montgomery*, 532 U.S. 757 (2001), holding that even though FED. R. APP. P. 3, requiring a timely-filed notice of appeal to commence an appeal, is "jurisdictional," a timely filed notice that was not signed did not have to be dismissed. The omission was curable because FED. R. APP. P. 3(c)(1), which details what the appeals notice must contain, does not include a signature requirement. That requirement derives from Rule 11, FED. R. CIV. P., and is not jurisdictional.

3. Making the time to appeal jurisdictional has come in for a great deal of criticism. *See, e.g.*, Paul D. Carrington, *Toward a Federal Civil Interlocutory Appeals Act*, 47 LAW AND CONTEMP. PROBS. 165, 170 (1984), Edward H. Cooper, *Timing as Jurisdiction: Federal Civil Appeals in Context*, 47 LAW AND CONTEMP. PROBS. 157 (1984), Mark A. Hall, *The Jurisdictional Nature of the Time to Appeal*, 21 GA. L. REV. 399 (1986) (arguing that because appeal periods involve primarily party interests, rather than societal interests, they should be subject to party waiver), and Maurice Rosenberg, *Solving the Federal Finality-Appealability Problem*, 47 LAW AND CONTEMPORARY PROBLEMS 171, 178 (1984) (all arguing, for varying reasons, against appealability requirements being "jurisdictional," that violations be treated as a procedural failure, not as competence-destroying, and that defects of appellate jurisdiction under 28 U.S.C. § 1291 *et seq.* or under rules of court be waivable). What reasons can you think of for making time-to-appeal requirements non-jurisdictional? or for retaining their jurisdictional character?

4. For details on the workings of the Federal Rules of Appellate Procedure, see 16A CHARLES A. WRIGHT, ARTHUR R. MILLER, EDWARD H. COOPER, FEDERAL PRACTICE & PROCEDURE §§ 3945-3994 (1999 & Supp. 2005).

5. Of necessity, state court systems also set time limits within which the initial appeal and additional appeals must be taken, and within which materials in support of the appeal must be filed.

IV.   SCOPE OF INTERLOCUTORY REVIEW: PENDENT APPELLATE JURISDICTION

SWINT v. CHAMBERS COUNTY COMMISSION
514 U.S. 35 (1995)

[After police raids on a nightclub in Chambers County, Alabama, two of the club's owners, an employee and a patron, sued the Chambers County Commission, the local municipality, and three police officers, seeking damages and other relief under 42 U.S.C. § 1983 for alleged civil rights violations. The District Court denied the summary judgment motions of all the defendants, ruling, *inter alia*, that the officers were not entitled to qualified immunity from suit, and that the sheriff who authorized the raids, although employed by the state, may have acted as the County's final policymaker for law enforcement and therefore rendered the County Commission potentially liable. The District Court said that it would rule on the County's liability before jury deliberations. Invoking the rule that an order denying qualified immunity is appealable before trial, *Mitchell* v. *Forsyth*, 472 U.S. 511(1985), the individual defendants immediately appealed. The Commission also appealed, arguing that the denial of its summary judgment motion was immediately appealable as a collateral order, and, alternatively, that the Eleventh Circuit had "pendent appellate jurisdiction" to decide the Commission's appeal. The Eleventh Circuit rejected the collateral order argument, but asserted pendent jurisdiction over the Commission's appeal. Determining that the sheriff was not a County policymaker, the Eleventh Circuit held that the Commission was entitled to summary judgment.

The Supreme Court held that the Eleventh Circuit lacked jurisdiction to rule on the County Commission's liability before final judgment and, accordingly, should have dismissed the Commission's appeal. The order denying the County Commission's summary judgment motion was not immediately appealable under the collateral order doctrine both because it was tentative, the District Court having announced its intention to revisit the issue, and because the order was effectively reviewable after final judgment: if the sheriff was not the County's policymaker, that would be a defense to liability, but did not give the County immunity from suit.]

JUSTICE GINSBURG delivered the opinion of the Court.

. . . [T]he Circuit Court reviewed that ruling [denying the county commission's summary judgment motion] by assuming jurisdiction pendent to its undisputed jurisdiction to review the denial of the individual defendants' summary judgment motions. Describing this "pendent appellate jurisdiction" as discretionary, the Eleventh Circuit concluded that judicial economy warranted its exercise. . . : "If the County Commission is correct about the merits in its appeal," the court explained, "reviewing the district court's order would put an end to the entire case against the County. . . ." 5 F.3d at 1450.[18]

Petitioners join respondent Chambers County Commission in urging that the Eleventh Circuit had pendent appellate jurisdiction to review the District Court's order denying the commission's summary judgment motion. Both sides emphasize that § 1291's final decision requirement is designed to prevent parties from interrupting litigation by pursuing piecemeal appeals. Once litigation has already been interrupted by an authorized pretrial appeal, petitioners and the county commission reason, there is no cause to resist the economy that pendent appellate jurisdiction promotes.

---

[18] [2] The Federal Courts of Appeals have endorsed the doctrine of pendent appellate jurisdiction, although they have expressed varying views about when such jurisdiction is properly exercised. (citations omitted)

Respondent county commission invites us to adopt a "'liberal'" construction of § 1291, and petitioners urge an interpretation sufficiently "practical" and "flexible" to accommodate pendent appellate review as exercised by the Eleventh Circuit.

These arguments drift away from the statutory instructions Congress has given to control the timing of appellate proceedings. The main rule on review of "final decisions," § 1291, is followed by prescriptions for appeals from "interlocutory decisions," § 1292. Section 1292(a) lists three categories of immediately appealable interlocutory decisions. Of prime significance to the jurisdictional issue before us, Congress, in 1958, augmented the § 1292 catalog of immediately appealable orders; Congress added a provision, § 1292(b), according the district courts circumscribed authority to certify for immediate appeal interlocutory orders deemed pivotal and debatable. Section 1292(b) provides:

> When a district judge, in making in a civil action an order not otherwise appealable under this section, shall be of the opinion that such order involves a controlling question of law as to which there is substantial ground for difference of opinion and that an immediate appeal from the order may materially advance the ultimate termination of the litigation, he shall so state in writing in such order. The Court of Appeals which would have jurisdiction of an appeal of such action may thereupon, in its discretion, permit an appeal to be taken from such order, if application is made to it within ten days after the entry of the order: *Provided, however,* That application for an appeal hereunder shall not stay proceedings in the district court unless the district judge or the Court of Appeals or a judge thereof shall so order.

Congress thus chose to confer on district courts first line discretion to allow interlocutory appeals.[19] If courts of appeals had discretion to append to a *Cohen*-authorized appeal from a collateral order further rulings of a kind neither independently appealable nor certified by the district court, then the two-tiered arrangement § 1292(b) mandates would be severely undermined.[20]

---

[19] [4] When it passed § 1292(b), Congress had before it a proposal, by Jerome Frank of the Court of Appeals for the Second Circuit, to give the courts of appeals sole discretion to allow interlocutory appeals. Judge Frank had opposed making interlocutory appeal contingent upon procurement of a certificate from the district judge; he advanced instead the following proposal:

"'It shall be the duty of the district judge to state in writing whether in his opinion the appeal is warranted; this statement shall be appended to the petition for appeal or, as promptly as possible after the filing of such petition in the court of appeals, shall be forwarded to said court by the district judge. The court of appeals shall take into account, but shall not be bound by, such statement in exercising its discretion."' Undated letter from study committee to the Tenth Circuit Judicial Conference, in S. Rep. No. 2434, 85th Cong., 2d Sess., 8-9 (1958).

[20] [5] This case indicates how the initial discretion Congress lodged in district courts under § 1292(b) could be circumvented by the "liberal" or "flexible" approach petitioners and respondent prefer. The District Court here ruled only tentatively on the county commission's motion and apparently contemplated receipt of further evidence from the parties before ruling definitively. In view of the incomplete state of the District Court's adjudication, including some uncertainty whether plaintiffs meant to sue the county as discrete from the commission members, it is unlikely that a § 1292(b) certification would have been forthcoming from the District Judge.

Two relatively recent additions to the Judicial Code also counsel resistance to expansion of appellate jurisdiction in the manner endorsed by the Eleventh Circuit. The Rules Enabling Act, 28 U.S.C. § 2071 *et seq.*, gives this Court "the power to prescribe general rules of practice and procedure . . . for cases in the United States district courts . . . and courts of appeals." § 2072(a). In 1990, Congress added § 2072(c), which authorizes us to prescribe rules "defining when a ruling of a district court is final for the purposes of appeal under section 1291." Two years later, Congress added § 1292(e), which allows us to "prescribe rules, in accordance with section 2072 . . . to provide for an appeal of an interlocutory decision to the courts of appeals that is not otherwise provided for under [§ 1292] (a), (b), (c), or (d)."

Congress thus has empowered this Court to clarify when a decision qualifies as "final" for appellate review purposes, and to expand the list of orders appealable on an interlocutory basis. The procedure Congress ordered for such changes, however, is not expansion by court decision, but by rulemaking under § 2072. Our rulemaking authority is constrained by §§ 2073 and 2074, which require, among other things, that meetings of bench-bar committees established to recommend rules ordinarily be open to the public, § 2073(c)(1), and that any proposed rule be submitted to Congress before the rule takes effect, § 2074(a). Congress' designation of the rulemaking process as the way to define or refine when a district court ruling is "final" and when an interlocutory order is appealable warrants the Judiciary's full respect.[21]

Two decisions of this Court securely support the conclusion that the Eleventh Circuit lacked jurisdiction instantly to review the denial of the county commission's summary judgment motion: *Abney* v. *United States*, 431 U.S. 651 (1977), and *United States* v. *Stanley*, 483 U.S. 669 (1987). In *Abney*, we permitted appeal before trial of an order denying a motion to dismiss an indictment on double jeopardy grounds. Immediate appeal of that ruling, we held, fit within the *Cohen* collateral order doctrine. 431 U.S. at 662. But we further held that the Court of Appeals lacked authority to review simultaneously the trial court's rejection of the defendant's challenge to the sufficiency of the indictment. 431 U.S. at 662-663. We explained:

> Our conclusion that a defendant may seek immediate appellate review of a district court's rejection of his double jeopardy claim is based on the special considerations permeating claims of that nature which justify a departure from the normal rule of finality. Quite obviously, such considerations do not extend beyond the claim of formal jeopardy

---

[21] [6] In the instant case, the Eleventh Circuit asserted not merely pendent appellate jurisdiction, but pendent *party* appellate jurisdiction: The court appended to its jurisdiction to review the denial of the *individual defendants'* qualified immunity motions jurisdiction to review the denial of the *commission's* summary judgment motion. We note that in 1990, Congress endeavored to clarify and codify instances appropriate for the exercise of pendent or "supplemental" jurisdiction in district courts. 28 U.S.C. § 1367 (1988 ed., Supp. V); see § 1367(a) (providing for "supplemental jurisdiction" over "claims that involve the joinder or intervention of additional parties").

and encompass other claims presented to, and rejected by, the district court in passing on the accused's motion to dismiss. Rather, such claims are appealable if, and only if, they too fall within *Cohen*'s collateral-order exception to the final-judgment rule. Any other rule would encourage criminal defendants to seek review of, or assert, frivolous double jeopardy claims in order to bring more serious, but otherwise nonappealable questions to the attention of the courts of appeals prior to conviction and sentence. *Id.* at 663 (citation omitted).

Petitioners suggest that *Abney* should control in criminal cases only. But the concern expressed in *Abney* — that a rule loosely allowing pendent appellate jurisdiction would encourage parties to parlay *Cohen*-type collateral orders into multi-issue interlocutory appeal tickets — bears on civil cases as well.

In *Stanley*, we similarly refused to allow expansion of the scope of an interlocutory appeal. That civil case involved an order certified by the trial court, and accepted by the appellate court, for immediate review pursuant to § 1292(b). Immediate appellate review, we held, was limited to the certified order; issues presented by other, noncertified orders could not be considered simultaneously. 483 U.S. at 676-677.

The parties are correct that we have not universally required courts of appeals to confine review to the precise decision independently subject to appeal. See, *e.g., Thornburgh* v. *American College of Obstetricians and Gynecologists,* 476 U.S. 747, 755-757 (1986) (Court of Appeals reviewing District Court's ruling on preliminary injunction request properly reviewed merits as well); *Eisen* v. *Carlisle & Jacquelin,* 417 U.S. 156, 172-173 (1974) (Court of Appeals reviewing District Court's order allocating costs of class notification also had jurisdiction to review ruling on methods of notification); *Chicago, R. I. & P. R. Co.* v. *Stude,* 346 U.S. 574, 578 (1954) (Court of Appeals reviewing order granting motion to dismiss properly reviewed order denying opposing party's motion to remand); *Deckert* v. *Independence Shares Corp.,* 311 U.S. 282, 287 (1940) (Court of Appeals reviewing order granting preliminary injunction also had jurisdiction to review order denying motions to dismiss). Cf. *Schlagenhauf* v. *Holder,* 379 U.S. 104, 110-111 (1964) (Court of Appeals exercising mandamus power should have reviewed not only whether District Court had authority to order mental and physical examinations of defendant in personal injury case, but also whether there was good cause for the ordered examinations).

We need not definitively or preemptively settle here whether or when it may be proper for a court of appeals, with jurisdiction over one ruling, to review, conjunctively, related rulings that are not themselves independently appealable. See *supra* (describing provisions by Congress for rulemaking regarding appeals prior to the district court's final disposition of entire case). The parties do not contend that the District Court's decision to deny the Chambers County Commission's summary judgment motion was inextricably intertwined with that court's decision to deny the individual defendants' qualified immunity motions, or that review of the former decision was necessary to ensure meaningful review of the latter. Cf. Riyaz A. Kanji, The Proper Scope of Pendent Appellate Jurisdiction in the Collateral Order Context, 100 Yale L. J. 511, 530 (1990) ("Only where essential to the resolution of properly appealed collateral orders should courts extend their *Cohen* jurisdiction to rulings that would not otherwise qualify for expedited consideration."). Nor could the parties so argue. The individual defendants' qualified immunity turns on whether they violated clearly established federal law; the county commission's liability turns on the allocation of law enforcement power in Alabama.

The Eleventh Circuit's authority immediately to review the District Court's denial of the individual police officer defendants' summary judgment motions did not include authority to review at once the unrelated question of the county commission's liability. The District Court's preliminary ruling regarding the county did not qualify as a "collateral order," and there is no "pendent party" appellate jurisdiction of the kind the Eleventh Circuit purported to exercise. We therefore vacate the relevant portion of the Eleventh Circuit's judgment and remand the case for proceedings consistent with this opinion.

NOTES

1. The courts of appeals generally have purported to follow the language in *Swint* indicating that it is proper to exercise pendent appellate jurisdiction when, but only when, the issue not supported by an independent basis of appellate jurisdiction is inextricably intertwined with a decision that is so supported, or when review of the former decision is necessary to ensure meaningful review of the latter. *See, e.g., Clinton v. Jones*, 520 U.S. 681 (1997) (approving exercise of pendent appellate jurisdiction over the question whether an equitable stay of trial was permitted in connection with review of a district court ruling that the President was protected, by a temporary immunity, from trial of suit for damages based upon events occurring before President's term began; reasoning that the stay issue was inextricably intertwined with the immunity decision and that review of the stay was necessary to ensure meaningful review of the immunity ruling); *Poulos v. Caesars World, Inc.*, 379 F.3d 654, 668-70 (9th Cir. 2004) (refusing to address issues including personal jurisdiction and abstention, holding them beyond appellate jurisdiction pendent to Rule 23(f) appeal); *compare Hendricks v. Bank of Am., N.A.*, 408 F.3d 1127 (9th Cir. 2005) (holding that upon § 1292(a)(1) review of a preliminary injunction, court had pendent appellate jurisdiction to decide objections of lack of personal jurisdiction over defendant and improper venue because they went to the authority of the court to grant any relief and thus were necessary to ensure meaningful review of the injunction).

On some occasions, the appeals courts also have held that, on interlocutory appeal, they could and should determine whether there was federal subject-matter jurisdiction over a case, *see, e.g., Poulos*, 379 F.3d at 662; *Hospitality House, Inc. v. Gilbert*, 298 F.3d 424 (5th Cir. 2002), despite the fact that they normally do not have jurisdiction to hear an interlocutory appeal from a district court's denial of a motion to dismiss for lack of subject-matter jurisdiction. Is this correct if the jurisdictional issue is not inextricably intertwined with a decision that is immediately appealable, and is necessary to ensure meaningful review of the immediately appealable ruling only in the sense that a court ought not to be rendering rulings in a case over which it lacks jurisdiction? For an argument that this is the correct approach, see Joan Steinman, *The Scope of Appellate Jurisdiction: Pendent Appellate Jurisdiction Before and After* Swint, 49 HASTINGS L.J. 1337, 1399-1409 (1998).

2. Few state courts have addressed pendent appellate jurisdiction, utilizing that rubric, but some have indicated openness to exercise of such jurisdiction, in an appropriate fact pattern. *See, e.g., District of Columbia v. Simpkins*, 720 A.2d 894 (D.C. Ct. App. 1998); *Darin v. Haven*, 437 N.W.2d 349 (Mich. Ct. App. 1989).

V. STANDING TO APPEAL AND THE RIGHT TO DEFEND JUDGMENTS

The preceding sections dealt with the timing of appellate review, the appropriate procedure for obtaining review, and the permissible scope of review (when, how and what). This section addresses the question of "who." Who is in a position to invoke the jurisdiction of the appellate court?

Common sense suggests that persons having no connection with a case would not be allowed to appeal or defend a judgment. Appellate courts do not sit to hear and decide questions put to them by persons having no stake in the matter being litigated. Like Anglo-American courts generally, they sit to resolve concrete disputes between adverse parties in live controversies, with consequences in the real world. In this respect, the question of who can appeal is similar to the question of who has standing to initiate a suit in the trial court, and the question of who can defend a judgment is similar to the question of who are proper defendants.

In reading the following case, consider what, if any, interest the would-be appellant had in the outcome, beyond the interest in the case shared by citizens generally. Why was he denied the opportunity to obtain appellate review?

A. Would-be Appellants

BENDER v. WILLIAMSPORT AREA SCHOOL DISTRICT
475 U.S. 534 (1986)

Justice Stevens delivered the opinion of the Court.

This case raises an important question of federal appellate jurisdiction that was not considered by the Court of Appeals: Whether one member of a School Board has standing to appeal from a declaratory judgment against the Board. We conclude that although the School Board itself had a sufficient stake in the outcome of the litigation to appeal, an individual Board member cannot invoke the Board's interest in the case to confer standing upon himself.

In September 1981 a group of high school students in Williamsport, Pennsylvania, formed a club called "Petros" for the purpose of promoting "spiritual growth and positive attitudes in the lives of its members." App. 46. The group asked the Principal of the high school for permission to meet on school premises during student activity periods scheduled during the regular schoolday on Tuesdays and Thursdays. The Principal allowed Petros to hold an organizational meeting that was attended by approximately 45 students. At that meeting passages of scripture were read and some students prayed. There is no evidence that any students, or parents, expressed any opposition or concern about future meetings of Petros. The Principal nevertheless advised the group that they could not hold any further meetings until he had discussed the matter with the School Superintendent. The Superintendent, in turn, advised the students that he would respond to their written request for recognition after he received "competent legal advice [from the School District's Solicitor] as to the propriety of approving establishment of the proposed prayer club" on school premises.

On November 16, 1981, the Principal and the Superintendent met with representatives of Petros and advised them that "based on the Solicitor's legal opinion, their request must be denied." 563 F. Supp. 697, 701 (M.D. Pa. 1983). The legal opinion is not a part of the record; nor does the record contain any evidence that the Principal, the Superintendent, or any other person except the Solicitor had voiced any opposition to the proposed meetings by Petros. Indeed, Petros was informed that it could meet off school premises and "would be given released time during the activity period" if it could secure "a location and an adult supervisor, preferably a clergyman" for their meetings.

The students thereafter wrote a letter to the Chairman of the Williamsport Area School Board appealing the Superintendent's decision. At a meeting held January 19, 1982, the Board upheld the Superintendent's decision and "denied the appeal on the basis of the Solicitor's opinion." . . .

On June 2, 1982, 10 of the students filed suit in the United States District Court against the Williamsport Area School District, the 9 members of the School Board, the Superintendent of the District, and the Principal of the high school. Although there is a general allegation in the first paragraph of the complaint that the action was brought against the defendants "in their individual and official capacities," App. 13, the specific allegation concerning each of the named members of the Board was in this form: "John C. Youngman, Jr., is a member of the Williamsport Area School Board and is sued in that capacity," *id.* at 16. The complaint alleged that the defendants' refusal to recognize Petros and to allow it to meet on the same basis as other student groups because of its religious activities violated the First Amendment. The complaint prayed for declaratory and injunctive relief.

One answer was filed on behalf of all the defendants. Although they admitted most of the material allegations of the complaint, they alleged that they had "requested and received in writing an opinion from the school district solicitor and legal counsel that it would be unlawful, improper and unconstitutional to recognize said group as a student organization."

After plaintiffs completed their discovery (defendants took no depositions), the parties filed cross-motions for summary judgment supported by affidavits, the deposition testimony, and statements of material fact not in dispute. On November 9, 1982, the District Court entered an order finding that the record was incomplete. It thereupon directed the parties to submit affidavits or other documentation concerning "the exact nature of the activity period, the type of activities or clubs that have been, and would be, approved, and what proposed groups, if any, have been denied approval." *Id.* at 101. After that additional information was supplied, and after the case had been fully briefed, the District Court on May 12, 1983, filed a detailed and carefully written opinion in which it stated:

> Presently before the court are the parties' cross-motions for summary judgment. . . . Although the case presents only a question of law, this is not to say that the facts are unimportant. On the contrary, the undisputed facts are of paramount importance to the resolution of the legal question presented in this case. A slight change in the facts could very well have dictated a contrary decision.
>
> After carefully reviewing those facts, and after giving full consideration to all pertinent legal authority, the court concludes that because the defendant school district is not constitutionally required to deny the plaintiffs the opportunity to meet, by doing so solely on constitutional grounds it has impermissibly burdened their free-speech rights. Accordingly, summary judgment will be granted in favor of the plaintiffs. 563 F. Supp., at 699-700.

The final order entered by the District Court was a ruling "in favor of the plaintiffs and against the defendants on plaintiffs' freedom of speech claim." No injunction was entered, and no relief was granted against any defendant in his individual capacity. The District Court, in effect, merely held that the Board's attorney was incorrect in his legal advice.

The School District did not challenge the judgment of the District Court in any way. It made no motion for a stay and took no appeal. Instead, it decided to comply with the judgment and to allow Petros to conduct the meetings it had requested.

However, John C. Youngman, Jr., who was then still a member of the Board, did file a timely notice of appeal.

In the Court of Appeals no one raised any question about Mr. Youngman's standing to appeal. The court did note that all of the original plaintiffs had graduated from high school, but it granted a motion to add additional plaintiffs who were currently enrolled students in order to prevent the case from becoming moot. Neither the majority nor the dissenting opinion even mentioned Mr. Youngman.

After repeatedly stressing "the crucial role which the particular facts play in every first amendment analysis," the majority of the Court of Appeals held "that the particular circumstances disclosed by this record and present at the Williamsport Area High School lead to the inexorable conclusion that the constitutional balance of interests tilts against permitting the Petros activity to be conducted within the school as a general activity program". . . .

After granting certiorari, however, we noticed that neither the Board nor any of the defendants except Mr. Youngman opposed the students' position and that only Mr. Youngman had challenged the District Court's judgment by invoking the jurisdiction of the Court of Appeals. We therefore find it necessary to answer the question whether Mr. Youngman had a sufficient stake in the outcome of the litigation to support appellate jurisdiction. The parties and the *amici* have identified three different capacities in which Mr. Youngman may have had standing to appeal — as an individual, as a member of the Board, and as a parent.

Before considering each of the standing theories, it is appropriate to restate certain basic principles that limit the power of every federal court. Federal courts are not courts of general jurisdiction; they have only the power that is authorized by Article III of the Constitution and the statutes enacted by Congress pursuant thereto. *See, e.g., Marbury v. Madison*, 1 Cranch 137, 173-180 (1803). For that reason, every federal appellate court has a special obligation to "satisfy itself not only of its own jurisdiction, but also that of the lower courts in a cause under review," even though the parties are prepared to concede it. *Mitchell v. Maurer*, 293 U.S. 237, 244 (1934). "And if the record discloses that the lower court was without jurisdiction this court will notice the defect, although the parties make no contention concerning it. [When the lower federal court] lack[s] jurisdiction, we have jurisdiction on appeal, not of the merits but merely for the purpose of correcting the error of the lower court in entertaining the suit." *United States v. Corrick*, 298 U.S. 435, 440 (1936).

This obligation to notice defects in a court of appeals' subject-matter jurisdiction assumes a special importance when a constitutional question is presented. In such cases we have strictly adhered to the standing requirements to ensure that our deliberations will have the benefit of adversary presentation and a full development of the relevant facts. . . .:

> The requirement of "actual injury redressable by the court," . . . serves several of the "implicit policies embodied in Article III," *Flast* [*v. Cohen*, 392 U.S. 83,] 96 [(1968)]. It tends to assure that the legal questions presented to the court will be resolved, not in the rarified atmosphere of a debating society, but in a concrete factual context conducive to a realistic appreciation of the consequences of judicial action. The "standing" requirement serves other purposes. Because it assures an actual factual setting in which the litigant asserts a claim of injury in fact, a court may decide the case with some confidence that its decision will not pave the way for lawsuits which have some, but not all, of the facts of the case actually decided by the court.

The first paragraph of the complaint alleged that the action was brought against the defendants "in their individual and official capacities." There is, however, nothing else in the complaint, or in the record on which the District Court's judgment was based, to support the suggestion that relief was sought against any School Board member in his or her *individual* capacity. Certainly the District Court's judgment granted no such relief. . . . Accordingly, to paraphrase our holding in *Brandon v. Holt*, 469 U.S. 464, 469 (1985), "[t]he course of proceedings . . . make it abundantly clear that the action against [Mr. Youngman] was in his official capacity and only in that capacity." Since the judgment against Mr. Youngman was not in his individual capacity, he had no standing to appeal in that capacity.

As a member of the School Board sued in his official capacity Mr. Youngman has no personal stake in the outcome of the litigation and therefore did not have standing to file the notice of appeal. As we held in *Brandon v. Holt, supra,* "a judgment against a public servant 'in his official capacity' imposes liability on the entity that he represents provided, of course, the public entity received notice and an opportunity to respond." *Id.* at 471-472. . . .

Mr. Youngman's status as a School Board member does not permit him to "step into the shoes of the Board" and invoke its right to appeal. In this case, Mr. Youngman was apparently the lone dissenter in a decision by the other eight members of the School Board to forgo an appeal. Generally speaking, members of collegial bodies do not have standing to perfect an appeal the body itself has declined to take. . . .

At oral argument Mr. Youngman advised the Court that he is the parent of at least one student attending the Williamsport Area High School and that as a matter of conscience he is opposed to prayer activities on school premises during regular school hours. The Solicitor General submits that Mr. Youngman's status as a parent provides an adequate predicate for federal appellate jurisdiction.

Mr. Youngman's status as an aggrieved parent, however, like any other kindred fact showing the existence of a justiciable "case" or "controversy" under Article III, must affirmatively appear in the record. As the first Justice Harlan observed, "the presumption . . . is that the court below was without jurisdiction" unless "the contrary appears affirmatively from the record." *King Bridge Co. v. Otoe County,* 120 U.S. 225, 226 (1887). That lack of standing was not noticed by either party matters not. . . Moreover, because it is not "sufficient that jurisdiction may be inferred argumentatively from averments in the pleadings," *Grace v. American Central Ins. Co.,* 109 U.S. 278, 284 (1883), it follows that the necessary factual predicate may not be gleaned from the briefs and arguments themselves. This "first principle of federal jurisdiction" applies "whether the case is at the trial stage or the appellate stage." P. Bator, P. Mishkin, D. Shapiro, & H. Wechsler, Hart and Wechsler's The Federal Courts and the Federal System 835-836 (2d ed. 1973).

There is nothing in the record indicating anything about Mr. Youngman's status as a parent. Nor is there anything in the record to indicate that he or his children have suffered any injury as a result of the District Court's judgment, or as a result of the activities of Petros subsequent to the entry of that judgment. For all that appears in the record, Mr. Youngman and his children might even be active supporters of Petros.

The reasons why Mr. Youngman may not take an appeal in his individual capacity also foreclose an appeal in his capacity as a parent. His interest as a parent in the outcome of the litigation differs from his interest as a member of the School Board which, as we have already noted, is legally that of a "different legal personage." Since Mr. Youngman was not sued as a parent in the District Court, he had no right to participate in the proceedings in that court in that capacity without first filing an appropriate motion or pleading setting forth the claim or defense that he desired to assert. . . .

We therefore hold that because the Court of Appeals was without jurisdiction to hear the appeal, it was without authority to decide the merits. Accordingly, the judgment of the Court of Appeals is vacated, and the case is remanded with instructions to dismiss the appeal for want of jurisdiction.

NOTES

1. Would the school board member who took this appeal be accorded standing, as a parent, to initiate an action challenging the school board's decision regarding the use of school facilities? If so, why was he not accorded standing to take an appeal from a judgment adverse to his position on the use of school facilities?

2. Does the Supreme Court's decision in this case rest on the lack of Art. III power in the court of appeals to entertain this appeal or is it a prudential decision reflecting a policy against entertaining appeals in these circumstances?

3. When there are no issues as to whether someone was a party to a case in the capacity in which he seeks to appeal, standing to appeal issues may arise because of questions as to whether the appellant has been aggrieved by the decision below. Ordinarily, prevailing parties cannot appeal, and courts review judgments, not opinions. *California v. Rooney*, 483 U.S. 307, 311 (1987) (so stating in refusing to review a pronouncement that a search of trash was unconstitutional, where the state, which sought to appeal, had won a judgment that its search warrant nonetheless was valid). Consequently, prevailing parties may not appeal courts' reasoning, unfavorable findings of fact, unfavorable conclusions of law, unfavorable applications of law to fact, or a failure of the lower court to rule on the ground preferred by the would-be appellant. *Mathias v. Worldcom Techs., Inc.*, 535 U.S. 682 (2002) (dismissing writ of certiorari as improvidently granted, citing facts that, "petitioners were the prevailing parties below, and seek review of uncongenial findings not essential to the judgment and not binding upon them in future litigation"). In *United States v. Accra Pac, Inc.*, 173 F.3d 630, 632 (7th Cir. 1999), Judge Easterbrook explained:

> Reluctance to review language divorced from results has a sound footing in the statutory requirement of an adverse effect — not to mention the constitutional requirement of a "case or controversy" — and has practical support too. Few victors in litigation . . . are thrilled with the opinion; almost everyone perceives that different language could have produced benefits — perhaps ammunition for some future dispute . . . perhaps psychic gratification. It is work enough to resolve claims made by losers; review of claims made by *winners* could double the caseload, and to what end? [The] [j]udicial time [it would take] . . . is time unavailable to resolve other, more concrete, disputes. No wonder appellate courts do not issue Writs of Erasure to change language in district judges' opinions. . . .

4. One controversial issue in recently decided cases is whether judicial criticism of an attorney's conduct in and of itself imposes an injury from which the attorney can appeal. There is a split in the circuits over whether a district

court's decision finding attorney misconduct but imposing no separate sanction can be appealed. *Compare, e.g., Walker v. City of Mesquite,* 129 F.3d 831 (5th Cir. 1997) (holding attorney to have standing to appeal verbal reprimand and finding of professional misconduct stated in court opinion, as injurious to his reputation and career prospects) *with Clark Equip. Co. v. Lift Parts Mfg. Co.,* 972 F.2d 817, 820 (7th Cir. 1992) (holding that attorney could not appeal from order finding misconduct but not imposing monetary sanction, despite potential, but speculative, effects on professional reputation; dismissing appeal as moot, vacating judgment to extent it imposed sanctions on attorney for other misconduct but declining to vacate opinions). The disagreement flows in part from the "black letter" principle that courts review judgments, not opinions, but it also turns in part on competing views as to when the injury inflicted engenders standing to appeal. Some courts have taken a middle-of-the-road position and find standing to appeal if, but only if, the trial court's action is tantamount to a formal reprimand or other sanction. *E.g., Precision Specialty Metals, Inc. v. United States,* 315 F.3d 1346, 1350-53 (Fed. Cir. 2003) (holding formal reprimand for misconduct to be appealable); *United States v. Talao,* 222 F.3d 1133, 1137-38 (9th Cir. 2000) (finding appealable sanction where district court found that attorney had violated specified state Rule of Professional Conduct, distinguishing between routine judicial commentary and that which is "inordinately injurious to a lawyer's reputation").

5. In *Diamond v. Charles,* 476 U.S. 54 (1986), the Supreme Court held that an intervenor's right to continue a suit in the absence of the party whose side it had taken is contingent on the intervenor showing that he fulfulls the requirements of Article III. Diamond, a pediatrician, had intervened as a defendant in a class action brought against the state of Illinois to challenge the constitutionality of a state law governing abortions. Dr. Diamond had cited his professional status, his status as the parent of a minor daughter, and his conscientious objections to abortion in support of his motion to intervene, which the district court granted. Ultimately, the district court permanently enjoined the enforcement of provisions of the law that imposed criminal liability on physicians for violation of particular statutory prescriptions. The Court of Appeals for the Seventh Circuit affirmed and permanently enjoined the enforcement of an additional, related, provision. Diamond alone appealed to the Supreme Court. While acknowledging that, under its Rules, Diamond could have "piggyback"ed on an appeal by the state, the Court held that he did not have standing to appeal by himself. Only the state had the direct stake necessary to entitle it to defend its statutes; Diamond, as a private individual, had no standing to defend the constitutionality of this state law. He suffered no injury in fact from the decision below: His contention that, if the law were upheld and enforced, he would gain patients was speculative; his conscientious objection to abortion was not a judicially cognizable interest; Diamond had failed to show that he was entitled to assert his daughter's interests; he was not entitled to assert the constitutional rights of unborn fetuses; and other interests he claimed were irrelevant because unrelated to the provisions of the state law that were at issue.

6. In *Devlin v. Scardelletti,* 536 U.S. 1 (2002), the Court held that an unnamed class member who, in a timely fashion, objects to a proposed class

action settlement at the fairness hearing on that proposal may appeal the court's approval of the settlement, without first intervening. The Court found standing to appeal to be a non-issue. It held that, as a member of the class that would be bound by the settlement, petitioner had an interest that created a case or controversy sufficient to satisfy Article III. In other words, he alleged an injury caused by the judgment and that the courts of appeals had the ability to redress. Moreover, there was no question that petitioner met all prudential standing requirements: "The legal rights he seeks to raise are his own [not those of third parties], he belongs to a discrete class of interested parties [he was not asserting a generalized grievance better addressed by a legislature], and his complaint clearly falls within the zone of interests of the requirement [of Rule 23(e), FED. R. CIV. P.] that a settlement be fair to all class members." *Id.* at 7. Having so held, the rest of the opinion dealt with prerequisites to absent class members' ability to appeal, *other than standing.*

The Court re-phrased the question presented as "whether petitioner should be considered a 'party' for the purposes of appealing the approval of the settlement." *Id.* at 2. Somewhat peculiarly, the Court then undercut this formulation of the critical question by stating that "We have never, however, restricted the right to appeal to named parties to the litigation."*Id.* It discussed cases in which the Court had permitted non-parties to appeal court orders, and concluded that "[p]etitioner's interest in the . . . approval of the settlement is similar."*Id.* at 8. Like appellants in those cases, he was being permitted to appeal only that aspect of the court's order that affected him, that is, its decision to "disregard his objections,"*id.* at 9, and his right to appeal could not be effectuated by the class representatives who had advocated the settlement, because his interests diverged from theirs. The Court concluded that petitioner was a party for purposes of appealing approval of the settlement because he was bound by it.

The Court rejected the argument that absent class members should be required to formally intervene as a prerequisite to appealing from a settlement approval. While acknowledging the contentions that allowing class members to appeal without having intervened would undermine the goal of avoiding a multiplicity of "suits" and make more difficult the management of class member appeals, the Court was persuaded that allowing such appeals would not be as problematic as claimed, so long as the power to appeal was limited to those who had objected during the fairness hearing. *Id.* at 11. The Court similarly was persuaded that little would be gained by imposition of an intervention requirement because unnamed class members who had objected at the fairness hearing easily could intervene, and that the situations in which an intervention requirement would be valuable would be few. Finally, it found that the structure of the Rules did not require intervention for purposes of appeal, noting that "[j]ust as class action procedure allows nonnamed class members to object to a settlement at the fairness hearing without first intervening, . . . it should similarly allow them to appeal the . . . decision to disregard their objections."*Id.* at 14.

7. For an examination of standing to appeal issues and the right to defend judgments on appeal, see generally, Joan Steinman, *Shining a Light in a Dim Corner: Standing to Appeal and the Right to Defend a Judgment in the Federal*

Courts, 38 Ga. L. Rev. 813 (2004), comparing plaintiffs and appellants, defendants and appellees, standing to sue and standing to appeal, the right to defend at trial and the right to defend judgments on appeal, and exploring the nature of grievances that entitle a litigant to appeal, the causation and redressability requirements of standing to appeal, as well as the interests that entitle a litigant to defend on appeal.

UNITED STATES v. CHAGRA
701 F.2d 354 (5th Cir. 1983)

[Several newspapers and a reporter appealed from a decision of the United States District Court for the Western District of Texas closing a pretrial bail reduction hearing in a criminal case on request of defendant.]

Rubin, Circuit Judge.

The first amendment to the Constitution accords the public and the press the right of access to a criminal trial. We here consider whether that guarantee forbids a district court's closure of a pretrial bail reduction hearing when the defendant, to protect his right to a fair trial, requests that the hearing be held in camera. . . .

We consider first several preliminary questions, starting with the appealability of the order, for it was, of course, interlocutory. . . .

The issue has not been rendered moot by the completion of the hearing to which access was sought. The controversy is capable of repetition under circumstances in which each repetition may evade review. We turn, then, to the question of the standing of the appellants to prosecute this appeal and, if they have the right to appeal, whether there are before us those adversary parties essential to the existence of a case or controversy.

The newspapers and reporter, none of whom was a party to the criminal case, seek relief only by appealing the trial court's order; they have not sought mandamus. [Defendant] Chagra disclaims further personal interest in restricting access to the transcript and exhibits of the closed bond hearing. He states only that "the rights to a fair trial of *other* defendants sought to be disclosed [sic] are involved." (Emphasis added.) Those other defendants have not sought to intervene or to appear in any fashion. Indeed, the murder trial of the [other defendants] has already resulted in a verdict of guilty. . . . The prosecution has never supported closure and has not opposed press access to the closed hearings or to the transcripts of those hearings.

"Ordinarily only a litigant *who is a party below* and who is aggrieved by the judgment or order may appeal." However, the right to appeal is not expressly limited to parties by the relevant statute, 28 U.S.C. § 1291 (1976): "[I]f the decree affects [a third party's] interests, he is often allowed to appeal."

Thus, a non-party may appeal orders for discovery if he has no other effective means of obtaining review. Similarly, non-parties have been allowed to appeal orders granting or denying further disclosure of documents already in the possession of a court or grand jury. Non-party creditors who assert rights in receivership proceedings may appeal orders affecting their legitimate interests.

If an injunction extends to non-parties, they may appeal from it. Similarly, a non-party may generally appeal an order holding him in civil contempt. Attorneys and experts, though non-parties, may sometimes appeal orders relating to their fees. Finally, unindicted co-conspirators may appeal an order refusing to strike their names from the indictment.

The courts differ on whether the media, though not parties to a case, may appeal closure orders or must seek other avenues of review. Some, including ours, have allowed such appeals. . . . Others allow an appeal after one of the media has "intervened" in the underlying action for the purpose of challenging the closure order. . . .

Other courts, noting that non-parties may not generally appeal, hold that closure orders are reviewable only on petition for writs of prohibition or mandamus. In the District of Columbia, a motion filed by the press objecting to a closure order is treated as initiating a separate miscellaneous civil proceeding. . . . Taking yet another approach, the [Supreme Court of Washington] . . . indicated that closure orders could be challenged by a separate action for declaratory judgment, mandamus, or prohibition.

The rule previously adopted by this circuit compels our adherence. This appeal is, therefore, properly before us. . . .

After Chagra lost interest in this case, the court was presented an issue without an opponent. . . . That their erstwhile contestant had retired from the field was not the fault of the appellants, but our jurisdiction is not predicated on the blamelessness of the party who invokes it.

The issue is, however, of continuing importance to the appellants, to the district court, and to other courts frequently presented with such problems. . . . [W]e, therefore, appointed counsel as amicus curiae to support the decision of the district court.

NOTES

1. Is the decision in *Chagra* on standing to appeal consistent with the Supreme Court's decision in the *Bender* case, *supra*?

2. In view of the absence in the appellate court of any party supporting the closure order in *Chagra*, why is there a case or controversy as required by Article III of the Constitution? Does the appointment of an *amicus* cure the defect, if any?

3. Can you formulate a general rule as to who will be allowed to appeal a trial court decision? As to who will be allowed to defend a decision that has been appealed?

4. A sues B and C. Judgment is entered in favor of A against both B and C, whom A has sued on the same legal theory. B appeals, but C does not. The appellate court reverses the judgment and orders a dismissal of the action on the ground that A has no cause of action under substantive law. Does the judgment against C remain in effect?

5. P sues D, a city, to enjoin D's enforcement of the city charter on the ground that it is unconstitutional. The court holds, as a matter of interpretation, that

the charter does not apply to P's specific activity and accordingly grants an injunction against its enforcement by D. P appeals, contending that the charter's enforcement should be enjoined on the ground that it is unconstitutional. Should the appellate court decide P's contention on its merits? *See Watson v. City of Newark*, 746 F.2d 1008 (3d Cir. 1984) (No).

6. Should non-intervening shareholders in derivative suits be recognized to have the right to appeal from an adverse judgment or a settlement of the action on terms they regard as adverse? *Compare Felzen v. Andreas*, 134 F.3d 873 (7th Cir. 1998), *aff'd by an equally divided Court sub nom. Cal. Pub. Employees' Ret. Sys. v. Felzen*, 525 U.S. 315 (1999) (holding that non-intervening shareholders may not appeal the approval of a settlement in a derivative action) *with Bell Atlantic Corp v. Bolger*, 2 F.3d 1304 (3d Cir. 1993) (holding that non-intervening shareholders may appeal from the approval of a settlement).

7. For an examination of the rights of persons who are not full-fledged parties to litigation to appeal or defend judgments on appeal, *see generally*, Joan Steinman, *Irregulars: The Appellate Rights of Persons who are Not Full-Fledged Parties*, 39 GA. L. REV. 411 (2005). It concludes, in part:

> [T]he general rule that nonparties have no standing to appeal from (or to defend) judicial orders or judgments may be useful to deter efforts to appeal (or to defend on appeal) made by total strangers to a litigation, but the rule is subject to so many exceptions as to be largely worthless and misleading. In fact, the federal legal system permits appeals . . . by many nonparties, including persons to whom court orders or judgments were addressed and as to whom injunctions were entered. . . ; persons who are adversely . . . affected by court orders, injunctions, or judgments entered against others; persons who were sanctioned by the trial court. . . ; and persons who were denied attorneys' fees or witness fees or awarded less of those fees than they believe they deserve. . . . [And the same is true with respect to nonparties who would be appellees.] Courts should change either their rhetoric or the legal reality so the two are congruent. If courts are to continue to allow nonparties to litigate on appeal — and I believe there are good reasons to do so — the courts should better articulate the circumstances in which they will permit nonparties to bring and defend appeals.

B. Would-be Cross-Appellants

Cross-appellants typically also are appellees. To the extent they are prevailing parties, the usual rule (and the exceptions to the rule) that prevailing parties may not appeal apply to them. However, appellees may file cross-appeals when they have been aggrieved in some measure by the lower court decision. For example, a defendant who prevailed on plaintiff's claim may have lost on counterclaims or cross-claims, and can cross-appeal his loss when plaintiff appeals her loss. Appellees who prevailed fully in the district court also may appeal contingently, asserting that they could be adversely affected by the disposition of the appeal and asserting a trial court error that would adversely affect them if a specified aspect of their win were reversed or vacated. For example, (1) when plaintiffs appeal a judgment on the merits for defendant, defendant may contingently cross-appeal the district court's grant of plaintiff-class certification. Such a defendant wants the court of appeals to reach the class certification issue if, but only if, it "takes away" defendant's win on the merits. *See, e.g., Council 31, Am. Fed'n of State, County & Mun. Employees v. Ward*, 978 F.2d 373, 380 (7th Cir. 1992) (stating that, "[n]ominally prevailing parties are entitled to filed . . . cross-appeals against the contingency that the court will reverse an otherwise thoroughly satisfactory judgment," and allowing defendant, whose win of summary judgment was reversed, to cross-appeal class certification and order permitting consultation among counsel for different parties); (2) If the trial court grants summary judgment to defendant on particular claims and dismisses without prejudice claims as to which the court declines to exercise supplemental jurisdiction, when plaintiffs appeal the grant of partial summary judgment, defendant may contingently cross-appeal the denial of summary judgment on the dismissed state law claims. *Jarvis v. Nobel/Sysco Food Servs. Co.*, 985 F.2d 1419 (10th Cir. 1993).

Various other doctrines concern cross-appeals. Among the most important are doctrines defining the kinds of arguments that an appellee will be heard to make without having cross-appealed. The classic statement was made in *United States v. American Ry. Express Co.*, 265 U.S. 425, 435 (1924): "[T]he appellee may not attack the decree with a view either to enlarging his own rights thereunder or of lessening the rights of his adversary, whether what he seeks is to correct an error or to supplement the decree with respect to a matter not dealt with below. But . . . the appellee may, without taking a cross-appeal, urge in support of a decree any matter appearing in the record, although his argument may involve an attack upon the reasoning of the lower court or an insistence upon matter overlooked or ignored by it." Thus, a winning defendant cannot, without cross-appealing, challenge a district court's denial of its motion to dismiss for lack of personal jurisdiction, *Hurchinson v. Pfeil*, 105 F.3d 562 (10th Cir. 1997), or a denial of attorneys' fees, *Montgomery v. City of Ardmore*, 365 F.3d 926 (10th Cir. 2004), but can defend the dismissal of a petition for habeas relief on the ground that the petition was untimely and that equitable tolling was not warranted, *Neverson v. Farquharson*, 366 F.3d 32 (1st Cir. 2004), or argue grounds that the district court rejected when defending the summary judgment that the appellee won. *Alberty-Velez v. Corporacion de Puerto Rico*, 361 F.3d 1 (1st Cir. 2004). If, on cross-appeal, a party merely asserts an alternative ground for affirming the judgment, the court may dismiss the cross-appeal, but it will consider the alternative grounds for affirming. *Elan Corp. v. Andrx Pharmas, Inc.*, 366 F.3d 1336 (Fed. Cir. 2004); *Alberty-Velez*, 361 F.3d 1.

Sometimes it is not altogether clear whether a cross-appeal is necessary. For example, the federal circuits are split on whether they have the authority to change a dismissal without prejudice to a dismissal with prejudice, where the claimant has appealed the dismissal and absent a cross-appeal. *Compare Coe v. County of Cook*, 162 F.3d 491, 497-98 (7th Cir. 1998) (while criticizing the jurisdictional nature of the rule that court of appeals lacks jurisdiction to enlarge a judgment in favor of the appellee unless the appellee has filed a cross-appeal, holding that appellees' brief did not give the appellant adequate notice of an intention to seek to alter the judgment in the appellees' favor) *with Marts v. Hines*, 117 F.3d 1504 (5th Cir. 1997) (en banc) (over a vigorous dissent, holding that the appeals court had authority to so change the nature of the dismissal with respect to a claim held to be frivolous under 28 U.S.C. § 1915(d)).

In federal court, an appellee must file a cross-appeal within 14 days of the date on which the appeals notice was filed, unless the Rules provide a longer time. FED. R. APP. P. 4(a)(3). The courts of appeals have been split over whether that deadline is mandatory, jurisdictional, and unwaivable, whether narrow exceptions nonetheless may be carved out, or whether it is a mere "rule of practice" that can be overcome in the appellate court's discretion, for good cause. The cases taking the view that the requirement is jurisdictional include *E.F. Operating Corp. v. American Buildings*, 993 F.2d 1046, 1049 & n.1 (3d Cir. 1993) and *Rollins v. Metropolitan Life Ins. Co.*, 912 F.2d 911, 917 (7th Cir. 1990). Cases that treat the absence of a cross-appeal as a rule of practice violation that can be overlooked in rare circumstances include *United States v. Tabor Court Realty Corp.*, 943 F.2d 335, 342-45 (3d Cir. 1991) and *Spann v. Colonial Village, Inc.*, 899 F.2d 24, 32-33 (D.C. Cir. 1990).

The Supreme Court had granted certiorari in a case that would have provided an occasion to resolve this split, but the Court dismissed the writ. *Zapata Indus. v. W.R. Grace & Co.-Conn.*, 537 U.S. 1025 (2002). The Court has indicated, however, that it regards the rule as jurisdictional. *See El Paso Natural Gas Co. v. Neztsosie*, 526 U.S. 473, 480-82 (1999) (characterizing the rule as "firmly entrenched," observing that, "in more than two centuries of repeatedly endorsing the cross-appeal requirement, not a single one of our holdings has ever recognized an exception to the rule;" and emphasizing the interests in "putting opposing parties and the appellate courts on notice of the issues to be litigated and encouraging repose of those that are not," among other things). Judge Posner of the Seventh Circuit disagrees, having concluded that, when the appellant has been adequately notified of the appellee's intentions — a critical condition — , rigid enforcement of the rule has bad consequences: It complicates federal law, increases paperwork, increases the number of remands because appellees are tripped up by the rule, and "multiplies the number of cross-appeals, because appellees frequently confuse defending a judgment on new grounds, which doesn't require a cross-appeal, with seeking to alter the judgment in their favor, which does." *Coe v. County of Cook*, 162 F.3d 491, 497 (7th Cir. 1998). Of course, when it is unclear whether a cross-appeal must be filed to assert one's position, it is better to err on the side of filing, even if one provokes the displeasure of the court, than to risk waiving one's argument.

Revisions of the Federal Rules of Appellate Procedure concerning cross-appeals became effective in December, 2005. These new Rules collect in one place, new Rule 28.1, all provisions regarding briefing in cases involving cross-appeals and fill gaps on this subject.

VI. HYPOTHETICAL APPELLATE JURISDICTION

May federal appellate courts merely assume, rather than determine whether, the district court had jurisdiction over a case and the appeals court has jurisdiction over it? Several courts had been doing just that when the merits questions would be more readily resolved than the jurisdictional questions and the prevailing party on the merits would be the same as the prevailing party were jurisdiction denied. This provoked the Supreme Court to denounce the practice in *Steel Co. v. Citizens for a Better Environment,* 523 U.S. 83 (1998). The Court said:

> We decline to endorse such an approach because it carries the courts beyond the bounds of authorized judicial action and thus offends fundamental principles of separation of powers. This conclusion should come as no surprise, since it is reflected in a long and venerable line of our cases. "Without jurisdiction the court cannot proceed at all in any cause. Jurisdiction is power to declare the law, and when it ceases to exist, the only function remaining to the court is that of announcing the fact and dismissing the cause." *Ex parte McCardle,* 74 U.S. 506 (1869). "On every writ of error or appeal, the first and fundamental question is that of jurisdiction, first, of this court, and then of the court from which the record comes. This question the court is bound to ask and answer for itself, even when not otherwise suggested, and without respect to the relation of the parties to it." *Great Southern Fire Proof Hotel Co. v. Jones, supra,* 177 U.S. 449 at 453 [(1900)]. The requirement that jurisdiction be established as a threshold matter "springs from the nature and limits of the judicial power of the United States" and is "inflexible and without exception." *Mansfield, C. & L. M. R. Co. v. Swan,* 111 U.S. 379, 382 (1884). . . .
>
> "Every federal appellate court has a special obligation to 'satisfy itself not only of its own jurisdiction, but also that of the lower courts in a cause under review,' even though the parties are prepared to concede it. *Mitchell v. Maurer,* 293 U.S. 237, 244 (1934). 'And if the record discloses that the lower court was without jurisdiction this court will notice the defect, although the parties make no contention concerning it. [When the lower federal court] lacks jurisdiction, we have jurisdiction on appeal, not of the merits but merely for the purpose of correcting the error of the lower court in entertaining the suit.' *United States v. Corrick,* 298 U.S. 435, 440 (1936)." *Arizonans for Official English v. Arizona,* 520 U.S. 43(1997), quoting from *Bender v. Williamsport Area School Dist.,* 475 U.S. 534, 541 (1986) (brackets in original). . . .
>
> [The Court then sought to distinguish several cases.] While some of the above cases must be acknowledged to have diluted the absolute purity of the rule that Article III jurisdiction is always an antecedent question, none of them even approaches approval of a doctrine of "hypothetical jurisdiction" that enables a court to resolve contested questions of law when its jurisdiction is in doubt. Hypothetical jurisdiction produces nothing more than a hypothetical judgment — which comes to the same thing as an advisory opinion, disapproved by this Court from the beginning. *Muskrat v. United States,* 219 U.S. 346 (1911); *Hayburn's Case,* 2 U.S. 409 (1792). Much more than legal niceties are at stake here. The statutory and (especially) constitutional elements of jurisdiction are an essential

ingredient of separation and equilibration of powers, restraining the courts from acting at certain times, and even restraining them from acting permanently regarding certain subjects. *See United States v. Richardson,* 418 U.S. 166, 179 (1974); *Schlesinger v. Reservists Comm. to Stop the War,* 418 U.S. 208, 227(1974). For a court to pronounce upon the meaning or the constitutionality of a state or federal law when it has no jurisdiction to do so is, by very definition, for a court to act ultra vires.

How does this affect the flexibility of federal appellate courts to assume their own jurisdiction? As observed in Joan Steinman, *After* Steel Co.: *"Hypothetical Jurisdiction" in the Federal Appellate Courts,* 58 WASH. & LEE L. REV. 855, 860-72 (2001)[22]:

> [A] great deal of language in the opinion suggests that the Court sought to ensure that lower federal courts [including intermediate appellate courts] will not reach merits questions without first determining that an Article III case or controversy is present. Insofar as only constitutional limitations on judicial jurisdiction are the Court's concern, lower federal courts may be free to resolve merits questions before jurisdictional questions that are of a merely statutory, prudential, or common law nature. But this is not entirely clear. Other language in the opinion, in particular that in which the Court stated that "[t]he statutory and (especially) constitutional elements of jurisdiction are an essential ingredient of separation and equilibration of powers, restraining the courts from acting at certain times, and even restraining them from acting permanently regarding certain subjects," suggests that the Court's denunciation of hypothetical jurisdiction extends to arguendo assumptions of jurisdiction that, while unquestionably constitutional, are doubtful as a statutory matter. Thus, the Court has laid the groundwork for playing *Steel Co.* either way.
>
> The majority opinion also raises questions about the scope of the denunciation of hypothetical jurisdiction by its embrace, rather than disavowal, of cases in which the Court itself "diluted the purity of the rule" that jurisdiction always is a threshold question. If [various of the] cases that lower federal courts had relied upon as legitimating hypothetical jurisdiction . . . remain good law, the line separating assumptions of jurisdiction that are forbidden from those that are permissible is blurry. . . .
>
> Even on the Court's own reading of *Chandler* [*v. Judicial Council of Tenth Circuit,* 398 U.S. 74 (1970)], that case can be read to permit one jurisdictional question to be avoided or assumed in favor of deciding another such question. As so interpreted, *Chandler* is a precursor of the Court's decision in *Ruhrgas AG v. Marathon Oil Co.,*[526 U.S. 574 (1999),] where the Court held that there is no "unyielding jurisdictional hierarchy" requiring a federal court to decide that it has subject-matter

---

22 Copyright © 2001. Reprinted with permission of Washington and Lee Law Review.

jurisdiction over a removed case before deciding whether it has personal jurisdiction over the defendant.

If issues concerning a court's subject-matter jurisdiction may be postponed, and perhaps permanently avoided, while the court addresses personal jurisdiction issues and other jurisdictional requirements, one may well ask what other issues are "jurisdictional" so that courts may give them sequencing priority over issues that bear upon subject-matter jurisdiction and so that courts must address *them* before reaching issues on the merits. The candidates include a defendant's Eleventh Amendment immunity from suit, [and] the argument that a federal court should abstain from deciding a case under the doctrine of *Younger v. Harris*[, 401 U.S. 37 (1971)] or other abstention doctrines. . . . Insofar as these issues are *not* jurisdictional in the relevant sense, courts will have to address "truly" jurisdictional issues before reaching them, but courts may continue to assume arguendo against them and address the merits first.

On the other hand, if there is a category of matters that may be addressed before (and even instead of) statute-based or even Article III-based subject-matter jurisdictional issues (the latter issues sometimes being entirely bypassed), the questions arise whether that category encompasses matters that are not jurisdictional in any sense and how broad that category is. It appears that Article III issues may be bypassed in favor of procedural issues, although theoretically not in favor of merits issues. . . . [T]here is some evidence that this is the Supreme Court's view of the law. In *Ortiz v. Fibreboard Corporation*, [527 U.S. 815 (1999),] the Court concluded that it could avoid addressing the argument that some of the members of a "limited fund" class, certified by the district court, had not suffered a cognizable injury in fact and thus lacked standing to sue, and could instead (first) address the propriety of the class certification, although "'mindful that [the Rule's] requirements must be interpreted in keeping with Article III constraints'."[*Ortiz*, 527 U.S. at 831, quoting *Amchem Prods., Inc. v. Windsor*, 521 U.S. 591, 612-13 (1997).] . . .

If federal courts sometimes may bypass Article III issues in favor of procedural issues, *which* procedural issues may be given such sequential preference, and under what circumstances, remain to be elucidated. More fundamentally, *why* federal courts should have authority to address such procedural issues without having first satisfied themselves of their subject-matter jurisdiction and related Article III and statutory requirements (including the standing of all plaintiffs seeking individual relief), when it would be ultra vires for them to resolve *merits* issues, has not been well-explained by the Court, although the Court has repeatedly *asserted* courts' authority to decide procedural issues before they address their jurisdiction. *See, e.g., U.S. Bancorp Mortgage Co. v. Bonner Mall Partnership*, 513 U.S. 18, 21 (1994). Intuitively, the notion that, if a court lacks subject-matter jurisdiction in a case, it ought not to resolve any issues, procedural or on the merits, has some appeal. Perhaps the answer lies in practicalities: A court may need to enter orders regarding pleadings and discovery before it can make a well-grounded determination as to whether subject-matter (or personal) jurisdiction exists. It may appropriately impose sanctions if such discovery orders are disobeyed. In light of the propriety of the courts' ruling upon procedural matters to enable the courts to determine their subject-matter (or personal) jurisdiction, the Court may implicitly have concluded that, as a matter of power, there are no limits on the procedural issues that a federal court can decide before determining its jurisdiction. I would suggest, however, that deciding procedural issues that have no bearing on the court's jurisdiction before determining that the court has jurisdiction might, in many circumstances, constitute an abuse of discretion.

NOTES

1. The federal appeals courts generally have read *Steel Co.*'s implications for them narrowly, to allow complex jurisdictional issues to be avoided when the merits can be easily resolved in favor of the party challenging jurisdiction, so long as no Article III requirement is implicated. *See, e.g., Cozza v. Network Assocs., Inc.*, 362 F.3d 12 (1st Cir. 2004).

2. *See also* Ely Todd Chayet, Comment, *Hypothetical Jurisdiction and Interjurisdictional Preclusion: A "Comity" of Errors*, 28 PEPP. L. REV. 75 (2000); Scott C. Idleman, *The Demise of Hypothetical Jurisdiction in the Federal Courts*, 52 VAND. L. REV. 235 (1999).

VII. WHERE TO APPEAL

Read 28 U.S.C. §§ 1294-95; 1407(e); 1631.

Ordinarily, the proper venue for an appeal is very clear: in the federal system, for example, appeals from decisions of the district courts must be taken to the court of appeals for the circuit embracing that district. However, the proper appellate venue is not so clear when an interlocutory appeal is sought in a case that has been transferred from a district court in one circuit to a district court in another circuit. Issues also arise concerning whether an appeals court whose jurisdiction is based upon subject-matter is the proper court to review trial court decisions or whether the case belongs in one of the courts of appeals whose jurisdiction is geographically-based. The cases that follow exemplify the kinds of issues that arise, and inform you how the courts have decided some of those issues.

FMC CORPORATION v. GLOUSTER ENGINEERING CO.
830 F.2d 770 (7th Cir. 1987)

POSNER, Circuit Judge

Three defendants in a suit pending in the federal district court in Massachusetts have asked us (in two applications) for permission under 28 U.S.C. § 1292(b) to appeal from the district court's order refusing to dismiss the complaint as to them. The request raises a question of first impression: whether, when the panel on multidistrict litigation transfers a case for consolidated pretrial proceedings (*see* 28 U.S.C. § 1407) and the district court to which the case is transferred makes an order and certifies it for appeal under section 1292(b), the court of appeals for the circuit in which the case was originally filed has jurisdiction to hear the appeal.

FMC Corporation filed this suit, an antitrust suit against several companies some of which are German, in the Northern District of Illinois. The German companies moved to dismiss the case against them on the ground that they did not transact business in the Northern District of Illinois. While the motion was pending, the panel on multidistrict litigation transferred FMC's lawsuit, for pretrial proceedings only, to the District of Massachusetts, there to be consolidated with the pretrial proceedings in a suit for patent infringement that FMC had brought against one of the domestic defendants in the antitrust suit. The district judge in Massachusetts denied the German defendants' motion to dismiss them from the antitrust case. He ruled that the Clayton Act's requirements for personal jurisdiction are satisfied if a defendant transacts business anywhere in the United States; it needn't be in the district where the suit is brought, as the defendants had argued. The judge certified his order denying the motion to dismiss for an immediate appeal under 28 U.S.C. § 1292(b). The German defendants have asked us to accept the appeal. At our request the parties have briefed the question whether we have jurisdiction of the appeal.

Section 1292(b) provides that

> When a district judge, in making in a civil action an order not otherwise appealable under this section, shall be of the opinion that such order involves a controlling question of law as to which there is substantial ground for difference of opinion and that an immediate appeal from the order may materially advance the ultimate termination of the litigation, he shall so state in writing in such order. The Court of Appeals *which would have jurisdiction of an appeal of such action* may thereupon, in its discretion, permit an appeal to be taken from such order, if application is made to it within ten days after the entry of the order. . . . [Emphasis added.]

Section 1294 provides so far as pertinent to this case that "appeals from reviewable decisions of the district and territorial courts shall be taken to the courts of appeals as follows: (1) From a district court of the United States to the court of appeals for the circuit embracing the district. . . ."

The order denying the German defendants' motion to dismiss the case was made by the district court in Massachusetts; so section 1294, read in isolation, would require that any appeal from that order be taken to the First Circuit rather than to us. However, the italicized words in section 1292(b) point the other way. For after pretrial proceedings are over, the antitrust case, unless terminated at the pretrial stage, will be remanded to the Northern District of Illinois, see 28 U.S.C. § 1407(a), and we will have jurisdiction over the "appeal of such [civil] action."

Added in 1984 by section 412(a) of the Technical Amendments to the Federal Courts Improvement Act of 1982, the italicized language was intended to make clear that appeals under section 1292(b) in patent-infringement cases would go to the Federal Circuit, which has exclusive appellate jurisdiction in such cases, rather than, as section 1294 read literally would have required, to the court of appeals covering the district in which the case was pending. Although the multidistrict statute does not say which court of appeals has jurisdiction over appeals from orders by the district court to which a case is transferred, most cases hold that it is the court of appeals covering the transferee court rather than the one covering the transferor court. However, none of the cases except [*Allegheny Airlines, Inc.*] v. *LeMay* [, 448 F.2d 1341, 1344 (7th Cir. 1971) (per curiam)] involves section 1292(b), which since the 1984 amendment has contained language suggesting a different conclusion for appeals under that section; and *LeMay* was decided long before the amendment. The amendment is not dispositive. Although written in general terms, it was responding to a specific and distinguishable problem — the anomaly of a system where the Federal Circuit would exercise exclusive jurisdiction over all appeals in patent-infringement suits except appeals under section 1292(b). Nevertheless, Congress's choice of general language may authorize us to deal with a lesser anomaly.

Confining appellate jurisdiction to the court of appeals for the region where the transferee court is located makes a great deal of sense in every situation we can think of — except possibly an appeal under section 1292(b). The court of appeals for that region is more convenient to the parties and knows the district judges. And many of the issues that arise in pretrial proceedings (and it is only for the pretrial stage of litigation that a transfer under section 1407, that is, an involuntary transfer, is allowed) will involve the practices and procedures of the local district court. Moreover, since most litigation never gets beyond the pretrial stage and most pretrial orders are not appealable, there is relatively little likelihood that appellate jurisdiction will be divided between two circuits if the court of appeals for the transferee circuit has jurisdiction over appeals taken while the case is in the transferee district court. There is some likelihood, admittedly. The court of appeals for the transferee district might reverse a judgment of dismissal (which the transferee court can enter, see last sentence of section 1407(a)) and order the case tried; and any appeal from the judgment entered after trial would be heard by the court of appeals for the transferor court, assuming that the case had been (but, as we shall see, it might not have been) returned to that court for trial.

The situation when appeal is taken under section 1292(b) is rather special. The usual case in which permission to appeal under that statute is requested and likely to be granted is where an immediate appeal may head off a trial. The discretionary judgment that the court of appeals must make is whether to hear the appeal or let the trial go forward and decide the issue later, on appeal (if any is taken) from the final judgment. The court that will have jurisdiction over any appeal from a judgment entered after trial is in a better position to make a responsible choice between appeal now and appeal later than a court that will not hear an appeal later because if the case is tried it will lose appellate jurisdiction. And since appeals under 1292(b) are permitted only when they present controlling questions of law — as to which appellate review is plenary — the reputation of the district judge for care and skill in resolving factual disputes and making the many discretionary determinations confided to trial judges — a reputation better known to the court of appeals for the transferee circuit than to the court of appeals for the transferor circuit — is not an important factor in deciding the appeal.

These considerations are substantial, but we consider them outweighed by others:

1. In part because most cases wash out one way or the other before trial, in part because the parties often consent to trial in the transferee court (which will have become familiar with the case during the course of the pretrial proceedings), few cases transferred under section 1407 are ever retransferred to the transferor court; a study some years ago found that fewer than 5 percent were retransferred. See Weigel, *The Judicial Panel on Multidistrict Litigation, Transferor Courts and Transferee Courts*, 78 F.R.D. 575, 583 and n. 62 (1978). The Clerk of the Judicial Panel on Multidistrict Litigation tells us that the figure is higher today, but how much higher is unclear. And of those cases that are retransferred only a fraction — we suspect a small one, but have no figures — generate appeals in the transferor circuit. The argument that the court with ultimate appellate jurisdiction should decide whether to accept an interlocutory appeal thus appears to have little practical significance in the setting of section 1407.

2. If the transferee court enters an order that affects more than one of the consolidated cases, and the cases affected had been transferred from different circuits, it is unclear which transferor circuit would have jurisdiction of an appeal from the order.

3. The previous point illustrates, what is anyway plain, that a rule which gives the transferee circuit exclusive appellate jurisdiction over all orders issued by the transferee district court is simple to administer and free from uncertainty, and these are important advantages in a rule governing jurisdiction. The statutory exception for § 1292(b) orders in patent cases is necessary to carry out Congress's wish to have all appeals in cases arising under the patent laws decided by a putatively expert body, the Court of Appeals for the Federal Circuit, and need not be interpreted to confer jurisdiction of 1292(b) appeals on courts of appeals for transferor circuits generally.

We conclude that we do not have jurisdiction, and the applications for permission to appeal are therefore DISMISSED.

The applicants have asked us in the alternative to exercise our power under 28 U.S.C. § 1631[23] to transfer their applications to the court of appeals that does have jurisdiction. That we believe is the First Circuit. It is true that the Federal Circuit has exclusive jurisdiction of appeals in cases

---

[23] [*] 28 U.S.C. § 1631 authorizes an appeals court lacking jurisdiction to transfer the action the appellate court, in the interest of justice. The action then proceeds as if it had been filed in the proper court on the date on which it was filed in the wrong court, so an appellate system altogether for failing to appeal to the right court.

arising in whole or part under the patent laws, 28 U.S.C. §§ 1295(a)(1), 1338, and that the case with which the pretrial proceedings in this suit have been consolidated in the District of Massachusetts is a patent case. However, the German defendants' motion to dismiss pertains only to the antitrust case, and not to the patent case, to which they are not even parties. The cases were consolidated for pretrial proceedings only; and if the antitrust case were to be tried separately, no appeal would lie to the Federal Circuit. Recall that the amendment to section 1292(b) made in 1984 was intended to give the Federal Circuit jurisdiction over appeals under section 1292(b) whenever it had ultimate jurisdiction over the action. It does not have ultimate jurisdiction over the antitrust case; the consolidation of the pretrial proceedings in that case with the pretrial proceedings in a patent case is adventitious.

It is possible that consolidation for pretrial purposes might be thought consolidation for purposes of appellate jurisdiction over orders made during pretrial proceedings. The First Circuit's view on this issue, as it happens, is to the contrary, *In re Massachusetts Helicopter Airlines, Inc.*, 469 F.2d 439 (1st Cir. 1972); the Federal Circuit's view is unknown. We do not want these applications for appeal to wander around the circuits like the Ancient Mariner. As we know that the First Circuit will assume jurisdiction of the applications (whether it will grant them is a separate question on which we express no view), transferring them to that circuit will assure that they have a home.

The applications for permission to appeal under section1292(b) are ordered TRANSFERRED to the First Circuit.

NOTES

1. In *Christianson v. Colt Industries Operating Corp.*, 486 U.S. 800 (1988), Christianson, a former Colt employee, brought an antitrust and tort action against Colt, alleging Sherman Act violations including conduct by Colt that drove Christianson out of business. Colt counterclaimed, alleging that Christianson had misappropriated some of its patents. The district court granted summary judgment to Christianson, based on a motion that argued against the validity of Colt's patents. The Court of Appeals for the Federal Circuit held that it lacked appellate jurisdiction, and transferred the appeal to the Seventh Circuit, which transferred the case back in the belief that the Federal Circuit was wrong that it lacked jurisdiction. The Federal Circuit then addressed the merits "in the interest of justice," and reversed the district court. Employing the "well-pleaded complaint" rule, the Supreme Court held that the Federal Circuit lacked jurisdiction over the appeal since the action did not arise under the patent statutes for purposes of 28 U.S.C. § 1338(a). Nor did the "law of the case" doctrine compel the Federal Circuit to accept the Seventh Circuit's view of which court had jurisdiction. If anything, law of the case required the Seventh Circuit to exercise jurisdiction, and given the flexibility available under that doctrine, once the Federal Circuit concluded that the Seventh Circuit was clearly wrong, it was obliged to decline jurisdiction. The Court vacated the Federal Circuit's holdings on the merits, and remanded for transfer of the case back to the Seventh Circuit.

2. In *Holmes Group, Inc. v. Vornado Air Circulation Systems, Inc.*, 535 U.S. 826 (2002), the Supreme Court rebuffed efforts to persuade it to abandon the well-pleaded complaint rule as the basis of the Federal Circuit's jurisdiction. Holmes Group sought a declaration that its products did not infringe on Vornado's "trade dress," and an injunction against accusations to the contrary. Vornado counterclaimed for patent infringement. The district court ruled for plaintiff and Vornado appealed to the Federal Circuit, which vacated the district court's judgment. On appeal by Holmes Group, the Supreme Court held that the Federal Circuit lacked jurisdiction because the well-pleaded complaint asserted no claim arising under the patent law, and the counterclaim could not confer jurisdiction upon the Federal Circuit. The Court refused to hold that the Congressional purpose of promoting uniformity in the patent law justified a departure from the statutory language of § 1338(a), which speaks of actions "arising under" federal law, as does § 1331.

There currently is pending in Congress a bill that would overturn *Holmes Group* and confer on the Federal Circuit jurisdiction of an appeal from a final decision of a district court "in any civil action in which a party has asserted a claim for relief arising under any Act of Congress relating to patents or plant variety protection." *See* Intellectual Property Jurisdiction Clarification Act of 2005, H.R. 2955, 109th Cong. (2005).

3. As noted above, not all issues of appellate venue involve the Federal Circuit. Issues also may arise as a result of the transfer of cases between district courts in different circuits. For example, if one court denies a motion for preliminary injunction and thereafter transfers the case out of circuit, which is the proper court of appeals to hear an interlocutory appeal from the denial of injunctive relief? In *Jones v. InfoCure Corp.*, 310 F.3d 529 (7th Cir. 2002), the Seventh Circuit, as the court of appeals for the transferor district court, held that it was the proper appellate venue, citing the language of 28 U.S.C. § 1294 — that appeals from reviewable decisions of the district courts shall be taken to the courts of appeals for the circuit embracing the district — , and distinguishing orders that may be appealed only after final judgment, which should go to the court of appeals for the district in which final judgment is entered. The Seventh Circuit declined to exercise pendent appellate jurisdiction over the transfer order, which ordinarily is not immediately appealable. *See also TechnoSteel, LLC v. Beers Constr. Co.*, 271 F.3d 151 (4th Cir. 2001) (holding the denial of a petition to compel arbitration to be reviewable by the court of appeals for the court that denied the petition and simultaneously transferred the case out of circuit), *but compare McGeorge v. Continental Airlines, Inc.*, 871 F.2d 952 (10th Cir. 1989) (holding that, as appeals court for the transferee district court, the Tenth Circuit lacked jurisdiction over a count dismissed by the transferor district court in a non-final order, notwithstanding that this would create a "jurisdictional hiatus" allowing some rulings to evade review).

Chapter 3

APPELLATE REVIEW: BREADTH AND DEPTH OF REVIEW

Assuming that a case is properly before the appellate court, the next question is the extent of the review to be afforded. There are two dimensions to this question: one of depth and one of breadth. The former involves how rigorous the appellate scrutiny should be, how deferential the appellate court should be to the trial judge's determinations. This inquiry is viewed as a matter of the applicable standard of review. The issue of breadth usually is spoken of as the scope of review. How broadly is the appellate net to be cast? What questions will be open for appellate review? We deal first with scope of review, and then consider standards of review.

I. SCOPE OF REVIEW

A. Introduction

Rules of procedure establish requirements for bringing an appeal. A litigant has to adequately object to trial court decisions that he wants to appeal; file a timely and otherwise sufficient notice of appeal; and see to the preparation of a record to be transmitted to the court of appeals. Subject to exceptions for issues of the trial and appellate courts' jurisdiction and for some issues of law (a subject that will be explored below in section II E.), courts of appeals — whether federal or state — generally will not address issues that were not presented to the trial court or rulings that the litigant did not challenge in a timely fashion and in a prescribed manner, such as by "taking an exception" to an adverse ruling, or by otherwise making known to the trial court the action that the party desired the court to take or the party's objection to the action that the court was taking. Rules of procedure may prescribe how particular issues must be preserved for appeal. For example, FED. R. CIV. P. 51 prescribes the circumstances under which an objection concerning jury instructions will be timely. It states that "A party who objects to an instruction or the failure to give an instruction must do so on the record, stating distinctly the matter objected to and the grounds of the objection." The rule also designates what a party may assign as error concerning the instructions. In many systems, a motion for judgment as a matter of law, or a motion seeking a new trial, is a prerequisite to challenging the sufficiency of the evidence to support a judgment.

Once trial is over, an aggrieved litigant who wants to appeal must file a timely notice of appeal. *See, e.g.*, FED. R. APP. P. 3(a). And every system requires the appellant to identify the issues on appeal, if not in the notice, then in the briefs or another document. Then, the appellate record has to be prepared and filed. It typically includes a copy of the docket entries in the trial court, all papers filed in the trial court, and a transcript of the trial court proceedings, either in its entirety or in its relevant parts. Preparation of trial transcripts can be a major cause of delay and expense in the appellate process. *See* RITA M. NOVAK & DOUGLAS K. SOMERLOT, DELAY ON APPEAL (1990). As a result, the governing rules may allow alternatives such as the filing of a less elaborate statement of the case, agreed to by the parties and certified by the trial court as the record on appeal, or a statement of the evidence, agreed upon by the parties, to be filed where no transcript is available. *See, e.g.,* FED. R. APP. P. 10 (b),(c),(d). Many states permit such an abbreviated record on appeal or statements in lieu of the record, showing how the issues presented by the appeal arose and were decided by the trial court and setting forth only so many of the facts proved or sought to be proved as are essential to a decision of the issues presented. Federal Rule of Appellate Procedure 30 exemplifies rules governing the appendix for use in an appeal.

J. Dickson Phillips, Jr., *The Appellate Review Function: Scope of Review*, 47 LAW AND CONTEMPORARY PROBLEMS 1, 2-3 (Spring 1984)[1]

The Formal Design for Limiting Scope

Scope is ultimately controlled by considerations of the specific functions that appellate courts serve. While there have been various formulations, most who have thought systematically about the matter identify the following basic functions: (1) correction of error (or declaration that no correction is required) in the particular litigation; and (2) declaration of legal principle, by new creation, clarification, extension, or overruling, etc. These are . . . respectively the corrective and preventive functions.

In the discharge of these basic functions several others of subsidiary but significant importance are also served. Among them are (a) ensuring principled decisionmaking in the trial courts; (b) diffusing accountability within the legal system; (c) ensuring uniformity of principle; and (d) making justice "visible" through the reasoned opinion.

The "proper" scope of review depends to a considerable extent upon one's view of the relative importance of the two basic functions. To the extent the corrective function is emphasized, scope will tend toward the narrow; to the extent the preventive, law-giving function is emphasized, it will tend toward the wide. The system itself is slanted by formal design toward the more constrictive attitude, emphasizing the corrective function. This reflects an historical preference for law's rather than equity's approach to the appropriate scope of appellate review.

In the evolution of our contemporary legal systems, we have borrowed from both sources. From the appeal in equity has come the notion that appellate review is simply a continuation of the same action rather than, as at law, a new proceeding against the trial judge or his judgment. But from the proceeding

---

[1] Copyright © 1984. Duke University School of Law and J. Dickson Phillips, Jr. Reprinted with permission.

in error at law has come the notion that the appellate court's function is not, as in equity, *de novo* review to give a right judgment on the same record, but is merely to correct errors of the trial court.

Strict adherence to the formal design that has developed would limit appellate review to the consideration of (1) specific first instance trial court actions or omissions (2) properly suggested as error to the trial court (3) and then properly presented for review to the appellate court (4) by an aggrieved party. The limitation on scope implied in (1) is realized by application of such judicial rules as that prohibiting "changing theories on appeal" and that prohibiting the exercise of "original" jurisdiction. . . . The limitation implied in (2) is embodied in specific rules of trial court procedure such as the "contemporaneous objection" requirements of Rule 46 of the Federal Rules of Civil Procedure and Rule 51 of the Federal Rules of Criminal Procedure. The limitation implied in (3) is specifically embodied in Rules 28(a)(2) and 28(b) of the Federal Rules of Appellate Procedure, which require that the issues for review be stated in briefs. The limitation in (4) is embodied directly in "aggrieved party" decisional law.

B.   Controlling Force of the Record

Ellis J. Horvitz, *Protecting Your Record on Appeal*, 4 LITIGATION 34 (Winter 1978)[2]

Justice Frankfurter once characterized appellate courts as forums in which "[d]isappointed litigants and losing lawyers like to have another go at it." *Ferguson v. Moore-McCormack Lines*, 352 U.S. 521, 524 (1957). . . . Unless a lawyer is careful, [however,] he will find not only that he has lost his case at trial but that his record reveals no errors for an appellate court to review. . . .

On appeal the record below is reviewed to determine whether there was prejudicial error that probably affected the outcome of the case. . . . The starting point for any appeal is the written record. Unless the appellant can demonstrate prejudicial error in the record, his cause is lost. Since the record is merely a written transcription of what occurred in the trial court, an appellant's counsel must be sure that any error will be preserved in the record before the trial court and that it is then incorporated in the appellate record. For the winning party protecting a record for appeal means taking the necessary action in the trial court to deprive the other side of a legal issue that might be asserted as grounds for reversal on appeal.

Protecting the record on appeal can occur at every stage in the trial court from the initial pleading through a motion for new trial and other post-judgment motions. At the pleading stage demurrers, motions to dismiss, motions to strike and motions for summary judgment are all useful and often necessary procedural tools for raising and preserving an issue for appeal. For example, defenses based on a statute of limitations, lack of personal jurisdiction, improper venue, insufficiency of process or service, to name a few, may

---

2 Copyright © 1978 by the American Bar Association and Ellis J. Horvitz. Reprinted with permission.

be waived and lost for appeal if not asserted in a motion or a responsive pleading.

Where a defect in a complaint or a defense may be correctable, conventional wisdom counsels against early identification to avoid educating the opponent to the defect in time to permit correction. Underlying this approach is the belief that the attorney who files a defective pleading can often be relied upon to prepare inadequately and to try the case poorly. A second reason why counsel frequently avoid summary testing of legal issues is that if the motion is successful all presumptions on appeal favor the losing side, thereby giving the opponent an appellate issue that might otherwise disappear if the case were tried on the merits.

New Varieties

In recent years, however, new varieties of cases have appeared where the conventional wisdom should not always apply. . . . In these cases, it may be helpful to both sides to test the new theory at the pleading stage.

. . . [T]he pretrial conference . . . may offer an important opportunity to raise and preserve issues for appeal and at the same time bury an opponent's issues. Where the pretrial conference order governs the subsequent course of the case, it may be useful to obtain rulings on a variety of issues, including the availability of causes of action and defenses, appearance of witnesses, admissibility of evidence, and right to jury trial. All matters on which the court has ruled should appear in the pretrial order or be reflected elsewhere in the record. Without such care, the record may not present the omitted issue for appeal.

To preserve any issue concerning the oral proceedings at trial, there must be a transcript of the proceedings. Otherwise, it will do about as much good on appeal as taking a photograph with a camera that has no film in it. Counsel should therefore determine in advance if a reporter is routinely furnished and, if not, request one. This applies to every stage of trial, starting with voir dire examination of jurors, and including all testimony, conferences at the bench or in chambers, instructions, closing argument and argument on motion for new trial.

Failing to Object

One of the easiest and most common ways to lose an issue for appeal is to fail to object before the trial court. Without an objection, the error is deemed waived. A close relative to waiver is the doctrine of invited error. A party cannot raise on appeal an error of his own making, such as challenging the admissibility of evidence he introduced, the correctness of an instruction he requested, or other error he caused. There is an exception to this rule where a party's error is simply a defensive tactic against a prior erroneous ruling. This may occur where a party is forced to offer evidence or request instructions on an irrelevant issue the trial court permitted the other side to raise over objection.

When he considers the introduction of evidence, a lawyer should be particularly careful in introducing evidence of limited admissibility. The record should show that the evidence was offered for a limited purpose only and that the jury was instructed accordingly.

Where a party is prevented from introducing evidence, it is critical that the record reflect an appropriate offer of proof. Counsel should state for the record precisely what evidence would have been forthcoming had the witness been permitted to testify. Without an offer of proof, it becomes virtually impossible to demonstrate prejudice as a result of the erroneous exclusion of evidence. There are two exceptions to this rule: (1) Where the question is asked of an adverse witness on cross-examination, many jurisdictions do not require an offer of proof, and (2) an offer of proof may be unnecessary where the substance of the disallowed evidence is apparent from the questions asked.

Where counsel seeks to exclude an opponent's offered evidence, a timely objection must be made along with a statement of the grounds for the objection. Where the question is answered before counsel has an opportunity to object, a prompt motion to strike will generally serve in lieu of an objection. Many able trial lawyers, to avoid antagonizing court and jury by repeated objections, allow opposing counsel to introduce harmless, inadmissible evidence. To avoid the need for repeated objections to a particular line of questioning, a lawyer may be able to make an early motion *in limine* or otherwise obtain a ruling that a single objection applies to the entire line of questioning.

Just as important as protecting your own record is suppressing the temptation to improve your adversary's record. All too often an essential element of the plaintiff's case in chief or the defendant's case is missing after direct examination, but the deficiency is then remedied by the meticulous cross-examination of opposing counsel. The message is clear: Never cross-examine adverse witnesses, particularly expert witnesses, merely to have them repeat their story. If you do not have a specific objective in mind and cannot think of any good reason to cross-examine an adverse witness, don't do it.

It frequently happens that significant conferences are held in chambers and are not reported. If rulings and stipulations are made that have a bearing on the case, the matter should be reflected in the record, either by having a reporter present in chambers or by repeating the ruling or stipulation for the record. Be certain that the record contains an adequate and accurate description of the ruling or stipulation.

In some courts, opening statement and closing argument to the jury are not reported unless specifically requested. If you anticipate the possibility of an appeal, request a reporter. Even if opposing counsel may not be guilty of misconduct, statements and arguments to the jury may contain valuable concessions.

Misconduct by counsel must be objected to at the time it occurs or it will be deemed waived. On the other hand, if objection is made and the court admonishes opposing counsel and instructs the jury not to consider the misconduct, thereby etching it even more deeply in the jurors' minds, it is deemed cured. Thus, in raising misconduct before the trial court, counsel is damned if he does and damned if he doesn't. On balance, it is more prudent to make the appropriate objection and take one's chances with the jury. If the verdict is unfavorable, counsel can move for a new trial before an appeal. Moreover, an unfavorable verdict may itself be some evidence of the prejudicial nature of counsel's misconduct. This is one of the many instantaneous judgment calls trial counsel must make, a burden that counsel on appeal is spared.

In the rare case where misconduct on the part of the trial judge occurs, even greater skill and judgment must be employed. If, for example, the judge has insulted or ridiculed counsel or a witness, or has indicated partiality toward one of the parties, counsel may take exception to the judge's remark and lodge an objection or motion for mistrial for the record. In some jurisdictions a motion for new trial based on misconduct may be required to preserve the issue for appeal.

Timely Objection

Jury instructions are treasure chests of reversible error. Therefore, counsel should think carefully before requesting the court to give instructions of dubious validity or application. This is particularly true where a lawyer has a strong case and the instruction involved is not likely to have a significant impact on the jury's deliberations. Several experienced trial lawyers have told me that they withdraw questionable instructions when they feel their case has gone well.

There is also a danger in requesting too many instructions. You may find yourself the victim of the invited error doctrine. This rule not only prevents a party from complaining about an instruction that he himself has requested, it also prevents him from challenging an erroneous instruction given at the request of opposing counsel or on the court's own motion if the party has requested a substantially similar instruction.

Most jurisdictions provide for special verdicts, special findings or interrogatories to the jury in support of a general verdict. These informative aids have found increasing favor in the appellate courts, spurred in part by the adoption of comparative negligence rules in over half of the states. These procedural tools may be helpful or even vital to effective appellate review by enabling the appellate court to understand exactly what the jury's decision was on specific issues of fact.

Treasure Chest

Where findings of fact and conclusions of law are prepared either by winning counsel or by the court, it may be necessary for the losing party to file timely objections and proposed counter-findings in order to preserve issues pertaining to the inadequacy of the findings. Conversely, the respondent will want to preserve victory by seeing to it that the findings and conclusions are properly drafted and support the judgment. Failure to make a factual finding on a material issue or other error in the findings or conclusions may be grounds for reversal.

A handful of jurisdictions require as a prerequisite to appellate review a motion for new trial which assigns as error the specific issues to be raised on appeal. Most jurisdictions have no such requirement. Nevertheless, in most jurisdictions it may be desirable to make a motion for new trial, particularly in a jury case. The trial court . . . generally has far broader discretion than an appellate court to grant or deny a new trial.

If you are unfortunate enough to receive an adverse verdict, but fortunate enough to have the court grant you a new trial, be sure that the court's statement of reasons or grounds for granting the new trial are adequate. If the court order granting a new trial is defective in any respect, seek correction by the trial court, but do so with great care. If the trial judge will not accept your suggestion, you may have presented your opponent with an issue on appeal from the order granting the new trial.

After you have done everything necessary in the trial court to preserve your issues on appeal, those issues must be included in the record on appeal. This is done by designating for inclusion in the written record all court documents, exhibits and testimony of oral proceedings that may be relevant to the issues on appeal. You can make all the right moves in the trial court, but it is useless if you fail to designate the proper record on appeal. On the other hand, if you inadvertently create or inherit a deficient record on appeal, check the court rules carefully. If the omission can be corrected, most appellate courts will permit correction or augmentation on a proper showing.

To succeed on appeal, an appellant must demonstrate reversible error in the record on appeal. This is accomplished by making all the right moves in the trial court to preserve error, assuring that the error is properly recorded in written documents filed in the trial court or in the reporter's transcript of oral proceedings, and in designating all necessary materials for inclusion in the record on appeal. From this foundation, you can then take your best shot at "having another go at it."

NOTES

For a recent practical guide, *see* Thom Hudson, *Preserving the Appellate Record: Five Common Traps to Avoid*, 40 ARIZ. ATT'Y., 32, 32 (Mar. 2004).

C. Facts Outside the Record

Facts not in the record generally are ignored by an appellate court — subject to two qualifications.

1. Counsel's statements during oral argument. At times, appellate courts have acted upon facts developed through statements of counsel made during oral argument, even though such facts did not appear in the trial record. *See, e.g., Jefferson County v. Acker*, 527 U.S. 423, 442 n.12 (1999) (citing representations of counsel at oral argument concerning matters not in the record in determining the constitutionality of an ordinance alleged to violate the intergovernmental tax immunity of federal judges); *Poe v. Ullman*, 367 U.S. 497, 507-08, 511-12 (1961) (relying on statement of counsel for the state that no prosecution under the statute involved had taken place for some eighty years to conclude that no case or controversy was presented by a challenge to the constitutionality of a state statute that prohibited the use of contraceptives and the giving of medical advice as to their use). Is reliance upon counsel's assertion of non-record facts inappropriate or ill-advised if opposing counsel does not contest the facts so asserted?

2. Judicial notice. Rule 201 of the Federal Rules of Evidence, set out below, provides for the taking of "judicial notice." Similar provisions exist in state practice.

Rule 201. Judicial Notice of Adjudicative Facts

(a) Scope of rule. This rule governs only judicial notice of adjudicative facts.

(b) Kinds of facts. A judicially noticed fact must be one not subject to reasonable dispute in that it is either (1) generally known within the territorial jurisdiction of the trial court or (2) capable of accurate and ready determination by resort to sources whose accuracy cannot reasonably be questioned.

(c) When discretionary. A court may take judicial notice, whether requested or not.

(d) When mandatory. A court shall take judicial notice if requested by a party and supplied with the necessary information.

(e) Opportunity to be heard. A party is entitled upon timely request to an opportunity to be heard as to the propriety of taking judicial notice and the tenor of the matter noticed. In the absence of prior notification, the request may be made after judicial notice has been taken.

(f) Time of taking notice. Judicial notice may be taken at any stage of the proceeding. [Subdivision (g) is omitted.]

PAUL MARK SANDLER & FRANCIS B. BURCH, JR., APPELLATE JUDICIAL NOTICE: OASIS OR MIRAGE?, APPELLATE PRACTICE MANUAL 154-57 (P. A. Schwab ed., 1992)[3]

The trial is over . . . [Y]ou lost . . . Your client insists on appeal . . . [Y]ou waste no time in reviewing [daily transcripts] in preparation for framing the issues on appeal. . . . Then it hits you. A fact, which you now think is crucial, was not proved or even proffered. [I]n our legal system . . . [s]cholars discuss it; lawyers occasionally attempt to use it; and, like obscenity, the courts know it when they see it; but the appellate advocate rarely knows whether [appellate judicial notice] is an oasis or a mirage until after the court has decided his case. . . .

Rule 201 regulates only judicial notice of adjudicative facts, and not legislative facts. Adjudicative facts are those that relate to the parties to the case. Legislative facts are facts that have relevance to legal reasoning and the law-making process in general. An example of an adjudicative fact is that the radar device used on the police vehicle accurately reflects the speed of a passing motorist. On the other hand, recognition by a court that adverse testimony by a spouse in a criminal case would likely destroy a marriage involves a legislative fact.

Subdivision f of Rule 201 says that judicial notice may be taken at any stage of the proceedings, and the Advisory Committee's Note . . . makes it clear that this includes the appellate level. As an abstract proposition, therefore, an

---

[3] Copyright © 1992 by the American Bar Association. Reprinted with permission.

appellate court may judicially notice any matter that the trial court could have noticed. As a practical matter, however, the appellate advocate must often overcome an additional hurdle: the instinctive disposition of many appellate judges not to consider a matter that is not part of the record.

Explain Why

The appellate advocate is invariably called upon to explain *why* the fact at issue was not proven or proffered for notice at the trial. Counsel's ability to justify the omission from the record may be an important factor in the appellate court's decision whether to notice the fact. For example, if the fact proffered was not proven at the trial because it did not come into being until after the trial, the appellate court may readily notice the fact. On the other hand, if the fact was not proved because of the lawyer's oversight or because it was thought to be unimportant at the time of the trial, the appellate court may be less forgiving.

Even in situations where a lawyer simply forgets to prove a fact, however, the dictates of logic may give way to the demands of justice, and the appellate court may accept and rely upon a fact, either legislative or adjudicative, not formally of record in the proceeding.

A good example of such a case is *James v. State,* 31 Md. App. 666, 358 A.2d 595 (1976), *cert. denied*, 278 Md. 725 (1976). During the trial the defendant took the stand, and on cross-examination the prosecutor elicited testimony that the defendant had been on parole and that the conditions of his parole prohibited possession of firearms. The prosecutor then introduced the order for release on parole, which revealed not only the conditions of parole but also that the defendant had been convicted in 1963 of robbery with a deadly weapon.

The prosecutor did not ask the defendant whether . . . at the time he had been convicted, he had the benefit of counsel, or had knowingly waived representation.

On appeal, the Maryland Court of Special Appeals determined that it was error for the prosecutor not to have established that the defendant either did not have or had waived representation in 1963. However, the court took judicial notice that in the Criminal Court of Baltimore in 1963 it was the standard operating procedure for the court to provide counsel or advise a defendant of the right to counsel. The conviction was, therefore, affirmed, and for the prosecutor judicial notice turned out to be an oasis. . . .

Courts will sometimes take judicial notice on their own of facts not in the record, leaving counsel dazed at judicial creativity. For example, in *Davidson v. Miller*, 276 Md. App. 54, 344 A.2d 422 (1975), the Maryland Court of Appeals took judicial notice of the fact that since the latter half of the nineteenth century there have been significant increases in shifts in Maryland's population to the extent that two counties are now almost as populated as the city of Baltimore. Therefore, the court held that differences in population statistics were no longer sufficient to justify distinctions between civil litigants in Baltimore City and those in the counties concerning the right to remove cases to other courts within the state. The court then proceeded to strike down a [state] removal statute that was more liberal for the city than for the surrounding counties. Neither party had requested that the court take judicial notice of any facts. . . .

In conclusion, judicial notice . . . is a concept that appellate counsel should understand and when appropriate utilize as another weapon in his or her arsenal of advocacy.

Thomas B. Marvell, Appellate Courts and Lawyers, Information Gathering in the Adversary system 160-66 (1978)[4]

The Prohibition Against Using Facts Outside the Record and Judicial Notice

The general and strongly espoused rule is that case facts either must be in the record or must be indisputable such that judicial notice is possible. The judicial notice standards, which are far from clear-cut, allow courts to use case facts outside the record only if there is little doubt about their accuracy and only if the facts are either generally known or can be found in some trustworthy reference book. . . .

What is the reason for the severe restrictions on the source of case facts? Most of the judges interviewed were asked why it is important to decide cases solely on the basis of facts in the record. They usually answered that appellate courts are not set up to find case facts: The record is the only means the judges have of knowing what has occurred; any information they receive outside the record is not subject to the safeguards of cross-examination, and if the attorneys were allowed to introduce new facts upon appeal, there would be never-ending disagreements between counsel [as to what occurred in the trial court] that the court could not resolve. . . . Thus the courts' difficulties in gathering information are seen as a reason for tightly restricting the source of the information. Furthermore, some judges worry about fairness to litigants, as they do in many aspects of appellate courts operations; a number said that they should not use facts that the parties have not had a chance to contest. . . . This reason, of course, applies only to facts assumed by the judges themselves and not brought out at the arguments. . . .

An interesting example of the uncertainty in this area concerns the use of technical advisers to help appellate judges understand the record in patent, environmental, antitrust, and similar cases involving complicated technical data. At present law clerks and staff attorneys in the Court of Customs and Patent Appeals [now the U.S. Court of Appeals for the Federal Circuit] have technical training, often advanced degrees in the physical sciences. They help the judges interpret engineering, chemical, and other types of evidence in the record; that is, they supply supporting case facts. Various suggestions have been made that other appellate courts be given similar advice when handling technical information that is above the judges' heads. So far these suggestions

[4] Copyright © 1978 by Thomas B. Marvell. Reproduced with permission with permission of Greenwood Publishing Group, Inc., Westport, CT.

have come to nothing; the judges are badly split over whether technical assistance of this sort should be in the record and, especially, whether counsel should be given a chance to answer the experts' contentions.

In all, the net result of the uncertainty in this area is probably that appellate judges have and use considerable discretion as to whether they will use or ignore supporting case facts not in the record and falling outside the judicial notice restrictions.

Reading Between the Lines of the Record

Because the record is only printed words, appellate judges often describe it as "cold" or "dead." But it need not be completely so; many judges, especially those with much trial court experience, enliven the transcript considerably while reading it. Their imaginations and memories allow them to embellish the printed words. . . .

Judges generally go a step further; they read between the lines and smell out facts beyond the actual words of the transcript. They use knowledge gained from their trial experience to impute motives to the trial judge and attorneys and to guess the effects of happenings in the courtroom on the jury. . . . [W]hen asked if he gets a feeling for what happens beyond the written words of the record, a circuit judge said:

> *Yes*, yes, I do. And I *believe* that this is the great advantage that the trial judge generally has *over* the man who has not been a trial judge. This is the *great* advantage. . . . [T]here's the record and if you read it with objectivity, but with an understanding of all the nuances, I think . . . you can more accurately assess what took place if you've had the experience yourself.

Also, Karl Llewellyn, who knew appellate judges well, said they have an "experienced 'feel' for what may lie, unspoken, underneath the record." Then in a footnote he continued, "We know that the court's 'smell' for the 'facts' beneath the officially given 'facts' is frequently, not just semi-occasionally, a factor in the deciding."

. . . In issues of incompetency of counsel, judges read between the lines of the record by attributing to counsel motives about trial tactics to explain away apparent mistakes. In harmless-error issues, they try to read the jury's mind, using their trial court experience to determine whether a particular error made by the trial judge was prejudicial in this case. And on a wide variety of questions they ascribe motives to trial judges and attorneys from the written record.

The nature of these issues makes reading between the lines necessary. The points were not contested or decided below; therefore, there is no evidence developed specifically aimed at the issues and no finding of fact by the trial judge or jury to rely on.

Here the judges decide issues on the basis of case facts not in the record — that is, the probability that a criminal defense counsel was concerned with trial tactics or the probability that the jury was affected by the trial judge's error — and these case facts are determined largely by supporting case facts, which also were not in the record, for example, the judges' impressions of defense attorneys' trial tactics in general or their impressions of how juries decide. Facts used in these situations certainly do not fall within the allowable limits of judicial notice.

Since the supporting facts come from the judges' experiences in the trial court, that experience is extremely important . . . [i]n the view of most judges except those who had had little such experience. . . .

In [some] cases the court seemed to ignore the facts outside the record. For example, the court reversed a criminal conviction for lack of speedy trial, largely on the ground that the record showed no reason for the delay — even though the prosecutor had explained (outside the record) that the delay was caused by an influx of cases following a riot. . . .

For the most part, as in these examples, the facts outside the record did not seem to be aimed at anything other than finding out what happened in the dispute. . . . Perhaps some were also used as social facts, that is, for lawmaking. . . . But . . . only several facts outside the record seemed obviously aimed at lawmaking. . . .

NOTES

1. What does the foregoing excerpt say about the kinds of persons who ought to be selected to be appellate judges? (Reconsider this question in Chapter 11.)

2. If, during the course of oral argument in the appellate court, a judge asks counsel about a fact not in the record, which of the following responses should counsel make: (a) state that the fact is not in the record and decline to disclose it; (b) state the fact and also state that it is not in the record; (c) state the fact but not reveal that it is not in the record?

3. Firmly established scientific theories that have attained the status of scientific "laws," such as the laws of thermodynamics, are subject to judicial notice, *Daubert v. Merrell Dow Pharms.*, 509 U.S. 579, 593 (1993), and courts can take judicial notice of facts that bear on issues other than the merits, such as issues of standing to sue. In *Maine v. Norton*, 257 F. Supp.2d 357, 373 (D. Me. 2003), for example, the court took judicial notice of the State's sovereign interests in deciding that the State had standing to challenge the federal government's listing of Atlantic salmon as an endangered species.

4. Judicial notice in state courts may work somewhat differently than it does in federal court. Lewis W. Beilin, *In Defense of Wisconsin's Judicial Notice Rule*, 2003 WIS. L. REV. 499, explains, for example, that whereas criminal juries in federal court are instructed that they may, but need not, accept as conclusive any fact judicially noticed, while federal civil juries are directed to accept any such fact as conclusive, under Wisconsin's rule both civil and criminal juries are instructed that they must accept as established any judicially noticed fact.

D. Resisting and Deciding "New" Questions and Theories on Appeal

The general rule is said to be that appellate courts will not consider arguments or theories raised for the first time on appeal. But there are exceptions

to this rule. The United States Supreme Court has declined to announce any
guidelines as to when appellate courts should consider arguments raised for
the first time on appeal, rather than in the trial court. It has left this decision
to the discretion of the courts of appeals. *Singleton v. Wulff*, 428 U.S. 106, 121
(1976). The same approach generally is taken in state appellate courts. Cases
presented below indicate the guidelines that courts of appeals have established
for themselves. Note that a related and logically prior question is whether an
argument has been sufficiently argued below that it will not be considered to
be "newly raised" on appeal. Out of respect for the trial court's function and in
fairness to opposing parties, appeals courts typically focus on whether opposing parties were sufficiently put on notice of the argument that they had a fair
opportunity to respond in the trial court and whether the trial court was sufficiently apprised of the argument that it had a fair opportunity to rule upon it.

ACCESS NOW, INC. v. SOUTHWEST AIRLINES COMPANY
385 F.3d 1324 (11th Cir. 2004)

MARCUS, Circuit Judge:

The plaintiffs, Access Now, Inc. and Robert Gumson, appeal the district
court's Rule 12(b)(6) dismissal of their claim against the defendant
Southwest Airlines Company ("Southwest") under the Americans with
Disabilities Act ("ADA"). The case centers around the inaccessibility of
Southwest's web site, Southwest.com, to individuals like Mr. Gumson who
are visually impaired and use the Internet through a special software program called a "screen reader." Some features of Southwest.com make it very
difficult for the visually impaired to access using a screen reader. The plaintiffs claim that this limitation places Southwest.com in violation of Title III
of the ADA, which requires privately operated "places of public accommodation" to be accessible to disabled individuals. Unfortunately, we are unable
to reach the merits of this case . . . because none of the issues on appeal are
properly before us. Accordingly, we are constrained to dismiss the appeal.

I.

. . . .

Mr. Gumson and Access Now, Inc., a nonprofit advocacy organization for
disabled individuals, brought suit . . . seeking a declaratory judgment that
Southwest.com violates [various provisions of the ADA]. They asked the district court to enjoin Southwest from continuing to violate the ADA, [and] to
order it to make Southwest.com accessible to the blind. . . . Southwest moved
to dismiss for failure to state a claim. . . . The district court . . . dismissed the
claim with prejudice, finding that Southwest.com is not a place of public
accommodation and therefore not covered under Title III. This appeal ensued.

II.

. . . .

However, we are unable to reach the merits of the plaintiffs' claim
because . . . they have presented this Court with a case that is wholly

different from the one they brought to the district court. As we see it, the plaintiffs have abandoned the claim and argument they made before the district court, and in its place raised an entirely new theory on appeal — one never presented to or considered by the trial court.

. . . [T]heir Title III claim was based on the simple idea that Southwest.com was itself a place of public accommodation. . . . The plaintiffs have not appealed from the determination made by the district court that Southwest.com is not a place of public accommodation under Title III. Rather, . . . [t]heir appellate brief, for the first time, argues that Southwest Airlines as a whole is a place of public accommodation because it operates a "travel service," and that it has violated Title III precisely because of the web site's connection with Southwest's "travel service." . . .

Our problem on appeal is that the new argument depends on critical facts (and a new theory) neither alleged in the complaint nor otherwise presented to the district court. . . . [T]he plaintiffs now contend that "there is a sufficient nexus between [Southwest's] physical 'facilities' and their off site internet use to prohibit discrimination." . . . The district court never had the opportunity to consider the merits of the new "nexus" claim, and, indeed, the defendant never had the opportunity to respond to the new allegations. . . . Thus, the claim presented to the district court — that Southwest.com is itself a place of public accommodation — appears to us to have been abandoned on appeal, and a new (and fact-specific) theory — that Southwest.com has a "nexus" to Southwest Airlines' travel service — has been raised for the first time on appeal. . . . [W]e believe it is improper for us to evaluate the merits of either.

III.

. . . [T]he law is . . . well settled in this Circuit that a legal claim or argument that has not been briefed before the court is deemed abandoned and its merits will not be addressed. . . . As we recently said in *United States v. Jernigan*, 341 F.3d 1273, 1283 n.8 (11th Cir. 2003): ". . . [This] stems from the obvious need to avoid confusion as to the issues that are in play and those that are not." If an argument is not fully briefed (let alone not presented at all) to the circuit court, evaluating its merits would be improper both because the appellants may control the issues they raise on appeal, and because the appellee would have no opportunity to respond to it. Indeed, evaluating an issue on the merits that has not been raised in the initial brief would undermine the very adversarial nature of our appellate system. . . .

IV.

Rather, on appeal, . . . the plaintiffs have advanced, for the first time, a very different theory and argument. . . . This Court has "repeatedly held that 'an issue not raised in the district court and raised for the first time in an appeal will not be considered by this court.'" *Walker v. Jones*, 10 F.3d 1569, 1572 (11th Cir. 1994). The reason for this prohibition is plain: as a court of appeals, we review claims of judicial error in the trial courts. If we were to regularly address questions — particularly fact-bound issues — that districts court never had a chance to examine, we would not only waste our resources, but also deviate from the essential nature, purpose, and competence of an appellate court.

. . . Plainly, as an appellate court with no fact finding mechanism, and, indeed, without any factual averments made in the trial court, we are naturally hesitant to consider this claim. We also observe that the plaintiffs had every opportunity to raise the new theory in district court, whether in their initial complaint or in an effort to amend their complaint. As best we can tell, at no time did the plaintiffs do so.

The argument that the plaintiffs have raised on appeal is not only new, but also one that is highly dependent on specific facts regarding Southwest Airlines' physical locations and "travel service," and their connections with the Southwest.com web site. . . . [T]hese facts were never alleged in a claim presented to the district court; were never explicated in any document or argument before that court; and no discovery was ever conducted about them. As a result, the district court never had an opportunity to make any findings as to the new allegations, and we have nothing to go on other than scattered (and unsupported) factual references in the appellants' brief before this Court. Thus, it would be improvident for us to try to grapple with the important question whether Southwest Airlines operates a "travel service" and whether Southwest.com has a sufficient "nexus" to that travel service to subject the site to Title III.

. . . We recognize that a circuit court's power to entertain an argument raised for the first time on appeal is not a jurisdictional one; thus we may choose to hear the argument under special circumstances. We have permitted issues to be raised for the first time on appeal under five circumstances:

> First, an appellate court will consider an issue not raised in the district court if it involves a pure question of law, and if refusal to consider it would result in a miscarriage of justice. Second, the rule may be relaxed where the appellant raises an objection to an order which he had no opportunity to raise at the district court level. Third, the rule does not bar consideration by the appellate court in the first instance where the interest of substantial justice is at stake. Fourth, a federal appellate court is justified in resolving an issue not passed on below . . . where the proper resolution is beyond any doubt. Finally, it may be appropriate to consider an issue first raised on appeal if that issue presents significant questions of general impact or of great public concern.

Wright v. Hanna Steel Corp., 270 F.3d 1336, 1342 (11th Cir. 2001).

. . . [N]one of these exceptional conditions is found in this case. . . . [T]he new theory is plainly not "a pure question of law," because it raises considerable questions of fact. The plaintiffs' argument hinges on whether there is a sufficient "nexus" between Southwest.com and a place of public accommodation to warrant a finding that the web site is covered by Title III. The questions whether and where various facilities (such as airport ticket counters, corporate headquarters, and rent-a-car offices) are owned and operated by Southwest, whether, in the aggregate, they qualify as a "travel service," and whether they are sufficiently connected to Southwest.com to subject it to Title III, are undoubtedly mixed questions of fact and law, and cannot be deemed to be covered by this exception. . . .

As for the second exception, the appellants have raised no objection to any order that they had no opportunity to raise before the district court. On the contrary, the record strongly suggests that they had every opportunity to raise the "nexus" theory before the district court. They chose not to do so. . . .

As for the third exception, we do not believe that, in this case, "the interest of substantial justice is at stake." Although this exception is theoretically broad, covering any case where a court genuinely concludes that the equities favor the party raising a new issue, as best we can tell, this Court has never once elected to evaluate a new argument on this basis.

. . . We can not discern any miscarriage of justice in this case. If the "nexus" argument was an overriding question involving substantial justice, it baffles us that the plaintiffs did not raise it in the district court. . . .

As for the fourth exception, the plaintiffs' "nexus" argument is plainly not one "where the proper resolution is beyond any doubt." First of all, . . . the argument depends on an evaluation of facts that were not alleged in the complaint. To resolve the question whether Southwest.com had a sufficient "nexus" to physical locations to subject it to Title III of the ADA, we would have to evaluate extensive factual records and testimony about Southwest Airlines' physical locations and their connection to the web site. Again, we are unable to do so because these matters were never presented to the district court. And again, this question is complicated further because many, if not all, of Southwest Airlines' physical facilities may be explicitly exempted from Title III, which does not cover the terminals or depots of aircraft. 42 U.S.C. § 12181(10). In short, this is a difficult question, and one about which there is considerable doubt.

Furthermore, even the purely legal question of the application of Title III to Internet web sites is far from "beyond any doubt." In addressing the question, we would be wading into the thicket of a circuit split on this issue. . . .

As for the final exception to the general rule — that an issue may be presented for the first time on appeal if it "presents significant questions of general impact or of great public concern" — we do not believe that this case is appropriate for application. The question raised before the district court — whether a web site is a place of public accommodation covered by Title III — is a question of substantial public interest, because it concerns the application of one of the landmark civil rights statutes in the country to a major new form of media that has only gained wide use in the past decade. However, the plaintiffs' argument before this Court that Southwest.com is covered by Title III because of its "nexus" with Southwest Airlines' "travel service" is narrower, and complicated by the specific exemption that Title III gives to airlines. Because of the special exemption Congress has given to the airlines, . . . any ruling we would make would likely be inapplicable to any future cases other than to challenges of airline web sites. And this case would shed little light even on Title III challenges to other airline web sites, because our ruling would necessarily be based on facts specific to the physical places owned and operated by Southwest Airlines.

Accordingly, we are constrained to conclude that this case is not one of the "exceptional" ones in which we should elect to entertain a new theory and argument never raised in the district court. Indeed, to evaluate it now, without the benefit of any record or district court ruling, invites disaster for an appellate court.

In declining to evaluate the merits of this case, we are in no way unmindful that the legal questions raised are significant. The Internet is transforming our economy and culture, and the question whether it is covered by the ADA — one of the landmark civil rights laws in this country — is of substantial public importance. Title III's applicability to web sites — either because web sites are themselves places of public accommodation or because they have a sufficient nexus to such physical places of public accommodation — is a matter of first impression before this Court. Unfortunately, this case does not provide the proper vehicle for answering these questions.

Thus, as we see it, there are no substantive questions properly before us. We will not address a claim that has been abandoned on appeal or one that is being raised for the first time on appeal, without any special conditions. Accordingly, we must dismiss this appeal.

MILLER v. AVIROM
384 F.2d 319 (D.C. Cir. 1967)

SPOTTSWOOD W. ROBINSON, III, CIRCUIT JUDGE.

Appellee, a licensed real estate broker, sued appellant . . . for a commission allegedly earned by appellee's negotiation of an offer, which appellant refused to accept, for the purchase of an apartment building. The District Judge, sitting without a jury, entered a judgment in appellee's favor on findings . . . that appellee had produced a purchaser ready, able and willing to buy on the conditions . . . established [by the parties].

Appellant resisted the action in the District Court principally on the ground that he never authorized appellee's activities, but also asserted the statute of frauds defensively. The case as submitted to us tenders two claims of error, one contesting the sufficiency of the proof to support the finding that the prospective purchaser was financially able to consummate his offer. We . . . are satisfied that the finding should not be disturbed.

Appellant's second and main argument on appeal is that the arrangements for the sale and payment of a commission were void because they were made orally. He directs our attention . . . to provisions in the statute regulating the licensing of real estate brokers and salesmen. As appellant reads them, the offering of realty for sale without the written consent of the owner or his authorized agent is both a ground for suspension or revocation of a license and an occasion for initiation of a criminal prosecution. On this analysis appellant insists that an oral sale listing is illegal, and cannot provide the basis for recovery of a commission.

. . . By our current appraisal, the question appellant poses is sufficiently substantial to command serious attention if properly presented for our decision. But because the issue was neither raised nor decided in the District Court, we do not address it on this appeal or intimate any view as to how it should be resolved.

In our . . . system, . . . review will normally be confined to matters appropriately submitted for determination in the court of first resort. Questions not properly raised and preserved . . . and points not asserted with sufficient precision to indicate distinctly the party's thesis, will normally be spurned on appeal. Canons of this tenor reflect, not obeisance to ritual, but "considerations of fairness to the court and the parties and of the public interest in bringing litigation to an end after fair opportunity has been afforded to present all issues of law and fact." The injunction that trial ventilation precede appellate exploration best subserves that policy. . . . "It requires the [litigants] to deal fairly and frankly with each other and with the trial tribunal. . . . It prevents the trial of cases piecemeal or in installments. It tends to put an end to litigation." . . . Appellant nowhere claimed that the licensing statute was involved until the litigation reached this court. Previously represented by different counsel, he did not advance that proposition in his pleadings or when the case was heard on the merits, nor are such singular omissions explained. Certainly appellant's secondary reliance upon the statute of frauds did not define for the District Court's decision the far-reaching contention his present approach incorporates. And . . . judicial action sought on one ground at trial does not suffice to enable a party to invoke another on appeal.

Sometimes even the salutary principle under discussion must give way . . . , but this is a course to be pursued sparingly and only in exceptional situations. Appellant has brought to our attention nothing to distinguish this case from a host of others in which that principle was conventionally applied. The dispensation appellant would have us grant "is a right to prevent a clear miscarriage of justice apparent from the record, and not a right to afford a defeated litigant another day in court because he thinks that if he were given the opportunity to try his case again upon a different theory he might prevail."

Affirmed.

NOTES

1. In the *Miller* case, would it be plausible for the appellate court to view the defendant's basic position to be that the contract was oral and hence unenforceable, to find that this defense was presented in the trial court, and to conclude that the defendant on appeal is simply presenting an alternative basis for that defense? Is this any different from defendant's citing a judicial precedent to the appellate court that it did not cite to the trial court? *Cf. Republic Tobacco v. N. Atl. Trading Co.*, 381 F.3d 717 (7th Cir. 2004) (holding that defendant had waived its defense to a defamation claim that its statement was a matter of opinion where its defense below had been the truth of its utterance). Would it be plausible for the appellate court in *Republic Tobacco* to consider the defendant's basic position to be that its statement was not actionable, that this defense was presented to the trial court, and that the defendant on appeal was simply presenting an alternative basis for that position? Is the situation in *Miller* any different?

2. What are the functional justifications for the general American appellate practice of refusing to consider on appeal issues not raised in the trial court? Is the customary refusal to consider arguments not presented to the trial court essential to efficiency and fairness and to preserve the essential function of

the trial court? If so, are any of the justifications for exceptions persuasive? Which ones?

For example, should it be enough that the issue put to the court of appeals poses a pure question of law? For a negative answer, see *Cavegn v. Twin City Pipe Trades Pension Plan*, 223 F.3d 827 (8th Cir. 2000) (refusing to decide whether an employee could recover retroactive disability retirement benefits under ERISA after reversing the district court's decision that plaintiff's claim was time-barred; rejecting the argument that because review of the district court's determination would be *de novo* it was unimportant which court first addressed the issue, stating that, "[a] standard of review does not equate with a grant of original jurisdiction" and allow the appellate court "to assume a role reserved for the district court").

3. In what kinds of circumstances would it be manifestly unjust to refuse to hear on appeal arguments that a party did not make in the trial court?

Would *Acree v. Republic of Iraq*, 370 F.3d 41, 58 (D.C. Cir. 2004), be a good example? There, American prisoners of war during the 1991 Gulf War sued Iraq under the Foreign Sovereign Immunities Act seeking compensatory and punitive damages for injuries allegedly suffered as a result of torture inflicted while captive in Iraq. A default judgment for over $959 million was entered against the defendants. After judgment, the United States sought to intervene to contest subject-matter jurisdiction, and appealed the trial court's denial of its intervention motion. The D.C. Circuit upheld federal jurisdiction after concluding that the trial court had abused its discretion in denying intervention, and reached the question whether plaintiffs had stated a claim on which relief could be granted, although no litigant had raised this issue. Citing the exceptional circumstances that appellees had "obtained a nearly-billion dollar default judgment against a foreign government whose . . . stability has become a central preoccupation of the United States' foreign policy," the court held that the question of law (whether plaintiffs stated a claim) was one it should reach. It then held that plaintiffs had no claim against Iraq.

4. When courts of appeals sua sponte consider their own jurisdiction or the jurisdiction of the trial court are they making another exception to the general rule not to consider arguments not raised below? *See* Robert J.Martineau, *Considering New Issues on Appeal: The General Rule and the Gorilla Rule*, 40 VAND. L. REV. 1023 (1987) (arguing that the general rule presupposes subject-matter jurisdiction and that the doctrine allowing jurisdiction to be raised at any time, and even sua sponte, is not an exception to the general rule but a precondition).

5. Should an appellate court be more likely to rely on a new theory to affirm a judgment than to reverse a judgment? In other words, can the appellate court properly hold that the trial court was "right for the wrong reason"? Why?

In *Russell v. SunAmerica Secs., Inc.*, 962 F.2d 1169 (5th Cir. 1992), plaintiffs brought an action against SunAmerica alleging securities fraud. SunAmerica set up several defenses, but not the defense of res judicata. The district court granted summary judgment for SunAmerica. Plaintiffs appealed. SunAmerica did not assert the defense of res judicata in the appellate court, but the court took notice of it on its own, relying on a prior judgment to foreclose the present action. It thus affirmed the summary judgment, saying:

> We begin by noting that SunAmerica did not plead the doctrine of res judicata as an affirmative defense. Under Federal Rule of Civil Procedure 8(c), the doctrine must be affirmatively pled. Failure to so plead usually precludes the district court and appellate courts from considering the doctrine. . . . We have held, however, that we may raise the issue of res judicata *sua sponte* "as a means to affirm the district court decision below." . . . In *American Furniture Co. v. International Accommodations Supply,* 721 F.2d 478, 482 (5th Cir. 1981), we noted as follows: "We are cognizant that *res judicata,* as such, has not been specially pled. FED. R. CIV. P. 8(c). In the posture of this case, however, where all of the relevant facts are contained in the record before us and all are uncontroverted, we may not ignore their legal effect, nor may we decline to consider the application of controlling rules of law to the dispositive facts, simply because neither party has seen fit to invite our attention to the issue by technically correct and exact pleadings. We do so *sua sponte.*" . . . In the instant case, the relevant facts are in the record before us and form an adequate basis for our invocation of res judicata.

Both in civil and in criminal cases, the general rule is that an appeals court may affirm a trial court decision on any ground for which there is record support, even grounds not relied upon by the trial court or argued on appeal. What policies underlie this rule? When the basis for affirmance is res judicata it is particularly clear that interests — not only of the parties but also of the court system — in finality and efficiency support that rule.

6. The question also may arise whether, without remand to the trial court, an appellate court should decide an issue that was properly raised in the trial court, but that was not decided by the trial court because it decided the case on other grounds. The Supreme Court had upheld the dismissal for lack of subject-matter jurisdiction of a class action insofar as it was brought by foreign vitamin purchasers who alleged a price-fixing conspiracy the foreign effect of which was independent of its domestic effect. The Court's decision left open whether an alternative theory of liability that linked the foreign and domestic harms was within federal jurisdiction. In *Empagran S.A. v. F. Hoffman-Laroche, Ltd.,* 388 F.3d 337, 339 (D.C. Cir. 2004), the appeals court held that because the issue posed a pure question of law, and its resolution by the appeals court would preserve judicial resources and "remain faithful to the integrity of the appellate process," the appeals court would rule on the sufficiency of the allegations to state a claim within federal jurisdiction. Was this appropriate? Do the same considerations that justify appellate consideration of arguments not made to the trial court also justify appellate courts' taking the first stab at issues whose resolution has become necessary by virtue of how other issues were resolved on appeal?

E. Plain Error

Appellate courts sometimes use words such as "plain error" and "manifest injustice" when they decide questions not raised below and sometimes not even raised by the parties in the appellate court. Consider the circumstances under which such concepts are properly invoked to justify a departure from the general rule of appellate practice.

1. Criminal Appeals

In criminal appeals, the plain error doctrine has been elaborated in the context of federal statutes and Federal Rules of Criminal Procedure. Rule 52(b) of the FED. R. CRIM. P. states that "Plain errors or defects affecting substantial rights may be noticed although they were not brought to the attention of the court." One of the most cited Supreme Court opinions on the subject is *United States v. Olano*, 507 U.S. 725 (1993). The defendants there were convicted of several charges in the federal district court, and they appealed. The defendants had not objected to the presence of alternate jurors during the jury's deliberations, but the court of appeals considered the presence of alternate jurors to be plain error and reversed, relying on Rule 52(b). The Supreme Court reversed. In speaking of the limitations on appellate authority under the Rule, the Court stated:

> [First,] . . . that there [must] indeed be an "error." . . . [Second,] . . . the error [must] be "plain." "Plain" is synonymous with "clear" or, equivalently, "obvious." . . . [Third,] . . . the plain error [must] "affec[t] substantial rights." . . . [I]n most cases [this] means that the error must have been prejudicial: it must have affected the outcome of the district court proceedings. . . . Normally, although perhaps not in every case, the defendant must make a specific showing of prejudice to satisfy the "affecting substantial rights" prong of Rule 52(b). . . . [T]he discretion conferred by Rule 52(b) should be employed " 'in those circumstances in which a miscarriage of justice would otherwise result.' " . . . The court of appeals should correct a plain forfeited error affecting substantial rights if the error "seriously affect[s] the fairness, integrity or public reputation of judicial proceedings.' " 507 U.S. 732-36.

The Court concluded that the error here did *not* affect substantial rights and that the court of appeals therefore erred in treating it as plain error.

The Court continues to adhere to this view of the plain error doctrine (see *United States v. Cotton*, 525 U.S. 625 (2002)), with the refinement added by *Johnson v. United States*, 520 U.S. 461 (1997). In *Johnson*, appellant had been charged with knowingly making a false material declaration under oath before a grand jury. It was settled at the time of Johnson's trial that the issue of materiality was to be decided by the court, not the jury, but by the time of appellate consideration the law had changed: materiality had become an issue for the jury. That was enough to warrant review under the plain error doctrine.

In *Nguyen v. United States*, 539 U.S. 69 (2003), the Court vacated a judgment without assessing prejudice to the defendant because a judge of an Article IV territorial court had served on a panel with two Article III judges, an error that violated a statute embodying strong policy concerning the proper administration of judicial business. *See also* Derrick A. Carter, *A Restatement of Exceptions to the Preservation of Error Requirement in Criminal Cases*, 46 U. KAN. L. REV. 947 (1998).

2. Civil Appeals

It is controversial whether the plain error doctrine even applies to civil cases. The position taken in *Goldfuss v. Davidson*, 679 N.E.2d 1099 (Ohio 1997), is probably typical, if more elaborately articulated than usual:

> . . . We do not hold that application of the plain error doctrine may *never* be appropriate in civil cases. However, we do reaffirm and emphasize that the doctrine is sharply limited to the *extremely rare* case involving *exceptional* circumstances where the error, left unobjected to at the trial court, rises to the level of challenging the legitimacy of the underlying judicial process itself.

> . . . The plain error doctrine should never be applied to reverse a civil judgment simply because a reviewing court disagrees with the result obtained in the trial court, or to allow litigation of issues which could easily have been raised and determined in the initial trial.

> We . . . hold that in appeals of civil cases, the plain error doctrine is not favored and may be applied only in the extremely rare case involving exceptional circumstances where error, to which no objection was made at the trial court, seriously affects the basic fairness, integrity, or public reputation of the judicial process, thereby challenging the legitimacy of the underlying judicial process itself. . . .

NOTES

1. In *Sibbach v. Wilson & Co.*, 312 U.S. 1, 16 (1941), an action to recover damages for personal injuries, the trial court ordered the plaintiff to submit to a physical examination pursuant to FED. R. CIV. P. 35. The plaintiff refused, and the trial court ordered her committed for civil contempt. No objection was raised to the contempt citation on the ground that this sanction was not authorized. The Supreme Court, however, took note of the point, saying:

> Neither in the Circuit Court of Appeals nor here was this action assigned as error. We think, however, that in the light of the provisions of Rule 37 it was plain error of such a fundamental nature that we should notice it. Section (b)(2)(iv) of Rule 37 exempts from punishment as for contempt the refusal to obey an order that a party submit to a physical or mental examination. The District Court was in error in going counter to this express exemption. . . . For this error we reverse the judgement and remand the cause to the District Court for further proceedings in conformity to this opinion.

2. In *Berry v. Patrick*, 2005 Ohio 3708 (2005), the court found plain error in a trial court's failure to rule in a timely manner on a motion for a civil stalking protection order. In *Maddux v. Maddux*, 475 N.W.2d 524 (Neb. 1991), the court found plain error in the imposition of a punitive sanction, rather than a coercive sanction, in a civil contempt proceeding. In *Meredith Co. Development Co. v. Bennett*, 444 S.W.2d 519 (Mo. App. 1969), the court held it plain error to enter a judgment against an entity that had not been sued. In *Rojas v. Richardson*, 703 F.2d 186 (5th Cir. 1983), the court held that the "fairness, integrity, or public reputation" of the proceedings were undermined by the

closing argument of defense counsel who introduced irrelevant and unproven allegations that Rojas was an illegal alien, thereby appealing to racial or ethnic bias. But these cases are exceptional. What interests justified applying the plain error doctrine in each of these cases?

3. Should the plain error rule apply at all in civil cases? *Compare Dillipaine v. Lehigh Valley Trust Co.*, 322 A.2d 114 (Pa. 1974) (abolishing the plain error rule in civil cases); Robert J. Martineau, *Considering New Issues on Appeal: The General Rule and the Gorilla Rule*, 40 Vand. L. Rev. 1023, 1052-55 (1987) (arguing that the rationale underlying the plain error rule does not apply to civil cases because of waivers and because the due process requirements applicable to criminal cases do not apply to civil cases, in which due process requires only notice and opportunity to be heard) *with* 1 Chrisopher B. Mueller & Laird C. Kirkpatrick, Federal Evidence § 22, at 119 (2d ed. 1994) ("[Fed. R. Evid.] Rule 103 makes the plain error principle fully applicable to civil cases, and pre-Rules case law makes clear that plain error was not new to civil cases."); David William Navarro, *Jury Interrogatories And the Preservation Of Error In Federal Civil Cases: Should The Plain-Error Doctrine Apply?*, 30 St. Mary's L.J. 1163, 1218 (1999) (urging courts to apply the plain error exception to errors arising from jury interrogatories and to provide analysis and justification for the courts' conclusions, to guide other courts).

F. Harmless Error

In sharp contrast to those trial court actions that prompt an appellate court to address "plain errors," there are errors committed in the trial court that have so little effect on the parties' rights and the outcome of the case that they do not justify setting aside the judgment. Every jurisdiction has some variety of a "harmless error" rule. The following rules are typical expressions of this concept.

Fed. R.Civ.P. 61: **Harmless Error**

No error in either the admission or the exclusion of evidence and no error or defect in any ruling or order or in anything done or omitted by the court or by any of the parties is ground for granting a new trial or for setting aside a verdict or for vacating, modifying or otherwise disturbing a judgment or order, unless refusal to take such action appears to the court inconsistent with substantial justice. The court at every stage of the proceeding must disregard any error or defect in the proceeding which does not affect the substantial rights of the parties.

Fed. R. Crim. P. 52(a): **Harmless Error**

Any error, defect, irregularity, or variance that does not affect substantial rights must be disregarded.

28 U.S.C. § 2111: **Harmless Error**

On the hearing of any appeal or writ of certiorari in any case, the court shall give judgment after an examination of the record without regard to errors or defects which do not affect the substantial rights of the parties.

Roger Traynor, The Riddle of Harmless Error 14-16 (1970)[5]

When appellate courts retreated from their responsibility, becoming instead "impregnable citadels of technicality," lawyers played the game accordingly. "So great was the threat of reversal, in many jurisdictions, that criminal trial became a game for sowing reversible error in the record, only to have repeated the same matching of wits when a new trial had been thus obtained." At long last the legal profession itself sought reform, which finally materialized in harmless-error statutes enacted by the federal government and many states. . . .

There is obvious need of guidelines to control appellate discretion in the evaluation of error. They are not to be found in the broad directives of the harmless-error statutes. The federal statute [28 U.S.C. § 2111], for example, simply directs appellate courts to disregard harmless errors that do not "affect the substantial rights of the parties." Such language, although adequate in the case of inconsequential errors, provides no standards for determining when non-technical errors are harmless. A determination that an error has affected a substantial right does no more than set the stage for the basic inquiry: Was the error harmless? There are countless possible variations of error. There are also countless possible exponential factors that may determine what effect, if any, an error in the course of litigation may have upon a judgment.

It is reasonable to suppose that the draftsmen of such harmless-error statutes as the federal one were preoccupied not merely with putting technical error in its place, but also with precluding reversals when the denial or impairment of a substantial right has caused no injury. Given that objective, it is also reasonable to suppose that what the draftsmen meant by "affect" was "injuriously affect." The statutes would have better reflected their objective had the phrase "affect the judgment" been used instead of "affect the substantial rights of the parties," since any effect on the judgment attributable to error would injuriously affect the substantial rights of the parties. The judgment completes the picture in a diptych that begins with the substantial rights, and whatever mars the judgment mars the whole picture.

NOTES

1. In Justice Traynor's view, "[u]nless the appellate court believes it highly probable that the error did not affect the judgment, it should reverse." *Id.* at 35. This accords with the old, but still widely accepted, view stated by Justice Rutledge in *Kotteakos v. United States*, 328 U.S. 750 (1946):

> If, when all is said and done, the conviction is sure that the error did not influence the jury, or had but very slight effect, the verdict and the judgment should stand, except perhaps where the departure is from a constitutional norm or a specific command of Congress. But if one cannot say, with fair assurance, after pondering all that happened without stripping the erroneous action from the whole, that the judgment

---

[5] Copyright © 1970. Reprinted with permission of Michael Traynor, Executor/Trustee of the Estate/Trust of Roger J. Traynor.

was not substantially swayed by the error, it is impossible to conclude that substantial rights were not affected. The inquiry cannot be merely whether there was enough to support the result, apart from the phase affected by the error. It is rather, even so, whether the error itself had substantial influence. If so, or if one is left in grave doubt, the conviction cannot stand.

2. In view of the liberty interest at stake in criminal, but not in civil cases, courts do not necessarily approach the question of harmless error in the same way in criminal and civil cases. They also may take a different view when constitutionally protected rights allegedly have been violated than when non-constitutional errors are claimed. Until 1967, many courts and commentators believed that violations of constitutional rights never could be regarded as harmless error. But in *Chapman v. California*, 386 U.S. 18 (1967), involving a state criminal conviction, the Supreme Court took a less extreme position, although still a rigorous one. It held that, in order for a court to treat a violation of the federal Constitution in the course of a criminal trial as "harmless," the court must determine that the error was harmless beyond a reasonable doubt, with the prosecution having the burden of establishing the harmlessness of the error. Reversal is required absent the required showing. *See generally* Harry T. Edwards, *To Err is Human, But Not Always Harmless: When Should Legal Error Be Tolerated*, 70 N.Y.U. L. REV. 1167 (1995) (arguing for reviewing courts to determine whether error contaminated a verdict rather than assessing the guilt or innocence of a defendant in light of the untainted evidence); Stephen A. Saltzburg, *The Harm of Harmless Error*, 59 VA. L. REV. 988 (1973) (arguing that the test for harmless error should complement, not undermine, the burden of proof, and therefore advocating a different standard in criminal than in civil cases).

LAVINDER v. COMMONWEALTH
407 S.E.2d 910 (Va. Ct. App. 1991)

BARROW, J.

A rehearing *en banc* was granted in this appeal to consider what test applies in measuring whether a non-constitutional error is harmless. We conclude that, if it plainly appears from the facts and circumstances of a particular case that a non-constitutional error did not affect the verdict, the error is harmless.

In Virginia, non-constitutional error is harmless "[w]hen it *plainly appears* from the record and the evidence given at the trial that the parties have had a fair trial on the merits and substantial justice has been reached." Code § 8.01-678 (emphasis added). "[A] fair trial on the merits and substantial justice" are not achieved if an error at trial has affected the verdict. Consequently, under Code § 8.01-678, a criminal conviction must be reversed unless "it plainly appears from the record and the evidence given at the trial" that the error did not affect the verdict. An error does not affect a verdict if a reviewing court can conclude, without usurping the jury's fact finding function, that, had the error not occurred, the verdict would have been the same.

Constitutional error, on the other hand, is harmless only when the reviewing court is "able to declare a belief that it was harmless beyond a reasonable doubt.". . . . The federal standard is not required, however, for a non-constitutional error . . . *Mu'Min v. Commonwealth*, 389 S.E.2d 886, 892 n.4 (1990), *aff'd*, [500 U.S. 415] (1991). While the federal standard expressly adopts "beyond a reasonable doubt" as the reviewing court's required level of confidence, the statutory standard for non-constitutional error does not.

Use of the "beyond a reasonable doubt" standard, while an appropriate measure of confidence in fact finding, is an unusual device to use in deciding questions of law. Like "preponderance of the evidence" and "clear and convincing evidence," "beyond a reasonable doubt" is a relative and subjective standard suitable for measuring the probability of the occurrence of a past event. But, in determining if an error is harmless, a reviewing court does not decide the probability of the occurrence of a past event, i.e., if, in fact, the defendant committed the crime charged. It determines, instead, whether, as a matter of law, this decision by the fact finder was affected by the error. If so, the error is not harmless; if not, the error is harmless.

In making this decision with respect to non-constitutional error, the level of confidence used by a reviewing court is not "beyond a reasonable doubt." It is, instead, whether "it plainly appears from the record and the evidence given at trial," a more absolute measure and one more suitable for application to questions of law.

This does not mean, however, that the burden of proof at trial is not a consideration in a harmless error analysis. Even though the burden of proof at trial is not part of the test for measuring whether non-constitutional error is harmless, a reviewing court must take into account the burden of proof applied at trial when evaluating the impact of an error upon a verdict. . . .

Code § 8.01-678 applies to both civil and criminal cases. By requiring a reviewing court to consider the applicable burden of proof at trial, the provisions of Code § 8.01-678 can be applied to both civil and criminal cases. . . . A civil case having a burden of proof with a lower degree of certainty than that required in a criminal case generally will not be tested for harmless error with the higher degree of certainty required by the burden of proof for criminal cases. Similarly, a criminal case requiring a higher degree of certainty in the burden of proof should not be tested for harmless error with the lower degree of certainty required by the burden of proof in civil cases. . . .

In criminal cases, the requirement of proof beyond a reasonable doubt is a constitutional requirement of due process. . . . Only by considering the burden of proof applied at trial when determining harmless error on appeal can this constitutional requirement be preserved.

In this case, in order to determine if it plainly appears that the error did not affect the verdict, we must review the record and the evidence and evaluate the effect the error may have had on how the finder of fact resolved the contested issues. The defendant was tried for robbery of a music store employee who was on his way to make a night deposit at a bank. . . .

During cross-examination, the defendant admitted that while he was a juvenile he had been found not innocent of two felonies. The trial court previously had ruled . . . over the defendant's objection, that the prosecutor could ask the defendant on cross-examination whether he had been found not innocent of these offenses.

This was error, but not one of constitutional dimension. . . . [T]he prosecution's cross-examination was limited by a policy of preserving a juvenile offender's anonymity as expressed in Virginia's juvenile law.

In determining whether this error could have affected the verdict, we must first determine whether the trial court gave a curative instruction. If it gave a curative instruction to the jury, the jury is presumed to have followed "an explicit cautionary instruction promptly given" unless the record shows otherwise. . . . If, however, the trial court did not give a curative instruction, the error is presumed to be prejudicial "unless it plainly appears that it could not have affected the result.". . .

In this case, there was no instruction to the jury directing them to disregard the defendant's juvenile record. In fact, the trial court instructed the jury that it could consider the evidence "as affecting his credibility." Consequently, we begin our analysis by considering the error prejudicial unless it plainly appears from the record and the evidence that the verdict was not affected by the error.

The decisive issue presented by the evidence at trial was whether the defendant was the perpetrator of the crime. The victim and a person who was with the victim said that the defendant was the robber. The other witnesses placed the defendant at the vicinity of the crime. These witnesses did not see any tattoos on the exposed arms of the robber even though the defendant has four tattoos on his arms. They did not see an injured ear on the robber even though the defendant had severely lacerated his ear eight days earlier which had required surgery and remained swollen and discolored. There were discrepancies in the testimony regarding height and hair color of the defendant. The defendant and three eyewitnesses testified that he was at home at the time of the robbery.

Only if the jury believed the eyewitnesses who said that the defendant was the robber or in the vicinity of the robbery and did not believe the defendant and the three witnesses who corroborated him, could it have found him guilty. The defendant's testimony was critical. If it believed the defendant or could not decide whom to believe, it would have had to acquit him. Impeachment of the defendant, therefore, may have been a basis upon which the jury chose not to believe him. In addition, had the jury found the defendant's testimony incredible, it was entitled to infer that he had lied to conceal his guilt. . . . Impeachment of the defendant, therefore, was an independent basis upon which the jury could have arrived at its verdict. We cannot say that impeachment of the defendant's exculpatory testimony was harmless.

In summary, evidence of the defendant's prior juvenile record offered to impeach his testimony, if successful in achieving its purpose, could have affected the verdict. We cannot say, therefore, that, in spite of the erroneous admission of this evidence, "it plainly appears from the record and the evidence given at trial that the parties have had a fair trial on the merits and substantial justice has been reached." Consequently, the judgment of conviction is reversed and the proceeding is remanded for a new trial.

Reversed and remanded.

KEENAN, J., concurring.

I believe that the test for review of non-constitutional error articulated by the majority is far more rigid than that provided by Code § 8.01-678. Further, while the majority expressly states that it does not apply the "harmless beyond a reasonable doubt" standard of *Chapman v. California* . . . to evaluate non-constitutional error, I believe that its standard is also more stringent than *Chapman*.

Code § 8.01-678 directs that the trial record be reviewed as a whole in determining whether trial error necessitates reversal of a cause. . . . This [statute] requires the reviewing court to consider the nature of the error committed, in the context of the entire case, to determine whether the parties have had a fair trial and substantial justice has been reached. In contrast, the majority opinion requires the reviewing court to consider the fact finder's original burden of proof in weighing the error and presume that the error is prejudicial unless the record affirmatively shows that it did not affect the result.

Code § 8.01-678, however, does not require that the record affirmatively show that the error did not affect the verdict. Nevertheless, the majority imposes this requirement. . . . I believe that such a requirement is more stringent than the *Chapman* standard . . . because this standard requires the reviewing court to find with certainty that the error had no effect upon the verdict, rather than simply finding beyond a reasonable doubt that the error was harmless. Even under the standard of review for constitutional error, "harmless beyond a reasonable doubt," the reviewing court is not required to disclaim every possibility that the error may have influenced a juror's consideration of the case, but only that no reasonable doubt exists upon the whole record that the verdict was affected by the error. Justice Traynor has said that non-constitutional error is harmless when it is "highly probable that the error did not affect the judgment." R. TRAYNOR, THE RIDDLE OF HARMLESS ERROR 34-35 (1976). I believe that is but yet another way of saying that it "plainly appears . . . the parties have had a fair trial on the merits and substantial justice has been reached."

An appellate court must consider the error and evaluate its effect, if any, upon how the fact finder weighed and balanced the evidence or resolved the credibility of witnesses. Thus, while the appellate court, in considering whether error is harmless, does not weigh and balance the evidence in the role of fact finder to determine whether guilt has been proven beyond a reasonable doubt, it does evaluate how the error may have affected the weight of evidence and credibility of witnesses in deciding whether, in accordance with the mandate of Code § 8.01-678, "the parties have had a fair trial on the merits and substantial justice has been reached." . . .

I would find that a fair trial was not had on the merits. . . . Accordingly, I concur in the majority's decision to reverse and remand. . . .

NOTES

In *Commonwealth v. Story*, 383 A.2d 155 (Pa. 1978), the court held that it would apply the federal standard for constitutional errors in criminal cases to determine whether state law errors were harmless:

[W]e hold that the proper standard for determining whether an error involving state law is harmless is the same as the standard this Court applies to federal constitutional error. . . .

Several considerations persuade us that the "beyond a reasonable doubt" standard is the proper standard to apply in determining the harmlessness of *any* criminal trial error. First, *this standard is commensurate with the standard of proof in criminal trials* — that an accused cannot be convicted unless the trier of fact is convinced beyond a reasonable doubt that the accused is guilty as charged. . . . In order to maintain the integrity of this standard, appellate courts should utilize a comparable standard in determining whether an error was harmless. . . .

Second, there are sound reasons for applying the same standard for determining harmless error whether the error violates state or federal law. State rules often implicate constitutional values, and the violation of a state rule may rise to the level of a federal constitutional violation. The protection of constitutional rights, as well as the development of a coherent doctrine of harmless error, militate in favor of the application of the same standard for constitutional and non-constitutional errors. Because it may be unclear whether a well established state rule is also constitutionally mandated, separate harmless error standards might prove to be unworkable. Moreover, a more relaxed harmless error standard for errors perceived as violations of state rules, but which might also be violations of the federal Constitution, would leave constitutional values inadequately protected.

Third, it is irrelevant whether an error is constitutional or non-constitutional in determining whether the error is prejudicial to the accused. Constitutional errors are not inherently more injurious to an accused than errors under state law. There is no reason why a state court should apply a stricter harmless error standard to federal constitutional rules than to state rules, especially since the purpose of most state rules is to assure a fair trial.

Finally, there is the danger that a lenient harmless error rule may denigrate the interests and policies which both constitutional and non-constitutional rules promote. We are convinced that the "beyond a reasonable doubt" standard reaches the proper balance of competing considerations implicated in the harmless error rule.

Id. at 164-65.

HADDAD v. LOCKHEED CALIFORNIA CORPORATION
720 F.2d 1454 (9th Cir. 1983)

NELSON, Circuit Judge:

Appellant Robert Haddad appeals from the district court's judgment on his [federal] national origin discrimination claim, and from the jury's verdict on his [federal] age discrimination in employment claim. Both claims arise from the same allegedly improper acts by appellee Lockheed. [Both claims were decided in favor of appellee Lockheed.] Despite the admission of improper evidence at trial, we affirm both the court's judgment and the jury's verdict. . . .

Appellant Robert Haddad worked for appellee Lockheed California Corporation from early 1969 until his resignation in July 1979. Appellant claims that while in Lockheed's employ he was subject to a variety of forms of disparate treatment. This treatment, appellant alleged below, was the product of discrimination on the basis of national origin and age. . . .

Appellant bases his appeal on purported errors in the district court's jury instructions and evidentiary rulings. . . . Appellant's third claim, involving the admission of testimony in violation of appellant's marital privilege, merits fuller consideration as it calls into question the proper standard for determining harmless error in a civil trial. . . .

Haddad next attacks the admission of certain testimony of his ex-wife, claiming that such evidence was protected by the confidential marital communication privilege. The privilege properly protects the marital communication about which the witness testified. Lockheed failed to overcome the presumption in favor of applying the privilege. Therefore, the district court should have excluded this testimony. Since this evidence is cumulative of other evidence in the record and the record contains no evidence to the contrary, we presume that the improper admission of this testimony had no effect on the court's decision rejecting Haddad's national origin discrimination claim. Thus, we affirm the court's decision on this claim.

The improper admission of Haddad's ex-wife's testimony poses a more serious problem for the jury verdict on Haddad's age discrimination claim. A jury, unlike a judge, cannot be presumed to have based its verdict only on properly admitted evidence. Our task, then, is to determine whether the evidentiary error committed below affected a "substantial right" of appellant and so requires reversal of the age discrimination verdict. 28 U.S.C. § 2111 (1976); FED. R. EVID. 103(a); FED. R. CIV. P. 61. . . .

As an initial inquiry, we must determine what standard to use to determine whether the error in this case was sufficient to require reversal. Some errors involve "constitutional rights so basic to a fair trial that their infraction can never be treated as harmless error." A second type of constitutional error does not involve the fundamental integrity of the judicial process but does implicate the constitutional rights of the criminally accused. These errors must be shown by an appellate court to be harmless beyond a reasonable doubt.

It would be possible to end our inquiry here merely by distinguishing the error in the case at bar from the constitutional errors discussed in *Chapman*. This court first stressed the importance of such a distinction in dicta, and suggested that the harmlessness of trial error might be gauged under two standards: harmless beyond a reasonable doubt for constitutional errors and more probably than not harmless for non-constitutional errors. . . .

Despite its convenience, we will not rely on the reasoning [above] to resolve the open question of what standard of harmlessness should prevail in a civil appeal.[6] Neither the distinction between constitutional and non-constitutional error nor the strictly bifurcated standard of harmlessness it creates has been uniformly accepted. Courts frequently avoid relying on the distinction by finding harmlessness under all standards. Commentators have cautioned against making the standard for harmless error turn entirely on a distinction between constitutional and non-constitutional error. Finally, we are not certain that application of the more lenient standard to errors involving the improper admission of evidence in a criminal trial can be reconciled with the Supreme Court's language in *Chapman:* "An error in admitting plainly relevant evidence which possibly influenced the jury adversely to a litigant cannot . . . be conceived of as harmless." 386 U.S. at 23-24. Because of our concern that courts' adoption of this bifurcated standard of harmlessness may have occurred through misinterpretation of *Chapman* and *Valle-Valdez*, we decline to perpetuate the mistake by extending the analysis to civil cases. We therefore put this distinction to one side, and address directly the question before us: How probable must the harm from an error in a civil trial be before it affects substantial rights and thus requires reversal?[7]

The purpose of a harmless error standard is to enable an appellate court to gauge the probability that the trier of fact was affected by the error. Perhaps the most important factor to consider in fashioning such a standard is the nature of the particular fact-finding process to which the standard is to be applied. Accordingly, a crucial first step in determining how we should gauge the probability that an error was harmless is recognizing the distinction between civil and criminal trials. This distinction has two facets, each of which reflects the differing burdens of proof in civil and criminal cases. First, the lower burden of proof in civil cases implies a larger margin of error. The danger of the harmless error doctrine is that an appellate court may usurp the jury's function, by merely deleting improper evidence from the record and assessing the sufficiency of the evidence to support the verdict below. This danger has less practical importance where, as in most civil cases, the jury verdict merely rests on a more probable than not standard of proof.

The second facet of the distinction between errors in civil and criminal trials involves the differing degrees of certainty owed to civil and criminal litigants. Whereas a criminal defendant must be found guilty beyond a reasonable doubt, a civil litigant merely has a right to a jury verdict that more probably than not corresponds to the truth.

The civil litigant's lessened entitlement to veracity continues when the litigant becomes an appellant. We conclude that a proper harmless error standard for civil cases should reflect the burden of proof. Just as the verdict

---

[6] [3] Which standard an appellate court selects depends on the type case on appeal — criminal or civil — or on the type of error committed in the trial court — constitutional or nonconstitutional. We agree with this general observation except that we believe that the inquiry should be described in the conjunctive, not the disjunctive. In other words, we will not treat the kind of error committed below as dispositive in establishing the standard of harmlessness in a civil case.

[7] [7] Where an error could have been and was the subject of an objection at trial, then appellate courts have three possible standards of review: harmless beyond a reasonable doubt; high probability of harmlessness; and more probably than not harmless. Our present task is to determine which of these standards properly applies to review of an evidentiary error in a civil case.

in a civil case need only be more probably than not true, so an error in a civil trial need only be more probably than not harmless. In other words, when an appellate court ponders the probable effect of an error on a civil trial, it need only find that the jury's verdict is more probably than not untainted by the error. . . .

In the case at bar, appellant had a "substantial right" to a jury determination as to whether the treatment accorded him by Lockheed was more probably than not the product of age discrimination. Our task on appeal is to determine whether the evidentiary error of which appellant complains has deprived appellant of the degree of certainty to which he is entitled. Although not beyond a reasonable doubt harmless,[8] the error in this case more probably than not had no effect on the jury's rejection of Haddad's age discrimination claim. We therefore hold the admission of privileged testimony in this case to have been harmless and we affirm the jury's verdict below.

Our assessment of the probable harmlessness of Mrs. Haddad's testimony rests partially on the relation between that testimony and the factual issues underlying Haddad's age discrimination claim. Mrs. Haddad improperly testified to the effect that in 1977 Haddad told her that he intended to resign from Lockheed and go into . . . business with his brother. This testimony might have harmed Haddad by tending to undercut his claim that he was constructively discharged in 1979 and by casting suspicion on his work attitudes during his last two years at Lockheed. However, constructive discharge was just a small part of appellant's disparate treatment claim. Moreover, although Haddad's "abrasive" personality was frequently discussed, Haddad's commitment to his work was not a point of contention. The eight-day trial focused primarily on the specific Lockheed employment practices described in Haddad's complaint.

Haddad's age discrimination claim recited a catalogue of grievances: no promotion in salary grade in ten-and-one-half years; improper distribution of merit raises to those within his salary grade; the imposition of travel restrictions and record-keeping requirements; the imposition of telephone use restrictions; the rejection of appellant's suggestions for company improvements; the referral of appellant to the company doctor. To each of these specific complaints of disparate treatment, Lockheed responded with non-discriminatory explanations. . . .

---

8 [8] We cannot say that Mrs. Haddad's testimony was harmless beyond a reasonable doubt. It is reasonably possible that the jury could have discredited Haddad's description of his work conditions if it suspected that Haddad had been planning to leave Lockheed two years before his actual departure. Still, we conclude that the testimony was more probably than not harmless. Although the credibility of a plaintiff undoubtedly has great impact on a jury verdict, in this case it was the credibility of Lockheed's witnesses that was crucial. Haddad had apparently made a *prima facie* case of age discrimination and the task of the jury was to determine whether . . . Lockheed's non-discriminatory explanations were mere pretext.

Mrs. Haddad's testimony was not only largely tangential to an evaluation of Lockheed's employment practices, it was also partially cumulative of other competent testimony regarding Haddad's attitudes towards Lockheed. Even without Mrs. Haddad's testimony, the jury was probably aware that Haddad was considering alternative careers in 1977. Many witnesses testified to Haddad's dissatisfaction with his salary during and prior to 1977. Haddad himself testified that he obtained a real estate license in 1977. Haddad also testified that he engaged in consulting and in the practice of real estate in 1979, immediately after leaving Lockheed. Mrs. Haddad's testimony may have reinforced the suspicion that Haddad was planning to leave Lockheed in 1977, but it probably did not create that suspicion.

The minimal extent to which counsel emphasized Mrs. Haddad's testimony to the jury supports our conclusion that the error in this case was more probably than not harmless. Counsel for Haddad and counsel for Lockheed had numerous discussions before the judge as to whether Mrs. Haddad was to testify at all. Nevertheless, these confrontations, although perhaps showing the value Lockheed placed on Mrs. Haddad's testimony, were out of the jury's hearing. Lockheed's counsel examined Mrs. Haddad for a very short period. The purpose of this examination seems to have been to show that Haddad was under substantial personal pressure during his last two years at Lockheed. In his closing argument, Lockheed's counsel mentioned Mrs. Haddad's testimony only briefly, suggesting that it showed Haddad's emotional strain in 1977. The overwhelming thrust of Lockheed's closing argument, like the overwhelming bulk of the trial, dealt with a point by point analysis of Lockheed's employment practices.

AFFIRMED.

NOTES

1. What policies underlie the harmless error doctrine?

2. Are you persuaded by the *Story* court's analysis? Do you think that the federal standard for determining the harmlessness of federal constitutional errors in criminal cases should be applied by state appellate courts to state law errors committed in criminal cases? What should the standard for determining the harmlessness of errors be in civil cases? How easy is it to capture the appropriate judgment in a word formula? Justice Rutledge in *Kotteakos v. United States*, 328 U.S. 750 (1946), wrote: "[T]he discrimination [that the harmless error doctrine] requires is one of judgment transcending confinement by formula or precise rule. . . . That faculty [judgment] cannot ever be wholly imprisoned in words, much less upon such a criterion as what are only technical, what substantial rights."

3. Claims of error in the admission or exclusion of evidence frequently are analyzed for the harmlessness of the errors. Errors in jury instructions also may be harmless, as may rulings on the wide range of matters that may come before trial courts. What circumstances can you imagine in which errors in jury instructions may be harmless? Would it be easier to demonstrate harmless error in the grant of a jury trial or in the denial of one?

II. STANDARDS OF REVIEW

J. Dickson Phillips, Jr., *The Appellate Review Function: Scope of Review*, 47 LAW AND CONTEMPORARY PROBLEMS 1 (1984)[9]

Although they operate within some legislatively imposed constraints on their powers of review, appellate courts basically control the timing, the standards, and the scope of review of trial court decisions. By these means of control, appellate courts effectively order the ongoing functional relationship between the trial and appellate levels of a judicial system. The resulting jurisprudence of appellate practice and procedure is obviously an important body of adjective law, but it is a surprisingly unsystematic and relatively obscure one. Only in the aspect touching the timing of interlocutory review — the appealability of nonfinal orders — is there a fairly well-developed and readily accessible jurisprudence comparable to that developed in most areas of trial court procedure.

The other two aspects (those concerned with the standards and scope of review) represent the two dimensions which actually define the appellate review function at large. Standards of review — "clear error," abuse of discretion, and *de novo* review, for example — define the depth or intensity with which trial court rulings of fact, law, and discretion are subjected to review. Scope of review — which specific trial court actions or omissions are properly subject to review on a given appeal — defines the breadth of the review function.

As between the latter two aspects of the review function, the jurisprudence of standards is relatively the more systematically developed and accessible. The jurisprudence of scope is the least systematically developed and readily accessible of the three aspects.

———

Implicit in the effort to formulate rational and workable standards of review is acceptance of the principle that the reviewing court should subordinate its own view and defer to the trial court's decision in some situations and to some degree. Thus, standards of review address two issues: whether the appellate court should defer to the trial court and, if so, to what extent. They produce a four-way classification of the nature of issues on appeal: questions of fact; questions of law; mixed questions; and questions of discretion. With regard to each category, the degree of deference accorded the trial judge is designed to promote the better functioning of the judicial process. In some circumstances, it has been believed, the trial judge is in a better position to make a correct decision than are appellate judges even though there normally are three appellate judges and only one trial judge. The various standards of review and their application in the federal appellate courts are analyzed at length in 1 CHILDRESS & DAVIS, FEDERAL STANDARDS OF REVIEW chs. 2-4 (3d. ed. 1999).

———

[9] Copyright © 1984 by Duke University School of Law and J. Dickson Phillips Jr. Reprinted with permission.

A. Distinguishing Questions of Law from Questions of Fact

On questions of law an appellate court's deference to the trial court is at its minimum. A typical statement appears in *Watzek v. Walker*, 485 P.2d 3 (Ariz. Ct. App. 1971): "This Court on appeal will normally not disturb a trial court judgment if there is any reasonable evidence supporting it. Yet, in reviewing questions of law, we are not bound by the findings of the trial court but are free to draw our own legal conclusions from the evidence presented." It often is said that appellate courts review questions of law "*de novo*," meaning that they give no deference at all to the trial court's decision. Why is this so?

By contrast, the Federal Rule set forth below is typical of the courts' approach to the review of fact finding by judges.

Fed. R. Civ. P. 52 Findings by the Court; Judgment on Partial Findings

(a) Effect. In all actions tried upon the facts without a jury or with an advisory jury, the court shall find the facts specially and state separately its conclusions of law thereon, and judgment shall be entered pursuant to Rule 58; and in granting or refusing interlocutory injunctions the court shall similarly set forth the findings of fact and conclusions of law which constitute the grounds of its action. Requests for findings are not necessary for purposes of review. Findings of fact, whether based on oral or documentary evidence, shall not be set aside unless clearly erroneous, and due regard shall be given to the opportunity of the trial court to judge of the credibility of the witnesses. . . .

Given this law-fact dichotomy, it becomes important for an appellate court to distinguish questions of law from questions of fact. The distinction has bedeviled the courts for decades. There are, of course, some clear-cut situations. But in many instances there is no bright line, and decisions are difficult to reconcile. As you study the cases below, consider why the particular question involved in the appeal is labeled as one of "fact," thus giving it a considerable measure of immunity from appellate reversal, or as one of "law" on which the appellate court is free to substitute its judgment for that of the trial judge.

VILLAGE OF WEYAUWEGA v. KRAMER
192 N.W. 452 (Wis. 1923)

[John P. Kramer suffered fatal injuries when he fell while painting a bridge located in Weyauwega and his widow claimed compensation. The village board had directed its road and bridge committee to hire someone to paint the bridge. Kramer submitted the most favorable bid and was given the job. The two parties did not sign a written agreement of any type. Kramer was merely directed to "go to it whenever he got around to it." Neither did the board discuss whether Kramer would do the work himself or employ assistants to help him.

The Industrial Commission decided that Kramer had been an employee of the village at the time of his death and granted compensation to his widow.

After the circuit court for Dane County affirmed, the village and the insurer appealed.]

OWEN, J.

In order to entitle the claimant to compensation, the relation of employer and employee must have existed between the village and Kramer at the time the injury was sustained. Appellant contends that the relation was not that of employer and employee, but that the relation of Kramer to the Village was that of an independent contractor. This is the sole question presented.

It is contended, on the part of the respondent, that the question presented is one of fact, that the evidence is such as to justify different inferences, and that the finding of the Industrial Commission is conclusive. If different inferences may reasonably be drawn from the evidence, even though it be undisputed, then a question of fact is presented, and the conclusion of the Industrial Commission cannot be disturbed. Whether under a given situation the relation is that of an employee or independent contractor is often a question of fact for the jury. Where the evidence is undisputed, it is not always easy to determine whether the conclusion to be drawn therefrom is one of fact or of law. Where the conclusion describes a legal status or condition, it is ordinarily denominated a conclusion of law. Whether a finding is an ultimate fact or conclusion of law depends upon whether it is reached by natural reasoning or by the application of fixed rules of law. . . . This court has held that, where there is no conflict in the evidence, the determination of the status of one who claims to have been an employee is a conclusion of law. . . . We are convinced that the evidence before the Commission did not present a question of fact. The terms of the employment were simple and undisputed. Kramer agreed to paint the bridge for $75. He was to do it in his own way and at his own convenience. Under the agreement he was at liberty to do the work himself or hire others to assist him. The village reserved no control over the details of the work. When the bridge was painted, Kramer was entitled to $75. He could not have been discharged at the whim or caprice of the village. Did this in law constitute him an independent contractor? . . .

Numerous tests have been suggested and applied by the courts to assist in the determination of whether a given status is that of an employee or independent contractor, perhaps the most significant of which is whether the employer has the right to control the details of the work. . . . The right to control the details of the work is to be distinguished from such supervision or inspection as may be necessary to secure the ultimate result. . . . It is clear from the record that the village reserved no right to control the details of the work. Not only that, but it appears the contract was let in this manner for the express purpose of relieving the members of the committee from any responsibility in that respect. Thus one of the members of the committee who made the arrangement with Kramer testified that —

> The bridge committee didn't care to be bothered to look after the day work, and that was the reason we asked to have it done by the job, to know what we was going to pay for it, and settled finally.

> Q. And you can tell us why it was you didn't hire day laborers to paint the bridge?

A. Why, because Mr. Reick and myself on the committee, we didn't want to look after the day labor part of it to keep account of it day by day, and that was the only reason we wanted to know what we was going to pay for the whole job, rather than be bothered looking after it by day labor.

And again:

The $75 charge was simply the plan selected by me and the other member of the committee, in order that we wouldn't be compelled to keep the hours on the work.

This indicates that the committee desired to give the job to a responsible person, one in whom they had confidence, and one over whom they would be required to exercise no detailed supervision. It appears that what was desired or required to be done was talked over before the agreement. This is shown by the following testimony of the same witness:

Well, I think all I told him was to clean the dirt off underneath the bridge, underneath the iron work there was a lot of dirt that had to be cleaned off first.

Q. And then painted?

A. That is all and he should scratch off the old scales, if there was any old paint.

Q. That was the understanding originally?

A. Yes sir.

Q. After that there were no more directions given?

A. No.

Q. He went ahead and started painting the bridge?

A. He went ahead and started painting the bridge; yes. . . .

Th[e] position [that the village had the right to control the details of Kramer's work] . . . is untenable, in view of the fact that the understanding was had prior to the execution of the contract, and prescribed the work which Kramer was expected to do. It is not contended that any power was reserved on the part of the committee or the village board to direct the manner in which the dirt should be cleaned off or the scales scratched off, or what part of the bridge should be painted first, or the kind of a brush that should be used, or any other detail that might arise in the prosecution of the work. That was all left to Kramer.

In *Madix v. Hochgreve Brewing Co.*, 154 Wis. 448, 143 N.W. 189, it is said:

Other significant characteristics of an independent contractor are that he is usually engaged in carrying on an independent employment or business, and customarily contracts to do a given piece of work for a specified sum of money, and is responsible for the result thereof, while a servant usually works by the hour, day, week, or month, and is not responsible for the result of the work, beyond performing his own labor in a workmanlike manner.

Here, Kramer undertook to do "a given piece of work for a specified sum of money." He was responsible for the result thereof. He was no doubt required to do the job in a good workmanlike manner, in order to entitle him to the stipulated compensation.

The village could no doubt quarrel with him about the result, but the record is barren of any evidence to indicate that it could interfere with or direct the manner of accomplishing the result. That it was customary for him to enter into such contracts is indicated by the testimony of the claimant, who said:

> He did other jobs on the basis of taking the work by the job. I do not know how many he might have had of such jobs. He always did the work himself. I never knew him in the last year prior to his death to take a job and have others help him with the work. I never knew that he took jobs on a contract basis where he hired helpers.

It is claimed that he was expected to do the work personally. We cannot see that that is very significant. Of course, where it appears that the nature of the work is such that the employment of others is necessary to accomplish it, the conclusion that one who undertakes to do the work is an independent contractor may be more readily reached, where other circumstances render the situation doubtful. However, we do not regard it as a weighty consideration in the present case. But, even though it were material, the testimony of one of the members of the committee who appeared, as before stated, on behalf of the claimant indicates that Kramer was at liberty to hire others if he desired. . . .

Cases involving facts very similar, if not identical, with those here presented, have frequently been before the courts, and the status of the one undertaking the employment under such circumstances has almost universally been held to be that of an independent contractor. . . .

Because it must be held as a matter of law that relation existing between the deceased and the village was that of proprietor and independent contractor and not that of employer and employee, it follows that the award cannot stand.

Judgment reserved, and cause remanded, with instructions to enter judgment vacating the award of the Industrial Commission.

NOTES

1. Suppose the witnesses had disagreed about what was said between Kramer and the village officials concerning whether the village was to exercise day-to-day supervision over the details of his work. Would the question as to whether Kramer was an employee or an independent contractor still be one of law and not of fact?

2. Litigated cases always have both factual and legal components. In *Village of Weyauwega*, what were the factual components? What was the court required to decide in order to resolve the case?

3. In *Village of Weyauwega* the court said that "[i]f different inferences may reasonably be drawn from the evidence, even though it be undisputed, then a question of fact is presented. . . ." Is this a reliable test for distinguishing

factual from legal questions? Consider this point again in connection with *United States v. McConney, infra.*

4. Assume this case were tried to a jury. At the close of all the evidence, the defendant moved for judgment as a matter of law under a rule like Rule 50 of the Federal Rules of Civil Procedure. How does the question presented by that motion compare with the question presented in the appellate court in the actual case?

5. Assume that, before the trial, the defendant moved for summary judgment, putting before the court the evidence described in the foregoing opinion. How would the question presented by that motion compare with the question presented in the appellate court in the actual case?

LONG v. SCHULL
439 A.2d 975 (Conn. 1981)

PER CURIAM.

The underlying facts in this case are as follows: The plaintiff's decedent, Ethel Mae Schull, entered the hospital in early March, 1975, for an ailment soon diagnosed as terminal cancer. On March 31, 1975, after she was informed of her condition and while still in the hospital, the plaintiff's decedent executed a power of attorney in favor of her stepson, the defendant, Andrea C. Schull. [The relevant portion of the power of attorney provided: "To do each and every act pertaining to my property or providing for my personal care and comfort and payment of the cost thereof, as fully as I might do if personally present and . . . sign and endorse checks, drafts, money orders, withdrawal orders and any other papers and documents in my name and for me and in my name to sign, seal, execute and deliver any and all deeds, mortgages, documents and papers of every description pertaining in any way to any of my property real or personal or to my safety deposit box, to hold and manage all my money and property of every kind, real and personal as fully as I might do if personally present and able."] The defendant obtained and presented the document, which was prepared by a legal secretary, to his stepmother at her request. Apparently, she desired to give the defendant the control of her possessions, but at the same time avoid any dealings with attorneys. After the plaintiff's decedent executed the power of attorney, she told the defendant where she had hidden her will and several savings account passbooks and instructed him to retrieve them. The defendant obtained possession of these items, and with the power of attorney, withdrew the funds from the savings accounts, depositing the money in accounts in his name, his wife's name, or both. He also disbursed funds from his stepmother's checking account. The parties stipulated that the total sum of money involved amounted to $25,001.64.

Both prior and subsequent to the plaintiff's decedent's death, a small amount of the money was disbursed from the checking account for the upkeep and maintenance of her home and to pay her outstanding bills. After her death, the defendants donated a large portion of the sum to religious organizations and for a holy spirit conference at the New Haven Coliseum. They expended the remainder for their own personal use, including a family trip to California.

On April 20, 1975, the plaintiff's decedent died, leaving a will, which had been executed on March 8, 1971. It named as executrix the plaintiff, Mary Long, sister of the testatrix and the primary beneficiary under the will. The plaintiff lived in Ohio and her contact with her sister consisted of letter writing, telephone calls and infrequent visits. The plaintiff, as the executrix of the estate of Ethel Mae Schull, commenced this action to recover the $25,001.64.

During the trial, conflicting testimony was offered by the parties. The defendants claimed that after the testatrix became aware of her condition, she intended to make a gift of her money to them. To support their position, they introduced the power of attorney and verbal expressions of her donative intent. On the other hand, the plaintiff attacked the credibility of the defendants and claimed that the defendants' right to the testatrix' funds was limited by the power of attorney and that they had wrongfully converted the money to their own use. The parties also offered conflicting versions of the relationship between the testatrix and the defendants, of the relationship between the testatrix and the plaintiff, and of the strength of the testatrix's religious faith. There was also a question whether the defendant closed out the testatrix's savings accounts before or after her death.

The trial court focused on the credibility of the witnesses and found the defendants' testimony "totally incredible and unworthy of belief." It concluded that no gift of the funds had been made to the defendants and that only $800 of the $25,001.64 had been spent within the authority of the power of attorney. It also concluded that the power of attorney terminated at the testatrix's death so that the balance of the money disbursed by the defendants actually belonged to the estate and had been wrongfully expended. Consequently, it rendered judgment in favor of the plaintiff in the amount of $24,201.64. The defendants have appealed from that judgment, raising three claims of error.

The first issue is whether the plaintiff's decedent had made a gift to the defendants. On appeal, the defendants argue that a gift had been made to them as a matter of law. When an estate is a party, the burden is on the person claiming the gift to prove the claim by clear and satisfactory proof. The question of whether a gift inter vivos or causa mortis has been made is within the exclusive province of the court. The determination of whether a gift has been made is not reviewable unless the conclusion of the court is one which cannot reasonably be made. The credibility of the witnesses and the weight to be accorded to their testimony is for the trier of fact. This court does not try issues of fact or pass upon the credibility of witnesses. The court's conclusion that no gift had been made to the defendants is not clearly erroneous in light of the evidence, the credibility of the witnesses, and the record. This conclusion cannot be overruled. . . .

There is no error.

NOTES

Why was the question of "independent contractor" deemed a question of law in *Village of Weyauwega*, while the question of "gift" in *Long* was deemed a question of fact?

PULLMAN-STANDARD v. SWINT
456 U.S. 273 (1982)

JUSTICE WHITE delivered the opinion of the Court.

Respondents were black employees at the Bessemer, Ala., plant of petitioner Pullman-Standard (the Company), a manufacturer of railway freight cars and parts. They brought suit against the Company and the union petitioners — the United Steelworkers of America, AFL-CIO-CLC, and its Local 1466 (collectively USW) — alleging violations of Title VII of the Civil Rights Act of 1964 and 42 U.S.C. §1981. As they come here, these cases involve only the validity, under Title VII, of a seniority system maintained by the Company and USW. The District Court found "that the differences in terms, conditions or privileges of employment resulting [from the seniority system] are 'not the result of an intention to discriminate' because of race or color," . . . and held, therefore, that the system satisfied the requirements of §703(h) of the Act. The Court of Appeals for the Fifth Circuit reversed:

> Because we find that the differences in the terms, conditions and standards of employment for black workers and white workers at Pullman-Standard resulted from an intent to discriminate because of race, we hold that the system is not legally valid under section 703(h) of Title VII, 42 U.S.C. § 2000e-2(h).

We granted the petitions for certiorari filed by USW and by the Company limited to the first question presented in each petition: whether a court of appeals is bound by the "clearly erroneous" rule of Federal Rule of Civil Procedure 52(a) in reviewing a district court's findings of fact, arrived at after a lengthy trial, as to the motivation of the parties who negotiated a seniority system; and whether the court below applied wrong legal criteria in determining the bona fides of the seniority system. We conclude that the Court of Appeals erred in the course of its review and accordingly reverse its judgment and remand for further proceedings.

Title VII is a broad remedial measure, designed "to assure equality of employment opportunities." *McDonnell Douglas Corp. v. Green*, 411 U.S. 792, 800 (1973). The Act was designed to bar not only overt employment discrimination, "but also practices that are fair in form, but discriminatory in operation." *Griggs v. Duke Power Co.*, 401 U.S. 424, 431 (1971). "Thus, the Court has repeatedly held that a prima facie Title VII violation may be established by policies or practices that are neutral on their face and in intent but that nonetheless discriminate in effect against a particular group." *Teamsters v. United States*, 431 U.S. 324, 349 (1977) (hereinafter *Teamsters*). The Act's treatment of seniority systems, however, establishes an exception to these general principles. Section 703(h), 78 Stat. 257, as set forth in 42 U.S.C. §2000e-2(h), provides in pertinent part:

> Notwithstanding any other provision of this subchapter, it shall not be an unlawful employment practice for an employer to apply different standards of compensation, or different terms, conditions, or privileges of employment pursuant to a bona fide seniority . . . system . . . provided that such differences are not the result of an intention to discriminate because of race.

Under this section, a showing of disparate impact is insufficient to invalidate a seniority system, even though the result may be to perpetuate pre-Act discrimination. In *Trans World Airlines, Inc. v. Hardison*, 432 U.S. 63, 82 (1977), we summarized the effect of §703(h) as follows: "[A]bsent a discriminatory purpose, the operation of a seniority system cannot be an unlawful employment practice even if the system has some discriminatory consequences." Thus, any challenge to a seniority system under Title VII will require a trial on the issue of discriminatory intent: Was the system adopted because of its racially discriminatory impact?

This is precisely what happened in these cases. Following our decision in *Teamsters*, the District Court held a new trial on the limited question of whether the seniority system was "instituted or maintained contrary to Section 703(h) of the new Civil Rights Act of 1964.". . . That court concluded, as we noted above and will discuss below, that the system was adopted and maintained for purposes wholly independent of any discriminatory intent. The Court of Appeals for the Fifth Circuit reversed.

Petitioners submit that the Court of Appeals failed to comply with the command of Rule 52(a) that the findings of fact of a district court may not be set aside unless clearly erroneous. . . .

The seniority system at issue here was adopted in 1954. Under that agreement, seniority was measured by length of continuous service in a particular department. Seniority was originally exercised only for purposes of layoffs and hirings within particular departments. In 1956, seniority was formally recognized for promotional purposes as well. Again, however, seniority, with limited exceptions, was only exercised within departments; employees transferring to new departments forfeited their seniority. This seniority system remained virtually unchanged until after this suit was brought in 1971. . . .

The [C]ourt [of Appeals] announced that "[h]aving carefully reviewed the evidence offered to show whether the departmental seniority system in the present case is 'bona fide' within the meaning of §703(h) of Title VII, we reject the district court's finding." . . .

In connection with its assertion that it was convinced that a mistake had been made, the Court of Appeals, in a footnote, referred to the clearly-erroneous standard of Rule 52(a). It pointed out, however, that if findings "are made under an erroneous view of controlling legal principles, the clearly erroneous rule does not apply, and the findings may not stand." *Id.* Finally, quoting from *East v. Romine, Inc.*, 518 F.2d 332, 339 (CA5 1975), the Court of Appeals repeated the following view of its appellate function in Title VII cases where purposeful discrimination is at issue:

> Although discrimination *vel non* is essentially a question of fact it is, at the same time, the ultimate issue for resolution in this case, being expressly proscribed by 42 U.S.C.A. §2000e-2(a). As such, a finding of discrimination or non-discrimination is a finding of ultimate fact. In reviewing the district court's findings, therefore, we will proceed to make an independent determination of appellant's allegations of discrimination, though bound by findings of subsidiary fact which are themselves not clearly erroneous.

Pointing to the above statement of the Court of Appeals and to similar statements in other Title VII cases coming from that court, petitioners submit that the Court of Appeals made an independent determination of discriminatory purpose, the "ultimate fact" in this case, and that this was error under Rule 52(a). We agree with petitioners that if the Court of Appeals followed what seems to be the accepted rule in that Circuit, its judgment must be reversed.

Rule 52(a) broadly requires that findings of fact not be set aside unless clearly erroneous. It does not make exceptions or purport to exclude certain categories of factual findings from the obligation of a court of appeals to accept a district court's findings unless clearly erroneous. It does not divide facts into categories; in particular, it does not divide findings of fact into those that deal with "ultimate" and those that deal with "subsidiary" facts.

The Rule does not apply to conclusions of law. The Court of Appeals, therefore, was quite right in saying that if a district court's findings rest on an erroneous view of the law, they may be set aside on that basis. But here the District Court was not faulted for misunderstanding or applying an erroneous definition of intentional discrimination. It was reversed for arriving at what the Court of Appeals thought was an erroneous finding as to whether the differential impact of the seniority system reflected an intent to discriminate on account of race. That question, as we see it, is a pure question of fact, subject to Rule 52(a)'s clearly-erroneous standard. It is not a question of law and not a mixed question of law and fact.

The Court has previously noted the vexing nature of the distinction between questions of fact and questions of law. Rule 52(a) does not furnish particular guidance with respect to distinguishing law from fact. Nor do we yet know of any other rule or principle that will unerringly distinguish a factual finding from a legal conclusion. For the reasons that follow, however, we have little doubt about the factual nature of §703(h)'s requirement that a seniority system be free of an intent to discriminate.

Treating issues of intent as factual matters for the trier of fact is commonplace. In *Dayton Board of Education v. Brinkman*, 443 U.S. 526, 534 (1979), the principal question was whether the defendants had intentionally maintained a racially segregated school system at a specified time in the past. We recognized that issue as essentially factual, subject to the clearly erroneous rule. In *Commissioner v. Duberstein*, 363 U.S. 278 (1960), the Court held that the principal criterion for identifying a gift under the applicable provision of the Internal Revenue Code was the intent or motive of the donor — "one that inquires what the basic reason for his conduct was in fact." *Id.* at 286. Resolution of that issue determined the ultimate issue of whether a gift had been made. Both issues were held to be questions of fact subject to the clearly erroneous rule. In *United States v. Yellow Cab Co.*, 338 U.S. 338, 341 (1949), an antitrust case, the Court referred to "[f]indings as to the design, motive and intent with which men act" as peculiarly factual issues for the trier of fact and therefore subject to appellate review under Rule 52.

Justice Black's dissent in *Yellow Cab* suggested a contrary approach. Relying on *United States v. Griffith*, 334 U.S. 100 (1948), he argued that it is not always necessary to prove "specific intent" to restrain trade; it is enough if a restraint is the result or consequence of a defendant's conduct or business arrangements. Such an approach, however, is specifically precluded by §703(h) in Title VII cases challenging seniority systems. Differentials among employees that result from a seniority system are not unlawful employment practices unless the product of an intent to discriminate. It would make no sense, therefore, to say that the intent to discriminate required by §703(h) may be presumed from such an impact. As §703(h) was construed in *Teamsters*, there must be a finding of actual intent to discriminate on racial grounds on the part of those who negotiated or maintained the system. That finding appears to us to be a pure question of fact.

This is not to say that discriminatory impact is not part of the evidence to be considered by the trial court in reaching a finding on whether there was such a discriminatory intent as a factual matter. We do assert, however, that under §703(h) discriminatory intent is a finding of fact to be made by the trial court; it is not a question of law and not a mixed question of law and fact of the kind that in some cases may allow an appellate court to review the facts to see if they satisfy some legal concept of discriminatory intent. Discriminatory intent here means actual motive; it is not a legal presumption to be drawn from a factual showing of something less than actual motive. Thus, a court of appeals may only reverse a district court's finding on discriminatory intent if it concludes that the finding is clearly erroneous under Rule 52(a). Insofar as the Fifth Circuit assumed otherwise, it erred.

Respondents do not directly defend the Fifth Circuit rule that a trial court's finding on discriminatory intent is not subject to the clearly-erroneous standard of Rule 52(a). Rather, among other things, they submit that the Court of Appeals recognized and, where appropriate, properly applied Rule 52(a) in setting aside the findings of the District Court. This position has force, but for two reasons it is not persuasive.

First, although the Court of Appeals acknowledged and correctly stated the controlling standard of Rule 52(a), the acknowledgment came late in the court's opinion. The court had not expressly referred to or applied Rule 52(a) in the course of disagreeing with the District Court's resolution of the factual issues deemed relevant under *James v. Stockham Valves & Fittings Co.*, 559 F.2d 310 (5th Cir.1977). Furthermore, the paragraph in which the court finally concludes that the USW seniority system is unprotected by §703(h) strongly suggests that the outcome was the product of the court's independent consideration of the totality of the circumstances it found in the record.

Second and more fundamentally, when the court stated that it was convinced that a mistake had been made, it then identified not only the mistake but also the source of that mistake. The mistake of the District Court was that on the record there could be no doubt about the existence of a discriminatory purpose. The source of the mistake was the District Court's failure to recognize the relevance of the racial purposes of IAM. Had the District Court "given the I. A. M.'s role in the creation and establishment of the seniority system its due consideration," it "might have reached a different conclusion."

When an appellate court discerns that a district court has failed to make a finding because of an erroneous view of the law, the usual rule is that there should be a remand for further proceedings to permit the trial court to make the missing findings:

> [F]actfinding is the basic responsibility of district courts, rather than appellate courts, and . . . the Court of Appeals should not have resolved in the first instance this factual dispute which had not been considered by the District Court. *DeMarco v. United States*, 415 U.S. 449, 450, n. (1974).

Likewise, where findings are infirm because of an erroneous view of the law, a remand is the proper course unless the record permits only one resolution of the factual issue. *Kelley v. Southern Pacific Co.*, 419 U.S. 318, 331-332 (1974). All of this is elementary. Yet the Court of Appeals, after holding that the District Court had failed to consider relevant evidence and indicating that the District Court might have come to a different conclusion had it considered that evidence, failed to remand for further proceedings as to the intent of IAM and the significance, if any, of such a finding with respect to the intent of USW itself. Instead, the Court of Appeals made its own determination as to the motives of IAM, found that USW had acquiesced in the IAM conduct, and apparently concluded that the foregoing was sufficient to remove the system from the protection of §703(h).

Proceeding in this manner seems to us incredible unless the Court of Appeals construed its own well-established Circuit rule with respect to its authority to arrive at independent findings on ultimate facts free of the strictures of Rule 52(a) also to permit it to examine the record and make its own independent findings with respect to those issues on which the district court's findings are set aside for an error of law. As we have previously said, however, the premise for this conclusion is infirm: whether an ultimate fact or not, discriminatory intent under §703(h) is a factual matter subject to the clearly-erroneous standard of Rule 52(a). It follows that when a district court's finding on such an ultimate fact is set aside for an error of law, the court of appeals is not relieved of the usual requirement of remanding for further proceedings to the tribunal charged with the task of factfinding in the first instance.

Accordingly, the judgment of the Court of Appeals is reversed, and the cases are remanded to that court for further proceedings consistent with this opinion.

NOTES

1. How is the determination of "intention to discriminate" in *Pullman-Standard* different from the determination of "independent contractor" in *Village of Weyauwega*?

2. Recall that Rule 52(a) provides that "[f]indings of fact, whether based on oral or documentary evidence, shall not be set aside unless clearly erroneous, and due regard shall be given to the opportunity of the trial courts to judge the credibility of the witnesses." All the evidence in *Pullman-Standard* was documentary. Why should an appellate court give any deference at all to a trial judge's finding based upon documentary evidence? Consider in this connection the functions assigned to appellate courts and the functions assigned to trial courts. What policies underlie Rule 52(a)? Do reasons of efficiency or other

policies justify continued deference to trial judges' fact-findings, even if trial judges are in no better position, and sometimes may be in a worse position, than appellate judges to accurately find facts?

3. Rule 52(a) requires the trial court to "find the facts specially and state separately its conclusions of law thereon." In practice, trial courts often ask counsel for the prevailing party to draft proposed findings of fact and conclusions of law. The opposing party is given an opportunity to object to the proposals and to submit alternatives. The trial court will then decide on its findings and conclusions. This sorting out of fact and law by the trial court can aid the appellate court in determining what is fact and what is law. However, the appellate court is not bound by the trial court's categorization. The appellate court can treat as law what the trial court considered as fact, and vice versa.

4. Some commentators have suggested that a functional approach should be adopted: They argue that the clearly erroneous standard should apply to categories of issues that it is most efficient to have a trial court decide finally, and *de novo* review should apply to issues that an appellate court can most efficiently decide. *See* Stephen A. Wiener, *The Civil Jury Trial and the Law-Fact Distinction*, 54 CAL. L. REV. 1867 (1966); Stephen A. Wiener, *The Civil Non-Jury Trial and the Law-Fact Distinction*, 55 CAL. L. REV. 1020 (1967). Would it be preferable for courts to choose their standard of review in this manner, rather than by a conceptual categorization of issues as issues of fact or issues of law?

5. Compare the remarks of the Supreme Court in *Miller v. Fenton*, 474 U.S. 104, 113-18 (1985):

> [T]he appropriate methodology for distinguishing questions of fact from questions of law has been, to say the least, elusive. A few principles . . . are by now well established. For example, that an issue involves an inquiry into state of mind is not at all inconsistent with treating it as a question of fact. Equally clearly, an issue does not lose its factual character merely because its resolution is dispositive of the ultimate constitutional question. But beyond these elemental propositions . . . the Court has yet to arrive at "a rule or principle that will unerringly distinguish a factual finding from a legal conclusion." *Pullman-Standard v. Swint*, 456 U.S. 273, 288 (1982).
>
> Perhaps much of the difficulty in this area stems from the practical truth that the decision to label an issue a "question of law," a "question of fact," or a "mixed question of law and fact" is sometimes as much a matter of allocation as it is of analysis. At least in those instances in which Congress has not spoken and in which the issue falls somewhere between a pristine legal standard and a simple historical fact, the fact/law distinction at times has turned on a determination that, as a matter of the sound administration of justice, one judicial actor is better positioned than another to decide the issue in question. Where, for example, as with proof of actual malice in First Amendment libel cases, the relevant legal principle can be given meaning only through its application to the particular circumstances of a case, the Court has been reluctant to give the trier of fact's

conclusions presumptive force and, in so doing, strip a federal appellate court of its primary function as an expositor of law. See *Bose Corp. v. Consumers Union of United States, Inc.*, 466 U.S. [485], at 503 [(1984)]. Similarly, on rare occasions in years past the Court has justified independent federal or appellate review as a means of compensating for "perceived shortcomings of the trier of fact by way of bias or some other factor. . . ." *Id.* at 518 (Rehnquist, J., dissenting).

In contrast, other considerations often suggest the appropriateness of resolving close questions concerning the status of an issue as one of "law" or "fact" in favor of extending deference to the trial court. When, for example, the issue involves the credibility of witnesses and therefore turns largely on an evaluation of demeanor, there are compelling and familiar justifications for leaving the process of applying law to fact to the trial court and according its determinations presumptive weight. . . . [T]he state trial judge is in a position to assess juror bias that is far superior to that of federal judges reviewing an application for a writ of habeas corpus. Principally for that reason . . . juror bias merits treatment as a "factual issue" . . . notwithstanding the intimate connection between such determinations and the constitutional guarantee of an impartial jury.

For several reasons we think that it would be inappropriate to abandon the Court's longstanding position that the ultimate question of the admissibility of a confession merits treatment as a legal inquiry requiring plenary federal review. . . . [W]e do not write on a clean slate. . . . [N]early a half century of unwavering precedent weighs heavily against any suggestion that we now discard the settled rule in this area. Moreover, . . . in the confession context we have the benefit of some congressional guidance. . . .

In addition . . . , the nature of the inquiry itself lends support to the conclusion that "voluntariness" is a legal question meriting independent consideration in a federal habeas corpus proceeding. Although sometimes framed as an issue of "psychological fact," the dispositive question of the voluntariness of a confession has always had a uniquely legal dimension. . . . [T]he admissibility of a confession turns as much on whether the techniques for extracting the statements, as applied to *this* suspect, are compatible with a system that presumes innocence and assures that a conviction will not be secured by inquisitorial means as on whether the defendant's will was in fact overborne. This hybrid quality of the voluntariness inquiry, subsuming, as it does, a "complex of values," itself militates against treating the question as one of simple historical fact. . . . [O]nce . . . underlying factual issues have been resolved, and the moment comes for determining whether, under the totality of the circumstances, the confession was obtained in a manner consistent with the Constitution, the state-court judge is not in an appreciably better position than the federal habeas court to make that determination.

Second, . . . the critical events surrounding the taking of a confession almost invariably occur in a secret and inherently . . . coercive environment. . . . [T]ogether with the inevitable and understandable reluctance to exclude an otherwise reliable admission of guilt, they elevate the risk that erroneous resolution of the voluntariness question might inadvertently frustrate the protection of the federal right. We reiterate our confidence that state judges, no less than their federal counterparts, will properly discharge their duty to protect the constitutional rights of criminal defendants. We note only that in the confession context, independent federal review has traditionally played an important parallel role in protecting the rights at stake when the prosecution secures a conviction through the defendant's own admissions.

Additional commentators have argued that there is no essential difference between law and fact; legal questions are a variety of fact questions, and the distinction between them must be decided functionally. They conclude, however, that the legal system should not necessarily "scrap the pretense that 'law' is conceptually distinct from 'fact'"; the fiction can be useful, and the Constitution may require it to be maintained. *See* Ronald J. Allen & Michael S. Pardo, *The Myth of the Law-Fact Distinction*, 97 Nw. U. L. Rev. 1769 (2003).

6. Not everyone agrees that appellate courts are incompetent or improper factfinders. *See* John C. Godbold, *Fact Finding by Appellate Courts — An Available and Appropriate Power*, 12 Cumb. L. Rev. 365 (1982). Judge Godbold wrote that nothing in the Constitution, in the U.S Code, or in historical practice precludes appellate courts from deciding factual issues or even from taking evidence in cases on appeal in non-jury cases. He argues that there need be little, if any, loss of accuracy when appellate courts find facts because multiple judges check one another, and the court often will have the benefit of a verbatim written record and attorneys' briefs, as compared with a trial judge who acts alone, and may not have a transcript or briefs. However, the appellate court should find facts only if the issues may be fairly resolved from the record. Moreover, for reasons of judicial economy and other policies, the appeals court should not find facts if the case has to be remanded in any event, nor should it repeat the work of the trial courts or find facts on issues that were not presented to the trial court. But appellate courts may find facts, without abusing their discretion, when, for example, a factual matter needs to be resolved because the appellate court is ruling on a different ground than that relied on by the trial court and the record permits resolution of the issue. The judge cites numerous contexts in which appellate courts routinely make fact findings, belying the notions that it is improper for them to do so or that they are incompetent to do so.

Judge Godbold similarly argues that, although considerations of fairness and judicial economy limit the circumstances in which appeals courts should take new evidence, they are empowered to do so, and in fact do so (in resolving issues such as whether a case has become moot) based upon affidavits and other sworn written testimony, undisputed assertions made by counsel, and party stipulations. As guiding principles, he offers that appeals courts should neither permit litigants to present evidence that they could not have presented at trial, nor address issues as to which non-documentary evidence is appropriate.

Stuart Minor Benjamin, *Stepping Into the Same River Twice: Rapidly Changing Facts and the Appellate Process*, 78 Tex. L. Rev. 269 (1999), argues for appellate courts to do their own factfinding when the factfindings of the trial court already are outdated by the time of appeal, the facts will continue to change so rapidly that the obsolescence of trial court findings would be a recurrent problem if the appellate court were to remand, and prospective relief is sought. The most common examples arise in cases involving rapidly changing technologies, although Judge Godbold cited similar experience with desegregation cases in which essential statistical data was in constant flux.

When, if ever, do you think it is appropriate for appellate courts to find facts on matters that go to the merits of a case, as opposed to matters of the court's jurisdiction or matters that the court is considering in original proceedings (for contempt, mandamus, petitions for stays, and the like)?

7. Consider Chad M. Oldfather, *Appellate Courts, Historical Facts, and the Civil-Criminal Distinction*, 57 VAND. L. REV. 437 (2004)[10], which challenges the conventional wisdom that appellate courts are not well designed to find facts, and argues that the greater need for accuracy in criminal, as opposed to civil, cases, demands closer scrutiny of trial court factfindings in criminal than in civil cases, while actual practice is precisely the opposite even though the Seventh Amendment restriction of reexamination of facts has no bearing in the criminal context. Oldfather writes:

> [Al]though appellate courts are far better at fact assessment than previously acknowledged, there remain costs associated with appellate factual review. . . . Our criminal justice system places an asymmetric premium on factual accuracy, such that avoidance of wrongful convictions is (at least in most accounts of the system) of paramount importance. As such, the value that would flow from effective appellate scrutiny of facts is relatively high. Our civil justice system, in contrast, places a comparatively low value on factual accuracy and a relatively high value on the role of the jury. That suggests . . . that appellate courts should . . . get involved in factual reconsideration . . . only in situations where they enjoy a clear competence advantage. . . . [T]he fact that the existing standards of review . . . fail to bring about this allocation of resources suggests a need to reconsider the standards and, more generally, the relationship between trial and appellate courts. *Id.* at 503-04.

Why do you suppose the appellate courts have been relatively reluctant to closely oversee the factfinding in criminal cases? Do we just pretend to be concerned that only those who have committed criminal acts are found guilty? Is the standard of review not up to the task of adequately policing juries, or of forcing appeals courts to confront the possibility that a convicted person may be innocent?

8. Once a court has decided that a particular issue is one of law, the appropriate standard of review is easy to understand. No deference is given to the trial court and the court answers the question of law by addressing it afresh.

---

10 Copyright © 2004. Reprinted with permission of Vanderbilt Law Review.

When a court has decided that a particular issue is one of fact, the meaning of the applicable standard of review is not so clear.

B. Trial Judge's Fact-Findings

The Meaning of Clearly Erroneous

Assuming the trial judge's determination is categorized by the appellate court as one of fact, by what test or standard does the appellate court determine whether it is "clearly erroneous" within the meaning of Rule 52(a)?

ANDERSON V. CITY OF BESSEMER
470 U.S. 564 (1985)

JUSTICE WHITE delivered the opinion of the Court.

In *Pullman-Standard v. Swint*, 456 U.S. 273 (1982), we held that a District Court's finding of discriminatory intent in an action brought under Title VII of the Civil Rights Act of 1964 . . . is a factual finding that may be overturned on appeal only if it is clearly erroneous. In this case, the Court of Appeals for the Fourth Circuit concluded that there was clear error in a District Court's finding of discrimination and reversed. Because our reading of the record convinces us that the Court of Appeals misapprehended and misapplied the clearly-erroneous standard, we reverse. . . .

[After pursuing appropriate administrative proceedings, petitioner Anderson filed this action in the U.S. District Court against the city under Title VII of the Civil Rights Act, alleging that she had been denied employment as Recreation Director because she was a woman. During a two-day trial the court heard testimony from the petitioner, Mr. Kincaid (who had been employed in the position), and the five members of the selection committee. The court thereafter made findings of fact and conclusions of law to the effect that the petitioner had been discriminated against because of her sex and entered a judgment in her favor for back pay. The city appealed.]

The Fourth Circuit reversed the District Court's finding of discrimination. In the view of the Court of Appeals, three of the District Court's crucial findings were clearly erroneous: the finding that petitioner was the most qualified candidate, the finding that petitioner had been asked questions that other applicants were spared, and the finding that the male committee members were biased against hiring a woman. Having rejected these findings, the Court of Appeals concluded that the District Court had erred in finding that petitioner had been discriminated against on account of her sex. . . .

Because a finding of intentional discrimination is a finding of fact, the standard governing appellate review of a district court's finding of discrimination is that set forth in Federal Rule of Civil Procedure 52(a). . . . The question before us, then, is whether the Court of Appeals erred in holding the District Court's finding of discrimination to be clearly erroneous.

Although the meaning of the phrase "clearly erroneous" is not immediately apparent, certain general principles governing the exercise of the appellate court's power to overturn findings of a district court may be derived from our cases. The foremost of these principles, as the Fourth Circuit itself recognized, is that "[a] finding is 'clearly erroneous' when although there is evidence to support it, the reviewing court on the entire evidence is left with the definite and firm conviction that a mistake has been committed." *United States v. United States Gypsum Co.,* 333 U.S. 364, 395 (1948). This standard plainly does not entitle a reviewing court to reverse the finding of the trier of fact simply because it is convinced that it would have decided the case differently. The reviewing court oversteps the bounds of its duty under Rule 52(a) if it undertakes to duplicate the role of the lower court. "In applying the clearly erroneous standard to the findings of a district court sitting without a jury, appellate courts must constantly have in mind that their function is not to decide factual issues *de novo.*" *Zenith Radio Corp. v. Hazeltine Research, Inc.,* 395 U.S. 100, 123 (1969). If the district court's account of the evidence is plausible in light of the record viewed in its entirety, the court of appeals may not reverse it even though convinced that had it been sitting as the trier of fact, it would have weighed the evidence differently. Where there are two permissible views of the evidence, the factfinder's choice between them cannot be clearly erroneous.

This is so even when the district court's findings do not rest on credibility determinations, but are based instead on physical or documentary evidence or inferences from other facts. . . .

The rationale for deference to the original finder of fact is not limited to the superiority of the trial judge's position to make determinations of credibility. The trial judge's major role is the determination of fact, and with experience in fulfilling that role comes expertise. Duplication of the trial judge's efforts in the court of appeals would very likely contribute only negligibly to the accuracy of fact determination at a huge cost in diversion of judicial resources. In addition, the parties to a case on appeal have already been forced to concentrate their energies and resources on persuading the trial judge that their account of the facts is the correct one; requiring them to persuade three more judges at the appellate level is requiring too much. As the Court has stated in a different context, the trial on the merits should be "the 'main event' . . . rather than a 'tryout on the 'road.'" *Wainwright v. Sykes,* 433 U.S. 72, 90 (1977). For these reasons, review of factual findings under the clearly-erroneous standard — with its deference to the trier of fact — is the rule, not the exception.

When findings are based on determinations regarding the credibility of witnesses, Rule 52(a) demands even greater deference to the trial court's findings; for only the trial judge can be aware of the variations in demeanor and tone of voice that bear so heavily on the listener's understanding of and belief in what is said. This is not to suggest that the trial judge may insulate his findings from review by denominating them credibility determinations, for factors other than demeanor and inflection go into the decision whether or not to believe a witness. Documents or objective evidence may contradict the witness' story; or the story itself may be so internally inconsistent or implausible on its face that a reasonable fact-finder would not credit it. Where such factors are present, the court of appeals may well find clear error even in a finding purportedly based on a credibility determination. But when a trial judge's finding is based on his decision to credit the testimony of one of two or more witnesses, each of whom has told a coherent and facially plausible story that is not contradicted by extrinsic evidence, that finding, if not internally inconsistent, can virtually never be clear error.

Application of the foregoing principles to the facts of the case lays bare the errors committed by the Fourth Circuit in its employment of the clearly-erroneous standard. In detecting clear error in the District Court's finding that petitioner was better qualified than Mr. Kincaid, the Fourth Circuit improperly conducted what amounted to a *de novo* weighing of the evidence in the record. The District Court's finding was based on essentially undisputed evidence regarding the respective backgrounds of petitioner and Mr. Kincaid and the duties that went with the position of Recreation Director. The District Court, after considering the evidence, concluded that the position of Recreation Director in Bessemer City carried with it broad responsibilities for creating and managing a recreation program involving not only athletics, but also other activities for citizens of all ages and interests. The court determined that petitioner's more varied educational and employment background and her extensive involvement in a variety of civic activities left her better qualified to implement such a rounded program than Mr. Kincaid, whose background was more narrowly focused on athletics.

The Fourth Circuit, reading the same record, concluded that the basic duty of the Recreation Director was to implement an athletic program, and that the essential qualification for a successful applicant would be either education or experience specifically related to athletics. Accordingly, it seemed evident to the Court of Appeals that Mr. Kincaid was in fact better qualified than petitioner.

Based on our own reading of the record, we cannot say that either interpretation of the facts is illogical or implausible. Each has support in inferences that may be drawn from the facts in the record; and if either interpretation had been drawn by a district court on the record before us, we would not be inclined to find it clearly erroneous. The question we must answer, however, is not whether the Fourth Circuit's interpretation of the facts was clearly erroneous, but whether the District Court's finding was clearly erroneous. The District Court determined that petitioner was better qualified, and, as we have stated above, such a finding is entitled to deference notwithstanding that it is not based on credibility determinations. When the record is examined in light of the appropriately deferential standard, it is apparent that it contains nothing that mandates a finding that the District Court's conclusion was clearly erroneous.

Somewhat different concerns are raised by the Fourth Circuit's treatment of the District Court's finding that petitioner, alone among the applicants for the position of Recreation Director, was asked questions regarding her spouse's feelings about her application for the position. Here the error of the Court of Appeals was its failure to give due regard to the ability of the District Court to interpret and discern the credibility of oral testimony. The Court of Appeals rested its rejection of the District Court's finding of differential treatment on its own interpretation of testimony by Mrs. Boone — the very witness whose testimony, in the view of the District Court, supported the finding. In the eyes of the Fourth Circuit, Mrs. Boone's testimony that she had made a "comment" to Mr. Kincaid about the feelings of his wife (a comment judged "facetious" by the District Court) conclusively established that Mr. Kincaid, and perhaps other male applicants as well had been questioned about the feelings of his spouse.

Mrs. Boone's testimony on this point . . . is certainly not free from ambiguity. But Mrs. Boone several times stated that other candidates had not been questioned about the reaction of their wives — at least, "not in the same context" as had petitioner. And even after recalling and calling to the attention of the court that she had made a comment on the subject to Mr. Kincaid, Mrs. Boone denied that she had "asked" Mr. Kincaid about his wife's reaction. Mrs. Boone's testimony on these matters is not inconsistent with the theory that her remark was not a serious inquiry into whether Mr. Kincaid's wife approved of his applying for the position. Whether the judge's interpretation is actually correct is impossible to tell from the paper record, but it is easy to imagine that the tone of voice in which the witness related her comment, coupled with her immediate denial that she had questioned Mr. Kincaid on the subject, might have conclusively established that the remark was a facetious one. We therefore cannot agree that the judge's conclusion that the remark was facetious was clearly erroneous.

Once the trial court's characterization of Mrs. Boone's remark is accepted, it is apparent that the finding that the male candidates were not seriously questioned about the feelings of their wives cannot be deemed clearly erroneous. The trial judge was faced with the testimony of three witnesses, one of whom (Mrs. Boone) stated that none of the other candidates had been so questioned, one of whom (a male committee member) testified that Mr. Kincaid had been asked such a question "in a way," and one of whom (another committeeman) testified that all the candidates had been subjected to similar questioning. None of these accounts is implausible on its face, and none is contradicted by any reliable extrinsic evidence. Under these circumstances, the trial court's decision to credit Mrs. Boone was not clearly erroneous.

The Fourth Circuit's refusal to accept the District Court's finding that the committee members were biased against hiring a woman was based to a large extent on its rejection of the finding that petitioner had been subjected to questioning that the other applicants were spared. Given that that finding was not clearly erroneous, the finding of bias cannot be termed erroneous: it finds support not only in the treatment of petitioner in her interview, but also in the testimony of one committee member that he believed it would have been difficult for a woman to perform the job and in the evidence that another member solicited applications for the position only from men.

Our determination that the findings of the District Court regarding petitioner's qualifications, the conduct of her interview, and the bias of the male committee members were not clearly erroneous leads us to conclude that the court's finding that petitioner was discriminated against on account of her sex was also not clearly erroneous. The District Court's findings regarding petitioner's superior qualifications and the bias of the selection committee are sufficient to support the inference that petitioner was denied the position of Recreation Director on account of her sex. Accordingly, we hold that the Fourth Circuit erred in denying petitioner relief under Title VII.

In so holding, we do not assert that our knowledge of what happened 10 years ago in Bessemer City is superior to that of the Court of Appeals; nor do we claim to have greater insight than the Court of Appeals into the state of mind of the men on the selection committee who rejected petitioner for the position of Recreation Director. Even the trial judge, who has heard the witnesses directly and who is more closely in touch than the appeals court with the milieu out of which the controversy before him arises, cannot always be confident that he "knows" what happened. Often, he can only determine whether the plaintiff has succeeded in presenting an account of the facts that is more likely to be true than not. Our task — and the task of appellate tribunals generally — is more limited still: we must determine whether the trial judge's conclusions are clearly erroneous. On the record before us, we cannot say that they are. Accordingly, the judgment of the Court of Appeals is

Reversed.

NOTES

1. *Anderson* may rest in part on the belief that trial judges are better able than appellate judges to determine what testimony is true. But empirical evidence suggests that judges, as well as other people, do not do well in distinguishing truthful testimony from falsehood, and there is some empirical evidence that people detect lies more successfully from reading a transcript than from hearing and seeing witnesses. *See* Olin Guy Wellborn III, *Demeanor*, 76 CORNELL L. REV. 1075, 1091 (1991) (concluding, contrary to long-standing assumptions, that available evidence indicates that transcripts are probably better than live testimony as a basis for predicting credibility because they eliminate distraction and unreliable nonverbal data and enhance verbal content, which is most reliable). If so, should appeals courts cease to defer to trial judges' findings of fact?

2. Returning to trial judges' superiority to find facts in non-documentary cases by virtue of the judges' presence in the courtroom, what should be the effect of our ability to enable appellate judges to largely replicate the experience of the trial judge? For example, what effect, if any, should a videotape of the trial have on the application of Rule 52(a)? *See* Robert C. Owen & Melissa Mather, *The Decisionmaking Process: Thawing Out The "Cold Record": Some Thoughts on How Videotaped Records May Affect Traditional Standards of Deference on Direct and Collateral Review*, 2 J. APP. PRAC. & PROCESS 411 (2000)[11]:

> The "coldness" of the written record of any trial has long provided the justification (or scapegoat, depending on one's point of view) for the deference appellate courts pay to the rulings of their colleagues on the trial bench. Reviewing judges . . . routinely recite their inability to second-guess the accuracy of the trial court's conclusion, given that only the trial judge actually "smelled the smoke of the battle." To hear the appellate courts tell it, they cannot hope to compete with the trial court's careful scrutiny of the demeanor of the witnesses and its attentive monitoring of the complex interplay among jury, witness, court, and counsel. . . .

---

[11] Copyright © 2000 by Robert C. Owen and Melissa Mather. Reprinted with permission.

Now, of course, trial court proceedings can be, and with increasing frequency are, captured on videotape. Video technology refutes the rhetoric of necessity. . . . Appellate courts, if they so choose, now can have access via video to the same "data" that presumably inform the discretionary decisions of trial judges, and that were heretofore impossible to examine on appeal. The advent of video technology makes de novo appellate review of such trial court rulings a real possibility for the first time.

The indications thus far, however, are that appellate courts . . . are extremely reluctant to take advantage of this newly available technology to evaluate, for example, witness credibility. . . . In some cases, appellate judges have refused even to watch available videotapes of disputed events, insisting that only the traditional "cold" record permits reasoned decisionmaking. Some judges, indeed, appear to think it dangerous even to consider reviewing the trial "as it happened," as if the prospect of exercising more substantive oversight somehow imperils the legitimacy of the whole enterprise of appellate review. . . .

[T]he appellate standard of deference has never been (solely) the regrettable, but necessary, consequence of technological constraints. Instead, deference represents a deliberate political/institutional choice — a preference for finality and economy, even at the possible expense of accuracy. Nothing demonstrates this point more clearly than the appellate courts' uncomfortable reaction to videotaped records and evidence. . . .

Once we understand the policies behind deferring to trial courts, we can evaluate the institutional concerns at stake without fearing a technology that might actually make the reviewing court's job easier and increase the accuracy of certain determinations on appeal. In contexts where more careful oversight makes sense as a constitutional matter (such as review of death penalty cases . . .), we can use available video technology to exercise that oversight as accurately as possible. Where greater deference makes sense as an institutional matter . . . , courts can justify the exercise of that deference honestly — by invoking values such as finality and judicial economy, rather than hiding behind no-longer-existent factual limitations. . . . In most routine civil cases, these institutional concerns of finality and judicial economy should prevail over any particular litigant's interest in a given outcome. Whether the record below is on paper or video, therefore, the factual findings and evidentiary rulings of most trial courts will continue to deserve and receive appropriate deference.

. . . Several states permit videotaped records, and at least one, Kentucky, requires no additional written transcript. . . . Complaints about the videotape procedure generally focus on the quality of the sound on some tapes, as well as the amount of time required to review lengthy trials. With regard to the standard of review, at least one state, Ohio, has expressed (in two unpublished opinions) a willingness to alter, at least slightly, the degree of deference it grants to trial judges when videotaped testimony is involved. Other states, such as Tennessee and Washington, have explicitly rejected attempts to alter the standard of review accorded to a trial court's factual determinations based on the availability of videotaped records. . . . [T]hese decisions cling to the rhetoric of necessity, noting that video cameras reveal "only a narrow view of the trial court proceedings" and do not "preserve the conduct of [all] participants in the trial."

. . . [But the irrevocability of death] supports requiring appellate judges who review capital cases to employ available video technology as an essential means for subjecting such proceedings to meaningful scrutiny. Simply put, where the constitution demands that appellate courts dispose of the cases before them as accurately as possible — as in death penalty cases — it is necessary that the courts use all available information in doing so. [The authors go on to illustrate how video technology could facilitate more reliable resolution of issues arising in connection with jury selection, closing argument, and claims of ineffective assistance of counsel in capital cases.]

MILLER v. MERCY HOSPITAL, INC.
720 F.2d 356 (4th Cir. 1983)

PHILLIPS, CIRCUIT JUDGE

In the Supreme Court's oft-cited elaboration of the "clearly erroneous" standard, we have been instructed that "[a] finding is 'clearly erroneous' when although there is evidence to support it, the reviewing court on the entire evidence is left with the definite and firm conviction that a mistake has been committed." *United States v. United States Gypsum Co.*, 333 U.S. 364, 395 (1948). Efforts at further refinement of this judgmental standard are not likely to give it much greater precision than does the *Gypsum Co.* formulation. Nevertheless, because in this case we *are* "left with a definite and firm conviction that a mistake has been committed" and because of the particular sensitivity of the standard's application to ultimate motivational issues in Title VII litigation, we elaborate briefly upon our understanding of the ways in which an appellate court may properly be "convinced" that a "mistake" in fact-finding has been made.

We start with the proposition that such a conviction may not be based simply upon a perception derived from *de novo* review of the record that the "actual" facts are other than those found. Closely related is the obverse proposition that the conviction of mistake need not rest upon any perception by the reviewing court that the "actual" facts are indeed different from those "found" (though it may obviously include such a subjective perception).[12] Thus, the conviction of

---

12 [5] Though in technical contemplation clearly erroneous review may rightly proceed with a completely neutral attitude toward what the "actual" facts may be, it is of course inevitable that a reviewing court's conviction of mistake may sometimes include a conviction that the actual facts are other than those "found." *See, e.g., Sanders v. Leech*, 158 F.2d 486, 487 (5th Cir. 1946) ("testimony considered as a whole convinces that the finding is so against the great preponderance of the credible testimony that it does not reflect or represent the *truth* and the *right* of the case") (emphasis added). Though occasionally they must exist, such convictions about the "truth" or "right" of a case are merely incidental to, not necessary predicates for, a reviewing court's conclusion that a finding is clearly erroneous. It is enough that the finding is "against the great preponderance of the evidence" in the record presented for review. A reviewing court's ability to discern the "truth" and "right" of a case presupposes that the record is also "true" and "right" (and complete) and this of course is beyond the court's ability and need.

mistake may properly be based upon a conclusion that, without regard to what the "actual" facts may be, the findings under review were induced by an erroneous view of the controlling legal standard, or are not supported by substantial evidence, or were made without properly taking into account substantial evidence to the contrary or are against the clear weight of the evidence considered as a whole. In sum, these establish that "clearly erroneous" review is properly focused upon fact-finding processes rather than directly upon fact-finding results. The appellate function is to insure that the process shall have been principled; the function is not authoritatively to find the "facts" first instance,[13] or to affirm or deny that the facts "found" by the trial court are the "actual" facts of the case.

NOTES

1. Consider whether an appellate court would hold a trial judge's factual findings to be clearly erroneous in each of the following circumstances: (a) where the trial judge had taken into account evidence that was legally inadmissible; (b) where the trial judge had excluded from consideration evidence that was legally admissible; (c) where the trial judge's finding was based on evidence that would be deemed insufficient to support a jury verdict if the case had been tried to a jury; (d) where the trial judge, in making the finding, was under a misapprehension about the governing law or premised the finding on an erroneous view of the law. Consider the bearing of the harmless error rule in (a) and (b).

2. The *Mercy Hospital* opinion stresses an appellate focus on the process of fact-finding in the trial court rather than on the correctness of the facts found. Is this distinction meaningful in applying the clearly erroneous standard? Is it sound or realistic?

3. When the appellate court determines that a finding is clearly erroneous, may it proceed to decide the fact itself, or should it remand the case to the trial court for a fresh factual determination? Does the answer to this question depend on the state of the evidence in the record?

4. The parties in *Parks v. McIntosh*, 361 P.2d 949 (N.M. 1961), owned ranches in neighboring counties consisting of both deeded and leased land. They agreed to exchange land, with defendants giving plaintiffs a secured promissory note, payable in annual installments. Defendants defaulted in the payments, claiming that the promissory note was void for lack of consideration because of plaintiffs' purported failure to deliver a Forest Service grazing permit for lands adjacent to the exchanged ranch. Plaintiff brought a lawsuit to recover on the promissory note and to foreclose the mortgage securing the note. The district court entered a judgment in favor of plaintiffs and defendants appealed. The New Mexico Supreme Court affirmed (*Id.* at 950):

---

[13] [6] Except perhaps in reviewing "constitutional" fact-finding, in taking judicial notice and, very occasionally and cautiously, when "facts" not found are manifest on the record.

The defendants testified that plaintiffs represented to them that they held a Forest Service grazing permit covering the area mentioned. On the other hand, the plaintiffs testified that they did not represent to the defendants that they had such a permit but had applied for one, and that they would waive their right thereto in favor of the defendants if their application therefor should be granted. In this situation, it was the province of the trial court to determine the weight of the evidence and the credibility of the witnesses. It follows, therefore, that the finding of the court, based on conflicting evidence, is conclusive on appeal.

If the trial court had found for the defendant, would that finding have been affirmed on appeal?

5. Assume that the existence of X is a material fact. Witness 1 testifies that X exists. Witness 2 testifies that X does not exist. Is the trial judge's decision on the existence or non-existence of X immune from appellate reversal, regardless of which way it goes?

6. In cases in federal court by virtue of diversity jurisdiction, federal courts must predict how state courts would resolve questions of state law. The federal appellate courts sometimes had deferred to the district courts, believing that the district courts were in a better position to make the prediction because of a supposed greater familiarity with state law. In so doing, the appeals courts, in effect, treated questions of state law like matters of fact, for purposes of appellate review. In *Salve Regina College v. Russell*, 499 U.S. 225 (1991), however, the Supreme Court directed the federal courts of appeals not to afford such deference and to review determinations of state law *de novo*. Does this seem sensible to you? Do the facts that appellate courts sit in multi-judge panels that must reach a collective judgment, that their "specialty" is deciding questions of law, that they will have received briefs on the legal issues, or other characteristics of appellate courts indicate that they would do a better job than federal trial courts of determining state law? In the Supreme Court's view, its decision in *Salve Regina* is supported by structural considerations such as these and by the risk that federal district courts will diverge in their interpretations of state law, leading to inequitable administration, contrary to the goals of *Erie R. Co. v. Tompkins*, 304 U.S. 64 (1938). *See* Jonathan Remy Nash, *Resuscitating Deference to Lower Federal Court Judges' Interpretations of State Law*, 77 S. CAL. L. REV. 975 (2004) (arguing for deference by the Supreme Court to state law determinations by courts of appeals, especially when affirming the trial court's determination).

C. Jury's Fact-Findings

I.M.A. v. ROCKY MOUNTAIN AIRWAYS, INC.
713 P.2d 882 (Colo. 1986)

LOHR, JUSTICE.

I.M.A., Inc. (I.M.A.) brought suit in Denver District Court against Rocky Mountain Airways, Inc. (Rocky Mountain) alleging that Rocky Mountain had breached a contract between the two parties. I.M.A. asserted that the alleged contract obligated Rocky Mountain to purchase all of the outstanding stock of I.M.A. and, as part of the purchase price, to assume I.M.A.'s liabilities. A jury returned a general verdict for I.M.A. and awarded $300,000 damages. The Colorado Court of Appeals reversed, holding that no contract existed. We granted certiorari in order to determine whether the court of appeals erred in concluding as a matter of law that the parties did not enter into a contract. We reverse the judgment of the court of appeals and remand with directions.

[I.M.A. encountered financial difficulties and ceased operations. It began negotiating with Aspen Airways to explore the possibility of a takeover.] . . . Rocky Mountain expressed interest in acquiring I.M.A. . . . I.M.A. discontinued its negotiations with Aspen Airways and concentrated on reaching an agreement with Rocky Mountain.

On August 1, 1978, the presidents of Rocky Mountain and I.M.A. signed a "Letter of Intent and Agreement," drafted by Rocky Mountain, the stated purpose of which was "to confirm [the parties'] recent understandings as to the acquisition of the assets of I.M.A. by Rocky Mountain Airways, Inc." According to the letter, Rocky Mountain intended "to acquire all of the assets of I.M.A. through acquisition of [all of I.M.A.'s outstanding stock]," and as consideration, Rocky Mountain agreed to assume I.M.A.'s liabilities and to pay a three dollar fee per passenger emplaning at Durango on the Denver to Durango route "to be credited . . . to the shareholders [of I.M.A.]." The fee was to be increased to four dollars per Durango passenger upon satisfaction of specified contingencies. Payment of the passenger fees was to continue for no longer than five years and was not to exceed $300,000. As part of Rocky Mountain's agreement to assume I.M.A.'s liabilities, the letter specified that Rocky Mountain would establish an escrow or trust fund in the amount of $20,000 within seven days for the purpose of providing assurance to taxing authorities that I.M.A.'s payroll tax obligations would be paid.

In the letter, I.M.A. represented that its liabilities totaled approximately $100,000 and its immediately redeemable assets were valued at approximately $45,000. I.M.A. promised to provide Rocky Mountain with a detailed list of its creditors and to update its accounting records for Rocky Mountain's inspection. The parties made no provision for the possibility that the accounting update might show I.M.A.'s assets or liabilities to be different from the approximate amounts represented. The letter also stated that "this Letter of Intent and Agreement is preliminary in nature, and . . . each party will work toward more definitive statements and the execution of agreements and resolutions and contracts, that may be required to consummate the overall purposes of this intent and agreement letter."

The letter listed five requirements upon which the "understanding and agreement and intent to acquire the assets" was contingent. [A letter on August 3, signed by both company presidents, modified the letter of August 1]. . . .

Following Rocky Mountain's refusal to proceed with the acquisition, I.M.A. commenced the present lawsuit. I.M.A. claimed damages for breach of contract, deceit, and unjust enrichment. It contended that the August letters constituted a binding contract and that I.M.A. had performed its obligations under the contract. It further averred that Rocky Mountain had never intended to consummate the transaction, but had allowed I.M.A. to rely on Rocky Mountain's representations that it would complete the acquisition. Finally, I.M.A. asserted that by using the PUC certificate and obtaining the attendant competitive advantages in serving the Denver-Durango market, Rocky Mountain had been unjustly enriched.

In response, Rocky Mountain contended that the August letters were merely preliminary and did not constitute a contract. Rocky Mountain further asserted that I.M.A. had materially misrepresented its financial position, that the parties were unable to resolve the new issues posed by the erroneous representations, and that, therefore, I.M.A. and Rocky Mountain were unable to "formalize" an agreement. Rocky Mountain also denied the averments of deceit and unjust enrichment.

At the close of the defendant's case, the trial court directed a verdict for Rocky Mountain on I.M.A.'s deceit claim, but it submitted the breach of contract and the unjust enrichment claims to the jury. The jury returned a general verdict of $300,000 for I.M.A. Rocky Mountain appealed, and I.M.A. cross-appealed the trial court's denial of prejudgment interest.

The court of appeals decided that the trial court erred when it denied Rocky Mountain's motion for a directed verdict on I.M.A.'s breach of contract claim. The court of appeals held that the trial court should have resolved the question of contract formation as a matter of law by looking at the two August letters. The court of appeals' own review of these two documents convinced it that Rocky Mountain and I.M.A. had contemplated further negotiations and had not entered into an enforceable contract. Because we conclude that the trial court properly allowed the jury to determine whether a contract between I.M.A. and Rocky Mountain existed, we reverse the judgment of the court of appeals.

The court of appeals concluded that no contract existed between Rocky Mountain and I.M.A., based on its own interpretation of the letters of August 1 and August 3. Although the interpretation of an established written contract is generally a question of law for the court . . . and thus subject to independent reevaluation by an appellate court, . . . we have stated previously that it is for the jury to determine whether the parties have entered into a contract. . . . More precisely, when the existence of a contract is in issue, and the evidence is conflicting or admits of more than one inference, it is for the jury to decide whether a contract in fact exists. . . . Appellate courts are bound by a jury's findings when the jury has been properly instructed by the trial court and there is competent evidence in the record to support the findings. . . . Application of these general principles to the present case yields the conclusion that the evidence and the law support a jury determination that I.M.A. and Rocky Mountain had entered into a contract.

In the present case, the evidence pertaining to the question of whether I.M.A. and Rocky Mountain had entered into a contract permitted a trier of fact to draw more than one inference. Thus, the trial court properly assigned the task of determining this question to the jury. . . .

Shareholders . . . attempted to renegotiate the Animas Air Park lease. I.M.A. apparently was cooperating fully with Rocky Mountain's efforts to obtain regulatory approval up to the time when Rocky Mountain announced its decision not to purchase I.M.A.'s stock. Thus, the jury could have found that I.M.A. satisfied all the contingencies within its control, and then could have concluded, in accordance with the trial court's instructions, that I.M.A. was excused for any nonperformance on its part since that nonperformance was caused by Rocky Mountain's conduct.

Because the evidence supports the jury's verdict for I.M.A. on breach of contract grounds, we do not address I.M.A.'s contention that the court of appeals should have considered I.M.A.'s unjust enrichment claim as a potential basis for upholding the jury's verdict.

NOTES

1. If I.M.A.'s case had been tried before a judge without a jury and the judge had found that there was a contract between the parties, how would the standard of review applied by the appellate court be different from that applied in the opinion above?

2. In ruling on motions for judgment as a matter of law under FED. R. CIV. P. 50 (formerly known as directed verdict and JNOV motions), either before or after submission of the case to the jury, the trial judge is deciding as a matter of law whether there is sufficient evidence to submit the matter to the jury. Assume that the verdict-loser has moved appropriately for judgment as a matter of law and that the motion has been denied. The verdict-loser then appeals, contending that the trial judge erred in denying the motion. What is the question that the appellate court must decide? What deference, if any, should the appellate court give to the trial judge's ruling?

In *Reeves v. Sanderson Plumbing Products, Inc.*, 530 U.S. 133 (2000), the Court explained that, although a trial court should review all of the evidence to decide a motion for judgment as a matter of law, that judge must give credence only to the evidence and reasonable inferences that tend to support the jury's findings and must disregard contrary evidence that the jury was not required to believe, that is, any evidence that is contradicted or has been impeached, or given by interested witnesses. But the jury is not free to disregard uncontroverted, unimpeached, testimony by impartial fact witnesses. The court is not to make credibility determinations or "weigh" the evidence. Courts of appeals review the propriety of a judgment as a matter of law under the same standard that is applied by district courts. *Peterson v. Kennedy*, 771 F.2d 1244 (9th Cir. 1985).

3. Jurors are drawn randomly from the community and typically are without training or experience in evaluating testimony and resolving disputes. What justification is there for immunizing jurors' fact-finding from appellate review to a greater extent than we immunize the fact-finding of a trial judge, a law-trained official experienced in making such determinations?

4. Contrary to general American appellate practice, the Louisiana appellate courts are authorized to review both law and fact in civil cases. LA. CONST., art. V, §10(B). This constitutional provision is implemented by Article 2164 of the Louisiana Code of Civil Procedure: "The appellate court shall render any judgment which is just, legal, and proper upon the record on appeal." *See Gonzales*

v. Xerox Corp., 320 So. 2d 163 (La. 1975). Pursuant to this authority, the appellate court can review the evidence *de novo* and make a finding contrary to the jury finding, and it also can independently compute the amount of damages. For example, in *Lanclos v. Rockwell Int'l Corp.*, 470 So. 2d 924 (La. App. 1985), the court reversed a jury verdict for the defendant in a products liability case, found the defendant liable, and entered judgment for the plaintiff in the amount of $276,083.23 for his personal injuries. Is the administration of justice better served by the Louisiana practice than by the general American practice? Could the federal appellate courts constitutionally adopt the Louisiana practice?

5. In further contrast to a federal appellate court's authority under the "clearly erroneous" standard of FED. R. CIV. P. 52(a), compare CAL. CODE CIV. PROC. tit. 13, §909:

> In all cases where trial by jury is not a matter of right or where trial by jury has been waived, the reviewing court may make findings of fact contrary to or in addition to those made by the trial court. Such findings may be based on the evidence adduced before the trial court either with or without the taking of evidence by the reviewing court. The reviewing court may for the purpose of making such findings of fact or for any other purpose in the interests of justice, take additional evidence of or concerning facts occurring at any time prior to the decision of the appeal, and may give or direct the entry of any judgment or order and may make any further or other order as the case may require. This section shall be liberally construed to the end among others that, where feasible, causes may be finally disposed of by a single appeal and without further proceedings in the trial court except where in the interests of justice a new trial is required on some or all of the issues.

In *Monsan Homes, Inc. v. Pogrebneak*, 258 Cal. Rptr. 676 (1989), the Sixth Appellate District stated that the power to make factual determinations contrary to those of the trial court should be used sparingly, usually only to affirm lower court decisions and terminate litigation, and in very rare cases where the record or new evidence compels reversal.

6. In *Gasperini v. Center for Humanities*, 518 U.S. 415 (1996), the Supreme Court held that a federal appeals court may review for abuse of discretion a trial court's decision not to set aside a jury verdict as excessive. In *Weisgram v. Marly Co.*, 528 U.S. 440 (2000), the Court recognized federal appellate power to instruct district courts to enter judgment as a matter of law and notwithstanding a jury verdict based on the appellate court's determination that expert evidence was not admissible, and the appeals court's re-weighing of the remaining evidence. The Court rejected the view that, in these circumstances, the appeals court was required to remand to allow the district court to decide whether a new trial should be afforded. Still more recently, in *Cooper Industries, Inc. v. Leatherman Tool Group*, 532 U.S. 424 (2001), the Court embraced *de novo* federal appellate review of a jury's punitive damages award, holding that the Ninth Circuit had erred in reviewing for abuse of discretion, on the ground that the "level of punitive damages is not really a 'fact . . . tried by a jury.'"

If these decisions recognize a greater capacity of the appellate courts to find facts than traditionally has been recognized, do these decisions represent a welcome development? Are the decisions permissible under the Seventh Amendment to the Constitution, which states in part that "no fact tried by a jury, shall be otherwise reexamined in any Court of the United States, than according to the rules of the common law"? *See* Debra Lyn Bassett, *"I Lost at Trial — in the Court of Appeals!": The Expanding Power of the Federal Appellate Courts to Reexamine Facts*, 38 HOUS. L. REV. 1129 (2001).

D. Administrative Agency's Fact-Findings

The standards for judicial review of agency fact-findings are different from those relating to review of jury and non-jury fact-findings. The generally applicable standard of review is "whether the finding is supported by substantial evidence on the record as a whole." That is the standard in the Administrative Procedure Act, 5 U.S.C. §706, and in statutes involving particular agencies such as the Federal Trade Commission, 15 U.S.C. §45(c). For useful treatments of the meaning and application of the standard, *see* RICHARD J. PIERCE, JR., ADMINISTRATIVE LAW TREATISE, Chap. 11 (4th ed. 2002) (discussing both the substantial evidence standard, which applies to formal adjudication and formal rulemaking, and the arbitrary and capricious test, which applies when agencies act through informal adjudication or informal rulemaking); RICHARD J. PIERCE, SIDNEY A. SHAPIRO & PAUL R. VERKUIL, ADMINISTRATIVE LAW & PROCESS §7.3.1-7.3.3 (4th ed. 2004) (also discussing both the substantial evidence standard and the arbitrary and capricious standard); Paul R. Verkuil, *An Outcomes Analysis of Scope of Review Standards*, 44 WM. & MARY L. REV. 679 (2002).

E. When Fact and Law are Intertwined

Issues in litigation often involve elements of both law and fact that are not neatly separable. Issues of this sort are variously referred to as involving mixed questions of law and fact, legal inferences from the facts, or the application of law to fact. They can present difficult problems for appellate courts determining the appropriate standard of review: whether to consider the issues to be questions of "law" and thus subject to *de novo* review, or to treat them as questions of "fact" subject to the clearly erroneous standard. FED. R. CIV. P. 52(a) provides for no hybrid or third category.

UNITED STATES v. MCCONNEY
728 F.2d 1195 (9th Cir. 1984)

JUDGE NORRIS delivered Parts I, II, and III of the opinion of the court.

JUDGE GOODWIN delivered Parts IV and V of the opinion of the court.

Winston McConney was convicted on stipulated facts of violating 18 U.S.C. §922(h) which prohibits a convicted felon from receiving firearms shipped in interstate commerce. His appeal challenges the denial of his timely motion to suppress evidence as illegally obtained. We took the case en banc for the specific purpose of resolving the issue of the appropriate standard of appellate review for the mixed question of law and fact of "exigent circumstances."

I

On June 12, 1979, an indictment was filed in the United States District Court for the Northern District of California accusing McConney, and thirty-one other defendants, of violating title IX of the Organized Crime Control Act of 1970. This title, commonly known as the Racketeer Influenced and Corrupt Organizations Act (RICO), prohibits conducting or participating in the conduct of an enterprise through a pattern of racketeering activity. 18 U.S.C. §1962. The indictment identified the RICO "enterprise" as the Hells Angels Motorcycle Club.

On the day after the indictment was filed, federal officers executed an "indicia" warrant authorizing a search of McConney's residence and seizure of any indicia of membership in or association with the Hells Angels Motorcycle Club. In addition to the indicia warrant, the searching officers possessed an arrest warrant and a *Prescott* warrant [which authorizes the search of a home of a person named in an accompanying arrest warrant].

On the evening of June 13, 1979, federal agents executed the arrest and search warrants at McConney's residence. When the agents approached the home at approximately 8:30 p.m., the solid front door was open but an inner screen door was closed. The lead agent, Olson, knocked on the door and announced his identity and purpose. He saw inside a person he recognized immediately as McConney. Between McConney and the door was a second person, sitting with his back to the door. Without waiting for a response or a refusal of entry, Olson opened the door and led the other agents into the living room. McConney and the other person were ordered to move several feet to a position on the floor next to a sofa in the same room. While the two men were being handcuffed, another agent discovered a loaded pistol beneath one of the sofa cushions. A subsequent search of the house made under the indicia warrant yielded a second weapon.

Following the discovery of the two firearms, a count was added in a superseding indictment charging McConney with violating 18 U.S.C. §922(h).

After the district court denied McConney's suppression motion, the government moved to drop the RICO charges against him and proceeded on the firearms charge. . . . The court found McConney guilty as charged. The appeal from the resulting judgment of confinement challenges the denial of the suppression motion.

McConney contends that the entry into his home violated the federal "knock-notice" requirement which provides that an officer, before opening a door of a house in order to enter, must give notice of his identity and purpose and be refused admittance by the occupant. 18 U.S.C. §3109. As this court recently stated, "section 3109 codifies a tradition embedded in Anglo-American law and declares the reverence which the law attaches to an individual's right of privacy in his house." . . .

In *Whitney*, this court addressed the problem of officers entering a house upon announcing their identity and purpose without first awaiting a refusal or admittance. The court recognized that compliance with section 3109's requirements may be excused by exigent circumstances. *Id.* at 908. The government's claim here, as in *Whitney*, is that exigent circumstances justified the agent's failure to await refusal of admittance.

The district court found that the agents had knocked and announced their identity, and that their simultaneous entry (without waiting for refusal of admittance) was justified by exigent circumstances. The district court also found that seizure of the first pistol was an incident of a lawful arrest.

We define exigent circumstances as those circumstances that would cause a reasonable person to believe that entry (or other relevant prompt action) was necessary to prevent either physical harm to the officers or other persons, the destruction of relevant evidence, the escape of the suspect, or some other consequence improperly frustrating legitimate law enforcement efforts.

II

We turn first to the question of what standard of review is applicable to the district court's determination that the federal agents' failure to comply with the requirements of section 3109 was excused by exigent circumstances. In *United States v. Flickinger*, 573 F.2d 1349, 1356-57 & n.2 (9th Cir.), this court held that the "mixed fact-law question" of exigent circumstances is factual in nature and therefore reviewable on appeal under the deferential, clearly erroneous standard. We took this case en banc to decide whether *Flickinger* should be overruled. . . .

[The] disarray in standard of review jurisprudence appears to be pervasive. The Supreme Court recently stated that "there is substantial authority in the circuits on both sides of [the question of the applicability of the rule 52(a) clearly erroneous standard to mixed questions of law and fact]." *Pullman-Standard v. Swint*, 456 U.S. 273, 289-90 n.19 (1982). The Court also acknowledged that, while it has usually reviewed mixed questions independently, its precedents are not entirely consistent and there is support in its decisions for clearly erroneous review of some mixed questions. . . .

The Supreme Court has defined mixed questions as those in which "the historical facts are admitted or established, the rule of law is undisputed, and the issue is whether the facts satisfy the [relevant] statutory [or constitutional] standard, or to put it another way, whether the rule of law as applied to the established facts is or is not violated." *Pullman-Standard v. Swint*. . . . Thus, there are three distinct steps in deciding a mixed fact-law question. The first step is the establishment of the "basic, primary, or historical facts: facts 'in the sense of a recital of external events and the credibility of their narrators. . . .'" The second step is the selection of the applicable rule of law. The third step — and the most troublesome for standard of review purposes — is the application of law to fact or, in other words, the determination "whether the rule of law as applied to the established facts is or is not violated." *Pullman-Standard*, 456 U.S. at 289 n.19.

The district court's resolution of each of these inquiries is, of course, subject to appellate review. The appropriate standard of review for the first two of the district court's determinations — its establishment of historical facts and its selection of the relevant legal principle — has long been settled. Questions of fact are reviewed under the deferential, clearly erroneous standard. *See* FED.

R. CIV. P. 52(a). Questions of law are reviewed under the non-deferential, *de novo* standard. These established rules reflect the policy concerns that properly underlie standard of review jurisprudence generally.

Rule 52(a)'s mandate that appellate courts not disturb a trial court's findings of fact unless clearly erroneous serves two policy objectives. First, it minimizes the risk of judicial error by assigning primary responsibility for resolving factual disputes to the court in the "superior position" to evaluate and weigh the evidence — the trial court. Rule 52(a) emphasizes that the trial judge's opportunity to judge the accuracy of witnesses' recollections and make credibility determinations in cases in which live testimony is presented gives him a significant advantage over appellate judges in evaluating and weighing the evidence: "findings of fact shall not be set aside unless clearly erroneous, and due regard shall be given to the opportunity of the trial court to judge of the credibility of the witnesses." FED. R. CIV. P. 52(a). Second, because under the clearly erroneous test, the reviewing court will affirm the trial court's determinations unless it "is left with the definite and firm conviction that a mistake has been committed," *Pullman-Standard v. Swint*, 456 U.S. 273, 284-85 n.14 (1982), it is relieved of the burden of a full-scale independent review and evaluation of the evidence. Consequently, valuable appellate resources are conserved for those issues that appellate courts in turn are best situated to decide.

The converse rule — that conclusions of law are subject to plenary or *de novo* review — reflects similar concerns. Structurally, appellate courts have several advantages over trial courts in deciding questions of law. First, appellate judges are freer to concentrate on legal questions because they are not encumbered, as are trial judges, by the vital, but time-consuming, process of hearing evidence. Second, the judgment of at least three members of an appellate panel is brought to bear on every case. It stands to reason that the collaborative, deliberative process of appellate courts reduces the risk of judicial error on questions of law. Thus, *de novo* review of questions of law, like clearly erroneous review of questions of fact, serves to minimize judicial error by assigning to the court best positioned to decide the issue the primary responsibility for doing so.

De novo review of questions of law, however, is dictated by still another concern. Under the doctrine of stare decisis, appellate rulings of law become controlling precedent and, consequently, affect the rights of future litigants. Rulings on factual issues, on the other hand, are generally of concern only to the immediate litigants. From the standpoint of sound judicial administration, therefore, it makes sense to concentrate appellate resources on ensuring the correctness of determinations of law.

Thus, we have a well developed standard of review jurisprudence for issues of fact and issues of law. Yet, when we review the third of the district court's determinations — its application of law to fact — we confront "a much-mooted issue" with "substantial authority in the circuits on both sides of th[e] question." *Pullman-Standard*, 456 U.S. at 289-90 n.19. We believe, however, that the well developed jurisprudence relating to questions of pure law and pure fact offers guideposts for working our way out of this confusion.

The appropriate standard of review for a district judge's application of law to fact may be determined, in our view, by reference to the sound principles which underlie the settled rules of appellate review just discussed. If the concerns of judicial administration — efficiency, accuracy, and precedential weight — make it more appropriate for a district judge to determine whether the established facts fall within the relevant legal definition, we should subject his determination to deferential, clearly erroneous review. If, on the other hand, the concerns of judicial administration favor the appellate court, we should subject the district judge's finding to *de novo* review. Thus, in each case, the pivotal question is do the concerns of judicial administration favor the district court or do they favor the appellate court.

In our view, the key to the resolution of this question is the nature of the inquiry that is required to decide "whether the rule of law as applied to the established facts is or is not violated." *Id.* If application of the rule of law to the facts requires an inquiry that is "essentially factual," *id.* at 288 — one that is founded "on the application of the fact-finding tribunal's experience with the mainsprings of human conduct," — the concerns of judicial administration will favor the district court, and the district court's determination should be classified as one of fact reviewable under the clearly erroneous standard. If, on the other hand, the question requires us to consider legal concepts in the mix of fact and law and to exercise judgment about the values that animate legal principles, then the concerns of judicial administration will favor the appellate court, and the question should be classified as one of law and reviewed *de novo*.

As the Supreme Court appeared to indicate in *Pullman-Standard*, 456 U.S. at 289 n.19, the concerns of judicial administration will generally favor the appellate court, justifying *de novo* review. This is so because usually the application of law to fact will require the consideration of legal concepts and involve the exercise of judgment about the values underlying legal principles. . . .

In summary, to classify mixed questions of law and fact for standard of review purposes, we adopt a functional analysis that focuses on the nature of the inquiry required when we apply the relevant rule of law to the facts as established. The analysis is not a precise one and does not offer any litmus test by which all mixed questions can be neatly categorized. It does not "unerringly distinguish between findings of fact and conclusions of law." *Pullman-Standard v. Swint*, 456 U.S. at 289 n.19. Nonetheless, we think that if we focus on the nature of the inquiry required in determining whether the established facts fall within the relevant legal definition, we employ a neutral test that accurately reflects the concerns that properly underlie standard of review jurisprudence.

III

Applying our functional analysis to the case at hand, we conclude that the mixed question of exigent circumstances is reviewable *de novo* as a question of law, and, consequently, we overrule *Flickinger*. . . .

The essential and difficult question raised by this balancing is how much risk police officers can reasonably be expected to assume before disregarding the rules society has adopted to otherwise circumscribe the exercise of their considerable discretionary authority in carrying out their vital law enforcement duties.

This is a question that no amount of factfinding will answer. The inquiry requires us to ask not merely whether the trial judge was correct in finding that Olson in fact had reason to believe, for instance, that McConney was a member of the Hell's Angels Motorcycle Club or that he had a prior felony conviction; it also requires a determination whether these facts and any other information Olson had about McConney's past are sufficient to satisfy the legal standard for exigency. We must decide, for instance, whether a reasonable belief that a suspect is a member of the Hell's Angels Club, without demonstration of a link to criminal activity, is relevant to the issue of exigency. . . . We must also decide how much weight may be given to an officer's knowledge that a suspect has previously been convicted of an unspecified felony.

When, as here, the application of law to fact requires us to make value judgments about the law and its policy underpinnings, and when, as here, the application of law to fact is of clear precedential importance, the policy reasons for *de novo* review are satisfied and we should not hesitate to review the district judge's determination independently.

In conclusion, we hold that the mixed question of exigent circumstances is not reviewable under the clearly erroneous test because it is not, like the question of intent, essentially factual. We do not at this juncture decide how any other mixed question should be reviewed. We do, it is true, adopt a functional analysis for the resolution of these questions. But our approach is an ad hoc one, permitting individual analysis and classification of each type of mixed question. Under it, we need only decide that the question of exigent circumstances is subject to *de novo* review.

IV

We have made the required review of the record, and we affirm the district court's holding that exigent circumstances excused the agents' failure to await refusal of admittance before entering McConney's home. . . .

SNEED, CIRCUIT JUDGE, concurring in judgment. . . .

The problem is essentially one of managing the allocation of appellate court resources. Those things the trial court does better we should not attempt to repeat. True, we should review the trial court's performance even with respect to those things it can do better to eliminate intolerable deviations. And, of course, those things the appellate court can do better we should not delegate to the trial court.

The problem is which things go where. Part II is a wise and intelligent attempt to formulate general principles that will provide the solution. My basic reservation is that I believe the process of deciding which things go where is more tentative, experimental, and ad hoc than even Part II suggests. What is a "fact" can never be satisfactorily fixed. . . . The precise level of abstraction deserving of being characterized as a fact, historical or otherwise, turns on the purpose being served. In the context of the standard of review with respect to exigent circumstances, I believe the trial courts, by employing the definition of such circumstances stated by the majority, can do a better job than we. Therefore, I would say whether a reasonable person would believe that entry was necessary to prevent "either physical harm to the officers or other persons," . . . is a question of fact. True, the definition employs a fairly high level of abstraction but it provides sufficient guidance to enable trial courts to bring to bear their unquestionably superior experience with police officers and defendants accused of crime. This superiority flows from their frequent opportunity to observe them face-to-face. Appellate courts can only read and classify cold records; trial courts confront the people whose actions they characterize.

For me this superior experience resolves the "which goes where" problem. *Flickinger* was properly decided. An appellate court cannot do as good a job in this area as the trial courts. This is said while recognizing, as I must, that our unrelenting duty is to protect constitutional rights. To me it better serves those rights to treat "exigent circumstances," as the majority defines them, as a question of fact subject to the "clearly erroneous" standard of review.

JUDGE GOODWIN, specially concurring in the judgment.

I concur in the majority opinion that the appellate review of a trial court's findings on the existence of exigent circumstances requires the application of a legal standard rather than the "clearly erroneous" standard of FED. R. CIV. P. 52 which we routinely apply to factual findings made by trial courts in the decision of purely factual questions.

I respect the scholarship, and agree with much of the reasoning of the majority. But I disagree with the majority's decision, stated in Parts II and III of the opinion, to leave a number of categories of suppression questions open to review under standards that will have to be developed for each of the categories by the separate weighing of the preponderance of facts or law in so-called mixed questions of law and fact. This exercise is likely to prove both time-consuming and uncertain in its results.

I agree that there is no simple, or bright line, test that will always steer this court to the appropriate characterization of a question, whether of law or fact. The difficulty in defining the difference between questions of law and questions of fact in a given formulation of a suppression question itself underscores the argument that we should adopt a rule that when the court is in doubt, it should treat the question as one of law. Judicial review in the doubtful, or complex law-fact questions would then be conducted as it should be, *de novo*, giving proper concern to underlying constitutional principles as the court makes certain that they were correctly applied to the historical facts. If reasonable lawyers and judges can't agree whether a given question is one of fact or one of law, then it is probably a question of law.

It is only in the close and debatable questions that arise when one invokes constitutional principles that anything important is likely to turn upon the way we characterize the question in any event. It is in precisely this type of case that we ought to proceed independently and examine the question of exigent circumstances as a question of law. Accordingly, I would be content to rest the debate that has for so long engaged this court upon a statement made by the Supreme Court, to which we look for leadership in such matters:

> While this Court does not sit as in *nisi prius* to appraise contradictory factual questions, it will, where necessary to the determination of constitutional rights, make an independent examination of the facts, the findings, and the record so that it can determine for itself whether in the decision as to reasonableness the fundamental — i.e., constitutional — criteria established by this Court have been respected. . . .

While *Sumner v. Mata*, 455 U.S. 591, 597 (1982), has limited the scope of federal court review concerning facts found by the state courts in proceedings that satisfied due process, we have found no Supreme Court case holding that federal appellate courts are bound by the district court's application of constitutional principles following the district court's designation of certain questions as questions of fact. We do, of course, defer to the district judge's findings when they deal with historical facts. But when the ultimate question involves both historical facts and their constitutional meaning, we have the duty to review the ultimate question independently. . . .

JUDGE BOOCHEVER, concurring in the judgment.

I agree with Judge Goodwin's concurrence on the assumption that the reasoning applies only to contentions that constitutional rights have been violated. In cases not implicating basic constitutional rights I believe that institutional values are better served by applying a clearly erroneous standard of review when a trial judge has applied a correct legal standard to established facts.

NOTES

1. How do "exigent circumstances" in *McConney* differ from "intention to discriminate" in *Pullman-Standard*? Can the two decisions be reconciled?

2. What are the "fact" components in *McConney*?

3. What "law" features does *McConney* display?

4. According to Maurice Rosenberg, *Standards of Review*, in ARTHUR D. HELLMAN, RESTRUCTURING JUSTICE 30, 41 (1991):[14]

> *McConney*'s functional analysis is the one most frequently applied by the courts of appeals. Because it requires subtle and complex judgments, the *McConney* approach is probably not much of a barrier to appealing. The temptation remains strong for the loser to present the mixed question as one of law only so that the panel, reviewing it independently, is freer to reverse than if the fact standard . . . applies. A brief list of typical cases will illustrate:

---

[14] Reprinted from RESTRUCTURING JUSTICE: THE INNOVATIONS OF THE NINTH CIRCUIT AND THE FUTURE OF THE FEDERAL COURTS, edited by Arthur D. Hellman. Copyright © 1990 by Cornell University. Used by permission of the publisher, Cornell University Press.

- Was the misstatement in the security offering "material" within the meaning of the statute?

- Were the motion picture clearances given to the competitor of the antitrust plaintiff "reasonable" restraints of trade?

- Was the suspect's consent to a warrantless police search "voluntary"?

In situations like those there clearly is an underlying matrix of facts. In each case these are imbedded in a context such that the court, while making findings of fact, could simultaneously resolve the ultimate, dispositive issues if it is so minded. Or it can instead treat the dispositive issue as a legal question, subject to the purposes and policies of the applicable rule of law. In each case the choice requires hard thought and close analysis; it is not susceptible to global solution.

5. 9A CHARLES ALAN WRIGHT & ARTHUR R. MILLER, FEDERAL PRACTICE AND PROCEDURE § 2589 (2d ed. 1995)[15]: "Mixed Questions of Fact and Law — In General":

Many issues in a lawsuit involve elements of both law and fact. Whether these be referred to as mixed questions of law and fact, or legal inferences from the facts, or the application of law to the facts, there is substantial authority that they are not protected by the "clearly erroneous" rule and are freely reviewable. . . .

It certainly is true that if an error of law has impaired the judgment of the trial judge on a mixed question of law or fact, then the court's finding should be set aside. It is less clear that it is very helpful to say generally that mixed questions of law and fact are entirely outside the "clearly erroneous" rule. In a long line of cases courts have held that that rule limited appellate review of matters that certainly seem to contain both legal and factual elements.

Thus the Supreme Court has treated as a question of fact, governed by Rule 52(a), an issue whether a payment to a taxpayer was a "gift," and lower courts have applied that principle to many other determinations relating to the tax laws. Other courts have applied the "clearly erroneous" rule to a tremendous variety of matters including: whether a party was guilty of laches; the existence and scope of an agency or fiducial relationship; questions involving contracts, including the existence of a contract, whether the parties had been under a mutual mistake, the nature or character of an instrument, and even in some instances the interpretation of a written contract; the eligibility of an alien for naturalization; the danger of consumer confusion with regard to trademarks and tradenames; whether a transaction was fraudulent; the existence of subject matter or personal jurisdiction and many other matters. . . .

6. In a state post-conviction hearing (a civil action) challenging the constitutionality of a conviction on the ground that it was obtained through the use of

---

[15] Copyright © 1995 by Thomson West. Reprinted with permission.

an involuntary confession in violation of the due process clause, the court takes the testimony of several witnesses. Assume that the testimony conflicts as to the circumstances under which the accused was interrogated, i.e., the number of hours interrogation lasted, the frequency of breaks, the amount of food and drink provided for the accused, the nature of statements made to the accused by the interrogating police officers, and so on. At the conclusion of the hearing the trial judge holds the confession to have been voluntary and hints that the conviction is valid. Is this conclusion one of fact or one of law? What standard of review should the appellate court apply in reviewing the decision? *See Miller v. Fenton*, 474 U.S. 104 (1985) (treating voluntariness as a question of law on federal habeas corpus review of a state conviction). Consider the following excerpt.

Ellen E. Sward, *Appellate Review of Judicial Fact-Finding*, 40 University of Kansas Law Review 1, 34, 35-36 (1991)[16]

The constitutional fact doctrine requires independent appellate review of fact-finding when a party claims denial of federal constitutional rights. It is an explicit exception to the clearly erroneous standard. The limits of the doctrine are not clear, and the doctrine is controversial. The constitutional fact exception to the clearly erroneous standard, however, does seem to reflect a confluence of the values that underlie both error correction and law declaration. Thus, it is not surprising that such an exception exists. Ultimately, the constitutional fact exception should probably be viewed as a special example of a mixed question.

. . . Beginning as early as 1935, the Supreme Court authorized independent review of constitutional facts found by state courts. The doctrine has recently been extended to review of judgments of inferior federal courts. The constitutional fact doctrine has become quite well-accepted in the First Amendment context. The leading case is *New York Times Co. v. Sullivan* [376 U.S. 254 (1964)], in which the Court required independent appellate review of a state trial court's findings of fact on the actual malice element of libel.

New York Times was a case that originated in the state courts. In *Bose Corp. v. Consumers Union of United States, Inc.,* [466 U.S. 485 (1984)], the Supreme Court affirmed the constitutional fact exception to the clearly erroneous standard for cases originating in the federal courts, holding that the clearly erroneous standard "does not prescribe the standard of review to be applied in reviewing a determination of actual malice in a case governed by *New York Times Co. v. Sullivan.*" [*Bose*, 466 U.S. at 514.] Consumers Union had published a review of some stereo speakers manufactured by Bose, and Bose claimed that the review was defamatory in its description of the way the sound moved about the room. The trial court evidently believed that anyone of modest capability in writing could have written an accurate description of the sound; therefore, the court inferred actual malice. The First Circuit reversed, holding that it was required to make a *de novo* review of the finding of actual malice and, upon making that review, holding that Bose had not

---

16 Copyright © 1991. Reprinted with permission of the Kansas Law Review.

proved actual malice by clear and convincing evidence, as was required under the *New York Times* standard.

The Supreme Court affirmed. The Court recognized that there was a conflict between the clearly erroneous standard of Rule 52 and the duty of independent review that the constitutional fact doctrine prescribes. The Court identified three relevant characteristics of the actual malice rule that suggest independent review of such determinations. First, the actual malice rule itself has a common-law heritage, and so gives a large role to the judge. Second, the rule is given meaning through the evolutionary process of case-by-case adjudication. Third, because constitutional values are at stake, judges have a duty to ensure that the rule is applied correctly.

This formulation of the constitutional fact doctrine is highly specific to First Amendment issues. There is, therefore, some question about the current scope of the constitutional fact doctrine. The doctrine could be applied to analogous issues, however, and given the fact that most legal doctrine, whether constitutional or not, is refined in case-by-case adjudication, the parameters of the doctrine could be quite broad.

NOTES

1. The constitutional fact doctrine is further explored in Henry P. Monaghan, *Constitutional Fact Review*, 85 COLUM. L. REV. 229 (1985).

2. The necessity of distinguishing between fact and law in civil litigation can arise in three ways: on a motion for summary judgment, on motions for judgment as a matter of law before and after jury verdicts, and on appeal following a non-jury trial. The following excerpt, although focused on summary judgments, reveals this common thread. Note that if an issue is considered one for the jury in a jury trial, an appellate court normally would consider a decision of that issue by the judge in a non-jury trial to be a determination of fact.

WILLIAM W. SCHWARZER, ALAN HIRSCH, & DAVID J. BARRANS, THE ANALYSIS AND DECISION OF SUMMARY JUDGMENT MOTIONS 13-21 (1991)[17]

Although judicial opinions frequently characterize a particular matter as one of fact or one of law, purporting to distinguish categorically between the two, these characterizations rarely provide much guidance for future cases. They are generally made in the factual context of the particular case. When a court says, for example, that the definition of the relevant market is a question of fact, it may have reached that conclusion because it sees evidentiary disputes in the case that must be resolved to define the market. Conversely, a court may reach the opposite conclusion when it considers the question as presented open to only one reasonable answer, thus calling it a question of law (although a more precise characterization might be a "non-genuine" issue of fact). . . .

Another difficulty is the lack of any line of demarcation, let alone a bright line, between fact and law. Instead, there is a spectrum ranging from fact to

---

[17] Published by the Federal Judicial Center.

law, in which a large continuum between the two extremes is occupied by mixed questions of law and fact and by questions of ultimate fact.

At one extreme of this spectrum lie so-called historical facts. A historical fact is a thing done, an action performed, or an event or occurrence. Some historical facts may be proved by direct evidence. Others, such as notice, intent, or other states of mind, are proved by inference from evidence of other facts. The resolution of disputes over historical facts or the inferences to be drawn from them is a jury function. A dispute over historical facts or inferences, if genuine and material within the meaning of Rule 56, precludes summary judgment.

At the other extreme of the spectrum lie issues of law. When the facts material to the application of a pure rule of law are undisputed, the application is a matter of law for the court, requiring no trial. For example, summary judgment is proper when undisputed facts establish that a requisite element of a claim or defense is lacking, as in *Celotex Corp. v. Catnett*, where the issue on summary judgment was whether plaintiff had adduced proof of exposure to products manufactured by defendant, an essential element of the claim. When there is no dispute over the sufficiency of evidence establishing the facts that control the application of a rule of law, summary judgment is the appropriate means of deciding the issue. Such issues include whether an action is barred by a statute of limitations, by res judicata, by collateral estoppel, or by lack of standing or jurisdiction. They also include issues turning on statutory interpretation and the evaluation of an administrative record, such as whether the findings of an agency are supported by substantial evidence.

When the application of a rule of law depends on the resolution of disputed historical facts, however, it becomes a mixed question of law and fact. Plaintiff's standing to sue, for example, may turn on activities of the plaintiff that are in dispute. Whether the statute of limitations has run may depend on a dispute over when plaintiff received notice. Such disputed facts normally preclude summary judgment.

Mixed questions of law and fact arise in a variety of other forms. Normally, the legal questions presented are resolved by the court and the fact issues by the jury. Contract disputes, though frequently questions of law, may present mixed questions; when the court determines that a document is ambiguous, for example, the jury resolves evidentiary disputes such as what the parties intended. Constitutional issues, though generally questions of law, may be mixed questions when they turn on factual determinations.

Although the terms are sometimes used interchangeably, it is useful to distinguish mixed questions of law and fact from questions of ultimate fact. Mixed questions generally require the resolution of disputes over historical fact. Ultimate facts present a different kind of "factual" inquiry, one involving a process that "implies the application of standards of law." Like some historical facts, ultimate facts are derived by reasoning or inference from evidence, but, like issues of law, they incorporate legal principles or policies that give them independent legal significance. They often involve the *characterization* of historical facts, and their resolution is generally outcome-determinative.

Ultimate facts occupy a broad segment of the spectrum between fact and law. Where on that spectrum a particular ultimate fact belongs depends on whether it is predominantly factual or legal. For example, whether a defendant used due care in the operation of a vehicle or was driving in the course of employment or whether that person's acts were the proximate cause of plaintiff's injuries are all questions of ultimate fact that are predominantly factual rather than legal and therefore clearly for the jury. Similarly, whether a person had reasonable cause, acted within a reasonable time, or can be charged with notice are predominantly factual (though outcome-determinative) questions. The resolution of such questions turns on an assessment of human behavior and expectations within the common experience of jurors. Concerning issues of this sort, traditionally resolved by juries, the Supreme Court said in 1873: "It is assumed that twelve men know more of the common affairs of life than does one man, that they can draw wiser and safer conclusions from admitted facts thus occurring than can a single judge."

Near the opposite end of the spectrum lie those ultimate facts that, though nominally facts, have a high law content. Their resolution (in the absence of evidentiary disputes) turns on matters of law and policy and on technical issues underlying the legal scheme. The administration of the rules under which they arise benefits from consistency, uniformity, and predictability. Whether an instrument is a security, whether a plaintiff is a public figure, whether a publication is not copyrightable as historical, whether an invention was reduced to practice, and whether a carrier operated as a common carrier are questions of ultimate fact calling for the interpretation and application of essentially legal standards.

Most of the difficulty is encountered in the middle range of the spectrum. Here considerations of public policy and individual justice overlap, making issues less susceptible to categorization. Although the decision involves the application of a legal (generally statutory) standard, the court must decide whether the context in which the question arises makes it more appropriate for decision by judge or by jury. For example, whether an employee whose duties bring him into contact with ocean-going vessels is a "seaman" within the meaning of the Jones Act is a question of ultimate fact because the finding has direct legal consequences, but in some circumstances it may be more appropriately decided by a jury. A court faced with making such an allocation between judge and jury should not reach that issue until it has determined whether historical facts material to the decision are in dispute. Thus, if a dispute exists over the terms or conditions of an employee's employment, summary judgment is generally inappropriate. However, when the dispute is not over historical facts but over their legal significance, such as whether an employee's position should be characterized as "policy-making" for purposes of a claim under the civil rights laws, the issue may be appropriate for summary judgment.

As noted, courts determining whether such a question should be treated as one of fact or law do not often find direct assistance in precedent. Not only do courts often fail to explicate reasoning on this aspect of summary judgment, but the question arises in the shadowy middle ground between fact and law where decisions may be too fact-driven to be entitled to much precedential weight. There are, however, a number of relevant factors and considerations that can provide useful guidance. Courts have generally used a functional test, assessing whether the question is more suitable for resolution by a court or a jury. The Supreme Court has endorsed such an inquiry in the allocation of functions between trial and appellate courts:

> [T]he appropriate methodology for distinguishing questions of fact from questions of law has been, to say the least, elusive.
>
> . . . Perhaps much of the difficulty in this area stems from the practical truth that the decision to label an issue a "question of law," a "question of fact," or a "mixed question of law and fact" is sometimes as much a matter of allocation as it is of analysis. At least in those instances in which Congress has not spoken and in which the issue falls somewhere between a pristine legal standard and a simple historical fact, the fact/law distinction at times has turned on a determination that, as a matter of the sound administration of justice, one judicial actor is better positioned than another to decide the issue in question.

As suggested above, the functional inquiry involves several factors, including whether the issue falls within the common experience of jurors, whether its resolution involves the kinds of decisions traditionally entrusted to jurors, and whether a judgment of peers is desirable. . . .

Where, on the other hand, a decision is likely to have significant precedential impact on the resolution of an issue imbued with the need for consistency and reasoned resolution, the balance tilts toward determination by the judge rather than the jury. The Supreme Court has stated, albeit in the context of allocation between trial and appellate courts, that "[r]egarding certain largely factual questions in some areas of the law, the stakes — in terms of impact on future cases and future conduct — are too great to entrust them finally to the trier of fact." If a decision will immediately affect a class of persons or groups, making it in the nature of judicial rule making, it generally should be treated as a question of law. For example, the question of whether homosexuals constitute a suspect or quasi-suspect class for purposes of the equal protection clause creates a widely applicable rule of law and should be decided by the court. Similarly, whether transportation of explosives on the highways constitutes ultrahazardous activity for purposes of imposing strict liability is an issue for the court to decide, but whether a particular driver's conduct in driving a truck loaded with explosives at speeds barely within posted limits is a violation is a question for the jury. The former has direct ramifications for many drivers and for society at large, whereas the latter is a fact-specific inquiry primarily affecting the one driver.

The policy implications surrounding an issue may make summary judgment the preferred means of resolution. In *Anderson v. Creighton*, for example, the Supreme Court ruled that whether a government agent was entitled to qualified immunity could be decided as a matter of law, even though the decision turns on a determination whether a reasonable person in the defendant's position could have believed his or her actions to have been lawful. The Court explained that the purpose of the rule is to protect government agents from having to submit to pretrial discovery, a public policy concern better addressed by courts than by juries. Similarly, although probable cause for arrest and reasonableness of force used are normally jury questions, where there are no material disputes over what transpired and the case turns on a policy determination, courts may resolve these questions on summary judgment. Causation, generally a jury issue, has been decided by a court in the context of a standing challenge as a mixed question primarily involving policy. And such antitrust policy issues as whether the exchange of price-related information or the maintenance of industry-wide licensing agreements constituted unlawful conspiracies have, in the absence of evidentiary disputes, been decided on summary judgment.

F. Trial Court's Exercises of Discretion

Patrick W. Brennan, *Standards of Appellate Review*, 33 DEFENSE LAW JOURNAL 377, 412-14 (1984)[18]

An appellate court may review a trial court's ruling when the judge below has abused the discretion vested in him. Discretion is simply the term employed to define the lower court's power or privilege to act. This discretion is exercised in many situations: rulings on motions, discovery, arguments of counsel, admissibility of evidence, instructions, and numerous other jury-related matters. . . .

The abuse of discretion standard of review will take on further meaning when compared to legal error and review intended to do justice. . . . It will be seen that the abuse of discretion standard allows great deference to the trial court unless its discretion was unreasonably or prejudicially exercised.

The abuse of discretion standard represents a compromise between the competing desires of affording power and flexibility to the trial court, yet at the same time minimizing arbitrary decisions. Since the lower court is in a better position to see and hear the participants for and against a cause, there is a need to allow rulings to be flexible so as to meet the varying rights of the litigants. This must be balanced against the danger of a lower court exercising this power arbitrarily or capriciously. The scales are tipped in favor of trial court flexibility.

There are a number of reasons for according discretion to the trial court. One justification is judicial economy: An appellate court could not begin to handle all of the cases that would be appealed if trial court rulings were a meaningless formality.

Another reason is judicial comity. Appellate courts should and do recognize the integrity and competence of the lower courts. The difficult task of making quick decisions in the heat of the trial should be, and is, respected.

Thirdly, trial courts have discretionary power in order to ensure that judgments are binding and final. The impetus to file an appeal from any adverse decision is avoided by dignifying the trial court's decisions with a high degree of finality.

---

[18] Reprinted from *Defense Law Journal* with permission copyright © 1984 Matthew Bender & Company, Inc., a member of Lexis Nexis Group. All rights reserved.

The final two reasons are interrelated. It is said that one of the strongest reasons behind according discretion to the trial court is the fact that the judge is in a better position to see and hear the witnesses. This superior position allows a better "feel of the case" that examination of the appellate court record does not afford.

Due to the great variety of factual situations that arise in court, this justification spawns another: formal legal rules are not practical instruments to use in reaching a just result at trial; only the principle of the abuse of discretion standard is adaptable enough to be applied to all types of cases.

[T]he practical reasons for trial court discretion — judicial economy, comity and finality — do not provide the guidance to a trial court that would allow it to know in advance which rulings are guarded by some discretionary immunity from review, and which are not. On the other hand, the trial court's "nether position" and the nonamenability of discretion to rule are both good reasons — they provide discriminatory guidance to the use of discretion. . . .

[T]he meaning of discretion can be narrowed to a single word: Choice. That is, a trial court has a choice in its decisions, and an appellate court is restrained in its review of the lower court's choice by the abuse of discretion standard. This description ultimately leads to the principle that a trial judge has a limited right to be wrong without fear of reversal on appeal.

Henry J. Friendly, *Indiscretion about Discretion*, 31 EMORY LAW JOURNAL 747, 760-62, 771-72, 783-84 (1982)[19]

One test for determining the amount of deference that should be accorded to rulings of trial courts which are neither of law nor of fact, is how closely the trial court's superior opportunities to reach a correct result approximate those existing in its determinations of fact.

Another principle supporting deference to rulings of the trial court is the absence of the benefits that ordinarily flow from appellate review in establishing rules that will govern future cases.

These principles support the deference traditionally accorded to many such rulings — such pretrial matters as discovery, continuances, allowing amendments of pleadings, permitting intervention or impleader, or holding pretrial conferences; such trial matters as the nature and extent of the voir dire of the jury, the conduct of counsel, the length of the trial day, or the denial of continuances; and such post-trial matters as the grant or denial of a motion for a new trial. . . .

Beyond all this, there is a limit on the capacity of the judicial system to entertain appeals and afford retrials. In addition to the obvious burden of a retrial, the retrial itself is likely to produce new grounds for appeal; the alleged errors simply will be different. Too perfectionist an attitude with respect to many sorts of claims of trial error involves the prospect of an infinite regress. There thus is a gray penumbra just beyond the boundaries of the

---

[19] Copyright © 1982 by Emory Law Journal. Reprinted with permission.

harmless error doctrine where the discretion rule may serve the purpose, at least in civil cases, of avoiding useless reversals where there is no real prospect that a different result should be forthcoming on a new trial. . . .

The case for full appellate review is particularly strong when a settled practice has developed in cases of the type *sub judice* and the trial court has departed from it. In *Noonan v. Cunard Steamship Co.*, the Second Circuit announced a principle that accumulated precedent at the trial court level may limit the scope of what initially was almost total discretion. Referring to Federal Rule of Civil Procedure 39(b), which says that "notwithstanding the failure of a party to demand a jury in an action in which such a demand might have been made of right, the court in its discretion upon motion may order a trial by a jury of any or all issues," we pointed to defendant's citation of eighteen reported decisions by district courts within our circuit that such a motion would not be granted when the moving party alleged nothing more than inadvertence, and plaintiff's failure to cite any to the contrary. We thought that "the settled course of decision had placed a gloss upon the Rule which a judge could no more disregard than if the words had appeared in the Rule itself." We then went on to hold that, with this as a given, a district judge could not allow a plaintiff to achieve the same objective by permitting dismissal without prejudice under Federal Rule of Civil Procedure 41(a)(2). We had this to say:

> [T]he fact that dismissal under Rule 41(a)(2) usually rests on the judge's discretion does not mean that this is always so. Several of the most important reasons for deferring to the trial judge's exercise of discretion — his observation of the witnesses, his superior opportunity to get "the feel of the case," and the impracticability of framing a rule of decision where many disparate factors must be weighed — are inapposite when a question arising in advance of trial can be stated in a form susceptible of a yes-or-no answer applicable to all cases.

We pointed also to three district court decisions denying leave to discontinue without prejudice under the same circumstances and none opposed save the one before us, and thought that "[t]he desirability of achieving consistency among district judges in the same circuit on such an issue and of avoiding judge-shopping outweighs that of appellate deference to a determination of the district judge on a preliminary procedural matter. . . ."

Since I wrote the opinion, naturally this seems very sound to me. The rulemakers gave the district courts discretion; but after enough of them had decided always to exercise it the same way, a way that the court of appeals deemed appropriate, the channel of discretion had narrowed, and a court of appeals should keep a judge from steering outside it rather than allow disparate results on the same facts. When the rulemakers have another go at the rule, as they should periodically, they can either adopt that construction or reject it. Meanwhile, parties will know where they stand and consistency will have been achieved. . . .

[T]here is not just one standard of "abuse of discretion" on the part of the trial judge. In those situations "where the decision depends on first-hand observation or direct contact with the litigation," the trial court's decision "merits a high degree of insulation from appellate revision." At the other extreme, when Congress has declared a national policy and enlisted the aid of the courts' equity powers in its enforcement, the Supreme Court has said that the fact that "the [trial] court's discretion is equitable in nature . . . hardly means that it is unfettered by meaningful standards or shielded from thorough appellate review." In some instances the need for uniformity and predictability demands thorough appellate review. In short, the "abuse of discretion" standard does not give nearly so complete an immunity bath to the trial court's rulings as counsel for appellees would have reviewing courts believe. An appellate court must carefully scrutinize the nature of the trial court's determination and decide whether that court's superior opportunities of observation or other reasons of policy require greater deference than would be accorded to its formulations of law or its application of law to the facts. In cases within the former categories, "abuse of discretion" should be given a broad reading, in others a reading which scarcely differs from the definition of error. Above all, an appellate court should consider whether the lawmaker intended that discretion should be committed solely to the trial judge or to judges throughout the judicial system.

A good note on which to end is Chief Justice Marshall's statement in the *Burr* case that discretionary choices are not left to a court's "inclination, but to its judgment; and its judgment is to be guided by sound legal principles." Although Marshall was there talking to himself as the trial judge, his remark embodies an appropriate standard for review of many "discretionary" determinations often claimed to lie beyond meaningful appellate scrutiny.

Review-limiting discretion in its stronger forms confers upon the trial judge unusual power with regard to many issues and, as a corollary, grave responsibility. The judge becomes a court of last resort on these issues, not because appellate machinery is lacking, but because the matters are not susceptible to firm legal rules and because the trial judge is thought to be in a better position than appellate judges to decide the matters wisely and justly.

Of course, it is important that a trial judge wielding such extraordinary power "play fair" with the system. To play fair, a trial judge relying upon discretion should place on the record the circumstances and factors crucial to her decision. The reasons should be spelled out clearly so that counsel and the reviewing court will know and be in a position to evaluate the soundness of the decision. If the appellate court concludes that the judge considered inappropriate factors or that the range of discretionary authority should be fenced in, it will be in a position to do this intelligently.

The obligation to behave in this fashion binds the common-law judge even in areas where discretion seemingly gives him choices. To "act in your considered judgment, with a resolve to decide in the same way if the issue arises again" also is an unspoken but inescapable command of our judicial system. To the extent that judges hear and obey this command, the potential for abuse of discretion is tempered.

The dilemma for judges is how to be sensitive to the need for even-handedness and constancy in their behavior and at the same time sensitive to the value of wielding judicial power flexibly. Very probably only the slow process of absorbing year after year the common law's values and ideals — beginning in law school — can produce the subtle blend of power and restraint that judges need.

NAPOLITANO v. COMPANIA SUD AMERICANA de VAPORES
421 F.2d 382 (2d Cir. 1970)

WATERMAN, CIRCUIT JUDGE.

Plaintiff-appellee, a longshoreman, commenced two actions against the defendant shipowner seeking to recover damages for personal injuries received on two separate occasions while working aboard defendant's vessels. After jury trials held one week apart judgments were rendered in plaintiff's favor in both cases by the United States District Court for the Southern District of New York. . . .

[In case one] plaintiff alleged that in 1963 he slipped on a newspaper which he claimed covered spilled oil or grease, and fell to the deck while loading cargo aboard the defendant's ship, SS COPIAPO, and that an injury to his left shoulder resulted. . . .

[In case two] plaintiff slipped from a Jacob's ladder (a rope ladder with wooden rungs), which was rigged to enable plaintiff and others to disembark from defendant's vessel SS MAIPO to a lighter (a large boat used to load and unload ships and to transport freight about a harbor) lying alongside. The cause of plaintiff's fall to the deck of the lighter, and the subsequent injury to his right shoulder, was allegedly the presence of oil or grease on a rung located about six rungs from the bottom of the ladder. . . .

Defendant-appellant raises similar issues in both appeals, and we treat both cases in this opinion. . . . Somewhat reluctantly we do not regard any of these contentions, viewed singly or in combination, sufficient to warrant a reversal and new trial in either case, and therefore affirm the judgments. . . .

The testimony of witnesses in case one started about 10:30 A.M. and concluded at 12:20 P.M. At that point defense counsel informed the court that a defense medical witness would not be available to testify until two o'clock that afternoon. Judge MacMahon refused to delay the proceedings to accommodate the defense witness and ordered counsel to sum up. The case was shortly thereafter submitted to the jury. Defendant claims that the trial judge abused his discretion by failing to recess until 2:00 P.M. It does not seem to us that a request to interrupt a trial for a period of approximately one and a half hours, the request coming at a time when courts normally recess for lunch, is unreasonable. Had any one of us been in a position to exercise the discretion committed to a trial judge when such a request is made, we have no hesitancy in stating that the decision would have been otherwise; but as appellate judges we cannot find that the action of the district judge was so unreasonable or so arbitrary as to amount to a prejudicial abuse of the discretion necessary to repose in trial judges during the conduct of a trial. Judge MacMahon's zeal in bringing to conclusion trials in which he has been the trial judge has prompted disappointed litigants to appeal on the ground that his rulings have been abuses of discretion; but, as we said in *Winston v. Prudential Lines, Inc.*, 415 F.2d 619 (2d Cir. Sept. 3, 1969), "We have permitted a great deal of latitude to be given to individual district judges who conscientiously labor to reduce calendar congestion." . . . We have also pointed out that litigants have alternative methods of protecting themselves if there is a possibility that a witness may not be available to testify when needed. First, counsel may take a deposition of such a witness and have it ready to introduce if his appearance at trial is in fact delayed. Second, while of little practical help in this case, application may be made to the Part I Judge under Calendar Rule 7(b)(1) of the Southern District of New York if a witness is not to be available on the day of trial, *Winston v. Prudential Lines, Inc., supra* at 621. While we hold that in the two cases presently before us Judge MacMahon did not overstep the bounds of his discretion, we quite frankly state that the court in case one did come dangerously close to causing "its zeal for a tidy calendar [to] overcome its duty to do justice." . . . [F]or it appears obvious that "very little by way of expeditious disposition of cases was gained by the judge's ruling." . . . Moreover, we do not think it amiss to indicate that if these recurrent occurrences which to date we have been constrained to view as not being abuses of discretion continue to recur we may find it necessary to consider such a pattern of conduct as detrimental to the administration of justice despite a trial judge's conscientious belief that he is facilitating it.

In case two, defense counsel also was deprived of defense testimony when witnesses present in court but who had not been named in defendant's pretrial memorandum were not permitted to testify. On the Friday before trial was to commence on Tuesday, defense counsel served on the plaintiff an amended pre-trial memorandum in which he named witnesses not previously mentioned in his original pre-trial memorandum. This memorandum was filed with the court on Monday. Prior to the start of defendant's case, plaintiff's counsel brought this to the court's attention. Judge MacMahon, noting that the action had been pending since 1965, declined to allow defendant's witnesses so named on June 20, 1969 to take the stand on June 24. Accordingly, unable to use the witnesses, the defense rested its case and counsel summed up. After the jury had been charged and had retired, defense counsel was given an opportunity to protect his position in opposition to the court's ruling. In the colloquy that ensued the court recited the protracted history of pre-trial hearings, pointing out that the first pre-trial conference was set for February 21, 1968; that conferences were had on February 26 and 27; that the pre-trial order was entered March 31, 1969; and that more hearings were held on April 24 and 30, 1969. In light of this history, Judge MacMahon was unmoved by counsel's efforts to have the adverse ruling reconsidered.

Rule 16 of the Federal Rules of Civil Procedure states in part that when a pre-trial order is entered it ". . . controls the subsequent course of the action, unless modified at the trial to prevent manifest injustice." Paragraph 5 of the pre-trial order controlling the "subsequent course" of case two reads:

> The parties agree that the witnesses whom each party now intends to call, along with the specialty of experts to be called, are those listed in

the memorandum heretofore filed pursuant to local Calendar Rule 13(b) III (h). Should any party hereafter decide to call any additional witnesses, *prompt* notice of their identity shall be given to each other party and to the Court by serving and filing a supplemental pre-trial memorandum. . . . [The supplemental pre-trial memorandum] shall set forth the reason why the witness was not theretofore identified. No witness may be called at trial unless identified in a pre-trial memorandum. (Emphasis in original.)

Defendant's amended pre-trial memorandum listed seven witnesses and stated as the reason for their belated identification that "their availability in this case was not previously known." Counsel was unable to expand upon the above reason at trial. Surely a diligent investigation which should have been conducted long before the eve of trial would have disclosed some, if not all, of the witnesses in question. Counsel's vague and incomplete "reason" is patently transparent. . . .

[I]t is a fundamental principle of pre-trial that this procedure be flexible, with power reserved to the trial judge to amend the order or permit a departure from strict adherence to the pre-trial statements of either party, when the interests of justice make such a course desirable. Otherwise a pre-trial order or pre-trial statements would hold the parties in a vise, and the result might be just about as bad as a return to the old sporting theory of justice.

While the pre-trial order is not a "strait jacket" binding the parties and court to an unwavering course at trial, there is a reasonable basis for Judge MacMahon's decision. Defense counsel listed only one witness, a medical doctor, in his pre-trial memorandum, being content to refer to other potential witnesses in general terms as e.g., "Officers and/or employees of the defendant who will be identified prior to the trial." Defendant's practice, in a case which had been pending for four years, of waiting until four days prior to the trial date to identify his witnesses by name clearly violates both the letter and the spirit of the rule. The defendant's failure to give "prompt" notice, therefore, precludes a finding of abuse of discretion on the part of Judge MacMahon. . . .

Finally, appellant claims that it was deprived of an impartial trial in each case because Judge MacMahon at times exhibited impatience and displeasure with defense counsel's handling of the defense. A reading of the records in these cases does tend to evoke sympathy for counsel. His back-to-back courtroom experiences before Judge MacMahon would tend to discourage even a tough skinned attorney's enthusiasm for trial work. While a good many of the court's unkind remarks indicate a harsh overreaction to counsel's performance, the more vitriolic of Judge MacMahon's displays of displeasure occurred out of the jury's presence. We are not prepared to hold upon a review of the records in these cases that what occurred before the jury so belittled counsel or so disparaged the defense as to deprive the defendant of fair trials. . . . However, our affirmance should not be construed as approving the trial judge's unnecessary sarcastic comments or his tongue lashing of defense counsel.

The judgments are affirmed.

NOTES

1. What is there about "discretion" that induced the court in *Napolitano* to affirm even though it "held its nose" in the process?

2. It has been said that where discretion of the review-limiting kind exists, neither side will be heard to argue on appeal that it is entitled to an opposite or different decision — i.e., a "correct" one. Does this mean that, as far as the appellate court is concerned, that the trial judge cannot be wrong?

3. What are the reasons for committing to the trial judge's discretion the matters dealt with in the *Napolitano* case?

4. What standards or guidelines determine whether there has been an abuse of discretion by the trial judge?

SKIDMORE v. BALTIMORE & OHIO RAILROAD CO.
167 F.2d 54 (2d Cir. 1948)

[Action under Federal Employers' Liability Act for personal injuries.]

. . . Defendant's counsel . . . asked that the jury be required to return a special verdict, answering the following questions: "(1) Was the defendant guilty of negligence which caused or contributed to the injury of the plaintiff (If your answer to question (1) is 'No' you should answer no further questions and you should return this paper to the Court.) (2) If the answer to question (1) is 'Yes,' was Buzzy Skidmore, the plaintiff herein, guilty of negligence which contributed to his injuries? (3) If the answer to question (1) is 'Yes,' and the answer to question (2) is 'No,' state in writing the amount of damages sustained by the plaintiff. (4) If the answers to both question (1) and (2) are 'Yes,' state in terms of percentage what proportion of the entire causal negligence is attributable to defendant and to Buzzy Skidmore separately. (___% by defendant) (___% by Skidmore). (5) If the answers to questions (1) and (2) are 'Yes, what is the total amount of damage (without the jury making any percentage computation in dollars and cents) sustained by Buzzy Skidmore."' This request was refused, and defendant's counsel excepted. In his charge, the judge covered the subject matter of the denied request, but directed the jury to bring in a general verdict. No exception was taken to the charge. The jury returned a verdict for plaintiff in the amount of $30,000. Defendant moved for a directed verdict or a new trial; the motion was denied. From a judgment on the verdict, defendant has appealed.

FRANK, CIRCUIT JUDGE.

. . . Defendant argues that the judge erred in denying its request for a special verdict. We cannot agree.

Undeniably, the verdict affords no satisfactory information about the jury's findings. But almost every general verdict sheds similar or even greater darkness. Such verdicts account for much (not all) of the criticism of the civil jury. . . .

But what many persons regard as its major defects can be mitigated. One device which will help to achieve that end is the special or fact verdict. . . .

We come, then, to this position, that the general verdict . . . confers on the jury a vast power to commit error and do mischief by loading it with technical burdens far beyond its ability to perform, by confusing it in aggregating instead of segregating the issues, and by shrouding in secrecy and mystery the actual results of its deliberations. . . . The record must be absolutely flawless, but such a result is possible only by concealing, not by excluding mistakes. This is the great technical merit of the general verdict. It covers up all the shortcomings which frail human nature is unable to eliminate from the trial of a case. In the abysmal abstraction of the general verdict concrete details are swallowed up, and the eye of the law, searching anxiously for the realization of logical perfection, is satisfied. In short, the general verdict is valued for what it does, not for what it is. It serves as the great procedural opiate, . . . draws the curtain upon human errors and soothes us with the assurance that we have attained the unattainable.

The general verdict enhances, to the maximum, the power of appeals to the biases and prejudices of the jurors, and usually converts into a futile ritual the use of stock phrases about dispassionateness almost always included in judges' charges. . . .

True, the common-law type of special verdict, when utilized in this country, frequently caused so many complications that it fell into disrepute. But in three states, North Carolina, Wisconsin and Texas, the special-verdict practice in civil cases was so modified as to avoid most of those complications. The Wisconsin and Texas procedures, apparently the most effective, seem to have been the model for Rule 49(a) of the Federal Civil Rules of Procedure, 28 U.S.C.A. following section 723c, which authorizes the trial judge to dispense with a general verdict and, instead, to require the return of special written findings. Rule 49(b) also authorizes the judge to call for a general verdict accompanied by written interrogatories. But, unlike the Texas trial judge, the federal district judge, under the Rule, has full, uncontrolled discretion in the matter: He may still require merely the old-fashioned general verdict.

Accordingly, we cannot hold that a district judge errs when, as here, for any reason or no reason whatever, he refuses to demand a special verdict, although we deem such a verdict usually preferable to the opaque general verdict. Perhaps some day soon Rule 49 will be amended to make compulsory either special verdicts or written interrogatories in civil jury cases. Meanwhile, we can but hope that, in such cases, the district judges will require one or the other, on their own motion or when asked to do so. . . .

Affirmed.

Maurice Rosenberg, *Standards of Review*, in ARTHUR D. HELLMAN, RESTRUCTURING JUSTICE 48-49 (1991)[20]:

There are wide variations in how "erroneous" by appellate lights the district judge's exercise of discretion may be and still escape reversal. Gradations of discretion can be calibrated, depending on how impervious

---

20 Reprinted from RESTRUCTURING JUSTICE: THE INNOVATIONS OF THE NINTH CIRCUIT AND THE FUTURE OF THE FEDERAL COURTS, edited by Arthur D. Hellman. Copyright © 1990 by Cornell University. Used by permission of the publisher, Cornell University Press.

to appellate revision the rulings will be. One area of lower-court discretion that is virtually invulnerable is the district judge's decision to hold or forego a pretrial conference. Another is the option of the trial judge to order special verdicts under Rule 49. . . . Allowing the jury to take notes during the trial for use in their deliberations is another example of "Grade A" discretion.

A slightly lower level of protection surrounds the district court's rulings on motions for a new trial or similar relief. In these situations the discretion is Grade B. The appellate court will show deference but will not be as tolerant as the "for any reason or no reason whatsoever" approach would require. The same is true on many rulings on admissibility of evidence. In *United States v. Solomon*, for instance, the court of appeals said, "The district court's evidentiary rulings will be upheld on appeal unless the court abused its discretion . . . or committed 'manifest error.'" A similar approach can be seen in the oft-repeated statement that the court of appeals reviews "strictly" a district court's exercise of discretion denying leave to amend a complaint.

At the lowest end of the scale is Grade D discretion, where little or no deference is accorded the trial court's ruling. Rulings on applications for declaratory judgments fall into this category. Many appellate courts treat discretion in declaratory actions as so dilute that a mere disagreement with the lower court's choice is enough to call for reversal. Rulings on motions to dismiss on *forum non conveniens* grounds are also examples of low-grade discretion. . . . Judge Skopil offers the following definition of "abuse of discretion": "Under the abuse of discretion standard, a reviewing court cannot reverse unless it has a definite and firm conviction that the court below committed a clear error of judgment in the conclusion it reached upon a weighing of the relevant factors."

NOTES

1. Note that Judge Skopil's formulation of the test for determining abuse of discretion is similar to the formulation in *United States v. United States Gypsum Co.*, discussed in *Anderson v. City of Bessemer*, for determining whether a trial judge's fact-finding is clearly erroneous. Isn't much greater deference due to a discretionary ruling than to a fact-finding?

2. Is the following formulation more meaningful? Judicial discretion is abused "when the judicial action is arbitrary, fanciful, or unreasonable, which is another way of saying that discretion is abused only where no reasonable man would take the view adopted by the trial court." *Denlo v. Market St. Ry.*, 124 F.2d 965, 967 (9th Cir. 1942).

3. Doesn't this latter formulation apply mainly to cases of what Professor Rosenberg called "Grade A discretion"? What sort of test should be formulated for lower grades of discretion?

4. In *Skidmore*, the court obviously disfavored general verdicts and exhibited a strong preference for special verdicts. Why, then, is the trial judge's choice of verdict being given such deference?

5. New trial motions are sometimes granted for errors of law made in the course of the trial, such as legal errors in instructions to the jury and underlying erroneous admission or exclusion of evidence. These legal grounds can be reviewed by the appellate court under a *de novo* standard like all other matters of law. However, new trial motions often are based on grounds such as alleged misconduct of jurors, prejudicial events occurring during the trial, or a contention that the verdict is against the weight of the evidence. The grant or refusal of a new trial on those grounds is a matter resting in the discretion of the trial judge; hence, appellate review is deferential.

What are the reasons for according discretion to the trial judge to grant or deny a motion for new trial asserting that the verdict is against the weight of the evidence? In Professor Rosenberg's terminology, what "grade" is this discretion?

6. Consider the extent to which the following factors justify a high degree of appellate deference to trial court rulings on discretionary matters:

a. The difficulty of formulating a general rule to govern the matter;

b. The inability of the appellate court, as a practical matter, to become adequately informed from the trial transcript of all the relevant circumstances taken into account by the trial court;

c. The undermining of the finality of trial court judgments that would result from non-deferential appellate scrutiny of the trial court's discretionary rulings;

d. Possible impairment of the status and authority of the trial judge in the absence of appellate deference to the judge's rulings;

e. Distraction of appellate judges' time and efforts from their primary work, if non-deferential review were accorded to discretionary rulings of the trial courts.

PIERCE v. UNDERWOOD
487 U.S. 552 (1988)

JUSTICE SCALIA delivered the opinion of the Court.

[This dispute arose out of a decision by a former Secretary of Housing and Urban Development not to implement a subsidy program authorized by Congress to offset rising utility expenses and property taxes. A nationwide class of tenants residing in subsidized Government housing brought suit, challenging the Secretary's decision. The trial court granted summary judgment in favor of plaintiffs, and entered a permanent injunction and writ of mandamus requiring the Secretary to disburse the accumulated operating-subsidy fund. After the Supreme Court granted the Secretary's petition for writ of certiorari, and before the Court reviewed the merits, a newly appointed Secretary settled with the plaintiffs. While the settlement was being administered, Congress passed the EAJA, 28 U.S.C. § 2412(d), which provided in relevant part that, "a court shall award to a prevailing party . . . fees and other expenses. . . , incurred by that party in any civil action . . . brought . . . against the United States . . . , unless the court finds that the position of the United States was substantially justified or that special circumstances make an award unjust. . . ." "Fees and other expenses" included reasonable attorneys' fees, and the amount of fees awarded was to be based on prevailing market rates but not exceed $75-per-hour unless the court determined that a special factor, such as the limited availability of qualified attorneys for the proceedings involved, justified a higher fee. The trial court awarded respondents attorneys' fees based on its finding that the position the Secretary took was not "substantially justified" within the meaning of the EAJA. The court also determined that "special factors" justified applying hourly rates ranging from $80 for work performed in 1976 to $120 for work performed in 1982. This produced a "lodestar" figure of $322,700 which the court multiplied by three-and-one-half, again because of the "special factors." The Court of Appeals for the Ninth Circuit held that the District Court had not abused its discretion in concluding that the Secretary's position was not substantially justified and that the special factors relied on justified increasing the hourly rates of the attorneys, but it reduced the award back to $322,700. The Supreme Court granted certiorari on the questions whether the Government's position was "substantially justified" and whether the courts below properly identified "special factors" justifying an award in excess of the statute's $75-per-hour cap on attorneys' fees.]

We first consider whether the Court of Appeals applied the correct standard when reviewing the District Court's determination that the Secretary's position was not substantially justified. For purposes of standard of review, decisions by judges are traditionally divided into three categories, denominated questions of law (reviewable *de novo*), questions of fact (reviewable for clear error), and matters of discretion (reviewable for "abuse of discretion"). The Ninth Circuit treated the issue of substantial justification as involving the last of these; other Courts of Appeals have treated it as involving the first. . . .

For some few trial court determinations, the question of what is the standard of appellate review is answered by relatively explicit statutory command. For most others, the answer is provided by a long history of appellate practice. But when, as here, the trial court determination is one for which neither a clear statutory prescription nor a historical tradition exists, it is uncommonly difficult to derive from the pattern of appellate review of other questions an analytical framework that will yield the correct answer. No more today than in the past shall we attempt to discern or to create a comprehensive test; but we are persuaded that significant relevant factors call for an "abuse of discretion" standard in the present case.

We turn first to the language and structure of the governing statute. It provides that attorney's fees shall be awarded "unless *the court finds* that the position of the United States was substantially justified." 28 U.S.C. §2412(d)(1)(A) (emphasis added). This formulation, as opposed to simply "unless the position of the United States was substantially justified," emphasizes the fact that the determination is for the district court to make, and thus suggests some deference to the district court upon appeal. . . . Moreover, a related provision of the EAJA requires an administrative agency to award attorney's fees to a litigant prevailing in an agency adjudication if the Government's position is not "substantially justified," 5 U.S.C. §504(a)(1), and specifies that the agency's decision may be reversed only if a reviewing court "finds that the failure to make an award . . . was unsupported by substantial evidence." §504(c)(2). We doubt that it was the intent of this interlocking scheme that a court of appeals would accord more deference to an agency's determination that its own position was substantially justified than to such a determination by a federal district court. Again, however, the inference of deference is assuredly not compelled.

We recently observed, with regard to the problem of determining whether mixed questions of law and fact are to be treated as questions of law or of fact for purposes of appellate review, that sometimes the decision "has turned on a determination that, as a matter of the sound administration of justice, one judicial actor is better positioned than another to decide the issue in question." *Miller v. Fenton*, 474 U.S. 104, 114 (1985). We think that consideration relevant in the present context as well, and it argues in favor of deferential, abuse-of-discretion review. To begin with, some of the elements that bear upon whether the Government's position "*was* substantially justified" may be known only to the district court. Not infrequently, the question will turn upon not merely what was the law, but what was the evidence regarding the facts. By reason of . . . pretrial activities, the district court may have insights not conveyed by the record, into such matters as whether particular evidence was worthy of being relied upon, or whether critical facts could easily have been verified by the Government. Moreover, even where the district judge's full knowledge of the factual setting can be acquired by the appellate court, that acquisition will often come at unusual expense, requiring the court to undertake the unaccustomed task of reviewing the entire record, not just to determine whether there existed the usual minimum support for the merits determination made by the factfinder below, but to determine whether urging of the opposite merits determination was substantially justified.

In some cases, such as the present one, the attorney's fee determination will involve a judgment ultimately based upon evaluation of the purely legal issue governing the litigation. It cannot be assumed, however, that *de novo* review of this will not require the appellate court to invest substantial additional time, since it will . . . have to grapple with the same legal issue on the merits. To the contrary, . . . where the Government's case is so feeble as to provide grounds for an EAJA award, there will often be (as there was here) a settlement below, or a failure to appeal from the adverse judgment. Moreover, even if there is a merits appeal, and even if it occurs simultaneously with (or goes to the same panel that entertains) the appeal from the attorney's fee award, the latter legal question will not be precisely the same as the merits: not what the law now is, but what the Government was substantially justified in believing it to have been. In all the separate-from-the-merits EAJA appeals, the investment of appellate energy will either fail to produce the normal law-clarifying benefits that come from an appellate decision on a question of law, or else will strangely distort the appellate process. The former result will obtain when (because of intervening legal decisions by this Court or by the relevant circuit itself) the law of the circuit is, at the time of the EAJA appeal, quite clear, so that the question of what the Government was substantially justified in believing it to have been is of entirely historical interest. Where, on the other hand, the law of the circuit remains unsettled at the time of the EAJA appeal, a ruling that the Government was not substantially justified in believing it to be thus-and-so would (unless there is some reason to think it has changed since) effectively establish the circuit law in a most peculiar, secondhanded fashion. Moreover, the possibility of the latter occurrence would encourage needless merits appeals by the Government, since it would know that if it does not appeal, but the victorious plaintiff appeals the denial of attorney's fees, its district-court loss on the merits can be converted into a circuit-court loss on the merits, without the opportunity for a circuit-court victory on the merits. All these untoward consequences can be substantially reduced or entirely avoided by adopting an abuse-of-discretion standard of review.

Another factor that we find significant has been described as follows by Prof. Rosenberg:

> One of the "good" reasons for conferring discretion on the trial judge is the sheer impracticability of formulating a rule of decision for the matter in issue. Many questions that arise in litigation are not amenable to regulation by rule because they involve multifarious, fleeting, special, narrow facts that utterly resist generalization — at least, for the time being. . . .

> The non-amenability of the problem to rule, because of the diffuseness of circumstances, novelty, vagueness, or similar reasons that argue for allowing experience to develop, appears to be a sound reason for conferring discretion on the magistrate. . . . A useful analogue is the course of development under Rule 39(b) of the Federal Rules of Civil Procedure, providing that in spite of a litigant's tardiness (under Rule 38 which specifies a ten-day-from-last-pleading deadline) the trial court "in its discretion" may order a trial by jury of any or all issues. Over the years, appellate courts have consistently upheld the trial judges in allowing or refusing late-demanded jury trials, but in doing so have laid down two guidelines for exercise of the discretionary power. The products of cumulative experience, these guidelines relate to the justifiability of the tardy litigant's delay and the absence of prejudice to his adversary. Time and experience have allowed the formless problem to take shape, and the contours of a guiding principle to emerge.

[T]he question whether the Government's litigating position has been "substantially justified" is precisely such a multifarious and novel question, little susceptible, for the time being at least, of useful generalization, and likely to profit from the experience that an abuse-of-discretion rule will permit to develop. . . . Application of an abuse-of-discretion standard to the present question will permit that needed flexibility.

It must be acknowledged that militating against the use of that standard in the present case is the substantial amount of the liability produced by the District Judge's decision. If this were the sort of decision that ordinarily has such substantial consequences, one might expect it to be reviewed more intensively. [H]owever, the present case is not characteristic of EAJA attorney's fee cases. The median award has been less than $3,000. We think the generality rather than the exception must form the basis for our rule.

In sum, . . . we are satisfied that the text of the statute permits, and sound judicial administration counsels, deferential review of a district court's decision regarding attorney's fees under the EAJA. In addition to furthering the goals we have described, it will implement our view that a "request for attorney's fees should not result in a second major litigation." *Hensley v. Eckerhart*, 461 U.S. 424, 437 (1983).

[The Court here addressed the meaning of "substantially justified" and concluded that it means justified to a degree that could satisfy a reasonable person, or, in the words of some other courts, a reasonable basis both in law and fact.]

We reach, at last, the merits of whether the District Court abused its discretion in finding that the Government's position was not "substantially justified." Both parties argue that for purposes of this inquiry courts should rely on "objective indicia" such as the terms of a settlement agreement, the stage in the proceedings at which the merits were decided, and the views of other courts on the merits. This, they suggest, can avoid the time-consuming and possibly inexact process of assessing the strength of the Government's position. While we do not disagree that objective indicia can be relevant, we do not think they provide a conclusive answer . . . for the present case.

Respondents contend that the lack of substantial justification for the Government's position was demonstrated by its willingness to settle the litigation on unfavorable terms. Other factors, however, might explain the settlement equally well — for example, a change in substantive policy instituted by a new administration. The unfavorable terms of a settlement agreement, without inquiry into the reasons for settlement, cannot conclusively establish the weakness of the Government's position. To hold otherwise would not only distort the truth but penalize and thereby discourage useful settlements.

Respondents further contend that the weakness of the Government's position is established by the objective fact that the merits were decided at the pleadings stage. We disagree. At least where . . . the dispute centers upon questions of law rather than fact, summary disposition proves only that the district judge was efficient.

Both parties rely upon the objective indicia consisting of the views expressed by other courts on the merits of the Government's position. Obviously, the fact that one other court agreed or disagreed with the Government does not establish whether its position was substantially justified. Conceivably, the Government could take a position that is not substantially justified, yet win; even more likely, it could take a position that is substantially justified, yet lose. Nevertheless, a string of losses can be indicative; and even more so a string of successes. Once again, however, we cannot say that this category of objective indicia is enough to decide the present case. Respondents emphasize that every court to hear the merits (nine District Courts and two Courts of Appeals) rejected the Government's position. The Secretary responds that the stays issued by the Court of Appeals for the Second Circuit and by this Court reflect a view on the merits and objectively establish substantial justification; and that it is "unlikely that [this] Court would have granted the government's petitions [for certiorari in two cases to review this issue] had the Secretary's argument" not been substantial. Respondents reply that neither the stays nor the grants of certiorari are reliable indications of substantial merit. We will not parse these arguments further. Respondents' side of the case has at least sufficient force that we cannot possibly state, on the basis of these objective indications alone, that the District Court abused its discretion in finding no substantial justification.

[Turning to the actual merits of the Government's litigating position, the Court summarized the arguments made by the Government and those made by respondents, both resting in large part upon statutory language, and concluded that the conclusion that the Government's position was substantially justified was not "commanded."Accordingly, it affirmed the Ninth Circuit's holding that the District Judge did not abuse his discretion when he found against the Government on this issue. With respect to whether the amount of the attorneys' fees award was proper, the Court announced that it was well established that the abuse-of-discretion standard applied, and vacated the judgment and remanded for proceedings consistent with its opinion.]

NOTES

1. In *Cooter & Gell v. Hartmarx Corp.*, 496 U.S. 384 (1990), the Court was asked to decide the standard of review of determinations made under FED. R. CIV. P. 11. Finding the governing considerations to be very similar to those that had been persuasive in *Pierce* and that the policy goals of Rule 11 also supported its conclusion, the Court purported to reject a three-tiered standard of review and held that "an appellate court should apply an abuse-of-discretion standard in reviewing all aspects of a district court's Rule 11 determination." The Court conceded, however, that, "A district court would necessarily abuse its discretion if it based its ruling on an erroneous view of the law or on a clearly erroneous assessment of the evidence."

2. The legal standard to be applied by the trial judge was expressly embodied in the provisions of a statute in *Pierce v. Underwood* and in the provisions of Rule 11 in *Cooter & Gell v. Hartmarx.* In such situations is the appellate court provided with more guidance in determining abuse of discretion than it is where no such standards are provided, as in the *Napolitano* and *Skidmore* cases, *supra*?

3. Adoption of an abuse of discretion umbrella standard of review that actually encompasses aspects of *de novo* review and aspects of clear error review is not limited to the area of sanctions. *See* Peter Nicolas, *De Novo Review in Deferential Robes?: A Deconstruction of the Standard of Review of Evidentiary Errors in the Federal System*, 54 SYR. L. REV. 531, 535 (2004) (finding that "the traditional tripartite standard of review is alive and well when it comes to reviewing evidentiary errors," despite frequent recitation of the notion that decisions to admit or exclude evidence are reviewed for abuse of discretion).

G.   Summarizing Observations for Appellate Counsel

George A. Somerville, *Standards of Appellate Review*, *in* APPELLATE PRACTICE MANUAL 17-25 (P.A. Schwab ed., 1992)[21]

At first glance, standards of review questions may seem obvious or boring. . . . In reality, however, complex and subtle questions — of both law and tactics — are present in considering standards of review. One good reason for assessing these issues carefully is that local rules in some federal circuits (the Third, Fourth, Ninth, Tenth, and Eleventh) require parties to state in their briefs the standards of review applicable to the issues presented. More important, a practical understanding will improve your written and oral presentations and enhance your chances of obtaining a favorable judgment on appeal. . . .

Going Up the Ladder

The reason for understanding and being able to use such standards is this: If you represent the appellant, you want to move the standard of review up the ladder to a strict ruling; if you represent the appellee, you want a standard more generous to the trial judge. More than that, you need to know that there are varying levels of review even within a single standard. They too may be used to your advantage.

To know how to move an issue up or down the review ladder, you must understand why review is structured as it is, and you must appreciate the variations within virtually every individual level of review.

Legal error is the standard of review the appellant wants. When an appellate court reviews on this basis, the theory is that it accords the trial court decision no presumption of correctness whatever. In practice, however, legal error review has its variations. Sometimes, even when the standard is legal error, the lower court opinion will have advantages. . . .

On a mundane level, for example, a well-written trial court opinion is every appellant's worst enemy and every appellee's best friend. It creates its own presumption of correctness by the force of its reasoning and the quality of its examination of law and precedent. If you are an appellant stuck with a good opinion, there is not much you can do about it except advise your client and press the attack.

The intensity of legal error review also will depend on what the appellate court is asked to do. Will the court have to select a legal rule? Interpret an existing rule? Or just apply recognized legal standards?

Most cases require only application of settled law to the facts. As cases, statutes, or regulations define an area of law, trial court decisions become more accurate and more predictable. Even though legal error is ostensibly the standard, decisions in such circumstances are more likely to be affirmed by *per*

---

[21] Copyright © 1992 by the American Bar Association. Reprinted with permission.

curiam opinions or unpublished orders. Appellate judges know that trial court errors occur less often in the application of settled law than in other kinds of cases where review for legal error is exercised. In effect, there is a presumption that the decision below is correct. Therefore, when you represent the appellee and face a legal error standard, you should try to argue that the case requires only application of settled law to the facts.

At the other end of the spectrum is the relatively rare case where a court must select or fashion a new legal precept, both for the case on appeal and as a precedent for future cases. Such cases ordinarily consume much of appellate judges' time and attention, and they tend to occupy many pages of the reports.

. . . Cases requiring the choice of a rule of law represent the core of the appellate function. As a result, this is the category of cases in which any deference to the trial court's rulings is likely to be a minimum. These cases also are those in which the quality of advocacy can be most influential, particularly when the trial court's opinion is weak or nonexistent. When new law must be fashioned, legal error review is truly *de novo*.

A final category of legal error review, interpretation, lies between application and choice. In this broad category is most of our statutory and constitutional jurisprudence. But, the lines between interpretation and its brothers are wide and gray. For example, when the question is which of two conflicting rules controls, choice and interpretation essentially merge. In the other direction, interpretation may become indistinguishable from application of the law in a particular case. The precise categorization is not critical, however. The point is that if what the trial judge did lies between the extremes of selecting a brand new rule and applying obvious law to obvious facts, then the legal error review will be intense, but there will be some deference to the trial court.

For an appellate advocate, the significance of these seemingly subtle distinctions lies in how the brief is written. Characterizations of what the lower court did, or what the appeals court should do, are often matters of opinion, or even semantics. How you describe what was done will depend on how intense you want the review to be. As appellant, for example, you would be better off saying that the trial judge adopted "an entirely new and erroneous legal standard" than to say the court applied the wrong rule of law to this case.

The standard that appellants fear is abuse of discretion. It often seems as if appeals courts think a decision left to a trial judge's discretion is none of their business. Even findings of fact, which are subject to a clearly erroneous review, seem to be scrutinized more closely than discretionary decisions.

Such fears are not always right. As with legal error, there are several varieties of discretion. Though review of discretion can be more forgiving than clearly erroneous review, some kinds of discretionary review are in fact stricter. Careful analysis of the particular exercise of discretion in a case may convince a court to apply a tougher standard.

A warning before proceeding: It is never easy to obtain reversal of a pure exercise of discretion. The odds are against you. The point is this: Do not give up — actually or emotionally — merely because a decision against you is discretionary. A careful and discriminating argument sometimes can overcome the unhelpful standard.

Consider a few examples: A ruling on a discretionary matter involving admission of evidence or discovery rarely is reversed. These kinds of questions — especially in discovery — are committed to the strong discretion of the trial court. That commitment is a recognition of the trial judge's superior knowledge of the issues, the record, the proceedings, and the personalities. It also is based on the tremendous variety of situations in which these questions arise, making formulation of legal rules difficult or impossible. Furthermore, there is the principle that a litigant is entitled to a fair trial but not to a perfect one; decisions on subjects such as discovery may be wrong, but they rarely affect the basic fairness of the trial.

Compare this with questions committed to trial court discretion, not because trial courts are in a better position to decide, but because such questions present novel issues. Committing certain decisions to trial court discretion provides a period of flexibility — almost experimentation — while appellate courts develop expertise from a series of cases. Sometimes, however, things change. Decisions move from the substantial to the limited discretion of the trial court, or even become prescribed by a rule of law. . . .

Close Review of Discretion

There are two other categories in which matters committed to trial court discretion may get meaningful review. In the first, the exercise of discretion must conform to standards announced in prior opinions; appellate courts may reevaluate lower courts' applications of the standards. In this category are cases seeking a preliminary injunction, a declaratory judgment, or an exercise of federal pendent jurisdiction. The second category involves subjects on which previous cases have established a preferred outcome. This includes motions for a voluntary dismissal or approval of a settlement. Even though ostensibly committed to trial court discretion, departures from the usual outcome are tolerated rarely, and only for good reasons persuasively articulated by the trial court.

There is another reason why almost all exercises of discretion may actually get meaningful review. A discretionary judgement often has legal components. Legal error can be embedded in an apparently discretionary decision when the trial judge fails to recognize that a question *is* discretionary; if he thinks himself bound by a rule of law, he should be reversed for legal error and instructed to exercise his discretion on remand.

More commonly, particularly in a developing area, a lawyer attuned to the substantive law may be able to persuade an appeals court that the trial court considered impermissible factors or failed to consider factors that should have been evaluated. Though appellate courts in such cases may say that the trial court did or did not abuse its discretion, in fact its choice of factors usually presents a question of law, subject to review for error and not for abuse of discretion. Once again, the aim for an appellant is to see through an apparently discouraging abuse of discretion standard, find a legal error, and make the review more intense. . . .

What about review of findings of fact? Most litigators know that appellate review of fact-findings is exceedingly forgiving. All of us have told clients that chances for an appeal are slim because the judge "killed us on the facts."

A common response to this is to try to characterize an issue of fact as a question of law. This happens very often with matters that are mixed questions of law and fact. But, the line between law and fact is not always sharp. It wavers and can be moved. Courts sometimes will characterize matters that appear factual as legal, usually to permit them to reach what they consider a just result. As an appellant you want to take advantage of this malleability.

Mixed Questions

What *is* the standard for findings of fact? In federal *civil* cases, Rule 52(a) forbids appellate courts from setting aside trial court fact-findings unless "clearly erroneous." . . .

This is a tough standard, and perhaps as a result, it has had exceptions and odd wrinkles. For example, until recently many federal courts employed a much stricter standard of review, often virtually *de novo*, of findings based on documentary evidence. The idea was that no credibility concerns were involved. This view was firmly put to rest in *Bessemer City* and by the adoption a few weeks after that case of the 1985 amendment to Rule 52. In *Bessemer City*, the Supreme Court observed that the clearly erroneous standard applies "even when the district court's findings do not rest on credibility determinations, but are based instead on physical or documentary evidence or inferences from other facts." 470 U.S. at 574. . . .

Review of fact-findings in federal *criminal* cases is not as well defined, because the Federal Rules of Criminal Procedure (unlike the Rules of Civil Procedure) do not prescribe a standard. Most courts apply the clearly erroneous standard in criminal cases, but sometimes they add the qualification that the "ultimate finding" of guilt will be reviewed only for "substantial evidence" to support it.

Given this law, what can you do if you are an appellant attacking a judgment based largely on factual considerations? First, learn to recognize lost causes. If your case arises in a settled area of the law and you lost at trial because the court found that the historical facts favored the other side, you have almost no chance on appeal. Such pure findings of fact generally can be attacked successfully only where they lack any rational connection to the record — where they seem to have materialized out of thin air — or occasionally when the vast weight of the evidence persuades the appellate court that a finding is surely wrong. Such circumstances are exceedingly rare. Appellate courts seem to take the view that while puzzling or questionable findings may reflect confusion or prejudice, they far more often are the product of the trial judge's hands-on familiarity with the case.

But clear errors do sometimes occur. Chiefly this happens in areas where the trial court's greater familiarity is a weakness and not an asset — for example, when a fact has been pleaded and asserted in briefs, and repeated so often it is almost second nature to the judge. The party asserting the fact may forget to support it with evidence, and the court may just assume it was proven. Absent such a special situation, however, you will have a hard time attacking the findings below. . . .

Better than attacking findings of fact is trying to turn them into conclusions of law. Isolating the legal components of the critical findings is what you want to do. Judge Aldisert described the process well in *Universal Minerals, Inc. v. C.A. Hughes & Co.*, 669 F.2d 98, 103 (3d Cir. 1981), where the issue was whether personal property had been abandoned:

> Abandonment is not a question of narrative or historical fact but an ultimate fact, a legal concept with a factual component. . . . It is "a conclusion of law or at least a determination of a mixed question of law and fact," . . . requiring "the application of a legal standard to the historical-fact determinations." . . . In reviewing the ultimate determination of abandonment, . . . we are therefore not limited by the "clearly erroneous" standard, . . . but must employ a mixed standard of review. We must accept the trial court's findings of historical or narrative facts unless they are clearly erroneous, but we must exercise a plenary review of the trial court's choice and interpretation of legal precepts and its application of those precepts to the historical facts. . . .

Many of the findings that burden appellants will, on close analysis, be seen to have a legal component. If a factual finding troubles you, look for the law.

Do not waste much time analyzing jury verdicts, however. Appellate challenges to jury findings rarely succeed. In federal courts, the Seventh Amendment's proscription of reexamination of jury findings except "according to the rules of the common law" limits review of jury verdicts even more than Rule 52 already restricts review of trial court findings. A jury's verdict should not be set aside unless it has no rational basis in the evidence. . . .

Chapter 4

JUDICIAL LAWMAKING

This chapter focuses on one important aspect of the work of appellate courts: the generation of substantive law. The other major appellate activity is reviewing trial court and administrative agency dispositions to insure that those tribunals are applying existing law correctly and administering justice fairly and evenhandedly. In appellate energy and time, that error correcting function looms far larger than the lawmaking function. Moreover, the error correcting function is essential to a regime of law and to public confidence in courts as the ultimate resolvers of disputes. The lawmaking function, however, also is profoundly important. It is not as well understood by the public or even by some lawyers. Yet, in this work, appellate courts contribute significantly to the governance of American society, and they do so in a distinctive manner and under special constraints, some of which will be examined in this chapter.

At first blush, the very idea of judicial lawmaking may seem inconsistent with the doctrine of separation of powers that is fundamental in American federal and state governmental structures. Under that doctrine, put in oversimplified terms, legislatures make law, executives enforce law, and courts apply and interpret law in order to adjudicate controversies. But in the Anglo-American legal world courts always have "made" law. For centuries in England, when parliament was enacting scarcely any statutes, the common-law and equity courts developed an entire legal corpus that was inherited by the American colonists and the later-formed states. Despite the rapid growth of legislation in our culture, common law or judge-made law continues to play an essential function in state and federal jurisprudence.

Historically, the judicial generation of substantive legal rules has been seen as a necessary by-product of adjudication. "[T]he essential aspect of the judicial function (indeed, an inescapable one in any regime of law) is that of authoritative application, in such particular situations as may be presented for decision, of general propositions drawn from preexisting sources. This function includes, as a necessary incident, the task of determining the facts of the situation and of resolving uncertainties about the content of the applicable general propositions." PAUL M. BATOR, DANIEL J. MELTZER, PAUL J. MISHKIN, & DAVID L. SHAPIRO, HART & WECHSLER'S THE FEDERAL COURTS AND THE FEDERAL SYSTEM 67 (3d ed. 1988). In other words, in order to decide a case before it, a court must identify and articulate the pertinent legal rules. If a rule is provided by an authoritative written text, such as a statute or constitution, the court must interpret and apply that text to the facts of the case. If there is no such text, under the doctrine of *stare decisis* the court must derive from its own prior decisions the rule that will serve as the starting point for reasoned decision. If there are no precedents on point, in the common-law tradition the court must formulate a rule under which it will decide the issue presented by the litigants ("Out of the facts the law arises."). Thus, American appellate courts make law. So long as they make law within the confines of a live case properly presented to them for resolution, and only to the extent required for disposition of that case, they do not transcend the judicial power. Controversy arises when courts go beyond the necessities of the case at hand in laying down rules. Then they may be perceived as acting "legislatively" and thus non-judicially. Even where the substantive rule at issue can be carefully tailored to the immediate case, there often remains a question whether it would be preferable, for a variety of reasons, for a rule on the matter to be formulated by the legislature rather than the court. Judicial-legislative tensions are frequently present when courts engage in law making.

In this chapter, we look first at the special position of an intermediate appellate court in relation to this lawmaking function. In three-tiered judicial systems the appellate power is divided between the intermediate level and the court of last resort, and this bifurcation gives rise to some problems as to the appropriate role of each. (Other aspects of the relationship between these two appellate levels are examined in Chapter 6.) We next survey some salient features of judicial lawmaking in common-law, statutory, and constitutional settings, followed by a consideration of the possible sources of information that courts can draw upon in devising legal rules. Finally we consider an avowedly legislative role that appellate courts perform: the making of procedural rules for lower courts.

I. LAWMAKING BY INTERMEDIATE APPELLATE COURTS

A. Overruling

JONES v. HOFFMAN
272 So. 2d 529 (Fla. Dist. Ct. App. 1973)

MAGER, JUDGE.

[T]he plaintiff has urged this court to reject the doctrine of contributory negligence in favor of a system of comparative negligence. . . . Briefly, the actions arose out of a car-truck collision resulting in the death of William Harrison Jones, Jr. One suit was a wrongful death action maintained by the plaintiff, in her individual capacity as widow; the other suit was maintained by plaintiff as administratrix of the Jones estate. Essentially, plaintiff alleged that the defendant Hoffman was negligent in operating a truck owned by defendant Pav-A-Way Corporation. Defendants filed a general denial and asserted the defense of contributory negligence. The court consolidated both lawsuits. The trial judge denied the plaintiff's requested instruction predicated upon comparative negligence of the parties and the jury returned a verdict in favor of the defendants.

The common law doctrine of contributory negligence which we are urged to reject provides in essence that there can be no recovery of damages for injuries negligently inflicted on one person by another if the injured person *by his own negligence* proximately *contributed* to the injury. Essentially this places upon one party the entire burden of the loss for which the two may be responsible. . . .

Under a comparative negligence system the relative *degree of negligence* of the parties is involved in determining whether, and the degree to which, either should be held liable; so that the plaintiff's negligence serves not to relieve the defendant entirely from liability but merely to diminish the damages recoverable.

Perhaps no rule of the common law has been more widely accepted *and* criticized than the general rule of contributory negligence. . . .

Beginning with the 1886 decision in *Louisville & Nashville R.R. Co. v. Yniestra*, 21 Fla. 700, 737, the doctrine of contributory negligence was enunciated and denunciated [sic] in Florida. In that case, Chief Justice McWhorter, speaking for the Supreme Court observed: . . .

> [I]n my opinion, and speaking for myself individually, the *operation of the principle of contributory negligence is unjust and inequitable.* . . .

Some eighty years later, Mr. Justice O'Connell similarly observed in *Connolly v. Steakley*, 197 So.2d 524, 537 (Fla. 1967):

> . . . I close with one last observation, which is solely my view. . . . Although I have stated herein that the last clear chance doctrine is intended to mitigate *the harshness of the rule of contributory negligence*, I do not suggest that it does so adequately or that it produces a just result. *The real fact is that the contributory negligence rule and the doctrine of last clear chance are both equally primitive devices for achieving justice as between parties who are both at fault.* All either does is to place the burden of an accident on one of the parties in the face of evidence that both are to blame.

> A better way to achieve justice in such cases is by the comparative negligence principle. . . .

> After nearly three-quarters of a century of urging, *see* opinion by Chief Justice McWhorter in *Louisville & Nashville R.R. Co. v. Yniestra*, 21 Fla. 700 (1886), it is time for Florida to face this problem squarely. Our legislature has attempted to do so at least once. Both houses of the 1943 Legislature passed a comparative negligence statute, S.B. 267. However, the bill was vetoed by the governor, and the legislature refused to override the veto. . . .

The doctrine of contributory negligence is a judicially created principle having originated in England in the 1809 case of *Butterfield v. Forrester*, 103 Eng. Rep. 926 (K.B. 1809). Virtually the whole of tort law has been the product of judicial action. Therefore, any modification of the doctrine of contributory negligence is within this judicial pattern and framework. As one writer observed:

> What the courts themselves have wrought to meet one set of circumstances, they may presumably undo or modify, when circumstances or prevailing values change, without treading on the toes of the legislature. *Comparative v. Contributory Negligence: Should the Court or Legislature Decide?* 21 Vand. L. Rev. 889.

In this vein, the Supreme Court of Florida aptly observed in *Gates v. Foley*, 247 So.2d 40, 43 (Fla. 1971):

> The law is not static. It must keep pace with changes in our society, for the doctrine of stare decisis is not an iron mold which can never be

changed. Holmes, in his *The Common Law* (1881), p. 5, recognizes this in the following language:

> "The customs, beliefs, or needs of a primitive time establish a rule or a formula. In the course of centuries the customs, belief, or necessity disappear, but the rule remains. The reason which gave rise to the rule has been forgotten, and ingenious minds set themselves to inquire how it is to be accounted for. Some ground of policy is thought of, which seems to explain it and to reconcile it with the present state of things; and then the rule adapts itself to the new reasons which have been found for it, and centers on a new career. The old form receives a new content, and in time even the form modifies itself to fit the meaning which it has received."

It may be argued that any change in this rule should come from the Legislature. *No recitation of authority is needed to indicate that this Court has not been backward in overturning unsound precedent in the area of tort law. Legislative action could, of course, be taken, but we abdicate our own function, in a field peculiarly nonstatutory, when we refuse to reconsider an old and unsatisfactory court-made rule.*

. . . The doctrine of contributory negligence . . . is a primitive device for achieving justice between parties who are both at fault. We think that the time has come to reject the doctrine of contributory negligence as being "at variance with modern-day needs and concepts of justice and fair dealing." . . .

With the advent of no fault automobile insurance in Florida whereby benefits are provided for bodily injury and property damage liability "without regard to fault" we would perceive no logical and just reason for the perpetuation of a principle which would preclude recovery because of *some* fault.

We therefore decide that contributory negligence should not bar recovery in an action by any person or his legal representative to recover damages for negligence resulting in death or injury to person or property, but any damages allowed shall be diminished in proportion (percentage) to the amount of the negligence attributable to the person bringing such action or on behalf of whom such action is maintained. . . .

Accordingly, the judgment of the trial court is reversed with directions to grant a new trial in accordance with this opinion.

We further conclude that because of the state-wide implications of the principle which we are here enunciating we deem it appropriate to certify this decision to the Supreme Court as one involving a question of great public interest, such question being:

> Whether or not the Court should replace the contributory negligence rule with the principle of comparative negligence?

Owen, Judge (dissenting):

I concur with the view that the doctrine of contributory negligence is fully deserving of the criticism leveled toward it, that replacing the doctrine with the principle of comparative negligence would in most cases reach a more equitable result, and that such a change can be accomplished by the judicial branch of government in view of the fact that the doctrine of contributory negligence was judicially created.

My disagreement with the majority lies simply in the fact that if and when such a change is to be wrought by the judiciary, it should be at the hands of the Supreme Court rather than the District Court of Appeal. . . . The majority decision would appear to flatly overrule a multitude of prior decisions of our Supreme Court, a prerogative which we do not enjoy.

. . . If affirmed, the question upon which the decision passes could be certified, thus affording the Supreme Court the opportunity to re-examine its position on contributory negligence vis-à-vis comparative negligence.

HOFFMAN v. JONES
280 So.2d 431 (Fla. 1973)

ADKINS, JUSTICE.

This cause is here on petition for writ of certiorari supported by certificate of the District Court of Appeal, Fourth District, that its decision . . . is one which involves a question of great public interest. . . .

The question certified by the District Court of Appeal is: "Whether or not the Court should replace the contributory negligence rule with the principles of comparative negligence?"

The District Court of Appeal answered the certified question in the affirmative and reversed the trial court in the case *sub judice* for following the precedent set down by this Court in *Louisville & Nashville R.R. Co. v. Yniestra*, 21 Fla. 700 (1886). This early case specifically held the contributory negligence rule to be the law of Florida, and it has uniformly been followed by the courts of the State ever since. The District Court of Appeal attempted, therefore, to overrule all precedent of this Court in the area of contributory negligence and to establish comparative negligence as the proper test. In so doing, the District Court has exceeded its authority.

In a dissenting opinion, Judge Owen stated well the position of the District Courts of Appeal when in disagreement with controlling precedent set down by this Court:

> [I]f and when such a change is to be wrought by the judiciary, it should be at the hands of the Supreme Court rather than the District Court of Appeal. . . . The majority decision would appear to flatly overrule a multitude of prior decisions of our Supreme Court, a prerogative which we do not enjoy. *Jones v. Hoffman*, 272 So.2d 529, 534.

. . . To allow a District Court of Appeal to overrule controlling precedent of this Court would be to create chaos and uncertainty in the judicial forum, particularly at the trial level. Ever since the District Court rendered its opinion there has been great confusion and much delay in the trial courts of the District Court of Appeal, Fourth District, while the attorneys and judges alike have been awaiting our decision in this case. . . .

This is not to say that the District Courts of Appeal are powerless to seek change; they are free to certify questions of great public interest to this Court for consideration, and even to state their reasons for advocating change. They are, however, bound to follow the case law set forth by this Court.

Prior to answering the question certified, we must also consider our own power and authority to replace the rule of contributory negligence with that of comparative negligence. It has been suggested that such a change in the common law of Florida is properly within the province only of the Legislature, and not of the courts. We cannot agree.

The rule that contributory negligence is an absolute bar to recovery was — as most tort law — a judicial creation, and it was specifically judicially adopted in Florida in *Louisville & Nashville R.R. Co. v. Yniestra, supra*. Most scholars attribute the origin of this rule to the English case of *Butterfield v. Forrester*, 103 Eng. Rep. 926 (K.B. 1809).

[I]n view of the fact that prior to *Butterfield* contributory negligence was a matter of judicial thought rather than judicial pronouncement, it cannot be said that the common law was "clear and free from doubt," so as to make it a part of the statute law of this State by virtue of Fla. Stat. § 2.01, F.S.A.

As we stated in *Duval v. Thomas*, 114 So.2d 791, 795 (Fla. 1959), it is "only when the common law is plain that we must observe it." We also said in this case,

> [W]hen grave doubt exists of a true common law doctrine . . . we may . . . , as was written in *Ripley v. Ewell, supra,* [61 So. 2d 420], exercise a "broad discretion" taking into "account the changes in our social and economic customs and present day conceptions of right and justice."

Even if . . . the present bar of contributory negligence is a part of our common law by virtue of prior judicial decision, it is also true from *Duval* that this Court may change the rule where great social upheaval dictates. . . .

This Court receded from the common law and held, in *Hargrove v. Town of Cocoa Beach*, 96 So. 2d 130, 132 (Fla. 1957), that a municipal corporation may be held liable for the torts of police officers under the doctrine of *respondeat superior*, saying:

> Tracing the rule to its ultimate progenitor we are led to the English case of *Russel v. Men of Devon*, 100 Eng. Rep. R. 359 (1788). . . .
>
> Assuming that the immunity rule had its inception in the *Men of Devon* case . . . , this case was decided in 1788, some twelve years after our Declaration of Independence. Be that as it may, our own feeling is that *the courts should be alive to the demands of justice. We can see no necessity for insisting on legislative action in a matter which the courts themselves originated.* (Emphasis supplied.)

The contemporary conditions must be met with contemporary standards which are realistic and better calculated to obtain justice among all of the parties involved, based upon the circumstances applying between them at the time in question. The rule of contributory negligence as a complete bar to recovery was imported into the law by judges. Whatever may have been the historical justification for it, today it is almost universally regarded as unjust and inequitable to vest an entire accidental loss on one of the parties whose negligent conduct combined with the negligence of the other party to produce the loss. If fault is to remain the test of liability, then the doctrine of comparative negligence which involves apportionment of the loss among those whose fault contributed to the occurrence is more consistent with liability based on a fault premise.

We are, therefore, of the opinion that we do have the power and authority to reexamine the position we have taken in regard to contributory negligence and to alter the rule we have adopted previously in light of current "social and economic customs" and modern "conceptions of right and justice.". . .

We find that none of the justifications for denying any recovery to a plaintiff, who has contributed to his own injuries to any extent, has any validity in this age.

Perhaps the best argument in favor of the movement from contributory to comparative negligence is that the latter is simply a more equitable system of determining liability and a more socially desirable method of loss distribution. The injustice which occurs when a plaintiff suffers severe injuries as the result of an accident for which he is only slightly responsible, and is thereby denied any damages, is readily apparent. The rule of contributory negligence is a harsh one which either places the burden of a loss for which two are responsible upon only one party or relegates to Lady Luck the determination of the damages for which each of two negligent parties will be liable. When the negligence of more than one person contributes to the occurrence of an accident, each should pay the proportion of the total damages he has caused the other party. . . .

Petitioners in this cause, and various amicus curiae who have filed briefs, have raised many points which they claim we must consider in adopting comparative negligence, such as the effects of such a change on the concept of "assumption of risk," and no "contribution" between joint tortfeasors. We decline to consider all those issues, however, for two reasons. One reason is that we already have a body of case law in this State dealing with comparative negligence, under our earlier railroad statute. Much of this case law will be applicable under the comparative negligence rule we are now adopting generally.

The other reason is that it is not the proper function of this Court to decide unripe issues, without the benefit of adequate briefing, not involving an actual controversy, and unrelated to a specific factual situation.

We are fully confident that the trial court judges of this State can adequately handle any problems created by our change to a comparative negligence rule as these problems arise. The answers to many of the problems will be obvious in light of the purposes for which we adopt the rule stated above:

> (1) to allow a jury to apportion fault as it sees fit between negligent parties whose negligence was part of the legal and proximate cause of any loss or injury; and

(2) to apportion the total damages resulting from the loss or injury according to the proportionate fault of each party.

In accomplishing these purposes, the trial court is authorized to require special verdicts to be returned by the jury and to enter such judgment or judgments as may truly reflect the intent of the jury as expressed in any verdict or verdicts which may be returned. . . .

Under the circumstances, we hold that this opinion shall be applied as follows:

1. As to those cases in which the comparative negligence rule has been applied, this opinion shall be applicable.

2. As to those cases already commenced, but in which trial has not yet begun, this opinion shall be applicable.

3. As to those cases in which trial has already begun or in which verdict or judgment has already been rendered, this opinion shall not be applicable, unless the applicability of the comparative negligence rule was appropriately and properly raised during some stage of the litigation.

4. As to those cases on appeal in which the applicability of the comparative negligence rule has been properly and appropriately made a question of appellate review, this opinion shall be applicable.

5. This opinion shall be applicable to all cases commenced after the decision becomes final.

The certified question having now been answered in full, this cause is remanded to the District Court of Appeal, Fourth District, to be further remanded to the Circuit Court for a new trial. . . .

ROBERTS, JUSTICE (dissenting).

[T]he sovereign powers of this State are divided into three coordinate branches of government — legislative, judicial and executive — by the Constitution of Florida, Article II, Section 3. Our Constitution specifically prohibits a person belonging to one of such branches from exercising any powers "appertaining to either of the other branches unless expressly provided herein." . . .

[T]he matter of changing statutory law is not one to be indulged by the Court, but is a legislative function. . . . [T]his Court also reaffirmed the principle that the common law, if not abrogated by statute or constitutional provision, is in full force and effect in this state. . . .

It is the statutory law of this state that,

> [t]he common and statute laws of England which are of a general and not a local nature, with the exception hereinafter mentioned, down to the fourth day of July, 1776, are declared to be of force in this state; provided, the said statutes and common law be not inconsistent with the constitution and laws of the United States and the acts of the legislature of this state. Fla. Stat. § 2-01, F.S.A.

. . . [T]he primary question is not whether or not the law of contributory negligence should be changed, but rather, who should do the changing.

Contributory negligence was recognized in the common law as far back as A.D. 1606 and made a part of the statute law of this State in A.D. 1829, and thus far not changed by statute. If such a fundamental change is to be made in the law, then such modification should be made by the legislature where proposed change will be considered by legislative committees in public hearing where the general public may have an opportunity to be heard and should not be made by judicial fiat. Such an excursion into the field of legislative jurisdiction weakens the concept of separation of powers and our tripartite system of government.

NOTES

1. Assuming that, in deciding appeals, the task of an intermediate appellate court (like the task of a trial court) is to apply the existing law of the jurisdiction, did the lower court do this in *Hoffman v. Jones*? The lower court was affirmed by its supreme court. Does this show that the court correctly applied existing law? If so, why did the Florida Supreme Court chastise the intermediate appellate court?

2. A similar set of recent cases involved the "pueblo rights doctrine," which provided that any municipality tracing its origins to a Spanish or Mexican pueblo has paramount right to all waters of nonnavigable streams flowing through or by the pueblo to the extent necessary to serve present needs and future growth. In *New Mexico ex rel. Martinez v. City of Las Vegas*, 880 P.2d 868 (N.M. Ct. App. 1994), the intermediate appellate court predicted that the state Supreme Court would invalidate the doctrine and held accordingly, despite a state Supreme Court opinion adopting the doctrine, because that state Supreme Court opinion had not been reaffirmed in its 36 year lifetime, scholars had uniformly criticized the doctrine as lacking historical support and as being incompatible with the state's water rights system, and the City could not have reasonably relied on the doctrine in the manner in which it claimed. The state Supreme Court affirmed in part, in *New Mexico ex rel. Martinez v. City of Las Vegas*, 89 P.3d 47, 55 (N.M. 2004), determining that the doctrine was flawed and needed to be overruled based solely on its incompatibility with the state's water rights system. The court emphasized that *stare decisis* requires intermediate courts of appeals to follow a state supreme court decision regardless of whether the high court has reconsidered or reaffirmed its decision, and regardless of scholarly criticism. The role of the intermediate appellate court, it advised, was to "explain any reservations it might harbor over its application of our precedent so that we will be . . . more informed." In deference to reliance interests, the court limited its overruling and remanded for the trial court to balance the City's reliance on overruled doctrine against other users' reliance on the overall state water allocation system.

3. In *Meeks v. Indiana*, 759 N.E.2d 1126 (Ind. Ct. App. 2001), the court declined appellant's invitation to overrule or even criticize state supreme court precedent that juries should not be instructed that they may refuse to enforce the law when justice so requires. Noting that the intermediate appellate court was authorized to criticize supreme court rulings, the IAC explained that it exercised the privilege rarely and solely to urge reconsideration of an issue. Where the state supreme court had analyzed the issue in depth and recently,

and repeatedly had adhered to its position, the IAC concluded that this was not an appropriate occasion to offer criticism. Is "obedience with a privilege to criticize" too timid a role for intermediate appellate courts?

4. In *Minersville School District v. Gobitis*, 310 U.S. 586 (1940), the Supreme Court upheld the constitutionality of a flag salute requirement for students in public schools. Thereafter, the constitutionality of such a requirement was again challenged in an action before a three-judge federal district court. Writing for that court in *Barnette v. West Virginia State Board of Education*, 47 F. Supp. 251, 252 (S.D.W.Va. 1942), Judge Parker held the requirement to be unconstitutional, despite the *Gobitis* decision, saying:

> Ordinarily we would feel constrained to follow an unreversed decision of the Supreme Court of the United States, whether we agreed with it or not. It is true that decisions are but evidences of the law and not the law itself; but the decisions of the Supreme Court must be accepted by the lower courts as binding upon them if any orderly administration of justice is to be attained. The developments with respect to the *Gobitis* case, however, are such that we do not feel that it is incumbent upon us to accept it as binding authority. Of the seven justices now members of the Supreme Court who participated in that decision, four have given public expression to the view that it is unsound, the present Chief Justice in his dissenting opinion rendered therein and three other justices in a special dissenting opinion in *Jones v. City of Opelika*, 316 U.S. 584. . . . Under such circumstances and believing, as we do, that the flag salute here required is violative of religious liberty when required of persons holding the religious views of plaintiffs, we feel that we would be recreant to our duty as judges, if through a blind following of a decision which the Supreme Court itself has thus impaired as authority, we should deny protection to rights which we regard as among the most sacred of those protected by constitutional guaranties.

The Supreme Court affirmed that decision. *W. Va. State Bd. of Educ. v. Barnette*, 319 U.S. 624 (1943).

Was Judge Parker's action consistent with his role as a lower court judge? Or should IACs and district court's leave it to the Supreme Court to overrule its own cases? Did the factors cited by Judge Parker make *Barnette* an exceptional case in which the federal district court was not obligated to follow *Gobitis*?

5. Consider the following statement from *Indianapolis Airport Authority v. American Airlines, Inc.*, 733 F.2d 1262, 1272 (7th Cir. 1984):

> [J]ust as an intermediate federal appellate court may properly decline to follow a U.S. Supreme Court decision when convinced that the Court would overrule the decision if it had the opportunity to do so, see, e.g., *Norris v. United States*, 687 F.2d 899, 902-04 (7th Cir. 1982), so may intermediate state appellate courts decline to follow earlier state supreme court decisions for the same reason — especially when almost a century has passed since the earlier decisions. And if we think the intermediate state appellate court has made a correct or even, perhaps, a just defensible prediction of what the state supreme

court would do if the question were put to it, then we are bound to follow its ruling in a diversity case or any other case where the issue is one of state law. . . .

Compare Hohn v. United States, 524 U.S. 236, 252-53 (1998) ("Our decisions remain binding precedent until we see fit to reconsider them, regardless of whether subsequent cases have raised doubts about their continuing vitality"); *Rodriguez de Quijas v. Shearson/Am. Express, Inc.*, 490 U.S. 477, 484 (1989) ("If a precedent of this Court has direct application . . . , yet appears to rest on reasons rejected in some other line of decisions, the Court of Appeals should follow the case which directly controls, leaving to this Court the prerogative of overruling its own decisions"). Does the view of the role of intermediate state appellate courts expressed in *Indianapolis Airport Authority* survive *Hohn* and *Rodriguez de Quijas*? Is the relation of state IACs to state supreme courts different from the relationship of federal IACs to the U.S. Supreme Court?

Suppose the state intermediate court had made no decision of the sort described in *Indianapolis Airport Authority*, quoted above. How should a federal court deal with the state law issue in that circumstance? Is a federal court more free or less free than a state intermediate appellate court to predict what the state supreme court would hold if it had the issue before it, and rule accordingly?

James D. Hopkins, *The Role of an Intermediate Appellate Court*, 41 BROOKLYN LAW REVIEW 459, 460-78 (1975)[1]

The intermediate appellate court is customarily cast into an error-correcting mold rather than into a rule-making model, the latter reserved for the highest court. Typically, the intermediate court is occupied with assignments of error which allege that existing rules were not followed; such role distinction properly insures that the highest court need not be called upon to expend its energies and capacities in reviewing that kind of appeal. Yet no three-tier system so divides appellate work that the intermediate court is exclusively engaged in the correction of errors without any involvement in the creative function, or that the highest court never corrects an error of either the *nisi prius* court or the intermediate court. There is, in brief, an interrelationship among the three that is continuing and unbounded during the decisional process. Once the highest court settles the point at issue, the relationship so far as that point is concerned, of course, terminates, but the relationship endures in the myriad appeals still pending and as the aspects of the law develop. . . .

[U]nless we are ready to say that the number of appeals must be sharply curtailed, it is undoubtedly more appropriate, and even inevitable, that the intermediate court should continue to bear the brunt of the ever-increasing load of appeals.

Two conclusions may be drawn from this observation. First, the general flow of litigation realistically is controlled by the intermediate courts of appeal. Only a small percentage of cases is finally determined by the third tier. . . . Hence, the

---

[1] Copyright © 1975. Reprinted with permission of the Brooklyn Law Review.

intermediate courts bear a heavy responsibility for the proper functioning of the system in terms of decision-making in accord with the existing law. To that end, it is desirable that the judges in that court constantly reexamine their work.

[S]econd . . . since the full flow of appeals is centered in the intermediate courts, it is those courts which are in a better position to determine in what areas of the law confusion is occurring and where reform or clarification is necessary. This suggests a second role for the intermediate court — to stimulate revision in the law, either by the highest court through common law doctrine or by the legislature through the enactment of statutes. The intermediate court may accomplish this purpose by several techniques.

First, the intermediate court may make a direct appeal to the legislature for a change in the law. Classically, the request takes the form of a direct or oblique statement to the effect that the existing law is ambiguous and should be made clear, or that it results in injustice under certain conditions, or that the policy of the existing law cannot be wholly effectuated because of loopholes or inadequate remedies. Classically, too, the court tactfully refrains from suggesting the remedy. More often than not, the statement to the legislature concerns statutes presently in effect.

. . . [T]he area in which an intermediate court operates with more facility is in adjective law, today almost entirely codified. The intermediate court is closer to the trial court; it reviews the procedural aspects of litigation more often and with greater influence than does the highest court; and it therefore deals in these areas with larger concern for the efficiency and justice of the process in disposing of cases.

Second, the intermediate court may make a direct statement to the highest court in support of a change in existing doctrine. Again, the statement may be couched in indirect terms, suggesting the unfairness or the inutility of the doctrine in the present setting of the community — a kind of polite nudge or, perhaps, even an outright plea for change. . . .

Beyond the technique of a direct statement to another authority, the intermediate court itself can effect change. In the hierarchal view of precedent, the act may take the form of either quiet usurpation of, or a bold challenge to, existing case law. Quiet usurpation occurs when the intermediate court consciously undermines doctrine by the process of distinction without expressly impugning the doctrine. This is, of course, the traditional common law technique which usually foretells the eventual overruling or modification of doctrine. But the process is customarily initiated by the highest court, with the intermediate court then following its lead. . . .

[T]he act of challenge does not avoid the doctrine; the intermediate court institutes the change by openly overruling the doctrine. Usually, it justifies its decision by claiming that the doctrine no longer fits contemporary circumstances; and it implies that it is taking the action which the highest court would itself have taken if given the opportunity.

Neither of these expedients seems to me to be appropriate. The highest court may indeed resent the destruction of the doctrine either by the slow erosion of distinction or by the straightforward method of overruling. . . .

More properly, it seems to me, the intermediate court's functions should be carried out by suggestion, by indicating the reasons for change, but not by infringing upon the prerogative of the highest court to make changes in the law. If stare decisis is to continue to hold any place in the judicial system as a control on the uniform and non-discriminatory determination of similar disputes, there cannot be two sources for the definition of the law to be applied. Any process other than the establishment of final power in one court — at the highest tier — results only in a distrust of the systems and in utter confusion among the bar and the trial courts. If the merit of the change is exposed by the statement of the intermediate court, we should expect that the highest court will give suitable consideration to the recommendation. . . .

When a question of fundamental importance is presented to the intermediate court, much may be done in the determination of the case to put it into proper perspective for the highest court. Usually, at or before the time of determination, the eligibility of the appeal for consideration by the highest court is apparent. On the assumption that the highest court will wish to lay down a definitive rule, the intermediate court should 1) make the determinations of fact necessary for the resolution of the appeal clearly and completely, 2) write on the issues of law so that, as far as possible, the varying positions of the parties and of the members of the court are fully delineated, and 3) make its disposition of the appeal plainly and without leaving undecided any issue critical to the rights of the parties.

When these three criteria are observed, the highest court is enabled to gauge the importance of the questions and to address itself to them without uncertainty as to the posture of the case before it. Moreover, if the discussion of the law in the intermediate court has been thorough and conforms to the view of the highest court, the latter's determination may be made by a simple affirmance without opinion or even by an affirmance on the opinion in the intermediate court.

Quite apart from these considerations, the intermediate court owes a duty to the system to present the merits and demerits of the possible solutions to a novel issue. Upon a study of the alternatives, the highest court is better informed to decide upon the course which it finds most appropriate for the determination of the problems. . . .

It is, of course, inevitable from the position of the intermediate court that it is for the great majority of cases the court of last resort. . . . Thus, a heavy responsibility is borne by the intermediate court. It must, for one thing, decide cases within the bounds of doctrine already enunciated by the highest court; distinctions said to call for a deviation from doctrine or for the choice of one doctrine as against another have to be carefully scanned to ensure that the force and spirit of the doctrine are not breached by the distinction. Not all errors of the intermediate court may be corrected at the highest level — the highest court cannot look at more than the merest fraction of the total unanimous decisions of the intermediate courts.

Moreover, the surging flow of cases through the intermediate court causes it to become more quickly aware of the need for change. Though the intermediate court cannot make an authoritative change (except in the fashioning of rules for the exercise of discretion), it does have the duty to assist the highest court to consider the change. It may do this, first, by focusing on the issue and putting it into perspective under the particular facts of the case. Second, it should analyze the reasons for change and indicate whether they are valid, again, in the perspective of the case. Third, a solution should be suggested. If the solution violates existing doctrine, it may not properly be adopted in the case, but the need for change may nevertheless be underlined.

It is within this process that the value of dissent at the intermediate stage is significant. The sharpening of the issue becomes especially prominent by the contrast of the majority with the minority view. In this sense, it is true that the intermediate court represents in effect a laboratory for the highest court. . . .

A function of the intermediate appellate court, sometimes overlooked, is its authority — at least in New York — to reverse or modify in the interests of justice. The power apparently also exists in some other jurisdictions. . . .

The three-tier system of appellate review has developed beyond the original purpose for which it was conceived. It now has the function not only to relieve the highest court of the burden of excessive caseload, but also to assist the highest court and legislature in making needed changes in common law doctrine and statutory provisions. As the court of last resort in the great majority of appeals, it has the duty of assuring uniformity of treatment, particularly in the area of discretionary rulings by the trial courts. Finally, as to that minority of cases which reach the highest court, it has the responsibility of sharpening the legal issues and determining the factual issues completely, so that the task of the highest court is made easier.

Benjamin Kaplan, *Do Intermediate Appellate Courts Have A Lawmaking Function?*, 70 MASSACHUSETTS LAW REVIEW 10-11 (1985)[2]

I have no trouble answering the question: the answer is Yes. Still, there is something heretical or paradoxical about the question itself, because everyone knows that an intermediate court is installed for the precise purpose of dealing in a routine way with routine cases, thereby releasing the highest court to think the highest thoughts and make law. This seems confirmed by the typical story of the founding of intermediate courts. The supreme court of a State finds that it is being inundated and overwhelmed by a tide of cases beyond the number it can handle by ordinary methods. This crisis, let us note, is contributed to by a notable increase in the volume of cases raising intricate, difficult, novel questions thrown up by massive social and economic changes. To meet the problem, the supreme court may experiment with speed-up devices such as abbreviating oral argument, writing midget rather than full-length opinions, or no opinions at all, splitting into divisions, using rotating panels, coopting commissioners or temporary or retired judges, relying heavily on staff, penalizing frivolous appeals, or otherwise trying to make do. All these

---

[2] Copyright © 1985. Reprinted with permission of the Massachusetts Bar Association.

methods turn out to be not enough to manage the flow, so the next device is to interpose, in the hierarchy of courts, a new court with appellate duties. This expedient has become popular — at somebody's late count, intermediate courts were found in thirty-six states [now thirty-nine]; and, of course, they have long been paralleled in the Federal system by the Courts of Appeals. [All of these measures taken in response to increased volume of appeals are examined in Chapters 6 through 9.]

When the intermediate courts are set up, it is on the plain understanding about where the run-of-the-mine or donkey work is to fall. The point is variously expressed, but the general sense is that the job of an intermediate court is to take on the mass of appeals that involve merely claimed errors of the trial courts in applying the settled legal rules, while the supreme court, picking up a smallish number of appeals selected in one way or another as being more exotic, is by its decisions to mold, develop, and change the law to satisfy emerging social needs and keep the law in tip-top, up-to-date working order. This conventional or orthodox view of the allocation of jobs as between the intermediate and supreme courts is enshrined in the ABA's Standards [STANDARDS RELATING TO APPELLATE COURTS (1977), Standard 3.00, commentary] and is set out and explained and modulated in so valuable a book as the one by Professors Carrington, Meador, and Rosenberg entitled *Justice on Appeal* [(1976)].

Now, I want to digress a bit. It may be objected that the question we are asking and trying to answer is but a phantom. I take the question to assume, implicitly, that there is such a thing as settled or established law, and that it can be and is followed or applied by judges; and the question asks, implicitly, whether intermediate courts, in addition merely to following and applying, do something else as well. But, according to the school of Legal Realism, in which many of us were nurtured, judges in fact follow their instincts in deciding cases, making sham references to rules of law; generally they are themselves unaware of what they are doing, and persist foolishly in believing that they are being obedient to precedent. . . . Critical Legal Studies . . . stresses the proposition that law is grievously and unavoidably indeterminate, so that, try as judges may, there is nothing out there that can in truth be followed or applied. On either view, . . . any purported allocation of functions in the hierarchy of courts must be a hollow hoax or mockery.

But I am going to reject these conceptions of law and judicial process which, I admit, I have described in somewhat exaggerated ways. Of course the law is to some considerable extent indeterminate rather than fixed; that is the price the law must pay for dealing with human material. And of course a judge to some considerable extent is the victim of his or her predilections. Yet I think there are legal rules than can be and are actually followed. There is such a thing as precedent that binds. When judges think they are following precedent, and that they are bound to do so, they are not, I believe, the captives of an illusion. The pioneer realist Karl Llewellyn had it about right when, in his final work, *The Common Law Tradition*, he acknowledged the fact and force of precedent, or rather the fact of a large number of steadying or stabilizing influences on the appellate process, including precedent. Or consider how that other pioneer realist, Jerome Frank, behaved in his actual encounters with precedent after he attained the Bench: he was highly conscious of it, and worked with it as the rest of us do. So I conclude my digression by saying that a sensible distinction — not a very sharp one, but a distinction nevertheless — can be maintained between applying law and making it, and our question stands, and remains to be answered.

Coming, then, to the nub — whether the work of intermediate courts conforms to the orthodox description — we must surely take account of the different organizational structures of these courts, which must have a bearing on their lawmaking potentialities. At one end of the spectrum are the courts resembling, for the present purpose, the Federal Courts of Appeals. Of all the multitudinous decisions of the Court of Appeals, only a minute fraction are ever reviewed by the Supreme Court of the United States, and those mostly upon applications for certiorari that the losing parties happen to file in their own interests, and not with a purpose to develop the law. At the other end of the spectrum are intermediate courts on a pattern resembling that of our intermediate court here in Massachusetts, our Appeals Court. Let me describe the Massachusetts pattern in general terms.

The highest court, the Supreme Judicial Court, is required to hear certain appeals — these are few. The big range of appeals from the trial courts are lodged as a formal matter in the Appeals Court. From this mass, the Supreme Court selects those appeals that it wishes to hear. First, the Supreme Court grants or denies applications by the parties for direct appellate review of the judgments of the trial courts, bypassing the Appeals Court. Second, the Supreme Court selects and takes appeals unto itself *sua sponte*, also bypassing the Appeals Court. As to the appeals remaining in the Appeals Court for determination by it, the parties after decision by the Appeals Court can petition the Supreme Court for further appellate review. . . .

I have now described two polar models. In the first, assimilated to the Federal model, the intermediate court is largely uncontrolled by its hierarchical superior, and it follows, does it not, that, besides merely correcting errors of the trial courts, the intermediate court must perforce be making a lot of fresh law, subject only occasionally to check from above. And if you look to the Federal Courts of Appeals, you do indeed find thirteen factories operating with intense energy to make law. Can we not say that it has been one aim of those who sponsor a National Court of Appeals . . . to channel or rationalize somewhat this vast power and exuberance.

In the opposite polar case, which I have located on my own home grounds, we see a system where the highest court has nearly complete control of the division of business between the intermediate court and itself. Hence one might expect that the conventionally prescribed allocation — routine correction of the trial courts assigned to the intermediate court, lawmaking assigned to the highest court — would be quite strictly achieved. . . .

I suggest, however, that, even in such a limiting situation as we find in Massachusetts, a situation of firm control from the top, the intermediate court will by no means be confined to the correction of the judgments of the trial courts for breach of established doctrines, but will make law, will contribute significantly to the evolution of law. . . .

NOTES

Is there a single correct answer to the question: What is the role of an intermediate appellate court? If not, what characteristics of the system in which such a court is situated might properly influence its role?

B. Recognizing New Causes of Action

SHACKIL v. LEDERLE LABORATORIES
530 A.2d 1287 (N.J. Super. Ct. App. Div. 1987)

[Claiming that their 14-year-old daughter had been severely brain-damaged by the administration of DPT vaccine nearly 13 years earlier, parents and their child sued a group of pharmaceutical manufacturers on product liability theories. Immunization with the vaccine was required by law to protect young children from diphtheria, whooping cough and tetanus. Each manufacturer used its own process in creating the vaccine. The trial court dismissed their complaint and the plaintiffs appealed. Not knowing which of the defendants had manufactured the vaccine administered to their child, the plaintiffs relied on a theory of collective responsibility and a market-share measure of liability.]

DREIR, J.A.D.

[T]his court in *Namm* [*v. Charles E. Frosst & Co.*, 427 A.2d 1121 [at 1125] (N.J. Super. Ct. App. Div. 1981)] stated:

> it is a fundamental principle of products liability law that a plaintiff must prove, as an essential element of his case, that the defendant manufacturer actually made the particular product which caused the injury.

. . . [I]n the usual case it is only "one who sells [i.e., a manufacturer, distributor or a retailer] any product in a defective condition" who is subject to strict liability under Restatement (Second) of Torts, § 402A, and there is an extensive series of Supreme Court cases adopting this general principle. We disagree, however, with *Namm's* finding that any Supreme Court case prohibits our holding each of those who sell substantially similar products (the effects of which after the passage of time cannot readily be distinguished from one another) collectively as "sellers" within the meaning of § 402A.

The *Namm* court next determined . . . that "traditional concepts and basic principles would of necessity be either distorted or abandoned altogether" if any theory of alternative liability was adopted. [427 A.2d at 1128.] Further, the court found, quoting a workers' compensation case, that an intermediate appellate court should "adhere to existing laws of the State and in the absence of appropriate amendatory legislation" should defer to the Supreme Court. *Ibid.* We fully subscribe to this principle where there is Supreme Court precedent or even dictum to the contrary, or where the Legislature has spoken and the matter is thus taken from the purview of the common law. The majority and dissent welcome the Legislature's entrance into this field. . . . But we note that the specific problem before us has not been addressed in the new Act.

If an intermediate appellate or trial court must decide an issue where there is no binding appellate authority or legislation, then it is within the authority of that court, and even its duty, to resolve the issue before it consistent with the court's understanding of the governing law. Here, where there is no indication of the Supreme Court's antipathy to collective responsibility, we perceive our role as one to determine what the Supreme Court would do if faced with the problem before us. . . . The denial of potential liability by *Namm* was as much a policy statement as our recognition, refinement and application of the recognized tort principles discussed herein. The rejection of these theories which have been developed in states with views of tort law similar to our own would be an unwarranted deviation from what we perceive to be a course already charted by our Supreme Court. Not to follow this course would constitute the very "policy shift" decried both in *Namm,* 178 N.J. Super. at 35, and the dissent. . . .

We look to the past decisions of our Supreme Court to determine whether some form of collective responsibility would be antithetical to principles applied in related fields. We note first that where the issue is not the identity of the manufacturer of a product, but rather the identity of the defendant which caused a particular injury, the Supreme Court has not hesitated to shift the burden of proof to defendants to exculpate themselves. . . . Similarly, where a plaintiff is unable to identify which of successive carriers damaged plaintiff's property, the Supreme Court placed the burden upon the carriers to come forward and exculpate themselves. *NOPCO v. Blaw-Knox Co.,* 59 N.J. 274 (1971). Also, in a recent toxic tort case, the Supreme Court in *Ayers v. Jackson Tp.,* 106 N.J. 557, 585-586 (1987), noted in dictum that in mass exposure litigation where identification of the culpable defendant presents a causation problem, resort might be had to the alternative liability theory expressed in *Summers v. Tice,* 199 P.2d 1 (1948), a case in which plaintiff could not prove which defendant was responsible for his injury, and under those special facts the burden of proof was placed upon defendants to disprove causation. Indeed, our Supreme Court has been in the forefront of jurisdictions to recognize and protect those injured by the wrongful acts of others. *See e.g., Kelly v. Gwinnell,* 96 N.J. 538 (1984); *Henningsen v. Bloomfield Motors,* 32 N.J. 358 (1960). We, therefore, have no reason to suppose that the Supreme Court would reject all theories of collective responsibility, provided the rights of the defendant manufacturers to exculpate themselves are scrupulously protected. . . .

Reversed and remanded.

NOTES

1. *Compare Brooks v. Brooks,* 680 N.W.2d 379 (Iowa Ct. App. Feb. 11, 2004) (table), 2004 Iowa App. LEXIS 225 (declining to decide whether Iowa should recognize a tort claim by a former husband against his former wife for fraud and intentional infliction of emotional distress based on a misrepresentation that the plaintiff fathered defendant's child, saying "[w]e leave it up to the legislature or our supreme court to establish new causes of action even when they appear to have merit"). Are *Shackil* and *Brooks* distinguishable? Did the intermediate appellate court act appropriately in each case?

2. It may be debatable whether a plaintiff is asking lower courts to recognize a previously unrecognized cause of action. In *Engler v. Wehmas,* 633 N.W.2d

868 (Minn. Ct. App. 2001), the parent of a child severely injured when hit by a car sued the driver for negligent infliction of emotional distress caused by fear for her son's safety and from witnessing her son's injury. The IAC found that it would be creating new law to hold that the parent could recover, and because creating new law is not the function of the IAC, it held that the parent could not recover for those injuries. The dissenting judge disagreed that a holding for the plaintiff required creation of new law, noting that Minnesota recognizes a claim for negligent infliction of emotional distress by plaintiffs within the zone of danger, who reasonably fear for their own safety and who suffer severe emotional manifestations with physical manifestations — all satisfied by the facts here. The dissent argued that this case presented a logical extension of existing case law, consistent with basic negligence principles. Is there a clear line between creating a new cause of action and merely extending existing authority? How should an IAC decide when extending existing case law would exceed the outer bounds of its functions?

II. JUDICIAL LAWMAKING BY SUPREME COURTS

Similar to the structure of section I above, the initial focus here is on the propriety of a supreme court's overruling its own prior common law decisions. We then turn to the concerns involved in a supreme court's recognition of a hitherto unrecognized cause of action.

A. Overruling

On the overruling problem, recall *Hoffman v. Jones*, in which the Florida Supreme Court decided to abandon the judge-made rule of contributory negligence and to adopt a rule of comparative negligence. That decision worked a change in the law by overruling the court's own prior decision. Such an action represents a drastic break with existing judicial precedent. In what circumstances is such overruling appropriate?

WISCONSIN v. PICOTTE
661 N.W.2d 381 (Wis. 2003)

SHIRLEY S. ABRAHAMSON, CHIEF JUSTICE.

[T]he circuit court . . . entered a judgment of conviction for first-degree reckless homicide (Wis. Stat. § 940.02), party to a crime, against Waylon Picotte, the defendant . . . The issue presented by this case is whether the defendant's conviction . . . is barred because the victim did not die within a year and a day of the infliction of the fatal injuries.

The defendant's postconviction motions asserted that his conviction . . . was barred because it violated the common-law year-and-a-day rule, which establishes an irrebuttable presumption that death occurring more than one year and one day after an accused's injury-inflicting act was not caused by the accused.

The circuit court denied the defendant's motions. . . . We disagree with the circuit court and hold that the defendant's conviction in this case is barred by the common-law year-and-a-day rule. In order to reach this conclusion, we must address four successive questions of law that this court decides independent of the circuit court but benefiting from the circuit court's analysis. The four questions and this court's answers to them are as follows:

1. Is the common-law year-and-a-day rule the law in Wisconsin? We agree with both the State and the defendant that the year-and-a-day rule has been the law of Wisconsin since statehood, preserved through Article XIV, Section 13 of the Wisconsin Constitution.

2. If the year-and-a-day rule is the law in Wisconsin, does this court have the authority to abrogate the rule? This court has the authority to develop the common law and therefore may abrogate the year-and-a-day rule.

3. If this court has the authority to abrogate the year-and-a-day rule, do sufficiently compelling reasons exist for this court to do so now? This court should abrogate a common-law rule when the rule becomes unsound. We conclude that the year-and-a-day rule is an archaic rule that no longer makes sense. Accordingly, the court abolishes the rule.

4. Should the abrogation of the year-and-a-day rule apply to the defendant in the present case? The court may change or abrogate a common-law rule either retroactively or prospectively. We conclude that purely prospective abrogation of the year-and-a-day rule best serves the interests of justice. Thus, prosecutions for murder in which the conduct inflicting the death occurs after the date of this decision are permissible regardless of whether the victim dies more than a year and a day after the infliction of the fatal injury. The prosecution for first-degree reckless homicide in the present case, however, remains subject to the year-and-a-day rule, and because the fatal injury in the present case was inflicted more than a year and a day before the death of the victim, the defendant's conviction for first-degree reckless homicide is reversed.

I

[Picotte was involved in a fight on September 26, 1996. During the fight, John Jackson was struck in the face and hit his head on a brick wall. Jackson suffered brain damage that left him in a coma. The defendant was charged with aggravated battery and substantial battery. He pled guilty and was sentenced to 15 years in prison. More than two years later, Jackson died from complications arising from the injuries sustained in the fight. Defendant was then charged with first-degree reckless homicide. After a jury trial, he was convicted and sentenced to 30 years in prison. Picotte filed postconviction motions asserting, among other issues, that his prosecution and conviction for first-degree reckless homicide violated the common-law year-and-a-day rule. The circuit court affirmed the conviction and the court of appeals certified the issues relating to the year-and-a-day rule for review by the state supreme court.]

II

. . . [W]e agree with both the State and the defendant that the year-and-a-day rule has been the law of Wisconsin since statehood, preserved through Article XIV, Section 13 of the Wisconsin Constitution.

Article XIV, Section 13 of the Wisconsin Constitution reads as follows:

Common law continued in force. Such parts of the common law as are now in force in the territory of Wisconsin, not inconsistent with this constitution, shall be and continue [to be] part of the law of this state until altered or suspended by the legislature. . . .

[W]e conclude that the year-and-a-day rule was incorporated into the laws of Wisconsin by Article XIV, Section 13 of the Wisconsin Constitution and has not been altered or suspended by the legislature.

III

We next consider whether this court has the authority to abrogate the year-and-a-day rule. The defendant asserts that Article XIV, Section 13 of the Wisconsin Constitution permits only the legislature to abrogate the common law and that this court does not have the authority to abrogate the common-law year-and-a-day rule. We disagree with the defendant. It is now well established that Article XIV, Section 13 did not usurp the traditional authority of the judiciary to develop the common law in Wisconsin.

. . . [T]he *Esser* decision [*State v. Esser*, 115 N.W.2d 505 (Wis. 1962)] . . . concluded that the Wisconsin Constitution vests this court, and other courts of this state, with "judicial powers," and that those judicial powers include the power to adapt and develop the common law through the judicial process. In light of this power, the *Esser* decision concluded as follows that Article XIV, Section 13 cannot be read to bar this court from changing the common law:

> We conclude that the function of sec. 13, art. XIV, Wis. Const., was to provide for the continuity of the common law into the legal system of the state; expressly made subject to legislative change (in as drastic degree within the proper scope of legislative power as the legislature might see fit) but impliedly subject, because of the historical course of the development of the common law, to the process of continuing evolution under the judicial power. [*Esser*, 115 N.W.2d at 514.]

This conclusion does not contravene the plain words of the constitutional provision because by definition, common law is law subject to continuing judicial development, including abrogation. "Inherent in the common law is a dynamic principle which allows it to grow and to tailor itself to meet changing needs within the doctrine of stare decisis, which, if correctly understood, was not static and did not forever prevent the courts from reversing themselves or from applying principles of the common law to new situations as the need arose." [*Bielski v. Schulze*, 114 N.W.2d 105, 110 (Wis. 1962)]. Thus, properly construed, Article XIV, Section 13 of the Wisconsin Constitution does not codify English common law circa 1776, but rather preserves law that by historical understanding is subject to continuing evolution under the judicial power. . . [T]he power to abrogate a common-law rule preserved by Article XIV, Section 13 is not limited to the legislature, but extends to the judiciary as well.

The defendant also argues that . . . this court may not abrogate the year-and-a-day rule in this case because the legislature has specifically refused to adopt such a change and thereby expressed a policy decision to maintain the rule as good law in Wisconsin. In light of this legislative history, the defendant asserts that abrogation of the common-law rule would be an improper exercise of judicial power by developing the law in contravention of the legislative policy.

We disagree with the defendant's assessment of the impact legislative history has on this court's authority to alter or abrogate the year-and-a-day rule. We have long rejected the doctrine that "legislative consideration coupled with inaction [is] indicative of preemption."

In *Holytz v. City of Milwaukee*, 115 N.W.2d 618 (1962), this court . . . announced that when the rule in question is a common-law rule, the court's responsibility for altering or abolishing that rule does not end due to legislative indifference or failure to enact a statute to the contrary. This important turning point has since been recognized in a number of decisions.

This court's post-*Holytz* decision, *Sorensen v. Jarvis*, 350 N.W.2d 108 (1984), is particularly on point. In *Sorensen*, this court abrogated the common-law rule barring a third party injured by an intoxicated minor from recovering damages from the retail seller who sold the intoxicating beverage to the minor. The defendant in *Sorensen* asserted that the court was prohibited from changing the common-law rule because a recent legislative attempt to do so "was allowed to die in committee" and by this inaction a declaration of the legislative will not to change the common law was announced. The *Sorensen* decision rejected this argument, concluding, "While in the past we have indicated that nonaction by the legislature could be so interpreted we have since stated that, even where there has been some evidence, arguably, of the legislature's will by its failure to act, we are not foreclosed from acting." [*Sorensen*, 350 N.W.2d at 112.]

 . . . [T]he decision not to treat a legislature's failure to enact a bill overriding the common law as indicative of legislative intent is further supported by considerations of the legislative process itself. As the *Sorensen* decision explains, "Nonpassage of a bill is not reliable evidence of legislative intent, for it may have failed" for a variety of nonpolicy reasons, such as insufficient time, the agenda-setting maneuverings of legislative leadership, the efforts of special interests, or lobbying efforts at a committee or floor level. [*Id*. at 112.]

It would be absurd to conclude that every time a bill to change the common law was introduced but not passed by the legislature, the relevant common law effectively freezes at that moment until further action by the legislature. Indeed, such a rule would result in an unwarranted encroachment on the judicial powers of the courts by individual legislators empowered with their own personal veto over development of the common law of Wisconsin.

We conclude, therefore, that the fact that the legislature declined to abrogate the year-and-a-day rule when it revised the criminal code in 1955 does not bar this court from doing so.

IV

Having decided that this court has the authority to abrogate the year-and-a-day rule, we must now determine whether the time has come to do so. Common-law rules are meant to develop and adapt to new conditions and the progress of society. In *Esser*, the court concluded that "whenever an old rule is found unsuited to present conditions or unsound, it should be set aside." [*Esser*, 115 N.W.2d at 513.] In *Antoniewicz v. Reszcynski*, 236 N.W.2d 1 [at 10] (1975), the court stated that "it is the tradition of common-law courts to reflect the spirit of their times and discard legal rules when they serve to impede society rather than to advance it."

We agree with the State that new conditions and the progress of society have rendered the year-and-a-day rule "unsuited to present conditions" and an impediment to society, and that the time has come to set it aside.

As the State points out, there are three traditional justifications for the year-and-a-day rule. The primary and most frequently cited justification is that because of the primitive state of medical knowledge in the thirteenth century it was not possible to establish causation beyond a reasonable doubt when a great deal of time had elapsed between the injury to the victim and the victim's death. Therefore, it was presumed that a death that occurred more than one year and one day after the assault or injury was due to causes other than the criminal conduct.

Second, it has often been said that the rule arose from the early function of the jury. In early English courts, jurors decided cases by relying upon their own knowledge of the matter at issue, and could not rely upon the testimony of fact witnesses or expert witnesses. Thus, even if expert medical testimony had been adequate to establish causation at common law, it would not have been admissible.

Third, the rule has occasionally been characterized as an attempt to avoid the harsh result of the common law of homicides: Those convicted of homicide in any form, from first-degree to manslaughter, were subject to the death penalty.

None of these justifications remain persuasive for maintaining the year-and-a-day rule in Wisconsin. Advances in medical science that permit causes of death to be identified with great certainty have undermined the first justification for the year-and-a-day rule. Modern rules of evidence giving jurors access to expert opinion testimony regarding the cause of death undermine the second justification for the rule. Finally, since Wisconsin does not have the death penalty, the third justification for the rule can have no sway in this state.

In addition to the lack of any justification for continuing the year-and-a-day rule in modern society, two affirmative reasons exist for abolishing the year-and-a-day common-law rule. First, the common-law rule raises the specter of a family's being forced to choose between terminating the use of a life-support system and allowing an accused to escape a murder charge. Second, it is unjust to permit an assailant to escape punishment because of a convergence of modern medical advances and an archaic rule from the thirteenth century.

Moreover, we agree with the State that the abrogation of the year-and-a-day rule would not deprive an accused of any fundamental right. The burden would remain "upon the prosecution to prove proximate causation — that death flowed from the wrongful act of the defendant.". . .

In short, we are persuaded that the year-and-a-day rule has outlived its various justifications and therefore now join the many states that have abrogated the rule.

V

Having abrogated the year-and-a-day rule, the remaining issue we address is the applicability of this abrogation of the common-law rule to the defendant in the case at hand.

The United States Supreme Court has made it clear that this court has the authority to abrogate the year-and-a-day common-law rule prospectively or retroactively. In *Northern Railway Co. v. Sunburst Oil & Refining Co.*, 287 U.S. 358, 364 (1932), Justice Cardozo, writing for a unanimous court, affirmed a decision . . . to apply [a] new rule only to future conduct — explaining: "We think the Federal Constitution has no voice upon the subject. A state in defining the limits of adherence to precedent may make a choice for itself between the principle of forward operation and that of relation backward."

More recently, Justice Sandra Day O'Connor, writing for a five-justice majority in *Rogers v. Tennessee*, 532 U.S. 451(2001), declared that the Tennessee Supreme Court had the authority to abrogate the year-and-a-day rule retroactively without violating the federal constitution.

These decisions make clear that state courts must decide for themselves whether to abrogate the common-law year-and-a-day rule prospectively or retroactively, and so we turn to Wisconsin case law for guidance.

This court has faced the question of prospective versus retroactive overruling of a common-law rule in several cases. The court has stated a number of times that it, like all courts, generally adheres to the "Blackstonian doctrine," which provides that "a decision to overrule or repudiate an earlier decision is retrospective in operation." The Blackstonian doctrine is based on the jurisprudential theory that "courts declare but do not make law. In consequence, when a decision is overruled, it does not merely become bad law, — it never was the law, and the later pronouncement is regarded as the law from the beginning."

The court, however, has also criticized the Blackstonian doctrine because it "leads to a strict and unyielding adherence to the rule of stare decisis and interferes with the progress of the law." Furthermore, inequities can arise when a court departs from precedent and announces a new rule. Accordingly, the court has recognized exceptions to the Blackstonian doctrine and has employed the technique known as prospective overruling, or "sunbursting," to soften or limit the impact of a newly announced rule.

In *Harmann v. Hadley*, 382 N.W.2d 673 [at 676] (1986), we explained that there are no easy-to-follow rules or consistent guidelines directing courts on whether or how to sunburst a decision. Courts must make the decision based upon the "equities peculiar to a given rule or case."

The decision to overrule a rule of law purely prospectively is therefore a "question of policy." The most common reason for prospective overruling is to protect the reliance interests of individuals and institutions that have ordered their affairs under the prior legal regime. Other interests, however, are also implicated when a court overrules past precedent. A free and democratic society requires stability in the law, and retroactive changes in the law jeopardize the courts' own institutional reliance on announced law. Our society also values the efficient administration of justice, and applying a new rule retroactively often imposes an added burden on the judicial institution. Moreover, retroactive application of criminal responsibility may be viewed as tarnishing the rule of law and institutional adherence to the law, thus tarnishing the "image of justice."

Purely prospective overruling frequently reduces the impairment of these interests and mitigates any hardships that result from a decision to change the law. . . . [T]he sunbursting technique relieves some pressure against departure from precedent and serves the same social interest in stability that is the root of stare decisis.

With respect to criminal cases, Wisconsin courts have expressed reservations about retroactive overruling of judge-made substantive criminal laws, making acts criminal that were not considered criminal when they occurred. In *Laabs v. Tax Commission*, 261 N.W. 404 [at 418] (1935), this court explained that the Blackstonian presumption of retroactivity should be abandoned where a criminal statute "which has received a limited construction by earlier decisions, has been so expanded in meaning by the later overruling decision as to make acts criminal which were not such under earlier decisions, and the later decision is sought to be applied to one whose acts were committed before the statute was given the enlarged construction."

Commentaries uniformly recognize the hardships created by retroactive application of judicial decisions expanding substantive criminal laws. Chief Justice Roger J. Traynor of the California Supreme Court (ret.) explained that the problem of "retroactive versus prospective application calls for the most sensitive balancing of competing claims to justice in the area of criminal law." [Roger J. Traynor, *Quo Vadis, Prospective Overruling: A Question of Judicial Responsibility*, 28 HASTINGS L.J. 533, 548 (1977).]

An argument can be made for retroactive application of the new rule to this case. The defendant here committed a criminal act, a battery against another person, ultimately resulting in death. Battery is recognized as criminal conduct regardless of the year-and-a-day rule, and the defendant cannot claim his conduct was lawful when he inflicted the injury. Furthermore, the criminal law accords high value to the preservation of individual life, and this defendant violently took a life.

We conclude, however, that a stronger argument can be made for purely prospective application of the new rule in this case. Our legal system accords high value to the rule of law and institutional adherence to the law. Although overruling the year-and-a-day rule does not mark the defendant's conduct in the case at hand as criminal for the first time, abrogating the year-and-a-day rule nevertheless creates criminal liability for a different crime, the crime of first-degree reckless homicide, where no such liability previously existed. By abrogating the year-and-a-day rule, we have altered the law after the defendant committed the crime. When the defendant battered the victim in this case, he was guilty of the crimes of aggravated battery and substantial battery, but not of violating Wis. Stat. § 940.02(1), which punished a person for recklessly causing the death of another human being within one year and one day of the conduct that showed utter disregard for human life.

In 1996, the defendant in the present case pled guilty to substantial battery and aggravated battery for his altercation with the victim and was sentenced to 15 years in prison. Then, more than two years later, the defendant was charged and convicted of first-degree reckless homicide for his part in that same altercation. Under the year-and-a-day rule in existence at that time, the State's prosecution was barred. The defendant in the present case was thus assured by the law that he was safe from the State's pursuit on a murder charge.

The bar on the State's ability to prosecute the defendant for murder is removed for the first time today, by this court's decision to abrogate the year-and-a-day rule. Thus, the decision today, if applied to the defendant, revives the State's ability to bring this second prosecution for murder. Judge Learned Hand artfully stated, when describing the problem with extending a criminal statute of limitation after it has already expired, that "for the state to assure a man that he had become safe from its pursuit, and thereafter to withdraw its assurance, seems to most of us unfair and dishonest." [*Falter v. United States*, 23 F.2d 420, 425-26 (2d Cir. 1928).]

As Chief Justice Roger J. Traynor ominously warned, permitting retroactive application of expanded criminal laws as a general proposition threatens the liberty interests of everyone within a free and open society:

> The first among them to be criminally prosecuted may be those whose offenses are so close to specified crimes as to seem properly punishable. But each such punishment broadens the area of prosecution and the number of those who may be caught in it. No one can forget that in our own time, in purportedly civilized countries, millions have thus been caught who have committed no greater offense than to be themselves. [Traynor, *Quo Vadis*, 28 HASTINGS L. J. at 550-51.]

Abrogating the year-and-a-day rule retroactively and thereby expanding the construction of § 940.02(1) — as well as all other homicide statutes in Wisconsin — undermines stability in the law and tarnishes the image of justice.

First, retroactive abrogation of the year-and-a-day rule would affect more than just the defendant in this case. There is no statute of limitations on a homicide prosecution in Wisconsin. Consequently, retroactive abrogation of the common-law rule will put many other individuals who committed similar crimes — some decades ago and some who have already served time for their crimes and been released — in jeopardy of new prosecutions.

Moreover, permitting the prosecution of these individuals for the same conduct for which they have already served time paints our criminal justice system with a brush of arbitrariness. Which of these individuals may actually be prosecuted could depend on a variety of arbitrary factors, including whether or not evidence has been preserved, the availability of resources in a given county to charge the accused again, and the age and health of the perpetrator. Liberty should not hinge on such chance events.

Consequently, we conclude that the year-and-a-day rule should be overruled purely prospectively. Prosecutions for murder in which the conduct inflicting the death occurs after the date of this decision are permissible regardless of whether the victim dies more than a year and a day after the infliction of the fatal injury. Although the defendant in the present case is not punished for the death of the victim and relatives and friends of the victim are not vindicated by our decision today, the defendant does not go unpunished. The defendant's conviction for aggravated battery and substantial battery stands. His sentence of 15 years imprisonment stands. Thus, important values in our society have been preserved.

In addition, we have expanded the construction of a statute through abrogation of the common-law year-and-a-day rule so that hereafter persons can be convicted of murder even though the death of the victim occurs more than a year and a day after the act inflicting the injury.

We recognize that there are different methods of prospective overruling and that one of the most common is to apply a change in the law prospectively in all cases except the one before the court that has served as the impetus for change. The reasons justifying this approach, however, are not present in the case at hand.

Courts and commentaries alike cite two reasons for applying a new rule of law to the parties in the case where the rule is announced and prospectively. The first is that to do otherwise would relegate the announced change in law to the status of mere dicta.

Wisconsin, of course, does not always recognize intentionally answered questions of law in judicial decisions as nonbinding dicta. "It is deemed the doctrine of the cases that when a court of last resort intentionally takes up, discusses, and decides a question germane to, though not necessarily decisive of, the controversy, such decision is not a dictum but is a judicial act of the court which it will thereafter recognize as a binding decision." [*State v. Kruse*, 305 N.W.2d 85 [at 88] (1981). . . .] Following this doctrine, prior decisions of this court have announced rules to be applied purely prospectively.

The second reason is that it is necessary to apply the new rule to the party that challenges the old law as a reward to encourage others to continue to bring claims to the courts. In the case at hand, it is the defendant who has raised the claim of the application of the common-law rule. It is hardly a reward to the defendant to abrogate the year-and-a-day rule in his case. Such a decision would uphold his conviction for first-degree reckless homicide.

Even if it is more accurate to recognize the State as bringing the claim in this case by prosecuting the defendant for conduct that caused death more than one year and one day later, the State does not need the encouragement to press claims that other litigants might. Ordinarily a private party who raises an issue is in court for that case only and gains nothing if the new rule does not apply to it. In contrast, the State litigates frequently and is a repeat player in criminal cases. The State gains even if the new rule applies only prospectively. While barred from prosecuting the defendant in this case, the State gets the benefit of the rule in the future from the ability to bring homicide prosecutions unencumbered by this archaic common-law rule.

For the reasons set forth, we conclude that the year-and-a-day rule should be overruled purely prospectively. Accordingly we reverse the judgment and order of the circuit court and remand the cause to the circuit court to dismiss the criminal complaint. . . .

Diane S. Sykes, J. *(concurring in part, dissenting in part)* [Justice Sykes disagreed with the majority's decision to abrogate the year-and-a-day rule prospectively only, noting that the majority discarded as obsolete each of the justifications for the common law year-and-a-day rule, and held it "unjust to permit an assailant to escape punishment because of a convergence of modern medical advances and an archaic rule from the thirteenth century," and yet allowed Picotte to escape responsibility for the reckless homicide he committed. She argued that, "It cannot seriously be suggested that persons who commit violent, ultimately fatal assaults 'order their affairs' around the year-and-a-day rule. The rule does not implicate any institutional reliance interests;" that "The 'image of justice' . . . is not a legal principle upon which to base an appellate judicial decision;" that "Stability in the law is an argument for adhering to an existing rule rather than refusing to apply a newly-declared one;" and that "The majority does not identify any equitable or policy factors that govern its use of sunbursting in this case. Such standardless appellate decisionmaking undermines rather than promotes the rule of law. . . ."]

Picotte inflicted serious, ultimately fatal head injuries on the victim, who was in a coma for over two-and-a-half years before he died. Picotte was convicted after a jury trial. The State proved causation (as well as the other elements of the crime) beyond a reasonable doubt. There are no claims of any constitutional or statutory violations.[3] Under these circumstances, I do not see any "hardship" in holding Picotte criminally responsible for reckless homicide. . . .

The majority claims that retroactive abrogation of the year-and-a-day rule will put "many other individuals who committed similar crimes" in jeopardy. Actually, retroactive abrogation would probably affect very few people — by its terms, the rule applied only in the highly unusual circumstance of a death occurring more than a year after the criminal infliction of injury. . . . More importantly, it is not at all uncommon for the criminal justice system to prosecute, convict, and sentence a defendant for several different crimes arising out of a single incident. Unless there is a double jeopardy bar, the law does not regard this practice as unfair or "painted with a brush of arbitrariness."

Ultimately, the majority's refusal to apply the general rule of retroactivity is itself quite arbitrary. . . . [T]he United States Supreme Court has held that retroactive abrogation of the year-and-a-day rule fully comports with due process. *Rogers v. Tennessee*, 532 U.S. 451 (2001). . . . If retroactive abrogation of the year-and-a-day rule does not offend due process, then it is not unfair to retroactively abrogate the rule in this case and apply that law to Picotte. . . . [I]n the end, the majority essentially holds that the "image of justice" prohibits what the federal and state constitutions and the applicable law permit. This,

---

3 [5] Picotte does argue that retroactive abrogation of the year-and-a-day rule (that is, applying the abrogation to his case) would violate the *Ex Post Facto* Clause of the state constitution. See Wis. Const., art. I, § 12 ("No. . . ex post facto law. . . shall ever be passed.") The state and federal *Ex Post Facto* Clauses prohibit only *ex post facto* legislative enactments. See also U.S. Const., art. I, § 9. . . .

then, is really just an act of judicial will. Applying the general rule of retro-activity, I would affirm the defendant's conviction for reckless homicide.

Paul J. Mishkin & Clarence Morris, On Law in Courts, 79-81, 85 (1965)[4]

Consider, then, the general question of whether courts should have *power* to overrule their own earlier precedents. The arguments for the existence of such power are . . . [that] [t]he earlier decision may simply have been wrong when decided — whether for reasons evident at the time or for others which have since become apparent[;] or conditions in the society may have changed, rendering an earlier sound rule ill-adapted to the circumstances or standards of a later day. In either event, following precedent would perpetuate what is currently seen as error.

What are the arguments to the contrary? Consider Bentham's reference to the "general utility which results from the adherence to established precedents." . . . [T]o the extent that the doctrine rests upon the time-saving aspects of simply repeating what has been done before or upon the desirability of utilizing inherited wisdom, does its force here go beyond urging care in discarding an earlier decision as "wrong"?

The "utility" of the doctrine of course goes further. As we have already seen, it helps to assure that evenhandedness of the law which a democratic society requires; it tends to prevent arbitrariness and willfulness on the part of judges, which is particularly important when courts are considered not merely as arbitrators of disputes between individuals, but as arbiters of when the society's force may be brought to bear upon individuals. But here again, does the assurance of impartiality and of the legitimacy of the use of such force call for total denial of power to overrule? Would not these ends be sufficiently served if overruling were done but only upon a strong, reasoned basis for overturning the earlier precedent, which basis in reason is fully explicated at the time of overruling?

But even with this limitation, overruling might disserve one other objective of *stare decisis* — the idea of reliability of the law, that law should be sufficiently stable so that individuals may plan their affairs for the future with the expectation of being able to carry them out. Certainly any society which seeks to utilize individual initiative and effort must assure parties that the law by which they act will remain substantially the same as at the time of action. But, once more, does this consideration require total negation of an overruling power? Is it not enough to meet this that only actual and justifiable reliance on the law be protected against disappointment by overruling?

To summarize, then, the considerations thus far examined would not call for total denial of power to overrule, but would rather demand that such power be exercised with care, only upon a strong basis in reason which is explicated at the time of action, and only when it does not upset justified reliance upon the old law.

---

[4] Copyright © 1965. Reprinted with permission of Foundation Press.

But one further dimension requires examination. Its kernel is contained in Aristotle's reference to "habit." The fact that courts might actually be careful, evenhanded and reliable is not enough. The operation of the society depends upon people acting habitually on the assumption that they are. Most people (including lawyers) do not stop to make a continuous examination of whether their courts in fact live up to the requirements indicated above. Rather they tend to accept the operation of courts "on faith." And it is essential that they do so. Contracts and other transactions cannot wait upon a fresh examination of the judicial system each time. Society, moreover, asks for and must receive obedience to decisions which individuals consider wrong; the use of force in the manner sanctioned by courts must be viewed as legitimate even by those who disagree with the particular decision.

This general "habit" of obedience conceivably might be purely the product of rational decision. Based upon an examination of courts' operations, individuals might come to the conclusion that law generally is sufficiently stable to be relied upon. They might similarly conclude that courts are normally impartial enough so that their franchise to authorize the use of society's force should be deemed legitimate. Or an analysis of the needs of organized society and a lack of alternatives might lead to the same conclusion. But in fact, the general habits of reliance on the law and obedience to judicial decision rest only in small part on such ratiocination. Much more strongly operative are the symbolic values attached to courts and the symbolic values attached to courts and the law. Herein lies the emotional strength which is the real foundation of the "habit" of obedience — in the symbol of the law as a fixed, certain body of authoritative rules which courts mechanically (and thus impartially) "apply" or "find." The symbol of a "government of laws and not of men" is a potent force in society.

The overruling of decisions weakens that symbol. By announcing the fact of change, it lessens the idea of certainty in the law. It demonstrates the element of choice and the humanity of the choosers.

But this is not to say that overruling should therefore be prohibited. To state the problem . . . is not to decide it. Indeed, it might even be argued that the very existence of this symbolism will help ensure that overruling power will not be abused. . . . At the same time, the importance of preserving the symbol should not be minimized. . . .

Consider the soundness of the following formulation: even if considered to embody an undesirable result, a precedent should not be overruled unless (a) upon careful examination and for good reasons (stated), the court is confident that the precedent is so unsound that the importance of its abolition outweighs the disadvantages involved in the overruling, including any uncertainty and instability thus introduced in the particular area of the law and in law generally; *and* (b) the overruling can be done without injury to someone who justifiably relied upon the precedent. . . .

NOTES

1. Were the courts' actions in *Hoffman v. Jones* and *Wisconsin v. Picotte* consistent with these considerations?

2. Factors listed by courts in deciding whether to extend "full retroactivity" to their decisions include:

— whether the issues involved a traditionally settled area of law and whether the new rule was clearly foreshadowed;

— whether the overruled decision dealt with procedural, rather than substantive, law;

— whether substantial public issues are involved, arising from statutory or constitutional interpretations that clearly depart from precedent;

— whether the new decision radically departs from previous law; and

— how other courts have handled the retroactive/prospective question as to similar areas of law.

How do each of these factors cut in deciding whether a decision should be fully retroactive?

3. Also note that there are at least four options along the dimensions of retroactivity/ prospectivity:

1) prospective only — applying [the new law] only to cases with operative facts that arise after the new rule is announced; (2) limited prospective application — applying the new law to future cases and to the parties in the case announcing the new law and applying the old rule to all other pending and post litigation; (3) limited retroactivity — applying [the new law] to the cases described in (1) and (2) and to all cases where the parties have not yet exhausted all avenues of direct review and (4) complete retroactivity — applying the [new] rule to all past, present and future cases. *State v. Bellamy*, 835 A.2d 1231, 1239 (N.J. 2003).

Do factors beyond those listed in n.2 need to be considered when a court decides which of these approaches to choose for the decision it is rendering?

4. Note that the second wing of the Mishkin-Morris formulation is concerned with protecting justifiable reliance. You see from *Wisconsin v. Picotte* that if a court is convinced that an overruling is in order, there is a way, namely prospective application, in which the court can avoid an adverse impact on those who may have relied upon the prior decision. Former Chief Justice of the California Supreme Court Roger J. Traynor, in a statement of a legal realist point of view, in *Quo Vadis, Prospective Overruling: A Question of Judicial Responsibility*, 28 HASTINGS L.J. 533 (1977), criticized the theory that judges merely discover law, as inducing judges to retroactively apply "decisions that they would have invalidated in statutes as contrary to the ex post facto clause, the impairment of contracts clause, or the due process clause of the Constitution." *Id.* at 535.

A court usually will not overrule a precedent even if it is convinced that the precedent is unsound, when the hardship caused by a retroactive change would not be offset by its benefits. The technique of prospective overruling enables courts to solve this dilemma by changing bad law without unsettling the reasonable expectations of those who relied on it. . . . In the hands of skilled judicial craftsmen, acting under well-reasoned guidelines, [this technique] can be an instrument of justice that fosters public respect for the law. *Id.* at 541-42.

But exclusively prospective application of judicial decisions is controversial. Much has been written about it.

5. The U.S. Supreme Court has said that *stare decisis* is "the preferred course because it promotes the evenhanded, predictable, and consistent development of legal principles, fosters reliance on judicial decisions, and contributes to the actual and perceived integrity of the judicial process," but that it is a "principle of policy" rather than "an inexorable command." *Payne v. Tennessee*, 501 U.S. 808, 827-28 (1991). Still, the Court sometimes does overrule its prior decisions. In *Planned Parenthood v. Casey*, 505 U.S. 833, 854-55 (1992), it explained:

> [W]hen this Court reexamines a prior holding, its judgment is customarily informed by a series of prudential and pragmatic considerations designed to test the consistency of overruling a prior decision with the ideal of the rule of law, and to gauge the respective costs of reaffirming and overruling a prior case. Thus, for example, we may ask whether the rule has proven to be intolerable simply in defying practical workability; whether the rule is subject to a kind of reliance that would lend a special hardship to the consequences of overruling and add inequity to the cost of repudiation [or, the Court later added, would do "significant damage to the stability of the society governed by it"]; whether related principles of law have so far developed as to have left the old rule no more than a remnant of abandoned doctrine ["a doctrinal anachronism discounted by society"]; or whether facts have so changed, or come to be seen so differently, as to have robbed the old rule of significant application or justification ["as to render its central holding somehow irrelevant or unjustifiable in dealing with the issue it addressed"].

Overrulings typically occur after the overruled decisions have been qualified or eroded by later decisions over a period of years. A good example is *Gideon v. Wainwright*, 372 U.S. 335 (1963), overruling *Betts v. Brady*, 316 U.S. 455 (1942), and holding that the due process clause of the Fourteenth Amendment guarantees a right to counsel in state felony cases. *Betts* had held that counsel was required only where "special circumstances" necessitated counsel in order to provide a fair trial for defendant. In decisions after *Betts*, the "special circumstances" became slimmer. The last step in eroding *Betts* came in *Chewning v. Cunningham*, 368 U.S. 443 (1962), where the Court held that the theoretical possibility of various defenses requiring the professional skills of a lawyer constituted "special circumstances" without regard to whether any of those defenses were available in the particular case. After that decision, virtually any criminal case could satisfy the "special circumstances" test, thus draining *Betts* of all meaning. The overruling that came in *Gideon* was clearly foreshadowed. The Court's opinion in *Gideon*, however, rested in large part on the proposition that *Betts* was out of line with pre-existing authority at the time it was decided. Should the Supreme Court have simply acknowledged that *Betts* had been eroded by experience and later decisions, and hence no longer provided a viable rule? What is the value of a chipping-away process prior to an overruling? In this respect, how does *Hoffman v. Jones* compare with *Gideon v. Wainwright*?

6. If a court believes that a prior decision is sufficiently unsound to be overruled, would it be appropriate for the court nevertheless to apply that decision to the case at hand while at the same time announcing in its opinion that the decision will be overruled the next time the question comes before it? For an argument that such a judicial technique is not only appropriate but desirable, *see* K. LLEWELLYN, THE COMMON LAW TRADITION: DECIDING APPEALS 299-309 (1960). Llewellyn asked: "[W]hy . . . do lawyers or judges go blind, see red, have kittens, stop thinking, gibber, and otherwise engage in scalene behavior at the proposal that it should become a standard tool of the judicial workbench to give explicit warning at a suitable juncture that a particular rotting tree of law is tottering to its fall?" *Id.* at 300. What is your answer to that question?

7. Where does a court get its authority to enunciate a rule of law that is prospective only? Is such authority consistent with the doctrine of separation of powers and with other constitutional principles, such as that affording equal protection of the law? Article III of the Constitution has been interpreted to prohibit federal courts from issuing advisory opinions. Does prospective overruling or the prospective creation of a common law cause of action by federal courts violate that prohibition?

8. In *Harper v. Virginia Dep't of Taxation*, 509 U.S. 86 (1993), federal civil service and military retirees sued the Virginia tax authority for a refund of taxes improperly assessed in violation of *Davis v. Michigan Dep't of Treas.*, 489 U.S. 803 (1989). The Court held that *Davis* would be given full retroactive effect in all cases still open on direct review. Although in the past the Court had permitted the denial of retroactive effect to a new principle of law under certain circumstances, it here announced that "When this Court applies a rule of federal law to the parties before it, that rule is the controlling interpretation of federal law and must be given full retroactive effect in all cases still open on direct review and as to all events, regardless of whether such events predate or postdate our announcement of the rule. . . . In both civil and criminal cases, we can scarcely permit 'the substantive law [to] shift and spring' according to 'the particular equities of [individual parties'] claims' of actual reliance on an old rule and of harm from a retroactive application of the new rule." *Id.* at 97 (quoting *James B. Beam Distilling Co. v. Georgia*, 501 U.S. 529 (1991)).

In his concurring opinion in *Harper*, Justice Scalia said (509 U.S. at 105-08):

> Prospective decisionmaking is the hand-maid of judicial activism, and the born enemy of *stare decisis*. It was formulated in the heyday of legal realism and promoted as a "techniqu[e] of judicial lawmaking" in general, and more specifically as a means of making it easier to overrule prior precedent. . . .
>
> Fully retroactive decisionmaking was considered a principal distinction between the judicial and the legislative power. . . .
>
> Prospective decisionmaking was known to foe and friend alike as a practical tool of judicial activism, born out of disregard for *stare*

decisis. In the eyes of its enemies, the doctrine "smack[ed] of the legislative process," "encroach[ed] on the prerogatives of the legislative department of government," removed "one of the great inherent restraints upon this Court's depart[ing] from the field of interpretation to enter that of lawmaking," caused the Court's behavior to become "assimilated to that of a legislature," and tended "to cut [the courts] loose from the force of precedent, allowing [them] to restructure artificially those expectations legitimately created by extant law and thereby mitigate the practical force of *stare decisis*." All this was not denied by the doctrine's friends, who also viewed it as a device to "augmen[t] the power of the courts to contribute to the growth of the law in keeping with the demands of society," as "a deliberate and conscious technique of judicial lawmaking," as a means of "facilitating more effective and defensible judicial lawmaking". . . . [citations omitted].

But other of the Justices (including Justices Kennedy, White, O'Connor and the Chief Justice) remained of the view that it sometimes is appropriate in the civil context to give only prospective application to a judicial decision. In the context of criminal law, the Court already had held that "[A] new rule for the conduct of criminal prosecutions is to be applied retroactively to all cases . . . pending on direct review or not yet final, with no exception for cases in which the new rule constitutes a 'clear break' with the past." *Griffith v. Kentucky*, 479 U.S. 314, 328 (1987).

Why distinguish between civil and criminal cases when it comes to the choice between retroactive and prospective application?

B.   Recognizing New Causes of Action

Another kind of judicial lawmaking can occur when the court recognizes a cause of action in circumstances where no cause of action had previously been recognized. Such a decision may or may not involve an overruling. The case may be one of first impression, or the case may present an opportunity to recognize a cause of action that the court refused to recognize in the past. When a court recognizes a new cause of action, issues of retroactive or prospective application can arise, as they do when precedent is overruled.

SORENSEN v. JARVIS
350 N.W.2d 108 (Wis. 1984)

HEFFERNAN, CHIEF JUSTICE.

These cases are before us on appeal from judgments . . . dismissing the complaints because they fail to state a claim upon which relief could be granted.

The question here is whether a third party injured by an intoxicated minor has a common law negligence action against a retail seller for the negligent sale of an intoxicating beverage to a person the seller knew or should have known was a minor and whose consumption of the alcohol was a cause of the accident. Based on a series of cases of this court holding that the cause of an accident involving an intoxicated driver was the consumption of the alcohol by the driver and not the sale or the furnishing of the alcohol to the driver by a vendor, the trial court held that no claim was stated upon which relief could be granted. We reverse and hold that, under facts which may be proved under the pleadings, a cause of action for common law negligence against the vendor has been stated. . . .

[A]s a part of our common law heritage, this court is free to amend the common law. True, as we have frequently stated, the legislature may amend or change our determinations of the common law, but we are not bound to adhere to the holdings of the common law as it existed in 1848.

A case upon which defendants rely, *Garcia v. Hargrove*, 176 N.W.2d 566 [at 569] ([Wis.]1970), makes it clear that this court is not bound to a common-law rule whether or not it existed prior to Wisconsin's reception into the Union. We said:

> The fact a common-law rule was in effect when the Wisconsin Constitution was adopted does not mean this court is "bound by the common law" and unable to change the law when it no longer meets the economic and social needs of society.

. . . [A]ccordingly, we hold that, where there is sufficient proof at trial, a vendor who negligently supplies intoxicating beverages to a minor and the intoxicants so furnished cause the minor to be intoxicated or cause the minor's driving ability to be impaired shall be liable to third persons in the proportion that the negligence in selling the beverage was a substantial factor in causing the accident or injuries as determined under the rules of comparative negligence. . . .

In respect to retroactivity of a new rule of law, the United States Supreme Court delineated the following as appropriate in making a determination where civil liability is imposed:

> First, the decision to be applied nonretroactively must establish a new principle of law, either by overruling clear past precedent on which litigants may have relied, or by deciding an issue of first impression whose resolution was not clearly foreshadowed. Second, it has been stressed that "we must . . . weigh the merits and demerits in each case by looking to the prior history of the rule in question, its purpose and effect, and whether retrospective operation will further or retard its operation." *Linkletter v. Walker*, [381 U.S. 618, at 629]. Finally, we have weighed the inequity imposed by retroactive application, for "[w]here a decision of this Court could produce substantial inequitable results if applied retroactively, there is ample basis in our cases for avoiding the "injustice or hardship" by a holding of non-retroactivity."

Cipriano v. City of Houma, [395 U.S. 701, at 706]. . . .

Applying these factors, we conclude that the rule of liability adopted herein, specifically overruling *Garcia* . . . which perpetuated the common-law rule of nonliability, should be prospective. By this, we mean that, with the exception of the claims at issue here, there shall be liability only for the acts of negligence of a vendor selling to a minor on or after September 1, 1984 [four months after the date of this decision].

We apply the rule of liability adopted herein to the parties in the cases before us. The judgments dismissing the complaints of the plaintiffs herein are reversed, and the causes are remanded to the circuit court for Racine county for further proceedings. . . .

NOTES

1. In *Sorensen v. Jarvis*, the court held the defendant vendor liable under the new rule announced in its opinion, but, as to all other vendors, made that rule applicable only to sales taking place in the future. Does this decision deny equal protection of the laws to the vendor in the *Sorensen* case? Would it have been better for the court in *Sorensen* to make its decision entirely prospective, so that it did not bind the parties before the court? Would the court have authority to make its decision entirely prospective?

2. Commentators have noted that the development of tort law in the United States has been almost entirely the province of the state appellate judiciaries, usually state supreme courts, whom the legislatures have left relatively free from competition and control. The clear tendency has been in the direction of expanding liability. *See, e.g.*, Lawrence Baum & Bradley C. Canon, *State Supreme Courts as Activists: New Doctrines in The Law of Torts*, 24 CONTRIBUTIONS IN LEGAL STUDIES 84-85, 102-03 (1982).

SOSA v. ALVAREZ-MACHAIN
542 U.S. 692 (2004)

JUSTICE SOUTER delivered the opinion of the Court.

[Plaintiff, a Mexican citizen, who had been acquitted of murder after having been abducted at the direction of the Drug Enforcement Administration and transported to the United States for prosecution, sued the United States and his abductors. The Court had to decide, among other things, whether plaintiff could recover under the federal Alien Tort Statute, which provides that "[t]he district courts shall have original jurisdiction of any civil action by an alien for a tort only, committed in violation of the law of nations or a treaty of the United States." This required the Court to decide whether that statute recognized the right of action asserted by plaintiff Alvarez. In the course of so doing, the Court addressed not only its approach to this particular question but also its approach to the creation of new common law causes of action generally.]

[T]he jurisdictional grant is best read as having been enacted on the understanding that the common law would provide a cause of action for the modest number of international law violations with a potential for personal liability at the time. . . . We assume, too, that no development . . . has categorically precluded federal courts from recognizing a claim under the law of nations as an element of common law; Congress has not in any relevant way amended § 1350 or limited civil common law power by another statute. Still, there are good reasons for a restrained conception of the discretion a federal court should exercise in considering a new cause of action of this kind. Accordingly, we think courts should require any claim based on the present-day law of nations to rest on a norm of international character accepted by the civilized world and defined with a specificity comparable to the features of the 18th-century paradigms we have recognized. This requirement is fatal to Alvarez's claim.

A

A series of reasons argue for judicial caution when considering the kinds of individual claims that might implement the jurisdiction conferred by the early statute. First, the prevailing conception of the common law has changed since 1789 in a way that counsels restraint in judicially applying internationally generated norms. When § 1350 was enacted, the accepted conception was of the common law as "a transcendental body of law outside of any particular State but obligatory within it unless and until changed by statute." *Black and White Taxicab & Transfer Co.* v. *Brown and Yellow Taxicab & Transfer Co.*, 276 U.S. 518 (1928) (Holmes, J., dissenting). Now, however, in most cases where a court is asked to state or formulate a common law principle in a new context, there is a general understanding that the law is not so much found or discovered as it is either made or created. . . .

Second, . . . [federal common law] largely withdrew to havens of specialty, some of them defined by express congressional authorization to devise a body of law directly. Elsewhere, this Court has thought it was in order to create federal common law rules in interstitial areas of particular federal interest. And although we have even assumed competence to make judicial rules of decision of particular importance to foreign relations . . . , the general practice has been to look for legislative guidance before exercising innovative authority over substantive law. . . .

Third, this Court has recently and repeatedly said that a decision to create a private right of action is one better left to legislative judgment in the great majority of cases. The creation of a private right of action raises issues beyond the mere consideration whether underlying primary conduct should be allowed or not. . . . While the absence of congressional action addressing private rights of action under an international norm is more equivocal than its failure to provide such a right when it creates a statute, the possible collateral consequences of making international rules privately actionable argue for judicial caution.

Fourth, the subject of those collateral consequences is itself a reason for a high bar to new private causes of action for violating international law, for the potential implications for the foreign relations of the United States of recognizing such causes should make courts particularly wary of impinging on the discretion of the Legislative and Executive Branches in managing foreign affairs. . . .

[Fifth], . . . [w]e have no congressional mandate to seek out and define new and debatable violations of the law of nations, and modern indications of congressional understanding of the judicial role in the field have not affirmatively encouraged greater judicial creativity.

B

. . . [A]s described before, we now tend to understand common law not as a discoverable reflection of universal reason but, in a positivistic way, as a product of human choice. And we now adhere to a conception of limited judicial power first expressed in reorienting federal diversity jurisdiction, *see Erie R. Co.* v. *Tompkins,* 304 U.S. 64 (1938), that federal courts have no authority to derive "general" common law.

Whereas Justice Scalia sees these developments as sufficient to close the door to further independent judicial recognition of actionable international norms, other considerations persuade us that the judicial power should be exercised on the understanding that the door is still ajar subject to vigilant doorkeeping, and thus open to a narrow class of international norms today. *Erie* did not in terms bar any judicial recognition of new substantive rules, no matter what the circumstances, and post-*Erie* understanding has identified limited enclaves in which federal courts may derive some substantive law in a common law way. For two centuries we have affirmed that the domestic law of the United States recognizes the law of nations. . . . It would take some explaining to say now that federal courts must avert their gaze entirely from any international norm intended to protect individuals. . . .

The First Congress, which reflected the understanding of the framing generation and included some of the Framers, assumed that federal courts could properly identify some international norms as enforceable in the exercise of § 1350 jurisdiction. We think it would be unreasonable to assume that the First Congress would have expected federal courts to lose all capacity to recognize enforceable international norms simply because the common law might lose some metaphysical cachet on the road to modern realism. Later Congresses seem to have shared our view. . . .

While . . . we would welcome any congressional guidance in exercising jurisdiction with such obvious potential to affect foreign relations, nothing Congress has done is a reason for us to shut the door to the law of nations entirely. . . .

C

. . . [W]hatever the ultimate criteria for accepting a cause of action subject to jurisdiction under § 1350, we are persuaded that federal courts should not recognize private claims under federal common law for violations of any international law norm with less definite content and acceptance among civilized nations than the historical paradigms familiar when § 1350 was enacted. . . . And the determination whether a norm is sufficiently definite to support a cause of action should (and, indeed, inevitably must) involve an element of judgment about the practical consequences of making that cause available to litigants in the federal courts.

. . . [W]hatever may be said for the broad principle Alvarez advances, in the present, imperfect world, it expresses an aspiration that exceeds any binding customary rule having the specificity we require. Creating a private cause of action to further that aspiration would go beyond any residual common law discretion we think it appropriate to exercise. It is enough to hold that a single illegal detention of less than a day, followed by the transfer of custody to lawful authorities and a prompt arraignment, violates no norm of customary international law so well defined as to support the creation of a federal remedy.

NOTES

The approach to the creation of new causes of action may be different under federal law than it is under state law, in part because the realm within which federal common law has been permitted is so limited. As Justice Scalia, concurring in part and concurring in the judgment in *Sosa* notes, "Because post-*Erie* federal common law is made, not discovered, federal courts must possess some federal-common-law-making authority before undertaking to craft it. 'Federal courts, unlike state courts, are not general common-law courts and do not possess a general power to develop and apply their own rules of decision.' *Milwaukee* v. *Illinois,* 451 U.S. 304, 312 (1981)." In areas of law as to which federal common law is recognized to have a proper place and that do not have implications for foreign relations, should the federal courts enjoy more latitude than the Court was willing to exercise in *Sosa* in creating new causes of action?

ALDISERT, OPINION WRITING, § 3.2 Rules, Principles, Doctrines 28-30 (1990)[5]

Legal precepts may be perceived as a hierarchy of various standards of conduct. . . . At the bottom of the hierarchy is the rule, a normative proposition making a certain legal result depend upon a certain situation involving a narrow range of facts. At common law, the sources of decision are . . . rules of specific cases. . . . These precepts provide "fairly concrete guides for decision geared to narrow categories of behavior and prescribing narrow patterns of conduct." [Hughes, *Rules, Policy, and Decision Making,* 77 Yale L.J. 411, 419 (1968).] The common law "creeps from point to point, testing each step" [A. Whitehead, Adventures of Ideas 25 (1956)], like an ice skater on a half-frozen pond, and is most characteristically a system built by gradual accretion from the resolution of specific problems. . . . The courts fashioned *principles* from a number of *rules* of decision, in a process characterized by experimentation. At common law, rules of case law are treated not as final truths, "but as working hypotheses, continually retested in those great laboratories of the law, the courts of justice."[M. SMITH, JURISPRUDENCE 21 (1909).] The common law has been described as . . . a method of "reaching what instinctively seem[s] the right result[ ] in a series of cases, and only later (if at all) enunciating the principle that explains the pattern — a sort of connect-the-dots exercise."[6] . . . The "dots" represent holdings of individual cases. . . .They are "connected" . . . to fashion broader precepts by techniques of induction. These techniques include the use of analogy, where resemblances are meticulously compared. . . .

Covering a broad range of facts, [legal principles] are assembled from publicly stated reasons for publicly stated rules in previously decided cases. Formulation of a principle is a gradual process, shaped from actual incidents

---

[5] Copyright © 1990. Reprinted with permission of West Publishing Company.

[6] [8] Ely, *The Supreme Court 1977 Term, Foreword: On Discovering Fundamental Values,* 92 HARV. L. Rev. 5, 32 (1978) (citing Amsterdam, *Perspectives of the Fourth Amendment,* 58 MINN. L. REV. 349, 351-52 (1974)).

in social, economic and political experience. It is a process in which counter-vailing rights are challenged, evaluated, synthesized and adjudicated . . . case-by-case. . . . For every rule [of] common law there is a publicly stated reason, the *ratio decidendi*. And for each principle that slowly emerges, there is a solid base of individual rules from particular cases and from the publicly stated reasons that support the decisions in those cases.

Principles in the law appear in statutes as well. . . . [M]ost statutes promulgate precepts that are broader than those that emerge from a single case. Instances are myriad, but consider, for example, the laconic declaration of federal antitrust law in the Sherman Act, 15 U.S.C. § 1. . . .:

> Every contract, combination in the form of trust or otherwise, or con-spiracy in restraint of trade or commerce among the several States, or with foreign nations, is declared to be illegal. . . .

15 U.S.C. § 2:

> Every person who shall monopolize . . . or combine or conspire with any other person . . . to monopolize any part of the trade or commerce among the several States, or with foreign nations, shall be deemed guilty of a misdemeanor. . . .

From these . . . statutorily created principles have emerged thousands of judicial opinions that interpret and apply precepts to the fact-specific scenarios presented to the courts . . . .

From broad principles, there is an even larger, more encompassing legal precept — the doctrine. . . . [A] doctrine is a very broad principle. It may be a collection of rules and principles or a systematic fitting-together of rules, principles and conceptions . . . in logically inter-dependent schemes.

. . . Does it really make a difference in the scheme of things whether we attach a proper label — a rule, principle or doctrine — to a particular legal precept? I think it does. This is more than a matter of nomenclature or writing style inasmuch as the precept is the raw material that goes into the multijudge decision-making mix.

INTERNATIONAL NEWS SERVICE v.
THE ASSOCIATED PRESS
248 U.S. 215 (1918)

MR. JUSTICE PITNEY delivered the opinion of the Court.

[Associated Press, an incorporated association of newspaper publishers, gathered news and for a fee, without applying for copyright, telegraphed it daily to its members throughout the country, for their publication. A rival corporation (International News Service (INS)) made a practice of obtaining this news through its early publication in newspapers and in bulletins produced by the AP's members, and of sending it by telegraph, either as taken or rewritten, to its own customers, thus enabling them to compete in the prompt publication of news that was obtained exclusively for the benefit of the customers of the AP and at their expense. The Court held that the AP and its members had an equitable *quasi* property right in the news, even after the early publications, and that appropriation of the news by the INS, for its own gain and to the damage of the AP and its members, amounted to unfair competition which should be enjoined. Justice Brandeis dissented, saying the following, in part.]

[T]he sole question for our consideration is this: Was the International News Service properly enjoined from using, or causing to be used gainfully, news of which it acquired knowledge by lawful means (namely, by reading publicly posted bulletins or papers purchased by it in the open market) merely because the news had been originally gathered by the Associated Press and continued to be of value to some of its members, or because it did not reveal the source from which it was acquired?. . .

The knowledge for which protection is sought in the case at bar is not of a kind upon which the law has heretofore conferred the attributes of property; nor is the manner of its acquisition or use nor the purpose to which it is applied, such as has heretofore been recognized as entitling a plaintiff to relief. . . .

The great development of agencies now furnishing country-wide distribution of news, the vastness of our territory, and improvements in the means of transmitting intelligence, have made it possible for a news agency or newspapers to obtain, without paying compensation, the fruit of another's efforts and to use news so obtained gainfully in competition with the original collector. The injustice of such action is obvious. But to give relief against it would involve more than the application of existing rules of law to new facts. It would require the making of a new rule in analogy to existing ones. The unwritten law possesses capacity for growth; and has often satisfied new demands for justice by invoking analogies or by expanding a rule or principle. This process has been in the main wisely applied and should not be discontinued. Where the problem is relatively simple, as it is apt to be when private interests only are involved, it generally proves adequate. But with the increasing complexity of society, the public interest tends to become omnipresent; and the problems presented by new demands for justice cease to be simple. Then the creation or recognition by courts of a new private right may work serious injury to the general public, unless the boundaries of the right are definitely established and wisely guarded. In order to reconcile the new private right with the public interest, it may be necessary to prescribe limitations and rules for its enjoyment; and also to provide administrative machinery for enforcing the rules. It is largely for this reason that, in the effort to meet the many new demands for justice incident to a rapidly changing civilization, resort to legislation has latterly been had with increasing frequency.

The rule for which the plaintiff contends would effect an important extension of property rights and a corresponding curtailment of the free use of knowledge and of ideas; and the facts of this case admonish us of the danger involved in recognizing such a property right in news, without imposing upon news-gathers corresponding obligations. A large majority of the newspapers and perhaps half the newspaper readers of the United States are dependent for their news of general interest upon agencies other than the Associated Press. The channel through which about 400 of these papers received, as the plaintiff alleges, "a large amount of news relating to the European war of the greatest importance and of intense interest to the newspaper reading public" was suddenly closed. The closing to the International News Service of these channels for foreign news (if they were closed) was due not to unwillingness on its part to pay the cost of collecting the news, but to the prohibitions imposed by foreign governments upon its securing news from their respective countries and from using cable or telegraph lines running therefrom. For aught that appears, this prohibition may have been wholly undeserved; and at all events the 400 papers and their readers may be assumed to have been innocent. For aught that appears, the International News Service may have sought then to secure temporarily by arrangement with the Associated Press the latter's foreign news service. For aught that appears, all of the 400 subscribers of the International News Service would gladly have then become members of the Associated Press, if they could have secured election thereto. It is possible, also, that a large part of the readers of these papers were so situated that they could not secure prompt access to papers served by the Associated Press. The prohibition of the foreign governments might as well have been extended to the channels through which news was supplied to the more than a thousand other daily papers in the United States not served by the Associated Press; and a large part of their readers may also be so located that they can not procure prompt access to papers served by the Associated Press.

A Legislature, urged to enact a law by which one news agency or newspaper may prevent appropriation of the fruits of its labors by another, would consider such facts and possibilities and others which appropriate enquiry might disclose. Legislators might conclude that it was impossible to put an end to the obvious injustice involved in such appropriation of news, without opening the door to other evils, greater than that sought to be remedied. . . .

Or legislators dealing with the subject might conclude, that the right to news values should be protected to the extent of permitting recovery of damages for any unauthorized use, but that protection by injunction should be denied, just as courts of equity ordinarily refuse (perhaps in the interest of free speech) to restrain actionable libels, and for other reasons decline to protect by injunction mere political rights; and as Congress has prohibited courts from enjoining the illegal assessment or collection of federal taxes. If a legislature concluded to recognize property in published news to the extent of permitting recovery at law, it might, with a view to making the remedy more certain and adequate, provide a fixed measure of damages, as in the case of copyright infringement.

Or again, a legislature might conclude that it was unwise to recognize even so limited a property right in published news as that above indicated; but that a news agency should, on some conditions, be given full protection of its business; and to that end a remedy by injunction as well as one for damages should be granted, where news collected by it is gainfully used without permission. If a legislature concluded . . . that under certain circumstances news-gathering is a business affected with a public interest, it might declare that, in such cases, news should be protected against appropriation, only if the gatherer assumed the obligation of supplying it, at reasonable rates and without discrimination, to all papers which applied therefor. If legislators reached that conclusion, they would probably go further, and prescribe the conditions under which and the extent to which the protection should be afforded; and they might also provide the administrative machinery necessary for ensuring to the public, the press, and the news agencies, full enjoyment of the rights so conferred.

Courts are ill-equipped to make the investigations which should precede a determination of the limitations which should be set upon any property right in news or of the circumstances under which news gathered by a private agency should be deemed affected with a public interest. Courts would be powerless to prescribe the detailed regulations essential to full enjoyment of the rights conferred or to introduce the machinery required for enforcement of such regulations. Considerations such as these should lead us to decline to establish a new rule of law in the effort to redress a newly-disclosed wrong, although the propriety of some remedy appears to be clear.

NOTES

1. Was the Court appropriately restrained in *International News Service*? What considerations led Justice Brandeis to conclude that the matter should be left to the legislative branch? How persuasive would Justice Brandeis's argument for legislative, instead of judicial, action be in relation to the questions presented in *Hoffman v. Jones* and in *Sosa v. Alvarez-Machain*?

2. Assume P sues D to recover damages for personal injuries resulting from D's negligence. The injuries occurred when D negligently ran his automobile over P's mother when she was six months pregnant with P. Under the governing state law, the courts never had recognized a cause of action for prenatally-inflicted injuries; no such case had been presented. Is the argument for leaving the matter to the legislature stronger or weaker in this hypothetical than in *International News Services*? *See Woods v. Lancet*, 102 N.E.2d 691 (1951) (overruling an earlier decision and recognizing a right of action for prenatal injuries to a viable fetus later born alive, with a dissenting opinion arguing that the matter should be left to the legislature).

3. Judge Henry Friendly in *The Gap in Lawmaking — Judges Who Can't and Legislators Who Won't*, 63 COLUM. L. REV. 787 (1963), placed at the head of the list of the legislatures' advantages over courts "the legislature's superior resources for fact gathering." He went on to list these additional advantages:

> [T]he ability to act without awaiting the adventitious concatenation of the determined party, the right set of facts, the persuasive lawyer, and the perceptive court, its power to frame pragmatic rules departing from strict logic, and to fashion a broad new regime or to bring new facts within an existing one, its practice of changing law solely for the future in contrast to the general judicial reluctance to [so] proceed; and, finally, the greater assurance that a legislative solution is not likely to run counter to the popular will.

Do Judge Friendly's remarks illuminate whether it was wise for the courts in *Hoffman*, *Sosa*, and *International News Service* to have made the decisions they did?

4. Consider the soundness of the following propositions:

Lawmaking by an appellate court can be justified as consistent with the doctrine of separation of powers (and within the proper role of an appellate court in the Anglo-American legal order) only if it occurs:

> a. in the process of deciding an actual, live legal controversy between adverse parties, properly before the court for a resolution;

> b. when the court's formulation of a legal rule is necessary for the disposition of the case and the rule formulated is no broader than necessary for the resolution of the specific controversy; and

> c. when the court states its reasons for and the justification for the rule that it formulates.

> d. Even if all these conditions are satisfied, the court must consider, in addition, whether formulation of the legal rule at issue should be left to the legislature.

5. A number of matters addressed in this chapter are insightfully surveyed in Roger J. Traynor, *Transatlantic Reflections on Leeways and Limits of Appellate Courts*, 1980 UTAH L. REV. 255 (1980).

C. Judicial Lawmaking in Cases Involving the Application of Statutory and Constitutional Provisions

Under some legal theories (sometimes called formalist or nineteenth century liberal theory) statutory decisions are entitled to particularly strong *stare decisis* effect for a number of reasons. Judicial construction becomes "as much a part of the statute as the text itself," *Douglass v. County of Pike*, 101 U.S. 677, 678 (1879); legislatures are able to overrule such precedents by amending the statute — and the courts may infer that their construction has the legislature's blessing and correctly effectuates legislative intent if the legislature does not change the statute; the legislature also may be in a better position to design an alternative regulatory scheme if the current construction is rejected — because the typical legislative mode of rulemaking operates prospectively, among other reasons; and both public and private decision makers rely on precedents interpreting statutes. State courts and federal courts share this reluctance to overrule statutory precedents; indeed, some state supreme courts are even more reluctant than the United States Supreme Court has been.

But they all sometimes do it. In *Rodriguez de Quijas v. Shearson/American Express, Inc.*, 490 U.S. 477, 484 (1989), cited above in relation to the role of intermediate state appellate courts, the Supreme Court overruled its own prior interpretation of a federal statute. It said:

> Although we are normally and properly reluctant to overturn our decisions construing statutes, we have done so to achieve a uniform interpretation of similar statutory language . . . and to correct a seriously erroneous interpretation . . . that would undermine congressional policy as expressed in other legislation.

In *Monell v. Department of Social Services*, 436 U.S. 658 (1978), in holding that municipal corporations are "persons" subject to suit under 42 U.S.C. § 1983 for depriving people of rights, privileges and immunities secured by the Constitution and laws of the United States, the Court overruled a decision it had rendered in *Monroe v. Pape*, 365 U.S. 167 (1961). Although the dissenters challenged each aspect of the majority's reasoning, the majority supported its overruling with arguments that the earlier precedent was clearly erroneous and inconsistent with other Supreme Court cases decided both before and after *Monroe*, and that other statutes evidenced Congress's nonacquiescence in *Monroe*. The concurrence argued the need for law to change in general and for this interpretation in particular to change in light of the reality that municipal corporations often were the real defendants in civil rights cases. *Id.* at 709 (J. Powell, concurring).

Generally speaking, the Rehnquist Court has been more willing to overrule statutory precedents than some earlier Courts have been, and has seemed to embrace the position, urged by some commentators, that statutory precedents should be afforded the ordinary level of *stare decisis* effect, not more. In *Payne v. Tennessee*, 501 U.S. 808 (1991), the Court said it would not be bound by decisions that are "unworkable or badly reasoned" and that it would be most constrained by *stare decisis* "in cases involving property and contract rights, where reliance interests are involved" and less constrained in cases involving procedural and evidentiary rules. The Court also has indicated that antitrust decisions deserve less respect under *stare decisis* than other statutory interpretations deserve because of the competing interest in "adapting to changed circumstances and the lessons of accumulated experience" and because Congress expects the courts to draw on the common law tradition in effectuating the statutes' broad mandate. *State Oil Co. v. Khan*, 522 U.S. 3, 20 (1997). Finally, in *Patterson v. McLean Credit Union*, 491 U.S. 164, 173-74 (1989), the Court declined to overturn *Runyon v. McCrary*, 427 U.S. 160 (1976), which interpreted 42 U.S.C. § 1981 to provide a remedy against private schools that excluded children on the basis of race but also declined to extend *Runyon* to hold that § 1981 provides a remedy against private employers. The Court wrote:

> [N]o special justification has been shown for overruling *Runyon*. In cases where statutory precedents have been overruled, the primary reason for the Court's shift in position has been the intervening development of the law, through either the growth of judicial doctrine or further action taken by Congress. Where such changes have removed or weakened the conceptual underpinnings from the prior decision, or where the later law has rendered the decision irreconcilable with competing legal doctrines or policies, the Court has not hesitated to overrule an earlier decision. Our decision in *Runyon* has not been undermined by subsequent changes or development in the law.

> Another traditional justification for overruling a prior case is that a precedent may be a positive detriment to coherence and consistency in the law, either because of inherent confusion created by an unworkable

decision, or because the decision poses a direct obstacle to the realization of important objectives embodied in other laws. In this regard, we
do not find *Runyon* to be unworkable or confusing. . . .

Finally, it has sometimes been said that a precedent becomes more vulnerable as it becomes outdated and after being "'tested by experience,
has been found to be inconsistent with the sense of justice or with the
social welfare.'" *Runyon*, 427 U.S., at 191 (Stevens, J., concurring), quoting B. CARDOZO, THE NATURE OF THE JUDICIAL PROCESS 149 (1921). . . .
[T]his consideration . . . offers no support for overruling *Runyon*. In
recent decades, state and federal legislation has been enacted to prohibit
private racial discrimination in many aspects of our society. Whether
Runyon's interpretation of § 1981 as prohibiting racial discrimination in
the making and enforcement of private contracts is right or wrong as an
original matter, it is certain that it is not inconsistent with the prevailing sense of justice in this country. . . .

The attitude toward overruling constitutional precedents is different. As
explained by Justice Brandeis, dissenting in *Burnet v. Coronado Oil & Gas
Co.*, 285 U.S. 393, 406-07 (1932):

Stare decisis is usually the wise policy because in most matters it is
more important that the applicable rule of law be settled than that it
be settled right. . . . This is commonly true even where the error is a
matter of serious concern, provided correction can be had by legislation. But in cases involving the Federal Constitution, where correction
through legislative action is practically impossible, this Court has
often overruled its earlier decisions.

In constitutional cases, an incorrect or outdated precedent may be overturned
only by the Court's own reconsideration of its decision or by constitutional
amendment. The Court that was led by Chief Justice Earl Warren in particular
(the Warren Court served from 1953 to 1969) prospectively applied a number of
decisions announcing new rules of constitutional law for criminal cases. That
Court also prospectively overruled decisions of constitutional law in civil cases
but the current Court has taken a more grudging attitude toward such decisions.

From your other law school courses, you are familiar with the work of the
courts and ultimately of the U.S. Supreme Court in deciding questions under
the federal Constitution. The authority of that Court to hold acts of the
Congress and state legislatures to be unconstitutional was established in
Marbury v. Madison, 5 U.S. (1 Cranch)137 (1803). State courts exercise similar authority. Subject to U.S. Supreme Court review, they can hold federal
statutes to be unconstitutional. Moreover, they can hold acts of state legislatures to be unconstitutional under state constitutions. The work of state
supreme courts in deciding state constitutional questions has received far less
attention than has the work of the U.S. Supreme Court, although that aspect
of the American constitutional order has received far more attention in the
last few decades than it received earlier. *See, e.g.*, Barry Latzer, *Whose
Federalism? Or, Why "Conservative" States Should Develop Their State
Constitutional Law*, 61 ALB. L. REV.1399 (1998); Margaret H. Marshall, *"Wise
Parents Do Not Hesitate to Learn from Their Children": Interpreting State*

Constitutions in an Age of Global Jurisprudence, 79 N.Y.U. L. Rev. 1633 (2004); Robert A. Schapiro, *Judicial Deference and Interpretive Coordinacy in State and Federal Constitutional Law*, 85 Cornell L. Rev. 656 (2000); G. Alan Tarr, *State Constitutional Interpretation*, 8 Tex. Rev. L. & Pol. 357 (2004); Clifford W. Taylor, *Construing the Text of Constitutions and Statutes*, 8 Tex. Rev. L. & Pol. 365 (2004) .

MINNESOTA v. RUSSELL
477 N.W.2d 886 (Minn. 1991)

Wahl, Justice.

We are asked, in this pre-trial appeal, to consider the following certified question:

Does Minnesota Statute § 152.023, Subd. 2(1) (1989), as it is applied, violate the equal protection clauses of the Fourteenth Amendment of the United States Constitution and the Minnesota Constitution, Article 1, Section 2?

. . . Pursuant to [Minnesota] statutes, possession of three grams of crack cocaine carries a penalty of up to 20 years in prison while possession of an equal amount of cocaine powder carries a penalty of up to five years in prison. Under the sentencing guidelines, the presumptive sentence for possession of three grams of crack cocaine is an executed 48 months imprisonment. The presumptive sentence for possession of an equal amount of cocaine powder is a stayed 12 months of imprisonment and probation.

Defendants, five African-American men who were charged with violating Minn. Stat. § 152.023, subd. 2, jointly moved the trial court to dismiss the charges on the ground that the statute has a discriminatory impact on black persons and violates the equal protection guarantees of the federal and state constitutions.

The trial court found that crack cocaine is used predominantly by blacks and that cocaine powder is used predominantly by whites.[7] As a result, a far greater percentage of blacks than whites are sentenced for possession of three or more grams of crack cocaine under Minn. Stat. § 152.023 with more severe consequences than their white counterparts who possess three or more grams of cocaine powder. The trial court concluded that the law has a discriminatory impact on black persons.

The trial court then determined that no rational basis supported the distinction between crack-cocaine and cocaine powder and that the law therefore violated constitutional guarantees of equal protection. The trial court granted the defendants' joint motion to dismiss and certified the question of the statute's constitutionality to the court of appeals. . . . We granted a joint petition for accelerated review. . . . We affirm.

---

7 [2] Among the many statistics provided to the trial court were those showing that of all persons charged with possession of cocaine base in 1988, 96.6% were black. Of all persons charged with possession of powder cocaine, 79.6% were white.

Review of an equal protection challenge under the federal rational basis test requires (1) a legitimate purpose for the challenged legislation, and (2) that it was reasonable for the lawmakers to believe that use of the challenged classification would promote that purpose.

The state . . . contends that the legislature has a permissible and legitimate interest in regulating the possession and sale of crack cocaine and cocaine powder and that it was reasonable for lawmakers to believe that the three grams of crack/ten grams of powder classification would regulate the possession of those drugs by the "street level" dealers at whom the statute was primarily aimed.

Even if we were to agree with the state's argument . . . under the federal test, we strike the statute as unconstitutional under the rational basis test as articulated under Minnesota law. Since the early eighties, this court has, in equal protection cases, articulated a rational basis test that differs from the federal standard, requiring:

> (1) The distinctions which separate those included within the classification from those excluded must not be manifestly arbitrary or fanciful but must be genuine and substantial, thereby providing a natural and reasonable basis to justify legislation adapted to peculiar conditions and needs; (2) the classification must be genuine or relevant to the purpose of the law; that is there must be an evident connection between the distinctive needs peculiar to the class and the prescribed remedy; and (3) the purpose of the statute must be one that the state can legitimately attempt to achieve. *Wegan v. Village of Lexington*, 309 N.W.2d 273, 280 (Minn. 1981) (quoting *Guilliams v. Commissioner of Revenue*, 299 N.W.2d 138, 142 (1980)).

. . . [W]here we have applied . . . the Minnesota rational basis analysis, we have been unwilling to hypothesize a rational basis to justify a classification, as the more deferential federal standard requires. Instead, we have required a reasonable connection between the actual, and not just the theoretical, effect of the challenged classification and the statutory goals. . . .

Nothing prevents this court from applying a more stringent standard of review as a matter of state law under our state constitutional equivalent to the equal protection clause. Moreover, there is every reason for us to continue to articulate and apply an independent Minnesota constitutional standard of rational basis review. To harness interpretation of our state constitutional guarantees of equal protection to federal standards and shift the meaning of Minnesota's constitution every time federal case law changes would undermine the integrity and independence of our state constitution and degrade the special role of this court, as the highest court of a sovereign state, to respond to the needs of Minnesota citizens. It is particularly appropriate that we apply our stricter standard of rational basis review in a case such as this where the challenged classification appears to impose a substantially disproportionate burden on the very class of persons whose history inspired the principles of equal protection.

We therefore hold that under our state constitutional standard of rational basis review the challenged statute cannot stand. First, the statute fails for lack of a genuine and substantial distinction between those inside and outside the class. In order to meet this standard, the state must provide more than anecdotal support for classifying users of crack cocaine differently from users of cocaine powder. The primary justification advanced by the state in support of the crack/cocaine classification is that it serves to facilitate prosecution of "street level" drug dealers.[8] . . .

The primary testimony before the legislature on the distinction between crack cocaine and cocaine powder in terms of the respective amounts of the drugs that indicate street-level dealing came from Mr. James Kamin of the Hennepin County Attorney's Office. He stated at legislative hearings that his knowledge of the quantities possessed by drug dealers did not come from study but "simply from talking with people like Sergeant Strauss and informants, people who have been convicted or are being prosecuted for drug offenses. My knowledge of these numbers comes from the streets." Minnesota Senate Criminal Law Subcommittee, 76th Minn. Leg., March 16, 1989.

This purely anecdotal testimony does not establish a substantial and genuine distinction. A statutory distinction that provides the basis for prescribing widely disparate criminal penalties is not sufficiently justified when based on the anecdotal observations of one expert witness. This is especially true in light of evidence presented that undermines the conclusion reached by the legislature. For instance, respondents point to a recent report by the Minnesota Department of Public Safety Office of Drug Policy [cited by the trial court] that states that police and prosecutors . . . are not persuaded by the "street dealer" distinction because they believe that most cocaine powder users are dealers as well. Without more factual support, the three grams of crack/ten grams of powder distinction appears to be based upon an arbitrary rather than a genuine and substantial distinction.

The second proffered basis for the disparate treatment of crack versus cocaine powder users is that crack is more addictive and dangerous than cocaine powder. The evidence on this point similarly fails to establish a genuine and substantial distinction between those inside and outside the class. The primary legislative testimony on this point was presented by Michael Strauss, an officer from the Minneapolis Narcotics Division, who testified from his experience and training in the Narcotics Division but who did not profess to be a trained scientist.

Further evidence on the chemical properties and physiological effects of crack and cocaine powder was presented to the trial court through the testimony of Dawn Speier, a chemist for the City of Minneapolis. She testified that there is a difference between crack and cocaine powder in the severity of the attack on the central nervous system and respiratory function, and, based on what she had read or heard, that a smaller amount of crack will produce the same effect as cocaine powder. She also testified, however, that the mood altering ingredient in both powder and base was the same — cocaine. Further,

---

[8] [4] In fact the state argues to this court that this purpose was the sole basis of the legislation and that any pharmacological difference between the substances is irrelevant to the constitutional analysis.

she testified that the difference in effect between the two was based on the way the drug was ingested (cocaine powder being generally sniffed through the nostrils, crack cocaine being smoked). In fact, Speier confirmed that if cocaine powder is dissolved in water and injected intravenously, the effect on the body is similar to the effect of smoking crack cocaine. Thus, as respondents argue, evidence as to the degree of dangerousness between crack and cocaine powder is based on testimony as to effects resulting from different methods of ingestion, rather than on an inherent difference between the forms of the drug. Disparate treatment of crack and powder cocaine users is not justified on the basis of crack's greater dangerousness when there is evidence that powder cocaine could readily produce the effects purported to justify a harsher penalty for possession of crack.

There is also evidence in the legislative record that there is more violence associated with the use of crack than with the use of cocaine powder. This evidence is not only anecdotal, but pales in light of official observation that if there is more violence associated with crack use, "that difference could be caused more by factors such as gang warfare and certain group behaviors than by the pharmacological effects of crack." Minnesota Department of Public Safety Office of Drug Policy, Minnesota Drug Strategy 1991, p. 14. Although under the more deferential rational basis test, we may not second guess the scientific accuracy of legislative determinations of fact absent overwhelming contrary evidence, the rational basis test under the Minnesota Constitution requires more factual support than is present here to establish a genuine and substantial distinction between the two substances.

The crack-cocaine distinction also fails because the classification is not relevant to the statutory purpose. Without more evidence to support the asserted dealership levels of drug possession, the . . . distinction does not further its statutory purpose of penalizing street level drug dealers. Without more evidence, it is as easily assumed that individuals jailed for possession of three grams of crack are mere personal users who were arbitrarily penalized as dealers. Furthermore, a statute which permits a person possessing less than ten grams of powder cocaine, which can be easily converted into more than three grams of crack [citing trial court findings], to be punished only for 5th degree possession of cocaine, is not only irrelevant to its purpose of penalizing drug dealers, it is also arbitrary and unreasonable.

Lastly, the crack-cocaine classification, while perhaps aimed at the legitimate purpose of eradicating street level drug dealers, employs an illegitimate means to achieve that purpose. The legislature determined that three grams of crack and ten grams of powder indicate a level at which dealing, not merely using, takes place. Once possession of the indicated amounts is proved, intent to sell is presumed, justifying a harsher penalty than that for mere possession. In effect, the statute punishes a person for possession with intent to sell without requiring the prosecution to prove, as an element of the crime, that an actual sale was intended, thus creating an irrebuttable presumption of fact. . . . [S]tatutes creating conclusive presumptions of law or fact have been almost uniformly declared unconstitutional as denying due process of law. Because the statute creates an irrebuttable presumption of intent to sell without affording the defendant an affirmative defense of lack of intent to sell, and on the basis of that presumption automatically metes out a harsher punishment, the means chosen to affect its purposes are constitutionally suspect.

We answer the certified question in the affirmative and affirm the decision of the trial court. Minn. Stat. § 152.023, subd. 2(1) (1989), violates the Minnesota Constitution, Article 1, Section 2.

COYNE, JUSTICE (dissenting).

I respectfully dissent: First, because the majority has abandoned the recognized rule for reviewing a facially neutral crime control statute in favor of an activist form of judicial review which allows the court to substitute its view of the basis for and efficacy of the statute for that of the legislature; and second, because, based on its assumption that crack cocaine and cocaine powder are identical substances — a matter on which experts disagree — the majority proceeds on the false premise that the legislature may not found a legislative distinction on differences in the form and marketing of the two substances.

I begin my analysis by emphasizing the limitations on this court's role vis-á-vis the legislature in matters relating to crime control and the punishment of crimes. . . . [T]he judicial branch of government in Minnesota has no inherent authority to set the terms or conditions of punishment for a criminal act. Instead, the power to define appropriate punishment for criminal conduct rests with the legislature. . . .

However, in reviewing the constitutionality of legislation under the equal protection clause we should remember the words of Justice Holmes . . .:

> Great constitutional provisions must be administered with caution. Some play must be allowed for the joints of the machine, and it must be remembered that legislatures are ultimate guardians of the liberties and welfare of the people in quite as great a degree as the courts.

Missouri, Kansas & Texas Ry. Co. v. May, 194 U.S. 267, 270 (1904) (fourteenth amendment equal protection case). We should not lightly or casually presume discriminatory purpose by the legislature.

Certainly, courts must subject any law that makes a classification based on race — any law that is not neutral on its face — to the "most rigid scrutiny" and must strike down the legislation as violative of equal protection unless the state can justify the law by demonstrating that the weightiest of considerations necessitated its enactment. . . .

. . . [T]he legislature was presented with evidence that crack cocaine and cocaine powder are not, as defendants contend and as the majority unjustifiably assumes, the same substance but different substances justifying dissimilar legislative treatment. . . . The unique characteristics of crack cocaine were discussed not only in the legislative hearings but also in the affidavit of defendants' own expert in this litigation, M. Dawn Speier, Public Health Chemist for the City of Minneapolis. According to her, smoking crack cocaine "delivers a highly concentrated dose — at least 3 times that delivered by snorting an equivalent dose of cocaine powder — to the brain" and "abusers lose control faster with crack smoking than with snorting [powder]." . . .

The legislature also considered evidence regarding customary units of sale and the sale price of such a unit. . . .

Finally, the majority assumes that the conversion ratio of pure cocaine powder to crack is 100%. It is not. The witness who testified to a conversion rate of about 90% in the laboratory stated that because the purity of cocaine powder varied . . . and because crack houses operated rather less efficiently than laboratories, 10 grams of cocaine powder produced about 6 grams of crack. Thus, there is no basis upon which it can be said that 10 grams of cocaine powder is the equivalent of 10 grams of crack.

. . . [I] disagree with the majority's conclusion that by declining to make intent to sell an element of possession crimes the legislature has in effect created an impermissible presumption. . . .

Here the record is barren of any evidence of discriminatory purpose by the legislature. . . .

I have no reason to doubt the assertion that . . . more African-Americans than white persons were prosecuted for possession of 3 grams or more of crack cocaine and 10 grams or more of cocaine powder. However, defendants have failed to establish either that those other defendants were selected for prosecution on the basis of their race or that they themselves have been selected for prosecution on the basis of race. Indeed, it appears that is not the case. . . .

Despite the utter absence of any evidence that the legislature acted with discriminatory intent or purpose or that law enforcement officers engaged in discriminatory enforcement, the majority, applying what it calls "the rational basis test as articulated under Minnesota law," has declared Minn. Stat. § 152.023, subd. 2(1) (1989) violative of . . . the equal protection clause of the Minnesota Constitution. Of course, this court may . . . construe the Minnesota Constitution to afford greater individual rights than are afforded by the United States Constitution. But this court has consistently ruled that the rational basis standard used in Minnesota equal protection analysis is the same as the standard used in federal equal protection analysis. The argument that Minnesota applies a rational basis test that differs from the federal standard has been put to this court before and emphatically rejected . . . .

What the majority has actually done here is to engage in substantive review — the kind of review epitomized by *Lochner v. New York*, 198 U.S. 45 (1905) — "criticized from its inception and . . . generally unmourned since its demise in the middle 1930s." One commentator, a prominent advocate of state constitutional theory, has defined substantive review as "judicial appraisal of the substance of laws directly under [the equal protection clause] . . . unaided by substantive values attributed to other provisions of the Constitution."

In short, substantive review replaces an appropriate standard of review, not with a stricter standard, but with no standard at all. That the majority has substituted its political judgment for that of the legislature is, perhaps, best illustrated by its cavalier dismissal of the testimony which the legislature heard. Th[at] testimony, although not of scientific precision, was certainly "empirical," . . . and the legislature was clearly entitled to credit that testimony. The majority's denigration of the testimony differs little in my opinion from a reviewing court's setting aside a jury's determination of credibility.

In conclusion, the power to define what act constitutes a crime and to fix the punishment for that crime rests with the legislature. This court has neither the obligation nor the right to interfere with legislation dealing with the control of crime without a very good reason. Absent some evidence of discriminatory intent or purpose, the fact that more black persons than white persons violate Minn. Stat. § 152.023, subd. 2(1) (1989) is not a basis for declaring the statute unconstitutional although it may well be indicative of deep-seated societal failings. . . . In my view, the cumulative evidence the legislature considered and the thoughtful remarks of the bill's authors and of other legislators exhibit only a commendable, concerted, and reasoned good faith effort to address a serious social problem.

Because I believe that Minn. Stat. § 152.023, subd. 2(1) (1989) meets the equal protection requirements of both the United States Constitution and the Minnesota Constitution, I would answer the certified question "no" and reverse the trial court.

NOTES

1. What is the answer, if any, to the assertion that six members of the Minnesota Supreme Court have substituted their judgment for that of a majority of the Minnesota legislature as to the appropriate sentencing policy?

2. Under the above decision, would it thereafter be open to the Minnesota legislature to hold new hearings, building a more substantial record showing the differences between crack and cocaine powder, and then reenact the statute? If so, does the court's decision amount to a holding that the Minnesota legislature was deficient in assembling an adequate factual basis for the statute?

3. It is often said that because federal judges are unelected and hold office for life they should be especially cautious in overturning acts of elected representatives of the people. The Minnesota Supreme Court justices are elected by the people for terms of six years. MINN. CONST. art. VI, § 7. Should this circumstance have any bearing on that court's ruling upon the constitutionality of state legislative action?

4. Note that this decision was placed solely on state constitutional grounds and is thus not reviewable by the United States Supreme Court. *See* 28 U.S.C. § 1257. If the decision had been placed expressly on both state and federal constitutional grounds, would the case be reviewable by the U.S. Supreme Court? See the discussion of the adequate and independent state ground doctrine in Chapter 12, below.

5. If a decision hinges on a constitutional interpretation, the court will be aware that, as a practical matter, only the courts can revise an unsound interpretation, unlike an incorrect construction of a statute, which the legislature could correct. What are the implications?

Michael Esler, *State Supreme Court Commitment To State Law*, 78 JUDICATURE 25, 31-32 (1994)[9]

Politics are not all that work against reliance on state law. Legal and institutional factors also provide important reasons for why state courts continue to rely on federal law for the majority of their decisions. The development and expansion of the incorporation doctrine throughout this century has transformed federal judicial relations in a fundamental way. As the number of incorporated provisions in the U.S. Bill of Rights reached its peak during the Warren years, the dominance of federal law became practically complete.

After decades of looking no further than federal requirements, state court reliance on federal law remains deeply entrenched. State courts continue to view federal law as the primary source for settling individual rights cases. Deference to the rule of precedent is decisive for many state courts. The sheer weight of years of U.S. Supreme Court decisions is reason enough to look no further than federal law. To depart from federal precedent could create uncertainty about legal issues that had been thought to be settled.

Moreover, many state court judges are unwilling to expend the resources, time, and effort to develop state law when an established body of federal law already exists. And, after so many years of neglect, some state courts lack the self-confidence to embark on an independent interpretation of their own law. As a result, most state court judges view the appropriate role of state law as "reactive" or "supplemental." Federal law is construed first, and state law is consulted only if federal law is found to be inadequate or when there are other reasons to justify turning to state law.

Textual similarities between the federal and state bills of rights also work against independent and innovative interpretations of state law. State court judges often feel they must justify interpreting identically worded provisions in state constitutions differently from their federal analogues. To do so could seem to undermine the idea that written law matters.

Some scholars have expressed concern that excessive concentration on state law could even retard development of federal law. It might "dampen the lively interaction between state and federal interpretations of the federal Bill of Rights . . . and thereby decrease the ability of the United States Supreme Court to select from a wide variety of innovative and well-considered interpretations of the federal charter." Along these lines, a state-centered approach might call into question the meaning and importance of federal law.

State courts especially are unlikely to turn to state law in the area of criminal procedure. Given the relative complexity of criminal law, state courts often find it difficult enough to apply standards mandated by federal law. If state courts were to turn to standards based on state law, their problems could multiply. Prosecutors and police especially might find it difficult to operate under an array of state and federal rules. At least one prosecutor called it "an open invitation to confusion-and-error on the enforcement front."

---

[9] Copyright © 1994. Reprinted with permission of the American Judicature Society.

Federal and state law enforcement officers often work together on the same cases. When this occurs, state officials usually prefer to prosecute under federal laws because they are generally tougher on criminal defendants. Sometimes state prosecutors are even deputized by federal officials so that they can more effectively pursue their cases. State courts may be reluctant to threaten these relationships by basing decisions on state law.

The powerful effect of decades of federal dominance retards development of state law in still another way. Even when state supreme courts are otherwise receptive to basing decisions on state grounds, institutional factors largely beyond their control often present significant obstacles to the development of state law. The general lack of historical records on the events and forces that shaped state constitutions creates problems for judges who wish to develop state law. Moreover, the paucity of precedents grounded in state law and the federal bias that characterizes the legal training of their clerks often means that judges will be presented only with federal cases when writing opinions.

Another factor is that attorneys often do not argue state grounds before state courts. When state grounds are not presented in legal arguments, it is difficult for judges to base their decisions on state law, since to do so they must develop their reasoning without benefit of counsels' briefs. However, there is an even more fundamental reason why the failure to raise state grounds often results in the underdevelopment of state law. Most state supreme courts refuse to base their decisions on legal grounds *sua sponte*, as a matter of principle. Thus, the type of arguments that attorneys present to state courts plays a central role in the relatively low level of development of state law. . . .

Placing the entire blame on attorneys, however, ignores the role of legal education in this process. Law schools focus scant attention on state law, much less offer courses in state constitutional law.Without training in the substance and procedures of state constitutional law, newly minted lawyers hardly can be expected to present adequate state legal arguments.

NOTES

It has been argued that judicial lawmaking, the creation of binding precedent, is subject to implicit "constitutional principles" (principles that "set forth the 'law' of judicial lawmaking," rather than principles that derive from a written constitution) that govern whether an act of judicial lawmaking is valid. Adam N. Steinman, *A Constitution for Judicial Lawmaking*, 65 U. Pitt. L. Rev. 545, 549 (2004). Professor Steinman posits that the distinction between dicta and holdings creates a constitutional limit on judicial lawmaking; that the doctrine governing whether panels of intermediate courts of appeals, or only the court en banc, may overrule prior panel decisions may be of constitutional magnitude; that *stare decisis* is a constitutional limit on lower courts while the supreme court of a system is free to change the law; that the authority of courts to deprive their decisions of precedential effect may be constitutional in the intended sense; and that doctrines (such as the "narrowest grounds" rule) governing whether a particular decision is supported by the minimum number of votes to constitute an act of judicial lawmaking also may be constitutional.

However one categorizes these matters, they are important features of court systems. The ways one might distinguish dicta from holding and the appropriate understanding of plurality opinions are left to other courses, however, as is the manner in which judges approach decisionmaking. Various approaches to attaining horizontal consistency across the panels at a particular level of a court system is addressed in Chapter 7, below, and issues raised by non-precedential opinions in Chapter 8, below.

III. LEGISLATIVE FACTS

A. Appellate Courts' Use of Legislative Facts Generally

"[When an agency or a court] finds facts concerning immediate parties — what the parties did, what the circumstances were — [it] is performing an adjudicative function, and the facts may conveniently be called adjudicative facts. When [an agency or a court] wrestles with a question of law or policy, it is acting legislatively, . . . and the facts which inform its legislative judgment may conveniently be denominated legislative facts." Kenneth Culp Davis, *An Approach to Problems of Evidence in the Administrative Process*, 55 HARV. L. REV. 364, 402 (1942).

MASSACHUSETTS MEDICAL SOCIETY v. DUKAKIS
637 F. Supp. 684 (D. Mass. 1986)

Keeton, D.J.,

. . . [N]o settled terminology has been adopted as a common label to designate all of the various kinds of facts that, together, stand in contrast with "adjudicative" facts. . . . I use the term "non-adjudicative" to refer to the whole array of facts that are relevant to determining a generally applicable rule of decision and not (or at least, not alone) to deciding a particular controversy between particular parties.

. . . [S]ome (though certainly not all) among the contrasting characteristics of adjudicative and non-adjudicative facts may be described in the following ways:

(1) Effect Generally of Fact Findings Upon Future Cases

An adjudicative fact finding in one case has no force as precedent and no effect in subsequent cases except to the extent determined by the law of *res judicata*, including issue preclusion. *Cf. Second Restatement of Judgments* §§ 17-29 (1982).

In contrast, a non-adjudicative fact finding does have force generally in later cases. Such a finding made by a legislature as a basis for enacting a statute ("legislative" fact) is reviewable in courts, if at all, only under standards developed in constitutional litigation. *E.g., Railway Express v. New York*, 336 U.S. 106, 109 (1949) (for purposes of due process challenge to state regulation the court will not itself weigh evidence to determine wisdom of regulation but will defer to the judgment of local authorities unless that judgment is shown to be "palpably false").

A non-adjudicative fact finding of a court as a reason for deciding an issue of law in a particular way . . . is effective not only in the case at hand (subject to review in higher courts) but also in future cases to the extent determined by the law of *stare decisis*.

. . . [A] court is not free to hold a legal rule inapplicable to [a] case . . . because the court disagrees with the fact determinations on which that rule was explicitly or implicitly based. Instead, a court must apply the legal rule unless it determines that the rule is to be abrogated generally. . . . A court may abrogate a rule by holding a statute unconstitutional, and a court may overrule its own precedents. If, for example, a court of last resort determines that the factual premises of a precedent are incorrect — either because circumstances have changed or because advances in knowledge have revealed error — the court may overrule.

(2) Characteristics of Findings in Jury Trials

In a jury trial, adjudicative fact findings of the jury on issues as to which, under the evidence, reasonable persons could differ, are binding upon the parties and cannot be set aside either by the trial court or on appeal merely because a court would find differently on the evidence.

In contrast, non-adjudicative fact disputes are not properly submitted to a jury; they are resolved in the same way in jury trials as in non-jury trials.

(3) Characteristics of Findings in Non-Jury Trials

A trial judge's adjudicative fact findings in a federal non-jury trial are reviewable under the standard prescribed in FED. R. CIV. P. 52(a) and are set aside on appeal only if "clearly erroneous." . . .

In contrast, . . . with respect to non-adjudicative fact findings higher courts owe no deference to a trial court's findings and may make their own determinations of such facts. . . .

. . . A question to which non-adjudicative facts are relevant "is not a question specifically related to this one case or controversy; it is a question of social factors and happenings which may submit to some partial empirical solution but is likely to remain subject to opinion and reasoning." [*Dunagin v. City of Oxford, Miss.*, 718 F.2d 738, 748 n.8 (5th Cir. 1983) (en banc).] It would thus be inappropriate to treat the findings reached by a particular judicial trier of fact on "social factors and happenings" with the same deference with which his or her findings on discrete occurrences between particular parties are treated. . . .[A]lso . . . the special role of the appellate courts in resolving issues of constitutional law . . . would be significantly eroded if the higher courts' determinations were made to "hinge on the views of social scientists who testify as experts at trial." [*Id.*] For these reasons and others stated in this Opinion, I conclude that higher courts will be free to examine non-adjudicative facts *de novo* rather than obliged to accept all but clearly erroneous findings of non-adjudicative facts by the trial court.

Of course, . . . neither a trial court nor an appellate court may set aside or disregard "legislative" determinations of fact on the basis of which a statute was enacted, except to the extent that the court determines that as a matter of constitutional law the legislature's reliance on those facts cannot withstand scrutiny.

An underlying theme of the three qualities thus far discussed is that adjudicative facts are specific to the case at hand ("case facts" or "discrete facts") and, in contrast, non-adjudicative facts bear upon the determination of what legal rule shall be applied to cases generally ("general facts"). Often, and perhaps typically, "general" fact findings are generalizations about human behavior or human institutions, including economic and social phenomena. However, "general" fact findings may be about other aspects of the broad context in which particular cases arise; they may be about "laws" of nature, for example.

(4) Historical and Evaluative (or Interpretive) Facts

A distinction may be observed between "historical" facts and "evaluative" (or "interpretive") facts.

Typical of disputes of "historical" fact . . . are disputes about who did what, when and where, and whether with or without a defined state of mind.

Typical of disputes of "interpretive" or "evaluative" fact are disputes about whether what was done violated a legal standard for evaluating conduct (such as the negligence standard or the "proximate" cause standard), or in some other way satisfied some prerequisite of liability. . . . [T]he kind of determination that contrasts with a finding of "historical" fact is often described as a finding on a "mixed question of fact and law."

In contrast with adjudicative fact disputes, which may involve either "historical" or "evaluative" ("interpretive") facts, non-adjudicative fact disputes rarely, if ever, concern "historical" facts. That is, disputes of non-adjudicative fact rarely center on happenings — who did what, when or where. Even when "data" are brought to bear, the emphasis of the dispute is not upon the . . . multitude of historical facts that constitute the data but instead upon disputed assertions as to whether the data are complete, or at least constitute an adequately representative sample, and upon what interpretive inferences or evaluative findings may properly be derived from or based upon them.

(5) Taking Judicial Notice

A court may take judicial notice of adjudicative facts "not subject to reasonable dispute." FED. R. EVID. 201(b).

It may reasonably be argued that the concept of "judicial notice" is inapplicable to non-adjudicative facts. In any event, if the phrase is used in relation to non-adjudicative facts, either its meaning must be sharply modified or else it applies to only a very small percentage of non-adjudicative facts. The reason is that non-adjudicative facts are typically in sharp dispute, as controversies over legislation well illustrate. Thus, if "judicial notice" is limited to facts "not subject to reasonable dispute," it is inapplicable to all reasonably disputable non-adjudicative facts. Sometimes, however, "judicial notice" is used in a very different sense, merely to indicate that the court determines relevant facts independently of evidence offered at trial. In this broad sense, of course, the phrase might be extended to all non-adjudicative fact finding.

(6) Applicability of Rules of Evidence

In making adjudicative fact findings, courts apply formal rules of evidence and, at least if timely objection is made, may not base findings on evidence that is inadmissible under those rules.

In relation to non-adjudicative fact finding, it is difficult to find authority precisely in point. I conclude, however, that on principle, and with . . . some suggestive support in judicial opinions, both trial courts and appellate courts, in making non-adjudicative fact findings, are free to draw upon sources of knowledge beyond evidence that is admissible under the formal rules of evidence that apply to adjudicative fact finding. An appellate court, in its decisionmaking, is not confined to the record of evidence presented to the trial court. It may consider additional sources referred to in appellate briefs, and may even resort to independent library research. For example, the Supreme Court did not confine itself to record evidence in considering the fundamental issues presented in *Brown v. Board of Education*, 347 U.S. 483, 494 n.11 (1954).

Although litigants may . . . present testimonial evidence of expert witnesses on disputed non-adjudicative fact questions . . . and trial courts may receive such evidence, it does not follow either that the parties must offer such evidence or that a trial court is bound to receive it, or having received it, is bound to consider it as if it were being presented in relation to a dispute of adjudicative fact.

In all but a small percentage of cases coming before the courts, disputes of fact . . . relate to adjudicative facts. Indeed, it is only a very small percentage of judicial opinions that even take note of a distinction between adjudicative and non-adjudicative facts. Partly for this reason, and partly . . . because of fundamental differences between adjudicative and non-adjudicative facts, some . . . of which are outlined here, . . . rules of evidence and procedure fashioned for resolving adjudicative fact disputes were not designed for resolving non-adjudicative fact disputes and, at the least, must be reexamined before being applied in resolving non-adjudicative fact disputes.

(7) Applicability of "Standing" Requirements

Are "standing" requirements, fashioned to determine one's qualifications for participating in an adversarial proceeding for resolving adjudicative fact disputes, applicable as well to participation in resolution of non-adjudicative fact disputes? . . .

Where the court is treating a question as one of adjudicative fact, . . . the requirements of "standing" . . . are appropriately stricter, at least in most circumstances, than where a question is treated as one of non-adjudicative fact. The underlying objective of assuring that a genuine case or controversy is before the court, with the adverse interests adequately represented, is more clearly implicated in adjudicative than in non-adjudicative fact disputes. Where the court is considering non-adjudicative facts — for example, the whole range of information on which a legislature did or might have relied — it is less important that the roles of who may present what information be sharply defined. Indeed, the court itself may go to reference books for enlight[en]ment with respect to this kind of information. . . .

NOTES

1. An early, celebrated use of legislative facts was in *Muller v. Oregon*, 208 U.S. 412 (1908), in which the Supreme Court upheld the constitutionality of an Oregon law limiting the hours of work for women. As counsel for the state, seeking to uphold the statute, Louis D. Brandeis included in his brief the findings of studies showing the deleterious effects of long hours of labor on women's health, thereby giving rise to the term, "Brandeis brief." Those studies were offered to show that there was a rational basis from which the legislature could have concluded as it did. Since then, courts often have cited such legislative facts in adjudicating constitutional questions and also in formulating common-law rules, as well as in connection with the interpretation of statutes. Among many examples that one might cite are the Supreme Court's use of a social science appendix detailing the deleterious effects of segregation on black children in *Brown v. Board of Education*, 347 U.S. 483 (1954), and the Maryland Supreme Court's use of governmental studies and other scholarly writings concerning the ethics of using children as research subjects for nontherapeutic research in *Grimes v. Kennedy Krieger Institute, Inc.*, 782 A.2d 807 (Md. 2001).

2. In reviewing a trial court's decision that relies on a finding of a legislative fact, ought the appellate court to defer to such a finding as it defers in reviewing a trial judge's findings of adjudicative facts? In *Menora v. Illinois High School Assocation*, 683 F.2d 1030 (7th Cir. 1982), after hearing evidence, the district court determined that insecurely fastened yarmulkes posed no substantial hazard to basketball players and invalidated the Association's ban on headwear while playing the sport. In denying a rehearing after reversing for further proceedings, the court of appeals said:

> We are accused of having failed to apply the clearly-erroneous rule to the district court's finding that insecurely fastened yarmulkes do not pose a substantial hazard to basketball players. That rule, however, is designed for the review of findings of "historical," not "legislative," fact. Legislative facts are those general considerations that move a lawmaking or rulemaking body to adopt a rule, as distinct from the facts which determine whether the rule was correctly applied. There is no question that insecurely fastened yarmulkes are within the scope of the Illinois High School Association's no-headwear rule; the question is whether the Association's concern with safety is substantial enough to support the rule as so interpreted; and a fact that goes to reasonableness of a rule or other enactment is a classic example of a legislative fact, to which, as we have said, the clearly-erroneous standard does not apply.

Id. at 1036. *Accord*, Robert E. Keeton, *Legislative Facts and Similar Things: Deciding Disputed Premise Facts*, 73 MINN. L. REV. 1, 41 (1988) (arguing that premise-fact disputes are decided by judges in both jury and nonjury trials and that "higher courts owe no deference to a trial court and may make their own determinations of such facts," citing in support *Lockhart v. McCree*, 476 U.S. 162 (1986), where the Court, although it did not decide the "standard of review" issue, commented that it was far from persuaded that the "clearly erroneous" standard of Federal Rule of Civil Procedure 52(a) applied to the kind of "legislative" facts at issue, from which the lower courts had reached the conclusion that "death qualification" produces "conviction-prone" juries).

3. As Professor Ann Woolhandler has noted, the judicial reception of legislative facts raises questions about the role of social science in law, the scope of judicial notice, and the process of judicial decisionmaking generally. Ann Woolhandler, *Rethinking the Judicial Reception of Legislative Facts*, 41 VAND. L. REV. 111, 112 (1988). The questions addressed in the following materials include these: To what extent is it proper for appellate courts to rely upon non-adjudicative facts? To what extent do judicial procedures disadvantage courts in acquiring important information when they make law? To what sources may the courts properly look for such facts? How should such facts be presented to or obtained by the courts?

Maurice Rosenberg, *Anything Legislatures Can Do, Courts Can Do Better?*, 62 AMERICAN BAR ASSOCIATION JOURNAL 587 (1976)[10]

Once upon a time the common law was an expanse of wide open space over which judges ranged freely and contentedly. Then the legislative hordes fell upon the open places, over ran them, and carpeted nearly the whole domain with wall-to-wall statutes. Not content, draftsmen in Congress and the state legislatures have kept stitching away at the seamless web. They appear to want to "civilianize" law and make it into something like the codes of the legally under-developed countries of Europe. Still, judges do manage to keep open at least these trails to active creativity: invalidation, interpretation, and obliteration.

The doom of invalidation may befall a statute that is found to be too broad, vague, narrow, or underinclusive. A label of unconstitutionality will be pinned on a law that divides people into groups and then deals with the groups unequally, if the legislature fails to show why creating the groups was necessary, the dividing line reasonable, and the objective legitimate. A further reason for invalidating a statute is a finding that it violates procedural due process. Lately, some laws have been struck down on the ground they offended notions of substantive due process. For a long time that basis for invalidation was in nearly total eclipse. Now, however, many observers side with . . . the view that substantive due process is riding again as a significant force. It gives judges a powerful set of constitutional jaws to rend asunder laws they believe are egregiously unsound.

But invalidation alone would not be sufficient to liberate courts from statutory shackles. After all, a surprising number of statutes are constitutional. This leads courts to their second form of creativity: interpretations.

A close reading of legislative statutes may reveal that the words have a squishy malleability invisible to the naked eye but lurking there all the same because of the legislative history. When the court realizes this, the revelation produces a decision with a happy ending for the judges.

---

10 Copyright © 1976 by the American Association. Reprinted with permission of the ABA and Gloria Rosenberg.

Another way to get to the happy ending is to approach the problem from exactly the opposite direction. This requires disregarding the legislative history, even though it contradicts the text, by invoking the "plain meaning" canon. Handy weapons, those canons — they fire from both ends of the barrel. It is required only that the judge know in which direction to point the artillery before pulling the lanyard.

Then there is obliteration. A prime example occurred in *Nga Li v. Yellow Cab Co.*, 532 P.2d 1226 (1975), in which the California Supreme Court said, in effect: True, a statute has been construed for 103 years as laying down the rule of contributory negligence. The statute, however, is only an extension of the common law. It ought not to tie our hands and prevent our decreeing a system of comparative negligence, considering that time has passed the old rule by.

Obsequies for judicial creativity, assertedly brought on by statutory suffocation, are premature. With so many ways to liberate themselves from statutory bonds and with so much readiness to use the available methods, courts are far from becoming merely ministerial agencies. It is one of the paradoxes of legal life that as statutory law proliferates, judicially declared law predominates. The volume of court work booms. The courts' reputation at potent agencies of government rises and rises.

Why? Perhaps the reasons are obvious. Courts have several great advantages over legislatures in resolving disputes over conflicting legal interests. One is conclusiveness. Citizens, as Carl McGowan has remarked, "appear to like the idea that there is one branch of government which can and will deal effectively with the shortcomings in the laws, or obtuseness in their administration."

A second is speed. Despite sluggishness here and there, courts operate in a blur of haste compared to the usual glacial pace of legislatures.

Third, there is focus. A lawsuit draws to a problem the rapt notice of authoritative eyes. The picture is sharp; the attention level is high.

No doubt the public shares with many lawyers a strong impression of judicial omnicompetence. This attitude propels more and more people into the courts. Judges, state as well as federal, come under greater and greater strain, and so does the very institution of the courts. Judge Kaufman stated it well when he told the *New York Times* in 1973: "I submit we are being smothered with confidence."

There has to be a better way. The answer to popular impatience with legislative un-responsiveness cannot be to confer an ever-expanding hegemony on the judicial branch. At any rate, it cannot be the answer unless we are ready to adopt drastic measures to assure that the courts are not only able to handle the burdens but also are able in some way to respond to the imperatives of a constitutional democracy.

On the other hand is the plain reality we may not disregard: a sharpened sense of legal entitlement is a pervasive fact of life in this society. Americans continue to define as legal problems more and more forms of the wounds, distresses, and anxieties they once regarded as the slings and arrows of outrageous fortune or as the responsibility of institutions other than courts. What is more, the courts have generously accepted, even invited, jurisdiction over new classes of controversy.

Judges are fully aware that the new breeds of cases are no longer in the classic bipolar mold of A suing B for damages. . . . They tend rather to be polycentric controversies, involving vast webs of interrelated interests. Deciding them inevitably affects the rights of large groups of people; many possible outcomes are conceivable; wide direct consequences radiate from them; large social or political stakes are often implicated in them.

Two related characteristics of these new types of disputes are striking. One is that many look much more like matters that legislatures, or even constitutional conventions, deal with than like classic bipolar lawsuits. The other is that they often require masses of complex data as predicates for decision. And neither the information resources, the rules for getting and presenting mass data in court, nor the understanding of how to use the data are equal to the demands the cases make.

The challenge is to reach a constructive accommodation that will render unto the legislatures and the constituents their constitutional due, that will assure the courts a healthy (but not boisterous) level of creativity, and that will equip them far better than they are now equipped to get information that is essential to performing wisely and well in their role as law-declarers.

My submission is that a way can be found to attain the increased informational capacity courts need. . . . The late Alexander Bickel held the view: "Courts are institutionally incapable of obtaining the empirical data necessary for making decisions on social policy."

The need for shedding light on the social impact of legal norms and on how legal problems work is growing by long leaps. If it were true that courts start out intellectually impoverished and as they proceed find themselves institutionally incapable of acquiring information, they and we should truly be in a bad way. I reject that estimate as too pessimistic. But it is worth something to be alerted to the need to think about how the courts' information gathering capacities can be enlarged.

Kenneth Culp Davis, *Judicial, Legislative, And Administrative Lawmaking: A Proposed Research Service For The Supreme Court*, 71 MINNESOTA LAW REVIEW 1, 3-10 (1986)[11]

[T]he law made by judges seems to me clearly inferior to statutes and administrative rules in clarity, reliability, and freedom from conflict. . . . Ideal procedure is hard to find, but easy to imagine. The lawmaking is solidly based on whatever scientific or professional understanding is relevant, and that is the main basis unless public opinion pulls toward something else. Ideal procedure may start with studies by qualified specialists of the appropriate kinds, and the one task may be to determine what parts of those studies must be modified in deference to the democratic element.

---

[11] Copyright © 1986. Reprinted with permission of Inger P. Davis.

Legislative procedure in the American government has evolved over two centuries . . . The first Congress probably legislated with hardly more facts than were already in the minds of Members of Congress . . . Some of the legislation of the Ninety-Ninth Congress is comparable, but most is not; most is based on investigation or studies, some extensive, nearly all openly available to the public in tentative form, along with ample opportunities to make comments and apply pressures. Lobbyists play a vital role. The staffs who help Congress are of higher and higher quality, including many who are among the leaders in their fields. The legislative committee system at its best is a superb procedure for the development of understanding and for the reflection of democratic desires.

Administrative rulemaking procedure has developed over the last half century, but the main development has been during the last twenty years. . . . Like legislative committee procedure, it is open and democratic, but it is also quicker and less expensive. With the help of its specialized staff, the agency prepares a proposed rule, which it publishes along with an invitation for written comments. Anyone at all may send in a written response, from a simple letter to a comprehensive study. The staff sifts the comments, and the agency heads may then have a sound foundation for preparing the final rule. Both the factual base and the democratic base usually are adequately developed.

The Supreme Court [of the United States] is a major lawmaker, but it has no procedure designed for lawmaking. Its only procedure is designed for adjudication. The Justices look at the record from the lower court, read the briefs, listen to oral arguments, confer with each other, sometimes look up law in a library or have their clerks do so, and prepare an opinion. The only significant change since the pattern became fixed in 18th century England is the use of law clerks, who are always young lawyers, never specialists in nonlegal fields. The Justices never openly consult specialists, either about law or nonlaw, and neither the Justices nor the law clerks are qualified to make studies or investigations of the kind that specialists in sciences or social sciences customarily make. The Court has no facilities for notice and comment procedure, no matter how much [such procedures] would sometimes improve the lawmaking. The procedure is essentially what it would be if it had been deliberately planned to make it as undemocratic as possible, for the Justices avoid lobbyists, take no opinion polls, make no inquiry about public opinion, and use no procedure of notice and comments. The weak spots are the insufficient factual or scientific base and the lack of a democratic base when one is needed.

Procedures used for lawmaking depend more on who is the lawmaker than on the needs of the particular lawmaking task. For the same lawmaking task, a legislator may consult lobbyists, sample public opinion, and call for a staff study of the relevant legislative facts; an administrator may have such a staff study and a notice and comment proceedings; and a judge listens to arguments. . . .

If choices among lawmakers were planned on the basis of relative advantages and disadvantages of each, as they never have been, courts would make no law except when neither a factual base nor a democratic base is needed for lawmaking.

The contrast between the way judges make policy and the way legislators make policy is a strong contrast. . . . Legislators do not protect themselves from informal influence by those who have interests at stake; judges do. Legislators do not insulate themselves from ex parte conferences with advocates; judges do. Legislators do not emphasize precedents created by their predecessors; judges do. Legislators have no problem about considering the way a policy may affect a non-party; judges usually focus mainly on parties, even when a decision may vitally affect nonparties.

The contrast between the way judges make policy and the way administrators make policy may be even stronger. Judges do not have specialized staffs; administrators usually do. Judges do not assign policy questions for special studies or investigation; administrators often do. . . .

No one has planned the present system under which the procedure of appellate courts, designed for *adjudication* of questions of law, is used for a large portion of all the *lawmaking* that is done in the whole society. No one would plan such a system. What has happened is that appellate procedure was originally planned for finding and applying law; and then appellate courts, without changing their procedure, have gradually increased their lawmaking activity. . . .

I believe that the procedure of appellate courts is exceedingly good procedure when it is used for the purpose for which it was designed, that is, finding and applying established law, but it is exceedingly poor procedure when used for a purpose for which it was not designed, that is, legislating new law. . . . Congressional procedure and administrative procedure have been designed for lawmaking. Procedure of appellate courts, including procedure of the Supreme Court, is not designed for lawmaking.

Of course, much judicial lawmaking does not require either a factual base or a democratic base. The Supreme Court is often at its best on complex thinking problems, on philosophical or ethical or moral issues, on analysis or reasoning, and on issues of interpretation. But the Court may often be at its worst on policy issues that are dependent upon understanding or instincts about legislative facts. Indeed, my impression is that, typically, the Court is basically baffled in trying to deal with legislative facts. . . . We may sympathize with the predicament of the Justices, but whatever our sympathy, it won't cure the inadequacy of the factual base and of the democratic base for lawmaking.

When the Supreme Court in deliberating about a case realizes that it needs legislative facts it does not have, what should it do? . . . The Supreme Court has no facilities either for a staff study or for a notice and comment procedure. What should the Supreme Court do? And what does it do? . . .

What the Supreme Court affirmatively does is quite various. It has no system. It tries one method after another, almost always with unsatisfactory results. I shall now list, with citations, seven solutions the Supreme Court has tried:

1) The Supreme Court sends the case back to the trial court for taking evidence on questions of legislative fact. *Borden's Farm Products Co. v. Baldwin,* 293 U.S. 194, 210 (1934). That idea has some merit, but it has failed to take hold, perhaps because the procedure is especially awkward.

2) The Supreme Court simply asserts an emphatic view of the legislative facts, with nothing to support its view. That is what the Court did when it called the agricultural dislocation of the 1930s "a widespread similarity of local conditions," contrary to the view of all economists of the time. *United States v. Butler,* 297 U.S. 1, 75 (1936).

3) Even worse is judicial notice of what the Supreme Court calls "common experience," without mentioning any facts, and directly in the face of a dissenter's abundant and convincing evidence to the contrary. *Jay Burns Baking Co. v. Bryan,* 264 U.S. 504, 517 (1924).

4) Another unfortunate way is to examine a published source and to find what is not there. The Supreme Court looked at a report of a 19-member investigating commission, which had divided 17-2. The majority of the commission said quite clearly that "empirical research . . . has found no evidence . . . that exposure to explicit sexual materials plays a significant role in the causation of . . . criminal behavior. . . ." *Paris Adult Theater I v. Slaton,* 413 U.S. 49, 108 n.26 (1973). The court completely ignored what the majority said, and relied only on what the minority said. On top of that, the minority did not all say what the Supreme Court said it said.

5) On the question whether government employees should be made liable for damages in some circumstances, even though they had previously enjoyed absolute immunity under Supreme Court decisions of 1845 and 1896, a main question was whether the change would cause "disruption of government." *Butz v. Economou,* 438 U.S. 478 (1978). Four dissenters plausibly asserted it would. But the Supreme Court imposed the new liability, while maintaining complete silence on the disruption question. The Court may have had no means of answering such questions as these: To what extent are offers of government positions rejected because of tort liability of officers? To what extent do officers resign on account of such liability? To what extent does Congress by private laws indemnify officers? How many judgments do officers pay, and in what amounts? Is insurance available? To what extent are officers insured? For all that appears, the Court had no information on such questions. Neither did the four dissenters.

6) One way the Court resolves questions about legislative facts without getting the facts is by imposing the burden of proof on one of the parties. In a challenge of state legislation, should the burden be on the challenger or on the defender? In 1973, the Court put the burden on the challenger; in 1977, it put the burden on the defender. In the 1977 case, it rejected the view of the 1973 decision without mentioning it.

7) In two major cases, the Supreme Court diligently did extrarecord research and made decisions based on its findings of legislative facts, but the Court in both cases failed to give the parties a predecision chance to challenge its extrarecord facts. *Ballew v. Georgia,* 435 U.S. 223 (1978); *Roe v. Wade,* 410 U.S. 113 (1973). Judge Friendly pointed out in an article that the Supreme Court decision in *Roe v. Wade* rested heavily on extrarecord abortion facts that the parties had had no chance to challenge, and he accurately asserted: "If an administrative agency, even in a rulemaking proceeding, had used similar materials without having given the parties a fair opportunity to criticize or

controvert them at the hearing stage, reversal would have come swiftly and inexorably." Friendly, *The Courts and Social Policy,* 33 U. Miami L. Rev. 21, 37 (1978).

Ann Woolhandler, *Rethinking the Judicial Reception of Legislative Facts*, 41 Vanderbilt Law Review 111 (1988)[12]

Because assumptions about disputable general facts are necessary to any reasoning process, the advisory committee on the Federal Rules of Evidence declined to prescribe formal rules for the reception of legislative facts when providing standards for judicial notice. The advisory committee believed that judicial absorption of general nonlegal knowledge should not be circumscribed by "any limitation in the form of indisputability, any formal requirements of notice other than those already inherent in affording opportunity to hear and be heard and exchanging briefs, and any requirement of formal findings at any level." Rather, according to the advisory committee, the process of judicial reception of legislative facts should parallel the court's methodology in determining domestic law, in which

> the judge is unrestricted in his investigation and conclusion. He may reject the propositions of either party or of both parties. He may consult the sources of pertinent data to which they refer, or he may refuse to do so. He may make an independent search for persuasive data or rest content with what he has or what the parties present. . . . [T]he parties do no more than to assist; they control no part of the process. . . .

[Some p]rofessors [including Professor] Davis . . . see a problem in the haphazard way in which courts receive legislative facts. They believe courts should embrace more openly their legislative functions by adopting procedures better suited to making general, prospective rules. These reformists claim that lawyers fail to understand the importance of presenting general data to assist courts in fashioning legal rules, and that courts are insensitive to the need to seek out facts about the general effects of the legal rules they create, rather than relying on unsupported assumptions or one-sided presentations. Their suggested remedies range from such unexceptionable proposals as increased sophistication on the part of lawyers and judges, and judicial requests for further presentations by parties and amici, to more ambitious goals such as adoption of formal rules of evidence, and appointment of independent experts and scientific panels.

Because it is difficult to argue against courts' knowing more about the effects of the legal rules they create, no one criticizes these proposals. But no one has followed them either, despite their twenty-seven year persistence. This Essay will first address why no one has followed these proposals, and then discuss why this is a good thing. . . .

A paradigmatic legislative fact is one that shows the general effect a legal rule will have, and is presented to encourage the decisionmaker to make a

---

[12] Copyright © 1988. Reprinted with permission of the Vanderbilt Law Review.

particular legal rule. . . . Examples of legislative facts include evidence that strict liability leads to efficient resource allocation, or that the death penalty does not deter crime, which is presented respectively to convince the court to adopt strict liability or strike down the death penalty. . . .

The line between adjudicative and legislative facts is indistinct, however, because decisionmakers use even the most particularized facts to make legal rules. . . . A court, for example, may view one indigent defendant's inability to defend himself without a court-appointed lawyer as representative of the plight of others, and conclude therefrom that due process requires court-appointment of lawyers for indigent defendants. In addition, once the decisionmaker finds even the most individual facts, lawmaking occurs in the application of a pre-existing, general legal standard to those facts. . . . [W]hen courts make law by applying a general standard to particular facts, the lawmaking is likely to be more interstitial and less self-conscious than when courts make law upon proof of general facts. In the latter case, the participants will have a greater sense of creating the framework of law rather than of merely filling in the gaps. . . .

[In addition], lawyers and judges continue to see the judicial process as one in which text, precedent, and principle still play a significant role. To the extent that nonpragmatic reasoning informs judicial decisionmaking, legislative factfinding is less important.

Even when pragmatism plays a significant role in judicial decision-making, however, the effect of a particular showing of legislative fact on a decision is inherently unpredictable. . . . Once an attorney proves legislative facts . . . these facts are balanced against the other social harms and benefits that the legal rule is shown or presumed to produce. . . .

This is not to deny . . . that showings of legislative facts may be important to particular cases. But there is no special need to adopt formal procedures for the judicial reception of legislative facts. Recommendations for solicitation of amici curiae and appointment of independent experts and scientific panels are aimed at giving courts a more balanced presentation to alleviate the effects of one-sided presentations that result from imbalances in litigation resources. But when lawyers perceive that a particular showing will affect the outcome in a case, they tend to make such a showing, which courts tend to receive. If the court relies on an imbalanced presentation in one case, attorneys with sufficient resources and sophistication are likely to respond in later cases with counter-presentations. Explicit judicial reliance on imbalanced information thus creates its own incentive for correction by showing attorneys what kinds of facts just might make a difference to the court. . . . [I]t is unlikely that over time a contestable scientific or social scientific study that is made the explicit basis of a court decision will remain unchallenged. . . .

The reformists maintain that courts should embrace more openly their legislative functions. . . . [T]heir reforms would make courts look more like administrative agencies, which combine rulemaking and adjudication. . . .

When the reformists claim that legitimacy will come from the increased accuracy of judicial decisions, they are claiming that science can neutrally answer legal questions. With processes for the courts to educate themselves about the general effects of legal rules in place, facts rather than discretion will determine the outcome of cases. . . .

[But t]he claims for legitimacy through the greater accuracy that more formalized reception of legislative facts is thought to entail ultimately fail . . . [because a]lthough legislative facts provide information for the pragmatic balancing of desirable effects, these "facts" cannot tell us what effects are desirable, or how to weigh them. . . .

[Insofar as the goal of proposed reforms is for courts to obtain the views of the unrepresented or underrepresented, there is reason to believe that] these interests are likely to receive better protection from principles and precedent rather than [from] ad hoc balancing of the effects of legal rules. If courts simply sought legitimacy through duplication of the legislative process, they ultimately would put themselves out of business. . . .

The current, haphazard method of receiving legislative facts, which creates its own incentives for counter-presentations over time, is preferable to a more rationalized approach to judicial reception of legislative facts that holds no promise of encouraging principled decisionmaking.

NOTES

1. What Professor Davis says about lawmaking in the U.S. Supreme Court also can be said about the state courts of last resort. What conclusion should be drawn from Professor Davis's description of the shortcomings of lawmaking in appellate courts?: That appellate courts should withdraw, to the extent possible, from any lawmaking, leaving issues whose resolution requires "legislative facts" to the legislature? That appellate courts should introduce radically revised procedures and staff assistance to help them ascertain legislative facts?

2. Professor Woolhandler takes a more sanguine view of the current state of affairs than that reflected in other excerpts presented above. In her view, can and should legislative or administrative procedures be adapted to the judicial function? Why or why not?

3. If courts of last resort pursued the implications of Professor Davis's article and adopted procedures and staffs of the type used by administrative agencies, would that undesirably blur the line between the judicial and legislative branches?

4. To what extent should a court's adjudication be grounded in a "democratic base"? Do we want courts deciding cases based on what the judges believe the majority view is? Isn't an independent judiciary intended to provide a mechanism for resolving controversies that will be unswayed by the popular will?

5. *See* Richard B. Cappalli, *Bringing Internet Information to Court: Of "Legislative Facts,"* 75 TEMP. L. REV. 99, 103, 120 (2002) (noting that "no rules block lawyers from passing on to the judges . . . by letter, email, attachments, cites to websites, and brief appendices (always with copy to opposing counsel) background information supporting the rules they need to win" and that "factual material from newspapers, journals, websites, government reports and so forth, cited within or appended to briefs or utilized during oral argument, is

always usable by the court once it understands that it is operating in a law-making and not a fact-to-law mode. The judicial problem then becomes one of controlling this informational inflow by creating internal or external (published law) standards to govern the accuracy of legislative facts;" citing writings that propose ways in which courts' discretion in gathering and eval-uating legislative facts can be controlled); Ellie Margolis, *Beyond Brandeis: Exploring the Uses of Non-Legal Materials in Appellate Briefs*, 34 U.S.F. L. REV. 197 (2000) (discussing the propriety of introducing non-legal materials at the appellate stage).

6. As indicated in the preceding materials, no codified rule now deals with judicial notice of legislative facts. Professor Peggy C. Davis, in *"There is a Book Out . . .": An Analysis of Judicial Absorption of Legislative Facts*, 100 HARV. L. REV. 1539, 1603 (1987), argues that codified rules of evidence concerning judi-cial notice should recognize the legitimacy of courts' consideration of *dis-putable* matters of fact in construing statutes, deciding constitutional issues, and formulating rules of law generally, and should codify "the authority . . . to entertain or solicit special briefs, arguments, affidavits or depositions of experts, or, in the rare case, hearings, as to the propriety of taking judicial notice of a disputable fact. A trial court's decision whether to exercise this authority should be reviewable and informed by standards." Scholars have dis-agreed as to whether it is best to present legislative facts to trial courts, or to reserve their presentation until the parties are before the appellate court, which may remand for further development of the legislative facts if that seems appropriate. *See* A.J. Stephani, *Therapeutic Jurisprudence: Issues, Analysis, And Applications: Therapeutic Jurisprudence in the Appellate Arena: Judicial Notice and the Potential of the Legislative Fact Remand*, 24 SEATTLE U. L. REV. 509, 525-26 (2000).

7. In *Hawkins v. United States*, 358 U.S. 74 (1958), the defendant was con-victed under the Mann Act of transporting a seventeen-year-old girl across state lines for immoral purposes. He argued for reversal on the ground that his wife had been used as a witness against him at the trial, in violation of the common-law rule of evidence that excludes one spouse's testimony against another.

The conviction was reversed. Justice Black wrote for the Court that the spousal privilege had to be upheld as a matter of "reason and experience" in the interests of domestic tranquility. He said:

> The basic reason the law has refused to pit wife against husband or husband against wife in a trial where life or liberty is at stake was a belief that such a policy was necessary to foster family peace. . . . Adverse testimony given in criminal proceedings would, we think, be likely to destroy almost any marriage.

Justice Stewart concurred on another ground but questioned Justice Black's empirical intuition based on "reason and experience." He urged:

> Before assuming that a change in the present rule would work such a wholesale disruption of domestic felicity as the court's opinion implies, it would be helpful to know the experience in those jurisdictions [some nineteen] where the rule has been abandoned or modified. . . .

Are there instances in which "reason and experience" provide appellate judges with an adequate basis for formulating a governing rule? Instances in which the formulation of the governing rule rests on value choices, making empirical data either irrelevant or of secondary importance? Recall *Woolhandler, supra p.* 353.

8. The courts have looked to social science in their making of law probably most frequently in the context of constitutional law, and particularly in decisions involving the First Amendment (obscenity), the Sixth Amendment (jury size and death-qualified juries, and as to the propriety of videotaping witnesses so as to avoid traumatizing abused children who otherwise might have to testify in the presence of their alleged abusers), the Eighth Amendment (deterrent effect of the death penalty), and the Fourteenth Amendment equal protection clause (race and sex discrimination). *See* JOHN MONAHAN & LAURENS WALKER, SOCIAL SCIENCE IN LAW: CASES AND MATERIALS 179-314 (4th ed. 1998). Courts also rely on social science in making common law, where it has influenced the rules of evidence and tort doctrine, among other things. *Id.* at 312-54.

B. Appellate Courts' Use of Research and Empirical Data

BALLEW v. GEORGIA
435 U.S. 233 (1978)

MR. JUSTICE BLACKMUN announced the judgment of the Court and delivered an opinion in which MR. JUSTICE STEVENS joined.

[In *Ballew* the Court faced the question whether a state criminal trial to a jury of only five persons deprived an accused of the right to trial by jury guaranteed to him by the Sixth and Fourteenth Amendments.]

Williams v. Florida [399 U.S. 78, 100 (1970)] and *Colgrove v. Battin*, 413 U.S. 149 (1973) (where the Court held that a jury of six members did not violate the Seventh Amendment right to a jury trial in a civil case), generated a quantity of scholarly work on jury size. These writings do not draw or identify a bright line below which the number of jurors would not be able to function as required . . . . On the other hand, they raise significant questions about the wisdom and constitutionality of a reduction below six. We examine these concerns:

Some of these studies have been pressed upon us by the parties.

We have considered them carefully because they provide the only basis, besides judicial hunch, for a decision about whether smaller and smaller juries will be able to fulfill the purpose and functions of the Sixth Amendment.

First, recent empirical data suggest that progressively smaller juries are less likely to foster effective group deliberation. At some point, this decline leads to inaccurate factfinding and incorrect application of the common sense of the community to the facts. Generally, a positive correlation exists between group size and the quality of both group performance and group productivity. A variety of explanations have been offered for this conclusion. Several are particularly applicable in the jury setting. The smaller the group, the less likely are members to make critical contributions necessary for the solution of a given problem. Because most juries are not permitted to take notes, memory is important for accurate jury deliberations. As juries decrease in size, then, they are less likely to have members who remember each of the important pieces of evidence or argument. Furthermore, the smaller the group, the less likely it is to overcome the biases of its members to obtain an accurate result. When individual and group decisionmaking were compared, it was seen that groups performed better because prejudices of individuals were frequently counterbalanced, and objectivity resulted. Groups also exhibited increased motivation and self-criticism. All these advantages, except, perhaps, self-motivation, tend to diminish as the size of the group diminishes. Because juries frequently face complex problems laden with value choices, the benefits are important and should be retained. In particular, the counterbalancing of various biases is critical to the accurate application of the common sense of the community to the facts of any given case. [The Court's citations to scholarly publications in support of these statements are omitted.]

Second, the data now raise doubts about the accuracy of the results achieved by smaller and smaller panels. Statistical studies suggest that the risk of convicting an innocent person . . . rises as the size of the jury diminishes. Because the risk of not convicting a guilty person . . . increases with the size of the panel, an optimal jury size can be selected as a function of the interaction between the two risks. Nagel and Neef concluded that the optimal size, for the purpose of minimizing errors, should vary with the importance attached to the two types of mistakes. . . . [T]hey concluded that the optimal jury size was between six and eight. As the size diminished to five and below, the weighted sum of errors increased because of the enlarging risk of the conviction of innocent defendants.

Another doubt about progressively smaller juries arises from the increasing inconsistency that results from the decreases. Saks argued that the "more a jury type fosters consistency, the greater will be the proportion of juries which select the correct (i.e., the same) verdict and the fewer 'errors' will be made." From his mock trials held before undergraduates and former jurors, he computed the percentage of "correct" decisions rendered by 12-person and 6-person panels. In the student experiment, 12-person groups reached correct verdicts 83% of the time; 6-person panels reached correct verdicts 69% of the time. . . .

Third, the data suggest that the verdicts of jury deliberation in criminal cases will vary as juries become smaller, and that the variance amounts to an imbalance to the detriment of one side, the defense. Both Lempert and Zeisel found that the number of hung juries would diminish as the panels decreased in size. [Details of studies followed.] . . .

Fourth, what has just been said about the presence of minority viewpoint as juries decrease in size foretells problems not only for jury decisionmaking, but also for the representation of minority groups in the community. The Court repeatedly has held that meaningful community participation cannot be attained with the exclusion of minorities or other identifiable groups from jury service. . . . The exclusion of elements of the community from participation "contravenes the very idea of a jury . . . composed of 'the peers or equals of the person whose rights it is selected or summoned to determine.'". . . [T]he opportunity for meaningful and appropriate representation does decrease with the size of the panels. Thus, if a minority group constitutes 10% of the community, 53.1% of randomly selected six-member juries could be expected to have no minority representative among their members, and 89% not to have two. Further reduction in size will erect additional barriers to representation. . . .

[T]hese studies, most of which have been made since . . . 1970, lead us to conclude that the purpose and functioning of the jury in a criminal trial is seriously impaired, and to a constitutional degree, by a reduction in size to below six members. We readily admit that we do not pretend to discern a clear line between six members and five. But the assembled data raise substantial doubt about the reliability and appropriate representation of panels smaller than six. Because of the fundamental importance of the jury trial to the American system of criminal justice, any further reduction that promotes inaccurate and possibly biased decisionmaking, that causes untoward differences in verdicts, and that prevents juries from truly representing their communities, attains constitutional significance. . . .

Methodological problems prevent reliance on the three studies that do purport to bolster Georgia's position. . . .

NOTES

1. As *Ballew* illustrates, social research and empirical data are sometimes pivotal in decisions. Earlier, in *Colgrove v. Battin*, 413 U.S. 149 (1973), upholding the six-member civil jury, Justice Brennan responded to the argument that, to be a "jury" within the meaning of the Seventh Amendment, a civil jury must number twelve persons by declaring that "the question comes down to whether jury performance is a function of jury size." In a long footnote he examined "four very recent studies" that, he wrote, "provided convincing empirical evidence that 'there is no discernable difference between the results reached' by the juries of different size." Dissenting Justice Marshall took issue with the majority on what the empirical data proved. Although he thought the matter ultimately depended on the historical meaning of the word "jury" as used in the Seventh Amendment, in footnotes he argued vigorously from the empirical evidence that a smaller jury does function differently from a twelve-member jury.

2. In John Monahan & Laurens Walker, *Social Authority: Obtaining, Evaluating, and Establishing Social Science in Law*, 134 U. Pa. L. Rev. 477 (1986), the authors argue that it is confusing and unsound to treat the sorts of data relied upon for the formulation of a rule of law as "facts." Rather, they argue that such empirical data should be analogized to "law" and denominated "social authority." Courts could then rely upon it, and cite it, in the way that they rely upon judicial precedents. Moreover, such "social authority" should be presented to the courts in the way that law is presented, i.e., in briefs or oral argument, and not by way of witnesses at trial. Do you see advantages and disadvantages to Monahans' and Walker's recommendations?

Maurice Rosenberg, *Improving The Courts' Ability To Absorb Scientific Information, in* SCIENCE AND TECHNOLOGY ADVICE TO THE PRESIDENT, CONGRESS AND JUDICIARY 480-83 (W. T. Golden ed., 1988)[13]

In an ever more complex world, the courts increasingly are asked to resolve disputes in which decision turns on scientific data. The case may depend on the results of:

- epidemiological studies of the health histories of veterans exposed to Agent Orange; or

- demographic studies bearing on racial or gender bias on the job; or

- consumer surveys showing the defendant has marketed a product so similar to the plaintiff's [that] the public is confused as to its source; or

- sociological studies on whether disqualifying persons with anti-capital punishment views produces juries that are too prone to vote "guilty"; or

- statistical data on the frequency of death, illness and injury from a growing list of products and contaminants; and so on.

The science advice the judiciary needs falls into two categories. In one, the court's scientific findings will affect the interests of the immediate parties and of almost no one else; in effect, their impact is limited to the single case. These findings are called "adjudicative facts." In the other category, the findings provide the factual basis for the way the court formulates a rule of law of general applicability. Those findings are called "legislative facts." They are the kind of facts an alert, responsible legislative body would seek to assemble before choosing a statutory solution to the problem addressed.

In both types of cases, the courts need evidence that experts can supply, but there the similarity ends. The two situations raise significantly different problems and require equally different solutions.

In recent times, various proposals to provide high-level courts with scientific experts as staff aides have not been well-received, despite the fact that "technical advisors" are firmly established and well accepted in the Court of Appeals for the Federal Circuit. The advisors in that court are trained in law and also hold advanced degrees in a scientific or technical specialty such as physics, chemistry or engineering. They assist the judges in patent cases and other lawsuits that turn on scientific proof. A major reason the technical advisor model has not been accepted for other courts is that the legal profession is generally wary of allowing in-court experts to speak inaudibly and anonymously to the judges in ways that may determine the results of sharply contested cases.

Even more urgent than improving the way courts obtain scientific data on case-specific issues of adjudicative fact is the need in the sphere of legislative

---

[13] Excerpted with permission from Maurice Rosenberg, *Improving The Courts' Ability To Absorb Scientific Information, in* Science and Technology Advice to the President, Congress and Judiciary 480-83 (W.T. Golden ed., 1988). Copyright © 1988 AAAS.

fact-finding. The judiciary's current method of absorbing scientific information on legislative facts is haphazard, unruly and unreliable. One study of appellate litigation reported that 40% of the cited references to the scientific literature came via the court's independent research, unaided by the lawyers or the record made in the lower court. (*See* Marvell, Appellate Courts and Lawyers, 192 [1978].) The appellate judges (including justices of the United States Supreme Court) simply took "judicial notice" of the materials they cited. That is, they or their law clerks found the materials in the library, read them, and used them.

To a large extent, the appellate courts have no alternative but to employ that kind of judicial notice, for the litigants are less likely to fill the information gaps in legislative-fact disputes than to help the court in adjudicative-fact situations. The parties' first priority, understandably, is to win the case. Assuring that the courts make "good law" in the process is not a vital objective. Except where it would induce a favorable decision, they have little incentive to spend great amounts of energy or money to provide the courts with the kinds of scientific data a responsible legislature would insist upon before making a law.

A major defect in the courts' self-help in this area is the tendency to use scientific studies, reports and data that are *methodologically* unfit for judicial consumption. Since neither the judges nor their clerks have been trained in scientific research methods, their use of flawed materials is not surprising.

A possible remedy suggests itself: creating a public agency to act as an information resource for the courts with regard to the methodological acceptability of scientific and technological research findings. The agency, probably at the national level, might be a consortium of scholars and scientists drawn from the National Academy of Sciences, the Library of Congress, the National Institutes of Health, the National Science Foundation, the National Endowment for the Humanities, and other entities. Its mission would be to receive and catalogue scientific studies that qualify for judicial attention. The criteria for determining whether a study qualifies for approval would not be agreement or disagreement with its content or recommendations, but only a finding that its design and methods fall within the range of accepted standards of scientific inquiry. . . .

Procedures would be developed to regulate the manner in which courts utilize studies on file in the depository. For example, a study found acceptable in its methods would be available for judicial notice if and only if timely notification were given to the parties and an opportunity afforded them to submit briefs supporting, contesting, or commenting on the material the court proposes to use. The comments could go both to the methods and the substance of the study. If a party so desired, it could submit any other relevant materials. Use by the court of studies found acceptable as to research methodology would not in the least inhibit resort to other materials.

Procedures would also be devised to assure a full and fair opportunity for researchers whose proffered studies were not at first approved to obtain a second review. Of course, the review process should not be unreasonably elaborated since the litigants will be free to offer studies not on file.

Although this proposal is not free from difficulties, it offers a way to improve the judiciary's ability to absorb scientific materials in discharging the courts' important law-declaring function. It deserves a trial run.

NOTES

1. Consider the following possibilities for informing appellate courts of legislative facts, each of which has been employed at various times:

a. Presentation as evidence by one or more parties in the trial court proceeding, thus becoming part of the trial record;

b. Presentation by one or more parties in briefs filed in the appellate court;

c. Independent library research by the appellate court;

d. Presentation in the brief of an amicus curiae.

What are the advantages and disadvantages of each method? Would it be preferable to provide the court with a trained staff, adequate to research the empirical data in all cases where such data would be significant in formulating a legal rule?

2. In *E. I. du Pont de Nemours & Co. v. Collins*, 432 U.S. 46, 57 (1976), the Supreme Court reversed the Eighth Circuit's decision rejecting an SEC determination, saying:

> We note that after receiving briefs and hearing oral argument, the Court of Appeals — over the objection of the Commission . . . and Du Pont — undertook the unique appellate procedure of employing a university professor to assist the court in understanding the record and to prepare reports and memoranda for the court. Thus, the reports relied upon by that court included a variety of data and economic observations which had not been examined and tested by the traditional methods of the adversary process. We are not cited to any statute, rule, or decision authorizing the procedure employed by the Court of Appeals.

Was the Eighth Circuit's reliance on data and observations reported by its professor assistant more objectionable than independent research by the appellate court would have been? If reliance on materials not tested by the adversary process was the problem, why isn't independent research by the court equally objectionable?

3. Presentation by amicus curiae of legislative facts has grown in frequency and importance in recent years, especially in the U.S. Supreme Court.

John Howard, *Retaliation, Reinstatement, And Friends Of The Court: Amicus Participation In* Brock v. Roadway Express, Inc., 31 HOWARD LAW JOURNAL 241, 253-54, 255-56 (1988)[14]

[P]articipating as an amicus is an alternative approach to affecting policy that is both less expensive than litigation and much more certain to be considered by the Court.

---

[14] Copyright © 1998. Reprinted with permission of the Howard Law Journal.

This reality has not been lost on those who attempt to influence policy through the judicial process. Amici involvement is pervasive. . . . Amicus participation is no longer an exception, it is now the rule. Since amicus briefs are filed in such a large percentage of all Supreme Court cases decided by opinion, and it is common for more than one amicus to participate in a given case, it is quite possible that the Supreme Court now reviews more briefs from amici than from parties. These briefs are from diverse organizations interested in the development of the law governing almost every facet of society. . . .

Although their historic functions have expanded, the amici's historical role of informing the court is still a very important function. Informing the Court is not limited to a restatement of record facts, but includes relating other circumstances that should be considered in resolving the controversy. Amici can supply nonrecord facts of which the court may take judicial notice. After marshalling these facts, the amicus then must explain how these circumstances necessarily affect the decision. This function, that of supplementing the record to help persuade the Court, is still one of the amicus's most important role[s].

NOTES

Is the filing of an amicus brief in an appellate court inconsistent with the adversary process? Does the use of amicus briefs create a risk of subjecting the court to undesirable external pressures? Is an amicus brief simply an obvious form of lobbying the Justices? Even if it is, may its benefits outweigh its risks?

For further discussion of amicus briefs, see Chapter 12, concerning the U.S. Supreme Court.

IV. MAKING RULES OF PROCEDURE FOR INFERIOR COURTS

When it comes to making rules of procedure for inferior courts, the roles of, and relationship between, the legislature and the courts may vary considerably among the states and between the state and federal courts.

A. Formal Rulemaking

WINBERRY v. SALISBURY
74 A.2d 406 (N.J. 1950)

VANDERBILT, C.J.

[Plaintiff brought suit to expunge an alleged libel on him from a report of a grand jury. The court dismissed the complaint as not stating a cause of action. When plaintiff served a notice of appeal, defendant moved to dismiss it as late, and the appeals court granted his motion. Article VI, Section II, paragraph 3 of the Constitution of 1947, directed that "the Supreme Court shall make rules governing the administration of all courts in the State and, subject to law, the practice and procedure in all such courts." The Appellate Division held that the Rules limiting to 45 days the time for an appeal from a final judgment prevailed over the statute that permitted an appeal within one year after judgment was rendered. In reviewing this decision, the New Jersey Supreme Court had to decide the meaning of the phrase "subject to law" in the above-quoted provision of the state constitution.]

[T]here can be no doubt in the mind of anyone familiar with the work of the Constitutional Convention or with the ensuing election at which the Constitution was adopted by the people that . . . there was a clear intent to establish a simple but fully integrated system of courts and to give to the judiciary the power and thus to impose on them the responsibility for seeing that the judicial system functioned effectively in the public interest. . . .

If "subject to law" were to be interpreted to mean subject to legislation, it would necessarily follow that once the Legislature had passed a statute in conflict with a rule of court, the rule-making power of the Supreme Court would be *functus officio,* for it would be intolerable to hold . . . that after the Legislature has passed an act modifying a rule of court, the Supreme Court might in turn adopt a new rule overriding the statute, and so on *ad nauseam.* Such an unseemly and possibly continuous conflict between these two departments of the State Government could never have been contemplated by the people. . . .

Article VI, Section II, paragraph 3 of the new Constitution not only gives the Supreme Court the rule-making power, but it imposes on the Supreme Court an active responsibility for making such rules — "The Supreme Court *shall* make rules.". . .

The only interpretation of "subject to law" that will not defeat the objective of the people . . . and which will at the same time give rational significance to the phrase is to construe it as the equivalent of substantive law as distinguished from pleading and practice.

. . . The phrase "subject to law" in Article VI, Section II, paragraph 3 of the Constitution thus serves as a continuous reminder that the rule-making power as to practice and procedure must not invade the field of the substantive law as such. . . . [T]he courts . . . are not to make substantive law wholesale through the exercise of the rule-making power. . . .

Rules of court for controlling practice and procedure . . . were the settled means of effecting changes and improvements in procedure, which had its origin in custom. That rules of court did not continue to be the exclusive means of developing practice and procedure in the courts is due to the gradual growth in England of the doctrine of parliamentary supremacy . . . and in the United States to the legislative hegemony in both the Federal Government and the states down to the Civil War . . . . These factors made possible, indeed, necessitated a century ago the adoption in New York and elsewhere of the Field Code of Civil Procedure. . . . But it must not be thought . . . that the courts generally abdicated their power to make rules governing practice and procedure. . . . New Jersey never adopted a code of civil procedure but instead short practice acts, and the exercise of the rule-making power here has been continuous, covering practice and procedure on a broad scale, so much so that our judges and lawyers would refer to the rules a hundred times to every time they looked at the Practice Act or the Chancery Act.

[T]he trend throughout the country has been to give the courts the power to regulate their own procedure and administration and then to hold them responsible for results. The reasons for this trend are obvious. Rules of court are made by experts who are familiar with the specific problems to be solved and the various ways of solving them.

In this State under the new Constitution the Supreme Court . . . designat[ed] the outstanding authorities on procedural law in the bar of the State to prepare a tentative draft of proposed rules of court . . . The tentative draft was distributed to the judges and lawyers of the State, who submitted hundreds of suggestions, all of which were examined by the experts appointed by the Court, and then appraised by the Court itself before the Rules of Court were finally promulgated by the Court on September 15, 1948. The rule-making process here has become a continuous one, the Court calling each spring for suggestions from the bench and bar and especially from committees appointed by the state and county bar associations. Their suggestions are considered every year . . . at the annual Judicial Conference made up of the judges, the legislative leaders, the Attorney General and the county prosecutors, the officers and trustees of the State Bar Association, the president of each of the county bar associations, and 60 delegates from the county bar associations, one representative from each law school in the State . . . , the Administrative Director of the Courts, and ten laymen appointed by the Chief Justice. Thus, in a very real sense . . . our Rules of Court are the product of the joint efforts of the bench and bar of the State, with the Supreme Court necessarily making the ultimate decision as to the contents of the rules. Rules of court, moreover, have the great advantage that not only are they made by experts, but they are interpreted and applied by judges who are sympathetic with them. Changes may be made whenever occasion may require without waiting for stated legislative sessions and without burdening already overworked legislators. Finally, procedure may be made subsidiary, as it should be, to the substantial rights of the litigants. The courts may avoid the snarls of procedural red tape and concentrate on the substantive questions at issue. . . . Our Constitution is one of the first to incorporate the rule-making power expressly along with principles of efficient judicial management. . . .

We therefore conclude that the rule-making power of the Supreme Court is not subject to overriding legislation, but that it is confined to practice, procedure and administration as such. In the present case Rules 1:2-5 and 4:2-5 apply. The appeal here was not taken within 45 days of the original order for judgment of May 25, 1948. . . .

The judgment appealed from is affirmed but without costs.

NOTES

Winberry has remained the law in New Jersey, subject to certain refinements. For example, in *Knight v. City of Margate*, 86 N.J. 374, 431 A.2d 833, 841-42 (1981), the Court explained:

Succeeding cases have made clear that while the judicial power is paramount and exclusive, it need not in every context or application be preclusive. . . . The cases show that, although the constitutional authority of the Supreme Court over the judicial branch of government is preeminent, this does not mean that this authority must invariably foreclose action by the other branches of government [,] . . . particularly where the judicial power has not been exercised or fully implemented, and where such action by the other branches serves a legitimate governmental purpose and, concomitantly, does not interfere with judicial prerogatives or only indirectly or incidentally touches upon the judicial domain. Thus, in . . . *State v. Deutsch*, 34 N.J. 190 (1961), this Court . . . held that the Court had the constitutional authority to impose requirements for the disqualification of judges which exceeded those enacted by the Legislature, but did not suggest that the statute [relating to the disqualification of judges] unconstitutionally invaded an area reserved exclusively to this Court. Rather, the clear implication was that the statute remained fully effective except to the extent the Court exercised its constitutional powers to impose different provisions for the disqualification of judges. . . . We conclude therefore that in the full enjoyment of its paramount and exclusive powers over the judicial branch, the Supreme Court has the authority, reasonably to be implied under the twin principles of the separation and interdependence of governmental powers, to permit or accommodate the lawful and reasonable exercise of the powers of other branches of government even as that might impinge upon the Court's constitutional concerns in the judicial area. The constitutional validity of such action by another branch of government, and the Supreme Court's ultimate power to accept or reject such action, turn upon the legitimacy of the governmental purpose of that action and the nature and extent of its encroachment upon judicial prerogatives and interests.

WHITE v. FISHER
689 P.2d 102 (Wyo. 1984)

THOMAS, JUSTICE.

The question which we shall address . . . is that of the constitutional propriety of the enactment of a statute by the legislature prescribing a rule of procedure in civil actions. In a civil action seeking money damages for medical malpractice the district court applied the provisions of § 1-1-114, W.S. 1977, which prohibit any allegation of the dollar amount of damages in "the ad damnum clause or prayer for damages incorporated in a pleading." The plaintiffs (appellants in this court) had alleged the dollar amount of their damages, and the district court dismissed their complaint. We hold the statute to be an invasion of the constitutional powers of the judicial branch of government, and we reverse the district court. . . .

Section 1-1-114, W.S. 1977, provides as follows:

The ad damnum clause or prayer for damages incorporated in a pleading which sets forth a claim for relief based upon personal injury or wrongful death shall not state any dollar amount as alleged damages or demand a sum as judgment other than an allegation that the damages are of an amount necessary to establish jurisdiction of the court. Nothing herein shall be construed to prevent any party from arguing to the court or jury the amount of his claim in money. In all cases the court shall inform the jury of the consequences of its verdict.

. . . [E]ven though these parties have not raised the question of constitutionality, this court has the power to dispose of that question. . . . [W]e are compelled to consider the constitutionality of the statute in this instance because of its apparent infringement upon the doctrine of separation of powers. . . .

The procedural tenor of the statute is perhaps best recognized by treating with the manner in which it conflicts with several rules of this court. Rule 8(a), W.R.C.P., requires a pleading which sets forth a claim to contain a short and plain statement of the claim, demonstrating that the parties are entitled to relief, and a demand for judgment for the relief claimed. . . . [I]n order to allege facts sufficient to constitute a cause of action a pleading normally must set out the amount of damages sustained in either a definite amount or afford a basis on which they may be estimated. Rule 54(c), W.R.C.P., dealing with default judgments, provides for the entry of default but it shall not be different in kind from or exceed in amount that prayed for, and in order to apply that rule the allegation of money damages is required. Rule 9(g), W.R.C.P., requires the specific statement of items of special damages claimed. . . . We also note that the official forms which accompany the Wyoming Rules of Civil Procedure reflect that specific money amounts for damages are to be included.

> Article V, § 2 of the Constitution of the State of Wyoming, provides: The supreme court shall have general appellate jurisdiction, co-extensive with the state, in both civil and criminal causes, and shall have a general superintending control over all inferior courts, under such rules and regulations as may be prescribed by law.

The general superintending control over all inferior courts granted to the supreme court by that provision encompasses the authority to prescribe rules of practice and procedure in those courts. More than fifty years ago this court, relying upon previous decisions, concluded "that the power of this court to control the course of litigation in the trial courts of this state is quite plenary." *State ex rel. Jones v. District Court of Ninth Judicial Dist.*, 263 P. 700, 703 (1928). . . .

As noted earlier . . . , the prescription of the form and content of pleadings which are to be filed in Wyoming courts is a procedural, not a substantive, matter. The form and content of pleadings is a function which the constitution ascribes to the Supreme Court of Wyoming. Article II, § 1 of the Constitution of the State of Wyoming provides:

> The powers of the government of this state are divided into three distinct departments: The legislative, executive and judicial, and no person or collection of persons charged with the exercise of powers properly belonging to one of these departments shall exercise any powers properly belonging to either of the others, except as in this constitution expressly directed or permitted.

The legislature is thus effectively prohibited from enacting statutes specifying the content of or foreclosing material from pleadings.

It is our conclusion that § 1-1-114, W.S. 1977, is unconstitutional in the present form. . . . [I]n any form it would constitute an attempt to prescribe the content of pleadings, a procedural function. The statute is a clear infringement upon the constitutional and inherent power of this court to make rules . . . . This holding leaves unaffected the last sentence of the statute. . . .

The judgment of the district court is reversed, and the case is remanded for further proceedings in accordance with this opinion.

NOTES

1. The Wyoming Supreme Court has continued to invalidate legislation as in violation of the principles enunciated in *White. See, e.g., Squillace v. Kelley*, 990 P.2d 497 (1999), striking down a statute that prescribed the practice and procedure for imposing sanctions for the signing and filing of papers with the courts for an improper purpose, holding this a procedural, not a substantive, matter, and hence beyond the legislature's power.

2. Consider the United States Supreme Court's rulemaking power.

28 U.S.C. § 2072. Rules of procedure and evidence; power to prescribe

(a) The Supreme Court shall have the power to prescribe general rules of practice and procedure and rules of evidence for cases in the United States district courts (including proceedings before magistrates thereof) and courts of appeals.

(b) Such rules shall not abridge, enlarge or modify any substantive right. All laws in conflict with such rules shall be of no further force or effect after such rules have taken effect.

(c) Such rules may define when a ruling of a district court is final for the purposes of appeal under section 1291 of this title.

28 U.S.C. § 2074. Rules of procedure and evidence; submission to Congress; effective date

(a) The Supreme Court shall transmit to the Congress not later than May 1 of the year in which a rule prescribed under section 2072 is to become effective a copy of the proposed rule. Such rule shall take effect no earlier than December 1 of the year in which such rule is so transmitted unless otherwise provided by law. The Supreme Court may fix the extent such rule shall apply to proceedings then pending, except that the Supreme Court shall not require the application of such rule to further proceedings then pending to the extent that, in the opinion of the court in which such proceedings are pending, the application of such rule in such proceedings would not be feasible or would work injustice, in which event the former rule applies.

(b) Any such rule creating, abolishing, or modifying an evidentiary privilege shall have no force or effect unless approved by Act of Congress.

BUSINESS GUIDES v. CHROMATIC COMMUNICATIONS ENTERPRISES, INC.
498 U.S. 533 (1991)

Justice O'Connor delivered the opinion of the Court.

In this case we decide whether Rule 11 of the Federal Rules of Civil Procedure imposes an objective standard of reasonable inquiry on represented parties who sign pleadings, motions, or other papers.

Business Guides, Inc., a subsidiary of a leading publisher of trade magazines and journals, publishes directories for 18 specialized areas of retail trade. In an effort to protect its directories against copying, Business Guides deliberately plants in them bits of false information, known as "seeds." . . . Business Guides considers the presence of seeds in a competitor's directory to be evidence of copyright infringement.

On October 31, 1986, Business Guides, through its counsel . . . filed an action in the . . . Northern District of California against Chromatic Communications Enterprises, Inc., claiming copyright infringement, conversion, and unfair competition, and seeking a temporary restraining order (TRO). The TRO application was signed by a Finley, Kumble attorney and by Business Guides' president on behalf of the corporation. Business Guides submitted under seal affidavits in support of the application. These affidavits charged Chromatic with copying, as evidenced by the presence of 10 seeds in Chromatic's directory. One affidavit, that of sales representative Victoria Burdick, identified the 10 listings in Business Guides' directory that had allegedly been copied, but did not pinpoint the seed in each listing. . . .

[T]he District Court, based on its discovery that 9 of the original 10 listings contained no incorrect information, denied the application for a TRO. More importantly, the judge . . . referred the matter to a Magistrate to determine whether Rule 11 sanctions should be imposed. . . . [T]he Magistrate [finding that Business Guides had not checked its information before signing the motion] recommended that both the law firm and the client be sanctioned. . . .

[The district court imposed sanctions only on the client. The court did not sanction the attorney because Business Guides' desire to seek an injunction immediately made it necessary for the attorney to rely on his client's factual representations.]

One issue remains: Business Guides asserts that imposing sanctions against a represented party that did not act in bad faith violates the Rules Enabling Act, 28 U.S.C. § 2072. . . . Business Guides argues that Rule 11, to the extent that it imposes on represented parties an objective standard of reasonableness, exceeds the limits of the Court's power in two ways: (1) it authorizes fee shifting in a manner not approved by Congress; and (2) it effectively creates a federal tort of malicious prosecution, thereby encroaching upon various state law causes of action.

We begin by noting that any Rules Enabling Act challenge to Rule 11 has a large hurdle to get over. The Federal Rules of Civil Procedure are not enacted by Congress, but "Congress participates in the rulemaking process." . . . Additionally, the Rules do not go into effect until Congress has had at least seven months to look them over. *See* 28 U.S.C. § 2074. A challenge to Rule 11 can therefore succeed "only if the Advisory Committee, this Court, and Congress erred in their prima facie judgment that the Rule . . . transgresses neither the terms of the Enabling Act nor constitutional restrictions." *Hanna v. Plumer*, 380 U.S. 460, 471 (1965).

This Court's decision in *Burlington N. R. Co. v. Woods*, 480 U.S. 1 (1987), presents another hurdle. There, the Court considered the Act's proscription against interference with substantive rights and held, in a unanimous decision, that "rules which *incidentally* affect litigants' substantive rights do not violate this provision if reasonably necessary to maintain the integrity of that system of rules." *Id.* at 5 (emphasis added). There is little doubt that Rule 11 is reasonably necessary to maintain the integrity of the system of federal practice and procedure, and that any effect on substantive rights is incidental. We held as much only last Term in *Cooter & Gell* . . . [496 U.S. 384, 393 (1990)].

Petitioner's challenges do not clear these substantial hurdles. In arguing that the monetary sanctions in this case constitute impermissible fee shifting, Business Guides relies on the Court's statement in *Alyeska Pipeline Serv. Co. v. Wilderness Soc'y*, 421 U.S. 240, 247 (1975), that, in the absence of legislative guidance, courts do not have the power "to reallocate the burdens of litigation" by awarding costs to the losing party in a civil rights suit; they have only the power to sanction a party for bad faith. *See id.,* at 258-259. The initial difficulty with this argument is that *Alyeska* dealt with the courts' inherent powers, not the Rules Enabling Act. Rule 11 sanctions do not constitute the kind of fee shifting at issue in *Alyeska.* . . . Finally, the Rule calls only for "an appropriate sanction" — attorney's fees are not mandated. As we explained in *Cooter & Gell:* "Rule 11 is not a fee-shifting statute. . . . 'A movant under Rule 11 has no entitlement to fees or any other sanction.'" 496 U.S., at 409, quoting American Judicature Society, *Rule 11 in Transition, The Report of the Third Circuit Task Force on Federal Rule of Civil Procedure 11*, p. 49 (Burbank, reporter 1989).

Also without merit is Business Guides' argument that Rule 11 creates a federal common law of malicious prosecution. We rejected a similar claim in *Cooter & Gell.* . . .

Affirmed.

JUSTICE KENNEDY, with whom JUSTICE MARSHALL and JUSTICE STEVENS join, and with whom JUSTICE SCALIA joins as to Parts I, III, and IV, dissenting.

The purpose of Federal Rule of Civil Procedure 11 is to control the practice of attorneys, or those who act as their own attorneys, in the conduct of litigation in the federal courts. Extending judicial power far beyond that boundary, the Court, relying only on its rulemaking authority, now holds that citizens who seek the aid of the federal courts may risk money damages or other sanctions if they do not satisfy some objective standard of care in the preparation or litigation of a case. . . .

In my view, the text of the Rule does not support this extension of federal judicial authority. Under a proper construction of Rule 11, I should think it an abuse of discretion to sanction a represented litigant who acts in good faith but errs as to the facts. . . .

II

Applied to attorneys, Rule 11's requirement of reasonable inquiry can be justified as within the traditional power of the courts to set standards for the bar. Our decisions recognize the "disciplinary powers which English and American courts . . . have for centuries possessed over members of the bar, incident to their broader responsibility for keeping the administration of justice and the standards of professional conduct unsullied." *Cohen v. Hurley*, 366 U.S. 117, 123-124 (1961). An attorney acts not only as a client's representative, but also as an officer of the court, and has a duty to serve both masters. Likewise, applying this duty of reasonable inquiry to *pro se* litigants, as amended Rule 11 does, can be viewed as a corollary to the courts' power to control the conduct of attorneys. Requiring *pro se* litigants to make the Rule 11 certification ensures that, in each case, at least one person has taken responsibility for inquiry into the relevant facts and law.

But it is a long step from this traditional judicial role to impose on a represented party the duty of reasonable inquiry prior to the filing of a lawsuit, measured by an objective standard applied in hindsight by a federal judge. Until now, it had never been supposed that citizens at large are, or ought to be, aware of the contents of the Federal Rules of Civil Procedure, or that those rules impose on them primary obligations for their conduct. This new remedy far exceeds any previous authority of a federal court to sanction a represented party. The rules we prescribe have a statutory authorization and need not always track the inherent authority of the federal courts. *See Sibbach v. Wilson & Co.*, 312 U.S. 1 (1941). At the same time, the farther our rules depart from our traditional practices, the more troubling becomes the question of our rulemaking authority.

NOTES

As the opinions in the New Jersey and Wyoming cases indicate, the supreme courts in those states were expressly authorized by the state constitutions to prescribe rules of procedure, thus leading to the corollary that the legislature was without authority to prescribe procedural rules for the courts. Given the Rules Enabling Act, is Congress likewise without authority to prescribe rules of procedure for the federal district courts? For example, in the wake of the *Business Guides* decision, could Congress validly enact a statute specifically prohibiting the federal courts from imposing sanctions on represented parties? For an argument that congressional authority over procedure is constitutionally circumscribed, *see* Linda S. Mullenix, *Unconstitutional Rulemaking: The Civil Justice Reform Act and Separation of Powers*, 77 MINN. L. REV. 1283 (1993). For arguments strongly to the contrary and that "[a] clear-eyed view . . . informed by precedent and history leaves little doubt that Congress holds the cards," see Stephen B. Burbank, *Procedure, Politics and Power: The Role of Congress*, 79 NOTRE DAME L. REV. 1677 (2004), a portion of which follows.

Stephen B. Burbank, *Procedure, Politics and Power: The Role of Congress*, 79 NOTRE DAME LAW REVIEW 1677, 1683-88 (2004)[15]

[T]he Court's decision in *Mistretta v. United States*, [488 U.S. 361 (1989),] . . . would appear to make legally untenable the notion that court rulemaking is an inherent judicial power. To the contrary, the Court was at pains to justify court rulemaking as not "inherently nonjudicial," and thus as capable of being delegated to the judiciary. "[R]ulemaking power," the Court acknowledged, "originates in the Legislative Branch and becomes an execu-

---

[15] Copyright © 2004 by Stephen B. Burbank. Reprinted with permission.

tive function only when delegated by the Legislature to the Executive Branch." By parity of reasoning, it becomes a judicial function only when delegated by the legislature to the judicial branch. . . .

Congress's power to prescribe procedure for the federal courts is shared with the federal courts to the extent that it covers matters subject to the power of the latter to make law when deciding cases, which is the only power that can without difficulty be deemed inherently judicial for these purposes under Article III. . . . (1) I am not aware that the federal courts have ever promulgated either local or supervisory court rules for civil cases without legislative authorization; [and] (2) the Supreme Court never exercised its delegated power to promulgate supervisory court rules for actions at law, first conferred in 1792, prior to the Rules Enabling Act of 1934. . . . [U]nlike the judiciaries of some states, the federal courts have very little inherent judicial power in the strong sense—power that prevails as against a conflicting legislative prescription. In order to qualify as such for a federal court the power must be "necessary to the exercise of all others." The federal courts do have substantial inherent power in the weak sense—power to make procedural law and "to provide themselves with appropriate instruments required for the performance of their duties"*in the course of deciding cases*, in the absence of congressional authorization. And it is true that one can find scattered assertions of inherent power to make procedural law by court rules, local and supervisory. Those assertions are toothless, however, both because they described a power in fact conferred by statute, and in any event because they never purported to describe a power to proceed in the teeth of a statute.

It is thus difficult, in light of history and doctrine, to justify federal local court rulemaking in civil cases as an exercise of inherent power even in the weak sense, both because court rulemaking ill fits within the category of judicial power to resolve cases or controversies under Article III, and because there have always been statutory authorizations when the federal courts have exercised such power. It is at least as difficult, but it has also never been necessary, to bring within that protection supervisory court rulemaking. It is quite impossible to carry an argument that either local or supervisory court rulemaking represents an exercise of inherent power in the strong sense and thus trumps a contrary legislative direction. To conclude otherwise is to ignore not only almost two centuries of Supreme Court precedent but also more than sixty years of experience under the Conformity Act of 1872. It is, moreover, to suggest that those who struggled so long and hard for the Rules Enabling Act of 1934 were wasting their time because the Court could have proceeded without congressional authorization and in the teeth of the Conformity Act.

If Congress chooses to exercise its power, it has the last word on matters of procedure, subject only to the specific limitations of the Constitution (i.e., in the Bill of Rights) and to a limitation that, although difficult to phrase precisely, prevents Congress, as a matter of separation of powers, from depriving the federal courts of powers that are necessary for them to act as such — to function as courts exercising judicial power under Article III — when deciding cases.

NOTES

1. *United States v. Wallace*, 377 F.3d 825 (8th Cir. 2004), held that a statute requiring de novo review of a downward departure from the federal sentencing guidelines was not constitutionally infirm because Congress's authority to regulate the hierarchical relationship among federal courts includes the authority to dictate standards of review. Do you find Congressional power to dictate standards of review to be problematic?

2. If there were no federal Enabling Act or any corresponding state legislation or constitutional provision authorizing courts to make rules of procedure, to what extent could appellate courts make rules of procedure for lower courts in the system or for themselves? Is there an inherent judicial power to prescribe procedural rules for the courts? See *Chambers v. Nasco, Inc.*, 501 U.S. 32 (1991), holding that a federal district court had inherent authority to impose a sanction on attorneys not specifically authorized by, but not prohibited by, FED. R. CIV. P. 11, finding that federal courts have inherent power to sanction the conduct of those who appear before them and act in bad faith, vexatiously, or wantonly, for purposes of oppressing other parties or to effect a fraud on the court, delay or disrupt the litigation. In general, however, the scope of inherent judicial power in the federal courts has been held to be quite limited. The Court has warned that, "The extent of these powers must be delimited with care, for there is a danger of overreaching when one branch of the Government, without benefit of cooperation or correction from the others, undertakes to define its own authority." *Degnan v. United States*, 517 U.S. 820, 823 (1996).

3. The Rules Enabling Act authorizes the promulgation of rules that will govern in federal district courts despite contrary state procedural rules. In *Hanna v. Plumer*, 380 U.S. 460 (1965), for example, the Court upheld Federal Rule of Civil Procedure 4 (d)(1), which conflicted with state service rules. The Court noted that, in prescribing the manner in which a defendant is to be notified that a suit has been instituted against him, the rule related to the "practice and procedure of the district courts." It continued,

> The test must be whether a rule really regulates procedure, — the judicial process for enforcing rights and duties recognized by substantive law and for justly administering remedy and redress for disregard or infraction of them." *Sibbach v. Wilson & Co.*, 312 U.S. 1, 14. . . . [N]either Congress nor the federal courts can, under the guise of formulating rules of decision for federal courts, fashion rules which are not supported by a grant of federal authority contained in Article I or some other section of the Constitution; in such areas state law must govern because there can be no other law. But . . . the constitutional provision for a federal court system (augmented by the Necessary and Proper Clause) carries with it congressional power to make rules governing the practice and pleading in those courts, which in turn includes a power to regulate matters which, though falling within the uncertain area between substance and procedure, are rationally capable of classification as either.

480 U.S. at 464, 471-72.

4. The Rules Enabling Act also can emasculate other acts of Congress. In *Henderson v. United States*, 517 U.S. 654 (1996), Henderson filed suit under the Suits in Admiralty Act for injuries he received as a seaman aboard a vessel owned by the United States. He served the United States within the time allowed by Federal Rule of Civil Procedure 4, but the United States moved to dismiss, arguing that Henderson had failed to serve process "forthwith" as required by § 2 of the Suits in Admiralty Act. The District Court dismissed Henderson's complaint for lack of subject-matter jurisdiction, based on Circuit precedent holding that service "forthwith" was a condition of the Government's waiver of sovereign immunity, and the Court of Appeals affirmed. But the Supreme Court held that the "forthwith" requirement of the Suits in Admiralty Act's was procedural, not jurisdictional, and was super-seded by Rule 4. Under the Rules Enabling Act, the Federal Rules govern mat-ters of "practice and procedure," and "all laws in conflict with such rules shall be of no further force or effect."

5. Do policy considerations favor exclusive judicial authority over procedu-ral rules? or exclusive legislative authority over procedural rules? Expertise and consensus among lawyers and judges as to what procedures are desirable are relevant, but when that consensus breaks down it becomes particularly clear that courts wield power through their procedures and that choices made by judges and lawyers in the formulation of rules and under the rules' author-ity are not necessarily neutral and can have significant consequences, even consequences that may threaten a legislature's prerogatives, given the inex-tricable entanglement of procedure and substance. *See* Burbank, *Procedure, Politics and Power*, 79 NOTRE DAME at 1710-11. A legislature may be better equipped than a rulemaking body such as the Judicial Conference to "hear" interest groups who are monitoring procedural rules' effects on them and, in the view of some commentators, "transparent policy choices by democratically accountable actors are preferable to buried policy choices by federal judges." *Id.* at 1713. Although the politics have changed over the last 15 years or so, compare the insights expressed by Professor Carrington in 1991.

Paul D. Carrington, *The New Order In Judicial Rulemaking*, 75 JUDICATURE 161 (1991)[16]

[S]ome contemporary literature questions whether judicial rulemaking does not rest on a false premise that procedure is apolitical or neutral. If that were its premise, then it would be subject to the popular contemporary criticism that nothing can be neutral, that all is politics. Let me begin, then, with a few words on procedure as politics.

Guarding against factionalism

[O]ur legislatures serve as forums of faction. In their corridors, it is, at least within undefined limits, appropriate and respectable to voice special interest. There, such interests can compete openly in a process of negotiation and com-promise. Resolution of factional conflict is, of course, an essential function of democratic government. I speak no ill of a politically accountable democratic

---

[16] Copyright © 1991. Reprinted with permission of the American Judicature Society.

legislature to say that it is responsive to opinions manifested through political organization. . . .

[F]actionalized democratic legislative bodies sometimes serve factional interests at the expense of the shared, public interest, and may be especially prone to do so when making laws governing legal institutions themselves. . . . Given a choice or an opportunity, most factions will try to claim the judiciary not only to control the selection of judges, but also to bend court administration and procedural rules to their own advantages. What vibrant political organizations want is not good procedure or due process, but victory for the interests they represent.

Concern for the public interest

Alas, there is on the other hand no natural and effective lobby for sound judicial administration, no political force that regularly favors impartiality or disinterest. . . .

Thus, American legislative codes of practice and procedure tend to be decorated with special-interest amendments reflecting momentary impulses of particular political organizations. And times of crisis for judicial institutions seldom call forth thoughtful legislative responses, not because legislators are indifferent to the welfare of the courts but because corrective action is often seen to jeopardize the interests of one or more organized factions. The influence of those factions overbears that of the mere do-gooders whose only stake in the matter is a concern for the public interest. That is why . . . judicial law reform is no sport for the short-winded. Moreover, for obvious reasons, legislative solutions to the problems of courts are prone to favor those factional interests that are best organized, thus reflecting the procedural preference of those whom Marc Galanter has aptly described as "repeat players." This adds to the advantage already held by such litigants.

There are, to be sure, moments when public attention can be focused on institutional matters, and political energy is available to correct critical shortcomings in our institutions. . . . The first acceptance of judicial rulemaking in America came in 1890 in the original Constitution of Wyoming. By 1934, many states had embraced the idea. In that year . . . a half century of effort by the ABA resulted in the enactment by Congress of the Rules Enabling Act.

There was, of course, resistance; it is doubtful that anyone ever regarded the judiciary as a perfect venue for making adjective law. . . . Those of populist bent were quick to recognize that court rulemaking removes issues of importance from the political arena, immunizing them in substantial measure from the control of organized factions. Also, it is likely that rules made by courts tend to be centered on the interests of the judges, interests that are not necessarily identical with the public interest. . . .

Most states have not only copied many or all of the [Federal R]ules, but have adopted judicial rulemaking if they had not previously done so. Congress quite thoroughly butted out for decades. . . .

The rise of interest groups

Meanwhile, . . . the openness of the process of rulemaking as conducted since 1985 may encourage factional politics. It does seem likely that one reason for the absence of factional politics in 1938 was that the rules were drafted in secret over 18 months and promulgated after only a brief period of public comment for which the public was scarcely prepared. There was not sufficient notice and time for interest groups then active to identify ways in which they might be adversely affected by the new rules and then organize to make their views known to Congress. Factional politics was defeated by an undemocratic fait accompli conducted in the name of the Supreme Court.

For better or worse, that can't happen anymore. A wide array of factional interests and organizations are actively watching our efforts and striving to influence the process. . . . There is a large benign consequence of this activity. . . . Many communications received from special interest groups are helpful to rulemakers, as they may be in any lawmaking context. This is especially so to the extent that comments are rooted in shared public concerns rather than particular interests. Many of the groups who study the rules and comment on published drafts are not organized around the interests of particular litigants and are themselves primarily interested in helping the rules committees pursue their aim of just, speedy, efficient determination of every case. . . .

The troublesome aspect of this process thus lies not in the flow of information from factions to the rulemakers, but in their relation to Congress. . . . If Congress is responsive . . . to every faction in the United States that detects a possible stake in a proposed amendment to the rules, the rulemaking tradition is doomed to disintegrate. Professor Mullenix suggests that by engaging in dialogue with all manner of factions and by giving them ample time to organize we may be in effect preparing those who are disappointed for a climb up Capitol Hill. . . .

If Mullenix is right, and she may well prove to be, then there is clearly needed at this time an organizational structure lending political support to the rulemaking process. Because the Rules Enabling Act requires affirmative steps by Congress to derail an amendment, the rulemaking process can be shielded from factional politics, provided that there are people and groups willing to stand up for it.

The one organization having the political clout to protect rulemaking from factional politics is the organization that called rulemaking into existence in 1934, the American Bar Association. . . .

NOTES

Be aware that, in addition to the rules promulgated by the highest court of any system, intermediate appellate courts and trial courts may be authorized to formally prescribe rules that govern within their respective jurisdictions. These rules can be lengthy and highly detailed. It is important to familiarize yourself with the local rules that govern in the particular courts where you will be practicing.

B. Supervisory Authority

In reviewing trial court actions, appellate courts apply law derived from constitutions, statutes, written rules of procedure, and controlling judicial precedents. A doctrine or rule from any of those sources can be the basis for reversal of the judgment under review. Beyond the reversing power stemming from those sources, however, is there some residual supervisory power under which an appellate court may reverse or otherwise control a trial court? Such a power often has been claimed by both state and federal courts. To the extent that there is some legitimate authority of that sort, it would appear to derive from inherent judicial authority over subordinate tribunals, in the service of the fair and effective administration of justice. But how far can such authority extend beyond that provided by the sources mentioned above?

The author of the following article, from which only a few excerpts appear here, undertakes to examine the exercise of this power in one court, the U.S. Court of Appeals for the Third Circuit. It is likely, however, that the questions and tensions encountered there exist in varying degrees in many state and federal appellate courts.

In considering supervisory authority, bear in mind that it, like all appellate authority, is not a self-starting power. It must be invoked through the initiative of one of the litigants through appropriate appellate procedure, by either appeal or petition for an extraordinary writ.

Murray M. Schwartz, *The Exercise Of Supervisory Power By The Third Circuit Court Of Appeals*, 27 VILLANOVA LAW REVIEW 506, 506-25 (1982)[17]

I. Introduction

During the last decade, the United States Court of Appeals for the Third Circuit . . . has dramatically expanded its use of supervisory power as a basis for decision. Courts in general have employed supervisory power in a broad range of cases. For example, the Supreme Court has used its supervisory power over lower federal courts to further the "fair administration of justice" by excluding various types of tainted evidence, establishing rules for the composition of federal juries, and overseeing activity of the executive branch. In the Third Circuit, supervisory power has been asserted, if not always exercised, in a wide variety of contexts in both the civil and criminal areas. The nature of supervisory power is amorphous and its doctrinal limitations are ill-defined. . . .

Defining supervisory power presents an initial problem. The Supreme Court generally refers to its "power of supervision over the administration of justice in the federal courts." This power has included such elements as "the formulation and application of proper standards for the enforcement of federal criminal law," including the "duty of establishing and maintaining standards of procedure and evidence;" the power to police and make certain that the Federal Rules of Criminal Procedure are honored by federal law enforcement agencies; the power under which evidentiary rules may be devised "governed by 'principles of the common law as they may be interpreted . . . in the light of reason and experience;'" the power to insure that "the waters of justice are not

---

17 Copyright © 1982 by the Villanova Law Review. Reprinted with permission.

polluted;" and, finally, the power to further the " 'two fold' purpose of deterring illegality and protecting judicial integrity." These phrases indicate the broad nature of the doctrine at the Supreme Court level.

This breadth is equally apparent at the intermediate appellate level. Occasionally, members of the Third Circuit have articulated their understanding of supervisory power. One member of the court has simply stated:

> Deciding a case in the exercise of a court's supervisory power means little more than ruling on a basis not specifically set forth in the Constitution, or by statute, procedural rule, or precedent. Although generally associated with the imposition of procedural safeguards for proper judicial administration, exercise of the supervisory power of the Supreme Court or the Court of Appeals is but a legitimate function of a court's law-making role. [*In re Grand Jury Proceedings* (*Schofield II*), 507 F.2d 963, 970 (3rd Cir. [1975]) (Aldisert, J., dissenting).]

Another judge has described his perception of supervisory power as enabling appellate courts to impose policy judgments on the lower federal courts, stating that "[a]ppellate courts, it appears, exercise their supervisory power over lower courts to impose procedural requirements that seem wise, but that are not compelled by the Constitution or statute." In fact, the court itself has cited with approval a statement by the Supreme Court asserting that "[o]ver federal proceedings we may exert a supervisory power with greater freedom to reflect our notions of good policy than we may constitutionally exert over proceedings in state courts." These statements indicate an expansive reading of supervisory power by members of the Third Circuit. It appears that supervisory power embraces any decision not based on the Constitution, statutes, procedural rules, or precedent, including decisions based on policy grounds. . . .

A brief examination of the Third Circuit cases involving supervisory power reveals the virtually unlimited scope of the doctrine. . . . Among the procedural matters affected by its exercise of supervisory power are the litany required under Rule 11, conditional plea agreements, enforcement of grand jury subpoenas, and other grand jury procedures, and enforcement of Internal Revenue Service summonses. Other directives have addressed the procedure to be employed in asking voir dire questions when there is a possibility of prejudicial pretrial publicity, the requirement of notice by the government of prior identification procedures, and the procedure to be followed in issuing gag orders. Third Circuit supervision of criminal justice has not been confined to matters of procedure. The court has used supervisory power to require certain jury instructions with prospective application only, as well as other substantive matters.

The Third Circuit has employed supervisory power in civil cases as well. Unlike criminal cases, where supervisory power is most frequently used to develop prospective rules, supervisory power holdings in the civil context are generally case-specific. There is a further difference between civil and criminal cases. In civil cases, with few exceptions, the court either openly acknowledges that it relies on supervisory power, or a dissenting opinion is quick to point out that fact. . . .

An examination of the cases in light of this analysis will demonstrate that the exercise of supervisory power by the Third Circuit often lacks a principled basis.

As to one area of frequent exercise, the establishment of procedural rules, . . . it is possible to classify such exercise into three categories and propose an analytic framework for determining the validity of exercise within each category. The first category encompasses situations in which Congress has developed a specific process for rulemaking, and that process has resulted in a formal rule. In these situations, any exercise of supervisory power by a court of appeals to establish contrary procedural rules is illegitimate. The second category contains instances in which a rulemaking mechanism has been created and a rule promulgated, but there is a perceived need to supplement the rule. Such supplementation, which goes beyond filling interstitial gaps through judicial construction, even if desirable, is illegitimate. The third category is comprised of situations in which there is a rulemaking mechanism in place, but no rule has been promulgated. In such cases, the courts of appeals must exercise supervisory power to fill the void created by the default. If such exercises are within the traditional competence of the courts or essential to the discharge of the appellate function, then the courts may exercise supervisory power. . . .

II.   Sources of Supervisory Power

. . . .

A.   *The Constitution as a Source of Supervisory Power*

The Constitution provides little support for the exercise of supervisory power by the courts of appeals. Article III does not itself create lower federal courts; it merely vests federal judicial power "in such inferior Courts as the Congress may from time to time ordain and establish." . . . It might be argued that[,] although Congress need not establish lower federal courts, once they are created under article III those courts have all the inherent powers that courts have historically possessed in Anglo-American jurisprudence. However, this argument does not advance the inquiry, for nowhere in the Constitution are these inherent powers defined. Moreover, beginning with the Process Act in 1789, Congress has explicitly governed matters traditionally regarded as being within the competence of the courts, in particular the procedures by which cases in law and equity should be tried. Thus, the mere assertion that a court created under article III has certain inherent powers cannot rise to the level of a constitutional justification for an exercise of supervisory power by a court of appeals.

B.   *Statutory Enactments as a Source of Supervisory Power*

Statutes as a source of supervisory power must be approached more cautiously. . . . A substantive statute placing some element of supervision in a federal court cannot be the source of supervisory power, because by definition the exercise of power under statute is not a use of supervisory power. . . .

1. *The Court of Appeals Act*

The Third Circuit has never attempted to justify its exercises of supervisory power on statutory grounds. Nevertheless, if supervisory power can be attributable to statute at all, it must stem from legislation establishing the intermediate appellate court system, and the function assigned to that system by Congress. Congress established the courts of appeals in 1891. . . .

Those exercises of supervisory power which aid a court of appeals in carrying out its traditional functions can be legitimized by reference to the Court of Appeals Act. In addition, exercises of supervisory power which further such traditional judicial functions as the regulation and improvement of the quality of the judicial process are within the courts' traditional sphere of competence, and can therefore be legitimized by reference to the congressional intent underlying the creation of the intermediate appellate courts. . . . By providing that the courts of appeal should be "courts of record," Congress bestowed a certain amount of that amorphous baggage known as the inherent power of the courts upon the new appellate courts. Supervisory power grounded in such an elusive, ill-defined concept is a fragile creature at best. It must give way to congressional act, court rule, and all other doctrinal limitations and principles which, in the ordinary course of events, would obviate the power. . . .

At times, however, the Third Circuit has strayed from its designated role and exercised its supervisory power in such a manner as to usurp functions of the district courts. Perhaps the most striking example of such an improper exercise is *Hoots v. Pennsylvania* [639 F.2d 972 (3rd Cir. 1981)]. In *Hoots*, the Third Circuit[,] impatient with the vagaries of litigation which had held up resolution of the remedial phase of a complex school desegregation case, ordered the district judge to complete all hearings and proceedings on the merits and issue a desegregation decree within ninety days. The decision is especially noteworthy because formulation of a desegregation decree is a discretionary function placed in the first instance in the district court. The dissent sharply questioned whether an appellate court had the power to enter such an order and noted the enormous difficulties created by the Third Circuit's action:

> [W]e have neither the right nor any power to order [a district judge] to complete his processing of this case within a time limit of 90 days. If there is such a right or power, I do not know from whence it stems, and absent such a power, there is no reason for a federal judge to give heed to our mandate.

> [If] he cannot, or does not, do we hold him in contempt? Do we subject him to some form of disciplinary proceeding? Do we remove his caseload? Do we hold a hearing and ask him to show cause why he has violated the 90 day mandate? What action can we take?

Although *Hoots* is by far the most dramatic example of a Third Circuit exercise of supervisory power in excess of its function, it is not a lone aberration. On three other occasions the court asserted its authority to remove district judges from further participation in particular cases. . . .

2. The "Trickle-Up" Theory

Although the Third Circuit has not attempted to justify its exercise of supervisory power by relying upon the statutory enactment which created the courts of appeals, it has occasionally pointed to a different statutory basis to support certain exercises of supervisory power. At times, the Third Circuit has asserted that statutory grants of power to district courts carry with them a related supervisory power vested in the courts of appeals. This "trickle-up" theory for the exercise of supervisory power was relied on in *In re Grand Jury Proceedings (Schofield I)* [486 F.2d 85 (3rd Cir. 1977)] where, in establishing flexible procedural requirements for contesting enforcement of a grand jury subpoena, the court stated that "[W]e impose this requirement both pursuant to the federal courts' supervisory power over grand juries and pursuant to our supervisory power over civil proceedings brought in the district court pursuant to 28 U.S.C. § 1826(a)." The court dispelled any latent ambiguity as to the source of the power relied upon when it later repeated and amplified its prior position in affirming a finding of contempt:

> Our supervisory power over grand juries is derived from several sources. Under 18 U.S.C. § 3331 and FED. R. CRIM. P. 6(a) *a district court* is given power to call a grand jury into existence; under FED. R. CRIM. P. 17(a), and 28 U.S.C. § 1826(a) respectively, *the district court* is given the power to issue and the duty to enforce grand jury subpoenas.

> But under our supervisory power over the grand jury and over the district court's enforcement of subpoenas, . . . we feel empowered to specify the particular way in which relevancy and proper purpose of a grand jury investigation shall be shown in this Circuit.

The Third Circuit thus transformed statutory and rule power vested in the district court into supervisory power at the appellate level. Inasmuch as these cases involve powers specifically allocated by Congress to the district courts, not the courts of appeals, the function of the appellate courts should be limited to a determination of whether the district court committed error. . . .

C.   *Supervisory Court Pronouncements as a Source of Supervisory Power*

The Supreme Court provides an additional potential source of intermediate appellate court supervisory power. The Supreme Court may be a source for this power either through a "trickle-down" theory, or by express statement. The "trickle-down" theory provides that if the Supreme Court has supervisory power over all lower federal courts, then the courts of appeals have supervisory power over the district courts. Although the Third Circuit has never expressly articulated this theory, on occasion it has cited cases in which the Supreme Court relied on its supervisory power to support its own assertions of supervisory power. However, the mere fact that the Supreme Court exercises supervisory power . . . over the federal court system as a whole cannot in and of itself justify even the more limited exercises by an intermediate appellate court. Moreover, given the structure of the federal court system, it is by no means self-evident that the existence of such a power in the Supreme Court, which is capable of imposing uniform, system wide standards, implies the existence of analogous powers in regional intermediate appellate courts. . . .

Unfortunately, although Supreme Court statements may establish the existence of intermediate appellate court supervisory power, they do not advance the inquiry as to whether any particular exercise of supervisory power is legitimate. This difficulty is compounded by the fact that the Supreme Court has never explained the basis for its assertion that the courts of appeals have supervisory power. The most recent Supreme Court case simply assumes the existence of supervisory power in the intermediate courts of appeal, and addresses instead the issue of whether the power was properly exercised.

NOTES

1. For other writings on the supervisory power of other appellate courts, see Bennett L. Gershman, *Supervisory Power of the New York Courts*, 14 PACE L. REV. 41 (1994); Gary E. O'Connor, *Rule(make)r and Judge: Minnesota Courts and the Supervisory Power*, 23 WM. MITCHELL L. REV. 605 (1997); and James E. Pfander, Marbury, *Original Jurisdiction, and the Supreme Court's Supervisory Powers*, 101 COLUM. L. REV. 1515 (2001).

2. Courts and commentators vary in how they define supervisory power, and even as to whether there properly is such power. One commentator has written:

> Supervisory power as such does not exist. The supervisory power label has been used to describe the exercise of several different forms of judicial power. Use of the term supervisory power has diverted attention from the nature, source, and limits of the authority being exercised in each case. . . . [I]t seems plain that the term supervisory power should be abandoned.

Sara Sun Beale, *Reconsidering Supervisory Power in Criminal Cases: Constitutional and Statutory Limits on the Authority of the Federal Courts*, 84 COLUM L. REV. 1433, 1520 (1984). While you would need greater familiarity with the specifics of the supervisory powers that have been upheld to enable you to judge whether these claims to power have been used for ill or good, do you think it appropriate for courts to exercise powers whose source and scope are so amorphous? Do reasons that justify the exercise of supervisory powers by the highest court of a system also justify the exercise of such powers by intermediate appellate courts?

3. Not all supervisory powers are rootless. A definition of supervisory power as a decision not based on a constitution, statutes, procedural rules or precedent (as Schwartz posited in the excerpt above) is inaccurate in the many states whose constitutions, statutes, or common law confer supervisory power. *See, e.g.*, COLO. CONST. art. VI, § 2(1) ("[The supreme court] shall have a general superintending control over all inferior courts. . . ."); IOWA CONST. art. V, § 4 "[The supreme court] shall exercise a supervisory and administrative control over all inferior judicial tribunals throughout the state."); OKLA. CONST. art. VII, § 4 ("The original jurisdiction of the Supreme Court shall extend to a general superintending control over all inferior courts. . . ."); PA. CONST. art. V, § 10(a) ("The Supreme Court shall exercise general supervisory and administrative authority over all the courts and justices of the peace. . . .");

WIS. CONST. art. VII, § 3(1) ("The supreme court shall have superintending and administrative authority over all courts."). Relevant state statutes include: HAW. REV. STAT. § 602-4 (1995) ("The supreme court shall have the general superintendence of all courts of inferior jurisdiction to prevent and correct errors and abuses therein where no other remedy is expressly provided by law."); MASS. GEN. LAWS ANN. ch. 211, § 3 (West 1988) ("The supreme judicial court shall have general superintendence of all courts of inferior jurisdiction to correct and prevent errors and abuses therein if no other remedy is expressly provided . . . ."); N.H. REV. STAT. ANN. § 490:4 (1983) ("The supreme court shall have general superintendence of all courts of inferior jurisdiction to prevent and correct errors and abuses . . . ."). Gary E. O'Connor, *Rule(make)r and Judge*, 23 WM. MITCHELL L. REV. at 617 n.62, 618 n.67. In these instances, the legitimacy of supervisory powers is clear, even if their scope remains ambiguous.

Iowa State Judicial Building, the newest state judicial building in the nation, completed 2003, houses the Supreme Court of Iowa, the Court of Appeals, and the State Court Administrator's Offices.

The Courtroom of the Supreme Court of Alabama, constructed 1987, is one of the newest and most distinctive state COLR courtrooms. A rotunda, encircled by 12 pairs of columns, replicating the limestone colums on the front of the bulding is surmounted by a 50-foot high skylighted dome, modeled after the Rotunda at the University of Virginia. The 40-foot long mahogany bench follows the contour of the wall.

Chapter 5

THE CRISIS OF VOLUME: PERCEIVED THREATS FROM DOCKET GROWTH

In Chapter 1, we took a preliminary look at the substantial increases in the quantity of appeals occurring in the United States between the 1960s and the 1990s. In this Chapter we examine this phenomenon of docket growth in greater detail. This subject deserves careful consideration because it underlies much of the remainder of the course. The "crisis of volume," as it is often called, already has worked major changes in both state and federal appellate courts. It is in this high-volume setting that appellate judges and lawyers must perform today. Thus, a study of appellate institutions apart from the problems of volume would be unrealistic and incomplete. Indeed, much of what currently goes on in appellate courts — contemporary norms of procedure and function — can be understood only in context as responses to the dramatic growth in the number of appeals. The Chapters following this one will address responses to this growth — responses in terms of structure, personnel, and process that already have been implemented, as well as proposals for further study and possible implementation in the future. As we begin, consider these big-picture themes:

- What is the magnitude of the appellate volume problem?

- What are the causes of the dramatic increases in appellate volume?

- How does the growth in volume impact the court system and threaten the process imperatives and systemic imperatives set out in Chapter 1?

Although litigation has increased at both trial and appellate levels, one curious aspect of this growth in volume is that the growth at the appellate level has been disproportionately greater than at the trial level. Over the last five decades, the rate of federal appeals increased five-fold, from 1 appeal out of every 40 district court terminations to 1 out of 8. The graph below illustrates this multiplier phenomenon in the federal courts.[1]

As you read the materials that follow in this Chapter, consider the important questions that are raised by these various reports of court statistics, caseload increases, and docket trends. For example, what possible explanations are there for the disproportionately higher rate of growth in the number of appeals compared with the growth in trial dockets? In reviewing the statistical data, note that there are several ways in which appellate growth can be measured: (a) overall, in number or percentage; (b) in relation to growth in other areas, such as population, trial court business, and judgeships;

---

[1] Copyright ©1990 by Cornell University. Used by permission of the publisher, Cornell University Press.

(c) in terms of appeals per judgeship. Consider which of these is most significant as a measure of appellate workload. Do we know enough about the causes and effects of appellate docket growth to craft policies and procedures to reduce the number of appeals or to lower the overall rate of appeals? Would lowering the overall rate of appeals or lowering the number of appeals of particular kinds of cases be legitimate public policy goals? Are there techniques to rid the system of "frivolous" or "unimportant" appeals? Or must we limit our responses only to developing procedures and structures for accommodating ever-increasing numbers of appeals? If so, what would those limited responses be? Are there limits on the number of judges or the size of appellate courts beyond which the system suffers diseconomies of scale?

Always keep in mind the appellate process imperatives, *i.e.*, the reasons we allow appeals in the first place and the traditional appellate procedures courts have used to hear and decide appeals. Do the requirements of constitutional due process or the statutory right to an appeal or just plain common sense suggest any limitations on procedural innovations that apportion less and less appellate judicial resources among more and more appeals? This Chapter describes the threat to the appellate courts posed by the crisis of volume. Succeeding Chapters will examine in more detail how the appellate courts have tried to cope with the dramatic increases in their dockets and how well the appellate courts have managed the threat. Again, be mindful of the "big picture" — how and why have appellate dockets increased so dramatically and how should the appellate courts respond? This Chapter is about understanding the perceived threats from docket growth.

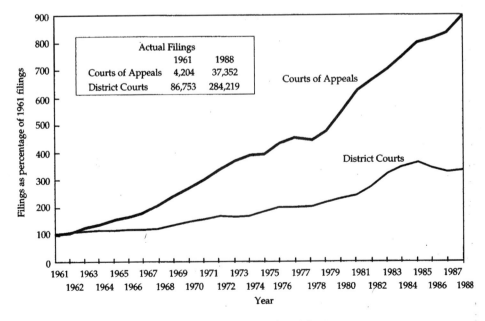

Figure 1.1. Caseload relative to 1961, courts of appeals and district courts
Source: Annual Reports, Director of the Administrative Office of the United States Courts.

Thomas B. Marvell, *Is There an Appeal From the Caseload Deluge?*, 24 JUDGES' J. 34 (1985)[2]

In recent years both civil and criminal appeals have increased rapidly — much faster than trial court caseloads, the number of judgeships, or any other factor one might associate with appellate volume. This article summarizes the results of a research project that explored the extent and causes of appellate caseload growth. . . . [I]t examines the factors that might be expected to affect the burgeoning number of appeals. Does appellate volume vary with trial court volume or with the number of trial judges? Do criminal appeals increase when crime rates or prison commitments increase? Do appeals increase when a new intermediate court is created or when the jurisdiction of an existing one is expanded? Does eliminating the requirement for printed briefs or records lead to more appeals? Do appellate settlement conferences attract more appeals? The answers to these and similar questions should help appellate judges predict whether, and roughly by how much, their caseloads will increase when changes are made in the courts.

Historical Trends: Long-term appellate caseload statistics, compiled from widely scattered reports and articles, show a clear nationwide pattern. Appellate caseloads grew during the 19th and early 20th centuries, reaching a high plateau in the 1920s. In the 1930s and 1940s appeals plummeted, dropping by 50 to 75 percent, even in fast-growing states like California. The nadir was reached just after World War II, with caseloads rising gradually for two decades thereafter. In the mid-1960s they began to skyrocket. First, criminal appeals shot up following the expansion of criminal procedural rights, especially a 1963 ruling [*Douglas v. California*, 372 U.S. 353 (1963)] that indigent defendants must be provided counsel on appeal. Within a few years civil appeals also shot up, although no causes can be singled out for this increase. This rapid caseload growth has continued unabated to the present day. . . .

Recent Appellate Filing Statistics: . . . Statistics for total appeals between 1973 and 1983, obtained for 43 states, show that the number of appeals increased by 112 percent (*see* Table 1). The number of criminal and civil appeals in the states with available statistics increased by similar amounts. Criminal appeals nationwide remained at about 45 percent of the total appellate volume throughout the decade, although the portion changed greatly in individual states.

Table 1. Increase in Appeals and Associated Factors, 1973-83

Total Appeals (43 states, including D.C.)	112%
Population	11%
Real Personal Income	16%
Appellate Judgeships	36%
Trial Judgeships	24%
Criminal Appeals (38 states)	107%
Criminal trial filings (28 states)	52%
FBI Crime Index	39%
Prison commitments (except D.C.)	113%
Civil Appeals (38 states)	114%
Civil trial filings (33 states)	43%

2 Copyright ©1985 American Bar Association. Reprinted with permission.

The appeals counted here are initial appeals of right from trial courts or administrative agencies. . . . Table 1 compares the growth of appeals to the growth of comparable social trends in states with appellate data. The appellate growth rate is more than 10 times that of the population, seven times that of real personal income, and three times that of appellate court judgeships. The average number of appeals per judgeship grew from 85 to 133 between 1973 and 1983. Criminal appeals grew faster than the FBI Crime Index but not quite as fast as prison commitments, which increased greatly in the past five years.

Table 2. Ten Year Appeals Growth, 1973-83

Alabama	156%	Missouri	97%
Alaska	305%	Montana	187%
Arizona	145%	Nebraska	68%
California	89%	Nevada	159%
Colorado	108%	New Hampshire	144%
Connecticut	265%	New Jersey	62%
Delaware	67%	New Mexico	86%
Dist. of Col.	57%	New York	87%
Florida	186%	Ohio	95%
Hawaii	201%	Oklahoma	85%
Idaho	72%	Oregon	212%
Illinois	129%	Pennsylvania	94%
Iowa	68%	Rhode Island	110%
Kansas	108%	South Dakota	156%
Kentucky	186%	Tennessee	62%
Louisiana	139%	Texas	140%
Maine	161%	Utah	116%
Maryland	53%	Vermont	137%
Massachusetts	154%	Virginia	60%
Michigan	167%	Washington	96%
Minnesota	172%	Wyoming	103%
Mississippi	38%		

Comparisons with trial court caseloads are more difficult because statistics are less often available and are less accurate. Civil trial filing statistics since 1973 were obtained in 33 of the 43 states with appellate data; these filings increased by 43 percent during the decade, less than half the growth rate for civil appeals. Criminal trial court filings, which are limited to felonies (and some misdemeanors in several states), grew 52 percent, again less than half as much as appeals.

One would expect appeals to be associated primarily with the number of cases decided by the trial courts, for with few exceptions only these cases can be appealed. Unfortunately, there is no adequate measure of trial court decisions. The only statistic available is the number of trials, which have increased much more slowly than trial court filings and show very little relationship to appellate volume. But no conclusions can be drawn because there are widespread problems with trial statistics, which often reflect disparate judgments by numerous local court officials as to what constitutes a trial.

The growth rate for appeals differs greatly from state to state, as can be seen in Table 2, which gives the ten-year growth for states with available statistics. Appellate caseloads also grew exceptionally fast in Alaska, Connecticut, Florida, Hawaii, Michigan, Montana, and Oregon.

Factors Behind Growth in Appeals: Although appeals have grown faster than most other factors listed in Table 1, those factors account for much of the appellate growth because they work together to push appellate volume upward. . . . In the analysis of criminal appeals, the crime rate and the number of general jurisdiction trial court judgeships stand out as particularly significant variables (*see* Table 3). Crime provides the raw material for proceedings that become appeals. The number of trial judgeships is important because more judges decide more cases, which then can be appealed. Interestingly, trial court filings are very slightly associated with criminal appellate volume.

Prison commitments (the number of defendants sent to prison for more than one year) are moderately related to appeals. A stronger relationship might be expected because a prison sentence provides more incentive to appeal than probation or a jail sentence. The great majority of prison commitments, however, follow guilty pleas, which are seldom appealed in most states.

On the civil side, three dominant background factors are economic conditions, trial court filings, and the number of trial court judgeships (*see* Table 4). There is no obvious reason for the much greater association between trial and appellate filings in civil cases than in criminal cases. Economic conditions have a tremendous impact on civil case filings at both the trial and appellate level. Trial filings tend to rise about two years after the economy improves and appeals about three or four years after an economic upswing.

Table 3. Factors Affecting Criminal Appeals

	Elasticity[a]
FBI Crime index (prior year)	.62
Number of Trial Judgeships	.78
Prison Commitments	.16

Other factors explored, but showing little or no impact:[b]
    Creation or expansion of an intermediate court
    Amount of backlog
    Trial court criminal filings
    New appellate rules
    New criminal code
    New criminal rules of procedure
    Record condensing — original papers or narrative
    Record duplication — whether printing is required
    Brief duplication — whether printing is required

[a]The elasticity roughly estimates the percent change in appeals filed that would result from a 1 percent change in the factor.
[b]These variables are not significant at the .05 level.

Court Features That Affect Appellate Volume: What happens to appellate volume when changes are made in appellate court procedures or structure? Their effects are measured by comparing caseloads within states before and after a particular change was made, while adjusting for the other factors discussed here.

Intermediate courts. Earlier research suggested that intermediate courts attract more appeals. The findings here, however, are that intermediate courts have little or no impact on the volume of filings. The use of intermediate courts is measured by the percentage of filings that go to those courts; this takes into consideration the great variety of dual appellate systems. After taking into account other changes — appellate jurisdiction, for example, is often expanded when intermediate courts are created — neither the creation nor expansion of intermediate courts was found to lead to more than a slight increase in filings.

Backlog. Whether delay affects appellate volume is the topic of many conflicting arguments. Delay might reduce criminal appeals because, for example, a defendant in prison with a two-year sentence gains little by appealing to a court with a two-year backlog. On the other hand, defendants on bail might wish to delay their prison commitment, but there are few defendants on bail pending appeal in most states. In civil cases, long delays may lead some defendants to appeal so they can delay payment of judgments; but other litigants may decide not to appeal because relief would take too long.

Table 4. Factors Affecting Civil Appeals

	Elasticity[a]
Economic conditions (real personal income, three and four years earlier)	.85
Trial court filings (one and two years earlier)	.53
Trial judgeships	.38
Amount of backlog	.06
Prehearing settlement conference (when used, appeals increase by roughly 29 per million population)	
Record duplication (when printing is required, appeals decrease by roughly 15 per million population)	

Other variables explored, but showing little or no impact:[b]
Creation or expansion of an intermediate court
New appellate rules
New civil rules of procedure
Record condensing — original papers or narrative
Brief duplication — whether printing is required
Difference between interest rates on judgments and money market rates

[a] The elasticity roughly estimates the percent change in appeals filed that would result from a 1 percent change in the factor. The elasticity for economic conditions and trial court filings is the sum of the elasticities for two years, which have roughly equal values.
[b] These variables are not significant at the .05 level.

Delay is measured by a "backlog index," which is the number of cases pending divided by the number of dispositions that year. This index estimates the length of time, in years, required to dispose of pending cases at the current disposition rate. The research found that there are a few more appeals, especially civil appeals, when delay is greater, but the impact is almost negligible. The various ways delay affects incentives to appeal seem to cancel each other out.

New rules and criminal codes. The research explored the impact of new trial court rules and new criminal codes. One might expect these to create interpretation problems and, thus, more issues to appeal. But there was no evidence of this in the research.

Appellate briefs and records. Appellate courts have been modernizing procedures by eliminating requirements for printed briefs, printed records, and narrative transcripts. One might speculate that these changes attract appeals by making them less expensive and time consuming. Our analysis, however, showed that this had little impact on the volume of civil or criminal appeals. Appeals did increase slightly when printed records were no longer necessary, but the impact was very slight.

Interest differential. A civil defendant who loses at trial can delay paying the adverse judgment by appealing. The interest paid on the judgment pending appeal is sometimes less and sometimes more than prevailing interest rates. When less, there is more economic incentive to appeal. Nevertheless, the research found virtually no relationship between the volume of civil appeals and the gap between the statutory interest rates and rates for three-month treasury bills.

Appellate court prehearing settlement conferences. Many of the courts studied have initiated conferences to persuade attorneys to settle cases. Some commentators claim that any settlements resulting from the conferences are outnumbered by new appeals from parties seeking to take advantage of the settlement opportunities. The research supports this contention: civil appeals increased moderately when settlement conferences were used.

Policy Consequences: These findings cannot provide exact forecasts of overall appellate volume, but they can help predict the impact of specific changes by analyzing which changes may be related to increased, reduced, or not appreciably affected appellate volumes. One clear conclusion is that more trial judges lead to more appeals. In fact, using the elasticity ratios in Tables 3 and 4, it can be predicted that a 10 percent increase in trial judgeships will lead to 4 to 12 percent more criminal appeals and 1 to 7 percent more civil appeals than would otherwise be filed.

In a similar manner, one can estimate that a 10 percent increase in a state's FBI Crime Index will mean roughly 8 percent more criminal appeals the following year. Ten percent more trial court civil filings in each of two years will probably translate to roughly 5 percent more civil appeals, while a similar change in real personal income will mean roughly 8 percent more appeals four years later. Finally, the analysis shows that settlement conferences in civil cases attract roughly 30 civil appeals per million population, which is almost a 10 percent increase in the average state.

It is also important to know that some changes have little impact on appellate volume. This is true of most of the factors studied, including creation or expansion of intermediate courts, the amount of backlog, modernization of appellate procedure, and increased interest rate on appeal. Judges and legislatures can make changes in these areas without fear that they will noticeably affect appellate volume.

Steven E. Hairston, Robert A. Hanson & Brian J. Ostrom, *The Work of State Appellate Courts — Where are the nation's state appellate courts headed? How consistent are the national patterns? And where does each state fit into that broad pattern?*, 17 STATE COURT J. 18 (1993)[3]

. . . Appellate court caseload statistics are important because the nature of appellate review is influenced by the volume of cases filed each year. In courts with rising caseload but no accompanying increase in the size of the judiciary or court staff, more cases mean less time for appellate judges to review the record, read the briefs, hear oral arguments, discuss the case, and prepare an order or opinion to resolve the case. The increased demands on judges and court staff prompt courts to seek new ways to handle cases more efficiently and productively. As caseload volume grows, however, many argue that the only way to maintain both quality and productivity is to increase the number of judges. If judges are not added, the argument goes, either quality is diminished or productivity drops and a backlog begins. Thus, appellate court caseloads and resources have a direct bearing on the courts' institutional responsibilities to correct lower court errors, ensure uniformity in the application of the laws, protect the constitutional rights of litigants, and clarify the meaning of laws. . . .

At the federal level, it has been asserted that a "crisis of volume" afflicts the U.S. Courts of Appeals. . . . At the State level, observers note a similar crisis, since "state appellate court caseloads have on average, doubled every ten years since the Second World War." Such long-term growth emerges from what may appear to be relatively modest year-to-year growth: an average annual increase of 7 percent will double the caseload volume in 10 years, an average growth rate of 5 percent will increase total volume by two-thirds, in 10 years, and an average growth rate of 3 percent will, over 10 years, cause caseload volume to rise by 34 percent. Moreover, appellate courts are not merely confronting more of the same: rather, "as the number of cases has grown, so has the range of complexity. Increasing number of complex cases, especially death penalty litigation, require substantial expenditure of judicial time." Volume and complexity combined to bring an intermediate appellate court to many states during the 1970s and to make the 1980s a period of significant institutional innovation, notably through streamlined appellate procedures, settlement conferences, and alternatives to full appellate review. . . .

The data . . . suggest that state courts of last resort and intermediate appellate courts operate under conditions of increasing caseload volume. Although

---

[3] Copyright ©1993 National Center for State Courts, Williamsburg, Virginia. Reprinted with permission.

only certain state[s] . . . continue to experience the rapid growth found in earlier decades, increases in caseload remain substantial. . . .

The consequences of these increases over time is that appellate courts are not able to keep up. Most simply do not dispose of as many appeals as are filed, as is clearly reflected in the number of courts with three-year clearance rates below 100 percent. The concern is most pronounced for the categories of cases that make up the bulk of the work load handled at each appellate level: Nearly three-quarters of the intermediate appellate courts had three-year clearance rates less than 100 percent for mandatory appeals and less than one-third of the courts of last resort had three-year clearance rates for discretionary petitions of more than 100 percent.

Therefore, the appellate courts are having only limited success in meeting the demands placed on them. Caseload pressures continue to confront state appellate courts and many are having difficulty keeping up with the demand.

Examining the Work of State Courts, 2003: A National Perspective from the Court Statistics Project 64-66 (National Center for State Courts 2004)[4]

Total appellate court caseloads include original proceedings and appeals over which the appellate courts have mandatory or discretionary jurisdiction. This trend shows annual filing data for state appellate courts for the last 10 years. Between 1993 and 1998 the number of appellate court filings increased 17 percent, from 254,000 to 297,000. Over the next five years, filings declined 6 percent to 278,000.

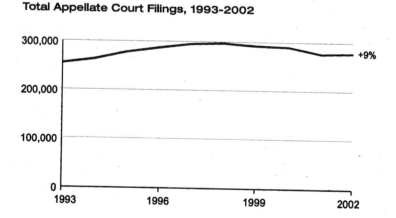

Total Appellate Court Filings, 1993-2002

---

[4] Copyright © 2004 National Center for State Courts, Williamsburg, Virginia. Reprinted with permission.

[Today, most states have divided their appellate systems into two levels: intermediate appellate courts (IACs) as a first level of review, and courts of last resort (COLRs) to handle the most important cases and appeals from the IACs. Caseload increases in the 1980s led to a proliferation of IACs. Only 10 states — all of them among the 14 states with the smallest populations — function without at least one IAC and a few large states — Oklahoma and Texas — have created more than one COLR.] Intermediate appellate courts provide first level review, while courts of last resort are the final arbiters of disputes. This structure results in intermediate appellate courts handling the majority of appeals. Where there is no intermediate appellate court, a state supreme court conducts first and final appellate review. The caseloads in IACs and COLRs are reported here as filings of mandatory appeals and discretionary petitions. Mandatory appeals in IACs outnumbered those in COLRs by a margin of 6 to 1. Conversely, there are more than two discretionary petitions filed in COLRs for every one filed in IACs.

Total Mandatory and Discretionary Caseloads in COLRs and IACs, 2002

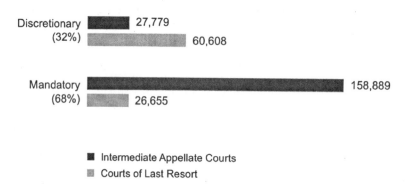

States in this table are divided into those with and without an intermediate appellate court and then ranked according to their number of appeals per 100,000 population. Caseloads are shown as percentages composed of mandatory appeals and discretionary petitions. When adjusted for population, Louisiana (population rank 24) reported the highest number of appeals (283 per 100,000 population) and North Carolina (population rank 11) reported the lowest (38 per 100,000 population).

Proportions of mandatory and discretionary caseloads vary dramatically, but several states show 100 percent mandatory or discretionary jurisdiction. These proportions were based upon the number of cases reported in each category rather than actual mandated jurisdiction. Hence, a 100 percent designation in one category could simply mean that there were no cases filed in the other category in 2002.

Total Appellate Caseloads by State, 2002

State	Appeals per 100,000 Pop.	Total Appeals	Mandatory Appeals	Discretionary Petitions	Pop. Rank
With Intermediate Appellate Court:					
Louisiana	283	12,706	29%	71%	24
Alabama	141	6,325	82	18	23
Florida	140	23,379	83	17	4
Puerto Rico	132	5,079	33	67	27
Pennsylvania	131	16,178	83	17	6
New Jersey	123	10,546	72	28	9
Oregon	120	4,213	83	17	28
Alaska	114	736	74	26	48
Ohio	113	12,952	88	12	7
Nebraska	106	1,830	82	18	39
Texas	103	22,413	86	14	2
Kansas	99	2,678	67	33	33
Illinois	95	11,985	78	22	5
Michigan	94	9,429	44	56	8
Washington	94	5,692	70	30	15
Idaho	93	1,248	85	15	40
Kentucky	92	3,783	78	22	26
Hawaii	92	1,146	94	6	43
Arizona	91	4,951	76	24	19
Colorado	90	4,041	69	31	22
California	89	31,296	45	55	1
Virginia	88	6,440	11	89	12
New York	86	16,386	76	24	3
Arkansas	83	2,256	74	26	34
Wisconsin	83	4,522	75	25	20
Missouri	80	4,519	86	14	17
New Mexico	78	1,440	58	42	37
Iowa	73	2,137	100	0	31
South Carolina	70	2,856	59	41	25
Tennessee	65	3,784	61	39	16
Maryland	63	3,453	63	37	18
Georgia	60	5,132	68	32	10
Minnesota	59	2,942	74	26	21
Massachusetts	57	3,694	60	40	13
Utah	55	1,264	100	0	35
Indiana	52	3,185	77	23	14
Connecticut	49	1,693	71	29	30
Mississippi	49	1,401	78	22	32
North Carolina	38	3,157	55	45	11
Without an Intermediate Appellate Court:					
D.C.	266	1,520	96	4	51
West Virginia	147	2,653	0	100	38
Delaware	89	715	100	0	46

Total Appellate Caseloads by State, 2002

State	Appeals per 100,000 Pop.	Total Appeals	Mandatory Appeals	Discretionary Petitions	Pop. Rank
Montana	88	798	73	27	45
Vermont	86	530	97	3	50
Nevada	79	1,723	100	0	36
Rhode Island	70	754	45	55	44
New Hampshire	64	813	0	100	42
South Dakota	60	457	84	16	47
North Dakota	57	363	94	6	49
Maine	57	738	76	24	41

Notes: Oklahoma and Wyoming were unable to provide data for 2002. States in bold are the nation's 10 most populous.

Most appeals are resolved by opinions, memoranda/orders, or pre-argument dismissals. While opinions can be rendered through a variety of means, the data here capture only two: signed opinions and *per curiam* affirmed opinions. In 2002, 17 courts of last resort issued almost 3,700 such opinions while 24 intermediate appellate courts issued over 34,500. During 2002, these courts also issued more than 23,000 memoranda/orders and dismissed approximately 27,000 cases.

The most common dispositions in intermediate appellate courts are signed opinions and pre-argument dismissals. Together, these two actions comprise about two thirds of all dispositions in IACs. Opinions typically include statements of fact, points of law, rationale, and dicta, while a pre-argument dismissal is based on a review of briefs rather than oral arguments. Nearly one-half of cases in appellate courts of last resort are resolved by a memorandum/order, which is a simple order based on a unanimous opinion. Pre-argument dismissals and signed opinions are the next

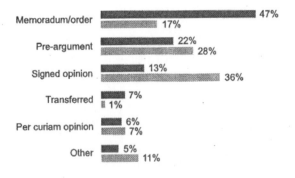

Manner of Disposition in COLRs v. IACs, 2002

Memoradum/order — 47% / 17%
Pre-argument — 22% / 28%
Signed opinion — 13% / 36%
Transferred — 7% / 1%
Per curiam opinion — 6% / 7%
Other — 5% / 11%

■ Courts of Last Resort   ▓ Intermdiate Appellate Courts

Manner of Disposition in 17 Courts of Last Resort and 24 Intermediate Appellate Courts, 2002

	Total Dispositions	Opinions Signed/P.C.	Non-Opinion Memo/Order	Dispositions Pre-Argument	Transferred	Other
COLRs (# Justices):						
Florida (7)	2,977	95/213	2,669			
Nevada (7)	2,454	38/61	1,767			
Iowa (8)	2,180	180/11	928	588	1,015	46
D.C. (9)	1,836	339/575	865			57
Colorado (7)	1,415	121	1,287		7	
Washington (9)	1,328	129	892	70	118	119
P.R. (7)	1,240	92/44	129	957		18
Indiana (5)	1,103	195/18	190	687		13
Hawaii (5)	847	191		257	258	141
R.I. (5)	818	75/105	70	290		278
Montana (7)	792	343	239	210		
Delaware (5)	713	71/19	546	77		
Vermont (5)	603	68	388	147		
Alaska (5)	516	182/68		95		171
South Dakota (5)	428	164	167	64		33
Oregon (7)	371	60/40	251			20
North Dakota (5)	345	189		71		85
IACs (no. of judges):						
Ohio (68)	10,627	6,992		3,389		246
PA Sup. (15)	8,152	5,315		2,835	2	
Michigan (28)	7,647	212/102	3,636	1,793		1,904

Manner of Disposition in 17 Courts of Last Resort and 24 Intermediate Appellate Courts, 2002

	Total Dispositions	Opinions Signed/P.C.	Non-Opinion Dispositions Memo/Order	Pre-Argument	Transferred	Other
New Jersey (34)	7,280	431/3,560	250	3,039	117	168
PA Comm. (9)	4,753	1,746		2,722	11	592
Washington (22)	4,306	1,846	264	1,593		190
Oregon (10)	3,844	393/118	1,483	1,660		190
Missouri (32)	3,661	1,686	103	1,200	92	580
Wisconsin (16)	3,486	761/523	867			1,335
Georgia (12)	3,389	1,401	643	567	69	709
Mass. (22)	2,869	363	1,071	618	76	741
AL Crim. (5)	2,748	122	1,673	578		375
Colorado (16)	2,463	291	1,330	834	8	
Maryland (13)	2,381	144/1,179		500	41	517
Minnesota (16)	2,007	1,324/3	61	609		10
Kansas (10)	1,742	1,246	292		204	
TN App. (12)	1,504	843	422	4		235
AL Civ. (5)	1,306	323	574	358	51	
TN Crim. (12)	1,304	890	288	17		109
Connecticut (9)	1,271	637		262	129	243
Iowa (9)	1,231	1,144/70		14		3
Arkansas (12)	1,200	629		43	80	448
N.M. (10)	855	152	541	145	8	9
Alaska (3)	302	55	172	31		44

most common at 22 percent and 13 percent, respectively. The remaining appeals are disposed of by *per curiam* opinions (usually a short opinion issued in the name of the court rather than specific justices), transfers to another court, or some other method.

Mandatory civil and criminal appeals in IACs, those cases that the courts are statutorily required to hear, have tracked consistently with one another for the last 10 years with civil appeals averaging about 8,000 more filings per year than criminal appeals. In 2002, mandatory civil and criminal appeals in the 36 intermediate appellate courts featured on this chart continued a decline that began in 1998, resulting in a 3 percent decrease in civil appeals and a 5 percent decrease in criminal appeals.

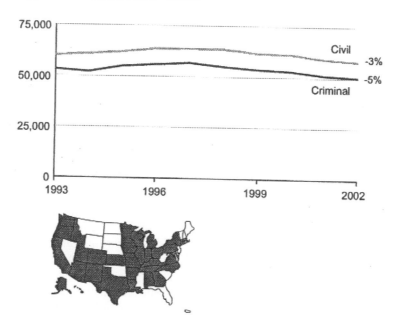

Mandatory Civil and Criminal Appeals in 36 Intermediate Appellate Courts, 1993 - 2002

Courts of last resort in 15 states were able to provide filing data for discretionary civil and criminal petitions from 1993 to 2002. For the ten-year period shown here, discretionary criminal petitions are up 20 percent despite a 4 percent decrease over the last two years. The number of discretionary civil petitions in the same 15 courts of last resort reached its peak in 1995; the number of filings then remained constant for three years. From 1997 to 2001, filings declined annually. The number of civil petitions filed in 2002 was virtually the same as in 2001. Overall, there has been an 8 percent decline in the last 10 years.

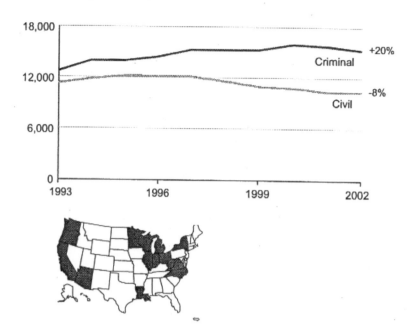

Discretionary Criminal and Civil Petitions in 15 Courts of Last Resort, 1993-2002

COMMISSION ON STRUCTURAL ALTERNATIVES FOR THE FEDERAL COURTS OF APPEALS FINAL REPORT 12-25 (Dec. 18, 1998)

Evolution of the Supreme Court's Discretionary Docket: Twentieth-century changes in the appellate system have in the main been functional, not structural. One such change [has been] the Supreme Court's transformation from a law-declaring and error-correcting court into a court almost exclusively for law declaring. . . . Table 2-1 shows that the Court's plenary docket has remained relatively steady, but courts of appeals' merits dispositions have grown by 1,000%. The result is a greatly reduced percentage of courts of appeals decisions reviewed by the Supreme Court. The Court has been able to develop as a national law-declaring court, while the courts of appeals have become the only federal error-correcting courts, for practical purposes, the federal appellate courts of last resort.

Table 2-1 Supreme Court Review of Federal Courts of Appeals Decisions

Year	Supreme Court Plenary Decisions in Cases from Court of Appeals	Courts of Appeals Decisions on the Merits	Percentage Supreme Court Plenary Review
1950	70	2,355	3.0%
1978	101	8,850	1.1%
1984	124	14,474	0.9%
1997	76	26,566	0.3%

Transformation of the Courts of Appeals and Their Work: The courts of appeals of 1998 are very different bodies from what they were 100 years ago. Changes in the nature and size of their workloads required courts to request more judges and to adapt their procedures to the changed circumstances.

1. Growth in judgeships and workload. The intermediate appellate courts grew gradually during the first part of the1900s and more rapidly since then. As displayed in Table 2-2, four decades after their creation, the modal number of judgeships in the courts of appeals had risen to four. As they grew, the courts began to sit in more than one panel of three, convening occasionally *en banc*, a practice approved by the Supreme Court and then codified in the 1940s. By 1950, the modal number of judgeships had risen to six. By 1984, the modal number had risen to twelve.

Table 2-2 Summary of Authorized Circuit Judgeships for Selected Years, 1892–1990

Year	Largest Court	Smallest Court	Modal Court	Total Judgeships
1892	3	2	2	19
1930	5	3	4	55
1950	9	3	6	75
1964	9	3	9	88
1978	26	4	11	144
1984	28	6	12	168
1990	28	6	12	179

Note: Years 1930-1978 combine the Court of Customs and Patent Appeals and Court of Claims;1984 and 1990 include the Court of Appeals for the Federal Circuit.

The work assigned to these courts, however, has increased disproportionately to the increase in judgeships, as shown in Table 2-3. Over the last 100 years, filings per appellate judgeship have increased by almost a factor of six. By contrast, filings per judgeship in the district courts have not even doubled.

Table 2-3 Authorized District and Circuit Judgeships and Filings per Judgeship

	District Courts			Courts of Appeals		
Year	Judges	Filings	Filings per Judgeship	Judges	Filings	Filings per Judgeship
1892	64	18,388	287	19	841	44
1930	139	135,630	976	55	3,532	64
1950	212	92,342	436	75	5,443	73
1964	301	98,663	328	88	6,736	77
1978	510	174,753	343	144	19,657	137
1984	571	298,330	523	168	32,616	194
1990	645	266,783	414	179	42,364	237
1997	646	314,527	487	179	53,688	300

Note: Years 1930-1978 combine the Court of Customs and Patent Appeals and Court of Claims; appellate filings and judgeships for 1984-1997 include the Court of Appeals for the Federal Circuit.

By any measure, the courts of appeals of today are handling more cases, and more work, than their predecessor courts. With only brief respites after new judgeship bills took effect, circuit judges have been faced with relentlessly increasing caseloads since the beginning of the upswing in appeals in the 1960s. Although increases in judgeships have been substantial, judgeships have not increased as rapidly as raw appellate filings. Since 1960, circuit judgeships have grown by roughly 160%, but appeals per judgeship have grown by 450%. Figure 2-D plots the increase in total filings and filings per judgeship since 1960.

Figure 2-D Appeals Filed and Appeals per Circuit Judgeship, Regional Courts of Appeals, 1960-1997

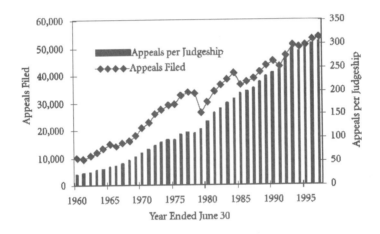

Perhaps as important as the increase in the number of appeals is the change in the nature of those appeals over time. As Table 2-4 shows, appeals of all types have increased, but the proportion of the courts' dockets accounted for by each type has changed. Most striking is the overall effect of the increase in appeals associated with the growth in criminal prosecutions. There has been substantial growth in direct criminal appeals over the past few decades, most dramatically since November 1987, the effective date of the sentencing guidelines developed and promulgated pursuant to the 1984 Sentencing Reform Act. After a slight decline in the 1970s and early 1980s, criminal appeals rose precipitously — from 4,377 in 1981 to 10,740 in 1997. There were several apparent causes — stepped up prosecutorial efforts, the sentencing guidelines themselves, the mandatory minimum sentences that became increasingly common in the 1980s, and the availability of appellate review of sentences even after a guilty plea. Along with the increase in direct criminal appeals came the growth in civil suits by incarcerated prisoners, including motions to vacate sentence and petitions for writs of habeas corpus (both technically considered civil actions), as well as suits alleging civil rights violations and unconstitutional conditions of confinement. Civil suits by prisoners made up about 8% of the docket in 1960, but more than 30% by 1997. All told, the "criminal-related" portion of the appellate docket grew from about 24% in 1960 to about 53% in 1997.

**Table 2-4 Appeal Types Filed in the Regional Courts of Appeals,
1960-1997**

1960	1970	1980	1990	1997
Criminal 623 (16%)	2,660 (23%)	4,405 (19%)	9,493 (23%)	10,740 (21%)
U.S. Prisoner 179 (5%)	818 (7%)	1,007 (4%)	2,263 (6%)	4,901 (9%)
Other U.S. Civil 609 (16%)	1,349 (12%)	3,647 (16%)	4,363 (11%)	3,809 (7%)
Private Prisoner 111 (3%)	1,622 (14%)	2,675 (12%)	7,678 (19%)	11,287 (22%)
Other Priv. Civil 1,423 (36%)	3,212 (28%)	7,525 (32%)	12,812 (31%)	15,429 (30%)
Bankruptcy 132 (3%)	205 (2%)	396 (2%)	1,087 (3%)	1,164 (2%)
Administrative 737 (19%)	1,522 (13%)	2,950 (13%)	2,578 (6%)	4,131 (8%)
Other 85 (2%)	274 (2%)	595 (3%)	624 (2%)	810 (2%)
Total filings 3,899	11,662	23,200	40,898	52,271

Note: Because of rounding, percentages may not total 100.

During the same time, the courts of appeals began to see increasing numbers of appeals brought by unrepresented litigants, as Table 2-5 reveals. In 1997, fully half of the filings in the courts of appeals that were not direct criminal appeals were appeals by unrepresented parties. Although we cannot tell how much *pro se* litigation went on in the courts of appeals in earlier decades, it was probably relatively uncommon until the growth in prisoner litigation described above. Much of the *pro se* docket is still accounted for by prisoners, but it is not uncommon for other litigants to lack legal counsel — about one-quarter to one-third of nonprisoner civil appeals from the district courts in 1997 were filed by unrepresented litigants.

**Table 2-5 Estimated Percentage of Appeals Filed by Unrepresented
Litigants, 1950-1997**

	1950	1960	1970	1980	1990	1997
Percentage of all filings	10%	7%	21%	16%	24%	42%
Percentage of non-criminal filings	11%	9%	27%	20%	32%	50%

Note: 1950-1990 figures are the number of civil appeals by prisoners as a percentage of the national appellate caseload. Reliable information about *pro se* status is available only for the last few years, so only the figures for the year ending Sept. 30, 1997, reflect a direct count of *pro se* cases.

Like many prisoner cases, appeals filed by unrepresented parties who are not incarcerated pose special challenges for the courts, but they generally do not involve as much work for judges as fully counseled cases because they typically are controlled by well-settled precedent or require a highly deferential standard of review.[5] In most courts, central staff attorneys prepare these cases for decision by a three-judge panel. Many such appeals, even when meritorious, do not require extensive legal research or conference time, and often they do not yield published opinions that take a lot of judicial time to craft. Accordingly, the number of filings, while important, is not a sufficient measure of judicial workload, and should not be taken alone as a sign that the courts are overwhelmed. Rather, the nature of the work done by the courts of appeals must be considered; it is likely that the above described changes in the nature of appeals at least partially account for the ability of the courts of appeals to cope with much larger caseloads without a commensurate increase in judgeships.

2. *Responses to growth in judgeships and workload.* Creating new circuits and courts of appeals: Since 1891, Congress has faced "insistent pressure for further subdivision" of the circuits. It has twice split circuits so as to create smaller courts of appeals that proponents of division said would be more effective. [In 1929, the new Tenth Circuit was carved out of the Eighth Circuit; in 1981, the new Eleventh Circuit was split off from the Fifth Circuit.] These actions reflected a view that the only way to deal with a court of appeals deemed to have grown too large was to reconfigure the circuit of which it was a part. Indeed, for the same reason, the current debate about the Ninth Circuit has centered on the question of whether the circuit should be split, even though in reality, the primary concern is about a court of appeals thought to be growing too large. . . .

New procedures and supporting personnel: The growth in the volume of appeals, in addition to necessitating more judges on each court, has wrought two other far-reaching, and related, innovations in the federal appellate courts in the last third of this century. One is the adoption of differentiated decisional processes, and the other is the employment of central staff attorneys. Both were inventions of necessity, pioneered by the courts to keep abreast of rising caseloads, but both have proven to be — for part of the docket — more efficient ways to deliver appellate justice regardless of docket pressures.

Differentiated decisional processes were adopted when courts recognized that not every appeal needs the same amount of judicial attention. Some appeals present difficult questions, or questions of great significance to the legal order, while other appeals present routine issues that are relatively easy to decide because the controlling law is well settled. For the latter, many courts began to find oral argument unnecessary or unhelpful, and the time spent in producing the traditional fully reasoned published opinion

---

5 [39] The current formula used in the assessment of circuit judgeship needs discounts *pro se* cases by two-thirds to reflect the generally lower judicial time requirements associated with such cases.

greater than judicial economy warranted. As cases of this type grew to represent a larger and larger proportion of appellate dockets, courts developed screening or tracking procedures to review appeals at an early stage and route them through the decisional process tailored to their difficulty and precedential significance. Under such tracking systems, some appeals continue to receive the traditional process — oral argument, conference by the panel, and fully reasoned opinion. Some are routed to a settlement procedure aimed at achieving an acceptable resolution of the dispute without expenditure of substantial judicial time. Still others are decided without oral argument and with a short, often *per curiam*, memorandum disposition or brief order, typically unpublished. The result, as Table 2-6 shows, is that in several of the courts fewer than a third of the cases decided on the merits are argued orally; in only three regional courts of appeals was the argument rate higher than 50% in 1997.

Table 2-6 Percentage of Cases Decided on the Merits in Which Oral Argument Was Heard in the Regional Courts of Appeals, FY 1997

1st	2d	3d	4th	5th	6th	7th	8th	9th	10th	11th	D.C.	Nat'l
All cases (%):												
61	65	30	30	35	50	51	46	39	30	30	47	40
Cases with Counsel (%):												
74	85	42	51	47	71	78	65	54	45	38	69	56

As the volume and nature of the appellate caseloads changed, so did the likelihood that an appellate court would publish an opinion explaining its decision, to the point where today, most courts issue published opinions in only a small percentage of the appeals they decide on the merits, as Table 2-7 reveals.

Table 2-7 Percentage of Cases Decided on the Merits that Resulted in a Published Opinion in the Regional Courts of Appeals, FY 1997

1st	2d	3d	4th	5th	6th	7th	8th	9th	10th	11th	D.C.	Nat'l
All cases (%):												
51	27	16	11	22	18	48	45	18	26	14	37	23
Cases with Counsel (%):												
61	39	22	19	29	25	71	62	24	36	17	55	32

For the most part, the decline in oral argument and publication is attributable to the influx of cases involving unrepresented litigants pursuing relatively simple appeals, many of which present the same issues. As the tables show, the percentage of cases with counsel that receive argument or published opinion is generally considerably higher. Because of changes in the nature of the caseload and in the significance of publication, lower rates of oral argument or opinion publication cannot automatically be interpreted as a sign of dysfunction in a court.[6]

Concurrently with the adoption of these abbreviated internal processes came the employment of central staff attorneys to help implement the new processes. Although judges have long had personal ("elbow") law clerks, the use of a central staff working for the court as a whole was genuinely new. Starting in the early 1970s with a handful of such attorneys, the courts of appeals have greatly increased their numbers. Although central staff attorneys were originally employed primarily to help the courts process cases filed by unrepresented prisoners, in most courts their duties now extend to other types of cases. In most (but not all) courts, staff attorneys perform a screening function, reviewing appeals as they become ready for the court's attention and routing them into either an oral argument track or a non-argument track. In all courts, any judge on the panel responsible for deciding the case may choose to schedule a case for argument, and the panel may unanimously determine that a case scheduled for argument does not need it. In addition to preliminarily determining whether a case will be decided with or without argument, staff attorneys generally review the briefs and records and prepare memoranda to assist the judges; in some courts they also recommend dispositions and draft proposed opinions, usually in the non-argued cases.

The number of central staff attorney "work units" allocated to each court of appeals, for the fiscal year beginning October 1, 1998, is shown in Table 2-8. The number of work units allocated is based primarily on raw filings, so courts with higher caseloads are entitled to more staff attorneys. However, the allocations do not precisely reflect the number of staff attorneys actually employed, because courts have considerable flexibility in how they use the funds allocated for this purpose.

Table 2-8 Central Staff Attorney Positions Allocated to the Regional Courts of Appeals, FY 1999

1st	2d	3d	4th	5th	6th	7th	8th	9th	10th	11th	D.C.
9	26	22	29	46	23	15	19	48	17	32	13

As central staffs grew, the number of personal law clerks for circuit judges also grew, and their functions expanded. At mid-century, each circuit judge had a single law clerk. Today an active judge may employ three law clerks and two secretaries or four law clerks and one secretary.

Collectively, this transformation of process and personnel in the courts of appeals over the last three decades has given rise to concerns among judges, lawyers, and legal scholars that the quality of appellate decision making may have been eroded and that there has been undue delegation of judicial work to non-judges. As to appeals decided without oral argument, the process has

---

[6] [57] Opinion publication rates declined when the federal judiciary began a deliberate effort to reduce the cost of law practice and legal services by refraining from publishing opinions that do not add anything new to the law or help attorneys better predict appellate outcomes. Although court publication and citation practices vary, "unpublished" opinions are increasingly accessible by electronic means and in some courts may be cited if no better precedent exists.

become less visible and, when combined with a less than fully reasoned opinion or cryptic judgment order, raises apprehensions as to the degree of attention those appeals actually receive from judges themselves. The apprehensions are intensified when the court uses staff attorneys to draft proposed dispositions, prompting claims by some critics of an "invisible judiciary," in addition to assertions of an invisible process, sometimes summarized in the claim that appellate courts have become "bureaucratized." The Commission has been made aware of these concerns through published writings, testimony at its public hearings, and written submissions. We have received suggestions that, to meet these concerns, the appellate courts hear oral argument in larger percentages of cases, issue a greater number of reasoned opinions, limit the number of staff attorneys they employ, and be supplied with a sufficient number of judges to minimize the likelihood of over-reliance on staff attorneys and law clerks. At the same time, responses to our survey of practicing appellate lawyers nationwide do not reveal a widespread discontent with current practices within the federal appellate courts.

We do not minimize the seriousness of these concerns and suggestions. Indeed, assertions about the decline of the appellate process were among the reasons [we] enlisted the cooperation of chief circuit judges in the preparation of profiles of each court of appeals' case-management procedures. After reviewing these profiles and survey results, we conclude that, in general, the courts have successfully accommodated their increased caseloads by stream-lining their processes and developing efficient methods of appellate case management. We believe, however, that most courts have streamlined their procedures as much as they can without unacceptably compromising their essential functions.[7] The use of nonjudicial staff, nonargument decision-making procedures, summary orders or unelaborated dispositions, and other procedural accommodations to caseload volume have made the courts more efficient, but at some cost to the appearance of legitimacy of the appellate process, and at some risk to the quality of appellate justice. Some courts have adopted these procedures in an effort to avoid requesting new judgeships, because their judges believe the deleterious effects of expanding the appellate bench outweigh its benefits. Courts can absorb caseload growth without large judgeship increases when that growth occurs largely in the types of cases that take little judicial time to resolve. There is no guarantee — and history does not support the assumption — that caseload growth will be restricted to these areas. . . .

Report of the Federal Courts Study Committee 4-9, 109-10 (1990)

At first almost all the nation's judicial business was handled by state courts; there were few federal judges and their jurisdiction was highly circumscribed. Even today, 90 percent of the nation's judicial business is handled by state rather than federal courts. With the expansion of the federal government — an expansion inaugurated by the Civil War, accelerated by Prohibition and

---

[7] [60] More than half of the 188 circuit judges who responded to a 1992 FJC survey agreed strongly or moderately with this view (*see* Planning for the Future: Results of a 1992 Federal Judicial Center Survey of United States Judges at 17).

then by the New Deal, and accelerated further during the burst of federal lawmaking that began with President Johnson's "Great Society" programs and has continued virtually unabated since — the federal courts were bound to grow, both absolutely and relatively to the state courts. And grow they did. But until the late 1950s the growth was extremely gradual (except for a blip during Prohibition), and was easily accommodated by such expedients as making the Supreme Court's jurisdiction primarily discretionary rather than mandatory (it is now almost entirely discretionary); creating (in 1891) a tier of regional appellate courts — the federal courts of appeals — in between the federal trial courts and the Supreme Court; and, from time to time, dividing the circuits (*i.e.*, the federal appellate regions) if they became unwieldy by reason of having too many judges.

The number of cases filed in federal courts began to surge as the 1950s drew to a close, and the surge has continued without surcease to this day. The causes are not fully understood but certainly include the continued growth of federal law and in particular the creation of many new federal rights both by Congress and by judicial interpretation of the Constitution, and a variety of procedural developments such as expanded use of class actions and "one-way" shifting of attorneys' fees. Whatever the causes of the case surge, the magnitude is not in doubt. We do not wish to numb the reader with statistics but we must point out that between 1958 and 1988, following decades of extremely slow caseload growth, the number of cases (both civil and criminal) filed in the federal district courts (*i.e.*, trial courts) trebled, while the number filed in the courts of appeals increased more than tenfold. . . .

At first glance it might seem puzzling why a growing, even a rapidly growing, number of cases should spell a "crisis." It might seem that any increase in the number of cases could be accommodated by a proportional increase in the number of judges and supporting personnel. But while adding judges is plainly necessary in the short term — and we recommend it — the federal courts cannot accommodate unlimited increases in the demand for their services by expanding their personnel. In this and other respects the federal courts cannot cope with a surge in the "demand" for their services in the way a business does. When a business firm experiences a surge in the demand for its product, this is cause for joy, not distress, since the firm can raise its price and at the same time begin the process, which may be gradual, of expanding its output to supply the higher demand. In principle, the federal court system could respond similarly to a surge in new cases. It could charge stiff filing or user fees that would discourage new filings, and it could go out and hire, at its leisure, as many more judges and other judicial staff as might be necessary to handle the growing but (by the increase in filing fees) moderated demand for its services. Among the objections that could be raised to the first solution, the most cogent is that it would drastically curtail federal rights. At first the rights holders priced out of the federal courts would turn to the state courts, but the states might decide to set their own stiff fees in order to prevent a flood of new cases; although the Constitution would not allow them to do that in a way that discriminated against federal claimants, a uniform increase in state court filings fees would not be discriminatory yet might have the effect of creating a large class of federal rights holders who could not find *any* tribunal in which to enforce their rights. Nor should the primary responsibility of the federal courts for resolving questions concerning federal rights be curtailed, notwithstanding the availability of state courts. . . .

Even if a highly competent federal judiciary consisting of thousands of judges could be created and maintained, the coordination of so many judges would be extraordinarily difficult. The more trial judges there are, the more appeals judges there must be; the more appeals judges there are, the higher the rate of appeal, because it becomes more difficult to predict the behavior of the appellate court; the more appeals there are, the more difficult it is for the Supreme Court to maintain some minimum uniformity of federal decisional law, because its capacity to review decisions of the lower federal courts is limited. Even the maintenance of the necessary minimum uniformity of law within a single circuit becomes problematic if there are a great many judges in that circuit, and while this problem can be alleviated by increasing the number of circuits, the result is to increase the number of intercircuit conflicts and hence the burden on the Supreme Court.

Thus the problems of the federal courts, at least as those courts currently are organized, cannot be solved by an indefinite expansion in the number of judges. If there were no appeals, expansion might be a tolerable if not ideal solution. There would be some dilution of quality and responsibility, but there would not be chaos. However, given appeals, continuous expansion of the number of judges at any level (and to expansion in the number of trial judges will lead inevitably to an increase in the number of appellate judges) will lead eventually to paralysis or incoherence, because of the judicial system's three-tier pyramidal structure.

There are subtler problems with indefinite expansion of the federal judiciary. Any such expansion is likely to come at the expense of the states, and thus to impair the fundamental constitutional concept of *limited* federal government. Keeping the federal judiciary relatively small increases the likelihood that federal intervention will be limited to those situations in which it is most clearly necessary. History teaches, moreover, that there are indeed situations where federal judicial intervention *is* clearly necessary. Many of these situations involve the protection of individual liberty against actions of the political branches of government. Such intervention is more likely to win public acceptance if the federal judiciary is perceived as a small and special corps of men and women whose talents are reserved for issues that transcend local concern, rather than as a faceless, omnipresent bureaucracy.

It becomes critical to assess how near the present federal court system is to the feasible limits on its growth. Perhaps quite near. Although most of the nation's judicial business continues to be handled by the state courts, the federal judiciary is the largest single court system in the nation if traffic and domestic relations cases are excluded. In 1987, for example, the number of appeals filed in Florida, the most in any state, were fewer than half the number filed in the federal courts. California, the state with the most appellate judges, had fewer than half as many appellate judges as the federal courts. The larger the federal court system becomes, the more difficult it becomes to expand it further without compromising the quality of federal justice. It has been suggested that 1,000 is the practical ceiling on the number of judges if the Article III judiciary is to remain capable of performing its essential functions without significant degradation of quality. There are now some 750 such judgeships, and if urgently needed additional judgeships are included, the number exceeds 800. So we may be approaching the limits of the natural growth of the federal courts, and yet the surge in case filings at both the trial and especially the appellate level continues with no cessation in sight.

We need not belabor the consequences for the nation of a federal judiciary rendered ineffectual by case overload.

We have tried to peer ahead and forecast the federal caseload, but have found the crystal ball opaque. The reasons for our inability to predict future demands for federal judicial services are twofold. First, it is extraordinarily difficult to predict any but the grossest social, economic, political, and demographic trends more than a few years in advance — if that far. By way of pertinent illustration, when this committee was formed fifteen months ago, the magnitude of the caseload impact of the federal war on drugs was not foreseen. Second, the relationship between those trends that can be foreseen and the caseload of the federal courts is largely unknown. No doubt the American population will continue to age, continue to expand, continue to experience improvements in the standard of living, but what effect these developments will have on the number of federal cases filed or appealed is unknown. The impossibility of responsibly forecasting federal caseload growth is underscored by the fact that, even with the rich benefits of hindsight, it is impossible to "postdict" (explain) the growth of the federal caseload from *known* developments in the past, such as changes in population and in income; these changes have been smaller in the last thirty years — years of rampant caseload growth — than they had been in the previous thirty years, which were years of slow growth for the federal courts. Although the growth of the federal caseload is due in part to the creation of new rights and remedies, this cannot be the whole story because areas of the federal docket controlled by state rather than federal substantive law (mainly the diversity jurisdiction, under which citizens of different states can litigate in federal court disputes over questions of state law) have also grown far more rapidly than population and income. All that is certain is that for thirty years the caseload has been growing rapidly and that there is no reason to expect a sudden abatement. But in a speculative vein we add that the Administrative Office of the United States Courts — whose predictions have been accurate in the past — forecasts that court of appeals caseloads will nearly triple in the next twenty-five years, while filings in the district courts will triple and filings in the bankruptcy courts will more than triple. . . .

However people may view other aspects of the federal judiciary, few deny that its appellate courts are in a "crisis of volume" that has transformed them from the institutions they were even a generation ago. Further and more fundamental change to the appellate courts would seem to be inevitable unless there is a halt to the climb in appellate workload. While it is impossible to read the future, we see little reason to anticipate such a halt.

If growth continues, the nation must ask how further changes in the appellate courts will occur. Will they be insidious and unplanned; will oral argument and reasoned opinions simply fade away, for example? Or will Congress and the courts fashion new structures and procedures specifically designed to preserve the hallmarks of our judiciary? Those hallmarks include that the judges do much of their own work, grant oral argument in cases that need it, decide cases with sufficient thought, and produce opinions in cases of precedential importance with the care they deserve, including independent, constructive insight and criticism from judges on the court and the panel other than the judge writing the opinion. These conditions are essential to a carefully crafted case law. Modern society requires no less.

Today's federal appellate courts have been able to provide these conditions only through increases in productivity that seem to be approaching their limit. Further attempts to raise productivity by the most commonly suggested and employed means, such as increases in staff and reducing opportunity for oral argument, could threaten the integrity of the process. Accordingly, although we make several proposals to enhance productivity, our emphasis in this Chapter is on more far-reaching analysis. We anticipate that within as few as five years the nation could have to decide whether or not to abandon the present circuit structure in favor of an alternative structure that might better organize the more numerous appellate judges needed to grapple with a swollen caseload. . . .

The crisis of volume is beyond dispute, even if the statistical measures of appellate workload still need refinement. The crisis is caused partly by an increase in district court cases but mainly by a heightened proclivity to appeal district court terminations. In 1945, litigants appealed about one of every forty district court terminations; they now appeal about one in eight. As a result, appellate filings have risen nearly fifteen-fold. ([T]hey have increased by tenfold since 1958.) The number of appellate judges, however, has increased since 1945 by a factor of less than three, from 59 to 168. Consequently, the caseload per judge has multiplied by nearly six over the same period. Circuit judges of the 1940s and 1950s would find today's caseloads unmanageable. Even in 1965, each appellate judge, sitting in panels of three, participated in an average of 136 terminations after hearing or submission. By 1989, that number had almost tripled, to 372 per judge. In all but two circuits it exceeds 255, which is the Judicial Conference standard for an appellate judge's annual workload. In the five busiest circuits, it ranges from 411 to 525. The 255 participation standard, furthermore, is too high according to most judges who responded to the committee's survey. The federal appellate caseload is higher than that of many state appellate courts even though the responsibilities of the federal circuit judges are generally greater.

To date, the courts of appeals have managed to avoid the worst effects of this growth. There has been no systemic breakdown in the quality of the courts' work. Moreover, pending cases as a percentage of terminations — the measure of "backlog" — has risen only from 55 percent in 1958 to 80 percent now. But the appellate courts have avoided major deterioration only by pushing productivity to maximum levels and by adopting truncated procedures that probably have reached the limits of their utility without compromising the quality of the process.

The appellate caseload explosion, moreover, threatens not only the courts of appeals as we know them. It also threatens the Supreme Court's role as the enunciator of national law. The Court is unable to give full review to more than about 150 cases per year. As court of appeals decisions increase in number, there is a corresponding decline in the percentage of those decisions that the Supreme Court reviews, thus making the thirteen intermediate appellate courts more and more the nation's courts of last resort. . . .

Structural and Other Alternatives for the Federal Courts of Appeals: Report to the U.S. Congress and the Judicial Conference of the U.S. 11-15 (Fed. Jud. Ctr. 1993)

Advocates for major structural change to the federal appellate system are responding to a volume of appeals that they believe threatens to overwhelm the appellate courts. Some consider the courts to be already enmeshed in a "crisis of volume" and doubt that the crisis will abate without major change either to the structure of the courts or to the accessibility of the courts. Other observers question the diagnosis of "crisis." Many of them believe the courts to be functioning effectively now, but see major problems on the horizon if judicial workloads continue to grow. Still others see the courts as fully capable of handling likely caseloads of the future by growing as needed and by streamlining their procedures.

Not every aspect of the courts' situation has been or can be empirically demonstrated. Our purpose is not to quibble over whether the federal court system is under stress — it is important enough that a substantial number of its members and at least some of its users perceive that it is. We believe the response to that perception — whether structural change, increased procedural flexibility, or a determination to retain the system largely in its current form — ought to be governed to the extent possible by an objective description and analysis of the current situation of the courts.

In light of recent efforts to reduce cost and delay in federal civil litigation, it is worth noting preliminarily that these factors do not appear to be driving current calls for [federal appellate] structural change. In any individual case, delay may work to the advantage of a party, but we assume general acceptance of one goal: Litigants should obtain a final decision as quickly and economically as possible, consistent with reasoned adjudication. There appears to be no groundswell of discontent with the cost, at least to litigants, of the appellate process. Some of the procedural changes adopted by the courts of appeals to expedite appeal processing have probably reduced overall costs to litigants. Indeed, it may reasonably be argued that appeals are so inexpensive relative to the entire cost of litigating a case that there is an insufficient economic deterrent to meritless appeals.

Whether appellate disposition times amount to a problem of delay is more difficult to assess. In our description of the work of the courts of appeals . . . , we present information about appellate disposition times and note that those times have in recent years stayed relatively stable, even as caseloads have grown. Absent a standard for the amount of time an appeal should take, we cannot say whether appellate disposition times are unacceptably long or not. If they are, it does not appear that the problem is one of court structure as distinct from other aspects of the system, particularly the volume of cases.[8] Structural changes of the sort generally proposed for the courts of appeals do not appear to be necessary to achieve delay reduction and may not contribute to achieving it. Indeed, some of the structural changes proposed, such as a new tier of appellate courts, could markedly lengthen the time to final disposition.

Thus, cost and delay are not the main factors spurring calls for change to the structure of courts of appeal. The major problems that judicial and legal commentators identify in the appellate system can be described and classified in different ways, but for analytical purposes we have divided the asserted problems into three major areas of concern:

(1) *Threat to just outcomes.* Some who observe or participate in the appellate system fear that conditions in the courts of appeals — in particular, the amount of work each judge must do to keep up with the caseload — threaten the ability of the judges to spend the time necessary for the deliberative work the courts of appeals have been known for, threaten the quality of life of the judges and the quality of the judiciary itself, and therefore threaten the quality of the product of the courts. In this view, loss of collegiality because of the press of business and the growth of the courts has diminished the quality of the appellate decision-making process for the judges themselves, with detrimental effects felt by the litigants, the bar, and the public.

(2) *Diminished quality of the appellate process.* Some observers of the work of the courts of appeals fear that the courts' extraordinary attempts to accommodate the caseloads of the past two decades have significantly diminished the quality of the appellate process. Certain screening practices, the decline of oral argument, the increased use of summary decision modes, restricted publication practices, and other procedural responses to volume have "transformed [the appellate courts] from the institutions they were even a generation ago."

(3) *Inconsistent interpretations of federal law.* Some who focus on the law-declaring function of the courts of appeals are concerned that the press of cases and the difficulties of keeping up with and reconciling decisions issued by a growing appellate bench have diminished the consistency and coherence of the national law, both within and among circuits. As a result, the same federal statute may be interpreted differently from one circuit to another, or even from one case to another in the same circuit. Some fear that the resulting

---

8 [34] As with civil litigation at the trial level, most of the time between when an appeal is docketed and when it is terminated is attributable not to the time judges spend deciding a matter but to the time spent preparing the matter for decision. Prior research suggests that about 85% of the elapsed time of an appeal occurs before the case reaches the panel that will decide it. Only about 15% of an appeal's life is spent in the hands of the judges themselves. . . . Thus, if the time required for an appeal is deemed to be too long by as-yet unspecified criteria, it may be most fruitful to focus delay reduction efforts on the period between when an appeal is filed and when it is submitted to a three judge panel for decision. Many courts have directed significant management efforts toward improving this stage of the appellate process. If the queue of cases ready for submission begins to lengthen, however, this may suggest insufficient judicial resources. Backlogs fluctuate. In recent years, some courts have been forced to cancel scheduled argument dates because there were no cases ready for submission; others, particularly courts with continuing judicial vacancies, have cases awaiting assignment to a panel.

uncertainty makes it difficult for citizens to conform their behavior to the law, complicates business transactions, and generates more litigation than would occur if the national law were uniform and predictable.

The major problems afflicting the courts can be linked to the volume of cases. For example, the problem of overwork is directly linked to caseload volume, at least with the current size of the judiciary. Keeping up with the work by truncating the appellate process, or by delegating more responsibility to nonjudicial personnel, or by giving cases less time than they deserve leads to perceived problems more or less directly attributable to too many cases and too much work. A perceived problem of inconsistency can be linked to too many judges (a proliferation of mind-sets, with decreasing collegial opportunities to know each other's minds) or too many opinions (too much law to keep up with). But the number of opinions and the number of judges are driven by the volume of cases.

Our findings about the primary problems identified are set out in brief here and developed throughout the report:

- *Threat to Just Outcomes.* Assessing the quality of the product of the courts of appeals is necessarily subjective. There is no adequate and generally accepted measure of the quality of appellate outcomes, so conclusions about the quality of current appellate performance and projections of the likely effects of change on quality must be considered speculative. We cannot conclude, as some assert, that the justness of appellate outcomes has been detrimentally affected by caseload volume. By prodigious effort and creativity, the courts of appeals have been able to keep relatively successfully with their rising caseloads without obvious harm to the quality of their opinions. The courts of appeals continue to develop and refine ways to handle their large caseloads without sacrificing the goal of just outcomes. At some point, especially if the workload of the courts of appeals continues to grow at its recent pace, changes in internal operating procedures may not be sufficient for the task. Some judges believe that point has been reached; others disagree. We cannot foretell the rate of caseload growth, but no major proposal for change to the structure of the courts would substantially reduce appellate filings in the near future.

- *Diminished Quality of Appellate Process.* Many proponents of structural change to the courts of appeals seek to reinstate traditions and procedures that were norm more than twenty-five years ago. They believe that whatever the evidence regarding the quality of individual outcomes in the short term, the incremental changes in the appellate system over the past few decades have damaged other fundamental values of our system, including the visibility and accountability that contribute to the legitimacy of the federal court system in the long term. Some of these values, if determined to be of continuing vitality and importance, might be reaffirmed and strengthened by nonstructural or procedural change. However, if it is determined to be in the national interest to restore or create a system that guarantees the full panoply of appellate procedures in all appeals, or even in all appeals decided on their merits, one of two courses must be adopted: (1) there must be substantially fewer appeals to decide, or (2) there must be a massive increase in judicial system resources, including judgeships, supporting personnel, and facilities. Moreover, restoring the former system by substantially or rapidly expanding the appellate judiciary in the current structure is likely to worsen some problems that are now relatively minor.

• *Inconsistent Interpretations of Federal Law.* Inconsistent interpretation and application of federal law by different courts of appeals is not at the present time a significant problem that warrants substantial structural change to the federal court system. Most important conflicts that reflect like cases being treated differently in different circuits are resolved within a reasonable period by the Supreme Court, by the courts of appeals themselves, or by intervening events such as legislative change. Intercircuit conflicts may be a problem in particular areas of the law (e.g., maritime law), but overall they probably represent a relatively small part of the legal uncertainty that affects the litigation and counseling functions of lawyers. Structural change to resolve intercircuit conflicts — for example, by creating a new court — is likely to provide relatively little benefit at relatively high cost. Nonstructural approaches such as encouraging consideration of the reasoning of other circuits may be beneficial. Proposals that would fundamentally change our system of precedent (such as national stare decisis) appear to be unpromising as solutions to any problem of inconsistency. Such proposals might be a necessary or desirable adjunct to a structural change made for other reasons, but do not in themselves seem likely to ameliorate any current problem.

Inconsistent interpretation and application of federal law by panels within circuits is reported to be a problem in some circuits in some areas of law. The only substantial empirical work on the issue found little evidence for intracircuit conflicts in the largest circuit. Although certain structural changes might reduce intracircuit inconsistency, nonstructural efforts to deal with the problem are already under way and show promise. Making structural changes solely to reduce current levels of intracircuit inconsistency — for example, by extensively restructuring the circuits to create courts of appeals of nine or ten judges — is likely to do more harm than good.

RUGGERO J. ALDISERT, WINNING ON APPEAL: BETTER BRIEFS AND ORAL ADVOCACY 7-10 (2d ed. 2003)[9]

The Avalanche of Appeals. Look for a moment at the paper storm that has descended on the West Publishing Company. The 27,527 published opinions that West received in 1929 represented approximately the same number it received in 1964 — some thirty-five years later. Yet by 1981, the volume had almost doubled to 54,104. By 1991, the number of published opinions peaked at 65,333. Although the number of published opinions has progressively dropped since then to a twenty-year low of 54,059 in 2001, this reduction is deceptive. With the rise in unpublished opinions over that same time, the total number of opinions — published and unpublished — has continued to increase.

Is case law churning and developing at the rate reflected by the increasing number of published and unpublished opinions? Of course not. Our common

---

9 Copyright © 2003 Reproduced with permission from the National Institute for Trial Advocacy. Further reproduction is prohibited.

law tradition requires unity of law throughout a jurisdiction and requires also the flexibility to incorporate legal precepts as they develop. Within this tradition is the concept of gradual change, with case law that creeps from point to point, testing each step, in a system built by accretion from the resolution of specific problems. Nevertheless, no one, not even the most fervent supporter of publication in every case, can seriously suggest that every one of these cases submitted for publication refines or defines the law or has precedential or institutional value. The reason for the avalanche is not only the expansion of trial and appellate litigation, but also because today there is no institutional inhibition against the paper storm.

Reasons why there was no such deluge of appeals as recently as forty years ago are easily identifiable. To be sure, we must recognize the general litigation increase attributed to the growth of population, commerce, industry, and the explosive effect of civil rights, environmental and securities regulation, products liability, the expanded concepts of torts, and the relatively untested realm of the Internet. But there are other reasons. At one time, most state and federal courts had a specialized appellate bar — experts in evaluating the prospects of relief on appeal. No such bar exists today, even at the level of the United States Supreme Court. Most lawyers now believe that they are competent to pursue and to win an appeal. However, even though you may be a good trial lawyer and know the rocky terrain of trial courtrooms, your expertise does not guarantee that you will successfully scale the slippery slopes of appellate advocacy. Experienced appellate judges despair when they examine the superficial preparation by some lawyers whose cases unreasonably crowd their dockets.

Moreover, we have seen a profound change in the lawyer-client relationship. Many lawyers are no longer able to control, or even to moderate, the demands of emotion-laden clients. Often, professional advice and wisdom are insufficient to curb the excess of losing parties in lawsuits. Persons who would never dare to instruct a cardiovascular specialist on heart surgery have no qualms about instructing their lawyers when and how to prosecute appeals of highly technical cases.

Such persons are everywhere. They are not restricted to any economic or social class. Appellants are rich or poor; from the east, west, north, and south; scarred by adverse jury verdicts or angered by judicial rulings. They are chief executive officers of multinational corporations who direct prestigious law firms on when to move and when not to move. They are impecunious defendants in criminal cases represented by court-appointed counsel who have nothing to lose by cluttering appellate dockets. Some appellants rationalize their actions thus: "I got a raw deal. Hey, it's just a crapshoot and maybe I will be lucky." Most people think cases are retried on appeal *de novo*. They simply cannot recognize that courts of appeals have limited review powers.

The Decision to Appeal. Then there are the lawyers. Some accede to the demands for appeal because they fear they may lose clients and earn reputations as "no-guts" lawyers. Others frankly and vulgarly resort to a self-interested, protective maneuver, taking appeals as calculated defenses against possible malpractice suits by clients for failure to exhaust all remedies. Others, unfortunately, take appeals to keep the fee meter running.

Another very important factor is economics. Until recently, taking an appeal required a substantial cash outlay. When I came to the bar, all appellate briefs and the entire record had to be commercially printed. This was a major expense that discouraged some unnecessary appeals. Now appeals are available at discount prices. New court rules no longer require professional printing, which means that the office photocopy machine may grind out briefs at a fraction of the former cost. The rules also allow the appellant to select those parts of the record necessary to support the brief. Appeal costs that formerly ran to substantial pre-inflation dollars are now reduced, in most cases, to a few hundred bucks. In addition, what does an appellant stand to lose if the appeal costs are assessed against him or her? In the majority of cases, the only expense is to pay minimal court costs and the opponent's costs in photocopying the brief and some pages from the record.

The high cost of delivering legal services at trial also has a direct bearing on the increase of appeals. Once a litigant has invested a substantial amount of money at trial, the additional expenses of taking an appeal do not appear extremely formidable. Unlike trial costs, where additional witnesses and depositions and prolonged court days make the legal costs an open-ended affair, there are discrete steps of processing an appeal that can be calculated with specificity in advance.

Even in the most borderline case, if the losing party has already invested $100,000 or $125,000 to present or defend a claim at trial, the costs of taking an appeal, by comparison, do not appear prohibitive. For another $10,000 to $20,000 investment, a respectable appeal may often be lodged and carried to fruition. Comparatively speaking, the appeal expenses are not high because your counsel can take the trial brief, cut and paste it for appellate court consumption, examine the record already prepared for post-trial argument, select parts for inclusion in the appendix or excerpts of record, and have it reproduced in-house or at the photocopy shop. Counsel can then take a few hours to prepare for oral argument, travel to the city (coach class) where the appellate court sits, deliver the fifteen-minute argument, and return home.

To be sure, these shortcuts do not produce the most desirable or effective advocacy . . . but taking an appeal today is relatively cost-effective when compared to massive trial expenses. And if you lose on appeal, unless the case involves a fee-shifting statute, generally speaking, as stated before, you only have to pay the minimal court costs and expenses your opponent incurred in photocopying its brief. Thus, the sheer cost-effectiveness at the appeal level when compared to the astronomical costs at trial is probably a major factor causing the dramatic recent increase of appellate filings. It is the exact opposite of the old adage, "In for a penny, in for a pound."

NOTES

1. "'Crisis' is a much overused word. Burgeoning caseloads are nothing new, nor is the sense that the system is on the verge of breakdown. What is new is the perception that the traditional remedies — enlarging the number of judgeship and auxiliary staff, creating new courts, or subdividing existing courts into smaller units — are no longer adequate." Arthur D. Hellman, *The Crisis in the Circuits and the Innovations of the Browning Years*, in RESTRUCTURING JUSTICE

— THE INNOVATIONS OF THE NINTH CIRCUIT AND THE FUTURE OF THE FEDERAL COURTS 4 (Arthur D. Hellman ed., 1990). *See also* J. Harvie Wilkinson, III, *The Drawbacks of Growth in the Federal Judiciary*, 43 EMORY L. J. 1147 (1994). What do you learn about the causes and cures of the "crisis of volume" when you read over these tables and statistics?

2. There are some skeptics who question the "crisis" characterization and proposed solutions — commentators who necessarily admit that appellate filings statistics have multiplied over the decades since the 1960s, but who nonetheless maintain that the caseload is being managed adequately and therefore proposals for far-reaching reforms ought to be resisted. Michael C. Gizzi, *Examining the Crisis of Volume in the U.S. Courts of Appeals*, 77 JUDICATURE 96 (1993) ("The exact nature of this crisis is not altogether clear, however. . . . Given the mixed measures uncovered about the crisis, it is probable that claims of impending doom might be exaggerations of problems that may only have the potential to reach crisis proportion."). *See also* George D. Brown, *Nonideological Judicial Reform and Its Limits — The Report of the Federal Courts Study Committee*, 47 WASH. & LEE L. REV. 973 (1986); Lauren K. Robel, *The Politics of Crisis in the Federal Courts*, 7 OHIO ST. J. ON DISP. RESOL. 115 (1991). Still others display a greater sense of panic and alarm to insist that things are worse than the judges and some reformers are letting on, so bad that drastic, even radical, changes in the appellate court systems are long overdue. William F. Rylaarsdam, *The Crisis of Volume in California's Appellate Courts: A Reaction to JUSTICE IN THE BALANCE 2020 and a Proposal to Reduce the Number of Nonmeritorious Appeals*, 32 LOY. L.A. L. REV. 63 (1998).

3. As an aside — wholly separate from appellate procedures — is it legitimate for a judge to consider the potential effects on caseload when deciding a case and making common law, *i.e.*, may a judge choose between two outcomes or two substantive rules of law based on which one will result in fewer cases and fewer appeals in the future? Donald P. Lay, *A Blueprint for Judicial Management*, 17 CREIGHTON L. REV. 1047 (1984); Toby J. Stern, Comment, *Federal Judges and Fearing the "Floodgates of Litigation,"* 6 U. PA. J. CONST. L. 377 (2003).

4. "Every lawyer is responsible for timely performance of obligations in the preparation and presentation of cases before an appellate court, and for properly performing the role of advocate with skill and professionalism and for prosecuting only those appeals raising issues of merit." A.B.A. STANDARDS RELATING TO APPELLATE COURTS, § 3.41, Responsibilities of Judges and Lawyers (1994). The *Commentary* to this Standard reads, in part: "Appellate courts observe that many cases before them lack merit. This suggests that the bar does not give sufficient attention to the lawyer's professional responsibility to refrain from prosecuting an appeal unless it rests on arguable grounds. Counsel has a duty to discourage an unwarranted appeal and, in extreme cases, except where appointed counsel is legally bound to present an appeal, to refuse services to a client who persists in prosecuting a frivolous appeal." What circumstance would trigger a lawyer's ethical duty to refuse to take an appeal? Do you agree with Judge Aldisert, that attorneys and litigants are partly to blame for the "crisis of volume"? What is the duty of the lawyer, as

an officer of the courts, to act in the best interest of the legal system? How might lawyers and bar associations come to the aid of beleaguered judges to work for court reforms? We will consider the role of appellate counsel in Chapter 10.

5. One of the leading experts on appellate courts believes the relentless docket growth reached a level of sustained crisis:

> The appellate caseload explosion and the resulting pressures on the courts are hard to exaggerate. Appeals have been doubling about every decade since World War II, placing extreme demands on judges to increase output. Judges have adopted a wide variety of responses, often radically changing court structure and procedure . . . : (1) adding judges; (2) creating or expanding intermediate appellate courts; (3) deciding cases in panels; (4) employing law clerks and staff attorneys; (5) curtailing opinion practices by deciding cases without opinion or with unpublished and memorandum opinion; (6) curtailing oral argument; and (7) using summary judgment procedures.

Thomas B. Marvell, *State Appellate Court Responses to Caseload Growth*, 72 JUDICATURE 282, 282 (1989). In Chapters 6 through 9, we will study these and other reforms to take the measure of the impact of the "crisis of volume" on the appellate courts.

6. In 1988, then-Chief Judge Howard T. Markey of the U.S. Federal Circuit compared the "before" and "after" of the crisis of volume. He lamented the long-term consequences from coping with decades of dramatic increases in the appellate dockets:

> As performed as recently as twenty years ago, the personally conducted federal appellate process comprised: (1) review of the record and briefs by the judge; (2) oral argument of thirty or forty-five minutes on a side; (3) preparation by the judge of a written opinion; (4) assistance in each chamber by one elbow law clerk and one secretary; and (5) frequent and adequate conferences of the judges on the cases.
>
> As performed today, the bureaucratically conducted federal appellate process comprises: (1) screening and track-setting by staff attorneys; (2) review of records and briefs by a law clerk or a staff attorney; (3) oral argument in less than one third of the cases, and then for fifteen or twenty minutes a side; (4) preparation of opinions by law clerks and staff attorneys; (5) dispositions without opinions in two-thirds of the cases; (6) assistance in each chamber by three law clerks and two secretaries and assistance to all chambers by a corps of staff attorneys; and (7) infrequent, short judicial conferences on the cases.

Howard T. Markey, *On the Present Deterioration of the Federal Appellate Process: Never Another Learned Hand*, 33 S.D. L. REV. 371, 376-77 (1988). This is the qualitative side of the "crisis of volume" — the perceived threats from docket growth and the transformative responses to docket growth taken together. We will examine this transformation of appellate courts and appellate procedures over the next several Chapters.

Chapter 6

STRUCTURAL RESPONSES TO THE CRISIS OF VOLUME: THE CREATION OF INTERMEDIATE APPELLATE COURTS

In Chapter 1, we sketched the origins and history of appeals and appellate courts. During the nineteenth century each American judicial system typically contained two tiers: a set of trial courts dispersed across the territory and a single reviewing tribunal. Having one supreme court as the sole appellate forum in a jurisdiction is perhaps the ideal arrangement because it provides maximum assurance of jurisdiction-wide uniformity in decisional law. But beginning in the late nineteenth century — and increasingly in the twentieth century — a single jurisdiction-wide appellate court came to be inadequate under the caseload pressure from the growing volume of litigation. This Chapter focuses on the early structural alterations in state judicial systems necessitated by this growth in demand for appellate decisions. A similar alteration was made in the federal judicial system in 1891.

Understandably, there is always reluctance to alter established judicial structures and to create new courts, and rightly so. Historically, in most states, responses other than structural alterations usually were tried first.

One early nonstructural response to caseload pressures taken by some state supreme courts was to appoint lawyers as "commissioners" to assist the court. These commissioners studied the briefs, researched the cases, and wrote opinions for the justices. The opinions were issued in the name of the court, typically as written by the commissioners. Thus, the concept of the appellate commissioner "envision[ed] an involvement in the appellate decisional process as deep and extensive as is possible for one not a judge," and various states relied on commissioners from the late nineteenth century until the middle of the twentieth century when they were phased out in favor of other arrangements and devices. Daniel J. Meador, Appellate Courts: Staff and Process in the Crisis of Volume 14-15 (1974).

The other common nonstructural response to growing caseloads was to divide the state supreme court into panels of fewer than all the justices. The typical arrangement was simply to have two panels, with the chief justice sitting on each. The appellate docket was divided evenly between the panels, but the panels had to be unanimous to decide an appeal. If one or more of the justices on the panel dissented, the appeal would be decided by the full court with all the justices sitting on the case. Sitting in panels allowed the courts to decide many more appeals. Again, this coping mechanism continued until it too was overrun by docket growth. Daniel John Meador & Jordana Simone Bernstein, Appellate Courts in the United States 16-17 (1994).

The appellate tier of the simple two-tiered court system eventually would have to be redesigned and reorganized to accommodate more and more appeals and, thus, the modern, more complex appellate court systems would come into being.

I. VERTICAL EXPANSION OF THE JUDICIAL PYRAMID

Nonstructural devices such as the use of commissioners and division of the state supreme court into panels eventually proved to be inadequate to meet the rising tide of cases. The seemingly ineluctable next step was the vertical expansion of the judicial pyramid by creating an altogether new tier of courts: the intermediate appellate courts. This generic name — often abbreviated "IAC" — derives from the simple fact that these courts were inserted between the trial courts and the court of last resort — often abbreviated "COLR." This Chapter focuses on the reasons for establishing such a new tier within the judicial structure, the typical forms these courts take, and the jurisdictional relationship between IACs and COLRs. While the emphasis in this Chapter is on state judicial systems, quite similar concerns were involved in the creation of the federal intermediate appellate courts in 1891 (discussed more fully in Chapter 14) and the same kinds of concerns about their proper functioning in the face of growing caseloads continue to the present day (as we shall learn in the intervening Chapters). The various states went about establishing IACs in fits and spurts, but having an intermediate appellate tier has become the national norm in the recent era of rising appellate caseloads.

STEPHEN L. WASBY, THOMAS B. MARVELL & ALEXANDER B. AIKMAN, VOLUME and DELAY IN STATE APPELLATE COURTS: PROBLEMS AND RESPONSES 51 (1979)[1]

. . . . The first intermediate court was established in New Jersey in the early 18th century. New York followed in 1846, Ohio in 1852, Missouri in 1865, Illinois in 1877, and Louisiana in 1879. These courts were not true appellate courts, though, because their judges, like those in early supreme courts, were mainly trial judges. The first intermediate court specializing in appellate work was established in Ohio in 1883. From then until 1911, 15 more states established true intermediate courts. Three later abolished the courts, however, and until 1958, when the Florida Courts of Appeal were established, only 13 states had intermediate courts. . . . [That signaled the modern era during which 26 other states did so, bringing the current total to 40 states with IACs. Currently, the only states without IACs are: Delaware, Maine, Montana, Nevada, New Hampshire, North Dakota, Rhode Island, South Dakota, Vermont, and Wyoming, plus the District of Columbia.]

---

[1] Copyright © 1979 National Center for State Courts, Williamsburg, Virginia. Reprinted with permission.

Paul D. Carrington, Daniel J. Meador & Maurice Rosenberg, Justice on Appeal 149-50 (1976)[2]

The Double Appeal Hierarchy. Typically, judicial systems which have been threatened with the problem of hyperextension of control have been modified by an extension of the appellate ladder. This is a forthright application of the hierarchical principle comparable to the techniques employed by military or business organizations which, as they outgrow one organizational system, are simply extended into an additional level of command or control. The federal legislation of 1891 [that created the circuit courts of appeals] is the exemplar, but a majority of the states have now followed the pattern of establishing an intermediate level of appeal. The American Bar Association has taken the position that this is the preferred first step to take when the simple one-high-court model has been outgrown.

There are, however, many models of three-level court systems, and they are not equal in their effectiveness in serving the needs of the public and of litigants. There are some adverse consequences associated with each as contrasted with the single appellate court system, but the adverse consequences vary in kind according to the particular features of the model used.

The most primitive hierarchical system is illustrated by the Circuit Court of Appeals Act of 1891 and by early developments in several states. This might be described as the double-appeal model, because most cases were permitted to proceed all the way up the system through two levels of appellate review, if the litigants were disposed to continue litigating. The intermediate tier served to buffer the volume reaching the highest court primarily by exhausting the litigants. The worst feature of this system is the burden it imposes on litigants in both delay and expense. Its advantage is that it effectively maintains uniformity in the system because the highest court retains potential control in virtually every case. Officials, litigants, and lower court judges can assume that any departure from the pattern established by the decisions of the highest court will be corrected by it.

ABA Standards Relating to Court Organization § 1.13 (1990)[3]

1.13 *Appellate Court.* The appellate court should fulfill the judicial functions of reviewing trial court proceedings and formulating and developing the law. Where the volume of appeals is such that the state's highest court cannot satisfactorily perform these functions, a system of intermediate appellate courts should be organized.

(a) *Supreme Court.* The supreme court, or highest appellate court, should have authority to review all justiciable controversies and proceedings, regardless of subject matter or amount involved. Where there is an intermediate court of appeals, appeal to the supreme court as of right should be available only in

---

[2] Copyright © 1976 Thomson West. Reprinted with permission.

[3] Copyright © 1994 American Bar Association. Reprinted with permission.

capital cases and in a limited number of other matters. The supreme court should have discretion to allow an appeal directly from the trial court in cases of great emergency and importance. Its authority should also include jurisdiction of original proceedings for mandamus, prohibition, injunction, and similar remedies, to protect its appellate jurisdiction and to effectuate its supervisory authority over courts below. It should also have ultimate disciplinary authority over members of the judiciary and the bar. The court should sit *en banc*, should have not fewer than five nor more than nine members, and its chief officer should be the chief justice.

(b) *Intermediate appellate courts*. The organization of appellate courts below the supreme court should be guided by the following principles:

(i) Jurisdiction. Every level and division of appellate court should have authority to hear all types of cases; appellate courts of specialized subject-matter jurisdiction should not be established. An appellate court should have jurisdiction of original proceedings for mandamus, prohibition, injunction, and similar remedies, comparable but subordinate to that of the supreme court, to protect its supervisory authority.

(ii) Right of appeal. Appeal as of right should be to the intermediate appellate court only, except as provided under paragraph (a).

(iii) Panels. The decision of an appeal should ordinarily be made by a panel of at least three judges. . . .

Commentary: Appellate courts perform two basic functions. . . . The reviewing function is normally performed at the instance of a party aggrieved by the result in the trial court and is, in any event, performed chiefly for that person's benefit. The function of developing the law is performed for the benefit of the community at large. In court systems with an intermediate appellate court, review by the highest court also serves to coordinate the decisions of the lower appellate courts. In either case, review after the first appeal is only incidentally for the benefit of the particular litigants.

The appellate court should be organized with these functions in mind. The highest appellate court should have authority to review all types of cases, regardless of subject matter or amount involved; important questions of substantive law and procedure can occur in cases of otherwise small significance. . . .

A supreme court should be constituted of an odd number of judges, so that decisions can be reached by majority vote. The number most common and generally satisfactory is seven. This number facilitates the working relationships required to establish concurrence of opinion on difficult legal questions, while at the same time being large enough to provide breadth of viewpoint and the personnel to prepare the opinions that are the principal work product of appellate courts. Nevertheless, some appellate courts have operated effectively with five judges, or nine, as the Supreme Court of the United States. . . .

Where a supreme court by reason of workload is unable to perform both of its principal functions, some additional mechanism of appellate review becomes necessary. This situation has long prevailed in states with large populations, and is becoming increasingly prevalent in states of smaller population. The immediate necessity for an intermediate appellate court may be met or postponed by such devices as use of per curiam and memorandum decisions in cases having limited general significance, by limiting oral argument in appropriate circumstances, and by improved efficiency in management of the highest appellate court's work. On the other hand, such expedients as dividing the highest appellate court into panels, using commissioners to hear cases, or eliminating oral argument dilute the appellate function, particularly that of developing the law. Adding judges to a highest court may actually slow down its operation rather than speed it up. Hence, when improvements in efficiency of operation in the highest court cannot be achieved without dilution of the appellate function, the appropriate solution is the creation of an intermediate appellate court. As there seems little prospect for a long-run decline in the volume of appellate litigation, once the surge of appellate cases has been felt in a state having only one appellate court, steps should be taken promptly to establish an intermediate appellate court rather than temporizing with substitute arrangements. . . .

ROBERT A. LEFLAR, INTERNAL OPERATING PROCEDURES OF APPELLATE COURTS 65-66 (1976)[4]

Advantages and Disadvantages. There can be no uniform rule for all jurisdictions as to what type of added appellate court is best if one is needed. Problems differ among states, just as problems of the federal courts differ from those of the state courts. Some systems, nevertheless, have virtues that others lack. A few years ago, state appellate judges throughout the nation were asked to list the advantages and disadvantages of intermediate courts. . . . In order of importance, the values of intermediate courts were identified as follows: (1) these courts constitute the best available method for dealing with large backlogs; (2) they can significantly decrease the number of appeals going to the highest court; (3) they make appeal available for more cases; (4) they provide a means of appeal at less expense to the litigant; and (5) local districts for appellate divisions reduce the inconvenience to litigants (and usually to their counsel) of traveling long distances to the site of a single central court.

In order of importance, the drawbacks of intermediate courts were listed as follows: (1) they increase the cost to litigants by making an extra appeal necessary in many cases; (2) they increase the length of time between initiation of litigation and its final disposition; (3) maintenance of a three-tier system of courts is more costly to the taxpayers; (4) the system undermines the certainty of precedent as law; and (5) the added court machinery and judicial personnel tend to lower the quality of the appellate judiciary of the state.

The size of appellate caseloads has been the principal factor in deciding whether intermediate courts should be established. Legal doctrine, in any event, is to be laid down by the existing top court. While the basic assumption is that every litigant losing at the trial level should be able to take an appeal, one appeal is enough as far as the interests of parties are concerned. It would be unfortunate to encourage an appeal in every lost case, but it is desirable to preserve the right to every loser who deems it worthwhile to seek review.

---

[4] Copyright © 1976 American Bar Foundation. Reprinted with permission.

Whether an intermediate court is needed depends on how well the top court can handle with fairness and efficiency the appellate business of the state.

ABA Standards Relating to Appellate Courts § 3.01 (1994)[5]

3.01 *Internal Organization of Appellate Courts.*

(a) *Supreme Court.* In hearing and determining the merits of cases before it, the supreme court should sit *en banc*. Except for those who may be disqualified for cause or unavoidably absent, all members of the court should participate in the decision of each case. The court should not sit in panels or divisions, whether fixed or rotating, or delegate its deliberative and decisional functions to officers such as commissioners.

(b) *Intermediate Appellate Courts.* In hearing and determining the merits of cases before it, an intermediate appellate court should sit in panels of at least three judges, with all judges participating in the consideration of each case before the panel of which they are members. Membership in the panels should be changed periodically, at least once a year. The court that sits in more than one panel should strive for decisional consistency, but the ultimate responsibility for it rests with the supreme court. . . .

NOTES

1. Suppose you were a member of a state supreme court in a state without an IAC. What factors would convince you to propose that the legislature create one? If you were a state legislator, what factors would convince you to create one? The menu of the different kinds of IACs is the subject of the next section.

2. A study of seven states found that while case filings and case processing times were reduced in the COLR in the years immediately following creation of the IAC that effect was only temporary: "[U]nless other measures were taken, such as increasing the size or jurisdiction of the intermediate court, the caseload of the court of last resort soon reached the same volume it would have reached if the intermediate appellate court had not been created. Indeed, the establishment of an intermediate court seems to encourage more initial appeals." Victor Eugene Flango & Nora F. Blair, *Creating an Intermediate Appellate Court: Does it Reduce the Caseload of a State's Highest Court?*, 64 Judicature 74, 84 (1980).

3. Concerns for judicial architecture and the effects of caseload growth must be ongoing. The law of unintended consequences applies to court reforms. For example, creating an IAC may solve the immediate caseload problem for the COLR but continued increases in the number of appeals can overload the IAC and create a bottleneck at that level of the state court system. Richard S. Brown, *Allocation of Cases in a Two-tiered Appellate Structure: the Wisconsin Experience and Beyond*, 68 Marq. L. Rev. 189 (1985); Matthew E. Gabrys, *A Shift in the Bottleneck: the Appellate Caseload Problem Twenty Years After the*

---

[5] Copyright © 1994 American Bar Association. Reprinted with permission.

Creation of the Wisconsin Court of Appeals, 1998 WIS. L. REV. 1547. Subsequent Chapters will deal with this scenario.

4. A study of state courts from 1968 to 1984 found that 98% of the growth in filings, decisions, and judges occurred in the IACs. Even if the COLRs' dockets remained stable, however, the supreme courts' actual workload necessarily increased because of the increased difficulty of the average case remaining after the more routine cases were shifted to the IACs. Thomas B. Marvell, *State Appellate Court Responses to Caseload Growth*, 72 JUDICATURE 282, 285 (1989).

5. All these structural developments are not without concern or controversy:

> Most states have accepted the idea that a supreme court should concentrate primarily on the most important cases, on articulating and elaborating principles of law. Some observers applaud this development and call it progress. Our society benefits, they say, when the states' highest courts are aware of issues, policies, and consequences and are responsive to changing circumstances and values. Others find the trend disturbing. The courts, they say, are ill-equipped to act as "roving commissions" in solving social problems. Because there are inevitable limits on the information available to supreme courts, and because of the piecemeal, case-by-case manner in which they act, it is dangerous, the critics charge, to let courts seek out big issues and change the law in big steps. Thus there are those who fear grave miscalculation and social disruption if a handful of judges, unrestrained by the ordinary electoral process, or the need to balance a budget, are encouraged to concentrate on important cases with incredible social impact.

Robert A. Kagan, Bliss Cartwright, Lawrence M. Friedman & Stanton Wheeler, *The Evolution of State Supreme Courts*, 76 MICH. L. REV. 961, 1000 (1978). What do you think? *See generally Symposium, A Tangled Tale: Studying State Supreme Courts*, 22 LAW & SOC'Y REV. 833 (1988).

II. VARIETIES OF INTERMEDIATE COURT STRUCTURES

State intermediate appellate courts can be organized in several ways. (1) There can be a single court of statewide jurisdiction. (2) The intermediate tier can be organized into geographical districts with an appellate court in each district having jurisdiction over trial court decisions in that district. (3) The intermediate tier can be organized into two or more appellate courts, each having jurisdiction over different types of cases. There is no single "best way" to organize state appellate courts. The readings in this section explore the basic options and some of their features.

ABA STANDARDS RELATING TO COURT ORGANIZATION § 1.13 (1990)[6]

Commentary. . . . In the creation of an intermediate appellate court, there are certain organizational aspects that cannot be reduced to formulae. One

---

6 Copyright © 1990 American Bar Association. Reprinted with permission.

is the question of whether the intermediate appellate court should be organized on the basis of geographic regions or as a single, centrally situated tribunal. This depends on such matters as the geographic size of the state, the
location and size of its principal population centers, the pathways in which
appellate litigation originates, and the cohesion of its political structure and
its bar. Related is whether the judges are to be selected statewide or from
regional districts. Another question is whether the judges of the intermediate appellate court should be organized in permanent divisions or should
constitute a single body from which panels are assigned docket by docket.
This depends on the considerations mentioned earlier, and also on such matters as whether the intermediate appellate court has any important administrative responsibilities concerning the trial courts, the degree of deference
which the intermediate appellate court judges are to give opinions by other
panels or divisions of that court, and the frequency and character of the
superintending review provided by the highest court.

There are successful intermediate appellate court systems that have important differences from one another in the respects referred to. At the same time,
. . . intermediate appellate courts should be organized in accordance with certain principles that implement their basic functions.

The first principle is that appellate courts of specialized subject-matter
jurisdiction should not be established. . . . It is, of course, true that many specialized appellate courts have performed honorable and effective judicial service. It is also true that any disestablishment of such courts should be done
with accommodation of the personal, professional, and institutional interests
that should characterize all court reorganizations. Nevertheless, the appellate
court function of developing the law cannot be performed in a coherent and
consistent way if jurisdictional divisions compel the law's fabric to be made in
a decisional patchwork.

A second principle is that a litigant should have only one appeal of right to
the intermediate appellate court in those matters where appeal is allowed,
except as provided in Standard 1.13(a). Review by the highest appellate court
is designed to serve the general public in the proper administration and development of the law and only secondarily the interest of litigants in having their
cases considered by the highest judicial authority. At the same time, the highest court should have authority to permit an appeal to bypass the intermediate appellate court where there is urgent public necessity to do so — for
example, in litigation involving impending elections or deadlocked disputes for
the authority of government officials.

A third principle is that the justices or judges for each level of appellate court
should be appointed or designated to serve in their offices either permanently or
for a substantial term. Maintaining the effectiveness of an appellate court structure requires recognition of the positions of authority held by the various elements of the structure. Rotation or short-term assignment of judges into
positions on an appellate court reduces the authority of each incumbent, and
thus ultimately weakens the authority of the court as a whole. Avoidance of this
consequence is especially important as to the appellate courts' function of
authoritatively expressing the applicable law. It is not inconsistent with observance of this general principle to provide for temporary assignment of judges

upward or downward within a court system. Assignment of trial judges to appellate courts, on a temporary basis and not to avoid creation of needed permanent appellate judgeships, provides valuable experience to the judges involved and an opportunity for assessing their proficiency in an appellate-judicial capacity.

A fourth principle is that an appeal should ordinarily be decided by a panel of at least three judges. This is both a long-established legal tradition and a recognition that an appeal is not merely the opportunity to substitute one judge's view of the law for another's. It does not follow that oral argument must be afforded in every appeal, or that cases on appeal may not be screened to differentiate between those that require fullest consideration and those for which a more summary hearing is appropriate. Procedures by which fewer than three judges make these screening decisions have been successfully adopted in several court systems. . . .

Marlin O. Osthus & Mayo H. Stiegler, State Intermediate Appellate Courts 5-6, 13-16 (rev. ed. 1980)[7]

It has been suggested that the most desirable organization is a single intermediate court with statewide jurisdiction. However, the main reasons cited in support of the single court system are administrative; and it is assumed that geographical districts necessarily entail independently-administered courts. Even with geographical divisions, however, a state intermediate court could be centrally administered, just as trial courts are often administered on a state or regional basis. The primary advantage of permanent districts of an intermediate court is the increased accessibility of the appeals process to state residents. Geographical districts can reduce travel, cost and the time involved in appealing a case from a trial court.

Whether an intermediate court is divided into geographical districts or is state-wide, it may also sit in panels. The majority of states apparently authorize their intermediate courts to sit in panels. The panels may be required to sit in a central location, or at various points in the state. Moreover, the panels may have permanent or rotating membership, although the majority of intermediate courts utilize rotating panels.

[W]hether an intermediate court should be divided into districts or whether it should sit in panels depends upon the peculiar situation of each state. The only generalizations that can be made are that no panel or district should have [fewer] than three judges, and that it is necessary to provide a mechanism to deal with conflicts between panels or districts. . . .

The danger in providing a model for a state appellate system is in reducing the structure to a formula which does not take into account the unique problems of a particular state. The model [below], therefore, is not necessarily the best alternative for a particular state in organizing an intermediate appellate court.

There are successful intermediate courts that significantly differ in jurisdiction, appellate procedure and internal organization. Rather, the purpose of the model is to suggest basic problems that each two-tiered appellate system

[7] Copyright © 1980 American Judicature Society. Reprinted with permission.

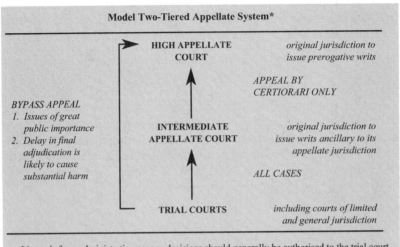

Model Two-Tiered Appellate System*

HIGH APPELLATE COURT — *original jurisdiction to issue prerogative writs*

APPEAL BY CERTIORARI ONLY

BYPASS APPEAL
1. *Issues of great public importance*
2. *Delay in final adjudication is likely to cause substantial harm*

INTERMEDIATE APPELLATE COURT — *original jurisdiction to issue writs ancillary to its appellate jurisdiction*

ALL CASES

TRIAL COURTS — *including courts of limited and general jurisdiction*

*Appeals from administrative agency decisions should generally be authorised to the trial court of general jurisdiction. However, important cases, such as rate-making decisions, could go directly to the intermediate appellate court.

must deal with, even though each state may attempt to deal with the problems in a unique way. . . .

[Five states — Alabama, Indiana, New York, Pennsylvania, and Tennessee — have divided intermediate appellate responsibilities along some kind of subject matter jurisdictional lines, *e.g.,* civil, criminal, tax. In Alabama and Tennessee the] two intermediate courts are labeled the court of civil and the court of criminal appeals. As the names of the courts suggest, the courts of civil appeals have jurisdiction to review civil cases and the courts of criminal appeals have the power to review criminal cases. . . . Pennsylvania's two intermediate courts are not divided into a civil court and a criminal court. The Pennsylvania Commonwealth Court has appellate jurisdiction of all violations of orders or rules of Pennsylvania administrative agencies and all appeals involving the affairs of political subdivisions, including planning or zoning codes or any home rule charter. Thus, the commonwealth court is an intermediate court with specialized or limited appellate jurisdiction. On the other hand, the Pennsylvania Superior Court has appellate jurisdiction from final orders of the court of common pleas [trial court of general jurisdiction], except for those cases within the exclusive appellate jurisdiction of the supreme or commonwealth courts. . . .

Even the simple division of the intermediate courts into a court of civil appeals and a court of criminal appeals may be problematical. Each court may develop its own judicial philosophy. If the ideology of the two courts conflict, civil cases may be treated differently philosophically from criminal cases. Even if the state high court can review both appellate courts' decisions, the high court may not be able to mold the conflicting philosophies into a satisfactory statewide approach. Moreover, the main reason for establishing a two-tiered appellate system is to relieve the congestion in the high court. If the high court must constantly "referee" between the two intermediate courts, the two-tiered system will probably be of limited effectiveness.

The problem of dividing the decision-making function has not been solved in Texas and Oklahoma, even though the supreme courts of the two states do not have the power to review decisions of the courts of criminal appeals. In fact the problem of lack of consistency in the appellate process may be exacerbated. Both states' courts of criminal appeals are courts of last resort in criminal cases. As a result the supreme court in each state decides the philosophical approach of the state for civil cases and the court of criminal appeals in each state sets the philosophical approach for criminal cases. There is not one body which can establish a unified, state judicial approach to cases.

DANIEL JOHN MEADOR, APPELLATE COURTS IN THE UNITED STATES (2nd ed. 2006)[8]

The subject-matter plan of appellate organization has not gained wide popularity in the states. It can be found in Pennsylvania, where the Commonwealth Court has jurisdiction over appeals in cases involving local government units and from state administrative agencies, while the Superior Court takes appeals in all other civil cases and in criminal cases. Alabama and Tennessee maintain separate intermediate courts for civil and criminal cases. Texas and Oklahoma have separate civil and criminal courts of last resort.

Subject-matter courts are inconsistent with the American Bar Association's standards on court organization, which assert that every appellate court should have jurisdiction over the entire range of appellate business. Many lawyers and judges agree with that view. Their apprehension about subject-matter organization seems to stem from their confusing it with specialization.

A subject-matter court need not be specialized. Appellate specialization occurs if a court entertains appeals in only one relatively narrow category of cases. For example, a court could properly be called specialized if its jurisdiction were restricted to deciding patent appeals or worker's compensation cases. The illustration most often cited in the federal system, usually with horror, is the Commerce Court, which existed for a few years just before the First World War. Its jurisdiction was confined to reviewing orders of the Interstate Commerce Commission. It exhibited, or at least suggested to observers, the dangers thought to accompany specialization: risk of capture by those with special interests in the court's work (there, the railroads), tendencies of the judges to lose contact with the general body of jurisprudence and develop esoteric legal views, and difficulty in attracting able lawyers to the bench. However, the U.S. Court of Appeals for the Federal Circuit shows that those dangers can be avoided while at the same time designated categories of cases are routed to a single court; the key to success is the variety of business given the court.

An appellate court with a caseload consisting solely of criminal matters is generally disfavored in the American legal world. In addition to some of the reasons against specialization just mentioned, it is thought that because of the peculiar human element in criminal matters and their special social importance, it is preferable to have criminal appeals decided by a court with at least some judges

---

[8] Copyright © 2006 Thomson West. Reprinted with permission.

who also decide appeals in other legal fields. Thus the scheme found in Texas, Oklahoma, Alabama, and Tennessee does not enjoy wide acceptance.

The subject-matter style of appellate organization has several advantages. It avoids conflicting decisions on the same legal issue — one of the major problems of co-equal regional courts — because only one court decides any given type of case. It also provides the optimum means of achieving coherent development of legal doctrine; a given group of judges dealing over time with a body of law within its exclusive jurisdiction develops a knowledge of the subject and its nuances that judges dealing only occasionally with issues cannot attain. This familiarity enhances efficiency and productivity because the judges do not need to re-educate themselves each time a particular legal issue comes before them. Continuity of decision makers also helps lawyers to predict the likely outcome of appeals and thus retards the filing of hopeless ones. The only disadvantages of subject-matter organization in the intermediate tier are encountered if a court's jurisdiction is defined too narrowly, thus making it a specialized court. The dangers of the specialization can be avoided by giving the court authority over a varied array of case types.

NOTES

1. Assume that you are a member of the legislature in a state in which the decision has been made to create an intermediate court or courts. The state is roughly the shape of a square, approximately 400 miles on each side. The population is approximately 4,000,000. The largest city, with a population of 600,000, is located in the eastern half of the state. The next largest city, with a population of 400,000, is located in the western half of the state. All other cities and towns have populations less than 100,000, and they are about equally distributed across the state. Which of the following would be preferable: (A) a single statewide court (of how many judges?) (sitting in panels or *en banc*?) or (B) more than one geographically organized courts (how many?) (how many judges each?) (sitting in panels or *en banc*?) Note that whichever choice is made, additional decisions must be made about size and organization. Do the answers to these questions depend on the anticipated volume of appeals? And the number of judges that will be required? Are there any advantages to be derived from geographically-organized courts that are not also provided by a single statewide court?

2. Geographically-organized intermediate courts exist in New York, Ohio, Illinois, California, Texas, and Florida. Do these states have anything in common that might explain why each has organized the intermediate tier in this way? Geographically-organized courts can also be found in Arizona, Louisiana, and Missouri. What explains this type of organization in those states?

3. Judicial architecture ought to be designed to accommodate future growth and shifts in population. In a geographically-organized system, new courts might have to be carved out of old courts, like area codes for phone numbers. In Texas, for example, one large city, Houston, has two intermediate courts of appeals, and several counties fall within overlapping appellate court jurisdictions, which creates a problem of forum shopping. And, some appellate courts have dockets so much larger than others that the state has a procedure for one court to transfer appeals to another court in another part of the state for decision. The state supreme court has recommended that the boundary lines

be completely redrawn, but the legislature has not acted to do so. Robert W. Higgason, *A History of Texas Appellate Courts: Preserving Rights of Appeal Through Adaptations to Growth*, HOUSTON LAW. 12 (Aug. 2002); Scott Brister, *Is It Time to Reform our Courts of Appeals?*, HOUSTON LAW. 22 (Apr. 2003). When, if ever, should a legislature be willing to just begin all over and redraw all the geographic lines of the courts in the state?

4. For a proposal to create separate federal criminal courts — district criminal courts, regional courts of criminal appeals, and a national court of criminal appeals — see generally Victor Williams, *A Constitutional Charge and a Comparative Vision to Substantially Expand and Subject Matter Specialize the Federal Judiciary: A Preliminary Blueprint for Remodeling Our National Houses of Justice and Establishing a Separate System of Federal Criminal Courts*, 37 WM. & MARY L. REV. 535 (1996). Are the policy considerations for redrawing the federal court boundaries different from the policy considerations for redrawing court boundaries within an individual state?

III. ALLOCATION OF JURISDICTION BETWEEN INTERMEDIATE COURTS AND THE COURT OF LAST RESORT

This section addresses the distribution of jurisdiction between the two appellate levels. The allocation of functions was earlier addressed in Chapter 4, relating to the lawmaking role of intermediate courts. As revealed there, the traditional view is that the intermediate courts are designed primarily to perform an error-correcting function, with the court of last resort reserved primarily for lawmaking and institutional functions. This perception of the appropriate allocation of functions influences — or should influence — the allocation of jurisdiction within a bi-level appellate structure.

An intermediate appellate court looks in two directions simultaneously — down to the trial courts under its jurisdiction, and up to the supreme court. The material in this section focuses on the jurisdictional relationships between the intermediate court and the supreme court. However, these necessarily involve the jurisdictional relationships between the two appellate levels and the trial courts. The intermediate court must be fitted into what otherwise would be a two-tiered judicial structure in a way that serves the system effectively and with minimum duplication and protraction of litigation. The variety of arrangements that have been developed in American judicial systems are described in this section. You should assess the advantages and disadvantages of each; at the end of this section, you should consider what arrangement seems best and why.

ABA STANDARDS RELATING TO APPELLATE COURTS § 3.00 (1994)[9]

Structure of Appellate Court System. Commentary. The appellate courts have two functions: to review individual cases to assure that substantial justice has been rendered, and to formulate and develop the law for general application in the legal system. In a court system having no intermediate

---

[9] Copyright © 1994 American Bar Association. Reprinted with permission.

appellate level, both functions are performed by the supreme court or a similar court with a different name. In systems having an intermediate appellate court, these functions are to an important degree differentiated. The intermediate appellate court has primary responsibility for review of individual cases and a responsibility, subordinate to that of the highest court, for extending the application of developing law within the doctrinal framework fashioned by the highest court; the supreme court exercises a function of selective review, to maintain uniformity of decision among subordinate courts and to reformulate decisional law in response to changing conditions and social imperatives.

To carry out its responsibilities, the supreme court should have authority to review all types of cases, regardless of subject matter or the amount in controversy. Thus, a supreme court should have authority to review and determine cases involving minor penal infractions or small claims, for they may present questions that should be resolved as a matter of public interest or because of their importance in the administration of justice. Such questions can be important even though they arise in cases that are otherwise of minor consequence because the law governing such cases often affects the interests of hundreds or thousands of citizens.

In court systems having an intermediate appellate court, appeals as of right to the supreme court should be available only in capital cases and in a limited number of other matters. The supreme court should have authority to review any case already determined by an intermediate appellate court, even if the decision in the latter court is unanimous and purports to accord with the law as previously announced by the supreme court. In some court systems with two appellate levels, attempts have been made to preclude supreme court review of intermediate appellate court decisions in certain circumstances. These attempts seek to eliminate the expense and delay involved in such further review. Absolute prohibition of further review is unnecessary to achieve this aim. When the volume of appellate litigation is sufficient to justify establishing an intermediate appellate court, the volume of cases in that court is generally very large in comparison to that of the supreme court, which has the capacity to review only a small proportion of the cases decided by the intermediate appellate court. This practical limitation forecloses successive review except in a relatively small number of cases. . . .

Where there is an intermediate appellate court, appeals should be taken initially to that court, except in capital cases and a limited number of other matters, and be subject to further review only at the discretion of the supreme court. Where the appellate structure consists only of a supreme court, review should be before that court. . . .

ROBERT A. LEFLAR, INTERNAL OPERATING PROCEDURES OF APPELLATE COURTS 70-78 (1976)[10]

In [one state], the state supreme court takes direct appeals from trial courts in equity cases and in cases at law in which the judgment is for more than $10,000, as well as appeals from the Public Service Commission; other appeals

---

[10] Copyright © 1976 American Bar Foundation. Reprinted with permission.

go to the court of civil appeals, from which review by the supreme court is discretionary. In two or three other states, no top-court review is permitted for intermediate decisions in certain types of cases, such as workmen's compensation appeals or cases in which less than a given amount of damages is involved.

It is quite proper for matters of major importance, such as constitutional issues and death-penalty cases, to go directly to the top court; they should go there eventually in any event. Little is gained by running them through the intermediate court first, and both delay and lost effort may ensue. Broader jurisdictional allocations, however, may miss the whole point of having two appellate levels. A case involving less than $10,000 may present basic legal issues that ought to be passed on by the top court, and one involving more than $10,000 may present no such issues. An equity case may or may not produce major issues. Similarly, Public Service Commission and workmen's compensation appeals vary. It is best not to make little supreme courts out of intermediate courts by making their decisions final in cases that fall within some arbitrary classification. Nor should the system be deprived of the economy of appellate [review] in intermediate courts because of a classification that may automatically require the top court to hear unimportant cases. Any type of case can be potentially important. Apart from a few areas such as constitutional law in which nearly all issues are important, it is best to let the intermediate court have jurisdiction over all kinds of appeals, subject to some discretionary authority that will enable the top court to take over the final adjudication of those that, for policy reasons, belong there. . . .

The key factor in the relationship between intermediate and top state courts is that one appellate review is enough to protect the interests of litigants. There would be only one if no intermediate court existed. The reason for establishing intermediate courts is not to increase the number of reviews but rather to see that every appeal is given one decent consideration. If we accept the principle that one appellate review is sufficient, the major problem remaining is what cases go up to the top court and how do they get there?

In general, it can be agreed that cases that involve the making of new law or that present major issues of public policy should go to the top court. . . . If such cases actually belong to the top court in any event, it saves time and avoids duplicative argument and decisional effort to send them there immediately. . . .

In most state systems, some method of select[ing which cases should be reviewed by the top court] at a . . . point [before they have been reviewed by an intermediate appellate court] is nearly always possible. It is true that the intermediate argument and decision that would serve as a preview might be attractive to judges on state supreme courts and induce some of them to encourage the creation of intermediate courts. The fact remains, however, that such a preliminary to the top-court hearing, however helpful, does not justify the delay, the extra expense to the parties of an intervening procedure, and the cost to the taxpayers of maintaining or enlarging an intermediate court to take care of the protracted litigation. The need for an intermediate court and the justification for putting cases on its docket are based on the quantity of appeals in the state. Intermediate state courts are not created to duplicate the work of the top court; they are created to take care of cases that cannot be adequately dealt with by the top court because of sheer bulk.

In a few states, the top court reviews any case in which the intermediate-court decision is not unanimous. That appears to be unnecessary. Appellate courts often are not unanimous; the top court is no more likely to be unanimous than the intermediate court. Unless the issue calls for top-court determination, a divided intermediate court can resolve the appeal as well as can a divided supreme court. Similarly, a loser's simple objection that the intermediate decision is wrong does not constitute a valid ground for additional review. Again, assuming that the nature of the issue does not call for top-court determination, the pragmatic answer is that from the point of view of the loser one appellate court is as likely to be wrong as another. . . .

It is important that the interrelationships between the intermediate court and the top court be intelligently planned and not allowed to develop haphazardly. The two courts should constitute a unified appellate system in which all the units work together to achieve the goals of individual justice and good law with maximum efficiency, with minimum delay, and at reasonable cost. The complete independence of districts and divisions, like the independence of a hog on ice, is inconsistent with orderly performance. The very fact that a state has enough appellate business to require an intermediate court attests to the manifest necessity for careful administrative planning. . . .

NOTES

Jurisdictional Relationships Between Intermediate Courts and the Court of Last Resort: As the foregoing extracts suggest, there are several ways of coordinating the jurisdictions of an IAC and the COLR. These are not mutually exclusive, and in each state (as well as in the federal system) several of them typically will be found in various combinations. The following is a list of the jurisdictional possibilities; examples of each are provided in the next set of Notes. Consider which combination of these would provide the optimum arrangement in relation to the functions to be assigned to the two appellate levels — the IAC and the COLR — and which will be the most efficient to minimize the cost and delay of litigation. (These terms admittedly are jargon, but they provide a useful nomenclature for our study of appellate court systems. Legislatures, courts, lawyers, judges, and commentators utilize these concepts but often without naming them or with different names.)

1. *Bypass*: (a) *Limited bypass:* Most initial appellate jurisdiction vested in the intermediate court, but with direct appellate jurisdiction in the supreme court for a designated few special types of cases; (b) *Extensive bypass:* Some appellate jurisdiction vested in the intermediate court, with a substantial array of direct appellate jurisdiction in the supreme court. Admittedly, the difference between limited and extensive bypass is a matter of degree and somewhat subjective.

2. *Shortstop*: Final jurisdiction vested in the intermediate court for some cases.

3. *Discretionary Double Review*: Initial appellate jurisdiction vested in the intermediate court, with discretionary jurisdiction in the supreme court to review the intermediate court's decisions.

4. *Double Appeals as a Matter of Right*: Initial appellate jurisdiction vested in the intermediate court with provision for appeal from the intermediate court to the supreme court as a matter of right, at least in some types of cases.

5. *Reference or Pour-over*: All direct appellate jurisdiction vested in the supreme court, with that court having authority to refer cases of its choosing to the intermediate court for decision, while retaining others for its own decision.

6. *Certification*: Authority in the intermediate court to certify any appeal lodged there — or sometimes a question in a pending appeal — to the supreme court for decision.

7. *Reach-down*: Authority in the supreme court on its own motion to take up for decision any case pending in the intermediate court.

8. *Leapfrog*: Discretion in the supreme court to grant a litigant's petition to review a case pending in the intermediate court, before judgment in that court.

PAUL D. CARRINGTON, DANIEL J. MEADOR & MAURICE ROSENBERG, JUSTICE ON APPEAL 151-52 (1976)[11]

Bypass and Shortstop. Some of the adverse consequences of vertical extension can be avoided or mitigated by partial eliminations of one step in the ladder. Thus, if the highest court can bear the burden of retaining jurisdiction to take some classes of matters directly from the trial courts, delay and expense can be avoided by means of a bypass of the intermediate court. The highest court then has at least some business which it handles by force of circumstance and not by its own preference. Bypass is used in several states. We favor the use of bypass where feasible. For example, in a state of medium size, it might well be preferable for the highest court to retain jurisdiction over appeals from agencies setting regional or statewide utility rates, or over appeals arising under contemporary environmental protection legislation. Various forms of bypass of intermediate courts are now in use in many state systems.

Two-level review can also be avoided by terminating the ladder at the intermediate level in some kinds of cases. Such a "shortstop" poses some threat to the pure theory of hierarchical control, but it may offer significant practical advantages, provided that the intermediate courts are organized in a manner which permits them to function coherently and uniformly. There are several states which use the intermediate court as a court of near-last resort in some kinds of matters. Workmen's compensation is one example. In all such cases, the highest court retains some narrowly defined power, perhaps only to control possible conflicts with its own exercise of authority; but within its defined range, the intermediate court is nearly always final.

STEPHEN L. WASBY, THOMAS B. MARVELL & ALEXANDER B. AIKMAN, VOLUME AND DELAY IN STATE APPELLATE COURTS: PROBLEMS AND RESPONSES 52-54 (1979)[12]

States have used three basic jurisdictional arrangements, with several variations, to apportion appeals between supreme courts and intermediate courts.

---

[11] Copyright © 1976 Thomson West. Reprinted with permission.

[12] Copyright © 1979 National Center for State Courts, Williamsburg, Virginia. Reprinted with permission.

The most common is to retain direct appeal to the supreme court for a substantial portion of first appeals, particularly those involving major felony convictions and constitutional issues, with the remainder going to the intermediate court(s). With this arrangement, double appeals (one case appealed to two courts) are less frequent because the types of cases for which it is most likely that review would be sought in the court of last resort go directly to that court. A drawback is that initial jurisdictional alignments, even if based on sound judgments about the importance of various types of appeals, only inexactly route to the supreme court on the first appeal the important issues on which that court should make law. Further, whenever the supreme court continues to have substantial mandatory jurisdiction, the division of jurisdiction may be unclear for many appeals, creating confusion among members of the bar and thus leading to the raising of additional jurisdictional issues that the supreme court must decide. More important, the jurisdictional division is very likely to result in uneven distribution of caseload between the supreme court and the intermediate court. (This should not cause delay, however, unless one level were underworked.) If initial jurisdictional distributions were based on the composition of the appellate caseload when the intermediate courts were established, they may later become unsuitable if certain types of appeals increase disproportionately. This problem must be addressed by action of the legislature.

[In t]he second type of jurisdictional arrangement, favored in the American Bar Association's standards, . . . [a]lmost all first appeals are to the intermediate court, leaving the supreme court with discretionary jurisdiction over intermediate court decisions and mandatory jurisdiction only over extraordinary writs. In this arrangement, the court of last resort can select for review, if it wishes, only those issues important for lawmaking, leaving error correction to the intermediate courts.

The third type of jurisdictional division, a relatively recent innovation, exists in only a few states [Hawaii, Idaho, Iowa, Oklahoma, Mississippi, and South Carolina]. . . . Appeals are sent initially to the supreme court, which retains some cases and refers the others to the intermediate court ["reference jurisdiction"]. The supreme court has discretionary jurisdiction over intermediate court decisions, but review is seldom granted, so double appeals are a minor problem. Apportionment of workloads between the two levels of appellate court can be adapted easily to resources available. The supreme court can retain the appeals containing issues important for lawmaking, permitting their prompt resolution. This third jurisdictional arrangement is not free of drawbacks, however. The supreme court judges must spend extra time reviewing and allocating the cases, necessarily adding an additional step that may contribute to delay. If the supreme court is not also sensitive about the caseload of the intermediate court, the intermediate court might become overloaded and then delayed.

Beyond these basic jurisdictional arrangements are several important variations that can affect the apportionment of appeals between intermediate and supreme courts and thus affect appellate court delay and backlog. In many states, appeals originally filed in the intermediate court can be transferred to the supreme court. Many states have provisions allowing the supreme court to bypass the intermediate court in cases containing major, important issues that need prompt resolution. The bypass mechanism also can be used to relieve overloaded intermediate courts whenever the supreme court can handle more than its regular caseload. In several states, intermediate courts can certify cases to the supreme court whenever the intermediate court believes the issues are of major importance. This greatly speeds the disposition of those issues. Certification may take considerable judge time, however, since both the intermediate and the supreme courts must review the case.

California has another variation. In addition to having the power to balance caseloads among district courts of appeal by reassigning cases from one district to another, the Supreme Court may take a case *sua sponte* after it has been decided by the court of appeal, even though no petition for further review has been filed. The high court can use this power to clarify the law and to reconcile rulings of the courts of appeal with its own rulings, either recently released or soon to be announced. This mechanism, clearly part of the court's lawmaking function, is seldom used, but can serve to protect the interests of parties in individual cases, too.

NOTES

Examples of Provisions Governing Jurisdictional Relationships: Examples of each of the eight previously listed types of jurisdictional relationships are set out below. When considering these, evaluate the merits and demerits of each of these arrangements. Every jurisdictional arrangement has advantages and disadvantages, benefits and costs. Consider whether a particular arrangement provides a net gain for the administration of justice that outweighs whatever disadvantages and costs may be involved. How does the likelihood of appellate review and its procedures affect lawyers' strategies and the logistics of litigation?

Provisions Permitting Only One Review

1. *Bypass*

a. *Limited Bypass*:

Illinois Constitution, art. 6, § 4(b):

> Appeals from judgments of Circuit Courts imposing a sentence of death shall be directly to the Supreme Court as a matter of right. The Supreme Court shall provide by rule for direct appeal in other cases.

Illinois Supreme Court Rule 302(a):

> Appeals from final judgments of circuit courts shall be taken directly to the Supreme Court (1) in cases in which a statute of the United States or of this State has been held invalid, and (2) in proceedings commenced [to compel compliance with the chief circuit judge's orders].

Georgia Constitution, art. 6, § 6, ¶ II:

> The Supreme Court shall be a court of review and shall exercise exclusive appellate jurisdiction in the following cases:

> (1) All cases involving the construction of a treaty or of the Constitution of the State of Georgia or of the United States and all cases in which the constitutionality of a law, ordinance, or

constitutional provision has been drawn into question; and (2) All cases of election contest.

b. *Extensive Bypass*:

Virginia Code § 17.1-406 (B):

> In accordance with other applicable provisions of law, appeals lie directly to the Supreme Court from a conviction in which a sentence of death is imposed, from a final decision, judgment or order of a circuit court involving a petition for a writ of habeas corpus, from any final finding, decision, order, or judgment of the State Corporation Commission, and from proceedings [for revocation of an attorney's license] and [for revocation of a professional law corporation's certificate of registration]. Complaints of the Judicial Inquiry and Review Commission shall be filed with the Supreme Court of Virginia. The Court of Appeals shall not have jurisdiction over any cases or proceedings described in this subsection.

2. *Shortstop*

Georgia Supreme Court Rule 40:

> A review on *certiorari* is not a right. A petition for the writ will be granted only in cases of great concern, gravity, and importance to the public. Subject to the foregoing, *certiorari* generally will not be granted: (1) To review the sufficiency of evidence; (2) Where the Court of Appeals has affirmed the denial of a motion to dismiss, denial of a motion for judgment on the pleadings, or a denial of a motion for summary judgment.

Virginia Code § 17.1-410:

> A. Each appeal of right taken to the Court of Appeals and each appeal for which a petition for appeal has been granted shall be considered by a panel of the court. When the Court of Appeals has (i) rejected a petition for appeal, (ii) dismissed an appeal in any case in accordance with the Rules of Court, or (iii) decided an appeal, its decision shall be final, without appeal to the Supreme Court, in:
>
> 1. Traffic infraction and misdemeanor cases where no incarceration is imposed;
>
> 2. Cases originating before any administrative agency or the Virginia Workers' Compensation Commission;
>
> 3. Cases involving the affirmance or annulment of a marriage, divorce, custody, spousal or child support or the control or disposition of a juvenile and other domestic relations cases arising, or involving adoption;
>
> 4. Appeals in criminal cases [by the Commonwealth in felony actions; cross-appeal by defendant.] Such finality of the Court of Appeals' decision shall not preclude a defendant, if he is convicted, from requesting the Court of Appeals or Supreme Court on direct appeal to reconsider an issue which was the subject of the pretrial appeal; and

5. Appeals involving involuntary treatment of prisoners.

B. Notwithstanding the provisions of subsection A, in any case other than an appeal [by the Commonwealth in felony actions] in which the Supreme Court determines on a petition for review that the decision of the Court of Appeals involves a substantial constitutional question as a determinative issue or matters of significant precedential value, review may be had in the Supreme Court.

Provisions Permitting Two Reviews

3. *Discretionary Double Review*

In most states the supreme court has a substantial measure of discretionary jurisdiction to review intermediate court decisions on the petition of a party. Those supreme courts typically have adopted rules governing the exercise of that discretion. The Louisiana Supreme Court rule provides a good example. That rule, and the rules of numerous other state supreme courts, are modeled after a rule of the Supreme Court of the United States governing the exercise of its *certiorari* jurisdiction, which we will study in Chapter 12.

Supreme Court of Louisiana, Rule X, § 1, Writ Grant Considerations:

(a) The grant or denial of an application for writs rests within the sound judicial discretion of this court. The following, while neither controlling nor fully measuring the court's discretion, indicate the character of the reasons that will be considered, one or more of which must ordinarily be present in order for an application to be granted:

1. Conflicting Decisions. The decision of a court of appeal conflicts with a decision of another court of appeal, this court, or the Supreme Court of the United States, on the same legal issue.

2. Significant Unresolved Issues of Law. A court of appeal has decided, or sanctioned a lower court's decision of, a significant issue of law which has not been, but should be, resolved by this court.

3. Overruling or Modification of Controlling Precedents. Although the decision of the court of appeal is in accord with the controlling precedents of this court, the controlling precedents should be overruled or substantially modified.

4. Erroneous Interpretation or Application of Constitution or Laws. A court of appeal has erroneously interpreted or applied the constitution or a law of this state or the United States and the decision will cause material injustice or significantly affect the public interest.

5. Gross Departure From Proper Judicial Proceedings. The court of appeal has so far departed from proper judicial proceedings or so abused its powers, or sanctioned such a departure or abuse by a lower court, as to call for an exercise of this court's supervisory authority.

When a court of last resort is vested with discretion, to any degree, to review decisions of the intermediate court, it is necessary to fix the number of judges required to grant review. As we will study in Chapter 12, the Supreme Court of the United States grants review if there are four votes among the nine Justices; thus, a minority of the Court can control the Court's docket to select less than 100 cases out of more than 5,000 petitions for review. In some states, a majority of the justices must concur in the grant of review. Which of these two procedures is preferable?

4. *Double Appeals as a Matter of Right*

Ohio Constitution, art. 4 § 2(B)(2):

> The supreme court shall have appellate jurisdiction as follows:
>
> (a) In appeals from the courts of appeals as a matter of right in the following:
>
> (i) Cases originating in the courts of appeals; (ii) Cases involving questions arising under the constitution of the United States or of this state.

Provisions for Switching Cases Between the Two Appellate Levels

5. *Reference or Pour-Over*

Hawaii Revised Statutes § 602-5(8):

> All cases addressed to the jurisdiction of the supreme court or of the intermediate appellate court shall be filed with the supreme court as shall be provided by rule of court. The chief justice or the chief justice's designee from any of the associate justices or the intermediate appellate judges, shall receive each case and shall assign the case either to the intermediate appellate court or to the supreme court within twenty days of the filing deadline for the last document permissible to be filed in the case pursuant to court rule.

Idaho Code § 1–2406:

> (1) Any provision of law to the contrary notwithstanding, the Idaho court of appeals shall have jurisdiction to hear and to decide all cases assigned to it by the Idaho supreme court; provided, that the supreme court shall not assign cases invoking the supreme court's original jurisdiction, nor appeals from imposition of sentences of capital punishment in criminal cases, nor appeals from the industrial commission, nor appeals from the public utilities commission.
>
> (2) In assigning cases to the Idaho court of appeals, the Idaho supreme court shall give due regard to the workload of each court, to the error review and correction functions of the court of appeals, and to the desirability of retaining for decision by the supreme court those cases in which there is substantial public interest or in which there are significant issues involving clarification or development of the law.
>
> (3) Upon motion of any party, or upon recommendation of the court of appeals, or upon its own motion, the supreme court may revoke assignment of a case to the court of appeals. In the event of such transfer or revocation of assignment, the case shall be heard and decided by the supreme court.

Idaho Appellate Rule 108(b):

> Generally, cases which involve consideration of existing legal principles will be assigned to the Court of Appeals. In assigning cases to the Court of Appeals, due regard will be given to the workload of each court, and to the error review and correction functions of the Court of Appeals. . . .Ordinarily, the Supreme Court will retain the following classes of cases:
>
> (1) Cases in which there is substantial public interest;
>
> (2) Cases in which there are significant issues involving clarification or development of the law, or which present a question of first impression;
>
> (3) Cases which involve a question of substantial state or federal constitutional interpretation;
>
> (4) Cases raising a substantial question of law regarding the validity of a state statute, or of a county, city, or other local ordinance;
>
> (5) Cases involving issues upon which there is an inconsistency in the decisions of the Court of Appeals or of the Supreme Court.

6. *Certification*

Georgia Constitution, art. 6, § 5, ¶ IV:

> The Court of Appeals may certify a question to the Supreme Court for instruction, to which it shall then be bound.

Ohio Constitution, art. 4 § 2(B) (2) (f):

> The supreme court shall review and affirm, modify, or reverse the judgment in any case certified by any court of appeals pursuant to section 3(B)(4) of this article.

Ohio Constitution, art. 4 § 3 (B) (4):

> Whenever the judges of a court of appeals find that a judgment upon which they have agreed is in conflict with a judgment pronounced upon the same question by any other court of appeals of the state, the judges shall certify the record of the case to the supreme court for review and final determination.

7. *Reach-down*

Illinois Supreme Court Rule 302 (b):

> Cases in Which the Public Interest Requires Expeditious Determination. After the filing of the notice of appeal to the Appellate Court in a case in which the public interest requires prompt adjudication by the Supreme Court, the Supreme Court or a justice thereof may order that the appeal be taken directly to it. Upon the entry of such an order, any documents already filed in the Appellate Court shall be transmitted by the clerk of that court to the clerk of the Supreme Court. From that point the case shall proceed in all respects as though the appeal had been taken directly to the Supreme Court.

Virginia Code § 17.1-409:

A. In any case in which an appeal has been taken to or filed with the Court of Appeals, the Supreme Court in its discretion, on motion of the Court of Appeals, or on its own motion, may certify the case for review by the Supreme Court before it has been determined by the Court of Appeals. The effect of such certification shall be to transfer jurisdiction over the case to the Supreme Court for all purposes.

B. Such certification may be made only when, in its discretion, the Supreme Court determines that:

1. The case is of such imperative public importance as to justify the deviation from normal appellate practice and to require prompt decision in the Supreme Court, or 2. The docket or the status of the work of the Court of Appeals is such that the sound or expeditious administration of justice requires that jurisdiction over the case be transferred to the Supreme Court.

Alabama Code § 12-3-15:

When it is deemed advisable or necessary for the proper dispatch of the business of the Alabama court of civil appeals, the chief justice of the supreme court, with the advice of the supreme court, and the presiding judge of the court of civil appeals, may in writing designate any case in the Alabama court of civil appeals to be transferred to the supreme court for a hearing and final determination by that court. Such written designation shall be entered upon the minutes of each of the courts, and the clerk of the court of civil appeals shall deliver to the clerk of the supreme court the transcript of the record and other papers in the cases so designated, together with copies of any orders that may be made in any of such cases by the court of civil appeals. Upon the making and entering of such designation, the jurisdiction and control of the court of civil appeals over the designated case shall cease and terminate. [In identical language, § 12-3-14 authorizes a similar transfer of cases from the court of criminal appeals to the supreme court.]

8. *Leapfrog*

28 U.S.C. § 1254:

Cases in the courts of appeals may be reviewed by the Supreme Court by the following methods: (1) By writ of *certiorari* granted upon the petition of any party to any civil or criminal case, before or after rendition of judgment or decree. . . .

U.S. Sup. Ct. R. 11:

A petition for a writ of *certiorari* to review a case pending in a United States court of appeals, before judgment is given in that court, will be granted only upon a showing that the case is of such imperative public importance as to justify deviation from normal appellate practice and to require immediate settlement in this Court.

For examples of cases in which the Supreme Court granted review without waiting for a court of appeals decision, see *Youngstown Sheet & Tube Co. v. Sawyer*, 343 U.S. 579 (1952) (steel seizure case), and *United States v. Nixon*, 418 U.S. 683 (1974) (Watergate tapes case).

9. *None of the Above.* Florida has a rather Byzantine arrangement in that the discretionary jurisdiction of its supreme court is circumscribed and confined to specified situations. FLA. CONST. art. 5, § 3 (b)(3)-(5). The state constitution provides that the supreme court may review a decision of one of the district courts of appeal — the five geographical regional IACs — only if the decision: (1) expressly declares a state statute valid, or expressly construes a provision of the state or federal constitutions; (2) expressly affects a class of constitutional or state officers; or (3) expressly and directly conflicts with a decision of another district court of appeal or of the supreme court on the same question of law. The supreme court also may review a district court of appeal decision that passes upon a question certified by the IAC to be of great public importance or to be in direct conflict with a decision of another IAC. In addition, the supreme court may review an order or judgment of a trial court certified by the district court of appeal in which the appeal is pending to require immediate resolution by the Supreme Court and either to be of great public importance or to have a great effect on the proper administration of justice. One consequence of this arrangement is that the IACs exercise a level of finality that is unique among the states. *See generally* Gerald B. Cope, Jr., *Discretionary Review of the Decisions of Intermediate Appellate Courts: A Comparison of Florida's System with Those of the Other States and the Federal System*, 45 FLA. L. REV. 21 (1993); Ben F. Overton, *District Courts of Appeal: Courts of Final Jurisdiction with Two New Responsibilities — An Expanded Power to Certify Questions and Authority to Sit En Banc*, 35 U. FLA. L. REV. 80 (1983).

10. *Federal Arrangements.* The statutes on federal appellate jurisdiction in Title 28 of the U.S. Code neatly illustrate how the various options and features sketched above can be combined and incorporated into one appellate court system. Basically, the federal scheme is in line with that endorsed by the ABA STANDARDS, *i.e.*, in almost all cases, appeals go directly from the district courts to the courts of appeals as a matter of right under 28 U.S.C. § 1291, with the Supreme Court exercising discretionary jurisdiction over the decisions of the courts of appeals. 28 U.S.C. § 1254(1) authorizes the Supreme Court to review, by writ of *certiorari*, any case in a court of appeals, before judgment or after judgment in that court (*leapfrog* and *discretionary*). 28 U.S.C. § 1254(2) authorizes a court of appeals to certify a case to the Supreme Court for review (*certification*). 28 U.S.C. § 1253 authorizes direct appeals from the district courts to the Supreme Court in cases heard and decided by a district court of three judges (*bypass*). Congress also can, and occasionally does, include a fast-track jurisdictional provision in an otherwise substantive statute that guarantees a direct mandatory appeal to the Supreme Court from a district court decision on the constitutionality of the particular statute (*bypass*). *E.g., United States v. Eichman*, 496 U.S. 310 (1990) (striking down the Flag Protection Act). The jurisdiction of the Supreme Court of the United States is more fully covered in Chapter 12.

IV. DOCTRINAL CONSISTENCY WITHIN THE INTERMEDIATE TIER

In a state that has created one or more intermediate appellate courts, it is generally assumed that the task of maintaining statewide uniformity in decisional law ultimately lies with the supreme court. But rampant inconsistency within the intermediate tier could exceed the capacity of the supreme court to achieve that supervisory goal. The volume of decisions at the intermediate level also could be so large that the supreme court would be unable to exercise a sufficient degree of control to eliminate appellate inconsistencies. Moreover, it is desirable that there be coherence and uniformity in the decisions rendered at the intermediate level. The appellate judiciary at each level should, to the greatest extent possible, speak with one coherent voice to articulate and apply the law of the state. If the state has a single statewide intermediate court, in which the judges are not too numerous, there generally will be little problem in maintaining decisional consistency because there is a continuity of decision-makers. When such a court grows in size and sits in multiple combinations of three-judge panels, however, the risks of inconsistency increase. Also, when the state's intermediate tier is divided geographically into districts, there is a risk of inconsistency between or among the districts. Risks of inconsistency increase still further when each district court consists of numerous judges sitting in panels of three. In that situation, there is a double threat of inconsistency in the decisional law of the state: first, between panels within the same district and second, between panels of one district and panels of other districts.

The intermediate appellate courts have developed various methods of policing their own decisions to maintain decisional harmony. The material in this section is concerned with the use of these methods within the intermediate tier of a relatively large system. The emphasis here is on state courts. Similar problems exist within the federal intermediate tier, however, and those special concerns will be considered in Chapter 14.

ABA STANDARDS RELATING TO APPELLATE COURTS § 3.01 (1994)[13]

Commentary. In an intermediate appellate court that sits in panels, membership in the panels should be rotated at least once a year. Intermediate appellate courts with permanently fixed panels tend to become substantially separate courts, with consequent problems of decisional inconsistency and discrepancy in procedural policies and practices. In some courts organized in this way, the dispositional time varies greatly among panels, resulting in further unequal treatment of litigants. Periodic and random rotation of panels reduces these problems and makes the court as a whole, rather than its panels or divisions, the focus of the loyalty and identity of its judges and court staff.

Some intermediate appellate courts rotate their panels for each day's argument calendar, often under a procedure in which the composition of the panel is not disclosed to the litigants until the time of argument. These procedures seek to eliminate any suggestion of favoritism or advantage in the designation

---

[13] Copyright © 1994 American Bar Association. Reprinted with permission.

of panels. This objective can be achieved equally well, however, by strict adherence to rules governing assignment of cases among panels. In some appellate courts, particularly those whose judges are geographically separated, continuous rotation of panel membership would complicate scheduling and communication among judges. . . .

An appellate court that sits in panels should have initial procedures by which to reduce the possibility that conflicting decisions will be rendered by different panels.

The federal courts of appeals, state intermediate appellate courts, and state supreme courts that sit in panels sometimes hear cases *en banc*. *En banc* hearings are held so that the court as a whole can authoritatively resolve a question on which there is or may be a difference of opinion between panels. The need for such a resolution is clear in a state supreme court that sits in panels. A similar need exists in the federal courts of appeals because of their responsibility for maintaining consistency in the law applied in the circuit and because the limited caseload capacity of the United States Supreme Court makes it difficult for it to perform that function satisfactorily. In a few state court systems, the relationship between the intermediate appellate court and the supreme court is such that the intermediate appellate court must assume responsibility for consistency of decision similar to that exercised by the federal courts of appeals. In most state court systems having an intermediate appellate court, further review by the supreme court is an adequate means of resolving decisional conflicts not only between separate geographical divisions of the intermediate appellate court but also between panels within such divisions. The extent to which *en banc* hearings may be necessary therefore depends on the organization of a particular appellate system, the size of the caseload within the system, and the allocation of responsibility for maintaining consistency in the law applied in the jurisdiction.

En banc hearings may be held before, and thus in lieu of, or after a panel has decided a case. A case should be heard initially *en banc* when preliminary consideration indicates that it involves an issue that might require *en banc* consideration in any event because of division of opinion within the court, or that it is of such importance that the court as a whole should participate in its decision. A case should be heard *en banc* following a panel decision if a conflict cannot be resolved by modification of the panel opinion after its circulation within the court. In any event, *en banc* hearings should be kept to a minimum because they impose a heavy burden on the court's time and, if held after a panel decision, impose an additional burden on litigants.

Consistency of decision by intermediate appellate courts can be furthered if the panels within such a court treat decisions of other panels as binding precedent and if each division or department (or circuit in the federal system) gives special deference to prior decisions of other such divisions or departments. According such effect to decisions of judges of coordinate authority does not require that difference of judicial opinion be stifled. Signaling disagreement, and inviting its resolution by the highest court, can be achieved equally well by appropriate statement in a court's opinion. This practice is particularly appropriate with regard to questions of statutory interpretation and the law governing the activities of administrative agencies.

John C. Godbold, *The Eleventh Circuit Court of Appeals — The First Ten Years,* 43 MERCER L. REV. 961, 969-70 (1992)[14]

Assignments of judges to panels and of cases to panels are made by separate sources, with neither source knowing what the other is doing. Judges are assigned by a committee of judges that does not include the chief judge. As far as feasible no judges sit regularly together or regularly at the same site. Panel assignments for a court year are completed about six months before the court year begins and are made known to the judges. The information is otherwise confidential, and assignments are not revealed to the clerk. Most panels are composed of two active judges with a senior or visiting judge as the third member.

The clerk puts together the argument calendars. After a calendar is formulated the names of the judges who will sit on the calendar are then delivered to the clerk. Under this system no case is assigned to a particular judge or judges, and no judge is selected to sit on a particular case. A judge cannot arrange to be assigned to a particular case.

COOK v. COOK
560 N.W.2d 246 (Wis. 1997)

SHIRLEY S. ABRAHAMSON, Chief Justice.

This is a review of the published decision of the court of appeals. . . . A recurring issue raised by the court of appeals in the present case and in other recent decisions and certifications to this court is whether the court of appeals has the power to overrule, modify or withdraw language from a previously published decision of the court of appeals. . . .

To answer the question posed we must examine the constitutional and statutory provisions defining the authority of the court of appeals. The court of appeals was created in 1977 by amendment to the Wisconsin constitution. Article VII, section 2 provides that the judicial power of the state is vested in a unified system consisting of one supreme court, a court of appeals, a circuit court, and trial and municipal courts. . . .

The constitution and statutes provide that the judges of the court of appeals are elected from districts, and that the districts of the court of appeals sit in different parts of the state. Nevertheless the constitution has been interpreted as establishing the court of appeals as a unitary court. "The constitutional and statutory provisions clearly set forth the mandate that the Court of Appeals function as a single court under a chief judge and not function as four separate courts." *In re Court of Appeals*, 263 N.W.2d 149 (1978). The statute provides that officially published opinions of the court of appeals shall have statewide precedential effect. Wis. Stat. § 752.41 (1995-96). *See also* Wis. Stat. (Rule) § 809.23 (1995-96) (publication of opinions).

Thus, the principle of *stare decisis* is applicable to the decisions of the court of appeals. The principle of *stare decisis* does not, however, answer the

---

[14] Copyright © 1992 Mercer Law Review. Reprinted with permission.

question before us because *stare decisis* contemplates that under limited circumstances a court may overrule outdated or erroneous holdings.

Judges of the court of appeals have responded differently to the question of the court of appeals' ability to overrule, modify or withdraw language from erroneous past precedent. Judge Gartzke in his concurring opinion in the present case opines that most judges of the court of appeals believe, as he does, that the court of appeals may not overrule a prior decision of the court of appeals. Judges Moser, Sullivan and Fine have concluded that even though the court of appeals had previously erred it was required to follow the erroneous opinion. Judge Eich [was] apparently persuaded in another case that a district has the power to withdraw language from or to overrule a statement in a previously published opinion but should apply the principles of *stare decisis*. Judge Brown has written that if a panel "feels that the written decision of another panel is wrong, it is probably better to write a decision following, although criticizing, that panel than to certify the issue."

Judge Dykman reports "an evolving consensus among court of appeals publication committee members that the court of appeals is powerless to overrule its erroneous decisions." Judge Dykman, disagreeing with this consensus and supporting the view that the court of appeals may overrule its prior published opinions, posits two reasons for the conclusion that the court of appeals cannot overrule, modify or withdraw language from its prior published opinions: First, a published opinion is binding. Second, the power to overrule, modify or withdraw language from a prior published opinion might "be abused, leading to a situation where the precedential effect of an opinion would last only until the issue arose before another panel." Judge Dykman is not persuaded by either reason. According to Judge Dykman, the statutory mandate that published opinions are binding does not resolve the question of the power to overrule. And, he believes, the stabilizing effect of precedent would not be lost because overruling erroneous past precedent would not "become everyday fare for the court of appeals." Judge Dykman argues that undesirable consequences flow from failing to recognize the power of the court of appeals to overrule, modify or withdraw language from a prior published opinion. The court of appeals has, he believes, avoided overruling cases by artificially limiting a holding, by drawing irrelevant distinctions or by ignoring prior rulings.

Judge Dykman's concerns are valid. Yet, we do not resolve this debate on these policy grounds. Rather, we believe the proper interpretation of the constitutional and statutory authority of the court of appeals lies in an analysis of the functions of the court of appeals and the supreme court. The court of appeals, a unitary court, has two functions. Its primary function is error correcting. Nevertheless under some circumstances it necessarily performs a second function, that of law defining and law development, as it adapts the common law and interprets the statutes and federal and state constitutions in the cases it decides.

In contrast, [this] supreme court's primary function is that of law defining and law development. The supreme court, "unlike the court of appeals, has been designated by the constitution and the legislature as a law-declaring court." The purpose of the supreme court is "to oversee and implement the statewide development of the law." *State v. Schumacher*, 424 N.W.2d 672

(1988). The supreme court is the only state court with the power to overrule, modify or withdraw language from a previous supreme court case.

If the court of appeals is to be a unitary court, it must speak with a unified voice. If the constitution and statutes were interpreted to allow it to overrule, modify or withdraw language from its prior published decisions, its unified voice would become fractured, threatening the principles of predictability, certainty and finality relied upon by litigants, counsel and the circuit courts. Further, with the ability to rely on the rules set out in precedent thus undermined, aggrieved parties would be encouraged to litigate issues multiple times in the four districts.

Four principles are clear: The court of appeals is a unitary court; published opinions of the court of appeals are precedential; litigants, lawyers and circuit courts should be able to rely on precedent; and law development and law defining rest primarily with the supreme court. Adhering to these principles we conclude that the constitution and statutes must be read to provide that only the supreme court, the highest court in the state, has the power to overrule, modify or withdraw language from a published opinion of the court of appeals. In that way one court, not several, is the unifying law defining and law development court.

The court of appeals, however, is not powerless if it concludes that a prior decision of the court of appeals or the supreme court is erroneous. It may signal its disfavor to litigants, lawyers and this court by certifying the appeal to this court, explaining that it believes a prior case was wrongly decided. Alternatively, the court of appeals may decide the appeal, adhering to a prior case but stating its belief that the prior case was wrongly decided.

For the reasons set forth we conclude that the court of appeals may not overrule, modify or withdraw language from a previously published decision of the court of appeals. The decision of the court of appeals is affirmed.

REPORT OF THE APPELLATE PROCESS TASK FORCE ON THE CALIFORNIA COURTS OF APPEAL 58-63 (August 2000)[15]

1. Stare Decisis in California Courts. As a general matter, *stare decisis* is the judicially-created principle that precedents should ordinarily be followed. This principle helps bring greater predictability and stability in the application and development of law by judges. Instead of every legal issue being decided anew with each case, judges ordinarily will apply the law as previously declared by other judges. *Stare decisis* does not imply rigidity in the law, however, since it is a doctrine that admits of exceptions when necessary to achieve justice and to move the law forward.

In California, one of the primary authorities discussing *stare decisis* is *Auto Equity Sales, Inc. v. Superior Court* (1962) which held:

> Under the doctrine of *stare decisis*, all tribunals exercising inferior jurisdiction are required to follow decisions of courts exercising superior jurisdiction. Otherwise, the doctrine of *stare decisis* makes no

---

[15] Available at http://www.courtinfo.ca.gov/reference/4_11courtscoa.htm.

sense. The decisions of this court are binding upon and must be followed by all the state courts of California. Decisions of every division
of the District Courts of Appeal are binding upon all the justice and
municipal courts and upon all the superior courts of this state, and
this is so whether or not the superior court is acting as a trial or appellate court. Courts exercising inferior jurisdiction must accept the law
declared by courts of superior jurisdiction. It is not their function to
attempt to overrule decisions of a higher court.

This discussion of *stare decisis* emphasizes the "vertical" aspect of the doctrine,
that is, the rule that courts of a lower jurisdiction are *bound* to follow decisions
from courts of higher jurisdiction. Thus, a decision by the Supreme Court of
California is binding on all lower courts. Similarly, a decision by a Court of
Appeal is binding on all lower courts so long as there is no conflicting Courts
of Appeal authority (as explained below, a Court of Appeal is *not* bound to follow other Court of Appeal decisions). When there is a conflict between two or
more Court of Appeal decisions, the trial courts may choose among the conflicting appellate decisions.

Stare decisis also has a "horizontal" component dealing with the question of
whether courts of equal jurisdiction are bound to respect and follow each other's
decisions. There is some authority for the proposition that a decision by one
panel of the Courts of Appeal is binding on all other panels of the Courts of
Appeal until the first decision is disapproved by the California Supreme Court.
The Supreme Court suggested as much in *Cole v. Rush* (1955), overruled on
other grounds in *Vesely v. Sager* (1971). Referring to an appellate decision as to
which the Supreme Court denied hearing, the court said: "[The Court of Appeal]
judgment stands, therefore, as a decision of a court of last resort in this state,
until and unless disapproved by *this court* or until change of the law by legislative action." This statement seems to say that even the panel of the Courts of
Appeal which made the decision could not later overrule it.

Some [older Court of Appeals] cases follow[ed] the suggestion in *Cole v.
Rush*. However, [the leading treatise] flatly states otherwise: "A decision of a
Court of Appeal is not binding in the Courts of Appeal. One district or division may refuse to follow a prior decision of a different district or division, for
the same reasons that influence the federal Courts of Appeals of the various
circuits to make independent decisions." 9 WITKIN, CAL. PROCEDURE, APPEAL,
§ 934, at 971 (4th ed. 1997). There are many cases supporting this statement
of the law, and it is clear that Courts of Appeal are following Witkin's interpretation of *stare decisis* instead of [the 1955 dictum] in *Cole v. Rush*.

Many reasons support this approach to *stare decisis*. First, permitting every
Court of Appeal to render its own interpretation of the law, relatively uncon-
strained by the opinions of other Court of Appeal panels, subjects the law to
constant reevaluation and testing in the crucible of individual cases. Second,
conflicts among Court of Appeal decisions are an important way in which new
ideas can be introduced into the law. Good ideas can flourish, while bad ideas
will ultimately whither. Third, conflicts create an ongoing, informed debate
that helps to inform the Supreme Court when it intervenes to resolve the conflict. Fourth, requiring one panel of the Courts of Appeal to follow another
might introduce an unhealthy element of competition within the Courts of

Appeal as one panel tries to rush to publication an opinion in an area where there may be multiple appeals pending raising the same or similar issues. Particularly in light of the Supreme Court's power and responsibility to resolve important conflicts between Court of Appeal decisions, a substantial majority of the Task Force members concludes that the benefits of California's approach outweigh the temporary confusion and risk of inconsistent results introduced into the law by permitting each Court of Appeal panel to follow its own conscience in stating and interpreting the law.

In summary, California law has fully embraced a strong concept of *stare decisis* in its vertical component, but has rejected *stare decisis's* horizontal component.

2. Criticism of California's Version of Stare Decisis and Proposals for Reform. There are critics of California's rejection of the horizontal components of *stare decisis* who raise two primary concerns. First, absent a doctrine of horizontal *stare decisis*, it is possible for conflicts to arise between districts and divisions that remain unresolved for many years (because the California Supreme Court may not intervene to resolve the conflict). Conflicts create confusion and disharmony in the law. Second, even absent clear conflicts, the absence of horizontal *stare decisis* fosters an undercurrent of uncertainty in the development of the law, over-emphasizing for each three-judge appellate panel its independence from other panels of the Courts of Appeal. Critics note that California's approach to horizontal *stare decisis* is unique among state courts.

These criticisms may, as a practical matter, be somewhat exaggerated. The number of conflicts between published Courts of Appeal opinions does not appear to be large, and the Supreme Court appears to be taking up most conflicts under its review jurisdiction. Moreover, conflicts permit an issue to be fully vented in the Courts of Appeal before being taken up by the Supreme Court. Thus, conflicts between districts and divisions have both positive and negative features.

As for the asserted undercurrent of uncertainty, although one panel of the Courts of Appeal is technically not bound to follow decisions from other panels, panels in practice appear to respect the view of other panels and to reject such views only for important reasons that are set forth in the court's opinion. In other words, an informal version of horizontal *stare decisis* may operate in practice, if not in theory.

There are essentially two versions of horizontal *stare decisis* that might be considered. First, California could adopt a state-wide doctrine, generally binding all three-judge panels in the State to follow the opinions of earlier panels. Second, California could adopt an intra-district doctrine, generally binding three-judge panels within a district to follow decisions from within that district. (This is similar to the rule followed in the federal circuit courts of appeal.)

The Task Force was nearly unanimous in concluding that there should be no change in California's doctrine of *stare decisis*. California has lived with its current doctrine for many decades, and there is no broad-based movement for reform of the doctrine coming from the bench or the bar. Although concerns about unresolved conflicts and simmering uncertainty are legitimate, a convincing case has not yet been made that the number of conflicts or the degree of uncertainty is so high that horizontal *stare decisis*, statewide or intra-district, has become necessary as an antidote.

3. En Banc Panels and Stare Decisis. Although there was no consensus on the Task Force that horizontal *stare decisis* should be introduced in California, there was general agreement that if a stronger version of horizontal *stare decisis* existed in California, it would be advisable to create some form of *en banc* procedures. An *en banc* procedure envisions calling together more than three Courts of Appeal justices to resolve an important legal question or a legal question where there exists a conflict in the Courts of Appeal. The decision of the *en banc* panel then becomes generally binding upon other panels of the Courts of Appeal (subject, of course, to contrary action by the Supreme Court).

It would be possible to create a doctrine of horizontal *stare decisis*, either statewide or intra-district, without creating *en banc* procedures. If conflicts between Courts of Appeal opinions developed notwithstanding *stare decisis*, or conflicts between districts developed in the context of intra-district *stare decisis, those conflicts* could still be resolved as they are today by the California Supreme Court. An *en banc* procedure is not logically necessary as an adjunct to horizontal *stare decisis*.

However, the Task Force sees significant advantages to having an *en banc* procedure if horizontal *stare decisis* is introduced. Under current law, three-judge panels can express their disagreement with the opinions of other three-judge panels by voting their conscience. If horizontal *stare decisis* were introduced, disagreements between panels might not be expressed as readily in published opinions, but the disagreements might persist below the surface and affect decision-making and opinion writing in subtle ways. The *en banc* procedure serves, in part, as a safety valve for the expression of these differing viewpoints. It permits difficult issues to be addressed by a large number of Courts of Appeal justices thereby reflecting the collective wisdom of a wider range of experiences and viewpoints.

The Task Force considered two types of *en banc*s, a statewide *en banc* to handle conflicts among districts and divisions, an intra-district *en banc* to handle conflicts only within a district. There was no interest in creating intra-district *en banc*s, which were viewed as excessively cumbersome in light of the relatively low payoff (*i.e.,* reducing conflicts only within a single district). The Task Force decided that a statewide *en banc* was not appropriate at this time. As noted above in the discussion of *stare decisis*, the Task Force is not convinced that there are enough important, unresolved conflicts among districts and divisions to justify the expense and additional bureaucratization required by an *en banc* procedure. Absent such conflicts, the primary justification for an *en banc* procedure disappears. If it appears that the number of unresolved conflicts starts to rise to a substantial and unacceptable level, the Task Force would recommend that a statewide *en banc* procedure be reconsidered.

Virginia Code Ann. § 17.1-402

D. The Court of Appeals shall sit *en banc* (i) when there is a dissent in the panel to which the case was originally assigned and an aggrieved party requests an *en banc* hearing and at least three other judges of the court vote in favor of such a hearing or (ii) when any judge of any panel shall certify that in his opinion a decision of such panel of the court is in conflict with a prior decision of the court or of any panel thereof and three other judges of the court concur in that view. The court may sit *en banc* upon its own motion at any time, in any case in which a majority of the court determines it is appropriate to do so. The court sitting *en banc* shall consider and decide the case and may overrule any previous decision by any panel or of the full court.

E. The court may sit *en banc* with no fewer than eight judges. In all cases decided by the court *en banc*, the concurrence of at least a majority of the judges sitting shall be required to reverse a judgment, in whole or in part.

FED. R. APP. P. 35, *En Banc* Determination

(a) When Hearing or Rehearing *En banc* May Be Ordered. A majority of the circuit judges who are in regular active service may order that an appeal or other proceeding be heard or reheard by the court of appeals *en banc*. An *en banc* hearing or rehearing is not favored and ordinarily will not be ordered unless: (1) *en banc* consideration is necessary to secure or maintain uniformity of the court's decisions; or (2) the proceeding involves a question of exceptional importance.

(b) Petition for Hearing or Rehearing *En banc*. A party may petition for a hearing or rehearing *en banc*.

(1) The petition must begin with a statement that either:

(A) the panel decision conflicts with a decision of the United States Supreme Court or of the court to which the petition is addressed (with citation to the conflicting case or cases) and consideration by the full court is therefore necessary to secure and maintain uniformity of the court's decisions; or

(B) the proceeding involves one or more questions of exceptional importance, each of which must be concisely stated; for example, a petition may assert that a proceeding presents a question of exceptional importance if it involves an issue on which the panel decision conflicts with the authoritative decisions of other United States Courts of Appeals that have addressed the issue.

. . . .

(f) Call for a Vote. A vote need not be taken to determine whether the case will be heard or reheard *en banc* unless a judge calls for a vote.

NOTES

1. Vertical *stare decisis*. Why must an inferior court obey a superior court and follow its precedents in the first place? Is it always required? The principle is so deeply ingrained that it is difficult to articulate its justifications. Are the justifications different for different levels of courts? In the classic three-tier hierarchical state court system, are the reasons a trial court must follow the precedents of the IAC and the COLR different from the reasons an IAC must follow the precedents of the COLR? Evan H. Caminker, *Why Must Inferior Courts Obey Superior Court Precedents?*, 46 STAN. L. REV. 817 (1994). Recall the discussion of judicial lawmaking in Chapter 4.

2. Horizontal *stare decisis*. As the materials in this section reveal, there are four standard means by which an intermediate appellate court may seek to achieve doctrinal uniformity in its own decisions to be consistent in the application of the decisional law over time, *i.e.*, to decide like cases alike: (1) adhering to the rule of precedent that a decision of one panel of the court is binding on all other panels of the court in subsequent cases; (2) providing for an *en banc* hearing before all the judges; (3) requiring that draft opinions be circulated to all judges of the court before issuance by a panel, affording the opportunity for non-panel judges to submit comments and suggestions to the panel; (4) requiring that panel composition be constantly altered so that each judge of the court sits with all other judges of the court on a relatively frequent basis to maintain a consensus. What are the costs and benefits of each of these means? Which works best? Can they be implemented in combination? In addition to these standard means, greater uniformity might be achieved through an internal subject matter organization of panels, although American appellate courts have not employed this means to any significant extent; this idea will be explored in Chapter 14.

3. Why do the Eleventh Circuit (*see* the Godbold excerpt above) and most other large appellate courts that sit in three-judge panels maintain such elaborate secrecy about panel composition and panel dockets? How does a system of constantly rotating panels promote consistency to a greater degree than permanent panels? *See generally* J. Robert Brown, Jr. & Allison Herren Lee, *Neutral Assignment of Judges at the Court of Appeals*, 78 TEX. L. REV. 1037 (2000).

4. In an intermediate appellate court in which the decision of one panel is binding on all other panels, in the absence of being displaced by an *en banc* decision or by the decision of the supreme court, suppose panel #1 decides the case of *A v. B*. Thereafter, the case of *C v. D* comes before panel #2. The legal issue in *C v. D* is identical to that decided in *A v. B*. The decision in *A v. B* is directly adverse to the position being asserted by the appellant in *C v. D*. The appellant argues that the inability of panel #2 to reexamine the issue and possibly overrule the prior decision of panel #1 deprives appellant of due process of law because it would bind the parties in the second case by a proceeding in which they had no opportunity to be heard. Is there any merit to this argument?

5. Like the current California approach described in the Task Force Report excerpted above, the Michigan Court of Appeals used to take the position that a panel decision was not binding on other panels of the court. This approach, however, resulted in a substantial and worsening confusion in the case law of the state. *See* Edward M. Wise, *The Legal Culture of Troglodytes: Conflicts Between Panels of the Court of Appeals*, 37 WAYNE L. REV. 313 (1991). That unsatisfactory situation eventually led to the adoption by the Supreme Court of Michigan of *Administrative Order 1990-6* (Oct. 1990), which provides:

> *Resolution of Conflicts in Court of Appeals Decisions*. A panel of the Court of Appeals must follow the rule of law established by a prior published decision of the Court of Appeals issued on or after November 1, 1990. The prior published decision remains controlling authority unless reversed or modified by the Supreme Court or a special panel of the Court of Appeals. . . . A panel which follows a prior published

decision only because it is required to do so shall so indicate in the text of its opinion, citing this Administrative order.

Which approach to precedent in a state IAC makes more sense: the California approach or the Michigan approach, and why?

6. Among the IACs in the fifty states, the rules of *stare decisis* vary considerably from state to state. *See generally* Brian E. Mattis & B. Taylor Mattis, *Erie and Florida Law Conflict at the Crossroads: The Constitutional Need for Statewide Stare Decisis*, 18 NOVA L. REV. 1333 (1994); Taylor Mattis, *Precedential Value of Decisions of the Court of Appeals of the State of New Mexico*, 22 N.M. L. REV. 535 (1992); Taylor Mattis & Kenneth G. Yalowitz, *Stare Decisis Among [sic] the Appellate Court of Illinois*, 28 DEPAUL L. REV. 571 (1979); Taylor Mattis, *Stare Decisis Among and Within Florida's District Courts of Appeal*, 18 FLA. ST. U. L. REV. 143 (1990); Taylor Mattis, *Stare Decisis Within Michigan's Court of Appeals: Precedential Effect of Its Decisions on the Court Itself and on Michigan Trial Courts*, 37 WAYNE L. REV. 265 (1991); Jennifer K. Anderson, Comment, *The Minnesota Court of Appeals: A Court Without Precedent?*, 19 WM. MITCHELL L. REV. 743 (1993); Paul W. Werner, Comment, *Navigating the Straits of Stare Decisis and the Utah Court of Appeals: The Scylla of Under-Application and the Charybdis of Over-Application*, 1994 BYU L. REV. 633.

7. The decisions of one of the twelve regional U.S. courts of appeals, panel or even *en banc*, are merely persuasive authority and are not binding precedent in the other courts of appeals — each court of appeals has its own "law of the circuit." But in all the U.S. courts of appeals the practice is to consider the decision of any three-judge panel to be the decision of the court and hence binding on all other subsequent three-judge panels. *See, e.g., Davis v. Estelle*, 529 F.2d 437, 441 (5th Cir. 1976) ("One panel of this Court cannot disregard the precedent set by a prior panel, even though it conceives error in the precedent. Absent an overriding Supreme Court decision or a change in the statutory law, only the Court *en banc* can do this."). This is sometimes called the "rule of interpanel accord." Chief Judge Friendly commented on the geographical hegemony of federal law:

> A presupposition of the "law of the circuit" concept is that a court of appeals is not overly impressed by the fact that another has reached a contrary conclusion. One circuit will follow another or others when it is persuaded, has no strong views either way, or considers immediate nationwide uniformity unusually important, but generally not when it firmly believes the other circuit or circuits have been wrong. The volume of precedents in each circuit and in the Supreme Court has become so great that only rarely is it necessary to rely on opinions of other circuits, and a district court opinion is not likely to have an impact merely as authority unless it comes from a judge enjoying special esteem. The circuits have become increasingly ingrown or, if one prefers a less pejorative term, self-contained.

Henry J. Friendly, *The "Law of the Circuit" and All That*, 46 ST. JOHN'S L. REV. 406, 413 (1972). If there happen to be two previous circuit precedents that are in conflict on the same issue of law, the general rule of *stare decisis* in the circuits is that the later panel is supposed to follow the earlier-in-time of the two previous panels; in that situation, however, the U.S. Eighth Circuit's unique rule of *stare decisis* permits the later panel to choose to follow either of the two previous conflicting panel decisions. *See United States v. Va Lerie*, 385 F.3d 1141, 1151 (8th Cir. 2004) (Riley, J., dissenting). Would it be possible to impose the general rule of interpanel accord across the entire country — on all 12 regional courts of appeals and on all their 168 judges — so that every panel in every circuit would be bound to follow a previous panel decision in any other circuit? Would it be a good idea? *See* Mary Garvey Algero, *A Step in the Right Direction: Reducing Intercircuit Conflicts by Strengthening the Value of Federal Appellate Court Decisions*, 70 TENN. L. REV. 605 (2003).

8. The Virginia statute excerpted above is representative of state statutes that authorize a state's IAC to sit *en banc* — the court has eleven judges sitting in three-judge panels. In other states, however, the IACs are not authorized to sit *en banc*. Those courts thus lack this particular mechanism for maintaining internal decisional harmony among their panel decisions and must rely on other mechanisms. What are the alternatives to *en banc* rehearings? *See generally* John V. Orth, *Why the North Carolina Court of Appeals Should Have a Procedure for Sitting En Banc*, 75 N.C. L. REV. 1981 (1997).

9. What are the kinds of cases that satisfy FED. R. APP. P. 35 above and therefore should be reheard *en banc*? If a three-judge panel is supposed to follow prior decisions of previous three-judge panels of the same court, when is it "necessary to secure or maintain uniformity"? If an appeal presents "a question of exceptional importance," then should not the Supreme Court be expected to grant the petition for a writ of *certiorari*? *See generally* Michael Ashley Stein, *Uniformity in the Federal Courts: A Proposal for Increasing the Use of En Banc Appellate Review*, 54 U. PITT. L. REV. 805 (1993).

10. The U.S. Ninth Circuit is unique among the federal IACs for its limited *en banc*:

> Traditionally, the determination whether to hear a case *en banc* has been made by the same group of judges that would decide the merits if the hearing is granted: all the circuit judges in regular active service. However, when Congress expanded the Ninth Circuit Court of Appeals from thirteen to twenty-three judgeships in the Omnibus Judgeship Act of 1978, it also made special provisions for large circuits. Section 6 of the act authorized any court with more than fifteen active judges to "perform its *en banc* function by such numbers of members of its *en banc* court as may be prescribed by rule of the court of appeals." Although [three] of the twelve circuits are now eligible to exercise this option, only the Ninth Circuit has done so. Under [Ninth] Circuit Rule 35-3 . . . the *en banc* court consists of the chief judge and ten additional judges drawn by lot from the active judges of the circuit. The power to select cases for *en banc* hearing remains, as the statute apparently requires, with the full court.

Arthur D. Hellman, *Maintaining Consistency in the Law of the Large Circuit*, in RESTRUCTURING JUSTICE: THE INNOVATIONS OF THE NINTH CIRCUIT AND THE FUTURE OF THE FEDERAL COURTS 63 (Arthur D. Hellman, ed. 1990). Is the Ninth Circuit's limited *en banc* court a good idea? What is gained and what is lost between having all the court's judges sit on the *en banc* court and having fewer than half of them chosen at random to sit *en banc*?

Interestingly, the Ninth Circuit has never held a "super" *en banc* rehearing from the limited *en banc* rehearing, in which all 28 judges would sit. Instead, the limited *en banc* has been used routinely in the Ninth Circuit — although it is suggestive of its controversial nature that other large courts of appeals have not implemented the congressional authorization to have an *en banc* court of fewer than all their judges. In 2005, the Ninth Circuit increased the size of its *en banc* court from eleven to fifteen, a majority of its twenty-eight authorized judges. This change was in part in response to criticisms of a court of less than a majority. But if the Judicial Conference's currently pending recommendations to add seven additional judgeships are approved by Congress, the Ninth Circuit would be obliged to increase its *en banc* court to eighteen members to maintain a majority of active judges.

Chapter 7

PERSONNEL RESPONSES TO THE CRISIS OF VOLUME

As we studied in Chapter 6, the first response of a judicial system to a marked increase in appeals that exceeds the decisional capacity of the supreme court typically has been to redesign the structure of the system by creating one or more intermediate appellate courts. This Chapter and the next deal with possible responses when the volume of appeals continues to grow apace and eventually outruns the additional appellate capacity of the intermediate court as originally designed. These responses have taken basically two forms: adding personnel, the subject of this Chapter, and altering internal processes and procedures, the subject of Chapter 8. The three types of added personnel discussed here are judges, law clerks, and central staff attorneys.

Our primary focus is on intermediate courts and how they have coped with the crisis of volume. The intermediate courts sometimes are referred to as the work horses or the front-line troops of the appellate system. These metaphors reflect the reality that intermediate courts bear the brunt of appellate business; they are the first and only forums for review in the great majority of cases, civil and criminal. Because their jurisdiction is mostly mandatory, they have relatively little control over their dockets; they must hear and decide all appeals brought to them by litigants complaining of trial court rulings. Thus, it is in these courts that the growth in appeals has been most dramatically felt, causing the judges and concerned legislatures to take novel steps that might have been deemed unacceptable absent a sense of crisis and a perceived threat to the function and design of the appellate court system. Each "reform" or "improvement" that has been taken or that could be taken — whether it be adding personnel or modifying traditional appellate procedure — has both advantages and disadvantages, costs as well as benefits. You should be alert to understand and appreciate what these are in each instance.

The problems of volume have afflicted both federal and state appellate courts, and the responses in all systems have a great deal in common. Thus in general we make no distinction between state and federal appellate courts in the materials that follow. Some of the distinctively federal problems and solutions will be addressed in Chapter 14.

I. JUDGES

As appeals increase and dockets grow in an intermediate appellate court, the judges tend to work harder and faster in an attempt to avoid the accumulation of an unseemly backlog. But when volume continues to rise, even the judges' extra efforts will not be sufficient. Backlogs will grow, and intervals from the filing of appeals to their disposition will lengthen. The typical first response to this problem is to consider adding judges to the court. This idea rests on the obvious premise that if the work is too much for the available hands, more hands are needed.

Yet there are significant concerns associated with this seemingly obvious solution. Creating new judgeships is not a cheap solution: besides the judge's salary, there are significant incidental expenses for the judge's chambers, secretary, law clerks, travel, library resources, and other necessary equipment and support services. There is an often-expressed concern for devaluing of the judicial currency by the multiplication of the number of judges. Having more judges creates greater stresses on collegiality, which is the subject of Chapter 9. And, as we have seen in Chapter 6, maintaining doctrinal consistency is both more important and more difficult the more judges there are sitting in more combinations on panels deciding appeals. Consider the advantages and disadvantages to the court system — the costs and benefits — of adding appellate judges.

STEPHEN L. WASBY, THOMAS B. MARVELL & ALEXANDER B. AIKMAN, VOLUME AND DELAY IN STATE APPELLATE COURTS: PROBLEMS AND RESPONSES 43-45 (1979)[1]

The appellate bench originally consisted of judges who spent much or most of their time riding circuit as trial judges. During the early and mid-19th century the states responded to increasing appellate caseloads by slowly abandoning circuit riding. The next step was to remove the judges' trial duties. [No comprehensive history of this trend is available, although there are many descriptions of specific states. The Alabama Supreme Court, for example, became a full-time appellate court in 1832. . . . The Pennsylvania Supreme Court made this change in 1874 after many years of gradual withdrawal from trial duty. . . . In Maryland the court of last resort consisted of trial judges from 1806-1851, appellate judges only until 1867, trial judges again until 1945, and appellate judges only from then on. . . . The Illinois Supreme Court made the final transition in 1848. . . .] Although the evidence is skimpy, it seems that the transition to specialized appellate courts was nearly complete by the turn of the century, and in recent years among the state supreme courts only judges of the Maine Supreme Judicial Court have retained a dual trial and appellate role.

The second major adaptation was to increase the number of judgeships. The vast majority of state supreme courts had three to five judges until the mid-1800s and then expanded by at least two judges by the turn of the century. Expansion slowed during the early 1900s and virtually stopped after the 1930s. On the other hand, the number and size of intermediate courts has increased greatly. There were 175 intermediate court judges in 1933 and 184 in 1956. [In 1979 there were 498. In 1991 there were 795. In 2003 there were 986.]

Adding judges would seem to be a way of reducing delay and, indeed, may be necessary simply to keep a court's backlog from getting worse. Caution

---

[1] Copyright © 1979 National Center for State Courts, Williamsburg, Virginia. Reprinted with permission.

must be exercised, however, in making the decision to add judges. One of the best statements on the possible effects of this action on delay was made in 1933: "Where the service is an individual one, a saving in time can be effected by increasing the number of judges, but where the service is collective no such gain is possible." This suggests the complexities of the problem. For one thing, the more judges on a court, the more the "managerial" or administrative problems. For example, a three-judge appellate court usually sits only *en banc*, while a seven-judge court might sit in panels that then must be set up and coordinated. Adding judges produces the problem of integrating new members of a court and raises the possibility of internal doctrinal conflict or inconsistency. When additions to the court are temporary, there is less opportunity for the new members to learn the norms and thought processes operative in the court, even if the new judges are conscientious in their efforts to absorb the court's ways of deciding its cases. As the size of a court increases, the use of and number of panels increases. This leads to increased problems of consistency of decision making among the panels. And large numbers of judges on a court makes convening of *en banc* courts difficult in terms of both the mechanics of convening the judges and the conduct of oral argument and conference. Finally, in those courts in which all opinions are circulated among all judges, increasing the number of judges operates to increase the time required to produce each opinion. . . .

The addition of judges also must be examined in relation to expected and actual individual judge productivity, defined as dispositions per judge. If judges already on a court "relax" when new judges are added, delay reduction may be less than expected. On the other hand, within limits, productivity can increase without the addition of judges if judges perceive backlog as a problem and adjust their work habits and procedures to improve productivity. (Ironically, such enhanced activity may make it difficult to convince legislators that more judges are necessary. This "Catch 22" situation may affect judges' incentives to increase productivity.)

Even if it is concluded that new judges are needed to achieve a reduction in delay, there clearly are a number of factors beyond the size of the caseload and the extent of delay that influence the decision of a court to seek additional judicial positions and of a legislature and executive to grant them:

- The short-term financial situation of the funding jurisdiction;

- The long-term financial impact of the new position(s), including pension and other fringe benefits, additional support staff, and additional office, library, and, perhaps, courtroom space;

- The present availability of office and courtroom space;

- Other needs and priorities of the court or of the judicial system;

- Concern about diluting the status of the position;

- Present political relations among the three branches of government;

- The public's support for or opposition to "the courts"; and, possibly,

- The present and anticipated methods of selecting new judges.

The influence of each of these factors varies considerably among states and over time within a state. Whether they operate independently of a court's caseload and delay situation or reinforce the need as shown by court statistics also varies, but all states share the reality that data alone do not determine the question.

Thomas B. Marvell, *Appellate Capacity and Caseload Growth*, 16 AKRON L. REV. 43, 49-52 (1982)[2]

[A]lthough additional judgeships can help supreme courts solve backlog problems, this solution quickly reaches an upper limit. Increasing the number of supreme court justices to nine or more suffers from a considerable weight of negative commentary and a lack of precedential models in the country. Intermediate courts, on the other hand, appear to have no upper limit in size although extremely large courts suffer from several practical problems. . . .

All 53 state high courts[3] have nine or fewer active judges. . . . [Seven] have nine judges, [twenty-eight] have seven, . . . eighteen have five. . . . More than nine judges seems to be out of the question for supreme courts. The available information indicates that during the nation's history only two state courts of last resort, New Jersey and Virginia, have ever had more than nine judges. Adding judgeships, moreover, has not been a favored means of increasing supreme court capacity in recent years; only 11 states have enlarged their top courts since 1950 in spite of the tremendous caseload increase everywhere. The ABA STANDARDS RELATING TO COURT ORGANIZATION support the existing state practices; Standard 1.13(a) states that the highest court "should have not [fewer] than five nor more than nine members." The commentary to this Standard suggests seven as the preferred number. . . .

[A]dditional judges do not necessarily relieve each judge of other decisional tasks. . . . The time required to maintain a collegial climate increases.

An exception occurs when the court sits in panels. Additional judges can be employed to form more panel sittings, and the output per judge should remain constant as long as decisions are not regularly reviewed by nonpanel members. *En banc* hearings are more unwieldy and time-consuming in larger courts; but, if *en bancs* are infrequent, the additional workload is relatively small compared with the relief accorded because panel sittings and opinion writing would be apportioned to a larger number of judges.

Consequently, the advisability of enlarging a court is closely connected with the advisability of the panel system. . . . [R]outine decision-making by panels, especially three-judge panels, is commonly considered objectionable in a high court. One major disadvantage is the possibility of inconsistent decisions. The probability of this result would increase proportionally with the enlargement

---

[2] Copyright © 1982 Akron Law Review. Reprinted with permission.

[3] [19] The fifty-three courts include the supreme courts in the fifty states, plus the District of Columbia Court of Appeals and the Oklahoma and Texas Courts of Criminal Appeals, which are courts of last resort.

of the court; the numeric basis for variation increases with the enlarged number of possible panel compositions.

The great majority of intermediate courts, on the other hand, sit in panels, generally of three judges. Consistency of decision is not as important in intermediate courts as in supreme courts because conflicts between panel decisions can be resolved upon further review. As a result, the number of intermediate court judgeships has increased substantially, more than doubling in the past fifteen years although increasing at a rate far slower than the caseload increase. The cost of new judgeships is probably the major factor limiting the expansion of intermediate courts. There may also be an upper limit at which the multiplicity of intermediate court panels would exceed the supreme court's ability to monitor the consistency of rulings below. The largest intermediate court systems are now in Texas, California, Ohio, Florida, New York, Louisiana, [and Illinois] with [80, 105, 68, 62, 70, 53, 52] judges respectively. These intermediate court systems are still considerably smaller than the federal system [179 circuit judgeships], where the issue of monitoring intermediate court decisions has been long debated.

PAUL D. CARRINGTON, DANIEL J. MEADOR & MAURICE ROSENBERG, JUSTICE ON APPEAL 138-46, 196-97 (1976)[4]

Obstacles to Enlargement of Appellate Court Systems. There are a number of reasons for caution in increasing the number of appellate judgeships. One familiar difficulty is the financial cost. All public budgets are finite; public money spent to provide appellate judgeships will not be spent on other important needs. . . . [However,] the cost of appellate justice is small in relation to other public expenditures. Indeed, appellate court expenditures are small even in relation to the other costs of law administration.

In response to these observations about the relative cost of appellate courts, it is sometimes said that court systems may be like highways in that the more we build, the busier they are. There is some reason to believe that this similarity may hold with regard to trial courts. It has been theorized that as trial justice becomes more available, fewer litigants settle privately and more remain in the queue to secure the service. But both observation and reason suggest that this theory, even if it is valid for trial courts, is inapplicable to appellate courts. Increases in appellate caseload, have not, in the experience of any system which publishes statistics, been shown to relate to increases in judgeships. And it should not be expected that there would be such a relationship; rather the effect of increased manpower in the appellate court should be to improve it. Moreover, litigants who have made the major investment of money, time, and emotional stress in a trial are unlikely to be easily affected in their appetite for appellate relief by marginal increases in the quality and availability of appeal.

It is unlikely that the minor financial cost of enlargement is the operative reason for the fact that many legislatures have not provided an adequate number of appellate judgeships. Natural inertia has sometimes been reinforced by

---

[4] Copyright © 1976 Thomson West. Reprinted with permission.

the failure of those directly involved — the judges themselves — to ask for adequate judgeships. In part, the judges may be motivated by a rational concern for the possible dilution of the status of the appellate judicial office.

Certainly it is not inappropriate to be concerned about the status of the judicial office. High status of judges is an essential element in the success of any judicial system in maintaining public esteem for its product. It is doubtful, however, that appellate judicial commissions would really be seriously cheapened by greater currency. The primary ingredients of the status of the office are tradition, method of selection, compensation, and working conditions. A legislature which maintains adequate levels of compensation and assures the judges of sufficient time and supporting services to exercise a high level of professional competence can be reasonably assured that it has done most of what can be done to attract persons of high quality to the appellate bench. Candidates of high quality are not so rare that a doubling or tripling, even, of most appellate court systems would necessitate a significant diminution of the quality of the judiciary.

The rational concern for status of judges may sometimes be enhanced by a less rational, but quite natural anxiety of the judges about the disturbance to their relations and habits caused by the introduction of numbers of new coworkers. Perhaps this feeling can be described as a variety of the territorial imperative. Without giving this attitude undue weight, responsible legislators should recognize it as real and take it into account in appraising the counsel of judges who recommend against new judgeships.

A more substantial obstacle to the enlargement of appellate court systems is presented by the problem of assimilating the additional judges. . . . [T]he addition of appellate judges is a more difficult matter than adding trial judges, each of whom functions autonomously as an additional unit of capacity at the trial level. Appellate judges do not function autonomously, but are expected to act in unitary collegia, and to serve as coordinators and harmonizers. Therein lies the problem. . . . [T]he problem is soluble, at varying costs; appellate judicial systems are expandable. But, as expansion increases, the system tends to be less effective and tends to require increasingly significant internal adjustments which affect the process. Therefore, our willingness to add judgeships should be to some extent influenced by the size of the system to be enlarged. . . .

IN RE CERTIFICATION OF NEED FOR ADDITIONAL JUDGES
863 So.2d 1191 (Fla. 2003)

Per Curiam. Each year Florida's Constitution requires this Court to certify the need for new judges throughout the state using uniform standards.[5] This is the sole constitutional mechanism for ensuring that every Legislature has

---

[5] [1] Article V, Section 9, Florida Constitution provides:

Determination of number of judges. The supreme court shall establish by rule uniform criteria for the determination of the need for additional judges except supreme court justices, the necessity for decreasing the number of judges and for increasing, decreasing or redefining appellate districts and judicial circuits. If the supreme court finds that a need exists for increasing or decreasing the number of judges or increasing,

an accurate system wide assessment of the judges needed to serve Florida's communities. The goal is to provide an effective and efficient justice system for Florida's growing population that will insure and protect the Rule of Law, the cornerstone of democracy in our state and our nation. The Rule of Law is the truest indicator of a healthy democracy. It is the idea that no person is greater than the law and that, under the law, no one is less important than any other. Key to the operation of the Rule of Law is a core belief: Justice must be timely dispensed to truly be justice. This in turn implies a judicial system with sufficient resources to make timeliness possible.

We continue to use established objective measures to determine judicial caseload and the corresponding need for additional judges. Our analysis in past years — and again today — has not only been conservative but has strongly emphasized the need to use less expensive alternatives and to maximize efficiency before seeking more judges. We have steadily moved toward court models that rely heavily on alternatives and skilled support staff. . . .

In the district courts of appeal, these models have included adding staff attorneys to conduct important research and to do preliminary screening and analysis of cases, thus freeing the judges to devote their important and more costly time to their most crucial duty — deciding appeals. [T]hese efforts are highlighted by a voluntary decision by the district court judges to increase their own recommended caseload by forty percent, in *lieu* of adding more judges. This decision reflects not only the dedication of these judges, but also the efficiencies they have achieved through the use of enhanced judicial staff. . . .

We also stress that our certification is not a statement of what Florida State Courts subjectively want. Rather, it is a statement of what the State Courts objectively need to meet their workload, using accepted standards of measurement. In order to ensure that the certification is as objective as possible, the constitutional framers reposed this duty in the Supreme Court, which itself neither benefits nor loses by the Legislature's final decision on the issue.

We also must acknowledge the very positive efforts of the Legislature in responding to the needs of the judicial branch. We understand the competing priorities lawmakers face in every session. Despite these pressures, the Legislature still has funded a number of new judgeships at the trial and

---

decreasing or redefining appellate districts and judicial circuits, it shall, prior to the next regular session of the legislature, certify to the legislature its findings and recommendations concerning such need. Upon receipt of such certificate, the legislature, at the next regular session, shall consider the findings and recommendations and may reject the recommendations or by law implement the recommendations in whole or in part; provided the legislature may create more judicial offices than are recommended by the supreme court or may decrease the number of judicial offices by a greater number than recommended by the court only upon a finding of two-thirds of the membership of both houses of the legislature that such a need exists. A decrease in the number of judges shall be effective only after the expiration of a term. If the supreme court fails to make findings as provided above when need exists, the legislature may by concurrent resolution request the court to certify its findings and recommendations and upon the failure of the court to certify its findings for nine consecutive months, the legislature may, upon a finding of two-thirds of the membership of both houses of the legislature that a need exists, increase or decrease the number of judges or increase, decrease or redefine appellate districts and judicial circuits.

appellate levels in recent years. It has also responded favorably to requests for additional resources that have greatly improved the efficiency of our courts. Florida legislators and their leadership deserve great credit for helping ensure that the Third Branch has been capable of providing a high standard of service to the communities of Florida. Our task today is to determine what is needed to maintain this standard of service to the people.

In summary, to fulfill our constitutional mandate we have considered judgeship requests submitted by Florida's five appellate districts and twenty judicial circuits. We have examined the requests for new trial judges using the Weighted Caseload System and have analyzed various other judicial workload indicators including the appellate judges' willingness to accept a higher workload. Based on our review of these factors, we conclude that there is a need for four new judges in the district courts of appeal, fifty-one circuit judges, and thirty-three county judges.

Under the federal system of government in the United States, our state courts are the primary vehicle for providing the Rule of Law to our people. As has often been noted, state courts account for well more than ninety-five percent of all judicial activity in the United States. State courts such as those in Florida protect democracy by upholding the law, ensuring individual rights and liberties, enforcing public order, and peacefully resolving disputes. Courts maintain public safety, settle costly business disputes, and protect our most vulnerable citizens. Of course, judges are crucial to the operation of this system. Their work helps our citizens and businesses resolve issues fairly and peaceably, in a way that promotes the well-being of all.

This Court fully understands the competing funding priorities that confront the Legislature. However, we also recognize the significant need for adequate funding of Florida's Third Branch of government in the face of unprecedented growth in this, the nation's fourth largest state. Just as growth places increasing demands on other public services, it has a direct relationship to the need for additional judicial resources in Florida's communities. Backlogs of cases would become inevitable without enough judges to preside over and dispose of cases, and without sufficient operating costs and resources to support them. In sum, justice itself would be delayed. Preventing this from happening deserves some priority. Without adequate funding for judges and other essential elements, the effective and efficient operation of the Florida State Courts System will be jeopardized. . . . Courts in other states have suffered devastating cuts in recent years, and their experiences demonstrate that inadequate funding can gravely impair court operations. . . . It is critical that Florida avoid similar harm to its justice system, and the fact that we have avoided problems as serious as these is largely due to the Legislature's efforts. Florida's judiciary has long been regarded as one of the finest in the nation. . . . Yet, Florida's budget for the Third Branch has consistently been well less than one percent of the state's budget. In short, while bearing an enormous caseload, Florida's courts have provided a genuine bargain to the people of Florida. Our judiciary's continuing tradition of excellence will now depend on whether its current standards continue to be funded. We are confident the Legislature will continue to provide these resources. . . .

[Omitted here is the Supreme Court's detailed evaluation of the judgeship needs of the state's trial courts.]

The district court of appeal workload has increased steadily over the last ten years.[6] Yet, the districts have been measured and modest in their requests for new judgeships. They have chosen to employ a variety of less expensive means of addressing increased workload. These have included the development of case management systems, the increased use of senior judge time,[7] the increased use of information technology to assist with legal research, and the expanded use of staff attorneys. In spite of these efforts, judicial workload in the districts is becoming too great.

In the face of this workload, the district court of appeal judges have voluntarily agreed to carry even higher caseloads before they seek additional judges on their courts. In 2002, this Court directed the Commission on District Court of Appeal Performance and Accountability to conduct an in-depth study of workload and related policy issues for the district courts of appeal. That Commission, with the support of district court of appeal judges, has recommended the adoption of a new and substantially increased appellate court workload standard — 350 primary assignment case filings per judge. This recommended standard is 100 more than the current standard of 250 case filings per judge as identified in Rule 2.035(b)(2), Florida Rules of Judicial Administration. It thus requires appellate judges to shoulder a caseload burden forty percent greater than before in determining the need for additional judges. This new standard further underscores the benefits of cost-saving measures now being used in the courts. The infusion of support staff and other resources over the last decade has enabled the district courts to keep pace with rising workload increases by achieving greater efficiency. . . .

Even under this increased standard, however, it is apparent that the Second, Fourth, and Fifth districts now require additional judges. In the district courts of appeal statewide, there was an average of approximately 389 case filings per judge in fiscal year 2002-2003. However, the Fourth and Fifth districts experienced approximately 423 and 420 case filings per judge, respectively, for the same time period. In fiscal year 2002-2003, approximately 430 cases per judge were filed in the Second District. Despite this significant increase in burden, the number of judges in the district courts has remained constant since the 1999 legislative session, although the number of annual filings has risen steadily. The 24,114 cases filed in the district courts in fiscal year 2002-2003 is an increase of approximately eleven percent over the 21,679 filings for fiscal year 1999-2000.

The Fifth District is projected to have the highest number of filings per judge, approximately 446, of any of the district courts for fiscal year 2004-2005. Traditionally, the Fifth District has resisted adding new judgeships to avoid the

---

6 [17] The 24,114 cases filed in the district courts in fiscal year 2002-2003 represent a thirty percent increase over the 18,549 filings in fiscal year 1992-1993.

7 [18] Senior judges are retired judges who, under the state Constitution, are eligible to serve as temporary judges. They are far less expensive to fund than traditional judgeships. Senior judges are paid at a fixed rate only for the days they actually serve.

costs and other burdens associated with creating larger courts. However, current workload necessitates the request for an additional judgeship. The chief judge of the Fifth District notes that even if that court is fortunate enough to receive a new judgeship, it will still exceed the new filings threshold standard of 350 by more than fifty filings per judge.

Since the 1993 Legislative Session, when the Second District was last authorized two additional judgeships, filings have increased by approximately thirty-two percent. During that time, the Legislature authorized thirty-one additional circuit judges for the Second District but no new district judges. The Second District remains the largest district in geographic size and now serves over 4.6 million residents — a more than twenty-two percent increase since fiscal year 1992-1993. The current ratio of circuit judges [trial courts of general jurisdiction] to district judges [intermediate appellate courts] in the Second District is ten to one and there are 142 circuit judges in the district, more than any other district.

These factors have begun to take their toll on the Second District's ability to keep pace with workload and maintain quality. As stated by Chief Judge Altenbernd in his letter of judicial needs, addressed to this Court:

> We have reviewed all of our procedures and implemented steps to prioritize the timely review of cases. I am personally very proud of the extraordinary effort of our dedicated staff. They have served above and beyond all realistic expectations to assure that all litigants receive a timely appeal. But this court simply cannot continue to operate at its current level of productivity without suffering a demoralized staff. Even more important, we cannot continue to dispose of cases at this rate without risking the quality of the review received by the litigants.

Under these circumstances, this Court is concerned that timely, high-quality appellate review is at risk of being compromised due to a lack of judges to handle the high workload.

Similarly, the Fourth District continues to experience significant growth in population, circuit judgeships, the number of practicing attorneys, and overall workload. The Fourth District was last authorized an additional judgeship during the 1988 Legislative Session, nearly sixteen years ago. The district's population currently exceeds three million people, which is more than a twenty-seven percent increase since fiscal year 1992-1993. Indeed, the three judicial circuits that constitute the Fourth District have some of the largest and fastest growing jurisdictions in Florida. . . . Since the 1993 Legislative Session, the Legislature has authorized sixteen additional circuit judges for the Fourth District. This represents an increase of approximately eighteen percent. The current ratio of circuit judges to district judges for the Fourth District is eight and one-half to one.

The chief judge of the Fourth District also notes that increases in the number of practicing attorneys, general litigiousness, and numerous filings within each case impact the district's judicial workload. Further, as with Chief Judge Altenbernd in his letter of judicial needs, Chief Judge Farmer cautioned that "we have significant concerns about our ability to continue the level of quality judicial performance the judges of this court have demonstrated since the last increase in judges." Like the Second, the Fourth District is concerned that excessive workload moves the courts perilously close to being unable to devote the necessary time to each case, potentially compromising effective appellate review.

District Court Certification: Given the high caseload, increases in population, and growth in the circuit courts within the Second, Fourth, and Fifth Districts, it is evident that efficiency measures implemented by them are no longer adequate to offset the need for additional judgeships.

Accordingly, utilizing the new and higher standard recommended by the District Court of Appeal judges, we certify the need for two additional district court judges for the Second District and one each for the Fourth and Fifth districts. This certification renews the requests for additional judgeships for the Second and Fourth Districts that were certified in last year's opinion, but not authorized by the Legislature.

Florida's State Courts System is at a critical juncture. Much is at stake. This is a time of great risk and great opportunity. We must take every step to minimize the risk and invoke every measure to ensure that we do not miss the opportunity to maintain a fair and effective justice system worthy of public trust throughout Florida. This opinion fulfills our constitutional mandate to certify those additional judgeships needed to maintain the fair and timely administration of justice in Florida's Court System.

We are confident that the Governor and the Legislature will respond to our concerns. . . . This will ensure that the courts continue to provide the citizens of Florida a justice system able to administer the Rule of Law — one that our nation and our state can continue to view as a model. We pledge our cooperation in every way to provide information and assistance to our coordinate branches of government to assure the continuation of effective and efficient judicial services to the people of Florida.

It is so ordered.

GORDON BERMANT, EDWARD SUSSMAN, WILLIAM W. SCHWARZER & RUSSELL R. WHEELER, IMPOSING A MORATORIUM ON THE NUMBER OF FEDERAL JUDGES: ANALYSIS OF ARGUMENTS AND IMPLICATIONS 23-26 (Fed. Jud. Ctr. 1993)

The argument for a moratorium begins with the assertion that any further significant increase in the size of the federal judiciary will change the institution's fundamental character to the serious detriment of the nation. The federal judiciary must not grow significantly larger if it is to protect its effective working relations, prevent undue inter- and intra-court conflicts, avoid an unacceptable number of mediocre appointments, and provide the public with an effective and respected forum. All these conditions are essential to maintaining a federal judiciary of the kind and quality that the country expects. Furthermore, as the judiciary grows, it must present increasingly unpalatable budget requests to Congress; a large court system will be unlikely to get the resources it needs to function effectively.

Without the drastic action of an explicit moratorium, however, the federal judiciary *will* grow significantly. A moratorium will prevent that growth in two ways. It will hold constant the number of judgeships, and it will force Congress to restrain the need for more judges by limiting the federal judicial workload to disputes that most need the federal forum. Finally, a moratorium is practical. It can work through a reapportionment approach somewhat analogous to that applied to the House of Representatives. More specifically, moratorium proponents make these arguments:

1. Continuing increases in the size of the federal judiciary will eventually create unacceptable problems:

a. Unchecked expansion of district and circuit judgeships vitiates the historic understanding, based on federalism, that the federal judiciary is a specialized body of limited jurisdiction.

b. Cohesiveness and efficiency will be impaired.

c. The quality of federal courts will decline because:

(1) As the number of judgeships increases, the ability of the office to attract the most qualified individuals will decline.

(2) As the number of vacancies to be filled increases, it will become increasingly difficult for executive and legislative branches to nominate and confirm with sufficient care.

d. A larger federal judiciary will require more resources than Congress will be willing to appropriate.

2. Without an explicit moratorium, the federal judicial workload will continue to grow, leading Congress to continue to add more judgeships to the system.

3. A moratorium will allow the courts to avoid growing larger because it will force Congress to control jurisdictional expansion and restrict unnecessary access to the courts, and it will force the courts to develop more efficient procedures.

4. A cap on the number of judgeships can be successfully implemented.

a. A statutory change can be effective.

b. Only an unequivocal cap, identified and argued for as such, will assist the federal courts.

c. Geographic shifts in demand for judicial services can be accommodated.

Opponents of a cap maintain that a ceiling on the number of circuit and district judgeships will exacerbate, not solve, the problems that moratorium supporters believe beset the federal courts. Whether or not a moratorium is in place, Congress will surely expand jurisdiction in response to new claims pressed by constituents, although its statutes will be empty gestures if there are insufficient judges to hear the cases that result. The federal caseload will increase, in fact, even if no new federal causes of action were created, simply because more people will turn to the federal courts as population grows.

Congress, though, would be incapable of the carefully calibrated adjustments to jurisdictional statutes that might otherwise restrain federal filings.

Unless the number of judges keeps relative pace with the legal problems needing their attention, meaningful access to the federal judicial forum will be denied to many citizens whose claims entitle them to that forum. The same number of judges will be forced to handle a greatly increased number of cases, to the point that few cases will get the judicial attention they require.

A moratorium would also impede efforts to increase gender, ethnic, and racial diversity on the federal bench. And a moratorium would require relocating judgeships geographically to accommodate the shifts of judicial business, threatening the historic sense that federal courts reflect local legal and social cultures, and thus creating additional legislative disincentives to make the moratorium work effectively.

These basic facts, opponents contend, demand rejection of the moratorium proposal but still accommodate more than one approach to ensuring an effective judiciary. One approach favors adding judges if and when necessary but would avoid large increases in judgeships by having the judiciary embark on a vigorous campaign of maximizing procedural innovations, promoting structural change where necessary, and working even more closely than at present with Congress and the executive to restrict federal judicial workload to disputes that truly need the federal forum. Another approach favors a significant expansion — perhaps a doubling or more — of the number of judgeships. In this view, the nation must invest the comparatively small sums necessary to provide judgeships sufficient to ensure fair hearings to all persons entitled to the federal forum, particularly those disadvantaged elements of society that tend to get inadequate attention when judicial resources are at a premium.

Jeffrey A. Parness & Jack E. Reagle, *Reforms in the Business and Operating Manner of the Ohio Courts of Appeals*, 16 AKRON L. REV. 3 (1982)[8]

[T]he general approach in Ohio to date has been to increase the numbers of judges as case volume grew, though there have been some experiments with other approaches initiated by local appeals courts. This general approach has failed as, particularly in the last twenty-five years, the additional volume of new cases has far outstripped the corresponding increase in new judgeships. But even if the number of new judgeships had kept pace with the growing case volume, continuing such an approach has severe shortcomings. As Judge Friendly has noted, a court of appeals is a collegial body where collegiality seemingly diminishes rather than increases with dramatic additions of new judges. The judge observes:

> Beyond all this is the desirability of judges of a collegial court really knowing each other, talking together, lunching together, even — perhaps particularly — drinking together. This promotes understanding,

---

[8] Copyright © 1982 Akron Law Review. Reprinted with permission.

prevents unnecessary disagreements, and avoids the introduction of personal animosity into those differences of opinion that properly occur. I believe that close personal relationships have been one of the sources of strength of the Supreme Court; when these have degenerated, so has the Court's performance. I thus agree again with Professor Geoffrey Hazard that "it will therefore be simply impossible, in the foreseeable future, to solve the problem of too many appeals by increasing the number of judges."

Assuming larger numbers of judges can still "drink together," the chance of one three-judge panel proceeding in ignorance of what another three-judge panel is doing inevitably rises as judicial numbers are increased.

Of course, the number of judges in any one appellate district can always be limited simply by expanding the number of appellate districts. In Ohio, this method has kept certain courts of appeals from becoming too heavily laden with judicial officers. Yet, the method has not been employed in districts embodying only one heavily populated county. Apparently, the General Assembly refuses to divide a single county into two appellate districts. Even assuming expansion of judicial districts can promote collegiality by limiting any one district to no more than a few judges, the method is still flawed. As the number of districts grows, the chance for inter-district conflicts increases, resulting in the possibility of numerous denials of equal protection and of certifications to the Ohio Supreme Court based on the "interest" in such conflicts.

Besides diminution in collegiality, knee-jerk increases in judgeships as case volume grows constitutes an expensive habit. As Judge Kaufman has observed:

> We do need more judges. But legislatures, sensitive to public displeasure with rising taxes and higher judicial outlays, are going to balk at the millions required to build new courthouses, create more judgeships, and hire the supporting personnel if we attempt to solve all our problems by simply increasing the number of judges. It is like adding more engineers to a railroad still operating with steam instead of diesel engines.

NOTES

1. What are the *qualitative* indicators that more appellate judges are needed? Consider this list of "symptoms of need:" "(1) A pattern of denial of oral argument without waiver by counsel; (2) A pattern of undue abbreviation of the length of oral arguments or of scheduling numerous arguments for the same time; (3) Use of internal operating procedures which make inadequate provision for conference and deliberation by the deciding judges; (4) Reliance on central staff attorneys in numbers greater than the judges of the court; (5) Regular use of more than two personal law clerks per judge; (6) Routine, substantial delay in making dispositions; and (7) Failure of the appellate system to provide even minimal explanation for its decisions." PAUL D. CARRINGTON, DANIEL J. MEADOR & MAURICE ROSENBERG, JUSTICE ON APPEAL 142 (1976). Evaluated by these objective indicators, all the U.S. Courts of Appeals and

almost all of the state IACs currently exhibit some degree of "symptoms of need" for additional judges, as we shall see in the rest of this Chapter and in the next Chapter.

2. Is there a way to *quantitatively* measure the workload of an appellate court to determine if and when more judges are needed? A generation ago, appellate court experts authoritatively declared:

> In fact, there is a finite limit to the number of decisions which any judge or panel of judges can make without jeopardizing the essential qualities of the process. Difficult though it be to define the limit, we have concluded that it should be this: if the mix of cases is not more nor less difficult than the usual mix for state intermediate courts where first appeals of right are heard, the limit is about 300 plenary dispositions per year for any one judge, or about 100 dispositions per judgeship if we assume that the judges sit in panels of three. . . . If 300 contested decisions a year is a sensible limit for a state appellate judge, a lower number must apply to federal judges. The federal appellate jurisdiction spans a wide gamut of complex matters. Given this greater complexity of much federal litigation and the high improbability of Supreme Court review, federal appellate judges must be expected to spend more of their own time and thought on each case than their state court counterparts. A rule of thumb imposing a limit of about 225 decisions on the merits each year seems prudent.

Paul D. Carrington, Daniel J. Meador & Maurice Rosenberg, Justice on Appeal 143, 196 (1976). As we have seen in the opinion excerpt above, in the face of raising caseloads the Florida Supreme Court increased the workload norm to 350 filings per judge for its IACs — in the process, raising the state's official threshold for determining whether to create a new appellate judgeship by 100 cases. Is there any empirical basis for setting these official numbers or are they chimerical figures? What explains how the appellate workload maxima have increased so dramatically over time, *i.e.*, how the official norm of how many appeals a judge and a court can realistically and effectively decide keeps going up and up?

3. In the federal system, the process for creating federal appellate judgeships relies on the Judicial Conference of the United States — not the Supreme Court. The Judicial Conference is the policy-making body of the federal courts and is composed of the Chief Justice of the United States and the chief judge of each of the 12 regional courts of appeals, the Chief Judge of the Court of Appeals for the Federal Circuit, the Chief Judge of the Court of International Trade, and 12 district judges, one from each of the regional circuits. The Conference is required to "make a comprehensive survey of the condition of business in the courts" and make recommendations to Congress. 28 U.S.C. § 331.

> Since 1964, the Judicial Conference has submitted periodic legislative proposals for additional judgeships. Those "judgeship bills" are based on surveys of judgeship needs conducted by the Judicial Conference Committee on Judicial Resources and, more particularly, its Subcommittee on Judicial Statistics. [The surveys were roughly

quadrennial from 1964 to 1980, when they became biennial.] The Conference has adopted a numeric standard [for the] desired workload for a circuit judge. . . . The Conference considers more than these standards in developing judgeship recommendations, however. [The Statistics Subcommittee also consults with judges and court managers, who may argue that filing data underestimate the true judicial burden in a court or conversely that, despite the need for additional judgeships based on formula, the court does not desire the additional judgeships because it believes any benefits they would provide are outweighed by their costs in efficiency and collegiality. This latter argument is most often made by appellate courts.] Of course, Congress is under no obligation to adopt the Judicial Conference recommendations, and it occasionally provides more or fewer judgeships and for different courts than those recommended by the Conference. Finally, Congress sometimes creates temporary judgeships to meet caseload pressures regarded as temporary. The judgeship is "temporary" in that a future vacancy (e.g., the first occurring after five years) will not be filled. The temporary judgeship thus creates no permanent increase in the court's authorized judgeships.

GORDON BERMANT, EDWARD SUSSMAN, WILLIAM W. SCHWARZER & RUSSELL R. WHEELER, IMPOSING A MORATORIUM ON THE NUMBER OF FEDERAL JUDGES: ANALYSIS OF ARGUMENTS AND IMPLICATIONS 8-9 (Fed. Jud. Ctr. 1993).

4. The current numerical standard of the Judicial Conference is that U.S. courts of appeals with "adjusted case filings" of 500 or more per three-judge panel may be recommended for one or more additional judgeships. The "adjusted case filings" workload measure counts all filings equally, with two significant exceptions: cases that were dismissed for procedural faults and later are reinstated — a relatively small number of appeals — are not counted and pro se cases in which one or both parties is not represented by an attorney (the vast majority of them prisoner appeals) — a relatively large number of appeals — are counted as only one-third of a case. Efforts to refine this workload measure have not proven successful. We usually are preoccupied with the seemingly inevitable growth of appellate courts, but what if a court approaches it from the other side to refuse bench growth, even though objectively more judges would seem to be needed? If the particular court resists or opposes any new judgeships, should the Judicial Conference and Congress defer to the judges even if the objective criteria are exceeded? In 2003, the Judicial Conference requested eleven new judgeships for four of the courts of appeals that had adjusted filings per judge ranging from 583 to 870. But no new judgeships were requested for the Fifth Circuit and the Eleventh Circuit, even though those two courts each had about 1000 adjusted filings — double the official benchmark of 500 filings per judge. If that standard were applied, the Fifth Circuit would grow from 17 judges to 28 judges and the Eleventh Circuit would grow from 12 judges to 22 judges. If a majority of the judges on a court of appeals does not want the court to grow, then under the present system, the court does not grow regardless of the statistical indicators. The judges on those two courts say they worry that if there were too many judges then the law of the circuit would become incoherent, unstable and so unpredictable that litigiousness would increase and deciding appeals would become

unduly complicated. But commentators respond that those arguments are more concerned with the law declaration function, rather than the error correction function which ought to be the primary concern. They worry, in turn, that courts with too few judgeships are more prone to over-rely on staff attorneys and law clerks and are more likely to abuse procedural shortcuts like eliminating oral argument and deciding appeals without an opinion. Arthur D. Hellman, *Assessing Judgeship Needs in the Federal Courts of Appeals: Policy Choices and Process Concerns*, 5 J. APP. PRAC. & PROCESS 239 (2003). If the Fifth and Eleventh Circuits are deciding twice as many appeals per judge as the other courts of appeals, then do the Fifth and Eleventh Circuit have too few judgeships or do the other courts of appeals have too many? How would you go about making that determination?

5. A comprehensive judiciary study of the federal procedures for creation of judgeships recommended: (1) Congress should delegate to the Judicial Conference the authority to create new judgeships; (2) the Judicial Conference should develop and follow explicit and public procedures; (3) a maximum of eight new judgeships be created each year; (4) judgeships might be taken away from one district or circuit and assigned to another district or circuit; (5) no judgeships be created in a year when overall case filings declined; (6) Congress might veto in whole or in part any decision of the Judicial Conference. CARL BARR, JUDGESHIP CREATION IN THE FEDERAL COURTS: OPTIONS FOR REFORM (Fed. Jud. Ctr. 1981). Between the two branches, the judiciary and the legislature, which branch is institutionally better-suited to assess the systemic needs of the courts in order to create new judgeships?

6. In the early 1990s, court experts and judges debated whether the federal judiciary should be capped, *i.e.*, whether there is some numerical limit on the number of judges that the system could support and maintain. Having read the official summary of their debate in the excerpt above, do you think that the proponents or opponents of imposing a moratorium on the creation of more federal appellate judgeships had the better arguments? The last increase was in 1990, when Congress increased the total of authorized circuit judgeships to 179. The Ninth Circuit is the largest federal appellate bench with 28 judgeships. The question whether there are too many federal appellate judges in total is separate and distinct from the question whether a particular court of appeals has grown too large. Do you think there is a limit to the number of judges that can serve together effectively and efficiently on one appellate court sitting in three-judge panels? *See* Richard A. Posner, *Is the Ninth Circuit Too Large? A Statistical Study of Judicial Quality*, 29 J. LEG. STUDIES 711 (2000); William M. Richman, *An Argument on the Record for More Federal Judgeships*, 1 J. APP. PRAC. & PROCESS 37 (1999); Jonathan D. Varat, *Determining the Mission and Size of the Federal Judiciary Via a Three-Branch Process: the Judges' Debate and a Reform Menu*, 27 CONN. L. REV. 885 (1995); J. Harvie Wilkinson, III, *The Drawbacks to Growth in the Federal Judiciary*, 43 EMORY L. J. 1147 (1994).

7. In the 39 states with IACs, there are a total of 947 judgeships. Alaska (3) and Idaho (3) have the fewest authorized judgeships; California (103) has the most. Among the largest intermediate appellate judiciaries are: Texas (80); Ohio (68); Florida (62); New York (57); Illinois (53); and Louisiana (52). Most

range from seven to fourteen judgeships. There is much variation. *See generally* DANIEL J. MEADOR, APPELLATE COURTS IN THE UNITED STATES (2nd ed. 2006).

8. By federal statute, if one of the judges on a three-judge panel is unable to continue, the remaining two judges constitute a quorum for deciding the appeal. 28 U.S.C. § 46(d). New Jersey has made the two-judge panel the appellate norm. N.J. CT. R. 2:13-2 provides:

> Appeals shall be decided by panels of 2 judges designated by the presiding judge of the part except when the presiding judge determines that an appeal should be decided by a panel of 3 judges. Such a determination may be made where the appeal presents a question of public importance, of special difficulty, of precedential value, or for such other special reason as the presiding judge shall determine. The panel of 2 judges to which an appeal is submitted for decision may elect to call a third judge to participate in the decision at any time before making its determination and shall do so if the 2 judges cannot agree as to the determination. In either case the appeal shall be reargued if it has already been argued unless reargument is waived. When an appeal is designated for decision by the full part, 3 judges shall constitute a quorum unless all parties consent to a quorum of 2 judges and, if only 2 of the 3 judges have heard the oral argument, the parties may consent to the participation in the court's decision by the third judge. Judges assigned to one part may be assigned to serve temporarily in any other part.

Do you think this is a good idea? If two judges agree on the decision, what, if anything, is lost by not having the participation of a third judge?

9. One technique to expand appellate judgepower is to designate a trial judge to sit as a third judge on appellate panels. In the federal system and in all the states there are many times more trial judges than appellate judges. Is this a good idea? James J. Brudney & Corey Ditslear, *Designated Diffidence: District Court Judges on the Courts of Appeals*, 35 LAW & SOC'Y REV. 565 (2001); Justin J. Green & Burton M. Atkins, *Designated Judges: How Well Do They Perform?*, 61 JUDICATURE 358 (1978); Richard B. Saphire & Michael E. Solimine, *Diluting Justice on Appeal?: An Examination of the Use of District Court Judges Sitting By Designation on the United States Courts of Appeals*, 28 U. MICH. J. L. REFORM 351 (1995).

10. How about using lawyers as substitute appellate judges? During the 1980s three state intermediate appellate courts experimented with the use of practicing lawyers as volunteer, part-time judges. In Arizona, one three-judge panel consisted of one regular judge of the court and two lawyers. In New Mexico, panels were constituted of three lawyers each, but the opinions written by these lawyers were circulated to three-judge panels and became the opinions of the court only after approval of the judges. In Oklahoma, numerous panels of three lawyers each were constituted with final decisional authority over appeals subject to discretionary review by the state supreme court. A study of these three programs is reported in Thomas B. Marvell & Carlisle E. Moody, *Research Note: Volunteer Attorneys as Appellate Judges*, 16 JUST. SYS. J. 49 (1992). As to the Oklahoma program, the study reports: "According to court staff, the program is successful, but it is costly in terms of

administrative time, mainly to arrange panel membership and to handle the frequent withdrawal of attorneys due to conflicts of interests." *Id.* at 54. As to the Arizona and New Mexico programs, the study concluded:

> In all, the research suggests that the volunteer attorneys have little impact. They did not reduce delay or increase decision output in the Arizona Court of Appeals. They did help the New Mexico Court of Appeals decide more cases and reduce backlogs, but the magnitude of the impact is very small — 2 percent more decisions and reduced backlog if attorneys panels decide 10 percent of the civil cases. Apparently, the help provided by attorney panels was counterbalanced by the time judges had to spend reviewing the attorneys' work. In addition, the courts encountered administrative problems with the attorney panels, especially persuading enough attorneys to volunteer their services and to finish draft opinions promptly. In all, we suggest that this example of volunteerism is not a helpful answer to appellate courts' problems.

Id. at 57. In addition to administrative problems and difficulties in obtaining qualified attorney volunteers, are there other concerns about using practitioners as appellate judges on a part-time basis?

11. With the steady upsurge of appellate filings since the 1960s, renewed attention was focused on the possibility of providing added assistance to the beleaguered judges. Sometimes referred to generically as para-judicial officials or judicial adjuncts or (derisively) sub-judges, such assistants are discussed in the remainder of this Chapter.

II. LAW CLERKS

This section sketches the history of law clerks and describes their function. Law clerks had been on the appellate scene long before the volume crisis of the late twentieth century. But their number has grown and their role has evolved significantly in response to workload. Also explored here are questions about their proper function and contemporary concerns that have been raised about their growing influence and power.

J. Daniel Mahoney, *Foreword: Law Clerks: For Better or Worse?*, 54 BROOK. L. REV. 321, 322-26 (1988)[9]

The institution of clerking began over a hundred years ago. It is largely undisputed that the first jurist to utilize legal assistants was Horace Gray [who first employed a law clerk in the summer of 1875 on the Massachusetts Supreme Judicial Court and who brought his clerk with him to Washington in 1882 when he was appointed to the U.S. Supreme Court]. . . .

The first official reference to the idea of employing assistants for the Supreme Court justices occurred in 1885, when Attorney General A.H. Garland suggested in his annual report that

---

[9] Copyright © 1988 Brooklyn Law Review. Reprinted with permission.

[i]t would greatly facilitate the business of the Supreme Court if each justice was provided by law with a secretary or law clerk, to be a stenographer, to be paid an annual salary sufficient to obtain the requisite qualifications, whose duties shall be to assist in such clerical work as might be assigned to him.

The notion of clerical help was a direct result of the increased workload the Supreme court faced at the time, and the associated delays in judicial action. [The Court began to experience a serious demand on the time and resources of its members around 1850, and was inundated by 1875, when it was churning out two hundred opinions a year.] On August 4, 1886, Congress acted upon Garland's recommendation and provided for a "stenographic clerk" for each justice of the Supreme Court at a salary of $1,600 a year.

While it might appear from this legislative description that Congress intended to circumscribe the duties that law clerks were to perform by limiting them to clerical work, Justice Gray continued to use his clerks in the same manner as he had in the past, which envisioned a much broader role. According to Samuel Williston, who served as one of Gray's law clerks, Gray used his assistants to review newly filed cases and opinions proposed by Gray's colleagues on the Court, engaged his clerks in vigorous colloquy, and had real interest in and respect for their views. They were sometimes asked to draft opinions, although the drafts served only as sources of discussion. It is fair to say that Justice Gray was not only the founder of the institution of "law clerking," but also the draftsman of the role a law clerk was thereafter to perform.

Despite the initial hesitance of the justices, all nine were using the allotted "stenographic clerk" by 1888. The justices typically found their law clerks through friends or relatives, or from the bar and law schools of the District of Columbia. [Nepotism was not unknown. John Harlan, for example, hired his son John Maynard Harlan. Other justices hired the sons of their colleagues.]

In 1919, Congress provided the justices with another clerical assistant. After some initial confusion, it became clear that Congress was authorizing a "law clerk" in addition to the previously authorized "stenographic clerk." It was not until 1921, however, that Chief Justice Taft became the first member of the Court to use both assistants. The other justices were slow to follow, but by 1939 all the justices were using both assistants.

In 1941, Harlan F. Stone became chief justice and employed four personal assistants; two law clerks and two secretaries. Again, the increased personal staff was a direct consequence of the increased workload associated with the position. In addition to being the chief administrative officer of the federal judiciary, Chief Justice Stone dealt with all *in forma pauperis* petitions personally, and their number increased greatly while he was chief justice. It was also during this time that the terms senior and junior clerk came into vogue, since Stone was the first justice to employ his law clerks for two-year, overlapping terms. When Chief Justice Vinson replaced Stone in 1946, he employed seven assistants: three law clerks, three secretaries, and a messenger. Around that time, many of the associate justices added a second law clerk to their staffs. Chief Justice Warren continued the Vinson practice.

The institution of "law clerking" became truly entrenched within the federal judiciary during the 1930s when law clerks were introduced to the lower federal courts. In 1930, Congress provided each circuit court judge with one law clerk, subject to the approval of the Attorney General. [The provision requiring approval of the Attorney General was removed when the Judicial Code was revised in 1948.] In 1936, district court judges were allowed to use law clerks, although the number of district court clerks was strictly limited until 1948, and required a certification of need by the appropriate senior circuit judge until 1959.

DANIEL J. MEADOR, APPELLATE COURTS: STAFF AND PROCESS IN THE CRISIS OF VOLUME 6-17 (1974)[10]

The appearance of law clerks in the state appellate courts has, on the whole, come later. A 1942 survey reported that law clerks were then provided for state supreme court justices in almost half the states. That report, by an American Bar Association Committee, endorsed the idea and suggested that "More of this kind of help would be of great value to assist busy courts and to aid them in perfecting opinions." By 1959, forty-nine state appellate courts had law clerks for their judges. In the majority of those courts, there was one clerk for each judge. In the California Supreme Court, however, each Justice had three clerks, the most per judge of any court at that time. A majority of the courts reported that the judges used their law clerks to prepare memoranda on entire cases or on specific problems, in addition to using them for various other mechanical and editorial duties. By 1968, the supreme courts of all but five states were provided with law clerks, as were two thirds of the state intermediate courts. . . .

Depending on the judge's desires, law clerks' work includes legal research, memorandum drafting, opinion drafting, cite checking, and editorial work. In addition, a clerk is often useful as a discussion partner and a sounding board for the judge.

The essential characteristic of the law clerk is that he [or she] is a personal assistant for a particular judge . . . is responsible solely to that judge, and takes directions from no one else. The Federal Judicial Center uses the term "elbow clerk" to express this idea. Some courts use other terms, such as research assistant or aide [or briefing attorney], but the concept and function of the position are the same.

J. Daniel Mahoney, *Foreword: Law Clerks: For Better or Worse?*, 54 BROOK. L. REV. 321, 326-35 (1988)[11]

II. *The Functions and Responsibilities of Law Clerks*

. . . .

[T]he Federal Judicial Center made an attempt to set forth in writing what a clerkship entails by publishing its LAW CLERK HANDBOOK. [A second edition

---

[10] Copyright © 1974 Thomson West. Reprinted with permission.

[11] Copyright © 1988 Brooklyn Law Review. Reprinted with permission.

was published in 1989.] Despite the detailed and comprehensive nature of that publication, the authors could only agree to the following general job description for law clerks:

> [A law clerk is a lawyer employed to assist a judge with as many administrative, clerical, and basic legal tasks as possible, so as to leave the judge more time for judging and critical decision-making. The clerk has no statutorily defined duties. Instead, the clerk carries out the judge's instructions. In doing so, the typical clerk is given a broad range of duties. Clerks are usually assigned to do legal research, prepare bench memos, draft orders and opinions, edit and proofread the judge's orders and opinions, and verify citations. Many judges discuss pending cases with their law clerks and confer with them about decisions. Frequently, clerks also maintain the library, assemble documents, serve as courtroom crier, and run errands for the judge.][12]

With respect to appellate clerks, the Law Clerk Handbook states that their primary function "is to research the issues of law and fact in an appeal and to draft a working opinion for the judge, pursuant to his directions." The problem with this broad assertion is self-evident. While it may be generally recognized that a majority of appellate law clerks today draft preliminary opinions, some may be confined to research, screening, and editorial or sounding board functions. And I believe it safe to assume that most clerkships entail certain more mundane tasks, such as proofreading and keeping a chambers' library up to date. Some judges, it is rumored, even make demands of a personal nature upon their law clerks. . . .

A. *One Judge's Use of Law Clerk*

My three law clerks play an active role in chambers. They assist me in virtually all aspects of the regular business of the [U.S. Court of Appeals for the Second Circuit]. Upon arriving in Milford, Connecticut, the clerks are immediately provided with a copy of my own *Law Clerk's Manual*. This manual details what the clerks' duties will be, and generally familiarizes them with the operations of my chambers and the court. It contains thirty-one instructive appendices, including law review articles and memoranda by some of my colleagues concerning the work of the court; the Code of Conduct for Law Clerks; sample bench memoranda and voting memoranda; a calendar for a typical "sitting" week; the *Federal Rules* of *Appellate Procedure* and the *Second Circuit Rules*; and an opinion history that traces one of our more complicated cases from the initial bench memorandum to the final opinion in the FEDERAL REPORTER. After the clerks have a few hours to settle in, the volume and complexity of the work before us requires them to roll up their sleeves and begin the tasks that will occupy most of their time for the next year.

1. *Preparation for and Attendance at Sittings.* The work of a Second Circuit judge's staff is cyclical in nature. The cycle centers around each "sitting," or the week during which we hear oral arguments. Much of the clerks' work

---

[12] [36] [ALVIN B. RUBIN & LAURA BARTELL, LAW CLERK HANDBOOK: A HANDBOOK FOR LAW CLERKS TO FEDERAL JUDGES § 1 (Fed. Jud. Ctr. rev. ed. 1989).]

consists of preparing cases for these sittings. Generally, each judge of the Second Circuit is assigned to hear arguments [in New York] one week during most months. Approximately five cases a day are heard. Accordingly, during a "full" five-day sitting, a panel of judges will typically hear argument on about twenty-five cases. Thus, each clerk should expect to be responsible for roughly eight cases for a five-day sitting week.

In order to prepare for a sitting, our chambers receives two sets of briefs and appendices for each case, one set for me and one for the clerk working on the case. In the normal course, the case materials arrive approximately two to three weeks prior to a sitting. Where there are expedited appeals or other extraordinary circumstances, however, these materials may arrive as late as a week or a few days beforehand. After the clerks select the cases on which each of them will work, the task of preparing bench memoranda begins.

A bench memorandum is designed to provide me with a brief factual and procedural history of a case, a summary and analysis of the arguments raised by counsel in their briefs, and a recommendation as to the disposition of the case. Its function is to pull the case together for me as briefly as possible without missing any essential matters. The amount of work a clerk should put into a bench memorandum depends primarily upon the complexity of the case, and secondarily upon the time available for preparation. Obviously, complex cases require carefully crafted memoranda, while simpler cases may call for no more than a one- or two-page summary. As a general proposition, I carefully read the briefs and the opinion below, if there is one, together with any leading cases or key documents or testimony in the appendix. It is the clerks' responsibility to dig more deeply into the record and the cases cited in the briefs. . . .

[I]t is extremely important for the clerk responsible for a particular case to attend oral argument and take notes. Immediately after oral argument, my colleagues on the panel and I discuss the cases just argued, especially with a view to ascertaining which cases can be resolved by a unanimous summary order and which will require more formal opinions. In most cases that will be decided by opinion, a voting memorandum is required. While the bench memorandum summarizes the law clerk's view of a case for me, the voting memorandum presents my view of a case to the other members of a panel. Sometimes I will ask a clerk working on a case to draft a voting memorandum, and sometimes I will write the draft and go over it with the clerk. Since the judges on the panel have read the briefs and heard oral argument, the voting memorandum is usually more succinct than the related bench memorandum. In addition, a voting memorandum will typically reflect the development of a case at oral argument.

2. *Opinion Writing.* At the end of a sitting week, the members of the panel hold a voting conference at which more or less tentative votes are cast as to the disposition of the cases heard during that week, and opinions are assigned to each judge. When an opinion is assigned to me, the law clerk assigned to the case prepares the initial draft of the opinion. Normally, the drafting law clerk and I will discuss the general direction and shape the draft is to take before the clerk undertakes this effort, although our prior collaboration on the case has usually been intensive enough to provide a fairly clear preview of the opinion. The law clerk must also review the voting memoranda, if any, to ensure

that the panel members' arguments, concerns and suggestions are adequately addressed in the draft.

It goes without saying that proposed opinions require extraordinary effort on the part of my law clerks. It is crucial that these drafts reflect close attention to detail, especially in the recitation of the factual background of a case, and contain a sound analytical framework with respect to the legal discussion. To this end, I ask that the clerks provide record, appendix, and any other required citations for the background section of a draft opinion, even though they will not ordinarily appear in the finished version. This practice enormously facilitates my review of the draft.

In most cases, I make substantial revisions to a draft opinion to ensure that the final opinion reflects precisely my views and analysis of the case. The drafting clerk is routinely provided with a xerox of my "mark up" of the original draft, a procedure useful to both of us. The law clerk can challenge the accuracy or soundness of my revisions, and it is my hope that the practice enhances the quality of the clerk's learning experience.

Once I am initially satisfied with my work on an opinion, my revised draft is circulated to all three law clerks. They review it, and then the four of us engage in a line-by-line editing session. Anything from the correction of grammatical or typographical errors to a questioning of the opinion's basic analysis is fair game for discussion. The fresh viewpoints of the clerks who had not worked on the opinion are especially useful. They often bring a perspective to the opinion that has escaped the drafting clerk and me, immersed as we are in the details of the case. This review also serves as a final check on the technical accuracy of the opinion. I suspect also that the substantial revisions that frequently result from this process are a source of some psychic satisfaction to clerks who have witnessed what they might deem unwarranted mutilation of their initial drafts.

Even after this process, however, it is still necessary that the opinion be cite checked one last time by a clerk other than the one who prepared the original draft. This should be done before the proposed opinion is circulated to the other members of the panel; in any event, it must be done before the opinion is filed with the Clerk of the Court. If other panel members respond with suggested corrections, additions or deletions, it is the drafting clerk's responsibility to see that they are incorporated into the draft before it is filed, assuming that I agree to the changes.

The process of reviewing opinions does not end with the filing of an opinion. Not long after an opinion has been filed, a slip opinion is issued by the Clerk of the Court. It is the law clerks' job to proofread all slip opinions against a copy of the opinion filed with the Clerk of the Court. Finally, the clerks must keep an eye on the FEDERAL REPORTER advance sheets for opinions on which they have worked. Once an opinion appears, a clerk must proofread the advance sheet opinion against the slip opinion. This is the last chance to catch any errors before an opinion is published in a bound volume of the FEDERAL REPORTER. These proofreading procedures obviously require a good deal of the clerks' time, but they are an essential part of the important task of releasing final opinions in as error-free a condition as human frailty will permit.

3. *Review of Orders and Opinions Written by Other Judges.* My law clerks are responsible for the initial review of proposed orders and opinions authored by other judges with whom I have heard an oral argument. Summary orders, not usually prepared by me, are often ready while [the court is] sitting in New York. The law clerk assigned to the case reviews the order to ensure that all citations are correct and that all authorities are properly cited for the related propositions in the text. The clerk should note any typographical or minor errors, and, of course, call to my attention any concerns of a more substantive nature.

The same procedure is followed when a draft opinion is forwarded to me by another panel member, but obviously more extensive work is required, and a memorandum of comments is more often necessary. It is important that the law clerk working on the case first review the voting memoranda, if any. If the draft opinion is at odds with my view of the case, and a mutually agreeable opinion cannot be negotiated, I may ask the clerk to draft a concurrence or dissent, although I am likely to write separate opinions myself and go over them with the clerk afterwards. In most cases, however, there is no need for a separate opinion, and I simply [agree to file the opinion] with or without a memorandum suggesting changes.

RICHARD A. POSNER, THE FEDERAL COURTS: CHALLENGES AND REFORM 139-57 (1996)[13]

The hiring of distinguished recent law school graduates to serve as federal judges' law clerks for a year or two became the general practice in the 1930s. Supreme Court justices and circuit judges each had one in those days (district judges got clerks in the 1940s). The justices were each given a second clerk in 1947. In 1965 the district judges got a second; in 1970 the circuit justices got a second and the justices a third; in 1978 the justices got a fourth, and in 1980 the circuit judges got a third. In the 1970s the courts of appeals began hiring staff attorneys; they have raised the current ratio of law clerks to circuit judges to approximately four to one. Thus, since 1960, the approximate beginning of the caseload explosion in the federal courts, the number of law clerks in the courts of appeals (including staff attorneys) has quadrupled. This increase is greater than in the other federal courts, and the difference parallels the greater increase in the courts of appeals' caseload. . . .

I am going to discuss with somewhat more candor than is usual for a sitting judge the costs of the heavy reliance on law clerks that is implied by the high ratio of clerks to judges in today's federal courts. But I hope I will not be misunderstood as criticizing this reliance. Many judges would like nothing better than to do their own research and writing; they did their own research and writing before the workload pressures became overwhelming. But except in the Supreme Court, which controls the major part of its workload (the hearing and decisions of cases that it accepts for plenary review), the caseload per federal judge has risen to the point where few judges can keep up with the flow

---

[13] Reprinted by permission of the publisher from "Consequences: The System Expands" in THE FEDERAL COURTS CHALLENGE REFORM by Richard A. Posner, pp. 139, 140-142, 143, 145, 146, 147-151, Cambridge, Mass.: Harvard University press, Copyright © 1985, 1996 by the President Fellows of Harvard College.

without relying heavily on law clerks, staff attorneys, and sometimes externs. My desire is not to deplore a practice that has been forced on many judges by circumstances but to highlight a cost of growing caseload, especially a growing appellate caseload.

If the judge has only one or two law clerks, problems of supervision and delegation are unlikely to be serious. But if like most federal appellate judges he has three or even four clerks, not only will he have to spend more time hiring clerks, additional secretarial assistance may also become necessary, in which event the judge will find himself presiding over a staff no longer of trivial size, though the computer is beginning to displace the judge's second secretary in some chambers. As more of the judge's time becomes taken up with supervision and coordination, leaving less time for conventional judicial duties, more judicial responsibilities must be delegated to the law clerks. The increase in delegation, by making the selection of each new law clerk a more consequential decision, in turn requires the judge to spend more time on each selection, as well as more total time because he is hiring more people. All of this comes at a time when the nondelegable judicial duties of responsible circuit judges — mainly reading briefs and petitions for rehearing, hearing oral arguments, conferring with other judges to decide cases heard (or submitted without argument), and reviewing opinion drafts circulated by other judges on his panels — have been increasing for many years and may continue to do so. The biggest "give" is in the time the judge devotes to the actual preparation of his opinions. It is here that the greatest delegation of judicial responsibilities to law clerks and staff attorneys can be expected to occur and has occurred.

The decisional function has not been delegated. But as the ratio of law clerks to judges has grown, the tendency has been for more and more of the initial opinion-drafting responsibility to be delegated to law clerks, transforming the judge from a draftsman to an editor. Judging from the length and scholarly apparatus of Supreme Court opinions, the transformation is all but complete there. This is not surprising. Not only do the justices have more clerks, but the ratio of law clerks to opinions is much higher in the Supreme Court than in the courts of appeals. In the court's 1994 term, the average justice wrote only 9 signed majority opinions, for which he or she had the assistance of four or even five law clerks, if wanted. This is fewer than 2 opinions per clerk. In the same period the average circuit judge wrote 41 signed majority opinions with the assistance of three law clerks (although staff attorneys occasionally assist judges in writing signed opinions).[14] This is a ratio of 13 opinions per clerk. . . . [T]he writing of separate opinions by the justices, especially concurring opinions (of which each justice wrote an average of 9), is optional; if the justices were groaning under a crushing workload, they would write fewer. The many differences between the two types of court make any quantitative comparison problematic. . . .

Although for a long time the polite fiction was maintained that law clerks were merely "gofers" and "sounding boards" — as indeed they were for some

---

[14] [29] A few court of appeals judges have only two law clerks, and an equally small number has four. A court of appeals judge has five staff positions, for law clerks and secretaries, and can shift positions between these categories. While most judges have three law clerks and two secretaries, some substitute a fourth law clerk for their second secretary. Chief circuit judges are entitled to six staff positions but usually substitute an administrative assistant for the fourth clerk. . . .

famous judges in times of yore — the role of law clerks in opinion writing is now discussed openly, as it should be in a government that claims to rule by consent rather than by mystery. (Even the handful of judges today who write all their own opinions are likely to depend heavily on their clerks for legal and factual research.) The dropping of this particular veil has caused no scandals. Americans do not respect writers anyway, take it for granted that every great figure has a ghostwriter, and in short could not care less whether Supreme Court justices or any other judges write their own opinions or have their clerks write them, provided the judges decide the outcome.

More than candor is involved in the new openness with which the role of the law clerk as judicial ghostwriter is discussed. There are no data but also no doubts that law clerks do more of the opinion writing today than they did thirty-five years ago (this is apparent from talking with older judges and with former law clerks). The judges have heavier workloads and more law clerks, and opinion writing is the most time-consuming of the delegable judicial tasks. And, as legal practice itself becomes more bureaucratic, fewer judges come to the bench with recent writing experience. Former supervisors in practice, they slip easily into the role of being judicial supervisors. . . .

The fact that a law clerk writes an opinion draft does not by itself enable one to measure the clerk's contribution to the opinion as eventually published. There is not only the judge's contribution as editor to be considered but also the marching orders that he gave the law clerk before the latter sat down to write. The structure, the ideas, and the style of the opinion may be the judge's even though much of the actual drafting is the law clerk's. But it is generally true that whoever does the basic drafting of a document will have a big impact on the final product. Opinions drafted by the law clerks tend to differ from opinions written by judges in several ways.

Style. Although . . . delegation of opinion drafting to law clerks may result in a change of literary style with every change of law clerks, the dominant effect is stylistic uniformity rather than variety. The greater variance among the opinions of the same judge is more than offset by the smaller variance among the opinions of different judges. The vast majority of law clerks are young, academically gifted, recent graduates of the nation's leading law schools, which provide a pretty uniform educational experience. The strongly marked individuality that traditionally characterized English and American judges and that makes the opinions of a Holmes, a Cardozo, or a Learned Hand instantly recognizable as their author's personal work is becoming a thing of the past. The result is not just a loss of flavor but a loss of information. A judge's style conveys a sense of the judge that can be used to help piece out his judicial philosophy from his opinions.

The standard opinion style that has emerged follows the style of the student-written sections of the law reviews — which is hardly surprising when one considers who the law clerks are. The style tends to be colorless and plethoric, and also heavily given to euphemism. . . .

Length. Opinions written by law clerks tend to be longer than those written by judges. The law clerk has more time to write than the judge does. There are more law clerks than there are judges and the judges have many demands on their time that the law clerks do not have. And as a recent and academically distinguished student, the law clerk may write more easily than the judge. Above all, the law clerk does not know what to leave out. Not being the judge, he is unsure what facts and reasons are essential and naturally tends to err on the side of inclusion. And since he is not an experienced lawyer, many things are new and fresh to him that are old hat to his judge, other judges, and other readers of the opinion. . . . [O]pinions today would probably be shorter if there were fewer clerks. . . .

Candor. Almost every appellate case worth deciding in a published opinion involves some novelty, and so cannot be decided by a mere recitation of authority. . . . [T]imid jurists still pretend that there is no such thing as a novel case, that is, a case that cannot be resolved by the straightforward application of settled principles, without changing any of those principles. Law clerks usually are timid jurists (and we can be thankful for that). They do everything they can to conceal novelty and to disguise imagination as deduction — hence the heavy reliance in opinions drafted by law clerks on string citations for obvious propositions (where they are superfluous) and novel propositions (for which they are inaccurate); on quotations (too often wrenched out of the context) from prior opinions; on canons of statutory construction that were long ago exploded as clichés; on truisms; on redundant adjectives and adverbs ("unbridled discretion," "inextricably intertwined," "plain meaning"); and on boilerplate of every sort.

Prolixity and lack of candor are not mere inelegances in judicial opinions. They increase the time required for reading an opinion — and most of the readers of judicial opinions are people whose time is valuable. And they reduce the opinion's usefulness as a guide to what judges are likely to do in future cases. . . . Law clerks, however, feel naked unless they are quoting and citing cases and other authorities. They do not understand that in any case involving a novel issue (and if it is not novel, why write an opinion at all? Why not just cite the controlling cases?), the most important thing is not the authorities, which by definition do not determine the outcome of the case, but the reasoning that connects the authorities to the result.

Research. Opinions written by law clerks often make an ostentatious display of the apparatus of legal scholarship — string citations, copious footnotes, and abundant references to secondary literature. Yet such opinions, except in the Supreme Court, where the ratio of law clerks to opinions is so high, tend actually to be less thoroughly researched than opinions written by judges. The time required to write the opinion presses on the time that the clerk would otherwise have to do research. If a circuit judge divides up the initial drafting of all his published and unpublished opinions among three law clerks, the bulk of each clerk's time will be taken up with opinion writing. And it is not to be supposed that while this is going on the judge is sitting hunched over his computer doing the original research for his opinion; he is busy supervising and editing the law clerks and performing his numerous other judicial duties. If the clerks do not do the original research, none will get done. If they lack the time, they will have to depend on the briefs. All too often this will mean dependence on inadequate research by the lawyers.

Even research is not fully delegable to law clerks. It is one thing (though not itself without perils) to rely on a law clerk to find the relevant precedents and another to delegate to him the reading of them as well. A judge who relies for his knowledge of cases entirely on what the parties' briefs, the opinion drafts circulated by his colleagues, and the opinions that his law clerks drafted for him told him about the cases will have only a meager knowledge of the law.

Credibility. The less that lawyers and especially other judges regard judicial opinions as authentic expressions of what the judges think, the less they will rely on judicial opinions for guidance and authority. A brilliant opinion written by a law clerk and acknowledged as such by the judge in the first footnote of the opinion would have a certain authority by virtue of its intrinsic quality, in the same way that some books and law reviews articles have authority with judges. But this kind of authority is different from and normally much less weighty than the authority of an opinion known to reflect, not refract, the thinking of the people who are doing the deciding and will continue to do so after the current crop of law clerks has vanished. The more the thinking embodied in opinions is done by law clerks rather than by judges, the less authority opinions have. . . .

Greatness. It is a curious feature of the American legal system that a handful of famous judges should have made a contribution to the law so greatly disproportionate to their number. But it is true; and it would be sad to think there will never be another great American judge. Yet one wonders whether an editor can be a great judge. It is not just a failure of imagination, I think, that makes me unable to visualize Oliver Wendell Holmes coordinating a team of law clerks and secretaries and polishing the drafts that the clerks submitted to him. The sense of style that is inseparable from the idea of a great judge in our tradition is unlikely to develop in a judge that does not do his own writing. People are not born great writers; they become great writers by hard work — as writers, not editors. And the struggle to compose a coherent opinion provides a more searching test of the soundness of one's ideas than performing an editorial function does. . . .

The average appointment to the federal bench is not inferior to what it was formerly. . . . But one wonders how many judges starting today with equal promise to that of judges of former days will turn out to be quite so good. Most will feel they just do not have the time to do their own opinion writing; they will conceive their role from the outset as an editorial and supervisory one.

I print these words about "greatness" just as they appeared in the first edition of this book, but I have come to doubt that they are true. I may be living in the golden age of the federal appellate judiciary. There may never have been a time when so large a fraction of federal judges were outstanding. Some of these judges write their own opinion drafts; others work from drafts prepared by law clerks. Some have their full complement of clerks; others have fewer. None is yet recognized as a peer of Holmes, Brandeis, Cardozo, or Learned Hand; of course, by definition none has yet completed his or her career. The growth in the size — and quality — of the federal judiciary will make it more difficult for any modern judge to achieve the prominence of the famous judges of earlier times. . . . Perhaps no living judge will be called "great," but many may be as good as the great judges of old.

The outstanding judge of today is not overwhelmed either by the caseload or by law clerks. Law clerks, like the computer, are a resource that earlier judges either lacked, lacked enough of, or didn't know how to use (Holmes). Unfortunately, only a minority of judges are outstanding. The law clerks are at once a great necessity for the majority and a greater danger to the integrity of these judges' output. In a recent survey, a solid majority of federal court of appeals judges (63 percent) reported "that they must rely on their clerks to do at least some work they believe they should do themselves."

This discussion sheds some further light on the issue of overwork. I do not think circuit judges worked as hard in 1960 as they do today, but they worked, and the increase in their output between then and now — the increase in terminations per judge, in signed opinions per judge, and in other measures of output — cannot be fully explained as a matter of taking up slack. Some of what judges did back then was work that was easily delegable — only it was not delegated, either for want of enough law clerks or because of inexperience in using them. Judges who "do all their own work" are not necessarily making good use of their time. I do think that bright appellate judges ought to write their own opinions (excluding unpublished orders, which can be left to staff to do) and use their clerks for other tasks. . . .

Fifty years ago a federal circuit judge knew that if he was unable or unwilling to write — himself — opinions in the cases assigned to him, he would not be able to hold his head up among his fellows. Today a circuit judge or Supreme Court justice who selects competent law clerks (or indeed just selects a competent selector of law clerks for him) can churn out quite impressive judicial opinions without personal effort. . . .

In emphasizing the costs of heavy reliance on law clerks, I do not mean to suggest that the sole *raison d'être* of a law clerk is to assist a judge in coping with a heavy caseload. Law clerks would be invaluable even if they were not necessary. Generally picked on a meritocratic basis, whereas the judges are not, they usually have better legal analytic capabilities, as well as more energy and freshness, than their judge. And a law clerk is the only person with whom a judge can discuss a case with complete freedom. Able judges can by rigorous direction and supervision of their law clerks infuse their opinions with their own distinctive insights, thereby marrying mature wisdom to youthful brilliance. The institution can be a splendid one, though its costs should not be overlooked.

U.S. JUDICIAL CONFERENCE CODE OF CONDUCT FOR LAW CLERKS (Mar. 13, 1982)

CANON 1.   A Law Clerk Should Uphold the Integrity and Independence of the Judiciary and the Office

An independent and honorable judiciary is indispensable to justice in our society. A law clerk should observe high standards of conduct so that the integrity and independence of the judiciary may be preserved. The provisions of this Code should be construed and applied to further that objective. The standards of this Code shall not affect or preclude other more stringent standards required by law, by court order, or by direction of the appointing judge.

CANON 2.   A Law Clerk Should Avoid Impropriety and the Appearance of Impropriety in All Activities

A law clerk should not engage in any activities that would put into question the propriety of the law clerk's conduct in carrying out the duties of the office. A law clerk should not allow family, social, or other relationships to influence official conduct or judgment. A law clerk should not lend the prestige of the office to advance the private interests of others; nor should the law clerk convey or permit others to convey the impression that they are in a special position to influence the law clerk.[15]

CANON 3.   A Law Clerk Should Perform the Duties of the Office Impartially and Diligently

The official duties of a law clerk take precedence over all other activities. Official duties include all the duties of the office prescribed by law, resolution of the Judicial Conference of the United States, the court in which the law

---

[15] THE CODE OF CONDUCT FOR LAW CLERKS OF THE SUPREME COURT OF THE UNITED STATES 2-3 (June 15, 1998) (Library of Congress Harry A. Blackmun Papers container 1568, folder 13) generally tracks the Code of the Judicial Conference set out in the text above, but goes on to provides the following additional elaborations under CANON 2:

Trustworthiness. The law clerk owes the appointing Justice, and all other Justices, and the Court as an institution duties of complete confidentiality, accuracy, and loyalty. Justices rely upon law clerks' assistance in exploring issue in pending cases. Justices rely on confidentiality in discussing the performance of their judicial duties and the work of the Court, and they expect and require complete loyalty from their own law clerks and the law clerks of all other Justices.

Conduct Expected of the Law Clerk. The law clerk plays an important role in the judicial process, and must strive to maintain the integrity of that system. Because of the close association between the Justices and the law clerk, the law clerk's actions, both professional and personal, reflect on the Justices, on the Court, and ultimately on the judiciary as a whole. The law clerk is therefore held to the very highest standards of conduct. The law clerk, like the Justices, holds a position of public trust and must comply with the demanding standards of that position.

The Justices and the Law Clerk. The relationship between the Justices and the law clerk has several facets: employer-employee, teacher-student, client-lawyer, and lawyer-lawyer. In all of these, the law clerk must be aware of the respect due the Justices. Respect does not mean acquiescence: a law clerk should not fear to express an opinion contrary to the Justice's, and most Justices expect and invite their law clerks to question their views. This exchange of ideas between the clerk and the Justices is at the heart of the Justice-clerk relationship. If, however, the appointing Justice should then reach a conclusion that differs from the law clerk's, the law clerk should carry out to the fullest and to the best of his or her ability the Justice's instructions. The ultimate responsibility for fulfilling the duties of the Justice's office always remains with the Justice.

The Court and the Law Clerk. Separate and apart from the duty owed by each law clerk to the appointing Justice is the duty owed by each law clerk to the Court as a body. Each law clerk is in a position to receive highly confidential circulations from the chambers of other Justices. All oral and written communications from the Justices or clerks in other chambers pertaining to the work of the Court are confidential. Examples of confidential matters include the outcome of the case; the vote in a case; the identity of the author of a majority, concurring, or dissenting opinion; the date on which an opinion is to be announced; and the positions or preliminary ideas or views of any Justice with respect to cases that have been before the Court, are pending before it, or are likely to come before it.

clerk serves, and the appointing judge. In the performance of these duties, the following standards apply:

A. A law clerk should respect and comply with the law and should conduct himself or herself at all times in a manner that promotes public confidence in the integrity and impartiality of the judiciary and of the office.

B. A law clerk should maintain professional competence in the profession. A law clerk should be dignified, courteous, and fair to all persons with whom the law clerk deals in the law clerk's official capacity. A law clerk should diligently discharge the responsibilities of the office. A law clerk should bear in mind the obligation to treat fairly and courteously the general public as well as the legal profession.

C. The relationship between judge and law clerk is essentially a confidential one. A law clerk should abstain from public comment about a pending or impending proceeding in the court in which the law clerk serves. A law clerk should never disclose to any person any confidential information received in the course of the law clerk's duties, nor should the law clerk employ such information for personal gain. This subsection does not prohibit a law clerk from making public statements in the course of official duties to the extent authorized by the appointing judge.

D. A law clerk should inform the appointing judge of any circumstance or activity of the law clerk that might serve as a basis for disqualification of the judge, *e.g.*, a prospective employment relation with a law firm, association of the law clerk's spouse with a law firm or litigant, *etc.*

CANON 4. A Law Clerk May Engage in Activities to Improve the Law, the Legal System, and the Administration of Justice [omitted]

CANON 5. A Law Clerk Should Regulate Extra-Official Activities to Minimize the Risk of Conflict with Official Duties [omitted]

CANON 6. A Law Clerk Should Regularly File Any Required Reports of Compensation Received for All Extra-Official Activities [omitted]

CANON 7. A Law Clerk Should Refrain From Political Activity

A law clerk should refrain from political activity; a law clerk should not act as a leader or hold office in a political organization; a law clerk should not make speeches for or publicly endorse a political organization or candidate; a law clerk should not solicit funds for or contribute to a political organization, candidate, or event; a law clerk should not become a candidate for political or public office; a law clerk should not otherwise engage in political activities.

NOTES

1. Students of a course on appellate courts can take some comfort that they will not graduate with the learning gap that a Ninth Circuit judge once described: "Some attributes of the decision-making process that the new clerk

finds difficult are institutional in nature. . . . The law clerk is also hampered by his introduction to the appellate process in the procedure casebooks used in law schools. A check on such casebooks indicates that most leave the materials on appeals until the end, with the treatment given the subject coming almost as an afterthought. As a result, incoming law clerks must spend valuable time learning rudimentary aspects of appellate procedure." Indeed, the Judge muses: "Maybe the law schools should offer a specialty course on the appellate process, making appeals co-equal with the trial. Surely appeals are as important and often as dispositive, and there is much to be learned about the nature of the judicial process in such a course." Eugene A. Wright, *Observations of an Appellate Judge: the Use of Law Clerks*, 26 VAND. L. REV. 1179, 1182 (1973).

2. What sort of background and experience should a person have to be well-qualified to serve as a law clerk? What sorts of tasks can be appropriately assigned to a law clerk and what tasks should be reserved to the judge? What are the costs and benefits of increasing the number of law clerks in chambers?

3. While admitting that "the number of variations in collaboration probably equals the number of appellate judges," a distinguished federal judge described three different modes of in-chambers relationship between judge and law clerk. FRANK M. COFFIN, ON APPEAL: COURTS, LAWYERING, AND JUDGING 74-75 (1994): (1) In the authoritarian mode, "work of very substantial importance is entrusted to a law clerk, but under a tight leash and with rather precise instructions. For example, the clerk is assigned to draft an opinion, but only after an outline has been approved by the judge. Or, the judge has in mind a theory and the intuition that there are cases to support it; the clerk is to put flesh on the bare bones"; (2) In the discretionary mode, "[w]hile the obviously basic decisions are made by the judge, there is room for minor decision-making by the clerk . . . [in] a creative collaboration which calls up in my mind the interaction between a master and his apprentices"; (3) In the collegial mode, "the collaboration takes on the collegial character of several colleagues devoting their entire efforts to the pursuit of a shared common objective. The bedrock responsibility of the judge is so understood that it needs no explicit expression. The ample discretion lodged in the clerk is a product of the trust earned by experience." If you were a judge, which of these three modes would your prefer? If you were a law clerk, which would you prefer? What are the implications from these different modes for appellate court values and imperatives?

4. How do you assess the costs and benefits of law clerks after reading Judge Posner's candid assessment? How is increasing appellate workload related to the increase in the number of law clerks and to the growing reliance upon law clerks? Judge Posner argues that lawyers should understand the fact that they are "writing for law clerks and not just, and in some cases not primarily, for judges." RICHARD A. POSNER, THE FEDERAL COURTS: CHALLENGES AND REFORM 158 (1996). How might this insight affect how you will practice law, specifically how you will write briefs and deliver oral arguments on appeals?

5. The typical U.S. Supreme Court chambers staff today consists of two secretaries, one messenger, and four law clerks who serve for a year; the maximum chambers staff of a U.S. circuit judge today is one secretary and four law clerks who serve for a year. If appellate workload is a growing problem, why

not simply keep adding law clerks to keep pace with increases in the docket? Is there some limit to the number of law clerks that a single judge can supervise? Consider this worry:

> Even defenders of elbow clerks must admit that increasing the number of law clerks eventually will result in diminishing marginal returns. The judge who remains a judge becomes something of a bottleneck as appeals move through chambers only as fast as the judge can review, evaluate, and act on recommendations and drafts from a large staff of sub-judges. When members of Congress — who are used to operating with large staffs — have offered to increase the number of law clerks at the Supreme Court, the Justices wisely have declined for this very reason. Many judges and court-watchers believe the [U.S.] Circuit Judges are at the same point. The worry that elbow clerks will become junior varsity judges is real.

Thomas E. Baker, *The Institution of Law Clerks in the U.S. Courts of Appeals*, 3 LONG TERM VIEW 71, 73 (Spring 1995). Does the reliance on law clerks provide cover for incompetent or mediocre judges? Does the reliance on law clerks allow judges appointed with life-time tenure to serve after becoming mentally or physically incompetent? Are there any ways to obviate these concerns?

6. Many law schools have large judicial internship programs that offer participating state and federal judges second or third year law students who work in chambers for a semester and earn academic credit. Often, these interns function as a *de facto* law-clerk-to-the-law-clerk. Stacy Caplow, *From Courtroom to Classroom: Creating an Academic Component to Enhance the Skills and Values Learned in a Student Judicial Clerkship Clinic*, 75 NEB. L. REV. 872 (1996); Elizabeth A. Kovachevich, *Federal Judicial Internship Programs: A Commitment to the Future of the Legal Profession*, 41 FED. B. NEWS & J. 680 (1994). Is this a good idea? What are the costs and benefits to the judge, the law clerk, and the student intern?

7. There has been an ongoing debate over the pros and cons of career law clerks, *i.e.*, "permanent" elbow clerks who are experienced lawyers and who serve in chambers indefinitely, as opposed to newly-graduated lawyers who serve one or two years and depart to be replaced by other newly-graduated lawyers. *Compare* BERNARD E. WITKIN, MANUAL ON APPELLATE COURT OPINIONS 12 (1977) *with* Eugene A. Wright, *Observations of an Appellate Judge: the Use of Law Clerks*, 26 VAND. L. REV. 1179, 1181-84 (1973). Occasionally, justices of the U.S. Supreme Court have kept law clerks for more than one year; the modern record is held by Eugene Gressman who served as law clerk to Justice Murphy for five years (1943-48) and earned the nickname (really a dig at Justice Murphy) of "Mr. Justice Gressman." Today, the norm for all nine justices is to rotate their clerks annually. For the most part, the annual rotation model also is followed throughout the U.S courts of appeals; however, two-year clerkships are common in the U.S. district courts. Many state supreme courts have a historical practice that persists to the present day to appoint permanent clerks who serve indefinitely, though at the pleasure of their justice, often for a decade or longer. Gerald Kogan & Robert Craig Walters, *The Operation and Jurisdiction of the Florida Supreme Court*, 18 NOVA L. REV.

1151, 1182 (1994). The practice varies from state to state, of course. In the California appellate court system, which is the largest appellate court system in the country, the judges on the state supreme court and the intermediate courts of appeals predominately employ career law clerks. *See generally* JOHN BILYEU OAKLEY & ROBERT S. THOMPSON, LAW CLERKS AND THE JUDICIAL PROCESS: PERCEPTIONS OF THE QUALITIES AND FUNCTIONS OF LAW CLERKS IN AMERICAN COURTS (1980). What are the pros and cons of permanent law clerks? From the perspective of the judge? From the perspective of the law clerk? From the perspective of the court system and appellate imperatives? Why do you suppose that state appellate judges are empirically more likely than federal appellate judges to employ career law clerks?

8. There was one notorious but obscure incident in which a Supreme Court law clerk resigned and was criminally prosecuted to no conclusion after allegedly conspiring with others to use court-insider knowledge to profit in the stock market. John B. Owens, *The Clerk, the Thief, His Life as a Baker: Ashton Embry and the Supreme Court Leak Scandal of 1919*, 95 NW. U. L. REV. 271 (2000).

9. There is a consensus that confidentiality during the actual term of the clerkship is critically important. The expression court insiders often use is that sensitive knowledge about the cases and the decisions — and even juicy gossip about the judges — ought to be "kept inside the court family." There is lots of controversy, however, about how the duty of confidentiality ought to play out after a clerkship is over and done. In modern times, the publication of two "clerk-and-tell" books generated more heat than light upon the issue. First, two reporters, Bob Woodward (of Watergate fame) and Scott Armstrong, wrote THE BRETHREN: INSIDE THE SUPREME COURT (1979) which provided an account of the 1969-1975 Terms based upon "interviews with more than two hundred people, including several Justices, more than 170 law clerks, and several dozen former employees of the Court." *Id.* at 3. This book led the Supreme Court to promulgate its code for law clerks excerpted above and many state supreme courts followed suit with codes of their own. Second, Edward Lazarus wrote CLOSED CHAMBERS — THE FIRST EYEWITNESS ACCOUNT OF THE EPIC STRUGGLES INSIDE THE SUPREME COURT (1998) an account of the internecine ideological struggles over high-profile issues like the death penalty, affirmative action, and abortion, that took place during his own clerkship. Lazarus issued this disclaimer: "I have been careful to avoid disclosing information I am privy to solely because I was privileged to work for Justice Blackmun. . . . I have reconstructed what I knew and supplemented that knowledge through primary sources . . . and dozens of interviews . . . with many people who spoke to me on the condition that I not reveal their names. . . . Justice Blackmun was not among them." *Id.* at xi-xii. To say that both of these books engendered considerable consternation and controversy would be an understatement. *See, e.g.*, Paul Bender, *Book Review: The Brethren*, 128 U. PA. L. REV. 716 (1980); David J. Garrow, *"The Lowest Form of Animal Life"?: Supreme Court Clerks and Supreme Court History*, 84 CORNELL L. REV. 855 (1999). The Compliance provision of the Supreme Court's code for law clerks states:

> The duty of confidentiality is a continuing one and for this purpose a former law clerk remains subject to the obligations set forth in this Code. Law clerks assume the obligations of this Code as conditions of

their employment, as attorneys, and as members or future members of the bar. Any breach of these provisions is prejudicial to the administration of justice and therefore will subject the law clerk to appropriate sanctions.

THE CODE OF CONDUCT FOR LAW CLERKS OF THE SUPREME COURT OF THE UNITED STATES 2-3 (June 15, 1998) (Library of Congress Harry A. Blackmun Papers container 1568, folder 13). What does this mean? Is it enforceable? How? Is it constitutional under the first amendment? Is it sound public policy? When and how does a former clerk's duty of confidentiality owed to the Court eventually give way to the scholar's duty to history? What about the justices and their own books and memoirs about the Supreme Court?

10. What qualities would you look for in a law clerk if you were an appellate judge? What objective criteria would you apply? Should judges take into account the value of diversity in race, gender, ethnicity, sexual orientation, geography, *etc.*? In 1998, Tony Mauro, a long-time reporter covering the Supreme Court, wrote a newspaper article bringing attention to the dearth of minorities among Supreme Court law clerks. The next year, civil rights groups staged protests at the Supreme Court and petitioned the Chief Justice. At subsequent congressional hearings on the Supreme Court's budget, the justices were questioned sharply about their law clerk hiring practices. Perhaps as a result, there is more diversity among the clerks than there was when the first reports were published, but the Court's critics are still not satisfied. *See generally* Robert M. Tony Mauro, *"In Other News. . . ": Developments at the Supreme Court in the 2002-2003 Term That you Won't Read About in the U.S. Reports*, 39 TULSA L. REV. 11, 17-22 (2003). State court judges are likewise cognizant of the diversity issue in law clerk hiring. Charles Toutant, *Minority Clerkships Holding Steady: New Jersey Judiciary Boasts Hiring Rate Upward of 22 Percent*, N.J. L. J., Feb. 25, 2002, at 1.

11. Perhaps, Judge Posner deserves the last word: "The law clerk is here to stay. We should accept that fact and move on." RICHARD A. POSNER, THE FEDERAL COURTS — CHALLENGES AND REFORM 158 (1996). *See generally Symposium: Law Clerks: The Transformation of the Judiciary*, THE LONG TERM VIEW (Spring 1995).

III. CENTRAL STAFF ATTORNEYS

Central staff attorneys are the newest personnel development to provide additional professional assistance to appellate judges. Unlike law clerks, who have a long institutional history, staff attorneys are a direct personnel response to the crisis of volume that began in the 1960s. The excerpts below present the history and development of the position, including descriptions of the types of work performed by staff attorneys.

Questions you should consider here include: What are the essential differences between central staff attorneys and law clerks? Are there tasks that should be assigned to staff attorneys and not to law clerks, or *vice versa*? What are the appropriate ratios of law clerks to staff attorneys to judges? What are the peculiar threats to appellate imperatives posed by staff attorneys, as opposed to law clerks? Are the appellate imperatives threatened more by one than by the other kind of judicial assistant? What relationship between judges and staff attorneys is most efficient and proper? How effective has this personnel development been in coping with the crisis of volume?

Daniel J. Meador, Appellate Courts: Staff and Process in the Crisis of Volume 12-13, 17-18 (1974)[16]

Central Staff in Historical Perspective. The primary purpose of a central staff of lawyers . . . is to assist judges in deciding appeals. While staff attorneys can perform a variety of other useful jobs in an appellate court, . . . their main mission as house counsel to the court — their *raison d'etre* — is to give professional help to the judges at the very heart of the decisional process. This role may suggest to some judges and lawyers an improper "delegation" of the ultimate judicial duty, or at least a kind of improper intrusion into decision making by one not a judge. Because apprehensions of that sort often surface in discussions of staff work, it is important at the outset to dispel the idea that there is something novel about judges' utilizing professional help in deciding cases. The contemporary concept of staff attorney, when viewed in historical perspective, is simply the most recently developed type of professional assistance for judges. Other varieties of such help have long been on the judicial scene. The totally unassisted appellate judge probably does not exist in the United States today. . . .

The Contemporary Concept of Central Staff Attorney. . . . [A] staff attorney is a legally trained person working for and assisting an appellate court as a whole. Various titles are used: research attorney, commissioner, *pro se* clerk, staff law clerk, and pool aide. If such persons in fact provide professional assistance for the court as an entity, they are staff attorneys, as that term is used in this [book]. A law clerk and a staff attorney are both lawyers providing professional legal help to appellate judges in the decision of cases. But the former works exclusively for a single judge in whatever way the judge wishes to use him [or her]; the job is highly personal. The latter has no special relationship to any individual judge but rather works for the court or a panel within it as a collective unit; the staff responsibility is institutional. This is a key distinction in understanding the roles of a central staff.

While this concept of central legal assistance has blossomed in very recent years, it is not totally new. . . . [T]he U.S. Court of Military Appeals has employed a central staff of lawyers[, called commissioners, since its creation in 1951]. It was probably the first appellate court in the United States to create such a staff, and it did so years before the idea became fashionable. Some of the U.S. Courts of Appeals began using *pro se* clerks or *habeas corpus* clerks in the early nineteen sixties. In England a central legal staff — the Criminal Appeal Office — has been used for many years to assist the Court of Criminal Appeal. The establishment of a central staff in the Michigan Court of Appeals in 1968 gave an impetus and a focus to the contemporary development . . . [s]preading to California, Minnesota, and other states. . . .

---

[16] Copyright © 1974 Thomson West. Reprinted with permission.

In addition to the *sine qua non* of working for the court as a whole, the staff attorney concept carries with it certain other features. One is that where there are multiple staff attorneys they are organized centrally as a group. This is a corollary of the proposition that they do not work for individual judges. In order to avoid drifting into individualized relationships with particular judges, central organization and procedures are essential. Another feature is a single responsible head presiding over the entire central pool of staff attorneys, responsible to the court for all staff personnel and activities. Although in theory this could be the presiding judge of the court, he [or she] is typically too busy and his [or her] interests and responsibilities are too dispersed. Common practice is to have a staff director who is one of the central staff lawyers but is typically more experienced than the others; he [or she] must also have administrative abilities. . . . Though a central staff with a staff director is a structural innovation resulting from the sharp rise in appellate volume since the mid-1960's, the concept is hardly novel when considered historically against the background of masters, commissioners, magistrates, and law clerks.

Donald P. Ubell, *Evolution and Role of Appellate Court Central Staff Attorneys*, 2 Cooley L. Rev. 157 (1984)[17]

. . . . Some say the first central staff attorneys were the court commissioners of the late 19th and early 20th centuries [*See supra* chapter 6]. . . . They were thought of as adjunct judges or magistrates who drafted opinions for a court once it made its decision. They were the first response to the cries for help that periodically emanate from appellate judges. As many as 19 states experimented with them before they went the way of the dinosaur. [The title has survived, however, and now is most often employed to describe staff attorneys assigned to research applications for leave to appeal and petitions for certiorari.]

In the late 1960s, two judges from intermediate courts of appeals, Michigan's T. John Lesinski and California's Winslow Christian, seized on this seed of an idea and brought it to institutional bloom. These two friends worked independently, but frequently compared notes to see what of each system could be successfully transplanted.

Both looked at their workloads and realized that their current judge level could not keep up if business were to be conducted as usual. Neither wanted more judges added to their courts because they feared institutional instability and weakened collegiality. So they looked to other solutions. They analyzed the tasks being performed by the individual judge's assistant, the law clerk, and recognized that there was a great deal of duplication of effort going on in those judges' chambers. Each law clerk would prepare his or her judge for oral argument by drafting a memorandum which would set forth the facts uncolored by advocacy, restate the issues in more useable form, and briefly suggest questions that needed clarification at oral argument. Some legal analysis might be done at that point. Why should three people do this work when the work of one would suffice, they thought.

---

[17] Copyright © 1984 Cooley Law Review. Reprinted with permission.

Justice Christian approached the development of a central staff by stripping each judge of his single law clerk. These attorneys did a report for each case scheduled for oral argument. In the screening process, the attorney was expected to identify cases suitable for routine disposition. He or she then presented the case orally to a panel of judges. If the panel agreed with the staff attorney, the case would be decided with a *per curiam* [opinion]. The concept of operating without an elbow clerk was startling, even though the elbow clerk had been around for only 40 years by then. The court found that it could operate more expeditiously in this way, however.

The Michigan story is somewhat different. The Legislature had just authorized a second law clerk per [appellate] judge. Chief Judge Lesinski convinced his colleagues to forego that second law clerk and pool them in the court's central office in Lansing under a senior attorney. . . . The pre-hearing attorneys, as they were called, were to prepare a report on every calendar case. The report was similar to the bench memo that the law clerk had been doing — a roadmap to decision. The facts were stated in non-argumentative form, the issues restated, and the arguments of counsel analyzed, with the pre-hearing attorney ultimately recommending a disposition and occasionally drafting a *per curiam* opinion if it were thought to be an appropriate disposition. This was not screening to determine whether the case should be orally argued, but simply to assist first the clerk [of court] in drawing up the calendar and secondly the judges with their eventual decision. The traditional [elbow] law clerk was left with the role of assisting in the disposition stage. The productivity increases realized over the next few years were outstanding. . . .

ABA Standards Relating to Appellate Courts § 3.62 (1994)[18]

(i) If an appellate court establishes a central legal staff for the court as a whole, it should be under the supervision of the Chief Justice or the Chief Judge respectively and in accordance with the court's internal operating procedures. . . . All staff attorneys, including supervisory staff attorneys, serve at the pleasure of the court.

(ii) A staff director should be appointed by the court. . . . The staff director should assist the Chief Justice or the Chief Judge in organizing and monitoring the work of the central legal staff.

(iii) The duties and responsibilities of a central legal staff may properly include, but need not be limited to:

(1) Monitoring, reviewing, and making preliminary classification of cases coming before the court in accordance with criteria established by the court and making recommendations for disposition of routine procedural matters;

(2) Assisting in the calendaring of cases containing similar or related issues;

---

[18] Copyright © 1994 American Bar Association. Reprinted with permission.

(3) Preparing analyses of cases, motions, and other matters coming before the court (including procedural history, facts, principal issues, parties' contentions, and applicable law) and presenting recommended dispositions as appropriate under criteria adopted by the court;

(4) Reviewing all matters presented in *propria persona* and taking measures necessary to put them in correct and intelligible form;

(5) Supplementing the research of the judge's individual law clerks, as required; and

(6) Acting for the court in supervising the preparation of complex records. . . .

Commentary. In many, if not most, appellate courts, staff attorneys play a vital role in case flow management and in serving as a link between the administrative functions performed by the clerk's office and the decisional and policy-making functions performed by judges. In addition, a central staff regularly exposed to recurring legal issues can provide informed and efficient processing of cases, as well as identification of conflicts and inconsistencies in decisions. Based on the practices of a variety of appellate courts, the duties of a central legal staff, in addition to those specified in this section, may include:

- Assisting the court in maintaining consistency of decisions by preparing standard order forms, summaries of recent decisions, digests, indices, and other materials for circulation within and, if appropriate, outside the court;

- Drafting proposed orders and opinions;

- Drafting proposed procedural rules or amendments to existing court rules;

- Assisting the court, as requested, in matters relating to bar admissions and discipline;

- Participating in the preparation or teaching of judicial or continuing legal education programs;

- Serving as court representatives on bar or other committees as designated by the court;

- Reviewing proposed opinions of the court to identify errors or inconsistencies;

- Participating in pre-hearing and settlement conferences.

U.S. CT. APP. 9TH CIR., LOCAL RULES (1999)

C. Judges and Supporting Personnel

. . . .

(4) Office of Staff Attorneys — This office consists of attorneys who work for the entire court rather than for individual judges. About half of the attorneys are court law clerks hired for one- or two-year periods. The others include the

staff director, attorneys assigned for up to five years to the civil and criminal motions units, case management attorneys who are permanent members of the court staff, and attorneys assisting in the administration of the office. The staff attorneys perform a variety of tasks for the court:

(a) *Inventory* — After appellate briefing has been completed, the case management attorneys review the excerpt of record and briefs in each case in order to identify jurisdictional defects and the primary issues raised in the appeal and to assign a numerical point designation to the case reflecting the relative amount of judge time that likely will have to be spent on the matter. Cases suffering from clear jurisdictional defects are processed through a motions panel as soon as the defects are noted.

(b) *Research* — Under the supervision of the staff director and supervising attorneys the court law clerks review briefs and records, research legal issues, and prepare memorandum dispositions for oral presentation to three judge panels, principally in cases in which no oral argument is calendared.

(c) *Motions* — Certain staff attorneys specialize in motions work. Except for procedural motions disposed of by the clerk, the motions attorneys process all motions filed in a case prior to assignment of a particular panel for disposition on the merits. Motions attorneys present all motions to three judge panels or the Appellate Commissioner. Criminal motions attorneys process motions arising from criminal actions, federal or state habeas corpus proceedings. Civil motions attorneys process all civil motions matters other than those defined as criminal motions. They also process attorney discipline matters where the attorney has initially been disciplined by another court. The civil and criminal motions attorneys also process emergency motions filed pursuant to Circuit Rules. . . , and motions for reconsideration, petitions for rehearing, suggestions for rehearing *en banc* for motions panels that initially decide the particular motions matter, and all requests for initial hearing *en banc*.

PAUL D. CARRINGTON, DANIEL J. MEADOR & MAURICE ROSENBERG, JUSTICE ON APPEAL 46-48 (1976)[19]

The use of central staff carries some of the same risks associated with excessive dependence on personal law clerks. If it is used in the wrong way, such a staff can become a sprawling bureaucracy which could dominate the court, and thus threaten the imperatives of identifiability, personal responsibility, collegiality, and inspiring working conditions. In fact, these risks seem greater in regard to the use of central staff, if central staff were to be used in precisely the same way that the more familiar personal law clerks are used, as a source of help in thinking. A central staff which acquired all the functions of the personal law clerks and provided the same service to all judges in every case would be quite likely to dominate the institution. The most powerful office in the court could come to be that of the staff director.

---

[19] Copyright © 1976 Thomson West. Reprinted with permission.

But this need not be. . . . [T]here are a number of steps which can be taken to abbreviate and accelerate the [appellate] process which do not require the full attention of all the judges. It is these functions which can be assisted efficiently by the central staff. The crucial step in the effective utilization of central staff is to alter the traditional appellate procedure which operates in all cases the same in favor of a differentiated procedure which measures the court's efforts to fit the needs of the particular case. It is in the operation of a differentiated procedure that the central staff can be used to substantial advantage. . . .

The adverse risks of the use of central staff are also less where the central staff functions are primarily associated with the routing procedures that are necessary to the differentiated process. Nevertheless, there is just reason for caution in the enlargement of the central staff. The staff functions are not, and cannot be, so clearly defined that there will be no danger of undue dependence, if there are a small number of judges served by a large central staff in a high volume situation. Prudence dictates that the central staff should not be permitted to become so large that it will be possible for it to compete for judicial functions. As a sound rule of thumb, we propose that no central staff be enlarged to include more professionals than there are judges to be served by the staff. To place this rule in relation to one previously suggested, we propose as a rule that not less than one professional of four serving in a high volume court should be a full-fledged judge; such a judge may be appropriately assisted by as many as two personal law clerks and the equivalent of one additional clerk serving in the central staff. To surround a judgeship in such a court with more supporting personnel would create risks we regard as excessive to the imperatives of appellate justice. As long as this rule is observed, there need be little concern about staff usurpation or the "bureaucratization" of the judiciary.

THOMAS E. BAKER, RATIONING JUSTICE ON APPEAL — THE PROBLEMS OF THE U.S. COURTS OF APPEALS 143-46 (1994)[20]

Staff attorneys . . . work for the court as a whole rather than for an individual judge. There is something of a paradox in this arrangement, however. Unless the staff attorneys are doing work that otherwise would be done by judges, they do not increase the overall productivity of the court. Yet, if they do perform some of the judge's duties, the judicial function is usurped. The philosophical resolution of this paradox assigns to staff attorneys tasks that in the past have been, but need not be, performed by judges. Such a resolution, however, is not easily accomplished. The various courts of appeals have experimented with the job description of the staff attorney. Many of the results of these experiments represent uncomfortable choices made in the face of the daunting workload. One judge explains that it is the staff attorney who:

> acquires a case at the moment the notice of appeal is filed, shepherds
> it through each procedural step until the closing brief is in, prepares
> legal memoranda, drafts a proposed opinion or other disposition,

---

[20] Copyright © 1994 Thomson West. Reprinted with permission.

recommends grant or denial of oral argument, and presents the complete package to the judges to be graded pass/fail.

The key assumption here is that these tasks need not be performed by judges. The motions process, for example, no longer simply sends along the matter for judicial consideration and action. Before the motion reaches a judge, a staff attorney writes a memorandum recommending a disposition and attaches a proposed order. Admittedly, these staff attorney evaluations save a substantial amount of judge time. Deciding whether a case deserves oral argument and how a case should be decided, however, lie at the core of the judicial function. The major concern frequently expressed is that the widespread dependence on staff attorneys has created a bureaucratic judicial process.

The premise of the staff attorney position is that one staff attorney does the work of three law clerks, one in each panel member's chambers. The number of staff attorneys and their duties vary considerably from circuit to circuit. Critics of the general expansion of central staff attorney responsibilities echo the concerns expressed about the expansion of law clerk responsibility in chambers. Both types of legal assistants potentially encroach on the judging responsibility, but the situation is worse with the staff attorney because the supervision characteristic of the in-chambers relationship with the "elbow" law clerk is lacking for the central staff attorney. Proponents, on the other hand, maintain that the harsh reality of caseload pressures prevents judges from doing everything they once did. Staff attorneys perform tasks low on the judicial scale, thus allowing judges to perform the important appellate tasks that require an Article III decisionmaker. Conceding this much departure from appellate traditions, proponents assert that, on balance, the wise use of central staff attorneys does more good than harm. Staff attorneys in most circuits play a prominent role in handling *pro se* appeals. In some appeals, staff attorneys may be performing the work that the advocates rightly ought to have done, but for whatever reason was not done or was not done adequately. Considered realistically, the capacity reform of central staff attorneys already has lasted too long to be deemed merely an experiment and today is an integral part of the appellate scene:

> Central staff attorneys are here to stay, without question. The reasons that gave birth to their existence remain. Filings continue to increase and the prospect for new judgeships is limited by political and economic reality. The only way to deal with that workload is to find more efficient ways to operate so that a judge's productivity may be increased.

While nearly everyone agrees that law clerks are necessary, there still is considerable disagreement over their proper role. The A.B.A. Standing Committee on the Federal Judiciary, for example, recently urged that if staff decisional personnel were inevitable, they should be made a formal and public part of the process so that the attorneys could review and respond to staff recommendations.

Judges have gone to great lengths to defend the level of delegation that already has taken place. Every study has concluded that the increases in law clerks over the years have "helped the circuit courts deal with the increasing volume of appeals without sacrificing the fundamental imperatives of appellate justice." The proponents of further expanded use of staff attorneys and law clerks, however, rest their arguments on an unstable foundation. With three law clerks and one staff attorney for each appeals judge, the judges are at the limit of their ability to supervise subordinate decisional personnel. Until recently, this was the official position of the Judicial Conference of the United States. The Judicial Conference had adopted guidelines in 1981 limiting the number of central staff attorneys in a circuit to the number of active judgeships authorized for that court. Then, in 1991, the Judicial Conference revisited the issue of limiting staff attorneys and adopted a more complex mathematical ratio for increasing the number of staff attorney positions in relation to the number of authorized judgeships, based on the computation of case filings in the court of appeals divided by full time equivalents of judgeships. [Today, by statute, 28 U.S.C. § 715 (b), the maximum number of staff attorney positions cannot exceed the number expressly authorized in the annual appropriations act for the federal courts.] Thus, adding more law clerks or more staff attorneys to the current deployment of decisional personnel no longer is as acceptable a method of coping with the caseload. Certainly, if not exceeded, limits have been reached for decisional staff in the courts of appeals.

Authorized Judgeships, Law Clerks per Judge, and Central Staff Attorneys in Selected Federal and State Appellate Courts[1]

Court	Judgeships	Law clerks per Judge	Central Staff Attorneys
— COLRs —			
US Supreme Court	9	4	2
CA Supreme Court	7	5	29
FL Supreme Court	7	2	8
LA Supreme Court	7	3	9
MI Supreme Court	7	3	17
NV Supreme Court[2]	7	2	21
NJ Supreme Court	7	2-4[3]	4
NY Court of Appeals	7	2	15
OK Supreme Court	9	2	26
OK Court Criminal Appeals	5	2	15
TX Supreme Court	9	2	12
TX Court Criminal Appeals	9	9	16
WV Supreme Court[2]	5	3	14
— IACs —			

US Court of Appeals for the 1st Circuit	6	3-4[4]	18
US Court of Appeals for the 5th Circuit	17	3-4[4]	46
US Court of Appeals for the 7th Circuit	11	3-4[4]	29
US Court of Appeals for the 9th Circuit	28	3-4[4]	54
US Court of Appeals for the 11th Circuit	12	3-4[4]	58
CA Courts of Appeals (6)	105	2	289
FL District Courts of Appeals (5)	62	2	31
LA Courts of Appeals (5)	54	2	68
MI Court of Appeals	28	1	70
NJ Appellate Division	32	1	33
NY Supreme Court Appellate Divisions (4)	55	1	107
OK Court of Civil Appeals	12	2	27
TX Courts of Appeals (14)	80	1	114

[1] This Table shows the number of authorized judgeships, law clerks per judge, and the total number of central staff attorneys for selected appellate courts. COLRs are courts of last resort; IACs are intermediate appellate courts. The data was compiled from: CAROL R. FLANGO & DAVID B. ROTTMAN, APPELLATE COURT PROCEDURES (National Center for State Courts 1998); SHAUNA M. STRICKLAND & BRENDA G. ONO, STATE COURT CASELOAD STATISTICS, 2002 (National Center for State Courts 2003); ABA COUNCIL OF STAFF ATTORNEYS, 2004-2005 DIRECTORY OF APPELLATE CENTRAL STAFF COUNSEL (http://www.abanet.org/jd/ajc/casa/home.html).

[2] Nevada and West Virginia have a COLR but do not have an IAC.

[3] Each justice has two or three law clerks and there may be up to two more law clerks assigned to death penalty cases.

[4] U.S. Circuit Judges can trade one of two secretarial positions for a fourth elbow law clerk and that is the recent trend.

NOTES

1. Do not confuse the work of "law clerks" and "staff attorneys" with the work performed in the "Office of the Clerk," the chief administrative officer of the court who maintains case files and court records. Consider this description:

The clerk's office began in 1981 with twenty-seven deputy clerks and increased to fifty-one by 1991. Case-handling is done on a "docket team" basis, with one or more teams responsible for all cases from a

state. The team handles filing and processing of case-related documents, monitors the progress of each case, and responds to requests for
case-related information. A separate deputy clerk handles death
penalty habeas cases.

The clerk's office is an activist office, not a mere filing facility. It
monitors the preparation of trial transcripts by court reporters, which
minimizes delays. It oversees the progress of appeals. It records the
status of opinions assigned to judges and the progress of cases on the
nonargument calendar and reports to the court each month the status
of each judge's work. The clerk's office makes up oral argument calendars, giving consideration to the ages of cases and the proximity of
case originations to the site for oral argument. The clerk is authorized
to act on many routine motions; others are referred to judges for
handling.

Automation is increasingly important to the court. In the clerk's
office automated systems have evolved from crude machines to an
office-wide network of personal computers using advanced software.
These computers keep track of each event in a case, transmit statistical data to the Administrative Office of Courts in Washington, and
support sophisticated word processing. They enable clerks in the
Atlanta headquarters, and judges and their staffs throughout the circuit, to obtain current information on most aspects of case status. All
judges' offices are connected with court headquarters, and with each
other, through E-mail, which transmits documents immediately in
hard copy form, supplemented by FAX machines.

Judges file their opinions with the court in a form that can be transmitted electronically to West Publishing Company without being
retyped or reformulated. West provides slip opinions, with headnotes
and *syllabi*, in the same form that the opinions will appear in the
FEDERAL REPORTER. The headnoted form is of great benefit to all users
of the slip opinions.

John C. Godbold, *The Eleventh Circuit Court of Appeals: the First Ten Years*
43 MERCER L. REV. 961, 968-69 (1992).[21]

2. Are there appellate court tasks that are better performed by a staff attorney than by an elbow law clerk? What appellate court tasks must be performed by an attorney and what tasks might be delegated to a non-lawyer
employee in the office of the clerk of court?

3. Do the A.B.A. STANDARDS and the sample court operating procedures
excerpted above clearly and adequately demarcate the boundary between
judicial decisionmaking and staff decisionmaking? How are the threats to
appellate imperatives from staff attorneys similar or different from the
threats from law clerks?

---

[21] Copyright © 1992 Mercer Law Review. Reprinted with permission.

4. As the excerpts above suggest, the position of central staff attorney first developed and then spread among state appellate courts. James Duke Cameron, *The Central Staff: A New Solution to an Old Problem*, 23 UCLA L. REV. 465 (1976). Interestingly, in some states, the more recent trend is to redesignate temporary elbow law clerk positions to permanent staff attorney positions. James T. Worthen, *The Organizational & Structural Development of Intermediate Appellate Courts in Texas, 1892-2003*, 46 SO. TEX. L. REV. 33 (2004). The justification has been the growing workload. But how do staff attorneys contribute more or better than elbow clerks to an appellate court's effort to cope with workload?

5. Among the U.S. Courts of Appeals, the Ninth Circuit, which is the biggest federal appellate court with the biggest caseload, has been a leader in the deployment of staff attorneys but the rest of the circuits also deploy them. Steven Flanders & Jerry Goldman, *Screening Practices and the Use of Para-Judicial Personnel in a U.S. Court of Appeals: A Study in the Fourth Circuit*, 1 JUSTICE SYSTEM J. 1 (1975); Timothy E. Gammon, *The Central Staff Attorneys' Office in the United States Court of Appeals, Eighth Circuit — A Five Year Report*, 29 S.D. L. REV. 457 (1984); Arthur D. Hellman, *Central Staff in Appellate Courts: the Experience of the Ninth Circuit*, 68 CALIF. L. REV. 937 (1980); Donald P. Ubell, *Report on Central Staff Attorneys Offices in the United States Courts of Appeals*, 87 F.R.D. 253 (1980).

6. Judge Posner notes an irony in the personnel development of the position of staff attorney:

> Federal administrative agencies traditionally had centralized opinion-writing staffs rather than giving each commissioner his own law clerks. This practice was heavily criticized, and the staffs have tended in recent years to be replaced with law clerks on the judicial model. With lovely irony this movement has intersected a contrary movement in the courts: the growth . . . of central staffs composed of what are called staff attorneys or staff law clerks. Although staff attorneys have other assignments besides opinion drafting (such as assisting the judges with motions), and although most of their drafting is of unpublished opinions, today a significant number of published court of appeals opinions are drafted by a staff attorney rather than by a judge or one of his law clerks. Several of the problems that I discussed in connection with opinion writing by law clerks are aggravated when it is done by staff attorneys.

RICHARD A. POSNER, THE FEDERAL COURTS — CHALLENGES AND REFORM 151-52 (1996).

7. What do you think of the ABA Committee's proposal that the staff attorneys and their work should be made a public and formal part of the appellate process so that attorneys could appear and argue before them and file written responses to their recommendations and draft opinions prior to the stage when the judges actually dispose of the case? REPORT OF THE ABA STANDING COMMITTEE ON FEDERAL JUDICIAL IMPROVEMENTS, THE UNITED STATES COURTS OF APPEALS: REEXAMINING STRUCTURE AND PROCESS AFTER A CENTURY OF GROWTH 36-38 (1989).

8. In various state appellate court systems, there have been due process objections and nondelegation doctrine challenges to officers called "commissioners" who perform case screening duties, write *per curiam* opinions, and decide certain motions without direct judicial supervision, but the objections and challenges have been rejected and the reliance of the judges on these quasi-judicial officers has been defended as a necessary accommodation to the growing workload. *See* Thomas C. Marvin, *Ignore the Men Behind the Curtain: The Role of Commissioners in the Michigan Supreme Court*, 43 WAYNE L. REV. 375 (1997).

9. The U.S. Court of Appeals for the Ninth Circuit created the office of "appellate commissioner" to process Criminal Justice Act vouchers for lawyer compensation, to rule on motions (usually those seeking counsel's appointment and withdrawal), and to act as a special master on certain matters, including attorney discipline and fee award requests in civil cases. 9th CIRCUIT LOCAL R., Introduction, C. (2) (1999). What are the proper limits of delegation to this kind of non-Article III, quasi-judicial officer, *i.e.,* what kinds of responsibilities must be handled only by a judge appointed by the President and confirmed by the Senate?

10. Consider three simple, abstract models for how an appellate court can organize its legal assistants: (a) all elbow clerks and no central staff attorneys; (b) no elbow clerks and all central staff attorneys; (c) a mixture of elbow clerks and central staff attorneys (what mixture and why?). Which of these arrangements do you find preferable? Would your answers change depending on whether the term of appointment was temporary (one or two years) or permanent?

11. Instead of adding more law clerks and more staff attorneys, reconsider the pros and cons of increasing the number of judges, at an increasing rate if necessary, to keep pace with increases in appellate workload? What are the public policy trade-offs? Charles E. Carpenter, *Having Faced the Circuit-Splitting Conundrum — What About More Judges, Less Staff?*, 15 J. L. & POL. 531 (1999).

Chapter 8

PROCEDURAL RESPONSES TO THE CRISIS OF VOLUME

In addition to creating more judgeships, multiplying the number of law clerks in chambers, and deploying legions of central staff attorneys, state and federal appellate courts, feeling pressures from growing increases in the number of appeals, have radically altered the traditional appellate procedures by which appeals are considered and decided — especially at the IAC level. Appellate practices and procedures that had prevailed throughout our country's history were discarded and revised by a generation of appellate judges who shared a sense of crisis, a kind of siege mentality that drastic times required drastic measures. They believed that otherwise their courts would be overwhelmed by the unprecedented increases in appellate filings. The sense of crisis prevailed from the late 1960s to the early 1990s.

In fact, the movement towards greatly truncated appellate processes has coincided with the introduction of central staff attorneys, although the two developments are not necessarily linked. In theory, an appellate court could adopt procedural short cuts without any changes in staffing. But the assistance of staff attorneys makes "new and improved" appellate processes more feasible and more effective by reducing the time and effort that the individual judge has to spend on individual appeals and increasing the rate and number of dispositions of the court as a whole. As a practical matter, therefore, the development of truncated appellate procedures and the deployment of central staff attorneys are closely related and the two developments reinforce each other. This Chapter focuses on the procedural responses to the increases in the volume of appeals, following upon the account of the advent and growing role of staff attorneys in the previous Chapter and anticipating the themes of collegiality and delegation in the next Chapter.

This Chapter is still another occasion to contemplate the systemic and process imperatives introduced in Chapter 1. To what extent do these reforms of traditional appellate procedures — considering each individual reform as well as the entire package of reforms and their cumulative effect — compromise or harm the imperatives of appellate justice? Have these reforms been successful solutions to the problems caused by the crisis of volume? Are there ways to tweak these reforms to make them more effective?

I. DIFFERENTIATED APPELLATE PROCESSES

A.B.A. STANDARDS RELATING TO APPELLATE COURTS § 3.50 (1994)[1]

Caseflow Management and Delay Reduction General Principle. An appellate court should supervise and control the preparation and presentation of all appeals coming before it. Its management procedures should:

(a) Take effect from the time the notice of appeal is filed and continue through final disposition of the appeal;

(b) Facilitate early differentiation of cases according to their urgency, complexity, common subject matter, common parties, and other relevant criteria;

(c) Permit resolution of cases within the time standards adopted specially by and for that court. . . .

(d) Conform to the rules of procedure and administrative regulations established for the court system as a whole; and

(e) Be established though consultation with affected staff and the bar, stated in writing, and made known to the bar and the public.

THOMAS B. MARVELL, APPELLATE COURTS AND LAWYERS — INFORMATION GATHERING IN THE ADVERSARY SYSTEM 243-44 (1978) (*Appendix B: Some Suggestions for Appellate Court Decision-Making Procedures*)[2]

At the outset it is best to have as a foundation a list of goals for appellate court decision-making procedures. The major, overriding problem is how best to inform the judges so that they can decide cases as well as possible within the time constraints. This involves numerous subsidiary goals, but the list that follows is limited to those that have traditionally been troublesome in appellate courts. These goals are obviously very interrelated, and the categorization must be somewhat arbitrary.

1. The judges should receive as much relevant information about the case as possible. It is more important that information pertaining to the court's lawmaking function be complete than that pertaining only to the dispute-deciding function, for lawmaking decisions ordinarily have a greater impact on society. But the information, however used, should be as free as possible from time-wasting extraneous material.

2. Each judge sitting on a case should know enough about it to make his own informed, independent decision. He should delegate as little as possible to the judge assigned the case and to law clerks and staff attorneys. This, of course, is a matter of degree; time

---

1 Copyright © 1994 American Bar Association. Reprinted with permission.

2 Copyright © 1978 by Thomas B. Marvell. Reproduced with permission of Greenwood Publishing Group, Inc., Westport, CT.

problems make delegation of independent research and study of the record necessary, and delegation of the search for information necessarily means some delegation of decision making.

3. Similarly, each judge should participate in the content of any opinion, especially if published, with which he concurs (except for the details of writing style). A number of minds can produce an opinion more serviceable to the bar than can one mind alone. So, again, each judge must understand the case, and he must study and comment on draft opinions as thoroughly as time and the preservation of friendly relations at the court allow. Also, the author of an opinion should be receptive to his colleagues' suggestions.

4. A judge should be open-minded in that he should withhold his final decision until he is fully informed and should weigh carefully arguments presented to support the opposing sides.

5. Appeals should be decided quickly, and judges should save time whenever possible without lessening the quality of their work. Judges' time is in short supply at many courts because of increased case loads and administrative duties.

6. Judges should get as much help as they can from counsel, both to save time and to improve their decisions and opinions. Judges believe that the quality of much appellate advocacy is low, and the trend now is to rely less on counsel and more on staff research. But, at least, judges should use counsel as much as they can if only to check the work done at the court.

John C. Godbold, *Improvement in Appellate Procedure: Better Use of Available Facilities*, 66 A.B.A. J. 863 (1980)[3]

The principles underlying our legal system, with its mixed common law and statutory heritage, require us to recognize the validity of drawing reasoned distinctions between cases. The theory of lockstep uniformity — that every appellate case either requires or deserves a full record, oral argument, a written explanation for the decision, and a published opinion — is inconsistent with acceptance of the legal system as an institution capable of making valid distinctions and operating under them. . . .

In performing its functions an appellate court spends much of its time and effort making distinctions and evaluating distinctions made by others. This role is familiar, expected, and indeed taken for granted. That same court can also rationally establish and apply procedures for selectively different handling of the cases before it. It may require a full record in some cases, abbreviated records in others. It may decide some cases without oral argument, schedule others for argument, and vary the time permitted for argument. Judges may confer face to face in one case and exchange views by memorandum or telephone in another. The court may enter a Grand Manner opinion in one case, a terse statement of reasons in another, and no written explanation

---

[3] Copyright © 1980 American Bar Association. Reprinted with permission.

in the next. An appellate court should not be denied the discretion to make these choices. . . .

The ceremonial aspects of adjudication serve both functional and symbolic purposes, each having value. Courts do need to be perceived as administering justice, but the activities observed must have substance and verity. Symbolism has no life of its own. Oral argument, a record of everything that occurred in the trial, face-to-face conference, and a full-scale opinion are tools in the administration of justice, not ends in themselves. Empty ceremony in a case predictably foreordained advances justice little more than wig or mace or a bailiff shouting "Oyez" on the courthouse steps. It is a cruel charade for lawyers and litigants. It is an abuse of judicial resources already insufficient to go around.

In a simple case in which the result is clear and no close or significant issues of law are involved, transporting counsel to the place of holding court and paying them for attendance is a waste of societal assets in a world where there are other priorities. Appellate courts do not contribute to the perception of justice in action merely by adding to the tidal wave of opinions that engulf us in meaningless factual minutiae and recitals of the rejection of propositions whose lack of merit is scarcely arguable. Perhaps most important of all, the appellate court's function and value are demeaned by requiring it to carry out acts merely ceremonial, while pretending that the façade is real.

RITA M. NOVAK & DOUGLAS K. SOMERLOT, DELAY ON APPEAL — A PROCESS FOR IDENTIFYING CAUSES AND CURES 14-16 (1990)[4]

Appellate Court Control of All Phases of the Appeal. Caseflow management starts from the premise that the appellate court has administrative authority over the progress of the case from the filing of the appeal to final decision. Neither counsel nor the trial court retains control over the pace of appellate litigation. . . .

Court responsibility for control of the caseflow is important not only from a management perspective; it also corresponds to the court's status as a public institution. As a public forum for the peaceful resolution of disputes, the court is charged with administrative as well as judicial responsibilities. From the citizens' perspective, these responsibilities belong to the court that will resolve the controversy in its current posture. When the caseload is appealed, the litigants and public hold the appellate court accountable for speedy and just resolution. The court's effectiveness is judged, therefore, from the time the appeal is filed until a decision is released. Early and continuous supervision of the appeal process evidences that court's acceptance of its responsibilities to the litigants and the public.

Differentiating Cases According to Processing Needs. Active case management requires the court to categorize cases and other matters according to their need for judicial attention and to develop procedures for handling cases in each category. Administrative matters that do not call for judicial discretion

---

[4] Copyright © 1990 American Bar Association. Reprinted with permission.

are more appropriately handled by staff following established court procedures. Cases involving questions of well-settled law demand less judicial
attention than novel issues presented in new circumstances. Proper case management means that distinctions be drawn between categories of cases along
rational, principled lines.

Case differentiation makes the appellate process more efficient.
Categorizing cases according to complexity, for example, allows schedules to
be tailored to the actual time required to complete each phase of the appeal,
avoiding repeated motions to extend time. Distinguishing tasks that may be
performed by staff from those that should be performed by judges permits
time and expertise to be allocated as needed. For instance, some courts have
delegated authority to the clerk to grant routine motions — extensions of
time or relief from default — under guidelines set by the courts. Similarly,
administrative and legal staff should structure their work so that responsibilities are delineated to reflect the functions each group performs within
the court.

Differentiated case management promotes justice as well as efficiency.
Equal treatment of like cases serves the interests of fairness and equality. All
cases do not require the same amount of time and thought, so when all matters are treated alike, judicial attention needed in more difficult cases is necessarily shortchanged. The results can be "procedural shortcuts that diminish
litigants' opportunity to be heard" or insufficient deliberation given to complex
issues of significant import.

NOTES

1. Professors Carrington, Meador, and Rosenberg have articulated the process imperatives that assure appellate justice in terms of how judges perform
their judicial functions:

> [J]udges who are impartial; are multi-partite; are identifiable, not
> anonymous, and not mere auxiliaries; think individually, but act
> collegially; respect the interest of adversaries in being heard, but
> inform themselves fully on the material issues, evidence, and law
> on which decisions are to be made; and announce their reasons for
> decisions.

PAUL D. CARRINGTON, DANIEL J. MEADOR & MAURICE ROSENBERG, JUSTICE ON
APPEAL 8-11 (1976). In other words, the overall appellate process must be visibly rational:

> [T]he system must provide uniform and coherent enunciation and appli-
> cation of the law; decisions that are expeditious, involving as few steps
> as possible; working conditions for judges which attract lawyers of high
> quality, who command professional respect; and working conditions for
> judges which will foster their humane concern for individual litigants.

Id. at 11-12. Keep these imperatives in mind as you study the various reforms
of appellate procedures in the remainder of this Chapter.

2. Today, as ABA Standard § 3.50 recognizes, the norm is to expect appellate courts to follow a caseflow management plan that categorizes individual

appeals and assigns them to different tracks for differentiated appellate procedures towards their resolution. The commentary to § 3.50 reads in part:

> *Case Classification.* Appropriate consideration of each case requires that court to make informed distinctions among cases, according to their complexity, common subject matter, common parties, and other relevant criteria, as they come before the court and move through processing. The court should have an internal information system for this purpose, beginning with a required docketing information statement for each case. It should have procedures for special supervision of complex cases. The underlying principle in the design and use of such procedures should be that the court accord each case the kind and extent of attention that is fitting for the case, not that it attempts to treat cases for administrative purposes as though they were all alike.

3. The excerpt above from Professor Marvel's book properly places the judge at the center of all appellate procedures. Any procedural reform should be measured in terms of how it helps judges to do more and to do better. But are there not limits, at least in theory, as to how much more and how much better a judge can do? The ultimate criterion for differentiated appellate processes is whether judges are ultimately responsible for the final decision in every case; the concern for untoward delegation is a topic in the next Chapter.

4. Professors Novak and Somerlot offer this elaboration on the concept of differentiated appellate processes:

> The term *caseflow management* originated in the early 1970's to describe a new method for conceptualizing the way courts should dispose of their caseloads. The word *caseflow* is intended to convey the notion that cases move though a series of discrete but interrelated events. Collectively, these individual events make up a process that is amenable to active management. Thus, the court can quicken disposition times not only by analyzing the individual events, but also by examining and improving the management of the interrelationships between events.
>
> In a sense, management of the court's caseload parallels the management of materials and operations necessary to complete a manufacturing process. Each manufacturing unit produces a component of the end product. Yet, the quality of that product depends upon the effectiveness of controls within each unit as well as procedures integrating each unit's work.
>
> The word *management* conveys another idea. A manager deals with what is routine, implementing systems designed to move the standard case through normal channels while establishing techniques to identify unusual situations and to deal with them for what they are — exceptions. This approach should be contrasted with the tack often taken by drafters of court rules, who design processing systems to respond to the problems raised by exceptional circumstances as though those circumstances represented the norm. . . .
>
> Although *caseflow* is intended to suggest smooth action, the movement of cases through the court is anything but a steady advance. The

individual events are separated by times, all too often long times, during which no activity occurs. The goal of managing the caseflow, and indeed the goal of court delay reduction activities generally, is to reduce the time between the individual court events, thereby creating a smoother flow of the cases through the court. . . .

Appellate *caseflow management* is, then, the art of controlling the progress of cases through the court's processes so that sufficient time is allowed to complete events but unnecessary time is eliminated.

RITA M. NOVAK & DOUGLAS K. SOMERLOT, DELAY ON APPEAL — A PROCESS FOR IDENTIFYING CAUSES AND CURES 77-78 (1990). What are the public policy justifications for requiring appellate courts to develop and implement caseflow management procedures?

5. In the excerpt above, Judge Godbold makes the conceptual argument against a "one-size fits all" appellate process; he insists that it would do more harm to the appellate imperatives not to have differentiated appellate processes because all appeals are not equal. Does it necessarily follow that because judges make other legal and factual distinctions in their actual decision-making of cases that they are also capable of making distinctions among categories of appeals to afford them more or less appellate process and judicial attention?

6. The *Appellate Caseflow Management Improvement Project* studied state IACs in Ohio, Maryland, New Mexico, and Washington to conclude:

American state intermediate appellate courts that succeed in handling their caseloads expeditiously have taken responsibility for the entire appellate process, beginning with the filing of the notice of appeal. They have recognized the public interest in minimizing delays, have committed themselves to deciding cases in a timely manner, and have mobilized themselves to pay sustained attention to effective case processing. While resources are important to an appellate court's effectiveness in handling its caseload, how the resources are actually *used* — i.e., what caseload management strategies and techniques are employed by the court — can make a significant difference in case processing time. Further, the traditions or culture of the court, as well as the leadership and commitment of the judge[s], play a very important role in the case processing time.

Richard B. Hoffman & Barry Mahoney, *Managing Caseflow in State Intermediate Appellate Courts: What Mechanisms, Practices, and Procedures Can Work to Reduce Delay?*, 35 IND. L. REV. 467, 470-71 (2002). *See also Symposium on Expedited Appeals in Selected State Appellate Courts*, 4 J. APP. PRAC & PROCESS 191 (2002) (District of Columbia, Indiana, Kentucky, Massachusetts, New Hampshire, New York, Ohio, Vermont, and West Virginia).

7. The topics and themes in this Chapter are extensively analyzed in THOMAS E. BAKER, RATIONING JUSTICE ON APPEAL — THE PROBLEMS OF THE U.S. COURTS OF APPEALS 106-50 (1994). *See also* Thomas E. Baker, *Intramural Reforms: How the U.S. Courts of Appeals Have Helped Themselves*, 22 FLA. ST.

UNIV. L. REV. 913 (1995); Thomas E. Baker, *Proposed Intramural Reforms: What the U.S. Courts of Appeals Might Do to Help Themselves*, 25 ST. MARY'S L. J. 1321 (1994).

II. SCREENING

The screening of appeals is the *sine qua non* of any system of differentiated appellate processes. Screening is the essential first step to all of the rest of the contemporary procedural modifications in the new generation of internal appellate processes. The philosophical assumption underlying all these changes is that appellate procedure should not be transubstantive: individual appeals differ in significant ways and do not all require or deserve the same consideration on appeal. This is a profound conceptual break with traditional appellate procedure of the past. Furthermore, the new approach maintains that to afford the same appellate process to every appeal today would be either impossible or unfair. It would be impossible to afford every appeal the old-fashioned traditional appellate procedures because of the caseload without creating unacceptable levels of delay. It would be improper and unfair to apply the new procedural shortcuts to the kind of cases that deserve and require the fuller, more judge-intensive, consideration on appeal that used to be afforded to every appeal but that today is saved for the more important and more difficult cases.

Are these sound assumptions? If they are — and all state and federal IACs operate from these assumptions today — then some means must be employed to sort the appeals into categories for the different procedural tracks, *i.e.*, to evaluate the individual appeal before it is decided on the merits in order to determine the amount of appellate process the appeal will get on its way to a final disposition. An important aspect of this determination is the self-conscious categorization of some appeals as complex or difficult or novel and other appeals as simple or easy or straightforward. Some appeals are thus more deserving of more time and attention of a panel of judges along the lines of the traditional appellate procedures, while other appeals can be disposed of with significantly less direct judge involvement by an appellate bureaucracy of law clerks and central staff attorneys functioning under internal operating procedures and supervised by judges.

"Screening" is the term used to describe the appellate procedures that determine how much additional appellate procedure an individual appeal should be afforded. Some courts use the term "inventorying" to describe this evaluating and routing stage. For screening to be effective and efficient, it must take place at the earliest stage of the appellate process and screening procedures themselves must be straightforward and consistently applied.

JUDITH A. MCKENNA, LAURAL L. HOOPER & MARY CLARK, CASE MANAGEMENT PROCEDURES IN THE FEDERAL COURTS OF APPEALS 8-14 (Fed. Jud. Ctr. 2000)

Case screening. The term "screening" has come to mean different things in different courts. At one time, screening meant diverting a case from the presumptive oral argument track to a nonargument track. Accordingly, "screened cases" or "screeners" typically referred to those cases decided by a three-judge panel without oral argument. Here, we use the term more broadly: "screening" means the process by which a court determines what treatment an appeal will receive and what path it will follow.

Appeals are screened for various purposes, but the most important screening function is to determine preliminarily whether the case will be orally argued or decided without argument. Screening models vary on two important dimensions: (1) who does the screening; and (2) what case types are screened into or out of the argument track.

As a formal — but important — matter, in all courts judges decide whether a case will be orally argued, because Fed. R. App. P. 34 permits decisions without oral argument only if the panel unanimously agrees that the case does not need oral argument. Nevertheless, as a practical matter, in almost all courts, cases that are screened at all are screened into the argument or nonargument track by staff, subject to panel review. Also, except for the Second Circuit, courts seldom or never allow *pro se* litigants to argue orally. Initial screening in some courts thus means finding out whether the parties are represented by counsel — if not, the case goes onto the nonargument track. (In some courts, staff attorneys may recommend that counsel be appointed if it appears the case warrants oral argument).

Screening by staff. In the most common arrangement, staff attorneys screen appeals into an argument or nonargument track. In some courts, certain types of appeal — *e.g.*, direct criminal appeals raising issues other than sentencing guideline application — are not subject to staff screening but go directly to the argument calendar or to a judge for screening. Staff used for screening may be central staff attorneys, attorneys in the clerk's office, or (in one court) the circuit executive. There is some variation, sometimes within courts, in whether the screening for argument occurs as soon as the appellant's brief is filed or after the case is fully briefed. Typically, courts that use a staff screening model have central staff attorneys screen cases and suggest whether the court would benefit from oral argument; in several courts, staff attorneys also recommend a decision on the merits of the case and draft an order or proposed opinion.

Screening by judges. In a few courts, judges play a large role in case screening. In the Tenth Circuit, judges do all the screening. In general, each active judge is on a "screening panel" at all times (these are reconstituted annually), and each member of the panel is primarily responsible for one-third of the cases assigned to that panel. That judge makes a preliminary decision to: (a) set the case for argument; (b) set it for nonargument disposition with staff workup; or (c) hold it in chambers and prepare a merits disposition for the rest of the screening panel to consider. Either of the other judges on the panel may disagree with (b) or (c) and call for argument, but disagreements are rare.

In the Third Circuit, judges screen counseled cases for argument or nonargument disposition, but do not sit on separate screening panels. Argument panels receive the briefs and other materials, and the panel members determine which cases will be argued (*pro se* cases are not argued).

Although the Fifth Circuit uses central staff for much screening, for some case types individual judges decide whether oral argument is necessary. The Fifth Circuit also has a "jurisdiction calendar" that meets every month to dispose of cases with jurisdictional defects; some courts perform the same function with motions panels.

Table 5 shows for each court the parties primarily responsible for initial screening for argument or nonargument disposition.

Table 5: Initial Screeners for Argument/Nonargument Disposition

	DC	1st	2nd*	3rd	4th	5th**	6th	7th	8th	9th	10th	11th	Fed*
Judges			–	X		X				X			–
Central Staff	X	X	–			X	X				X	X	–
Clerk's Office			–		X				X				–
Circuit Exec.			–					X					–

*All cases are scheduled for oral argument in the Second Circuit unless they involve an incarcerated *pro se* litigant. All counseled cases, but no pro se cases, are scheduled in the Federal Circuit.

**Individual judges serve as screening judges for certain case types in the Fifth Circuit, including diversity, Title VII, bankruptcy, some tax, and some agency cases. Staff attorneys do initial screening for *pro se* cases, prisoner cases challenging conditions of confinement, habeas corpus cases, civil federal question cases, immigration cases, cases in which the United States is a party, civil rights cases other than Title VII, and Social Security cases.

What cases get oral argument? Circuit standards for granting argument are formally similar, with local rules and internal operating procedures generally restating in more or less detail the minimum standard set down by Fed. R. App. P. 34(a): Oral argument must be allowed unless a three-judge panel unanimously determines that: (1) the appeal is frivolous; or (2) the dispositive issue or issues have been authoritatively decided; or (3) the facts and legal arguments are adequately presented in the briefs and record, and the decisional process would not be significantly aided by oral argument. Any judge on the panel may decide that the case should be orally argued and direct the clerk to place it on the oral argument calendar. No national statistics are kept on how often cases initially screened for nonargument decision get rerouted for argument. We did not systematically canvass the courts on this point, but anecdotal evidence suggests that the frequency is low and probably varies with the type of screening program used, e.g., where only *pro se* cases are screened, the preliminary decision is unlikely to be changed; where all counseled cases are screened as well, some are likely to present issues that judges, but not staff, identify as needing argument — and vice versa.

Case characteristics that courts often identify as likely to trigger oral argument include presence of counsel, novel issues, complex issues, extensive records, and numerous parties. For a look at how the criteria affect different case types, Tables 6 and 7 show the percentage of cases in various categories that were decided after oral argument in FY 1998. As Table 6 shows, whether the litigants have counsel plays an important role in whether the court hears oral argument — most courts rarely or never allow unrepresented litigants to argue, and in all courts the percentage of cases in which argument occurs is higher for counseled cases.

Table 6: Percentage of Cases Decided after Oral Argument, FY 1998

	D.C.	1st	2nd	3rd	4th	5th	6th	7th	8th	9th	10th	11th	Nat'l
All	54	58	68	29	25	38	51	59	43	37	35	34	41
Counseled	73	69	85	41	41	52	74	83	65	54	50	43	57

Table 7 shows that case type also makes a difference in whether oral argument will occur, with counseled private civil cases being more likely, in most courts, to be decided with oral argument than other counseled cases.

Table 7: Counseled Cases Decided After Oral Argument, as a Percentage of Counseled Cases Decided on the Merits, FY 1998

	D.C.	1st	2nd	3rd	4th	5th	6th	7th	8th	9th	10th	11th	Nat'l
Criminal	65	62	81	29	27	37	63	80	53	47	52	29	45
Agency	88	67	85	27	44	56	68	75	68	29	45	44	50
U.S. civil	69	53	83	39	54	40	60	76	58	58	22	36	51
Private civil	62	83	92	56	77	59	86	89	76	73	58	62	72
Other	17	67	46	24	66	51	48	49	51	41	44	39	44

What other assessments are made during the screening process? In addition to screening for whether oral argument should be heard, many courts assess the following attributes while screening a new appeal:

- jurisdictional defects warranting dismissal without determination on the merits by a three-judge panel;
- suitability for diversion to the court's settlement or mediation program;
- whether counsel should be appointed for an unrepresented party;
- whether the litigants have complied with the court's requirements regarding brief format and other procedural matters;
- whether a certificate of appealability should issue in habeas corpus cases;
- whether an appeal in habeas corpus matter is successive;
- whether a *pro se* appeal is frivolous;
- indicators of the amount of judge time required to dispose of the appeal, i.e., the "weight" that should be attached to the appeal in light of the complexity or novelty of the issues;
- whether an appeal presents an issue already being considered by a panel of the court, and whether the case should be routed to that panel or held in abeyance pending the decision;
- whether the appeal presents an issue that is currently before the high court for decision; and
- how much time should be allotted for oral argument.

Table 8: Models of Nonargument Decision Making

Cir.	Argument panels also Decide submitted cases	Judges meet as nonargument panel	Judges confer by telephone	Judges review appeals serially
D.C.	Some cases that argument Panels unanimously decide do not need argument	Most nonargued cases decided by special panels	Occasional cases	
1st				All nonargued cases
2nd	All nonargued cases			
3rd	All nonargued cases			
4th			Simplest cases	All but the simplest nonargument cases. Lead judge reviews draft opinion and notifies other judges of intention to adopt or reject it; invites responses.
5th	Conference calendar: simple cases that are more not fact-intensive. Each judge reviews			Summary calendar: Cases that are more complex than on conference calendar yet do not warrant

Table 8: Models of Nonargument Decision Making

Cir.	Argument panels also Decide submitted cases	Judges meet as nonargument panel	Judges confer by telephone	Judges review appeals serially
6th	All nonargued cases	30 cases the night before or morning of conference; panel disposes of approximately 90 cases with staff-prepared dispositions.		argument. Initiating judge reviews staff-proposed disposition and sends to next panel judge, and so on.
7th		Some nonargued cases	Some non-argued cases	
8th		All nonargued cases		
9th		All nonargued cases		
10th		Some panels use	Some panels use	
11th				All nonargued cases. First judge reviews staff memorandum and proposed order with briefs/record; sends to next judge, and so on.
Fed.	All nonargued cases			

Table 9: Models of Staff in Nonargument Decision Making

Circuit	Staff prepared materials distributed to judges consideration	Staff role in panel
D.C.	General: Proposed judgments, memoranda to the litigants, and bench memoranda analyzing the arguments, case law, and record Simple: Proposed orders	Staff present case/discuss with merits panel (both case types)
1st	*Pro se* cases: Memorandum and draft disposition	None
2nd	Bench memorandum in *pro se* cases only	None
3rd	Simple *pro se* cases only: Draft *per curiam* opinion	None
4th	Simple cases: Draft opinion and supporting documentation go to panel More complex: Memorandum and draft opinions; these go with supporting documentation to panel	Staff present case/discuss with merits panel by phone None
5th	Summary calendar: For many cases, in-depth research memorandum; for about half of these, proposed disposition Conference calendar: Memorandum and short *per curiam* opinion	None Staff present case/discuss with merits panel
6th	*Pro se* cases and cases where counsel waive oral argument research memorandum and proposed dispositive order	None
7th	Draft memorandum order (not bench memorandum)	Staff meet with full panel, then work with authorizing judge

Table 9: Models of Staff in Nonargument Decision Making

Circuit	Staff prepared materials distributed to judges consideration	Staff role in panel
8th	Memorandum and precise proposed dispositive order	Further research as directed by authorizing judge
9th	Draft memorandum disposition; supplemental research memorandum if necessary	Staff present case/discuss with merits panel
10th	Draft dispositional document (usually order and judgment) and detailed analytical memorandum; these are approved by mentor judge before distribution to other panel members	Staff attorney works with "mentor" judge, then meets with full panel
11th	Some classes of cases: memorandum and proposed order	Court is experimenting with oral presentation to special panel of senior judges in some appeals
Fed.	None	None

Decision without argument. Nonargument decision-making practices are closely tied to the screening process. Courts use one, or a combination, of two fundamental processes: (a) contemporaneous, collegial deliberation; and (b) serial review by the panel judges. Table 8 summarizes the primary models used.

Within the types of nonargument decision making, the role of staff varies, as Table 9 shows. In most courts the central staff attorneys draft memoranda and proposed dispositions of some type. A few courts have the staff attorney prepare a neutral memorandum. Most have the attorney draft an order that will (if adopted) dispose of the case and, if necessary, an opinion explaining the order. These opinions are not routinely published, but some courts make exceptions. In a few courts, the staff attorney works with one judge to draft a disposition for the remaining two judges to review. In several courts, the staff attorneys present cases to the merits panel, either in person or by telephone.

Jerry Smith, *Foreword: Fifth Circuit Survey,* 25 TEX. TECH L. REV. 255, 255-58 (1994)[5]

Readers of opinions from the United States Court of Appeals for the Fifth Circuit may have noticed that a new designation, "Conference Calendar," has appeared in a few captions in recent opinions. The Conference Calendar is a new means devised by the court for facilitating the disposition of cases in an effort to handle the increasing volume on our court.

One of the more dramatic innovations by the Fifth Circuit, more than twenty years ago, was the practice of placing certain cases on the so-called "Summary Calendar" for disposition without oral argument. That process has proven successful, despite early doubts expressed by many members of the bar to the effect that every appealing party, with the possible exception of *pro se* litigants, deserves to be heard orally before a court of appeals. So workable has been the "Summary Calendar" that about two-thirds of the cases fully submitted on briefs have been disposed of in this fashion during the past few years. Still, the per-judge caseload has increased unabated. . . .

Given the imposition of the increasing number of cases on a relatively fixed number of active judges, the court in 1991 began casting about for a mechanism for handling the less burdensome cases in a more efficient manner without sacrificing the quality or accuracy of the decision-making process. Under the Summary Calendar procedure, almost all cases that are fully briefed are assigned to screening panels, each consisting of three judges who serve on such a panel for a full court year. The briefs and record from the case are mailed from the clerk's office to one of the three judges, who decides whether the case is to be orally argued. If not, he or she then prepares a proposed opinion and sends it, along with the briefs and record, to the second judge on the screening panel, who then has the option of designating the case for oral argument or sending the package with the proposed opinion to the third judge, who repeats the process and sends the record and briefs to the clerk, usually with the proposed opinion, which is then issued as an opinion of the court. Such opinions, not submitted on oral argument, receive the designation "Summary Calendar."

---

[5] Copyright © 1994 Texas Tech Law Review. Reprinted with permission.

By 1991, the court had reached the consensus that some cases not only do not deserve oral argument, but also do not merit the separate attention of each of three screening judges individually in chambers. Given that our thirteen active judges are spread among seven cities, and none is in New Orleans where the clerk's office is located, the physical burden, time, and expense of shipping records and briefs from the clerk to and among the three judges on a screening panel, then back to the clerk, is substantial. While that process is necessary and workable in regard to cases that are properly classed for Summary Calendar treatment, we were convinced that a more efficient means could be utilized to identify those cases that could be handled in a less cumbersome fashion.

Thus was born the Conference Calendar, first implemented in February 1992. Approximately once every two months, three active judges go to New Orleans for the sole purpose of serving on the Conference Calendar. They meet for three or four days and consider approximately thirty cases per day that have been designated by the Fifth Circuit Staff Attorney's Office as appropriate for Conference Calendar disposition.

The staff attorneys prepare memoranda for the judges on each case, giving factual and legal background and providing a proposed disposition of the case. Staff counsel also prepare a proposed written opinion, usually about two pages in length, for the three judges' consideration. A typical Conference Calendar week might consist of 120 cases to be considered over four days. In New Orleans, the judges consider the cases one day at a time, taking approximately one-half day to review that day's designated cases before meeting together to discuss them.

For each of those cases, one of the three judges is designated as the initiating judge. Each judge is then responsible as initiating judge for approximately ten cases each day. He or she is provided with the full record on appeal for each of those cases and studies the record in addition to the briefs of the parties, the staff attorney's memorandum, and the proposed opinion. The other two judges on the panel review all such materials but do not have immediate access to the original record.

After the half day of preparation, the three judges meet together for the remaining half day to consider that day's cases. Each case is addressed separately, and the judges receive an oral presentation by a staff attorney, who is available for questions. The judges then discuss that case and either agree to the opinion proposed by the staff attorney or request that revisions be made. In a few instances, the judges may decide that the case is not appropriate for decision on the Conference Calendar but should be sent through the normal screening process either for decision on the Summary Calendar or for assignment to the oral argument calendar.

Through August 1993, nine Conference Calendar sessions have been completed, resulting in decisions in 804 cases and the referral of twenty-nine cases to the customary screening process. Of those 833 cases, 361 were civil rights cases, including a large number of prisoner *pro se* complaints regarding jail conditions; 238 were direct criminal appeals; 149 were habeas corpus cases; 58 were fully briefed civil cases; and 27 were motions requiring a three-judge order. The fully briefed civil cases included such matters as maritime, employment discrimination, property forfeiture, social security, the Fair Labor Standards Act, the Carriage of Goods by Sea Act, the Freedom of Information Act, and FDIC cases.

The cases that are selected by staff counsel for Conference Calendar disposition are those involving one or two simple issues, usually a very short record, and an obvious result. They are cases that a judge can review in a short time without sacrificing thoroughness or accuracy. Almost without exception, these are cases that make no new law and have very few essential facts to explicate in an opinion. Only about one percent of the Conference Calendar opinions are deemed appropriate for publication.

The result of the Conference Calendar process has been salutary, and, despite initial misgivings by some, it has generally received high marks from the active judges of the Fifth Circuit, all of whom by now have participated in one or more Conference Calendar panels. The Conference Calendar procedure has certain advantages over the screening process: whereas in the screening procedure each judge considers the case alone in his or her chambers, the Conference Calendar judges actually confer at a conference table. This has the advantage of collegial interchange of ideas between and among the judges that can be helpful in maintaining uniformity of decisions and in understanding one another's approach to decision-making.

Moreover, the physical presence of staff attorneys has been helpful in explaining cases to the judges and in acquainting the staff attorneys with the decision-making process, including the actual deliberations of the judges, to which the staff attorneys otherwise would not be privy. This has been a morale boost to the dedicated corps of staff attorneys who work for the Fifth Circuit in New Orleans and has enabled them to meet and get to know the court's judges better than they otherwise would.

[T]he Conference Calendar has become a means of disposing of large numbers of cases in an expeditious way without sacrificing quality. It uses judges' time efficiently by isolating three of them from other court duties for three or four days in order to dispose of large volumes of relatively simple cases that otherwise would be obscured by more difficult and complex matters in the ordinary course of the court's proceedings.

Like the Summary Calendar, the Conference Calendar is a means of identifying a category of cases that deserve a level of scrutiny that is different from that accorded cases of other kinds. Thus, it is a means of focusing the court's attention in different ways for different types of cases and of using scarce resources most productively. Undoubtedly, as the caseload of the Fifth Circuit continues to increase, the court should and will devise further means of increasing its efficiency as a decision-making tribunal.

NOTES

1. *Getting the appellate process started.* To implement screening, mediation, and other pre-decision phases of appellate case management, most courts have adopted some formal requirements for information to be submitted in the early stages of an appeal. The most common vehicle is the "docketing statement," in

which the filer states the basis of the court's jurisdiction, identifies related cases, and provides certain information about the issues and procedural posture of the case. This information helps the court staff determine whether the case is suitable for an appellate mediation program, whether it is likely to require oral argument, and whether the transcript procurement process is on track.

JUDITH A. MCKENNA, LAURAL L. HOOPER & MARY CLARK, CASE MANAGEMENT PROCEDURES IN THE FEDERAL COURTS OF APPEALS 7-8 (Fed. Jud. Ctr. 2000). Consider the information available to the screener and the nature of the evaluation that must be made at this preliminary point.

2. In 1968, the Michigan Court of Appeals created the first central staff attorney positions and in that same year the U.S. Court of Appeals for the Fifth Circuit adopted a judge screening process. These two reforms, one staffing and the other procedural, developed together, reinforced each other, and spread to most state and federal IACs. The changes were dramatic. Before 1968, oral arguments had been afforded in every appeal; just four years later the Fifth Circuit was deciding three out of five appeals without oral argument. DANIEL J. MEADOR, APPELLATE COURTS: STAFF AND PROCESS IN THE CRISIS OF VOLUME 10-11 (1974). The Fifth Circuit has never looked back: currently, it grants oral argument in only one out of five cases (18.8 % in 2004). *See infra* Section V.

3. In *Huth v. Southern Pacific Co.*, 417 F.2d 526, 527-31 (5th Cir. 1969), the Fifth Circuit described the court's prototype program of judge screening developed in 1968 that has been replicated since then in many IACs with minor procedural variations:

> Every case upon the filing of the last brief (or expiration of time in which to file briefs) is referred to one of four standing panels composed of Judges in active service of the Fifth Circuit. The case is judicially screened by Judges. This results in a classification as one of four categories. Class III is for limited oral argument (15 minutes). Class IV is for full argument (30 minutes). Class II covers those cases in which the Court has determined that the case is of such a character as not to justify oral argument. On the Court making such determination, the parties are notified in writing that the case has been put on the Summary Calendar. Class I, now small in numbers, covers frivolous cases. The parties are notified that the case is on the Summary Calendar prior to the time any opinion is filed.

> [F]or a case to go on the Summary Calendar there must be unanimous action of the panel members, and in disposing of it, the decision must likewise be unanimous. The experience of the Court has been both informative and productive. The figures covering the first six months are revealing. Although it is too early to tell for a certainty the extent to which the Summary Calendar practice enhances the productivity of Judges and the Court, the fact is that in the fiscal year just closed, during the last six months of which we had the Summary Calendar, our output was markedly increased and more than kept up with our ever expanding increase of input.

4. If A's appeal is afforded oral argument and receives a full-length published opinion, while B's appeal is denied oral argument and receives only a short unpublished memorandum opinion or only an entry in a table of cases with the single word "affirmed," does appellant B have any basis for claiming a denial of the equal protection of the laws? What about procedural due process? Looking over the statistics in the Federal Judicial Center report above, what types of cases get short-shrift appellate procedures? Do *pro se* cases deserve less appellate process *per se*? What kinds of assessments are made during the screening process? What might explain the variations in the models of screening adopted by the various U.S. Courts of Appeals? How about the variations in the involvement and responsibilities of central staff attorneys?

5. The Fifth Circuit has continued to innovate with the *Conference Calendar,* described above by Judge Smith, that takes screening to the next level of efficiency. *See generally Graves v. Hampton*, 1 F.3d 315 (5th Cir. 1993). Notice, however, how central staff attorneys participate alongside the judges. Back when screening began, the Fifth Circuit emphasized, "The important thing is that this screening is a judicial one performed by Judges, not the Clerk or other non-judicial staff. It is done through a series of standing panels of three Judges, made up of active Fifth Circuit Judges only." *Murphy v. Houma Well Service*, 409 F.2d 804, 806 (5th Cir. 1969). Compare the Conference Calendar with the original Summary Calendar in terms of the process imperatives and Professor Marvel's goals for judges from the previous Section's introduction to differentiated appellate processes. What are the pros and cons of this latest generation of screening procedure? One senior Fifth Circuit judge is so enthusiastic about the Conference Calendar that he would have his court make it the norm rather than the exception and have all judges spend six weeks out of the year on Conference Calendar panels. Thomas M. Reavley, *The Appeals Process*, 24 PEPP. L. REV. 899, 902 (1997). Would that be a good idea?

6. In the Supreme Court of Rhode Island (a COLR without an IAC), parties file a short summary of the appellate issues presented before any briefing takes place. The parties are then required to attend a pre-briefing conference with a single justice who has read the record and the parties' summaries of issues. After hearing the comments of counsel, the justice may order the case to be fully briefed and argued (and specify the schedule), remand the case for specific action by the trial court, or enter a show cause order for "either attorney to appear before the full court prior to the briefing to show cause why the judgment . . . should not be summarily affirmed or reversed without further briefing or argument." R.I. S.CT. PROVISIONAL ORDER 16. Each side is allowed ten minutes in the show cause hearing. The full court may then order the judgment affirmed or reversed without further briefing or argument, may order the case to be fully briefed, and may determine issues to be added to or withdrawn from the court's consideration. *See* Lynae K. E. Olson & Joy A. Chapper, *Screening and Tracking Criminal Appeals: The Rhode Island Experience*, 8 JUST. SYS. J. 20, 24-28 (1983); Joseph R. Weisberger, *Appellate Caseload: Meeting the Challenge in Rhode Island*, 16 U. MICH. J.L. REF. 527 (1983). Could this form of single-judge screening work on an IAC that sits in three-judge panels?

7. Staff Screening. In contrast to the judge-screening model developed in the Fifth Circuit, screening may be done by central staff attorneys, a model pioneered in California's IACs. In the late 1960s several districts of the California Court of Appeal began employing staff attorneys to perform both a screening and research function. In the Court of Appeal for the First District, which sits in San Francisco, when the appellee's brief is filed, the clerk sends the briefs to the principal staff attorney, who then performs a screening function to examine the briefs quickly to determine whether the appeal is routine, with the outcome readily predictable and likely to be uncontroversial. Appeals assigned to this track are channeled through expedited dispositional routes and typically are decided without the traditional steps of oral argument, conference, and an elaborately written opinion. If the case is not deemed appropriate for the truncated processes, the briefs are returned to the clerk's office; the appeal then is dispatched to a three-judge division for hearing and decision as though no central staff existed. This is an amalgam of the innovation of the Michigan Court of Appeals of deploying central staff attorneys and the innovation of screening appeals first developed in the U.S. Court of Appeals for the Fifth Circuit. The deployment of central staff attorneys in screening has become commonplace in the U.S. Courts of Appeals and most state IACs. *See* DANIEL J. MEADOR, APPELLATE COURTS: STAFF AND PROCESS IN THE CRISIS OF VOLUME 9, 11-12 (1974). Thus, the question no longer is judge screening *or* central staff screening, but rather the question is how central staff attorneys and judges should interact in screening procedures.

8. The most widespread feature of the differentiated appellate processes that has emerged since the deployment of central staff attorneys in the screening of appeals is the staff attorney-drafted memorandum. Ideally, staff memoranda "provide a roadmap to decision; they help subsidize the uneven quality of appellate practice; they give the court an accurate background of the case uncolored by advocacy." Donald P. Ubell, *Evolution and Role of Appellate Court Central Staff Attorneys*, 2 COOLEY L. REV. 157, 165 (1984). For what types of appeals should the central staff prepare a memorandum? What functions can or should a staff memorandum serve? What is the difference in utility or effect between a memorandum prepared by a staff attorney and one prepared by the judge's in chambers law clerk? A staff memorandum on a case can be neutral. It can provide a summary of the facts and of the legal arguments but take no position on the merits and make no recommendations for its disposition. Alternatively, the memorandum can evaluate the merits and propose a disposition and even draft a brief opinion for the judges to consider. What are the arguments in favor of these different ways of relying on central staff attorneys? Which would be more likely to be helpful to the judges? Which is more likely to speed up the decisional process? Which poses greater threats to the appellate imperatives? What kinds of cases should be decided with truncated procedures? Consider these suggested criteria for routing appeals to central staff attorneys for the preparation of a memorandum: "(1) The issues involve no more than the application of well-settled rules of law to a recurring fact situation; (2) The issue is whether the evidence is sufficient, and it clearly is; (3) Disposition of the appeal is clearly controlled by a prior holding and no reason appears for questioning or qualifying the holding; or (4) The decision

reviewed is accompanied by a full opinion which is essentially correct." PAUL D. CARRINGTON, DANIEL J. MEADOR & MAURICE ROSENBERG, JUSTICE ON APPEAL 48-51 (1976). What proportion of the docket should be decided with truncated procedures, *i.e.*, is there any desirable limit?

9. A study of the U.S. Court of Appeals for the Ninth Circuit concluded that the screening of cases with central staff attorney participation had no apparent effect on the actual outcome of appeals, *i.e.*, whether a case ultimately was affirmed or reversed. Jerry Goldman, *Appellate Justice Economized: Screening and Its Effect on Outcomes and Legitimacy* in RESTRUCTURING JUSTICE — THE INNOVATIONS OF THE NINTH CIRCUIT AND THE FUTURE OF THE FEDERAL COURTS 138, 162 (Arthur D. Hellman ed., 1990). A study of the Michigan Court of Appeals found that the judicial outcome agreed with the central staff screening recommendation 89% of the time. Mary Lou Stow & Harold J. Spaeth, *Centralized Research Staff: Is There a Monster in the Judicial Closet?*, 75 JUDICATURE 216 (1992). However, "[g]iven the role of appellate courts, the routine nature of cases they hear, and the limitations of standards of review, the more appropriate response might be surprise that the court disagreed with the research staff as often as it did." David J. Brown, *Facing the Monster in the Judicial Closet: Rebutting a Presumption of Sloth*, 75 JUDICATURE 291, 292 (1992).

10. Just how little actual judge-time is the minimum per appeal? Judge Edith Jones, from that push-the-procedural-envelope Fifth Circuit, sorts appeals into three categories of cases defined by how much judge-time they require: "light" — one hour or less; "medium" — one to three hours; and "heavy" — more than three hours. Edith H. Jones, *A Snapshot of a Fifth Circuit Judge's Work: Boutique Justice*, 33 TEX. TECH L. REV. 529, 533 (2002). How much time do you prepare for class? Is preparing for a law school class comparable to judging a federal appeal?

III. ORAL ARGUMENT

Since "time whereof the memory of man runneth not to the contrary" — in the quaint expression of that far distant past — the American appellate tradition called for the parties to present their case to the court through two procedural means: a carefully crafted document of legal research known as a brief followed by counsel's appearance in a formal colloquy of oral argument before the deciding panel of judges. In the late 1960s, as the untoward effects of exponential increases in appellate filings were beginning to accumulate, one of the early reforms taken by appellate courts to alter the decisional processes was to reduce the time allowed for oral argument in all appeals. Soon thereafter the next step taken was to eliminate oral argument altogether in selected appeals. As we have seen in the previous section, the U.S. Court of Appeals for the Fifth Circuit was the first court to routinely screen large numbers of appeals onto a nonargument calendar, but since then most every appellate court has followed this approach in various ways for a significant portion of its docket.

Of course, it is one thing to reduce or eliminate oral argument across the board in all appeals, but it is quite another thing to do so only in certain types of screened cases. This distinction is not always made, however, in the discussions of appellate oral argument. Consider to what extent, if at all, views about oral argument may be influenced by views concerning how judges best function in theory or views about the actual competence of appellate advocates and the quality of oral argument. Consider also how the treatment of oral argument relates to how screening procedures are performed and by whom, *i.e.*, how central staff attorneys participate in the screening and ultimate disposition of cases. This section considers what is lost and what is gained by the elimination of oral argument, both in systemic terms of process imperatives and in terms of informative and effective appellate decision-making in particular appeals. Like most other aspects of appellate procedure, there are varying views on the importance and need for oral argument that deserve to be taken into account.

Robert J. Martineau, *The Value of Appellate Oral Argument: A Challenge to the Conventional Wisdom*, 72 IOWA L. REV. 1, 11-30 (1986)[6]

Institutional Purposes. A principal justification for oral argument is stated in terms of the appellate court's importance as an institution of government in democratic society. The premise underlying this approach is that the governmental processes should, to the extent possible, be conducted in public, to assure the public and the participants in the process that decisions are based on publicly acknowledged considerations and interests. . . . For the judicial system, accountability is crucial, since it depends on public confidence and acceptance of the results of its processes. . . . This imperative lies behind the often-stated principle that it is essential not only that justice be done but that it appear to be done.

Accepting all of the foregoing as true does not mean, however, that oral argument must be heard on every aspect of every case, or on the merits of every case, or even on a substantial majority of cases. The starting point of the analysis should be an awareness that, in order for the judicial process to satisfy the demands for accountability, it has never been a requirement that all proceedings be conducted in public or that the participants have the right to make oral presentations. Instead, the essentials for accountability are: (1) interested parties must be able to present their views to the decision-maker; (2) the factors that serve as the basis for the decision — the record — must be available to the public; (3) the decision must be publicly announced and become part of the record; and (4) the process must appear fair to the parties and the public. . . .

Orality and visibility, however, have never been absolute requirements for every step in the appellate process. The confidentiality of the court's conference room, draft opinions, and communications among judges and their staffs is virtually unquestioned. Many decisions on motions, both substantive and procedural, and on whether to have oral arguments, written or published opinions, or rehearings are made on written submissions to the court without oral

---

[6] Copyright (1986) Iowa Law Review. Reprinted with permission.

arguments, even though many of these decisions may be "outcome determinative." The question then becomes when will orality be required. That question should be the focus of debate, rather than the question of how to preserve oral argument in every case.

To say that oral argument is not required in all cases does not mean that it should not be held in a substantial number of cases, even some in which the judges may have concluded that briefs are adequate to decide the case properly. There are some cases which, by virtue of the importance of the issues involved, or the public interest in those issues, demand the full panoply of the traditional appellate process, including oral argument and a full, signed published opinion. If these cases and those in which the judges think oral argument would be helpful are not sufficient to legitimate the appellate process, then the judges should assign additional cases for oral argument to satisfy those institutional interests. With a large caseload, the need for oral argument to satisfy these interests becomes particularly important when the court utilizes different features of the appellate process such as dispositions on motion, an enlarged central staff, disposition without opinion, and unpublished opinions. When oral argument is held for reasons other than to assist judges in deciding cases, this fact should be acknowledged by judges, counsel, and litigants.

The Judge's Purposes. Many proponents of oral argument cite its usefulness to the appellate judge as one of the principal reasons for having it in virtually every case. The core justification, stated in various ways by different commentators, is that oral argument can assist judges in understanding issues, facts, and arguments of the parties, thereby helping judges decide cases appropriately. According to this theory, assistance comes in several ways, depending on the nature of the case or the quality of the briefs. For example, there may be matters that are unclear or omitted from the briefs that can be clarified only by questioning opposing counsel, particularly in cases with complicated facts or novel legal issues. Moreover, some ideas are better transmitted orally than by written means.

Other justifications for oral argument are based on the nature or practices of the individual judge. It is contended that some judges, for example, assimilate ideas more effectively through oral rather than written communication.

Another justification concerns the judge not so much from the standpoint of the individual case, but from that of the judge's role in the judicial process. Oral argument helps judges avoid becoming too isolated, and serves to remind them that they are not the only participants in the judicial process, and that their decisions directly affect individual lives. Moreover, it is important for judges to have direct personal contact with the litigant's attorney. Without this contact, a judgeship would be reduced merely to processing paper and thus, fewer well-qualified persons may be attracted to the bench. . . .

In examining the first justification — that oral argument facilitates the judge's understanding of the issues, facts, and arguments — it is clear that the usefulness of oral argument in a particular case depends on the quality of the briefs, and the extent to which the judges and their staffs study the briefs and the record, and use means other than oral argument to clarify ambiguities. To suggest that most cases involve issues and facts so complicated and briefs so poorly written that oral argument is virtually indispensable ignores a basic fact about most appellate cases: they are not exceedingly complicated. By reading the briefs and the relevant portions of the record, judges are usually provided a sufficient basis to decide a case.

On the other hand, if briefs are so bad that even after careful scrutiny confusion still remains over the facts, issues, or contentions of the parties, it is doubtful whether a fifteen- or twenty-minute oral argument will do much to clarify matters, particularly when there is no advance notice as to the matters on which the judges seek clarification. Attorneys who cannot write an adequate brief are not likely to be better at oral argument; thus, oral argument may be a wasted effort. The idea that an attorney can respond better orally to an unanticipated question, under the pressures of a personal appearance in a public courtroom, relying exclusively on memory, than in a written brief over which the attorney has had thirty or more days to prepare, with full access to the record, and to the texts of relevant cases, simply defies the realities of the situation.

This is not to suggest that oral argument will never be helpful. Among other things, exploring the limitations of precedent and the implications of a decision, as well as the public's interest in the decision, may all justify oral argument in a particular case. Such exploration, however, does not justify a general policy in favor of oral argument, particularly in the usual case that involves only error correction issues.

The two remaining justifications for oral argument — one relating to the nature of the case and the other to judges' abilities — are closely related and yet are opposite sides of the same coin. The first justification is that some ideas or arguments are better communicated by oral rather than written means, while the second justification is that some judges assimilate ideas more effectively when they are transmitted orally. What validity there may be to either of these arguments, when comparing oral versus written communication generally, is without merit when applied to oral argument as it is conducted in most appellate courts.

Oral arguments are fifteen or twenty minutes in length per side. During that period attorneys hope to summarize one or two of their best points set forth in the briefs and to answer questions from the judges. Some attorneys have a sufficient command of the record and the relevant law, and are competent enough at public speaking, to make effective oral argument succinctly and coherently and to respond competently to questions from the judges. Most attorneys, however, do not make good use of oral argument, whether for lack of skill, insufficient knowledge of the purposes of oral argument, or inadequate preparation for the particular argument. It simply flies in the face of common sense that the transitory, spontaneous, and soon forgotten oral statement can communicate an idea better than a carefully prepared brief that can be studied as long as necessary.

Communicating emotion is one aspect of advocacy that is unquestionably done more effectively in oral form. This emotive quality is achieved by making what is essentially a jury argument to the appellate court, emphasizing the equities of the case. Judges, however, do not respond well to this kind of argument; although they are concerned with doing justice, they are more concerned with rendering justice on a principled basis, not on an emotional basis induced, in part, by counsel's rhetoric. Consequently, the ability to communicate emotion should not justify preference for oral argument over the written brief. Furthermore, the idea that some judges assimilate ideas better from oral presentations than from written documents ignores the limitations of oral argument and the generally accepted principles on the amount that can be absorbed orally at one time.

Notwithstanding these inherent weaknesses of oral argument, it must be acknowledged that oral argument does allow judges to explore their ideas of the case with counsel. In recognizing this fact, however, the question must be asked whether oral argument is the most effective means for judges to test their ideas. This function is usually served by the judge's meeting with the staff and other judges on the panel. Often they are just as conversant as counsel on the strengths and weaknesses of the judges' ideas, particularly as they may be affected by the record or other cases. Furthermore, a short oral argument is hardly the most appropriate time to obtain a thoughtful response from counsel about a novel idea. Attorneys will be far more likely to give a reasoned response if given an opportunity to reflect on the idea, review the record, and do additional research. If put in this position at oral argument, the wise advocate will ask for permission to submit a short memorandum on the idea, avoiding a spur of the moment response.

There is no doubt that participation in oral argument on occasion can be important to the appellate judge for all of the reasons suggested by its supporters. Likewise, this fact supports oral argument in some, but not in all cases, and not even in some predetermined percentage of cases. It proves only that it is important for an appellate court to hear oral argument in some cases. The key question is in which cases. . . .

Criticisms of Oral Argument. Until recently, most appellate judges accepted the desirability of oral argument in every case. Today, oral arguments have been shortened dramatically, and in some cases eliminated, to foster judicial expediency. The explanation given for these changes is that oral argument is one of the bottlenecks of the appellate process, that it takes substantial time, and that by eliminating or shortening oral argument, appellate courts could dispose of more cases faster. . . .

If the length of oral argument is shortened, more oral arguments can be heard each day. Likewise, eliminating oral argument in some cases will increase the number of cases decided by the appellate court. In either situation, the time for disposition of cases will be reduced, and the productivity of the court will be increased.

Although this rationale has an appealing logic, it is difficult to prove its accuracy, primarily because changes in oral argument practices are seldom made in isolation. Usually, they are accompanied by other measures designed to increase the court's productivity. . . .

In contrast, some commentators have compared the time spent on the bench hearing oral argument in an individual case, usually between thirty and sixty minutes, with the total time spent on the case. These observers suggest that oral argument represents such a small proportion of the total time spent on a case, that little time would be saved by its elimination in any case in which one of the parties had requested oral argument. This conclusion, however, is misleading. A case that is argued orally does in fact consume substantially more of the court's time than one decided solely on the briefs. This is because of the nature of the preparation involved, travel time, and the fact that on a day when a judge hears oral arguments, both the judge and staff have little time to accomplish anything else. Moreover, an appellate court's schedule typically shows that a judge who hears oral arguments one week out of each month for nine or ten months a year must also spend approximately one additional week each month preparing for and recovering from oral arguments. The judge and staff thus spend approximately one-half of their time on oral argument. The time spent on the bench is, consequently, only the tip of the oral argument iceberg.

Even this enormous expenditure of judge and staff time is not, however, the most significant effect that oral argument has on an appellate court's capacity to dispose of cases. For each panel of the court, whether the court sits in three-judge panels or *en banc*, it is generally accepted that a judge should hear a maximum of five or six cases a day, and sit for no more than five days during each month. This is because a judge cannot adequately prepare for or absorb the arguments of more than five cases per day, and given the other duties of the judge, cannot sit for more than ten months of each year if he or she is to have one month for vacation, and another month for participating in judicial conferences and educational programs, and in other types of official and professional activities.

In addition to these official duties, the judge must prepare for the next month's arguments. This means that each three-judge panel (or the entire court if it always sits *en banc*) can dispose of only 250 to 300 cases per year, if it hears oral argument in virtually every case. The burdensome caseload of most appellate courts today renders inadequate this rate of review if a court is to dispose of cases within any reasonable time limits. A court that insists on hearing oral argument in almost all cases must either accept this number as its maximum output or adopt other means of increasing it, such as deciding cases by order rather than opinion or by oral decisions from the bench immediately following oral argument. . . .

The Value of Oral Argument. Notwithstanding the generally accepted view that oral argument is a valuable and perhaps essential part of the appellate process, its real contribution to sound decision-making is questioned by an increasing number of commentators. The heart of the criticism is a realization that, in many if not most cases, oral argument adds little or nothing to the judge's understanding of a case that was not previously obtained through a study of the briefs and the record by the judges and their staffs. Simply stated, oral argument is not cost-effective.

Diminution of the value of oral argument is based on two separate but related contentions. The first is cogently expressed by Chief Judge Ruggero Aldisert of the Third Circuit and concurred in by others. He compares the time judges and their staffs work with briefs in an individual case with the time spent hearing the oral argument — usually less than an hour for both sides combined — and concludes that briefs have a far greater impact on the decisional process than oral argument. . . .

The second principal contention, recently expressed by [Judge Alvin Rubin of the Fifth Circuit] and several other appellate judges, is that oral argument has no significant effect in most cases, and that there is no substantial difference in the outcome of cases argued orally and those decided only on the briefs. Opposing this view, however, are two judges of the Eighth Circuit [Judges Arnold and Bright] who claim that oral argument for them is decisive in between a third and a half of the cases in which it is heard.

Measuring the value of oral argument by comparing the amount of time spent with the briefs with the time spent in oral argument has an apparent logic. It would not be persuasive, however, if, in fact, oral argument were decisive in a large number of cases. But who is more accurate in reflecting the experiences of most judges — Judges Aldisert and Rubin, who put the decisive effect of oral argument at no more than ten percent, or Judges Arnold and Bright, who claim a much higher percentage? The different percentages are a product of the four judges' own experiences; essentially, the matter comes down to one of expectation and approach.

If judges study the briefs and preargument memoranda in hopes of deciding cases without the aid of oral argument, it is likely that oral argument will seldom be decisive. Judges will attempt to resolve questions by further examining the briefs and records or by additional research. If, however, judges prepare for oral argument by using the briefs and staff memoranda, not as a means of resolving doubts and questions, but as a source for generating questions at oral argument, the briefs and staff memoranda are far less likely to have a decisive effect for those judges.

In the latter situation, a decision to have oral argument will most likely be made on the basis of a preliminary screening either by staff members or by a judge. Thus, oral argument is a foregone conclusion. It is also likely that a judge reading briefs and other material in preparation for oral argument will simply defer any questions until the time of the argument.

Regardless of the percentage of cases in which oral argument is decisive, this number would be reduced even further if oral argument were not scheduled automatically or solely on the basis of a preliminary screening. An alternative would be to have the case assigned to a panel of judges. The panel would read the briefs and record with the intent of deciding the case based only on the written material. It would direct oral argument only if the judges concluded that it was necessary to decide the case properly. In such a case, oral argument would often be decisive, but the number of cases requiring oral argument would be substantially reduced.

The value of oral argument must also be considered in light of counsel's ability to make an effective oral argument. Some appellate judges, in more candid moments, have acknowledged that many, if not most, appellate attorneys do not use the opportunity for oral argument. There are many possible explanations for this including that they have not been trained properly, they are not aware of the different nature of oral argument today compared to several decades ago, and they do not handle a sufficient number of appeals to become expert at it. It is more likely, however, that these weaknesses are inherent in the very nature of oral argument in its traditional format.

Realistically, one should not expect the average attorney to respond effectively to unanticipated questions, relying solely on memory, without an opportunity to reflect on either the question or the response. . . . Should the parties' rights and the development of the law turn upon a precise phrasing of a question and the attorney's understanding of that question, or upon the attorney's ability to recall relevant portions of the record or of statutes or cases, or upon the attorney's immediate response and the judge's understanding of the reply? In all likelihood, there is bound to be a misunderstanding of the question or the response, or the attorney will fail to recall the precise portion of the record or the precise language of a statute or opinion that would supply the best answer to the question. Consequently, oral argument, rather than being an excellent means of communication, is in fact a highly unreliable one, at least in its present format.

The weaknesses of oral argument are exacerbated by the tradition of holding the decision conference immediately following oral argument. Generally, if oral argument does influence the result in a case, it is largely because of its temporal proximity with the decision conference. Thus, this procedure gives the weakest link in the appellate process its potentially outcome determinative character. . . .

On the other hand, the temporal relationship between oral argument and the decision conference is justifiable to the extent that knowledge gained through oral presentations is only retained for a short period of time. If the decision conference were not held immediately following oral argument, the likelihood that oral argument would have any effect on the result would be diminished. In sum, when there is a close temporal relationship between oral argument and the decision conference, the effect of oral argument is too great, but, when there is no close temporal relationship the lack of effect destroys the justification for having the oral argument. . . .

The threshold question is not whether oral argument is necessary, but whether the judges to whom the case is assigned need any additional information from counsel concerning the facts, the relevant law, or counsel's views on matters relating to the case. . . . Since only the judges assigned to decide a case on the merits can determine this threshold question, there is no need for preliminary screening of cases for oral argument by a screening panel or staff. Instead, the judges to whom a case is assigned for decision should read the briefs from the standpoint of whether they contain everything necessary for a reasonable and fair decision on the merits or whether anything additional is needed from counsel. It would be helpful in this regard for each brief to contain a section stating counsel's view on whether oral argument is necessary or desirable and, if so, the reasons why.

If this initial reading of the briefs or subsequent work on the case indicates that there are questions, ambiguities, or general concerns that the judges want counsel to address, then a decision should be made as to how that information can best be obtained. Should the judges solicit written comments or some type of oral presentation, either by telephone or in person? The written response could be a letter, a memorandum, or even photocopies of portions of the record or other documents. Once the initial response has been reviewed, a decision should be made as to whether a session with both counsel and judges is necessary. The advantages of first seeking written responses are twofold. First, the information can be obtained in a short period, usually no more than seven to ten days, and it does not involve the delays inherent in scheduling cases for oral argument. Second, the procedure avoids one of the major weaknesses of oral argument (*i.e.*, spontaneous responses) by giving the attorney time to prepare a well-thought-out response to the query. . . .

Oral argument can and should continue to have a significant role in the appellate process. However, unless its real purpose is understood and it is used only in those cases in which that purpose can be served, it will delay the disposition of cases and increase expenses. . . . [and] continue to be little more than a waste of time.

A.B.A. STANDARDS RELATING TO APPELLATE COURTS § 3.35 (1994)[7]

Oral Argument. A party to an appeal should have the opportunity to request oral argument on the merits of the appeal. The time allowed each side for oral arguments should be of reasonable length. The opportunity for oral argument may be subject to qualifications, established by court rule, as follows:

(a) The time allowed for argument may be shortened or extended by order of the court.

(b) Oral argument may be denied if the court concludes from a review of the briefs and record of the case that its deliberation would not be significantly aided by oral argument. When the court advises the parties that it does not believe that oral argument would be useful, it should permit the parties to submit a written statement of reasons why oral argument should be allowed.

(c) The Court may order oral argument, even if the parties waive it.

Commentary. Oral argument historically has been an essential part of the appellate process. It is a medium of communication that may be superior to written expression for many appellate counsel and judges, particularly in complex, novel, and difficult cases. It can provide a fluid and rapidly moving method of getting at essential issues. It contributes to judicial accountability, enlarges the public visibility of appellate decision-making, and is a safeguard against undue reliance on staff work. Oral argument should not ordinarily be allowed on applications to grant discretionary review or on motions or other procedural matters. When an appeal is considered on its merits, however, oral argument should never be discouraged routinely and should be denied only if

---

[7] Copyright © 1994 American Bar Association. Reprinted with permission.

the court is convinced that argument would not be useful. Waiver or denial of oral argument does not mean that counsel or the court considers the case unimportant.

Some appellate courts are so overburdened that they have felt compelled to deny opportunity for oral argument in a substantial proportion of the cases before them. In some situations this practice may be unavoidable and should be treated as a symptom of the need to restructure the court's organization or jurisdiction. In any event, the practice should be adopted only as an extreme measure when other means of keeping the court abreast of its caseload are insufficient. . . .

The time allowed for oral argument should be sufficient to permit probing discourse. . . . The time allowed for oral arguments should be extended when the issues are unusually complex and shortened when they are few and relatively simple. . . .

INTERNAL OPERATING PROCEDURES OF THE UNITED STATES COURT OF APPEALS FOR THE THIRD CIRCUIT (July 1, 2002)

Chapter 2. Oral Argument.

2.1. Determination in Panel Cases. The panel determines whether there will be oral argument and the amount of time allocated. There is oral argument if it is requested by at least one judge. Each judge communicates his or her views to the other panel members. No later than eleven (11) days before the first day of the panel sitting, the presiding judge furnishes the Clerk with the panel's determinations in accordance with the maximum request, up to 20 minutes per side, of any single judge. Usually, 15 minutes per side is allotted. A request for oral argument beyond 20 minutes a side is determined by a majority of the panel. . . .

2.4. Suggested Criteria for Oral Argument.

2.4.1. Experience discloses that judges usually find oral argument unnecessary when: (a) The issue is tightly constrained, not novel, and the briefs adequately cover the arguments; (b) The outcome of the appeal is clearly controlled by a decision of the Supreme Court or this court; or (c) The state of the record will determine the outcome and the sole issue is either sufficiency of the evidence, the adequacy of jury instructions, or rulings as to admissibility of evidence, and the briefs adequately refer to the record.

2.4.2. Experience discloses that judges usually vote for oral argument when: (a) The appeal presents a substantial and novel legal issue; (b) The resolution of an issue presented by the appeal will be of institutional or precedential value; (c) A judge has questions to ask counsel to clarify an important legal, factual, or procedural point; (d) A decision, legislation, or an event subsequent to the filing of the last brief may significantly bear on the case; or (e) An important public interest may be affected.

2.4.3. The foregoing criteria shall not be construed to limit any judge's discretion in voting for oral argument.

REPORT OF THE DIRECTOR OF THE ADMINISTRATIVE OFFICE OF THE UNITED STATES COURTS **Table S-1,** *U.S. Courts of Appeals – Appeals Terminated on the Merits After Oral Hearings or Submission on Briefs during the 12 — Month Period Ending September 30, 2004* **(2004)**

Circuit	Oral Hearing			Submission on Briefs	
	Total	Total	Percent	Total	Percent
ALL	27,438	8,645	31.5	18,793	68.5
DC	492	262	53.3	230	46.7
First	683	380	55.6	303	44.4
Second	1,777	1,047	58.9	730	41.1
Third	2,047	503	24.6	1,544	75.4
Fourth	2,424	413	17.0	2,011	83.0
Fifth	4,018	752	18.7	3,266	81.3
Sixth	2,490	1,050	42.2	1,440	57.8
Seventh	1,411	738	52.3	673	47.7
Eighth	1,860	649	34.9	1,211	65.1
Ninth	5,783	1,805	31.2	3,978	68.8
Tenth	1,349	390	28.9	959	71.1
Eleventh	3,104	656	21.1	2,448	78.9

Editor's note: This table does not show the breakdown of *en banc* cases that totaled only 51 cases for all twelve Courts of Appeals during this period.

NOTES

1. An oral argument was traditionally and universally seen as a necessary part of presenting an appeal. *See* KARL N. LLEWELLYN, THE COMMON LAW TRADITION: DECIDING APPEALS 240 (1960). After conceding that oral argument is still the ideal, however, one U.S. Circuit judge remarked, "I'll be frank about it, it is not possible with this caseload to practice the ideal." JOE S. CECIL & DONNA STIENSTRA, DECIDING CASES WITHOUT ARGUMENT: AN EXAMINATION OF FOUR COURTS OF APPEALS 133 (Fed. Jud. Ctr. 1987).

2. According to the summary CASE MANAGEMENT PROCEDURES IN THE FEDERAL COURTS OF APPEALS, excerpted in section II above, what kinds of cases are being afforded oral argument? What are the factors that distinguish appeals that are decided on the briefs from appeals that are afforded oral argument? The subject matter of the appeal? The size of the record on appeal? The number of litigants? Whether the litigants are represented or unrepresented? Are there more intangible factors like the difficulty or complexity of the legal and factual issues? The importance of the legal issues beyond the case? What should be the screening criteria for deciding an appeal without an oral argument?

3. The question we should ask ourselves is: Are we so superior to those who preceded us that we can resolve a more complex case in a better fashion by devoting less time and effort to it? My own supposition is that while the abilities of the bench and bar are perhaps improved they have not changed substantially and that we could benefit by a return to longer oral arguments. While the reduction in oral argument may have been a response to an increase in case load, it is also interesting to note that that reduction parallels an increasingly technological society in which everything from the telecast of war to the evening meal is instantaneous. I suspect that culturally we have lost our patience for listening to others carefully and for thoroughly developing arguments in even important cases. It appears that the reduction in oral argument is part of the quest for the "instant judicial decision" as the companion of this morning's instant breakfast.

Richard L. Aynes, *Maintaining the Integrity of the Ohio Appellate System*, 16 AKRON L. REV. 115, 130-31 (1982).

4. There are a good many articles extolling the importance and value of oral arguments on appeal — Professor Martineau's provocative article excerpted above stands out for taking a more skeptical point of view. Does he persuade you? Does its importance and function require oral argument in every case or in most cases or only in some cases? Beyond possibly assisting the judges who must decide the appeal, what are the advantages or benefits of oral argument from the standpoint of the litigants and lawyers? Are there some types of cases in which oral argument should be held even though the judges would be willing to dispense with it? What might possess an attorney to waive an oral argument, if given the opportunity?

5. While appellate judges as a group, state and federal, dispense with oral arguments in a majority of their actual cases, many individual judges are willing to wax eloquently about the value of oral arguments. How do you explain this seeming contradiction? Do you suppose it is merely nostalgia? For the most part, the testimonials provide only personal endorsements and anecdotal evidence. Joseph W. Hatchett & Robert J. Telfer, III, *The Importance of Appellate Oral Argument*, 33 STETSON L. REV. 139 (2003); Myron H. Bright & Richard S. Arnold, *Oral Argument? It May Be Crucial!*, 70 A.B.A. J. 68 (1984); Stanley Mosk, *In Defense of Oral Argument*, 1 J. APP. PRAC. & PROCESS 25 (1999). A rare empirical study concluded that the lawyer's common wisdom ("You cannot win an appeal with a good performance, but you can lose an appeal with a bad performance") seriously understates the importance and impact of oral argument on the court. The study found that Supreme Court justices gather specific information about a case at the oral argument that they in fact rely on to make their substantive decisions. Timothy R. Johnson, *Information, Oral Arguments, and Supreme Court Decision Making*, 29 AMER. POLITICS RESEARCH 331 (2001).

6. In 1974, the American Bar Association House of Delegates adopted the following resolution: "Be It Resolved that the American Bar Association expresses its opposition in an appropriate manner to the rules of certain United States Courts of Appeals which drastically curtail or entirely eliminate

oral argument in a substantial proportion of non-frivolous appeals, and, *a fortiori*, to the disposition of cases prior to the filing of briefs." What might explain the ABA's endorsement of the nonargument calendar twenty years later in Standard § 3.50 excerpted above?

7. The U.S. Court of Appeals for the Third Circuit was the first appellate court to adopt and publish a written standard in its internal operating procedures regarding when there should be an oral argument. Numerous appellate courts now do so. What does the Third Circuit standard mean? Does it cabin the judicial discretion to grant or deny oral argument — or is that too much to expect from a written standard? *See also* FED. R. APP. P. 34 ("Oral argument must be allowed in every case unless (A) the appeal is frivolous; (B) the dispositive issues have been authoritatively decided; or (C) the facts and legal arguments are adequately presented in the briefs and record, and the decisional process would not be significantly aided by oral argument.")

8. IACs in Arizona, California, and New Mexico have adopted a variation on the nonargument calendar. The court sends a "tentative" draft opinion before the scheduled oral argument along with a request that the parties waive oral argument. Thomas E. Hollenhorst, *Tentative Opinions: An Analysis of their Benefit in the Appellate Court of California*, 36 SANTA CLARA L. REV. 1 (1995); Mark Hummels, Note, *Distributing Draft Decisions Before Oral Argument on Appeal: Should the Court Tip Its Tentative Hand? The Case for Dissemination*, 46 ARIZ. L. REV. 317 (2004). Do you think this is a good idea? The Supreme Court of California ruled that the IAC's notice and waiver form were improper, however, because the documents had the potential to discourage defendants from asking for oral argument and the language suggested too strongly that the tentative opinion was final. The case was remanded with instructions to make appropriate changes in the documents. *People v. Pena*, 83 P. 3d 506 (Cal. 2004). Try your hand at drafting the new form notice and request for waiver of oral argument: what should it say?

9. Appellate courts have been experimenting with technology to make oral arguments more efficient and more cost effective. Many state appellate courts, both COLRs and IACs, as well as more than half the U.S. Courts of Appeals have developed video-conferencing capability that allows attorneys, parties, and judges to participate in oral argument from remote locations. Fredric I. Lederer, *The Effect of Courtroom Technologies on and in Appellate Proceedings and Courtrooms*, 2 J. APP. PRAC. & PROCESS 251 (2000). Argument by these means is endorsed in the commentary to A.B.A. STANDARDS RELATING TO APPELLATE COURTS § 3.35 (1994).

10. One of the premises underlying the move to eliminate oral argument, at least in some jurisdictions, is a sense of redundancy, *i.e.*, that it is not necessary that counsel present their arguments in briefs and at oral argument; one opportunity for advocacy often ought to be adequate. It generally has been assumed that if only one means of advocacy were allowed, then that means should be the written brief. Consider the out-of-the-box thinking that the one means of advocacy could as well, or perhaps better, be oral argument. *See* Suzanne Ehrenberg, *Embracing the Writing-Centered Legal Process*, 89 IOWA L. REV. 1159 (2004); Daniel J. Meador, *Toward Orality and Visibility in the Appellate Process*, 42 MD.

L. Rev. 732 (1983). Why do you suppose that American appellate judges have been reluctant to move in the direction of greater orality?

11. The statistics above from the Administrative Office of U.S. Courts reveal that in all the federal IACs oral argument is provided in less than a third of the cases (31.5%), so a little more than two thirds of the cases are decided without oral argument (68.5%). The breakdown circuit-by-circuit goes from a high of 58.9% oral arguments in the Second Circuit to a low of 18.7% in the Fifth Circuit, which first developed the nonargument calendar in the late 1960s. What might account for the variations circuit-by-circuit? The experience in the state IACs mirrors the federal experience in that there has been a gradual but steady decline in the frequency of oral arguments over the last four decades. It is estimated that the typical state intermediate court hears oral arguments in only approximately 25% of its appeals. Warren D. Wolfson, *Oral Argument: Does it Matter?*, 35 Ind. L. Rev. 451 (2002). That means that three out of four state appeals are now being decided without oral argument. Do these percentages make you pause, knowing that up until 1968 every appeal in every appellate court was afforded an opportunity to present an oral argument?

IV. COURT CONFERENCES

Before American intermediate appellate courts transformed themselves and their procedures in response to the crisis of volume, the long-standing tradition was for the deciding panel of judges to read the briefs in preparation for oral argument and then hold a collegial conference after argument to discuss and vote on each case. This face-to-face conference focused on the legal and factual issues presented and reached a collective decision, at least tentatively, in anticipation of a full-blown written published opinion, circulated and approved by each of the judges. That appellate process still obtains, but only for a small fraction of the cases.

As we have seen, dockets exploded and the judges initiated triage procedures to screen cases and assign some appeals to decisional tracks characterized by truncated appellate procedures. Indeed, as we have seen in the previous section, today most appeals are decided without an oral argument, an appellate procedure that once was a *sine qua non* of an appeal. Consequently, the decisional conference has been replaced in the typical nonargument calendar cases with a serial, or round-robin system: a central staff attorney culls the nonargument cases and prepares a research memorandum, perhaps along with a draft opinion, which is forwarded to the "initiating judge." The initiating judge may adopt the proposed opinion with or without changes. That judge then forwards the materials to a second judge on the panel, who reviews the case and the proposed opinion and, if in full agreement, the second judge sends the appeal on to the third judge for review. If all three judges sign-on to an opinion, the decision is released; any one judge can reclassify the case onto the oral argument calendar and it will be heard and decided by an argument panel of judges who will hold the traditional in-person conference. Otherwise, there may be some back and forth over the telephone among the participating judges, but only rarely; in most courts, the *seriatim* procedure is usually conducted exclusively in writing and through the mail. Thus, there is never an occasion when the three judges are in the same room at the same time to decide the case. The various U.S. Courts of Appeals adhere generally to this nonargument calendar paradigm with local variations of screening procedures, like the Fifth Circuit's conference calendar previously described in section II. There is considerably more variation among state IACs, depending on their jurisdiction and how they are organized and structured. But the bottom line is that judicial conferencing on cases has mutated along with the other appellate procedures in response to increasing docket pressures.

A.B.A. STANDARDS RELATING TO APPELLATE COURTS § 3.36 (1994)[8]

Decisions and Opinions.

(a) Conferences by the Court. The judges who are to decide a case should confer after argument is completed and before a decision is formulated. The process by which an opinion is prepared may appropriately vary, but all participating judges should join in its formulation. . . .

Commentary. Decisional process. An appellate court's decisional process should be collegial. Each case should be dealt with in conference joined by all participating judges.

When oral argument has been heard, conference deliberations should give due regard to matters raised at argument that might not have appeared in the briefs. When the case is to be decided without oral argument, there should be searching consideration of the arguments advanced by the briefs and special inquiry among the participating judges to assure that they share a common conception of what the case involves and how it should be decided.

Decisional conferences are strengthened by the presence of the participating judges. When the judges are separately headquartered, however, they may appropriately exchange views by memoranda, telephone, or e-mail, unless the complexity of the matter under consideration makes those forms of communications inadequate. . . .

FRANK M. COFFIN, ON APPEAL: COURTS, LAWYERING, AND JUDGING 149-61 (1994)[9]

The Judges' Conference. Although the conferences held by judges after oral argument are as much beyond the ken of advocates as are the deliberations of a jury, it is important to have an idea of the nature and variety of these conferences — partly to appreciate how narrowly focused many are, and partly to be able to anticipate issues that might well determine the nature, scope, and consequences of the ruling, if not the very essence of it. . . .

---

[8] Copyright © 1994 American Bar Association. Reprinted with permission.

[9] From On Appeal: Courts, Lawyering, and Judging by Frank M. Coffin. Copyright © 1994 by W.W. Norton & Company,Inc. Used by permission of W.W. Norton & Company, Inc.

A Critical and Unique Stage. Whether the judges' conference is a more structured one or seemingly casual conversation among three judges, it is the most significant step in what I have characterized as a process of graduated decision-making. All the participants have read, discussed, listened, and asked questions about the case. They have absorbed insights from their clerks, the lawyers, and their own colleagues. They have already seen their own initial impressions change, perhaps several times. And they know that although their ideas might now be fairly well seasoned, they could change their minds again. The judges come to conference fresh from the most intense and concentrated exposure of oral argument. Most important, this is generally the only time when all judges will be discussing the case together. Even though their tentative disposition of the case in conference may change, it is safe to say that at least 90 percent of the decisions made at conference will stand.

The judges' conference, as a method of group decision-making, is unique. The outsider would find it remarkable that, notwithstanding the bundle of questions of fact and law that must accompany most cases deemed worthy of an appeal, case conferences are very often abbreviated, telescoped conversations hitting only a few issues. All judges are by now so immersed in the case that most questions have been answered. They know the points that bother them. Their talk is plain and to the point, cutting through the lengthy legalese of many of the briefs. There is generally no "hype" or salesmanship in their comments, no guile, simply a statement of how each judge reacts to the point being discussed, and perhaps some reference to a fact or case authority deemed crucial, and reasoning about policy implications. The tenor of comments is usually not combative or final. A judge who finds her initial views disputed by colleagues may say, " I didn't think this through very deeply. I will probably go along with both of you." Or a possible dissenter will end his comments by saying, "I'll listen. If you find some cases or show me in the record something to support your position, I'll be open."

During all these exchanges, no one knows who will be writing the opinion. Each judge carefully notes the concerns of colleagues; if he or she is to write the opinion, it is important to address those concerns and heed the nuances expressed in the conference. . . . Much of the conversation may bear little relation to what was said at oral argument. Indeed, some issues may not be touched upon at all. Sometimes, because of failure to consider or deal adequately with a "sleeping" issue, the writer of the opinion may run into a roadblock and find that a quite different opinion must be written. . . . Because of this always present possibility, the decisions at conference are not engraved in stone. . . .

[T]he judges' conference breaks all the rules. It has no fixed agenda for any case, staff, minutes, rules, or press release. It consists of informal conversation on the issues the judges find important. It is nonadversarial. It is nonbinding. No one stands to gain or lose prestige, position, or power by what he or she says or does not say. No one is trying to take advantage of another. Each has trust in the motives of the others.

A Spectrum of Case Conference Types. To convey something of the focus and flavor of appellate case conferencing, I have drawn upon my own rudimentary conference notes of the past several years. . . . I think the following

impressionistic survey of types or models of case conferences is fairly representative of what goes on. . . . I list conference models beginning with the
simplest and working toward the more complex, full-scale conferences. . . .
Perceptive counsel can anticipate the nature of some of these conferences,
but the very nature of the process we are dealing with — an evolving case
analysis in which, as in peeling an onion, new layers of facts, issues, interpretation, and legal theory are revealed — more often defies prediction.

(1) "Rope of Sand" Cases. There are cases in which the judges in conference
quickly agree, without detailed discussion, to affirm. Frivolous cases . . . are of
course, primary candidates for this treatment. But there are many nonfrivolous cases which merit the same disposition. Whatever persuasiveness
may have initially appeared in appellant's claims has, after much reading of
brief and listening to argument, been dissipated — like a rope of sand before
a rising tide. . . .

(2) "Cafeteria" Cases. These are cases presenting the judges with a choice of
grounds on which to rest their decision — such as jurisdiction, procedural
waiver, standing, the merits, and harmless error. Sometimes the choice is left
to the writer of the opinion. But quite often judges feel strongly that the choice
is important and needs discussion. . . .

(3) "Technical Weighing" Cases. Slightly more discussion . . . takes place
when facts are to be weighed against a legal standard. . . . In such cases there
is initially likely to be room for differences as judges try to assemble all relevant facts and see if they measure up to the legal standard. Generally the discussion is not carried to the point where a final vote is taken; judges are likely
to be content to await a more complete review of the trial record by the judge
who ultimately is assigned to draft an opinion. When the draft opinion is later
circulated, unanimity is highly likely. . . .

(4) "Abuse of Discretion" Cases. Offering a wider range for discussion are cases
where the issue is whether the trial judge, the hearing examiner, or the administrative agency abused the discretion granted by the law. . . . Abuse of discretion
is a fuzzier question than whether the facts meet a legal standard. Each judge is
not asking whether the action in the agency or lower court was correct or not. The
judge begins with the assumption that the action below was not that which he
would have taken; the question is then whether it was so wrong, arbitrary, or
irrational that an abuse of discretion was committed. The question arises in myriad forms. . . . Appellate judges generally are reluctant to find abuse of discretion.
. . . Sometimes the discussion over a judge's abuse is brought to a head by the
question: if we don't reverse for this conduct, when would we ever reverse?

(5) The Dispositive Fact. Once in a while a complicated case may eventually
be found to run on one fact — whether a paper was signed, whether a conversation took place, whether a notice was given. The briefs may range widely
and miss such a fact. . . . But oral argument, aided perhaps by the assiduous
record-reading of a judge, may highlight the gap in the facts. In such cases, the
conference is brief, although there is always the caveat: let the writing judge
check the record thoroughly to be sure we are right.

(6) The Dispositive Legal Issue. Sometimes a case focuses to the point where
all judges recognize the dominance of a stark legal issue. . . . When legal

doctrine is involved, judges are loath to decide quickly. They realize that much research needs to be done on the case law. So here, too, the decision is really to await the analysis of the writing judge.

(7) The Value-Added Weighing Decision. The values of judges creep into the discussion of many cases. . . . Values probably all stem from personal experience in some generalized sense. But some values may be traceable to the rather specific experience of a judge. . . . Similarly, when, as often happens, trial judges sit on appellate panels, they bring quite a different perspective, as do appellate judges who have once served as trial judges. Sometimes this results in a plea for deferring to the trial judge; but sometimes it results in a searching review, the former trial judge feeling strongly that any sensible trial judge would never have acted as the judge below did. Judges being human, the "value-added" component of judicial balancing sometimes exceeds professional bounds. Once in a while a judge will give vent to spleen . . . [or] *ad hominem* remarks. . . . Once such a statement is made, it appears to be what it is, a remark that has no place in the decision process. It reflects a value judgment . . . but nothing about the law, the facts, or the process of reaching a just decision in accordance with the law. In its very utterance, the remark generally seals its own doom. It is not unusual that a judge who has "sounded off" in unjudicial irritation will join or even write an opinion running contrary to her initial comments.

(8) Judicial Creativity. Some of the most interesting conferences turn not on what the briefs and arguments have discussed but on some additional input from one of the judges. It might take the form of a novel theory that could dispose of the case in a more satisfactory manner than either side has suggested. . . . Though the law might appear to foreclose such a result, it is likely that the other judges will at least give their colleague head room to try out her idea. . . . My admiration of moments of creativity is tempered by a word of caution. Such moments often reflect a judge's independent research of the law, or perhaps a detailed scrutiny of critical testimony or exhibits, placing the case in a new light. Or even a remedy that the parties did not consider. While such new insight is always welcome, a court is wise to pause at this juncture. It may be that somewhere in the lengthy history of the litigation the newly discovered "insight" was considered and either rejected or found irrelevant by the parties and the trial judge. Or the point may simply not have been raised on appeal and thus not be available as a basis for decision. So prudence often dictates that the new idea be broached to the parties and supplemental memoranda solicited.

(9) "Blockbuster" Cases. At the "heavy" end of the spectrum of case conferences is the case which obviously will require a great deal of work by the opinion writer. A case may be a blockbuster for any one of several reasons. . . . A conference on such a case usually generates vigorous and lengthy discussion, for the issues have long been clear and views of all the judges have had a chance to become focused and refined. Some judges come to such a conference with their opposing views deeply entrenched. The excitement lies in seeing which way the "swing" judges, those who have been on the fence, lean. Usually the conference ends with two opinions assigned, one to represent the views of the putative majority and the other to represent the

minority. I say "putative" because a draft minority opinion has been known eventually to command a majority. Another blockbuster is the case which, because of the multiplicity of issues and huge record, will require an enormous investment of time. . . . Of the dozen issues raised, none may prove troublesome in the final analysis, but reading the transcript, analyzing and researching all the issues, and organizing and writing a manageable opinion make the task a formidable one. At conference, however, there will seldom be extended discussion. A few issues which look close may be highlighted; the judges will note that the disposition is probable affirmance, and the writer is charged to "read the record." Then there is the occasional case involving complex issues of both law and fact. . . . Once in a while, if a judge has had the time and inclination to do some early digging into the record, he will provide his colleagues with insights which may guide decision. Or oral argument may succeed in distilling from a welter of contentions and facts a succinct, luminous, and compelling capsule that goes far to tip the balance. Generally, however, the conference is not lengthy, the judges knowing that they will not have any reliable "feel" until an in-depth, systematic, and comprehensive analysis has been accomplished. So they put down in their notes a big "?" and leave the initial job to the judge who will shortly be assigned to write the opinion.

PAUL D. CARRINGTON, DANIEL J. MEADOR & MAURICE ROSENBERG, JUSTICE ON APPEAL 29-31 (1976)[10]

As volume pressure has mounted, another measure adopted by appellate courts has been the elimination of conferences among the judges in selected cases. This short-cut is said to have advantages in saving judicial time and in speeding up dispositions.

Many judges argue that after they have examined the briefs and the record and have exchanged memoranda with each other they often find there is nothing further that needs to be said in order to dispose of the case. They may already have recorded their unanimous agreement on both the disposition and a draft of an explanatory opinion. Typically in these cases the issues are seen to be simple, routine, or not fairly controvertible. Also, this view is most likely to be taken where the court has a central staff and that staff has prepared a memorandum and draft opinion. . . . The judges in these situations have a natural tendency to ask: Why hold a conference to ratify the inevitable? Doing so, it is asserted, uselessly absorbs judge time and slows down the disposition rate, to no good purpose.

Nevertheless we believe that the complete by-passing of conference poses too large a threat to the imperatives. The conference is an important assurance of collegiality and also reinforces the individual judge's sense of personal responsibility. Moreover, the conference can in some cases contribute to the quality of the result. The group is sometimes greater than its parts; conferring may yield synergistic results. Accordingly, we advocate the following rule: A conference will be held on every appeal. If there is oral argument, the conference may be held at that time, on or off the bench.

---

10 Copyright © 1976 Thomson West. Reprinted with permission.

If no oral argument has been heard, a case should go on the conference list. Some cases on the list may not in fact be discussed. But calling each case will at least provide a "moment of silence" — in other words, an interval in which the minds of all participating judges are directed specifically to that case. Cases that have earlier been categorized as hopeless or unanswerable can be indicated as such on the conference list. A moment of silence could still be accorded each such case; at least the presiding judge might ask whether any judge had anything to say about any one of them.

The essence of appellate collegiality is that all the deciding judges give simultaneous consideration in each other's presence to the particular case. Unless there is a place and time at which this can occur, assurance is lacking that the decision is genuinely collegial. Not taking up the case at a conference, where there has been no oral argument, removes the opportunity for interaction and exchange of views by the judges participating in the decision.

Whether the oral argument can, in a particular case, serve as an acceptable substitute for the closed conference depends on how it is conducted. If the judges participate actively, the oral argument will involve substantial interchange. . . . When arguments are often scheduled to allow not more than 20 minutes . . . it is illusory to suppose that the colloquy probes deeply into the issues and illumines the path to decision. . . . In any event, a case might be disposed of at oral argument without being listed for further conference if all participating judges agree at the conclusion of the argument that no purpose would be served by further discussion. In this situation, if the judges are in agreement on both the outcome of the appeal and the reasons for reaching the result, their presence together on the bench and participation simultaneously in consideration of the case during the argument, would have provided sufficient opportunity for collegial deliberation to justify dispensing with a further formal conference consideration. Such a mutual decision is, in effect, a conference.

Pressures of volume cause courts not only to bypass conferences but also to overload the conference agenda when a conference is to be held. This pressure must also be resisted. This is somewhat similar to the problem of human capacity in connection with oral argument. . . . There is a limit to the amount of material and number of matters on which an individual can be fully prepared in a single day.

NOTES

1. Begin with the ultimate question: on balance, does by-passing a court conference provide significant benefits? What are the costs? Does it come down to a trade-off between efficiency and appellate process imperatives?

2. Judge Coffin provides a rare insider's account of how judges behave at the judges' conference, characterized by another judge as "the most sacred and secretive of all aspects of the appellate process." James H. Coleman, Jr., *Appellate Advocacy and Decision-making in State Appellate Courts in the Twenty-First Century*, 28 SETON HALL L. REV. 1081 (1998). Conferences tend to be brief, votes are tentative, difficulty and uncertainty are deferred to the writing process. What do you think of Judge Coffin's typology of nine types of case conferences? Note that under most screening procedures some of his

categories would never be put on the oral argument calendar and therefore never be subjected to a conference.

3. Writing in 1976, in the excerpt above, Professors Carrington, Meador, and Rosenberg insisted that eliminating the court conference was an unacceptable expedient that was harmful to appellate process imperatives. Today, screening cases to a nonargument calendar for disposition by judges acting *seriatim* is commonplace. Is there any way of knowing whether the current situation is a necessity or simply is an expediency or both? They went on to put forward a ten-case-a-day absolute limit to estimate the outer capacity of a judge to meet and decide appeals. What do you suppose they would say about the Fifth Circuit's "Conference Calendar," described by Judge Smith in the excerpt in section II, that expects a three-judge panel to dispose of 120 cases over four days? Does the Fifth Circuit have super-judges? That many junk cases?

4. Conference practices vary considerably according to local traditions. Some courts hold a conference prior to oral argument to identify and discuss the important issues in advance. Various state and federal appellate judges have experimented with the practice of sending the attorneys written questions in anticipation of oral argument to provide some focus. One of the most interesting local variations is the Second Circuit's custom for the members of a panel to exchange written "voting memos" shortly after oral argument or submission of the appeal that state the judge's vote and reasoning, usually in a few sentences and no more than a couple of pages. This memo helps to focus the judges, informs the conference discussion of the case, and memorializes the panelists' views for the benefit of the opinion writer. Wilfred Feinberg, *Unique Customs and Practices of the Second Circuit*, 14 HOFSTRA L. REV. 297 (1986).

5. There is a different dynamic to the conference on a COLR, on which all the members hear and decide all the cases *en banc*, as opposed to an IAC which usually is composed of many combinations and permutations of three-judge screening and hearing panels. The Supreme Court of the United States is *sui generis* in many respects, but the High Court has a family resemblance to state supreme courts. "The Conference" refers to the private meeting of the justices when they convene to conduct their judicial business, screening petitions to grant review and voting to resolve cases on the merits after briefing and argument. The Court also refers to itself as "the Conference" as a collective policymaker on administrative matters concerning the budget, staff, and building. Although the Court is a highly-ritualized place — everything is done by seniority, the justices shake hands with each other at the beginning of the conference, the junior justice acts as doorkeeper — the style and tone of the conference is established by the Chief Justice who is *primus inter pares* ("first among equals"). For example, Chief Justice Rehnquist took a no-nonsense approach to briefly summarize each case himself and then, going around the table, the justices briefly announced their views in order of seniority. He discouraged cross-talk and there was little give-and-take. When he was an associate justice, and spoke last in this order, he chaffed at this ritual and expressed his disappointment, as have others, about the lack of debate and discussion or opportunity to persuade. But upon his elevation to be Chief Justice, he changed his mind: "[M]y years on the Court have convinced me that the true purpose of the conference discussion of argued cases is not to

persuade one's colleagues through impassioned advocacy to alter their views, but instead, by hearing each justice express his own views, to determine therefrom the view of the majority of the Court." WILLIAM H. REHNQUIST, THE SUPREME COURT 258 (2001). *See generally* DEL DICKSON, ed., THE SUPREME COURT IN CONFERENCE (1940-1985) — THE PRIVATE DISCUSSIONS BEHIND NEARLY 300 SUPREME COURT DECISIONS (2001) (reconstructing conference discussions from the collections of papers of the justices). The Supreme Court is the subject of Chapter 12.

V. OPINIONS — PUBLISHED AND UNPUBLISHED

In American appellate courts, an "opinion" is defined as "a court's written statement explaining its decision in a given case, usually including the statement of facts, points of law, rationale, and *dicta*." BLACK'S LAW DICTIONARY 1125 (Bryan A. Garner, ed., 8th ed. 2004). This definition says nothing, however, about the dissemination of the document. Today, opinions may be (officially or unofficially) published or unpublished and an opinion may or may not be awarded precedential authority as a preliminary matter at the time of decision.

Opinions are "handed down" — or issued, along with a "mandate," *i.e.*, a brief court order formally entering the appellate judgment — at the time the court releases its decision to the parties and the public. Its author usually is identified by name, but an opinion may be *"per curiam,"* meaning that it was issued in the name of the court as a whole with no particular judge being identified as its author. *Per curiam* opinions often are abbreviated to leave out some or all of the elements of the traditional appellate opinion. Until the truncating of processes began in response to the perceived crisis in volume, there had been no systematic procedure for designating certain types of appeals to be decided by a short opinion. But now that has become a widely-adopted procedure in state and federal IACs. Court insiders refer to the short forms of opinions by many different names. We use the term "memorandum opinion" to indicate a short opinion that is significantly different from the traditional appellate opinion, which is usually more lengthy and involved. We refer to the latter as a "full opinion." A memorandum opinion also is to be distinguished from a "staff memorandum." Considered previously in this Chapter, a staff memorandum is an internal document prepared by a central staff attorney for the judges' use in screening the case and deciding how to dispose of the appeal. Central staff attorneys sometimes do draft memorandum opinions for consideration by the court, however, much the same way that a chambers law clerk might prepare a draft full opinion for a judge's consideration. Opinions also can be "published" or "unpublished" in the case reporters, although this distinction is being undone by computer-assisted research databases like LEXIS, WESTLAW and others. There also has been considerable debate over the propriety of designating some opinions — usually unpublished memorandum opinions — as being non-citable in subsequent cases — sometimes these are referred to as "non-precedential precedents [sic]."

The written opinion is the most labor intensive feature of the appellate process — studies have found that judges spend over half their time working on opinions, so the opinion process has attracted the attention of reformers. This section focuses on the purpose and function of the appellate opinion in all its contemporary variations. What are the distinctions in form between a full opinion and a memorandum opinion? When is each form appropriate or necessary — what are the criteria? When, if ever, is it appropriate to dispense with an opinion altogether in deciding an appeal? What appellate imperatives and public policy issues are involved in court rules that authorize published and unpublished opinions? What are the practical distinctions between these categories? What are the pros and cons of the various rules found in many appellate courts that designate unpublished opinions as non-binding decisions? What is the difference between citable and noncitable opinions? Behind the debate over opinion forms, nonpublication, and noncitation are some subtle yet rather profound questions about the nature of the appellate process and the role of appellate judges.

Ruggero J. Aldisert, Opinion Writing 9 (1990)[11]

The Purpose of an Opinion. A judicial opinion may be defined as a reasoned elaboration, publicly stated, that justifies a conclusion or decision. Its purpose is to set forth an explanation for a decision that adjudicates a live case or a controversy that has been presented before a court. This explanatory function of the opinion is paramount. In the common-law tradition the court's ability to develop case law finds legitimacy only because the decision is accompanied by a publicly recorded statement of reasons.

Announcing a rule of law of the case is nothing but a by-product of the court's adjudicative function. It is acceptable only because the public explanation sets forth the grounds for the decision. Without this explanation, commonly called the statement of reasons, the court's decision would merely resolve that particular dispute presented by parties to the court. Thus, in our tradition, the critical by-product of the decision survives long after the dispute between the litigants has been resolved.

The by-product promulgates a legal precept describing the legal consequence that flows from the adjudicative facts set forth in the opinion. It forms the bedrock of the common-law doctrine of *stare decisis* because the consequence attached to the relevant or material facts becomes case law which is binding on all future cases that come before the court containing identical or similar facts. Case law possesses the same power and force as a legislative act until or unless subsequently changed by the court or modified by the legislature.

Frank M. Coffin, The Ways of a Judge 57-58 (1980)[12]

The Constraint of Writing. A remarkably effective device for detecting fissures in accuracy and logic is the reduction to writing of the results of one's thought processes. The custom of American courts of embodying decisions in a written opinion setting forth facts, law, logic, and policy is not the least of their strengths. Somehow, a decision mulled over in one's head or talked about in conference looks different when dressed up in written words and sent out into

---

[11] Copyright © 1990 Thomson West. Reprinted with permission.

[12] Copyright © 1980 Frank M. Coffin. Reprinted with permission.

the sunlight. Sometimes the passage of time or a new way of looking at the issue makes us realize that an opinion will simply not do, and back we go to the drawing board. Or we may be in the very middle of an opinion, struggling to reflect the reasoning all judges have agreed on, only to realize that it simply "won't write." The act of writing tells us what was wrong with the act of thinking.

One can canvass other kinds of deciders who come to mind and find few who accompany their routine decisions with written explanations. If explanations there are, they are likely to be incomplete, informal, oral, and perhaps meant to be forgotten. Or, if in writing, there is little guarantee that they reveal the real reason for decision. A legislature may vote down a tax increase, invoking impressive economic data; one may suspect that the prospect of an impending election had more to do with the result. A chief executive may announce a policy decision and marshal sophisticated reasons in support; in reality he may have been reacting to interest groups or congressional pressures.

What makes the "in writing" tradition a demanding one for appellate courts is that judges do not write on a clean slate. Prior decisions in other cases of different degrees of similarity demand to be reconciled with, or distinguished from, the present one. If results differ, the court must explain why. While conscientious and competent judges may disagree, the rigors of dealing honestly with facts, of recognizing and respectably treating precedent, and of reasoning logically, reduce the occasions for differences and narrow the gulf of such as remain.

NATIONAL LABOR RELATIONS BOARD v. AMALGAMATED CLOTHING WORKERS OF AMERICA, AFL-CIO, LOCAL 990
430 F.2d 966 (5th Cir. 1970)

Per curiam: ENFORCED. See Local Rule 21.

Brown, C.J. It may seem incongruous that a one-word disposition should have this rather extended opinion as a part of the Court's action. But the purpose of this opinion is not to discuss the merits, or more accurately the lack of merits, in the case under review.[13] Rather it is to advise litigants, parties and the Bar about the Fifth Circuit's most recent Rule 21 [now 5th Cir. Local Rule 47.6].[14]

---

13 [1] The instant case is a run-of-the-mill Board Order finding that the Union had violated § 8(b)(1)(A) of the Act by threatening employees with loss of employment if they did not join the Union. It turns wholly on credibility choices which are amply supported.

14 [2] Rule 21 provides:

When the Court determines that any one or more of the following circumstances exists and is dispositive of a matter submitted to the Court for decision: (1) that a judgment of the District Court is based on findings of fact which are not clearly erroneous; (2) that the evidence in support of a jury verdict is not insufficient; (3) that the order of an administrative agency is supported by substantial evidence on the record as a whole; (4) that no error of law appears; and the Court also determines that an opinion would have no precedential value, the judgment or order may be affirmed or enforced without opinion. In such case, the Court may in its discretion enter either of the following orders: "AFFIRMED. See Local Rule 21," or "ENFORCED. See Local Rule 21."

As was this Court's system for judicial screening of cases [see *Huth v. Southern Pacific Co. supra* Section B] — now rounding out a year and three quarters' experience which continues to demonstrate its fairness and workability — Rule 21 is another response of this Court to the ever-growing explosive increase in the amount of its judicial business.

What is worse, the future both for the Fifth Circuit and for the Federal Courts of Appeals nationwide is portentous, as witness the surveys of the United States Courts of Appeals made by [the former] Deputy Director of the Administrative Office of the United States Courts. These reflect that actual experience in the short space of four years proves that all projections err on the low side. The increases are spectacular for the Fifth Circuit and for that matter foreboding for the Courts of Appeals as a whole.

But even more foreboding, for the Fifth Circuit, we have had to continually revise these nationwide projections upward because of our own demonstrated experience. Within but a year — tomorrow — we will have 2,000 cases and a couple of years more — day after tomorrow — we will have 2,500 cases.

We need not here canvass the causes for this local and nationwide increase. A core cause undoubtedly is the like increase in the nation's population from 150 million to 205 million in the short space of 20 years — a growth which this area more than shares. More directly related to Court operations, quite obviously it is due to the increase in Federal Court business generally. But of unusual significance is the fact that the percentage of appeals taken in both civil and criminal cases markedly exceeds the percentage of increase in trials in the District Courts. For the Fifth Circuit, total District Court trials have increased 78% against an increase of 168% for appeals in the period 1961-1969, and, whereas criminal trials have increased 48%, criminal appeals have increased 210%.

With this staggering prospect now upon us, we can see it is our duty to exercise imaginative, inventive resourcefulness in fashioning new methods and in adapting or modifying older ones, to enable us to at least stay abreast of this flood tide. This means that with safeguards which will assure the proper handling of cases, the Court and its members, up to the maximum physical and mental capacity of each of the Judges, must increase output.

Experience again demonstrates that cases in which an opinion really serves no useful purpose falls into several well recognized groups. Rule 21 undertakes to identify them broadly as (1) through (4). The factor (1) deals with the familiar situation in which the correctness of the Judge-tried case turns on fact findings. Of course, sometimes judicial judgment will persuade the panel that an articulate discussion of factual details is desirable if not necessary. On the other hand, from the standpoint of the function of an appellate court opinion, little is to be served by an elaborate discussion or for that matter a discussion at all on the underlying facts which the Court, after mature study, is convinced are not demonstrated to be clearly erroneous under F. R. Civ. P. 52(a). Closely akin and for the jury trial is factor (2) where the Court concludes the evidence warranted jury submission. There is seldom any need for discussion of the legal standard. And in many cases the law receives no benefit from any discussion of the evidence which the Court concludes is sufficient. These same considerations are carried over into the field of administrative law by factor (3) for cases in which the legal standard is well known and in which the facts are often of a kind which are non-repetitive and completely uninstructive with respect to the illumination of legal principles or as a guide for future conduct by parties or judicial action by administrative agencies or Courts. Factor (4) covers that broad group of cases in which no error of law appears.

As the Rule points out, its application depends upon the Court determining judicially "that any one or more of the following [(1) through (4)] circumstances exists and is dispositive. . . ." But of decisive significance in each of these factors, singly or collectively, is the further judicial determination by the Court "that an opinion would have no precedential value."

It is here that the Court faces a heavy obligation. For as a part of the time-proved hierarchical system, this Court and each of its Judges must constantly bear in mind the distinctive role of an appellate court, particularly a United States Court of Appeals. Foremost, we are a court of review and in the Federal system a court of review of cases in which appeal is nearly always a matter of right, not a *certiorari*-type discretion. That means, of course, that we must determine in each case whether the outcome under review meets acceptable legal standards. But our role does not stop there even though to the parties it is the result we ordain which counts the most.

A most important function is the writing of opinions. Opinions are to serve a number of purposes at least two of which are highly significant. One is that an articulated discussion of the factors, legal, factual or both, which lead the Court to one rather than to another result, gives strength to the system, and reduces, if not eliminates, the easy temptation or tendency to ill-considered or even arbitrary action by those having the awesome power of almost final review. The second, of course, is that the very discursive statement of these articulated reasons is the thing out of which law — and particularly Judge-made law — grows. It is an essential part of the process of the creation of principles on which predictions can fairly be forecast as a basis for conduct, accountability, or the like. All Judges know that in some cases this latter factor may almost completely transcend the importance of the case which is the vehicle bringing the questions forward.

By Rule 21 the Court not only implicitly assumes the responsibility for evaluating this factor, but also is specifically commanded to make the conjunctive judicial determination that an opinion would have no precedential value. Having to make unanimously that explicit decisive determination, and implicitly, the further one that circumstances or factors, other than precedential value, do not make an opinion essential or appropriate, the Court, by the adoption of the Rule, affirms that it must be carefully and selectively employed.

The Court recognizes that it must — the word is must — never apply the Rule to avoid making a difficult or troublesome decision or to conceal divisive or disturbing issues. This means that while Rule 21 should make a real contribution toward the goal of avoiding delays which can often amount to a denial of justice, it must be sparingly used.

The Court itself must be vigilant. We believe we are sensitive now to the factors which would make application of the Rule wrong or unwise or inappropriate.

It is the Court's purpose to heed them and in our own survival assure survival of the system we cherish.

PAUL D. CARRINGTON, DANIEL J. MEADOR & MAURICE ROSENBERG, JUSTICE ON APPEAL 31-35 (1976)[15]

Indispensability of Statements of Reasons. The integrity of the process requires that courts state reasons for their decisions. Conclusions easily reached without setting down the reasons sometimes undergo revision when the decider sets out to justify the decision. Furthermore, litigants and the public are reassured when they can see that the determination emerged at the end of a reasoning process that is explicitly stated, rather than as an imperious *ukase* without a nod to law or a need to justify. Especially in a case in which there is no oral argument, the opinion is an essential demonstration that the court has in fact considered the case. In many circumstances, appellate courts have required administrative agencies to write opinions [to facilitate judicial review]. It is paradoxical for appellate courts to claim the power now to do without them.

On the other hand, it is advantageous that beleaguered courts not expend undue energy and time on opinion writing. It is clearly established that this is the most time-consuming and expensive phase of the traditional American process. Some judges are prone to write more than is necessary and to polish and refine the literary style at considerable cost in time and with insignificant gain for the judicial function. Refined editing is particularly likely when the opinion is destined to be preserved in print between hard covers under the author's name.

The pressures of heavy workloads have led some appellate courts to overreact by curtailing too sharply the explanation that accompanies the decision. Some have adopted the practice of issuing curt or perfunctory rulings that say nothing more than "Judgment affirmed." These and other cryptic styles of judgment orders tend to give an impression of an imperious judiciary that acts without the need to justify its judgments. They should not be used. But this does not mean that lengthy opinions must be employed in every case. A reasonable accommodation is possible.

The Memorandum Decision. A short form of opinion can, in many cases, serve both of the interests involved: It can give reasons sufficient to explain the decision, while at the same time avoiding the expenditure of undue energy or time in trying to lay out a full exposition of the facts and the analysis in deathless legal prose for posterity — and pride. Thus we recommend much more use of the short form.

Memorandum decisions can vary in style and in length. . . . Whatever the length, it is essential that the memorandum decision convey at least three elements: (1) the identity of the case that the judges were deciding; (2) the ultimate result or disposition; and (3) the reasons for the result. In addition, it is often desirable that the issues — or the appellant's contentions — be explicitly stated. . . .

---

[15] Copyright © 1976 Thomson West. Reprinted with permission.

An opinion that contains these elements, even though it be less than a page in length, adds assurances that the judges did in fact bring their minds together on the same matter, and it tells the parties what the judges considered and why they decided as they did. Less than this raises doubts about collegiality and the degree of attention that the judges gave the case.

The full opinion, by contrast, would typically set forth the facts and the procedural history at greater length, and it would spell out the reasoning as well as give the reasons. This latter point is a key difference between the opinion forms. A memorandum decision gives only the reasons; it does not lay bare the reasoning. The full opinion presents both. This important distinction bears on the question of publication or non-publication. . . .

LOCAL RULES OF THE UNITED STATES COURT OF APPEALS FOR THE NINTH CIRCUIT (2004)

36-1. Opinions, Memoranda, Orders; Publication. Each written disposition of a matter before this Court shall bear under the number in the caption the designation Opinion, or Memorandum, or Order. A written, reasoned disposition of a case or motion which is designated as an opinion under Rule 36-2 is an Opinion of the Court. It may be an authored opinion or a *per curiam* opinion. A written, reasoned disposition of a case or a motion which is not intended for publication under Rule 36-2 is a Memorandum. Any other disposition of a matter before the Court is an Order. A memorandum or order shall not identify its author, nor shall it be designated "Per curiam." All opinions are published; no memoranda are published; orders are not published except by order of the court. As used in this rule, the term publication means to make a disposition available to legal publishing companies to be reported and cited.

36-2. Criteria for Publication. A written, reasoned disposition shall be designated as an opinion only if it:

(a) Establishes, alters, modifies or clarifies a rule of law, or

(b) Calls attention to a rule of law which appears to have been generally overlooked, or

(c) Criticizes existing law, or

(d) Involves a legal or factual issue of unique interest or substantial public importance, or

(e) Is a disposition of a case in which there is a published opinion by a lower court or administrative agency, unless the panel determines that publication is unnecessary for clarifying the panel's disposition of the case, or

(f) Is a disposition of a case following a reversal or remand by the United States Supreme Court, or

(g) Is accompanied by a separate concurring or dissenting expression, and the author of such separate expression requests publication of the disposition of the Court and the separate expression.

36-3. Citation of Unpublished Dispositions or Orders.

(a) Not Precedent: Unpublished dispositions and orders of this Court are not binding precedent, except when relevant under the doctrine of law of the case, *res judicata*, and collateral estoppel.

(b) Citation: Unpublished dispositions and orders of this Court may not be cited to or by the courts of this circuit, except in the following circumstances:

(i) They may be cited to this Court or to or by any other court in this circuit when relevant under the doctrine of law of the case, res judicata, or collateral estoppel;

(ii) They may be cited to this Court or by any other courts in this circuit for factual purposes, such as to show double jeopardy, sanctionable conduct, notice, entitlement to attorney's fees, or the existence of a related case;

(iii) They may be cited to this Court in a request to publish a disposition or order made pursuant to Circuit Rule 36-4, or in a petition for panel rehearing or rehearing *en banc*, in order to demonstrate the existence of a conflict among opinions, dispositions, or orders.

(c) Attach Copy: A copy of any cited unpublished disposition or order must be attached to the document in which it is cited, as an appendix.

A.B.A. STANDARDS RELATING TO APPELLATE COURTS § 3.37 (1994)[16]

Publication of Opinions.

(a) Public Access. Opinions of an appellate court should be a matter of public record. Parties should be provided copies of a decision or opinion when it is filed, even if general dissemination is withheld until the opinion is in printed form.

(b) Formal Publication. An opinion of an appellate court should be published in the series of printed volumes in which the opinions of the court appear if, in the judgment of the judges participating in the decision, it is one that:

(i) Establishes a new rule of law, alters or modifies an existing rule, or applies an established rule to a novel fact situation;

(ii) Involves a legal issue of continuing public interest;

(iii) Criticizes existing law; or

(iv) Resolves an apparent conflict of authority.

(c) Citation of Opinions Not Formally Published. Rules of court should provide that an opinion which is not formally published may not be cited, but may be used to establish *res judicata*, collateral estoppel, law of the case, or other similar purposes. . . .

---

16 Copyright © 1994 American Bar Association. Reprinted with permission.

Commentary

Publication of Opinions. The opinions of an appellate court are customarily published in official and *quasi*-official series of bound volumes. The publication of these series, or electronic access to the opinions are the primary means by which the trial courts, bar, and general public are kept apprised of current decisional law. However, routine publication of all opinions involves substantial expense and results in publication of many decisions that are of little interest or use to anyone other than the immediate parties. The total cost includes not only printing, distribution, and storage, but also, ultimately, the rapidly increasing expense of legal research resulting from the proliferation of published reports. Where the point is reached in an individual jurisdiction that these costs outweigh the value of routine publication of all appellate opinions, procedures should be adopted that limit publication to those opinions having some apparent precedential significance. . . .

Citation of Unpublished Opinions. Most jurisdictions that have adopted a limited publication procedure also have adopted a rule that an opinion not formally published may not be cited either before the court that rendered it or any other court. Allowing citation of unpublished opinions creates pressures to make such opinions generally available, resulting in a secondary system of unofficial publication which to some extent frustrates the purpose of the non-publication rule. A rule against citation can reduce but not totally eliminate this problem, because it does not prevent compilation and use of unpublished opinions in negotiation and for other out-of-court purposes.

On the other hand, a no-citation rule permits courts to refuse to consider previous decisions that a litigant desires to cite as having some precedential significance. It also means that lawyers who have access to compilations of unpublished opinions will know of prior decisions that cannot be brought to the court's attention under a no-citation rule.

Vincent M. Cox, Note, *Freeing Unpublished Opinions from Exile: Going Beyond the Citation Permitted By Proposed Federal Rule of Appellate Procedure 32.1,* 44 WASHBURN L. J. 105, 107-14 (2004)[17]

The United States appellate courts have erected a barrier around a large number of opinions by creating rules that allow courts to issue unpublished opinions and then limiting or eliminating the citation of these opinions. For years, some judges and lawyers have been attempting to eliminate the issuance of unpublished opinions. At the very least, these judges and lawyers advocate for unpublished opinions to be freely cited in briefs and arguments to the courts. The most recent attempt to remove the barrier surrounding unpublished opinions is PROPOSED FEDERAL RULE OF APPELLATE PROCEDURE 32.1 [reproduced below].

Beginning in 1974, each federal circuit court began implementing rules that enabled the courts to issue unpublished opinions. Since implementing these

---

[17] Copyright © 2004 by Washburn Law Journal. Reprinted with permission.

rules, the federal circuit courts produce more unpublished opinions than published opinions. Each year, the federal appellate courts label a vast majority of the opinions they issue "unpublished." The state appellate courts also engage in the practice at the same rate as the federal circuit courts.

The negative impact of unpublished opinions is becoming increasingly evident each year. The lack of uniformity in the practices of the federal circuit courts and the state appellate courts creates a conundrum. There is a lack of uniformity, not only as to when an opinion will be published, but also as to how an opinion that is labeled "unpublished" is treated.

The development of the concept of unpublished opinions lends clues to the controversy. The courts introduced unpublished opinions to improve the efficiency of the judicial system. A simple thought produced the original idea: eliminate mundane and unnoticed appellate opinions from those that are published, thereby relieving the appellate system of the extra pressures created by publishing every opinion. Since that original idea, case law, appellate judges, developing technology, and public policy changed the way the utility of unpublished opinions is viewed.

It is necessary to put the term "unpublished" into perspective. The term appears to ring of inaccessibility, but when used in the context of appellate court opinions, "unpublished" simply indicates that a court's opinion will not be placed in an official reporter. For example, the official reporter for the federal circuit courts is the FEDERAL REPORTER; thus, an "unpublished" opinion of a federal circuit court is an opinion that does not appear in the FEDERAL REPORTER. Although an "unpublished" opinion cannot be found in an official reporter, there are several other sources where such an opinion can be obtained. Copies of all opinions are always available with the clerk of the court, and most circuits are now providing their "unpublished" opinions to different internet databases, most notably LEXIS and WESTLAW. Further, the *E-Government Act of 2002* [Pub. L. No. 107-347 § 205(a), 116 Stat. 2899] requires that each federal circuit court maintain a website containing their judicial opinions.

Prior to the 1970s, the federal courts of appeals uniformly published all opinions. This changed, however, as the tide of growing case loads in the appellate courts caused many to rethink the system. . . . By 1974, every federal circuit had created and implemented a publication plan. [E]ach circuit created individual rules. Through 2003, the federal circuit courts continue to operate with independent publication rules.

The problem with the lack of consistent publication and citation rules throughout appellate courts in the United States is painfully clear. Nine of the thirteen federal circuits permit the citation of unpublished opinions. Of those nine, the D.C., Fourth, and Sixth Circuits allow the citation of unpublished opinions for full precedential value. The First, Fifth, Eighth, Tenth, and Eleventh Circuits allow the citation of unpublished opinions for persuasive value only. The Third Circuit permits the citation of unpublished opinions but does not clarify the specific value assigned to unpublished opinions. On the other hand, the Second, Seventh, Ninth, and Federal Circuits do not allow the citation of unpublished opinions for any purpose.

In state appellate courts, the plague of inconsistency continues in the same fashion. There are five identifiable categories into which all fifty states and the District of Columbia fall. The first category contains states that do not have restrictions involving unpublished opinions. States are included in this category because they do not have unpublished opinions or do not have rules against the citation of unpublished opinions.[18] The second category includes the states that allow the citation of unpublished opinions as binding precedent.[19] The next category consists of states that allow the citation of unpublished opinions for persuasive value only.[20] The fourth category is comprised of states that prohibit citation of unpublished opinions.[21] Finally, some states have conflicting approaches which sometimes allow citation, and sometimes prohibit it.[22] Oklahoma, for example, prohibits unpublished opinions issued by its supreme court to be cited for any reason, but permits unpublished opinions of the court of criminal appeals to be cited in some circumstances.

Thus, while twenty-two states allow the citation of unpublished opinions, twenty-three states and the District of Columbia do not. The remaining five states are too close to call to fit cleanly into either category. Although the slim majority of states still do not allow the citation of unpublished opinions, within the last two years at least six states have changed from prohibiting the citation of unpublished opinions, to permitting the citation of these opinions. Therefore, there seems to be a trend in favor of allowing the citation of unpublished opinions.

The debate surrounding unpublished opinions created significant case law across the country. *Anastasoff v. United States*[23] originated much of the controversy. *Anastasoff* involved a tax dispute between a taxpayer and the Internal Revenue Service. The case was before the Eighth Circuit Court of Appeals on the appeal of the taxpayer. In *Anastasoff*, the taxpayer made an argument that had been rejected in a previous Eighth Circuit case. The taxpayer argued that the court did not need to follow its holding in [the previous case]. Controversy ensued because [the previous case] was an unpublished opinion, and in the Eighth Circuit, "[u]npublished opinions are not precedent" but may be cited if "the opinion has persuasive value on a material issue and no published opinion . . . would serve as well. . . ." The fact that [the previous case] was the only case directly on point further complicated the situation. As a result, in *Anastasoff*, the Eighth Circuit held that the rule prohibiting the use of unpublished opinions as precedent was unconstitutional.

In the year following *Anastasoff*, the Ninth Circuit Court of Appeals addressed the issue of unpublished opinions and non-citation rules in

---

18 [40] [Connecticut, Mississippi, New York, and North Dakota]
19 [41] [Delaware, North Carolina, Ohio, Texas, Utah, and West Virginia]
20 [42] [Alaska, Georgia, Iowa, Kansas, Michigan, Minnesota, New Jersey, New Mexico, Tennessee, Vermont, Virginia, and Wyoming]
21 [43] [Alabama, Arizona, Arkansas, California, Colorado, Florida, Idaho, Kentucky, Louisiana, Maryland, Massachusetts, Missouri, Washington, Wisconsin, and the District of Columbia]
22 [44] [Hawaii, Illinois, Maine, Oklahoma, and Oregon]
23 [51] 223 F.3d 898 (8th Cir. 2000).

Hart v. Massanari.[24] In *Hart*, Judge Kozinski directly defended the Ninth Circuit's rule that prohibited the citation of unpublished opinions [which is reproduced above]. Judge Kozinski addressed the rationale articulated by Judge Arnold in *Anastasoff* and found it to be flawed. The Ninth Circuit held that the non-citation rule was proper on two bases: a historical and constitutional basis; and a current policy basis.

On the constitutional front, Judge Kozinski stated that *Anastasoff* was incorrect in concluding that the Framers had the same concept of precedent because "our concept of precedent today is far stricter than that which prevailed at the time of the Framing." The opinion continued that "[t]he Constitution does not contain an express prohibition against issuing non-precedential opinions because the Framers would have seen nothing wrong with the practice."

Addressing current policy, Judge Kozinski argued that although making all opinions binding authority may appear to be a good idea, to do so would eliminate any flexibility in the law. In addition, Judge Kozinski stressed that although binding authority creates predictability and consistency, a court should not be bound by judicial opinions it believes were wrongly decided. Further, he contended that several other practical considerations, most notably the court's lack of resources and time, made the idea of universal precedential value a poor one. . . .

The controversy raised by [these] court cases and the recent visibility of the differences in which the federal circuit courts treat unpublished opinions led to proposed federal reform. In 2002, the Federal Advisory Committee on the Rules of Appellate Procedure announced that it would consider a rule that would uniformly require all of the circuit courts to allow the citation of unpublished opinions. Six months later, the Advisory Committee released the proposed language of [the new FEDERAL RULE OF APPELLATE PROCEDURE 32.1. The Judicial Conference approved the new Rule — which follows — to apply only to decisions issued on or after January 1, 2007].

FEDERAL RULE OF APPELLATE PROCEDURE 32. 1
(Approved to apply only to decisions issued on or after January 1, 2007)

Citation of Judicial Dispositions.

(a) Citation Permitted. No prohibition or restriction may be imposed upon the citation of judicial opinions, orders, judgments, or other written dispositions that have been designated as "unpublished," "not for publication," "non-precedential," "not precedent," or the like, unless that prohibition or restriction is generally imposed upon the citation of all judicial opinions, orders, judgments, or other written dispositions.

(b) Copies Required. A party who cites a judicial opinion, order, judgment, or other written disposition that is not available in a publicly accessible

---

[24] [72] 266 F.3d 1155 (9th Cir. 2001).

electronic database must file and serve a copy of that opinion, order, judgment, or other written disposition with the brief or other paper in which it is cited.

NOTES

1. What are the purposes and functions of a written opinion? How does an opinion further the appellate imperatives? If there were no crisis of volume, would there be some appeals that did not require or deserve a written opinion? Is the crisis of volume alone enough justification to dispense with a written opinion?

2. In the U.S. Courts of Appeals, the one-word "Affirmed" dispositions accounted for 6% or 1524 of the 25,020 merits terminations in 1998. It was used sparingly or not at all in most of the federal IACs, but the device accounts for significant percentages of appeals in a few of the circuits: Third (23.4%); Eighth (20.9%); and Eleventh (16.6%). William C. Smith, *Big Objections to Brief Decisions*, 85 A.B.A. J. 34 (1999). *See also* JUDITH A. McKENNA, LAURAL L. HOOPER & MARY CLARK, CASE MANAGEMENT PROCEDURES IN THE FEDERAL COURTS OF APPEALS 20 (Fed. Jud. Ctr. 2000). The state courts, by and large, have not borrowed the device of the one-word affirmance. Although many states have statutes or court rules that allow for non-published opinions, more often than not they require some memorandum opinion and specifically do not permit an affirmance without opinion. Melissa M. Serfass & Jessie Wallace Cranford, *Federal and State Court Rules Governing Publication and Citation of Opinions: An Update*, 6 J. APP. PRACTICE & PROCESS 349 (2004). When is a one-word affirmance appropriate in an appeal? Why do you suppose this device is neither widely-adopted nor frequently used? Should it be abolished or does it serve some valid purpose?

3. What are the features of a "memorandum opinion" as described by Professors Carrington, Meador and Rosenberg? Is their distinction between "reasoning" and "reasons" meaningful and workable? The NINTH CIRCUIT LOCAL RULES distinguish between a published "opinion of the court" and an unpublished "memorandum disposition" ("memodispos" in insider's slang). The Ninth Circuit judges have developed the following template for memodispos:

> If a panel decides not to publish its disposition (memorandum) every effort should be made to shorten the length of the disposition. Consistent with the objective of informing parties of the court's reasoning, the dispositions should include: (1) Statement of the court's reason(s) for accepting or rejecting the appellant's contention(s), with the appropriate citation(s); and (2) Statement of the result.

> The disposition may but need not contain: (3) Statement of the nature and posture of the case; and (4) Statement of appellant's contention(s) on appeal.

> Thus the following is acceptable: "Smith appeals from her conviction for transporting illegal aliens. Defendant argued that statements she made after her arrest were admitted in violation of her *Miranda* rights. Defendant's statements were volunteered, rather than made in response to police questioning, and were therefore admissible. *United States v. Cornejo*, 598 F. 2d 554, 557 (9th Cir. 1979). AFFIRMED."

But only the following is necessary: "Defendant's statements were volunteered rather than made in response to police questioning, and were therefore admissible. *United States v. Cornejo*, 598 F. 2d 554, 557 (9th Cir. 1979). AFFIRMED."

Professor Wasby reviewed hundreds of unpublished memoranda dispositions from the Ninth Circuit and from other courts of appeals over many years and concluded that there was no single type of unpublished memorandum disposition. Rather, they varied from court to court, from judge to judge, and from case to case. They described a continuum from a few cryptic sentences to far more elaborate documents that were difficult to distinguish from published opinions in style, content, length, and attention to detail. Their content was affected by central staff screening memoranda, oral argument, and the difficulty and complexity of the individual case. Stephen L. Wasby, *Unpublished Court of Appeals Decisions: A Hard Look at the Process*, 14 S. CAL. INTERDISC. L. J. 67 (2004).

4. The Ninth Circuit Rules excerpted above designate opinions to be published and memorandum dispositions not to be published; unpublished memorandum dispositions are designated "not precedent" and their citation is prohibited except in limited situations. These distinctions follow the ABA STANDARDS RELATING TO APPELLATE COURTS § 3.37. What is the rationale for non-publication? What is the rationale for non-citation? How do non-publication and non-citation rules affect the appellate imperatives?

5. In 2004, 81% of all written opinions went unpublished in the U.S. Courts of Appeals. The circuit-by-circuit breakdown was as follows: D.C. (51%); First (45.5%); Second (76.1%); Third (84.4%); Fourth (90.8%); Fifth (89.7%); Sixth (81.5%); Seventh (56.9%); Eighth (62.3%); Ninth (87.2%); Tenth (75.8%); Eleventh (87.8%). ADMINISTRATIVE OFFICE OF THE UNITED STATES COURTS, JUDICIAL BUSINESS OF UNITED STATES COURTS Table S-3 (2004). Thus, the norm for every appeal in the 1960s has become something of a *rara avis* — an opinion is published in only about one-out-of-five cases today. But does it really make much sense to distinguish between "published" and "unpublished" opinions given the availability of "unpublished opinions" on-line on LEXIS or WESTLAW or the court's homepage and in print in the new FEDERAL APPENDIX? Is the concept of "unpublished" anachronistic in the age of the internet? Is it not passing strange that the "unpublished" opinions of the D.C. Circuit can be cited to the Seventh Circuit, but the "unpublished" opinions of the Seventh Circuit cannot be cited to the Seventh Circuit, D.C. Cir. R. 28; 7th Cir. R. 53? More broadly, how can the judges justify a system that permits parties to bring to a court's attention virtually every written or spoken word in existence *except* those contained in the court's own "unpublished" opinions?

6. The state experience with published and unpublished opinions in many respects mirrors the federal experience. *See generally* Arthur G. Scotland, *The Filing and Publication of Appellate Opinions: A Survey of the Council of Chief Judges of Courts of Appeals*, 42 JUDGES' J. 31 (2004).

The pattern of publication for state courts varies from state to state; however, in many instances, the pattern resembles that in federal courts. In other words, very few trial decisions are published; the only

ones that make their way into the reporters are those that are submitted by the deciding judge and are deemed significant enough to
publish. A greater proportion of intermediate state court decisions get
published, although, for some states there is not a policy of publishing
all such decisions. All of the decisions of the state's highest court are
typically published.

Joseph L. Gerken, *A Librarian's Guide to Unpublished Judicial Opinions*,
96 LAW LIBR. J. 475 (2004). Two novel state practices deserve mention. First,
California (along with Arizona and Hawaii) practices "depublication": the
state supreme court can refuse to review a case but then can enter an order
that the opinion of the state intermediate court previously published in the
advance sheets not be published in the permanent edition of the official state
reporter. The rationales are that this summary procedure is efficient to avoid
briefing, argument, and a published opinion in undeserving cases of mere
error correction, not law-making. *Id.* at 487-90. *See also* Michael A. Berch,
Analysis of Arizona's Depublication Rule and Practice, 32 ARIZ. ST. L. J. 175
(2000). Second, the Supreme Court of Illinois promulgated a rule that sets a
cap on the number of appellate opinions that can be published by the state's
IACs district-by-district and established strict page limits for their majority,
concurring, and dissenting opinions. IL S. Ct. R. 23. Mark Hansen, *Illinois
Caps Appellate Opinions*, 80 A.B.A. J. 36 (1994). Are these kinds of caps a good
way to deal with the crisis of volume?

7. Reconsider the account of unpublished opinions and citation rules in the
U.S. Courts of Appeals summarized in the excerpt above by Vincent Cox.
Between Eighth Circuit Judge Arnold in *Anastasoff* and Ninth Circuit Judge
Kozinski in *Hart*, who has the better argument on the constitutionality of
court rules that prohibit the citation of previously decided cases? Are there *any*
constitutional limits on the authority of appellate courts to pursue efficiency
to create procedural shortcuts? Which of the two judges has the better public
policy argument, *i.e.,* assuming *arguendo* that it is constitutional, is it a sound
public policy for a court to prohibit the citation of previously decided cases?
Why? When? Which cases? What about the appellate imperatives? How can
judges tell in advance which ones should not be cited? Should judges be able
to change their minds and re-classify a case from non-citable to citable? *See
also Symbol Technologies, Inc. v. Lemelson Medical*, 277 F.3d 1361 (Fed. Cir.
2002) (choosing sides with the Ninth Circuit).

8. Judge Arnold had written about his views in an earlier article that
squarely anticipated the position he took in *Anastasoff*. Richard S. Arnold,
Unpublished Opinions: A Comment, 1 J. APP. PRAC. & PROCESS 219 (1999).
Four months after the panel decision, Judge Arnold authored an opinion for
the Eighth Circuit on rehearing *en banc* that ruled the case moot and vacated
the panel opinion. However, he was careful to write that the constitutional
issue "remains an open question in this Circuit." *Anastasoff v. United States*,
235 F.3d 1054, 1056 (8th Cir. 2000) (*en banc*). Judge Kozinski likewise has
persisted in his beliefs. Alex Kozinski, *In Opposition to Proposed Rule of
Appellate Procedure 32.1*, FED. LAWY., June 2004, at 36.

9. What does the new FEDERAL RULE OF APPELLATE PROCEDURE 32.1 mean?
How does the new rule address the constitutional and policy questions

concerning appellate court procedures governing the citation of unpublished opinions? *See generally* Jessie Allen*, Just Words? The Effects of No-Citation Rules in Federal Courts of Appeals*, 29 VT. L. REV. 555 (2005); Stephen R. Barnett, *No-Citation Rules Under Siege: A Battlefield Report and Analysis*, 5 J. APP. PRAC. & PROCESS 473 (2003); Dean A. Morande, *Publication Plans in the United States Courts of Appeals: The Unattainable Paradigm*, 31 FLA. ST. U. L. REV. 751 (2004); Martha Dragich Pearson, *Citation of Unpublished Opinions as Precedent*, 55 HASTINGS L. J. 1235 (2004); Amy E. Sloan, *A Government of Laws and Not Men: Prohibiting Non-Precedential Opinions By Statute or Procedural Rule*, 79 IND. L. J. 711 (2004).

10. The COLR is faced with something of a logistical problem when it is called upon to review an unpublished opinion of the IAC — and in many jurisdictions that means in the majority of IAC decisions. The unpublished status of the opinion indicates the IAC's considered judgment that the case does not present any significant issue, so must the COLR automatically deny review? How can the COLR effectively review an unpublished opinion that, as might be expected, is conclusory or superficial, *i.e.*, an inadequate explanation of the IAC's reasoning? Should an unpublished opinion count as creating a split in the IACs that deserves to be resolved by the COLR? Michael Hannon, *A Closer Look at Unpublished Opinions in the United States Courts of Appeals*, 3 J. APP. PRAC. & PROCESS 199 (2001).

VI. APPELLATE ADR

FED. R. APP. P. 33 (1994)

Appeal Conferences. The court may direct the attorneys — and, when appropriate, the parties — to participate in one or more conferences to address any matter that may aid in disposing of the proceedings, including simplifying the issues and discussing settlement. A judge or other person designated by the court may preside over the conference, which may be conducted in person or by telephone. Before a settlement conference, the attorneys must consult with their clients and obtain as much authority as feasible to settle the case. The court may, as a result of the conference, enter an order controlling the course of the proceedings or implementing any settlement agreement.

Robert J. Niemic, *Mediation Becoming More Appealing in Federal and State Courts*, 5 DISP. RESOL. MAG. 13-17 (1999)[25]

For various reasons, including overcrowded dockets, many courts turn to alternative dispute resolution ["ADR"] to resolve civil disputes at the appellate level. . . . The courts of appeals in all federal circuits have some form of mediation or settlement program; about half of the states have some form of appellate ADR process, mostly at the intermediate appeals level. . . .

[25] Copyright © 1999 American Bar Association. Reprinted with permission.

Primary focus is settlement. Pursuant to Federal Rule of Appellate Procedure 33, all 13 federal courts of appeals have implemented processes to help parties resolve issues on appeal . . . in mediation-like processes facilitated by a nonjudicial court employee or other third-party neutral.

While these neutrals have different titles in different courts, their role is primarily that of a mediator. These mediation processes — also called conferences — usually precede the filing of appellate briefs and, in nearly all cases, occur before oral argument. Local procedures identify criteria for determining whether a mediation session should be scheduled. While the first of these programs began in the 1970s, seven started after 1990.

The primary focus of the programs is settlement of cases. An underlying assumption is that lawyers at the appeals level are frequently reticent about initiating settlement negotiations. Without Rule 33 conferences, the appellate process, unlike pretrial and trial proceedings, would present few opportunities for parties to discuss settlement.

Appellate mediation conferences are structured to help parties communicate their interests, identify the strengths and weaknesses of their legal positions, explore the consequences of not settling, and generate settlement options. Mediation might stimulate the development of creative solutions that could not be achieved through traditional appellate processes or by the parties acting on their own. Mediation might also help parties expand settlement discussions by going beyond the legal issues in controversy. Such creative settlements sometimes even resolve disputes not on appeal in that court, as part of global settlements of two or more cases or controversies.

The programs have the potential to benefit the courts as well as the parties. Many courts started their programs to help conserve scarce judicial resources. Settling a case early without judicial action helps reduce appellate docket pressures. This becomes especially important as appellate filings increase while many judges and others are reluctant to increase the number of appellate judgeships.

While most programs focus mainly on settlement, they also address procedural issues and case management. They often help parties simplify or clarify issues and may, without motions, resolve procedural matters. These steps have the potential to streamline the appellate process. Even when cases do not settle, effective case management at the conclusion of mediation can improve the quality of briefs and oral arguments, which can expedite decisions.

Basic program features. Although the programs go by various names, most are essentially mediation programs. Confidentiality is a key element of the programs. The administration and operation of each program is separate from the court's decision-making process. Local rules usually prohibit mediators, attorneys and parties from disclosing the substance of mediation sessions to any judge or nonparty. Generally not considered confidential, however, are the facts that the mediation took place, the bare results of the mediation (for example, settled, not settled, or continued), and any resulting post-mediation filing entered on the docket.

No federal appellate mediation program covers criminal cases. The programs differ, however, in their civil case-selection processes. Because some program managers find it difficult to predict which types of cases are likely to settle, they schedule nearly all civil cases for mediation or select cases by random draw. Other program managers have developed criteria to select cases. For example, some programs exclude certain cases in which a public agency is a party because government attorneys often cannot secure sufficient authority to settle a case. . . . *Pro se* cases are rarely scheduled for mediation because a *pro se* party might view the mediator as an advisor or as imposing a settlement. Prisoner petitions and original proceedings are likewise rarely mediated.

In the 1st and 2nd Circuits, nearly all civil cases docketed (including administrative agency cases) are eligible and scheduled for mediation. In the 6th, 10th and Federal Circuits, settlement discussions are held in nearly all civil cases that meet eligibility requirements. The 3rd, 4th, 5th, 8th, 9th and DC Circuits schedule mediation only in cases in which it appears that program efforts are likely to contribute toward settlement. For instance, cases in which one or more of the parties require a judicial resolution of the issues on appeal might not be deemed likely to settle. These six programs also may consider the parties' expressed interest in mediation, the complexity of the case, the parties' underlying interests insofar as they are identifiable, or the amount of monetary relief requested. In some of these courts, before assigning a case to mediation, mediation staff not only review case documents but also contact appellate counsel by telephone to evaluate the possibility of settlement and suitability for the program. The programs in the 7th and 11th Circuits use other selection techniques, after reviewing all civil cases that meet basic eligibility requirements.

Conference logistics. Most mediation conferences occur at an early stage in the appeal. An underlying assumption by some program designers is that parties' incentives for settlement often decrease as their briefing and oral argument preparation progresses. Early scheduling gives parties an opportunity to settle before they incur the expense of filing briefs and appendices. Some programs have procedures that allow a party to request mediation at any time during a civil appeal, even if the case is otherwise ineligible under the court's selection criteria. Such requests are often granted in any civil case where all parties are represented by counsel.

The scheduling of mediation generally does not automatically toll the running of time periods for filing briefs, transcripts or other matters. If the need arises, the mediator, or the parties by motion, may arrange for enlargement of the time for such requirements. In some programs, the court's mediation office is authorized to dispose of a wide variety of procedural motions that arise in a case.

Generally, mediators work with counsel to schedule a location for mediation convenient for all participants. Where the circuit boundaries encompass large states, as in the 5th, 6th, 9th and 10th Circuits, a large percentage of conferences take place over the telephone. Proponents of teleconferences note their convenience, efficiency, and cost-effectiveness, while proponents of in-person mediation maintain that face-to-face interactions help promote settlement. In the four most geographically compact circuits — 1st, 2nd, 3rd and the DC — most conferences are held in person. However, even in those programs, distant locations of participants or other factors may preclude in-person conferences, and teleconferences are scheduled when appropriate.

Mediation techniques. Most federal programs use facilitative mediation or a combination of facilitative and evaluative techniques. The mediator usually discusses settlement jointly with all parties and their counsel and often also meets separately with each party and that party's counsel. In the 1st and 2nd Circuits, mediators also may make predictions about the likely court outcome or, when appropriate, recommend a specific negotiated settlement. These predictions or recommendations are non-binding advisory opinions of the mediator — not those of the court.

In nearly all programs, once mediation is scheduled, parties — or at least their counsel — must participate. Although participation is mandatory, the mediation is non-binding. No settlement can be reached unless all parties fully consent. A few courts provide for removal of a case from mediation at a party's request or at the discretion of the mediator. In the 8th Circuit, however, participation in mediation is completely voluntary, meaning all parties must consent to participate and a party has the right to cancel a scheduled mediation.

Pursuant to Rule 33, attorneys attending an appellate mediation must obtain from their clients "as much authority as feasible to settle the case." In many programs, clients — not just their counsel — are strongly encouraged to attend. When the client is a corporation or other entity, the client often sends a company representative in addition to legal counsel. Some programs have guidelines governing settlement authority in these situations. For example, a company representative who attends should have authority to settle or, if circumstances do not provide for delegation of full settlement authority, the representative should have readily available the means to obtain approval of a settlement from company officials. Some mediators ask that the person with full settlement authority be reachable during the mediation by telephone.

The mediators. In nearly all of the programs, attorneys employed by the court conduct the mediations. Most of these attorneys had prior experience or training in mediation techniques before coming to the program. The courts also frequently provide additional training. In some courts, senior federal judges or retired state judges mediate some cases.

In the District of Columbia Circuit, the director of the mediation program routinely assigns cases to volunteer attorney-neutrals who meet the court's qualifications. The volunteers are experienced members of the local bar approved by the court for participation in the program and trained in mediation skills. The program director also mediates cases. Although the use of volunteer mediators is quite common in trial courts, this program is unique in the federal courts of appeals. The Federal Circuit requires settlement discussions in certain types of cases, with the parties' counsel scheduling and conducting the discussions. The court's local rule does not require a third-party neutral. The court staff's involvement is limited to issuing notices of the local rule's requirement. This design is also unique among the federal courts of appeals.

For the most part, the mediation programs are available at no charge. Each court funds the administration of the program. In at least one court, the costs for teleconferences are typically borne by the party initiating the call, usually the appellant. In the District of Columbia Circuit, volunteer mediators are reimbursed for out-of-pocket expenses.

State programs. State courts in about half the states currently have appellate ADR programs, generally mediation or mediation-like settlement conferences. The oldest program still in existence began in the late 1970s.

In 17 states, programs are found only at the intermediate courts of appeals. Certain states — including California, Florida and Ohio — have programs at more than one intermediate appellate court. Connecticut, Hawaii, Idaho, Ohio and Oregon have ADR both at the supreme court and intermediate (or court of appeals) level. Montana, Nevada and Rhode Island have programs at the supreme court only; these three states have no intermediate appellate level. The New Hampshire and Vermont Supreme Courts have rules governing pre-hearing settlement conferences but the rules are used infrequently.

State court programs cover a broad range of civil cases, but most courts exclude certain categories of civil cases they deem inappropriate for their program. For example, *pro se* cases are eligible for settlement conferences in only about five programs. The volume of cases selected for ADR varies from nearly all civil appellate cases in some states to only certain cases selected by the program administrator in others. About half of the programs use neutrals employed by the court and about half use outside attorneys as neutrals with some using a combination of in-house and outside neutrals. Fewer than 10 state courts have voluntary programs. For the rest, the parties are required to attend the ADR conference if their case is selected under the program. A small percentage of courts with mandatory programs allow eligible parties who are not selected to opt in.

There are many variations in the state programs. Some details about the programs in Connecticut, Hawaii and Oregon illustrate the types of characteristics found in many other programs. While Connecticut's neutrals use evaluative mediation, Hawaii's and Oregon's mediators generally use a more facilitative approach. All three states' programs make attendance mandatory for cases selected for the program. Except for habeas, juvenile and *pro se* cases, Connecticut's program has covered nearly all civil and family appeals at the supreme court and intermediate court of appeals since the late 1980s. The pool of neutrals consists of retired supreme court justices and retired appellate court judges. Both the attorney and client on each side must be present for the conference. The Hawaii Supreme Court established an appellate conference program in 1995. All civil cases, with certain limited exceptions, are eligible for the program; however, only cases selected by the program administrator or where the parties opt-in are sent to mediation. Volunteer retired judges or justices or volunteer retired attorneys trained in appellate mediation comprise the neutral pool. Each party prepares a pre-mediation statement prior to the mediation. Oregon established a mediation program for its intermediate court of appeals in 1995 and approved a program for its supreme court in 1999. As in Hawaii, the program director screens eligible cases and selects those to be mediated. The mediators are mostly private attorneys but also include sitting trial court judges and some retired judges. All mediators must take a course in appellate mediation. Each party to the mediation shares in the payment of the neutral's fee when a private practitioner conducts the mediation.

Use likely to increase. Appellate mediation and settlement programs have grown over the last 10 years, both in federal and state courts. . . . As litigants get more accustomed to court-based ADR at the trial level, they increasingly may come to expect that similar programs will be available at the appellate level.

NOTES

1. How do the prospects for success of alternative dispute resolution at the appellate level differ from those prospects at the trial level? What are the characteristics of appeals that get settled as compared with the characteristics of those that cannot be readily settled? In designing an appellate settlement program, at least three questions must be addressed. Consider how each should be answered. Who should conduct the conference: a judge on the court; a trial judge; a retired judge; a central staff attorney or some other appellate court staff lawyer; or a practicing lawyer designated by the court who is either paid or a volunteer? What types of cases should be assigned to the program? What ADR procedures should be adopted for conducting the conferences — what approach or variety of mediation fits best?

2. What training, experience, characteristics, and skills make for an effective neutral mediator? What advantages might flow from a conference for the litigants, lawyers, and the court even when a settlement does not result? How can the mediator make a meaningful prediction of the outcome on appeal, if that is important to the parties or their attorneys? Does an ADR program save appellate resources? Is there a concern for undue delegation of judicial authority to the mediator? Is it a good idea to make mediation mandatory? Should it be mandatory in all cases?

3. What is an acceptable settlement rate? How do we measure whether a mediation program is successful? "It is fair to say that the appellate mediation program in the [U.S.] Ninth Circuit has been very successful. In 2003, for example, of the 878 cases mediated, the program resolved 803 of them — a success rate of ninety-one percent. In practical terms, mediators therefore assumed the workload of approximately one and two-thirds appellate judges." J. Clifford Wallace, *Improving the Appellate Process Worldwide Through Maximizing Judicial Resources*, 38 VAND. J. TRANSNAT'L L. 187, 207 (2005). That level of settlement has more to do, perhaps, with the highly-selective criteria for determining which appeals go to mediation. State appellate court settlement rates vary as the features of the programs themselves vary from state to state. But it is not unusual to achieve settlement rates between one-third and one-half of the cases among those that are selected for appellate mediation. Ignazio J. Ruvolo, *Appellate Mediation— "Settling" the Last Frontier of ADR*, 42 SAN DIEGO L. REV. 177 (2005).

4. Relating back to the previous section, private litigants may seek to effectuate a depublication themselves, by reaching a settlement on appeal with the condition that the appellate court vacate a published lower court opinion. *See* Howard Slavitt, *Selling the Integrity of the System of Precedent: Selective Publication, Depublication, and Vacatur*, 30 HARV. C.R. — C.L. L. REV. 109 (1995). The Supreme Court has disfavored the procedure for the federal courts. *U.S. Bancorp Mortgage Co. v. Bonner Mall Partnership*, 513 U.S. 18 (1994). However, state courts still permit it. *E.g., Neary v. Regents of the University of California*, 834 P. 2d 119 (Cal. 1992); *Panterra Corp. v. American Dairy Queen*, 908 S.W. 2d 300 (Tex. Ct. App. 1995).

Chapter 9

COLLEGIALITY, DELEGATION, AND THE DOCKET DILEMMA REDUX

The three previous Chapters have described the structural, personnel, and procedural responses of the state and federal appellate courts to the dramatic growth in their caseloads over the last several decades that was chronicled in Chapter 5. Some judges, lawyers, and court experts were troubled by the wholesale experimentation with the familiar and were uncomfortable with the many permanent changes in the received appellate traditions that took place during this remarkably transformative period. Others characterized the changes as "necessary evils" — emergency measures that were accommodations necessary to the very survival of the appellate courts. Still others championed the changes on their own terms, as positive reforms and improvements that effectively redesigned and modernized the appellate court system for the 21st century. Between the 1960s — when the docket growth began — through the 1970s and 1980s — the peak of the "crisis of volume" — until the 1990s — when the widespread reforms were largely completed — the appellate courts were indeed transformed.

This Chapter seeks to evaluate and assess those various reforms, on their own terms and in terms of the appellate imperatives that are the starting point and the ending point of our study of the appellate court system — the purposes and functions for which we have appeals, appellate courts, and appellate judges in the first place. We must avoid a *faux* nostalgia for some halcyon era that existed only in our romanticized ideas of the past. We must avoid the mistake of modernity to pretend that everything new and different is necessarily better or improved. As we have seen in the previous three Chapters, there has been sea change in our state and federal courts over the last generation. We have drawn a sharply contrasting comparison "before" and "after" the crisis of volume. Thus, the ultimate question is whether on balance the overall quality of appellate justice in the United States today has been improved or impaired by these myriad developments in structure, personnel, and procedure.

The concerns on which this Chapter focuses are collegiality among the judges of an appellate court and delegation of the judicial function to staff attorneys or law clerks. Collegiality and delegation are closely intertwined, and discussion of the two often cannot be neatly separated. Basic questions considered here are these: What is meant by "collegiality" in an appellate court and what is its value? Where is the philosophical dividing line between that which can appropriately be assigned to professional staff assistants and that which must be done only by judges themselves? These questions return us to the beginning of our study to understand the functions and purposes of appellate courts.

There has been a great deal of critical writing and hand-wringing about how the appellate judiciary is turning into a "bureaucracy." But that is a loaded term. What does it mean? Is it necessarily a bad thing? We certainly rely on government bureaucracy in other important areas of public policy. Perhaps our courts are best understood as government agencies that resolve disputes and dispense justice. Admittedly, however, justice is a fundamental public good and profoundly important to the individual and to society. Indeed, as a nation we realize the Preamble's aspiration to "establish justice" by ordaining and establishing the courts. This Chapter considers what is unique about appellate courts and what is special about what appellate judges do.

All those additional law clerks and all those new central staff attorneys are doing something. They are justified by the argument that they are doing things that judges need not do. Therefore, law clerks and central staff attorneys are performing tasks today that a generation ago were being performed by judges without such extensive staffs. Perhaps there was an excess of judicial capacity in the appellate courts before the advent of the "crisis of volume." The question to consider is whether the older division of labor was an inefficient use of judges or whether the new division of labor goes too far in the other direction. Delegation issues get broken down further. The cumulative and subtle effects of deploying legions of central staff attorneys seem to be more troubling to judges, lawyers, and court experts than the multiplying of elbow law clerks in chambers that has taken place over the same period. Why is this so? Is the distinction between "judging" and staff work sufficiently well-defined and adequately administered? Is the background concern that the weak judge or the lazy judge will become overly-reliant on law clerks and staff attorneys a valid worry? Are the best ways to prevent that from happening to create adequate numbers of judgeships to deal with caseload and to select capable and scrupulous lawyers to go on the bench? In Chapter 7, we have seen how the state and federal courts have increased the number of judgeships up to a point, to meet the demands of caseload. Chapter 11 will consider the qualifications and selection of appellate judges. But even a brilliant judge who is also a hardworking judge can come to rely on staff out of necessity and overwork. And what of the fact that sometimes it is the law clerk or staff attorney who knows more of the relevant law or is more familiar with the record on appeal than the judge?

We will imagine the long term future of appellate courts in Chapter 14, to consider the court system we might have some day. This Chapter focuses us on the here and now: the appellate courts we have in the aftermath of the "crisis of volume" — a crisis that seems to have been postponed or avoided, at least for now. This Chapter ends with a return to the docket dilemma: was there any alternative to the structural, personnel, and procedural responses to the "crisis of volume"? In retrospect, perhaps the fact that court after court, state and federal, implemented similar reforms is proof enough of their inevitability. Perhaps the appellate dilemma is a true dilemma in the sense that the appellate courts had no good choice and chose the lesser of the evils. But as students of the courts, we might usefully ask how and why all these courts chose these reforms in common over the possible alternatives. Beyond these considerations, have the reforms caused unintended consequences and a new set of problems for the appellate courts? Are there additional possible reforms in appellate procedures that can be implemented without violating the imperatives? Do some of the reforms deserve to be undone? In Chapter 14, we will reconsider some of these questions by looking into the future of the appellate courts.

The ultimate question in this Chapter is whether our state and federal appellate courts have evolved into a higher form or devolved into a mutated form of their historic past. We have very different appellate courts today than we had four decades ago, to be sure, but do we have better appellate courts as a result of all these reforms? Are the contemporary appellate courts adequate to their important responsibilities? Do they fully realize our appellate imperatives and due process values? Or have the judges struck a Faustian bargain to achieve too much "efficiency" by rationing justice on appeal?

I. COLLEGIALITY

FINAL REPORT OF THE COMMITTEE ON CIVILITY OF THE SEVENTH FEDERAL JUDICIAL CIRCUIT, 143 F.R.D. 441, 452 (1992)

Judges' Duties to Each Other

1. We will be courteous, respectful, and civil in opinions, ever mindful that a position articulated by another judge is the result of that judge's earnest effort to interpret the law and the facts correctly.

2. In all written and oral communications, we will abstain from disparaging personal remarks or criticisms, or sarcastic or demeaning comments about another judge.

3. We will endeavor to work with other judges in an effort to foster a spirit of cooperation in our mutual goal of enhancing the administration of justice.

FRANK M. COFFIN, ON APPEAL — COURTS, LAWYERING, AND JUDGING 213-15, 218 (1994)[1]

Appellate Collegiality: Its Characteristics. "Collegiality" descends from the Latin word *collegium*, meaning a body of colleagues or coworkers. The term fits appellate courts with exactness, for the judges on such a court are a small band of brothers and sisters. They are all peers, having no real superior, their chief judge or chief justice bearing heavy administrative responsibilities but having no more than one vote in any case. Their association with each other is long-lasting, often for the duration of their professional lives. They have differing values and philosophies, but they share the common discipline of the law and fidelity to their court.

I can think of no other contemporary institution that brings to every decision this degree of intimate, equal, permanent, independent, and single-minded collegiality. . . . And although trial judges in a multi-judge court may lunch

---

1 From On Appeal: Courts, Lawyering, and Judging by Frank M. Coffin Copyright © 1994 by W.W. Norton & Company, Inc. used by permission of W.W. Norton & Company, Inc.

together, share experiences with each other, and govern their court in a collegial manner, each is alone in carrying out his or her judicial duties. All of these modes of collegiality are, I think, transcended by that of appellate judges.

Collegiality at its best has several qualities. One is intimacy — intimacy beyond affection, resulting in a deep if selective knowledge of one another. Nobody knows one's societal values, biases, and thought ways better than a colleague. This intimacy is fed from the spring of our common enterprise and manifests itself in an abiding concern for each other and, above all, for the court. There is no instinct for competition; at oral argument there is no desire to appear to outperform colleagues. There is no envy and no sense of inferiority or insecurity. Openness characterizes the relationship. By openness I mean an absence of dissimulation, maneuvering, or exploitation. We say what we mean, and though much of our energy is spent in trying to persuade each other, we rely on the words that clothe the thought. On the whole, there is as little pettiness and enmity as one can expect among strong-minded people working together.

All this is not to say that there are no costs or burdens in the collegial life. Appellate judges lack the autonomy of trial judges, who preside with undivided authority over their own courtrooms. Not only must appellate judges be prepared to live with a certain restraint on their style, but they must compromise on many matters of substance. They write for not just themselves but others also. In doing so, they may chafe under the constraint of consensus. And occasionally they may be outvoted on a significant issue on which they feel strongly. It is during these dark moments that they muse over the paradox of collegiality. They know that they enjoy the respect of all their colleagues. But it is a generalized respect. In any given case, there is no such thing as a respect for one's specific opinion that will carry any weight whatsoever with another judge who has invested enough effort to develop and feel deeply about contrary views. There is absolutely nothing one can do to convince a colleague of the error of his or her ways. And the only way to survive with serenity is to don and wear proudly the sheltering cloak of civility that we call collegiality. I therefore would describe appellate judicial collegiality in hornbook fashion:

> *The deliberately cultivated attitude among judges of equal status and sometimes widely differing views working in intimate, continuing, open, and noncompetitive relationship with each other, which manifests respect for the strengths of the other, retains one's pride of authorship, while respecting one's own deepest convictions, values patience in understanding and compromise in nonessentials, and seeks as much excellence in the court's decision as the combined talents, experience, insight, and energy of the judges permit.*

. . . . A skeptical reader, after reading what I have said about collegiality and conscious efforts to nourish it, may ask whether the endeavor is justified. I think I have said enough to indicate that the opinions of a truly collegial court are bound to be better in substance, style, and tone than the effusions of one judge supporting a result commanding the votes of a majority without any effort to harmonize nuanced differences of view.

What has so far been unsaid is that collegiality is not only a guaranty of top judicial work, it is also a cherished source of joy in the life of an appellate judge. Even though judges may disagree on basic issues, they still — in a collegial court — relish the company of their colleagues and look forward to sitting on another case with them. But the pressures of the times — the escalation of caseload, the emotional overtones of some of the issues, the occasional reporting of internal disagreements by the press — threaten collegiality. It can no longer be taken for granted. It may someday be regarded as a quaint relic of simpler times. If so, we shall surely be the poorer. In the meantime, the paradox of collegiality among independent peers is eminently worth thinking about, planning for, and struggling to maintain.

Harry T. Edwards, *The Effects of Collegiality on Judicial Decision Making*, 151 U. PA. L. REV. 1639, 1644-52, 1666-70, 1683-86 (2003)[2]

The Principle of "Collegiality" Briefly Stated. When I speak of a collegial court, I do not mean that all judges are friends. And I do not mean that the members of the court never disagree on substantive issues. That would not be collegiality, but homogeneity or conformity, which would make for a decidedly unhealthy judiciary. Instead, what I mean is that judges have a common interest, as members of the judiciary, in getting the law right, and that, as a result, we are willing to listen, persuade, and be persuaded, all in an atmosphere of civility and respect. Collegiality is a process that helps to create the conditions for principled agreement, by allowing all points of view to be aired and considered. Specifically, it is my contention that collegiality plays an important part in mitigating the role of partisan politics and personal ideology by allowing judges of differing perspectives and philosophies to communicate with, listen to, and ultimately influence one another in constructive and law-abiding ways.

What is at issue in the ongoing collegiality-ideology debate is not whether judges have well-defined political beliefs or other strongly held views about particular legal subjects; surely they do, and this, in and of itself, is not a bad thing. Instead, the real issue is the degree to which those views ordain the outcomes of the cases that come before the appellate courts. Collegiality helps ensure that results are not preordained. The more collegial the court, the more likely it is that the cases that come before it will be determined solely on their legal merits.

The Mitigating Effects of Collegiality on Partisanship, Disagreement, and Dissenting Opinions. In an uncollegial environment, divergent views among members of a court often end up as dissenting opinions. Why? Because judges tend to follow a "party line" and adopt unalterable positions on the issues before them. This is especially true in the hard and very hard cases that involve highly controversial issues. Judges who initially hold different views tend not to think hard about the quality of the arguments made by those with whom they disagree, so no serious attempt is made to find common ground. Judicial divisions are sharp and firm. And sharp divisions on hard and very

---

[2] Copyright © 2003 University of Pennsylvania Law Review. Reprinted with permission.

hard issues give rise to "ideological camps" among judges, which in turn beget divisions in cases that are not very difficult. It is not a good situation.

I should be clear again that, when I speak of collegial decision making, I am not endorsing the suppression of divergent views among members of a court. Quite the contrary. In a collegial environment, divergent views are more likely to gain a full airing in the deliberative process — judges go back and forth in their deliberations over disputed and difficult issues until agreement is reached. This is not a matter of one judge "compromising" his or her views to a prevailing majority. Rather, until a final judgment is reached, judges participate as equals in the deliberative process — each judicial voice carries weight, because each judge is willing to hear and respond to differing positions. The mutual aim of the judges is to apply the law and find the right answer.

Some commentators worry that, when members of a court have strong collegial relationships, judges may be reluctant to challenge colleagues and may join opinions to preserve personal relationships. . . . In my view, it is collegiality that allows judges to disagree freely and to use their disagreements to improve and refine the opinions of the court. Strong collegial relationships are respectful of each judge's independence of mind while acknowledging that appellate judging is an inherently interdependent enterprise.

Social science studies on group composition and decision making offer some support for the idea that collegiality may make disagreement more comfortable and more likely, not less. These studies indicate that group members who are familiar to each other feel less of a need to conform and to suppress alternative perspectives and judgments. Unfamiliar group members, by contrast, are likely to be concerned with social acceptance within the group. . . .

Familiarity is one of the major components of collegiality, and these insights on the effect of familiarity in groups resonate, to a certain degree, with my experience on the D.C. Circuit. Through the experience of working as a group, one becomes familiar with colleagues' ways of thinking and reasoning, temperaments, and personalities. All of this makes a difference in how smoothly and comfortably group members can share, understand, and assimilate each other's ideas and perspectives.

One of the reasons I believe collegiality encourages the sharing of ideas is that I know the difference between serving on a court that is collegial and serving on one that is not. During my extended tenure on the D.C. Circuit, now in its third decade, I have seen the court go through many different phases and express a number of different moods. It has gone from a divided and divisive place, to one stamped with the blessings of collegiality. . . . On my first day as a member of the court, I was greeted by one of the liberal judges. This judge's first words to me, after saying "hello," were: "Can I count on your vote?" I knew very little of the inner workings of the D.C. Circuit in those days, so I was shocked by the question. I responded by telling my colleague that he could count on my vote only on those occasions when we agreed on how a case should be decided. In short order, however, I came to understand that, in those days, the D.C. Circuit was ideologically divided on many important issues. In those bad times, if two or three so-called "liberal" or "conservative" judges were randomly assigned to sit together, they might use the occasion to tilt their opinions pursuant to their partisan preferences.

In my early days on the D.C. Circuit, judges of similar political persuasions too often sided with one another (say, on petitions for en banc review) merely out of partisan loyalty, not on the merits of the case. In fact, judges might have voted together to hold their allegiances even in cases that had no ideological or political component. The point was that you were not supposed to "break ranks" if a colleague asked for your allegiance. At that time, I believe, the absence of collegiality made it more likely that judges would walk in lock step with other judges with whom they shared political or ideological views. There was pressure to conform along those lines, because there were ideological "camps" on the court. The absence of a genuine sense of being involved in an institutional enterprise contributed, I believe, to a feeling that one was not really free to disagree except along the predictable party lines. When a court is bereft of collegiality, judges become distrustful of one another's motivations; they are less receptive to ideas about pending cases and to comments on circulating opinions; and they stubbornly cling to their first impressions of an issue, often readily dismissing suggestions that would produce a stronger opinion or a more correct result. Judges on our court in those days did not like to receive comments on draft opinions from other judges. In the end, these tendencies do damage to the rule of law. They make the law weaker and less nuanced.

In my experience, judges on a collegial court do not seek advantage in panel composition. When a court is operating collegially, panel members focus on what each person brings to conference in terms of intellectual strength, preparation, and background. . . . In some instances, when a judge on a panel is struggling with a difficult issue, he or she may seek the expertise of another judge who is not on the panel. In other words, in a collegial environment, judges will check their substantive knowledge against a nonvoting colleague's expertise. This process of seeking and giving expert advice has nothing to do with partisanship.

On a collegial court, the overarching mission of a panel is to figure out where a particular case fits within the law of the circuit. The goal is to find the best answer (not the best "partisan" answer) to the issues raised. The judges also think carefully about writing too much on an issue and about deciding issues that are not before the panel. Our mutual aim is to avoid these things. The consequences of alternative approaches are also openly discussed, so that all members of the panel are equally informed. We are looking for a sound basis for decision making, not a strategy for achieving one's preferred result.

The mental states of judges who are engaged in collegial deliberations are entirely different from those of judges on a court that is not operating collegially. On the D.C. Circuit of today, judges not only accept feedback from colleagues on draft opinions, they welcome it, and might even be disappointed if none is forthcoming. When a judge disagrees with the proposed rationale of a draft opinion, the give-and-take between the commenting judge and the writing judge often is quite extraordinary — smart, thoughtful, illuminating, probing, and incisive. Because of collegiality, judges can admit and recognize their own and other judges' fallibility and intellectual vulnerabilities. No judge, no matter how smart and confident, can figure out everything perfectly on his or her own. To be able to admit that one is not perfect and to look to one's colleagues to provide a safety net and a check against error is a wonderful thing in a work environment. The result is a better work product. If one's reasoning or writing admits of ambiguities that one did not intend or legal consequences that one did not foresee, these can be cured through the give-and-take of collegial deliberation. When such flaws are addressed during the drafting of the opinion for the court, dissenting and concurring opinions are rarely required. . . .

Through careful, collective exploration and consideration of the different views of each judge, a product that reflects consensus can emerge. The freedom to disagree with one's colleagues, which is fostered by collegiality, enables judges accurately and honestly, and without hesitation, to identify what is common ground and what is not, all the while remaining open to revising their views. Instead of asking each other, "What is your vote?," judges inquire, "What makes sense to you?"

On a collegial court, if there is to be a dissent in a case, judges will help one another to make dissenting opinions as effective as possible. Dissents become more precise, focused, and useful to the development of the law. In a collegial environment, a dissenting judge can more effectively identify and articulate what exactly bothers him or her about the majority position, because other judges on the panel participate in playing that out. The simple truth, however, is that most cases in the lower appellate courts do not warrant a dissent. The Supreme Court's practice of issuing multiple opinions in a relatively large percentage of their cases is an entirely inappropriate norm for the courts of appeals. We hear too many cases, most of which admit of a best answer. What the parties and the public need is that answer, not a public colloquy among judges. A multiplicity of opinions in a single case can contribute to confusion about what the law is. These days, the trend on the D.C. Circuit is to dissent less and less, because the members of the court can see that collegiality enables all judges' views to be aired and routinely taken into account in the court's judgments. When dissenting opinions are written, they are more likely to indicate the presence of truly important competing legal arguments that ought to be presented to the legal community, the legislature, and the public at large. . . .

Diversity on the Bench in Furtherance of Collegiality. The term "collegiality" may evoke the clubbiness, exclusivity, and homogeneity found among certain privileged classes of people and elite institutions in society. The idea of collegiality among judges perhaps conjures up images of wood-paneled chambers in which judges make plans to play golf. The collegiality which I have thus far described is obviously very different from this. The collegiality of which I speak embodies an ideal of diversity and envisions judges drawing on their differences in the process of working together to get the law right.

There are two major types of "diversity." Researchers on group decision making typically focus on diversity in terms of variations in expertise or information. Researchers on organizational demography focus on characteristics such as age, race, and sex. . . .

The research on diversity in organizations suggests a diversity paradox. Under several major theories, the bulk of the evidence suggests that diversity is likely to impede group functioning in organizations. However, information and decision-making theories posit that variance in group composition can make for better decisions because of an increase in the skills, abilities, information, and knowledge that diversity brings. Diversity is thus valuable when it brings a rich range of information and perspectives. Yet, the same heterogeneity that provides for different perspectives and the "cognitive conflict" that can lead to better decisions may also result in increased emotional conflict, which impedes group functioning.

Research on the interaction between informational diversity and member familiarity in groups suggests another paradox: "[T]he more familiar group members are with one another, the less likely they are to possess unique knowledge or different points of view. Thus, while familiar groups may be better equipped psychologically to resolve conflicts effectively, they may be less likely than stranger groups to experience the knowledge asymmetries from which cognitive conflicts arise. On the other hand, groups of strangers are likely to know different facts and have different perspectives, but they may lack the social ties and interpersonal knowledge to tap into the spoils of their diversity." This suggests that the ideal group performance could be expected from groups composed of diverse yet familiar members. In other words, without familiarity, it is difficult for the group to take advantage of the unique knowledge and perspectives that each diverse member may have to share.

I have experienced the benefits of diversity in expertise, knowledge, and information among my colleagues on the bench. It is clear to me that when the court has been collegial, this diversity has improved our decision making. Differences in professional and personal background, areas of expertise, and ideological perspectives make the deliberative process more lively, rich, and thorough. In a judicial environment in which collegial relations are fostered, diversity among the judges makes for better-informed discussion. As I have written elsewhere, diversity in a collegial setting "provides for constant input from judges who have seen different kinds of problems in their pre-judicial careers, and have sometimes seen the same problems from different angles. A deliberative process enhanced by collegiality and a broad range of perspectives necessarily results in better and more nuanced opinions — opinions which, while remaining true to the rule of law, over time allow for a fuller and richer evolution of the law."

Recognizing the importance of diversity can undermine some reductive assumptions that inform certain scholars' work on judging. For example, judges who are assigned to a particular political category, such as "liberal" or "conservative," or Democratic or Republican, are often assumed to be of like mind and to have policy preferences on most substantive legal issues that are indexed with these political labels. This is likely to be accurate in an uncollegial environment, because judges are more likely to flatten out their differences and allow themselves to be grouped into the most obvious categories available. Just the opposite happens on a collegial court. As our court has become more collegial, I have seen my colleagues become familiar with each other along a variety of dimensions. As a result, the party of the appointing President recedes in importance and the multitude of other characteristics differentiating each judge comes to the fore. When this multidimensional diversity became visible, judges began to encounter each others' differences without the battle mentality that existed in my earlier days on the D.C. Circuit. As judges come to see each other as multidimensional people with a variety of reasons for their different views, it is more likely that they will present and consider a greater variety of legal arguments without regard to whether the arguments are associated with a "liberal" or "conservative" perspective.

The existence of collegiality on a court, then, greatly affects whether the judges on that court will be able to capitalize on their diversity. A court that can use the diversity of its members productively will make better decisions than a court that cannot. I have found that, as my court became more collegial, the judges came to enjoy what made them different. I have thus far been speaking of "diversity" in the sense of differential expertise, experience, and professional background — that is, diversity that denotes the possession of unique knowledge, information, or perspectives by group members. Demographic diversity on a court — such as race, sex, age, and socioeconomic and geographic background, for example — raises different issues. It is more difficult to explain how the race or sex of judges affects collegiality in judicial decision making. Do these diverse voices make it easier or harder to attain and maintain a collegial environment?

Research on demographic diversity in organizations suggests that increased diversity of race, ethnicity, and gender can have negative effects on group functioning because it leads to increased stereotyping and makes communication more difficult and conflict more likely. But, as noted earlier, diversity research also shows that diverse groups have access to diverse information, which may enhance group processes.

My own experience suggests that demographic diversity enhances collegiality. The studies that suggest otherwise are not focused on judicial settings, where judges are equal in status, pay, authority, and position. Most judges on the federal bench are very smart and accomplished, so they are not vying for recognition on these terms. Indeed, we appreciate and admire unique feats of scholarship among our colleagues, because it aids us in our work and brings respect and prestige to the court. I see no reason why race, sex, or ethnic diversity should be disruptive in this context, and I have not experienced it as a disruptive force on my court. If anything, demographic diversity lends to the richness of deliberation among members of a court. In my experience, increased demographic diversity often fosters the informational diversity that promotes improved appellate decision making.

I believe that a collegial court becomes greater than the sum of its diverse parts and that demographic diversity can promote, not impede, collegiality. Why? Judges are whole people who have multiple identities and experiences. But judges also serve as equals who are obliged to enforce the law no matter their distinctive perspectives. "A more diverse judiciary . . . reminds judges that all perspectives inescapably admit of partiality. With this understanding, judges are less likely to fall prey to the temptations that trouble scholars and members of the public who believe that judicial decision making is mostly a product of personal ideology". . . .

Collegiality in Furtherance of Judicial Authority, Judicial Restraint, Principled Decision Making, and Better Decisions. What scholars and other commentators often miss in their assessments of appellate decision making is that shared authority is an essential component of the judicial function. Thus, even in the worst of times, an appellate court must function collegially, because the judges must act pursuant to "shared authority" in the performance of their work.

Although three judges sit together on a panel, they must arrive at one disposition of a case. Whatever their different perspectives, they must channel their views into a collective effort. This is not optional. It is a formal requirement of legal authority. A circuit judge has no individual authority. His or her authority consists solely in joining a collegial product. If an appellate judge does not persuade or agree with at least one other judge, his or her position simply does not become the law. The area of overlap between the positions of panel members is the common ground that becomes the court's holding. Legal authority on the circuit courts thus depends on judicial consensus.

Because finding common ground is a condition of legal authority, judges must invest in building trust and respect among colleagues. Panel judges cannot easily go their separate ways on their own intellectual paths, for they are bound together by the nature of their job. They are quite literally constrained by the consensus imperative. They must find common ground in a case and maintain it, as the tentative agreements reached in conference are translated into the written word.

[O]ver time and over the experience of repeatedly working together, judges become more mature and balanced as they internalize the need for group consensus. They can become temperamentally more flexible, open to persuasion, and less entrenched. They also learn to remain mindful of the partiality of all perspectives. In other words, judges, like other professionals, evolve in their thinking, and we are aided by the wisdom and insights given to us by our seniors, as well as by our time on the bench. After having seen my court evolve over the years, I see collegiality's moderating effect, not only on the decisions of panels, but on the judges themselves, so that as a judge becomes more experienced, he or she develops habits of mind that reflect the constraints of collegiality.

It is my explicit contention that the quality of judges' decisions improves when collegiality filters their decision making. I think there are several qualitative measures suggesting that collegiality enables courts to reach better decisions. First, if, as I argue, collegiality has the effect of removing the determinism of politics and ideology, then collegial decisions are necessarily better in terms of the rule of law. Such decisions are less likely to admit of judges' personal ideological preferences. Judges are more likely to focus only on matters that properly should affect decision making, such as positive law, precedent, the record in a case, and the parties' arguments. Second, since collegiality enables smart people to lend fully what they have to offer to the process of deliberation, judicial decisions made in a collegial environment invariably will benefit from the full range of expertise, experience, intellectual ability, and differing perspectives that exist on a court. The deliberative process is richer and fuller because of collegiality, so the decisions are the product of more rigorous, challenging, and thorough discussion. Third, since collegiality fosters better deliberations, collegial judges are more likely to find the right answer in any given case. Most cases heard in the courts of appeals, both "easy" and "hard," admit of a best answer if judges do their work correctly. It is only in a very small percentage of appeals, involving "very hard" cases, that no "right" answer can be found. Collegiality prevents judges from going astray in "hard" cases and facilitates the process of finding right answers. . . .

Conclusion. The D.C. Circuit has changed dramatically in the years that I have been on the bench. In that time, it has gone from an ideologically divided court to a collegial one in which the personal politics of the judges do not play a significant role in decision making. In reflecting on this over the years, I have come to understand that there are a number of factors that may affect appellate decision making, some that should and some that should not. Among these factors are the requirements of positive law, precedent, how a case is argued by the litigants, the effects of the confirmation process, the ideological views of the judges, leadership, diversity on the bench, whether a court has a core group of smart, well-seasoned judges, whether the judges have worked together for a good period of time, and internal court rules. My contention is that decision making is substantially enhanced if these factors are "filtered" by collegiality. There are cross-fertilizing effects between collegiality and certain of these factors (such as internal court rules, leadership, and diversity), so that the factors both promote collegiality and enhance decision making when they are filtered by collegiality. In the end, collegiality mitigates judges' ideological preferences and enables us to find common ground and reach better decisions. In other words, the more collegial the court, the more likely it is that the cases that come before it will be determined on their legal merits. . . . I also hope I have been able to convey the vital importance of collegiality to the judicial function. For, in my view, collegiality invokes the highest ideals and aspirations of judging.

FRANK M. COFFIN, ON APPEAL — COURTS, LAWYERING, AND JUDGING 224-28 (1994)[3]

General Considerations. Why should dissenting and concurring opinions be discussed in a chapter on collegiality? Because they are ruptures in the cloak of consensus ordinarily worn by collegiality. To the extent that separate opinions are deemed necessary by the writers, to that extent is collegiality diluted. It is therefore the obligation of each member of an appellate court to give serious thought to when, why, and how to indulge oneself in a separate opinion in order to minimize any corrosive effect on underlying collegiality. In over a quarter of a century I have authored some 2300 opinions; in that period I have written only twenty-seven dissents and twenty-one concurrences. That may signal a craven yielding to a majority, but I prefer to think it is rather a testament to the efficacy or real collegial interaction in reaching a result all can accept.

Nevertheless, even in the most collegial of courts, just because they consist of different individuals with different perspectives and values, there will be occasions for the recording of separate views. The values of consensus and independence are in constant tension. . . .

There are several general propositions that can safely be advanced about separate opinions — concurring, dissenting, and *"dubitante"* (a very gentle

---

3 From On Appeal: Courts, Lawyering, and Judging by Frank M. Coffin Copyright © 1994 by W.W. Norton & company, Inc. use by permission of W.W. Norton & clmpany, Inc.

way of dissenting.) The first is: consider a separate opinion only after making efforts to persuade colleagues or concluding, after deep thought, that such efforts would be futile. The second is: before forging ahead, weigh the time involved and decide whether a separate opinion is worth the sacrifice to your regular opinion load. Third, if a separate opinion still seems worthwhile, be brief; a dissenter can usually make his point without assembling a massive scholarly apparatus. And the final caution is: after writing, let the product simmer, then eliminate all the unflattering innuendoes and pejorative words. What follows is a brief listing of subordinate propositions for concurring and dissenting opinions that would generally be accepted by the judicial-legal community.

Concurring Opinions. They are justified:

1. When a judge strongly prefers *a different theory or ground* to support the result, e.g., the judge would not reach the merits because of a procedural bar.

2. When a judge wishes to limit the holding, e.g., the judge concurs in this case involving the interstate transfer of prisoners but would not extend this to apply to an intrastate transfer.

3. When a judge wishes to expand a holding, e.g. the judge points out that the instant case by its reasoning and holding effectively overrules a precedent.

4. When a judge wishes to *expand the majority's reasoning* on a particular point, e.g., the judge wishes to drive home a point to the bar or the trial courts, or to address a dissenter's argument in a more thorough manner than would fit the court's opinion.

A judge should never merely declare that she concurs. This is no more illuminating and less quotable, than two examples: "I concur in the result and so much of the opinion as supports the result." And this gem, delivered by an Irish chief justice, after hearing the view of his two colleagues: "I agree with the decision of my brother on the right for the reasons stated by my brother on the left."

Dissenting Opinions. A concurrence is like a fencing foil; it elegantly makes its usually bloodless points. A dissent, on the other hand, is more like a broadsword. It takes more resolution and commitment to wield it and there is the expectation of drawing at least a little blood. In any event, there is a feeling of unjudicial glee as one shucks off the normal restraints of writing for a panel and proceeds to thrust and parry with gay abandon. For this very reason, we judges are well advised to resist the temptation unless we find a compelling interest and no more effective alternative. Sometimes, however, a dissent is the precise instrument that should be used. This occurs:

1. When the dissenter feels that a *serious mistake of the law* has been made *on a significant issue* that is *likely to recur*. I have noted three prerequisites: a mistake that is serious, not minor; an issue that is significant, not trivial; and an issue that is likely to recur, not one relating to a law that has just been repealed. The dissent in such a case alerts the non-panel members of the court of a likely petition for rehearing *en banc* and serves also as a flag to the Supreme Court if further review is sought.

2. When all the judges on the panel feel that the *issue is close* and that a dissent will sharpen the focus and reflect the closeness. In such a case the dissenter is acting with his colleagues' blessing.

3. When the dissenter feels that her panel colleagues have *erred as to the facts*, *e.g.*, in finding a sufficiency or insufficiency of evidence to support a verdict, or *erred as to procedure*, *e.g.*, in considering the merits of an issue in the absence of an adequate objection or request. In such cases, the dissenter's motive may be solely to keep her colleagues honest or at least deter their transgressions.

4. When the dissenter feels strongly enough about the *injustice of a rule* or precedent that he wishes to send a signal to bench and bar, the state courts, the legislature, the law schools, and commentators underscoring the inequity, anomaly, or inconsistency and calling for change.

5. When the dissenter feels strongly enough about the *conduct of the judges or lawyers* involved in the case to issue her own warning to the prosecutor, plaintiff's or defense counsel, or trial court. Even though the majority may not have found reversible error in the proceedings, the unvarnished indignation of a dissenter may serve a useful purpose.

NOTES

1. What is "collegiality" and why is it important to appellate judges and appellate courts? Why is it so important to Judge Frank Coffin in the reading above? In his book, he lists several "do's" and "don'ts" for judges. Don'ts: hardening attitudes about a case or issue prematurely; taking too long to circulate a draft opinion or taking too long to respond to another's draft; using corrosive language and *ad hominem* arguments in concurring and dissenting opinions; lobbying for judicial favors and votes; expecting too many additions or deletions or rejecting an approach without offering a substitute. Do's: being aware of personal strengths and weaknesses as well as the strengths and weaknesses of colleagues; anticipating and being sensitive to others' sensibilities; and responding respectfully and in kind to others and their work product. All this is pretty much the Golden Rule. What is there about the nature of appellate courts and the work of appellate judges that places such a premium on collegiality? *See generally* Deanell Reece Tacha, *The "C" Word: On Collegiality*, 56 OHIO ST. L. J. 585 (1995).

2. Recall the discussion in Chapter 7, about adding judges as one of the personnel responses to the crisis of volume. The number of U.S. circuit judgeships increased 275%, from 65 to 179, between 1950 and 1990. When he was first appointed to the bench, Judge Coffin was one of only three judges on the U.S. First Circuit who sat together, today he is one of ten judges who sit together in various combinations of three-judge panels. That increase made an "enormous" difference to him, yet his court of appeals is still the smallest bench among the federal IACs:

> The difference in the collegial atmosphere between sitting with all of one's colleagues each month and sitting with each only once or twice or even three times a year is enormous. How much knowledge, conscious and unconscious, of each other's strengths, biases, and foibles I present in the first situation and how little in the second. How much motivation is present to establish the most harmonious relationships,

to cater to particular habits and tastes, to minimize differences in the first situation and how little in the second. If we have to deal with someone all the time, unadulterated self-interest leads us to try to make the experience enjoyable. But if we sit with another judge only once or twice a year, there is less incentive to try to forge an open, relaxed, and trustful relationship. In such event, each sitting of a court approaches the convening of a panel of polite strangers.

FRANK M. COFFIN, ON APPEAL — COURTS, LAWYERING, AND JUDGING 216 (1994). Consider the improvement of collegiality from downsizing a court. The former U.S. Fifth Circuit (26 judges) was split in 1981 to create the new U.S. Fifth Circuit and the new Eleventh Circuit. Judge Tjoflat served on the jumbo former Fifth Circuit and then the Eleventh Circuit, which is less than half the size of his former court. From his experiences, he is convinced that degraded collegiality is a significant diseconomy of scale in large courts that render them overall less efficient and less coherent. Gerald Bard Tjoflat, *More Judges, Less Justice*, 79 A.B.A. J. 70, 72 (1993). Also reconsider the common practice in the federal IACs of relying on visiting judges from other circuits and from the district courts to fill-in on three-judge panels. Are there potential harms to collegiality from this practice?

3. How is Judge Harry Edwards' understanding of collegiality reflected in the reading above different from Judge Coffin's? How is it similar? Judge Edwards claims it has almost magical powers: collegiality mitigates partisanship, disagreement, and dissent; collegiality amplifies the positive aspects of diversity; collegiality furthers judicial authority, judicial restraint, and principled decisionmaking. Do you believe his claims? What do you think about the following example he gives for how collegiality affects judicial decision-making:

A very good example of what I am talking about is the recent decision of the D.C. Circuit in *United States v. Microsoft Corp.* [253 F.3d 34 (D.C. Cir. 2001) (*en banc*)] I cannot discuss the merits of the case or any of its substantive details, but I can say that the work of the court was a model of collegial decision making. The issues in the case were as difficult as any that I have seen in my twenty-three years on the bench, and, at least when measured by public attention, the case was one of the most important ever heard by the D.C. Circuit.

After many months of deliberations, the court sitting *en banc* issued a unanimous, unsigned, 125-page opinion. There was great irony in this. Months before we heard argument, THE WASHINGTON POST had published an article on the likely outcome of any appeal in the D.C. Circuit. The headline read, "A Game of Judicial Roulette: Microsoft's Fate Could Hinge on Which Judges Hear Appeal," and the article predicted that the court's decision would be a matter of "dumb luck," "judicial lotto," and "blue-bucket bingo," clearly implying that the political leanings of the judges would outweigh any other considerations in the court's ruling. In July of 2001, following the issuance of our opinion, the POST published a very different story. The POST article stated:

Seven judges of extremely diverse politics took on a politically divisive case that involved a complex record and had significant implications for the national economy. Defying almost all predictions, they put ideology aside and managed to craft a ruling that every member of the court could sign in its entirety. The D.C. Circuit did not look much like a partisan battleground last week. Rather, its judges looked, well, like judges — neutrally applying complicated precedents to even more complicated facts and striving successfully to get the right answer.

A decision like Microsoft is forged as much out of *productive disagreement* as out of agreement. Through careful, collective exploration and consideration of the different views of each judge, a product that reflects consensus can emerge. The freedom to disagree with one's colleagues, which is fostered by collegiality, enables judges accurately and honestly, and without hesitation, to identify what is common ground and what is not, all the while remaining open to revising their views. Instead of asking each other, "What is your vote?," judges inquire, "What makes sense to you?"

Harry T. Edwards, *The Effects of Collegiality on Judicial Decision Making*, 151 U. PA. L. REV. 1639, 1650-51 (2003). *See also* Lewis A. Kornhauser & Lawrence G. Sager, *The One and the Many: Adjudication in Collegial Courts*, 81 CAL. L. REV. 1 (1993).

4. In the excerpt above, Judge Edwards discusses the interplay between diversity and collegiality. Would you expect judges to take different approaches to deciding an appeal and to reach different results as a consequence of their ideology or gender or race or other demographic indicators? *See, e.g.*, Heather Elliot, *The Difference Women Judges Make: Stare Decisis, Norms of Collegiality, and "Feminine Jurisprudence" a Research Proposal*, 16 WIS. WOMEN'S L. J. 41 (2001); Tracey E. George, *Court Fixing*, 43 ARIZ. L. REV. 9 (2001); Cass R. Sunstein, *et al.*, *Ideological Voting On Federal Courts of Appeals: A Preliminary Investigation*, 90 VA. L. REV. 301 (2004).

5. According to Judge Coffin's criteria in his second excerpt above, when is it appropriate for a judge to publish a separate concurring opinion or dissenting opinion? If you were an appellate judge, what personal guidelines would you follow? What should be the tone of such judicial exchanges? Do some of the Supreme Court opinions in your constitutional law casebook violate Judge Coffin's standards or your own standards? Judge Winter gives two pragmatic reasons for avoiding writing opinions in purple prose:

Intemperate dissent has two *sequelae* which are extremely undesirable. When the dissenting language becomes excessive, it can easily be construed as a personal attack on a fellow judge, the judge whose vote you hope to capture tomorrow. Personal animosity makes future agreement more difficult. An even more important consideration, however — and this I think is the overriding one — is that a court is a very fragile institution. We couldn't possibly go out and enforce all of our decrees and all of our judgments. We don't have the staff; the marshals could not do it. Our effectiveness depends upon people accepting our judgments and abiding by our decisions willingly. We rely on public confidence and public acceptance. When the public sees that we're hurling words that verge on insult, especially on a point about which there can legitimately be an intellectual difference, we destroy the very basis on which we must ultimately depend.

Harrison L. Winter, *Goodwill and Dedication*, in THE FEDERAL APPELLATE JUDICIARY IN THE 21ST CENTURY 167, 169 (Cynthia Harrison & Russell R. Wheeler, eds., Fed. Jud. Ctr. 1989).

6. Does modern technology, like teleconferencing or e-mail, etc., increase or decrease the quality of collegiality among appellate judges? Does authentic collegiality depend on "quality time" judge-to-judge? Michael R. Murphy, *Collegiality and Technology*, 2 J. APP. PRAC. & PROCESS 455, 455 (2000) ("Some innovations may benefit communications with speed or cost containment, but they do not necessarily advance the quality of communication and can even generate friction with collegiality.").

7. The patterns of dissent in state COLRs during the period of the crisis of volume present some interesting trends:

> The most important studies of dissent including all fifty state supreme courts were conducted using data from the early to mid-1960s, but during this period, there was not much variation in dissent. Fewer than ten states produced dissents in 20 percent or more of their cases, and only the supreme courts in Michigan, Pennsylvania, and New York produced dissents at or above the 40 percent mark. . . .

> [V]ery high levels of dissent still are the exception in the fifty states. Only thirteen states had dissent rates at or above 25 percent, although three others were very close. Comparisons across the years, however, show considerable growth in the level of dissent. In 1974-75, only eight state supreme courts produced dissents in 25 percent or more of their cases. In 1966, there were seven, in 1941, five, and in 1916 only two states had dissent levels at or above 25 percent.

> The mean percentage of cases involving dissents also has risen from approximately 12 percent in 1941 and 1966 to nearly 15 percent in 1974-75 and to over 18 percent in 1980-81. Variation among states in dissent rates increased a little in 1980-81, but . . . the figures suggest a general upward shift in the level of dissent in most of the states. Comparison of individual states between 1966 and 1980-81 confirms a general pattern toward more dissents: thirty-eight state supreme courts experienced increased levels of dissent between 1966 and 1981 and only ten experienced decreased levels of dissent.

> On a number of state supreme courts, levels of dissent rose dramatically between 1966 and 1980-81, suggesting that important changes have occurred in state judicial politics. For example, the New Jersey Supreme Court, described in the 1970s as very harmonious and cohesive, increased its level of dissent from 7.1 percent in 1966 (1.6 percent in 1974-75) to slightly more than 30 percent in 1980-81. Courts in about a dozen other states have doubled or nearly tripled their rates of dissent since the 1960s.

> Yet there are a few large changes in the opposite direction. A remark-able decrease occurred in the Michigan Supreme Court, often described

as a partisan, contentious, and divided court. In 1980-81, it had a dissent rate of 24 percent and ranked sixteenth, compared with its rank as number one in dissents in 1966 at 46.5 percent. The New York and Pennsylvania supreme courts, also often described as very contentious with high levels of dissent, have decreased their levels in 1966 of around 40 percent to 25.3 and 32.8 percent, respectively, in 1980-81.

Henry R. Glick & George W. Pruet, Jr., *Dissent in State Supreme Courts: Patterns and Correlates of Conflict* in JUDICIAL CONFLICT AND CONSENSUS: BEHAVIORAL STUDIES OF AMERICAN APPELLATE COURTS 199, 200-203 (Sheldon Goldman & Charles M. Lamb, eds. 1986).[4] What factors might explain the increase in the number and frequency of dissents in state COLRs that seems to coincide with the crisis of volume? What about some of the factors we have been studying: workload pressures, creation of IACs, discretionary jurisdiction, changes in the makeup of the caseload, increased staffing, etc.?

8. Finally, consider collegiality in the larger context of workload and workplace, *i.e.*, the quality of judicial life: "In the face of suffocating caseloads, swelling bureaucracy, and proliferating error, the major constraint on appellate discretion is probably judicial collegiality, which involves the 'unremitting criticism' by one judge of another's 'perceptions, premises, logic and values.'" Patricia M. Wald, *Some Thoughts on Judging as Gleaned from One Hundred Years of the Harvard Law Review and Other Great Books*, 100 HARV. L. REV. 887, 905 (1987).

II. DELEGATION

RICHARD A. POSNER, THE FEDERAL COURTS: CHALLENGES AND REFORM 139-51 (1996)

[Reread this excerpt in Chapter 7, Section II, at page 483]

Wade H. McCree, Jr., *Bureaucratic Justice: An Early Warning*, 129 U. PA. L. REV. 777, 787-94 (1981)[5]

When I first became a judge, we were still operating with one clerk. Later, we had two. While I never served under the present system of three clerks, I am not sure that I could really use three clerks and still believe that I was the one . . . "who had the last word." In any event, it seems to me undesirable that we move beyond three clerks. There are inherent limits to the amount and types of work that can safely be delegated to clerks. Perhaps of greater importance, there are limits to the amount of time and energy that any one person can be expected to devote to the supervision of even the brightest of law clerks. It is not enough that the judge be sufficiently satisfied with the clerk's work that he is willing to sign it. The judge must make the critical decisions in the analysis and the execution

---

[4] Copyright © 1986 The University Press of Kentucky. Reprinted with permission.

[5] Copyright © University of Pennsylvania Law Review. Reprinted with permission.

of the work. Clerks are certainly helpful in relieving judges of some of the burden, but it is the judge who was appointed to weigh the issues in every case, and there are limits to the number of cases he can personally judge. Finally, the increase in the number of clerks may significantly alter the role of the clerk. Rather than critiquing and testing judicial work, clerks may come to perform this work themselves. All of these considerations raise doubts in my mind as to the wisdom of further increasing the role of law clerks in the judicial process.

A development that I regard with even greater concern, however, is the growth — I might say cancerous growth — of central staff attorneys' offices. . . . Central staff attorneys perform a variety of functions, including several that are grounds for some concern. They make initial recommendations whether cases warrant oral argument and how they should be decided. In some cases for which they deem oral argument unnecessary, they prepare draft opinions for consideration by a panel of judges. These arrangements, while contributing generally to the development of a more bureaucratic judicial process, are at odds in several specific respects with traditional notions of the judicial office. [W]e have long expected that the judge "will do his own work," and that he will be directly involved in the decisionmaking process. Similarly, we have expected that judges hear whatever claims are brought before them. The widespread use of staff attorneys creates the possibility that these expectations will not be realized.

While I have no statistics to support my conjecture, I would not be surprised if the press of business might tempt some judges to give the briefs in cases deemed unworthy of judicial attention a cursory look at best. Indeed, I have seen many opinions in the last few years that contain substantial internal evidence of cursory judicial examination. It is not at all rare to see unpublished, *per curiam* opinions containing obvious logical — and even grammatical — flaws, all carried beneath the names of three judges whose published opinions generally demonstrate clear thinking and precise writing. One explanation of this phenomenon is that such opinions are not authored in chambers and receive only the most fleeting consideration when they reach the judge's desk. This phenomenon gives substance to fears that the use of staff attorneys will alter our traditional expectation that judges hear whoever comes before their court. More obvious, perhaps, is the stark contrast between poorly reasoned and written opinions and our fundamental expectation that judicial decisions will be accompanied by reasoned justifications.

Delegation of some aspects of the judge's work is essential, as is no doubt true of much of the work of many other public officials. Such delegation appears particularly desirable against the background of overloaded dockets. But we must not lose sight of the fundamental changes in the nature of the judicial enterprise that may accompany delegation of too many or too critical aspects of the judge's work.

On one level, excessive delegation results in a product shaped by people other than the men and women chosen because of their "wisdom, uprightness, and learning." We might well repose considerably less "trust and confidence" in a group of faceless assistants than we do in the appointed judge. On another level, excessive delegation poses a threat to the traditional institutional structure of the judicial office. We can no longer count on receiving the personal attention of a judge who is insulated by layers of staff.

Elimination of time-consuming oral argument and considered opinions in cases deemed meritless is another of the palliatives increasingly used to reduce the burden of the caseload. . . . Such summary justice may be necessary in our society today. But in my judgment it is efficiency achieved at too great a cost. My experience as a judge of the Sixth Circuit Court of Appeals leads me to believe that oral argument, although sometimes fruitless, is often useful for both the bench and bar. Points not clearly made in briefs can often be forcefully made in oral argument, or at least adequately explained as a result of persistent questioning. Cases that clearly seem to be "predestined . . . to affirmance without opinion," to use Cardozo's phrase, sometimes seem less predestined after oral argument. Oral argument is the most visible, and often the most effective, form of "dialogue" between judge and litigant. Curtailment of this type of exchange further alters our perception of the judicial office as a personal one.

Little need be said about the desirability of opinions. All of us have had seemingly brilliant ideas that turned out to be much less so when we attempted to put them to paper. Every conscientious judge has struggled, and finally changed his mind, when confronted with the "opinion that won't write." We can only guess at the number of decisions "affirmed without opinion" that might have been reversed had a judge attempted to write an opinion explaining the announced result. Moreover, a five- or ten-word opinion provides neither the litigants nor the rest of us with the reasoned analysis central to the judge's enterprise. This development, together with the use of staff attorneys to screen cases, the reductions in oral arguments, and the increasing delegation of responsibilities to law clerks, seems to strike close to the heart of traditional notions of the judicial process. These changes subtly alter what I have termed the "personal" character of the judicial office. Judges may no longer hear every case, but only the important ones. They may no longer engage in genuine dialogue with litigants nor be expected to give reasons for the decisions they announce. These changes ultimately may prove unimportant. In light of the traditional importance of the personal character of the judicial office, however, a miscalculation might prove costly. I recognize that there is room for considerable difference of opinion on this issue. My point is simply that these are costs that must be weighed against the benefits of the changes in the federal courts system.

Lest my uneasiness be thought the mere speculations of a curmudgeon, a judge turned lawyer, let me briefly describe the experience of one state appellate court, which may serve, if not to reveal the difficulties that are present in the federal courts today, at least to highlight the difficulties that await the federal court system. In a recent article, political scientist John Wold reported on his study of the California Court of Appeal. [John T. Wold, *Going Through the Motions: the Monotony of Appellate Court Decisionmaking*, 62 JUDICATURE 58 (1978).] Professor Wold and a colleague interviewed forty-one of the fifty-six judges of the California Court of Appeal, the state's intermediate court, which sits in thirteen divisions in five districts. The court, like many others, has experienced an explosive increase in litigation. . . . The candor with which the judges discussed their work is commendable; what they had to say is frightening. For instance, one judge remarked, "We have chances for creativity a couple of times a year, maybe. But we're too busy to think that much. We give each case full consideration, but this is essentially an assembly line."

Apparently, the only way that the system works at all is through a procedure whereby incoming cases are screened by permanent central staff attorneys who weed out appeals that they consider non-meritorious. The staff then prepares memorandum opinions in those cases. As Professor Wold said in his article: "The staff product does not become the decision of the court until the judges themselves adopt it. But judicial adoption, perhaps with minor modifications, is typically perfunctory, and the memoranda are eventually handed down as 'By-the-Court' opinions." Significantly, some judges complained that not enough cases were delegated to the staff.

With respect to the opinions that they wrote, the judges noted that they did not receive credit under the court's "unofficial quota system" for writing separate concurrences or dissents, thereby creating an institutional bias in favor of unanimous decisions even in concededly difficult cases. With disarming candor, one judge said, "I hate to say this, but just the workload alone may encourage one judge to agree with the others, because otherwise he or she would have to write a dissenting opinion." The judges also noted that a callousness had developed out of boredom, and that "they constantly had to remind themselves that all cases deserved their close scrutiny, since appeals sometimes proved to be much more deserving of attention than they appeared at first glance."

I would venture to guess that the situation that is developing in the federal courts of appeals is not different in kind from that which is portrayed in Professor Wold's study. The remedies with which we are experimenting in the federal courts have been tested in California, and they have clearly failed to solve the problem. The system of churning out staff-generated *per curiam* opinions in the intermediate appellate court was recently described by Chief Justice Bird of the California Supreme Court as "turning our appellate justices into administrators processing paper in a large bureaucracy, rather than judges writing opinions."

In the eyes of a number of observers, the changes in judicial administration adopted in California have altered the character of the judicial office. It is difficult, if not impossible, to square the image of "administrators processing paper in a large bureaucracy" with the traditional view of judging as a "personal" business centering on dialogue and reasoned analysis. To return to Justice Brandeis for a moment, can the judges who hand down these *per curiam* opinions say that they "do their own work"? And if they cannot, will they continue to command our respect?

Harry T. Edwards, *The Rising Work Load and Perceived "Bureaucracy" of the Federal Courts: A Causation-Based Approach to the Search for Appropriate Remedies,* 68 IOWA L. REV. 871, 879-90 (1983)[6]

The Bureaucratization Thesis. The recent growth in the size and complexity of the federal judiciary has generated concern among judges and commentators that the federal courts, like the executive and legislative branches of

---

[6] Copyright © 1983 Iowa Law Review. Reprinted with permission.

government, may become bureaucratic organizations. In the face of an onslaught of cases, we have seen significant increases in the number of federal judges and in the size of their personal staffs, the creation of new central legal staffs to screen cases and otherwise assist in the decision-making process, expanding reliance on "subjudges" — for example, special masters and magistrates — and the emergence of centralized administrative structures like the Judicial Conference and the Administrative Office. These changes, many observers fear, threaten to displace our traditional conception of the judging function, characterized as it is by solitary craftsmanship and collegial arbitration. There is also concern that these changes are the seeds of destruction of our traditional system of judicial administration, the hallmarks of which are independence, decentralization, and individualism, and will cause it to be replaced with some form of institutionalized or bureaucratic justice.

A reference to bureaucratization, however, can encompass a host of divergent problems, and the phrase "bureaucratic justice" has thus become an epithet for critics of many different trends in judicial administration, some of which are quite unrelated to organizational size and complexity. Professor Owen Fiss attempts to bring some order to the debate by grounding an analysis of the bureaucratization problem in two very different intellectual traditions. [Owen M. Fiss, *The Bureaucratization of the Judiciary*, 92 YALE L. J. 1442 (1983).] [T]he first such tradition, associated with the work of Max Weber, views bureaucratic behavior as excessively rigid rule-governed conduct. This conception of bureaucracy . . . is not strongly implicated by either the expansion of the federal judiciary or the recent changes in judicial administration. Although it is possible to imagine the degeneration of current appellate screening mechanisms into overly programmed, rule-governed assembly lines . . . bureaucracy in the sense of "Rule by Rules" is unlikely to overtake the federal judiciary.

There is a second intellectual tradition concerned with bureaucratization, however, reflected principally in the works of Hannah Arendt, that has far greater relevance in the context of the federal courts. It is this Arendtian conception of bureaucracy that . . . warrants serious consideration.

Diffusion of Responsibility and Loss of Control. The Arendtian conception of the pathology of bureaucratization rests on the diffusion of responsibility and the ultimate "Rule by Nobody." In an Arendtian bureaucracy, no one individual assumes responsibility for institutional output. Applying this concept to the federal courts . . . to the extent that law clerks, central staff attorneys, and subjudges participate in the decision-making process, judges can no longer be viewed as individually responsible for their decisions.

Several adverse consequences might flow from the situation. . . . The first potential consequence — the loss of a valuable check on the judicial power — poses, in my mind, no real danger. . . . "[F]ew judges will defend their mistakes by explaining that it was the work of a law clerk, in part because it would constitute an admission of a dependence on the clerk, and in part because the judge would then have to answer for the selection and supervision of the clerk." [H]owever, central legal staffs and sub-judges must be distinguished from judges' personal law clerks . . . but I would maintain that a similar conclusion holds. Ultimately, it is the judges who will be held responsible for decisions issued in their names, and admitting dependence on faceless central staff attorneys would be just as damning — if not more so — than admitting dependence on personal law clerks whom the judges had carefully selected and groomed. . . .

A second potential consequence of the loss of individual responsibility is more fundamental and thus more troubling. By significantly changing the allocation of actual decision-making responsibility, bureaucratization may lead to "the degeneration of the intellectual process by which judges come to know the law and a judicial decision achieves its intellectual authority." The legitimacy of courts, like any societal institution, depends not only on the "consent" of the citizenry, but also "on the courts competence, on the special contribution they make to the quality of our social life." In the case of the federal courts, that contribution is assumed to rest in the exercise of their peculiar ability to give meaning to our constitutional values and otherwise to interpret federal law. But our confidence in courts' ability to perform these functions does not rest on a belief in [judges'] moral expertise, or on a denial of their humanity. Judges are most assuredly people. They are lawyers, but in terms of personal characteristics they are no different from successful businessmen or politicians. Their capacity to make a special contribution to our social life derives not from any personal traits or knowledge, but from the definition of the office in which they find themselves and through which they exercise power.

Our confidence in courts derives, in other words, from the existence of a process that requires judges to hear (or perhaps read) a litigant's claims, study the issues, and reach and justify a decision regarding those claims. To the extent that bureaucratization results in "division and delegation of [judges'] decisional powers," the resulting "fractionation and compartmentalization" of the process from which courts' competence and our confidence in them arise will destroy that process.

That conclusion is, to be sure, an alarming one, but I believe that the premise on which it rests is demonstrably incorrect. Courts do not conform precisely to any of the extant models of bureaucratic behavior, and increases in the size of judicial support staffs or the complexity of the judicial system need not result in either the division of judges' decision-making authority or the delegation of functions critical to the proper exercise of that authority. These adverse effects could come about in any of three ways, one of which is strongly linked to mere increases in organizational size and complexity, one of which is weakly tied to such increases, and one of which is unrelated to these structural factors.

An increase in the size and complexity of judicial support staffs would be most troubling if judges were unable to prevent staff members from usurping decisional authority or if the ability of judges to declare the law as they see it was impeded by the values and needs of their subordinates. The judiciary would then come to resemble modern public service bureaucracies, which are characterized less by excessively rigid rule-governed behavior or diffusion of responsibility than by the frustration of organizational goals that occurs when lower-level employees attempt "to mitigate the immediate and persistent pressures of their working environment." . . . In short, the modern bureaucracy is characterized both by substantial gaps between the goals of the designated policy makers and those of street-level operatives, and by a working environment that allows, even encourages, lower-level employees to pursue their own goals to such an extent as to frustrate official agency policy.

Neither of these characteristics, which so adequately explain the persistent failure of efforts to reform public service bureaucracies, are present in the judiciary. The daily experiences of personal law clerks, central staff attorneys, and even sub-judges — their working environments if you will — do not diverge sharply from those of judges. There are, of course, aspects of the decision-making process in which these individuals do not participate and of which they may be only vaguely aware, but neither their job descriptions nor their working environments are likely to be such as to give them a "radically different view of the task" of deciding cases. And, while law clerks, staff attorneys, and sub-judges often hold views on various political, economic, and social issues that differ from those of the judges for whom they work, it will be a rare staff member who attempts to usurp a judge's decisional authority or subvert the judge's decision-making process. Attempts at persuasion based on case law, logic, morality, public policy, and other authority are commonplace (and valuable to the judge's deliberations), but professionalism is the norm and the standard by which staff members are judged, and efforts to do more than persuade, I would guess, are infrequent indeed.

Courts are unlike modern bureaucracies in the second critical respect as well: unlike the heads of public service agencies, whose organizational missions almost inevitably require them to define goals broadly, and sometimes ambiguously, and to vest considerable discretion in lower-level operatives, judges possess the ability, if they so choose, to retain relatively complete control over the decision-making process. . . . Courts are different, for a qualified and conscientious judge can delegate tasks to staff members without losing control over the "output" of the court. Not only are judicial goals more clearly definable than the goals of public service bureaucracies, but the performance of a judge's mission does not require the vesting of broad discretion in his assistants. While there may be valid reasons to limit or reduce the number of personal law clerks and the size of central legal staffs, the possibility that the supporting casts will somehow wrest control of the decision-making process from the hands of judges who are unwilling to surrender that control is not one of them.

A second, and more subtle, way in which an increase in the size and complexity of judicial support staffs might lead to a division of judges' decisional powers pertains to the delegation of functions that inheres in the efficient utilization of personnel. "Institutional decision-making," however "productive" it may be in the terms of number of cases "processed," is not an adequate substitute for personal judgment by the individual judge based on his own careful reflection and wrestling with the issues. If judges, in the course of delegating tasks that they perceive to be properly performable by staff members, assign away functions that actually are critical to the exercise of their decision-making authority, we would indeed have cause for concern.

But few would argue, I take it, that all delegation of responsibility — no matter how trivial — undermines the process by which judges come to know the law and by which judicial decisions achieve their intellectual authority. I also assume that few would seriously contend that a judge must read every case cited in every brief or write every word of every opinion in order properly to discharge his obligation to litigants and society. The decision-making — dialogic if you will — process that gives legitimacy to the judiciary is not as rigidly structured. Judges' special competence and society's trust in that competence derive, I submit, less from the fact that they produce from scratch every jot of every opinion that leaves their chambers than from the fact that their opinions communicate the decisions and reasoning of the judges on the panel, who have allowed themselves to be fully educated by the adversarial process and ultimately have reached their own conclusions on the merits of particular claims. A judge who merely rubber-stamps staff recommendations obviously lacks that competence and does not deserve society's trust. But, and this is the critical point, delegation and division of decision-making, as opposed to decision-enhancing, functions is not an inevitable result of the availability of law clerks, central staff attorneys, or sub-judges.

This discussion has foreshadowed a third way in which the growth of judicial support staffs might lead to a division of decision-making authority and undermine the legitimacy of the judicial process: judges might, for whatever reason, voluntarily choose to delegate responsibility for particular decisions or parts of decisions to various staff members. I doubt, however, that the mere existence of these staffs or even the press of rising case loads could accurately be cited as causes of such renunciations of a judge's duty. What staff members cannot legitimately do and, I suggest, cannot possibly do without judges' acquiescence is to make up judges' minds for them. Those few judges who actually allow subordinates to exercise decision-making authority would likely succumb to this practice no matter what the size of the support staff. Every profession has its "weak links," and the judiciary is no exception. I would maintain, however, that judges who abdicate decision-making authority constitute a miniscule minority among those now serving on the federal bench.

Bureaucratic Writing. Even if the Arendtian analysis does not hold and judges manage to retain control of the decision-making process, one might also decry the spread of "bureaucratic writing," another possible consequence of diffusion of responsibility in the judicial system. It has been suggested that, as judicial staffs grow and their role in the drafting of opinions becomes more substantial and more widely acknowledged, lawyers' "confidence that through reading an opinion or set of opinions they can reach a mind behind those opinions must begin to fail within them." Should this confidence dissipate, the judiciary may well come to be perceived as a "mindless system," the work product of which — like the work product of the opinion-writing bureaus of the large administrative agencies — cannot fruitfully be dissected with the tools of traditional legal analysis. Courts' constituents, of course, will continue to react to judicial decisions and remain "interested in what a court might do to them. But they will not internalize a court's purposes, or listen really to what it says to them."

To the extent that this concern rests — as it seems in part — on the low quality of the legal reasoning or the lack of lucidity of judicial opinions of recent vintage, I see no cause for alarm. Not only can I find no measurable differences between the quality of the opinions of, for example, the [current Supreme Court] and its predecessors, but I also think that one must recognize that law clerks often may clarify "patchwork" draft opinions of overworked

Justices or judges. The model of the judging function to which some critics compare current practice is, of course, best typified by Learned Hand, one of the most competent and respected jurists our country has known, who "wouldn't even let a law clerk write a sentence, not one sentence." But . . . adherence to the perceived traditional model is no guarantee of consistent brilliance. [S]everal former Supreme Court justices, who are now recognized for their superb "craftsmanship" in opinion writing, are reputed to have relied extensively on their law clerks to prepare drafts of written opinions.

The bureaucratic writing problem, however, has another, more subtle aspect: no matter how high the quality of staff-written opinions, such opinions may fail to reflect the thinking of the decision-making judges. If so, traditional legal analysis — in its most probing and refined sense at least — might fail, and the process by which lawyers come to know the law might change radically. . . . A similar situation could arise in the use of central legal staffs to draft *per curiam* opinions. At least in terms of the perceptions that it creates of a loss of judicial control over the decision-making process, courts' growing use of unsigned opinions is indeed problematic.

But, those perceptions aside, the problem is somewhat overstated. The fact that an opinion is unsigned, for example, does not necessarily mean that it was drafted outside the chambers of individual judges. That an opinion was drafted by a central staff attorney, moreover, does not mean that it does not accurately reflect the thinking of the judges who made the decision. And, because *per curiam* opinions are used only when those judges have determined that the matter in question has occasioned no need for a fuller statement of their views, they are likely to be issued primarily in cases requiring the application of settled law to particular, often recurring, factual situations. As a result, there is no reason to suppose that *per curiam* opinions — so long as they are not overused — make judges' reasoning opaque, frustrate the orderly development of bodies of law, or render useless the traditional tools of legal analysis.

Critics of bureaucratic writing are concerned, I assume, less with the prevalence of *per curiam* opinions — a possibly overused expedient for simple, fact-bound cases — than with the use of personal law clerks in the opinion-writing process. . . . [T]here can be little doubt that in general, Learned Hand's view of the judge-clerk relationship — "I write, you criticize" — seems to be fading in favor of increasing reliance on law clerks and staff for research and writing. [T]he Hand model may never have predominated because judges and justices have always used their law clerks in a wide variety of ways. It has also been observed — correctly I think — that drafting opinions is "not the same as deciding the outcome of appeals." But, even conceding these points, the critic of bureaucratic writing may still raise a colorable argument that such writing will reduce both judges' ability to declare the law and lawyers' ability to know it.

I believe, however, that the argument is flawed; if a judge is competent and conscientious, lawyers will be able to hear him "speaking through" his opinions and to uncover "the sense of mind behind them" even when those opinions are drafted in part by a law clerk. . . . [D]ifferent judges use law clerks differently and attempt to draw on their clerks' particular talents. All judges, I assume, write some opinions with little or no assistance from their law clerks. But the volume of work and litigants' need for speedy resolutions of their disputes make it practically impossible for most judges to draft every word in every opinion without assistance. Some judges, therefore, work on first drafts and then turn them over to their clerks for editing and polishing; others have clerks prepare first drafts and rewrite or edit those drafts themselves. But all careful judges will confer at length with their clerks and give them fairly specific instructions concerning the content of opinions. And, more important, careful judges will not allow an opinion to issue in their name until the words constituting the opinion precisely reflect their views on the proper disposition of the case. Those who would believe otherwise either do not fully understand the judicial process or underestimate the competence and dedication of the majority of the judges now serving on the federal courts.

As long as there is intimacy in the judge-clerk relationship, little or nothing need be lost in these optional approaches to opinion drafting. Clerks who have a close working relationship with their judge will look at cases with his sensitivities in mind and will likely draft opinions that hew as closely as possible to both the judge's preliminary analysis of the case and his preferred style. Even without an intimate judge-clerk relationship, most judges so completely control decision-making that this invariably determines the style of opinion drafting. Thus, during the opinion-drafting stage, a clerk's discretion is substantially limited. Clerks may, and often do, discover problems with the court's tentative approach to a case that require the judge to rethink the proposed disposition. But clerks are rarely, if ever, given unbridled discretion or told to justify a decision with any arguments they can dream up.

It seems unlikely, moreover, that clerks will ignore the judge's decision, his desired line of argument, or even his stylistic preferences. Not only are clerks aware of the nature and limits of their professional responsibilities, but there is also a socialization process within judges' chambers, bolstered by frequent communications between judge and clerk, by which clerks are encouraged at the opinion-drafting stage to develop and refine the judge's arguments and to express them in the way the judge would express them were he writing the opinion from scratch. The net result, assuming that the judge takes care in studying case precedents, briefs, and record evidence, and takes adequate time to rework any drafts produced by his clerks, is that "most opinions [will] accurately reflect the style and thinking of the authoring judge.". . . In the opinions of a careful judge, as in other fields, sentences, forms of expression, even ideas that are not originally the author's own become his by adoption, because he actually, and I emphasize actually, considers them, sentence by sentence, phrase by phrase, thought by thought, comma by comma, and makes them his own after deliberation. As a result, law clerks' participation in the opinion-drafting process should not undermine the authoritative nature of judicial declarations of law.

Conclusion. When examined carefully, then, the most commonly cited elements of the bureaucratization thesis appear less serious than at first glance. This does not mean, however, that we can continue to increase the size of judicial support staffs without changing the nature of the judicial process. If we have not already reached the limit on the number of useful law clerks for each judge or justice, we are certainly approaching it. Further increases in the size of judicial staffs may "strain the supervisory ability and energy of the judge.

At some point, which will vary greatly among individual judges, the judge cannot know what his subordinates are doing and will become dependent on them to do some or all of his thinking for him." Increases in the size of personal staffs, moreover, may reduce the collegiality that has characterized our Supreme Court and courts of appeals. One group of commentators has noted, for example, that "the larger the judge's personal retinue becomes, the greater is the tendency for the judge to confer with his staff rather than with his judicial colleagues. He may become less receptive to peer argument in conference." The possibility that these problems and others I have discussed will manifest themselves more prominently as judicial staffs grow is a real one, and we should thus look elsewhere than to increases in the number of law clerks and central staff attorneys to solve the case-load problem.

Lauren K. Robel, *Caseload and Judging: Judicial Adaptation to Caseload*, 1990 B.Y.U. L. Rev. 3, 44-47[7]

Judges' Perceptions on Delegation: Survey Responses. Appellate judges were asked a number of questions about whether caseload required them to delegate judicial work to clerks or central staff. The question of excessive delegation is initially complicated by the ambiguity surrounding what constitutes "judicial work": that is, what tasks can be delegated without fear that the judge's responsibility for the ultimate decision has been compromised? The questions in the survey required judges to consider and define for themselves the boundaries of proper delegation. Judges were initially asked how frequently they are forced to rely on law clerks to do things "that [the judges] believe [they] should do themselves." Judges who responded that such reliance occurred were then asked to describe the nature of the delegated work.

The majority of judges (63%) responded that they must rely on their clerks to do at least some work they believe they should do themselves, and 30% of respondents must do so "often" or "usually."[8] Many of the judges (113) took the opportunity to describe the delegated work. The variety of their responses indicates that judges may have different beliefs about the boundaries of "judicial work."[9] Some judges, for example, seem uncomfortable with any reliance

---

[7] Copyright © 1990 Brigham Young University Law Review. Reprinted with permission.

[8] [170] The complete question and responses were: How frequently are you forced to rely on your law clerks to do some things that you believe you should do yourself?

Response	Number	%
Never:	18	11.46%
Almost never:	37	23.57%
Sometimes:	50	31.85%
Often:	41	25.11%
Usually:	9	5.73%
No response:	2	1.27%

[9] [9] The complete question and responses were: If you are forced to rely on your clerks to do some things that you believe you should do yourself, what is the nature of that work?

Number of judges responding with written comments: 113

Drafting opinions: 62

on work done by their clerks, even in checking case citations. The tasks mentioned most frequently by respondents, however, were opinion drafting, research, and reading the trial or administrative record.

Answers to other questions confirm that clerks play a large role in opinion drafting. In response to a question about opinion drafting practices, for instance, only 14 judges (9%) report that they prepare the first draft in all cases. Most respondents (115 or 73%) reported preparing the first draft in some cases, and 21 judges (13%) reported that they never prepare the first draft. Many judges wrote that caseload required they delegate much opinion writing to clerks:

> In this circuit, a judge has to turn out 150 opinions a year to stay current. It is not possible to do that without excessive reliance on the law clerks.

> . . . .

> Keeping current with the docket has to be a high priority for any judge. I am unable to keep my work current if I read the records and do the writing and take time for thinking in those cases where is it needed. I spend time moving mail with little decisions (protecting the law clerks from being interrupted) and editing the work of clerks.

Many of the judges also mentioned their reliance on the clerks' reading and interpretation of precedents required for a decision of a case:

> Sometimes I rely on a law clerk's reading of cases when I am pressed.

> . . . .

> I am now forced to rely on my clerks for record examination and for research I would prefer to conduct myself. In the past I would draft all written materials. I now find that I am obliged to "plug in" memoranda or research that the clerks conducted.

Finally, judges often mentioned using clerks to read trial and administrative records, and many judges mentioned that they are required to rely on the clerk's reading, rather than their own.

Judges are less troubled by their use of the staff attorneys than by their reliance on their own clerks. Only 5% of the respondents believed they must

---

Research (reading and analyzing cited cases, finding relevant authority): 57
Reviewing the record: 44
Reviewing petitions for en banc and rehearing: 5
Reading briefs: 4
Checking cites, legislative history, etc.: 6
Motions: 2
Bench memos/review of bench memos: 2
Editing: 2
Work on time-sensitive cases (extraordinary writs, death penalty): 2
Reading court's slip opinions: 2
Reading cases to prepare for argument: 2
Reading court's unpublished opinions: 1

"often" or "usually" rely on central staff to do work they should be doing,[10] even though almost 20% of respondents rely greatly on staff draft opinions in non-argued cases.[11] In response to a question about the nature of work delegated to staff, some of the respondents volunteered that the work done by central staff was "appropriate" or "not a problem."[12] One judge captured the view of several: "Central staff, in my opinion, does things that judges should not be doing, which is the reason for the staff."

The judges' responses provide some foundation for the critics' fears about delegation. Judges themselves worry that caseload forces excessive reliance on law clerks for opinion writing and for both the research required to make an opinion sound and the record-checking required to make it accurate. Moreover, the judges' responses justify some of the concerns about the use of central staff. While judges feel the staff's work is appropriate, they rely heavily on the work of staff attorneys in cases for which those attorneys are given

---

[10] [170] The complete question and responses were: How often are you forced to rely on central staff to do things that you believe you should do yourself?

Response	Number	%
Never:	13	8.28
Almost never:	74	47.13
Sometimes:	53	33.76
Often:	7	4.46
Usually:	1	.64
No response:	9	5.73

[11] [175] The complete question and responses were: In non-argued cases:

Response	Number	%
I rely on the staff draft opinion greatly:	31	19.75
I almost always go through the record and law thoroughly myself:	43	27.39
I sometimes go through the record and law thoroughly myself:	48	30.57
My law clerks usually go through the record and law for me:	20	12.74
No response:	15	9.55

[12] [176] The complete question and responses were: If you are forced to rely on central staff to do things that you believe you should do yourself, what is the nature of that work?

Number of judges responding:	61
Reading/checking record:	19
Drafting opinions/orders:	18
Motions:	13
Research:	11
Pro se/habeas/prisoners:	8
Administrative:	4
Jurisdictional issues:	4
Screening:	3
Bench Memos:	3
"Case development Work":	1
Their work appropriate/ "not a problem":	4

responsibility. In some circuits, staff attorneys are responsible for a very large number of cases, many of which judges do not find intellectually challenging. As one judge stated, "The problem in handling the cases that occupy the staff attorneys' time is not our delegation of authority but rather the often trivial nature of those cases." If judges perceive it is the nature of the cases that is the problem, rather than the lack of time to devote to them, it is likely that many judges will continue to rely on central staff to alleviate this aspect of caseload pressures.

THOMAS E. BAKER, RATIONING JUSTICE ON APPEAL — THE PROBLEMS OF THE U.S. COURTS OF APPEALS 143-46 (1994)

[Reread this excerpt in Chapter 7, Section III, at page 500]

Mary Lou Stow & Harold J. Spaeth, *Centralized Research Staff: Is There a Monster in the Judicial Closet?*, 75 JUDICATURE 216 (1992) [13]

[T]he Michigan Court of Appeals has consistently ranked first among the nation's appellate courts in the number of filings per judge. It has also ranked among the top three such courts in the number of dispositions per judge. This court, in 1988, saw 8,559 filings. This meant 476 filings per judge, and a backlog of 1,717 cases at the end of that year. (The court has defined "backlog" as those cases that are awaiting submission to a panel of judges.) By 1990, total filings had grown to 13,083, with new filings per judge reaching 545. In addition, by the end of 1990, backlogged cases had more than doubled, to 3,853. Given such prodigious increases, there is no insurance that the judges treat staff "recommendations" as such in all cases. In other words, there is no guarantee that the decision in a given case really is made by a three-judge panel, after careful review. In fact, the reverse may be true: judges may hurriedly accept staff recommendations, transforming a staff attorney's case evaluation into the decision of the court.

Our study, then, focuses on this question: Who really makes the decision: the judges, or the centralized staff? . . . Though the scope of our study is much too narrow to provide a definitive answer, even for Michigan, it is the first systematic, empirical consideration of this question. We focus on the Michigan Court of Appeals, analyzing a random sample of 603 cases submitted during the years 1989 and 1990, which for the most part were decided in 1990 or 1991. . . .

Until the summer of 1991, oral arguments were allowed in all appeals on final review, if parties to the case requested them and complied with court rules. Now cases may be decided without oral arguments "if the judges determine that arguments would not help them decide the merits, if the issue had recently been resolved or if the appeal is frivolous." . . .

---

[13] Copyright © 1992 American Judicature Society. Reprinted with permission.

With central staff, a very large group of nonjudicial employees is supervised and monitored by an administrator, the research director. This research director is an experienced attorney who is charged with supervision of the central staff, yet he is no closer to being a *judge* than are any of the staff. . . .

By relieving judges of some of their duties, any type of research attorney will necessarily exercise some judicial responsibility. A centralized, institutional staff removes responsibility farther still from each individual judge. Reliance by the courts on such staff is therefore more problematic than judicial use of more traditional, personal clerks. . . .

Therefore, to gain insight into judicial dependence on the centralized research staff, we undertake a comparison of staff recommendations with the judges' final decisions. . . .

We consider first the extent of agreement between the recommendations of prehearing staff and final dispositions. We identified two types of agreement in the 307 cases in our prehearing sample: opinion type and outcome. While agreement on outcome is obviously of much greater significance, it is worth noting that the recommended opinion type plays an important role. It serves as a screening mechanism, signalling to judges how much time should be spent on a case. . . .

Agreement on the type of opinion a case deserved was found in 224 cases, or 73.0 per cent of the sample. As might be expected, it was more likely that the prehearing attorney believed the case he or she was reviewing deserved full blown treatment than it was for the panel of judges to think so. . . . The most frequent disagreement over opinion type occurred when the staff attorney recommended an authored, published opinion, but the panel opted for an unpublished *per curiam* or memorandum decision.

More specifically, in 307 sampled cases, authored opinions were recommended in 17 per cent, with the panels choosing this option in 7 per cent. *Per curiam* opinions were recommended in 81 per cent, while the panels so opted in 83 per cent. Memorandums were recommended in 2 per cent, and used in 10 per cent. . . .

Agreement on the actual disposition of the case was higher than agreement on opinion type, occurring in 274 of the cases examined. Of these 274, we found agreement in both opinion type and outcome in 196 cases (71.5 per cent). In 78 cases, the judges differed on the opinion type chosen, but agreed with the staff person's recommended result. The two categories combined produced agreement in 89.3 per cent of the cases in the sample. . . .

The modal disposition recommended was to affirm. Fully 78.2 per cent of sampled cases contained such a recommendation, while 79.5 per cent produced this outcome. There was no appreciable difference here between criminal and civil cases . . . .

The scope of our analysis does not warrant definitive conclusions about the Michigan Court of Appeals' reliance on central staff. However, it does show high levels of agreement between staff recommendations and the judges' decisions, strongly suggesting that the judges rely almost entirely on staff recommendations to reach their decisions. Most surprising is the level of agreement on discretionary matters. The judges seemed to rely most on staff (commissioners, specifically) when deciding whether or not to grant full review. One possible explanation for this is that commissioners are tenured staff, and experience very low turnover. Prehearing staff, on the other hand, are generally freshly graduated from law school, and usually remain with the court no more than two years. . . .

Whatever the reason for higher correspondence in recommendations regarding discretionary review, the high level of agreement in both categories is disturbing. It is far from conclusive, however. Agreement may merely reflect high caliber attorneys who almost always please the panels with a careful, objective and thorough analysis of each case. Even after full review of party briefs and the record, judges may find little reason to deviate from the staff recommendation. Alternatively, but less plausibly, most appeals may be so "open and shut," in the sense that no other outcome is credible, that both the staff and the judges are exactly right. It is also possible that judges, provided with a ready-made decision and analysis for each case, and haunted by an ever growing docket, are rarely able to bless cases with more than perfunctory review. Or it may very well be that the actual situation reflects a combination of these possibilities. . . .

At any rate, further research is needed to determine precisely what the Michigan court's closet contains. . . .

Judges must decide cases that come before them. They must not serve a function that amounts only to review and approval of staff decisions. . . .

With the Michigan Court of Appeals displaying such high levels of agreement between central research staff and outcomes, the basic question is simply this: Do we trust our judges? If we hope to base our notions of justice on something more substantial than faith in their integrity and devotion to duty, we must pull this mysterious "monster" out of its closet, and have a better look at it.

David J. Brown, *Facing the Monster in the Judicial Closet: Rebutting a Presumption of Sloth,* 75 JUDICATURE 291 (1992)[14]

There is a myth about the role of intermediate appellate judges and the power they wield. These mythical judges have the power of unfettered discretion to weigh, review, reject, or affirm any trial court decision, merely on whim and an arcane rule of law or two. In Kansas, and I suspect in Michigan, this myth has no relation to reality. The judges on the Kansas Court of Appeals are indeed overburdened, but they are rarely called on to do anything more than routine. After reading Stow and Spaeth's article, I reviewed 53 of my own memoranda, prepared while I served on the central research staff for the Kansas Court of Appeals. I was surprised to discover the court adopted my case-by-case recommendations about as often as Stow and Spaeth found the Michigan court adopted its central staff recommendations. I was not startled, however, when I determined the judges agreed with me most often simply because they had no choice — there was only one answer possible. . . .

---

[14] Copyright © 1992 American Judicature Society. Reprinted with permission.

It is time to explode the myth of midlevel appellate court judges with the power to do as they choose. Intermediate-level courts hear predominantly routine, boring matters by legislative fiat. And, as they do so, they are not free to use their own judgment in a majority of cases. As one scholar explains: "Appellate judges operate in a world not of their own making: they review cases that have already been decided. In performing that review, they are constrained by rules — standards of review — that often require substantial deference to the lower court's decision."

Another scholar has defined the role of standards of review in appellate decision making as setting "the height of the hurdles over which an appellant must leap in order to prevail on appeal." Unfortunately, the role left for intermediate appellate judges is often just to see if an appellant has jumped high enough to clear the hurdle. If the answer is yes, appellant wins. If the answer is no, appellant loses. Thus, intermediate courts are left to struggle not with questions of justice but with dispositive questions of substantial competent evidence, abuse of discretion, failure to preserve an issue for appeal, harmless error, and other variations on this theme. As the late Justice Benjamin N. Cardozo [then a justice on the New York Court of Appeals] lamented in 1921: "Of the cases that come before the court in which I sit, a majority, I think, could not, with semblance of reason, be decided in any way but one. The law and its application are plain." In 1924, Cardozo estimated that 90 percent, and maybe more, of the cases heard are "predetermined — predetermined in the sense that they are predestined — their fate preestablished by inevitable laws that follow them from birth to death. The range of free activity [for judges] is relatively small.". . .

I reviewed all the issues raised on appeal in each of 53 cases [during my tenure as a central staff attorney at the Kansas IAC]. I attempted to determine whether those issues would be governed by dispositive standards of review, or whether they involved questions of law that would allow the appellate court to conduct a *de novo* review. . . .

Of 53 cases studied, 30 involved only issues governed by various dispositive standards of review. This means that in 56.6 percent of the cases, the appellate judges had to give considerable deference to the trial court's ruling and had no issues on which they were free to ignore other judges' thoughts. Of the remaining 23 cases in which questions of law were raised, 9 were directly controlled either by court of appeals or supreme court precedent. In other words, in 9 cases, or about 17 percent of the total studied, the judicial panels had to give complete deference to another appellate court's opinion. Thus, in about 73.5 percent of the cases, court of appeals judges were forced to give deference to the actions and rulings of other judges. In other words, judges were only free to make *de novo* determinations in 14 cases, or about 26.5 percent of the total cases studied. . . .

My recommendations were not followed in only 5 cases. The judges, therefore, agreed with my recommendations in 94.3 percent of the cases. Nevertheless, all of the disagreements were in cases that involved questions of law. Indeed, all the disagreements were on specific questions of law. When the judges were free to make up their own minds and apply a *de novo* standard of review, they agreed with me in 9 cases out of 14, or 64.3 percent of the time.

The concerns Stow and Spaeth express about judicial independence are important. Judicial opinions should reflect judicial thinking and judges should not blindly accept the legal work of research attorneys. But there are other more important concerns that should be addressed. Why are our intermediate appellate courts spending so much time addressing routine cases? If any competent legally trained person can review the cases before an intermediate court and determine the outcome, and the outcome will be the same no matter who reviews those files, why must the cases be considered by a three-judge judicial panel? If the standards of review make any result other than affirmance unlikely, why are appeals filed? Isn't it possible that the valid, critical concerns of worthy appellants get lost in the shuffle? Why are we wasting the time of our most respected and learned jurists with cases whose fates have been predetermined?

. . . . Stow and Spaeth are naive in thinking central research staffs are the monsters in the judicial closet. They insult judges by suggesting the judiciary is too harried, or too lazy, to write its own opinions. The problem is that appellate panels face a press of cases — many of which, at best, are mundane, easily resolved, not worth one judge's time, let alone three, and at worst, are frivolous and should never have been appealed. Central staffs are an excellent tool to use in separating the wheat from the chaff. The question that must be resolved is why we keep sending the chaff to our appellate judges expecting them to make bread.

Alex Kozinski, *The Real Issues of Judicial Ethics*, 32 HOFSTRA L. REV. 1095, 1097-1100, 1105-06 (2004)[15]

The first ethical issue I want to examine has to do with work allocation — the amount of time and effort judges spend on cases, particularly small cases. Judicial caseloads have increased tremendously over the last few decades, and they continue to do so. When I graduated from law school in 1975 I clerked for the Ninth Circuit, and at that time each judge disposed on the merits of approximately 210 cases per year. In 2002, the number stood at 492 cases per active judge, and the Ninth Circuit is far from the busiest court of appeals in the country. That dubious honor goes to the Eleventh Circuit, which decided 843 cases per judge in 2002. Just imagine what that means: Every judge of the Eleventh Circuit signed off on the merits disposition of 2.3 cases a day, every day of the year — weekends and holidays included.

Add to this the fact that not all cases are created equal. Most judicial work is routine and dull, involving issues that are of no consequence to anyone other than the parties. Only a few cases raise difficult and interesting issues — the kind of issues that make for an important judicial opinion. When lawyers seek appointment to judicial office, they generally think of the interesting cases as the core of judicial work; none I know seeks judicial office so he can spend his days, nights, weekends and holidays slogging through an unending stack of routine, fact-intensive and largely (in the grand scheme of things) inconsequential cases.

---

[15] Copyright © 2004 Hofstra Law Review. Reprinted with permission.

Human nature being what it is, there is a strong tendency to devote a disproportionate amount of judicial time to the big cases and to give short shrift to the small ones. There's actually a lot to be said for this. Preparing a precedential opinion requires a significant amount of time because such an opinion not only decides the dispute between the parties, but also sets the course of the law for innumerable cases to come. So you are justified in spending most of your time on the big cases, because you really do have a serious responsibility: A rushed and sloppy opinion can cause major problems for a lot of people down the road. Yet, the small cases, too, have a legitimate claim to a fair share of judicial time and attention.

An important part of the judicial function thus consists of allocating one's time between the big and small cases — and this is a decision judges make almost implicitly and with no possibility of complaint by the parties affected. In fact, no one knows precisely how judges allocate their time among the cases assigned to them, but the risk that small and seemingly unimportant cases will be given insufficient attention is ever-present.

People might assume, if they think about such issues at all, that there's no real problem — because most cases are, in fact, easy. This points to an important paradox in the process of judging. In one sense, most cases are very easy. In a different sense, though, there are no easy cases. Most cases are easy in that, if you took any three judges in the federal judiciary, no matter how diverse their judicial philosophies, and asked them to look closely at the record, the applicable case law and the arguments of the parties, you'd get a unanimous result every time. But all cases are difficult in the sense that it takes time and attention to get to the point of decision. You have to make sure you know the record and the arguments; you have to be confident that you have the latest case law and understand exactly what it says. All of this takes a fair degree of concentration and effort, even in the easy cases.

Most of the time — nine times out of ten, maybe more — when you're done, you reach the obvious result. And so it seems almost pointless to go to the trouble again and again and again, only to come up with the result you could have guessed from the beginning. It's a bit like banging your head against a padded wall. But then, once in a while, it turns out that what looked like an easy case is actually quite difficult, because of a small fact buried in the record, or a footnote in a recent opinion. After more than two decades of judging I have found no way to separate the sheep from the goats, except by taking a close look. But how close a look any one judge takes in a particular case is strictly a matter of the judge's own conscience. It's one of the embedded ethical issues that no one ever talks about.

A closely related issue is the tendency to delegate essential aspects of the judicial function to staff. At the time I clerked, each federal circuit judge had one secretary and two law clerks. Then, in the early 1980s, the staff complement was increased to five, made up of two secretaries and three law clerks. Sometime in the 1990s, judges were allowed to substitute a law clerk for one of the secretarial positions; I believe most circuit judges take advantage of this option, so that now judges generally have four clerks. In the Eleventh Circuit, by special dispensation, judges have been allocated an additional clerk, apparently because they have not sought the increase in judicial positions that their caseload would justify.

During the same quarter-century, there has been a steep increase in the number of central staff attorneys. In 1975, our court had a skeletal central staff whose function was largely to process motions; all merits cases were handled in chambers by judges and their elbow clerks. Today we have something like seventy staff attorneys, all located in our headquarters in San Francisco, and they process approximately forty percent of the cases in which we issue a merits ruling. When I say process, I mean that they read the briefs, review the record, research the law and prepare a proposed disposition, which they then present to a panel of three judges during a process we call "oral screening" — oral, because the judges don't see the briefs in advance, and because they generally rely on the staff attorney's oral description of the case in deciding whether to sign on to the proposed disposition. An oral screening panel meets for two or three days each month and during that time disposes of a hundred and fifty cases, sometimes more.

The increase in caseload coupled with the proliferation of staff creates a constant temptation for judges to give away essential pieces of their job. The pressure is most severe in the small and seemingly routine cases, especially those handled through the screening process. After you dispose of a few dozen such cases on a screening calendar, your eyes glaze over, your mind wanders and the urge to say okay to whatever is put in front of you becomes almost irresistible. The temptation is heightened by the fact that the staff attorneys who present these cases are very experienced and usually get it right. It often takes a frantic act of will to continue questioning successive staff attorneys about each case, or to insist on reading key parts of the record or controlling precedent to ensure that the case is decided by the three judges whose names appear in the caption, not by a single staff attorney.

A similar temptation exists as to the bigger cases. Writing opinions is a difficult, time-consuming, exacting process. It is a reality of current judicial life that few judges draft their own opinions from scratch. Generally, the judge will give instructions about how a case is to be decided and what points the opinion should make, but the initial drafting is almost always left to a clerk. The draft opinion, when it lands on the judge's desk some weeks later, is generally pretty good — after all, we pick only the best law students as clerks. On reading the opinion, the judge may be able to detect any obvious flaws in reasoning, and he'll certainly be able to make some word edits. But this casual read is a far cry from the time and effort required to study the opinion closely, deconstruct its arguments, examine key portions of the record and carefully parse the precedents — all the things a judge must do before he can call the opinion his own. Nevertheless, if the judge chooses merely to fiddle a bit with an opinion drafted by his clerk and then circulate it, nobody is the wiser. And we do occasionally get opinions circulated that look like they were written by someone a year out of law school with no adult supervision. The only guarantee one can have that judges are not rubber-stamping their law clerks' work product is each judge's sense of personal responsibility. . . .

[T]he internal temptations that I described above are ones I confront every day. Giving short shrift to small cases, signing on to the work of staff and calling it my own . . . and the dozens of other ways in which I feel the pressure to do something unethical, yet wholly undetectable by anyone other than me — all these temptations I must fight off many times every single day. . . . A judge can appear to act ethically and still betray his responsibility in essential respects, and in ways that no one will ever know about. . . . Judicial ethics, where it counts, is hidden from view. . . . Ultimately, there is no choice but to trust the judges. . . .

NOTES

1. In *Dorsey v. Kingsland*, 173 F.2d 405, 414 (D.C. Cir. 1949) the court observed by way of *dicta*:

> An attorney who had occasion to quote from Washington's Farewell Address would be guilty of no breach of faith if he failed to mention the fact that it is generally believed that a considerable part of the actual penmanship was done by Alexander Hamilton. One who quotes from Andrew Jackson's majestic Nullification Proclamation is not to be criticized for fraud if he fails to set out the fact that while written from Jackson's notes the stately diction is actually the result of the penmanship of Edward Livingston. It is generally known that most Presidents and candidates for President employ assistants who not only engage themselves in preparing data and making suggestions for the speeches and state papers of their chiefs but frequently participate extensively in the actual draftsmanship. Yet seldom, if ever, in the delivery of the speech is attention called to the portions actually written by the deliverer and the portions supplied by the assistants. It is not wholly unknown that the judges of even the highest courts have law clerks and that these law clerks are engaged not only in research but frequently make most valuable suggestions as to the preparation of opinions and not infrequently participate largely in the actual draftsmanship of the opinion. Yet when these opinions are handed down no specific mention is called to the paragraphs actually written by the judge rendering the opinion and those written by the law clerk or those inserted as a result of the suggestions of other judges who may or may not have sat in the case.

But is there a considered difference between an elected official's having assistance in the writing of a speech and an appellate judge's having someone else research and draft an opinion? Professor Witkin thinks not:

> The fact that a justice's research attorney digests the facts, or digs the issues out of partisan briefs, or extracts the relevant law from reported decisions or textbooks, or states the legal reasons for a decision by applying the law to the facts and issues does not mean that the court has delegated judicial functions to a non-judge. In government, business, and the academic world, the writing down of significant thoughts is often done by someone with special skills in expression and plenty of time to devote to the task, working for someone who initiates or acquiesces in those thoughts but has only limited time to phrase them. Thus, courts need not seek excuses for delegating part of the opinion-writing function to talented experts, with superior legal training and experience in writing. It is the task of stating the reasons for the decision, not the authority to decide, that is delegated. No matter

how elaborate or polished the draft opinion may be, the justice must make the final version his own opinion, because he is responsible for what it says.

BERNARD E. WITKIN, MANUAL ON APPELLATE COURT OPINIONS 14-17 (1977). What do you think?

2. Judge Richard Posner, in the "reread" excerpt in Chapter 7, Section II, provides a candid behind-the-scenes description of the contemporary judge-law clerk relationship. Judge Wade McCree sounds an alarm that there already is too much delegation and too little supervision, more so with central staff attorneys than elbow law clerks, and he fears that the courts are morphing into bureaucracies characterized by excessive delegation to staffers. Judge Edwards seeks to refute the "bureaucracy" charge by breaking down the theory of bureaucracy as it applies to courts, but even he is careful to qualify his argument to admit that judges are at their full capacity to supervise law clerks and central staff attorneys. With whom do you agree? What light is shed on this debate by Professor Lauren Robel's summary of the survey of judges conducted by the Federal Courts Study Committee on the effects of caseload? If, as she explains, the judges strongly believe that the unworthy nature of the cases is the problem, rather than the lack of judge time to devote to them, then we should assume that the judges see nothing problematic with delegation to law clerks and central staff attorneys to handle those kinds of cases. Is there some other way to simply be rid of all those junk cases in the system while still being mindful of the appellate imperatives? (Apart from the whole delegation issue, an alternative to increasing the number of law clerks and central staff attorneys, of course, is to increase the number of judges, a response considered in Chapter 7, Section I.)

3. Professor Daniel Meador points out this logical dilemma:

The extent to which a court agrees with and accepts the recommendations of its staff attorneys in the decisions of appeals is an indicator of (1) the value to the judges of the staff assistance and (2) the degree to which the judges are retaining and exercising their judicial responsibilities or, instead, are over-relying upon the staff. Unless the staff recommendations are acceptable to the judges in a large percentage of the staff cases, the staff is not helping the court significantly. From that standpoint, a 100% judicial acceptance of staff work would show that staff is of maximum help. Yet the higher the percentage of judicial acceptance the greater the danger of judicial abdication of the independent decision-making responsibility. In other words, the same indicator points in two quite different directions.

DANIEL J. MEADOR, APPELLATE COURTS: STAFF AND PROCESS IN THE CRISIS OF VOLUME 11 (Supp. 1975). The readings explore this dilemma. The "reread" excerpt from Professor Baker restates this dilemma. In their excerpt, Professors Stow and Spaeth ask if there is a delegation monster in the judicial closet and their study of the Michigan Court of Appeals raises some concerns for untoward delegation by judges to central staff attorneys. In his excerpt, former-Staff Attorney David Brown seeks to rebut their implication of untoward delegation by emphasizing the narrow parameters within which appeals of right are decided. He insists that judges are not lazy and central staff attorneys are not usurping the judicial role. What do you think? What about the larger issue Mr. Brown raises: if he is right that there are too many automatic, routine, and meritless cases in the appellate court system, what can be done to be rid of them most efficiently so that the important, complex, and difficult cases receive more time and attention from the judges?

4. Professor Fiss states these postulates of judicial modernity: (1) the history of the twentieth century was largely the history of increasing bureaucratization; (2) virtually every phase of American life has come to be dominated by a large-scale, complex organization — corporations, labor unions, universities, state and national government agencies, etc.; (3) today the nostalgic focus on the agony of the lonely, isolated judge is outdated and irrelevant because the judiciary has become another large-scale, complex organization. Owen M. Fiss, *The Bureaucratization of the Judiciary*, 92 YALE L. J. 1442 (1983). Do you disagree with any of these postulates? If not, what are the implications from them for our study of appellate courts? Is the crisis of volume — and the attendant high volume of routine cases — the cause of the bureaucratization of the appellate courts or were the judges' responsive personnel and procedural reforms the cause of the bureaucratization? *See* Frank H. Easterbrook, *What's So Special About Judges?*, 61 U. COLO. L. REV. 773 (1990); Richard B. Hoffman, *The Bureaucratic Spectre: Newest Challenge to the Courts*, 66 JUDICATURE 60 (1982); John T. Wold, *Going Through the Motions: The Monotony of Appellate Court Decisionmaking*, 62 JUDICATURE 58 (1978).

5. Professor Paul Carrington helps us understand what is ultimately at stake in the abstract and philosophical debate over appellate court delegation with this provocative thought-experiment to imagine an appellate court process based on a complete and total delegation:

> Doubtless we can stand a little judicial delegation. But surely there is a point at which this becomes undesirable, and sufficiently so that we should look elsewhere for the means to cope with the caseload.

> Let me emphasize this by asking you to consider the ultimate in delegation. It would be possible to manage an entire judicial system, however large, with one panel of judges, indeed with a single judge. What would be required is a very large and reasonably talented staff. I dare to suggest that one of our largest law firms could easily manage the appellate business of all the federal courts. They would need a good deal of internal discipline and efficiency. In order to maximize their efficiency, they might find it most useful to hold oral arguments before a single associate in the firm, or perhaps without any hearing officer at all, and tape record the arguments for use by those more senior associates and partners who might review the decision as it floated upward through the office and out, over the signature of the senior partner. My guess is that such an operation would produce very craftsmanlike decisions, perhaps significantly better than what we now read in the FEDERAL REPORTER, even though that publication is already my favorite periodical. I fancy that there would be very few "splits in the circuits" and no confusing dissents or concurrences. The *corpus juris* would probably be as certain as we have ever known it.

Indeed, it might become so stable and certain that appeals would be less speculative and the gambling appellant would be deterred from wasting his money and our time.

What would be lost in the change to that kind of system of appellate review? . . . I would describe it as the human component of the process of review. No longer would we make the commitment which we now make to every individual in our society that his grievance will be heard and answered by high government officials. Instead, we would promise only that his grievance would go into the same large institution as all other grievances of a like class. Each individual would receive the same impersonal treatment as everyone else.

Paul D. Carrington, *The Dangers of Judicial Delegation: Concluding Remarks*, 52 F.R.D. 76, 77-78 (1971). *See also* DANIEL J. MEADOR, APPELLATE COURTS: STAFF AND PROCESS IN THE CRISIS OF VOLUME 123-37 (1974).

6. In the last excerpt, Judge Kozinski makes two provocative admissions: first, judges have built-in temptations to shirk their duty by giving short shrift to cases and by abdicating their judicial authority to their staff and, second, judges can get away with it, because these abuses are hidden and beyond regulation. He insists that the rest of us can only trust judges. Do you trust judges? Why or why not?

III. THE DOCKET DILEMMA REDUX

Thomas B. Marvell, *State Appellate Court Responses to Caseload Growth*, 72 JUDICATURE 282 (1989)[16]

The appellate caseload explosion and the resulting pressures on the courts are hard to exaggerate. Appeals have been doubling about every decade since World War II, placing extreme demands on judges to increase output. Judges have adopted a wide variety of responses, often radically changing court structure and procedure. . . .

The information presented here comes from a study of 45 states from 1968 to 1984. In 1968, appellate courts were just beginning to make structural and procedural changes to meet the caseload pressures; by the 1980s, almost all courts had made major changes. . . .

Factors that enable appellate courts to decide more appeals. Which of the many changes described here helped appellate courts tackle their rising caseloads? There is abundant speculation about the effectiveness of efficiency measures courts have taken, but no usable evidence. Determining what causes what in the courts is notoriously difficult because so many factors are involved and they change so rapidly. For example, a finding that courts with central staffs decide more cases per judge than courts without staff would not show that staffs help get more cases decided. The finding may well result from variables that affect both staff use and decision volume, such as programs to

[16] Copyright © 1989 American Judicature Society. Reprinted with permission.

screen cases for decision without argument or published opinion. More important, the causal direction may be the other way; courts with high caseloads may be more likely to create central staffs.

Another common mistake is to assume that a program works because it is followed by an increase in decision output. Again, many other factors may have intervened. If a court increases decisions after a central staff is created, one must determine that the increase is not due to the numerous other changes that probably occurred at the same time — usually an impossible task. Moreover, for various reasons, appellate courts usually decide more appeals each year, such that almost any change made to increase output will seem successful. As a practical matter, a judge can probably never determine whether changes help his or her court decide more appeals. Evaluating the impact of changes requires that one study the experiences of many courts. . . .

Filings. The strongest conclusion is that the volume of filings has a very strong impact on the volume of decisions. If filings increase 10 per cent, the number of cases decided increases about 5 to 7 per cent — even if no judges are added and none of the efficiency measures are adopted. The implication is that appellate judges adapt their work habits to the demands made on them, but far from enough to meet the demands fully.

Adding judges. There are "constant returns to scale;" for example, if one judge is added to a ten-judge court, the number of decisions goes up by roughly the same 10 per cent, assuming that filings also increase. An exception is that in states having only supreme courts, without IACs, adding judges does not produce a correspondingly large increase in appeals decided. Likewise, adding temporarily assigned trial judges or retired judges usually does not produce as many additional cases decided as the extra judicial manpower would suggest.

Intermediate courts. Creating or expanding intermediate courts helps increase decision volume. The output per judge in an appellate system becomes noticeably greater when jurisdiction is shifted to an IAC, even after controlling for other changes commonly associated with IACs, such as use of panels and unpublished opinions.

Staff aides. Adding law clerks has a moderate impact: when judges are given an additional law clerk, they decide one to five more cases a year. Adding staff attorneys has no discernible impact on decision volume, except possibly in large IACs. A likely explanation is that their work products add to the amount of information the judges consider; so they spend more time on some cases. That is, the staff's work goes less towards increasing productivity than towards increasing decision quality. . . .

Opinions. Deciding cases without opinion greatly enhances judicial productivity. For example, if a court decides to stop writing opinions in half its cases, the annual decision output should increase by 10 to 15 appeals per judge. Curtailing opinion publication and issuing unsigned opinions have smaller impacts: the same 50 per cent use would increase the decision output per judge by roughly five to ten appeals a year.

Panels. A surprising, but clear, conclusion is that reducing the average panel size does not increase productivity. A likely reason is that the assigned judge does most of the work, and smaller panels do not reduce opinion assignments.

Oral arguments. Limiting oral arguments has a moderate impact: for each 10 per cent of cases decided without argument, there should be 1 or 2 per cent more appeals decided.

Conclusion. Adding judges and deciding cases without opinion are the two most effective means to increase appellate output. They are also among the least popular with judges and legislators. Also effective are using temporary judges, curtailing oral argument, using unpublished or memorandum opinions and creating or expanding IACs. Changes that usually have little or no impact on decision output include reducing panel size and adding staff attorneys.

THOMAS E. BAKER, RATIONING JUSTICE ON APPEAL: THE PROBLEMS OF THE U.S. COURTS OF APPEALS 44-49 (1994)[17]

Median Time Intervals on Appeal (months)

Year	Filing Record to Last Brief	Last Brief to to Hearing or Submission	Hearing or Submission to Decision or Final Order	Filing Record to Final Disposition
1950	3.7	0.7	1.5	7.1
1960	3.6	0.8	1.5	6.8
1970	3.5	1.8	1.6	8.2
1980	2.8	2.9	1.6	8.9
1990	4.5	3.1	2.5/1.1	10.1

What comparisons can be teased from this Table? It is quite remarkable that collectively the Courts of Appeals remain virtually current despite sustained off-the-chart level of growth in their caseload. . . . Look at the sum of the second column (the interval between the last brief and the hearing or submission) plus the third column (the interval between the hearing or submission and the decision or final order). These two appellate intervals added together comprise the period during which an appeal is lodged with the judges, that is, how long it takes the Court of Appeals to perform its appellate review function. In 1950, the median time an appeal was lodged with the court was 2.2 months. By 1990, the median time had more than doubled to a figure of 5.6 months in argued cases and 4.2 months in nonargument summary calendar cases.

It is important to keep in mind that over this same forty-year period the Courts of Appeals implemented numerous procedural shortcuts, various intramural reforms — such as the nonargument summary calendar and the decision without opinion — designed to cope with dramatic caseload growth. These intramural reforms were designed to allow the Courts of Appeals to process many more appeals more efficiently and faster than the more traditional procedures would have allowed and, therefore, presumably had the cumulative effect of shortening these appellate time intervals. . . .

---

[17] Copyright © 1994 Thomson West. Reprinted with permission.

There has been a significant quantitative increase in the appellate time intervals it takes the Courts of Appeals to hear and decide an appeal. The Courts of Appeals took 255% longer to decide an orally argued appeal in 1990 (5.6 months) than they took to decide an appeal in 1950 (2.2 months). Even an appeal on the nonargument summary calendar, the most significant of the appellate efficiency reforms of the last forty years, took 190% longer (4.2 months) in 1990 than an appeal took in 1950 (2.2 months). It should be remembered that in 1950 an oral argument and a written opinion were afforded in all federal appeals as of right.

Of course, the argument can be made that overall the Courts of Appeals continue to perform at capacity and their capacity is adequate and their efficiency is sufficient. It can be observed that the Courts of Appeals continue to decide roughly the same number of appeals each year as are being filed, although the precise numbers demonstrate some slippage. And it might be argued, perhaps even more soundly, that the per appeal intervals of 5.6 months in argued cases and 4.2 months in nonargued cases — representing additional delays of "only" 3.4 months and 2.0 months respectively over the forty year period — are not very large when considered relatively or absolutely. There are two levels of response to this argument.

First, it should be pointed out that these are median figures and that they are for all the Courts of Appeals. Therefore, there are equal numbers of appeals in the federal appellate system being decided in longer and in shorter appellate time intervals; some particular appeals take more time than others; and some particular Courts of Appeals take more time than other Courts of Appeals. This may be a statistical way of saying nothing more than that things actually could be better or worse than these figures suggest and, because it is difficult to know, one should not make too much out of median statistics. The purpose here is to make the most of these statistics, but not too much.

Second, there is a more interesting way to consider the increases in the appellate intervals systemically, which takes into account the increase in the volume of appeals during the last four decades and, while somewhat novel, which arguably is more revealing for this Chapter discussion on the crisis of volume. The idea is to multiply the length of the median appellate intervals times the total number of appeals decided during the year to compute a figure of the aggregate median appellate time interval. This yields an aggregate measure of how long the Courts of Appeals took to decide all the appeals for that year. Then compare this systemic aggregate measure of decision time for the years 1950 and 1990. This will provide a comparison of roughly how long the Courts of Appeals took to hear and decide a year's worth of appeals before and after what has been called the "crisis of volume". . . .

In 1950, the courts of appeals decided 2,355 appeals with a median appellate interval of 2.2 months, for an aggregate of 5,181 months of appellate decision time for that year. In 1990, the courts of appeals decided 21,006 appeals; screening the appeals for different appellate procedural tracks complicates the mathematics somewhat but the aggregate for that year was 88,456 months of appellate decision time.

This increase in the aggregate decision time for the appellate year represents an increase of one full order of magnitude in the total number of months it took to decide a year's worth of federal appeals. Measured in years, the 1990 aggregate is just over 17 times the 1950 aggregate, an increase from four cen- turies to more than seven millennia, an added difference of Biblical propor- tions. Keep in mind that these aggregations of appellate delay are annual figures. This is the total for each calendar year. Beyond peradventure, these numbers must be considered significant, relatively or absolutely.

The comparison seems even worse considered backwards. In 1990, the Courts of Appeals decided 21,006 cases on the merits and took 88,456 months in the aggregate to decide them. If the Courts of Appeals of 1990, with all their new-fangled appellate procedures and added resources and personnel were as efficient as the 1950 courts of appeals (2.2 months appellate interval), the same caseload would have been decided in 46,231 months, closer to half the time they actually took, and each case would have been orally argued with a published opinion. And again, it should be remembered, the appellate interval in the control of the attorneys has not changed appreciably over the same period of comparison. Either the 1990 Courts of Appeals are half as efficient as they were in 1950 or the crisis of volume has them doubled over. . . .

Certainly, everything about the Courts of Appeals is bigger in the 1990s. There are more judges deciding more appeals, of course. But it is most note- worthy that the time it takes the Courts of Appeals to hear and decide all the cases on their annual docket is so much appreciably longer than it was one generation ago. 1950 represents a typical year before the deluge of appeals and before intramural reforms of appellate procedures. 1990 represents the after- math of the "crisis of volume." That the aggregate increase is so huge is even more significant given the wholesale reforms of appellate practice and proce- dure that have taken place over the same period. The computations compar- ing 1950 with 1990 most assuredly would be wholly unacceptable as a "trend" in other areas of federal public policy performance.

Russell R. Wheeler, *Intermediate Courts of Appeals and Their Relations with Top-Level Courts: the US Federal Judicial Experience*, in Andrew Le Sueur, ed., Building the UK's New Supreme Court — National and Comparative Perspectives 262-63 (2004)[18]

To perform their functions, the U.S. courts of appeal must be able to adapt procedures that provide different types of cases with different levels of attention, depending on the nature of the cases. The types of cases that have been respon- sible for the increased caseload in the courts of appeals are largely those that permit abbreviated procedures. As Table 11.8 shows, petitions by state and fed- eral prisoners seeking review of their convictions or changes in their conditions of confinement have increased much more rapidly than the overall caseload. Such petitions (combining the categories in the first and second rows) went from less than 20% of the appellate docket in 1985 to over 30% in 2000, and the trend over longer periods is even more dramatic. Nevertheless, . . . those cases

---

[18] Copyright © 2004 by permission of Oxford University Press.

Table 11.8: Changes in caseload composition

Type of Appeal	1985		1990		1995		2000*		1985-2000
US prisoner petitions	1,492	4.5%	2,246	5.5%	3,453	6.9%	4,955	9.1%	232.1%
Private prisoner petitions	5,052	15.1%	7,749	19.1%	11,527	23.0%	12,297	22.5%	143.4%
Criminal	4,998	14.9%	9,608	23.6%	10,147	20.3%	10,707	19.6%	114.2%
Administrative Appeals	3,179	9.5%	2,532	6.2%	3,298	6.6%	3,237	5.9%	1.8%
Bankruptcy	1,051	3.1%	1,110	2.7%	1,662	3.3%	1,007	1.8%	-4.2%
Other private civil	11,935	35.7%	12,630	31.0%	14,749	29.5%	14,788	27.0%	23.9%
Other US Civil	5,125	15.3%	4,213	10.4%	4,460	8.9%	3,740	6.8%	-27.0%
Original proceeding	618	1.8%	589	1.4%	740	1.5%	3,966	7.3%	541.7%
Total	33,450		40,677		50,036		54,697		63.5%
Per authorized judgeship	199.1		242.1		279.5		305.6		53.5%

Table 11.9: Changing procedures in the US Courts of Appeals

Type of disposition	1985		1990		1995		2000		1985-2000
All terminations	**32,536**		**38,790**		**49,805**		**56,512**		**73.7%**
By consolidation	2,888	8.9%	3,390	9.9%	3,177	6.4%	2,740	4.8%	-5.1%
Cross appeal	1,080		893		770		713		
Consolidated appeal	1,808		2,946		2,407		2,027		
Procedural termination	12,704	39.0%	14,008	36.1%	18,856	37.9%	26,256	46.5%	106.7%
By judge	5,076		5,581		6,817		12,330		
By staff	7,628		8,427		12,039		13,926		
Termination on the merits	16,944	52.1%	20,943	54.0%	27,772	55.8%	27,516	48.7%	62.4%
After oral hearing	9,537	56.3%	9,434	45.0%	11,080	39.9%	9,752	35.4%	
After briefs submitted	7,407		11,509		16,692		17,764		
Oral Opinion	177	40.8%	93	31.9%	99	24.1%	63	20.2%	
Written published opinion	6,921		6,690		6,689		5,558		-19.7%
Written unpublished opinion	9,846		14,160		20,984		21,895		122.4%
All terminations	32,536		38,790		49,805		56,512		73.7%
Per authorized judgeship	193.7		230.9		278.2		315.7		63.0%
Termination on the merits	16,944		20,943		27,772		27,516		62.4%
Per authorized judgeship	100.9		124.7		155.2		153.7		52.4%

"generally do not involve as much work for judges as fully counseled cases because they typically are controlled by well-settled precedent or require a highly deferential standard of review."

Some of the changes that courts of appeals have adopted since the 1960s to help accommodate more cases per judge are highlighted in Table 11.9, showing changes over time in the types of dispositions used by the courts of appeals. These changes [case screening, central staff attorneys, settlement conferences, nonargument calendar, unpublished opinions, noncitation rules, one-word affirmances] have not been unanimously blessed. As the Federal Courts Study Committee put it in 1990, "'the crisis of volume'. . . has transformed [the federal appellate courts] from the institutions they were even a generation ago."

NOTES

1. How effective have the various procedural reforms been to increase the productivity of the state and federal appellate courts? Which reforms have not been successful? Which reforms might be pursued more? Are there still other reforms that might be considered? Or have the procedural shortcuts been taken to their limits? Are there limits to the procedural shortcuts, either constitutional due process limits or policy limits in terms of the appellate imperatives? What would have happened to the state and federal courts if they had not developed and implemented these various procedural responses to the "crisis of volume"? One of the greatest judges of the era before the "crisis of volume" and its aftermath, Judge Learned Hand once said, "If we are to keep our democracy, there must be one commandment: Thou shalt not ration justice." Learned Hand, Address Before the Legal Aid Society of New York, *Thou Shalt Not Ration Justice* (Feb. 16, 1951), in LEGAL AID BRIEF CASE, Apr. 1951, at 3, 5. Have our state and federal courts broken this commandment?

2. Consider the two extreme modes of appellate process: at one extreme is the full, traditional appellate process — attorneys, written briefs, oral argument, conference among the judges, lengthy published opinions that elaborate a body of precedent — and at the other extreme is the complete truncation of process — no printed transcript, no briefs, no oral argument, no conference among the judges, a one-word affirmance or possibly a memorandum opinion prepared by a central staff attorney that cannot be cited. Like most court insiders, suppose you agree that every appeal does not require or deserve the full traditional appellate process. But suppose, like some court insiders, you are concerned that the complete truncation mode is lacking basic attributes of fairness and decisional integrity that are fundamental to an appeal as of right. Considering the various procedural shortcuts described in Chapter 8, and taking into account the possibilities for adding judges, law clerks, and central staff attorneys described in the Chapter 7, try to design an optimum internal process for a busy intermediate appellate court that maximizes efficiency and provides adequate assurance of fair and just results.

3. Judge Posner relies on economic theory to help understand the political motives behind the pattern of responses to the "crisis of volume:"

[W]ithout ever clearly acknowledging their policy, the people who control the federal court system (members of Congress, executive branch officials, judges, and judicial administrators) have acted consistently as if they had an unshakable commitment to accommodating any increase in the demand for federal judicial services without raising the price of those services directly (as by filing fees) or indirectly (as by imposing delay), in the short run or the long run. . . .

The political appeal of this response is evident. It shifts the cost of dealing with the increase in demand for federal judicial services from current users (realistically, the . . . lawyers as well as the actual litigants) — who could be expected to protest vociferously if they had to pay more for using the federal courts, whether in the form of explicit user fees, queues, or restrictions on the federal courts' jurisdiction — to a diffuse group consisting of the taxpayers who have to pay for a larger federal court system, and, to the extent that the measures taken to accommodate the increased demand adversely affect the quality of the justice meted out by the federal courts, of the public at large.

RICHARD A. POSNER, THE FEDERAL COURTS: CHALLENGE AND REFORM 128-29 (1996). If the demand for appellate court decisionmaking exceeds the supply, why not simply allow the price to rise by raising the direct cost, *i.e.*, charge higher and higher filing fees? What about the other path not taken to raise the indirect cost: maintain all the traditional process, true to the appellate imperatives, to have an oral argument and a full published opinion, *etc.* in every case (pretty much the way appellate courts functioned until the late 1960s) with the consequence that cases would queue up and the time for deciding appeals would lengthen and lengthen with the increases in the caseload? Do your answers to these questions change between federal appellate courts and state appellate courts?

4. One response to the "crisis of volume," as we learned in the Chapter 7, has been to increase the supply of judges — but only up to a point — and to increase the staff of judges by adding law clerks and deploying central staff attorneys. Yet, over the same time, as we learned in Chapter 8, there has been a radical truncation of process at every phase of federal appellate procedure. Why not consider an equally radical supply-side solution to greatly increase the size of the federal judiciary in order to maintain, really to restore, the important hallmarks of traditional appellate process? In a plea to Congress to create more federal judgeships, a Ninth Circuit judge made this admission:

> I speak primarily about the courts of appeals. Those who believe we are doing the same quality work that we did in the past are simply fooling themselves. We adopt more and more procedures for "expediting" cases, procedures that ensure that individual cases will get less attention. In place of the traditional oral argument and written opinions that we used to provide in most instances, we now all too often give cases second-class treatment. We merely look at the files and then issue unpublished memorandum dispositions or orders.

The use of these makeshift procedures ensures that many cases do not get the full attention they deserve, and the quality of our work suffers. It is a most unsatisfactory way for us to have to do our job.

Stephen Reinhardt, *A Plea to Save the Federal Courts — Too Few Judges, Too Many Cases*, 79 A.B.A. J. 52 (1993).

5. Judge Wallace of the U.S. Ninth Circuit recognizes the reality that these procedural reforms are here to stay:

> [T]here will always be commentators who argue that widespread adoption of appellate case management and mediation techniques signals not a ratification of the approach, but rather the acceptance of a necessary evil — that is, that oppressive workloads are corrupting more and more courts to prize efficiency over quality. I could not disagree more with such an assessment. To me, each time a judiciary embraces appellate court case management and mediation, more credence is lent to the practices. Indeed, not only is case management becoming pervasive, but courts readily recognize that increasing efficiency does not necessarily compromise core judicial principles.
>
> . . . . Due process, literally, is the amount of process due — that is, the proceedings to which a party is entitled to protect its rights in the face of the law's coercive power. Flexibility inheres in this concept; surely not every appeal is "due" extensive procedures. . . .
>
> In fact, if the legal system channeled all appeals to judges and expected them to reflect deeply on every case no matter how facially unmeritorious, it would risk depriving litigants of the right to due process in other cases, especially those that raise difficult or complex issues or confront the court with a question for the first time. . . .
>
> In sum, as more demands are placed on scarce appellate judicial resources . . . more courts are recognizing that case management and mediation efforts are not inimical to due process. Rather, these courts are coming to understand that the opposite holds true: streamlined case management and mediation mechanisms actually ensure that this lofty principle remains intact.

J. Clifford Wallace, *Improving the Appellate Process Worldwide Through Maximizing Judicial Resources*, 38 VAND. J. TRANSNAT'L L. 187, 212-13 (2005).

6. "The history of procedure is a series of attempts to solve the problems created by the preceding generation's procedural reforms." Judith Resnik, *Precluding Appeals*, 70 CORNELL L. REV. 603, 624 (1985). Looking back over all the previous generation's reforms in appellate procedures responding to the crisis of volume, what new problems have been created and how might they be solved? Are there ways to insure against the concerns that some appeals are getting second-class consideration?

Chapter 10

THE CONTEMPORARY
ROLE OF APPELLATE COUNSEL

I. INTRODUCTION

This chapter invites reflection on the impact on the work of appellate lawyers of the developments sketched in Chapters 7 and 8. An astute appellate lawyer must be aware of the changes in use of personnel and in process, because they call for an altered style of presentation by advocates, at least in some subtle ways. Before considering what the alterations might be, it is useful to review the steps typically involved in lawyers' appellate work.

A lawyer representing a litigant dissatisfied with the trial court result and considering an appeal needs to: (1) study the trial court proceedings and disposition to determine whether there are plausible grounds for a successful appeal; (2) advise the client whether an appeal would be worthwhile and ascertain whether, in light of that advice, the client wishes to pursue the appeal; (3) if an appeal is to be taken, prepare and file the notice of appeal and any other papers necessary to perfect the appeal; (4) assemble the required record and timely file it in the appellate court; (5) prepare and file the appellant's brief; (6) if oral argument is to be heard, appear in court and present the argument.

A. The Decision Whether to Appeal

In studying the trial court record and considering whether an appeal would be worthwhile, a number of factors come into play. (How many can you think of, before you read what follows?) The considerations include:

a) the likely costs, including attorneys' fees and expenses such as paralegal time, the cost of transcript and record-preparation, docketing fees, copying charges, costs of reproducing the brief and appendix or record-excerpts, and travel for oral argument;

b) the client's interest in resuming a normal business relationship with the litigation adversary, and the intangible interests at stake in the litigation such as an emotional investment in the principles at issue, the stress of uncertainty, and other personal considerations. The time it will take for an appeal to run its course may be significant in appraising whether it is worthwhile;

c) the odds that filing the appeal would lead to a settlement more favorable than the present judgment;

d) the odds that filing an appeal will provoke a cross-appeal, and the risks attendant upon that possibility;

e) the odds of winning on appeal. This determination entails evaluating the existence and significance of errors in the trial court as reflected in rulings on motions, on the admissibility of evidence, in jury instructions and the like.

Reaching a sound judgment as to the odds of winning on appeal includes consideration of whether the trial attorney properly preserved errors on the record, and what the standard of review will be on any alleged errors. It may require a judgment as to how likely the appellate court would be to modify or abandon old precedent. Research into the reversal rate of the particular appellate court in general, in the specific kind of case, or as to the specific kind of issue involved may be appropriate.

An arguable error in the trial court proceedings that might have produced a reversal when appellate courts were less pressed for time might not do so today. The types of issues and alleged trial errors likely to elicit the serious interest of appellate judges will vary from one jurisdiction to another. Appellate advocates must know the jurisprudence of the particular appellate courts in which they practice in order to accurately analyze the chances of success on appeal. That is, lawyers must understand the substantive rules likely to be applied by the court, as well as the particular court's position on trial court discretion and supervision of trial courts. All of this is summed up in one of the most venerable maxims of appellate practice: Know your court.

Professional responsibility, to the client and to the courts, calls for a lawyer not to recommend an appeal unless the lawyer believes in good faith, after study of the case, that there is at least an arguable likelihood of prevailing in the appellate court. The ultimate decision whether to appeal is for the client to make, after receiving the lawyer's advice, although professional ethics constrain the lawyer, as will be discussed later in this chapter.

f) the likely consequences of a win. The likely consequences might include having to retry the case, but the value of that opportunity would depend on the probability and benefits of winning that retrial as compared with its financial and other costs. Or a successful appeal might result in an immediate judgment in the appellant's favor. Another likely consequence might be a sense of vindication or other intangible benefits. It is vital to define the objectives of an appeal so that one can appraise their attainability;

g) the likely consequences of a loss. Losing might mean having an adverse decision on the law become a matter of precedent, with adverse consequences for the future, rather than having merely a non-precedential decision by a trial judge, affecting this dispute only;

h) how the costs of appeal (financial and otherwise) compare with the likely benefits of appeal, considering both the probability and the meaning of success; and

i) the pros and cons of alternatives to appeal such as filing post-trial motions in the trial court.

The lawyer representing the party that prevailed in the trial court ordinarily is not concerned with initiating an appeal, so that lawyer usually does nothing unless the other side takes an appeal. Then, as lawyer for the appellee, that attorney will have to prepare and file a brief for the appellee and present oral argument if argument is to be heard. Of course, the appellee's lawyer must be sure that all pertinent material in support of the appellee's position is included in the record. If the appellee has any grounds to cross-appeal, counsel for the appellee also must make the kind of calculations that any appellant's lawyer must make in deciding whether an appeal is worth taking. All of these steps for both parties are governed by procedural rules of the particular appellate court, and it is essential that a lawyer follow these rules meticulously. A representative set of such rules is the Federal Rules of Appellate Procedure, applied in the United States courts of appeals.

NOTES

1. As Professor Robert Martineau has pointed out, attorneys are well advised to make the possibility of appeal part of their strategy from the outset. The possibility of appeal can influence where an action is filed and whether it is removed, in terms of the choice between federal and state court when litigants have that choice, and in terms of the state of filing, because the differences between systems' appellate procedure may be significant to the parties. The possibility of appeal also may affect how the issues are framed in the pleadings and at trial, and attorneys' conduct during trial, because procedural steps may be prerequisites to taking an appeal. ROBERT J. MARTINEAU, MODERN APPELLATE PRACTICE-FEDERAL AND STATE CIVIL APPEALS § 2.1 (1983).

2. As noted in the text, the reversal rate of the appellate court to which one is appealing may be a consideration in the decision whether to appeal. The Administrative Office of the U.S. Courts reports the federal appellate reversal rate for each circuit except the Federal Circuit and overall for the included circuits. For the twelve months ending March 31, 2004, of the total appeals and original appellate proceedings terminated on the merits (27,222), 21,444 were affirmed, 2,377 were dismissed and 2,162 — only 8.7% of the total — were reversed. In private civil litigation, of the 6,421 appeals terminated on the merits, 271 were dismissed and 793 (12.4%) were reversed. In private civil litigation, the reversal rate ranged from a low of 0.9% in the Second Circuit to 18.6% in the Seventh Circuit. For information about the individual circuits and data as to criminal, bankruptcy, administrative, and other categories of appeals, see http://www.uscourts.gov/caseload2004/tables/B05Mar04.pdf.

The National Center for State Courts data on reversal rates in 11 states [Alabama, Alaska, Delaware, Illinois, Massachusetts, Minnesota, New Mexico, New York, North Carolina, North Dakota, Texas], and Puerto Rico for 2002 (its most recent, but unpublished, data) show reversal rates ranging from 1.4% by the Illinois Appellate Court to 17.65% by the Minnesota Supreme Court. Data for particular courts may be available on their websites. See also the reversal rates reported in Chapter 1, Section IV.

State	Reversing Court	Total Dispositions	Reversed Decisions	Reversal Percentage
Alabama	Court of Civil Appeals	1,306	145	11.10
Alabama	Court of Criminal Appeals	2,748	39	01.42
Alaska	Supreme Court	516	50	09.70

State	Reversing Court	Total Dispositions	Reversed Decisions	Reversal Percentage
Alaska	Court of Appeal	302	31	10.26
Delaware	Supreme Court	713	42	05.89
Illinois	Appellate Court	9,419	133	01.41
Massachusetts	Appeals Court	2,869	178	06.20
Minnesota	Supreme Court	204	36	17.65
Minnesota	Court of Appeals	2,007	235	11.71
New Mexico	Court of Appeals	855	103	12.00
New York	Appellate Div. of Sup. Ct.	19,109	1,457	07.62
New York	Appellate Terms of Sup. Ct.	1,928	305	15.82
North Carolina	Supreme Court	732	30	04.10
North Dakota	Supreme Court	345	43	12.46
Puerto Rico	Supreme Court	1,240	165	13.31
Texas	Courts of Appeals	12,399	777	06.27

3. A recent study of losing civil litigants in urban Illinois, urban/rural mixed Minnesota, and mostly rural Mississippi found that those litigants often had different objectives in appealing than their lawyers had. While the lawyers focused on the likely outcome, their clients often were more focused on process values. They sought the opportunity to show a higher court how their opponents or the trial court had wronged them. "The belief that the appellate court would treat their claims seriously seemed to vindicate the appellants' perceptions of the appropriateness of their claim." They sought an opportunity to be heard by an authoritative decision maker — to have their stories told to and taken seriously by an appellate court; and they hoped to be a force in eventually bringing about change, whether or not they personally benefitted from that change. Thus, many clients were not deterred by the information that they had a slim chance of prevailing on their appeals. *See* Scott Barclay, *A New Aspect of Lawyer-Client Interactions: Lawyers Teaching Process-Focused Clients to Think about Outcomes*, 11 CLINICAL L. REV. 1, 6 (2004).

How should this disjunction between an attorney's goals and the client's goals be reflected in the decision whether to appeal? Should an attorney try to disabuse a client (1) of a belief that the mere fact that an appellate court will entertain the appeal vindicates the client's stance in the litigation? or (2) of a belief that the appeal is another opportunity to tell the client's story? Are the objectives of a client who holds these beliefs inappropriate reasons to appeal? Should the appellate system change to better fulfill such clients' objectives in appealing?

B. Effects on Appellate Advocacy of Changes in Appellate Personnel and Process

All of the steps in appellate practice that were noted in the text preceding Section A above have obtained for decades. The primary questions considered in this chapter are the manner and extent to which the work of appellate advocates has been affected by changes made in appellate courts as the result of the substantial increase in the number of appeals. How have the developments concerning the use of judicial personnel and the changes in internal processes altered the work of lawyers presenting appeals?

For purposes of examining this question, we assume that we are dealing with the initial appeal from a trial court, an appeal on the merits as a matter of right. We assume that the appeal is to the intermediate appellate court (provided, as is usually the case, that the judicial system has an intermediate level). We also assume that this is a high-volume court in which there are numerous three-judge panels, a central staff of substantial size, and internal processes involving screening and differentiated decisional tracks. In this hypothesized court, a large number of cases are decided without oral argument and with unpublished memorandum opinions.

Once a decision is made to appeal, the filing of the notice and possibly other papers will proceed, as will the assembling and filing of the record. Unless the court's rules provide otherwise, the next step normally will be preparation and filing of the appellant's brief. In constructing the brief, the appellant's counsel needs to know and understand the court's internal processes and to bear them in mind.

In the appellate court assumed here, the first person to read the brief will be one of the central staff attorneys. That staff attorney's principal task will be to decide, at least tentatively, whether the case should be routed to oral argument or designated for decision without argument. Realizing this, and realizing also that the affirmance rate for non-argued cases is quite high, the appellant's advocate must frame the issues and argument in a way that is likely to lead the staff attorney to conclude that the case fits the court's standards for oral argument. How this is to be done will depend on the nature of the issues and the lawyer's creative imagination. Of course, the lawyer must work within the record and the applicable law, and these constraints may make it difficult to accomplish this objective. Nevertheless, the lawyer should construct the brief with a keen awareness that it will be the basis for this critical staff routing action. At the same time, the lawyer must be aware that the case may not be orally argued; in some courts, fewer than half the appeals are scheduled for argument. (In 2004, in the federal courts of appeals collectively, excluding the Federal Circuit, only 32% of appeals terminated on the merits were decided after oral hearing, rather than after submission on briefs. *See* http://www.uscourts.gov/ judicialfactsfigures/table1.08.pdf. Most states do not publish the percentage of cases in which appellate courts hear oral arguments, but what statistics there are indicate that a far higher percentage of cases are orally argued in some states. In 2001 or 2002, of nine states that published these figures, the lowest percent argued was 14.5% in Rhode Island and the highest was 98.9% in North Carolina. *See* RUGGERO J. ALDISERT, WINNING ON APPEAL: BETTER BRIEFS AND ORAL ARGUMENT 16 (2d ed. 2003).) Because the brief may be the only communication from the lawyer to the judges, the lawyer must present a fully developed argument.

At the same time, the brief should be true to its name and be kept as short as possible. Courts typically impose page limits. Beyond that, the staff attorney, beset with many appeals to process, may be persuaded more effectively by a short, well-written brief than by a verbose document. Moreover, busy appellate judges with central staff attorneys preparing memoranda may give a brief only a cursory examination. The shorter the brief, the more likely it is that the judges will actually read it, or at least substantial portions of it. If judges are reading briefs from their computer screens, the need for conciseness is no less, in consideration of tired eyes. Key statutory provisions and portions of documents should be set out in an appendix to the brief so that they will be immediately accessible.

If the case is scheduled for oral argument, the advocates must prepare and present an argument that takes account of the high-volume circumstances under which the judges are functioning. The length of argument has been reduced in most courts; fifteen minutes per side is now not unusual. This time limitation means that a lawyer must get immediately to the crucial one or two points in the case. Almost all appellate courts today function as "hot courts." That is, the judges will have prepared themselves in advance of the oral argument. Typically each judge will have read either a staff memorandum or a bench memorandum prepared by his law clerk. Thus, it is not likely to be necessary for the appellant's counsel to trace the proceedings below. However, counsel is well advised to be prepared to do this in case the judges express interest in that history. In any event, it is appropriate for appellant's counsel to open the presentation with a few sentences of explanation as to the general nature of the case, the court from which it comes, the decision below, and the key question presented on appeal. But unless there are questions from the judges, counsel should move immediately to the main and strongest point for reversal. The appellee's counsel will want to put forth, without preliminary meanderings, the strongest argument for affirmance.

While much traditional advice about effective brief writing still holds true, traditional advice as to oral argument techniques is less helpful because oral argument has been more affected by the changed circumstances in appellate courts. Time-tested techniques of appellate advocacy have to be applied with attention to the altered decisional processes in particular appellate forums.

Some writings on appellate advocacy are focused on the presentation of cases in the United States Supreme Court. Although some of the techniques recommended in these writings would be useful in any appellate court, an attorney must recognize that because of the different function of the Supreme Court some arguments one would make to that Court would not be suitable in any lower court.

Entire law school "skills" courses may be devoted to appellate advocacy. It is not the objective of this chapter to offer a "crash" course that supplants such courses. The extracts that follow, from the writings of experienced appellate judges and lawyers, and addressing appellate advocacy in contemporary circumstances, are intended to highlight points that are especially responsive to today's altered appellate setting. In addition, recall the material presented in Chapter 8, Section C, concerning the debate over oral argument's value to judges; it too contains insights as to effective oral presentations amidst the crisis of volume.

NOTES

1. Useful books for law students, written with an awareness of the contemporary appellate setting, include RUGGERO J. ALDISERT, WINNING ON APPEAL: BETTER BRIEFS AND ORAL ARGUMENT (2d ed. 2003); APPELLATE PRACTICE

MANUAL (Patricia Anne Schwab ed., 1992); MICHAEL R. FONTHAM, DAVID W. MILLER, MICHAEL VITIELLO, PERSUASIVE WRITTEN AND ORAL ADVOCACY: IN TRIAL AND APPELLATE COURTS (2002); MICHAEL E. TIGAR & JANE B. TIGAR, FEDERAL APPEALS: JURISDICTION AND PRACTICE (3d ed 1999); FREDERICK BERNAYS WIENER, BRIEFING AND ARGUING FEDERAL APPEALS (rev. ed. 2001). *See also* Andrew L. Frey & Roy T. Englert, Jr., *How to Write a Good Appellate Brief*, 20 LITIG. 6 (1994); Luther T. Munford, *Appealing to a Deluged Court*, 5 PRAC. LITIG. 61 (1994). Older writings still worth consulting include: ADVOCACY AND THE KING'S ENGLISH (George Rossman ed., 1960); COUNSEL ON APPEAL (Arthur A. Charpentier ed., 1968); Whitman Knapp, *Why Argue an Appeal? If So, How?*, 14 REC. N.Y.C.B.A. 415 (1959); Karl N. Llewellyn, *A Lecture on Appellate Advocacy*, 29 U. CHI. L. REV. 627 (1962).

2. Be aware, however, that appellate practice has increasingly become a specialty. This is evidenced in part by the establishment of two professional organizations of appellate lawyers: the American Academy of Appellate Lawyers (membership in which is by invitation) and the Council of Appellate Lawyers, which operates under the aegis of the ABA Appellate Judges Conference and is open to ABA members who are appellate practitioners. The periodical, *Journal of Appellate Practice and Process,* also has been established.

II. TECHNIQUES FOR A NEW SETTING

A. Views from the Bench

North Dakota Supreme Court Appellate Practice Tips

http://www.ndcourts.com/court/filing/tips.htm

General

. . .

- When your client wants to appeal as a matter of principle, tell the client how much principal it will take. . . .
- Seek to persuade, not to show how much you know.
- You serve your client by maintaining your own credibility. . . .
- Acknowledge obvious weaknesses in your case and explain why you should win anyway . . .
- Drop the hyperbole!!!
- Cheap shots at the other side will only hurt your case.
- "Civility is not too much to expect in a civilized society . . ." *Jacobson v. Garaas*, 652 N.W.2d 918.
- Not every lawyer excess is justified by the mantra of zealous representation.
- A lawyer is not always protected by following the client's specific directions.
- Summary judgment can't be reversed on appeal based on what you wish you had presented in the trial court, only on what was presented as competent evidence in the trial court. . . .

- When you discover you are riding a dead horse, the best strategy is to dismount.

- "The best arguments are those that tell us how you believe we can do justice and maintain the integrity of the law at the same time." — former Justice Robert Vogel

. . .

Briefs

. . .

- Don't make your brief a mystery. Tell the reader what the case is about right up front. . . .

- Statements of the facts should be placed in chronological order, not in the order of testimony. . . .

- The word "clearly" is no substitute for authority or logic.

- Arguing in favor of the position taken in a recent dissent is almost never successful. . . .

- Cite only cases you have actually read. . . .

- Make sure cases and statutes are cited correctly. Make sure cases cited are still good law.

- Read the cases cited by your opponent.

- Avoid "legalese." Don't use "pursuant to," "hereinafter," "herein." Never use "said" as an adjective or an article. Clear language — not pompous or ponderous language — is most effective.

- The possessive "its" has no apostrophe, just as there is no apostrophe in "his," "hers," "theirs," "yours," and "ours." "It's," with the apostrophe, means "it is." . . .

- "Always use your computer's spell check, and never trust it." Steve Wilbers, Minneapolis Star Tribune . . .

- "Error" is a noun. "Err" is a verb. A party errs by saying "The trial court did not error. . . ." "Time period" is redundant. . . .

- At the end of your brief, state clearly and concisely what specific action you are seeking from the appellate court. For example, if you are the appealing party, it's not enough to ask the court to say the trial court was wrong, you must say what you are asking the appellate court to do about it. . . .

- Briefs should have a binding allowing them to lie open without having to be held down. Justices often have more documents open than they have hands. . . .

- Proofread. Then proofread again.

Appendix

- Only material actually in the trial court record may be included in the Appendix. . . .

Oral Argument

- The primary purpose of oral argument is to answer the court's questions. . . .

- Prepare, prepare, prepare. Review the record and your cases and your opponent's cases before oral argument. Check this website for opinions issued since you filed your brief. If you didn't handle the case in the trial court, you are still expected to be familiar with the record.

- Be prepared to discuss each case you cite and each case your opponent cites.

- Start off oral argument on the right foot. The traditional opening is "May it please the court". . . . In North Dakota, the Supreme Court has a "Chief Justice" and "Justices," not "Associate Justices." . . .

- Answer [a] question when it is asked.

- Don't evade.

- Don't answer a question with a question.

- If you don't know the answer to a question, say so.

- If the premise of a question is wrong, politely say so.

- If a Justice throws you a life preserver, don't bat it away. . . .

- Remember, the Justice asking the question isn't the only audience for your answer.

- Oral argument is not the time to present a list of cases that could have and should have been in your brief.

- Don't talk faster than the Justices can listen. . . .

- Watch the podium time lights.

- When your time is up, your time is up. Stop.

- Don't ask, "May I briefly conclude?"

Petitions for Rehearing

. . .

- Don't file a petition for rehearing if the real audience is the client. . . .

- A Petition for Rehearing will not succeed by simply parroting the dissent.

- A Petition for Rehearing merely repeating the argument previously made is pointless . . .

Shirley Hufstedler, *The Art of Oral Argument*[1]

Oral argument is an art, but it is not a gentle art, nor can it be, because oral argument is an integral part of decision making and nothing about making hard decisions is gentle.

---

[1] Based on a speech delivered at the Henry M. Campbell Memorial Competition Banquet, University of Michigan Law School, *in* Law Quadrangle Notes, March 12, 1974. Copyright © 1974. Reprinted with permission. Judge Hufstedler served on the U.S. Court of Appeals for the Ninth Circuit from 1968-79.

Moot court arguments, both in brief and in oral advocacy, are superb teaching devices. Yet, I have some reservations about them. . . .

[T]he combination of moot court competitions and casebooks bulging with opinions from rarefied appellate courts may lead neophyte lawyers to believe that arguments before trial courts and the earthier appellate courts are not much different from those appropriate in the Supreme Court of the United States. In fact, a lawyer who makes the same kind of arguments to each level of the state and federal hierarchies is going to turn up a loser, unless the advocate has an archangel on his or her shoulder — preferably Moses, with tablets, suitably inscribed. That is not because the intellectual girth of judges automatically expands with each rise in the judicial ladder and not because a case in the Supreme Court did not begin in a trial tribunal. Rather, it is because the institutional roles and functions of each court are different, and effective argument must be addressed to the institutional concerns and restraints of each level of courts.

Argument before a trial court is supposed to fit the evidence into a unified composition, to brush in the lights and shadows, to throw the images into perspective, and to press the whole into a legal theory supported by statutes or case authority that leads the court irresistibly to the advocate's predetermined result. While not fudging the facts nor obscuring pertinent statutory and appellate law, the advocate leans hard on any existing law favorable to his cause and seeks distinguishing features of every authority that looks the other way. Unless he is writing on a totally clean precedential slate, the advocate has little or no occasion to expound his views of policy. He gets nowhere by attacking an opinion of a higher court, to which the trial court is bound, on the ground that the precedent is aging and wrong, because it is a brave trial judge or a foolhardy one — depending on your point of view — who thinks his task is to overrule the law laid down by a court that can reverse him. Of course, the trial advocate must know how to lay the appropriate challenge in the trial court to preserve his points for the higher courts who have the power to correct their bygone brothers' mistakes.

Intermediate appellate courts have functions very different from either trial courts or courts of last resort. Their duties are a mixture of error correction in the individual case and institutional functions, by which latter term I mean supervising lower courts, filling interstitial spaces in statutory and case law, and, from time to time, striking out a few paces on a new jurisprudential path. Broad-gauge policy making is only rarely a part of these courts' institutional concerns. Arguments addressed to these courts are most effective when the advocate can persuade the courts that existing precedent controls, or if it does not, that it need be nudged only a little to reach his conclusion.

Arguments addressed to courts of last resort exercising discretionary review are very different creatures because the function of these courts is to establish overarching precedents and policy for every level of the judicial system below their lofty perches. Here's the place to topple the eroded cases. Here's the place to argue your legal and social philosophies — at least to the extent that you have reason to believe a majority of the court may find your arguments convincing. In these courts, the advocate must realize that he would not be there unless some of the judges believed that prior law was inadequate to dispose of the case. The concern of these courts is not so much where the law has been as where it should be going. The function of courts of last resort, exercising powers of discretionary review, is not correcting error in individual cases. The overriding function is setting precedent and policy, although such courts may perform incidental error correction.

Apart from shaping arguments to the functions of each level of courts, a successful advocate must know how the particular appellate court handles oral argument. It is essential to learn about the internal operating procedures of each court in order to frame an effective argument. In the unimaginative cant of appellate courtese, there are "hot and cold" benches. "Hot" benches are those in which all of the judges always read the briefs before argument. "Cold" benches are those in which the judges never read the briefs before argument. Among the hot courts, some are scorchers and others are tepid. Scorchers like the United States Supreme Court do a good deal of independent work on the case before oral argument. Woe to the advocate whose preparation quit before the Court's did. Obviously, the kind of argument the advocate makes depends enormously upon what kind of temperature that court runs. Cold bench enthusiasts are not slothful; the judges who practice the method defend it on a basis of the joys of free-wheeling advocacy. I confess that I have never been an adherent of the benefits from ignorance. . . .

The attitudes of different appellate courts towards oral argument are as varied as Darwin's singular group of finches. As you are aware, oral argument is highly valued in the Supreme Court, if it is well done. Questioning from desultory to devastating must be anticipated. The same attitude prevails in most federal appellate courts. Other appellate courts may simply tolerate oral argument as quietly as possible. No appellate lawyer is worth his fee if he has not done the basic research to determine how the particular court conducts argument and the role which that court assigns to oral advocacy.

Diane P. Wood, *Judicious Advice for the Occasional Appellate Lawyer*, 11 Chicago Bar Association Record 16 (1997)[2]

Appellate practice is only as hard as you make it. You must . . . learn[] the court's rules and internal practices. And, you must . . . take a cold hard look at your case as it was shaped in the trial court and bear in mind . . . the perspective the appellate judges will have. . . .

Know The Basics

. . . Know your appellate court, inside and out. . . . Do the judges call themselves "Judge" or "Justice" as a title? (If you're in federal court, the answer is "Judge," . . . ; if you're in Illinois state court, the answer is "Justice.") What is the final action in the trial court that starts the clock on your time to appeal, and how long will you have to file your notice of appeal? What should be included in the record on appeal? Are you admitted to practice before the court of appeals?

---

2 Copyright © 1997 by the Chicago Bar Association. Reprinted with permission. Judge Wood serves on the U.S. Court of Appeals for the Seventh Circuit.

If the court to which you are appealing is the Seventh Circuit, . . . obtain a copy of the . . . *Practitioner's Handbook for Appeals to the United States Court of Appeals for the Seventh Circuit*. . . .

Once . . . your oral argument date is coming up, . . . visit the courthouse, find the courtrooms and familiarize yourself with the layout. Talk with someone who knows the scene: for example, in our court when the white light turns on at the podium during oral argument, it means the appellant has finished the initial time and is now cutting into his or her own rebuttal time; we give no two-minute warning that the initial time itself is about to expire. I have seen a distressing number of lawyers look shocked after the appellee is finished when they learn that they have already used up all their rebuttal time. Forewarned is forearmed: do everything you can to avoid those kinds of unpleasant surprises.

Begin The Appellate Process With The Complaint

. . . The legal issues that you may wish to bring before the appellate court should, at a fundamental level, be something you have been developing since the outset of the litigation. . . . If you don't know what your theory is at trial, there is a real risk that you will not build the kind of record you need to win on appeal.

Conversely, when the trial lawyer has taken a long-term view of the case and litigated it with clear legal theories in mind, the appellate brief practically writes itself.

The Harmless Error Rule

. . . [F]rom our perspective as an appellate court the crucial word is "prejudice:" did the ruling about which you are now trying to complain have a significant impact on your case, or was it just "harmless error?"

Standards Of Review

. . . Federal Rule of Appellate Procedure 28(a)(6) requires the argument section of each brief to include "for each issue a concise statement of the applicable standard of review." It is important to take great care in identifying exactly what the appeal is about for this purpose. Is the real problem the facts? Is it a legal error in instructions? Should the district court have admitted certain expert testimony? Advocates gain nothing by attempting to recharacterize a dispute over the facts found below as a legal problem, and they risk losing the confidence of the judges who are reading the briefs. By the same token, if the real dispute is over the interpretation of a statute, for example, it doesn't help much when an appellee assumes the statute means what that side would prefer and argues from that premise that only the facts were disputed. There is no avoiding the fact that it is difficult, though certainly not impossible, to prevail on appeal when the only points that can be raised are factual. Often a party will argue in the alternative that certain independently reviewable errors occurred, and that in any event the facts found were clearly erroneous (perhaps because they were internally inconsistent, perhaps because critical evidence was excluded, perhaps because they flatly contradicted agreed facts).

Errors: Identification, Evaluation

As you . . . identify[ ] errors that might form the basis of an appeal, . . . keep in mind which ones are errors of fact and which are errors of law. From a pragmatic stand-point, this will help you to assess your chances of obtaining a different result on appeal (and thereby will help your client decide whether an appeal makes sense).

. . . FED. R. APP. P. 38 allows a court of appeals to award "just damages and single or double costs to the appellees" if it determines that the appeal was frivolous. . . . [Y]ou should be especially alert to this possibility if your review of the trial proceedings turns up no errors of law, discretionary rulings that could reasonably have gone either way, and factual findings which . . . have support in the record. A "Hail Mary" pass may be worth it for legal errors, especially if you are frank with the court about the need to reconsider some prior precedent in the light of intervening Supreme Court decisions, legislation, Seventh Circuit decisions or something equally important, but it is very unlikely to work for purely factual problems.

Another important point . . .[:] Normally, the appellate court will not consider matters raised for the first time on appeal, for . . . this would lead to sloppy trial court practice [and] . . . deprives the trial judge of the opportunity to take immediate corrective action. Thus, the identification of errors itself should entail . . . reviewing everything to which you objected below, and deciding which of these points survives the final judgment. With that . . . overview before you, you can decide which ones arguably merit the appellate court's attention, what standard of review will apply . . . , and what your chances of prevailing would be.

The Issues On Appeal

. . . [I]t is almost never good practice to present a plethora of issues on appeal. Far better to choose a limited number — three or four, if possible — that are central to the case. . . . It is especially dismaying from the judge's perspective to pick up a brief that lists 10 issues on appeal, in *prolix* wording, typed all in capital letters, without any indication of the relative importance of each one. Although you might be concerned about preserving a point for possible further appeal to the Supreme Court, . . . you don't need a proliferation of issues to preserve your right to further review. To the contrary, your chances of further review are normally enhanced if you focus your arguments carefully at the court of appeals stage of the case and present your points carefully and concisely.

With your limited number of issues on appeal, you will have the space to develop each one sufficiently. . . . Issues should be stated with enough detail to let the court know what the dispute is about — i.e. Which law is involved? What is the nature of the issue under that law? What is the essential context for the issue? You should avoid writing issues that are so detailed that they amount to a repetition of your "summary of the argument." The *Handbook* offers several examples of issues that are not well stated:

Did the district court err in granting [failing to grant] a directed verdict? Was summary judgment properly granted? Was there sufficient evidence to support the jury's verdict? Did the order obtained by the prosecutors after indictment requiring defendant Doe to furnish evidence directly to the prosecutors grant the government a mode and manner of discovery not sanctioned by the law and in violation of the Fourth, Fifth, Sixth and Fourteenth Amendment rights of defendant Doe, thereby rendering evidence relating thereto as inadmissible?

The first three tell the court virtually nothing about why this particular case is on appeal. If the problem relates to summary judgment, it helps to have a hint about which issues of material fact are alleged to be disputed, and under what law the case arises. The last, obviously, is filled with unreadable legalese and offers a scattershot condemnation of the actions of the police. The *Handbook* also offers several examples of well drafted issues, which I commend to your attention.

Final Thought

. . . When I pick up a set of briefs, I begin by looking at the issues presented, as they are phrased by both (or all) parties, and I then turn to the lower court's opinion. . . . I read the rest of the materials . . . only after I know what the lower court has done, and what the parties are focusing on for the appeal.

. . . [I]f you are going to handle an appeal successfully, you must select, rank and state your issues effectively. If you know the two or three points on which you must convince the appellate court, and you organize . . . your written and oral presentation around them, your client, the court and you yourself will all be well served.

John C. Godbold, *Twenty Pages and Twenty Minutes,* 15 Litigation 3 (Spring 1989)[3]

Appellate practice . . . is . . . changing. Bench and bar are learning to get to the bare bones of disputes with less concern for the fat. There is an overall air of "no nonsense." At the same time, the picture of the typical appellate advocate — a wily veteran of many cases and a master of rules, tactics, and wit — is changing. . . . I do not imply that today's advocates are less effective than their predecessors. Many are superb. But all of them need all the help they can get.

Nowadays, the written brief in particular must aim for maximum effectiveness. A brief may be the only shot that counsel gets at the appellate court. . . . Today's advocate must use to his full potential the tools available to him.

My comments are from the side of the bench that reads what advocates write and listens to what they say. I therefore cover both brief writing and oral argument. . . .

Presentation of an appellate case calendared for oral argument involves assembling a group of actors at a formal meeting place under the rules of a highly structured system. Gathered together are (1) the lawyers (and the parties if they want to come); (2) the record of the case; (3) advance written statements of the parties' positions (the briefs); and (4) a body of official deciders (the judges). . . .

Counsel's role in this assembly is communication and persuasion, first by the briefs and then by oral argument. When the meeting occurs, the judges ordinarily will have done their homework. They will be sufficiently acquainted with the matters under discussion that they can understand what is said and perhaps participate in the dialogue. Counsel's participation is specifically defined and rigidly constricted. His skills of communication and persuasion must be brought to bear in a few pages and a few minutes.

---

[3] Copyright © 1989 by the American Bar Association. Reprinted by permission.

Inform and Persuade

There are two steps in counsel's task of convincing the court that what he advocates is correct. . . . But there is a preliminary step. Before counsel can convince, he must inform. . . .

It is not enough that counsel understands perfectly what he writes and speaks. All is in vain unless the court understands. But in many cases, the advocate is so intent upon . . . persuasion that he overleaps the threshold step of making clear to the court what he complains of, how it came about, what he wants the court to do about it, and why. I recall with pain and amusement the comment of a colleague, seated beside me, after 15 minutes of argument by an impassioned lawyer in a significant *en banc* case: "Do you have the remotest idea what he is talking about?"

. . . True, cases are won on the facts and the law, not on the eminence, polished writing, oratory or personality of counsel. A lawyer can, and often does, lose with a good performance and win with a poor one. . . .

Nonetheless, judges need help. They are neither all-wise nor all-seeing. . . . [T]he judge is trying with every ounce of his capacity to traverse the path from issue to answer. Every intellectual pore is open to receive help and guidance from what the lawyers say and write. This help is most effective when there are no artificial obstacles and irrelevant diversions impeding communication. Unfortunately, lawyers erect their own obstructions to the judge's progress from issue to answer.

Courtroom lawyers are endowed with at least a bit more ego than the average person. . . . [T]he loser is tempted to use the appellate court as a forum to soothe his bruised self-esteem. The winner is equally tempted to seek additional elevation of his already triumphant ego. Each attorney wants the approval of the appellate body for his position. . . .

Ego building and esteem repairing, however, are counterproductive when they interfere with the essential tasks of communication and persuasion. And sometimes they do interfere. . . . I keep a file of examples of poor appellate advocacy. One . . . is a 58-page brief, of which 19 pages — one-third of the brief — are devoted to complaints about rulings and events before and at trial, followed by a statement that *none* of these matters is claimed to be reversible error. The crucial question in the case, the basis for appellate decision, is given three pages of superficial and incomplete discussion. Counsel squandered his time and his client's money to compose and print a litany of bruises to his emotions. The court lost the benefit of the guidance and assistance it wanted, needed, and should have had in those wasted pages.

Picking Issues

Each year I tell my law clerks that the most valuable by-product of clerking is grasping the fact that the dispositive issues in appeals are highly predictable. As Justice Robert H. Jackson wrote:

> One of the first tests of a discriminating advocate is to select the question, or questions, that he will present orally. Legal contentions, like the currency, depreciate through over-issue. The mind of an

appellate judge is habitually receptive to the suggestion that a lower court committed an error. But receptiveness declines as the number of assigned errors increases. Multiplicity hints at lack of confidence in any one. [Justice Robert H.] Jackson, *"Advocacy Before the Supreme Court: Suggestions for Effective Case Presentation,"* in ADVOCACY AND THE KING'S ENGLISH 216 (G. Rossman ed., 1960).

It is a lawyer's job to pick with a dispassionate and detached mind the issues that common sense and experience suggest will likely be dispositive. Other issues must be rejected or given short treatment. In oral argument, counsel may have to be even more selective. Eight or ten issues cannot be treated in 20 or 30 minutes. . . .

I recall an especially effective presentation by a young lawyer . . . who walked to the podium and said simply: "My name is So & So, from Houston, Texas. The issue in this case is whether *Chambers v. Maroney* is retroactive." The effect was electric. In two sentences, he had identified himself and precisely targeted the dispositive issue on which discussion would be centered and the case decided. The room came alive. Everyone was mentally on the edge of his chair. In seconds, counsel had riveted the attention of all on the critical question.

. . . .

Clear and Simple

The need to be selective is just one aspect of a more general requisite: You must communicate with the court, by pen and by voice, in terms as simple and as easily understood as the subject matter permits. . . . Write and talk that way to judges. Some are brilliant, some are bright, some pedestrian. But all want to understand, and understanding is the condition precedent to persuasion.

Speak to the court in conversational tones. The day of oration is gone. . . . Argument is more and more a Socratic dialogue between informed and interested persons. . . .

Pointless Jargon

Like other professionals, lawyers love, or fall into, professional jargon. Some words of the profession carry their own credentials and are invaluable: "proximate cause," "self-incrimination," and "impeachment." Other jargon adds nothing and can obscure meaning. In this "no value" category is the following example from my file:

> Without waiving any point heretofore made but expressly relying upon each and all of them, separately, severally and collectively, and without reflecting upon the able judge below, The Honorable _____, United States District Judge for the _____ District of _____, who ordinarily is fair, able and well informed but nevertheless is subject to normal human error, I am constrained to say, respectfully but firmly, that the District Judge committed error to the substantial prejudice of the plaintiff when he declined to accept the argument made in Part IV of plaintiff's trial brief relating to par. 7 of the complaint and instead accepted the contrary argument of the defendant and ruled accordingly.

This is irrelevant nonsense, except for the concluding effort to describe the error, and that effort conceals rather than describes the point. Only when the reader reaches into the body of the actual argument is he able to piece together what the writer means.

Snarled Prose

. . . . [A] corollary to the principle of "tell it short and plain" . . . is "tell it once — or twice at most." Erosion by repetition is a poor way to convince. Most judges will catch the point the first time it is developed. . . . They are more likely to understand if told early. The court blesses the lawyer who steps to the podium and, zap, like an arrow to the center of the target, strikes the heart of the controversy.

Many lawyers also spend too much space and time framing alternative arguments. Every appellate court understands the use of an alternative argument. Judges know that by suggesting an alternative, the advocate does not waive his initial contention. "Even if" or "alternatively" is enough. Using a phrase like "without waiving anything heretofore said to the contrary by specifically insisting thereon" is a trite formalism. It almost implies that the court has neither good sense nor good faith.

Tell the Whole Truth

Besides writing simply, every appellate advocate must state facts and law candidly and accurately. This is an uncompromising absolute. Every sentence must shine with the whole truth. Even when it has been misled, the court may find the correct path, but an attorney who is inaccurate or less than candid interferes with the objective of persuasion. He comes to the court saying "please believe me and be persuaded," but if what he says cannot be believed, he forfeits the confidence that he seeks to create.

Telling the facts accurately does not mean stopping with just those facts favorable to your side. It especially does not mean stating inferences as though they were facts. In an appeal in which everything turned on whether the accused was inside or outside a car when he was arrested, the statement of facts in the defendant's brief said, without qualification or reference to pages of the record, that he was inside the car. The government's brief, with equal assurance and without reference to what the defendant had asserted, baldly stated that the defendant was outside the car. This sent me to the record to read pertinent testimony. I discovered, as you might expect, that some witnesses said the defendant was inside the car, and others said he was outside.

Inferences Aren't Facts

Both counsel misled the court. Neither told us that the evidence was in conflict and that the real issue was whether permissible inferences had been drawn from the conflicting testimony. This is inexcusably bad advocacy.

Both brief and argument should reflect the dignity and professional competence of the spokesman and a respect for the courts, trial and appellate. Improper tone is a self-created impediment. Courts are uncomfortable with a lawyer who recklessly accuses his adversary of misleading the court or misstating the facts. Casting aspersions on an adversary casts a shadow on a lawyer's own standards and on the strength of his presentation. No one expects a good lawyer to roll over and play dead. But firmness and preservation of one's own points and rights seldom require stridency or discourtesy.

Besides keeping the court comfortable, appropriate moderation is also persuasive. I say "appropriate" because a case may call for forceful hard-hitting statements. But not every mosquito must be killed with a sledgehammer. Appellate judges, except brand-new ones, have already heard, and rejected, more *ad hominem* arguments than any one lawyer can think up. A judge who has normal sensibilities and loves the law will react on his own to events that call for outrage.

Answers to Questions

Finally, there is the matter of responding to questions from the bench. In an assemblage where the purpose is to inform and persuade, it should be like manna from heaven for the potential persuade to say to the persuader: "Here is what troubles me about the subject on which you are trying to convince me." This is an opening into the mind of the listener. It is the most valuable piece of information the persuader can get. Most advocates understand this principle and welcome questions from the bench. They know how to capitalize on them. Other counsel unwisely resent questions as intrusions into a carefully prepared and organized presentation. But the court has its own responsibility to reach the correct decision, and only the judge knows what still troubles him.

I have been surprised at the number of experienced advocates who believe that they are overquestioned during oral argument. Though questioning sometimes is overdone, and the judge may ask for help too soon, usually it is essential and inevitable. Judges enjoy lively dialogue, but they too can, and do, impede the communicative process. The solution lies, I believe, in moderation on both sides of the bench. Counsel can recognize and accept why questions are valuable to the court. The court can exercise restraint through fewer and better-thought-out questions, and can be a little less quick on the trigger.

In the written words in his brief and his spoken words at the podium, the advocate should try to leave some parting impression fixed in the minds of the judges who have read and listened. There is no better impression to leave than this: "I understood what he said. He did not say too much. I have confidence in what he said. I am persuaded by it and am compelled to rule with him."

NOTES

1. Other recent writings by judges emphasize the importance of properly framing the issues, knowing the language of relevant statutes, the relevant principles of statutory construction, and the legislative history, knowing the state constitution where it is relevant (Robert J. Cordy, *Voice of the Judiciary: a Practical View from the Appellate Bench*, 46 BOSTON BAR JOURNAL 8 (2002)); knowing the applicable codified rules of appellate procedure and circuit or state court rules, determining which facts are material and what legal principles govern, reviewing the record for possible grounds of error if you represent the appellant, and to that end reading, in its entirety, the transcript of an evidentiary hearing or trial, and writing concisely, precisely, accurately and

clearly. (Joel F. Dubina, *How to Litigate Successfully in the United States Court of Appeals for the Eleventh Circuit*, 29 CUMB. L. REV. 1 (1998/1999)).

2. Judge Dubina's 16 simple suggestions that should help a lawyer achieve success in orally arguing a case are to:

> (1) Be courteous and polite. (2) Get right to the issues. (3) Don't dwell on the facts. (4) Answer the judges' questions directly and precisely. (5) Learn to overcome fear. (6) Cite to Supreme Court authority and Eleventh Circuit authority. (7) Check slip opinions the day before oral argument to see whether recent law impacts your case. (8) Keep in mind that the brief is critical. (9) Know the standards of review. (10) If you represent the appellee, track the argument of the appellant. (11) Know the record. (12) Don't make a jury argument. (13) If you represent the appellee and the district judge committed error, you will do better to admit it and argue that it was harmless. (14) When concluding your argument, tell the court what you want. (15) Educate and teach the court. (16) PREPARE!

Joel F. Dubina, *How to Litigate Successfully in the United States Court of Appeals for the Eleventh Circuit*, 29 CUMB. L. REV. 1, 8-9 (1998 /1999).

3. See also David M. Ebel, Michael R. Murphy, Andrew G. Schultz, *What Appellate Advocates Seek from Appellate Judges and What Appellate Judges Seek from Appellate Advocates*, 31 N.M.L. REV. 255 (2001),[4] where Judge Murphy gave this advice for establishing one's credibility as an appellate advocate:

> First, be obsessive. . . . Be obsessive about adherence to every rule there is, whether it is a rule of court, rule of grammar, or rule of spelling. . . . If there are misspellings, typos, or if it is sloppy, these things are an indication of the quality of the arguments. They destroy any likelihood that you are going to create an aura of credibility. . . .

> Second, you need to create a sense of readability. . . . You need to make your brief easy to read. Use short paragraphs and subdivisions; all of this will help to avoid creating a visual fog of text.

> Third, limit your factual statement to a readable and fairly chronological listing of the important and salient facts. Do not make it a digest of what the witnesses said.

> Fourth, make your product truly brief. There is a psychological message in brevity and it goes somewhat like this: my case is so simple that it doesn't take me 14,000 words. . . .

> Fifth, make only sound arguments and eliminate the weaker ones. Justice Frankfurter, reflecting on this point, once said that it's like a clock striking thirteen. It puts all the other ones in doubt.

> Sixth, be selective with the issues you present, whether you are an appellant or a cross appellant. Adhere to Justice Jackson's admonition that legal contentions, like currency, depreciate through overuse.

---

[4] Copyright © 2001 by New Mexico Law Review. Reprinted with permission. Judges Ebel and Murphy serve on the U.S. Court of Appeals for the Tenth Circuit.

B. Views from the Bar

Brian L. Porto, *The Art of Appellate Brief Writing, 29 Vermont Bar Journal & Law Digest* 30 (2003)[5]

LAWYERS AS PROFESSIONAL WRITERS

The Essentials of an Effective Appellate Brief

A. Preliminary Considerations

The first subject that a brief writer ought to think about is whether the court to which appeal will be . . . made has jurisdiction to hear the case . . . The first query prompts additional questions. Have all the parties been named or identified in the appeal papers? Is the order or judgment below final or an interlocutory order that one can appeal? Have all time deadlines been met? Have events since the decision below made the whole case moot? Brief writers must anticipate these questions, and, if necessary, address them in writing. The failure to do so will make painstaking research and careful drafting on other issues all for naught if the court bases its decision on the threshold jurisdictional issue.

The second subject that a brief writer should ponder is the rules of the court that will hear the appeal. Even the veteran appellate lawyer can always use a brief refresher course. . . .

B. Statement of the Issues

A successful appellate brief begins with a statement of the issues that helps to convince the court to decide the case in your client's favor. . . . [T]he statement of the issues is an opportunity to begin convincing the court of the correctness of your position. Therefore, your statement should not be merely informative; it should be influential too. This advice applies equally to Appellant and Appellee. Therefore, the Appellee's counsel should almost never accept the issues as they are framed in the Appellant's brief, but instead, should rework them to favor the Appellee. State the issues as questions to which the only reasonable response would be: "Well, yes, of course."

It is not easy to produce [such] a question . . . while using relatively few words. Therefore, do not try to do so until you are certain that you understand the pertinent issue and the standard of review that the court will apply to it. If you represent the Appellant, satisfy yourself that any claimed error by the trial court was harmful to your client's case. Otherwise, you may waste time raising an issue that the court will dispatch quickly as harmless error. Besides, appellate courts look askance at briefs that present more than four issues, often assuming that the more issues raised, the less merit each one has. Therefore, you cannot afford to argue marginal issues when you also have *real* issues to argue; a good brief usually argues between one and three real issues.

---

[5] Copyright © 2003. Reprinted with permission of the Vermont Bar Association and Brian L. Porto.

If you represent the Appellant, state first the issue that is most likely to trigger a reversal of the judgment below. This will ensure that the court regards your claims as worthy of the most careful consideration. The only exception . . . applies when, logically, a weaker argument must precede a stronger argument. For example, a procedural issue about the appellate court's jurisdiction should precede a substantive issue. . . .

The statement of an issue should include both facts and law, and it should identify the appropriate standard of review. . . . Three methods of stating an issue are available to the brief writer. One method is the incomplete sentence that begins with "whether." . . . The second method is the full-sentence question. . . . The third method is the multi-sentence question. It identifies pertinent facts and legal principles in one or more declarative sentences, then, . . . it concludes by asking the court a question. . . .

I prefer the second method because a question tends to arouse my curiosity, hence, command my attention, more than an incomplete sentence does. . . . On the other hand, [one should] prefer the multi-sentence format in a case so complex or fact-laden that one cannot present each issue in a full sentence without writing sentences that are as long as paragraphs. William Faulkner notwithstanding, paragraph-long sentences inhibit understanding and prevent persuasion.

Whichever method you use, present each issue in a way that suggests how you want the court to resolve it. . . . [A]sk, "Did the Family Court abuse its discretion when it concluded that Mr. Jones had the present ability to meet his spousal-maintenance and child-support obligations, despite his showing that his only source of income was his wages and tips from tending bar, and that his income was substantially less than the total amount of his monthly support and maintenance obligations? " . . .

It may require considerable rewriting to produce an issue statement that is narrow, clear, and focused. Do not fear or bemoan rewriting, though; it is the birthplace of understanding, and without understanding, there is no persuasion.

C. Statement of the Case

The path . . . to persuasion runs directly through the statement of the case. . . . The statement of the case offers you an opportunity to persuade [the court] that your client is entitled to relief. Seize this opportunity. . . . [I]n your first sentence . . . identify[] plainly the subject of your case. . . . Then weave facts and procedural history into a *balanced and fair account* of the events that led up to the appeal. Heed the words of Senior Circuit Judge Ruggero Aldisert, formerly of the U.S. Court of Appeals for the Third Circuit, . . . that statements of fact and procedural history should be "scrupulously accurate and free of argumentativeness. . . . " [RUGGERO J. ALDISERT, WINNING ON APPEAL: BETTER BRIEFS AND ORAL ARGUMENT 177 (1992).] . . .

The easiest and clearest way to relate facts and procedural history is chronologically. Identify the subject of the case, note what the Appellant is appealing from, then . . . describe pertinent facts and procedural history, beginning with the event(s) that spawned the litigation and ending, if you represent the Appellant, with a brief indication of what your client will argue on appeal. If you represent the Appellee, summarize the Appellant's main argument accurately, then indicate briefly how you will refute it. The following example illustrates.

> On appeal, Mr. Smith argues that the Family Court abused its discretion when it issued its final order because the evidence did not show that his conduct placed Mrs. Smith 'in fear of imminent serious physical harm' within the meaning of 15 V.S.A. § 1101(1)(B). Mrs. Smith rejects this view of the evidence, and will argue that she is a victim of 'abuse' under that statute because Mr. Smith's conduct toward her has indeed placed her 'in fear of imminent serious physical harm.' Thus, Mrs. Smith contends that the Family Court acted well within its discretion when it granted her petition for relief from abuse. Her argument follows.

. . . [T]his example names the parties instead of referring to their legal status (i.e., Appellant or Appellee). This reminds the lawyers and the court that the parties are human beings who deserve a fair and expeditious resolution of their dispute, and it makes your narrative more enjoyable to read. Notice, too, that the example signals to the court the essence of the legal argument to follow. . . .

Regardless of how well you set up your argument, your credibility will suffer if you fail to support statements of fact and procedural history with references to the pages in the printed case or appendix . . . where each statement can be found. . . . You cannot afford to make appellate judges' blood boil, so . . . include page references to the record in your statement of the case.

D. Summary of the Argument

. . . The most important things to remember are what *not* to do. Do not address in the summary subjects that the argument does not address. Do not write a summary until after you have written and edited the argument. It is difficult and dangerous to summarize that which is incomplete and/or not fully understood. Therefore, . . . it is best to write the summary [after you write] the argument. . . .

E. Argument

Appellate brief writing . . . is an art, not a science. There are no "iron laws" that, if followed scrupulously, will make your argument a winner every time. Yet, helpful hints . . . can improve the quality of briefs and the odds of victory considerably.

A persuasive argument is the product of careful research. Whenever you read a case, consider how it relates to cases you read earlier and how it might fit into an argument. Consider also whether the cases reveal anything about the judges' respective judicial philosophies. How do they treat precedents? Are they quick to find an abuse of discretion or to conclude that factual findings below were clearly erroneous? Do they see themselves as deciding narrow issues only or as instruments of social change? Begin constructing an argument . . . as your research proceeds, and write the gist of it down so that you will be able to make a smooth transition to writing when your research is finished. . . .

The transition should begin with a heading that sums up the argument that follows it. A heading should include facts, law, and a conclusion. . . . [I]t must be argumentative. "The question of laches" is a topical heading. "This suit is barred by laches" is an assertive heading. Neither one will make an appellate court want to rule in your favor. So convert them into an argumentative heading, namely, "This suit is barred by laches because it was filed 25 years after the issuance of the original certificate. " If you do this properly, a judge can glean the essence of your argument merely by glancing at the headings that appear in the table of contents.

Begin with your best argument — that is, the one that is most likely to persuade the court to rule in your client's favor. A topic sentence should lead off, and should encapsulate, the argument without . . . repeating the heading that preceded it. . . . A discussion of pertinent precedents should follow, and the precedents must support the legal conclusion stated in the topic sentence. Show how and why these precedents support your legal conclusion. Quote the court's own words to it in order to emphasize that the result you seek is consistent with the precedents. . . . After discussing the precedents, marry them to the facts of the case, and show how this union naturally, if not inevitably, begets the result that you seek. Do your best to depict that result as narrow, safe, and conservative.

Do not neglect the applicable standard of review. . . . Identify it early on in your argument . . . because it is of utmost concern to appellate judges. Indeed, it is likely to be the first question that judges and their law clerks will ask themselves about each argument as they read a brief. Moreover, no matter how creatively you mesh facts and law, you are likely to lose if you assume that review is *de novo* when, in fact, the "abuse-of-discretion" or the "clearly erroneous" standard governs. In order to win, you must show why, under the governing standard of review, the law, as applied to the facts, commands the result that you seek.

If you represent the Appellant, you have the advantage of being able to introduce the court to the case. Use this opportunity to explain how the rule that you propose will affect society. Do not make emotion-laden jury arguments. . . . You also have the burden of showing the appellate court how the trial court erred, which you should do as early on as possible. If you represent the Appellee, you have two advantages; first, the Appellant's brief may offer a large target at which to shoot, and second, a trial court or administrative agency has already agreed with your position. The second advantage means that your client will usually win if the decision below was reasonable (i.e., neither clearly erroneous nor an abuse of discretion).

The brief will be a large target if the Appellant failed to preserve below each of the arguments raised on appeal. Consider whether the Appellant objected properly at trial to the jury instructions that are at issue on appeal, and whether the reasons that the Appellant cites for overturning evidentiary rulings by the trial court were the same reasons cited in timely objections at trial. If not, you have a potential winning argument; namely, that . . . the Appellant waived [its contentions] by failing to preserve them for appeal. After addressing jurisdiction, proceed to rebut the Appellant's substantive arguments. Either attack the reasoning of his authorities directly or show that they do not apply to the facts of the case at hand.

Whether you represent Appellant or Appellee, direct the court's attention to inconsistencies between the documentary and testimonial evidence that your opponent offered below. Confront adverse authority directly; do not try to hide or to avoid cases or statutes that run counter to the rule that you propose. Finally, indicate the result that you seek. For the Appellee's counsel, this may be simply an affirmance of the trial court's decision. For the Appellant's counsel, it may include a request beyond reversal, such as to release the client from custody or to dismiss an indictment.

F.   Conclusion

In brief writing, less is more and small is beautiful. Small words, economical sentences, and short briefs are generally advisable. The exception to this rule is the conclusion, where lawyers' custom is to write less than they should. . . . [B]egin with two or three sentences that remind the judges of your reasoning and of why it should prevail. Make the request for relief the last sentence of the conclusion, not the first.

Editing the Brief

If you are satisfied with your brief after the first draft, your standards are too low. . . . [G]ood editing is as important to the success of your brief as good legal research is. Plan to edit, for both style and substance, at least twice. . . . If you [can], . . . see if a brief hiatus enables you to view your work with a fresh eye. . . . [T]ry to replace clumsy or dull prose with sharp prose that is likely to hold the reader's interest.

This is not the place to present a full menu of stylistic recommendations. . . . Nevertheless, a few key tips deserve mention. Build word bridges to ensure that the narrative moves easily from one paragraph to the next. . . .

Omit surplus words. . . . [W]rit[e] in the active voice. . . . Avoid compound constructions too. . . . Write short sentences that use short words. . . . By and large, confine your sentences to one main thought, and try to keep average sentence length under twenty-five words. Avoid dreadful "lawyerisms," such as "hereinafter," "heretofore," "on point," and "on all fours." Shun double negatives too. . . . Reject sarcasm, vitriol, and hyperbole, but look for opportunities to grab the court's attention with an interesting turn of phrase or an offbeat word that makes your point in an engaging way. . . . Like the late Professor Fred Rodell of Yale Law School, "I am the last one to suppose that a piece about the law could be made to read like a juicy sex novel or a detective story, but I cannot see why it has to resemble a cross between a nineteenth century sermon and a treatise on higher mathematics." [Fred Rodell, *Goodbye To Law Reviews — Revisited,* 48 VA. L. REV. 279, 282 (1962).]

Parting Thoughts

After drafting and editing your brief, ask a colleague to check citations, quotations, and references to the record for accuracy, as your eye is likely to see what you intended, not what is actually on the page. If you practice alone, you will have to perform these tasks yourself, but other people can help you assess the clarity of your arguments. Explain them to a nonlawyer orally; if you stumble through the oration, you do not understand your case as well as you should, and the brief will reflect that. Alternatively, ask a nonlawyer to read the brief and assess its clarity. Partners and spouses perform this role well because they are secure enough to offer honest critiques. If no reviewer is available, read the brief minus the cases, and see whether the fact statement and the policy discussion are convincing all by themselves. If not, revisions are probably in order.

If you represent the Appellant, a reply brief may be in order too. When the briefs present the pertinent issues clearly and the Appellee's brief contains no surprises, do not file a reply. If, however, the Appellee muddies the legal waters, or makes an argument or cites pertinent authorities that your main brief did not address, you should file a reply. Confine your reply to new matters; it should not be a reprise of your main brief.

. . . [T]he key to successful brief writing is to seize the opportunities that appellate writing offers you to be creative. Revel in these opportunities because the more you do, the better your briefs will be.

C. What the Future Holds

Fredric I. Lederer, *An Environment of Change: the Effect of Courtroom Technologies on and in Appellate Proceedings and Courtrooms,* 2 JOURNAL OF APPELLATE PRACTICE AND PROCESS 251 (2000)[6]

Introduction

. . . [O]ur appellate courts now are beginning to experience the effects of the technological age — the age of visual information.

. . . As appellate courts necessarily review the conduct of trials and their results, . . . appellate judges must now review the effects of technology at trial. However, legal technology is also changing the nature of appeals themselves.

In one sense the most sweeping change facing the appellate courts is the likely change in the record of trial from text to multi-media, a change that presents at least the possibility of affecting the standard of appellate review. Yet . . . technology may also affect appellate practice, as courts consider electronic hyperlinked briefs and receive appellate argument in the form of electronic, perhaps even multi-media, presentations. Even our expectations about the nature of appellate hearings are likely to change as judges and counsel appear from remote locations by two-way video.

---

6 Copyright © 2000 by The Journal of Appellate Practice and Process. Reprinted with permission.

. . . In the new evolving age of technology-augmented appeals, . . . pictures [that lawyers draw] will no longer be figurative, but actual.

I. The Case Below — The Court Record

The traditional court record consists of a paper text transcript with the necessary supporting exhibits and ancillary papers. . . . Lawyers have the primary initial responsibility to direct the judges' attention to the appropriate parts of the transcript. Ordinarily, it is for the lawyers to search the transcript for error. . . .

Text transcripts present, of course, only a small part of what actually happened at trial. Neither voice nor image is present, and their absence can be extraordinarily misleading. Even when described in the record, witness gestures and demeanor often are inadequately set forth in text. Voice intonations are absent, and except for word choice, all witnesses "sound" alike in the text transcript. . . . At the same time, . . . lawyer and judicial misconduct can be shielded by text.

As of 1993, only eight states permitted non-transcribed videotaped records on appeal. . . . Anecdotal reports indicate . . . that a large majority of judges and lawyers are hostile to audio/video records. This may be because, as lawyers and judges, we are used to the written word. It may also stem, however, from the fact that text can be browsed quickly and the transcript opened to any necessary point while audio and videotapes must be viewed in real time. Accordingly, for appellate purposes, most jurisdictions ordinarily require that recordings be turned into text transcripts. At first blush, the perceived need for a text transcript would seem to necessarily result in rejection of an audio/video record. The dichotomy is false, however. Modern technology now makes available the combined text-central, multimedia court record.

II. The New Court Record

Computer-assisted transcription uses computerized court reporting equipment to create a computerized version of the stenographic court reporter's record. . . . Trial lawyers have used multi-media depositions for some time. When conducting a deposition, counsel videotape the examination, often with concurrent computer-assisted transcription . . . , and then create an integrated multi-media transcript, usually on a CD-ROM. The deposition record consists of an electronic text transcript with synchronized audio and video that appear when the text is clicked appropriately with the computer mouse. The text can be searched, and the audio and video only appear when wanted. Appropriate exhibits are also made part of the visual part of the disk. A multi-media court record works the same way that a multi-media deposition does.

A comprehensive multi-media appellate court record consists of . . . the electronic text, along with the accompanying digitalized audio and video of the entire proceeding, further augmented by the proffered evidentiary exhibits. . . .

Given inexpensive durable electronic multi-media records, records that could be transmitted by Internet nearly instantaneously to all parties and the appellate court, the question becomes how, if at all, such records would affect appellate practice.

III. Effect on Appellate Practice

A. Appellate Deference To Trial Court Factual Findings

. . .

B. The "Appellate Record"

The appellate court reviews the actions of the trial court below. No evidence is presented on appeal, and accordingly no true appellate record exists. However, if appellate argument is actually valued by the court, it might be useful for the appellate court to make a record of oral argument. Although any form of recording or reporting would be satisfactory, appellate courts would do well to consider realtime reporting. Realtime would not only give the court a transcript of the argument but would also permit contemporaneous publication of the argument to the Internet for the edification of the bar and public.

C. The High-Technology Appellate Brief

Like the court record, the traditional appellate brief ordinarily has been a paper document. Because computer media can store the equivalent of a vast number of paper pages it was only a matter of time before appellate counsel attempted to file briefs in computer format. What one did not necessarily expect in the early days of computer technology was the advent of the "hot-linked" multi-media brief.

Today's high-technology briefs consist not only of the brief's text, but also all referenced law — case, statutory, and rule — as well as the trial transcript, the exhibits, and appropriate ancillary papers. All are available by hyperlinks. One clicks on the hyperlink and is taken immediately to the cited reference. The court, and opposing counsel, has on one disk the equivalent of the traditional brief, the court record, and what can be a surprisingly large law library, all of which can be accessed on a single notebook computer.

. . . On one level, the new electronic briefs can be regarded as simply more efficient and environmentally sound versions of traditional briefs. . . . [A] "judge need no longer put down a printed brief to pull a lawbook from a library shelf. No longer will he or she have to dig through a multivolume appendix to find a documentary exhibit or set up a VCR to play a videotaped excerpt of testimony. " [Francis X. Gindhart, *Documents, Transcripts, Exhibits Are on Hand in Hypertext Briefs*, 217 N.Y. L.J. 5, 10 (Apr. 15, 1997).] On another level, they may be regarded as the unavoidable method for providing meaningful appeals from today's increasing number of high technology courtrooms. A paper record is an inadequate mechanism for showing appellate judges what actually happened in technology-augmented trial level litigation.

The process of creating a CD-ROM brief, especially one without multi-media, is simple. Indeed, both Corel WordPerfect and Microsoft Word include the basic technology to create the necessary hyperlinks. It is the access to the necessary legal authorities that may be problematic. Neither West nor LEXIS/NEXIS may own the cases and statutes, but obtaining easy access to reliable legal authority outside their systems may be troublesome. At the same time, compilation of any necessary exhibits, supporting papers, and the transcript, especially if a paper transcript needs to be scanned, may be especially time-consuming.

In 1997, Professor Moy argued that "the cost [of electronic legal materials] is much higher than that of printed materials. Is it right to build into the appellate review system the ability of wealthy parties to outstrip opponents' persuasive power, through the use of the communication medium itself?" [Francis X. Gindhart & Carl R. Moy, *High-Tech Appeals: Can Hypertext Briefs Aid Justice without Changing the System?*, 83 A.B.A. J. 78, 79 (1997).] This concern may be significant. However, the cost of preparing such a brief has . . . fallen since 1997. The cost of a contemporary electronic brief is hard to estimate. . . . [T]he cost depends upon the features chosen. The basic brief with authorities is no longer a significant matter. . . . The potential need to scan massive paper transcripts and allied papers can create, however, a very large bill indeed. Should increased efficiency and potentially significant storage savings be halted by resource disparity concerns? The same issue is presented not only by all forms of technology use, but even by the basic availability of counsel in our adversarial legal system.

Electronic briefs must be viewed by computer. . . . It is not unreasonable to assume that the near or mid-future will bring us a leather-covered portfolio that when opened will show two pages of electronic text, left and right. Indeed, multi-media may prove possible even in such a small "package."

. . . [T]he new briefs may hold transformative possibilities. It is not so much that a CD-ROM or otherwise formatted electronic brief provides enhanced efficiency and ease of information access, but it also permits visual argument.

D. Visual Argument

As Daniel Webster observed, "The power of clear statement is the great power at the bar."[7] In an appellate context, counsel are arguing facts, law, and policy. . . . How best should counsel present clear statements?

Although traditional appellate argument is entirely oral, when people are presented with both aural and visual matter concurrently they better understand and remember its content. When arguing law, it may be helpful for counsel, or the court, to accompany oral presentation with the visual image of the authority argued. . . . The court may reply in kind, displaying the judge's view of the law to counsel at counsel's podium. This interactive exchange of law holds promise for eliminating confusion or mis-citation. At the same time, . . . only counsel or judges highly comfortable with computer use can or will use it effectively. Always concerned about the limited time available for oral argument, . . . counsel are loathe to risk loss of time by inefficiently searching for authority. . . . The hyperlinked brief presents counsel with an already prepared "menu" of authorities ready at an instant's need.

. . . If counsel can argue law visually, what of the rest of the case? In February, 1999, the United States Court of Appeals for the Armed Forces heard the case of *United States v. Rockwood* [52 M.J. 98 (Armed Forces App. 1999)][,] . . . the most technologically sophisticated appeal known to have taken place anywhere in the world. . . . Five . . . law students, acting as amicus curiae, filed an electronic CD-ROM brief, . . . and two of the student counsel argued. Amicus counsel presented their arguments visually. The primary

---

[7] [42] FRED R. SHAPIRO, THE OXFORD DICTIONARY OF AMERICAN LEGAL QUOTATIONS 10 (Oxford U. Press 1993) (quoting Letter to R.M. Blatchford, 1849, *reprinted in* PETER HARVEY, REMINISCENCES AND ANECDOTES OF DANIEL WEBSTER 118 (1878)).

amicus argument was presented using a computer slide show that contained counsel's talking points, key quotes from legal authority, and a photograph illustrating policy concerns. Counsel also displayed a critical portion of the CD-ROM brief to the judges as well. In short, an appellate argument was presented much as a trial court opening or closing might be. To equate trial and appellate argument is novel and perhaps heretical. Is it also troublesome?

. . . Ultimately, the key questions are . . . "Is the argument helpful to the court?" and . . . "Does it help persuade the court?" Absent formal study . . . we cannot be sure that visual, multi-media argument consistently is helpful to either judge or counsel. However, both subjective anecdotal experience and concededly tangential studies suggest the probability that it is. Ultimately, as at trial, visual argument is a tool that should be available in the appellate hearing when useful.

E. Remote Appearances by Judges and Counsel

Modern video-conferencing permits easy and inexpensive two-way interactive video appearances. . . . The appellate courts have seen the greatest use . . . of remote judges and lawyers.

Several federal courts, including the United States Courts of Appeals for the Second, Tenth, and District of Columbia Circuits, have used videoconferencing for remote judicial appearances. The . . . Second Circuit provides remote locations for counsel appearances. The court first experimented with live, remote video oral argument in October, 1996. The court then . . . established video links in four locations. . . . [T]he advent of remote oral argument has proved to be a significant benefit to attorneys who previously had to travel all day for a ten-minute argument. . . . The circuit executive has noted that the judges do not feel there is an advantage to personal appearances in court.

. . . There is every reason to believe that remote appearances in appellate cases will increase in number. Appellate hearings arguably lack the need for public attendance and participation that may attend trials. . . . [A]ppellate courts are often significant distances from the advocates. The judges may reside and have their offices far from the appellate hearing. Indeed, many intermediate appellate courts ride circuit in an effort to compensate for distance. Why can we not use video conferencing both for oral argument and judicial conference?

The availability of remote appearances and the potential need to review multi-media court records and electronic briefs and to receive visually presented law and argument necessarily raise the question, how will these technologies affect our appellate courtrooms?

III. The High Technology Appellate Courtroom

A. The Effect of Remote Appearances

. . . Remote appearances present interesting questions of human interaction and policy. If remote appearances are to be used, the court must decide whether it wishes to duplicate to the extent possible the physical courtroom setting. If so, remote participants should be made to appear as if they were actually present . . . to the extent . . . that is reasonably possible. . . . There are two primary ways in which remote appearances take place: Counsel appears in the courtroom while one or more judges appear remotely, or one or more judges appear in the courtroom while counsel appears remotely.

In the first scenario, each remote judge is presented in the courtroom via a separate life-size image behind the appellate bench. Counsel experiences a multi-judge court nearly identical to the traditional one. In the second scenario the appellate courtroom receives argument from remote counsel. The lawyer is presented in the courtroom via a large plasma screen in the podium location. The judges in the courtroom thus experience counsel as if she or he were physically present. . . . Remote counsel should see three distinct images of the courtroom judges so that counsel's appellate experience is similar to normal argument. At the same time, remote counsel must be able to see opposing counsel's argument as well.

B. A Virtual Appellate Courtroom?

. . . [I]f we can have remote judges and remote counsel, we may not need the courtroom at all. Indeed, it would not be difficult to move the entire appellate argument to the World Wide Web. Each participant would see and hear all the others as appropriate. . . . Accordingly, . . . modern courtroom technology can change the appellate courtroom — it can eliminate it wholesale.

The courtroom is the very center of the legal system. The long American tradition of substantial courthouse architecture recognizes the people's need to give justice a pride of place and to enshrine it in physical form. . . . [M]oving trials from the local courthouse to the virtual world would raise enormous questions of both law and public policy. A trial is not, however, an appeal. Indeed, our stark time constraints on appellate oral argument suggest that we give it only limited importance. It is by no means clear that the public would care . . . if at least ordinary appellate arguments occurred outside a courthouse, especially if the public were given full electronic access to them.

IV. Conclusion

. . . Appellate courts will be forced to adopt the technology necessary to adequately review the case below, if only because they review the actions of trial courts . . . that increasingly are hosting technology-augmented litigation. Multi-media text-central electronic court records will provide appellate courts with unprecedented information in order to better review proceedings below. At the same time, many of the technologies that are changing trial practice lend themselves to appellate practice. Whether through the . . . electronic brief or the visually augmented appellate argument, courtroom technologies may enrich appellate practice. The nature of appellate practice stands on the brink of change. Visually based argument alone would be a significant departure from traditional practice. . . . [H]owever, the massive time and cost savings to court and counsel inherent in remote appearances presents the possibility of moving oral argument from the physical courtroom to the virtual world. The basics of appellate practice have existed unchanged for generations. We must now expect significant changes to occur. Our traditional assumptions about the nature of appellate practice and the courtrooms in which it takes place surely will not outlast the twenty-first century.

NOTES

1. How will the kinds of technologies discussed by Lederer further alter the work of the appellate advocate, and the skills that such an advocate will need to master?

2. An excellent article on electronic briefs and the technical and pragmatic issues they raise is Maria Perez Crist, *The E-brief: Legal Writing for an Online World*, 33 N.M.L. Rev. 49, 92-93 (2003).[8] Professor Perez Crist concludes:

> In response to an increasingly technologically sophisticated judiciary, the practicing attorney must understand the advantages and constraints of the electronic environment. Because the outline of the brief's argument may well become the brief's key navigational tool, logical and concise point headings are more vital to the brief's effectiveness. In addition to providing the reader with a clear organizational scheme, the brief itself must be attentive to the constraints of online reading. The online reader needs efficient and focused paragraphs, clear sentence structures, the judicious use of links, and a favorable online reading environment. A writer's ability to craft an effective legal argument in an electronic media will depend upon time-tested advocacy skills coupled with a keen understanding of the capabilities of the online environment.
>
> As the legal community continues to experiment with the role of technology in the court infrastructure, the judiciary, the parties, the lawyers, and the public can all benefit from the reasoned and effective use of electronic communication in the courts. Although the initial motivation for electronic communication was a concern for efficiency and the need for storage space, the electronic platform is increasingly becoming the media of choice where briefs will be read and evaluated. As the judicial community becomes more acclimated to this electronic platform, the legal community must respond with electronic submissions that effectively tap into the resources of the technology and meet the needs of the judicial reader. This means providing a clear and pervasive organizational blueprint for the brief. It means using hypertext effectively to aid both in navigation and to access materials outside the document as needed. It means writing in a style that understands both the constraints and the possibilities inherent in the technology. It means the birth of tech-rhetoric.

D.   Timeless Considerations: Ethics for the Appellate Lawyer

Roger J. Miner, *Professional Responsibility in Appellate Practice: A View From the Bench,* 19 Pace Law Review 323 (1999)[9]

Ethical considerations first come into play for the appellate lawyer in the decision on whether to undertake representation on appeal. . . . The Code [of Professional Responsibility in force in New York] prohibits unwarranted appeals, and frivolous appeals are sanctionable under the Federal Rules of Appellate Procedure. On the other hand, the Code requires diligent and zealous prosecution of arguably meritorious appeals. My own view . . . is that far

---

[8] Copyright © 2003 by New Mexico Law Review. Reprinted with permission.

[9] Copyright © 1999. Reprinted with permission of the Pace Law Review. Judge Miner is a Senior Judge of the U.S. Court of Appeals for the Second Circuit.

too many frivolous appeals and far too many non-meritorious issues are pre-sented to appellate tribunals.

. . . Why do attorneys go forward with appeals they know they cannot win? I can suggest several reasons, none of which contributes to the good reputation of the legal profession. Some attorneys pursue these appeals out of the desire to demonstrate to the client that they are willing to fight to the end; some fear that another lawyer may take the case on appeal if they do not and [that the lawyer will thereby loss the client]; some think it is necessary to appeal in order to avoid malpractice claims or, in criminal cases, to be accused of inef-fective assistance; some are guided solely by their client's wishes; and some, most unfortunately, are interested only in the billable hours involved.

The Code prohibition against advancing claims unwarranted under existing law carries exceptions for claims that "can be supported by good faith argu-ment(s) for an extension, modification, or reversal of existing law." The exception is an important one. Without it, *Brown v. Board of Education* would never have been brought to the Supreme Court. We must take care, however, not to let the exception swallow the rule, especially in cases where a change in existing law might diminish individual rights. . . . [But] an attorney faced with a decision whether to appeal must be concerned with the rules of ethical conduct, and must recognize that the Code sometimes requires that employment be declined.

I turn now to the ethical duty of candor to the appellate court. It should go without saying that counsel must not misrepresent the facts or the law when arguing an appeal. . . . It certainly is rare, since counsel fully understand that a violation of this rule is not only sanctionable but may be fatal to an appeal. More problematical for some, but not for me, is the rule requiring the citation of adverse authority.

The Code . . . provides that "in presenting a matter to a tribunal, a lawyer shall disclose . . . controlling legal authority known to the lawyer to be directly adverse to the position of the client and which is not disclosed by opposing counsel." [N.Y. Code of Professional Responsibility DR 7-106(b)(1).] The American Bar Association Model Rules of Professional Conduct puts it just a bit differently. . . . [T]he result is the same: The duty to the tribunal supersedes the duty to the client in connection with the disclosure of adverse authority.

Many lawyers are not happy with this rule of conduct. Their contention is that duty to client is primary and that they should have no obligation to bring forward anything that may work to the benefit of the other side. Professor Monroe Freedman . . . agrees. . . . I strongly disagree. No matter how enam-ored we are of the adversary system as the great engine in the search for truth, we must recognize its limitations and cabin it . . . to maintain as even a playing field as possible. These rules must include certain responsibilities to the appellate tribunal.

Not all attorneys are equal in skill, and there is no reason to permit the stronger to play the hidden ball trick with the weaker. . . . [A]n overly adver-sarial system is what has led the legal profession into such a sorry state that rules of civility are specifically required. . . . The trend must be reversed! We must not lose sight of the fact that the purpose of our enterprise is justice under the law and that anything that moves us away from that purpose, including the non-disclosure of legal precedent, is to be condemned.

My own view is that candor to the tribunal should require even more than the Rule requires. I think that a lawyer should cite pertinent authority from other jurisdictions to help the court in its labors, even if the adversary fails to do so. I also think that there is no reason to say that it is wrong only for the lawyer to omit the citation of contrary authority known to him or her. With modern computer research techniques, precedent cases are easily knowable to all lawyers. Beyond all this, it may very well be counterproductive to one's case to omit the citation of authority, whatever its source. . . . Obviously, a lawyer cannot argue to distinguish, modify or overrule an adverse precedent not mentioned in the brief but discovered by the court on its own.

. . . It is not enough to be zealous in advancing a client's cause. The Code specifies that "[a] lawyer should represent a client competently." [N.Y. Code of Professional Responsibility Canon 6.] Among other things, lawyers are prohibited by the Code from handling legal matters "without preparation adequate in the circumstances." [DR 6-101(A)(2).] I have become alarmed in recent years by the increase in the number of briefs and oral arguments that appear to be lacking in adequate preparation on the law and on the facts. . . . [I]t is surprising how often parties fail to raise the issue of subject matter jurisdiction. I remember a case not long ago when we pressed the jurisdictional question during oral argument, and both counsel insisted on arguing the merits of the appeal. . . . They just did not get the point, although they may have grasped it when the appeal was dismissed, sua sponte, for lack of subject matter jurisdiction. . . . The Federal Rules of Appellate Procedure require that briefs contain a statement of subject matter and appellate jurisdiction. . . . [O]ften very little thought is given to the importance of this provision.

The Federal Rules of Appellate Procedure also require that briefs "include for each issue a concise statement of the applicable standard of review." The competent attorney will ponder long and hard over the standard of review applicable to the issues raised. . . . [I]t is in the appellate attorney's interest to argue for a standard that is most favorable to his or her case. And yet we see, time after time, counsel struggling unsuccessfully to overcome such standard of review barriers. . . . On innumerable occasions, we have stopped counsel for appellant during oral argument and asked whether findings of fact are under attack. . . . [C]ounsel inevitably presses forward with unwinnable arguments regarding the weight of the evidence. Basic competence dictates close familiarity with the standards of review. If those standards cannot be met, [the case should not be on appeal].

Most oral arguments are made by attorneys who "wing it." The lack of preparation is apparent. . . . Counsel often seem to be taken by surprise at a question from the court. A frequent response is "I'll get to that[,]" by attorneys who never do. An attorney once responded to my question this way: "Why do you ask that question, Judge?" A frequent answer to a question from the court is: "That is not this case." . . . A properly prepared attorney is ready to distinguish the facts and the law in the question from those in his or her case.

I think that the waiver of oral argument demonstrates a lack of professional competence. . . . As a practitioner at the appellate bar, I would never waive oral argument. Although its importance has been downplayed in recent times, oral argument presents an unparalleled opportunity to discuss the case with the court, to get an idea of how the judges are thinking, . . . to hear the judges think out loud and debate the merits among themselves through the medium of counsel. Many articles have been written about how attorneys should conduct oral argument, but it seems to me that most attorneys who argue before us never have read any of them.

While competence in oral argument is greatly to be desired, competence in the techniques of brief writing . . . is even more desirable . . . because we have the briefs in hand before, during and after oral argument, and the impressions they convey are longer-lasting than oral argument. ! . . . All too often, we see briefs that are poorly organized, that wander off the point being made, that make too many points, that have too many citations and quotations, that are deficient in the citation of authority and that are highly repetitive. The purpose of a brief, like the purpose of oral argument, is to persuade. Unfortunately, too many briefs fail to deliver.

. . . There is no reason why counsel should demonstrate incompetence in appellate practice. . . . My view . . . is that the competence culprit is usually lack of preparation. . . . [T]he result of procrastination is diminution in the time for preparation. Poor performance inevitably results. . . . When my students come to my classes unprepared, I always give the same admonition: "An unprepared student becomes an unprepared lawyer, and that works to the detriment of client, court and justice system."

I would hold appellate attorneys to a high degree of competence. . . . I agree with my colleague, Judge Aldisert, that competent representation should be the very first rule of professional responsibility.

The Code tells us that "a lawyer should assist in maintaining the integrity and competence of the legal profession." . . . [This admonition] requires complete honesty to the appellate tribunal. To me, maintaining the integrity of the legal profession also requires that lawyers adhere to ethical and moral principles in their dealings with each other. . . .

In the United States Courts of Appeals, as in many state appellate courts, the parties file an appendix containing those parts of the record that are considered pertinent to the appeal. The Federal Rules of Appellate Procedure state [that]: "The parties are encouraged to agree as to the contents of the appendix." More and more, we are seeing parties unable to agree on a joint appendix. As a result, there is a separate appendix filed by each party and a concomitant necessity for judges to flip back and forth between two separate submissions. . . . When counsel refuse to cooperate, additional burdens are imposed upon the court. . . .

A profession lacking in collegiality is a profession lacking in integrity. Lawyers are engaged in a joint enterprise. . . . Lawyers are responsible for each other, and what one does reflects on all. When I see briefs that seek sanctions against other lawyers for bringing or defending appeals that are clearly meritorious, when I see unfounded accusations of conflict of interest . . . , when

I hear arguments in which attorneys spend their allotted time in criticizing each other rather than in arguing the merits, I worry about the integrity of the legal profession.

. . . In the discharge of the duty to maintain the competence of the Bar as regards appellate practice, it seems to me that the Bar should take a greater interest in educational programs devoted to appellate practice. . . . Lawyers may assist in maintaining the professional competence of the Bar in other ways. In olden times, lawyers helped each other by reviewing briefs and listening to proposed oral arguments, and I am not referring here to lawyers in the same firm. . . . They saw it as helping to maintain the competence of the profession. In those days, young lawyers were welcomed to the Bar and helped by older members in all phases of practice.

I am given to understand that that is not the case today. . . .

. . . It seems to me that the closer the relationship between appellate judge and appellate lawyer, the greater will be lawyer awareness of the Rules of ethical conduct required in appellate practice. Appellate judges have an important duty here. Judicial ethics compel the performance of a great number of other duties as well. But that is a Lecture for another day.

NOTES

1. Compare J. Thomas Sullivan, *Ethical and Aggressive Appellate Advocacy: The "Ethical" Issue of Issue Selection*, 80 DENV. U.L. REV. 155 (2002). Professor Sullivan argues that the conventional wisdom to refine the appeal to include only the issues most likely to be meritorious is fraught with problems. The narrowing of issues displeases the client, particularly criminal defendants; it presupposes that counsel can accurately assess which issues would not be successful on appeal; and it often distorts the trial which gave rise to the claims of error. Moreover, while counsel may choose to urge narrow issues, urging broad policy issues in addition might enhance the chances of success and "if judges are not afforded the opportunity to debate broader questions, or if they are not forced to consider policy consequences, the chance that reform will be forced on the justice system from the appellate courts is minimized. . . ." *Id.* at 174. Professor Sullivan also argues that there are legitimate reasons to include issues that have little prospect of success. These include making the case for cumulative error that made the trial unfair; enabling the court to resolve additional issues that are likely to arise on re-trial, should the court reverse on other grounds; allowing one's client to benefit from a change in law; and having the appellate court recognize error or decide an issue that may be important in the future even if it does not provide grounds for reversal in the particular case.

Can you reconcile the views of Judge Minor and Professor Sullivan on this aspect of an appellate attorney's role? With whom do you agree?

2. Judge Miner opines that the waiver of oral argument demonstrates a lack of professional competence. Do you agree or, in light of the pressures on the courts of appeals, is it appropriate for counsel to waive oral argument if counsel believes that the briefs fully address the issues and the issues are not of particular public interest?

III. SUPREME COURT PERSPECTIVES

William H. Rehnquist, *Oral Advocacy*, 27 South Texas Law Review 289, 297-300 (1986)[10]

. . . [T]he most important message I can convey to you is that appellate advocacy consists of two instruments to be employed by counsel: first, the brief, and second, the oral argument. Many able lawyers seem to regard these as the functional equivalent of one another, as you will observe from this account of an oral argument which one of the presiding judges of the Appellate Division in New York City told me a number of years ago. The court had a rule prohibiting counsel from reading their briefs, and this particular lawyer was not long into his argument before it was apparent that he was violating the rule. The presiding judge cautioned him, . . . but he nonetheless persisted in simply reading his brief, albeit in a rather florid way. The presiding judge finally interrupted to say: "Counsel, . . . we have read your brief." Whereupon counsel righteously replied: "Yes, but you have not heard it with gestures."

The Supreme Court gets more advocates than it should who regard oral argument as a "brief with gestures." Actually, the brief in an appellate court has about the same relation to oral argument as the pleadings in a case do to arguments before the trial judge or even a jury. The oral arguments you make must necessarily be structured by what is covered by your brief, but under no circumstances should you simply recite, summarize, or selectively read from your brief and consider it a satisfactory oral argument.

You naturally try to make your brief readable, even interesting if possible; but you are hampered . . . by the commonsense dictate that your brief must cover every point you wish to preserve within a limited number of pages. A brief may often be top-heavy with citations to cases or quotations from them, quotations from portions of statutes, and the like. There is no help for this. But when it comes to oral argument, the more flesh and blood you can insert into it, as opposed to a dry recitation of principles of law or decided cases, the more . . . effective that argument can be. The difference in the two may perhaps be summarized by the difference between a "preview" of a movie and the movie itself. The "preview" consists solely of scenes from the movie, but the preview selects dramatic or interesting scenes that are apt to catch the interest of the viewer and make him want to see the entire movie.

Lawyers who practice before our Court, or for that matter before any appellate court, should also consider the different contexts in which oral argument and brief reading occur. Brief reading is a solitary occupation; . . . it is something you must do yourself, and in a relatively quiet environment.

Oral argument, on the other hand, is an essentially collegial function. It is one of only two occasions on which the judges get together to consider the case. As an oral advocate you should take advantage of this opportunity to be present with the Court when it collegially concentrates on your case. [One hopes that] the judges will have read the briefs, and are now ready to begin hearing

---

10 Copyright © 1986 by South Texas Law Review. Reprinted with permission.

your explanation of both your strong points and your weak points, and to ask you some questions. Because of the different nature of an oral presentation from a written one, your oral argument can be more "freeform" than your brief. But you must not let the greater latitude of oral argument produce any sloppiness in your presentation.

Robert H. Jackson, *Advocacy Before the United States Supreme Court,* 37 Cornell Law Quarterly 1, 5-7, 10, 13, 16 (1951)[11]

If you are called in after assignments of error have been filed, or feel impelled to raise many in your brief, at least forego oral argument of all but one or two. The impact of oral presentation will be strengthened if it is concentrated on a few points that can be simply and convincingly stated and easily grasped and retained. . . .

The petitioner should never dodge or delay but give priority to answering the reasons why he lost below. The respondent should ask himself what doubts probably brought the case up and answer them. They will then be covering the questions that the Justices are waiting to hear answered. To delay meeting these issues is improvident; to attempt evasion of them is fatal. . . .

I used to say that, as Solicitor General, I made three arguments of every case. First came the one that I planned — as I thought, logical, coherent, complete. Second was the one actually presented — interrupted, incoherent, disjointed, disappointing. The third was the utterly devastating argument that I thought of after going to bed that night. . . .

It would surprise you to know how frequently counsel undertake to expound a recent decision to the very men who made it. If the exposition is accurate, it adds nothing to the Court's knowledge and if it is not, it discredits counsel's perception or fairness. . . .

If making an argument is not a great day in your life, don't make it; and if it is, give it everything in you.

By all means leave at home the associate who feels constantly impelled to tug at your coattails, to push briefs in front of you, or to pass up unasked-for suggestions while you are speaking. These well-meant but ill-conceived offerings distract the attention of the Court, but they are even more embarrassing and confusing to counsel. The offender is an unmitigated pest, and even if he is the attorney who employed you, suppress him. . . .

No toleration, however, can repeal the teaching of Polonius that "The apparel oft proclaims the man." You will not be stopped from arguing if you wear a race-track suit or sport a rainbow necktie. You will just create a first impression that you have strayed in at the wrong bar. . . .

---

[11] Copyright © 1951 by Cornell Law Quarterly. Reprinted with permission. Address to the California State Bar (August 23, 1951). Justice Jackson was an Associate Justice of the Supreme Court of the United States from 1941 until his death in 1954.

To participate as advocate in supplying the basis for decisional law-making calls for vision of a prophet, as well as a profound appreciation of the continuity between the law of today and that of the past. He will be sharing the task of reworking decisional law by which every generation seeks to preserve its essential character and at the same time to adapt it to contemporary needs. At such a moment the lawyer's case ceases to be an episode in the affairs of a client and becomes a stone in the edifice of the law.

Seth P. Waxman, *The Office of Solicitor General: In the Shadow of Daniel Webster: Arguing Appeals in the Twenty-First Century*, 3 JOURNAL OF APPELLATE PRACTICE AND PROCESS 521 (2001)[12]

Sixty years ago, John W. Davis, a storied Solicitor General and a brilliant appellate star, observed that any lecture on the argument of an appeal should come from a judge, rather than from an advocate. As he explained, ". . . Who would listen to a fisherman's weary discourse . . . if the fish himself could be induced to give his views on the most effective methods of approach. For after all, it is the fish that the angler is after. . . ." [John W. Davis, *The Argument of an Appeal*, 26 A.B.A. J. 895 (Dec. 1940).] . . . [J]ust like Davis, [the Solicitor General] is a fisherman, not a fish. . . .

Daniel Webster . . . is widely regarded as the greatest advocate ever to argue in an American court. . . . Inspiring though it is to recall Webster's towering achievements, we might as well admit that we could never equal them. That is true not only because few mortals can claim the blessing of Webster's gifts. It is also true because no advocate today will ever have the opportunity to perform in the arena Webster commanded. The days of oral advocacy as declamation, of unlimited time and no page limits, are over. Can anyone now imagine the luxury of an oral argument stretching for hours, or even for days, without interruption by questions? For Webster, though, that was routine: the *Dartmouth College* argument spanned three days, and that in *McCullough v. Maryland*, four. . . . Yet, . . . we, like the lawyers of Webster's day, find ourselves on our own at oral argument. And while we no longer live in a world that otherwise much resembles Webster's, the principles evident in the Master's work apply with equal force today.

Passion

This first principle is the most fundamental. If you want to be a great oral advocate, you must care passionately about your work. . . . Webster . . . saw complete dedication as the key to his work — dedication to his client, to his craft, and to the principles to which he believed his profession should aspire. As Chief Justice Fuller once observed, ". . . [I]n Mr. Webster's arguments fidelity to the Court is as conspicuous as fidelity to his client. It is not the client first and the conscience afterwards, but duty to both together, one and inseparable." [Quoting Chief Justice Fuller's remarks at the Webster

---

[12] Copyright © 2001 by the Journal of Appellate Practice and Process. Reprinted with permission.

Centennial.] That passionate devotion to duty has continued to resonate with judges and lawyers from generation to generation. . . .

Preparation

. . . Webster acknowledged . . . the absolute importance of comprehensive preparation. Lawyers who are merely earning a living . . . will prepare enough to get by, and if they are lucky they will perform well. But . . . [f]or lawyers building a cathedral, every argument demands what others might deride as over-preparation. "Accuracy and diligence," Webster said, "are much more necessary to a lawyer than great comprehension of mind, or brilliancy of talent." To be a great lawyer, he recognized, one "must first consent to be only a great drudge." [Both from *Letter from Daniel Webster to Thomas Merrill* (Nov. 11, 1803), *in* VOL. 17 THE WRITINGS AND SPEECHES OF DANIEL WEBSTER, 148-49 (Fletcher Webster ed., 1903).] As Webster understood, the goal of preparation is simply this: When you walk into the courtroom to make your oral argument, you should know every aspect of the case better than anyone else does. Certainly you should know it far better than any judge. You must know the entire factual record. You must comfortably understand all of the relevant law, whatever its source. And finally . . . you must understand the implications of every principle upon which your case depends.

. . . I generally try to do this in two ways. First, I think about questions. I attempt to identify every question a judge could reasonably ask. I think as hard as I can about what the best possible answer is. And finally I consider what further questions might follow from that answer, and what the answers to those questions should be. This is, for me at least, hard, hard work. It is generally easy to think of a few difficult questions; it is impossible to think of them all. How far down the list of conceivable questions you get, though, is a pretty good indicator of how well prepared you are.

The other thing I often do is to try to explain the case to a non-lawyer. . . . I find that explaining the case to someone who is not a lawyer helps me to discern whether there is a basic flaw in my reasoning, and whether I am really able to distinguish what is fundamental about my case from what is not. Preparing to answer all sorts of doctrinally tricky questions is essential, but it may also obscure the forest for the trees. You must be able to see both very clearly when you stand up to argue.

Planting the Kernel

. . . Because oral argument is now so very different from what it was in Webster's day, it is difficult to translate the principles for appellate advocacy that might have been used in his time into precepts that will apply today. In all but the rarest of modern appellate courtrooms, for example, we litigate in an environment of interruption, not oration. But even in this very different world, there is a fundamental principle from Webster's day that still prevails, and it is this: When you stand up to present your oral argument, facts and law at your command and head crammed with answers to every conceivable question, something else must be at the forefront of your mind. . . . It is the kernel of the case — the one, two, or at the very most, three points that you must impress upon the court before you sit down.

These points may or may not be those you emphasized in your briefs. Sometimes . . . the thorough preparation you make for oral argument leads you to see the fundamentals of your case in a different way. I once came to reconceptualize a case on the very night before oral argument, because, although I had conducted two moot courts in the case, each using a different theme, neither had worked to my satisfaction. My last-minute change worked beautifully in that case, but I would never counsel brinksmanship . . . for its own sake, for it is fraught with risk. But my own experience in this unusual case does demonstrate . . . that however difficult the kernel may be to discern, and however late it reveals itself, you must have it in mind when you appear before the court.

Once you have found the kernel, polish and refine it into its purest, simplest form. And consider carefully how best to present it to the court. . . . In Webster's day the kernel was often planted only after hours spent carefully tilling the judicial mind. Nowadays, the best strategy before a fully prepared court may be to make your point, pellucidly, as soon as you begin. But however you plan to do it, you must be absolutely clear in your mind about what the essentials are, and you must also be confident that when you sit down, the judges will understand both what they are and why they are important. . . .

Questions will come — in the Supreme Court they come in a torrent. You should welcome and embrace questions, not be annoyed by them. An oral argument punctuated by questions may not be as transiently satisfying as a perfectly declaimed speech. Almost certainly, it will not be studied with admiration through the generations. But if those are your objectives, stick to giving speeches or lectures. The oral advocate's job is to convince judges, and questions provide the clearest window of insight into what will accomplish that. Treat each question as a sincere effort to understand your point — even if that might not be the judge's true reason for asking. And answer every question frankly, respectfully, and directly. If you are sufficiently well-prepared, you will often see how a judge's question can lead you to a point you need to make in order to help the court understand the kernel of your case. Fish are more assertive today than they were in Webster's time; they will not simply jump into your pocket at the sight of your fishing rod. But once judges start to nibble with questions, with direct and thoughtful answers you can still hope to reel them in. . . .

Richard H. Seamon, *Appellate Advocacy: Preparing for Oral Argument in the United States Supreme Court*, 50 South Carolina Law Review 603 (1999)[13]

I. Introduction

Many articles offer excellent advice on how to present oral argument in the United States Supreme Court. This Article offers advice on how to prepare for the argument. . . . My preparation method reflects the current Court's practice

---

[13] Copyright © 1999 by South Carolina Law Review. Reprinted with permission. Mr. Seamon is a former Assistant to the Solicitor General of the United States who, in that position, orally argued 15 cases in the United States Supreme Court.

of drilling most oral advocates with questions for most of their argument time. Because it is rare to encounter a cold Court these days, it makes no sense . . . to spend time preparing a canned, linear spiel. The advocate should instead spend his time anticipating the Justices' questions and preparing answers to them. . . .

[T]he advocate must identify the small handful of key points that have to be made during oral argument . . . [and] should be able to express each key point in one simple and memorable phrase or sentence. . . . [and] to answer each question in a way that steers the Court to one of those key points. . . .

II. Anticipating Questions

. . . When a lawyer begins preparing for oral argument, she may . . . reread the record from cover to cover and the relevant cases from start to finish. . . . It is not enough for the advocate to know the record and the precedent; she must be able to use them at oral argument to answer questions and make affirmative points. To do so, the advocate must systematically identify what questions from the Court the material is likely to generate and what oral responses will be most effective.

. . . I initially . . . review[ed] every single line of [my] brief with the objective of thinking up questions that each line might prompt the Justices to ask. . . . Especially at the beginning of the process, I devoted my time to generating questions in this way, rather than answering them.

As the list of questions grows, the advocate will see that most of the hard questions clump around a limited number of issues. Those are the issues at the heart of the case. They are the matters for which the advocate must compose key points. . . .

The reason that preparation should revolve around the advocate's brief is that the brief is what the Justices have with them. . . . Before the argument, the Justices . . . no doubt found things that they did not understand, things that they agreed with, and things that they disagreed with. The Justice may well have marked up the brief . . . so that he could ask about various passages at the oral argument. After the argument, a Justice may use the brief in deciding how to vote and write an opinion.

. . . One objective of . . . oral argument is to convince the Justices that they can confidently rely on that advocate's brief. The advocate can achieve that objective with an argument that lifts the key points out of the brief, impresses them into the Justice's minds, and leaves them with an impression that the advocate's position is coherent and workable.

When the advocate picks up his brief on the first day of preparation, he must scrutinize it. . . . [T]he advocate should actively attempt to recall the decisions that he made when writing the brief. He should remember . . . the unfavorable facts that were smoothed over; the ambiguous statutes, regulations, or constitutional provisions that were claimed to be unambiguous; and the gap between the precedent that was cited and the case at hand. This is the retrospective, essentially deconstructive part of one's scrutiny. To write the brief, the advocate had to simplify and shape the facts and the law into a coherent whole. Now the process should be reversed, so that the brief is disassembled into the sometimes unruly facts and uncooperative legal principles that were woven together.

The toughest questions from the bench often concern matters that were elided in writing the brief. Therefore, as the advocate recollects the factual and legal elements of the case, he should imagine how they might be turned into questions from a Justice. The imagining should encompass both what was included in the brief and what was left out. Facts that were omitted from the brief's statement of facts may well be the subject of questions; so may lines of precedent that, the advocate's research revealed, led nowhere. The imagining should encompass both easy and hard questions, friendly and hostile ones, innocent ones and ones with ulterior motives.

. . . [T]he Justices often require advocates . . . to answer questions that do not pertain directly to the relevant facts and the relevant law. Moreover, questions about the record and precedent often range beyond what is set forth in the brief. Nonetheless, those questions usually are prompted by the . . . the briefs. Accordingly, the advocate should use the brief to anticipate the questions that must be answered by going outside the brief.

. . . The caption may prompt questions about . . . who the parties are (including their domicile, their occupation, and their history); how they are related to one another . . . ; why they brought this suit or were named as defendants; when they entered the lawsuit; why certain parties dropped out of the case; why entities or individuals whom one might have expected to be named in the case were not named; and whether the alignment of the parties reflected in the caption accurately reflects the various interests. . . .

The first page of the brief, which sets forth the question or questions presented, can be another fruitful source of questions. Is there a dispute about what questions are properly before the Court? Were the questions properly raised below? Where in the record is it indicated that the questions were presented? How did the courts below rule on the questions presented? Where does the record reflect those rulings? Have the respondents restated the question presented? If so, what is the significance, if any, of that restatement? Have any amici curiae attempted to inject additional issues into the case? If so, what is counsel's position about whether and how those issues should be addressed? Are there any factual wrinkles that might prevent the Court from squarely addressing the questions presented? Are there potential legal barriers, such as the existence of an adequate and independent state ground for the judgment below? If the case presents more than one question, how are the questions related? Is it necessary for the Court to decide all of the issues? How might its ruling on one issue affect its ruling on another?

The next major section of the brief, the statement of jurisdiction, also can generate questions. The advocate should anticipate questions about the statutes and the procedural rules (including the timing rules) that governed the jurisdiction of each court below. Particular care is warranted for cases from a state-court system. Each such system has distinct features that may . . . strike a Justice as peculiar or, at least, sufficiently unfamiliar to prompt a question.

In reviewing the statement of facts, an advocate should do at least five things for each factual assertion. First, review the parts of the record that support the assertion. Second, recall whether the evidence supporting the assertion is weak or disputed. Third, identify what, if anything, the opponent (or its amici) says about that factual assertion. Fourth, determine how the assertion is relevant to the case. Fifth, consider how the legal analysis might change if the fact asserted were changed or omitted. Going through these steps will spark additional questions. . . .

The steps just described entail preparation of a defensive nature. The advocate must also scrutinize the statement of facts to devise an affirmative strategy. In particular, the advocate should decide which factual issues she should downplay and which she should play up. Facts to be downplayed will not be raised at oral argument except in response to questions from the bench, and those responses should be brief. Facts to be played up may well be raised before the Justices pose questions about them; or, if they are raised in response to questions, the advocate will dwell on those facts to the extent necessary to buttress a key point. . . .

The process of reviewing the argument section resembles that for reviewing the statement of facts. For each legal assertion, the advocate should reread the judicial opinion, statutory provision, regulatory provision, or constitutional provision that was cited in support. . . . For each source, the advocate should develop a one- or two-sentence description of the source; an explanation of how it supports the advocate's overall position . . .; responses to questions challenging the advocate's reliance on that source; responses to questions about the original reasoning underlying the source (including judicial decisions, which, notwithstanding stare decisis, are always open to reexamination); and responses to what the opponent or its amici have to say about the cited source or the assertion for which the advocate has cited it.

. . . [T]he advocate must think strategically. Specifically, she must begin to identify the weakest and strongest points in her argument. . . . [T]his identification process can be accomplished primarily by determining, respectively, which arguments are most likely to draw the most numerous and difficult questions and which responses will most effectively answer those questions.

Finally, the advocate should not ignore the "conclusion" section of the brief. . . . [T]he advocate should hope to be asked what disposition is appropriate if the Court rules in her favor. The Court usually remands a case for further proceedings of some sort. The advocate should anticipate questions about what issues would remain to be sorted out if the Court decides the case favorably to the advocate; whether there is any dispute about which issues should be left for remand; how the Court's ruling on the issues before it might affect the resolution of issues left for remand; whether (and, if so, why) the Court should include in its opinion any instructions for the courts below on remand; and whether the Court might need, in further proceedings or in a future case, to address any of the issues left for remand.

. . . An advocate can anticipate questions most effectively by putting himself in the shoes of the Justices. . . . [T]he Justices function both as a group and as individuals. Both the group and each Justice have a history that the advocate should learn as much about as possible. Those functions and that history account for many of the questions at oral argument.

. . . The task most immediately at hand at the time of oral argument is to decide the case correctly. Then comes . . . writing an opinion that is persuasive and leads to appropriate results in future cases. In approaching these tasks, the Justices' collective disposition is independent-minded and skeptical. . . .

The collective skepticism generates questions to this effect: "Aren't you sugar coating the facts when you say. . . ?" or "Isn't there a critical difference between the case you have cited and yours. . . ?" The weight of their decision as precedent in the future prompts questions such as: "If we rule in your favor in this case, how do we decide the next case that comes down the pike, with the following slightly different facts?" The weight of past precedent generates questions such as: "If we decide this case in your favor on this rationale, what do we say about our prior decision X v. Y?" Justices' opinion-writing duties lead to questions the essence of which is: "How do we state the holding in this case?" In short, a large proportion of the Justices' questions simply reflect their desire to do their jobs as well as possible.

The advocate should also try to anticipate questions from individual Justices. Each Justice has his or her own jurisprudence. . . . The Justices know that academics will scrutinize their jurisprudence for coherence and consistency. Each Justice expects or hopes that the advocate who appears before the court will be able to explain how a ruling in the advocate's favor will square with the Justice's own jurisprudence.

To predict questions from individual Justices, the advocate should determine how each one voted in all relevant precedent. The advocate must . . . read that precedent carefully and . . . bear in mind that the Justices remember their past opinions with varying degrees of clarity. For that reason, the advocate should anticipate both straightforward and sophisticated questions about the precedent — ranging from the simple question "What did we hold in that case?" to more subtle ones concerning, for example, the voting alignments and the distinguishing facts.

An advocate can greatly enhance his ability to predict questions from individual Justices by listening to oral arguments. This has become much easier now that so many oral arguments are available on the Internet. An advocate will benefit even by listening to cases that concern issues unrelated to those presented in the case for which he is preparing because certain Justices favor certain questions. Justice White, for example, liked to ask questions that took this form: "If we reject the argument you just made, do you lose?" Chief Justice Rehnquist likes to ask: "What's your best case [for the argument that you have just made]?" Justice Scalia likes to ask questions about how the text of statutes or regulations supports an advocate's position. Justice Kennedy likes to ask questions related to ensuring that individuals are treated fairly by the legal system. . . .

It is better to anticipate questions that never get asked . . . than to hear questions at oral arguments that one never anticipated. . . . [A]nticipating the questions is half the battle. . . .

III. Composing Answers to Anticipated Questions

. . . Only after the advocate has identified these key issues can she prepare effective answers to all of the questions. An effective answer leads the Court to the advocate's statement of her position on the key points. . . .

Every answer to a Justice's question may have as many as three parts: (1) a response of three words or fewer; (2) an explanation of item (1); and (3) a transition to a key point. For each anticipated question, the advocate should decide which parts the answer must include and what each part will contain. . . . [S]ome questions will warrant only the first item . . . ; the rest will require all three items.

Questions warrant only an answer of one to three words when they are wholly and obviously incidental to the case. Examples . . . include most questions about geography or the identity of the judges who decided the case below. After the concisest-possible response, the advocate should immediately return to the point that she was making. . . . The advocate should . . . show, by her succinctness and rapid return to the original point, appropriate control over her presentation. This is a small but easy way of gaining credibility. It depends, of course, on a complete knowledge of the case's trivia.

Most questions sufficiently relate to the case that they deserve . . . an explanation. . . . [S]ome transition back to the affirmative presentation will be needed. The best transitions follow the explanation seamlessly. Making such transitions is most likely when the advocate has . . . anticipated the question. . . . In general, the advocate should plan to jump from the explanation to the most closely related key point. . . .

IV. Rehearsing Questions and Answers

Before the argument the advocate should spend as much time as possible talking about the case while on his feet. Well before the advocate feels ready to do so in front of others in a moot court, he should rehearse before an imaginary set of Justices. Indeed, the advocate can use this process not only to refine, but also to compose the substance of his presentation. . . .

This process . . . helps the advocate get feelings of nervousness and self-consciousness out of his system. It helps him determine the best way to argue the case with the spoken word[, and] . . . become fast on his feet by anticipating directions that questioning might take and developing the appropriate footwork.

After the rehearsal time ends, the advocate should . . . analyze the argument[,] . . . write down any additional questions that he anticipated[, and] . . . the answers that he composed during the rehearsal. Most importantly, the advocate should begin to identify the key points — the small handful of assertions to which the answer to all questions must lead in order for the Court to decide the case in the advocate's favor. . . .

[H]e should then prepare and rehearse . . . the presentation that he would make if uninterrupted by questions. As a rule, the presentation should last not much longer than half of the time allotted for argument, which usually means fifteen minutes. Although this might seem too short, it is not. If the Court does not consume the additional time with questions, the advocate will win its gratitude by ending early.

The advocate should incorporate the affirmative presentation into his later rehearsals . . . while answering anticipated questions. This process forces the advocate to make his key points in different orders and with appropriate transitions. It also should enable the advocate to learn the affirmative presentation well enough not to need a script of it. Although the advocate may wish to have such a script at the argument, the advocate should rely primarily on a one- or two-page outline limited to key phrases and cases.

NOTES

How much of the advice in Mr. Seamon's article is relevant to appellate advocacy generally, and how much is peculiar to arguments before the United States Supreme Court?

IV. FRIVOLOUS APPEALS AND COUNSEL'S SCREENING ROLE

In this section three questions should be considered: (1) what is the definition of a frivolous appeal? (2) what is the responsibility of a lawyer in relation to frivolous appeals? (3) what procedures are available in appellate courts to deal with and retard the filing of frivolous appeals?

In every jurisdiction these problems are addressed by statutes, rules of court, or decisional law. The federal provisions set out below were invoked in the cases that follow and are discussed in the text thereafter.

28 U.S.C. § 1912. Damages and costs on affirmance

Where a judgment is affirmed by the Supreme Court or a court of appeals, the court in its discretion may adjudge to the prevailing party just damages for his delay, and single or double costs.

28 U.S.C. § 1927. Counsel's liability for excessive costs

Any attorney or other person admitted to conduct cases in any court of the United States or any Territory thereof who so multiplies the proceedings in any case unreasonably and vexatiously may be required by the court to satisfy personally the excess costs, expenses, and attorneys' fees reasonably incurred because of such conduct.

Federal Rule of Appellate Procedure 38. Frivolous Appeal — Damages and costs

If a court of appeals determines that an appeal is frivolous, it may, after a separately filed motion or notice from the court and reasonable opportunity to respond, award just damages and single or double costs to the appellee.

NOTES

1. "Examples of actions deemed sanctionable [under Rule 38] include, but are not limited to, relitigating issues already finally adjudicated; failing to explain

how the trial court erred or to present cogent or clear arguments for reversal; failing to cite authority and ignoring opponent's contrary cited authority; citing irrelevant or inapplicable authority; distorting cited authority by omitting language from quotations; making irrelevant and illogical arguments; misrepresenting facts or law to the court; failing to reference or discuss controlling precedents; or raising an appeal when the issue is moot." *Abbs v. Principi*, 237 F.3d 1342, 1345 (Fed. Cir. 2001).

2. Most states also have statutes that authorize their courts to impose penalties for frivolous appeals, unfounded appeals, appeals found to have been brought solely for delay, in bad faith, and the like. The articulation of the standard varies somewhat. What is meant by "bad faith" in bringing an appeal? What kinds of conduct by an attorney in connection with an appeal should be considered abusive?

3. Note that the "damages" that Federal Rule of Appellate Procedure 38 and similar rules speak of often include attorneys' fees.

4. In addition to provisions like these concerning a court's authority, rules of professional conduct and a lawyer's obligations as an officer of the court come into play in connection with the frivolous appeal problem.

MODEL RULE OF PROFESSIONAL CONDUCT 3.1. Meritorious Claims and Contentions

A lawyer shall not bring or defend a proceeding, or assert or controvert an issue therein, unless there is a basis in law and fact for doing so that is not frivolous, which includes a good faith argument for an extension, modification or reversal of existing law. A lawyer for the defendant in a criminal proceeding, or the respondent in a proceeding that could result in incarceration, may nevertheless so defend the proceeding as to require that every element of the case be established.

5. Numerous other ethical considerations enter into appellate practice. Appellate advocates must be candid with the court, adhere faithfully and accurately to the trial record, disclose all pertinent proceedings relating to the case and any other matters that might reasonably be thought pertinent by the appellate court, and observe appropriate standards of decorum and good taste. *See* Janis L. Harwell, *Truth, Lies, and Consequences in Appellate Advocacy*, 5 PRAC. LITIG. 31 (1994); Kay Nord Hunt & Eric J. Magnuson, *Ethical Issues on Appeal*, 19 WM. MITCHELL L. REV. 659 (1993) (discussing the responsibilities of appellate counsel to ensure their competence and to avoid unmeritorious appeals, conflicts of interest and conflicting positions on issues on appeal, and raising issues of candor and demeanor, with emphasis on the Minnesota appellate system).

COLLINS v. AMOCO PRODUCTION CO.
706 F.2d 1114 (11th Cir. 1983)

BY THE COURT:

This is an attempt by plaintiffs to appeal from an order denying their motion to disqualify opposing counsel in a civil case.

In 1981 the Supreme Court settled a conflict between the circuits by deciding that an order denying a disqualification motion is not appealable as a final decision within 28 U.S.C. § 1291. *Firestone Tire & Rubber Co. v. Risjord*, 449 U.S. 368 (1981). In view of this decisive Supreme Court authority the effort to appeal is palpably frivolous.

The appeal is DISMISSED. The trial court is directed to assess damages to the appellee caused by the appeal, to include a reasonable attorney's fee. Appellee is also awarded double costs. FED. R. APP. P. 38.

NOTES

1. An intermediate court is, of course, bound by the highest court's decisions. Thus, the *Collins* court properly viewed the *Firestone* decision as foreclosing the question presented. By contrast, the Supreme Court itself can modify or overrule its own prior decisions. Does this mean that the Supreme Court would not have considered appellant's argument in *Collins* to be frivolous? Is frivolousness to be judged differently at the intermediate appellate level and in the court of last resort?

2. For a somewhat different kind of frivolousness, consider *Schlessinger v. Salimes*, 100 F.3d 519 (7th Cir. 1996), in which a restaurant patron, dissatisfied with how his steak was cooked, sued the restaurant owner, a policeman, and "everyone else in or out of sight" after having been told by the police, whom plaintiff had called, to pay and leave. He sued for a seizure of his person in violation of the Fourth Amendment and on state law theories. His various claims were dismissed for lack of the jurisdictional amount for diversity jurisdiction or failure to state a claim, or rejected on the basis of qualified immunity. Judge Easterbrook wrote, "Frivolous at the outset, and likely maliciously retaliatory as well, the case has deteriorated on appeal"; "Schlessinger . . . never attempted to articulate a theory of liability for the chief of police, the chairman of the Town's board, and like defendants"; "What the Town's unconstitutional 'policy' might be remains a mystery"; and "Instead of addressing the reasons he lost, Schlessinger argues that a district court's order denying a motion under Rule 60(b)(6) should be reviewed de novo by the court of appeals. The contention is nutty. At all events, the contention is beside the point: by omitting any argument that the district court's decision in favor of these defendants was mistaken, Schlessinger has rendered the standard of review irrelevant." The court therefore directed Schlessinger and his attorney to show cause why they should not be penalized under FED. R. APP. P. 38 and the local Circuit Rule 38 for pursuing a frivolous appeal.

3. "An appeal is held to be 'frivolous as filed' when an appellant grounds his appeal on arguments or issues 'that are beyond the reasonable contemplation of fair-minded people,' and 'no basis for reversal in law or fact can be or is even arguably shown.'" (internal citations omitted). . . . An appeal is . . . 'frivolous as argued' when an appellant has not dealt fairly with the court, has significantly misrepresented the law or facts, or has abused the judicial process by repeatedly litigating the same issue in the same court.' [An appeal also may be held to be frivolous as argued when a party fails to address the authority against his position, cites inapplicable authority, or seriously misrepresents the record and applicable law.] 'An appeal which is frivolous as filed must also be frivolous as

argued, since any arguments made in support of it are, by definition, frivolous.'" *Abbs v. Principi*, 237 F.3d 1342, 1345 (Fed. Cir. 2001) "'As filed' appeals [also] have been described as existing 'when the trial court's disposition was so plainly correct . . . that no reasonable person could believe that there is an appealable issue.'" *Finch v. Hughes Aircraft Co.*, 926 F.2d 1574, 1579 (Fed. Cir. 1991). And 'as argued' appeals have been described as appeals in which, "although there *may* be grounds for appeal, the particular arguments advanced lack any basis either in law or fact." S. Jay Plager, Leif R. Sigmond, Jr., Lawrence M. Kaplan & Jennifer M. Swartz, *The Federal Circuit and Frivolous Appeals*, 13 FED. CIR. B.J. 373, 375 (2003).

4. How is the nature of the alleged frivolousness of the appeals different in the various cases that follow?

LEPUCKI v. VAN WORMER
765 F.2d 86 (7th Cir. 1985)

PER CURIAM.

Our system of jurisprudence is designed to insure that all disputants with colorable claims have access to the courthouse. Relatively low barriers to entry have, however, generated an undesirable result — a deluge of frivolous or vexatious claims filed by the uninformed, the misinformed, and the unscrupulous. These claims clog court dockets and threaten to undermine the ability of the judiciary to efficiently administer the press of cases properly before it. Perhaps the greatest safeguard against this danger is the integrity and good sense of practicing lawyers who, as officers of the court, have both an ethical and a legal duty to screen the claims of their clients for factual veracity and legal sufficiency. Model Rule of Professional Conduct 3.1 (1983); FED. R. CIV. P. 11. Lawyers have a unique opportunity to counsel restraint or recklessness, to craft imaginative arguments or to press empty challenges to well-settled principles. Because of our reluctance to constrain the discretion of attorneys in the vigorous advocacy of their clients' interests, we penalize them only where they have failed to maintain a minimum standard of professional responsibility. But we will not overlook such a failure when it occurs, in part because it evidences disdain for the public, whose claims lie dormant because frivolous suits have diverted away scarce judicial resources, disdain for adversaries, who must expend time and money to defend against meritless attacks, and disdain for clients, whose trust is rewarded with legal bills, dismissals, and court-imposed sanctions. We have consolidated the following two appeals by attorney John A. Hyde as examples of irresponsible advocacy falling below minimum professional standards and deserving of penalty.

In *Pazdur v. Blaw-Knox Foundry and Mill Machinery* (No. 84-3041), appellant John A. Hyde represented various plaintiffs who sought, among other things, (1) an injunction barring their employer from "using or tendering various federal reserve notes as any purported payment for a debt obligation unless the creditor expressly consents to receive them," (2) an injunction barring the circulation of federal reserve notes, (3) a return of all of their wages withheld pursuant to the Internal Revenue Code and Treasury Regulations, and (4) costs and fees.

. . . Defendant orally moved to award costs and fees against appellant pursuant to FED. R. CIV. P. 11 and 28 U.S.C. § 1927. The court assessed costs of $2,139.97 against appellant and costs of $50 each against the six party plaintiffs. John A. Hyde appeals from the $2,139.97 award alone.

His primary argument is that "as there are no dollars and a court can enter judgment only in dollars, no court can enter a valid judgment for money today." This outrageous contention is so absurd that it merits no response. In any event, we summarily rejected a nearly identical claim in a recent appeal in which appellant served as plaintiffs' counsel. *Edgar v. Inland Steel Co.*, 744 F.2d 1276, 1278 n. 4 (7th Cir. 1984). Appellant also argues that he never received notice that penalties could be imposed against him and that he is entitled to a hearing before any penalty can be imposed.

We initially note that courts require notice and a hearing before they impose costs and fees against an attorney. While the Notes of the Advisory Committee on Rule 11 point out that the procedure followed must comport with due process, it goes on to state that "[t]he particular format to be followed should depend on the circumstances of the situation and the severity of the sanction under consideration. In many situations the judge's participation in the proceedings provides him with full knowledge of the relevant facts and little further inquiry will be necessary." While appellant did not have explicit notice that the court would consider imposing costs and fees against *him* at the October 25, 1984 hearing, he knew that the court would consider generally the imposition of penalties. Such notice was sufficient under the circumstances of this case, and appellant, having voluntarily chosen not to attend the hearing, cannot now complain that he is entitled to additional process. The decision of the district court is affirmed.

The second appeal, *Lepucki v. Van Wormer* (No. 84-2304), involved an employee of Inland Steel Co. ("Inland"), who filed a Form W-4 Withholding Allowance Certificate claiming exemption from withholding. Inland sent the form to the Internal Revenue Service (the "IRS"), which, following an investigation, ordered Inland to resume withholding federal income taxes from plaintiff's wages. It also imposed a $500 penalty plus interest on plaintiff for providing false information on the W-4 form. Richard Smulevitz, then payroll supervisor of Inland, informed plaintiff that the penalty would be deducted from his wages pursuant to the directions of the IRS.

Plaintiff retained attorney John A. Hyde, who filed a complaint in Indiana state court asserting that IRS officials defamed plaintiff when they communicated to Inland that he was being penalized for providing false information on his W-4 form, that defendant Smulevitz repeated the slander when he relayed the information to plaintiff, and that defendants Smulevitz and Inland wrongfully withheld his wages to satisfy the IRS directive. Defendants removed the action to federal court. After the district court denied plaintiff's motion for remand, it dismissed the action against the named IRS officials, finding them absolutely immune from suit for defamation. The slander action against Smulevitz was dismissed after the court determined his statement to plaintiff to be true. The court also dismissed the claim for recovery of allegedly wrongfully withheld wages by Smulevitz and Inland, finding such an action barred by statute. 26 U.S.C. § 3403. Last, the court imposed costs and fees against plaintiff "because it is patently obvious that this action was instituted not for the good faith reparation of an actual wrong but, rather, as a device for asserting certain philosophical beliefs regarding the tax laws of the United States and their implementation. Though plaintiff has every right to the free expression of his beliefs in this area, he does not have the right to exploit the judicial system of the United States, and resources of individual and corporate defendants thereof, to that end." [*Lepucki,*] 587 F. Supp. 1390, at 1395. This appeal followed.

Plaintiff first challenges the district court's denial of his motion for remand to state court. His complaint, among other things, seeks damages for libelous comments allegedly made by federal officials in the course of their employment. Such actions are removable to federal courts. 28 U.S.C. § 1442(a)(1). . . . Moreover, . . . a defendant . . . can remove the entire action, including pendent state law claims. . . . Thus, the district court had jurisdiction to consider all of plaintiff's claims and did not abuse its discretion in refusing to remand the dispute back to state court. Neither did the district court abuse its discretion by awarding costs and fees to defendants for the filing of this patently frivolous suit. The rest of plaintiff's appeal consists of attorney John A. Hyde's familiar litany about the evils of federal reserve notes and other non-meritorious arguments. We affirm the district court's order.

We will no longer tolerate abuse of the judicial process by irresponsible counsel who obstinately continue to use the courts in bad faith as forums for expression of philosophic beliefs and not for the resolution of *bona fide* disputes. We have repeatedly cautioned against the filing of frivolous appeals such as these and have no hesitation imposing costs and reasonable attorney's fees, pursuant to FED. R. APP .P. 38, against attorney John A. Hyde as appellant in No. 84-3041 and as lawyer for appellant in No. 84-2304. . . . We also impose costs against appellant Lepucki in No. 84-2304.

Last, we are referring attorney John A. Hyde to the appropriate state disciplinary bodies for investigation because of his pattern of abuse of the judicial process. . . .

NOTES

1. In *Grimes v. Commissioner of Internal Revenue*, 806 F.2d 1451 (9th Cir. 1986), Grimes appealed the Tax Court's dismissal of his petition for a tax deficiency redetermination concerning his 1981 income taxes for failure to state a claim upon which relief may be granted and the Tax Court's award of $5000 in damages to the government predicated upon its finding that Grimes' petition was frivolous, completely without merit, and initiated primarily for reasons of delay. In his petition, Grimes had argued that he was constitutionally entitled to an exemption for expenditures to provide his family with the "American Standard of 'good living,'" and that, applying this purported exemption, he owed no taxes as his "gross receipts" were "entirely consumed" in providing for his family. The government sought sanctions on the grounds that Grimes's appeal was frivolous. The Ninth Circuit affirmed and imposed further sanctions pursuant to 28 U.S.C. § 1912 and FED. R. APP. P. 38.

The appeals court reasoned that the Internal Revenue Code specifically sets forth the exemptions allowed for a taxpayer and the taxpayer's family; it does not authorize exemptions of the kind that Grimes claimed. Moreover, 26 U.S.C. § 262 expressly prohibit[ed] deductions for 'personal, living, or family expenses.' Because there is no statutory provision for the deduction Grimes claims, his income in the form of wages is subject to taxation. Grimes's claim that the statute relates only to deductions and not to the "principle of exemption," which he argues is constitutionally protected by the United Nations Charter[,] is preposterous. Grimes failed, therefore, to present any justiciable error in his petition for redetermination. . . . The Tax Court thus correctly dismissed his case for failure to state a claim upon which relief can be granted. . . .

[Noting that the court had discretion to impose sanctions for a frivolous appeal pursuant to 28 U.S.C. § 1912 and FED. R. APP. P. 38, it continued:] We are sensitive to the obligation of the courts to provide access for petitioners seeking in good faith to avail themselves of the protection of the law, and we do not impose sanctions lightly. We are also aware that an appeal that lacks merit is not always frivolous. These principles do not, however, inhibit the court from imposing sanctions when presented with unsupportable appeals, presenting no colorable claim of error. Sanctions are appropriate when the result of an appeal is obvious and the arguments of error are wholly without merit. . . . Grimes's arguments regarding the "principle of exemption" lack any semblance of merit. They are contrary to specific and unambiguous statutory provisions and to clearly established principles of law. . . . [T]he result of this appeal was obvious. . . . Groundless litigation of the kind pursued here by Grimes diverts the resources of the judicial system from more serious claims, and imposes unnecessary costs on other litigants. Even though Grimes is proceeding pro se, sanctions are appropriate. We award damages to the government in the amount of $1500.

2. Note that in *Lepucki* the court of appeals affirmed the district court's imposition of sanctions and also imposed sanctions of its own under Rule 38. If a plaintiff's case is frivolous at the trial level and is thus dismissed, it would seem to follow that an appeal in that case likewise would be frivolous. Might it be, however, that a case *not* frivolous at the trial level could be frivolous on appeal?

3. Should the standard of review applicable to the appeal on the merits influence whether an appeal is regarded as frivolous?

4. While some commentators believe there has been an increase in sanctions for frivolous appeals, others see a reduction, at least in some circuits. *Compare* Scott A. Martin, *Keeping Courts Afloat in a Rising Sea of Litigation: An Objective Approach to Imposing Rule 38 Sanctions for Frivolous Appeals*, 100 MICH. L. REV. 1157 (2002) (asserting increased imposition of sanctions for frivolous appeals) *with* S. Jay Plager, Leif R. Sigmond, Jr., Lawrence M. Kaplan & Jennifer M. Swartz, *The Federal Circuit and Frivolous Appeals*, 13 FED. CIR. B.J. 373, 391 (2003) (finding an 85% decline in the number of appeals declared frivolous by the Federal Circuit in the ten years from 1982-92). If there is a reduction, what reasons might explain it?

5. Is there, or should there be, any subjective scienter requirement for an appeal to be frivolous? Or should bad faith and the like be relevant only to whether a sanction is imposed and what that sanction should be?

6. Note that MODEL RULE 3.1 permits a lawyer to pursue an appeal on any basis "that is not frivolous." Consider the following civil action to recover damages for assault and battery. Plaintiff testified that she was struck and injured by defendant. Witness X testified that he was present at the time and that defendant struck plaintiff. Defendant testified that he did not strike plaintiff. Witness Y testified that she was present and that defendant did not strike plaintiff. The jury returned a verdict for plaintiff. You represent the defendant. He is irate, contending that the plaintiff and her witness are lying; he insists on appealing to correct this injustice. You have studied the record carefully and find no errors of law committed by the trial judge. As defendant's attorney, could you properly pursue an appeal? Suppose the case had been tried to a judge without a jury and that the judge had made a finding that defendant struck plaintiff. Would the propriety of an appeal be any different? Suppose that the defendant is wealthy and offers to pay you five times your normal fee to take the appeal. Would that alter your view of the matter?

7. Based on the foregoing cases and the other material in this section, how would you define a "frivolous appeal"? Not every appeal that lacks merit is frivolous.

MCKNIGHT v. GENERAL MOTORS CORP.
511 U.S. 659 (1994)

PER CURIAM

After petitioner appealed the dismissal of his employment discrimination claim, respondent moved for dismissal of the appeal and for sanctions. Respondent argued that the appeal was frivolous in light of controlling decisions of the Court of Appeals for the Seventh Circuit holding that § 101 of the Civil Rights Act of 1991, 2 U.S.C. § 1981 (1988 ed., Supp. IV), does not apply to cases arising before its enactment. *See Luddington v. Indiana Bell Tel. Co.,* 966 F.2d 225 (1992). In an order dated September 30, 1992, the Court of Appeals granted respondent's motion, dismissed the appeal, and imposed a $500 sanction on petitioner's attorney.

The Court of Appeals correctly rejected petitioner's argument that § 101 applies retroactively. *See Landgraf v. USI Film Products,* 511 U.S. [244] (1994). However, if the only basis for the order imposing sanctions on petitioner's attorney was that his retroactivity argument was foreclosed by circuit precedent, the order was not proper. As petitioner noted in his memorandum opposing dismissal and sanctions, this Court had not yet ruled on the application of § 101 to pending cases. Filing an appeal was the only way petitioner could preserve the issue pending a possible favorable decision by this Court. Although, as of September 30, 1992, there was no circuit conflict on the retroactivity question, that question had divided the District Courts and its answer was not so clear as to make petitioner's position frivolous.

Accordingly, the petition for a writ of certiorari is granted, the order imposing sanctions is vacated, and the case is remanded for further proceedings consistent with this opinion.

NOTES

1. Consider the relationship between the concept of "frivolousness" and the concept of "substantiality" in the law of federal court jurisdiction. In *Zucht v. King*, 260 U.S. 174 (1922), the plaintiff sought an injunction against enforcement of a city ordinance requiring a smallpox vaccination as a condition for attendance in public schools, contending that the ordinance violated the Due Process and Equal Protection Clauses of the Fourteenth Amendment. The state courts denied relief, and the plaintiff sought review in the Supreme Court. The Court held that in view of its previous decision sustaining the constitutionality of a compulsory vaccination statute, the question presented was not "substantial in character," and it dismissed the appeal. Before 1988, appeals to the Supreme Court from state courts were authorized as a matter of right, and the *Zucht* decision was viewed as holding that a substantial federal question was essential to the Supreme Court's jurisdiction. If a case contains no substantial federal question for purposes of federal appellate jurisdiction, should the case be considered frivolous?

2. Compare *Maher v. Hyde*, 272 F.3d 83 (1st Cir. 2001), dismissing an appeal as moot and ordering counsel to show cause why sanctions should not be imposed because of the frivolous nature of the appeal, deriving in part from its mootness.

3. Appeals can be frivolous only in part, and still justify sanctions. *See, e.g., Breneman v. United States ex rel. FAA*, 381 F.3d 33 (1st Cir. 2004). And the sanctions courts impose for frivolous appeals are not limited to money. *See Iwachis v. N.Y. State DMV*, 396 F.3d 525 (2d Cir. 2005), threatening that, if appellant filed further appeals in the several actions he had pending, the court would enter an injunction directing the court clerk to refuse to accept the filings unless appellant first obtained leave of the appellate court.

Robert A. Martineau & Patricia A. Davidson, *Frivolous Appeals in the Federal Courts: The Ways of the Circuits,* 34 American University Law Review 603, 604-06, 657-60 (1985)[14]

One tool long available to the courts of appeals, but seldom used, is the power to impose sanctions on litigants and attorneys for taking frivolous appeals or for employing abusive tactics in the appellate courts. Sections 1912 and 1927 of the United States Judicial Code and Federal Rule of Appellate Procedure 38 provide express authority for a range of sanctions in various circumstances. Conflict has developed among the circuits, however, concerning the proper application of these statutes and rules. Courts have differed regarding such issues as the definition of a frivolous appeal, the relationship between the merits of an appeal, conduct on appeal, and the sanction, the necessity for showing bad faith, the procedures followed in imposing a sanction, and the type and appropriateness of the sanction.

. . . [I]t is important for both lawyers and litigants to know how the various circuits currently apply sections 1912 and 1927 and Appellate Rule 38.

---

[14] Copyright © 1985 by Robert H. Martineau and Patricia A. Davidson. Reprinted with permission.

Appellants and their attorneys should be familiar with the risks they may run by taking an appeal that the court might characterize as frivolous or by engaging in tactics on appeal that the court might consider abusive. It is also important for appellees and their attorneys to be familiar with the attitude of each circuit on these matters so that they may know when they are likely to receive an award of damages from an appellant or opposing counsel.

    . . . [T]he various circuits fall into three broad categories. The first category is best characterized as the "reluctant circuits." Rather than expressly stating any reluctance to impose sanctions, the circuits in this category have demonstrated their reluctance by imposing sanctions only in a small number of cases. At the other end of the spectrum are the . . . "aggressive circuits." These circuits either have used sanctions consistently as a deterrent to frivolous appeals or have begun to do so more frequently in the past several years. The final category, the "uncertain circuits," is so denominated because different panels of judges in each of these circuits have expressed conflicting views as to whether bad faith is a requirement for imposition of a sanction. It is thus impossible for litigants to know in advance which approach a panel will take in any particular case. . . .

Sanctions can be an effective deterrent to frivolous appeals only if courts impose them under a reasonable and predictable standard, if the sanctions are of a substantial nature, and if their imposition is given widespread notice. . . .

[A]nalysis of the various circuits' treatment of frivolous appeals indicates, however, that courts rarely use sanctions for frivolous appeals in a manner to enhance their effectiveness. The cases reflect a disparity of treatment that has no justification in the different caseloads facing the various circuits. Moreover, there is no legitimate disagreement regarding the proper interpretation or application of the relevant statutes or rule. Only three circuits — the First, Fifth, and Ninth — consistently have been alert to the problem of frivolous appeals and have used their authority to impose sanctions over the period when the caseload of the federal appellate courts grew so dramatically. The Sixth, Eleventh, and Federal Circuits recently have joined these three circuits in an aggressive approach to sanctions for frivolous appeals. Their classification as aggressive can only be tentative at this point, however, because of the limited number of cases in which they have imposed sanctions. The Sixth Circuit appears simply to have recognized the problem of frivolous appeals and the importance of dealing with them, whereas the Eleventh and the Federal Circuits are still of very recent origin.

    Four circuits — the Third, Fourth, Eighth, and District of Columbia — are demonstrably reluctant to impose sanctions. The Second, Seventh, and Tenth Circuits take an approach that is different from the reluctant circuits but which has the same effect on deterrence. This article has classified these circuits as uncertain because on occasion they have required a clear showing of bad faith to justify imposition of a sanction, while at other times they have imposed sanctions without referring to the necessity of a showing of bad faith.

    This disparity among the circuits . . . may have emanated from judicial reluctance to impose sanctions or from different views regarding the type of proof required for a finding of frivolousness. Another cause of the disparity among circuits and between cases in the same circuit may be confusion regarding the appropriate source of authority to use in imposing sanctions on an appellant's attorney. The authorities themselves contribute to this confusion. Section 1927 is directed at attorneys who prolong proceedings "unreasonably and vexatiously," but it does not expressly mention frivolous appeals. Conversely, section 1912 and Appellate Rule 38 both provide sanctions for delay or for frivolous appeals, but neither provision expressly subjects the attorney to those sanctions. . . .

This disparate situation is clearly undesirable. At the very least, each circuit should determine when an attorney can be found liable for a sanction, and under which authority. Each circuit should also determine expressly whether the standard for an attorney is the same as the standard for an appellant, and whether the standard varies depending upon which section or rule it applies. Absent such clarification, attorneys have no idea when and under what circumstances a federal appellate court will compel them to pay a frivolous appeal sanction.

Robert J. Martineau, *Frivolous Appeals: The Uncertain Federal Response,* 1984 Duke Law Journal 845, 847-49, 870-71, 879-86[15]

The courts of appeals have set forth three principal purposes to be achieved by the imposition of sanctions [for frivolous appeals]. The immediate objectives are to compensate the opposing party for the time and expense that he has incurred and to punish the offending person for wasting the limited time and resources of the appellate court. The long-term objective is deterrence — reducing the number of appeals taken to the courts of appeals and the amount of time spent on appeals. Deterring frivolous appeals serves another purpose — protecting litigants in other cases whose appeals are delayed because the court is spending time on the frivolous appeals. Compensation will more likely be the objective when the appellee files a motion seeking a monetary award, while deterrence will be cited more often when the court raises the issue sua sponte.

The use of sanctions to penalize appellants and their attorneys is not without difficulty. The fear of a sanction may discourage a person with a valid claim from pursuing it on appeal. Although this danger may exist even if it were clear when and under what circumstances a sanction would be imposed, it is heightened substantially when there are several different sources of authority for imposing a sanction, when there are multiple purposes for the sanction, when varying standards are used in judging whether an appeal is frivolous, when the relationship between frivolous appeal sanctions and abusive litigation tactics is unclear, when the sanction is imposed without notice or an opportunity to be heard, and when the procedure varies for initiating consideration of a sanction.

Because of these uncertainties, it is imperative that when courts impose sanctions for frivolous appeals, they do so in accord with a procedure that is consistent with due process requirements. It is also essential that courts develop a clearly articulated definition of frivolous appeals, indicating, in particular, whether an objective or subjective standard is used. Further, they

---

[15] Copyright © 1984 by Robert J. Martineau. Reprinted with permission.

must clearly distinguish between (1) a sanction imposed for taking a meritless appeal, and (2) a sanction imposed for abusive litigation tactics during the pendency of an appeal with merit. Unless these procedural and substantive requirements are met, it is unlikely that the sanctions imposed by the courts of appeals will reduce the number of frivolous appeals and abusive litigation tactics. . . .

Confusion Over Defining Frivolous Appeals and Determining When to Impose a Sanction

The courts of appeals have often confused two distinct issues. The first issue is whether an appeal should be classified as frivolous because of its lack of merit. The second issue is whether, given that an appeal is frivolous on its merits, the conduct of the appellant or the attorney is such that a sanction should be imposed on one or both. Often courts determine that an appeal is frivolous by examining the conduct of the appellant or attorney, rather than by looking at the merits of the appeal. This conduct is then used as the basis for determining the necessity for the sanction and the type to be imposed. This approach causes the courts to vacillate between objective and subjective standards and obscures the extent to which the intent of the appellant or the attorney determines whether an appeal is frivolous.

Even though an appeal does have some merit, it may still be frivolous if the appellant's conduct indicates that his primary purpose is to delay enforcement of the judgment, to cause the appellee to incur unnecessary expense, to be vexatious, or if the conduct otherwise demonstrates bad faith by abuse of the judicial process. There is no case in which a court has found that an appeal had merit and yet was conducted in such a way as to call for a frivolous appeal sanction. What the courts have done, however, is to look at the conduct of the appellant as evidence of whether the appeal is without merit and thus frivolous. This type of analysis creates confusion. A frivolous appeal should be one that has no merit when viewed objectively and should not be defined by the beliefs or intent of the appellant or attorney.

This does not mean, however, that the conduct of the appellant or the attorney is irrelevant to the frivolous appeal sanction. What it does mean is that the conduct is significant for another purpose — to determine the nature and extent of the sanction to be imposed. This is the real reason the courts look to the conduct and the intent it demonstrates. The more flagrant the conduct, the clearer it is that the intent or motive of the person is culpable and the larger the sanction should be. Thus, the conduct or intent should be the measure of the sanction, not the measure of the merit of the appeal. . . .

There may be some concern that the deterrent effect of a sanction will discourage the good faith appellant or attorney from filing a legitimate appeal or motion. This is, at most, a theoretical problem. . . . The history of the use of sanctions by appellate courts does not suggest that the courts will misuse or overuse this authority. If anything, the record demonstrates that the threat of sanctions has had minimal effect because the courts have been so reluctant to use them.

Because of the problems associated with the current piecemeal approach to frivolous appeals, a single new statute or rule should be established as the exclusive basis for sanctioning frivolous appellate conduct. A rule that attempts to reduce both the number of meritless appeals and abusive tactics should deal with four main areas: (1) frivolous appeals; (2) abusive appeal tactics; (3) the range of sanctions; and (4) procedures for initiating consideration of a sanction.

A. *Frivolous Appeals*

The first section of an amended Appellate Rule 38 should simply authorize the imposition of a sanction for the taking of a frivolous appeal. The first section should not attempt to define precisely a frivolous appeal, but should simply state that it is an appeal with no reasonable legal or factual basis. A frivolous appeal must meet some objective standard, but that standard is best left to the courts to address on a case-by-case basis. The standard applied should be objective and not subjective; issues of a subjective nature, such as the intent of the appellant, are relevant only to the sanction to be imposed.

. . . [Making] the imposition of the sanction [ ] mandatory [but] the type and size of the sanction [ ] discretionary [is the] . . . philosophy [that] should be followed when imposing a sanction for taking a frivolous appeal.

The bad faith of the appellant, as demonstrated by his conduct at the trial, on appeal, and in prior or other pending litigation, becomes significant only when the court considers the type of sanctions to be imposed, and should not be used to determine whether the appeal is frivolous in the first place.

The rule should apply to attorneys as well as to parties. The attorney, rather than the party, may be the principal actor in taking the appeal. Attorneys are expressly the subject of 28 U.S.C. § 1927 and have also been held liable when sanctions are imposed under other sources of authority. Again, revised Federal Rule of Civil Procedure 11, which provides for the imposition of a sanction upon a party, the attorney or both, is the model for the appellate rule. It will be up to the court to ascertain who, in any particular case, is the person at fault.

The rule should include a reference to initiating a proceeding as well as to taking an appeal. In a court of appeals, parties often file petitions for supervisory writs as a substitute for appeal. These proceedings can be frivolous in the same way as an appeal and thus should be included in the section. Furthermore, if a legitimate appeal becomes frivolous as a result of later developments,[16] continuing the appeal should be sanctioned. . . .

B. *Abusive Appeal Tactics*

The fact that appellants and their attorneys abuse the appellate process by various tactics has long been recognized. When these tactics are used in connection with an appeal that can be objectively defined as frivolous, the tactics used . . . are relevant in determining the sanction imposed for taking the frivolous appeal. If an appeal does in fact have some merit and thus cannot properly be classified as frivolous, it does not follow that a sanction cannot or should not be imposed for the improper conduct. This is the thrust of 28 U.S.C.

---

16 [210] If, during the pendency of an appeal, there is a retroactive change in the relevant law, adverse to the appellant, continuing the appeal may be frivolous.

§ 1927, but that section applies only to attorneys and not to parties. It is also the thrust of the *Roadway Express* decision. [*Roadway Express, Inc. v. Piper*, 447 U.S. 752 (1980).] Some courts, in an effort to penalize this type of conduct, use the conduct to conclude that an appeal is frivolous. This confusion can best be avoided by including in an appellate rule a provision . . . [that] would make it clear that whether or not an appeal is found to be frivolous, abusive appeal tactics should be penalized.

. . . The language of the section should be virtually identical to that of Rule 11, so that the same type of improper conduct will receive equal treatment in the court of appeals and in the district court. Cases interpreting one rule may serve as precedent for interpretations of the other.

. . . Because present Appellate Rule 25 already deals with filing and service of papers, adding the signature requirement and its status as a certification in Rule 25(a) with a cross reference to Appellate Rule 38, where the penalty for filing a paper in violation of the certification is stated, is preferable. . . .

Moreover, . . . the new appellate rules would apply to conduct beyond the filing of papers. Although that is the type of activity most likely to fall within the meaning of "abusive appeal tactic," it is not necessarily the only abusive tactic. The new Rule should also sanction the failure to file or the late filing of a paper such as a record or brief; failure to order the transcript in a timely manner; failure to appear for a settlement conference or oral argument; a dilatory response to an order or request from the court or a request from the other party; or any act of commission or omission that has the same improper purpose mentioned in Rule 11 — delay, harassment, or causing needless expense. Consequently, the appellate rule must include a general reference to any abusive appeal tactic which would include, but not be limited to, filing a paper with an improper purpose. . . .

C. *Available Sanctions*

The section on sanctions should, to the extent possible, give flexibility to the court while . . . giving some advance warning to litigants and attorneys. This can best be achieved by listing the most common types of sanctions, but allowing the court to fashion a different sanction when appropriate.

One sanction that should be included is the power to dismiss the appeal. Although dismissal is not actually a sanction for a frivolous appeal, a dismissal will not necessarily occur in a case of abusive tactics absent its use as a sanction. The inclusion of dismissal as a sanction for abusive tactics is supported by *Roadway Express* and by its customary use as a sanction for discovery abuses pursuant to Federal Rule of Civil Procedure 37.

Fines payable to the court are not included as a sanction in any present statute or rule. Monetary sanctions have been used by the courts of appeals as a means of compensating the opposing party for the delay or additional expense caused by the appellant or his attorney. The court itself, however, may have been put to additional expense because of the conduct of a party or attorney even though the opposing party has not been directly harmed. It may also be that the harm is borne primarily by other litigants who suffer delay in the disposition of their cases. In those situations, deterrence is the principal reason for a sanction, and a fine payable to court rather than damages payable to the opposing party is the most appropriate sanction. . . .

D. *Procedure*

Prior notice of the possibility of a sanction must be given either by a motion filed by an opposing party or by an order to show cause issued by the court. The only opportunity to be heard required by due process guarantees is the opportunity for the party or attorney to present his views in writing to the court prior to the court's decision on whether to impose a sanction. . . .

Conclusion

. . . Until recently, the failure of the federal appellate courts to define clearly the type of appeal or conduct that would subject a party or attorney to a sanction and their reluctance to impose sanctions had no great effect on their caseload. In the past two decades, however, increased litigation has had a dramatic impact on the federal appellate courts with a concomitant increase in the number of meritless appeals and actions taken by appellants or their attorneys that have no purpose other than to harass or delay. It has now become a matter of priority for the federal appellate courts to recognize clearly the type of conduct that should be prevented and to use their powers to impose sanctions to achieve that goal.

. . . Rule 38 of the Federal Rules of Appellate Procedure should be revised to read as follows:

(a) A court of appeals shall impose a sanction upon a party or attorney or both for taking or continuing an appeal or initiating a proceeding in the court that the court finds to be frivolous. For purposes of this rule, a frivolous appeal is one that has no reasonable legal or factual basis.

(b) A court of appeals shall impose a sanction upon a party or attorney or both for filing a paper in violation of Rule 25(a) or for any act of commission or omission that has an improper purpose such as to harass or to cause unnecessary delay or needless increase in the cost of litigation.

(c) A court of appeals may impose one or more of the following sanctions:

    (1)   dismissal of the appeal;

    (2)   striking a paper, pleading or motion;

    (3)   a monetary sanction including but not limited to (i) double costs, (ii) a penalty not to exceed ten percent of the judgment, (iii) damages occasioned by delay, (iv) reasonable attorney fees, (v) a fine payable to the court.

(d)(1) A party may by motion request that a sanction be imposed upon another party or attorney pursuant to this rule.

(2) If a court on its own initiative considers that a sanction pursuant to this rule may be appropriate, the court shall order the party or attorney to show cause in writing why a sanction should not be imposed on the party or attorney or both.

Rule 25 of the Federal Rules of Appellate Procedure should be amended to include a new section (a) to precede the present section (a). The new section should read:

> (a) A party or attorney who files a paper in a proceeding conducted pursuant to these rules shall sign the paper. The signature of the party or attorney or the filing of a paper without a signature constitutes a certification that: the document is well grounded in fact; is warranted by existing law or a good faith argument for the extension, modification, or reversal of existing law; and is not filed for an improper purpose such as to harass or to cause unnecessary delay or needless increase in the cost of the litigation. A party or attorney who files a paper in violation of these rules, or the party on whose behalf the paper is filed, is subject to a sanction in accordance with Rule 38.

NOTES

1. If an appellate court were authorized to impose sanctions on an attorney for bringing an appeal that was not "well-grounded in fact" or not "warranted by existing law" could the court impose a sanction in an appeal that was not frivolous? That is, could a non-frivolous appeal fail to meet the requirements of the appellate version of Rule 11 proposed by Professor Martineau? Would that be good policy?

2. Commentators writing more recently have continued to observe a lack of uniform approach and splits among the circuits as to issues such as whether bad faith is a prerequisite to the imposition of sanctions. *See, e.g.*, Scott A. Martin, *Keeping Courts Afloat in a Rising Sea of Litigation: An Objective Approach to Imposing Rule 38 Sanctions for Frivolous Appeals*, 100 MICH. L. REV. 1156 (2002). Some practitioners bemoan appellate courts' reluctance to impose sanctions, arguing that "it may take substantial effort to reveal the frivolous nature of the appeal," and that "to those who have been forced to bear the expense of defending against a frivolous appeal, sanctions [in the form of the full extent of the costs reasonably incurred in responding] are as important to providing complete justice as the affirmance itself." Mark R. Kravitz, *Unpleasant Duties: Imposing Sanctions for Frivolous Appeals*, 4 J. APP. PRAC. & PROCESS 335 (2002). Are there any countervailing arguments that support or at least explain judicial reluctance to find appeals to be frivolous, or even reluctance to impose "the full extent of the costs reasonably incurred in responding" once a court has found an appeal to be frivolous, or is such reluctance inexplicable?

3. Although not necessarily categorized as a "sanction," some states have an automatic "affirmance penalty" under which a statutorily prescribed penalty is assessed against a defendant-appellant when a money judgment is affirmed on appeal. In *Burlington Northern R.R. v. Woods*, 480 U.S. 1 (1987), an Alabama statute prescribing an automatic 10% affirmance penalty was attacked as violating the Fourteenth Amendment. The question arose on appeal to a federal court of appeals from a district court judgment in a case in federal court by virtue of diversity jurisdiction. The Supreme Court held that FED. R. APP. P. 38 applied and that the Alabama statute therefore would not

be applied. In view of that holding, the Court did not reach the constitutional question. What is the argument that an automatic affirmance penalty is unconstitutional? If and when that question is reached by the Supreme Court, what should its decision be?

4. The foregoing material concerning frivolousness addresses this problem in the context of civil appeals. The problem has been dealt with quite differently in criminal appeals, at least in those cases involving court-appointed counsel for indigent defendants. The remainder of this chapter addresses that problem.

V. COURT-APPOINTED COUNSEL IN CRIMINAL APPEALS: THE FRIVOLOUS-MERITLESS DISTINCTION

ANDERS v. CALIFORNIA
386 U.S. 738 (1966)

Mr. Justice Clark delivered the opinion of the Court.

We are concerned with the extent of the duty of a court-appointed appellate counsel to prosecute a first appeal from a criminal conviction, after that attorney has conscientiously determined that there is no merit to the indigent's appeal.

. . . [A]fter a study of the record and consultation with petitioner, the appointed counsel concluded that there was no merit to the appeal. He so advised the court by letter and at the same time, informed the court that petitioner wished to file a brief in his own behalf. At this juncture, petitioner requested the appointment of another attorney. This request was denied and petitioner proceeded to file his own brief *pro se*. The State responded and petitioner filed a reply brief. . . . [T]he District Court of Appeal unanimously affirmed the conviction.

On January 21, 1965, petitioner filed an application for a writ of habeas corpus in the District Court of Appeal in which he sought to have his case reopened. In that application he raised the issue of deprivation of the right to counsel in his original appeal because of the court's refusal to appoint counsel at the appellate stage of the proceedings. The court denied the application on the same day, in a brief unreported memorandum opinion. The court stated that it "ha[d] again reviewed the record and [had] determined the appeal [to be] without merit." The court also stated that "the procedure prescribed by *In re Nash*, 61 A.C. 538, was followed in this case. . . ."[17]

On June 25, 1965, petitioner submitted a petition for a writ of habeas corpus to the Supreme Court of California, and the petition was denied without opinion

---

17 [2] *In re Nash*, 393 P. 2d 405 (1964), held that the requirements of *Douglas v. California*, 372 U.S. 353 (1963), are met in the event appointed counsel thoroughly studies the record, consults with the defendant and trial counsel and conscientiously concludes, and so advises the appellate court, that there are no meritorious grounds of appeal; and provided that the appellate court is satisfied from its own review of the record, in light of any points personally raised by the defendant, that appointed counsel's conclusion is correct. The appeal then proceeds without the appointment of other counsel and decision is reached without argument.

by that court on July 14, 1965. Among other trial errors, petitioner claimed that both the judge and the prosecutor had commented on this failure to testify contrary to the holding of this Court in *Griffin v. California*, 380 U.S. 609 (1965). We have concluded that California's action does not comport with fair procedure and lacks that equality that is required by the Fourteenth Amendment.

. . . In *Gideon v. Wainwright*, 372 U.S. 335[, 344] (1963), the Sixth Amendment's requirement that "the accused shall enjoy the right . . . to have the Assistance of Counsel for his defence" was made obligatory on the States by the Fourteenth Amendment, the Court holding that "in our adversary system of criminal justice, any person haled into court, who is too poor to hire a lawyer, cannot be assured a fair trial unless counsel is provided for him." We continue to adhere to these principles.

In petitioner's case, his appointed counsel wrote the District Court of Appeal, stating:

> I will not file a brief on appeal as I am of the opinion that there is no merit to the appeal. I have visited and communicated with Mr. Anders and have explained my views and opinions to him. . . . [H]e wishes to file a brief in this matter on his own behalf.

The District Court of Appeal, after having examined the record, affirmed the conviction. We believe that counsel's bare conclusion, as evidenced by his letter, was not enough. . . . Here the court-appointed counsel had the transcript but refused to proceed with the appeal because he found no merit in it. He filed a no-merit letter with the District Court of Appeal whereupon the court examined the record itself and affirmed the judgment. On a petition for a writ of habeas corpus some six years later it found the appeal had no merit. It failed, however, to say whether it was frivolous or not, but, after consideration, simply found the petition to be "without merit." The Supreme Court, in dismissing this habeas corpus application, gave no reason at all for its decision and so we do not know the basis for its action. We cannot say that there was a finding of frivolity by either of the California courts or that counsel acted in any greater capacity than merely as *amicus curiae*. . . . Hence, California's procedure did not furnish petitioner with counsel acting in the role of an advocate nor did it provide that full consideration and resolution of the matter as is obtained when counsel is acting in that capacity. The necessity for counsel so acting is highlighted by the possible disadvantage the petitioner suffered here. In his *pro se* brief, which was filed in 1959, he urged several trial errors but failed to raise the point that both the judge and the prosecutor had commented to the jury regarding petitioner's failure to testify. In 1965, this Court in *Griffin v. California*, *supra*, outlawed California's comment rule, as embodied in Art. I, § 13, of the California Constitution.

The constitutional requirement of substantial equality and fair process can only be attained where counsel acts in the role of an active advocate in behalf of his client, as opposed to that of *amicus curiae*. The no-merit letter and the procedure it triggers do not reach that dignity. Counsel should, and can with honor and without conflict, be of more assistance to his client and to the court. His role as advocate requires that he support his client's appeal to the best of his ability. Of course, if counsel finds his case to be wholly frivolous, after a conscientious examination of it, he should so advise the court and request permission to withdraw. That request must, however, be accompanied by a brief referring to anything in the record that might arguably support the appeal. A copy of counsel's brief should be furnished the indigent and time allowed him to raise any points that he chooses; the court — not counsel — then proceeds, after a full examination of all the proceedings, to decide whether the case is wholly frivolous. If it so finds it may grant counsel's request to withdraw and dismiss the appeal insofar as federal requirements are concerned, or proceed to a decision on the merits, if state law so requires. On the other hand, if it finds any of the legal points arguable on their merits (and therefore not frivolous) it must, prior to decision, afford the indigent the assistance of counsel to argue the appeal.

This requirement would not force appointed counsel to brief his case against his client but would merely afford the latter that advocacy which a nonindigent defendant is able to obtain. It would also induce the court to pursue all the more vigorously its own review because of the ready references not only to the record, but also to the legal authorities as furnished it by counsel. The no-merit letter, on the other hand, affords neither the client nor the court any aid. The former must shift entirely for himself while the court has only the cold record which it must review without the help of an advocate. Moreover, such handling would tend to protect counsel from the constantly increasing charge that he was ineffective and had not handled the case with that diligence to which an indigent defendant is entitled. This procedure will assure penniless defendants the same rights and opportunities on appeal — as nearly as is practicable — as are enjoyed by those persons who are in a similar situation but who are able to afford the retention of private counsel.

The judgment is reversed and the case is remanded for further proceedings not inconsistent with this opinion.

NOTES

1. The dissenters in *Anders* (Justice Stewart, joined by Justices Black and Harlan) noted that under the system that had been in use in California for handling indigent appeals counsel was appointed to represent the defendant on appeal, thoroughly studied the record, and consulted with the defendant and trial counsel. If counsel conscientiously concluded that there were no meritorious grounds of appeal and the appellate court was satisfied from its own review of the record, in the light of any points raised by the defendant personally, that counsel's assessment was correct, the court could decide the appeal without oral argument, without appointing other counsel. Does *Anders* reflect a lack of confidence by a majority of the Supreme Court justices in either the competence or diligence of court-appointed counsel in criminal cases? Was such a lack of confidence justified?

2. The dissenters also pointed out that if an appeal is frivolous, by definition there is nothing to argue; yet the majority opinion requires a lawyer who has deemed the appeal to be frivolous to file a brief referring to anything of record that arguably might support an appeal. What can a lawyer say in a brief in support of an appeal that the lawyer has concluded is frivolous? Was the

procedure that the Court commanded in *Anders* constitutionally superior to the system followed in California before this decision? Did the Court imply that the procedure it prescribed in *Anders* is the only way that a state can accord equal protection to indigent criminal appellants?

3. The Supreme Court sought to place indigent defendants on the same footing as non-indigent defendants, i.e., to make counsel available to indigents so that they could obtain the same quality of appellate review as non-indigents could obtain through retained counsel, despite the absence of any constitutional right to an appeal. Does *Anders* provide indigents with more than non-indigents can obtain on appeal? If a non-indigent retains counsel, may that counsel properly argue a frivolous appeal?

4. The *Anders* opinion makes a distinction between frivolous appeals and meritless appeals. Is this a meaningful, workable distinction? What is the difference?

5. Does an appellate court have a responsibility and a burden in deciding an indigent's appeal that it does not have in deciding a non-indigent's appeal?

JONES v. BARNES
463 U.S. 745 (1983)

CHIEF JUSTICE BURGER delivered the opinion of the Court.

[When David Barnes appealed from a criminal conviction for robbery and assault, the New York Appellate Division appointed Michael Melinger to represent him. In a letter to Melinger, Barnes asked that several claims be raised on appeal, and enclosed a pro se brief he had written. Melinger found flaws in some of Barnes' suggestions and discovered some additional contentions. In the end, Melinger submitted his own brief, claiming three points of error, and also submitted Barnes' pro se brief. The Appellate Division upheld the conviction by summary order. Barnes continued to seek to overturn his conviction, petitioning the U.S. District Court for habeas corpus, claiming ineffective assistance by appellate counsel.]

The District Court concluded that respondent had exhausted his state remedies, but dismissed the petition, holding that the record gave no support to the claim of ineffective assistance of appellate counsel on "any . . . standard which could reasonably be applied." The District Court concluded:

> It is not required that an attorney argue every conceivable issue on appeal, especially when some may be without merit. Indeed, it is his professional duty to choose among potential issues, according to his judgment as to their merit and his tactical approach.

A divided panel of the Court of Appeals reversed, 665 F.2d 427 (1981). Laying down a new standard, the majority held that when "the appellant requests that [his attorney] raise additional colorable points [on appeal], counsel *must argue the additional points to the full extent of his professional ability.*" *Id.* at 433 (emphasis added). In the view of the majority, this conclusion followed from *Anders v. California*, 386 U.S. 738 (1967). In *Anders*, this Court held that an appointed attorney must advocate his client's cause vigorously and may not withdraw from a nonfrivolous appeal. The Court of Appeals majority held that, since *Anders* bars counsel from abandoning a nonfrivolous appeal, it also bars counsel from abandoning a nonfrivolous issue on appeal.

. . . The Court of Appeals went on to hold that, "[h]aving demonstrated that appointed counsel failed to argue colorable claims at his request, an appellant need not also demonstrate a likelihood of success on the merits of those claims." *Id.* at 434.

The court concluded that Melinger had not met the above standard in that he had failed to press at least two nonfrivolous claims. . . .

We granted certiorari, 457 U.S. 1104 (1982), and we reverse.

In announcing a new *per se* rule that appellate counsel must raise every nonfrivolous issue requested by the client, the Court of Appeals relied primarily upon *Anders v. California, supra.* There is, of course, no constitutional right to an appeal, but in *Griffin v. Illinois*, 351 U.S. 12, 18 (1956), and *Douglas v. California*, 372 U.S. 353 (1963), the Court held that if an appeal is open to those who can pay for it, an appeal must be provided for an indigent. It is also recognized that the accused has the ultimate authority to make certain fundamental decisions regarding the case, as to whether to plead guilty, waive a jury, testify in his or her own behalf, or take an appeal, see *Wainwright v. Sykes*, 433 U.S. 72, 93, n. 1 (1977) (Burger, C.J., concurring); ABA STANDARDS FOR CRIMINAL JUSTICE 4-5.2, 21-2.2 (2d ed. 1980). In addition, we have held that, with some limitations, a defendant may elect to act as his or her own advocate, *Faretta v. California*, 422 U.S. 806 (1975). Neither *Anders* nor any other decision of this Court suggests, however, that the indigent defendant has a constitutional right to compel appointed counsel to press nonfrivolous points requested by the client, if counsel, as a matter of professional judgment, decides not to present these points.

This Court, in holding that a state must provide counsel for an indigent appellant on his first appeal as of right, recognized the superior ability of trained counsel in the "examination into the record, research of the law, and marshalling of arguments on [the appellant's] behalf," *Douglas v. California, supra*, at 358. Yet by promulgating a *per se* rule that the client, not the professional advocate, must be allowed to decide what issues are to be pressed, the Court of Appeals seriously undermines the ability of counsel to present the client's case in accord with counsel's professional evaluation.

Experienced advocates since time beyond memory have emphasized the importance of winnowing out weaker arguments on appeal and focusing on one central issue if possible, or at most on a few key issues. . . .

There can hardly be any question about the importance of having the appellate advocate examine the record with a view to selecting the most promising issues for review. This has assumed a greater importance in an era when oral argument is strictly limited in most courts — often to as little as 15 minutes — and when page limits on briefs are widely imposed. Even in a court that imposes no time or page limits, however, the new *per se* rule laid down by the Court of Appeals is contrary to all experience and logic. A brief that raises every colorable issue runs the risk of burying good arguments — those that, in the words of the great advocate John W. Davis, "go for the jugular," Davis, *The Argument of an Appeal*, 26 A.B.A. J. 895, 897 (1940)....

This Court's decision in *Anders*, far from giving support to the new *per se* rule announced by the Court of Appeals, is to the contrary. *Anders* recognized that the role of the advocate "requires that he support his client's appeal to the best of his ability." 386 U.S. at 744. Here the appointed counsel did just that. For judges to second-guess reasonable professional judgments and impose on appointed counsel a duty to raise every "colorable" claim suggested by a client would disserve the very goal of vigorous and effective advocacy that underlies *Anders*. Nothing in the Constitution or our interpretation of that document requires such a standard. The judgment of the Court of Appeals is accordingly reversed.

[Justice Blackmun, concurring, agreed that attorneys should make all non-frivolous arguments upon which the client insists, but found the source of that obligation to be in professional ethics, rather than inhering in the constitutional guarantee of effective assistance of counsel.]

JUSTICE BRENNAN, with whom JUSTICE MARSHALL joins, dissenting.

The Sixth Amendment provides that "[i]n all criminal prosecutions, the accused shall enjoy the right . . . to have the *Assistance* of Counsel for his defence" (emphasis added). I find myself in fundamental disagreement with the Court over what a right to "the assistance of counsel" means. The import of words like "assistance" and "counsel" seems inconsistent with a regime under which counsel appointed by the State to represent a criminal defendant can refuse to raise issues with arguable merit on appeal when his client, after hearing his assessment of the case and his advice, has directed him to raise them. I would remand for a determination whether respondent did in fact insist that his lawyer brief the issues that the Court of Appeals found were not frivolous.

NOTES

1. Compare the Supreme Court's view of court-appointed appellate counsel (in terms of competence, diligence, professional responsibility, etc.) that arguably underlies the opinion in *Anders v. California* with the Court's view of counsel that arguably underlies its opinion in *Jones v. Barnes*. Is there a difference? To what might this be attributed?

2. *Smith v. Robbins*, 528 U.S. 259 (2000), took the next big step in this series of cases. After *Anders*, in *People* v. *Wende,* 25 Cal. 3d 436 (1979), California adopted a new procedure under which counsel is to review the record; counsel who finds no arguable issues neither states that review has led him to conclude that an appeal would be frivolous nor requests leave to withdraw. Instead counsel is silent on the merits and offers to brief any issues the court indicates. The appellate court is to review the entire record; it affirms if it finds the appeal frivolous, and orders briefing of issues it finds arguable. Robbins was convicted of second-degree murder and grand theft. His appointed counsel on appeal concluded that appeal would be frivolous and filed with the State Court of Appeal a brief that complied with the *Wende* procedure. Agreeing with counsel's assessment, the Court of Appeal affirmed.

The California Supreme Court denied review. After exhausting his state post-conviction remedies, Robbins sought federal habeas relief, arguing, *inter alia,* that he had been denied effective assistance of appellate counsel because his counsel's *Wende* brief did not comply with the *Anders* requirement that the brief refer "to anything in the record that might arguably support the appeal." The District Court agreed, concluding that there were at least two issues that arguably might have supported Robbins's appeal and finding that his counsel's failure to include those issues in his brief deviated from *Anders'* dictates and amounted to deficient performance. (Rather than requiring Robbins to prove prejudice from this deficiency, the court applied a presumption of prejudice.) The Ninth Circuit agreed, concluding that *Anders* set forth the exclusive procedure by which appointed counsel's performance can be constitutional, and that counsel's brief failed to comply with that procedure.

In a 5-4 decision, in the majority opinion written by Justice Thomas, the Supreme Court held that the *Anders* procedure is not the only method of satisfying the Constitution's requirements for indigent criminal appeals, and that states are free to adopt different procedures, so long as those procedures adequately safeguard a defendant's right to appellate counsel. The Court had, since *Anders,* rejected a challenge to a Wisconsin variant of the *Anders* procedure, even though it, in at least one respect, provided less effective advocacy for an indigent. *McCoy* v. *Court of Appeals of Wis., Dist. 1,* 486 U.S. 429 (1988). And in *Pennsylvania* v. *Finley,* 481 U.S. 551 (1987), the Court had explained that the *Anders* procedure is not an independent constitutional command, but a prophylactic framework, and the Court had not said that it was the only framework that could adequately vindicate the right to appellate counsel. Moreover, the *Smith* Court said, to view the *Anders'* procedure as a straitjacket would contravene the Court's practice of allowing the states wide discretion, subject to the minimum requirements of the Fourteenth Amendment, to experiment with solutions to difficult policy problems. Thus, the Ninth Circuit erred in concluding that the procedure set forth in *Anders* was obligatory upon the States.

The Court then held that California's *Wende* procedure did not violate the Fourteenth Amendment. It reasoned that a procedure affords adequate and effective appellate review to indigent defendants so long as it reasonably ensures that the appeal will be resolved in a way that is related to the merit of that appeal. Focusing on the goals of ensuring that those indigents whose appeals are not frivolous receive the counsel and merits brief required by past decisions, and of enabling a state to protect itself so that frivolous appeals are not subsidized and public moneys needlessly spent, the Court concluded that the *Wende* procedure afforded indigents the adequate and effective appellate review required by the Fourteenth Amendment. It reasoned that that procedure was far better than the procedures the Court had found inadequate. Unlike them, it did not require merely a determination that the defendant was unlikely to prevail on appeal. *Wende,* by contrast, required both counsel and the court to find the appeal to be lacking in arguable issues, i.e., frivolous. It did not permit an appellate court to allow counsel to withdraw and then decide the appeal without appointing new counsel. Under *Wende,* counsel does not move to withdraw and the court orders briefing of issues it finds arguable. The procedure disapproved in *Anders* required counsel to file a mere one-paragraph "bare conclusion" that the appeal had no merit, while *Wende* required counsel to provide a summary of the case's procedural and factual history, with citations to the record, to ensure that a trained legal eye had searched the record for arguable issues and to assist the reviewing court in making its own evaluation. Finally, by providing at least two tiers of review, the *Wende* procedure avoided a flaw found in some other cases.

The Court also concluded that the *Wende* procedure was at least comparable to procedures the Court had approved. Moreover, by neither requiring the *Wende* brief to raise legal issues nor requiring counsel to explicitly describe the case as frivolous, California had made a good-faith effort to mitigate one of the problems that critics had found with *Anders,* namely, the requirement that counsel violate his ethical duty as an officer of the court (by presenting frivolous arguments) as well as his duty to further his client's interests (by characterizing the client's claims as frivolous). *Wende* also attempted to resolve another *Anders* problem — that it apparently adopted gradations of frivolity and used two different meanings for the phrase "arguable issue" — by drawing the line at frivolity and by defining arguable issues as those that are not frivolous. It was enough that the *Wende* procedure, like the *Anders* procedure, afforded adequate and effective appellate review for criminal indigents.

The Court then remanded the case for the Ninth Circuit to evaluate Robbins's ineffective-assistance claim, opining that it might be that his appeal was not frivolous and that he was therefore entitled to a merits brief. The Court instructed that the proper standard for evaluating Robbins's claim on remand was that enunciated in *Strickland* v. *Washington,* 466 U.S. 668 (1984): He had to show that his counsel was objectively unreasonable in failing to find arguable issues to appeal and filing a merits brief; and, if Robbins succeeded in making that showing, he then had to demonstrate prejudice, for his claim did not warrant a presumption of prejudice, for reasons the Court explained. Having given this guidance, the Court reversed and remanded.

Four Justices dissented, criticizing the Court's reliance on the need for an appellate court to review the full record as insufficient, and the *Wende* procedure's failure to require attorneys to provide representation of "adversarial character" which addresses the legal issues lurking in the record:

> A simple statement by counsel that an appeal has no merit, coupled with an appellate court's endorsement of counsel's conclusion, gives no affirmative indication that anyone has sought out the appellant's best arguments or championed his cause to the degree contemplated by the adversary system. . . . [N]othing in the scheme requires counsel to show affirmatively, subject to evaluation, that he has made the committed search for issues and the advocate's assessment of their merits that go to the heart of appellate representation in our adversary system. . . . On like reasoning, *Wende* is deficient in relying on a judge's nonpartisan review to assure that defendant suffers no prejudice at the hands of a lawyer who has failed to document his best effort at partisan review. . . . *Wende*'s reliance on judges to start from scratch in seeking arguable issues adds substantially to the burden on the judicial shoulders. While I have no need to decide whether this drawback of the *Wende* scheme is of constitutional significance, it raises

questions that certainly underscore the constitutional failing of relying on judicial scrutiny uninformed by counsel's partisan analysis.

Smith, 528 U.S. at 294-99 (Stevens, J., dissenting).

For further criticism of the *Wende* procedure, *see* David M. Majchrzak, *The Impropriety of a Constitutional Doctrine: Why* Wende *Review Should Be Terminated*, 23 T. JEFFERSON L. REV. 267 (2001).

3. Compare ABA STANDARDS FOR CRIMINAL JUSTICE 4-8.3 (3d ed. 1993):[18]

STANDARD 4-8.3 COUNSEL ON APPEAL (a) Appellate counsel should not seek to withdraw from a case solely on the basis of his or her own determination that the appeal lacks merit. (b) Appellate counsel should give a client his or her best professional evaluation of the questions that might be presented on appeal. . . . Counsel should advise on the probable outcome of a challenge to the conviction or sentence. Counsel should endeavor to persuade the client to abandon a wholly frivolous appeal or to eliminate contentions lacking in substance. (c) If the client chooses to proceed with an appeal against the advice of counsel, counsel should present the case, so long as such advocacy does not involve deception of the court. When counsel cannot continue without misleading the court, counsel may request permission to withdraw. (d) Appellate counsel has the ultimate authority to decide which arguments to make on appeal. When appellate counsel decides not to argue all of the issues that his or her client desires to be argued, appellate counsel should inform the client of his or her pro se briefing rights. . . .

Commentary

. . . The responsibility of counsel assigned to represent a person unable to afford representation requires that the lawyer provide his or her client with effective, quality representation as an advocate. It is inappropriate for counsel to act simply as amicus curiae or as adviser to the court. . . . [T]he defendant is entitled to the zealous advocacy of a lawyer in fact as well as in name.

. . . [C]ounsel has a primary obligation to give the client sound professional advice. . . . If a convicted defendant wants to appeal on entirely frivolous grounds, trial counsel should attempt to dissuade the defendant from so appealing and appellate counsel should seek to persuade the defendant to withdraw the appeal. Such advice should be given freely and forcefully. Assigned counsel has a special responsibility to develop a relationship of trust and confidence with the client so that the client will appreciate that the lawyer knows the case and has the client's best interests clearly in mind.

Counsel, however, should not conclude too quickly that an appeal is frivolous. A defendant is entitled to more than merely a reflexive or negative reaction to the supposed errors that the convicted defendant thinks are present in the case. The lawyer, whether retained or appointed, should closely examine and analyze the record. In some instances, even when the

---

[18] Copyright © 1993. Reprinted by the permission of the American Bar Association.

existing doctrine does not support a case for reversal on appeal, there may be a sound basis for arguing for an extension, modification, or reversal of existing law. In such a case, the appeal ground is not frivolous.

While counsel has the professional duty to give to his or her client fully and forcefully a candid opinion concerning the case and its probable outcome on appeal, counsel's role, however, is only to advise. The decision whether to appeal must be made by the client. When a client seeks to prosecute an appeal against the advice of counsel that there is no hope for success, counsel should present the case but cannot deceive or mislead the court on behalf of the client. Counsel should . . . bear in mind that if the ground upon which the client seeks relief lacks any legal support or is contravened by existing law, counsel may nonetheless argue for extension, modification, or reversal of existing law.

. . . In an appeal that is not entirely frivolous in counsel's estimate, the problem may arise of the appellant's insisting upon including in the appeal a particular point despite counsel's protest that it is frivolous or otherwise inappropriate or unwise to make such argument. In this situation, it is proper for the lawyer to brief and argue only the points he or she believes are supportable and tactically or strategically advisable to make and to omit the others. However, the client should be promptly advised in advance of argument which points the client wanted to make that are not going to be included in counsel's presentations on appeal. The client should also be advised of his or her right to file a supplemental pro se brief raising such points, although counsel may attempt to dissuade the defendant from so filing if counsel believes that a pro se brief or the points to be made therein might or would prejudice the client's chances of success on appeal. In any event, counsel must never knowingly argue an issue orally or in a brief which works against the interests of his or her client.

Commentary to Standard 21-3.2. Counsel on Appeal of those same ABA STANDARDS FOR CRIMINAL JUSTICE[19] further states in part:

> . . . Withdrawal is an extreme step that should not be taken by counsel for a defendant-appellant on the ground that the client wishes to proceed with an appeal that appears hopeless to the attorney. It is not the lawyer's role to pass judgment on a client's cause. The Supreme Court of the United States has declared that it is counsel's duty to the client and to the court to prepare and file a brief referring to anything in the record that might arguably support the appeal; only then, said the Court, may counsel consider asking for permission to withdraw.

> . . . Under the standards set forth here for criminal appeals, . . . [i]f the appellate court is adequately informed as to the questions presented and the factual basis in the record, it can determine whether the legal issues merit plenary consideration by the court. Employing the flexibility of procedures for processing appeals espoused by these standards, an appellate court will not list a case for oral argument if it does not perceive potentially valid contentions or other countervailing policies justifying oral argument.

---

[19] Copyright © 1980. Reprinted by the permission of the American Bar Association.

Is ABA Standard 4-8.3 consistent with *Anders* and *Jones*? If you think it departs from *Anders* or *Jones*, in what respects does it do so? Would it pass muster under *Smith v. Robbins*?

4. James E. Duggan & Andrew W. Moeller, *Make Way for the ABA*: Smith v. Robbins *Clear a Path for* Anders *Alternatives*, 3 J. APP. PRAC. & PROCESS 65 (2001),[20] observes:

> The ABA approach eliminates the two most controversial steps that *Anders* added to the appellate process. Appellate counsel is not required to inform the court that in her opinion the appeal is frivolous, and the court is not required to undertake an independent review of the record. . . . [C]ounsel must determine the overall strength of the appeal and the various issues presented. She must give the defendant her professional judgment as to the benefits and likelihood of success on appeal. . . . If counsel determines that the appeal is wholly frivolous, ethically she must advise the defendant to withdraw the appeal. . . . From the client's perspective, there is little or nothing to be gained by abandoning the appeal. . . . [I]f the defendant decides not to withdraw the appeal, the ABA procedure allows counsel to continue in her traditional role. . . . To the individual defendant, the mere fact that his lawyer does not withdraw . . . may improve the quality of the representation. . . . [Moreover,] [r]equiring counsel to brief what appears to be unbriefable will sometimes result in an unexpectedly persuasive argument. . . . On the other hand, . . . there is no check on counsel's performance because there is no independent judicial review of the record. . . . But . . . the very presence of independent judicial review may encourage counsel not to scrutinize the record as closely as counsel who knows that she has to write a brief. At the same time, if the court assumes that counsel has scrutinized the record with the utmost of care and has found nothing to argue, there is at least a risk that the defendant will not receive the full benefit of either's expertise.
>
> . . . [T]he issue remains as to the appropriateness of an appellate court reviewing the record on the defendant's behalf. Requiring a court to take on the mantle of the defendant's advocate is at odds with the neutrality of the court. . . . The court is not looking simply for error, but rather, is looking for ways that a creative criminal defense lawyer can argue that reversible error exists. This involves thinking about precedent with one eye towards extending it in favor of a defendant's rights. But the judge who is reading the record . . . may have purposely worked to de-program himself of this method of thinking when he moved from the bar to the bench. In fact, the arguments that an experienced criminal defense attorney may consider plausible, a judge may regard as at odds with the direction he thinks the law should take. Thus, for a court to assume the role of defense counsel is undermined by its usual, natural role.

---

[20] Copyright © 2001 by the Journal of Appellate Practice and Process. Reprinted with permission.

Moreover, the judge who must review the record and cull out meritorious issues must later decide the issues. The same court must then switch back to its neutral role and declare whether the issue which it found to be meritorious merits reversal. . . . [This] puts the judge in the position of arguing against himself.

Ultimately, the value of independent review must be measured against the goals of the appellate process. One goal is to identify those cases where reversible error has occurred. The traditional method for achieving that goal relies on the effective advocacy of appellate counsel. The *Anders* procedure allows counsel to abandon her advocacy without requiring counsel to attempt to write a merits brief. Counsel can simply decide an appeal is frivolous and assume the court will act as a safety net. The court of course assumes that defense counsel has thoroughly reviewed the record and found no issues. Neither defense counsel nor the court is acting as normally envisioned by the adversary system. This structure — far from ensuring effective assistance of counsel — may create a risk that counsel is less effective and that reversible error remains uncovered in the process.

. . . The procedure suggested in the ABA Standards overcomes many of the deficiencies present in *Anders* and strikes the closest balance between counsel's duty to her client and ethical duties as an officer of the court. It is arguably more efficient because it eliminates independent judicial review, is certainly more consistent with the traditional roles of appellate counsel and appellate judges, and may improve the quality of representation afforded to indigent appellants.

The Court's decision in *Smith* liberates states that have followed *Anders* . . . under the misconception that they were required to do so and frees them to serve as laboratories for alternative procedures, such as the ABA approach. . . .

The ABA approach, or something like it, has been adopted in a number of states, starting with Missouri, Colorado, and Idaho. *See id.* at 95-96. *But see* Jeffrey A . Weber, *Supreme Court of Arkansas Rule 4-3(J): No Merit Briefs in Arkansas and the Need to Amend the Rule*, 24 U. ARK. LITTLE ROCK L. REV. 313 (2002) (arguing that the ABA proposal unacceptably requires counsel to act unethically by proferring frivolous arguments, allows counsel to abrogate the duty to use professional judgment, and may inundate appellate courts with frivolous issues).

5. In death penalty cases, the necessity of raising every argument, including contentions that are likely to be frivolous, is even greater. Guideline 10.8 of the ABA GUIDELINES FOR THE APPOINTMENT AND PERFORMANCE OF DEFENSE COUNSEL IN DEATH PENALTY CASES (2003) takes this position. Its commentary states in part:

Because of the possibility that the client will be sentenced to death, counsel must be significantly more vigilant about litigating all potential issues at all levels in a capital case than in any other case. . . . [C]ounsel also has a duty . . . to preserve issues calling for a change in existing precedent; the client's life may well depend on how zealously counsel discharges this duty. Counsel should object to anything that appears unfair or unjust even if it involves challenging well-accepted practices.

As Professor Monroe Freedman has written, in *The Professional Obligation to Raise Frivolous Issues in Death Penalty Cases*, 31 HOFSTRA L. REV. 1167, 1168-69,1173, 1175-80 (2003):[21]

Criminal defense lawyers are rarely disciplined or otherwise sanctioned for asserting frivolous positions in advocacy. . . . As stated in the comment to Model Rule 3.1, which relates to frivolous arguments:

> The lawyer's obligations under this Rule are subordinate to federal or state constitutional law that entitles a defendant in a criminal matter to the assistance of counsel in presenting a claim or contention *that otherwise would be prohibited by this Rule.*

. . . [As the Ninth Circuit stated in *In re Becraft*, 885 F.2d 547 (9th Cir. 1989):]

> [W]e are hesitant to exercise our power to sanction under Rule 38 against criminal defendants and their counsel. . . . [S]uch reluctance . . . primarily stems from our concern that the threat of sanctions may chill a defense counsel's willingness to advance novel positions of first impression. Our constitutionally mandated adversary system of criminal justice cannot function properly unless defense counsel feels at liberty to press all claims that could conceivably invalidate his client's conviction. . . .

The court added that because significant deprivation of liberty is often at stake in a criminal prosecution, "courts generally tolerate arguments on behalf of criminal defendants that would likely be met with sanctions if advanced in a civil proceeding."

. . . Behind every innovative judge, therefore, is a lawyer whose creative (and, arguably, frivolous) litigating opened up that small range of judicial opportunity, thereby making the precedent-shattering decision possible.

. . . Recognizing how creative lawyering can dispel "old ignorance" and impart "new wisdom" to judges, the American Bar Association has taken care in its ethical rules not to discourage lawyers from challenging established precedent or otherwise seeking to make new law on behalf of their clients. . . . Thus, a lawyer contemplating a novel legal argument, or even one that has been rejected by the court in previous litigation, can nevertheless act ethically in presenting that argument despite her own professional opinion that the argument will be rejected. In other words, a lawyer can make an argument in "good faith" . . . even if the lawyer has no faith that the argument will prevail. . . . It is therefore crucial that in any capital case, "any and all conceivable errors" be preserved for review. The alternative is that a client may be put to death by the state, despite reversible error, because counsel has waived the issue or defaulted on it.

---

[21] Copyright © 2003. Reprinted with permission of the *Hofstra Law Review Association.*

. . . The conclusion is therefore clear. Counsel in a capital case must, as a matter of professional responsibility, raise every issue at every level of the proceedings that might conceivably persuade even one judge in an appeals court or in the Supreme Court, in direct appeal or in a collateral attack on a conviction or sentence. . . . [A]ssertion of a claim (even a "frivolous" one) might increase the chances of a desirable plea agreement or might favorably influence a governor or other official in making a decision regarding clemency.

In short, in a capital case, the lawyer for the accused has a professional obligation to assert at every level of the proceedings what otherwise might be deemed a frivolous claim.

6. Indigent criminal defendants' right to appointed counsel for purposes of appeal is applicable only to the first level of appeal. In *Ross v. Moffitt*, 417 U.S. 600 (1974), the Court held that a state has no obligation to appoint counsel to assist a poor person seeking to pursue a discretionary appeal to the state's highest court or seeking to file a petition for writ of certiorari in the U.S. Supreme Court. At those stages, error correction is not the courts' main function, and the defendant would have the assistance of the papers filed in the first-level appeal.

In *Halbert v. Michigan*, 125 S. Ct. 2582 (2005), the Court made clear however that the fact that an appeals court has discretion whether to hear an appeal is not the factor that distinguishes the situations in which an indigent has the right to appointed counsel from those in which the indigent does not. In Michigan, the state IAC hears appeals of right from criminal convictions except when a defendant has been convicted on a guilty or nolo contendere plea; such a defendant must seek leave to appeal. Halbert pleaded nolo, was not permitted to withdraw his plea, and was denied appointed counsel despite his pleas that he had learning disabilities, was mentally impaired, and needed assistance of counsel. The Supreme Court held that the due process and equal protection clauses of the Fourteenth Amendment required the state to appoint counsel for him, for the first tier of review. The Court relied primarily on the facts that (1) in ruling on an application for leave to appeal, the IAC looks to the merits of the appellant's claims because it is an error-correcting court, and (2) indigent defendants usually are ill-equipped to represent themselves, so that "a pro se applicant's entitlement to seek leave to appeal . . . may be more formal than real." Does *Halbert* persuasively distinguish *Ross*?

7. In *Roe v. Flores-Ortego*, 528 U.S. 470 (2000), the Court addressed how courts should approach claims that counsel was constitutionally ineffective for failing to file a notice of appeal in a criminal case. Respondent's counsel failed to timely file an appeal, and respondent ultimately filed a federal habeas petition, alleging constitutionally ineffective assistance of counsel based on his attorney's failure to file the notice after promising to do so. The Court held that its decision in *Strickland* v. *Washington,* 466 U.S. 668 (1984), provides the proper framework for evaluating such a claim. Under *Strickland,* a defendant must show that counsel's representation "fell below an objective standard of reasonableness" based on the facts of the case, judging counsel's performance deferentially, and prejudiced the defendant.

The Court rejected the view that failing to file a notice of appeal without the defendant's consent is *per se* deficient. Courts should ask whether counsel consulted with the defendant about an appeal, meaning: Did counsel advise the defendant about the advantages and disadvantages of taking an appeal and make a reasonable effort to ascertain the defendant's wishes? The Court opined that counsel who so consult perform in a professionally unreasonable manner only if they then fail to follow the defendant's express instructions concerning appeal. If counsel has not consulted, the court must ask whether that failure itself constitutes deficient performance. The better practice, the Court said, is for counsel routinely to consult with the defendant about an appeal, but counsel has a constitutional duty to consult only when counsel has reason to believe that a rational defendant would want to appeal, or that this particular defendant demonstrated to counsel an interest in appealing. (The Court noted that whether the conviction follows a trial or a guilty plea will be highly relevant, because a plea both reduces the scope of potentially appealable issues and may indicate that the defendant seeks an end to judicial proceedings. Even then, a court must consider such factors as whether the defendant received the sentence bargained for and whether the plea expressly reserved or waived some or all appeal rights.)

When a defendant contends that his counsel's deficient performance led to the forfeiture of his appeal, prejudice must be presumed because no presumption of reliability can be accorded to judicial proceedings that never took place and because "the adversary process itself" has been rendered "presumptively unreliable." However, the defendant must demonstrate that there is a reasonable probability that, but for counsel's deficient failure to consult with him about an appeal, he would have timely appealed. Evidence that there were nonfrivolous grounds for appeal or that the defendant expressed a desire to appeal will be highly relevant in determining the "but for" proposition. (The Court noted that the evidence in support of a performance deficiency and the evidence supporting prejudice may overlap because both may be satisfied if the defendant shows nonfrivolous grounds for appeal, although the two are not always coextensive.)

Because the court below did not do a *Strickland* inquiry and the record did not provide the Court with sufficient information to determine whether respondent's counsel rendered constitutionally inadequate assistance, the Court remanded for a determination whether counsel had a duty to consult with respondent (either because there were potential grounds for appeal or because respondent had expressed interest in appealing), whether counsel satisfied her obligations, and, if counsel did not, whether respondent was thereby prejudiced.

Do the hurdles that *Roe* places in the path of defendants whose counsel have altogether failed to file an appeal seem consistent with the stringent standards the Court has imposed on attorneys for criminal defendants for whom an appeal has been filed? Was *Roe* wrong to graft the *Strickland* framework onto this issue? How else would you approach it? For a critical view of *Roe, see, e.g.,* Kimberly Helene Zelnick, *In Gideon's Shadow: The Loss of Defendant Autonomy and the Growing Scope of Attorney Discretion,* 30 AM. J. CRIM. L. 363 (2003).

Paul D. Carrington, Daniel J. Meador, & Maurice Rosenberg, Justice on Appeal 91-96 (1976)[22]

The Hopeless Appeal Problem

[H]opeless appeals can clog the judicial system and cause an erosion of the process which results in less adequate justice for those appellants who do have substantial questions to raise. Hopeless cases tend to produce unreadable briefs, soporific arguments, and impatient decisions. They are demoralizing to counsel and to judges. While it is perfectly true that they require less time and energy for disposition, this fact itself represents a basic cheapening of the process. Every care must be taken to observe all of the imperatives of appellate justice in dealing with every case having any plausible merit, but this goal can scarcely be achieved without taking some care to manage the tide of hopeless cases.

. . . The only other alternative [to reestablishing defense counsel as a filter of hopeless cases] appears to be to provide some counterincentive which might influence the decision of the defendant to initiate an appeal. Much of the problem lies in the fact that the indigent is in a no-lose situation, which provides every inducement to appeal, however forlorn the hope.

Creating valid counterincentives under our Constitution is not easy. As the due process and equal protection clauses have been construed, indigents cannot be subjected to handicaps that are not laid on non-indigents. Courts cannot deal with indigents' cases in ways that are less favorable than the ways in which they deal with non-indigents' cases. But from this constitutional development, sound enough in principle, a reverse inequality has in fact emerged. Indigents now are not treated equally; they are given preferred treatment.

The indigent's preferential treatment derives from the no-lose position; non-indigents are in no such position. . . . The key to our proposal for equalizing all criminal appellants is to give the indigent defendant something to lose in the appeal similar to that which the non-indigent has. The following scheme aims to do that by creating a monetary stake that will cause the defendant to appraise his case, with the aid of counsel, and decide whether there are any appealable issues that make the appeal worthwhile when balanced against the economic loss that will be involved.

A monetary stake can be created by establishing a fund that might be called the Criminal Defense and Rehabilitation Fund.

This fund, supplied out of tax money, would be used to defray the expenses of appeals for indigents who do take appeals. However, the defendant would be given an option: he could pursue his appeal at public expense (as he can now) or he could elect instead to take a specified amount of money from the fund, either for himself or to be paid to persons he would designate. This amount of money could be based on some estimate of the expense involved in the average criminal appeal. It would be a one-time payment of a fixed figure of at least several hundred dollars; the amount could be recalculated

22 Copyright © 1976. Reprinted from PAUL D. CARRINGTON, DANIEL J. MEADOR & MAURICE ROSENBERG, JUSTICE ON APPEAL 91-96 (1976), with permission of Thomson West.

periodically by an appropriate state official to conform to changing economic conditions. The persons whom the defendant could designate to receive the payment might be limited to his spouse, members of his family, bona fide creditors, charitable institutions or providers of goods or services useful to a self-rehabilitation program.

This plan would force the defendant to think about his case as a non-indigent must. The plan would not treat indigents less favorably. Indeed it would afford them a financial benefit not now available. If the defendant elected to take the money, he would forever forego his right to take an appeal or to pursue collateral procedures at public expense. Of course he would remain free to pursue such litigation thereafter at his own expense.

The plan makes sense in that often a sum of money would be more useful to a defendant or his family, as well as to society, than the pursuit of a fruitless appeal. Indigents and their families are by definition not affluent. This arrangement would be an indirect means of affording financial assistance to needy persons while at the same time providing salutary counterincentives to filing meritless appeals.

Some observers find this plan unattractive in that it favors convicts with a transfer of money. This objection should be weighed in light of the alternatives. The present system of no counterincentive is a bigger waste of the public fisc than the gift to convicts. It is a waste of expensive but useless services associated with frivolous appeals. And non-monetary incentives, such as requiring additional time to be served, are either ineffective or cruel. Nevertheless, we do call attention to the fact that our purpose could be served by a rule which reduced the sentence of a convict by a fixed percentage as a reward for a waiver of appeal.

An additional counterincentive could be provided by creating a routine administrative review for all criminal cases in which no appeal is taken. This idea draws on the review practices for courts martial in the armed services and also to an extent from practices in the Home Office in England. Basically the idea is to provide an office staffed by lawyers — it might be called the Criminal Review Office — charged with doing a comprehensive review of every conviction where no appeal is taken.

One purpose of the Criminal Review Office would be to give additional incentives to a defendant not to appeal. For the indigent, it would make more attractive the option of taking a sum of money instead of appealing; the defendant would know that his case would not go unreviewed even though he took no appeal. For the non-indigent, whose money is at stake, it would likewise make more attractive the option of not appealing. The office would provide these inducements not to appeal by providing a thorough, objective review of the entire case by an independent group of lawyers.

To present an attractive alternative to an appeal, it is important that this Criminal Review Office be independent to a high degree. It should in no way be identified with the prosecution. It should not be under the control, directly or indirectly, of the state attorney general. Its staff should be selected through procedures that are not entangled in politics. The staff should have a high degree of job security. Perhaps the legislation establishing the office should create a non-partisan board, similar to some of those that control public defender offices, that would be responsible for appointing and discharging lawyers in the office. The office should have unquestionable competence and integrity.

Of course the review office, not being a judicial body, would have no authority itself to set aside a conviction or sentence entered by a court. But the review office would identify errors of substance and would be authorized to certify those points to the appellate court for decision. The Home Office in England has this kind of authority; it may certify a case to the Court of Appeal, Criminal Division, and that court must decide the question. Creating a non-judicial office in each state would provide a mechanism for screening cases, thus submitting to the appellate court only those which have been identified as presenting substantial issues by an independent, professional review. Once a case is certified to the appellate court, it would be treated in all respects as though an appeal had been taken. The appellate court would be required to decide the certified issues, but it could also decide any other issues in the case and either affirm or remand to the trial court.

This scheme comes close to establishing an automatic review in every criminal case, something like that in the military justice system. Under that system, every court martial conviction is reviewed either in a Court of Military Review or in the office of the judge advocate general. Under the proposed plan every case would likewise be reviewed, but not necessarily in the appellate court. The defendant would be given a choice of review — either in the appellate court or by the Criminal Review Office. In the latter, the case may still get to the appellate court on certification. In addition to creating an alternative to appeal, this plan would enhance justice in criminal law administration by assuring that every conviction for crime was reviewed somewhere beyond the trial court.

NOTES

1. The relative costs of continuing the present system of indigent criminal appeals and of adopting the proposal of Carrington, Meador, & Rosenberg which would allow convicts to choose between a lump sum and an appeal or post conviction proceeding, are discussed in Myron Moskowitz, *Indigent Criminal Defendants Should Pay for Their Appeals*, 2 CAL. LAWYER No. 5, 8 (May 1982) (concluding that such a program would save California taxpayers more than $1.3 million per year).

2. What do you think of this proposal? Would it equalize the position of indigent and non-indigent convicted criminals? Would it be constitutional? How would one draw the line between those eligible to receive the benefits of this system, and those not eligible? Would that line-drawing create potential denials of equal protection of the laws from the perspective of those ineligible to trade their appeal rights for money, or from the perspective of those who were lured out of taking an appeal by the enticement of money? How would one determine the appropriate amount of money to offer in this program? Should it vary with the offense, the sentence, or some other parameter? To the degree it was successful in deterring appeals, would this proposal undermine

the development of the law by removing from the appellate court system cases that might have provoked changes in the law? What other aspects of the proposal, if any, trouble you?

3. The functions of the Home Office in England described in the foregoing piece now are exercised by the Criminal Cases Review Commission, established by Act of Parliament, and described in Chapter 13, Section I, below.

Chapter 11

APPELLATE JUDGES

Earlier chapters of the book have considered how the crisis of volume has altered how appellate judges do their work and addressed the nature and importance of collegiality among judges who serve on the same court. Here we examine the qualifications appellate judges do and should have, the various systems for selecting appellate judges and issues each of those systems raise, how individuals are educated to be good appellate judges, and some of the rules of conduct that govern appellate judges.

I. QUALIFICATIONS FOR APPELLATE JUDGESHIPS

Ruggero J. Aldisert et al., *What Makes A Good Appellate Judge? Four Views*, 22 JUDGES' JOURNAL 14 (Spring 1983)[1]

Ruggero J. Aldisert[2]

What should be the qualities of an ideal appellate court judge? This is a difficult question for there is always a great risk in attempting to reduce the intangible to the tangible, to translate hypothetical ideals into specific, objective criteria. One . . . must make value judgments, and the very exercise of these judgments destroys any claims to complete objectivity.

Acknowledging this internal inconsistency I boldly suggest that an ideal appellate judge should possess the following six characteristics:

1. *The quality of fairness, justness, and impartiality.* This means regarding people and circumstances without using one's own interests as a reference point; adhering strictly to a standard of what has been determined as right, true, or lawful; and being impartial toward both parties. Negatively, this means not deciding a case because of a personal (not just monetary) interest in its outcome or because of a personal interest in the parties or their counsel; not deciding a case as a favor or convenience to a judicial colleague on your court, a court superior, or an inferior court; and not showing favor for or prejudice against one side over the other. Being just means more than being fair. It means communicating your humanity by feeling compassion for . . . the concerns of the litigants as persons. It also means that to achieve justice for the litigants before you, you must do more than slavishly adhere to the dictates of mechanical jurisprudence.

---

[1] Copyright © 1983 by ABA Publishing. Reprinted by permission.

[2] Judge Aldisert is a senior judge for the U.S. Court of Appeals for the Third Circuit. He served as chief judge of that Circuit from 1984-86, and assumed senior status in 1986.

2. *The twin qualities of devotion and decisiveness. Devotion* means being industrious, attentive, and thorough. . . . But the quality of devotion must be tempered with decisiveness. *Decisiveness* means the ability to make decisions without unduly prolonging the litigation in the court or interfering with the work schedules of colleagues. An appellate judge can be industrious without being unduly assiduous. To research without deciding is as much a sin as to decide without research. Hard decisions are not made easier by postponement. The judge must have intellectual courage and confidence to meet the responsibilities of office without procrastination.

3. *The quality of clear thought and expression.* This means reasoning lucidly and having a sense of order and arrangement. The model judge must instinctively know the difference between the important and the merely interesting. He or she must know well the material fallacies of reasoning and avoid them. A judicial opinion is an utterance that is performative; in the common law tradition it serves as a basis of future law. As an opinion utters a statement of reasons today, it performs for the future. Because the characteristic of "writtenness" is all-pervasive in our tradition, a judge's writing must be free from obscurity, ambiguity, and the danger of being misunderstood; its meaning must be quickly and easily recognized.

4. *The quality of professional literacy.* This means being learned in the law in the sense of possessing a general familiarity with the substantive law of the jurisdiction and a highly developed knowledge of all the court's procedural rules. Moreover, being professionally literate requires a thorough understanding of the common law tradition — specifically, recognizing that the holding of every case sets forth only a detailed legal consequence for the specific facts adjudicated in that case and no more. It means adhering to precedent in order to afford predictability or reckonability in the law but departing from precedent when the reason for the previous decision is no longer valid. Where reason stops, so stops the rule.

5. *The quality of institutional fidelity.* This means a loyalty to the court as an institution that adjudicates a dispute, yet interprets and refines the law for the future guidance of society within the court's jurisdiction. Judges must understand, however, that their commission requires them to decide specific cases and not to ruminate constantly over the state of the law. A court is not a forum for the publication of legal essays. We have law reviews and professional publications for that purpose. The opinion of the court is designed only to explain the decision publicly; it is not primarily an educational instrument or a stage for polemics. It is not the personal statement of the author but a reflection of a collegial input, for which every member of the court or panel must assume responsibility.

To respect the institutional integrity of the court, a separate opinion, concurring or dissenting, should be written only when absolutely necessary. The quality of institutional fidelity recognizes that an American appellate court reviews only the law; the substantive fact finding of the court or tribunal of the first instance must always be respected. Reviewing the law may mean reviewing the choice, interpretation, and application of controlling legal precepts; such review is plenary. It may also mean reviewing an exercise of discretion; such review is limited. In sum, the quality of institutional fidelity is a recognition of the internal structure of a public collegial body, as well as a recognition of the real responsibility of the appellate court in terms of the entire judicial hierarchy.

6. *The quality of political responsibility*. This means understanding that the legislature and the executive have primary responsibility to fashion public policy, and that this responsibility falls to the courts only when legislative or executive action is absent or inadequate. Judicial interpretation may be needed, for example, if a bill or regulation is not relevant to the precise facts before the court or if provisions are obscure, enigmatic, ambiguous, or equivocal.

When fashioning judge-made law, the refinement of legal precepts must not be an exercise to establish rules for their own sake. Scientific symmetry in the law is not an aim in itself. Cardozo said that the "final course of law is the welfare of society." Professor Harry W. Jones has taught that "a legal rule is a good rule when and to the extent that it contributes to the establishment and preservation of a social environment in which the quality of life can be spirited, improved, and unimpaired."

A judge, however, must understand that he is primarily a settler of disputes and not a political scientist. The resolution of the immediate dispute takes priority over one's desire to fashion a novel facet of public policy. The means must not be devised to dominate the end. In every judicial decision the sole objective is for the immediate parties to receive justice based on the facts presented before the court; this objective may not ever be subordinated to a judge's desire to promulgate some nuance of a personal, political, or ethical philosophy.

To adjudicate properly, a judge must sometimes legislate, but judicial legislation is only a means to an end. It is never justified as an end in itself; rather, it is merely an adjunct to the resolution of a dispute on the basis of justice between the parties. When judicial law making ceases to become an adjunct and assumes the dominant role in the decision-making process, it runs counter to the quality of political responsibility.

William H. Erickson[3]

A good judge:

1. Should be dedicated to the law and to the court in the expression and support of his or her opinions on an issue.
2. Should reflect humility and abhor arrogance.
3. Should have compassion, a sense of fundamental fairness, and a sense of humor.
4. Should be courteous and understanding not only to the litigants, but to all lawyers and judges.
5. Should be willing to accept and fairly consider criticism.
6. Should avoid procrastination, the infectious disease which all judges are exposed to and sometimes impose on suffering litigants.

---

[3] Judge Erickson was a Justice of the Supreme Court of Colorado from 1971 to 1996, and served as Chief Justice of that court from 1983-1985.

7. Should maintain inviolate the confidences of the courts and to all matters which pertain to the court's business.

8. Should have integrity and abide by the ethics of the legal profession, the code of judicial conduct, and the judicial process.

9. Should have the ability to recognize and avoid conflicts which might compromise the integrity of the court or bear even the slightest suggestion of impropriety.

10. Should avoid *ex parte* communications about pending cases with litigants, lawyers, judges, and all other persons.

11. Should require that no case be resolved without adequate and full preparation.

12. Should have the ability to listen and not prejudge a case or reach a result until all parties have had the opportunity to present their sides.

13. Should possess the strength to avoid political and public pressure in reaching a result or decision in any case.

14. Should be willing to follow the law unswervingly without permitting personal predilections to dictate the result.

15. Should have the ability to avoid personality disputes among the members of the court, and maintain a collegial relationship with his or her colleagues.

16. Should have the ability to write clearly, concisely, coherently, and analytically.

17. Should recognize that loose language and dictum in an opinion is the scourge of the bench and bar and creates problems for the appellate court, and that a treatise on the law is far worse.

18. Should be willing to carry out the collegial duty of fairly setting forth the views stated by the members of the court whom he or she represents in the preparation of an opinion.

19. Should be willing to participate meaningfully in the collegial appellate court drafting practice to the extent of sacrificing some of his own personal views on procedural or even substantive issues when compromise produces unanimity.

20. Should be willing to live outside the ivory tower of judicial seclusion by participating in community and bar activities which assist the court in its business.

21. Should be willing to work assiduously to improve the law and maintain his or her competence in the law by continuing study.

22. Should have the engrained desire to make the quest for truth and justice through the adversary system attainable by application of the rule of law and not by the application of a personal sense of justice or injustice.

Robert A. Leflar[4]

There is no one description of goodness for an appellate judge. Good judges come in more than one mold. Although there can be a fairly acceptable description of a good court, the quality of a multi-judge court depends on the unique

---

[4] Judge Leflar was a justice of the Supreme Court of Arkansas from 1949-50. He also served as a professor of law at the University of Arkansas School of Law and New York University School of Law, where he directed the Appellate Judges Seminars for 30 years.

characteristics of the individual judges who comprise it. Five, seven or nine ideal judges on one court, all with identical characteristics, would not make a very good court. Diversity is needed. Not only diversity in legal and social points of view but also diversity in methods of work, study, and even personalities.

Good judges may well have some common characteristics. None would be lazy. All would be honest, intelligent, conscientious, respectful of their court, serious in their work, and reasonably learned in the law. One or two would be real students of the law. None would have a divinity complex. They would work together well. Common courtesy always would be present among them but would not interfere with strongly held views. No judge would be intimidated by another, but each could be persuaded by reason and wise judgment. Dissent induced by personal obstinacy or self-importance would never occur. Every judge would attempt to keep up with current developments, both in the law and in society, and would read and think outside the formal topics of the law, as well as in law books. Every judge would regard the judiciary as his or her career, and while sitting on the bench would not actively seek a nonjudicial office or a more financially profitable position, political or private. Each judge would be able to write clearly and understandably.

The judges on a good court would differ in age and length of judicial experience. Not all would be old-timers, but some would be young enough to become old-timers, when the next generation comes along. The values inherent in continuity could thus be preserved but with no deadening adherence to a particular legal past for its own sake. The judges' pre-appellate experiences would vary to assist the court in better understanding the diversity of issues before it and, more important, to assure a better correlation of views on social policy. Some judges would enjoy mixing with the public more than others, and almost all would maintain social and professional contacts outside the court. In their elevated roles, they would all still see themselves as human beings.

Whether a judge is a good judge certainly does not depend on whether I, or you, agree with his or her opinions. The quality of the opinions, however, does have a great deal to do with whether a person is a good judge. If opinions are disorganized, illiterate, marred by fallacies of logic, or lengthened by wordy irrelevances, an appellate judge is not good at performing one of the major jobs. Mere avoidance of these vices, though, does not alone make one a good judge.

Quality, whether in opinions or in judicial performance, depends ultimately on sound reasoning. In this regard, Professor Harry Jones' description of Dean Roscoe Pound's test of quality is worth noting:

> When one asked Pound whether a recent Supreme Court decision was a "good" decision or a "bad" one, [he] had a way of answering not in terms of the correctness or incorrectness of the Court's application of constitutional precedents or doctrine but in terms of how thoughtfully and disinterestedly the Court had weighed the conflicting social interests involved in the case and how fair and durable its adjustment of

the interest-conflicts promised to be. [Harry W. Jones, *An Invitation to Jurisprudence*, 74 COLUM. L. REV. 1023, 1029 (1974).]

The point is that a good opinion-writing judge is one who concerns him or herself, necessarily, with formal law and precedents, but simultaneously considers the societal effects of the law promulgated or predicted by the opinion.

Reaching decisions and writing opinions are only some of the tasks appellate judges must perform. There are always administrative tasks, chores, and burdens of a dozen kinds, some more psychological than legal. Each judge should do his or her share to see that these get done even though the bulk of them belongs to the chief justice. The question "What makes a good appellate judge?" applies to the chief justice as well as to associates, but for a chief justice additional criteria may apply as well.

In summary, there is no single description of goodness in a judge. A good appellate judge is one who effectively assists in the making of a good court.

Samuel J. Roberts[5]

A good appellate judge should come to the court by fair means, beholden to no one — not to the governor, legislators, trial lawyers, or special interest groups. His professional conduct should demonstrate a strong commitment to the indispensable goal of an independent and impartial judiciary. He should not ascend to the appellate bench by waging an unfair attack on the court and its administration of justice. As Canon 7 of the Code of Judicial Conduct mandates, a good judge makes no pledges or promises of conduct in office "other than the faithful and impartial performance of the duties of the office," nor does he "announce his views on disputed legal or political issues."

Ideally, a good appellate judge comes to the court with prior trial experience, either as a trial judge, an advocate, or both. He understands not only the theory of the adjudicatory process but also its practice.

After ascending to the bench, a good appellate judge must be conscientious and hard working. He strives to improve the administration of justice. Because judicial resources are both scarce and costly, a good judge seeks maximum efficiency in whatever his court does, though *never* at the expense of fair and equal justice for all.

A good appellate judge is willing to be both a scholar and a teacher, to help new colleagues, and to learn from older ones. He keeps abreast of current judicial and legal scholarship and participates in professional activities that concern the bench, bar, and community.

A good appellate judge recognizes that he is part of a greater whole, which is itself part of a process. Thus, he cares about the quality of all decisions rendered by his court, not simply his own opinions. To that end, a good judge is skilled in the art of compromise — making and taking suggestions — but

---

[5] Judge Roberts was a justice of the Supreme Court of Pennsylvania from 1963 to 1987, and served as Chief Justice from 1983-84.

never compromising his principles. A good appellate judge reviews colleagues' opinions as carefully as possible and when, ultimately, he disagrees, expresses that disagreement. He circulates all of his opinions, including dissents, as promptly as possible, knowing that there is no excuse for unnecessary judicial delay.

A good appellate judge is aware that courts are not designed to be popular institutions and does not make decisions with one eye on the media, or on public opinion polls, or on chances for retention or reelection, or on opportunities after leaving the bench. He is quick to defend the court and the judicial process when they are subjected to unfounded attacks, and he urges colleagues, members of the bar, and fellow citizens to do the same.

A good appellate judge regards the Canons of the Code of Judicial Conduct as only the minimum, nonnegotiable standards of judicial performance. His goal must be to embody in his judicial conduct the highest ethical standards of a free society. He knows that the American sense of justice and fair play is satisfied only when every person is accorded the same rights that we claim for ourselves. To that end, in the daily pursuit of impartial and equal justice for all, he bears in mind Thomas Jefferson's wise admonition that "a society that trades a little liberty for a little order will deserve neither and lose both."

A good appellate judge exercises thoughtful influence on the rule-making and administrative functions of the court. He opposes those so-called advances that in fact further no important judicial end but are merely excess baggage piled on the system — weight without substance. A good judge respects and defends the separation of powers. He does not intrude unnecessarily into the provinces of the other coequal branches of government, yet he does not hesitate to confront the legislative and executive branches when necessary to defend against unwarranted intrusion into the function of the judiciary.

On the bench, a good appellate judge always gives counsel a fair opportunity to explain their positions. If a closed-minded colleague should attempt to end an advocate's argument prematurely, a good judge makes certain that the argument continues until the court is truly satisfied.

Just as a good court enhances the judicial competence and efficiency of all of its members, so the efforts of an individual judge can contribute greatly to the improvement of the court's entire judicial product. Thus, a good judge opposes unreflected, knee-jerk decision making wherever it appears, for he knows, as Professor Arthur Sutherland so well put it, that "[t]he soul of a government of laws is the judicial function; and that function can only exist if adjudication is understood by our people . . . to be — as it is — the essentially disinterested, rational, and deliberate element in our democracy."

With these qualities, together with a devout commitment to the integrity and fairness of the judicial process — plus a touch of humility — an appellate judge can be not simply good but great: he will bring honor to himself and to his court, and fair, equal, and prompt justice to the society he serves.

Lawrence B. Solum, *A Tournament of Virtue*, (Sept. 7, 2004), University of San Diego Legal Studies Research Paper No. 05-16, http://ssrn.com/abstract=588322[6]

I. INTRODUCTION: THE MEASURE OF MERIT

How ought we to select judges? One possibility is that each of us should campaign for the selection of judges who will transform our own values and interests into law. An alternative is to select judges for their possession of the judicial virtues — intelligence, wisdom, courage, and justice. . . .

II. WHAT IS JUDICIAL EXCELLENCE?

. . . B. The Thin Judicial Virtues

. . . In recent years, judicial selection has largely been driven by the preference of political actors for certain outcomes on key issues (abortion, affirmative action, and so forth), and hence ideology has played a major role in judicial selection. Nonetheless, it may be possible to identify a set of judicial excellences on which there is likely to be widespread agreement. . . . [T]he "judicial virtues" include both the human virtues that are relevant to judging and any particular virtues that are associated with the social role of judge. . . .

1. Incorruptibility and Judicial Sobriety

. . . [T]here is widespread consensus on . . . features that make judges truly awful. One . . . is "corruption." Judges who sell their votes undermine the substantive goals of the law, because corrupt decisions are at least as likely to be wrong as they are to be substantively correct. Moreover, corrupt decisions undermine the rule of law values of productivity and uniformity of legal decisions and likewise undermine public respect for the law and public acceptance of the law as legitimate.

If corruption is a vice, then incorruptibility is a virtue. We want judges who will be able to resist the temptations of corruption in its many forms, both subtle and blatant. . . . [I]ncorruptibility summarizes a variety of particular virtues. . . .

One such vice is graspingness . . . , the defect of wanting more than one deserves. Judges (like the rest of us) can [view wealth as] a good that is worth pursuing for its own sake. . . . Once this mistake is made, it is all too easy for humans of great talent and ability to become resentful if their income and wealth is not as great as their peers who are less talented. This vice may take

---

6 Copyright © 2004 by Lawrence B. Solum. Permission is hereby granted to duplicate this paper for scholarly or teaching purposes, including permission to reproduce multiple copies for classroom use, subject only to the requirement that this copyright notice, the title of the article, and the name of the author be prominently included in the copy or excerpt. In addition, permission is granted to incorporate any part of this paper in an open source compilation on the Internet; so long as the compilation is governed by an open source license (including, but not limited to, the Creative Commons license), no attribution of authorship is required.

on a special poignancy for judges, who frequently forgo the opportunity for large incomes in order to take the bench. . . . [I]ncorruptibility is the corrective. . . .

But not all corruption is motivated by the desire for undeserved wealth as a final end. A judge . . . who lacks the virtue of temperance . . . might become corrupt in order to support the taste for . . . the finer things of life. . . . Thus, temperance . . . is a virtue for judges. . . . [W]e name this virtue "judicial sobriety". . . .

2. Civic Courage

Judges are sometimes faced with physical danger, and so . . . they need the virtue of courage. But judges are more frequently faced with a different sort of threat that induces a different kind of fear. . . . When justice conflicts with the desires and opinions of one's fellows, this creates a temptation — to act unjustly in order to preserve good opinion. . . . [J]udges need the virtue of civic courage — the disposition to put the regard of one's fellows in proper place and to take it into account in the right way on the right occasions for the right reasons. A judge with this virtue will not be tempted to sacrifice justice on the altar of public opinion. A courageous judge does not see the good opinion of his fellows as a relevant reason in the context of making a judicial decision.

3. Judicial Temperament and Impartiality

. . . Intemperate judicial behavior may lead the judge to misapply the law — misinterpreting the applicable legal standards in "the heat of anger." Moreover, a hot-headed judge may become partial — pulling against the party who is the object of anger and displaying favoritism to that party's opponent. The corrective for bad temper is temperateness, and we traditionally call the judicial form of this virtue "judicial temperament." . . . [J]udges with the virtue of a judicial temperament will not display their anger by ruling against an offending party on issues that are close or exercising discretion on incidental matters so as to disfavor the anger-provoking party.

Because anger can produce bias, the virtue of judicial temperament is closely related to another judicial virtue, which we might call "judicial impartiality." . . . Judges should neither be cold-blooded nor hot-tempered . . . because the role of judge requires insight and understanding into the human condition. The impartial judge is not indifferent to the parties that come before her. Rather, the virtue of impartiality requires even-handed sympathy for all the parties to a dispute. . . . [T]he virtue of impartiality requires both sympathy and empathy without taking sides or favoring the legitimate interests of one side over those of the other.

4. Diligence and Carefulness

In systems where judges are given life tenure and a guarantee against diminished compensation (as in the United States federal system), judges may be tempted by the vice of sloth. Slothful or lazy judges are tempted to take the easy way out. Such a judge might delegate too much to judicial clerks, substituting the judgment of the clerk for the judge's own intellectual engagement with the case. Or such a judge might be tempted to rule in ways that reduce the judge's workload — choosing the ruling that requires the lesser rather than the greater effort. The slothful judge might also be tempted to put inappropriate pressures on the parties to a dispute to enter into a settlement agreement.

The dangers of judicial sloth are readily apparent. . . . [S]ince [judicial] clerks are usually hired directly out of law school, they usually lack both the knowledge of the law and the sound practical judgment that is required for good decision making. Overreliance on clerks is likely to lead to poor decisions. When a judge rules so as to avoid work, then there is a real danger that the easy decision will . . . work[] a substantive injustice to one or more of the parties to the dispute. And substantive injustice can also be the result of inappropriate settlement pressures.

The corrective . . . is diligence. Ideally, this virtue is reflected in the attitude of the judge towards judicial work. Excellent judges should enjoy their work; they should find judicial tasks engaging and rewarding. . . . The diligent judge will be hard working, putting in the required hours and sweating out the difficult tasks. Such a judge will not over-rely on clerks or assistants and will put in the effort required to insure that her decisions and opinions are the product of her own judgment and not the judgment of subordinates.[7] Such a judge will not hesitate to make the right decision, even if that makes more work for the judge. It may well be appropriate for judges to attempt to facilitate settlement, but a diligent judge will not do this for the wrong reason. Aiming for just settlements is one thing; aiming for convenient settlements is another.

Closely related to diligence is carefulness, the corrective for the vice of judicial carelessness. The slothful judge is tempted to . . . avoid the burdens of meticulous attention to details. Thus, a slothful judge will be tempted to avoid . . . mastering the structure of a complex statute or . . . making sense of [a] tangled body of precedent. Likewise, a slothful judge may avoid. . . drafting an opinion in which each and every sentence is worded with careful appreciation of the importance of precision and accuracy. The careful judge must be meticulous, with an eye for detail and devotion to precision.

5. Judicial Intelligence and Learnedness

Judges . . . need to be able to comprehend complexity in both the law and the facts. . . . [U]nintelligent judges are likely to make decisions that are incorrect. . . . Excellent judges can . . . make findings of fact that [are] true (or best supported by the evidence) and conclusions of law that are correct, even in the face of powerful attempts at obfuscation.

---

7 [5] Judging is not a managerial task. Good judges are not expected to hire good clerks and then manage them efficiently. Such delegation may be appropriate for other officials. Executives and even legislators may well deserve praise for delegation of responsibility to others. But judges are expected to exercise sound practical and legal judgment on the issues they are required to decide. Of course, some tasks may be delegated, and research is the paradigm case of proper delegation. Even here, however, diligence may require that the judge actually read the key sources and form her own independent judgment as to their proper interpretation.

... A virtuous judge must be learned as well as smart. ... Good judges must have a good legal education and must immerse themselves in the law, reading widely and deeply in the fields of law that are relevant to their jurisdiction. ... [W]ide and deep legal knowledge is likely to result in better comprehension of the law and the avoidance of mistakes about what the law actually requires.

6. Craft and Skill

So far, I have been discussing ... moral and intellectual virtues, dispositions of character and mind that make for human excellence. Good judging also requires craft and skill. ... A treatise on judicial craft and skill could consume volumes. ... Nonetheless, one particular aspect of judicial craft and skill deserves special comment.

Good judges (and especially good appellate judges) need to be skilled in the use of language. ... Written communication is especially important for appellate judges in a common law system, because of the doctrine of stare decisis. Appellate opinions set precedent, and a badly written opinion can fail to communicate the intended decision in a manner that will provide clear guidance to parties in future litigation. A really well-written opinion, on the other hand, can do tremendous good — illuminating the law where it was murky and settling questions that were up in the air. ...

C. The Thick Judicial Virtues

... 1. The Virtue of Justice: ...

An excellent judge is just. ... But what does the virtue of justice require? ... [W]e might say that the good judge must have the virtue of fidelity to law and concern for the coherence of law. ...

2. The Virtue of Judicial Wisdom: ...

But ... there are surely extraordinary cases — cases where we think of justice not as lawfulness but instead as fairness. ... [I]n the context of a society — like our own — which is characterized by deep and persistent pluralism about fairness ... if each judge follows her own notions of fairness, then law will simply not be able to do the job of coordinating behavior and avoiding conflict. Judges will disagree about the content of the law; hence that content will be uncertain and unpredictable. [Nonetheless] ... [a] virtuous judge ... needs to have a keen sense of fairness, so as to be able to do justice in the cases where simply following the rules laid down would lead to absurd and unintended consequences. ... [D]oing equity is being true to the spirit of the law, even when we depart from the letter of the law. ... Doing equity requires both a sense of a fairness and a grasp of the ... laws, norms, and customs generally accepted by the community.

III. Discerning Excellence

Excellent judges possess the judicial virtues. They are incorruptible and sober, courageous, good tempered, impartial, diligent, careful, smart, learned, skilled, just, and wise. But how can we tell which candidates for high judicial office possess these virtues? . . .

A. Screening for Judicial Vice

. . . The first screen for judicial excellence eliminates candidates who are vicious — corrupt, ill-tempered, cowardly, unintelligent, or foolish. Screening for these vices is already a large part of the judicial selection process. Background investigations, conducted at the federal level by the FBI, seek to ferret out the moral vices. The solicitation of comments by peers (lawyers and judges) is designed to elicit evidence of more subtle defects in character of intellect.

If we want to effectively screen for vice, we want to select judges . . . from candidates who have a track record that is likely to expose the vices if they exist.

B. Detecting [Practical Wisdom]

The absence of the worse vices is not enough. A good judge must possess the virtue of practical wisdom . . . . [D]etecting [such wisdom] is likely to be both more difficult and more controversial. . . . [However,] . . . [p]ersons of practical wisdom . . . are recognizable by those who know them and interact with them. [Therefore,] . . . the process of selecting judges should rely heavily on the recommendations of those who are in a position to know whether the candidate possesses practical wisdom.

. . . Given the separation of powers and the code of judicial ethics, judges may become cloistered — isolated from everyone but their friends and family, judicial colleagues, and law clerks. Opinions give evidence of craft and the intellectual virtues, but provide an imperfect window on the practical wisdom. For this reason, it is especially important that judges — at least those who would be willing to serve on the Supreme Court — engage in practical activities that expose them to public life. Civil activities and service on judicial commissions are two obvious opportunities for judicial immersion in a public life of practical activity. Supreme Court Justices should be selected from among those who have demonstrated their possession of practical wisdom, both from the bench and in wider public life.

C. Recognizing [Dedication to the Rule of Law]

. . . [J]udicial opinions . . . [indicate] which judges are lawful and which are results oriented. . . . [A] persistent pattern of lawfulness is truly difficult to conceal. In sum, we have good reason to believe that we can screen for vice, discern the possession of practical wisdom, and recognize true dedication to the rule of law. . . .

David B. Saxe, *Selecting Younger Judges — A Critique*, 77 AMERICAN BAR ASSOCIATION JOURNAL 66 (November 1991)[8]

[J]udges are younger than they used to be. . . .

To many, this is a positive trend. . . . [T]hey believe younger, more vibrant, more alert individuals ought to be selected and encouraged to seek a lengthy stay on the bench.

There is, no doubt, some merit to this view. . . .

Now, at the ripe-old-age of 48 and recently elected to the state supreme court, I have some serious doubts about whether this trend toward youth is good. . . . [B]eing younger doesn't necessarily mean being better. . . .

[L]awyers who barely meet minimum post-bar-admission requirements for becoming judges (generally 10 years) are often not sufficiently accomplished in the profession to operate as effective judges. It's not that they are not smart enough or sufficiently motivated; it's that lawyering is a craft that takes a long time to become proficient at. . . .

[R]equiring prospective judges to accumulate more experience to enhance their intellectual capital is not unreasonable. . . .

In addition, those who barely meet the minimum time qualification are often limited in life experience as well. . . . [B]eing effective requires an understanding of human nature and a motivation that is often the product of life's seasoning and even some gray at the temples. . . .

. . . I also believe that older judges are less likely to take umbrage at motions to reargue or renew, but, rather, see them as vehicles to correct errors prior to appellate review — not as a means to embarrass. Also, older, more seasoned judicial aspirants are more likely to understand the problems facing lawyers in their everyday practices, and be more understanding about the need for an unavoidable delay or postponement. Less seasoned jurists often take their scheduling as written in stone and view legitimate requests for delays as challenges to their authority.

Then, too, judges who are elected or appointed at an early age find themselves looking at a future of 25 years or more at the job. They may face judicial burnout, a factor . . . that can have a deleterious effect on the administration of justice. It used to be that a judge rarely served longer than one term before reaching retirement. That's not true now.

Additionally, . . . [y]ounger judges are less likely to accept the institutional constraints of the profession. Younger people may find the slower, more deliberate pace of judging to be disconcerting, preferring instead the charged-up maelstrom of private practice. They may find that the judicial lifestyle is unpleasurable, with its often prolonged periods of solitude.

---

[8] Copyright © 1991 by the American Bar Association. Reprinted by permission.

Young judges also may find it difficult getting the respect of older, more seasoned lawyers . . . especially . . . in settlement conferences, where a young judge's lack of experience may be glaring. I remember the looks of incredulity that, in my younger days, greeted my damage assessments in personal injury cases.

. . . I submit that more experience ought to be required, perhaps as much as 20 years' worth, before an individual may be considered for a judgeship.

ABA STANDARDS RELATING TO COURT ORGANIZATION (1990)[9]

1.21 Selection of Judges. . . .

(a) Personal and professional qualifications. . . .

. . .

(ii) Appellate judges. The selection of appellate judges should be guided by the aim of having an appellate bench composed of individuals having a variety of practical and scholarly viewpoints, including some with substantial experience as trial judges. Persons selected as appellate judges preferably should have high intellectual gifts and experience in developing and expressing legal ideas and facility in exchanging views and adjusting differences of opinion.

NOTES

1. How do the qualifications necessary for effective appellate judging differ from those necessary for effective trial judging?

2. Diversifying the bench in gender, age, race, ethnicity and socio-economic background can help to obtain a variety of viewpoints on the bench, and enhance the legitimacy of judicial decisions, at least among some populations. The methods by which judges are selected can affect the diversity of the bench. For thoughts on the values of diversifying our judiciaries and the influence of selection methods on such diversification, see Theresa M. Beiner, *How the Contentious Nature of Federal Judicial Appointments Affects 'Diversity' on the Bench*, 39 U. RICH. L. REV. 849 (2005); Herma Hill Kay & Geraldine Sparrow, *Workshop on Judging: Does Gender Make a Difference?* 16 WIS. WOMEN'S L. J. 1 (2001); Becky Kruse, *Luck and Politics: Judicial Selection Methods and Their Effect on Women on the Bench*, 16 WIS. WOMEN'S L. J. 67 (2001); Susan Moloney Smith, *Diversifying the Judiciary: The Influence of Gender and Race on Judging*, 28 U. RICH. L. REV. 179 (1994); James Andrew Wynn, Jr. & Eli Paul Mazur, *Perspectives: Judicial Elections Versus Merit Selection: Judicial Diversity: Where Independence and Accountability Meet*, 67 ALB. L. REV. 775 (2004).

3. The materials on selection of appellate judges, which follow, at times refer to the qualities of appellate judges that have been regarded as important by persons who think about judicial selection. As you read, see whether you find

---

[9] Copyright © 1990 by the American Bar Association. Reprinted with permission.

any ideas about desirable qualities of judges that have not already been illuminated by the writings presented above.

II. SELECTION OF APPELLATE JUDGES

A. STATE APPELLATE JUDGES

Although American appellate judges have widely varying backgrounds, they share two experiences. All have attended law school, and all have become lawyers. The extract below provides information about the pool from which appellate judges come and presents an overview of the processes by which they come to the bench.

Daniel J. Meador, American Courts 49-56 (2d ed. 2000)[10]

Because American judges sit on courts of widely varying types and come from a variety of backgrounds and experiences, it is difficult to generalize about them. Two generalizations, however, are possible. First, judges in the United States initially come to the bench from other lines of legal work and after a substantial number of years of professional experience. Second, once on the bench they do not, generally, follow a promotional pattern through the ranks of the judiciary. In these respects American judges differ from judges of the common-law and civil-law systems in other parts of the world. . . .

[T]he [selection] methods used in the United States are quite varied. These procedures generally lack means of assuring professional quality. . . . With the relatively minor exception of some lay judges on state courts of limited jurisdiction, all American judges have studied law and been licensed to practice law.

Although most judges have actually practiced law, the nature of that practice can be quite varied. Many judges have been litigators, but some have been office lawyers or counsel to organizations such as corporations or private associations. The types of law practice that judges have experienced range from small-town general practice to specialized fields in large metropolitan firms. Numerous judges have been lawyers in government service as prosecuting attorneys or counsel to government agencies, either state or federal. Some judges are former law professors, but not very many. Many judges have earlier been active in political affairs, often as legislators, political campaign managers, or party committee members or chairmen. Indeed, many American judges can be described as former lawyer-politicians.

Another feature of the American judiciary that sharply distinguishes it from that of civil-law countries and other common-law countries is that persons can enter the judicial system at any level . . . in either a state or the federal system. Lawyers who come on the bench at the trial or intermediate appellate levels have no real promise of moving to a higher court, although some may have hopes in that regard. In practice, some judges are elevated to higher courts, but most spend their entire judicial careers on the same court. There is no

---

[10] Reprinted from Daniel J. Meador, American Courts 49-56 (2d ed. 2000) with permission of Thomson West.

system of promotion and no substantial sentiment among American lawyers, judges, or politicians that such a system would be desirable. There is, however, a body of opinion to the contrary. Views about judicial promotion vary from state to state. In Virginia, for example, there is a tradition of selecting appellate judges from among trial judges, but such tradition is not widespread. During the last quarter of the twentieth century, it has been common for Presidents to nominate judges of appellate courts to be Justices on the U.S. Supreme Court, but that has not been the dominant pattern historically.

Lawyers become judges in the United States through four methods: (1) by nomination of the chief executive with confirmation by a legislative body, (2) by appointment of the chief executive from a short list of persons certified by an independent commission to be qualified for the position, (3) by popular election, and (4) by election in the legislature. Terms of office vary considerably from one system to another. They range from terms of years — some as short as four or six and a few as long as twelve to fifteen — to "good behavior," usually spoken of as a term "for life."

The federal system is the best known example of executive nomination with legislative confirmation. All judgeships on the district courts, courts of appeals, and the Supreme Court are filled in this manner. The filling of district judgeships usually involves a significant amount of participation by members of the Senate, the confirming body. Senators view district judgeships in their states as being of special importance to them and their supporters. Officials in the Department of Justice are key executive branch participants in the selection process, along with the White House staff. All of these participants must discuss and often negotiate with each other in order to arrive at a mutually agreeable choice — a person acceptable to them both professionally and politically. While the President ultimately selects the nominee, he is constrained as a practical matter by all these forces.

In making nominations for the U.S. courts of appeals the President and the Department of Justice have generally had a somewhat freer hand, with less involvement by the Senators. Judges on each of these courts are drawn from several states, so no Senator is likely to have as strong an interest in the vacancy as he usually does in a district court position in his own state, although there have been instances in recent years in which Senators have shown special concern about these appointments. In selecting Supreme Court nominees, the President has even more leeway, but he still must take into account sentiment in the Senate, as that body has in effect a veto power over the nomination.

Only a handful of states employ a judicial selection method similar to the federal. In most states the commission nominating method is used for at least some courts. In some states all judges are appointed through this process. In others it is used only for appellate judges. In still others it is used only for trial judges in certain cities or counties.

This so-called "merit plan" involves the use of an independent nominating commission, typically consisting of nine to fifteen members, a mixture of lawyers, judges, and nonlawyers. Efforts are usually made to constitute the body in a bipartisan or nonpartisan way to diminish as much as possible the aura of partisan politics in the selection process. When a judicial vacancy occurs, the commission invites suggestions from the bar and the public as to suitable nominees. It also receives applications from interested lawyers. The commission will then review all available information about each prospect and will often interview those who appear most promising. In the end it will submit to the Governor a short list of those it considers best qualified, supposedly without regard to political affiliation. In some states the list consists of three names; in other states as many as five names may be submitted. From this list the Governor makes the appointment.

Often known as the "Missouri Plan" because it was first used in that state in 1940, this system is praised for providing a buffer against pure partisan politics, giving some assurance that judges will possess the requisite character and solid professional qualifications, and, at the same time, allowing leeway to the chief executive to make a choice, taking into account his policy judgments.

Despite the spread of this commission nominating system in the last half of the twentieth century and the continual campaign for its adoption, many states still choose judges at popular elections. This method of judicial selection, unknown in England, in civil law countries and in the first decades of the United States, was introduced during the presidency of Andrew Jackson as an aspect of "Jacksonian democracy." In some states candidates for judgeships run under party labels like candidates for all other offices. In others they are on the ballot without party identification. Running for a judgeship under either arrangement raises special problems. A candidate for judicial office cannot have a "platform" or an agenda for action. The nature of the office requires that its holder be objective and above all that he not take a position in advance on any issue; judges must decide cases on the basis of the facts and the law as they appear when the case is before them for decision. That being so, there is little of significance that a judicial candidate can appropriately say. Another major problem is campaign financing. Campaigns for judgeships have become increasingly expensive, a condition exacerbated by the high cost of television advertising, considered essential to a successful race. Candidates must raise these funds from others, chiefly lawyers who will be appearing before them in the future. The damage to judicial objectivity and to the appearance of objectivity is obvious.

It is interesting that in many states where the law provides for the election of judges, the majority of judges are in fact appointed by the Governor. This is because the Governor is authorized to fill vacancies that occur between elections or legislative sessions, and many vacancies come about at those times through death, resignation, or retirement.

At the time of the formation of the Union, over half of the states chose their judges by election in the legislature. Now this method is employed only in Virginia and South Carolina and, in a modified way, in Connecticut. While legislative election has disadvantages in that the decision often turns on partisan political factors, it has an advantage over popular election in that it does not involve extensive and costly campaigning by prospective judges, nor does it entail the evils associated with fundraising for judicial campaign purposes.

In the United States, the concept of judicial independence resting on the separation of powers means that in deciding cases judges are free from control by the executive and legislative branches of government as well as from control by the popular will of the moment. In other words, judges act free of extrajudicial controls in determining the facts, ascertaining and enunciating the law, and applying the law to the facts to arrive at decisions of cases. Although this concept is widely accepted and supported in the United States, it does not mean, and has never meant, an absolute and complete independence of the judiciary. That would not be tolerable in a democracy. Under democratic theory the people are sovereign. The judiciary, like the rest of government, must be ultimately accountable to the people. However, too much accountability can unduly impair independence.

The tension between judicial independence and accountability cannot be altogether resolved. What one finds among the American judicial systems, therefore, are varying degrees of independence. The key element is tenure of office.

The highest degree of judicial independence is found in the federal system. All federal judges appointed under Article III of the Constitution hold office during good behavior and can be removed only through impeachment by Congress. In an impeachment proceeding the House of Representatives must bring charges against the judge by a majority vote, and the Senate must try the judge on those charges. The judge can be removed only if the Senate finds him guilty by a two-thirds vote. Impeachment is a formidable procedure, not easily invoked.

At the other end of the spectrum, affording the smallest degree of independence, are those state judicial systems in which judges hold office for terms of years, at the end of which they must stand for reelection by the voters. A judge with a term as short as four or six years, no matter how conscientious he may be, can hardly be unaware that his judicial decisions could become a political issue in the next election, never more than a few years away. Even if the judge himself can perform judicial duties without regard to such considerations, public suspicion of political influence will be a lurking threat to the appearance of justice. Short terms of office and popular election seem inconsistent with the concept of judicial independence. Yet such arrangements exist in many states in which, paradoxically, judicial independence is praised.

Judges whose terms are substantially longer are less likely to be influenced by political concerns. Longer terms also strengthen the appearance of judicial independence. Terms of twelve or fifteen years, found in some states, provide a higher degree of independence than terms of four or six years, but not as high a degree as tenure during good behavior. . . .

In some states the reelection of judges is by a "retention election." The judge runs on his own record without any opponent. The people are asked simply to vote "yes" or "no" on whether that judge shall be retained in office. That system normally works to afford a somewhat higher degree of independence than does a contested election. A judge knowing that he can be challenged by any lawyer who cares to pay the filing fee to become a candidate is likely to be more attentive to political currents and popular sentiment than a judge running only for retention on the record made.

Short terms and political elections are not the only threats to judicial independence. Independence can be impaired, or at least the appearance of independence damaged, in the process of executive appointments with legislative confirmation if the prospective appointees are required to indicate the positions they would take on legal issues likely to come before the court.

Although long terms of office and difficult processes of removal are the principal elements that heighten judicial independence, also of great importance are the customs and understandings relating to judges and their work. It is, for example, well-understood in the United States that it is improper for anyone to communicate with a judge concerning a pending case, other than the litigants and their lawyers acting through established procedural channels. It is universally acknowledged to be highly improper for anyone — a member of the legislature, an executive official, or a private citizen — to contact a judge in an effort to influence the judge's decision in any case. Such an action would be widely condemned, and, in fact, such improper contacts rarely occur. This deeply embedded understanding as to appropriate behavior in relation to the judiciary is itself a powerful protection of the judges' independence.

AMERICAN JUDICATURE SOCIETY TABLES

Judicial Selection in the States
Appellate and General Jurisdiction Courts
"Initial Selection: Intermediate Appellate Courts"[11]

Merit Selection (18)	Partisan Election (6)	NonPartisan Election (11)	Gubernatorial Appointment (2)	Legislative Appointment (2)
Alaska	Alabama	Arkansas	California	South Carolina
Arizona	Illinois	Georgia	New Jersey	Virginia
Colorado	Louisiana	Idaho		
Connecticut	Ohio[12]	Kentucky		
Florida	Pennsylvania	Michigan		
Hawaii	Texas	Minnesota		
Indiana		Mississippi		
Iowa		North Carolina		
Kansas		Oregon		
Maryland[13]		Washington		
Massachuh setts[13]		Wisconsin		
Missouri				
Nebraska				
New Mexico				
New York[13]				
Oklahoma				
Tennessee				
Utah				

[11] Copyright © 2004. Reprinted with permission of the American Judicature Society.

[12] [1] Candidates appear on the general election ballot without party affiliation but are nominated in partisan elections.

[13] [2] Merit Selection is established by executive order.

Judicial Selection in the States
Appellate and General Jurisdiction Courts
"Initial Selection: Courts of Last Resort"

Merit Selection (24)	Partisan Election (8)	NonPartisan Election (13)	Gubernatorial Appointment (4)	Legislative Appointment(2)
Alaska	Alabama	Arkansas	California	South Carolina
Arizona	Illinois	Georgia	Maine	Virginia
Colorado	Louisiana	Idaho	New Hampshire	
Connecticut	Michigan[14]	Kentucky	New Jersey	
Delaware[15]	Ohio[16]	Minnesota		
District of	Pennsylvania	Mississippi		
Columbia	Texas	Montana		
Florida	West Virginia	Nevada		
Hawaii		North Carolina		
Indiana		North Dakota		
Iowa		Oregon		
Kansas		Washington		
Maryland[15]		Wisconsin		
Massachusetts[15]				
Missouri				
Nebraska				
New Mexico				
New York				
Oklahoma				
Rhode Island				
South Dakota				
Tennessee				
Utah				
Vermont				
Wyoming				

Justice in Jeopardy, Report of the American Bar Association Commission on the 21st Century Judiciary (2003)[17]

Executive Summary

. . . The judicial systems of the United States at the beginning of the 21st Century remain unparalleled in their capacity to deliver fair and impartial justice, but these systems are in great jeopardy. . . . Increased political involvement in the judiciary, diminished public trust and confidence in the justice system, and uncertain resources supporting the courts place burdens on the judiciary's capacity to provide fair and impartial justice. Indeed, the

---

[14] [1] Candidates appear on the general election ballot without party affiliation but are nominated at political party conventions.

[15] [2] Merit Selection is established by executive order.

[16] [3] candidates appear on the general election ballot without party affiliation but are nominated in partisan primary elections.

[17] Copyright © 2003 by the American Bar Association. Reprinted with permission.

escalating partisanship and corrosive effects of excessive money in judicial campaigns, coupled with changes in society at large and the courts themselves, have served to create an environment that places our system of justice, administered by independent and impartial judges, at risk. . . .

The Commission recognizes that effective, independent and impartial judicial systems require the trust and confidence of the public, which must understand and care about its courts. A set of enduring principles underscores the importance of an independent, impartial judiciary to uphold the rule of law in a constitutional, democratic republic. Challenges to these enduring principles are identified. Recommendations serve as a framework for the ABA and the states to address and counteract the developments that are adversely affecting the fair and impartial administration of justice.

Eight enduring principles should be central components to each state's understanding of the role of the judiciary as a co-equal branch of government. These principles recognize that judges should uphold the rule of law and be impartial and independent, while possessing the appropriate temperament and character, as well as appropriate capabilities and credentials. Moreover, . . . the justice system should be diverse, reflecting the society it serves. Finally, judges should be constrained to perform their duties in a manner that promotes public trust and confidence in the courts.

A number of factors and trends have led to the excessive politicization of state courts. Among these are the proliferation of controversial cases generally; the rediscovery of state constitutions as a basis to litigate constitutional rights and responsibilities; the increases in caseload; the interposition of intermediate appellate courts between trial courts and courts of last resort; the spread of the two-party system; the emergence of single-issue groups; and the presence of a skeptical and conflicted public. Additional challenges for the judiciary include changes in classes of litigants, including a trend towards pro se litigation . . . ; changes in the demographic composition of America, with concomitant impact on the public's confidence in the courts; and changes in the role of the courts, including the rise of problem-solving courts.

. . . Increasingly expensive state judicial campaigns focus on narrow issues of intense political interest, contributing to the public's perception that judges are influenced by their contributors. Some of the most partisan and misleading campaign related speech comes in the form of "issue advertising." The viability of judicial ethical standards are at risk, especially in light of recent judicial decisions, including that by the U.S Supreme Court in *Republican Party of Minnesota v. White*, limiting some ethics rules. The pronounced lack of diversity in the judicial system inhibits public trust and confidence in the courts, as do apparent trends in the relationships between courts and legislatures that too often have been problematic, manifested by attempts to cut the judiciary's budget, curb court jurisdiction, remove judges from office, and constrain courts' constitutional interpretations.

. . . [T]he Commission . . . provides a call to action that will maintain independent, impartial state judiciaries, functioning as effective, co-equal branches of government, for generations to come.

Principles and Conclusions
August 2003

I. ENDURING PRINCIPLES

A. Judges should uphold the law.
B. Judges should be independent.
C. Judges should be impartial.
D. Judges should possess the appropriate temperament and character.
E. Judges should possess the appropriate capabilities and credentials.
F. Judges and the Judiciary should have the confidence of the public.
G. The judicial system should be diverse and reflective of the society it serves.
H. Judges should be constrained to perform their duties in a manner that justifies public faith and confidence in the courts.

II. PRESERVING THE JUDICIARY'S INSTITUTIONAL LEGITIMACY

A. Judicial Qualifications, Training and Evaluation

- States should establish credible, neutral, non-partisan and diverse deliberative bodies to assess the qualifications of all judicial aspirants so as to limit the candidate pool to those who are well qualified.
- The judicial branch should take primary responsibility for providing continuing judicial education, [which] should be required for all judges, and . . . appropriations should be sufficient to provide adequate funding for continuing judicial education programs. . . .
- States should develop judicial evaluation programs to assess the performance of all sitting judges.

III. IMPROVING JUDICIAL SELECTION

A. The preferred system of state court judicial selection is a commission-based appointive system, with the following components:

- The governor should appoint judges from a pool of judicial aspirants whose qualifications have been reviewed and approved by a credible, neutral, non- partisan, diverse deliberative body or commission.
- Judicial appointees should serve until a specified age. Judges so appointed should not be subject to reselection processes, and should be entitled to retirement benefits upon completion of judicial service.
- Judges . . . not . . . subject to reselection, nonetheless [should] remain subject to regular judicial performance evaluations and disciplinary processes that include removal for misconduct.

B. Alternative Recommendations on Systems of Judicial Selection

- For states that cannot abandon the judicial reselection process altogether, judges should be subject to reappointment by a credible, neutral, non-partisan, diverse deliberative body.

- For states that cannot abandon judicial elections altogether, elections should be employed only at the point of initial selection.
- For states that retain judicial elections as a means of reselection, judges should stand for retention election, rather than run in contested elections.
- For states that retain contested judicial elections as a means to select or reselect judges, all such elections should be non-partisan and conducted in a non-partisan manner.
- For states that continue to employ judicial elections as a means of judicial reselection, judicial terms should be as long as possible.
- For states that use elections to select or reselect judges, states should provide the electorate with voter guides on the candidate(s).
- For states that use elections to select or reselect judges, state bars or other appropriate entities should initiate a dialogue among affected interests, in an effort to deescalate the contributions arms race in judicial campaigns.
- For states that use elections to select or reselect judges, state bars or other appropriate entities should reach out to candidates and affected interests, in an effort to establish voluntary guidelines on judicial campaign conduct.
- For states that do not abandon contested elections at the point of initial selection or reselection, states should create systems of public financing for appellate court elections.
- For states that retain contested judicial elections and do not adopt systems of public financing, states should impose limits on contributions to judicial candidates. . . .

NOTES

1. The ABA Commission Report reflects a belief in the importance of freeing judges from political accountability to an electorate while assuring accountability within the judicial hierarchy. It would accomplish this through performance assessments and disciplinary mechanisms. The Report also reflects a belief in fostering judicial independence and the appearance of such independence through such means as long terms of service, non-partisan elections, elections based on up-or-down retention ballots rather than against other candidates, and public funding rather than funding by lawyers or interest groups. Where state law provides for contested elections, the ABA urges the creation of guidelines to govern judicial campaign conduct, and voter education. While these views enjoy wide support, they are far from uncontroversial. There are arguments to be made for contested popular elections, for relatively short terms of office, for partisan elections between candidates, and for continuation of the tradition of having interested persons finance elections, subject perhaps to campaign finance disclosure rules. What are some of the arguments to be made for judicial elections with these characteristics?

2. Recently, two of the most controversial issues concerning judicial elections have been how freely candidates for judicial office should be able to state their views on issues of the day, including issues that might come before them, and to what degree judicial bodies or other government entities may limit the speech of those candidates. The U.S. Supreme Court addressed these subjects in the following case.

REPUBLICAN PARTY OF MINNESOTA v. WHITE
536 U.S. 765 (2001)

JUSTICE SCALIA delivered the opinion of the Court.

The question presented in this case is whether the First Amendment permits the Minnesota Supreme Court to prohibit candidates for judicial election in that State from announcing their views on disputed legal and political issues.

I

[Minnesota's election of state judges was subject to a legal restriction that a "candidate for a judicial office, including an incumbent judge," shall not "announce his or her views on disputed legal or political issues," a prohibition based on Canon 7(B) of the 1972 American Bar Association (ABA) Model Code of Judicial Conduct, and known as the "announce clause." Both incumbent judges and lawyers running for judicial office who violated it were subject to discipline. In 1996, one of the petitioners, Gregory Wersal, ran for associate justice of the Minnesota Supreme Court. In the campaign, he distributed literature criticizing several Minnesota Supreme Court decisions on issues such as crime, welfare, and abortion. A complaint against Wersal challenging the propriety of this literature was filed with the agency charged with investigating and prosecuting ethical violations of lawyer candidates for judicial office. The agency dismissed the complaint. Nonetheless, Wersal withdrew from the election. In 1998, when Wersal ran again for the same office, he sought an advisory opinion from the agency, the Lawyers Board, with regard to whether it planned to enforce the announce clause. The Board responded equivocally. Wersal filed suit seeking a declaration that the announce clause violated the First Amendment and an injunction against its enforcement, alleging that the clause forced him to refrain from announcing his views on disputed issues. Other plaintiffs alleged that, because of the clause, they were unable to learn Wersal's views and support or oppose his candidacy accordingly. The parties filed cross-motions for summary judgment, and the District Court held that the announce clause did not violate the First Amendment. The Eighth Circuit affirmed. The Court granted certiorari. It first discussed the meaning of the announce clause.]

II

. . . The prohibition extends to the candidate's mere statement of his current position, even if he does not bind himself to maintain that position after election. . . . There are . . . some limitations that the Minnesota Supreme Court has placed upon the scope of the announce clause that are not (to put it politely) immediately apparent from its text. . . . The Judicial Board issued an opinion stating that judicial candidates may criticize past decisions. . . . In light of the constitutional concerns, the District Court construed the clause to reach only disputed issues that are likely to come before the candidate if he is elected judge. The Eighth Circuit accepted this limiting interpretation . . . , and in addition construed the clause to allow general discussions of case law and judicial philosophy. The Supreme Court of Minnesota adopted these interpretations as well when it ordered enforcement of the announce clause in accordance with the Eighth Circuit's opinion.

It seems to us, however, that . . . these limitations . . . are not all that they appear to be. First, . . . statements critical of past judicial decisions are *not* permissible if the candidate also states that he is against *stare decisis*. Thus, candidates . . . may state their view that prior decisions were erroneous only if they do not assert that they, if elected, have any power to eliminate erroneous decisions. Second, limiting the scope of the clause to issues likely to come before a court is not much of a limitation at all . . . [because] "[t]here is almost no legal or political issue that is unlikely to come before a judge of an American court, state or federal, of general jurisdiction." Third, construing the clause to allow "general"discussions of case law and judicial philosophy turns out to be of little help in an election campaign. . . . [T]he announce clause would prohibit the candidate from exemplifying his philosophy. . . . Without such application to real-life issues, all candidates can claim to be "strict constructionists" with equal (and unhelpful) plausibility [for example].

In any event, it is clear that the announce clause prohibits a judicial candidate from stating his views on any specific nonfanciful legal question within the province of the court for which he is running, except in the context of discussing past decisions — and in the latter context as well, if he expresses the view that he is not bound by *stare decisis*.[18]

III

. . . [T]he announce clause both prohibits speech on the basis of its content and burdens a category of speech that is "at the core of our First Amendment freedoms" — speech about the qualifications of candidates for public office. The Court of Appeals concluded that the proper test . . . to determine the constitutionality of such a restriction is what our cases have called strict scrutiny; the parties do not dispute that this is correct. Under the strict-scrutiny test, respondents have the burden to prove that the announce clause is (1) narrowly tailored, to serve (2) a compelling state interest. . . . [Respondents] must demonstrate that it does not "unnecessarily circumscribe protected expression.". . .

A

. . . We think it plain that the announce clause is not narrowly tailored to serve impartiality (or the appearance of impartiality) in th[e] sense [of the lack of bias for or against either *party* to a proceeding]. Indeed, the clause is barely tailored to serve that interest *at all*, inasmuch as it does not restrict speech for or against particular *parties*, but rather speech for or against particular *issues*.

B

. . . "[I]mpartiality" mean[ing] lack of preconception in favor of or against a particular *legal view* . . . may well be an interest served by the announce clause, but it is not a *compelling* state interest, as strict scrutiny requires. A judge's lack of predisposition regarding the relevant legal issues in a case has never been thought a necessary component of equal justice, and with good

---

[18] [5] [T]he ABA Judicial Code 50 (1992) . . . prohibits a judicial candidate from making "statements that commit or appear to commit the candidate with respect to cases, controversies or issues that are likely to come before the Court." ABA Model Code of Judicial Conduct, Canon5(A)(3)(d)(ii) (2000). . . . [T]he Minnesota Supreme Court was urged to replace the announce clause with the new ABA language, but, unlike other jurisdictions, declined. . . . We do not know whether the announce clause (as interpreted by state authorities) and the 1990 ABA canon are one and the same. No aspect of our constitutional analysis turns on this question.

reason. For one thing, it is virtually impossible to find a judge who does not have preconceptions about the law. . . . Indeed, even if it were possible to select judges who did not have preconceived views on legal issues, it would hardly be desirable to do so. "Proof that a Justice's mind at the time he joined the Court was a complete *tabula rasa* in the area of constitutional adjudication would be evidence of lack of qualification, not lack of bias." The Minnesota Constitution positively forbids the selection to courts of general jurisdiction of judges who are impartial in the sense of having no views on the law. Minn. Const., Art. VI, § 5 ("Judges of the supreme court, the court of appeals and the district court shall be learned in the law"). And since avoiding judicial preconceptions on legal issues is neither possible nor desirable, pretending otherwise by attempting to preserve the "appearance" of that type of impartiality can hardly be a compelling state interest either.

C

. . . [O]penmindedness . . . in a judge demands, not that he have no preconceptions on legal issues, but that he be willing to consider views that oppose his preconceptions, and remain open to persuasion, when the issues arise in a pending case. . . . It may well be that impartiality in this sense, and the appearance of it, are desirable in the judiciary, but we need not pursue that inquiry, since we do not believe the Minnesota Supreme Court adopted the announce clause for that purpose. . . .

[S]tatements in election campaigns are such an infinitesimal portion of the public commitments to legal positions that judges (or judges-to-be) undertake, that this object of the prohibition is implausible. Before they arrive on the bench (whether by election or otherwise) judges have often committed themselves [in opinions written while on the bench or outside the context of litigation, in classes that they conduct, and in books and speeches] on legal issues that they must later rule upon. . . . As a means of pursuing the objective of open-mindedness that respondents now articulate, the announce clause is so woefully underinclusive as to render belief in that purpose a challenge to the credulous. . . . The proposition that judges feel significantly greater compulsion . . . to maintain consistency with *nonpromissory* statements made during a judicial campaign than with such statements made before or after the campaign is not self-evidently true. It seems to us quite likely, in fact, that in many cases the opposite is true. We doubt, for example, that a mere statement of position enunciated during the pendency of an election will be regarded by a judge as more binding — or as more likely to subject him to popular disfavor if reconsidered — than a carefully considered holding that the judge set forth in an earlier opinion denying some individual's claim to justice. In any event, it suffices to say that respondents have not carried the burden imposed by our strict-scrutiny test to establish this proposition (that campaign statements are uniquely destructive of openmindedness) on which the validity of the announce clause rests.

Moreover, the notion that the special context of electioneering justifies an *abridgment* of the right to speak out on disputed issues sets our First Amendment jurisprudence on its head. "Debate on the qualifications of candidates" is "at the core of our electoral process and of the First Amendment freedoms," not at the edges. "The role that elected officials play in our society

makes it all the more imperative that they be allowed freely to express themselves on matters of current public importance." *Wood* v. *Georgia,* 370 U.S.
375, 395 (1962). "It is simply not the function of government to select which
issues are worth discussing or debating in the course of a political campaign."
Brown [v. Hartlage], 456 U.S. [45] at 60 [(1982)] (internal quotation marks
omitted). We have never allowed the government to prohibit candidates from
communicating relevant information to voters during an election. . . .

[W]e neither assert nor imply that the First Amendment requires campaigns for judicial office to sound the same as those for legislative office. What
we do assert . . . is that, *even if* the First Amendment allows greater regulation of judicial election campaigns than legislative election campaigns, the
announce clause still fails strict scrutiny because it is woefully underinclusive,
prohibiting announcements by judges (and would-be judges) only at certain
times and in certain forms. . . .

IV

. . . [A] "universal and long-established" tradition of prohibiting certain conduct creates "a strong presumption" that the prohibition is constitutional. . . .
The practice of prohibiting speech by judicial candidates on disputed issues,
however, is neither long nor universal. By the time of the Civil War, the great
majority of States elected their judges. We know of no restrictions upon statements that could be made by judicial candidates (including judges) throughout
the 19th and the first quarter of the 20th century. Indeed, judicial elections
were generally partisan during this period, the movement toward nonpartisan
judicial elections not even beginning until the 1870's. Thus, not only were judicial candidates (including judges) discussing disputed legal and political
issues on the campaign trail, but they were touting party affiliations and
angling for party nominations all the while.

The first code regulating judicial conduct was adopted by the ABA in 1924.
It contained a provision akin to the announce clause: "A candidate for judicial
position . . . should not announce in advance his conclusions of law on disputed
issues to secure class support. . . . " ABA Canon of Judicial Ethics 30 (1924).
The States were slow to adopt the canons, however. "By the end of World War
II, the canons . . . were binding by the bar associations or supreme courts of
only eleven states." Even today, although a majority of States have adopted
either the announce clause or its 1990 ABA successor, adoption is not unanimous. Of the 31 States that select some or all of their appellate and general-
jurisdiction judges by election, 4 have adopted no candidate-speech restriction
comparable to the announce clause, and 1 prohibits only the discussion of
"pending litigation." This practice . . . does not compare well with the traditions deemed worthy of our attention in prior cases.

There is an obvious tension between the article of Minnesota's popularly
approved Constitution which provides that judges shall be elected, and the
Minnesota Supreme Court's announce clause which places most subjects of
interest to the voters off limits. . . . The disparity is perhaps unsurprising,
since the ABA, which originated the announce clause, has long been an opponent of judicial elections. . . . That opposition may be well taken . . . , but the
First Amendment does not permit it to achieve its goal by leaving the principle of elections in place while preventing candidates from discussing what the

elections are about. . . . If the State chooses to tap the energy and the legitimizing power of the democratic process, it must accord the participants in that process . . . the First Amendment rights that attach to their roles.

The Minnesota Supreme Court's canon of judicial conduct prohibiting candidates for judicial election from announcing their views on disputed legal and political issues violates the First Amendment. Accordingly, we reverse the grant of summary judgment to respondents and remand the case for proceedings consistent with this opinion.

[JUSTICE O'CONNOR, concurring, wrote separately to express her concern that the very practice of electing judges undermines a state's interest in an actual and perceived impartial judiciary. She wrote in part:]

[I]f judges are subject to regular elections they are likely to feel that they have at least some personal stake in the outcome of every publicized case. Elected judges cannot help being aware that if the public is not satisfied with the outcome of a particular case, it could hurt their reelection prospects. . . . Even if judges were able to suppress their awareness of the potential electoral consequences of their decisions and refrain from acting on it, the public's confidence in the judiciary could be undermined simply by the possibility that judges would be unable to do so.

Moreover, contested elections generally entail campaigning. And campaigning for a judicial post today can require substantial funds. . . . Unless the pool of judicial candidates is limited to those wealthy enough to independently fund their campaigns, a limitation unrelated to judicial skill, the cost of campaigning requires judicial candidates to engage in fundraising. Yet relying on campaign donations may leave judges feeling indebted to certain parties or interest groups. . . . Even if judges were able to refrain from favoring donors, the mere possibility that judges' decisions may be motivated by the desire to repay campaign contributors is likely to undermine the public's confidence in the judiciary. . . .

Despite these significant problems, 39 States currently employ some form of judicial elections for their appellate courts, general jurisdiction trial courts, or both. . . . Judicial elections were not always so prevalent. . . . From the 1830's until the 1850's, as part of the Jacksonian movement toward greater popular control of public office, this trend accelerated. . . . By the beginning of the 20th century, however, elected judiciaries increasingly came to be viewed as incompetent and corrupt, and criticism of partisan judicial elections mounted. . . .

In response to such concerns, some States adopted a modified system of judicial selection that became known as the Missouri Plan (because Missouri was the first State to adopt it for most of its judicial posts) . . . . [J]udges are appointed by a high elected official, generally from a list of nominees put together by a nonpartisan nominating commission, and then subsequently stand for unopposed retention elections in which voters are asked whether the judges should be recalled. If a judge is recalled, the vacancy is filled through a new nomination and appointment. This system obviously reduces threats to judicial impartiality, even if it does not eliminate all popular pressure on judges. . . . The Missouri Plan is currently used to fill at least some judicial offices in 15 States. . . .

Thirty-one States, however, still use popular elections to select some or all of their appellate and/or general jurisdiction trial court judges, who thereafter run for reelection periodically. Of these, slightly more than half use nonpartisan elections, and the rest use partisan elections. Most of the States that do not have any form of judicial elections choose judges through executive nomination and legislative confirmation. . . .

Minnesota has chosen to select its judges through contested popular elections. . . . In doing so the State has voluntarily taken on the risks to judicial bias described above. As a result, the State's claim that it needs to significantly restrict judges' speech in order to protect judicial impartiality is particularly troubling. If the State has a problem with judicial impartiality, it is largely one the State brought upon itself by continuing the practice of popularly electing judges.

NOTES

1. Justice Ginsburg, with whom Justices Stevens, Souter, and Breyer joined, dissenting, in *White* argued that, "[t]he balance the State sought to achieve — allowing the people to elect judges, but safeguarding the process so that the integrity of the judiciary would not be compromised — should encounter no First Amendment shoal." She contended that the majority had misconstrued and mis-portrayed the Announce Clause as barring more speech than, rightly understood, it did, and had ignored the significance of the Announce Clause in the context of the integrated system of judicial campaign regulation that Minnesota had developed. In particular, the Court had ignored the fact that "[b]y targeting statements that do not technically constitute pledges or promises but nevertheless 'publicly make known how [the candidate] would decide' legal issues, the Announce Clause prevents [an] end run around the letter and spirit of its companion provision [in Minnesota's Code of Judicial Conduct, prohibiting candidates from 'making pledges or promises of conduct in office other than the faithful and impartial performance of the duties of the office']." She concluded, "Judges are not politicians, and the First Amendment does not require that they be treated as politicians simply because they are chosen by popular vote. Nor does the First Amendment command States who wish to promote the integrity of their judges in fact and [in] appearance to abandon systems of judicial selection that the people, in the exercise of their sovereign prerogatives, have devised." *White,* 536 U.S. at 808-09, 821.

2. The decision in *White* was roundly criticized by some. Insofar as it left the bounds of permissible speech and permissible regulation of speech unclear, some commentators predicted that further legal challenges would follow. Some have. *See, e.g., Family Trust Found. of Ky., Inc. v. Ky. Judicial Conduct Comm'n,* 388 F.3d 224 (6th Cir. 2004) (denying the stay pending appeal of an injunction prohibiting enforcement of the Kentucky Supreme Court Rule prohibiting judicial candidates from making pledges other than of faithful and impartial performance of their duties, where the district court had found that the State had used the clause to reach content covered by the "announce clause" struck down in *White* and the appeals court concluded that the State was therefore unlikely to succeed in its challenge to the injunction).

Can any speech by a judicial candidate now be constitutionally restricted? Is it clear what a candidate for judicial office meaningfully can say during a campaign?

3. Others feared the effects of the *White* decision. Lynn A. Wardle, then co-chair of the ABA Section of Litigation's Task Force on the Judiciary was quoted as saying that "Judicial candidates will now be forced to cast about for votes by signaling how they might rule on cases, undermining the actual and perceived impartiality of the judiciary and encouraging sound-bite campaigning." 28 LITIG. NEWS #1, Nov. 2002, at 2. Deborah Goldberg, then Deputy Director of the Democracy Program at the Brennan Center for Justice, New York University School of Law, added that, "To get elected, candidates will be pressured by special interest groups to indicate how they will rule on hot-button issues." *Id.* Law professor Steven Lubet wrote in the *Chicago Tribune*: "Judges . . . are supposed to rule according to the law, no matter what the public wants. Therefore, campaign commitments are contrary to the very premise of judging, and threaten to undermine the due process rights of litigants. . . . [Moreover,] special-interest groups press candidates for answers to questionnaires, or even for outright commitments during the campaign. . . . [T]he pressure to make campaign statements may result in the multiplication of 'opinions,' far beyond the judicial candidates' previously settled ideas." Steven Lubet, *Bad Policy Headed for Courtrooms*, CHI. TRIB., July 2, 2002, § 1, at 17. Assuming that the *White* decision was not demanded by the First Amendment (as four of the nine Justices believed), do you think the *White* decision's undesirable effects on judicial campaigns outweigh its desirable effects?

4. The ABA's Joint Commission to Evaluate the Model Code of Judicial Conduct is working on a draft of proposed revisions. As of June 1, 2005, its draft of a revised Canon 5 would permit candidates for judicial office to publicly identify themselves as candidates of a political organization but only in partisan elections, and to seek and use endorsements from individuals and organizations including political organizations. However, it would command judicial candidates and judges (among other things) not to "make any comment that might reasonably be expected to affect the outcome or impair the fairness of a proceeding while it is pending or impending in any court; . . . [or] with respect to cases, controversies, or issues that are likely to come before the court, make pledges, promises or commitments that are inconsistent with the impartial performance of the adjudicative duties of the office." If adopted, will this language make clear what a candidate for judicial office will be able to say during a campaign?

The draft Commentary explains, that "judicial ethics rules may not prohibit judicial candidates from announcing their views on disputed legal and political issues. Rule 5.01(m) . . . does not proscribe a candidate's public expression of personal views on disputed issues. . . . [W]here the law differs from the candidate's personal belief, however, candidates are encouraged to emphasize their duty to uphold the law regardless of their personal views." Similarly, "candidates who choose to respond [to questionnaires or requests for interviews from organizations seeking to learn their views] should make clear their commitment to keeping an open mind while on the bench, regardless of their personal views." Does this go far enough? Does it go too far in delimiting what judicial candidates may or may not, should or should not, say?

5. The distinctive features and peculiar nature of political campaigns for judicial office are discussed in Hans A. Linde, *The Judge As Political Candidate*, 40 Clev. St. L. Rev. 1 (1992). For a survey of *White*'s consequences thus far, *see* Rachel Paine Caufield, *In the Wake of* White: *How States Are Responding to* Republican Party of Minnesota v. White *and How Judicial Elections Are Changing*, 38 Akron L. Rev. 625 (2005).

Roy A. Schotland, *Elective Judges' Campaign Financing: Are State Judges' Robes the Emperor's Clothes of American Democracy?*, 2 Journal of Law & Politics 57, 73-76 (1985)[19]

Prelude: Perspective on Judicial Campaigns

A. Scope of the Problem . . .

The number of judges involved [in elections] is quite large. . . . [As of 1984, according to Schotland, approximately 7,425 judges were subject to elections of some type.] [In 2001, Schotland wrote that "Of the nation's 1243 state appellate judges, for initial terms, . . . 40% face partisan elections, and 13% [that is, 659 of 1,243] face nonpartisan elections. . . . For subsequent terms: . . . 43% face retention elections, 32% face partisan and 13% face nonpartisan elections . . . [based on the U.S. Dept. of Justice, Bureau of Justice Statistics, State Court Organization 1998]." The figures given do not include elected trial court judges. Roy A. Schotland, *Summit on Improving Judicial Selection; Introduction: Personal Views*, 34 Loy. L.A. L. Rev. 1361, 1365 & n.9 (2001).]

Assuming that our state court norm of judicial elections will continue to be the case for judges in most states, the crucial issue becomes the conduct of such elections. . . .

1. *Changes in Judging and in the Bar*

Judges and the judicial role have changed in three pertinent ways: impact, policy and proliferation. Judges' decisions have far greater impact on people's daily lives today than a generation ago. They affect more people more weightily, or at least more visibly, than in the past: consider the political flares lit in the communities affected by judicial decisions on criminal, environmental and school bussing issues alone, and it is easy to understand why the public has been more interested in judicial elections and why these elections have been more hotly contested recently.

Judges have assumed a larger role in the nation's policy-making process. The literature on judicial selection contains straight-faced explanations that judges make law rather than discover it; and so, it is said, judges' range of discretion in shaping policy explains why the public wants judges to be electorally accountable. . . . Whatever our past, Professor Chayes has shown us the extent to which we are in the era of "The Public Law Judge": (a) more constitutional law and broader remedial reach; (b) an explosion of statutes imposing more official intervention and more delegation to resolution by judges, whether by

[19] Copyright © 1985 by the Journal of Law & Politics. Reprinted with permission.

legislative design, legislative oversight, or legislative buck-passing; and (c) a flowering of common-law creativity in such areas as product liability, making legislative change look modest in comparison. With such forces propelling judges into more policy-shaping adjudication, in subjects that affect so many people, it is not surprising that the public's interest in the occupants of these policy-shaping seats has intensified. . . .

The last change in judging that may spur increased attention to judicial elections may be termed "proliferation." When there were fewer judges, their sheer rarity may have evoked a measure of respect. Today's larger number of judges may coincide with a drop in the quality of the bench which in combination with the rise of the quantity of judges fosters decreasing respect for the bench. Less respect and more vulnerability yield more contests. The other side of "proliferation" is the great increase in the size of the bar. So great an increase in lawyers competing with one another is bound to result in more lawyers either looking to the bench as a means of job security, or looking to judicial campaigns simply as good advertising.

NOTES

Along with the content of the campaign, the cost of campaigning is another critical aspect of the debate over the best method for selecting judges.

Mark Hansen, *The High Cost Of Judging*, 77 AMERICAN BAR ASSOCIATION JOURNAL 44 (September 1991)[20]

It's been nearly 20 years since Washington Supreme Court Justice Robert F. Utter first complained about the high costs and long hours involved in elections to the bench.

Utter lamented the fact that spending had topped the $35,000 mark in two 1970 supreme court races, which, he said, forced judges into selling their homes to pay for the costs of their campaigns.

And he bemoaned the extensive amount of time that a judge had to spend getting himself reelected, which in Utter's experience was cutting the court's productivity by as much as a third.

Worse than the time or the money, though, he deplored the outright assault on the integrity of the judiciary by subjecting judges to periodic political campaigns.

"Lawsuits must . . . be won in court on the merits of the particular case, leaving no room for the subtle and not-so-subtle political pressures inherent in an elective judiciary system," Utter wrote in 1973. "In the face of such pressure, our country's rule by law rather than men could become the ultimate victim, seriously threatening the concept that 'in our courts all men are created equal.'"

At the time, in a *Washington Law Review* article, Utter supported a proposed state constitutional amendment to replace Washington's nonpartisan judicial elections with a merit selection system.

---

20 Copyright © 1991 by the American Bar Association. Reprinted by permission.

That question never made it to the ballot. But Utter, who last faced opposition in 1980, is even more resolute now in his conviction that a contested election is no way to pick a judge.

The financial burden imposed on judges by an elective process concerns Utter. Twice he has had to take out a second mortgage on his home to retire a campaign debt. And the veteran jurist, who is up for re-election in 1992, figures that a contested race to keep his seat the next time around will cost at least $200,000.

"Not much has changed in the last 20 years," said Utter, who recently headed an 18-month study of judicial elections by the American Judicature Society. "Merit selection isn't a total answer, but I still feel it's the lesser of two evils."

In his disdain for an elective judiciary, Utter has a lot of company on both sides of the bench. But the judges in Washington should consider themselves lucky.

In last fall's partisan race for three contested seats on the Texas Supreme Court, the six candidates spent a combined total of nearly $6 million. Two years earlier, when six seats were up for grabs, the 12 contenders together spent more than $10 million.

While Texas may be ahead of the pack in judicial campaign spending, it is not alone. In 1989, the winning candidate for a seat on Pennsylvania's supreme court spent more than $1.4 million, a half-million of which went to his Democratic primary race alone. His Republican opponent in the general election raised only a third as much.

And the 1986 non-partisan race for chief justice of Ohio's supreme court cost more than $2.7 million, up from less than $100,000 six years earlier. The incumbent, who had spent about $80,000 to win his seat in 1980, poured $1.7 million into his losing bid for re-election six years later. . . .

The national spending record in a judicial race still belongs to California, where three supreme court justices were defeated in a 1986 merit-retention campaign that cost $11.4 million. And only last fall, Leander Shaw Jr., the chief justice of Florida's supreme court, spent $300,000 to keep his job in the face of an organized campaign by anti-abortion forces to oust him from the bench.

Nor is the phenomenon confined to big, urban states where partisan politics long have played a role in judicial elections. Even rural states in the nation's heartland aren't immune to the trend.

In Montana, the 1986 campaign for chief justice cost nearly $250,000, up 320 percent from the $59,000 race waged six years earlier. And spending in last year's campaign for a supreme court seat in Arkansas topped $500,000 for the first time.

"There's an obvious conflict-of-interest problem when you have judges, who are supposed to be not only independent but insulated, raising huge amounts of money for their own campaigns," said Roy Schotland, a professor at Georgetown University Law Center and one of the country's leading scholars on judicial elections. "If anything, [the problem is] worse now than ever."

It wasn't that long ago, according to Schotland and other election researchers, that judicial campaigns were regarded as a model of civility in the American political process. Incumbent judges rarely encountered opposition. When they did, those contests generally were conducted in a quiet, dignified and relatively inexpensive manner.

These days, it's usual for judicial hopefuls to employ image builders and media consultants, conduct sophisticated polling and mass mailings, sound their names over the airwaves, and come out swinging on the stump. In some states, candidates for the bench have begun raising money for their next campaign as soon as they have finished their last.

What went wrong?

The concept of electing judges involves a balancing act between two competing interests: The notion that judges, like other public officials, should be accountable to the electorate, and the idea that judges, as impartial dispensers of justice, should be independent.

But experts say the ante has gone up considerably during the past two decades, when big money and special interests discovered the courts. Their deep pockets and political agendas have helped turn judicial campaigns into the kind of high-priced and hard-fought free-for-alls that one associates with, say, congressional elections.

"Judicial elections have entered a new era, one which I like to characterize as noisier, nastier and costlier than ever before," Schotland said. "That doesn't mean that it's happening everywhere, but it is happening in places where you wouldn't expect it."

Some people believe that any time a lawyer makes a contribution to a judge's campaign, it creates the potential for conflict somewhere down the road. "Lawyers don't contribute to judicial campaigns for altruistic reasons. They do it to gain influence," said Durham, N.C., lawyer Robert Baker. "I don't care where you are. When a case goes to trial, if lawyer A contributed to the judge's campaign and lawyer B didn't, it's going to cause problems."

Others say the level of concern rises with the amount of money involved. "Nobody really gives a damn if a judge gets a $100 contribution from a law firm," Schotland said. "But if a judge receives $10,000 from one lawyer or a fund raiser brings in $50,000, are we as confident that nothing is expected in return? What doesn't matter when it amounts to peanuts becomes very troublesome when big money is involved."

The changing nature of judicial elections is alarming for many reasons, but none has received more attention than the increasing role that lawyers, potential litigants and other single-minded interest groups have come to play in the process. Critics of an elective judiciary say it has fueled the perception, if not the reality, that modern justice may be going to the highest bidder.

"Special-interest groups have come to believe, correctly or not, that they can buy results simply by spending a lot of money," said Leslie Jacobs, a Cleveland lawyer and past president of the Ohio State Bar Association. "A cynic might say that we've reached the stage where it's cheaper to buy four out of seven supreme court justices than an entire legislature."

Countless studies have shown that contributions by lawyers generally account for less than half of the money raised in judicial elections, although lawyers often represent the largest single source of campaign funds. Political action committees, representing doctors, unions, big business and other special-interest groups, often make up the next biggest bloc of campaign contributors.

An analysis of the 1986 California merit-retention campaign, for example, showed that insurance, oil, agricultural and real estate interests contributed more than $356,000 to defeat three supreme court justices. Lawyers and law firms spent more than $641,000 to retain them in office.

Another study showed that in Ohio's 1986 supreme court race, labor unions contributed $350,000 to Chief Justice Frank Celebrezze's losing bid for re-election. But business and medical interests chipped in more than $50,000 toward the $1 million war chest of the victor, Thomas Moyer.

In Pennsylvania's 1989 supreme court race, law firms contributed more than $800,000, or 57 percent, of winning candidate Ralph Cappy's $1.4 million campaign fund.

And in Texas, where supreme court races tend to pit plaintiffs' lawyers against the defense bar, the state's top 50 law firms and the Texas Medical Association contributed more than one-third, or nearly $3.5 million, of all funds raised in the 1988 election.

In certain instances, the influence of lawyers and potential litigants in the judicial-elections process may even be higher. In 1982, Woodrow Wilson Bean, an unsuccessful candidate for a supreme court seat in Texas, received more than $200,000 from a single contributor — more than 90 percent of his entire campaign contributions. And Gerald Stern, administrator of the New York State Commission on Judicial Conduct, said he believes that 90 percent of the money contributed to judicial elections in that state comes from lawyers.

Widespread concern over the soaring costs and potential conflicts in judicial elections had led to a number of proposed reforms by the AJS, state and local bar officials, and a host of "good government" groups like Common Cause and the League of Women Voters. . . .

[O]ne recent tactic in election reform seeks simply to educate voters and keep the candidates in line. Last year, bar officials in North Carolina created a statewide Committee on Judicial Campaigns, which monitored campaign practices, sponsored a series of televised debates between candidates, and published a voter's guide to the fall election.

Baker, the Durham lawyer who chaired the project, said the committee was created to head off the name-calling and other below-the-belt tactics that have become standard practice in other states. For that limited purpose, the effort was a success, he said.

"It was a lot of work, but I recommend it," Baker said. "We ran out of money along the way or we could have done a lot more. But what we did do was pretty effective. We didn't get any complaints."

Bar officials in Ohio are studying the North Carolina example with an eye toward taking the reform process one step further, according to Columbus lawyer Denis Murphy, a founding member of that state's Committee for Judicial Election Reform. The committee, a joint project of the state bar and the Metropolitan Bar Leaders Conference, will begin to monitor judicial campaign practices statewide this fall, Murphy said. Later, the committee will pursue a legislative agenda possibly including a requirement that judges disclose campaign contributions that exceed a nominal amount, he said.

"Recognizing that Ohio is not going to have merit selection anytime soon, we're looking for ways to improve the system we've got," Murphy said. "It's a slow process, but I think we'll see some meaningful reform come out of it."

NOTES

1. Since Mark Hansen wrote in 1991, spending on judicial elections has exploded. The Justice at Stake campaign (described below) reports that in state supreme court judicial elections alone in 2004:

— candidates raised $46.8 million;

— interest groups contributed at least $10 million;

— in one Illinois race, the candidates raised more than $9.3 million, which represents more fundraising than was done in 19 of the 34 races for seats in the United States Senate. This was the most expensive state court race in American history;

— in West Virginia, candidates for judicial office raised in excess of $2.8 million, and groups spent at least an additional $5.5 million, in a successful effort to defeat an incumbent state supreme court justice;

— half of the 18 states that held privately financed, contested elections broke records for total candidate fundraising (AR, GA, IL, MT, NM, NV, OH, WA, WV).

In addition, network television ads for these races were broadcast in 16 states in 2004, as compared with 9 in 2002 and 5 in 1999-2000. The cost of this advertising, by both groups and candidates, exceeded $24 million, more than double the previous record of $10.7 million, spent in 2000.

Candidate questionnaires, urging state supreme court candidates to take stands on controversial issues and threatening political retribution, were utilized in more states than previously. And, in the 42 contested elections for state supreme court seats, only one woman was added (that was in Alabama), two women Justices were defeated (one in Kentucky, one in Alabama), and six women successfully defended their seats in contested elections. Justice at Stake campaign, State Supreme Court Summary, updated as of 5/25/05.

The Justice at Stake campaign describes itself as "a nationwide, nonpartisan partnership of more than thirty judicial, legal and citizen organizations . . . [whose] mission is to educate the public and work for reforms to keep politics and special interests out of the courtroom." Its members include the ABA, American Judicature Society, and the Brennan Center for Justice at NYU School of Law.

The website of the Brennan Center notes that of the 28 races with television advertising, 25 of the winners had more such advertising than did their opponents, and that nearly one-quarter of the "spots"were negative in tone, with attack ads quadrupling as compared with 2002 and almost doubling as compared with 2000. Ads paid for by interest groups as well as those paid for by political parties were negative more than half the time. Deborah Ginsberg, Director of the Democracy Program at the Brennan Center, is quoted as saying that "Negative ads are known to depress voter turnout, which allows special interest groups to assert even more influence over judicial elections," and that "High spending by candidates means that special interest groups are giving substantial amounts directly to judicial candidates, furthering the impression that justice is for sale." http://www.brennancenter.org.

2. If this picture represents a dangerous situation, what can be done? Ideas (some of which have been enacted in some states) include making easily available to voters nonpartisan voter guides that seek to present accurate, positive, candidate-supplied information; imposing contribution limits and disclosure requirements concerning contributions; placing and enforcing provisions in codes of judicial conduct that prohibit judges from personally soliciting or accepting contributions (although allowing campaign committees to do the soliciting and accepting); and having public financing replace private financing of judicial campaigns. Are these good ideas? Are they, individually or collectively, sufficient to solve the various problems caused by the current systems for electing judges?

3. Thomas R. Phillips, a former Chief Justice of the Supreme Court of Texas, has endorsed several of the ideas proposed in note 2, above, and also has suggested that we reduce the number of judicial elections by lengthening judicial terms, "elevate the tenor of judicial campaigns by clarifying our codes of judicial conduct, . . . creat[e] citizens' campaign monitoring groups," and encourage media and other groups to sponsor candidate forums and debates, to help educate voters in ways that reduce the need for campaign contributions. Thomas R. Phillips, *Keynote Address: Electoral Accoutnability and Judicial Independence*, Symposium: *Perspectives on Judicial Independence, Elections and the Challenge to Judicial Autonomy*, 64 OHIO ST. L. J. 137 (2003). What objections might there be to Judge Phillips' recommendations?

ABA MODEL CODE OF JUDICIAL CONDUCT (2004), as amended[21]

CANON 3

A judge shall perform the duties of judicial office impartially and diligently.

. . . .

E. Disqualification.

(1) A judge shall disqualify himself or herself in a proceeding in which the judge's impartiality might reasonably be questioned. . . .

---

[21] Copyright © 2004 by the American Bar Association. Reprinted with permission. Copies of ABA *Model Code of Judicial Conduct, 2004 Edition* is available from Service Center, American Bar Association, 321 North Clark Street, Chicago, IL 60610, 1-800-285-2221.

CANON 5

A judge or judicial candidate shall refrain from inappropriate political activity.

A. All Judges and Candidates

. . .

    (3) A candidate for a judicial office:

. . .

      (d) shall not:

        (i) with respect to cases, controversies, or issues that are likely to come before the court, make pledges, promises or commitments that are inconsistent with the impartial performance of the adjudicative duties of the office; . . .

B. Candidates Seeking Appointment to Judicial . . . Office.

    (1) A candidate for appointment to judicial office . . . shall not solicit or accept funds, personally or through a committee or otherwise, to support his or her candidacy.

    (2) A candidate for appointment to judicial office . . . shall not engage in any political activity to secure the appointment except that:

      (a) such persons may:

        (i) communicate with the appointing authority, including any selection or nominating commission or other agency designated to screen candidates;

        (ii) seek support or endorsement for the appointment from organizations that regularly make recommendations for reappointment or appointment to the office. . . .

C. Judges and Candidates Subject to Public Election.

    (1) A judge or candidate subject to public election may, except as prohibited by law:

      (a) at any time

        (i) purchase tickets for and attend political gatherings;

        (ii) identify himself or herself as a member of a political party; and

        (iii) contribute to a political organization;

      (b) when a candidate for election

        (i) speak to gatherings on his or her own behalf;

        (ii) appear in . . . advertisements supporting his or her candidacy;

        (iii) distribute . . . campaign literature supporting his or her candidacy; and

(iv) publicly endorse or publicly oppose other candidates for the same judicial office. . . .

(2) A candidate shall not personally solicit or accept campaign contributions or personally solicit publicly stated support. A candidate may, however, establish committees of responsible persons to conduct campaigns for the candidate. . . . Such committees are not prohibited from soliciting and accepting reasonable campaign contributions and public support from lawyers. . . .

NOTES

1. Under Canon 3(E), should a judge be disqualified from sitting on a case in which one of the lawyers or one of the parties has made a financial contribution to the judge's election campaign?

2. Is an elected judiciary compatible with judicial objectivity and independence? Does the ABA Code of Judicial Conduct satisfactorily deal with this problem?

3. Are the restrictions that the ABA Code imposes on judicial candidates' solicitation and acceptance of funds to support their candidacy and on publicly stated support of judicial candidacies sufficient to ensure judicial independence and the appearance of such independence? What further restrictions or other measures would you suggest to bolster those objectives?

The ABA's Joint Commission to Evaluate the Model Code of Judicial Conduct is working on a draft of proposed revisions. As of December, 2005, its draft of a revised Canon 5 would continue to provide that a judge or candidate for judicial office shall not "personally solicit or personally accept campaign contributions" but would permit candidates for judicial office to establish a campaign committee. The draft would make the candidate responsible for ensuring that the committee complies with applicable law including the regulations set forth in the Canons. The draft Canons would prohibit the committee from soliciting or accepting contributions for a judicial candidate's campaign more than a year prior to the election and for some months thereafter; would impose a dollar limit on the aggregate contributions that the committee could accept from any donor; and would require public disclosure of contributions from a given donor in excess of a designated amount. Would you support these provisions?

4. What method of judicial selection is most likely to place on the state appellate bench persons having the qualities that are desirable in appellate judges?

Frank K. Richardson & Joseph R. Grodin, *Judging Judges: How We Choose Our Federal and State Judges*, 1 JOURNAL OF CONTEMPORARY LEGAL ISSUES 147, 148-61 (1988)[22]

[Following the failure of the Reagan Administration's attempt to appoint Robert Bork or Douglas Ginsburg to the Supreme Court, and the elections

---

[22] Copyright © 1988 *The Journal of Contemporary Legal Issues*. Reprinted with the permission of The Journal of Contemporary Legal Issues.

which removed Rose Bird, Joseph Grodin, and Cruz Reynoso from the California Supreme Court, Justice Richardson[23] and former Justice Grodin of the Supreme Court of California made the following remarks.]

Richardson:

The 1986 California Supreme Court experience, the Bork and the Ginsburg hearings, have focused attention on the issues of judicial retention and judicial selection. They have left lingering echoes and scars, and they have also left a series of unanswered questions as well. How much does politics enter into the matter of the nomination and confirmation process? To what extent do the judge's personal character and philosophy affect the process? Is the federal system of lifetime appointments a desirable and preferable system? What changes, if any, should we make in the process? These questions are broad but, beyond a few unsatisfactory generalizations, are not susceptible of easy or pat answers. . . .

[B]etween the years 1906-1913 . . . largely through the impetus of the American Judicature Society, a . . . plan was introduced which involved the appointment of judges by an elected official from a select panel or list of names submitted by an impartial, non-partisan nominating body. The judge was to go before the voters at stated intervals thereafter on the sole question of his or her retention in office.

With minor variations, it is this fundamental pattern of executive appointment, commission approval, and popular confirmation which California voters approved by their adoption in 1934 by a constitutional amendment. Under this amendment, appellate court judges nominated initially by the Governor are subject to approval of a three-member confirmation commission, with periodic appearances before the voters on the sole issue of their retention in office. Today, Article VI § 16(d) provides for nomination or appointment of all appellate judges by the Governor effective upon confirmation by the Commission on Judicial Appointments, which is composed of the Chief Justice, the Attorney General, and the Senior Presiding Justice of the affected district. The term of office is twelve years except that the Justice shall run for the unexpired term of his predecessor at the next gubernatorial election after his or her appointment.

How has this system worked in California in the 50 years since its adoption? To what degree do politics and considerations of philosophy or attitude in their cruder forms intrude into the process? Are there better ways?

In an illuminating article in the University of Southern California Law Review a few years ago,[24] Dorothy Nelson, presently on the Court of Appeal, Ninth Circuit, and former Dean of the University of Southern California Law School, quotes the following sage observation of earlier scholars and cites a principle which you and I should bear in mind when we think in terms of politicization of the judicial office:

> Whether judges should be elected or appointed is a political question
> and in all honesty ought to be treated as such. You may take the

---

[23] Frank K. Richardson was an Associate Justice of the Supreme Court of California from 1974-1983.

[24] The article to which reference is made is Dorothy W. Nelson, *Variations on a Theme — Selection and Tenure of Judges*, 36 S. Cal. L. Rev. 4 (1962).

controlling power of selection from one group or individual and vest it in another but you cannot abolish it. There simply is no such thing as automatic selection of any public officer except where the office is hereditary. Any system which places the power of selecting judges or other officials in the hands of the human being or a group of humans is political. Every person who is or hopes to be in office is in politics.

. . . The arguments for and against the selection of judges by popular election were readily marshalled by Judge Nelson. She noted that the primary objections to an election process are:

1. The election campaign places judges in the untenable position of forfeiting both the appearance and the reality of impartial neutrality when soliciting either votes or campaign funds.

2. Campaigning by sitting judges is distracting and diverts time and attention from official duties to the disadvantage of the public.

3. Judges may tend or appear to tend to tailor their judicial decisions to accommodate the perceived current of public opinion.

4. The public has no realistic basis upon which to judge or evaluate the abilities of judicial nominees.

5. Supporters of or contributors to a judge's campaign have a continuing claim on the judge which may affect the impartial, judicious discharge of his or her duties.

6. A combination of these reasons.

She listed some arguments favoring the retention of the election system:

1. Democracy itself rests upon "faith" in the ultimate judgment and wisdom of the people.

2. Popular elections assure a more representative court, including multinational judges of different faiths.

3. For policy reasons, judges should not be "frozen" into office.

4. Judicial decisions should reflect contemporary yet changing opinions, economic conditions and public mores.

5. The security of tenure is founded on the belief that a person cannot be relied upon to act rightly regardless of his or her personal consequences.

Essentially, our goal is to seek a satisfactory answer to the question which may be broadly put — in a democratic society how can we obtain and retain judges with an optimum of quality and a minimum of political or partisan influence?

In the words of Judge Nelson, "Once an honest and competent judge has been put on the bench, he ought to be allowed to remain indefinitely until incompetency, death, retirement or resignation." She quotes from an article in the *Journal of the American Judicature Society:* "If there was some way of protecting the tenure of good judges by dropping out the worthless, incompetent and dishonest ones, it would surely be an improvement over a system of keeping the bad in order to avoid losing the good."

A strong argument for a federal lifetime appointment system can be made in furtherance of the independence of the judiciary. Whatever partisan or political influence has been exercised in the initial selection process presumably thereby has been exhausted. The judge's position, barring incompetency, is impregnable. The judge's loyalty to his oath is undiluted. He or she cannot be reached or threatened. This is a plus, for, as was said in 1961 in an American Bar Association report: "There is no harm in turning a politician into a judge. He may become a good judge. The curse of the elective system is that it turns almost every elective judge into a politician."

If, however, the people are not to have a direct voice in the selection and retention of judges, what are the alternatives? Several have been suggested. Some have thought that a nominee should be chosen by a legislature or at least subject to its confirmation, but legislatures have been known to act politically, too. It is suggested, though, that the United States is not a true and pure democracy but a representative one in which the people act through their representatives. . . .

It's almost an historic truism that both presidents and governors tend consciously or unconsciously to choose appointees whose records on the whole are harmonious with the attitudes, the approaches and the philosophy of the appointing power. To put the question boldly — does politics in some sense enter into the nomination, confirmation and retention process of California judges, federal and state? The answer, I fear, must be a resounding "yes."

At this point, however, the discussion inevitably turns into pure and unadulterated speculation. The variables of character, of philosophy, of attitude, of sense of responsibility of the appointing power, and time of appointment are not quantifiable. To attempt to trace the inner motivations and thought processes behind individual judicial appointments is to venture into never-never land. Governor A of whatever party looks on the power to appoint judges as a golden opportunity to bring into public service able, dedicated and sincere men and women who are gifted, intellectually balanced, fair, calm and dispassionate. Governor B of whatever party views the power of judicial appointment consciously or unconsciously as an opportunity to reward his or her friends and supporters. Then there is Governor C of whichever party whose judicial appointments are an interesting but random mix of all of the above, unpredictable and not susceptible of easy assessment.

This is an area in which both accurate prediction and careful measurement simply fail. Latent talent frequently remains dormant until awakened by appointment. Moreover, the potential for growth cannot safely be ignored. People sometimes rise to challenges in surprising ways. A Hugo Black can arise from a Ku Klux Klan background as a youth to become a towering, legendary figure on the nation's highest court.

Having said all of this, it cannot be denied that presidents and governors usually nominate as judges those who are perceived as philosophically at home or comfortable with the philosophy, the attitude, the approach of the appointing authority. 'Twas ever thus, and perhaps 'twill ever be. . . .

[Justice Richardson then discussed popular judicial elections in general and the 1986 California Supreme Court election in particular, in which three Justices were voted out of office.] To what degree, if at all, should the people be permitted to vote for the confirmation of judges? I personally favor public participation. In a representative democracy, the people should be permitted periodically to express their views directly on judicial performance. The ultimate authority is theirs, even though they may make mistakes. Under our Constitution, the people are the basic source of political power. . . .

I could support enthusiastically the three proposed changes suggested by Dean Uelmen:

1. Newly appointed Supreme Court appointees would face voters at the next general election after their appointment rather than at the next gubernatorial election.

2. A justice who wins confirmation would be elected to a full twelve-year term rather than for the unexpired term of his or her predecessor.

3. At the conclusion of the twelve-year term, a justice would continue in office only after reappointment by the Governor and confirmation by the people for a new twelve-year term. . . .

Grodin:

Justice Richardson's perspective is of the dispassionate scientist. Mine is more the perspective of the rat in the maze being studied. I owe my present relative leisure to an overenthusiastic electorate and the process which Justice Richardson has with characteristic judiciousness examined so objectively. You will have to evaluate my remarks in that light. . . .

In the course of the hearings of the nomination of Robert Bork, some of my friends who supported me enthusiastically during the last campaign talked to me as if I would find particular vindication in the spectacle of some of those who opposed my candidacy finally getting theirs, being treated to some of the same medicine, as it were. And to be honest with you, I can't say the thought didn't cross my mind. But truth to tell, I felt considerable discomfort during the course of the Bork campaign, and without regard to the question whether or not Judge Bork should have been confirmed. My discomfort stemmed rather from the procedure and the criteria implicit in the process that was brought to bear.

I was uneasy, for example, about the extent to which some of Judge Bork's opponents characterized his opinions in statistical terms, looking at them in categories rather than as individual opinions, and looking at the results, rather than the reasoning. It reminded me of the kind of argument that was waged during the course of the 1986 California campaign based upon our respective statistics in the area of death penalty judgements.

I was uneasy about the extent to which portions of Judge Bork's record were distorted by his opponents. I was uneasy with the 30-second television spot that represented a simplistic attack on Judge Bork's views, the kind of attack to which no rational response, given the nature of the media, was readily available.

I was disturbed by the extent to which Judge Bork was asked and responded to very specific questions about his views regarding particular decisions of the United States Supreme Court and about how he would vote as a judge on those issues. And I was disturbed overall by the degree of politicization that surrounded the atmosphere of that campaign.

Having said all of that, I think it is important to recognize the distinctions which exist between the federal model of Senate confirmation and the state model of retention elections.

In the case of the federal model, instead of an election, we have a dialogue in a Senate Judiciary Confirmation Hearing, in which at least some rational discourse can take place and in which the candidate has an opportunity in front of a surprisingly interested and alert television audience to confront questions and explain views. An election is not like that. Also in the federal system we have a situation in which the nominee confronts that process before appointment to a vacant position.

By contrast, in a state like California, a judge who has served for some period of time is being looked at on the basis of the decisions he or she has made in that position. Evaluation inevitably focuses upon the results of those decisions. That is a substantial difference between the state retention process and the federal appointment process.

There is another difference as well. A justice of the United States Supreme Court participates in the making of decisions which are, for all practical purposes, irreversible except to the extent that they may be reversed by some future court or in the extremely unlikely event that there is an amendment to the federal Constitution. At the state level, there is nothing that a state court justice does that cannot be "corrected," if that is the proper word, either by the United States Supreme Court in the case of decisions involving the federal Constitution or federal statutes, or by the state legislature, or by the people acting through initiative. . . . Federal court decisions are more difficult to change, and on that basis one might argue that if any judges should be subject to election, it should be federal judges. And yet for the reasons that Justice Richardson has set forth — historical reasons based upon populism — we have, unlike every other democratic system in the world, a system of electing or subjecting state court judges to retention or confirmation elections.

Justice Richardson has indicated some of the problems that flow from such a system and I want to elaborate on those briefly.

He has talked about the serious problem of campaign funding. . . .

Even more serious . . . is what I have called the pollution of the atmosphere which results from a judicial campaign in which attention inevitably focuses upon the results of judges' decisions in particular cases. The public is invited to vote for or against the judge on the basis of the same criteria involved in the election of a candidate for a legislative or executive office.

It may very well be that 91 percent of the judges of the State of California believe such a system has had no effect upon their decisions. I would like very much to believe that myself. In fact, I used to say in the course of the election that it was my goal to be able to go to bed election night knowing that I did not vote any differently on account of the pendency of the election than I would otherwise have voted. And I think that that's true, but to be quite honest with you, I cannot be sure. . . .

In a situation in which the governor of the State of California and others were saying that the candidates should be evaluated on the basis of their votes in death penalty cases, and in which records were being compared on the basis of how many cases we had voted to reverse and how many cases we had voted to affirm, I have to tell you quite honestly that I cannot be sure in my own mind whether I bent over backward or bent over forward or stood straight up with respect to difficult death penalty cases that were pending in the court at the time. Despite whether the campaign influenced me . . . or any other judge and whether we think that it did, the public perception that it did was certainly there. . . .

There has been too little discussion of the relationship between judicial elections and what it is that we expect of judges, our notion of the judicial function. . . . We know that judgments entail sometimes difficult policy considerations to which reasonable people will differ. We do not pretend that judges are "the living oracles"of the law, as Blackstone put it, or that they interpret the body of principles in some esoteric way the common folk are not capable of understanding. Judges are human beings and they inevitably bring to the decision of cases something of their own background and outlook.

At the same time we have the notion, or if we do not we should, that the process of judging is a great deal more than bringing to bear one's personal predilections. We have the notion that there is such a thing as a rule of law. We have the notion that judges are supposed to reach decisions at times with which they would disagree if they were in the legislature; that they have an obligation to interpret statutes in good faith to match the legislative intent or implement the legislative purpose; that they have an obligation to interpret and apply common law principles in good faith in order to continue a tradition and not make an idiosyncratic breakthrough. We have the notion that even in the arena of constitutional law, when dealing with the most flexible and furry-edged concepts of the Constitution, that judges have an obligation not simply to look within their hearts or spirits or emotions but to bring to bear as best they can the spirit of the law as reflected in the history of interpretation of the constitutional provision and the values that can legitimately be found to be expressed there. We expect judges at times to make decisions with which they themselves disagree in terms of the results. And even more significantly, we expect judges at times to make decisions with which a majority of the people, at least at the moment, will disagree because that too is part, and perhaps the most important part, of the constitutional function of judicial review.

What I am talking about is not simply a matter of fairness to candidates for judicial office. . . . We are talking about the integrity of the process. We are talking about the integrity of the judicial function and that is what is threatened by an election system characterized by the quick fix, statistics, 30-second television spots, and the focus upon results.

Where do I come out? . . . Would I prefer to substitute a system of lifetime appointments if I could? Yes, I suppose I would. At least for the appellate bench. The trial bench is characterized by different considerations. The trial bench confronts the public, it confronts lawyers and litigants who have a right to expect they will be treated with decency. A trial judge acts alone and does not have the constraints imposed by the collegial process. Many of his decisions do not require explication or justification by opinion as we require of appellate courts. So I make no argument concerning getting rid of elections for trial judges. As to appellate judges, I would prefer that we conform our state system to the federal system and to the system of every other democratic country in the world which regards the election of judges as something of an anomaly and a joke. But I do not think that is going to happen, so that is not something that I am going to spend a lot of time worrying about. . . .

ABA STANDARDS RELATING TO COURT ORGANIZATION (1990)[25]

1.21 Selection of Judges. . . .

(b) Procedure for selecting judges. Judges should be selected through a procedure in which for each judicial vacancy as it occurs (including the creation of a new judicial office) a judicial nominating commission nominates at least three qualified candidates, of whom the governor appoints one to office.

(i) The judicalicial nominating commission should be constituted of eight members as follows: The chief justice of the highest court, or a justice of that court designated by the chief justice, should be a member ex officio, and should be the commission's presiding officer, but should not have a vote. Four public members, who are neither judges nor lawyers, should be appointed to the commission by the governor, for staggered terms of at least three years. Three members of the legal profession should be appointed to the commission for staggered terms of at least three years. Lawyer members should not be eligible for nomination to a judicial position during their service on the commission and for three years thereafter. The lawyer members should be selected by a mandatory bar association that includes all active members of the bar in its membership, or by an election of all active members of the bar where there is no such bar association. In states with large or geographically separate populations, a nominating commission should be established on a statewide basis for appellate judges, and separate commissions on a regional basis for judges of the trial courts. The judicial member of a district nominating commission should be a supreme court justice or intermediate appellate court judge designated by the chief justice and chosen on the basis of special familiarity with the bench and bar of the district involved. When a judge is a candidate for reappointment or for higher judicial office, the judge should recuse sua sponte or on motion of opposing counsel in every case before that judge in which a nominating commission member is a party or counsel.

---

[25] Copyright © 1990 by the American Bar Association. Reprinted with permission.

(ii) The commission should be provided with training and staff assistance. It should maintain an inventory of qualified nominees by actively and continually soliciting names of persons suggested as potential nominees or persons who have expressed their interest in being nominated. The appointment procedure should be as follows: Within 30 days after the occurrence of a vacancy in a judicial office with respect to which it has nominating authority, the commission should submit to the governor, and simultaneously make public, the names of at least three persons qualified for appointment to the office. Fewer than three names may be submitted if the commission certifies that there are not three persons with the requisite qualifications, but at least two names should be submitted for each vacancy. The governor should appoint one of those nominated; if the governor fails to do so within 30 days after the list of nominations has been submitted, the chief justice should select an appointee from the list of nominees.

(iii) The person so selected should hold office: (A) for a preliminary term of two years and until the next general election thereafter when the judge's name should be submitted, without opposing candidates, for confirmation or rejection by the electorate in the area served by the court to which appointed, and, if confirmed should serve an initial and subsequent terms, until reaching retirement, of a specified number of years, subject to confirmation by the electorate at the end of each term in the same manner as the initial confirmation; or (B) subject to periodic review, until reaching the age of retirement, of the judge's fitness to hold office; or (C) during good behavior until reaching the age of retirement.

NOTES

1. In states where judicial nominating commissions are used (the so-called Missouri Plan), the composition of the commissions varies in size and types of members. Some commissions are larger and have more lawyers than the commission recommended in the foregoing standard. Is it a good idea for lawyers to outnumber lay members on a judicial nominating commission? What is the argument for having a majority of law members?

2. As of August 2004, "Twenty-one states hold elections for judges serving on courts of last resort: 8 use partisan elections, 13 use nonpartisan elections. In 23 states and the District of Columbia, judges are appointed to the highest court by the governor with the assistance of a judicial nominating commission. In [four states] the governor appoints these judges without the aid of a nominating commission [and in two states] Supreme Court judges are chosen by the legislature. . . . Of the 41 states that have intermediate appellate courts, 17 elect appellate judges: 6 states use partisan elections and 11 states use nonpartisan elections. Four states use appointments without a nominating commission (2 allow the governor to appoint judges and 2 allow the legislature to select judges). Twenty states use a judicial nominating commission to help the governor appoint judges to intermediate appellate courts." Larry C. Berkson, updated by Rachel Caufield, *Judicial Selection in the United States: A Special Report*, at 6-7 http://www.ajs.org/js/berkson_2005.pdf.

3. In *Chisom v. Roemer*, 501 U.S. 380 (1991), registered black voters sued under the Federal Voting Rights Act, challenging the method of electing Justices for the Louisiana Supreme Court on the grounds that the election of two Justices at-large from the New Orleans area impermissibly diluted minority voting strength. One aspect of the case required the Court to decide whether a particular sentence of the Act applied to the election of judges. That sentence stated that a violation of the act is established "if, based on the totality of circumstances, it is shown that the political processes leading to nomination or election in the State or political subdivision are not equally open to participation" by members of a class of citizens based on race or color in that those citizens "have less opportunity than other members of the electorate . . . to elect representatives of their choice." The Court held that the above-quoted section of the Voting Rights Act did apply to these judicial elections. It relied in part on its conclusion that where each of several members of a court were required to reside in a district different from that in which other court members resided, and had to be elected by the voters of that district, "it was reasonable and realistic to characterize the winners as representatives of that district." The Court also relied in part on the anomaly that would exist if a state could not implement a new voting procedure that would have discriminatory effects in judicial elections but could not be challenged for maintaining a similarly discriminatory system. Apart from the interpretation of the Voting Rights Act, is there anything troubling about the concept of judges as "representatives"?

4. Is the decision in *Chisom* likely to motivate states to adopt a nominating commission system for the selection of judges?

5. The New Jersey Constitution provides that "the governor shall nominate and, by and with the consent of the senate, shall appoint judges of the superior court." N.J. CONST. art. VI, § 6,¶ 1. The state senate has a long standing custom of "senatorial courtesy," under which the senator from the district that includes part of the nominee's home county or judicial district may in effect veto the nomination by refusing to consent; the senate thereupon declines to consent simply by not acting on the nomination. That practice was judicially challenged on the ground that senatorial courtesy violated the above quoted provision of the state constitution. The trial court dismissed the action on the ground that it presented a political, and thus non-justiciable, question. On appeal, the Supreme Court of New Jersey affirmed the judgment by an equally divided court and without an opinion of the court. *DeVesa v. Dorsey*, 634 A.2d 493 (N.J. 1993).

In a concurring opinion, joined by two others, Justice Stewart Pollock explained that the state constitution committed to the state senate the procedure through which that body gives or withholds its "consent" to judicial nominations. He relied in part upon the U.S. Supreme Court's decision in *Nixon v. United States*, 506 U.S. 224 (1993). In *Nixon*, a federal district judge who had been removed from office by a vote of the Senate finding him guilty on impeachment articles preferred by the House of Representatives brought suit challenging the Senate's procedure of appointing a special committee of twelve to receive evidence and report its findings to the Senate, which then debated the case on the floor and took a vote of the entire Senate. The removed judge contended that this committee hearing system was in violation of article I, section 3, of the Constitution requiring the Senate to "try all impeachments." The Supreme Court held that the action should be dismissed because it presented a political question.

B.   FEDERAL APPELLATE JUDGES

The process for appointing federal appellate judges has become so contentious in recent years that it is easy to regard it with a jaundiced eye. Recognizing that danger, we present here first some writings from not so long ago that reflect how the system worked over a considerable number of years. Then we will address some of the problems that are afflicting the system today.

Larry Berkson, Scott Beller & Michele Grimaldi, *Judicial Selection In The United States: A Compendium Of Provisions* 7-8 (1981)[26]

Unlike the wide variation in state methods for selecting judges, the federal scheme has remained relatively stable until quite recently. At the Constitutional Convention of 1787, there was considerable disagreement among the delegates about how to appoint justices of the supreme court and judges of other courts that might be established. In the final days of the Convention they settled upon a method that had been proposed by Alexander Hamilton. The President was granted authority to nominate and, with the advice and consent of the Senate, to appoint justices of the supreme court. As a matter of practice, the President has appointed lower federal court judges as well.

From the very beginning, however, senators played the dominate role in selecting federal judges. They were quick to realize that judgeships could be used to reward loyal political supporters. In one of the first confirmation cases, President Washington's nomination of Benjamin Fishbourn to be an officer of the Port of Savannah was defeated when the two Georgia senators opposed him. Ultimately, Washington nominated the senators' choice and the senate then gave its consent to the nomination. This practice, known as senatorial courtesy, was soon extended to judicial confirmations. To avoid invocation of courtesy, Presidents were required to consult with senators from the state in which an appointment was to be made and to nominate a person acceptable to the senators of that state.

[As with the original methods of selecting state judges, the federal system has been constantly challenged.] Four amendments were proposed in Congress to alter the process during the first 90 days of the Constitution's existence and more than 40 were offered between 1889 and 1944. During the past two decades, attention to the process has increased even more dramatically. It has been primarily criticized for allowing mediocre and unqualified individuals to ascend the bench solely because of their political connections.

---

[26] Copyright © 1981. Reprinted with permission of the American Judicature Society.

In 1974 the first major change took place in the selection of federal judges. That year Democratic Senators Lawton Chiles and Richard Stone created a nominating commission to aid them in recruiting and screening candidates for the federal district bench in Florida. Two years later the Democratic senators from Kentucky implemented a similar system. [In 1980], 47 U.S. senators in 29 states use[d] commissions to aid them in selecting federal district judges.

In 1977 President Carter created the United States Circuit Judge Nominating Commission to aid him in selecting federal circuit judges. Historically, senators have not acquired complete control over the selection of these judges because the circuits cover more than one state and thus no senator or pair of senators can reasonably claim that they should have the right of veto. The Commission [wa]s composed of 13 panels, one for each judicial circuit with two for the geographically large Fifth and Ninth Circuits. It recruit[ed], screen[ed], interview[ed] and recommend[ed] approximately five candidates to the President for each vacancy. Through May 1980, the President had appointed 50 circuit judges who had been recommended by the Commission.

[After his inauguration in 1981, President Reagan discontinued the United States Circuit Judge Nominating Commission.]

Rayman L. Solomon, *The Politics of Appointment and The Federal Courts' Role In Regulating America: U.S. Courts of Appeals Judgeships From T.R. to F.D.R.*, 1984 AMERICAN BAR FOUNDATION RESEARCH JOURNAL 285, 290-93[27]

B. *The Mechanics of the Politics of Appointment*

1. Senatorial Levers

. . . Article II, section 2 describes only the formal structural prerequisites of the appointment of a federal judge: the president should place the name of the candidate before the Senate, and a majority of the Senate must approve the nomination before the candidate may receive his commission. The ideal of presidential autonomy in selecting lower federal court judges — the heart of an effective Hamiltonian system of checks and balances — could not survive the realities of American political development.

. . . The Senate's predominance in the federal government after the Civil War stood the Hamiltonian system on its head and saw the Senate virtually dictating lower federal court appointments to the president. Political scientists who have studied the politics of appointment have noted that in the twentieth century presidents have reasserted some control over appointments of court of appeals judges. They have described the political factors and institutional arrangements that determine the ability of a senator or a president to influence selection of appellate judges. To exercise control over an appointment a senator must be from the president's own party and from the state where the vacancy occurs. The more senior a senator is or the greater his power in the

---

[27] Copyright © 1984. Reprinted with permission of the University of Chicago Press.

Senate (such as being chair of the Judiciary Committee) or in the national party hierarchy, the more influential he will be in the selection process.

Senatorial courtesy and its corollary "the blue slip" are the procedural mechanisms by which senators seek to exercise their power in the selection process. As the Senate's only formal power in the process comes from its ability to block a judicial nomination, a senator who does not accept a presidential choice can attempt either to prevent a nomination from clearing the Judiciary Committee or to defeat it on the Senate floor. The blue slip provides a way to accomplish the former: A nomination is not reported favorably out of committee unless the senior senator of the president's party from the nominee's home state has signed and returned the blue slip indicating he has no objection to the nomination. Senatorial courtesy, which apparently developed during the high-water mark of the Senate's power in the late nineteenth century, is an informal custom among senators that originally required senators to vote against a presidential nominee when a senator from the president's own party and from the nominee's state declared that the nominee was "personally obnoxious" to him.

2. *Presidential Levers*

The president has several major weapons to use in resisting a senator's attempts to nominate a court of appeals judge. First, he has the advantage of timing. Since only the president has the constitutional power to nominate, he can simply refuse to send a senator's choice to the Senate, thus trying to create public pressure on the senator to eliminate the impasse and allow the nomination of a new judge for an overworked court. The president can also attempt to use timing to his advantage by making a recess appointment, which requires no immediate Senate approval. He can hope that by the time the Senate convenes, his candidate will have proved himself so worthy that failure to confirm would be difficult. Second, the president can attempt to move a court of appeals judgeship from one state to another. When a senator insists on a candidate unacceptable to the president, the president may try to select a judge from a neighboring state. This is possible because U.S. statutes allocate court of appeals judgeships to a circuit, not to a particular state. A circuit judge need only be a resident of one of the states within the circuit. A third tactic available to the president (but also to the senator) is to use negative evaluations by either the FBI or American Bar Association's Standing Committee on Federal Judiciary to try to block the choice. A president can expect that a finding by the ABA that a candidate is unqualified will cause the senator to drop his support because he will not want to try weathering the publicity storm associated with backing an "unqualified" nominee.

The preceding discussion has concerned *how* a president or a senator attempts to impose or block a choice for judge of the U.S. Courts of Appeals. *Why* a senator does so appears obvious. Senators seek to maximize their influence over selections of federal appellate court judges because those judgeships are an important component of the federal patronage available to a senator. The positions are coveted by many influential lawyers, and a skillful judicial selection offers a senator the opportunity to expand or reinforce his political coalition.

But little attention has been paid to exploring why a president would not simply defer to senatorial recommendations. After all, a president dependent on state electoral votes provided by his party's state organization should welcome a chance to bolster his standing with the highest elected federal office holder in the state by nominating the senator's choice for a judgeship. In addition, going along with the senator's selection usually rewards a member of the president's party who will have to vote on the president's legislative program. However, there are three typical situations in which the president may become more active in the selection process. The first exists when there are intraparty splits within the state. If two senators are from opposite factions of the president's party, or if there is only one senator from the president's party and he is from a faction opposing the president, the president will intervene in the selection process in an effort to reward those from his faction of the party by denying the opposing senator the opportunity to select the court of appeals judge. Second, a president may be convinced that a senator's choice is not qualified for the position of federal appellate judge, either because the candidate lacks the ability (*e.g.*, intelligence, training) or character (*e.g.*, honesty, temperament) to be a judge. A third situation exists when the administration perceives that the decisions the judge will probably be called on to render will have an effect on the administration's pursuit of policies. In other words, when lower federal courts assume a significant enough role in the administration of federal policy that a president perceives this nexus, the president will attempt to achieve a major role in determining who the judges are.

C. *The Patterns of Appointment*

The three situations described above represent different presidential motivations. The first situation evidences presidential concern with patronage; the second, concern with professional standing; the third, concern with policy. These concerns are related to presidential ideas about the role of the federal government and the role of the courts.

In an administration that has a minimalist view of the federal government's responsibility for effecting economic, social, and political change and that views the work of the federal courts as unimportant to its ability to carry out this minimalist view, patronage considerations will tend to dominate the selection of court of appeals judges. In such an administration the president will either generally defer to the senator's choice or will intervene only to choose between factions. When patronage considerations dominate, the president's primary concern is not a candidate's position on issues or his standing among professional groups but who supports the candidate. The immediate political impact of a nomination receives the most scrutiny.

However, in an administration that perceives the role of the federal government as limited but sees court of appeals judges as potentially important (if limited) policy makers, concern about professionalism will dominate. The judicial model for such administrations was the common law ideal; judges were to be trained experts in the law who decided cases by closely reasoning from precedent, not by politics. Policy making by judges was to be incremental and essentially conservative. This model of professionalism places great importance on perceptions of a candidate's potential judicial abilities. Judicial experience, intelligence, and craftsmanship are the qualities sought. A candidate's reputation as a "lawyer's lawyer" counts more than the political value of the appointment or the appointee's views on public issues. Recommendations are sought from elites in state and local bars and from bar associations.

Finally, when administrations attempt to use the federal government to effect economic, social, and political change — and thereby involve the courts of appeals in deciding cases whose outcomes influence the programs the administration favors — policy considerations dominate. When this occurs, a judicial candidate's attitudes toward public policy issues will be investigated. The candidate's policy orientation will determine selection more than political recommendation or professional standing.

Mitchel A. Sollenberger, *The Law: Must the Senate Take a Floor Vote on a Presidential Judicial Nominee?* 34 PRESIDENTIAL STUDIES QUARTERLY 420 (2004)[28]

. . . [On October 30, 2002, President George W. Bush proposed a plan to enforce mandatory confirmation votes on his judicial nominees.] [T]he plan called on every sitting federal judge "to notify the President of their intention to retire at least a year in advance" if at all possible. After the notification . . . the president would have up to 180 days to submit a nomination to the Senate. The Senate Judiciary Committee would then have 90 days . . . to hold a hearing. Finally, the Senate would be required to hold "an up-or-down floor vote on each nominee no later than 180 days after the nomination is submitted.". . .

The fundamental argument . . . that the Senate has a duty to take floor votes on all judicial nominations does not have . . . clear-cut benefits for the Senate as an institution. . . . [M]andatory votes preclude the Senate from functioning as a check on the executive branch if a president seeks to aggrandize his power in the confirmation process. . . .

This article details how the Senate conducts its advice and consent responsibility and evaluates whether its current handling of the confirmation process follows a well-ordered constitutional design. . . .

The Lower Court Confirmation Process

The process for making lifetime appointments to judgeships in the U.S. district courts and U.S. circuit courts of appeals involves a number of formal and informal steps that are not widely known or thought of as being constitutionally mandated. . . . [S]enators exercise a great deal of control over the fate of judicial nominees. Most of that power is derived from the concept of senatorial courtesy, a long-held Senate tradition, which promotes deference of one senator to another. Additionally, . . . [v]arious steps have been created not only to restrain the executive branch but also to serve as a final review of those who may ultimately be given powerful lifetime appointments. . . .

[T]he concept of senatorial courtesy goes beyond the confines of the Senate and, at times, represents the courtesy a president extends, or arguably should

---

[28] Copyright © 2004 by Blackwell Publishing. Reprinted with permission.

extend, to senators. . . . By tradition, senators of the state where there is a vacancy to either a U.S. circuit or district court judgeship have a strong say in the selection for that position. Presidents often give great weight or even defer to home-state senators of their own party in the selection of federal judges. In recent years, senators of the minority party have at times been given the opportunity to become involved in the selection stage. . . . [P]olitical scientist Harold Chase does well in describing its basic origin:

> Senators . . . must continuously nurture their political support back home; . . . senators from the First Congress on have recognized that one or two senators have a much greater stake in a particular appointment than others. It is, of course, exceedingly helpful to a senator to be able to reward supporters with good posts in the federal government. Conversely, it is enormously damaging to a senator's prestige if a president of his own party ignores him when it comes to making an appointment from or to the senator's own state. What is even more damaging to a senator's prestige and political power is for the president to appoint to high federal office someone who is known back home as a political opponent to the senator. It was easy for senators to see that if they joined together . . . to protect their individual interests in appointments, they could to a large degree assure that the president could only make such appointments as would be palatable to them as individuals. Out of such considerations grew the custom of senatorial courtesy.

The courtesy a president extends to senators is now augmented by closer legislative oversight of the federal judiciary. Senators are increasingly willing to block judicial nominees they see as being outside the mainstream of legal thinking. . . .

Senatorial courtesy, in this respect, provides home-state senators with a real veto power well before a nomination is submitted. Despite this power, however, some believe that senators cannot force the president to make a selection he does not want. . . .

Once the president submits the nomination in writing to the Senate, he . . . places his selection at the mercy of the Senate. The process in the Senate is rather straightforward. On the same day the nomination is received, it usually is referred by the Senate executive clerk to the Committee on the Judiciary. . . . Following referral, the Judiciary Committee will send out a number of documents relating to the nomination. The blue slip, committee questionnaire, and financial disclosure statement are all tools used by the Judiciary Committee to primarily gain information about a nomination; however, the documents can also serve as devices to delay and prevent committee action as well.

Blue Slips

One of the oldest devices used by the committee, the blue slip, is a central component in the confirmation process. The blue slip is used by the Judiciary Committee chairman to seek the assessment of senators concerning judicial nominees from their home states. . . . The blue slip . . . is issued by the committee counsel to the senators of the state where the president has nominated the individual. For a period of over 20 years (1956-1979), the blue slip gave senators absolute control in preventing confirmation of their home-state nominations. All a home-state senator had to do to stop committee action was to fail to return the blue slip or return it with a negative response. This effectively stopped the nomination from moving in committee and in turn prevented a Senate confirmation vote as well.

Although the committee does not presently permit home-state senators to have absolute control, recent history shows that the committee still gives due consideration to the assessments of home-state senators. In fact, if a negative blue slip is returned, action almost always slows or stops. . . . The blue slip has the power to prevent committee action even when the presidency and the Senate are controlled by the same party. . . .

[C]ritics charge that a few individual senators have improperly taken the Senate's advice and consent role and used it for their own political benefit. . . . Yet, the blue slip . . . is a mechanism that encourages the president to consult with senators about their home-state nominations. . . .

Numerous Judiciary Committee chairmen have defended the blue slip because it gives balance to the otherwise disproportionate relationship between the president and a senator. . . . [T]he blue slip offers home-state senators a means to enforce senatorial courtesy on a president. Such a courtesy by the committee does not offend constitutional requirements, but in fact works to promote the advice and consent function. Without a blue slip policy, the president would have little incentive to consult with the Senate, and its individual members would be cut out of the advice phase by being effectively excluded from the selection process.

Questionnaires, Financial Disclosure Reports, and Outside Sources

The Judiciary Committee also uses questionnaires and financial disclosure reports. Unlike the blue slip, the questionnaire and financial disclosure report are based primarily on the Senate's review function. . . . The questionnaire, first instituted in the late 1970s by Chairman Edward Kennedy, has given the committee an added layer in the review process to investigate judicial nominations without the aid of the executive branch or the need to rely solely on home-state senators.

Unlike questions submitted by individual senators, the questionnaire remains largely unchanged from congress to congress. For example, besides the standard background information concerning name, address, and other personal history, the committee asks the nominee to provide if he or she was a judge a summary of . . . the ten "most significant opinions you have written" and "all rulings of yours that were reversed or significantly criticized on appeal." In addition, the committee looks at the litigation history of each nominee while they were in public service or private practice. Finally, the questionnaire addresses the circumstances that led to the nominee's selection. In the last question in the section, the committee asks whether . . . :

> anyone involved in the process of selecting you as a judicial nominee discussed with you any specific case, legal issue or question in a manner that could reasonably be interpreted as asking or seeking a commitment as to how you would rule on such case, issue, or question.

This question was first instituted . . . several years ago to ensure that neither the executive nor legislative branches violates the separation of powers principle when screening candidates for the judiciary. Although this question cannot provide an absolute guarantee that improper influence is not sought by the president or members of the Senate, it does show that the committee is at least concerned with this problem and tries to provide a corrective measure.

In addition to the questionnaire, the financial disclosure report provides the committee with another investigative tool. . . . Required by the Ethics in Government Act of 1978, the report . . . calls for the nominee to provide information concerning his or her income, assets, and liabilities. Unlike the executive branch's standard form 278 (Public Financial Disclosure Report), the report for judicial nominees has various restrictions on public access. . . .

Over the years, important information on nominees has also come from outside sources [including the Justice Department.] . . . Other outside sources tend to be nongovernmental organizations such as interest groups. Although these groups have no formal role in the confirmation process, they help committee and individual senators' staff investigate the various judicial nominees' backgrounds. For instance, the Alliance for Justice played a key role in voicing concern over President Bush's judicial nominations. . . . On the Republican side, members of the Federalist Society have worked in the executive branch in aiding in the selection of judicial nominations. . . .

ABA Reports

The American Bar Association's reports on judicial nominations are another important factor in committee review. Even though both political parties have attacked the ABA over the years, the organization's reports have become a valued part of the confirmation process. Traditionally, if questions have been raised by the ABA or the legal community, the Judiciary Committee will often look seriously at the charges raised. The committee has a history of not reporting a nomination to the full Senate if the ABA submits a negative review. . . .

Committee Hearings

Except for the blue slip, the devices used to review judicial nominees usually do not stop a nominee from receiving a hearing. . . . If important information is discovered during committee review then a hearing is often the only time the nominee will be able to publicly answer the charges raised. At the hearing, committee members have the opportunity to ask the nominee questions and, in turn, the nominee is permitted to clarify his/her record. The pro forma quality of most hearings produces little public attention. At times, however, the controversial nature of a nominee or the manner in which a nominee answers a senator's questions may have a substantial effect on how the committee moves forward. . . .

In addition to the questions asked during a committee hearing, senators might want the nominee to submit a more detailed explanation in writing. . . . Another variant of such a request occurs when a senator submits to the nominee detailed written questions. . . .

Committee hearings are not required by either Senate or Judiciary Committee rules. Over the last 20 years the Judiciary Committee has not acted on a number of nominees. In the 106th Congress, 19 of President

Clinton's circuit court nominations did not receive a hearing. In the 107th Congress, President Bush did not fare much better. Twelve of his circuit court nominations did not receive hearings. If a hearing is not held, the nominee will usually not be voted out of committee. Yet even if a hearing is held, it may prove inadequate. Although rare, the chairman may call for an additional hearing if he or other senators feel an issue has not been fully addressed. . . .

Committee Votes

Once the chairman determines that all relevant issues have been covered, a vote on whether to report the nominee is usually scheduled. Sometimes, for various reasons, a committee vote is not taken. The most common reason a vote is not taken relates to the legislative agenda of Congress. At the end of a session of Congress, the Senate is often trying to pass important bills before it recesses. Therefore, if a nominee is submitted well into a Congress, the committee and Senate may not have the time or ability to move through all of the procedural steps required to confirm the nominee. . . . [T]he blue slip, committee questionnaire, financial disclosure, or outside sources can also keep a nominee in committee. Nothing in the Senate or committee rules requires the chairman to schedule a vote on a judicial nominee.

If a vote is called, committee rules permit a delay of that vote (usually for one week) at the request of any committee member (Judiciary Committee 2003, Rule 1, Part 3). . . . [W]hen a vote does occur, in most instances the outcome will be to report favorably. . . . [If] the committee . . . vote[s] other than favorably . . . , the committee can choose . . . : (1) to table the nomination, (2) to report without recommendation, or (3) to report unfavorably. The nomination moves on to the Senate floor if the committee agrees to report favorably, to report without recommendation, or to report unfavorably. If a motion to table the nomination is passed, or if the committee decides not to report, the nomination remains in committee.

. . . In the last 50 years, only one nomination . . . has been tabled. A total of eight judicial nominations have failed to reach the Senate floor because of a negative vote to report out of committee. . . .

Executive Calendar

If reported out of committee, the nomination will be listed on the Executive Calendar. At this point, the majority leader has the discretion to determine when and even whether a nomination will receive a confirmation vote. Senate rules do not require him to schedule a nomination for consideration. . . . For the most part, such delays are the result of Senate rules and customs that prevent the majority leader from bringing a nomination to vote.

Holds

One of the means a senator can use to stop a confirmation vote is through use of a hold. . . . [A] hold is an informal device that blocks action on measures scheduled for floor consideration. The majority leader decides whether he will honor the hold and for how long. Holds are generally honored because . . . senatorial courtesy plays an important part in conducting Senate business. Each senator has the ability to create a lot of mischief, and without the consent of all its members, no measure would be passed easily in the Senate.

Traditionally, holds have not been used on judicial nominations, but in recent years they have become an important tool in confirmation battles. Indeed, to varying degrees a hold can be used as a strategic leverage against the president. . . . [I]n 1989 Senator Jeffords used a hold to force President George H. W. Bush to select his choice to a district court judgeship. More often, a hold will be used to delay or even prevent confirmation of a judicial nomination. . . .

Filibusters

. . . [T]he power of the device [the filibuster] is largely founded on the threat of senators speaking for as long as they wish — thus bringing to a halt Senate business, and in the case of judicial nominations, preventing an up-or-down vote. The right to debate is based on Senate Rule XIX, which states that "No Senator shall interrupt another Senator in debate without his consent." Usually senators cannot be forced to cede the floor, or even be interrupted, without their consent. Couple this right with the lack of time limits on debate and this creates the possibility of filibusters.

The only exception is if Senate Rule XXII, referred to as the cloture rule, is invoked. The rule permits a senator to submit a motion, signed by 16 other senators, "to bring to a close the debate." A vote on the cloture motion cannot be held until two days after it is presented. After the motion has ripened, the Senate will vote on the motion to end debate. It takes three fifths of the Senate, or 60 senators, to invoke cloture.

Filibusters are rarely used to prevent the confirmation of judicial nominations. The first filibuster of a judicial nominee occurred in 1968 when Supreme Court Justice Abe Fortas was being elevated to the chief justice position by President Lyndon Johnson. . . . [The] filibuster . . . led to a presidential withdrawal of the nomination later in the congress. This was the only successful filibuster of a judicial nominee until the 108th Congress, when President Bush withdrew his DC Circuit nominee, Miguel Estrada, after several attempts of invoking cloture had failed. . . .

The filibuster, along with the above-stated Senate rules and precedents, creates the possibility to delay or even prevent a confirmation vote. What the filibuster or even a threat of one produces is a reality that a confirmation vote cannot occur without the tacit consent of each senator. This permits even the party out of power to wield substantial power over the fate of each judicial nominee the president submits to the Senate. Supporters of mandatory up-or-down votes argue that the founding fathers did not envision that 60 votes would be needed to fulfill the Senate's advice and consent duty. Yet, the plain words of the Constitution do not indicate a limit on senatorial consent. One must remember that the ability of three fifths of the Senate to cut off debate was not even an established rule in the Senate during its first 100 plus years. Not until 1917 could even two thirds of the Senate stop its members from preventing an up-or-down vote from occurring, and before that time any piece of legislation could be blocked by just one senator.

The Constitution does not dictate how the Senate shall handle a president's judicial nominations. Neither do the core Senate rules relating to voting override Senate Rule XIX, which governs the application of unlimited debate. Only under a cloture vote can a filibuster be overridden. Still, supporters of a mandatory up-or-down vote state that this super-majority requirement of 60 votes is unconstitutional because the Constitution expressly dictates when there should be super-majority votes, such as the two-thirds requirement on treaty ratifications. As with most parts of the Constitution, the Framers created vague language that is not easily interpreted. . .

Judicial Nominations and the Right to a Vote

In terms of how the Senate has traditionally applied its advice and consent duty, the presumption that a Senate vote must occur does not survive the weight of evidence. Neither Senate rules nor precedents support the assumption that a president's nomination must receive a timely up-or-down vote. The record demonstrates that confirmation votes are neither timely nor absolute. . . . The Constitution is not clear on whether the Framers required up-or-down votes. Two centuries of Senate procedure offer little support for that proposition [that the Senate should conduct business under majority rule].

. . . As the president has stated, "[b]ecause of the Senate's failure to hold timely votes, the number of judicial vacancies has become unacceptably high. When the Federal courts are understaffed, they cannot act in a timely manner to resolve disputes that affect the lives and liberties of all Americans." However, . . . the judicial branch is only 44 judges from reaching maximum capacity. Even if more judges are required than currently called for by statute, that is a question that should be addressed through legislation, not constitutional conflict. . . .

The Sovereign Power of the Senate

. . . Senate rules that permit a senator to delay or stop a confirmation vote are currently under attack because some believe that majority rule would serve the Senate better. The problem is that majority rule has rarely been a working concept within the Senate. For all practical purposes, the Senate works to strengthen, not weaken, minority power. That understanding goes back to the original design of the Senate. . . . [T]he devices used to block judicial nominations are rooted in history. Senators, because they represent sovereign states, still hold a measure of power that affords them the ability to block measures that would have a substantial effect on their states. An offshoot of such power is the ability to balance the president's role in the confirmation process and prevent an unchecked attempt to unilaterally control the selection and confirmation of judicial nominations. Therefore, any attempt to take away the institutional devices that promote both presidential and senatorial courtesy would most likely upset the balance of power between the two branches.

Conclusions

. . . By calling for [up-or-down votes on every judicial nominee], both the president and his supporters are in effect doing away with important constitutional principles such as checks and balances and separation of powers. The constitutional responsibility of advice and consent should not be dispensed with because it may be politically expedient. . . . [But t]he ability to protect the constitutional integrity of the Senate and the minority rights of its members serves to show that keeping the various devices that prevent up-or-down votes is best for the Constitution and the confirmation process.

NOTES

1. Rayman Solomon's description of the federal appointments process, while certainly recognizing the political nature of that process, sounds relatively tame. But as Sollenberger's article indicates, the process has become far more partisan and acrimonious in recent years than it sometimes has been. That acrimony is reflected in the scholarly writing of the day: it focuses on such matters as the propriety of filibusters of judicial nominations, how great a role ideology should have at both the nomination and the confirmation stages of the process, and the propriety of the President's making of recess appointments to temporarily escape Senatorial blocks of those whom the President wants to appoint. (Article II, Section 2, Clause 3, of the Constitution says that "The President shall have Power to fill up all Vacancies that may happen during the "Recess of the Senate, by granting Commissions which shall expire at the End of their next Session." In *Evans v. Stephens*, 387 F.3d 1220 (11th Cir. 2004) (en banc), the Eleventh Circuit upheld the applicability of this clause to judicial appointments, as the Ninth and Second Circuits had done in the past. The Eleventh Circuit refused to interpret "recess" narrowly and held the clause to apply when vacancies exist during a recess, although they predate it.)

Does the "ugliness" of this process in its current incarnation imply that a process in which the executive nominates and the legislature confirms (or refuses to confirm) judicial nominees is less desirable than popular election of judges? Or is the current contentiousness of the process merely a cautionary tale that even systems that are very good in theory can be "mucked up" by participants who are excessively partisan and "play the game" in too "hardball" a fashion? Is the federal appointments process still better than the alternatives? It has been observed that "The shift to direct election was an effort to escape the 'politics' of appointments and to improve the quality of those serving as judges, just as the shift away from elections is also argued as a necessary response to the 'politics' of elections and a quest for the qualified." Judith Resnik, *Judicial Selection and Democratic Theory: Demand, Supply, and Life Tenure*, 26 CARDOZO L. REV. 579, 594 (2005). What "tweaks" to the system might improve it?

2. Are you persuaded by Sollenberger's arguments that blue slips, committee votes, holds, and filibusters all are valuable aspects of the Senate's advise and consent role?

3. Professor Judith Resnik has noted that conflict over life-tenured judgeships has a very long history in this country dating back to the events that gave rise to *Marbury v. Madison*, 5 U.S. (1 Cranch) 137 (1803), and has argued that that conflict is neither surprising nor necessarily inappropriate in light of the power such judges hold, and the allocation of power to the President to nominate and to the Senate to confirm Article III judges. However, because of "the swelling ranks [of such judgeships] and information technologies making visible both the attitudes of nominees and voting patterns of appointees, politicians have come to see seats on the federal judiciary as an opportunity for . . . 'partisan entrenchment,' . . . [an opportunity] to extend temporally that party's authority to change the governing

legal regime." Resnik, *Judicial Selection and Democratic Theory*, 26 Cardozo L. Rev. at 587. (One might consider in this connection the role of the appointment of young judges who, as a practical matter, can have particularly long life-terms.) Thus, the stakes have become so high that some changes in the system might be appropriate.

Professor Resnik argues for requiring a super-majority to approve a nominee, as appropriate for our democracy, helpful in reducing presidents' sense of entitlement to appoint whom they like, and reflective of the kind of consensus that is appropriate to the unusual nature and duration of the power of life-tenured judges. She also argues for the creation of financial incentives for federal judges to step aside, or even the re-interpretation of Article III to permit fixed retirement times. *Id.* at 584, 588, 638, 641. What do you think of these suggestions?

4. In 1996 the Commission on the Selection of Federal Judges, established under the aegis of the Miller Center for Public Affairs at the University of Virginia, issued a report entitled 'Improving the Process of Appointing Federal Judges.' The report recommended numerous steps designed to expedite and simplify the process of nominating and confirming federal judges, including time tables for the various steps and the use of a single questionnaire for the prospective judge. Thus far, the report seems to have had little effect on the process.

5. As indicated in the reading above, the screening and evaluation of candidates by the ABA Standing Committee on Federal Judiciary sometimes has helped to provide common ground for Presidents and Senators. A description of that Committee's composition and how it has operated follows.

The ABA Standing Committee on Federal Judiciary: What it is and How it Works (2002)[29]

What it is and How it Works

The Standing Committee on Federal Judiciary of the American Bar Association consists of fifteen members — two members from the Ninth Circuit, one member from each of the other twelve federal judicial circuits and one member-at-large. . . . The members have varied backgrounds and professional experience and are appointed for staggered three-year terms by the President of the ABA. No member serves more than two terms.

The Committee evaluates the professional qualifications of persons nominated for appointment to the Supreme Court of the United States, courts of appeals, district courts, [and other federal tribunals]. . . . The Committee . . . restricts its evaluation to issues bearing on professional qualifications and does not consider a nominee's philosophy or ideology. . . .

. . . The ABA's Board of Governors, House of Delegates and Officers are not involved in any way in the work of the Committee. . . . Confidentiality in the Committee's evaluation procedures is a cornerstone of its effective operation.

---

[29] Copyright © 2002 by the American Bar Association. Reprinted with permission.

As a condition of appointment, each member agrees while on the Committee and for at least one year thereafter not to seek or accept federal judicial appointment and agrees while on the Committee not to participate in or contribute to any federal election campaign nor engage in partisan political activity. . . .

I. Appointments to Federal Courts Other than the Supreme Court

. . .

A.   Evaluation Criteria

The Committee's evaluation of nominees to these courts is directed to professional qualifications: integrity, professional competence and judicial temperament.

. . . The nominee's character and general reputation in the legal community are investigated, as are his or her industry and diligence.

Professional competence encompasses such qualities as intellectual capacity, judgment, writing and analytical ability, knowledge of the law and breadth of professional experience.

The Committee believes that ordinarily a nominee to the federal bench should have been admitted to the bar for at least twelve years and should have been engaged in the practice of law. In evaluating the experience of a nominee, the Committee recognizes that opportunities for advancement in the profession for women and members of minority groups may have been limited. Substantial courtroom and trial experience (as a lawyer or a trial judge) is important for nominees to both the appellate and the trial courts. Additional experience that is similar to in-court trial work — such as appearing before or serving on administrative agencies or arbitration boards, or teaching trial advocacy or other clinical law school courses — is considered by the Committee in evaluating a nominee's trial experience. Significant evidence of distinguished accomplishment in the field of law may compensate for a nominee's lack of substantial courtroom experience.

Recognizing that an appellate judge deals primarily with records, briefs, appellate advocates and colleagues (in contrast to witnesses, parties, jurors, live testimony and the theater of the courtroom), the Committee may place somewhat less emphasis on the importance of trial experience as a qualification for the appellate courts. On the other hand, although scholarly qualities are necessary for the trial courts, the Committee believes that appellate court nominees should possess an especially high degree of scholarship and academic talent and an unusual degree of overall excellence. The abilities to write lucidly and persuasively, to harmonize a body of law and to give guidance to the trial courts for future cases are considered in the evaluation of nominees for the appellate courts.

The Committee considers that civic activities and public service are valuable experiences, but that such activity and service are not a substitute for significant experience in the practice of law, whether that experience be in the private or public sector.

In investigating judicial temperament, the Committee considers the nominee's compassion, decisiveness, open-mindedness, courtesy, patience, freedom from bias and commitment to equal justice under the law.

B.   The Investigation

After a judicial vacancy occurs and a nomination is announced, the investigation of the nominee is usually assigned to the circuit member of the Committee in the judicial circuit in which the judicial vacancy exists, although it may be conducted by another member or a former member.

The Attorney General's office sends to each nominee a questionnaire (called the "Senate Judiciary Committee Questionnaire") that seeks wide-ranging information related to fitness for judicial service. The responses are sent to the U.S. Department of Justice, which then forwards the nominee's response to the public portion of the questionnaire to the ABA Committee Chair. (The non-public portion . . . solicits financial information . . . .) . . . [R]eceipt . . . is usually the starting point for the investigation. The circuit member makes extensive use of it in the investigation. . . .

The circuit member examines the legal writing of the nominee and personally conducts extensive confidential interviews with those likely to have information regarding the integrity, professional competence, and judicial temperament of the nominee including, where pertinent, federal and state judges, practicing lawyers in both private and government service, law school professors and deans, legal services and public interest lawyers, representatives of professional legal organizations, community leaders and others who are in a position to evaluate the nominee's integrity, professional competence and judicial temperament. In addition, comments from groups involved in the merit selection or evaluation of nominees for the federal judiciary may be received and considered.

Interviews are conducted under an assurance of confidentiality. If information adverse to the nominee is discovered, the circuit member will advise the nominee of such information if he or she can do so without breaching the promise of confidentiality. If not, the Committee will not consider those facts in its evaluation unless the persons disclosing them authorize disclosure, or the information is otherwise known by, and discussed with, the nominee. Sometimes a clear pattern emerges early in the interviews, and the investigation can be briskly concluded. In other cases, conflicting evaluations of professional competence may be received, or questions may arise regarding the nominee's integrity or temperament. In those instances, the circuit member takes whatever further steps are necessary to reach a fair and accurate assessment of the nominee. This may involve a large number of interviews as well as the examination of transcripts and other relevant records.

. . . [T]he circuit member, and in appropriate cases one or more other members of the Committee, meet with the nominee. . . . [T]he circuit member discusses with the nominee his or her qualifications for a judgeship and raises any adverse information discovered during the investigation. The nominee is given a full opportunity to rebut the adverse information and provide any additional information bearing on it. . . . [T]he circuit member may need to conduct additional interviews in order to complete the investigation.

If information concerning the health of the nominee arises . . . , the Committee's evaluation of the candidate may take that information into consideration.

In certain circumstances, one or more additional circuit members may be assigned to the investigation. For example, if the nominee's career has extended geographically over more than one circuit . . . , it is customary to ask the circuit member in each such circuit to conduct the relevant interviews in his or her own circuit. All information is exchanged among the participating members. A second investigator also may be appointed where it appears at any time during the evaluation process that the nominee may receive a "Not Qualified" rating. As a matter of fairness to the nominee, another member of the Committee may be asked to participate in the investigation, interview or reinterview the nominee and conduct whatever supplemental inquiries he or she feels appropriate. In some particularly difficult cases, more than one additional committee member may be asked to participate.

Upon conclusion of the investigation, the circuit member prepares a written informal report to the Chair containing a description of the nominee's background, summaries of all interviews conducted, including the interview with the nominee, an evaluation of his or her qualifications and a recommended rating.

The Chair receives the informal report and reviews it for thoroughness with the circuit member. The circuit member then prepares a formal or final written report and sends it to all members of the Committee, together with the nominee's response to the public portion of the questionnaire and copies of any other relevant information. If questions are raised, the Committee may discuss the nominee. . . . After careful consideration of the formal report and its enclosures, each member submits his or her rating vote to the Chair.

Once all votes are tallied, the Chair, by letter, advises the White House, the Office of the Attorney General, the Senate Judiciary Committee and the nominee of the Committee's rating. If the Committee has been unanimous in its rating, the Chair so states. Otherwise the Chair discloses that the nominee received the specific rating from a majority or substantial majority of the Committee, noting that a minority gave the nominee another stated rating or ratings. The majority rating is the official rating of the Committee.

C. Ratings

To merit a rating of "Well Qualified," the nominee must be at the top of the legal profession in his or her legal community, have outstanding legal ability, breadth of experience, the highest reputation for integrity and either have demonstrated, or exhibited the capacity for, judicial temperament. The evaluation of "Qualified" means that the nominee meets the Committee's very high standards with respect to integrity, professional competence and judicial temperament and that the Committee believes that the nominee will be able to perform satisfactorily all of the duties and responsibilities required by the high office of a federal judge.

When a prospective nominee is found "Not Qualified," the Committee, based on its investigation, has determined that the nominee does not meet the Committee's standards with regard to professional competence, judicial temperament or integrity. In that event, the Committee opposes the nomination in such ways as appear appropriate under the circumstances. This has traditionally taken the form of testimony by the Committee's Chair, presented upon the request of the Senate Judiciary Committee, at the nominee's confirmation hearing.

[A section concerning appointments to the U.S. Supreme Court is omitted.]

NOTES

1. The Standing Committee has not been without its critics. For example, Laurence H. Silberman, *The American Bar Association and Judicial Nominations*, 59 GEO.WASH. L. REV. 1092 (1991), criticized the Committee in a number of respects. The author had worked with the Committee as Deputy Attorney General, and later had been the object of its scrutiny when he was nominated for a federal appellate judgeship.

(a) Although Judge Silberman believed that the Committee performed valuable service in blocking efforts to place unqualified persons on the bench, he criticized the Committee for unduly emphasizing extensive trial experience and undervaluing other kinds of legal work (transactional, scholarly) and nonlegal work in the legislative and executive branches. *Id.* at 1093, 1099-1100. He attributed this distortion to the over-representation of litigators on the Committee and perhaps to a belief he attributed to many litigators that "those who ponder too much about the law are undesirable judges." *Id.* at 1100.

(b) Related, but more profoundly, Judge Silberman believed that the Committee had become a political factor in the process, despite its purpose to "restrain the influence of partisan politics in judicial selection." *Id.* at 1092. In particular, he pointed to use of the criterion of "judicial temperament" to rebuff nominees whose political views conflicted with those on the Committee. He pointed in particular to a period when "judicial temperament" was used "to rebuff those nominees whose political views were identified with the conservative wing of the Republican party or with notions of judicial restraint," and suggested that the controversial political positions taken by the ABA might disqualify the Standing Committee from performing a nonpolitical role. *Id.* at 1094-95.

(c) Judge Silberman found objectionable the confidential solicitation of the views of sitting judges on nominees, as inducing sitting judges to take an inappropriate role. *Id.* at 1097-98.

(d) And he criticized the Committee's overzealousness in evaluating nominees' integrity, opining that the Committee should vouch for nominees' reputation for integrity and leave it to the FBI to investigate the underlying truth. *Id.* at 1099.

2. *In Public Citizen v. United States Department of Justice*, 491 U.S. 440 (1989), the Washington Legal Foundation brought suit against the

Department of Justice after the ABA Standing Committee on Federal Judiciary, from which the DOJ regularly sought advice regarding potential nominees for federal judgeships, refused WLF's request for the names of potential judicial nominees it was considering and for the ABA Committee's reports of its meetings. The questions to be decided were whether the Federal Advisory Committee Act (FACA), as amended, applied to these consultations and, if it did, whether its application would interfere unconstitutionally with the President's prerogative under Article II to nominate and appoint officers of the United States, violate separation of powers doctrine, or unduly infringe the First Amendment right of members of the ABA to freedom of association and expression. If FACA were applicable, the ABA committee would have been required to make its records and reports available to the public, unless they fell within a Freedom of Information Act exemption. The Court held that FACA did not apply to this advisory relationship, and therefore did not reach the constitutional questions.

The Court relied, in substantial part, on Congressional intent and purpose in concluding that the ABA Committee was not an advisory committee "utilized" by the President or the DOJ in the intended sense, and in concluding that FACA did not apply to the DOJ's solicitation of the Committee's views on prospective judicial nominees. What tipped the balance for the Court on what it found to be a close statutory question was that "construing FACA to apply . . . would present formidable constitutional difficulties," some of which concerned separation of powers, that the Court was unwilling to resolve unnecessarily.

Judge Silberman's view was that if FACA had been held to apply, it would have "put the Standing Committee out of business." At the same time, he thought that the behind the scenes role that sitting judges play in the deliberations of the Standing Committee made the rationale of the Court and concurring Justices ironic: "Three Justices concurring in the judgment thought the application of FACA to the ABA would interfere unconstitutionally, albeit indirectly, with the President's appointment power, whereas the majority based its imaginative construction of the statute in part on the desirability of avoiding that constitutional question. In my view, the Standing Committee has become another check on the President's appointment power — one in which the judiciary plays an important, if unofficial, role." Silberman, 59 GEO. WASH. L. REV. at 1098.

3. During the 1976 presidential campaign, candidate Jimmy Carter promised to create a nominating commission for the selection of federal judges. After his election, President Carter and Attorney General nominee Griffin Bell negotiated with the then-chairman of the Senate Judiciary Committee an agreement to establish a commission to assist the President in nominating judges for the courts of appeals. Nominations for the district courts would continue to be handled as in the past, through a process in which senators exercised considerable influence in the selection of nominees.

President Carter's Executive Order of February 14, 1977, created the United States Circuit Judge Nominating Commission, to consist of a panel of eleven persons in each circuit, with two such panels in the Fifth and Ninth Circuits. The following extracts from the Order prescribe panel procedures and the criteria for selecting prospective nominees.

ESTABLISHING THE UNITED STATES CIRCUIT JUDGE NOMINATING COMMISSION
Exec. Order No. 11,972, 3 C.F.R. 96 (1978)

. . . .

Sec. 3. Functions of Panels.

A panel shall begin functioning when the President notifies its Chairman that he desires the panel's assistance in aid of his constitutional responsibility and discretion to select a nominee to fill a vacancy on a United States Court of Appeals. Upon such notification, the panel shall:

(a) Give public notice of the vacancy within the relevant geographic area, inviting suggestions as to potential nominees;

(b) Conduct inquiries to identify potential nominees;

(c) Conduct inquiries to identify those persons among the potential nominees who are well-qualified to serve as a United States Circuit Judge; and

(d) Report in confidence to the President, within sixty days after the notification of the vacancy, the results of its activities, including its recommendations as to the five persons whom the panel considers best qualified to fill the vacancy.

Sec. 4. Standards for Selection of Proposed Nominees.

(a) Before transmitting to the President the names of the five persons it deems best qualified to fill an existing vacancy, a panel shall have determined:

(1) That those persons are members in good standing of at least one state bar, or the District of Columbia bar, and members in good standing of any other bars of which they may be members;

(2) That they possess, and have reputations for, integrity and good character;

(3) That they are of sound health;

(4) That they possess, and have demonstrated, outstanding legal ability and commitment to equal justice under law;

(5) That their demeanor, character, and personality indicate that they would exhibit judicial temperament if appointed to the position of United States Circuit Judge.

(b) In selecting persons whose names will be transmitted to the President, a panel shall consider whether the training, experience, or expertise of certain of the well-qualified individuals would help to meet a perceived need of the court of appeals on which the vacancy exists.

(c) To implement the above standards, a panel may adopt such additional criteria or guidelines as it considers appropriate for the identification of potential nominees and the selection of those best qualified to serve as United States Circuit Judges. . . .

Following the issuance of the President's Executive Order, the Department of Justice and the White House collaborated in selecting members for the various circuit panels. The Department of Justice then issued instructions to the panels, elaborating on the procedures and criteria contained in the Executive Order.

This experiment was successful in some respects, and disappointing in others, as indicated in the following excerpt, which is taken from a study of the work of the United States Circuit Judge Nominating Commission during its short life. The commission ceased to function after 1980, when President Reagan terminated it by Executive Order. Jonathan C. Rose, Assistant Attorney General for Legal Policy, who played a significant role in judicial selection under President Reagan, reported that he recommended against maintaining the Commission because he thought it would delay appointments without necessarily removing political considerations and because he questioned whether the Commission was "designed to find high quality, capable people to go on the bench." He did credit the Commission with having added diversity to the federal appellate bench. *Rose Defends Reagan's Judicial Appointment Record*, Legal Times, Nov. 8, 1982, at 6.

Larry C. Berkson & Susan B. Carbon, *The United States Circuit Judge Nominating Commission: Its Members, Procedures And Candidates* 81 (1980)[30]

Merit Selection

The Commission as a whole has been successful in expanding the pool of individuals considered for positions on the courts of appeals. The panels have demonstrated a commitment to this objective throughout their work. One of the panels modified the applicant questionnaire for the express purpose of seeking a broader range of applicants with less traditional and more diverse professional experience. The questionnaire also elicited information tending to reveal desirable personal qualities, rather than only professional credentials.

Publication of the notices of vacancy has also served to make more persons aware of the vacancies, thereby encouraging a larger number of individuals to apply. The Sixth Circuit, for example, disseminated the notice to nearly 250 media sources, judges, attorneys, and interested groups. Thirty-eight percent of the candidates indicated that they had become aware of the vacancies by reading a printed notice.

Publicizing the notices is also intended to encourage the public, including senators, to recommend qualified applicants to the panels for consideration. Again the Commission has been successful in this regard: 43% of the candidates learned of the vacancy from friends or other nonpanel sources.

---

[30] Copyright © 1980. Reprinted with permission of the American Judicature Society.

Another effective way of encouraging public participation is by inviting representatives of interest groups to address the panels at their organizational meetings. However, only one panel expressly did so. Absent such an invitation, few concerned parties are likely to appear.

More important to the success of the commission system is active recruitment by the panels. The data revealed that more candidates learned about the vacancies from a panel member than from reading one of the printed notices. However, the commissioners have not demonstrated uniform enthusiasm for personal recruitment. Some of the panels were decidedly more active than others. The collective efforts of only three panels' members could be characterized as vigorous. An equal number of panels were relatively inactive.

When the efforts of individual panelists were examined, a much more revealing picture emerged. Only 60% of the panelists made any attempt to recruit applicants; a much smaller percentage engaged in active recruitment. This means, of course, that 40% of the panelists virtually abdicated their recruitment responsibilities. Information obtained from the candidates confirms this low level of activity: 27% learned of the vacancy *only* from sources (friends or other) not directly related to the Commission's efforts. The order and instructions clearly require the panels to "seek out" likely candidates. Passive involvement simply has no place in a nominating commission system.

. . . [A] low level of activity typically produced a relatively small number of applications. Active recruitment by one panel generated approximately 70 applications for one vacancy, whereas two other panels which actively recruited produced approximately 20 applications per vacancy. Fortuitous circumstances sometimes adversely affect even the most vigorous recruitment. Examples include a lack of women and minorities with sufficient experience in certain parts of the country, and restrictions on geographic representation to meet existing needs of the court. However, a limited number of applications can almost always be expected when panels delegate recruitment responsibilities to those members from the state where the vacancy exists, when panels include members who believe that recruitment is *not* a function of the Commission, or when individual commissioners believe that recruitment is unnecessary because applicants "already know."

Only one panel intentionally attempted to recruit individuals from both major political parties, probably because the executive order and supplemental instructions do not contain any language which encourages, or even refers to, bipartisan recruitment. However, historically presidents have made the vast majority of judicial appointments from members of their own political party. . . . Thus one would hardly expect Republicans to apply to a largely Democratic commission on their own initiative during a Democratic administration. The credibility of the Commission can be attacked when good faith efforts are not made to encourage all qualified persons to apply, regardless of party. . . .

[A]t least two panels apparently did permit politics to affect the selection process. In one circuit, applicants were invited for interviews if the members believed "political protocol" warranted their invitations. One federal judge and one past president of a state bar association were reportedly interviewed for this reason. In another circuit, all state and federal judges were invited largely because of "party affiliation and political ideology." These practices are contrary to those recommended by advocates of judicial merit selection. . . .

The extent to which panels have operated openly depends at least partially upon which stage of their proceedings is examined.

Conclusion

The Commission operated in substantial compliance with the fundamental precepts of merit selection throughout the interview and evaluation stages. The pool of applicants from which the panels made recommendations to the President was greatly enlarged. Unlike the traditional system where consideration is given to only a few hand-picked allies, an average of 11 persons were interviewed for each vacancy. Most of the commissioners were satisfied with the number of applicants their panels interviewed; very few thought that more persons should have been interviewed.

The commissioners consistently demonstrated a commitment to seek those best qualified for the bench. Nearly all panelists thoroughly scrutinized the applicants' questionnaires and supplementary materials. Many panels prepared questions prior to the interviews to ensure that all necessary information would be obtained. . . .

Both panelists and candidates were generally pleased with the scope and propriety of the interview questions. Most thought that the panels had asked all the necessary questions. The candidates reported that no one had asked about their party affiliation or activity. However, a small percentage of both groups believed that some unnecessary and improper questions were asked. Some of the candidates were troubled by the apparent emphasis on their personal positions on contemporary social issues, and nearly one-quarter believed that political biases had clouded the interviews. Although most did not find the bias objectionable, the evidence raises some doubts about whether the Commission is functioning in a nonpartisan manner.

It is apparent from the data that the panelists wanted to recommend highly competent professionals who exhibited admirable human qualities. Regardless of the commissioners' sex, race, occupation, or whether they were early Carter supporters, they generally worked to achieve a complementary balance of attributes in the candidates recommended to the President.

The panels consistently placed greatest emphasis on character and personality traits along with professional experience. Concern with an applicant's physical and mental health followed closely. Religion and party affiliation were of least importance. The same hierarchy emerged when panelists were asked how important these factors *should* be in evaluating candidates. The only exception was that approximately one-third of the early Carter supporters would have preferred that greater emphasis be placed on an applicant's party affiliation. This clearly violates the stated purpose of a judicial merit plan. To advocates of merit selection, those who are responsible for recruitment and recommendations should not be concerned with party activity. Rather, the goal should be to recommend the best qualified persons irrespective of partisan politics. Only the appointing body, the President in this case, may take into consideration the candidates' political background when choosing a nominee. Even then, advocates claim, party activity should not be a primary reason for selection.

The Commission has at times permitted increased participation of outsiders in the selection process. A university affirmative action officer gave an oral presentation in one circuit on the need for recommending women. In another circuit, several public interest groups and private citizens joined together in lobbying for candidates who were sensitive to civil rights matters and who had demonstrated a commitment to equal justice.

Other forms of lobbying have generally not been effective. The commissioners consciously disregarded most improper political lobbying efforts and refused to bow to political or personal pressures directed at the candidacy of unqualified individuals. On several occasions political officials attempted to influence panel recommendations, but in only a few instances did they appear to have any effect.

The Presidential Nominees

By May, 1979, all but one of the first round nominees had been chosen by the President, and all but one of these had been confirmed by the Senate. . . . Fourteen were men and two were women. . . . There were 11 Caucasians, four blacks and one Asian American. All were Democrats. The President appointed six attorneys, six federal judges, two state judges and two academics.

Additionally, 12 of the second round candidates had been nominated. . . . Five were women, and three were members of minority groups (two blacks and one Hispanic). Eight were Democrats, three were independent and one was a Republican, six were federal judges, five were attorneys, and one was an academic.

Most of President Carter's nominees to the court of appeals have been white (71%), male (75%), Democrats (86%), and were serving as federal judges (43%) at the time of nomination.

The educational backgrounds of the nominees varied greatly. No two first round nominees attended the same undergraduate college, and only two attended the same law school. The Ivy League schools did not dominate. However, a greater number of second round nominees attended prestigious undergraduate universities and law schools. . . .

A smaller number of second round nominees had ties to the Democratic Party. . . .

Only one second round nominee had sought political office during the preceding five years and only three had made campaign contributions to the Democratic party. It may be that the President satisfied most of his patronage debts during the first round and was therefore able to select nominees who are less closely connected with the Democratic Party during the second.

NOTES

1. According to JUSTICE HELD HOSTAGE, *Politics and Selecting Federal Judges*, The Report of the Citizens for Independent Courts Task Force on

Federal Judicial Selection, UNCERTAIN JUSTICE: POLITICS IN AMERICA' COURTS (The Century Foundation, Inc. 2000):[31]

> From 1977 to 1998, the mean number of days from vacancy to nomination [of all Article III federal judges] was 277; for the same period, the mean number of days from nomination to confirmation or other final action was 100. In these years, the greater increase in delay occurred during the interval from nomination to confirmation or other final action. During his first six years in office, President Clinton took an average of 75 more days to nominate a candidate for the federal judiciary than President Carter took. During the 105th Congress of 1997-98, the Senate took an average of 163 more days to act on a nomination (or to let it expire) than the Senate did in the 95th Congress of 1977-78.

> The average number of days for Presidential action on nomination for the federal courts of appeals was 224 for President Carter, 230 for President Reagan, 292 for the first President Bush, and 329 for President Clinton. *Id.* Table 3. The average number of days between nomination and final action is reflected in this bar graph from that report.

FIGURE 10. SENATE ACTION: AVERAGE NUMBER OF DAYS BETWEEN NOMINATION AND FINAL ACTION,[a] BY PRESIDENT AND TYPE OF COURT, 1977-98

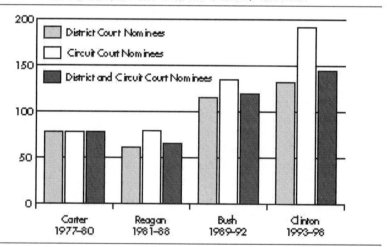

[a] Final action is the confirmation, return to the president, or withdrawal of a nomination.

Source: Prepared by the Program for Law and Judicial Politics at Michigan State University.

According to the Congressional Research Service, (http://www.constitution-project.org/ci/reports/justice_held_hostage.pdf):

---

[31] Copyright © 2000. Reprinted with permission of The Century Foundation.

TABLE 8. SENATE ACTION: AVERAGE NUMBER OF DAYS BETWEEN NOMINATION AND FINAL ACTION FOR CIRCUIT NOMINEES BY CIRCUIT AND CONGRESSIONAL TERM, 1977-98 (CONT.)

Congress	Circuit													All Circuits
	1st	2nd	3rd	4th	5th	6th	7th	8th	9th	10th	11th	DC	Federal	
103rd	61 (1)	88 (4)	115 (2)	111 (3)	124 (4)	84 (2)	—	71 (1)	63 (1)	86 (1)	202 (1)	111 (2)	98 (1)	103 (23)
104th	65 (1)	—	—	287 (2)	240 (1)	149 (3)	100 (2)	—	282 (5)	63 (3)	199 (1)	395 (1)	169 (1)	194 (20)
105th	164 (1)	251 (4)	200 (2)	279 (3)	454 (1)	283 (3)	—	185 (1)	310 (10)	—	136 (2)	71 (1)	204 (2)	258 (30)
95th through 105th	66 (11)	119 (22)	110 (19)	147 (22)	109 (38)	114 (28)	68 (14)	81 (14)	157 (50)	90 (16)	149 (13)	108 (22)	121 (18)	118 (287)

Note: Numbers in parentheses indicate the number of nomination for each category.

[a] Final action is the confirmation, return to the president, or withdrawal of a nomination.

Source: Prepared by the Program for Law and Judicial Politics at Michigan State University.

Daniel J. Meador, *Unacceptable Delays in Judicial Appointments*, 6 JOURNAL OF LAW & POLITICS 7, 9-11, 14 (1989)[32]

There is . . . a glaring flaw in the process [for appointing federal judges] . . . : the extraordinarily long period of time that it takes to fill a vacancy on the federal bench. It is almost certain that in no other nation does such an extended period of time elapse between creation of a judicial vacancy and the installation of a judge. . . .

The Senate's record in confirming nominees, once the nominations are received from the President, is better. . . . It is understandable — and is to be expected — that the Senate's confirmation time would be significantly less than the President's nominating time. It is much easier to review the qualifications and fitness of a person already selected for a judgeship than it is to make an initial selection of such a person. Moreover, the Senate receives a wealth of information about the nominee, including the FBI report, the completed questionnaire secured from the nominee by the Department of Justice, and the American Bar Association committee report. The Executive has already undertaken the time-consuming process of assembling that data. . . .

Before setting out . . . suggestions [for reducing the time in this process], I wish to underscore the obvious reason why it is important that the time involved in this process be substantially reduced. The federal courts are heavily burdened with litigation. . . . From time to time Congress has created new judgeships to enable the judiciary to cope with this extraordinary growth in business. But the creation of new judgeships never seems quite to keep pace with the growth in litigation. Congress is slow to react to recommendations from the Judicial Conference of the United States for new judgeships. Often years pass between the time the Judicial Conference communicates to Congress the need for a new judgeship and the congressional authorization of that position. Thus, there is a persistent shortfall in the number of authorized judgeships. Moreover, vacancies inevitably occur constantly . . . as a result of death, resignation, or retirement. These circumstances mean that the federal judiciary is chronically undermanned and would likely continue to be so even if the appointment process were handled at maximum speed. To permit delays [of the magnitude that we have] in the face of these circumstances is to impair further the ability of the federal judiciary to handle the nation's adjudicatory business. Indeed, it may not be unfair to characterize such a pattern of official activity as public irresponsibility. To say the least, it is a situation that cries out for attention. . . .

The most promising steps, closely intertwined with each other, would be the creation of a permanent office on judicial nominations, the staffing of such an office with an adequate number of high level civil servants, and the establishment of a system in that office for monitoring every federal judicial position and developing files of potential nominees to fill those positions before vacancies actually occur.

---

[32] Copyright © 1989 by The Journal of Law & Politics. Reprinted with permission.

. . . The lack of any permanent location for this responsibility within the Justice Department exacerbates the traditional lack of continuity resulting from the clean break made at each change of administration.

The first step, therefore, toward greater expedition is to introduce continuity and stability of personnel and procedure into the judicial nominating process by establishing a permanent judicial appointments office within the Department of Justice. Inasmuch as experience suggests that not much is likely to be accomplished in this regard through the voluntary actions of successive Attorneys General, Congress should move to create this office by statute, just as it has created other entities within the Justice Department. This office would be specifically charged by statute with monitoring all federal judicial positions, identifying and developing information about persons suitable to fill each such position when a vacancy does occur, and maintaining permanent files of all such prospects. . . .

In the end, the most effective cure for the unseemly delay that we now have in this process lies in an activated public and professional pressure that makes it clear to the nominating authorities and to the Senate that these protracted times are unacceptable. This is not the kind of subject about which the public is likely to be well informed or to become excited. Thus, it is the bar that must take the leadership and bring to bear, in a nonpartisan way, its full influence on all those public officials involved in this process, insisting that vacancies be filled expeditiously. The situation portrayed [here] cripples the federal judiciary and impairs its ability to do the job that the Congress has called upon it to do.

NOTES

1. The recommendations made by Professor Meador in 1991 have not been followed. As of September, 1, 2005, there were twelve vacancies on the U.S. Courts of Appeals, and five nominees pending for those vacancies. In June, 2005, in an effort to push through President Bush's remaining and future nominees, Senate Majority Leader Bill Frist had threatened to exercise "the nuclear option," a change in Senate rules that would allow senators to end judicial nomination debates with the support of a simple majority of senators rather than the 60 required under current rules. Do you think this would be a positive change? This step might be taken out of concern about the filibuster of nominees to the Supreme Court, even more than out of concern about filibusters of nominees to the courts of appeals. A Supreme Court Justice may postpone retirement or take retirement strategically, with a view to the philosophy of the President who will nominate his or her successor. Is this a problematic feature of the federal appointments process?

2. In 2005, Professors Roger Cramton and Paul Carrington advanced a proposal that Supreme Court justices hold office for staggered terms of eighteen years, one new appointment to be made every two years, thus giving each president two appointments to the Court for each term the President serves. The proposal was prompted by concerns over the length of service on the Court, largely the result of extended life spans and reluctance of justices to retire, and by the disproportionate influence some presidents have on the makeup of the

Court through the fortuitous timing of deaths and retirements. A collection of papers analyzing all aspects of this proposal is published in REFORMING THE COURT: TERM LIMITS FOR SUPREME COURT JUSTICES (Roger C. Cramton & Paul D. Carrington eds., 2006). What do you think of this proposal? Could it be implemented by statute, or would a constitutional amendment be necessary? Article III, Section 1, of the Constitution says in part: "The Judges, both of the supreme and inferior Courts, shall hold their Offices during good Behavior, and shall, at stated Times, receive for their Services, a Compensation, which shall not be diminished during their Continuance in Office."

III. JUDICIAL EDUCATION FOR APPELLATE JUDGES

Programs for the education and training of judges of all sorts in the United States began in a small way in the 1950s. They grew in number and acceptability during the 1960s and have now become well-established parts of the American judicial scene for judges at all levels. Initially, some judges resisted such educational programs in the belief that they implied that the judges were not already sufficiently educated for their jobs. Judges now generally recognize that, regardless of how much experience they have, there always are new subjects to be mastered, including new developments in statutory and case law, newly emerging fields that become involved in litigation, and changing conditions that call for new ways of conducting judicial business. Today it is a rare judge who does not regularly pursue educational programs of one kind or another.

In the United States judicial education is especially important because of the general lack of uniform quality controls over the selection of judges. Some persons come to the bench with legal and professional experiences that equip them superbly for the judicial task. Others come from backgrounds that leave them ill-prepared for their judicial tasks. Judicial education programs attempt to ensure at least a minimum level of competence and knowledge of judicial work.

The first program of judicial education for appellate judges — and one of the first judicial education programs of any kind — was the Seminar for Appellate Judges, begun in 1956 by the Institute of Judicial Administration at the New York University Law School. That program continues today, now conducting a one week-long program for new appellate judges, both state and federal, and a two-day long program for appellate judges with 3 or more years of experience, alternating annually between programs for state judges and those for federal judges. Law professors and appellate judges act as the instructors. The 2005 New Appellate Judges Seminar covered such subjects as oral argument, conferencing, judicial decision-making, ethical judging, issues of accountability and independence, opinion writing, the craft of judging, elections, statutory interpretation, theories of constitutional interpretation, and current problems in criminal law. The advanced seminars' topics change from year to year. Recent topics have been state constitutional law and employment law, and international law and federalism.

In 1980 the University of Virginia Law School, in collaboration with the ABA Appellate Judges Conference, established the Graduate Program for Judges, an academically oriented program for state and federal appellate judges, and the only judicial education program in the United States conducted by a law school and leading to the award of a university degree: Master of Laws (LL.M.) in the Judicial Process. Each class of thirty judges attended two six-week summer sessions at the Law School, and each judge had to write a thesis under faculty supervision. The courses in the curriculum included Anglo-American Jurisprudence, Law and Economics, Courts and Social Science, Law and Biomedical Science, Courts and Federalism, Contemporary Legal Thought, English Appellate Courts, and German Appellate Courts. Written examinations were required in all courses. These courses were taught by the University of Virginia Law School faculty, supplemented occasionally by visiting lecturers from other university departments and institutions. Through 2004, a total of 297 judges had completed the program, mainly state supreme court judges and federal and state intermediate appellate court judges. This program has been dependent upon Congressional appropriations. Because of a reduction in those appropriations in 2005, the future of the program is in doubt.

For many years, the Appellate Judges Conference (AJC) of the American Bar Association conducted four or five three-day seminars annually for appellate judges. These seminars were attended mainly by state appellate judges, but some federal appellate judges also attended. The seminars met at different locations around the United States. Typically each half day was devoted to a different topic, including matters such as recent U.S. Supreme Court decisions and recent developments in various legal fields. This educational function of the AJC is now administered by the Appellate Judges Education Institute (AJEI), which is located at the SMU Dedman School of Law. Educational seminars are co-sponsored by the AJEI, the ABA and the law school.

Today, judicial education is offered by a number of organizations, both public and private. The National Association of State Judicial Educators has promulgated Principles and Standards of Continuing Judicial Education. The National Judicial College in Reno, Nevada, an independent organization, has offered programs for both trial and appellate judges since 1963. Appellate judges' seminars and conferences often last from one to three days, and often are offered on a regional basis or for the judges of a single state. Some programs are offered by universities and organizations concerned with particular aspects of the justice system; these frequently bring appellate judges and trial judges together, often from both state and federal courts. When judicial education is offered by private organizations, it has come to raise a number of issues, as the following excerpt by Senior Judge Jack B. Weinstein indicates.

Jack B. Weinstein, *The Contribution of Henry G. Manne Towards the Education of the American Judiciary*, 50 CASE WESTERN RESERVE LAW REVIEW 421 (1999)[33]

. . . [J]udicial education is essential in any sophisticated system of justice. . . . The need for post-appointment education has become more urgent since the Supreme Court has emphasized recently the courts' obligations to exercise better control over scientific, medical, economic, technical and other specialized expert testimony. Education through lectures, face-to-face conferences, satellite

---

[33] Copyright © 1999 by Case Western Law Review. Reproduced with permission via the Copyright Clearance Center.

conferences, literature, audiocassettes, and videotapes is now supplied by many organizations. These organizations include the Federal and State Judicial Centers, the ABA Center for Continuing Legal Education and Law Schools and Bar Associations. . . .

After appointment, judges should, to the extent that their arduous time-consuming duties permit, enhance their understanding of life and theory. As generalists they need to continue to acquire new information about the changing world — much as any intelligent, well-educated person does. . . . We cannot make intelligent fact decisions or evaluate the effect of our legal decisions on society unless we have some degree of understanding about that society as it currently exists.

. . . One form of judicial education that has recently drawn public attention is conferences and privately sponsored classes for judges. This method of education developed in part from the training sessions for federal judges sponsored by Professor Manne and the Federal Judicial Center.

The Center is funded through the judicial branch of the federal government. Private foundation money supplements the federal budget on some projects. The Center was created primarily to assist newly appointed judges . . . , but the Judicial Center's mission has expanded enormously to include continuing education courses for judges, preparation of training materials and research on the operation and improvement of the courts. In 1984, Congress created the State Justice Institute, which is a similar organization designed to improve the administration of justice in state courts.

Other legal institutions have followed the Judicial Center's and Professor Manne's lead, initiating judicial conferences and seminars of their own. Universities, foundations, bar associations, special interest groups, and corporations sponsor these sessions.

Ethical issues for judges arise, and such conferences may cause concern, when the sponsor is a group that participates regularly in litigation or because the program may be perceived as biased. . . . A good practice would be to routinely provide payment for judge's expenses at such seminars only by the law school or by funds from the federal Administrative Office or Judicial Center. . . . [J]oint sponsorship, where appropriate, should be encouraged since it extends the Judicial Center's resources beyond its limited budgetary restrictions. Were sufficient funding available, it would be best to have much of the training of judges paid for by the most neutral source of all — the government. How this can be accomplished depends on management decisions of state and federal training centers and legislatures, which tend to emphasize more directly useful instruction in current substantive and procedural developments.

Generally, judges should be entitled to rely on the neutrality of government bodies such as the Judicial Center, the Court Administrative Office, the State Justice Institute, the Federal Judicial Conference, and the Administrative Conference of the United States. Yet, even reliance on government agencies has its own dangers. The view of a government agency may itself be slanted. . . .

A useful model . . . is that of the Carnegie Commission on Science, Technology, and Government. . . . Cooperative efforts with the Federal Judicial Center have culminated in a project at the Judicial Center to create a

Science and Technology Resource Center that focuses on judicial education in science and technology. . . . [A] continuing program of general training in science was devised. . . . The jointly sponsored seminars and training materials cover topics ranging from the use of DNA evidence, to computer generated evidence, to proving causation in toxic tort litigation, to basic problems in science such as those in astrophysics.

. . . Where non-suspect, non-criticizable funding from a foundation without any apparent axe to grind is available, it seems appropriate to use joint arrangements of official groups such as the Federal Judicial Center, ALI/ABA, and national and local bar associations. If sponsorship by a narrower bar association such as the Association of Trial Lawyers of America is used, balancing by the Defense Research Institute, if possible, is desirable.

. . . [C]riticism of the lush settings for the courses is not, in my opinion, entitled to weight. . . . Spouses are discouraged from coming and the readings are intensive, constituting the equivalent of a college course in a week. While classes are conducted only from 8:00 a.m. to 12:00 noon, with an occasional night session, the readings require a great deal of homework. Given the age of the students, these courses can hardly be characterized as junkets.

Providing comfortable settings for education may be objectionable if carried to an extreme, since the public believes it pays us enough and perks are resented by taxpayers. "Junkets" with judges' expenses paid may cement bar and bench healthy relationships, but they could be subject to understandable lay criticism since judges affect lawyers' livelihoods.

Both Yale Law School's conferences and the Law & Economics Center seminars originated by Professor Manne have been criticized by the Alliance for what it perceived to be an ideological bias. . . . Professor Manne had a long and distinguished history as an advocate of law and economics. At the seminars I attended there were no overt attempts to proselytize. After attending some of the seminars, I have become more sensitive to economic analysis. As a result, my thinking on torts may have shifted somewhat. It has moved toward a regime of court and bureaucratic protections in the field of mass torts that might not be congenial to either corporate or plaintiffs' lawyers' interests.

Mature and experienced judges' thoughts can seldom be re-channeled by an instructor's bias. Judges should not be deterred from attending conferences that espouse a certain viewpoint as long as the funding of the programs is balanced, and any potential bias is disclosed. . . .

In general, a judge ought to be able to attend any lecture or public meeting. Judges' civil liberties remain in force during their tenure. Nevertheless, discretion is prescribed. Pending cases need special sensitivity, lest the judge give the impression that his or her private views will have some influence on the case. Even in the absence of a pending case, . . . [t]he public's view of neutrality by the judge needs to be considered by the judge.

Judicial education conferences have made a significant contribution in promoting collegiality among the judiciary, and between judges and experts in other fields. The educational sessions of federal judges meeting in intense small groups under distinguished professors, with excellent materials in pleasant surroundings, have done much to improve the morale of the federal bench. . . .

Conferences and other educational opportunities have become especially important in bringing federal judges together as the number of judges has increased. . . . It has become increasingly difficult for the judges to get to know each other. Consequently, they are less likely to consult with each other and involve themselves in the fellowship so important to morale. . . . [Then,] as much disclosure as is practicable is desirable. Judges could open their calendars to the public so that their attendance at meetings, seminars, and lectures is disclosed. . . . Any paper delivered by a judge should be sent to the pressroom. Judges are currently required to disclose all reimbursements they receive for travel and related expenses, as well as the source of the funds, a brief description of the travel itinerary, and the nature of the expenses provided.

More care and discretion by the judge needs to be shown if the knowledge is being acquired for a specific case. Here it is important that all sides be informed as soon as possible about what the judge is reading, hearing, or seeing. The judge should create a record of all material the judge reads and hears that is related to the facts of a pending case. . . .

The key in this area is openness and balance. . . . Parties must have the opportunity to counter these extra-judicial sources of knowledge.

NOTES

1. At first glance, continuing judicial education might seem to be as uncontroversial a subject as one could think of. But, as the above excerpt indicates, it raises all sorts of issues. For example, who should pay for it, and how are legislators and others to be persuaded of the need to allocate scarce resources to this task? How worrisome is it that judges may receive "slanted" information? Judge Weinstein tells us that his thinking has been influenced, but also insists that "Mature and experienced judges' thoughts can seldom be re-channeled by an instructor's bias." Is it really enough that the bias of an educational program is disclosed to the attending judges?

2. The October 5, 2004 draft of revisions to Canon 4 of the Model Code of Judicial Conduct provides in pertinent part (Rule 4.14):

(a) A judge may receive reimbursement or accept a waiver of charges from sources other than the judge's employing entity for the expenses of necessary travel, food and lodging associated with the judge's participation in extra-judicial activities permitted by this Code, if such receipt or acceptance does not cast reasonable doubt on the judge's capacity to act with impartiality, integrity, or independence.

[(b) commands disclosure under specified circumstances.]

The Commentary states in part:

A variety of factors may affect the propriety of attendance at such seminars, including the educational nature of the seminar, the sources of funding, the identity of the seminar sponsor, and the reasonableness of the expenses paid or reimbursed. The judge should consider whether the sponsor or the funding source . . . is currently appearing, or likely to appear, before the judge in a matter . . . [and] should determine whether attendance may create a conflict of interest, may result in disqualification or recusal in matters coming before the judge, may give rise to a judge's independence being questioned, or may interfere with the judge's performance of his or her judicial duties. . . . [T]he judge should undertake a reasonable inquiry to obtain the information necessary to make an informed judgment.

. . . [A] judge should take reasonable steps to ensure that information concerning his or her participation in seminars and other events, as well as reasonable information regarding the nature and circumstances of such events, are available to the public. A judge should therefore promptly and publicly disclose participation in extra-judicial events at which the judge's expenses are paid by sources other than the judge's employing governmental entity.

3. One commentator has concluded:

The public's concern is that federal and state judiciaries are being transformed as institutions, as private entities with a conservative ideological cast have coopted the process of educating judges. The appearance, if not the reality, is that, by taking over the function of judicial education, these private entities have greatly influenced decision making by the judiciary as a whole, if not by all judges individually, in a direction favorable to the legal interests and preferences of the corporations that fund the programs. Whether the concern is a fair one is debatable. But it seems clear that this is a concern that the judiciary ought to address on an institutional basis.

Bruce A. Green, *May Judges Attend Privately Funded Educational Programs? Should Judicial Education be Privatized?: Questions of Judicial Ethics and Policy*, 29 FORDHAM URB. L.J. 941 (2002).

4. Under what circumstances should a judge recuse him- or herself after attending an expenses-paid seminar sponsored by interests with a stake in litigation before the judge? In *In re Aguinda*, 241 F.3d 194, 203-06 (2d Cir. 2001), plaintiffs contended that defendant Texaco had caused environmental damage and personal injuries in Ecuador and Peru. While dismissal of the complaint was on appeal, the trial judge attended an expenses-paid seminar on environmental issues sponsored by an organization to which Texaco contributed, and a former Texaco executive spoke at the seminar. Upon remand for further proceedings, after the Second Circuit reversed dismissal of the complaint, the judge refused to disqualify himself, and the Second Circuit affirmed, relying on Texaco's contribution having been small. Even assuming that the seminar had provided an unbalanced perspective on policy issues, the court presumed that the judge would follow the law, rather than his personal beliefs. The Second Circuit indicated that where a party or lawyer's financial contribution was significant, or the presentation addressed legal issues that were material to disposition of the claim, the result might have to be different. *See generally*, Douglas T. Kendall & Jason C. Rylander, *Tainted Justice: How Private Judicial Trips Undermine Public Confidence in the Judiciary*, 18 GEO. J. LEGAL ETHICS 65 (2004); Douglas T. Kendall & Eric Sorkin, *Nothing for Free: How Private Judicial Seminars Are Undermining Environmental Protections and Breaking the Public's Trust*, 25 HARV. ENVTL. L. REV. 405 (2001).

IV. EVALUATION AND REGULATION OF APPELLATE JUDGES WHILE IN OFFICE

We have talked of qualifications of appellate judges, of approaches to selecting them and of mechanisms for educating appellate judges. Particularly in the last few years, increasing attention has been paid to the evaluation of judicial performance, especially in state courts where judges need not be retained indefinitely. In February 2005 the American Bar Association published Guidelines for the Evaluation of Judicial Performance. The guidelines encourage judicial evaluation programs to improve judges' performance and to aid those responsible for assigning judges and deciding whether individual judges should be continued in office, while avoiding the impairment of judicial independence.

The criteria that the ABA guidelines propose are:
– "legal ability"including "legal reasoning ability;" knowledge of — and keeping current on developments in — substantive law, rules of procedure and evidence;

– "integrity and impartiality," including avoiding impropriety and the appearance thereof; "treating all people with dignity and respect;" not favoring or disfavoring anyone, including on the basis of "race, sex, religion, national origin, disability, age, sexual orientation, or socioeconomic status;" giving individual consideration; considering both sides of an argument; "basing decisions on the law and the facts, without regard to the identity of the parties or counsel, and with an open mind . . . ;"and "ability to make difficult or unpopular decisions;"

– "communication skills," including "clear and logical oral communication while in court"and in written decisions;

– "professionalism and temperament," including "acting in a dignified manner," treating people courteously, "acting with patience and self-control," "dealing with pro se litigants . . . fairly and effectively," "participating . . . in professional development activities and in . . . court improvement and judicial education activities," and "promoting public understanding of and confidence in the courts."

– "administrative capacity," including such matters as punctuality, preparation, "fostering a productive work environment . . . ," and utilizing practices to ensure a broad and diverse staff.

The guidelines propose that appellate judges be evaluated on the quality of their preparation for and participation in oral argument and on their effectiveness in working with other judges on the court. Commentary notes that "it is essential for [appellate] judges to be able to resolve differences with their colleagues, to consider the views of others, and to offer constructive criticism with respect to each other's draft opinions."

The guidelines also advise that experts be used to design approaches, instruments, and techniques to be used in these evaluation programs.

NOTES

1. The ABA Guidelines offer a selected bibliography of writings on judicial evaluation. *See also* Stephen J. Safranek & Diana Azzopardi, *Judging the Justices: A Statistical Review of the Record of the Judges for the Michigan Supreme Court*, 75 U. DET. MERCY L. REV. 621 (1998) (considering the reversal rates of opinions and vindication of dissent to determine whether a judge's rulings were approved as correct by the state supreme court). For ideas as to how empirical studies of judicial performance should be done, evaluations of some such efforts, and consideration of behavioral and institutional implications of those studies, see Symposium, *Empirical Measures of Judicial Performance*, 32 FLA. ST. U. L. REV. 1001 (2005).

2. One commentator has found that most examples of bad judging (to be distinguished from merely poor judging) fall into the following categories: "(1) corrupt influence on judicial action; (2) questionable fiduciary appointments; (3) abuse of office for personal gain; (4) incompetence and neglect of duties; (5) overstepping of authority; (6) interpersonal abuse; (7) bias, prejudice, and insensitivity; (8) personal misconduct reflecting adversely on fitness for office; (9) conflict of interest; (10) inappropriate behavior in a judicial capacity; (11) lack of candor; and (12) electioneering and purchase of office." Geoffrey P. Miller, *Bad Judges*, 83 TEX. L. REV. 431 (2004). To assist appellate judges to be "good"and to punish them when they are "bad," there are ethical rules and sanctions. Canons that address judges who seek reelection and candidates for judicial office were noted earlier, in the section on selection of appellate judges. Other canons deal with other aspects of judicial conduct. A study of those canons is beyond the scope of this course. You can find an example of such canons, however, in the Model Code of Judicial Conduct, which is available online at www.abanet.org/judicialethics. Notice the degree to which the ABA Guidelines for the Evaluation of Judicial Performance track the qualities reflected in Professor Miller's identification of the respects in which judges can be bad and the matters dealt with in the Model Code. A general resource on judicial ethics is JEFFREY M. SHAMAN, STEVEN LUBET, & JAMES J. ALFINI, JUDICIAL CONDUCT AND ETHICS (2000).

3. Appellate judges have to police their own impartiality through recusal. In the federal courts, recusal is the only procedure available to combat partiality of appellate judges, because the federal judicial disqualification statute, 28 U.S.C. § 144, applies only to district court judges. For a review of the law and recommendations for strengthening the protections against bias and prejudice, see Debra Lyn Bassett, *Judicial Disqualification in the Federal Courts*, 87 IOWA L .REV. 1213 (2002). For treatment of the law governing disqualification and recusal in both the state and federal courts, see RICHARD E. FLAMM, JUDICIAL DISQUALIFICATION: RECUSAL AND DISQUALIFICATION OF JUDGES (1996 & 2005 Supp.).

Chapter 12

THE SUPREME COURT OF THE UNITED STATES

The Supreme Court of the United States ("SCOTUS") is unique. No other appellate court in the world has ultimate jurisdiction over so many appellate courts from so many different court systems. The Supreme Court, of course, is the COLR for all questions of federal law — constitutional, statutory, or federal common law — with jurisdiction to review not only the decisions of the thirteen U.S. Courts of Appeals but also decisions of the U.S. Court of Appeals for the Armed Forces, the fifty state court systems, and the courts of the District of Columbia and the Commonwealth of Puerto Rico. *See* 28 U.S.C. §§ 1254, 1257, 1258 & 1259.

The Supreme Court's supervisory authority over the federal courts of appeals is plenary; the latter are subordinate tribunals within the same sovereign's judicial system. Therefore, the Supreme Court can review all cases in those IACs, either before or after judgment, and all issues in the case, both state and federal; although as a matter of practice it rarely reviews a state law question in a case from a lower federal court. Cases coming from state courts, however, are a different matter. The Supreme Court's statutory jurisdiction in cases from the courts of the sovereign states is limited to federal questions, specifically to those federal questions that are controlling of the judgment. Thus, in our federalism the state and federal courts articulate together as a judicial system: a state supreme court is the COLR within its own state judicial system with final authority over questions of state law, but on federal questions it performs more like an IAC with its decisions subject to review and reversal by a higher court — the SCOTUS.

There is no further appellate review from a decision by the justices of the Supreme Court. The High Court's papal-like authority was once aptly described by Justice Jackson: "We are not final because we are infallible, but we are infallible only because we are final." *Brown v. Allen*, 344 U.S. 443, 540 (1953) (Jackson, J., concurring).

In Chapter 6, we focused on the design of the judicial architecture: the vertical expansion of the appellate structure and the allocation of jurisdiction between IACs and COLRs. This Chapter examines the Supreme Court *qua* appellate court — inside and close-up. In successive sections, we will examine its appellate jurisdiction, how it manages its docket, and its case selection practices. We will focus on its policies and processes concerning the exercise of its discretionary jurisdiction at the apex of the judicial pyramid of the federal and state court systems in the United States. Consequently, we will better understand the COLRs in the several states that have been patterned after the SCOTUS. Likewise, our study will help inform our understanding of the appellate courts more generally.

Why do we have a Supreme Court? What functions does it serve? How does it perform its functions? What are its practices and procedures? Why have critics been heard to complain at various times that the High Court is taking "too many" cases or "too few" cases or "not the right" cases? How would we rate its appellate performance? What benchmarks should we apply? How might we tweak its features to improve its efficiency and effectiveness? In all of this, however, we must be mindful of the rich history and deep traditions that make this court such a unique American institution, which, truth be told, is the envy of the world judicial order.

I. JURISDICTION

U.S. CONST. art. III, §§ 1 & 2

§ 1. The judicial Power of the United States, shall be vested in one supreme Court, and in such inferior Courts as the Congress may from time to time ordain and establish. The Judges, both of the supreme and inferior Courts, shall hold their Offices during good Behaviour, and shall, at stated Times, receive for their Services, a Compensation, which shall not be diminished during their Continuance in Office.

§ 2. The judicial Power shall extend to all Cases, in Law and Equity, arising under this Constitution, the Laws of the United States, and Treaties made, or which shall be made, under their Authority; — to all Cases affecting Ambassadors, other public Ministers and Consuls; — to all Cases of admiralty and maritime Jurisdiction; — to Controversies to which the United States shall be a Party; — to Controversies between two or more States; — between a State and Citizens of another State; — between Citizens of different States; — between Citizens of the same State claiming Lands under Grants of different States, and between a State, or the Citizens thereof, and foreign States, Citizens or Subjects.

In all Cases affecting Ambassadors, other public Ministers and Consuls, and those in which a State shall be Party, the supreme Court shall have original Jurisdiction. In all the other Cases before mentioned, the supreme Court shall have appellate Jurisdiction, both as to Law and Fact, with such Exceptions, and under such Regulations as the Congress shall make.

28 U.S.C. § 1254. Courts of appeals; *certiorari*; certified questions

Cases in the courts of appeals may be reviewed by the Supreme Court by the following methods:

(1) By writ of *certiorari* granted upon the petition of any party to any civil or criminal case, before or after rendition of judgment or decree;

(2) By certification at any time by a court of appeals of any question of law in any civil or criminal case as to which instructions are desired, and upon such certification the Supreme Court may give binding instructions or require the entire record to be sent up for decision of the entire matter in controversy.

28 U.S.C. § 1257. State courts; *certiorari*

(a) Final judgments or decrees rendered by the highest court of a State in which a decision could be had, may be reviewed by the Supreme Court by writ of *certiorari* where the validity of a treaty or statute of the United States is drawn in question or where the validity of a statute of any State is drawn in question on the ground of its being repugnant to the Constitution, treaties, or laws of the United States, or where any title, right, privilege, or immunity is specially set up or claimed under the Constitution or the treaties or statutes of, or any commission held or authority exercised under, the United States.

(b) For the purposes of this section, the term "highest court of a state" includes the District of Columbia Court of Appeals.

Sup. Ct. R. 10. Considerations Governing Review on *Certiorari*

Review on a writ of *certiorari* is not a matter of right, but of judicial discretion. A petition for a writ of *certiorari* will be granted only for compelling reasons. The following, although neither controlling nor fully measuring the Court's discretion, indicate the character of the reasons the Court considers:

(a) a United States court of appeals has entered a decision in conflict with the decision of another United States court of appeals on the same important matter; has decided an important federal question in a way that conflicts with a decision by a state court of last resort; or has so far departed from the accepted and usual course of judicial proceedings, or sanctioned such a departure by a lower court, as to call for an exercise of this Court's supervisory power;

(b) a state court of last resort has decided an important federal question in a way that conflicts with the decision of another state court of last resort or of a United States court of appeals;

(c) a state court or a United States court of appeals has decided an important question of federal law that has not been, but should be, settled by this Court, or has decided an important federal question in a way that conflicts with relevant decisions of this Court.

A petition for a writ of *certiorari* is rarely granted when the asserted error consists of erroneous factual findings or the misapplication of a properly stated rule of law.

Sup. Ct. R. 14. Content of a Petition for a Writ of *Certiorari*

1. A petition for a writ of *certiorari* shall contain, in the order indicated:

(a) The questions presented for review, expressed concisely in relation to the circumstances of the case, without unnecessary detail. The questions should be short and should not be argumentative or repetitive. If the petitioner or respondent is under a death sentence that may be affected by the disposition of the petition, the notation "capital case" shall precede the questions presented. The questions shall be set out on the first page following the cover, and no other information may appear on that page. The statement of any question presented is deemed to comprise every subsidiary question fairly included therein. Only the questions set out in the petition, or fairly included therein, will be considered by the Court.

(b) A list of all parties to the proceeding in the court whose judgment is sought to be reviewed (unless the caption of the case contains the names of all the parties), and a corporate disclosure statement as required by Rule 29.6.

(c) If the petition exceeds five pages, a table of contents and a table of cited authorities.

(d) Citations of the official and unofficial reports of the opinions and orders entered in the case by courts or administrative agencies.

(e) A concise statement of the basis for jurisdiction in this Court, showing:

(i) the date the judgment or order sought to be reviewed was entered (and, if applicable, a statement that the petition is filed under this Court's Rule 11);

(ii) the date of any order respecting rehearing, and the date and terms of any order granting an extension of time to file the petition for a writ of *certiorari*;

(iii) express reliance on Rule 12.5, when a cross-petition for a writ of *certiorari* is filed under that Rule, and the date of docketing of the petition for a writ of *certiorari* in connection with which the cross-petition is filed;

(iv) the statutory provision believed to confer on this Court jurisdiction to review on a writ of *certiorari* the judgment or order in question; and

(v) if applicable, a statement that the notifications required by Rule 29.4(b) or (c) have been made.

(f) The constitutional provisions, treaties, statutes, ordinances, and regulations involved in the case, set out verbatim with appropriate citation. If the provisions involved are lengthy, their citation alone suffices at this point, and their pertinent text shall be set out in the appendix referred to in subparagraph 1(i).

(g) A concise statement of the case setting out the facts material to consideration of the questions presented, and also containing the following:

(i) If review of a state-court judgment is sought, specification of the stage in the proceedings, both in the court of first instance and in the appellate courts, when the federal questions sought to be reviewed were raised; the method or manner of raising them and the way in which they were passed on by those courts; and pertinent quotations of specific portions of the record or summary thereof, with specific reference to the places in the record where the matter appears (e.g., court opinion, ruling on exception, portion of court's charge and exception thereto, assignment of error), so as to show that the federal question was timely and properly raised and that this Court has jurisdiction to review the judgment on a writ of *certiorari*. When the portions of the record relied on under this subparagraph are voluminous, they shall be included in the appendix referred to in subparagraph 1(i).

(ii) If review of a judgment of a United States court of appeals is sought, the basis for federal jurisdiction in the court of first instance.

(h) A direct and concise argument amplifying the reasons relied on for allowance of the writ. See Rule 10.

(i) An appendix containing, in the order indicated:

(i) the opinions, orders, findings of fact, and conclusions of law, whether written or orally given and transcribed, entered in conjunction with the judgment sought to be reviewed;

(ii) any other relevant opinions, orders, findings of fact, and conclusions of law entered in the case by courts or administrative agencies, and, if reference thereto is necessary to ascertain the grounds of the judgment, of those in companion cases (each document shall include the caption showing the name of the issuing court or agency, the title and number of the case, and the date of entry);

(iii) any order on rehearing, including the caption showing the name of the issuing court, the title and number of the case, and the date of entry;

(iv) the judgment sought to be reviewed if the date of its entry is different from the date of the opinion or order required in sub-subparagraph (i) of this subparagraph;

(v) material required by subparagraphs 1(f) or 1(g)(i); and

(vi) any other material the petitioner believes essential to understand the petition.

If the material required by this subparagraph is voluminous, it may be presented in a separate volume or volumes with appropriate covers.

2. All contentions in support of a petition for a writ of *certiorari* shall be set out in the body of the petition, as provided in subparagraph 1(h) of this Rule. No separate brief in support of a petition for a writ of *certiorari* may be filed, and the Clerk will not file any petition for a writ of *certiorari* to which any supporting brief is annexed or appended.

3. A petition for a writ of *certiorari* should be stated briefly and in plain terms and may not exceed the [30] page limitation specified in Rule 33.

4. The failure of a petitioner to present with accuracy, brevity, and clarity whatever is essential to ready and adequate understanding of the points requiring consideration is sufficient reason for the Court to deny a petition.

5. If the Clerk determines that a petition submitted timely and in good faith is in a form that does not comply with this Rule or with Rule 33 or Rule 34, the Clerk will return it with a letter indicating the deficiency. A corrected

petition received no more than 60 days after the date of the Clerk's letter will be deemed timely.

NOTES

1. The SCOTUS is the only federal court created by the Constitution. Article III, § 1 requires that there be "one supreme Court" and authorizes Congress to "ordain and establish" other "inferior courts" as it deems appropriate. *See also* U.S. CONST. art. I, § 8, cl. 9 (Congress authorized "[t]o constitute Tribunals inferior to the supreme Court"). The Constitution also provides for the selection of the justices, guarantees their tenure in office subject only to impeachment by the House of Representatives and removal by the Senate, and provides them salary protection to assure their independence. *See also* U.S. CONST., art. II, § 2, cl. 2 (presidents appoint the judges of the Supreme Court with the "advice and consent" of the Senate); U.S. CONST. art. II, § 4 (impeachment and removal). *See generally* Chapter 11, *Appellate Judges*.

2. Review the constitutional and statutory provisions above that provide for the SCOTUS's subject matter jurisdiction. The emphasis of this Chapter is on the Court's discretionary jurisdiction and how the Court exercises that discretion — how the justices decide what cases to decide on the merits. What are the official "considerations governing review on *certiorari*" provided in the SUP. CT. R. 10? Read over the "content of a petition for a writ of *certiorari*" set out in SUP. CT. R. 14. What criteria are the justices applying? How specific are the criteria? Do the Rules provide the justices or their law clerks with sufficient guidance? What information do the justices have before them when they are determining whether or not to grant the writ, *i.e.*, whether the case is "certworthy"? Is it realistic to expect the petition to be written exclusively in terms of the *certiorari* standard and not get into the merits of the case?

3. Earlier jurisdictional statutes elaborately distinguished between two alternative bases for obtaining Supreme Court review. First, some cases were heard by "appeal" — using the word in the narrow technical sense to mean a guaranteed statutory right to have the merits decided and the lower court decision reviewed. Second, some cases were heard by the Court granting a "writ of *certiorari*" — by which the losing litigant in the court below asks permission and the Supreme Court exercises its discretion to grant review. One other distinction under the former statutory scheme was that every affirmance and reversal of an appeal was a decision on the merits and carried some precedential effect. Even so, in reality the justices managed to avoid deciding a considerable proportion of appealed cases on jurisdictional grounds, such as a dismissal for want of a substantial federal question, a procedural finesse to be rid of the case even though it technically satisfied the statutory criteria, a practice that had the look and feel of a discretionary writ. In 1988, responding to this reality and to the justices' entreaties for more formal control over their docket, Congress all but did away with Supreme Court appeals. *See* Act of June 27, 1988, Pub. L. No. 100-352, 102 Stat. 662. Appeals are still technically a matter of right only in cases decided by a three-judge District Court, which is nearly an extinct creature of the federal court system now pretty much limited by statute to Voting Rights Act challenges to the constitutionality of the apportionment of congressional districts and statewide legislative districts. 28 U.S.C. §§ 1253 & 2284(a).

Consequently, true appeals — cases which the Supreme Court is obliged to hear and decide — arise rather infrequently, and now they show up on the Supreme Court's docket mostly on the ten-year census-and-redistricting cycle. *E.g., Easley v. Cromartie*, 532 U.S. 234 (2001). Congress rarely, but occasionally, will include a particular designated grant of Supreme Court jurisdiction in a controversial statute that is sure to be challenged on constitutional grounds, like the federal anti-flag burning act of 1989 that provided for an automatic appeal from the federal trial court directly to the Supreme Court, bypassing the IAC. *United States v. Eichman*, 496 U.S. 310 (1990). *See generally* Robert L. Stern, Eugene Gressman & Stephen M. Shapiro, *Epitaph for Mandatory Jurisdiction*, 74 A.B.A. J. 66 (1988). When reading opinions from before 1988, students must be generally aware of these developments in SCOTUS jurisdiction to appreciate the then-prevailing distinction between a review as of right on appeal and a review as a matter of discretion on a writ of *certiorari*.

4. While the emphasis of this Chapter is on the Supreme Court's appellate jurisdiction, note that Article III, Section 2, Clause 2 also provides for the original jurisdiction of the Supreme Court that is implemented by a jurisdictional statute, 28 U.S.C. § 1251. The most famous decision of the Court was in fact a case of original jurisdiction that established the power of judicial review — the power of the Supreme Court to review and strike down unconstitutional acts of the legislative and executive branches of the state and national governments. *Marbury v. Madison*, 5 U.S. (1 Cranch) 137 (1803). Cases are filed directly in the SCOTUS sitting as a *nisi prius* trial court only in the most limited circumstances, however. The most common type of original jurisdiction cases involve a dispute between two states, for example, a boundary dispute or a suit over water rights in an interstate river. *E.g., Virginia v. Maryland*, 540 U.S. 56 (2003). Here the Court's jurisdiction is original and exclusive; therefore, it is the only court that can hear the case. The Supreme Court itself does not hold a trial; instead, the matter usually is referred to a special master, a retired judge or a distinguished lawyer, who conducts a hearing and then makes formal written recommendations to resolve the dispute. In some other specified classes of cases, including controversies between the United States and a State, the Supreme Court's jurisdiction is original but not exclusive so that the Court can and usually does merely stand by and allow the matter to be resolved in the first instance in a lower federal court. *E.g., California v. Nevada*, 447 U.S. 125 (1980). For present purposes, it is enough to point out that the original jurisdiction cases do not amount to a large or an important part of the Supreme Court's docket today.

5. An historical note: The structure of the federal court system has evolved along the lines of development studied in Chapter 6 — an intermediate tier was added to expand a two-tiered structure in response to caseload overload — the federal IACs were created in response to dramatic docket increases at the SCOTUS. *See generally* THOMAS E. BAKER, RATIONING JUSTICE ON APPEAL: THE PROBLEMS OF THE U.S. COURTS OF APPEALS 3-12 (1994). The Judiciary Act of 1789, Act of Sept. 24, 1789, ch. 20, 1 Stat. 73, originally established a two-tiered structure of trial courts (district courts with limited jurisdiction and circuit courts with general jurisdiction) with the Supreme Court acting as the principal appellate court. In the period after the Civil War, the nation's geographic expansion,

population increase, and commercial development all contributed to a dramatic increase in federal court litigation that was compounded by congressional extensions of the federal court subject matter jurisdiction. Between 1870 and 1880 the Supreme Court caseload nearly doubled, and by 1890 the Court had nearly three times its 1870 caseload and the backlog of cases exceeded fifty thousand. After a considerable period of uncertainty and delay, Congress eventually enacted the Circuit Court of Appeals Act of 1891, Act of Mar. 3, 1891, ch. 517, 26 Stat. 826, commonly known as the Evarts Act, that created an intermediate tier of nine appellate courts — arranged geographically — and authorized somewhat limited second appeals to the Supreme Court. The next phase of this structural reform was a reallocation of jurisdiction; the famous Judges' Bill of 1925, Act of Feb. 13, 1925, ch. 229, 43 Stat. 936, afforded the justices of the Supreme Court considerably more discretion over their appellate docket. *See supra* Note 3. That basic three-tiered structure has remained intact, with a few minor modifications. A tenth circuit was carved out of the eighth circuit in 1929. In the 1948 Judicial Code, Congress formally added the District of Columbia Circuit and renamed the "circuit courts" to call them the "courts of appeals for the [relevant] circuit." In 1981, the Fifth Circuit was split into the new Fifth Circuit and the new Eleventh Circuit; in 1982, the Court of Appeals for the Federal Circuit was created with national jurisdiction over specified subject matters. All in all, the federal court structure has been remarkably stable, considering the changes that have taken place in the nation over this period. *See also* FELIX FRANKFURTER & JAMES M. LANDIS, THE BUSINESS OF THE SUPREME COURT: A STUDY IN THE FEDERAL JUDICIAL SYSTEM (1927); ERWIN C. SURRENCY, HISTORY OF THE FEDERAL COURTS (1987). The future design of the federal court structure is the subject of Chapter 14.

6. The statutes reproduced above describe an elaborate jurisdictional relationship between the federal IACs and the SCOTUS. 28 U.S.C. § 1254 (2) provides for "certified questions," a review procedure by which the U.S. Courts of Appeals can identify a particular legal issue and ask the Supreme Court for a binding decision on the issue. The Supreme Court then has discretion either to answer the question or to call the entire case up for review or to refuse to do anything. This device is common among state court systems and is commonly used. Although this procedure is still "on the books" it is never used in the federal system. One reason is that the Supreme Court must agree to hear and decide the question being certified. *See Wisniewski v. United States*, 353 U.S. 901 (1957). The same statute also provides for the extraordinary procedure of the Supreme Court taking up a case for review before the Court of Appeals has had the opportunity to rule, a procedure that the Supreme Court is somewhat more willing to use, albeit in rare and historic cases when an expeditious and final decision is a matter of "imperative public importance" and an intermediate appeal would serve no judicial purpose. 28 U.S.C. §§ 1254(1) & 2101(e); SUP. CT. R. 11. *E.g., United States v. Nixon*, 418 U.S. 683 (1974). *See generally* Chapter 6.

7. The statutes reproduced above likewise map the jurisdictional boundary between the SCOTUS and the state appellate court systems. 28 U.S.C. § 1257

requires a "final judgment" from "the highest court of a state." Thus, the finality doctrine of appellate jurisdiction of the courts of appeals covered in Chapter 2 likewise comes into play in the Supreme Court. *See* 28 U.S.C. § 1291. The "highest court" requirement, however, is qualified. Final judgments from the COLR of the state — usually called a supreme court but called a court of appeals in a few states — satisfy the requirement. If under state procedures the case is not within the jurisdiction of the highest state court but it presents a constitutional issue, the Supreme Court can hear and decide an appeal from a lower state court. *E.g., Brown v. Texas*, 443 U.S. 47 (1979). The SCOTUS will not consider a constitutional issue if the case has been disposed of in the state court on some non-constitutional ground which is sufficient to justify the final decision. The non-constitutional ground can be procedural or substantive, but it must be "independent and adequate." It must be independent of the federal constitutional ground and not be entwined with it either explicitly or implicitly. It must be adequate in the sense of being *bona fide* and broad enough to sustain the judgment and dispose of the case, *i.e.*, of sufficient legal significance to decide the case and to justify the Supreme Court's declining to reach the federal constitutional issue. The holding in *Michigan v. Long*, 463 U.S. 1032 (1983), announced the prudential rule that a state supreme court must clearly state in its opinion that it is deciding a case on the independent and adequate state law ground and then the SCOTUS will not hear the case. Otherwise, without the plain statement, the federal constitutional issue will be deemed still in play and subject to judicial review by the Supreme Court. In close and difficult cases, the Supreme Court may remand the case to the state supreme court for clarification of the basis of its decision. *See generally* Thomas E. Baker, *The Ambiguous Independent and Adequate State Ground in Criminal Cases: Federalism Along a Möbius Strip*, 19 GA. L. REV. 799 (1985).

8. Alexis De Tocqueville observed that the SCOTUS performs an almost-mythic role, as a judicial body and as an institution of constitutional self-government, a role that is at once profound and subtle, a role that is as difficult to understand as it is impossible to overstate:

> The peace, prosperity, and the very existence of the Union rest continually in the hands of these [nine] judges. Without them the Constitution would be dead letter; it is to them that the executive appeals to resist the encroachments of the legislative body, the legislature to defend itself against the assaults of the executive, the Union to make the states obey it, the States to rebuff the exaggerated pretensions of the Union, public interest against private interest, the spirit of conservation against democratic instability. Their power is immense, but it is power springing from opinion. They are all-powerful so long as the people continue to obey the law; they can do nothing when they scorn it. Now, of all powers, that of opinion is the hardest to use, for it is impossible to say exactly where its limits come. Often it is as dangerous to lag behind as to outstrip it.

ALEXIS DE TOCQUEVILLE, DEMOCRACY IN AMERICA 150 (J.P. Mayer ed., 1969).

II. PRACTICES AND PROCEDURES

H.W. PERRY, JR., DECIDING TO DECIDE: AGENDA SETTING IN THE UNITED STATES SUPREME COURT 41-51 & 64-69 (1991)[1]

The Process: A Generic Description. Petitions for *certiorari* are either mailed or hand-delivered to the Clerk of the Court. [T]he petitioning cases must fulfill certain jurisdictional and procedural requirements. The Clerk screens the petitions for various types of technical errors such as page length and timeliness, but few are culled for such reasons. From the Clerk's office, the petitions and any accompanying papers (such as responses or appendices) are not sent to each chamber on a "rumbling cart." From this point on, there are actually two different general processes.

Pool Chambers. With the number of *cert* petitions increasing almost geometrically, Chief Justice Burger and several of his colleagues formed what has come to be known as the "*cert* pool." Current members are Chief Justice [Roberts] and Justices Scalia, Kennedy, [Souter, Thomas, Ginsburg, Breyer, and Alito]. Justices Powell, [White, Blackmun O'Connor and Chief Justice Rehnquist] also were members. The pool was designed to reduce the workload by eliminating duplication of effort. Rather than have each chamber review every petition, the petitions are randomly assigned for evaluation among the [eight] chambers in the pool. Each chamber then divides its [one-eighth] of the petitions randomly among the clerks in that chamber. A clerk will review the petitions assigned to her and then write a *cert* pool memo for each of her petitions.

The pool memo follows a standard form. It lists the following basic information: whether the case is on *cert* or appeal; if it is timely (in a jurisdictional sense); the court below; the name of the judges on the panel below; who wrote the opinion; and who dissented or concurred. The memo then summarizes the issues, the facts and the opinion(s) below, followed by a cursory analysis and a recommendation to grant or deny. The pool memo runs anywhere from one to ten pages but usually is two to five. The completed memo is sent to the chief's chambers. Copies of the pool memo are then forwarded to all chambers in the pool. There, a second clerk examines the memo and "marks it up" for his justice. The markup memo may simply note that it agrees with the pool memo; or, it may analyze the case more thoroughly and disagree with the pool memo. The pool memo and the clerk's markup are then given to the justice along with the *cert* petition and any accompanying papers. In most cases, the justice reads only the memo and the markup. For those cases where a decision to grant or deny is more difficult, the justice may read parts of the petition.

Nonpool Chambers. Justice[] Stevens is not in the pool, nor were Justices Brennan, [Marshall,] and Stewart. Generally, each of these chambers evaluates every petition, and there is no formalized sharing of information between chambers. The process in nonpool chambers is much more informal. Petitions are divided randomly among the clerks within a chamber, and a memo is written only for one's own justice. These memos contain much of the same

---

[1] Reprinted by permission of the publisher from DECIDING TO DECIDE: AGENDA SETTING IN THE UNITED STATES SUPREME COURT by H.W. Perry, pp. 41-44, 46-47, 48-50, 64-67, 69, Cambridge, Mass.: Harvard University Press, Copyright © 1991 by the President and Fellows of Harvard College. [Bracketed edits reflect changes in SCOTUS membership as of 2005].

information that is in the pool memo, but they are usually shorter and much less formal, particularly as the term progresses. An extreme example of informality was recounted by one nonpool clerk, who recalled one memo that simply said, "this is the draft cases — deny." Most cases require more than that, of course, but it indicates a type of informality that does not exist in a pool memo.

There is a good deal of variation among the nonpool chambers, however. For example, Justice Brennan [used to do] most of his own *cert* work, and Justice Stevens has a different procedure altogether. The processes used in these two chambers are described in more detail below.

Discuss List. After the memos have been written and the markups have been done, the chief justice prepares a list of those cases he believes worthy of discussion at the conference. He circulates this "discuss list" to all nine chambers. Any justice can add cases to the list simply by informing the administrative clerk in the chief's chambers. The other chambers are then informed of the additions. All cases not making the discuss list are automatically denied *cert*.

Conference. On Friday, conference day, the morning is spent discussing cases that have already been argued. The justices break for lunch, and they return in the afternoon to dispense with the requests for *certiorari*. Each justice has already developed a fairly firm idea of how he will vote prior to the conference and so goes into the conference room carrying a copy of the discuss list with each case marked as to how he plans to vote on *certiorari*. He also brings a cart into the room loaded with all the petitions and the memos written by his clerks with any annotations that he himself has made.

The chief justice begins discussion of the first cases on the discuss list. Each justice, in order of seniority, gives his comments on the case and usually announces his vote at that time. If a case receives four votes — the "rule of four" — it is granted *cert*. Though formal votes are rare, if one is required, it, too, is taken in order of seniority. Traditionally, it was thought that the justices "discussed down and voted up" that is, discussion proceeded from the most senior to the most junior justice, and voting, from the most junior to the most senior. Indeed, most books on the Court report the procedure as such, and I had always assumed it to be so. During an interview with a justice, however, I learned that the common wisdom is not so wise as common. . . . One wonders how many other "silly" notions we outsiders have. Were justices not so secretive about innocuous details, maybe scholars would not perpetuate these errors. It is easy to understand how such misinformation spreads, because rarely do justices speak out on internal procedures. . . . Allowing the public to know the order of the voting procedure is innocuous. That does not mean it is unimportant. For social scientists engaged in theory building through formal modeling, for example, the ordering of decisional steps is crucial. It is also important to scholars who are trying to evaluate the Court in ways other than formal modeling. . . .

The traditional explanation for voting up is that it was done so that the junior justices would not be influenced or intimidated by their senior brethren. Justice Goldberg, however, once characterized the notion that junior justices would be influenced or intimidated by their colleagues as "ridiculous." The justices with whom I spoke would agree with Justice Goldberg, at least as far as *cert* votes are concerned. Even so, order remains important. Recall that a justice's vote is announced at the time he discusses the case and that there is no formal vote *per se*. Since the discussion and vote usually occur simultaneously, the order of voting has at least one interesting consequence. As one justice pointed out: "[The order] does raise a question in that while theoretically all we are doing is taking a tentative vote when we are discussing a case, it is rare that anyone ever changes, so sometimes as a junior justice one doesn't have the chance to speak to convince others." I asked all the justices in one form or another to describe what went on in conference.

> *Justice:* [Of the typical conference] The chief justice [Rehnquist] is really a past master at this. He succinctly summarizes the cases he's put on, unless it's an issue that particularly troubles him. Then we discuss in order of seniority. . . . I generally would say, "I don't think this is a case that we need to hear; I deny," and nothing more than that. Or, "I'd hear the case for these reasons"; or sometimes, "I would deny for these reasons". The chief begins the discussion for the cases he has listed. Now if I have listed a case, then he'll turn to me to discuss it, and I'll lay it out. I'll give my reasons and I'll say, "therefore I would grant," although there are some times I will put a case on and I will wind up suggesting to deny it because it is not ripe. . . . Obviously I go in with an agenda. I have the discuss list on the left, and inside the case I have my vote. I may get to conference intending to deny, yet later vote to grant because of something a colleague said on something I hadn't considered, and he might be right. But most times, though, I vote as I had planned to when I went in there. There are enough times that I change, though, to suggest that it happens.

Finally, one justice put it this way: "There wouldn't be much need for a conference if we were all firm in our opinions. But we generally have a tentative view. We do have some discussion, but it varies from case to case in terms of how intense or what the discussion is about."

As described by the justices, then, there is usually little discussion in conference on *cert*. They come to the conference with their minds made up for most cases, and they will usually vote to grant or deny on the spot.

Another vote that a justice can announce, however, is that he will "join three." Obviously, it means that if there are three others who are voting to grant, the justice will give them a fourth vote. There is also a vote calling for a summary disposition. Some justices will say, "I will vote to reverse, but not to hear." This latter practice has caused controversy, some of which has been aired publicly. . . . [J]ustices have criticized the Court in specific instances for disposing of a particular case in summary fashion. Nevertheless, as with the "rule of four" to grant *cert*, an informal operating rule of the Court has developed which says that a case may be treated summarily if six justices agree. The decision is often made at the time of the *cert* vote.

Relisting. Not all cases are disposed of the first time they appear on the conference list. For various reasons, cases are sometimes relisted. One of the most common reasons to relist is to "call for a response." If the winning party below did not file a response brief in opposition to the petition for *certiorari* — an "opps" as they are commonly called — then the Court sometimes requests one before making a *cert* decision. When that happens, the case is "put over," or "relisted," which means that it is put on the agenda for a future conference after the response has been filed. If at the original conference there are only one or two votes to grant, there is probably no reason to call for a response. However, if any justice calls for a response, or asks that a case be relisted, it is done automatically regardless of the initial vote.

One variant of calling for a response is to call for the views of the solicitor general, or the "SG" as he is commonly called. He is the person who represents the United States in the Supreme Court. Until recently, the SG always filed a brief in opposition when a ruling was being appealed against the United States, but that is no longer so. The Court, then, may ask him for a response. Usually, however, calling for the views of the SG refers to a situation where the United States is not a party to the case, but where the case has a potentially significant impact upon the government. Here, the SG is asked to file an amicus brief on *cert*.

The justices will also relist a case from time to time to "call for the record." In order to sort out issues to determine certworthiness, the justices, or their clerks, sometimes need the entire record from the courts below, most particularly the court of first instance. Poring over the record is very time consuming, however, so if certworthiness cannot be determined by the petition alone, the case is usually just denied. Finally, a justice will sometimes request that a case be put over because he is contemplating writing a dissent from denial of *certiorari*.

A new norm has recently developed with regard to relisting. Although the rule of four means that a case is granted review if it receives at least four votes, when a case has only four votes, the chief justice may ask if the case can be relisted to see if any of the four want to reconsider. This practice has resulted from the increasing caseload; it has not been used as an attempt to undercut the rule of four. If the four granting justices want the case reviewed, it shall be. Likewise, there is no attempt to dissuade any of the granting justices. This new procedure is simply an effort to make sure that a case is really considered certworthy even though it was only able to muster four votes. . . .

In sum, relisting is not a favored practice unless it is to call for the views of the SG, or when a case has only gathered four votes. One justice put it this way: "There is only so much time that the conference has as a body, and there is not much time to debate *cert* on a case more than once. The consensus of the conference is that you vote it up or down on the spot."

The Stevens Process. Justice Stevens is not a member of the pool, and the process used in his chambers is quite different from that used in other nonpool chambers. As he has stated publicly, beginning in October Term 1977, he had his clerks write memos only on those cases that the clerks thought should be granted or discussed. If a case appeared on the discuss list for which no memo had been written, a clerk would prepare one prior to conference. I asked the Stevens clerks the percentage of cases requiring memos.

Clerk: We wrote no memo on about 40 to 50 percent of them. We started out by writing many more, but soon you learn the standards the Justices use. To get *cert*, a case almost has to be perfect.

Clerk: I would say that we didn't on about half the unpaid [*in forma pauperis*] list.

Perry: How many memos did you write on the paid cases?

Clerk: I'd say that on about 25 to 30 percent of the paid cases there were no memos written.

Perry: Now am I to assume that many of the memos you did write were still cursory?

Clerk: Oh yes. We'd only write about this much [he held his fingers about two inches apart]. We'd simply say, "here is another such and such case."

Clerk: Incidentally, we would automatically write a memo if the SG was petitioning.

In spite of Stevens' instructions to write only on cases the clerks deemed cert-worthy, some clerks suggested that they often wrote cursory memos on cases that were obvious denies. I asked them why.

Clerk: That's a really good question. To a certain extent, it was a prag-matic consideration. You were interested in protecting yourself because if you knew that another justice was going to put it on the dis-cuss list, you might as well go ahead and write the memo. . . . Another criteria was if you could do a quick one, you just went ahead and did it. That in a sense could protect you. I don't think that was Justice Stevens' concept, but that's part of the way it worked. . . . Some of the things that I thought were obvious denies and I knew that Justice Stevens wouldn't be interested in, I knew by now that other justices were interested in it. . . . Again, the process evolved. In the beginning it was real difficult for me to tell what was an obvious deny. Everything looked like it deserved to be heard.

It is not clear why Justice Stevens uses this method. Perhaps it is explained by his [earlier] lack of seniority and the fact that he rarely has the responsi-bility to lead a *cert* discussion. More likely, it has something to do with Justice Stevens' strong belief that the Court takes far too many cases for review. He is probably the most vocal critic of the Court in this regard. Perhaps he believes that allowing clerks to devote their time to other tasks outweighs any benefit from a process that would only serve to increase the likelihood of a case being accepted.

Brennan: "The Wizard of Cert." During the summer preceding the first con-ference, Brennan clerks would prepare *cert* memos for Justice Brennan. But once the term began, Justice Brennan read every *cert* petition himself; more precisely, he glances at each one. Justice Brennan has said publicly that he feels that he can make most *cert* decisions based solely on reading the "Questions Presented" section in the petition. He has stated how important he thinks the case selection process is and that it is a responsibility that clearly cannot be ceded to another court. Yet the reason he did not have his clerks work on *cert* cannot be that he thought it too important to let them do it, since he had them do the *cert* work in the summer. Rather, it seems to be because he liked doing the work, and he could do it very fast. . . .

Sometimes before the decision, Brennan would ask his clerks to do some research on a petition. I asked several Brennan clerks what this research might involve.

Clerk: The easiest is when it is a technical problem. . . .

Clerk: . . . I'd say maybe fifteen or twenty the whole term.

It was unclear if Justice Brennan's particular procedure made any substantive difference. No one seemed to think he was either better or less well prepared for *cert* discussions in conference. That Brennan could handle the cases as he did and that Stevens never sees many of the cases at all, suggests that the *cert* decision can frequently be made on very little information.

John Paul Stevens, *The Life Span of a Judge-made Rule*, 58 N.Y.U. L. Rev. 1, 10-21 (1983)[2]

Whenever four justices of the United States Supreme Court vote to grant a petition for a writ of *certiorari*, the petition is granted even though a majority of the Court votes to deny. Although the origins of this so-called Rule of Four are somewhat obscure, it was first publicly described by the justices who testified in support of the Judges' Bill that became the Judiciary Act of 1925. That Act enabled the Supreme Court to cope with the "utterly impossible" task of deciding the merits of every case on its crowded docket. The Act alleviated the Court's problem by giving it the power to refuse to hear most of the cases on its docket. Since 1925, most of the cases brought to the Supreme Court have been by way of a petition for a writ of *certiorari* — a petition which requests the Court to exercise its discretion to hear the case on the merits — rather than by a writ of error or an appeal requiring the Court to decide the merits.

In their testimony in support of the Judges' Bill, members of the Court explained that they had exercised discretionary jurisdiction in a limited number of federal cases since 1891 when the Circuit Courts of Appeals were created, and also in a limited number of cases arising in the state courts since 1914. They described in some detail the procedures they had followed in processing their discretionary docket and made it clear that they intended to continue to follow those practices in managing the enlarged *certiorari* jurisdiction that would be created by the enactment of the Judges' Bill.

Several features of the Court's practice were emphasized in order to demonstrate that the discretionary docket was being processed in a responsible, nonarbitrary way. These four are particularly worthy of note: (1) copies of the printed record, as well as the briefs, were distributed to every justice; (2) every justice personally examined the papers and prepared a memorandum or note

---

2 Copyright © 1983 New York University Law Review. Reprinted with permission

indicating his view of what should be done; (3) each petition was discussed by each justice at conference; and (4) a vote was taken, and if four, or sometimes just three, justices thought the case should be heard on its merits, the petition was granted. [Reading the legislative history in its entirety, I gain the impression that the principal emphasis in the presentation made by the justices concentrated on the individual attention given to every petition by every justice and the full discussion of every petition at conference, and that significantly less emphasis was placed on the Rule of Four.] In his testimony, Justice Van Devanter pointed out that in the 1922 and 1923 Terms the Court had acted on 398 and 370 petitions respectively. Since these figures indicate that the Court was processing only a handful of *certiorari* petitions each week, it is fair to infer that the practice of making an individual review and having a full conference discussion of every petition was not particularly burdensome. Indeed, at that time the number was so small that the Court was then contemplating the possibility of granting an oral hearing on every petition for *certiorari*. Times have changed and so have the Court's practices.

In the 1947 Term, when I served as a law clerk to Justice Rutledge, the practice of discussing every *certiorari* petition at conference had been discontinued. It was then the practice for the Chief Justice to circulate a so-called "dead list" identifying the cases deemed unworthy of conference discussion. Any member of the Court could remove a case from the dead list, but unless such action was taken, the petition would be denied without even being mentioned at conference.

In the 1975 Term, when I joined the Court, I found that other significant procedural changes had occurred. The "dead list" had been replaced by a "discuss list"; now the Chief Justice circulates a list of cases that he deems worthy of discussion and each of the other members of the Court may add cases to that list. In a sense, the discuss list practice is the functional equivalent of the dead list practice, but there is a symbolic difference. In 1925, every case was discussed; in 1947 every case was discussed unless it was on the dead list; today, no case is discussed unless it is placed on a special list.

Other changes have also occurred. It is no longer true that the record in the court below is routinely filed with the *certiorari* petition. It is no longer true that every justice personally examines the original papers in every case. Published dissents from denials of *certiorari* were unknown in 1925 but are now a regular occurrence. Today law clerks prepare so-called "pool memos" that are used by several justices in evaluating *certiorari* petitions. The pool memo practice may be an entirely proper response to an increase in the volume of *certiorari* petitions from seven or eight per week when the Judges' Bill was passed in 1925 to approximately 100 per week at the present time. It is nevertheless noteworthy that it is a significant departure from the practice that was explained to the Congress in 1924.

The rule that four affirmative votes are sufficient to grant *certiorari* has, however, survived without change. Indeed, its wisdom has seldom, if ever, been questioned. Perhaps it is time to do so. . . .

I am neither persuaded myself nor prepared to shoulder the burden of persuading my colleagues, that the Rule of Four should be abandoned — either temporarily or permanently. I am, however, prepared to demonstrate that it would be entirely legitimate to reexamine the rule, that some of the arguments for preserving the rule are unsound, and that there are valid reasons for a careful study before more drastic solutions to the Court's workload problems are adopted.

First, I would put to one side any suggestion that the representations made to Congress when the 1925 Judges' Bill was enacted created some sort of estoppel that would make it dishonorable for the Court to change the Rule of Four. The Justices' testimony in 1924 contained a complete and candid explanation of the practices then being followed and a plain expression of an intent to continue to follow essentially the same practices in the future. The purposes of the testimony were to demonstrate that the selection of cases for review would be based on neutral and relevant considerations, rather than the arbitrary choice of particular justices, and that the Court would continue to hear an adequate number of cases. The testimony, however, contained no representation or even suggestion that the Court might not make various procedural changes in response to changes in the condition of its docket. I have found nothing in the legislative history of the 1925 Act that limits the Court's power to modify its internal rules governing the processing of its *certiorari* docket.

But even if I have misread that history, ample precedent supports the proposition that the Court has the authority to modify the *certiorari* procedures that were being followed in the 1920's. The Court has already eliminated the record filing requirement; it has abandoned the practice of individual discussion of every petition at conference; there have been substantial changes in the way each individual justice evaluates each *certiorari* petition. In my judgment, each of those procedural modifications was an entirely legitimate response to a dramatic change in the character of the docket. They are precedents that establish the legitimacy of making such other internal procedural changes — specifically including a possible modification of the Rule of Four — as may be appropriate to cope with a problem whose present dimensions were not foreseen in 1925.

During most of the period in which the Rule of Four was developed, the Court had more capacity than it needed to dispose of its argument docket. The existence of the rule in 1924 provided a persuasive response to the concern — expressed before the Judges' Bill was enacted — that the Court might not accept enough cases for review if its discretionary docket were enlarged. In my judgment, it is the opposite concern that is now dominant. For I think it is clear that the Court now takes far too many cases. Indeed, I am persuaded that since the enactment of the Judges' Bill in 1925, any mismanagement of the Court's docket has been in the direction of taking too many, rather than too few, cases.

In his talk on stare decisis in 1944, Justice Jackson noted that the substitution of discretionary for mandatory jurisdiction had failed to cure the problem of overloading because judges found it so difficult to resist the temptation to correct perceived error or to take on an interesting question despite its lack of general importance. In a letter written to Senator Wheeler in 1937 describing the workload of the Supreme Court, Chief Justice Hughes, after noting that less than twenty percent of the *certiorari* petitions raised substantial questions, stated: "I think that it is the view of the members of the Court that if any error is made in dealing with these applications it is on the side of liberality." In a recent letter Paul Freund, who served as Justice Brandeis' law clerk in 1932, advised me that the Justice "believed the Court was granting review in too many cases — not only because of their relative unimportance for the development or clarification of the law but because they deprived the Court of time to pursue the really significant cases with adequate reflection and in sufficient depth."

It can be demonstrated that the Rule of Four has had a significant impact on the number of cases that the Court has reviewed on their merits. A study of Justice Burton's docket book for the 1946 and 1947 Terms reveals that, in each of those Terms, the decision to grant *certiorari* was supported by no more than four votes in over twenty-five percent of the granted cases. It is, of course, possible that in some of those cases a justice who voted to deny might have voted otherwise under a Rule of Five, but it does seem fair to infer that the Rule of Four had a significant impact on the aggregate number of cases granted.

A review of my own docket sheets for the 1979, 1980, and 1981 Terms confirms this conclusion. No more than four affirmative votes resulted in granting over twenty-three percent of the petitions granted in the 1979 Term, over thirty percent of those granted in the 1980 Term, and about twenty-nine percent of those granted in the 1981 Term. In my judgment, these are significant percentages. If all — or even most — of those petitions had been denied, the number of cases scheduled for argument on the merits this Term would be well within the range that all justices consider acceptable.

Mere numbers, however, provide an inadequate measure of the significance of the cases that were heard because of the rule. For I am sure that some Court opinions in cases that were granted by only four votes have made a valuable contribution to the development of our jurisprudence. My experience has persuaded me, however, that such cases are exceptionally rare. I am convinced that a careful study of all of the cases that have been granted on the basis of only four votes would indicate that in a surprisingly large number the law would have fared just as well if the decision of the court of appeals or the state court had been allowed to stand.

The Rule of Four is sometimes justified by the suggestion that if four justices of the Supreme Court consider a case important enough to warrant full briefing and argument on the merits, that should be sufficient evidence of the significance of the question presented. But a countervailing argument has at least equal force. Every case that is granted on the basis of four votes is a case that five members of the Court thought should not be granted. For the most significant work of the Court, it is assumed that the collective judgment of its majority is more reliable than the views of the minority. Arguably, therefore, deference to the minority's desire to add additional cases to the argument docket may rest on an assumption that whether the Court hears a few more or a few less cases in any term is not a matter of first importance.

History and logic both support the conclusion that the Rule of Four must inevitably enlarge the size of the Court's argument docket and cause it to hear a substantial number of cases that a majority of the Court deems unworthy of review. It has been argued that because the Court now grants a smaller percentage of *certiorari* petitions than it did in the past, it is not granting enough. But that argument rests on the untenable assumption that the correct standard was set at some unspecified time in the past — an assumption that simply ignores the impact of the Rule of Four.

Reflection about the impact of the Rule of Four on the size of the docket demonstrates that the Court has a greater capacity to solve its own problems than is often assumed. We might, for example, simply abandon the Rule of Four, or perhaps refuse to follow it whenever our backlog reaches a predetermined point. But there are reasons to beware of such a procedural change. Even if the Rule of Four had nothing more than a distinguished parentage, an unblemished reputation, and a venerable age to commend itself to posterity, it has additional redeeming virtues. It gives each member of the Court a stronger voice in determining the makeup of the Court's docket. It increases the likelihood that an unpopular litigant, or an unpopular issue, will be heard in the country's court of last resort. Like the danger of awakening a sleeping dog, the costs of change are not entirely predictable. Surely those costs should not be incurred if less drastic solutions to the Court's problems are available.

In the processing of our *certiorari* docket we are often guilty of ignoring the teachings of the doctrine of judicial restraint; if we simply acted with greater restraint during the case selection process, we might be able to manage the docket effectively under the Rule of Four. But we may find it necessary to acknowledge that the Rule of Four is a luxury we can no longer afford. In conclusion, I will merely note that my primary objective has been neither to praise nor to bury the Rule of Four, but rather to suggest that one may legitimately ask questions about its future life span.

MARYLAND v. BALTIMORE RADIO SHOW, INC.
338 U.S. 912 (1950)

Petition for a writ of *certiorari* to the Court of Appeals of Maryland denied.

Opinion of Mr. Justice Frankfurter respecting the denial of the petition.

. . . The sole significance of such denial of a petition for writ of *certiorari* need not be elucidated to those versed in the Court's procedures. It simply means that fewer than four members of the Court deemed it desirable to review a decision of the lower court as a matter "of sound judicial discretion." A variety of considerations underlie denials of the writ, and as to the same petition different reasons may lead different Justices to the same result. This is especially true of petitions for review on writ of *certiorari* to a State court. Narrowly technical reasons may lead to denials. Review may be sought too late; the judgment of the lower court may not be final; it may not be the judgment of a State court of last resort; the decision may be supportable as a matter of State law, not subject to review by this Court, even though the State court also passed on issues of federal law. A decision may satisfy all these technical requirements and yet may commend itself for review to fewer than four members of the Court. Pertinent considerations of judicial policy here come into play. A case may raise an important question but the record may be cloudy. It may be desirable to have different aspects of an issue further illumined by the lower courts. Wise adjudication has its own time for ripening.

Since there are these conflicting and, to the uninformed, even confusing reasons for denying petitions for *certiorari*, it has been suggested from time to time that the Court indicate its reasons for denial. Practical considerations preclude. In order that the Court may be enabled to discharge its indispensable duties, Congress has placed the control of the Court's business, in effect, within the Court's discretion. During the last three terms the Court disposed of 260, 217, 224 cases, respectively, on their merits. For the same three terms the Court denied, respectively, 1,260, 1,105, 1,189 petitions calling for discretionary review. [In the 2004 Term, the Court granted review in 87 cases and denied 7,697 petitions.] If the Court is to do its work it would not be feasible to give reasons, however brief, for refusing to take these cases. The time that would be required is prohibitive, apart from the fact as already indicated that different reasons not infrequently move different members of the court in concluding that a particular case at a particular time makes review undesirable. It becomes relevant here to note that failure to record a dissent from a denial of a petition for writ of *certiorari* in nowise implies that only the member of the Court who notes his dissent thought the petition should be granted.

Inasmuch, therefore, as all that a denial of a petition for a writ of *certiorari* means is that fewer than four members of the Court thought it should be granted, this Court has rigorously insisted that such a denial carries with it no implication whatever regarding the Court's views on the merits of a case which it has declined to review. The Court has said this again and again; again and again the admonition has to be repeated.

RICE v. SIOUX CITY MEMORIAL PARK CEMETERY, INC.
349 U.S. 70 (1955)

[This was an action brought by the widow of a member of the Winnebago Tribe to compel a private cemetery to permit burial of the deceased on the legal basis that a provision in the cemetery's standard contract limiting burial privileges to Caucasians was void and unenforceable under both the Iowa and the U.S. constitutions. An Iowa trial court found the clause was unenforceable but held that it nevertheless could constitute a defense to this action and entered judgment for the defendant cemetery. The Iowa supreme court affirmed. The SCOTUS granted *certiorari*, received briefs, heard oral argument, and affirmed the judgment by an equally divided court with a *per curiam* opinion. 348 U.S. 880 (1954). Thereafter, a petition for rehearing was filed and this opinion followed.]

Mr. Justice Frankfurter delivered the opinion of the Court.

. . . In our consideration of this petition our attention has now been focused upon an Iowa statute enacted since the commencement of this litigation. Though it was in existence at the time the case first came here, it was then not seen in proper focus because blanketed by the issues of "state action" and constitutional power for which our interest was enlisted. This Iowa statute bars the ultimate question presented in this case from again arising in that State. In light of this fact and the standards governing the exercise of our discretionary power of review upon writ of *certiorari*, we have considered anew whether this case is one in which "there are special and important reasons" for granting the writ of *certiorari*, as required by SUPREME COURT RULE 19 ["compelling reasons" under current SUP. CT. R. 10].

This Rule, formulated thirty years ago, embodies the criteria, developed ever since the Evarts Act of 1891, by which the Court determines whether a particular case merits consideration, with due regard to the proper functioning of the limited reviewing power to which this Court is confined, decisively restricted through the creation of the intermediate Courts of Appeals and more largely confined by the Judiciary Act of 1925. In illustrating the character of reasons which may be deemed "special and important," the Rule refers to cases: "Where a state court has decided a federal question of substance not theretofore determined by this court, or has decided it in a way probably not in accord with applicable decisions of this court."

A federal question raised by a petitioner may be "of substance" in the sense that, abstractly considered, it may present an intellectually interesting and solid problem. But this Court does not sit to satisfy a scholarly interest in such issues. Nor does it sit for the benefit of the particular litigants. "Special and important reasons" imply a reach to a problem beyond the academic or the episodic. This is especially true where the issues involved reach constitutional dimensions, for then there comes into play regard for the Court's duty to avoid decision of constitutional issues unless avoidance becomes evasion.

In the present case, *certiorari* was granted, according to our practice, because at least four members of the Court deemed that despite the rather unique circumstances of this case Iowa's willingness to enforce this restrictive covenant rendered it "special and important." We were unmindful at the time of Iowa's corrective legislation and of its implications. While that statute had been cited in the opinion of the Iowa Supreme Court, without quotation, in tangential support of a substantive argument, and while similar passing references appear in respondent's briefs in opposition to the petition and on the merits, it was not even suggested as a ground for opposing the grant. Its importance was not put in identifying perspective, and it did not emerge to significance in the sifting process through which the annual hundreds of petitions for *certiorari* pass. Argument at the Bar was concerned with other issues and the even division of the Court forestalled that intensive study attendant upon opinion-writing which might well have revealed the crucial relevance of the statute.

These oversights should not now be compounded by further disregard of the impact of this enactment when viewed in the light of settled Iowa law, not previously brought to our attention, concerning its effect upon private litigation. . . .

Had the statute been properly brought to our attention and the case thereby put into proper focus, the case would have assumed such an isolated significance that it would hardly have been brought here in the first instance. Any adjudication of the constitutional claims pressed by petitioner would now be an adjudication under circumstances not promotive of the very social considerations which evidently inspired the Iowa Legislature to provide against the kind of discrimination of which complaint is here made. On the one hand, we should hesitate to pass judgment on Iowa for unconstitutional action, were such to be found, when it has already rectified any possible error. On the other hand, we should not unnecessarily discourage such remedial action by possible condonation of this isolated incident. Moreover, the evident difficulties of the case suggest that, in the absence of compelling reason, we should not risk inconclusive and divisive disposition of a case when time may further illumine or completely outmode the issues in dispute.

Such factors are among the many which must be weighed in the exercise of that "sound judicial discretion" which Rule 19 requires. We have taken this opportunity to explain their relevance, when normally, for obvious reasons in view of our volume of business, no opinion accompanies dismissal of a writ as improvidently granted, because of the apt illustration here provided of the kinds of considerations, beyond those listed by Rule 19 as illustrative but not exhaustive, which preclude adjudication on the merits of cases which may have the surface appearance of public importance.

We are therefore of the opinion that this Court's order affirming by an equally divided Court the decision of the Iowa Supreme Court, must be vacated and the writ of *certiorari* dismissed as improvidently granted. There is nothing unique about such dismissal even after full argument. There have been more than sixty such cases and on occasion full opinions have accompanied the dismissal. The circumstances of this case may be different and more unusual. But this impressive practice proves that the Court has not hesitated to dismiss a writ even at this advanced stage where it appears on further deliberation, induced by new considerations, that the case is not appropriate for adjudication. In the words of Mr. Chief Justice Taft, speaking for a unanimous Court:

> If it be suggested that as much effort and time as we have given to the consideration of the alleged conflict would have enabled us to dispose of the case before us on the merits, the answer is that it is very important that we be consistent in not granting the writ of *certiorari* except in cases involving principles the settlement of which is of importance to the public as distinguished from that of the parties, and in cases where there is a real and embarrassing conflict of opinion and authority between the circuit courts of appeal.

The petition for rehearing is granted. The order of this Court of November 15, 1954, affirming by necessity the judgment of the Supreme Court of Iowa is vacated and the writ of *certiorari* is dismissed as improvidently granted. It is so ordered.

Mr. Justice Black, with whom the Chief Justice and Mr. Justice Douglas join, dissenting.

We think that only very unusual circumstances can justify dismissal of cases on the ground that *certiorari* was improvidently granted. Our objections to such dismissals are stronger when, as here, a case has already been argued and decided by the Court. We do not agree that the circumstances relied on by the Court justify this dismissal. We granted *certiorari* because serious questions were raised concerning a denial of the equal protection of the laws guaranteed by the Fourteenth Amendment. Those questions remain undecided.

The Court dismisses the case because the Iowa Legislature has provided that every person in Iowa except one who has already filed a suit can prosecute claims like this. Apparently this law leaves everyone in Iowa free to vindicate this kind of right except the petitioner. This raises a new question of denial of equal protection of the laws equally as grave as those which prompted us to take this case originally. We cannot agree that this dismissal is justified merely because this petitioner is the only one whose rights may have been unconstitutionally denied.

LAWRENCE v. CHATER
516 U.S. 163 (1996)
&
STUTSON v. UNITED STATES
516 U.S. 193 (1996)

[In *Lawrence v. Chater*, a child was seeking Social Security survivors' benefits but a majority did not reach the merits and entered a grant of *certiorari*, *vacatur*, and remand (GVR) after Chater, the Commissioner of the Social Security Administration, abandoned the interpretation of the Social Security Act which she had successfully argued in the U.S. Fourth Circuit. The first *per curiam* opinion from that case follows. The majority entered a second GVR the same day in a second *per curiam* opinion in *Stutson v. United States*, a federal criminal case, after the Government abandoned an argument it had made before the U.S. Eleventh Circuit about the lack of timeliness of the defendant's appeal. That second *per curiam* — which merely applied the same basic analysis as the first *per curiam* — is omitted here. Justice Stevens' concurring opinion and the Chief Justice's concurring and dissenting opinion also are omitted. Justice Scalia's dissenting opinion, which responded to the two GVR's in the two *per curiam* opinions, appears below. Note that the Government, which was the respondent in both cases, abandoned the arguments it had made to prevail in the lower courts but did not concede error in either case before the Supreme Court — did not seek reversals of the lower courts. Instead, the Solicitor General invited the Supreme Court to enter a GVR in both cases, and the Court did so, resulting in the following two opinions debating the propriety of GVR dispositions in general.]

Per Curiam.

Without conceding Lawrence's ultimate entitlement to benefits, the Solicitor General invites us to grant *certiorari*, vacate the judgment below, and remand the case (GVR) so that the Court of Appeals may either decide it in light of the Commissioner's new statutory interpretation or remand the case to the Commissioner for reconsideration in light of that interpretation. We conclude both that we have the power to issue a GVR order, and that such an order is an appropriate exercise of our discretionary *certiorari* jurisdiction.

Title 28 U.S.C. § 2106 appears on its face to confer upon this Court a broad power to GVR: "The Supreme Court or any other court of appellate jurisdiction may . . . vacate . . . any judgment, decree, or order of a court lawfully brought before it for review, and may remand the cause and . . . require such further proceedings to be had as may be just under the circumstances." In his dissent issued today in this case and in *Stutson v. United States*, another case in which we issue a GVR order, Justice Scalia contends that "traditional practice" and "the Constitution and laws of the United States" impose "implicit limitations" on this power. We respectfully disagree. We perceive no textual basis for such limitations. The Constitution limits our "appellate Jurisdiction" to issues of "[federal] Law and Fact," *see* Art. III, § 2, but leaves to Congress the power to "ordain and establish . . . inferior Courts," Art. III, § 1, and to make "Exceptions" and "Regulations" limiting and controlling our appellate jurisdiction. Insofar as Congress appears to have authorized such action, we believe that this Court has the power to remand to a lower federal court any case raising a federal issue that is properly before us in our appellate capacity.

Our past practice affirms this conclusion. Although the exercise of our GVR power was, until recent times, rare, its infrequent early use may be explained in large part by the smaller size of our *certiorari* docket in earlier times. Regardless of its earlier history, however, the GVR order has, over the past 50 years, become an integral part of this Court's practice, accepted and employed by all sitting and recent Justices. We have GVR'd in light of a wide range of developments, including our own decisions, State Supreme Court decisions, new federal statutes, administrative reinterpretations of federal statutes, new state statutes, changed factual circumstances, and confessions of error or other positions newly taken by the Solicitor General.

This practice has some virtues. In an appropriate case, a GVR order conserves the scarce resources of this Court that might otherwise be expended on plenary consideration, assists the court below by flagging a particular issue that it does not appear to have fully considered, assists this Court by procuring the benefit of the lower court's insight before we rule on the merits, and alleviates the "[p]otential for unequal treatment" that is inherent in our inability to grant plenary review of all pending cases raising similar issues. Where intervening developments, or recent developments that we have reason to believe the court below did not fully consider, reveal a reasonable probability that the decision below rests upon a premise that the lower court would reject if given the opportunity for further consideration, and where it appears that such a redetermination may determine the ultimate outcome of the litigation, a GVR order is, we believe, potentially appropriate. Whether a GVR order is ultimately appropriate depends further on the equities of the case: If it appears that the intervening development, such as a confession of error in some, but not all, aspects of the decision below, is part of an unfair or manipulative litigation strategy, or if the delay and further cost entailed in a remand are not justified by the potential benefits of further consideration by the lower court, a GVR order is inappropriate. Used in accordance with this approach, the GVR order can improve the fairness and accuracy of judicial outcomes while at the same time serving as a cautious and deferential alternative to summary reversal in cases whose precedential significance does not merit our plenary review.

Our differences with Justice Scalia's dissent should not overshadow the substantial level of agreement shared by all Members of this Court. On the one hand, all are agreed that a wide range of intervening developments, including confessions of error, may justify a GVR order. On the other hand, all are agreed that our GVR power should be exercised sparingly. This Court should not just GVR a case "because it finds the opinion, though arguably correct, incomplete and unworkmanlike; or because it observes that there has been a post-judgment change in the personnel of the state supreme court, and wishes to give the new state justices a shot at the case." Respect for lower courts, the public interest in finality of judgments, and concern about our own expanding *certiorari* docket all counsel against undisciplined GVR'ing. It remains to apply these principles to the facts of this case.

The feature of this case that, in our view, makes a GVR order appropriate is the new interpretation of the Social Security Act that the Solicitor General informs us that the Social Security Administration, the agency charged with implementing that Act, has adopted. Here the Solicitor General has recommended judicial reconsideration of the merits, while not conceding the petitioner's ultimate entitlement to statutory benefits, based on a new statutory interpretation that will apparently be applied, and will probably be entitled to deference, in future cases nationwide. Here our summary review leads us to the conclusion that there is a reasonable probability that the Court of Appeals would conclude that the timing of the agency's interpretation does not preclude the deference that it would otherwise receive, and that it may be outcome determinative in this case. A GVR order is, therefore, appropriate, subject to the equities.

As to the equities, it seems clear that they favor a GVR order here. That disposition has the Government's express support, notwithstanding that its purpose is to give the Court of Appeals the opportunity to consider an administrative interpretation that appears contrary to the Government's narrow self-interest. And the Government has informed us that it intends to apply that interpretation to future cases nationwide. Giving Lawrence a chance to benefit from it furthers fairness by treating Lawrence like other future benefits applicants. We believe, therefore, that the equities and legal uncertainties of this case together merit a GVR order.

Accordingly, the motion for leave to proceed *in forma pauperis* and the petition for a writ of *certiorari* are granted. The judgment is vacated and the case is remanded to the United States Court of Appeals for the Fourth Circuit for further consideration in light of the position taken in the brief for respondent filed by the Solicitor General, August 17, 1995.

Justice Scalia, with whom Justice Thomas joins, dissenting.

I dissent because I believe that the dispositions in both No. 94-8988 and No. 94-9323 are improper extensions of our limited power to vacate without first finding error below.

It sometimes occurs that, after having considered the lower court decision and found error, an appellate court merely reverses or vacates and then remands — that is, it sets the judgment aside and sends the case back to the lower court for further proceedings, rather than entering or directing entry of judgment for the appellant or petitioner. That is the appropriate course whenever the finding of error does not automatically entitle the appellant or petitioner to judgment, and the appellate court cannot conduct (or chooses not to conduct) the further inquiry necessary to resolve the questions remaining in the litigation. Our books are full of such cases.

What is at issue here, however, is a different sort of creature, which might be called "no-fault V & R": vacation of a judgment and remand without any determination of error in the judgment below. In our discretionary *certiorari* system of review, such an order has acquired the acronym "GVR" — for the Court grants *certiorari*, vacates the judgment below, and remands for further proceedings. The question presented by today's cases is whether there is any limitation (other than the mandate "do what is fair") upon this practice. The Court's *per curiam* opinions answer "no"; I disagree.

The Court today seeks to portray our no-fault V & R practice as traditionally covering a kaleidoscopic diversity of situations. That is in my view a misportrayal; the practice has always been limited to a few discrete categories of cases. . . . Today's cases come within none of these categories of no-fault V & R.

What is more momentous than the Court's judgments in the particular cases before us — each of which extends our prior practice just a little bit — is its expansive expression of the authority that supports those judgments. It acknowledges, to begin with, no constitutional limitation on our power to vacate lower court orders properly brought before us. This presumably means that the constitutional grant of "appellate Jurisdiction" over "Cases . . . arising under [the] Constitution [and] Laws of the United States," Art. III, § 2, empowers the Court to vacate a state supreme court judgment, and remand the case, because it finds the opinion, though arguably correct, incomplete and unworkmanlike; or because it observes that there has been a post-judgment change in the personnel of the state supreme court, and wishes to give the new state justices a shot at the case. I think that is not so. When the Constitution divides our jurisdiction into "original Jurisdiction" and "appellate Jurisdiction," I think it conveys, with respect to the latter, the traditional *accoutrements* of appellate power. There doubtless is room for some innovation, particularly such as may be necessary to adapt to a novel system of federalism; but the innovation cannot be limitless without altering the nature of the power conferred.

Not only does the Court reject any constitutional limitation upon its power to vacate; it is unwilling to submit to any prudential constraint as well. Even while acknowledging the potential for "unfair[ness] or manipulat[ion]" and professing to agree that "our GVR power should be exercised sparingly," the Court commits to no standard that will control that power, other than that cloak for all excesses, "the equities." The power to "revis[e] and correc[t]" for error, *Marbury v. Madison* (1803), has become a power to void for suspicion. Comparing the modest origins of the Court's "no-fault V & R" policy with today's expansive dénouement should make even the most Pollyannish reformer believe in camel's noses, wedges, and slippery slopes.

The Court justifies its approach on the ground that it "alleviates the potential for unequal treatment that is inherent in our inability to grant plenary review of all pending cases raising similar issues." I do not see how it can promote equal treatment to announce a practice that we cannot possibly pursue in every case. If we were to plumb the "equities" and ponder the "errors" for all the petitions that come before us — if we were to conduct, for example, in all cases involving summary decisions, today's balancing of the "burden" to the Court of Appeals against the litigant's "interests" in having clarification of the ruling, or today's calculation of "the overall probabilities and equities," we would have no time left for the cases we grant to consider on the merits. Of course we do not purport to conduct such inquiries, not even the basic one of whether the decision below is probably in "error" — which is why we insist that our denial of *certiorari* does not suggest a view on the merits. Moreover, even if we tried applying the Court's "totality-of-the-circumstances" evaluation to all the petitions coming before us, we would be unlikely to achieve equal treatment. Such a plastic criterion is liable to produce inconsistent results in any series of decisions; it is virtually guaranteed to do so in a series of decisions made without benefit of adversary presentation (whether we should GVR is rarely briefed, much less argued — as it has not been here) and announced without accompaniment of a judicial opinion (we almost never give reasons as the Court has done today). The need to afford equal treatment argues precisely against the "totality-of-the-circumstances" approach embraced by the Court, and in favor of a more modest but standardized GVR practice.

Henceforth, I shall vote for an order granting *certiorari*, vacating the judgment below without determination of the merits, and remanding for further consideration, only (1) where an intervening factor has arisen that has a legal bearing upon the decision, (2) where, in a context not governed by *Michigan v. Long* (1983), clarification of the opinion below is needed to assure our jurisdiction, and (3) (in acknowledgment of established practice, though not necessarily in agreement with its validity) where the respondent or appellee confesses error in the judgment below. (I shall not necessarily note my dissent from GVR's where those conditions do not exist.) As I have discussed, neither of the present cases meets these standards. Accordingly, I respectfully dissent from today's orders and would deny both petitions.

NOTES

1. Consider Professor Perry's description of the *certiorari* processes. *See also generally* Doris Marie Provine, Case Selection in the United States Supreme Court (1980). Why is the case selection process so important? How has the SCOTUS adapted to the dramatic increases in the number of petitions for review? Have the justices delegated too much of the case selection process to their law clerks? Does this process remind you of how the U.S. courts of appeals perform their screening function? What do you think of the *cert* pool? Does it perform a function similar to the function performed by the office of central staff attorneys in the state and federal IACs? Compare how Justices Stevens and Brennan individually review petitions with how the rest of the justices review petitions by relying on the pool. Contrast how Justice Brennan personally reviewed every petition with how Justice Stevens reviews only some of them. Would the appellate process imperatives be better served if the rest of the justices adopted the Brennan approach or the Stevens approach? Is there some process value to have some of the justices opt out of the pool? If you were a justice, would you opt in or opt out? Why?

2. What kind of "rule" is the "Rule of Four"? It is not expressly provided for in the jurisdictional statutes or the SUPREME COURT RULES. *See generally* Joan Maisel Leiman, *The Rule of Four*, 57 COLUM. L. REV. 975 (1957). Justice Stevens briefly describes its origins and how it operates. He was writing at a time when the SCOTUS was deciding upwards of 150 cases a Term and some of the justices and many commentators were calling for more radical structural changes to provide relief for an overworked Supreme Court. *See infra* section III. What is the effect of the Rule of Four? Why give a minority of the justices the authority to decide what cases the full Court will decide when for every other purpose appellate courts operate under a majority rule? If a majority of the justices agree on most grants of review today (so the rule affects only a relatively small number of cases — only an estimated 2% of all petitions), is the Rule of Four still useful? *See* David M. O'Brien, *Join-3 Votes, the Rule of Four, the* Cert. *Pool, and the Supreme Court's Shrinking Plenary Docket*, 13 J.L. & POL. 779 (1997); Richard L. Revesz & Pamela S. Karlan, *Nonmajority Rules and the Supreme Court*, 136 U. PA. L. REV. 1067 (1988).

3. Justice Frankfurter's opinion above in *Maryland v. Baltimore Radio Show, Inc.* is the classic version of the official explanation that "a simple order denying a petition for a writ of *certiorari* is not designed to reflect the Court's view either as to the merits of the case or as to its jurisdiction to hear the matter." ROBERT L. STERN, EUGENE GRESSMAN, STEPHEN M. SHAPIRO & KENNETH S. GELLER, SUPREME COURT PRACTICE §5.07 at 306 (8th ed. 2002). In *Brown v. Allen*, 344 U.S. 443 (1953), the majority repeated this common wisdom, but Justice Jackson provided this bit of Zen:

> The Court is not quite of one mind on the subject. Some say denial means nothing, others say it means nothing much. Realistically, the first position is untenable and the second is unintelligible. How can we say that the prisoner must present his case to us and at the same time say that what we do with it means nothing to anybody. We might conceivably take either position but not, rationally, both, for the two will not only burden our own docket and harass the state authorities but it makes a prisoner's legitimate quest for federal justice an endurance contest.

> True, neither those outside of the Court, nor on many occasions those inside of it, know just what reasons led six Justices to withhold consent to a *certiorari*. But all know that a majority, larger than can be mustered for a good many decisions, has found reason for not reviewing the case here. Because no one knows all that a denial means, does it mean that it means nothing? Perhaps the profession could accept denial as meaningless before the custom was introduced of noting dissents from them. Lawyers and lower judges will not readily believe that Justices of this Court are taking the trouble to signal a meaningless division of opinion about a meaningless act. It is just one of the facts of life that today every lower court does attach importance to denials and to presence or absence of dissents from denials, as judicial opinions and lawyers' arguments show. . . .

> I agree that, as *stare decisis*, denial of *certiorari* should be given no significance whatever. It creates no precedent and approves no

statement of principle entitled to weight in any other case. But, for the case in which *certiorari* is denied, its minimum meaning is that this Court allows the judgment below to stand with whatever consequences it may have upon the litigants involved under the doctrine of res judicata as applied either by state or federal courts.

344 U.S. at 542-43 (Jackson, J., concurring). *See also United States v. Kras,* 409 U.S. 434, 443 (1973) (commenting on an earlier denial). However, "the Court is aware that the bar and the lower courts do not fully believe that the denial of *certiorari* indicates nothing as to the Supreme Court's reaction to the merits of a case." SUPREME COURT PRACTICE, *supra* § 5.07 at 308. Does this skepticism or disbelief make any sense considering: (1) the criteria for granting a writ of *certiorari*; (2) the internal processes of the Court; (3) the number of petitions; and (4) the percentage of petitions that are granted?

4. Over the last fifty years, the practice of dissenting from the denial of *certiorari* has become more acceptable among the justices. SUPREME COURT PRACTICE, *supra* § 5.6 at 303-06. Some dissents are motivated to attract three more votes, but presumably some dissents get suppressed when they succeed in a grant. Dissents might signal that there is something wrong with the particular case but there is some willingness among the justices to reconsider the legal issue or to rethink settled doctrine. Partly to protest the *cert* pool and partly to campaign for more annual grants, towards the end of his career Justice Douglas published all his dissents. Justices Brennan and Marshall, and later Justice Blackmun, dissented from the denial of *certiorari* in every death sentence case. Among recent justices, all but one dissent from denials of *certiorari* from time to time. Only Justice Stevens has expressed a principled objection to the practice — in what could be labeled a "dissent" from a dissent from a denial of a *certiorari*:

> One characteristic of all opinions dissenting from the denial of *certiorari* is manifest. They are totally unnecessary. They are examples of the purest form of dicta, since they have even less legal significance than the orders of the entire Court which have no precedential significance at all.

> Another attribute of these opinions is that they are potentially misleading. Since the Court provides no explanation of the reasons for denying *certiorari*, the dissenter's arguments in favor of a grant are not answered and therefore typically appear to be more persuasive than most other opinions. Moreover, since they often omit any reference to valid reasons for denying *certiorari*, they tend to imply that the Court has been unfaithful to its responsibilities or has implicitly reached a decision on the merits when, in fact, there is no basis for such an inference. . . .

> Admittedly these dissenting opinions may have some beneficial effects. Occasionally a written statement of reasons for granting *certiorari* is more persuasive than the Justice's oral contribution to the Conference. For that reason the written document sometimes persuades other Justices to change their votes and a case is granted that would otherwise have been denied. That effect, however, merely justifies the

writing and circulating of these memoranda within the Court; it does not explain why a dissent which has not accomplished its primary mission should be published.

It can be argued that publishing these dissents enhances the public's understanding of the work of the Court. But because they are so seldom answered, these opinions may also give rise to misunderstanding or incorrect impressions about how the Court actually works. Moreover, the selected bits of information which they reveal tend to compromise the otherwise secret deliberations in our Conferences. . . . In my judgment, the importance of preserving the tradition of confidentiality outweighs the minimal educational value of these opinions. In all events, these are the reasons why I have thus far resisted the temptation to publish opinions dissenting from denials of *certiorari*.

Singelton v. Commissioner, 439 U.S. 940, 944-45 (1978) (Stevens, J.).

5. *Rice v. Sioux City Memorial Park Cemetery, Inc.* excerpted above is an unusual exercise of a common SCOTUS practice to dismiss a case as improvidently granted ("DIG"). What is the rationale for DIGing this case on rehearing? Why not just leave alone the affirmance by the equally divided Court? What appellate values are being honored by such an inefficient and seemingly unjust outcome at such a late procedural stage? How could the justices and their law clerks have overlooked the procedural problem with this case? Is the Court's own *certiorari* negligence being blamed on the petitioner to deprive her of her hard-fought court victory and, in effect, relegating her to litigation limbo as a class of one? Should the Court be expected always to publish an opinion to justify DIGing a case? The reasons for DIGing a case are as varied as the reasons for granting or denying *cert*. SUPREME COURT PRACTICE, *supra* §5.15 at 328-32. The five justices who do not vote for *cert* could in theory dismiss as improvidently granted any case granted by the other four justices, and thus subvert the Rule of Four:

> Some Justices have indicated that once the writ has been granted, absent new considerations which were not known to the court prior to the grant of *certiorari*, the case should be determined on the merits. Other Justices have indicated that dismissal can be warranted under any circumstances. Some have argued that dismissal requires one of the Justices who originally granted the writ to change his or her position. At least one Justice indicated that a writ should not be dismissed as improperly granted except in exceptional situations with unanimity. Although the historical basis for the utilization of the dismissal of a writ for being improvidently granted seems to indicate that only where new factors were raised should it be employed, there exist logical reasons to dismiss it any time up until a decision is rendered.

James F. Fagan, Jr., *When Does Four of a Kind Beat a Full House? The Rise, Fall and Replacement of the Rule of Four*, 25 NEW ENG. L. REV. 1101, 1108 (1991). What do you think are good reasons to DIG a case?

6. SUP. CT. R. 16, governing the dispositions of petitions for *certiorari,* provides that "an appropriate order . . . may be a summary disposition on the merits." The grant-vacate-remand or GVR disposition debated in the *Lawrence*

and *Stutson* opinions above is the most common summary disposition used today. It also is a matter of considerable controversy among the justices. What kind of petitions and issues deserve a GVR disposition? Why would the justices want to GVR a case instead of using one of their other standard procedural options: deny the *cert* petition outright or grant the *cert* petition and set the case for full briefing and argument? Why do you suppose that by convention and custom among the justice a GVR requires six votes, *i.e.,* there is a Rule of Six? H.W. PERRY, JR., DECIDING TO DECIDE: AGENDA SETTING IN THE UNITED STATES SUPREME COURT 99-102 (1991). A frequent use of the GVR device is to remand a case to the lower court for reconsideration in light of an intervening Supreme Court decision or when the Government has confessed error in a case, meaning the Government as respondent officially and formally admits to the Court that the petitioner should prevail on the merits. The typical GVR obliges the lower court to reconsider the case being remanded, and the same case may later percolate back up to the SCOTUS on a subsequent petition for *certiorari.* But the SCOTUS also sometimes grants the petition and summarily affirms or reverses the judgment below to decide the case once and for all. These summary affirmances or reversals — reversals are more common — are decisions on the merits sometimes with and sometimes without a *per curiam* opinion, although the opinion might be merely a sentence or two with a couple of citations. They have precedential value and are binding on the lower courts as Supreme Court decisions. The SCOTUS decision on the merits is thus reached on the considerably truncated basis of the petition and the brief in opposition without the benefit of full merits briefing, without oral argument, and without a full opinion. Commentators have criticized the practice in the abstract as being an ill-informed appellate process, and members of the Court often have been heard to dissent that the particular decision in a case is uninformed. SUPREME COURT PRACTICE, *supra* §5.12 at 314-26. *See generally* Arthur D. Hellman, *The Supreme Court's Second Thoughts: Remands for Reconsideration and Denials of Review in Cases Held for Plenary Decisions,* 11 HASTINGS CONST. L.Q 5 (1983); Shaun P. Martin, *Gaming the GVR,* 36 ARIZ. ST. L.J. 551, 551 (2004) ("The Supreme Court has GVR'd over 2,500 cases since 1960, and the pace at which the Court has employed this procedure has only increased in recent years.").

7. The Solicitor General confesses error by filing an admission in the Supreme Court that the lower court has erroneously decided the case for the Government, *i.e.,* that the Government should have lost below. It is up to the Court ultimately whether to reverse the judgment or to deny review. One estimate is that this has happened "approximately 250 times in the past 100 years, or two or three times per Term on average." David M. Rosenzweig, Note, *Confession of Error in the Supreme Court by the Solicitor General,* 82 GEO. L.J. 2079, 2081 (1994). What factors should inform the SCOTUS's discretion on how to deal with a confession of error?

8. There is a common tendency, reflected in this Chapter, to treat the SCOTUS as a unique judicial entity. In many ways it is unique, but it also is an appellate court with many qualities in common with other appellate courts trying to cope with caseload demands along the themes of the previous Chapters concerning structure, jurisdiction, staffing, summary procedures, *etc.* Indeed, the study of appellate jurisdiction and procedures cuts across the

levels of the court system: For example, there is a family resemblance between the way the SCOTUS exercises its *certiorari* discretion and the way the federal IACs screen appeals with differentiated summary procedures. Stephen L. Wasby & Martha Humphries Ginn, *Triage in Appellate Courts: Cross-Level Comparison*, 88 JUDICATURE 216 (2005).

9. This section has examined how the SCOTUS manages its docket, *i.e.*, the practices and procedures that have built up around the *certiorari* jurisdiction such as the *cert* pool, the Rule of 4, DIGs, GVRs, etc. The next section examines how the justices actually have exercised their discretion to select cases, *i.e.*, identifying the factors that have influenced whether a petition gets granted or denied and examining how and why the overall number of grants has ebbed and flowed over time resulting in complaints that the justices are granting "too many" or "too few" cases.

III. CASE SELECTION

A. The Influence of the Solicitor General

REBECCA MAE SALOKAR, THE SOLICITOR GENERAL: THE POLITICS OF LAW 12-14, 22-32 (1992)[3]

Responsibilities. The solicitor general of the United States wears many hats in the Department of Justice. In addition to being a part of the organizational chain of command for the department, the officeholder is tasked with a broad range of responsibilities that include work before the Supreme Court as well as any other court in the nation. The solicitor general must authorize the United States attorneys to proceed with an appeal in every case that the government loses in a lower court. Although this basic appellate work requires a significant amount of manpower within the office, most members of the solicitor general's staff see their work before the Supreme Court as the most important.

There are a variety of tasks managed by the solicitor general's office with respect to Supreme Court litigation. These responsibilities include the following:

– Deciding which cases warrant a petition for *certiorari* to the Supreme Court.

– Writing and revising briefs in support of or opposition to *certiorari*.

– Writing and revising briefs for cases selected by the Supreme Court for a decision on the merits in which the government is a participant.

– Presenting oral arguments in the Supreme Court, or authorizing another party to present arguments.

– Submitting *amicus curiae* briefs to the Supreme Court when the United States is an interested party.

---

[3] Material excerpted from 12-24, 22-32 from *The Solicitor General: The Polotics of Law* by Rebecca Mac Salokar. Used by permission of Temple University Press. © 1992. All rights reserved.

- Authorizing others to intervene as *amicus curiae* in cases where the United States is a party.

- Deciding on intervention where the United States has a technical right to intervene.

- Mediating interdepartmental disputes that arise over matters of legal policy.

In short, the solicitor general is responsible for any and all actions on behalf of the United States government before the Supreme Court. Although some rare exceptions have been made to allow certain agencies of the government to argue cases without the solicitor general's assistance, the agencies will have had at least the solicitor general's approval to present their cases.

These mandated responsibilities are accomplished not only by drawing on the expertise of the staff within the solicitor general's office but through close cooperation with the various staff attorneys assigned to the other divisions of the Department of Justice (for instance, Civil, Civil Rights, or Antitrust Divisions), the senior counsels of governmental departments (Labor, Transportation, *et cetera*) and with the lawyers for independent agencies (such as the National Labor Relations Board, Interstate Commerce Commission, or Federal Trade Commission). Because these other agencies have been working on the cases since the trial stage, they often provide the solicitor general with a thorough history of the cases, as well as insight on the contested legal issues. As Solicitor General Charles Fried noted, "We do not sit on the fifth floor of the Department of Justice, scan the legal universe, and then decide what will happen. Rather, they, divisions and departments of Government with pro-grammatic responsibilities come to us with recommendations, which we approve, and then proceed, in the Supreme Court, to brief and argue for them." In essence, the Office of the Solicitor General is not insulated from other areas of government in accomplishing its work. Rather, it is subject to a range of influences from the executive branch, Congress, and even the Supreme Court itself. . . .

A closer examination of the total workload of the solicitor general sheds light on both the frequency with which the government appears before the Supreme Court and its overwhelming success in this arena. By focusing on the 1959 to 1989 Supreme Court terms, it is evident that the government is a decisive presence before the Court. More important, however, is the substantial success that this small "law firm" enjoys before the highest court in the nation. . . .

The Successful Litigant. The Supreme Court's jurisdiction, its power to hear cases and decide controversies, is rooted in constitutional, legislative, and self-imposed rules and practices. This quagmire of standards permits the Court a wide range of discretion in deciding which cases it will hear each term. It is within this rather tentative and unpredictable scheme that the solicitor general of the United States must select the cases the government will pursue. Additionally the government's attorney must also respond to suits in which a private litigant attempts to take the government to the Supreme Court. Just how successful is the government in getting on the Court's agenda when acting as a petitioner, getting off the Court's agenda when named as a respondent, and, most important, how often does the government prevail when the case is decided on the merits? The answers to these questions confirm that the office of the Solicitor General is an exceptionally successful litigant before the Supreme Court.

Agenda Success. Most of the Supreme Court's workload involves cases appealing a lower-court decision, and the key means of gaining the Court's review is through the petition for a writ of *certiorari*. . . .

The most frequent form of government participation in *certiorari* cases was as respondent, responding to a suit brought by an aggrieved private litigant or state against the United States. The solicitor general responded to 38,412 *certiorari* cases during the 1959 to 1989 terms. . . . The government was quite successful in having these cases dismissed early in the *certiorari* process. Over 96 percent of the cases naming the United States as respondent were eliminated at the first stage with the decision by the Court to deny *certiorari* or review. This is not surprising considering that the Court routinely dismisses 91 percent of all *certiorari* requests with or without government involvement. The government, although successful as a respondent at this first stage of litigation, does not seem to enjoy any special advantages over the private respondent.

As petitioner, however, the solicitor general has a significant advantage over private litigants. As the attorney for the United States, the solicitor general has available a large pool of possible *certiorari* requests and selects only a small number of cases that will most likely meet the standards of the Court in granting review and, subsequently, result in a decision favoring the government. And even if the government is denied review, it is likely that cases raising similar issues will flow into the office at a later time providing other opportunities for Supreme Court review. Private litigants, on the other hand, are usually involved in only one case and do not enjoy the same selection of opportunities. A denial of *certiorari* by the Court generally means the end of the litigation for the private petitioner.

The advantage that the solicitor general enjoys in his capacity as a petitioner is clear. The solicitor general sought *certiorari* in 1,294 cases between 1959 and 1989, and was successful in obtaining the Court's review 69.78 percent of the time. *Certiorari* requests were granted in only 4.9 percent of the private litigation. Given such poor odds, it is no wonder that private litigants seek the government's support through an *amicus* brief.

The *amicus curiae* or "friend of the court" brief permits the government (and other litigants) to participate in a case in which the United States is not formally named as a party. *Amicus* briefs may be filed either at the petition stage, when the Court is deciding whether or not to review a case, or at the stage when the justices are considering the merits or issues of a case. By filing an *amicus* brief, the solicitor general has the opportunity to present the government's views on a range of issues. The government may wish to express its support for, or opposition to, a petition for a writ of *certiorari*. Additionally, the solicitor general is likely to address the potential impact a decision will have on federal law and federal agency operations and programs or simply provide additional information and legal considerations not contained in the litigant's documentation. Finally, the *amicus* brief has served as a vehicle to express the administration's policy positions and goals on issues that have historically been considered outside the scope of the federal law. . . .

It is clear that the solicitor general's *amicus* support of petitioners significantly benefits the private litigant. When the government filed an *amicus* brief on behalf of the appellant or petitioner, the Court granted review in 87.6 percent of the cases. Surprisingly, this success is even greater than when the government sought the Court's review of its own cases.

More curious, however, is the government's apparent influence as an *amicus* on behalf of respondents. Of the 484 cases in which the United States sided with the respondent or appellee, the private litigant had only a 60 percent chance of getting the most favorable outcome, a denial of review. When we consider that nearly 95 percent of all *certiorari* cases and over 79 percent of appellate cases without government involvement are routinely denied review, the *amicus* support of the solicitor general appears to be detrimental to the private litigant trying to stay out of court. . . .

These findings support the argument that the government's participation serves as a cue or signal to the Court in its search for cases that merit review. Unfortunately for private respondents, the cue is also used for their cases. The court may view the government's intervention as a red flag indicating executive interest or that the case is controversial and involves legal issues important enough to merit the solicitor general's attention and that, therefore, perhaps the Court should also give the case serious consideration.

An alternative explanation for the government's support of respondents and the apparently negative impact on those litigants may hinge on the Court's *amicus* invitation to the government, an invitation that is seen as an order. . . . Nearly half of the solicitor general's *amicus* cases were the result of a Court request.

Success in Merit Decisions. During the 1959 to 1989 terms, the Court decided 8,926 cases on the merits. The government participated either as a party to the suit or as an *amicus* in 4,329 (47.5 percent) of these cases. On the average, it participated in almost 140 cases per year that were resolved through the complete administration of the Supreme Court's judicial process.

The success that the solicitor general enjoys at the early stages of the Court's decision making continues in decisions on the merits. The government's position prevailed in 2,961 (67.6 percent) of the cases in which it participated. There were 1,159 decisions (26.8 percent) between 1959 and 1989, that were clearly against the government's position and 209 decisions (4.8 percent) that were unclassifiable. The decisions on the merits in favor of the government were the result of the solicitor general actually "going to the mat" with an opposing litigant and being declared the victor by the Supreme Court. . . .

More revealing is to consider all of the "first-round knockouts" that the government enjoys, the early dismissals rendered by the Court through denials of *certiorari* and refusals to grant jurisdiction. The success rate of the government increases substantially when these early victories and losses are tabulated in conjunction with the decisions on the merits.

When all of the "quick" victories and losses are considered, the government is successful in nearly 96 percent of the cases in which it participates. The core of this success rests on the more than 36,000 cases brought by private litigants against the government that were subsequently denied *certiorari* by the Supreme Court. . . .

In this respect, the United States enjoys unrivaled success. On the average, only one of every twenty-five private claims docketed before the Supreme Court against the United States is accepted for the Court's review. And even when these private cases are decided by the justices on the merits, only one of every four are held in favor of the private litigant. In essence, private litigants win a mere 1 percent of their cases against the United States before the Supreme Court.

The Definitive "Repeat Player." . . . The Repeat Player enjoys a substantial measure of success over the less frequent litigant. . . . Solicitors general [are] the definitive repeat players. They enjoy the numerous advantages of the Repeat Player including advance intelligence, access to specialists, a wide range of resources, expertise, opportunities to build informal relations with the Supreme Court, and a high degree of credibility before the Court. In addition, the government is more interested in the long-term development of the law and rules than in the immediate success of a particular case.

Institutional overload also favors the Repeat Player. "Typically there are far more claims than there are institutional resources for full dress adjudication of each." The sheer number of cases on the Court's docket favors the solicitor general over . . . the infrequent litigant who attempts to take her case before the Supreme Court. Lastly, rules, "a body of authoritative normative learning," also favor Repeat Players since these litigants have "successfully articulated their operations to pre-existing rules."

The complicated nature of the rules further requires the resources of legal experts. . . . The solicitor general has access not only to a staff of professional lawyers who are skilled in the intricacies of Supreme Court adjudication, but to issue experts scattered throughout the Department of Justice and the executive branch. The solicitor general, Repeat Player *par excellence*, is highly successful before the Supreme Court.

Rex E. Lee, *Lawyering for the Government: Politics, Polemics & Principle,* 47 OHIO ST. L. J. 595, 596 (1986)[4]

. . . . The reason that the Solicitor General of the United States has the greatest lawyering job in the world is that one of his two responsibilities is to handle litigation for only one client, the United States of America, before only one court, the United States Supreme Court. In other words, he represents the world's most interesting client before the world's most interesting court.

The Supreme Court in any given year will consider about 160 cases on the merits [in more recent years the average has been eighty cases]. The Solicitor General's client is a party in about sixty of those cases. In addition, his client

---

[4] Originally published at 47 OHIO ST. L. J. 595, 596 (1986). Reprinted with permission.

will participate as *amicus curiae* both in the briefing and the oral argument of about twenty-five or thirty more cases. Those numbers alone render unique the relationship of this particular little twenty-three member law firm to the only court before which it practices. I know of no other court of general jurisdiction in the world in which one law firm appears in more than half of its cases.

There are some other numbers that make this relationship even more remarkable. First, the national average for winning cases before the United States Supreme Court is fifty percent. (Now if you poll the lawyers it will come out slightly higher than fifty percent, but I will assure that by any objective measurement it is fifty percent.) But this particular firm rather consistently wins seventy percent or more.

Next, the national average for persuading the Court to consider the case on the merits — that is to note jurisdiction of appeals or to grant *certiorari* — is about three percent to five percent. For the Solicitor General's office, it is somewhere between sixty percent and seventy percent. A final example, and perhaps the most significant of all, is this: About two dozen or more times each year, the United States Supreme Court will enter an order asking the Solicitor General to express the views of the United States in a case in which the United States is not involved as a party.

Those numbers are only part of the story. Beyond the numbers there is a widely held, and I believe substantially accurate, impression that the Solicitor General's office provides the Court from one presidential administration to another — and largely without regard to either the political party or the personality of the particular Solicitor General — with advocacy which is more objective, more dispassionate, more competent, and more respectful of the Court as an institution than it gets from any other lawyer or group of lawyers.

The relationship I have just described is one that has great advantages for both institutions. The advantage to the Court is that in more than half of its cases it has a highly-skilled lawyer on whom it can count consistently for dependable analysis rendered against the background of an unusual understanding and respect for the Court as an institution.

The benefit to the Solicitor General and his clients is obvious. What lawyer would not value a relationship in which the court before which he appears with frequency, asks him, "what should we do about this case in which you are not involved?" I think that it is not only proper for the Solicitor General to use the adversarial advantages that result from that kind of relationship; it would be a breach of obligation to the President who appointed him to fail to do so. But it must be done with discretion, with discrimination, and with sensitivity, lest the reservoir of credibility which is the source of this special advantage be diminished, with adverse consequences not only to the government's ability to win cases, but also to an important institution of government itself.

Let me give you three examples of temptations that exist to consume the Solicitor General's capital in the interest of particular cases. It would be an exaggeration to use the metaphor of killing the goose that laid the golden egg, but there are some similarities.

The first of my examples concerns the filing of petitions for *certiorari*. I mentioned a moment ago that of the 160 cases that the Court considers each year, about sixty or so are cases in which the government is a party. How do those cases get there? About five or ten of them get there over the government's opposition; they are filed by opposing parties in cases that the government won in the lower courts. But most of them are there because the Solicitor General makes a conscious decision to file a petition for *certiorari*. Since about two-thirds of the Solicitor General's petitions for *certiorari* are granted, the sixty or so cases reviewed on the merits are the product of some eighty to ninety petitions for *certiorari*. Those eighty to ninety filings represented a culling from about five or six times that many recommendations from cabinet heads, U.S. attorneys, and assistant attorneys general and general counsel of the various departments and agencies. Thus, after an initial screening we would have about 300 to 350 recommendations to file petitions for *certiorari*, and we would file about one-sixth that number.

There is great pressure to file more. Put yourself in the position of a cabinet head, or the chairman of an independent regulatory commission. You have lost a case in a Court of Appeals and you want to take it to the United States Supreme Court. Assume also that you have come from private industry where you have been accustomed to dealing with lawyers. In the private sector, when you want to file a petition for *certiorari* you go to a lawyer and he or she asks only two questions: is it a responsible position, and are you willing to pay the fee? If the answer to both questions is yes, he will file the petition for *certiorari*.

Not, so, if you work for the United States of America. Even if the position is meritorious, the chances are only about one in six that the United States Supreme Court will even see a *cert* petition. And the judgment whether to file will not be made within your department or your agency, even though the issue is crucial to your program. The judgment will be made by someone in the Department of Justice. And what makes it even worse, the person tells you no, (as he will five times out of six) not because he disagrees with your position, but solely because he perceives that filing that case might affect his relationship with the Court.

I have heard this question many times: "What possible difference can it make to this nebulous thing you call your credibility with the Court if we file just this one more *cert* petition?"

Well, let us just assume that there was a change in the approach I have described. Assume that the Solicitor General did change his standards for filing *cert* petitions and he filed not seventy-five per term, but twice that many. Or, assume that he simply applied the same standards that the private practitioner applies. The result would probably be that about 400 petitions for *certiorari* would be filed for the federal government each year. (That assumes that the same kind of screening would still go on within each department and agency.)

What would be the consequence? I believe that over the first year the number of the Solicitor General's *certiorari* petitions granted would increase dramatically. Concomitantly, the percentage of the Supreme Court's decisional capacity consumed by the United States of America would probably increase from around forty percent to something higher. But I also believe that if the members of the Court consciously faced the issue, most of them would probably share my view that something in the range of forty percent of its decisional capacity is about what the United States is entitled to. Thus, over a longer period (probably about three or four years) we would settle back to just about the same number of government *cert* petitions that were granted before the Solicitor General changed his policy.

Two things would have happened in the process. First, the government would file 400 petitions instead of eighty in order to get the same number of grants. This would increase the Supreme Court's work load; the justices, rather than the executive branch, would be doing the screening. Second, the executive branch itself would be disadvantaged. Any given administration ought to be in a better position than the Court to make a judgment as to the comparative importance to its total program of a petition from one department or another.

The second example of temptations that can consume the Solicitor General's capital concerns the selection of cases in which to file as *amicus curiae*. Return to our numbers for just a moment. Each year there are about ninety to 100 Supreme Court merits cases in which the government is not a party. By definition these are important cases. Almost every one of them involves questions in which I either have an interest or could easily develop one. And I will tell you that in every single case the Court would be better off if it had the benefit of my views. That is true today, and it was also true when I was Solicitor General. But I started from the premise that if I filed in every single case, the Court would not have taken me as seriously. It is almost as though I had a certain number of chips that I could play. Where was the best place to play them? If you assume that you are going to file as *amicus* in about twenty-five or thirty cases (and that is probably about right), how do you select those twenty-five or thirty?

These are the guidelines that I used. I divided the non-government cases into two categories. The first class of cases — the easier one — consisted of those that involved direct federal law enforcement interests. Examples are Title VII cases, antitrust cases, securities cases, voting cases, or criminal cases, in which the federal government did not happen to be one of the litigants, but the holding in the case would probably have a larger impact on the interests of the United States than it would have on the immediate parties.

The harder cases fall in the second category: cases that have nothing to do with any federal law enforcement responsibility, but which fall right at the core of the current administration's broader agenda. For me these included cases involving obscenity, the religion clauses, and abortion. There are people who argued with great force during my four years in office that the Solicitor General should never file in this kind of case. They believed that pursuing the President's social agenda was not a legitimate objective for the President's Supreme Court lawyer. There were others who argued that I should file in virtually every one of them because the only person who can speak for the President in the United States Supreme Court is the Solicitor General. If he does not speak, then the President's views will not be heard on those important issues; and since most important changes that will occur in the law of abortion, obscenity, and freedom of religion will be changes in judge-made law, the President's view must be made known to those who have final decisional authority in those areas.

My own view is an intermediate one and it is this: It is not only all right to file in a few of those non-federal enforcement issue cases, it is a part of your job, but it is a mistake to file in too many. This is one instance where precedent actually works in reverse. The fact that I had already filed several *amicus* briefs in these "category two" cases during a particular term was a strong argument against doing it again. The reason is that while I think it is proper to use the office for the purpose of making my contribution to the President's broader agenda, a wholesale departure from the role whose performance has led to the special status that the Solicitor General enjoys would unduly impair that status itself. In the process, the ability of the Solicitor General to serve any of the President's objectives would suffer.

I come now to the third and final example of a temptation to consume the Solicitor General's capital. Should the Solicitor General make arguments that he knows the Court will reject? There are two arguable reasons for taking a position which you know the Supreme Court will reject. First, even though the Court will disagree now, you may start a dialogue (either within the Court or in other quarters) which might eventually contribute to the Court's adopting your view. If I ever found a case in which I really thought that that chain of events was a reasonable possibility, I would not hesitate to make an argument knowing that the Court would reject it. But, in my opinion, such cases are extremely rare. In my four years of experience as Solicitor General, I found no such case. The more probable result is this: the assertion of a position that the Solicitor General knows will be rejected will lead not only to its rejection, but also to a more strongly-worded opinion. The result is that at some later time, with a Court more favorably disposed to your view, the job of getting the position accepted will be even more difficult because the earlier experience led to more formidable adverse precedent.

The other argument in favor of taking positions that the Solicitor General knows will be rejected takes as its premise that the nine members of the Court do not constitute the Solicitor General's only audience. There are other people who read his briefs and have an interest in what the Solicitor General says. It is very proper, even required (so the argument goes), to take this broader audience into account. If you don't believe in the President's program, you shouldn't be the Solicitor General. And if you do believe in it, why don't you say so? If you get a chance to say what you believe, you should say it. To decline to do so is not only unwise, but borders on dishonesty.

That argument profoundly misunderstands the Solicitor General's office and function. The audience for his briefs and arguments consists of nine people and nine people only. To the extent that his efforts to persuade those nine people also yield some other benefits, that is fine, but that is not his job. Public relations and mass communications are not what he was trained for and not what he does well. He is not the pamphleteer general nor the neighborhood essayist.

During my tenure, for example, it was seriously urged that we advance — as one argument in support of the constitutionality of Alabama's moment of silence statute — that the first amendment generally and the establishment clause in particular were not binding on the states. As a matter of historical and legal analysis, a respectable argument along those lines can be made. As a practical matter, however, it comes forty years too late. If, as the Solicitor General of the United States, I had advocated that the first amendment was not binding on Alabama, I would have destroyed — with one single filing — the special status that I enjoyed by virtue of my office. I would have also acquired a new status, equally special. The Court would have written me off as someone not to be taken seriously.

There has been built up, over 115 years since this office was first created in 1870, a reservoir of credibility on which the incumbent Solicitor General may draw to his immediate adversarial advantage. But if he draws too deeply, too greedily, or too indiscriminately, then he jeopardizes not only that advantage in that particular case, but also an important institution of government. The preservation of both — and striking just the right balance between their sometimes competing demands — lies at the heart of the Solicitor General's stewardship.

NOTES

1. Of all the nation's legal officials, including the Attorney General and the Supreme Court justices, the Solicitor General is the only official who is required by statute to be "learned in the law." 28 U.S.C. § 505. The Solicitor General ("SG") often is called the "Tenth Justice" because of his unique relationship and responsibility to the SCOTUS. *See generally* LINCOLN CAPLAN, THE TENTH JUSTICE: THE SOLICITOR GENERAL AND THE RULE OF LAW (1987). The SG is an executive branch official and an advocate, however, not the Supreme Court's central staff attorney. Professor Salokar's excerpt describes the SG's duties and the remarkable influence that office wields over the case selection and merits decisions of the SCOTUS. The Rex E. Lee excerpt offers the perspective of a former SG who served 1981-85. *See Transcript of the Conference on the Office of the Solicitor General of the United States*, 2003 BYU L. REV. 1. What does account for the remarkable influence of the SG over the *certiorari* process and the decisionmaking of the SCOTUS? If a particular case is otherwise certworthy, what other factors might influence the SG's decision whether or not to petition for review on behalf of the Government? What role should politics play in the SG's performance of the office's responsibilities?

2. Other institutional litigators besides the SG also try to leverage some advantage from being repeat players before the SCOTUS. The practice has evolved in recent years, particularly since the Court has been taking fewer cases, for these organizations and associations to file *amicus curiae* briefs with the Court to try to influence the justices at the *cert* stage and the merits stage. There has been an 800% increase over the last 50 years. Today, *amicus curiae* briefs are filed in 85% of the cases and sometimes dozens are filed in a single case. The all-time record of 107 *amicus* briefs — many of them signed by multiple organizations and individuals — was set in the university affirmative action cases from 2003, *Gratz v. Bollinger*, 539 U.S. 244 (2003), and *Grutter v. Bollinger*, 539 U.S. 306 (2003). A comprehensive study found: *amici* of

respondents enjoy greater influence than do *amici* of petitioners; small dispar-ities in the number of briefs for one side tend to coincide with success but larger disparities do not necessarily do so; *amicus* briefs on the winning side get cited more often; *amicus* briefs filed by seasoned practitioners are more successful; the Solicitor General is among the most influential filer of *amicus* briefs, but other repeat players before the Court, like the American Civil Liberties Union and the States, also enjoy some success as *amicus* filers. Joseph D. Kearney & Thomas W. Merrill, *The Influence of* Amicus Curiae *Briefs on the Supreme Court*, 148 U. PA. L. REV. 743 (2000). These numbers and this measure of influ-ence have significant implications for the SCOTUS's case selection process and case decisionmaking process, as well as for its workload.

3. The symbiosis between the SG and the SCOTUS includes how the SG manages the litigation and appeals agenda of the Government to create, main-tain, and percolate "conflicts" in the federal law. In *United States v. Mendoza*, 464 U.S. 154 (1984), the Supreme Court formally sanctioned the Government's practice of nonacquiescence by holding that the doctrine of offensive nonmu-tual issue preclusion does not apply to the United States Government. This doctrine permits federal agencies to relitigate issues of law that have been resolved adversely to them in prior proceedings in other courts with other lit-igants. Consider one example of this practice: before the Supreme Court finally answered the "yes-or-no" question whether the U.S. Postal Service is immune from state court garnishment proceedings, the Government had urged its view twenty times in district courts and eight times in different courts of appeals. *Franchise Tax Bd. v. United States Postal Serv.*, 467 U.S. 512, 519 n.12 (1984). *See generally* Samuel Estreicher & Richard L. Revesz, *Nonacquiescence by Federal Administrative Agencies*, 98 YALE L.J. 679 (1989). Justice White used to dissent from the denial of *certiorari* in every case pre-senting a conflict because he believed they had a compelling claim on the Court's discretionary jurisdiction. J. Thomas Sullivan, *Justice White's Principled Passion for Consistency*, 4 J. APP. PRAC. & PROCESS 79 (2002). A study of the 1988 and 1990 terms determined that the number of conflicts in cases denied review exceeded 200 a term. ARTHUR D. HELLMAN, UNRESOLVED INTERCIRCUIT CONFLICTS: THE NATURE AND SCOPE OF THE PROBLEM 34-64 (Fed. Jud. Ctr. 1991). SUP. CT. R. 10(a) announces an official priority for granting *certiorari* to resolve "conflicts" between the federal courts; however, the rule further states that the conflict must be "important." SUPREME COURT PRACTICE, *supra* § 4.4 at 226-32. What is an "important" conflict? When might a conflict be unimportant or tolerable?

B.   The 1980s: Too Many Cases?

REPORT OF THE STUDY GROUP ON THE CASELOAD OF THE SUPREME COURT, 57 F.R.D. 573 (1972)[5]

While the progressive spirit, which prompts us to search continually for greater knowledge and better ways of doing things, would alone justify these various studies, the current and anticipated rate of growth in the amount of

---

[5] Copyright © 1972 Thomson West. Reprinted with permission.

business brought to the federal judiciary strikes a note of urgency. . . . [T]he recent growth of Supreme Court business has been equally dramatic. For example, during Chief Justice Stone's tenure (1941-1946), the docketed cases in the Supreme Court increased only 158 cases from 1,302 to 1,460. In marked contrast, cases increased 956 during the past five years from 3,559 in the 1967 Term to 4,515 in the 1971 Term. . . . In the fall of 1971 Chief Justice Burger appointed a Study Group [known as the Freund Committee], under the auspices of the Federal Judicial Center, to study the case load of the Supreme Court and to make such recommendations as its findings warranted.

I. Nature and Dimensions of the Problem

The bare figures of the Court's workload present the problem most vividly. Approximately three times as many cases were filed in the 1971 Term as in the 1951 Term. The growth between 1935 and 1951 was gradual and sporadic, from 983 new filings to 1,234. But by 1961 the number was 2,185, an increase of 951, and by 1971, 3,643 new cases were filed, an increase of 1,458 in ten years. The most dramatic growth has been in the number of cases filed, *in forma pauperis* (IFP) by persons unable to pay the cost of litigation, mostly defendants in criminal cases. The regular appellate filings (the non-IFP cases) have also steadily increased, only a little less explosively.

A number of factors have contributed to this trend. The population of the nation will have grown from 132 million in 1940 to 210.2 million at the end of 1972. More and more subjects are committed to the courts as the fields covered by legislation expand. Civil rights, environmental, safety, consumer, and other social and economic legislation are recent illustrations. And lawyers are now provided to a markedly increasing extent for persons who cannot afford litigation. Changes in constitutional doctrines have also contributed, as the reapportionment and school desegregation cases, as well as the criminal cases, attest.

Of course, no one can foresee how future events, laws or cases will affect the Supreme Court's docket. The lesson of history teaches that, independent of other factors, the number of cases will continue to increase as population grows and the economy expands.

With no substantial difference in the number of cases argued, the percentage of petitions for *certiorari* granted has sharply dropped as the filings have increased. In 1971, 5.8% were granted, in contrast to 17.5%, 11.1% and 7.4% in 1941, 1951 and 1961 respectively. This diminution is in part attributable to the fact that a much larger proportion of the IFP cases lacks any merit. But the decline also in the percentage of paid petitions granted would seem to reflect, not a lessening of the proportion of cases worthy of review, but rather the need to keep the number of cases argued and decided on the merits within manageable limits as the docket increases. One result is that a conflict between circuits is not as likely to be resolved, at least as speedily, by the Supreme Court as when the docket was much smaller.

The number of cases argued and decided by opinion has not changed significantly despite the rising flood of petitions and appeals. Since 1948 the number of arguments has ranged between 105 in 1954 and 180 in 1967. In recent years the number of arguments rose from 144 in the 1969 Term to 177 in 1971, but in some still earlier years, when the total case load was less than one-third of what it is now, there were more oral arguments. The number of cases decided by full opinion has ranged from 84 in 1953 to 199 in 1944. At the 1971 Term 143 cases were so disposed of, with 129 opinions of the Court; during the preceding 15 years the average was 120 cases, with 100 opinions.

The statistics of the Court's current workload, both in absolute terms and in the mounting trend, are impressive evidence that the conditions essential for the performance of the Court's mission do not exist. For an ordinary appellate court the burgeoning volume of cases would be a staggering burden; for the Supreme Court the pressures of the docket are incompatible with the appropriate fulfillment of its historic and essential functions.

Over the past thirty-five years, as has been seen, the number of cases filed has grown about fourfold, while the number of cases in which the Court has heard oral argument before decision has remained substantially constant. Two consequences can be inferred. Issues that would have been decided on the merits a generation ago are passed over by the Court today; and, second, the consideration given to the cases actually decided on the merits is compromised by the pressures of "processing" the inflated docket of petitions and appeals. There is no basis to foresee anything but an intensification of this trend in the period ahead, and with a larger and active bar, increasing legal assistance, and the possibility of an increase in the number of federal judicial circuits, the prospects of a still further increase in the number of review-worthy cases reaching the Court cannot be gainsaid. The Courts of Appeals have encountered a dramatic rise in their own business, with a proportionate outflow to the Supreme Court; and the task of coping with the discretionary jurisdiction on *certiorari* overhangs all of the Court's work.

We are concerned that the Court is now at the saturation point, if not actually overwhelmed. If trends continue, as there is every reason to believe they will, and if no relief is provided, the function of the Court must necessarily change. In one way or another, placing ever more reliance on an augmented staff, the Court could perhaps manage to administer its docket. But it will be unable adequately to meet its essential responsibilities.

II. Jurisdictional Changes

. . . .

B. Recommended: A National Court of Appeals

Our own recommendation builds on the Judiciary Act of 1925. Its aim is twofold. It deals first with that part of the solution embodied in the Act of 1925 which has since itself become a problem, namely the screening of a mass of petitions for review; and, second, with the pressure exerted on the Supreme Court by cases of conflict between circuits that ought to be resolved but that are otherwise not of such importance as to merit adjudication in the Supreme Court.

We recommend creation of a National Court of Appeals which would screen all petitions for review now filed in the Supreme Court, and hear and decide on the merits many cases of conflicts between circuits. Petitions for review would be filed initially in the National Court of Appeals. The great majority, it is to be expected, would be finally denied by that court. Several hundred would be certified annually to the Supreme Court for further screening and choice of cases to be heard and adjudicated there. Petitions found to establish a true conflict between circuits would be granted by the National Court of Appeals and the cases heard and finally disposed of there, except as to those petitions deemed important enough for certification to the Supreme Court.

The composition of the National Court of Appeals could be determined in a number of ways. The method of selection outlined here draws on the membership of the existing courts of appeals, vesting the judges of those courts with new functions in relation to the new Court. The National Court of Appeals, under this plan, would consist of seven United States circuit judges in active service. Assignment to this Court should be for limited, staggered terms. Thus the opportunity to serve on the National Court of Appeals would be made available to many circuit judges, the Court would draw on a wide range of talents and varied experience while not losing its identity and continuity as a court, and the burden of any personal inconvenience would not fall too heavily on any small group of judges. Appointments should be made by a method that will ensure the rapid filling of vacancies, and itself tend to provide the court with the widest diversity of experience, outlook and age, in order to help secure for it the confidence of the profession, of the Supreme Court, and of the country.

Assignment of circuit judges to the National Court of Appeals could be made for three-year staggered terms by a system of automatic rotation, as follows. A list of all United States circuit judges in active service would be made up in order of seniority. All judges serving as chief judges, or who would have succeeded to a chief judgeship during their term of service on the National Court of Appeals had they been selected, and all judges with less than five years' service as United States circuit judges would be struck from the list. Appointments to the National Court of Appeals would be made from the resulting list by alternating the judge most senior in service and the most junior, except that each judge would have the privilege of declining appointment for good cause; no two judges from the same circuit could serve at the same time on the National Court of Appeals, and no judge who had served once would be selected again until all other eligible judges had served. It is to be noted that some additional circuit judgeships would have to be created. . . .

The threshold jurisdiction of the National Court of Appeals would be co-extensive with the present appellate jurisdiction of the Supreme Court. We assume, as we shall urge, that access to that jurisdiction will be entirely by *certiorari*. . . . We recommend that all cases now within the Supreme Court's jurisdiction, excepting only original cases, be filed initially in the National Court of Appeals. . . . The National Court of Appeals would have discretion to deny review, governed by the considerations now mentioned in the *certiorari* Rules of the Supreme Court, or in such further Rules of the Supreme Court as may be made, or in Rules of the National Court of Appeals made subject to the supervening rule-making power of the Supreme Court. Denial of review by the National Court of Appeals would be final, and there would then be no access to the Supreme Court.

The National Court of Appeals would also have discretion, similarly governed, to certify a case to the Supreme Court for disposition. Possibly the concurrence of three judges (one less than a majority) of the National Court of Appeals might suffice for a decision to certify a case to the Supreme Court. In cases where a court of appeals has rendered a decision in conflict with a decision of another court of appeals, the National Court of Appeals would certify the case to the Supreme Court for disposition if it finds the conflict to be real and if the issue on which the conflict arises, or another issue in the case, is otherwise of adequate importance. In all other cases of real conflict between circuits, the National Court of Appeals would set the case down for argument, and proceed to adjudication on the merits of the whole case. Its decision would be final, and would not be reviewable in the Supreme Court.

It should be plain on the face of the proposal, and if found necessary could be made plain by statement, that where there is serious doubt, the National Court of Appeals should certify a petition rather than denying review. The expectation would be that the National Court of Appeals would certify several times as many cases as the Supreme Court could be expected to hear and decide — perhaps something of the order of 400 cases a year. These cases would constitute the appellate docket of the Supreme Court, except that the Court would retain its power to grant *certiorari* before judgment in a Court of Appeals, before denial of review in the National Court of Appeals, or before judgment in a case set down for hearing or heard there. The expectation would be that exercises of this power would be exceptional.

Once a case had been certified to it, the Supreme Court would, as now, have full discretion to grant or deny review or limited review, to reverse or affirm without argument, or to hear the case. In cases of conflict among circuits, the Supreme Court would, in addition, be able to grant review and remand to the National Court of Appeals with an order that the case be heard and adjudicated. This would be the disposition indicated in a case in which the Supreme Court agreed that the conflict was a true one, but did not view the issue involved as being of sufficient comparative importance to warrant a hearing in that Court.

In no instance would the parties need to file additional papers. A certified petition and the brief in opposition would come forward to the Supreme Court, and in the rare event of a remand of a conflict to the National Court of Appeals, the papers would simply go back. . . .

We are aware of objections that can be raised against this recommendation. But relief is imperative, and among possible remedies, none of which is perfect, this appears to us to be the least problematic.

Undoubtedly some room is opened up for the play of the subjectivity of the judges of the National Court of Appeals in the exercise of discretionary judgments to deny review. But someone's subjectivity is unavoidable. We believe our recommendation minimizes the chances of an erratic subjectivity. There are safeguards in the method of designation of the judges; and if the vote of three of the seven judges were to suffice for certification to the Supreme Court the concurrence of five of the seven would be required to deny the certification. We believe that a National Court of Appeals such as we propose would succeed in gaining the confidence of the country, the Supreme Court and the profession.

Again, some measure of loss of control by the Supreme Court itself is inevitable if the Court's burden is to be lessened. We believe this recommendation involves the least possible loss of control. The Supreme Court would select cases for decision on the merits from a docket of several times the number it would be expected thus to decide. *Certiorari* before final action in the court below, though not a procedure to be encouraged, remains available. Finally, the Supreme Court's readiness to reopen what had seemed to be settled issues, its impatience with, or its interest in, one or another category of cases — all this, we think, would communicate itself to the National Court of Appeals, and would be acted upon. We suggest, however, that the Supreme Court would be well-advised to return to the early practice of writing an occasional opinion to accompany a denial or dismissal of *certiorari*, and to offer a sentence or two in opinions on the merits by way of explanation of the grant.

We know of no way to quantify the relief that this recommendation would provide for the Supreme Court. Obviously, the chaff on the docket is less time-consuming than the marginal cases that hover between a grant and a denial, and of the latter the Court would still see some few hundred. But when the chaff is counted in the thousands, the burden is bound to be considerable. We are confident that a substantial amount of Justices' and law clerks' time would be conserved, and more imponderably, that there would be an appreciable lessening of pressure. We think that the costs of the proposal recommended — not merely the material ones, and not merely to litigants, but in terms of the values of the legal order and of the judicial process — are minimal. Balancing these costs against probable benefits, we are entirely persuaded that the proposal is worth adopting. An incidental advantage is that it would allow for experimentation for a period of years without a commitment to a permanent new tier of judicial review and a permanent new judicial body. It may turn out merely to palliate, or it may serve as a cure for at least as long as the reforms of 1891 and 1925 did in their time. Only experience will tell. We believe it should be allowed to tell.

William J. Brennan, Jr., *The National Court of Appeals: Another Dissent,* 40 U. CHI. L. REV. 473, 475-85 (1983)[6]

[M]y now almost seventeen years service as an Associate Justice of the Supreme Court does afford me an unusual perspective on the [Freund Committee] proposal, and I am anxious to describe to you what seem to me two glaring defects in the plan. First, its fundamental premise that "consideration given to the cases actually decided on the merits is compromised by the pressures of processing the inflated docket of petitions and appeals" is entirely unsupportable. Contrary to the Study Group's assumption, the Supreme Court is not overworked. Indeed, my law clerks tell me each year that the burden on the District and Circuit Courts with which they served before coming to me is no less substantial than the burden on the Supreme Court. Our docket has

---

6 UNIVERSITY OF CHICAGO LAW REVIEW by WILLIAM J. BRENNAN, JR.. Copyright 1983 by UNIV OF CHICAGO LAW SCH. Reproduced with permission of UNIV OF CHICAGO LAW SCH in the format Textbook via Copyright Clearance Center.

most definitely not swollen to a point where the burden of screening cases has impaired our ability to discharge our other vital responsibilities. Second, the Study Group has regrettably misconceived both the nature and the importance of the screening process. Even if it were as time-consuming and difficult as the Study Group believes, that would underscore, not diminish, its importance. It is a task that should, I am convinced, be performed only by the Members of the Court. I hope I can demonstrate to you [that] the removal of seven-eighths of that function from the Supreme Court would substantially impair our ability to perform the responsibilities conferred on us by the Constitution.

At the outset, I want to examine the Study Group's assumptions concerning the present work load of the Supreme Court. They observe, and I fully agree, that "the indispensable condition for discharge of the Court's responsibility is adequate time and ease of mind for research, reflection, and consultation in reaching a judgment, for critical review by colleagues when a draft opinion is prepared, and for clarification and revision in light of all that has gone before.". . .

The method of screening the cases differs among the individual Justices, and thus I will confine myself to my own practice. That practice reflects my view that the screening function is second to none in importance. . . . For my own part, I find that I don't need a great amount of time to perform the screening function — certainly not an amount of time that compromises my ability to attend to decisions of argued cases. In a substantial percentage of cases I find that I need read only the "Questions Presented" to decide how I will dispose of the case. This is certainly true in at least two types of cases — those presenting clearly frivolous questions and those that must be held for disposition of pending cases. Because of my familiarity with the issues of pending cases, the cases to be held are, for me, easily recognizable. . . . Similarly, with other cases I can conclude from a mere reading of the question presented that for me at least the question is clearly frivolous for review purposes. For example, during recent weeks, I thought wholly frivolous for review purposes questions such as: "Are the federal income tax laws unconstitutional insofar as they do not provide a deduction for depletion of the human body?" "Is the 16th Amendment unconstitutional as violative of the 14th Amendment?" and only last week, "Does a ban on drivers turning right on a red light constitute an unreasonable burden on interstate commerce?"

Nor is an unduly extended or time-consuming examination required of many of the cases that present clearly nonfrivolous questions. For very often even nonfrivolous questions are simply not of sufficient national importance to warrant Supreme Court review. And after a few years of experience, it is fair to say that a Justice develops a "feel" for such cases. For example, when the question is whether a court of appeals in a diversity case correctly applied governing state law, or correctly directed entry of a judgment notwithstanding the verdict, the question of error, if any, ordinarily does not fall within the area of questions warranting Supreme Court review. As to cases where my initial reading of the questions presented suggests to me that the case may merit Supreme Court review — the special "feel" one develops after a few years on the Court enables one to recognize the cases that are candidates for such review. I need not spend much time examining the papers in depth when the questions strike me as worthy of review, or at least as warranting conference discussion. . . .

I should emphasize here that the longer one works at the screening function, the less onerous and time-consuming it becomes. I can state categorically that I spent no more time screening the 3,643 cases of the 1971 Term than I did screening half as many in my first Term in 1956. Unquestionably, the equalizer is experience, and for experience there can be no substitute — not even a second court. I subscribe completely to the observation of the late Mr. Justice Harlan that "Frequently the question whether a case is 'certworthy' is more a matter of 'feel' than of precisely ascertainable rules." . . . I fear that the Study Group gave insufficient weight to this vital fact in assuming that inflated numbers of appeals and petitions must inevitably make the screening function a more onerous and time-consuming burden. . . .

Similarly, an artificial limitation of the Supreme Court's docket to only 400 cases per year would seriously undermine the important impact dissents from denial of review frequently have had upon the development of the law. Such dissents often herald the appearance on the horizon of a possible reexamination of what may seem to the judges of the National Court of Appeals to be an established and unimpeachable principle. . . . The creation of a National Court of Appeals that would certify the 400 "most reviewworthy" cases to the Court each Term would inevitably sacrifice this invaluable aid to constitutional adjudication by denying certification in cases that might otherwise afford appropriate vehicles for such dissents.

Moreover, the assumption that the judges of the National Court of Appeals could accurately select the 400 "most reviewworthy" cases wholly ignores the inherently subjective nature of the screening process. The cases docketed each Term cannot simply be placed into a computer that will instantaneously identify those that are "most reviewworthy." And this is particularly true with respect to distinctions among the 1,100 or so cases presently deemed to be of sufficient "reviewworthiness" to merit discussion at one of our weekly conferences. Indeed, a question that is "substantial" for me may be wholly "insubstantial" to some, perhaps all the rest, of my colleagues.

For the more statistically oriented, the subjective nature of the decision whether a particular case is of sufficient "importance" to merit plenary consideration is amply demonstrated by the voting pattern of the Justices in the screening process. Under our rules, a case may be granted review only if at least four of the nine Justices agree that such review is appropriate. It is noteworthy that, of the cases granted review this Term, approximately 60 percent received the votes of only four or five of the Justices. In only 9 percent of the granted cases were the Justices unanimous in the view that plenary consideration was warranted. Thus, insofar as the key determinant is the "substantiality" of the question presented, there can be no doubt that the appraisal is necessarily a subjective one. . . .

In response to these objections, it might of course be suggested that the National Court of Appeals certify to the Supreme Court, not 400 cases per Term, but, rather, all 1,110 or so cases normally placed on the "Discuss List."

As I have already indicated, however, by far the greatest portion of the Court's time and energy presently devoted to the screening process is concentrated, not in the selection of cases to be discussed at conference, but, rather, in the selection from that group of cases of the 150 to 200 cases that will be granted plenary review each Term. Thus, even if the judges of the National Court of Appeals could accurately identify all or most of the cases that normally would be placed on the "Discuss List," such a scheme would inevitably prove virtually useless in terms of administrative efficiency.

Finally, it should be noted that the Study Group's recommendation that the breadth of the Court's screening function be curtailed rests in part upon what I consider to be the mistaken assumption that the screening function plays only a minor and separable part in the exercise of the Court's fundamental responsibilities. In my view, the screening function is inextricably linked to the fulfillment of the Court's essential duties and is vital to the effective performance of the Court's unique mission "to define the rights guaranteed by the Constitution, to assure the uniformity of federal law, and to maintain the constitutional distribution of powers in our federal union."

The choice of issues for decision largely determines the image that the American people have of their Supreme Court. The Court's calendar mirrors the ever-changing concerns of this society with ever more powerful and smothering government. The calendar is therefore the indispensable source for keeping the Court abreast of these concerns. Our Constitution is a living document and the Court often becomes aware of the necessity for reconsideration of its interpretation only because filed cases reveal the need for new and previously unanticipated applications of constitutional principles. . . .

Justice Goldberg has rightly said that "[t]he power to decide cases presupposes the power to determine what cases will be decided." I agree too that "[a]lso presupposed [is] the more subtle power to decide when, how, and under what circumstances an issue should or should not be accepted for review. . . . Delegating to an outside body any significant exercise of the Supreme Court's discretionary power conceivably could injure the delicate interplay of the discretionary forces that underlie virtually every aspect of the Court's jurisdiction. Power once lodged in a given court must be totally retained, not divided, not delegated." [A]s two members of the Study Group, Professors Freund and Bickel, have reminded us, when Justice Brandeis was asked how he explained the great prestige of the Court, he replied, "Because we do our own work."

NOTES

1. When the 1972 Freund Committee Report excerpted above was released, the perception was that the SCOTUS's workload had grown beyond its capacity to function effectively as a COLR, *i.e.*, that the High Court was facing a "crisis of volume." The Freund Committee considered and rejected several alternative reforms: a constitutional court; exclusion of certain classes of cases; specialized courts of administrative appeals; a court of criminal appeals; a central staff to screen petitions; and a new national court of appeals between the courts of appeals and the SCOTUS. The 38-page Report also included a great deal of statistics and went on to assess: the SCOTUS's other jurisdictions, internal case selection processes, the rule of four, the

court calendar, and staffing patterns. Justice Brennan promptly filed his "dissent" from the Report that immediately follows the excerpt from the Committee's Report above. Likewise, Justice Stevens insisted that that the better solution to the *certiorari* problem was to grant fewer cases, advice that he and his colleagues have followed in earnest. John Paul Stevens, *Some Thoughts on Judicial Restraint*, 66 JUDICATURE 177 (1982). Indeed, as the rest of the readings in this Chapter describe, the current concern is not that the SCOTUS is deciding "too many" cases but that it is deciding "too few." What was this debate really about? Why is it important for the justices to select the cases they will decide? If that is at once so important and so subjective, so critical a matter of "feel," as Justice Brennan is convinced, what does that suggest about the legitimacy of the *cert* pool, from which Justice Brennan himself opted out?

2. In the aftermath of the failed Freund Committee proposal, Congress created the Commission on the Revision of the Federal Court Appellate System, popularly-known as the Hruska Commission after its chair, Senator Hruska. In 1975, that Commission issued a report, 67 F.R.D. 195 (1975), recommending that a new national court be created between the Supreme Court and the courts of appeals. This proposed court would decide cases referred from the Supreme Court and transferred from the courts of appeals, but the Supreme Court itself would perform all *certiorari* screening. The Hruska Commission proposal is discussed in Chapter 14.

C. The 2000s: Too Few Cases?

ROBERT L. STERN, EUGENE GRESSMAN, STEPHEN M. SHAPIRO & KENNETH S. GELLER, SUPREME COURT PRACTICE § 1.20 at 55-64 (8th ed. 2002)[7]

The Growth of the Court's Workload. During the first decade of its existence, 1791-1800, the Supreme Court had fewer than 100 cases on its docket. In contrast, during the last decade of the twentieth century, 1990-1999, nearly 76,000 cases appeared on the Court's docket.

But it is more meaningful to contrast the workloads of the Court during the last half of the twentieth century, from 1950 to 2000. That was a period in which the Court's dominant weapon in controlling and disposing of its rising workloads was its discretionary *certiorari* power. It was a power whose effectiveness was not significantly blunted by the declining presence of mandatory appeal jurisdiction.

Moreover, the latter half of the twentieth century witnessed improvements and refinements in the Court's internal docket control procedures. The Justices employed more law clerks to help in the initial screening of *certiorari* petitions. And most of the Justices agreed to pool and share their law clerk

---

[7] Reprinted with permission. Supreme Court Practice, Eighth Edition, Section 1.20 (pages 55-64), by Robert L. Stern, Eugene Gressman, Stephen M. Shapiro and Kenneth S. Geller. Copyright © 2003 The Bureau of National Affairs, Inc., Washington, DC 20037. For BNA Books publications call toll free 1-800-960-1220 or visit www.bnabooks.com.

screening resources, thereby avoiding unnecessary duplication in each chamber of such law clerk screening assistance.

In addition, as Chief Justice Hughes once noted, at least 60 percent of the petitions for which filing fees have been paid "are wholly without merit and ought never to have been made," while "about 20 percent or so in addition . . . have a fair degree of plausibility but which fail to survive critical examination." [The Chief Justice went on to say "the remainder, falling short, I believe, of 20 percent, show substantial grounds and are granted." But today, with many more cases on the docket, fewer than 20% of the *certiorari* petitions are being granted.] That is as true today as it was in 1937, when the Chief Justice made that remark. And with respect to *in forma pauperis* petitions, more than 90 percent fit the "wholly without merit" category. [In recent years, the number of grants of *in forma pauperis* petitions constitutes about two-tenths of 1% of the more than five or six thousand *in forma pauperis* petitions filed.]

The point has been made many times that counting the number of cases on the docket, or counting the number of pages of the petitions and briefs that must be read during the screening process, is an "illusory basis" for any outside critique of the screening process. The Justices are quite capable of establishing their own screening techniques; and if they find some intolerable obstruction — such as an overload of mandatory appeal cases — they have not hesitated to ask Congress to provide appropriate relief.

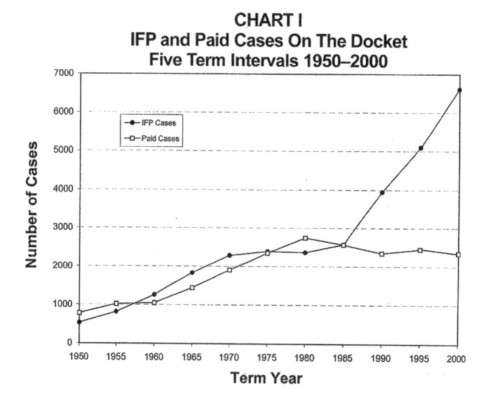

CHART I
IFP and Paid Cases On The Docket
Five Term Intervals 1950–2000

But the practitioner should be aware of the increasing numbers of cases that are entering the Court's docket, each of them competing for the Court's plenary attention. Chart I compares the 2000 Term workload with the workloads before the Court in five-Term intervals over the past 50 years. Chart I divides the workload figures into the two major components thereof: (1) the paid cases, cases in which a filing fee has been paid; and (2) the *in forma pauperis* cases, cases filed by prisoners or by any person who cannot afford to pay the filing fee or to prepare a petition in booklet form. Several observations can be drawn from these figures:

(1) The 1999 and 2000 Term dockets contained more cases than any other Term in the history of the Supreme Court. The 1999 docket was composed of 6,024 *in forma pauperis* cases and 2,413 paid cases, making a total of 8,437 cases (not counting 8 original cases on the docket). The 2000 docket was composed of 6,651 *in forma pauperis* cases and 2,305 paid cases making a total of 8,956 cases (not counting 9 original cases on the docket).

(2) The *in forma pauperis* cases are now the dominant part of the docket, accounting for about three-fourths of the cases on the 1999 and 2000 Term dockets. While always a significant part of the dockets since the 1950 Term, the *in forma pauperis* cases began a spectacular rise in numbers following the 1985 Term. This dramatic increase may be due, at least in part, to the nationwide increase in prison population, as well as legislative creation of new crimes and longer punishments.

(3) The paid cases have not exhibited the spectacular rise in docket numbers that have marked the *in forma pauperis* cases. Yet it is from these paid cases that the court selects the most cases for plenary review on the merits. At a time when there are growing numbers of cases being resolved by federal courts of appeals, as well as increasing litigation involving federal statutory and constitutional matters, the number of paid cases on the Court's docket has remained remarkably stable. Never has there been as many as 3,000 such cases on the docket. In recent years, the number has hovered around 2,400 per Term.

(4) Whatever the reasons for the rise in the *in forma pauperis* docket numbers, the court remains in complete control of its docket as it enters the twenty-first century. The court's administration of its docket continues to be "prompt, adequate, and efficient," with "no congestion of cases upon our [argument] calendar."

The Decline of the Argument Calendar. The foregoing summary of the Court's administration of its docket is not of mere historic or academic interest to the practicing lawyer. It provides the background for understanding why the Court cannot be a court of errors and appeals, and why the Court must confine itself to resolving only those relatively few critically important federal questions that emerge from the lower judiciary. And it provides a basis for estimating the mathematical odds of any given case being given plenary review by the Court.

Lawyers advising clients, in determining whether or not to seek Supreme Court review, should advise that the odds are, and always have been, strongly against a grant of review, and that the ruling of the lower federal or state court is likely to be final in all but a small minority of cases. But there are several different factors that enter into any calculation of the odds.

(1) In an *in forma pauperis* case, the odds that *certiorari* will be granted are always low, less than 1 percent. And as the *in forma pauperis* caseload gets larger, as it has in the last few years, the odds become ever lower. In the 1997, 1998, 1999, and 2000 Terms — a period during which the *in forma pauperis* workload soared to historic heights — the percentage of *in forma pauperis* petitions granted fell far below 1 percent each Term. The *in forma pauperis* statistics for those three Terms, as calculated by the *Harvard Law Review* from the Clerk's annual statistical statements, document this downward spiral:

The *In Forma Pauperis* (IFP) Docket

	IFP Petitions Considered	IFP Petitions Granted	Percent Granted
1997 Term	4,600	14	0.3%
1998 Term	4,946	9	0.2%
1999 Term	5,269	14	0.3%
2000 Term	5,773	14	0.2%

While the literal number of successful petitions has not significantly declined, the percentage decline is largely traceable to the soaring numbers of *in forma pauperis* cases filed and considered.

(2) The docket of paid cases, from which most of the successful petitions are drawn, has remained fairly constant over the past 30 years. As Chart I indicates, during that time period and up to the present, the paid case docket has consistently remained below 2,500 cases per Term, including the 2000 Term when 2,305 paid petitions were on the docket. That docket has never witnessed the dramatic case increases that have marked the *in forma pauperis* case docket in recent years.

During the 1970-1988 period, the Court granted plenary review of about 150 cases each Term, drawn mainly from the paid case docket. Percentage wise, that meant that the Court was granting review of about 6 to 8 percent of the cases on the paid case docket. As a result, the Court was "hearing and deciding an average of 147 cases each Term."

(3) But, starting with the 1989 Term, the Court began to reduce the number of cases taken for plenary consideration. This reduction, which continues in effect in current Terms, is highlighted not only by a reduction in absolute numbers but also by a significant percentage drop of cases from the paid case docket that are accepted for plenary review. Where once the *certiorari*-granted rate for paid cases was 6 to 8 percent, the rate has fallen to about 3.5 percent.

This downward trend is evidenced in the paid docket statistics for the 1997, 1998, and 1999 Terms:

The Paid Case Docket

	Paid Petitions Considered	Paid Petitions Granted	Percent Granted
1997 Term	2,106	75	3.56%
1998 Term	2,056	72	3.50%
1999 Term	2,070	78	3.70%
2000 Term	1,990	85	4.30%

It appears, therefore, that the decline in cases accepted for plenary review is at the statistical expense of the paid case docket. The statistical odds that a paid petition for *certiorari* will be granted have fallen to an historic low.

(4) But even those lowered odds, approximating 3.5 percent, do not tell the full story of the mathematical odds that confront a private or non-governmental petitioner who files a petition on the paid case docket. The above statistical odds of any petition on the docket being granted are based on counting all kinds of petitions that are considered and granted during a given Term. But included within that count are petitions filed by the Solicitor General of the United States, who files each Term a mathematically significant number of petitions that present important issues of national importance and are therefore likely to be accepted for plenary review. Indeed, the rate of success for petitions filed by the Solicitor General is consistently far greater than the overall rate of granted petitions. By so eliminating the Solicitor General's petitions from the mathematical odds computation for private practitioners, the odds that any private party petition filed on the paid case docket will be granted fall significantly below the overall 3.5 percent odds, barely reaching the 1 percent mark.

(5) Another variable factor that may have some relevance in understanding this fall in the plenary docket is that the Court may be engaging in something of a reversal strategy. That is, it may want to hear more cases that it might wish to reverse, but at the same time such reversible cases may be declining in number.

The Decline in Supreme Court Decisions. This ongoing numerical retreat in accepting cases for plenary review necessarily means that the Court is deciding fewer cases per Term. Before that retreat began in 1989, about 150 cases were decided each Term by full or *per curiam* opinions. Now, as Chart II illustrates, fewer than 90 cases are being decided each Term, a number that declined again in the 2000 Term. The reasons for this sharp reduction in the number of Court opinions are not immediately obvious. Academic commentators differ about the significance of and the reasons for this "shrunken docket". . . . [*See infra* section III.]

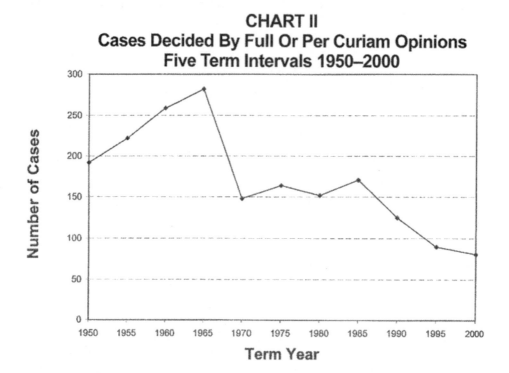

CHART II
Cases Decided By Full Or Per Curiam Opinions
Five Term Intervals 1950–2000

The Effect of the Workload on the Practitioner. There is not much that the practitioner before the Court can do about these workload problems. Indeed, a private counsel's concern "should not be so much in terms of the Court's workload; rather, it must be premised on a complete awareness of the fact that the Court is not a tribunal of general errors and appeals, that it is a *national* tribunal that can afford to listen only to issues of *national* significance," and "once that fundamental fact is understood, the lawyer can more effectively draft his [or her] *certiorari* or appeal papers.". . .

Moreover, the Court's ability to perceive the true nature of the case, no matter how much the practitioner may try to overstate its importance or hide its parochial nature, is one of the means by which the Court is able to eliminate the unmeritorious cases and thus reduce its heavy workload to a manageable size.

Counsel should not be too discouraged by the fact that a petition for *certiorari*, no matter how short or persuasive, may well be read by only one or possibly two law clerks, or by the additional fact that the petition, if it survives a law clerk reading, may be read by only a few Justices. Law clerks are quickly educated in what the Court deems to be either certworthy or uncertworthy. Moreover, nothing that a clerk may write about the uncertworthiness of a case can prevent a Justice from acquiring a "feel" that this kind of case, having been shown to have important *national* implications, does merit the Court's plenary attention. Such are some of the ways in which the Court executes its discretion in controlling and reducing its workload. All the practitioner can do is to follow [the] Rules and do so in the most persuasive and honest manner possible.

Margaret Meriwether Cordray & Richard Cordray, *The Supreme Court's Plenary Docket*, 58 Wash. & Lee L. Rev. 737 (2001)[8]

Twenty-five years ago, controversy raged over the size of the Supreme Court's docket. Two very different concerns animated the critics: first, that the Court's workload was unmanageably large; and second, that the Court's capacity for deciding cases was no longer adequate in light of the burgeoning caseload in the lower courts. These concerns were considered so pressing that scholars and legislators developed serious proposals to institute a national court of appeals to relieve the Court's burden and to expand the total appellate capacity.

At that time, the Court was issuing about 150 plenary decisions per Term. Just over a decade later, the Court's docket began to plunge, reaching its modern nadir of 76 cases in the 1999 Term. With the plenary docket reduced so dramatically, concerns about the Court's workload understandably abated. Commentators, however, have remained strangely silent about the second concern — whether the limited size of the Court's docket enables it adequately to supervise and guide the lower courts. This silence is all the more surprising, given that the Court's production has now fallen so far below the levels that alarmed commentators in the Burger Court era.

We think that issues concerning the appropriate size and shape of the Supreme Court's plenary docket warrant further consideration. But in order to have an informed discussion on those issues, it is first essential to develop a more complete understanding of the causes of the dramatic change that occurred between the Burger and Rehnquist Courts. . . .

The Recent Decline in the Plenary Docket. Beginning in the 1989 Term, the Court's docket — which had remained fairly constant at about 150 plenary decisions for the past decade — suddenly began to decline. In the 1988 Term, the Court issued 145 plenary decisions; in the 1989 Term, the number fell to 132; and in the 1990 Term, it fell to 116. It dropped slightly to 110 in the 1991 Term, held steady at 111 during the 1992 Term, then plunged to 90 in the 1993 Term. At present, the number of plenary decisions seems to have come to rest at a remarkably low plateau, ranging from 76 to 92 over the seven most recent Terms.

This unexpected development surprised and puzzled both participants and observers. At his confirmation hearings in 1986, then-Justice Rehnquist said, "I think the 150 cases that we have turned out quite regularly over a period of 10 or 15 years is just about where we should be at." Indeed, in response to questioning about whether the size of that caseload might be too great for effective administration, he stated more pointedly, "[m]y own feeling is that all the courts are so much busier today than they have been in the past, that there would be something almost unseemly about the Supreme Court saying, you know, everybody else is deciding twice as many cases as they ever have before, but we are going to go back to two-thirds as many as we did before."

---

[8] Copyright © 2001 Washington and Lee Law Review. Reprinted with permission.

Justice Souter, who arrived at the Court in the midst of this dramatic decline, said he has been "amazed" at the trend, which he suggests has "just happened" without any conscious decision on the Justices' part.

Commentators also recognized and were perplexed by the marked decline. Although some offered possible explanations for the decline, most of that discussion was tentative and came too soon to benefit from the kind of detailed investigation of additional data that is necessary to test the various hypotheses adequately. Some commentators on the decline expressed frustration that the Court's already precious resources were not being fully utilized, whereas others dispensed praise or blame, according to their views about the proper role of the Supreme Court in national life. The individual Justices who noted the phenomenon offered only vague and uncertain rationales for what may have happened to bring it about. . . .

Possible Explanations for the Recent Decline. Lawyers, commentators, and even the Justices themselves have hypothesized a variety of causes for the drop in the Supreme Court's plenary docket over the past decade. For the most part, however, these theories have remained mostly speculative and have not been satisfactorily evaluated in light of numerical data that would allow them to be either verified or falsified. This problem occurs because the close secrecy of the Court's internal deliberations makes it difficult to quantify the Justices' voting behavior in conference. In the discussion that follows, we attempt to draw upon the available data in new ways to amass the kinds of information that make it possible to test hypotheses more carefully and to draw more definite conclusions. In addition, one must consider the timing of each proposed explanation because a theory can be ruled out if its application does not correspond to the actual rise and fall of the plenary docket.

(A) Elimination of the Court's Mandatory Jurisdiction. [O]ne obvious (but ultimately unpersuasive) candidate is the almost wholesale repeal of the Court's mandatory jurisdiction. Prior to 1988, the Supreme Court enjoyed discretion to determine whether to review most of the cases coming before it, but several important statutes gave litigants a right of appeal to the Supreme Court. In 1988, at the Court's urging, Congress eliminated virtually all of these mandatory appeal provisions, substituting instead discretionary review on *certiorari*. . . . Although this first explanation cannot be ruled out entirely, it is implausible. Far more likely is the possibility that some variable (or variables) independent of the legislative amendments was simultaneously depressing the number of cases granted plenary review in both the traditional *certiorari* and "appeal" categories, to approximately the same degree. This strongly suggests that in the mid-1980s the Court was not giving plenary consideration to appeals that did not warrant *certiorari* review, except in perhaps one or two cases per Term, because it had already implemented internal procedures that led it to evaluate appeals and petitions for *certiorari* in similar fashion when deciding whether to grant review on the merits. The 1988 legislative changes thus seem to have had little or no effect on the Court's plenary docket.

(B) Fewer Actions Filed in Particular Subject Areas. Justice Souter has suggested that the declining docket may be partly attributable to fewer cases being filed in particular subject areas that are highly susceptible to

Supreme Court review, such as antitrust and civil rights. Yet a careful examination of the actual case filings reveals that this theory cannot account for the decline. . . . It remains possible, of course, that petitioners filed fewer meritorious applications for review in recent years, as litigation continues in certain areas without generating the kinds of significant "agenda" cases that lend themselves most naturally to Supreme Court review. Yet even here, the Court is demonstrably more likely to grant review in cases in which *amicus* briefs are filed at the petitioning stage, presumably because they indicate the general importance of the issue raised. As the number of cases in which *amici* filed such briefs has increased in recent years, this fact tends to cut against the notion that fewer important cases are now making their way to the Court than in previous years.

(C) Federal Government Seeking Review Less Frequently. A factor that is contributing to the declining docket is the smaller number of cases in which the Solicitor General has been seeking plenary review on behalf of the United States. The Solicitor General is by far the most frequent Supreme Court litigant and the most successful applicant in obtaining plenary review. Indeed, the proportion of the Solicitor General's petitions for *certiorari* that the Court grants is consistently over fifty percent, whereas paid petitions filed by other parties are granted at a rate of only about three percent. . . . Statistics from the Office of the Solicitor General demonstrate that the United States has been seeking plenary review in fewer cases in recent years. . . . The Solicitor General's pullback in seeking review accounts for a drop of approximately 15 cases per Term in the Court's plenary docket. In addition, the Solicitor General's less active involvement as *amicus* at the *certiorari* stage explains the loss of about 10 more cases per Term because the federal government is just about as successful in supporting another party's application for review as it is in seeking review in its own right. These figures indicate that the drop in filings by the Solicitor General, which occurred over essentially the same period as the decline in the plenary docket, is an independent factor that made a substantial contribution to the decline.

But this fact prompts an even more interesting question: What has caused this decline in the Solicitor General's activity? Three hypotheses, which are not mutually exclusive, warrant examination. First, the Justice Department may have changed its internal petitioning policies or criteria, and as a result may be seeking review in a smaller percentage of cases. Second, the Justice Department may be applying the same criteria, but the federal government may be involved in less litigation than in the past. Third, the Justice Department may be applying the same criteria to fewer cases simply because the federal government is winning more of its cases in the lower courts. . . .

(D) Greater Homogeneity Among the Courts. Another suggested explanation, which we credit in part, is greater homogeneity among the lower courts. According to this theory, a broad judicial realignment resulting from the steady appointment of like-minded federal judges has contributed to the declining docket. Justice Souter describes this homogeneity as one legacy of "the Reagan-Bush era," and he speculates that it is a "rare" phenomenon that probably will be short-lived.

Advocates of this view focus on the possibility that changes within the lower courts have led them to agree more frequently with one another, which we call a "philosophical realignment." This concept is related to but distinct from what we call a "control realignment," which occurs when the Supreme Court exerts greater control over the lower courts by providing clearer guidance that brings them more squarely in line with the direction of its own decisions. . . . Either type of realignment would have clear repercussions for the Court's docket: a philosophical realignment would reduce the need to grant review to resolve decisional conflicts, and a control realignment would reduce the need to grant review to correct perceived errors.

There are . . . empirical reasons to doubt the extent to which a philosophical realignment can explain the shrinking plenary docket. . . . Nonetheless, the discussion above in (C) suggests that one particular form of judicial realignment may have had a tangible effect on the Supreme Court's docket. That is, an apparent realignment in the lower federal courts toward more "pro-government" results — i.e., a "statist realignment" — has led the Solicitor General to seek review less often in civil cases, with a corresponding decline in such cases granted. Once again, this realignment seems to have made itself felt both by deterring lawsuits against the federal government and by affording less opportunity for it to seek review of adverse decisions. Consequently, the number of plenary decisions in civil cases involving the federal government has sunk dramatically: it averaged 40 cases per Term from 1983-1985, but only 19 cases per Term from 1993-1995. A similar development is manifest in federal litigation that involves state and local governments. Indeed, it is striking that the number of plenary decisions in federal civil cases involving state and local governments has fallen even more steeply than in cases involving the federal government: from an average of 35 cases per Term from 1983-1985 to fewer than 11 cases per Term from 1993-1995. Outside the arena of government litigation, however, any theory of realignment confronts mixed results.

(E) Changes in Personnel on the Supreme Court. One of the most compelling explanations for the recent decline in the Supreme Court's plenary docket stems directly from changes in personnel. [W]hen a similar decline occurred fifty years ago, the primary cause was the retirement of Justices who had voted aggressively to review cases and their replacement by new Justices who were far less inclined to do so. . . . Around the period of the most recent decline there were six retirements: Chief Justice Burger in 1986, Justice Powell in 1987, Justice Brennan in 1990, Justice Marshall in 1991, Justice White in 1993, and Justice Blackmun in 1994. The question posed here is whether these changes in personnel, taken singly or together, caused any systematic change in the frequency with which the Court decides to grant review.

The difficulty in gauging the impact of changes in personnel stems from the secrecy of the Supreme Court's internal deliberations in disposing of applications for review. Although Justice Douglas urged otherwise, the Court does not publish even the votes cast in cases not accepted for argument. Thus, in order to get a sense of whether certain Justices are more prone to grant review than others, it is necessary to read such tea leaves as are available. . . . These signs must be read with caution, however, because there is no necessary correlation between a willingness to vote for plenary review and a willingness to register that vote publicly.

The availability of the private papers of some of the recently retired Justices, which include the conference votes recorded in their docket books, offers new opportunities to compile grant rates at least for those Justices who served on the Court before Justice Marshall's retirement at the end of the 1990 Term. Although these sources do not allow calculation of grant rates for all of the current Justices, they offer ample information to enable us to draw much more definitive conclusions than have previously been possible. . . . The cumulative data suggests that the grant rates of individual Justices, relative to one another, tend to remain fairly constant over time, reflecting a general outlook that does not vary appreciably from one Term to the next. . . .

The data on conference votes demonstrates that changes in the Court's personnel have had a dramatic effect on the recent decline in the plenary docket. In the last decade of the Burger Court, the two Justices who consistently voted most frequently to grant plenary review were Justices White and Rehnquist, sometimes by a wide margin over their colleagues. Justices Blackmun, O'Connor, and Powell (usually in that order) were in the middle of the Court, followed by Chief Justice Burger; throughout this period, Justices Brennan, Marshall, and Stevens uniformly voted least often to grant review. The figures for Justice Blackmun and Chief Justice Burger are regularly fortified by their more frequent use of the Join-3 vote. . . . In 1986, Chief Justice Burger retired and Justice Scalia replaced him on the Court. . . . The next year, Justice Powell retired and was replaced by Justice Kennedy. . . . The numbers reveal that each of these three changes on the Court played a discernible part in shrinking the docket. Over the course of the next several Terms, both Justice Scalia and Justice Kennedy settled into abnegating roles in the discretionary review process, voting to grant review less often than any other Justice, including Justices Brennan, Marshall, and Stevens. . . . At this point, two more retirements occurred: Justice Souter replaced Justice Brennan after the 1989 Term, and Justice Thomas replaced Justice Marshall after the 1990 Term. The erosion of the Court's docket had continued even before these events occurred, as approximately half of the argument calendar for the 1990 Term was already set before Justice Brennan's retirement, and the number of plenary decisions declined again to 116 in that Term. . . . The final round of retirements came in 1993, when Justice Ginsburg replaced Justice White, and in 1994, when Justice Breyer replaced Justice Blackmun. Although no data is available yet to enable us to calculate individual grant rates for these new Justices, it is clear that these two changes had a profound influence on the shrinking of the docket. For many years, Justice White had been the Court's most outspoken advocate for granting review in more cases, particularly those involving conflicts among the lower courts. His voting behavior mirrored his public comments; throughout the first five Terms of the Rehnquist Court, he consistently had far and away the highest grant rate on the Court, routinely casting almost twice as many such votes as the average for the other Justices. Justice Blackmun had always been at the high end of the Court's middle tier, making far more frequent use of the Join-3 vote than his colleagues. By the 1990 Term, he was voting for review more often than any Justice other than Justice White.

The retirement of these two Justices caused an immediate further decline in the number of plenary decisions, to levels never before seen in the Court's modern era. The Court issued 90 plenary decisions in the 1993 Term, 85 in the 1994 Term, and only 78 in the 1995 Term. The numbers have remained at this level as the composition of the Court has remained unchanged, eventually reaching a new low of 76 plenary decisions in the 1999 Term. In light of the conference data now available, these unprecedented results are understandable. Justice White's voting behavior was so extraordinary that replacing him by someone with even an average grant rate would be tantamount to eliminating the votes cast by a typical Justice for plenary review in a given Term. At the same time, it is highly unlikely that the retirement of Justice Blackmun led to any increase in total grant votes, as he had become firmly established toward the high end of the spectrum. In addition, the tenor of their academic writings suggests that neither Justice Ginsburg nor Justice Breyer would press for any expansion in the Court's plenary docket. Aggregated with the effects of the 1986-87 retirements, therefore, the effect of these changes was to squeeze the Rule of Four even further, as if it were now being made to operate on a court composed of fewer than six of the former members of the Burger Court.

The cumulative effect of these changes in the Court's membership thus appears to have been dramatic. Quite apart from issues about who was winning and losing in the lower courts, and what parties were seeking review in which cases from one Term to the next, it is now evident that the Court's personnel changes over this decade were a substantial independent cause of the remarkable decline in its docket.

(F) Growth of the "*Cert* Pool." The foregoing analysis also helps dispel another explanation that has been offered for the declining docket — the allegedly excessive influence of law clerks in screening out cases through operation of the "*cert* pool." . . . The mechanism of the *cert* pool was controversial from its inception, and it remained so for years. . . .

It seems unlikely, however, that the *cert* pool has had much systematic influence on the votes cast by individual Justices to grant or deny plenary review, at least when compared to the dominant factor of the Justices' own predispositions. All of the Justices had individualized screening mechanisms in place prior to the *cert* pool, which made varying use of the law clerks. Such supplemental procedures also remained after the pool was in place, and it appears that the varying levels of scrutiny that individual Justices give to the applications does not correlate with their participation in the pool. Moreover, the actual voting behavior of the Justices in the pool has been far from uniform. . . . The supposed boundary between those Justices who do and do not belong to the *cert* pool is further blurred by frequent consultations among their law clerks.

Indeed, for the first fifteen years after the *cert* pool made its debut, the number of cases granted plenary review remained in the range of 150 cases per Term. . . . It is more likely that the clerks' initial screening simply helps in weeding out the great mass of cases that are universally viewed as marginal and in focusing attention on the remainder. . . . It thus seems virtually certain that the number of Justices in the *cert* pool has had little or nothing to do with the Court's declining docket.

Conclusions About the Changing Docket. The above analysis thus points to a multifaceted explanation for the recent decline in the Supreme Court's plenary docket. At the outset, the much-anticipated legislation restricting the Court's mandatory jurisdiction appears to have had little or no effect on the caseload. Changes in the Court's personnel, however, have played a substantial role in shrinking the docket. To begin with, the substitution of Justice Scalia for Chief Justice Burger and Justice Kennedy for Justice Powell, along with Justice Rehnquist's promotion to Chief Justice, provided a considerable impetus to reduce the docket. This was followed in short order by the retirements of Justices Brennan and Marshall, which had less impact than might have been expected, even though it cost the Court two votes and a more extensive lobbying effort for granting review in certain kinds of cases. The final substantial shift occurred with the retirements, soon afterwards, of Justices White and Blackmun. By their votes at conference, as well as by Justice White's frequent prodding both in public and private statements, these two Justices had strongly supported the Court granting review on the merits in more cases. When Justices who appear to have more moderate viewpoints on this issue replaced Justices White and Blackmun, the docket immediately plunged. . . .

In addition, an important influence that has independently contributed to the decline is the changing pattern of federal civil litigation involving government parties. Over the same period, the federal government was winning more of its fewer civil cases in the lower courts and thus was seeking plenary review less frequently. Similar factors were also at work in civil litigation involving the state and local governments and in criminal cases (though the numbers here were partially offset by a rising tide of federal criminal prosecutions), as for a generation the Supreme Court had asserted its control over the direction of the lower courts and presided over some version of a judicial realignment. Our analysis indicates that these factors — even apart from any changes in the Court's personnel — may have been responsible for as much as half of the overall reduction in the plenary docket.

Given these explanations for the declining docket, it is likely that the current situation will endure for some time to come, unless or until significant changes occur from new appointments to the Court. The consequences of the changes in personnel to date have been so great that it would take a real and sustained shift in the Court's direction to reverse them. Barring the appointment of a jurist whose approach to *certiorari* is cast in the highly unusual mold of a Justice White or a Justice Douglas, it will take several new members with a definite inclination to grant more cases to effect a substantial increase in the Court's caseload. At the same time, the confirmed pattern of government attorneys bringing fewer cases to the Court is likely to persist, for though they can anticipate paddling into rougher waters again at some point in the future, there is no apparent reason to believe that this will happen any time soon. For the time being, therefore, the Supreme Court's plenary docket has stabilized at levels that are unprecedented in the modern era.

Arthur D. Hellman, *The Shrunken Docket of the Rehnquist Court,* 1996 SUP. CT. REV. 403, 403-05, 425-38[9]

How can we explain the Supreme Court's shrunken docket? One possible source of enlightenment is the Justices themselves. From time to time, members of the Court have offered their views about why the Court is taking so few cases. . . . Experience has shown, however, that the Justices do not always have an accurate picture of the Court's practices. Nor can we rely on the impressions or speculations of those who watch the Court from the outside. If we want to know why the docket has shrunk so drastically, we must identify the changes that have taken place in the cases selected for plenary review and analyze them in a systematic fashion.

That is the approach taken in this article. Specifically, I shall compare the composition of the plenary docket during the three most recent Terms (1993 through 1995) with the docket 10 years earlier, during the height of the 150-case era. Using these data, I shall test five hypotheses that have achieved special prominence, either because they have been cited frequently by outside observers or because they have been endorsed by one or more Justices. They are:

1. The virtual elimination of the Supreme Court's mandatory appellate jurisdiction allows the Court to deny review in some cases that would have received plenary consideration under the pre-1988 regime.

2. After the retirement of its three most liberal Justices, the Court took fewer cases in which lower courts had upheld convictions or rejected civil rights claims.

3. Twelve years of Reagan-Bush judicial appointments brought greater homogeneity to the courts of appeals, resulting in fewer intercircuit conflicts that the Supreme Court had to resolve.

4. The Federal Government was losing fewer cases in the lower courts and therefore filed fewer applications for review in the Supreme Court.

5. The 12 years of Reagan-Bush appointments made the courts of appeals more conservative, resulting in fewer "activist" decisions of the kind that a conservative Supreme Court would choose to review.

[N]one of these theories fully explain why the Court is accepting only half as many cases for review as it did a decade ago. But they do offer clues. And a comprehensive analysis of the plenary docket of today, compared with that of the 1983-85 period, suggests that while external developments have played a part, the principal agent of change has been internal — a shift in the Supreme Court's own view of its role in the American legal system. . . .

None of the narrowly focused theories fully explains the shrinkage in the plenary docket. . . . Looking at the composition of the docket of the 1980s, one *leitmotif* stands out. With a single exception — governmental powers cases

---

[9] Copyright © 1996 The University of Chicago Press. Reprinted with permission.

from state courts — case selection was skewed in what would generally be viewed as a conservative direction.

The plenary docket of the 1990s presents a dramatically different picture. In every category of federal-court litigation, "liberal" and "conservative" grants appear in numbers that are virtually equal. This pattern can be seen in the governmental powers segment of the docket; it also holds true for issues of statutory interpretation. . . . The only imbalance is found in state-court cases involving governmental powers. But the imbalance favors litigants asserting federal rights, not those defending state official action. . . .

These data suggest that [the] Court no longer leans to "the right" in selecting cases for plenary consideration; rather, it has moved close to complete neutrality. Indeed, apart from maintaining the Court's traditional role of overseeing compliance with federal law by state courts, the docket reflects a balance that may well be unique in the Court's modern history.

What explains the new approach to case selection? One obvious possibility is that the Court of today is not the Court of 10 years ago. Six of the Justices who sat on the Court in the 1983-85 period have retired, and one of the remaining three serves as Chief Justice rather than as an Associate Justice. . . .

Justice Antonin Scalia . . . has provided the most detailed jurisprudential justification for a stripped-down plenary docket. Justice Scalia explicitly disavowed the common-law approach of "gradually closing in on a fully articulated rule of law by deciding one discrete fact situation after another until . . . the truly operative facts become apparent." Rather, he would extend "the law of rules . . . as far as the nature of the question allows," then leave the rest to the lower courts, even if this means "tolerating a fair degree of diversity" in the rules' application.

In short, the Justices who have joined in the Court in the last 10 years take a substantially different view of the Court's role in the American legal system than the Justices of the 1980s. They are less concerned about rectifying isolated errors in the lower courts (except when a state-court decision threatens the supremacy of federal law), and they believe that a relatively small number of nationally binding precedents is sufficient to provide doctrinal guidance for the resolution of recurring issues.

The influence of this philosophy can be seen most readily in the statutory segment of the docket. . . . [I]n this segment of the docket, the Court relies almost entirely on two strong indicia of the need for a nationally binding decision: the presence of an intercircuit conflict or an assertion of importance backed by the unique credibility of the Solicitor General. In the governmental powers segment of the docket, the Court's criteria are somewhat more flexible, but, outside the realm of the Supremacy Clause, the emphasis remains on articulating rules rather than on filling in the interstices of existing doctrines. . . . In both segments of the docket, the patterns I have described demonstrate a substantial narrowing of the criteria that the Court applied during the 1980s.

The new philosophy is also reflected in the 1995 revision of the Supreme Court's rules. For example, in describing the criteria for a grant of certiorari, the rules now tell petitioners that the existence of an intercourt conflict, without more, is not sufficient; the conflict must involve a question of importance. In addition, for the first time, the rules explicitly state that a petition "is rarely granted when the asserted error consists of . . . the misapplication of a properly stated rule of law."

An Olympian Court?

From Taft and Hughes onward, the Justices of the Supreme Court have emphasized that the Court's function is not to correct errors in the lower courts, but to "secur[e] harmony of decision and the appropriate settlement of questions of general importance." Under Chief Justice Rehnquist, the Court has moved closer than at any time in its history to acting upon that vision. It resolves direct conflicts between circuits; it responds to pleas by the Solicitor General that vital interests of the Federal Government are at stake; and it guards the supremacy of federal law against apparent violations by state courts. The Court also addresses issues of obvious importance in the realm of governmental powers. Beyond that, with only occasional exceptions, the Court stays its hand.

Many judges and lawyers will see his as a positive development. They share the concern of Justice Ginsburg that centralization of judicial authority tends to carry the "'imperial' judiciary to its logical limits." In this view, the Court can best serve the needs of the national law by laying down broad principles, leaving their application and elaboration largely to the federal courts of appeals and the state appellate courts. Nor is there any need for the Supreme Court to iron out every wrinkle of statutory interpretation, even some that give rise to apparent intercircuit conflicts. From this perspective, the shrunken docket of the Supreme Court can be seen as the judicial counterpart to the devolution that is taking place in the political branches of the national government.

But there is also a less benign way of viewing this development. The Court, if not imperial, has now become Olympian. The Justices seldom engage in the process of developing the law through a succession of cases in the common-law tradition. Rather, Court decisions tend to be singular events, largely unconnected to other cases on the docket and even more detached from the work of lower courts.

This approach may pose a threat to the effective performance of the Court's functions that is no less serious than that created by an "imperial judiciary." At the simplest level, the Court runs the risk that the paucity of decisions will leave wide gaps in the doctrines governing important areas of law. . . .

Some will see these gaps as symptomatic of a larger problem in the legal system: an insufficient number of nationally binding precedents. Others will argue that when it comes to expounding the national law, more is not necessarily better. Certainly it is not difficult to find areas and issues that have received sustained attention from the Court, but which continue to generate confusion and conflict.

In any event, the Court's Olympian stance raises concerns that go beyond the adequacy of the doctrinal guidance that the decisions provide. Quite apart from any gaps in precedent, paring the docket may impair the quality of the Court's work in the cases that it does take. When the Court addresses a particular statute or doctrine only in isolated cases at long intervals, the Justices may not fully appreciate how the particular issue fits into its larger setting. They may lose sight of the practical aspects of adjudication that emerge only when judges actually apply their rules to resolve disputes in a variety of factual contexts. The cases that attract the Court's attention may well be ones that involve extreme facts or idiosyncratic lower-court rulings. The resulting decisions, if not tempered by precedents deriving from more routine controversies, may skew the law in a way that would be avoided if the Court regularly adjudicated cases in that area.

Detachment from the work of lower courts gives rise to concerns of a different kind. . . . The Supreme Court need not acknowledge the work of lower courts in every one of its decisions, or even most of them. Nor need the Court attempt to replicate the common-law method in all of the many areas of its jurisprudence. But if the Court recurrently ignores the efforts of lower-court judges to address the issues on its docket, while remaining aloof from the day-to-day operation of the rules it lays down, two consequences can be anticipated. Lower-court judges will no longer feel the spirit of goodwill and cooperation that comes from participation in a shared enterprise. Without that spirit, it is hard to see how a hierarchical judiciary can function effectively. What is worse, the Justices themselves, engaged in work that is increasingly distinct from that of other courts, will have ever greater difficulty in adhering to the line that separates the judicial role from the legislative. The result, ironically, may be a Court that is even more "imperial." The Court has already moved in that direction. During the same period that the Justices have reduced their role as a source of precedential guidance for lower courts, they have cut a wide swath through controversial issues of public policy, enhancing judicial power and setting at naught the resolutions reached through majoritarian processes.

Philip Allen Lacovara, *The Incredible Shrinking Court; If Their Productivity Were Measured by Private Sector Standards, the Supremes Might Receive Pink Slips,* AMERICAN LAWYER, December 2003, at 53[10]

I yield to no one in my admiration of the Court as an institution. It is, after all, the apex of the legal system that now features more than a million law school graduates. A major part of my professional career has been wrapped up with the Supreme Court. But that experience just raises a nagging question: Why don't the justices produce more justice?

I am not questioning the soundness of their decisions on any particular topic of controversy. I just wish the justices would do more. The Court's business is to decide important cases. Despite growing resources and an expanding

---

[10] Reprinted with permission from the December 2003 edition of American Lawyer. Copyright © 2003 ALM Properties, Inc. All rights reserved. Further duplication without permission is prohibited.

market for dispositive decisions, the Court's market share is shrinking — as a matter of deliberate but ill-conceived choice. The justices inexplicably have decided not to do as much as the taxpayers pay them to do.

Every term the Court generates a handful of blockbuster decisions — perhaps half a dozen, rarely as many as ten — that make the evening news. Sometimes those blockbuster cases actually have broad impact. . . . [O]thers are largely symbolic. . . .

The tiny handful of blockbusters tend to obscure the real work of the Court. They may lead even lawyers to assume that a large iceberg of less notorious cases is being resolved, even though the public notices only the prominent tip that generates the fuss. Unfortunately, the iceberg is really just an ice cube. The Court is not doing much to resolve the important, workaday disputes of federal commercial law that it should be addressing. The numbers tell a compelling story. In the term that ended in [June] 2003 . . . measuring the Court's actual output in performing its constitutional function of deciding "cases and controversies," the Court produced a total of only 80 decisions.

By any measure, this is a shockingly low performance record. Look at the Court's productivity as measured either by the trend of its decision making or by the percentage of cases decided by the lower federal and state courts and subjected to Supreme Court review. By either comparison, taxpayers, lawyers, and litigants may fairly ask: "What are the justices doing with all the resources given to them?" . . .

The numbers are far more dramatic and revealing if one looks at what the Court used to accomplish as recently as a generation ago. . . . [W]ithin the lifetime of even the newest members of the bar, the Supreme Court has settled into a pattern of resolving barely half as many cases as it once did.

Indeed, these figures do not tell the full story of the Court's dramatic decline in disposing of the nation's judicial business. Before Congress acceded to the Court's request in the late 1980s to remove virtually all of its "mandatory" jurisdiction . . . . [t]hose summary dispositions were treated as decisions "on the merits" and had precedential force. Thus, a generation ago the Court actually was deciding the merits of almost 400 cases in a typical term. It is not an oversimplification to say, therefore, that the Court today is deciding barely 20 percent of the cases it resolved in the relatively recent past.

Of course, it is not as if the lower courts have experienced a dramatic decline in their caseloads, so that fewer cases are available for Supreme Court reexamination. Quite the contrary; the dockets of the federal and state appellate courts have exploded over this period. Those courts are resolving several times as many cases as they did a generation ago, and the caseloads per individual judge have escalated dramatically. . . .

Someone looking for a benign explanation of the Supreme Court's incredibly shrinking docket will point out that the Court is disposing of more *certiorari* petitions than ever before. That is true, but it is also misleading and irrelevant. . . . One could speculate that the Court is distracted by these additional *cert* petitions and cannot get around to deciding many cases on the merits.

I do not think that this is a fair explanation, for two reasons. First, virtually the total growth in the number of cases presented to the Court has come in the swelling of the *in forma pauperis* docket. With few exceptions, these are applications by indigent criminal defendants and prisoners (reflecting our nation's burgeoning criminal justice machinery and bulging prisons). Almost all of these petitions are frivolous on their face, and very few are ever granted.

By contrast, the number of cases on the "paid" docket has remained remarkably stable over the years. . . . [I]t is the paid docket that features the litigations among government agencies and regulated enterprises as well as securities, antitrust, employment discrimination, and other private commercial cases. These are the cases in which the party who lost below believes there is enough at stake to justify the substantial expense of paying the fees and legal expenses involved in asking the Supreme Court to review the case. While the number of paid cases has remained in the same range (2,100-2,500) for more than a generation, the Supreme Court has reduced by half its willingness to decide these cases.

The other reason the "escalating workload" argument does not wash can be summed up in two words: law clerks. In earlier times (within the lifetime of lawyers practicing today), each justice had one or perhaps two law clerks. Now each has four. So their resources have doubled or quadrupled. . . .

Moreover, in that same era not so long ago, each justice read (or at least glanced at) most of the petitions before deciding whether to vote to grant review. Often that consideration was informed by a short memorandum written by the justice's own law clerk, but many *cert* petitions actually received personal attention from the justices.

During the past 20 years, however, that process has become bureaucratized through the mechanism of the "*cert* pool". . . . Many justices never touch the actual petition, much less read it.

This is, of course, quite efficient. Only one person (a very recent law school graduate) does the work that used to be done by nine justices and perhaps nine law clerks reviewing a particular *cert* petition. And three or four times as many law clerks are available to perform this potentially decisive screening.

Two simple but disquieting facts emerge from this: First, the Court has dealt with the increase in the total number of requests for its attention by instituting procedures that dramatically reduce the consideration actually given to each request, whether frivolous or substantial. Second, the Court's productivity in achieving what it was created to do — decide important cases and controversies — has slipped substantially both in absolute terms and by every relative measure.

What explains this precipitous drop in judicial output by the nation's highest court? Structurally, Congress helped make it possible by removing almost all types of cases that the Court once had a duty to decide. Everything now falls in the discretionary category. . . .

There are a couple of problems with this policy of giving the justices absolute discretion over whether to review a case. One is that the number of fractious cases actually decided illustrates that it is often hard to get several justices to agree on anything. In recent years the number of separate opinions filed has risen substantially. It is not uncommon for a single case to spark three or four or five opinions reflecting highly individualized commentary that necessarily dilutes the force of a collegial body's decisions. Sometimes the quibbles get as minuscule as one justice's refusal to concur in a single footnote of another justice's opinion, although it is more common to disavow some subsection of another opinion. With this growing discord, it is harder and harder to get four justices to agree on so basic a question as whether a case should be reviewed in the first place.

Another factor that contributes to the refusal to cast a vote in favor of review is defensive strategizing: A justice is less likely to vote for review in an important case if the justice fears that a majority may come out the "wrong way."

Another contributing factor is more delicate to address. All of the justices are hardworking. They put in full days during most of the period when the Court is in session, from the first Monday in October until the end of the following June. A couple even show up in chambers on weekends from time to time. But human nature builds in a certain inertia that cannot be gainsaid. If there is a choice whether to take on a difficult task and the question is a close one, it is reasonable to surmise that the "default" position is "vote to deny."

A change in the way the justices see their role also accounts for some of the decline. Throughout most of its history, the Court addressed important issues of federal commercial law, especially those arising under the regulatory statutes that began to proliferate in the late nineteenth century. Now, with bizarre exception[s] . . . the Court disdains ordinary commercial law issues as unworthy of the justices' time. Instead, if a case is not one of the relatively few that pose intriguing questions of social policy, the chance of interesting four justices approaches zero.

One other institutional innovation compounds the problem. This is the phenomenon of the *cert* pool, which . . . inevitably builds into the memorandum on which eight of the justices heavily rely a strong bias to recommend turning down cases. Law clerks fresh from policy-laden Socratic classroom discussions are far more likely to be interested in the relatively few abortion, gay rights, and free speech cases than the host of commercial disputes.

Moreover, a new law clerk starts with the knowledge that the Court always turns down at least 98 percent of the cases presented for review. . . . Any decision to review a case is extraordinary and so is a law clerk's recommendation to do so. It takes a good deal of self-confidence for a recent law school graduate, even the kind of high achiever who makes it to clerking for a Supreme Court justice, to go out on a limb and say: "Take this one."

Sometimes the mistakes in making such a recommendation become embarrassingly public. A couple of times a year, after getting full briefs and hearing oral argument, the Court "DIGs" a case that it had been persuaded to review. . . . No law clerk wants to be on the line having recommended *certiorari* to the Court, including seven justices in other chambers, only to have the Court later decide, after investing a lot of time and effort, that it was "improvident" to do. Even if the clerk's judgment was innocent and reasonable, the embarrassment is palpable.

The safer course is to recommend against review except in the most compelling case. Since the Court itself regularly reminds the bar that review is a matter of discretionary privilege, disappointed litigants and their counsel may grumble, but the Court feels no sense of having deprived them of a right. There is no public record of an improvident denial of review. There is no second-guessing a denial, only a grant. So, apart from the sheer weight of other cases competing for the Court's attention, litigants must recognize that the deck is stacked against them when they seek Supreme Court review.

The problem is not a lack of resources. I emphasize that this figure does not include the other federal courts, just the Supreme Court itself. . . . In 2003 alone, the total federal budgetary allocation for the Supreme Court's salaries [for 396 employees including the nine justices] and facilities is $86 million. All of this public money buys about 75 decisions. These figures give new meaning to the term "the high cost of justice."

Another possible view of the "limited resources" thesis looks not to money but to time. The premise of this argument is that the Court does not have the time to decide more cases "judiciously." The circular reasoning goes like this: The Court takes a full term to rule on the number of cases it currently decides; therefore, it would have to give slipshod attention to its caseload if it tried to decide more cases.

Both history and common sense belie such a contention. With far fewer resources, the Court used to decide more than twice as many cases as it now does. I know of no empirical or scholarly basis to conclude that those decisions were less well-reasoned than contemporary decisions. It is true that today's opinions tend to be longer and that the multiplication of separate concurrences, dissents, and combination partial concurrences and dissents consume a huge amount of the justices' time. . . . The prolixity of the contemporary opinions is hardly a compelling reason for not deciding more cases.

Instead, this is a self-inflicted constraint. With more self-discipline, opinions could be shorter. One easy way to impose that self-discipline is, paradoxically, to decide to review more cases. . . . If the Court undertakes to decide only 75 cases a year, then one can predict with absolute certainty that those 75 opinions will take up all of the time of the justices and their clerks until the Court recesses for its three-month vacation in June.

But history and common experience demonstrate that if the Court undertook to decide 100 cases or 150, the justices and their clerks once again could decide that number within the same nine-month term. They would produce twice as many opinions, but probably no more total pages. Everyone would be better for the change.

The final question one may ask is whether the declining productivity of the Supreme Court matters. Are there cases that should be reviewed and decided by the Court that are lost in the morass of the 9,000 denials? Put another way, are there only 75 or 80 cases a year coming out of the 12 federal circuits and the highest courts of 50 states and the District of Columbia that merit the Supreme Court's attention?

To believe that the Court is actually deciding all — or even most — of the cases it should be addressing, one would also have to believe one of several very dubious propositions. One is that there are fewer difficult legal issues than there were a generation or more ago. Dramatic growth in the caseloads of the lower federal and state appellate courts suggests that this proposition is unsound. Indeed, the number of parties asking the Supreme Court to intervene has not declined. That the number of "paid" petitions has remained relatively constant also illustrates that serious litigants believe the Court should be resolving at least as many cases as it once did, not 50 percent or even 20 percent of its former productivity.

Moreover, commentators regularly publish lists of "circuit conflicts" on issues of federal law. Scores of those conflicts are left unresolved, even though one of the Court's principal responsibilities under the Constitution is to assure that the law is the same for all persons, regardless of the circuit in which they happen to live or litigate.

At the very least, the current Court should try an experiment: Consciously undertake to grant review in a larger number of cases. If necessary, modify the rule of four into a rule of three, so that any three justices could conclude that a case justifies the full Court's attention. See whether there is some inherent reason why these high achievers with life tenure cannot be as productive as their predecessors. If the justices do not manifest the self-discipline to exercise their discretion to decide more cases, then Congress should restore some categories of cases the Court must address.

NOTES

1. The excerpt from SUPREME COURT PRACTICE carefully documents the two dramatic and opposite trends in workload over the last two decades: in the 1980s the SCOTUS was deciding upwards of 150 cases and in the 2000s the SCOTUS was deciding downwards of 80. Do the statistics offer any insights into the workload demands on the justices and how they have responded? What might explain these up and down cycles of *certiorari* grants?

2. Professors Meriwether Cordray and Cordray present the most comprehensive multi-factor statistical analysis of the decline in the plenary docket. What factors help to explain why the SCOTUS went from granting 150 cases a year to only 80 cases a year? What factors have not affected the number of grants, according to their research? The same researchers have sharply contrasted the secrecy of the *certiorari* process to select cases with the transparency of the plenary process to decide cases:

> The contrast between the processes that the Court has devised for case selection and for plenary decisionmaking is thus quite stark. At the threshold stage, decisions are made atomistically, with little collegial deliberation, and are based on a very brief review of the documentation submitted in support of and opposition to a petition for certiorari. At the merits stage, decisions are made after extensive study and consideration and are based on a more explicit and intensive presentation of views and collective exchange that occurs both in public — at oral argument — and in the Justices' private conference. At the threshold

stage, decisions can be, and often are, made with a mere plurality vote; whereas a precedential decision at the merits stage requires majority support. At the threshold stage, decisions are made based on criteria that are designed to preserve immense discretion; at the merits stage, there are elaborate procedural and interpretive norms that often influence and channel the Justices' decisionmaking. Finally, at the threshold stage votes typically are kept secret — meaning not only that the Court's *certiorari* decisions are largely unexplained, but also that the Justices' individual decisions lack accountability in the particular case and from one case to the next. At the merits stage, the Justices publish both their individual votes and the reasons for the Court's holding; indeed, any Justice may issue a written account explaining his or her vote. Moreover, at the merits stage the accepted principle of *stare decisis* exerts further pressure on each Justice to justify his or her position in light of the Court's prior precedents, which are understood, from an institutional standpoint, to merit great respect in the process of deciding subsequent cases. This striking disparity between the Court's decisionmaking process at the *certiorari* stage and its more familiar process at the merits stage reinforces one Justice's comment that "[i]t is really hard to know what makes up this broth of the *cert* process."

Margaret Meriwether Cordray & Richard Cordray, *The Philosophy of Certiorari: Jurisprudential Considerations in Supreme Court Case Selection*, 82 WASH. U. L.Q. 389, 405-06 (2004). Should the *certiorari* processes be changed to make them more public? Why or why not? If so, how? If the conclusion of this study is that the secret and subjective preferences of the individual justices, aggregated under the Rule of Four, determine the number of grants and the kinds of cases that are granted, are we then back to the standardless discretion to review "important conflicts" and "important federal questions"? *See* SUP. CT. R. 10. What is a certworthy issue? Is it for the justices to know and for the rest of us to find out? Do the justices really know? Is the nature of *certiorari* jurisdiction, for lack of a better word, "discretionary," an example of the proverbial "black box" in social science — the petitions are known inputs and the grants are known outputs, but what happens inside the SCOTUS is unknowable?

3. Professor Hellman admits in his excerpt above that various factors offer partial explanations of the shrunken docket, but he believes the best explanation is that the current justices share a different vision of the role and function of the SCOTUS than did their predecessors. Do you agree with his "Olympian Court" thesis? What are the problems he associates with this mindset? Do you share his concerns? What are the costs and benefits to the SCOTUS deciding eighty cases a year versus 150 cases a year?

4. Philip Lacovara, a former deputy solicitor general and counsel to the Watergate special prosecutor, is a prominent appellate lawyer who has argued seventeen cases in the Supreme Court. He threatens the justices with a "pink slip." Would you vote to "fire" the "supremes"? Should Congress restore some of the formerly mandatory categories of cases and require the Court to hear and decide more cases? What kinds of cases might deserve this statutory pri-

ority? If the justices wanted to implement Mr. Lacovara's proposed experiment to grant more cases, if they set a goal to double their plenary docket to take 150 cases, how would they go about doing it within the existing *certiorari* processes?

5. As we have seen, in the 1980s, critics complained that the Court was deciding "too many" cases and in the 2000s, critics complained that the Court is deciding "too few" cases. How do these critics know the optimum number of cases that the Court should be deciding? Is it a function of workload demand? Is it a function of institutional capacity? Is it a consequence of the competing visions of the role of the Court? Is it ideological? Is there really some Pareto optimality of *certiorari*?

6. Justice Jackson summed up the mystery of *certiorari* this way: "neither those outside the Court, nor on many occasions those inside of it, know just what reasons led six Justices to withhold consent to a *certiorari*." *Brown v. Allen*, 344 U.S. 443, 542 (1953) (Jackson, J., concurring).

Chapter 13

COMPARATIVE PERSPECTIVES

This chapter affords an opportunity for a comparative examination of appellate courts, processes, and judges in two foreign countries: England (mother of the common law system) and Germany (a representative civil law system). Several reasons call for such a comparative excursion. First, knowledge of the legal systems of other countries is increasingly important for American lawyers in light of the growing internationalization of law practice. The global village is bringing with it ever more global legal work. Second, studying the legal system of another country enables us to see our own system in a new light and can inspire useful ideas for improvement. Here, though, a caveat is in order. As in the biological world, where a plant that thrives in one environment may not thrive in another, so transplanting a procedure, practice, or doctrine from one legal system to another may not be successful. Nevertheless, improvements in the American justice system might be made by creative adaptations from other legal environments. Finally, apart from the practical advantages of comparative study, all lawyers, as a matter of their general and well-rounded education, should have some understanding of how courts and law function in other legal orders.

I. ENGLISH APPELLATE COURTS AND JUDGES

The American and English appellate judiciaries share the same ancestry: the English common-law and equity systems of the eighteenth century. Two centuries of separate development, however, have resulted in numerous differences. Yet significant similarities remain, including a common core of underlying premises and concepts.

In studying this subject, students should try to evaluate the advantages and disadvantages of the corresponding English and American procedures and whether there might be some gain in fairness or efficiency in American appellate courts by adopting or adapting some facets of the English process. It is, of course, possible that the English might find something in American appellate practice that would improve their system, and students should be alert to such possibilities. As will be explained later, from an American standpoint, the most useful English appellate procedures for comparative purposes are those employed in criminal appeals, and they are the focus here.

A. The Judicial System of England and Wales[1]

The appeals examined here are appeals in the court system for England and Wales. Scotland and Northern Ireland have their own separate courts; they

---

[1] The information in this section comes from JUDICIAL STATISTICS ANNUAL REPORT 2003 (Dept. of Constitutional Affairs, 2004).

are not dealt with here. The entire United Kingdom, however, is linked together judicially at the top in the House of Lords, the highest court in the Kingdom. (Without disrespect to Wales, for simplicity we use the terms "English courts" and "English judges.")

To an American, the English judiciary seems unnecessarily complicated. It is roughly a pyramid, but not a tidy one; there are bulges and irregular indentations. The judges present a confusing picture; they sometimes have strange titles, and they have mixed duties. In contrast, American judges are rather clearly identified with respect to court and function. In the main, American judges stay in their own identifiable slots and perform one kind of judicial work. In England there is more fluidity between trial and appellate positions, and there are changing combinations of judges who come together from time-to-time to exercise a special jurisdiction. To an outsider it all seems unduly complicated and without good reason. The explanation seems to be the same explanation that underlies many English institutions — history combined with contemporary utility. Following is a brief description of the system, from bottom to top, as illustrated by the diagram on page___. No more is said of this complicated structure than is necessary to place the appellate courts in perspective. Details of the system can be found in JACKSON'S MACHINERY OF JUSTICE (J.R. Spencer ed., 1989), although it needs updating in some respects.

Trial Courts

Magistrates Courts. Magistrates' courts form the judicial base of the criminal justice system. All criminal proceedings are commenced in these courts. They have jurisdiction to dispose of what Americans would consider misdemeanors. They commit the serious cases, *i.e.*, felonies, to the Crown Courts for trial and sentencing. Well over 90% of all criminal cases in the country are finally disposed of by magistrates' courts. These courts are presided over by some 28,000 lay magistrates, about half of whom are men and half women, called Justices of the Peace. They are citizens, broadly representative of their communities, recommended by local advisory committees and appointed by the Lord Chancellor. In large urban areas, district judges preside. They are full-time, law-trained professionals (formerly called stipendiary magistrates). There are 436 in the country, many of whom also sit on county courts, as indicated below.

Crown Courts. These are the major criminal courts. They sit at locations all across the country and are usually presided over by circuit judges, of whom there are 609. But many cases are presided over by High Court judges, as mentioned below, and by recorders, who are practicing barristers appointed by the Lord Chancellor to serve part-time. More than 1,400 such part-time recorders serve on the crown courts. Trial is by jury, with sentencing by the judge.

County Courts. These courts have original trial jurisdiction over certain tort and contract actions and over numerous other types of civil cases. They sit at 90 locations throughout the country. Each county court is assigned one district judge and one circuit judge. Circuit judges generally sit on cases involving larger amounts or of special importance.

High Court of Justice. This court consists of 107 High Court judges, addressed as "Justice," the major trial judges in the system. They are based in the Royal Courts of Justice in London. The court is organized into three divisions: Queen's Bench (72 judges), Chancery (17 judges), and Family (18 judges). The QB judges sit on the more important civil actions. They also serve on Crown courts, presiding over the most serious criminal cases. In addition, they sit on criminal appeals, as will be explained below. The Lord Chief Justice heads the Queen's Bench Division; the vice-chancellor heads the Chancery Division. The Family Division is headed by a President.

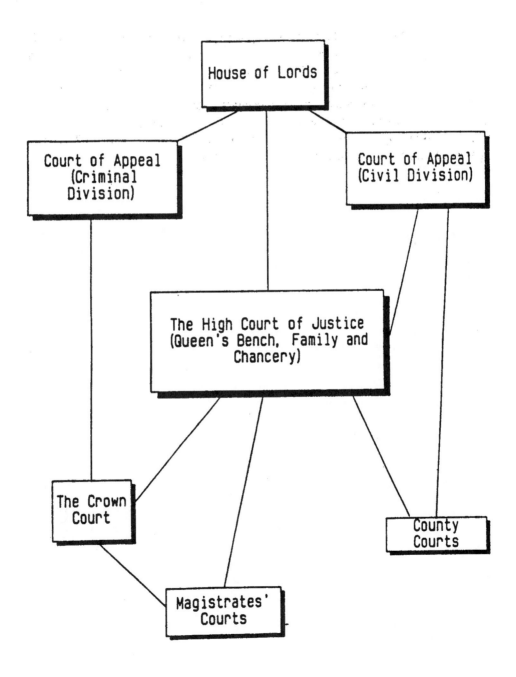

Appellate Courts

Court of Appeal. This purely appellate court is the major subject of this study and will be dealt with in detail hereafter.

House of Lords. Although the House of Lords is the upper house of the British Parliament, it also serves, through its "Appellate Committee," as the court of last resort, the highest judicial entity in the United Kingdom. As described in section E of this part, this court will be replaced in 2008 by a Supreme Court of the United Kingdom.

B. The Court of Appeal and its Judges

The Court of Appeal is the single appellate court for England and Wales. Cases come to it for review by various means from the trial courts described above. It is organized into a Criminal Division and a Civil Division. The latter is presided over by the Master of the Rolls, the second highest judge in the English judiciary, the highest being the Lord Chancellor. The Criminal Division is headed by the Lord Chief Justice, the third ranking judge (who also heads the Queen's Bench Division of the High Court). In addition to the Master of the Rolls and Lord Chief Justice, the Court of Appeal has 37 judges, all housed in the Royal Courts of Justice, each with the title of "Lord Justice of Appeal."

1. The Setting

Daniel J. Meador, *English Appellate Judges from an American Perspective,* 66 GEO. L. J. 1349-51, 1353-54, 1356, 1359, 1361-62 (1978)[2]

In London along the Strand, where it joins Fleet Street at Temple Bar, is sprawled a cavernous Victorian edifice officially known as the Royal Courts of Justice. . .[informally as the "Law Courts"] To the casual tourist it would not be a noticeable attraction. Inside, however, the architecture and the activities that can be observed suggest that this is no ordinary place . . .

As one walks through its front portals, escaping the rumble of traffic on the Strand, he emerges into a vast room — a concourse stretching into the distance, surmounted by a soaring roof. The size, shape, windows, and milky gray color of the stone combine to give the immediate impression of a Gothic cathedral. Stairways and corridors lead in all directions from this central concourse, and along those corridors are many courtrooms . . . Much human activity goes on here, with sittings of the Court of Appeal taking place daily in many of these rooms. In each, a massive judges' bench of mellow wood stretches across the front, higher than the head of anyone standing on the floor. Bookshelves filled with buckram-bound law reports line the walls on both sides up to a height that only a stepladder can reach. In banked array facing the bench are pew-like wooden seats, the front two rows for barristers, the next for solicitors, and the rear two or three rows for the public. High above the bookshelves and everything else are cathedral-like windows, or in some rooms sky lights,

---

[2] Copyright © 1978 GEORGETOWN LAW JOURNAL. Reprinted with permission. Updated information is shown in brackets.

through which filters the muted light of an English sky. Chandeliers dropping from the extraordinarily high ceilings add to the soft illumination of the scene.

The principal actors in the dramas that take place here day after day are not dressed in ordinary clothes. The three judges sitting behind the bench wear wigs and robes. The barristers likewise dress in robes and wear wigs, though of a different style from those of the judges.

. . .

. . . [The Court of Appeal] is the principal appellate court of the country and, for all but that handful of litigants who go on to the House of Lords, it is the court of last resort. Indeed, it is the only strictly appellate court in the country apart from the House of Lords. In function it resembles an American state supreme court of a state in which there is no intermediate appellate court . . .

. . . The judicial manpower in the Criminal Division [of the Court of Appeal] is regularly augmented by trial judges from the High Court, the highest level of trial court in the country. [Two High Court judges from the Queen's Bench division typically sit with one Lord Justice of Appeal to hear criminal appeals.] . . .

. . .

. . . The English courts have no authority to pass on the constitutional validity of legislation. Unlike the United States, England has no written constitution under which the validity of the acts of the legislature or of government officials can be tested . . . In short, there is Parliamentary supremacy; whatever Parliament enacts is binding law on everyone, including the judges, and the courts are bound to enforce it . . .

. . .

Despite the great age of the country and of the courts, the body of relevant English precedent is not large. In the Court of Appeal the majority of the cases are unreported . . . [However, many unreported decisions are collected in the growing number of specialist law reports. Furthermore, all judgments of the Court are transcribed, and indexed copies are kept in the Court library and are available to practitioners. Furthermore, commercial organizations electronically preserve the judgments which can be retrieved and printed out at terminals] . . .

. . . [O]ne of the most distinguished English appellate judges, Lord Devlin, a [former] Law Lord, asked in a recent lecture, "What is the function of the judge?" He answered by quoting Professor Jaffe, "The disinterested application of known law.". . .

That statement captures well the English appellate judges' view of their role: the courts decide legal controversies in accordance with existing law. Law is viewed as a relatively fixed array of rules, derived from cases and statutes, and the court's task is to ascertain the law and to apply it to the facts of the case at hand.

NOTES

1. As a result of developments in European law, English courts now exercise something like the kind of judicial review exercised by American courts. That is, English courts may now hold an act of Parliament to be contrary to

European law and thus void. For a description of the European courts and the effect of European law on national courts, see Part III of this chapter.

2. Generally speaking, the English appellate courts appear to be more committed than American courts to the doctrine of *stare decisis*. Indeed, it was not until 1966 that the House of Lords assumed authority to overrule its prior decisions. *See* T. Prime & G. Scanlan, *Stare Decisis and the Court of Appeal: Judicial Confusion and Judicial Reform*, 23 CIVIL JUSTICE QUARTERLY 212 (2004).

2. The Judges and the Road to the Appellate Bench

Daniel J. Meador, *English Appellate Judges from an American Perspective*, 66 GEO. L. J. 1349, 1371-78, 1380-83, 1402-03 (1978)[3]

Sitting in a courtroom in the Royal Courts of Justice as appeals are being heard, one sees behind the bench three judges who seem by casual observation to be almost identical. Each is wearing an identical robe and wig. Each appears to be about the same age. The demeanor of each is similar, and in some threesomes even the eyeglasses are identical. Indeed, the picture is one of three almost depersonalized figures, three figurines cast from the same mold. This has been said to be a salutary feature of wigs and gowns; they conceal individual variances of physical appearance and personality, thus heightening the sense that it is the law and not individual human personalities speaking. The judge is perceived as a mere conduit for the law; as the expression goes, he is the embodiment of the law. The entire physical setting works to import an aura that the judgments being rendered are those of the law and not those of mortal men.

The identity of judicial appearance and demeanor turns out to reflect something else — an identity of background. These judges not only look alike when they are sitting on the bench, but they are in fact similar in education and experience and indeed in every significant respect. Each of these [37] appellate judges served as a trial judge in the High Court immediately before his [or her] appointment to the Court of Appeal. Before appointment to the High Court, each was a practicing barrister, and all but [four] had been accorded the added status of Queen's Counsel. Those [four] had been "Junior Counsel to the Treasury," thus serving as advocate for the government in the High Court. With [few exceptions], each studied at either Oxford [17] or Cambridge [16] . . .

The road to the appellate bench is thus clearly marked. There is a career pattern, a professional progression, that is unvarying. The steps in chronological order can be stated thus: Call to the bar, active practice as a barrister, appointment as Queen's Counsel or service as Treasury Counsel, appointment to the High Court as a trial judge, and finally, appointment to Court of Appeal. Appellate judicial selection, in other words, is made from a pool that has been progressively narrowed — from barristers, to Queen's Counsel, or Treasury Counsel, to High Court judges. In numbers this shrinkage of the pool is huge: there are some [100,000] lawyers in England and Wales, of which only about

---

[3] Copyright © 1978 GEORGETOWN LAW JOURNAL. Reprinted with permission. updated information is shown in brackets.

[10,000] are barristers; of these, some [1,000] are Queen's Counsel, and there are [107] judges on the High Court. Under this system when a vacancy occurs on the Court of Appeal, the appointing authority does not have to survey the entire legal profession of . . . barristers and . . . solicitors, nor even the . . . Queen's Counsel; he looks only to the High Court judges . . .

Because the road to the appellate bench begins with the call to the bar and because the barristers form the exclusive pool from which appellate judges ultimately come, it is necessary to say something about the peculiarities of that professional body . . . [T]he English legal profession is divided into two distinct groups (barristers and solicitors. Each has its own admission requirements, its own rules of professional conduct, and its own governing authority . . . Not only is the work of the two groups different; their whole professional lifestyles, so to speak, are also different . . .

. . . Solicitors' work and working arrangements seem much like that of a typical American law firm. They practice in partnerships of various sizes, and ordinary citizens come to their offices as clients seeking legal advice or legal assistance of all kinds. Solicitors are entitled to appear and try cases in some of the lower trial courts, and many of them do so regularly. [Under late twentieth century reforms, solicitors who meet certain qualifications may also appear in the High Court, just as barristers do. In other words, barristers no longer have the exclusive right of audience in the High Court as they once did.]. . .

Most barristers devote their entire professional lives to litigating in court, either trying cases — both civil and criminal — in a trial court, or arguing cases in the Court of Appeal or the House of Lords . . .

. . . [T]his generalization does not convey the full dimensions of a barrister's peculiar way of operating, which differs sharply from the way solicitors and American lawyers practice. Barristers cannot form partnerships; each practices alone and independently. Although they share "chambers" — a suite of rooms with some common employees — the American style, and solicitor's style, of "law firm" does not exist among barristers. They are prohibited from holding any other employment while in active practice. Specifically, they may not be directors of corporations or banks or be involved in any sort of commercial enterprises. Complete independence is the tradition of the bar and is viewed as impaired by any entanglements in other activities. A barrister's independence is heightened by the absence of a permanent or continuing relationship with any client; every representation he undertakes is brought to him by a solicitor. Thus, he is unlikely to become a representative of a "cause" or to become biased in favor of certain types of clients.

One of the most important distinctions between a solicitor and a barrister is that the latter never deals directly with lay clients. The barrister deals only with solicitors; solicitors are their immediate clients. A person with any kind of legal problem must go first to a solicitor. If litigation in the High Court is necessary, the solicitor will then pick a barrister to handle the matter in court. The barrister gets "instructions" from the solicitor, who alone investigates a case and assembles the evidence to be presented in court. The solicitor['s] . . . work is embodied in a "brief" which he provides the barrister and that is the basis for the barrister's conduct of the case in court.

There is still another distinctive feature in a barrister's life — his membership in one of the four Inns of Court. To become a barrister one must pursue a training program offered jointly by the Inns of Court. These Inns date back to the Middle Ages. In those early centuries of the common law they provided the only legal education available. It was an apprenticeship system, a highly vocational type of training. A period of apprenticeship — "pupilage" — is still required, in addition to the Inns' formal course of lectures and examinations. A would-be barrister may or may not have studied law in a university; it is not required. University legal education does not occupy and never has occupied the place in England that it has come to enjoy in the United States . . .

The four Inns — Middle Temple, Inner Temple, Lincoln's, and Gray's — still perform the function of "calling to the bar." Every barrister is a member of one of the Inns; he must be, because that it is the only door to the bar. Each Inn has its own complex of buildings and gardens covering several acres each, lying within a short walk of the Royal Courts of Justice. Barristers' chambers occupy the buildings of the Inns, and some of the judges actually live there. The central feature of each Inn is a great medieval style dining hall. Here many members gather for lunch every day, as do some of the judges, each of whom, having been a barrister, is a member of an Inn. In order to be eligible for the call, candidates for the bar must eat a certain number of dinners in the Inn annually. More importantly, candidates must pursue a substantial course of instruction offered jointly by the four Inns through their common organization, the Council of the Bar.

All this gives the bar the appearance of being a large club, or, more precisely, four closely related clubs. An outside observer cannot resist the conclusion that a barrister, at least compared with many American trial lawyers or English solicitors, is shielded from much of life. He does not, as part of his professional work, talk with ordinary people about their legal, business, or personal problems, nor does he go out to investigate matters, to interview witnesses, and to discover the facts of a case. He talks only to solicitors and fellow barristers and judges. He typically eats lunch with fellow barristers within their own dining hall where only other barristers eat, and though he comes into contact with a variety of persons when he examines or cross-examines witnesses in court, such contact is limited and in a formal setting. As the behavioral scientists might say, there is a high degree of socialization within the English bar; barristers would be described in current jargon as an "elite" group.

After a barrister becomes a High Court judge his life becomes even more regimented. He spends his days sitting alone on the bench hearing cases. If he is sitting in London, as he will be much of the time, he associates almost exclusively with his fellow judges and with barristers in his Inn. If he is sitting on circuit away from London, as many High Court judges do for a number of weeks each year, he lives in comfortable but isolated "judge's lodgings" provided especially for him and staffed with personal servants.

From this setting the High Court judge is picked to become a judge on the Court of Appeal.

. . .

The Office of the Lord Chancellor [now known as the Department for Constitutional Affairs] selects all judges in England. In no state or other jurisdiction in the United States is judicial selection so well organized, so tightly structured, and so centrally based. Because this office is one of key importance in the administration of justice in the United Kingdom, the selection of judges in England cannot be comprehended without understanding it.

The Lord Chancellor himself is an avowedly political appointee. Named by the Prime Minister from his party, he is a part of the government of the day [now holding also the title of Secretary of State for Constitutional Affairs]. To Americans he represents a curious mixture of powers. The Lord Chancellor is a member of the cabinet and of the executive branch of government. He is also speaker of the House of Lords, and he often speaks for the government in debates; thus he is a part of the legislature. In addition, he is the presiding judge in the House of Lords when it acts as a court; thus, he belongs to the judiciary, although he actually sits judicially in only a few cases annually. He is also entitled to sit ex-officio as a judge in the Court of Appeal, but in practice he almost never does. He is a unique link between the judicial and the political branches of the government. As Lord Kilmuir put it, "the Lord Chancellor is the personified contradiction of Montesquieu's theory of the separation of powers." In England, however, the office works.

In these various capacities the Lord Chancellor is responsible for the operations of the entire judicial system. In fact, his main duties concern the management of the courts and the selection of the judges. Some of the post-World War II Lord Chancellors have said that judicial selection is the most important duty of the office. The Lord Chancellor himself actually appoints the judges for all courts below the central royal courts [High Court, Court of Appeal, and House of Lords]. For the High Court and the appellate courts, the Prime Minister is formally charged with selecting the judges, but in practice he relies almost totally on the recommendations of the Lord Chancellor.

By custom the Lord Chancellor must have been a barrister and a Queen's Counsel. Well regarded among bench and bar, he bears little resemblance to the American politician-lawyer who might, for example, be elected state attorney general with only slim professional standing at the bar . . . Next to the Lord Chancellor himself, the most important figure in that office is the Permanent Secretary, and he also plays a key role in judicial selection. As those familiar with English government know, a permanent secretary is the highest rank in the civil service and typically is a person with long experience and competence in his field. He remains in the position despite changes in the government. In the Lord Chancellor's office the Permanent Secretary is, and has been for many years, a barrister, like the Lord Chancellor; he resembles other members of the bar and bench in professional status and associations.

The process of judicial selection in England is not an episodic affair, activated only when a vacancy occurs on some court. It is a continuous, on-going process. Because the Lord Chancellor sits over the entire judicial establishment from the magistrates' courts through the House of Lords, his office is in position to administer a system-wide selection process and to maintain a kind of judicial career planning. He is responsible for the appointing of lawyers to dozens of lower trial court judgeships as well as to the higher courts.

The career path to the High Court and the Court of Appeal begins for a barrister with the application to become a Queen's Counsel. The Lord Chancellor's responsibility for considering and passing on these "applications for silk" — so called because of the silk gowns worn by Queen's Counsel — places his office in a unique position in relation to the entire bar. The formal appointment of a Queen's Counsel is made by the Queen, but it is always on the Lord Chancellor's recommendation. There is no counterpart anywhere in the United States to this application procedure and to the status that comes with the appointment. The grant or denial of this application is probably the single most important event in the entire professional career of a barrister. If the application is granted, the way is open for higher income, less onerous and more selective work, greater prestige, and a future appointment to the higher courts . . .

. . .

When and whether to apply for silk is a decision that is left entirely to each barrister. Typically a barrister needs to be well established and well regarded in order for the application to have any chance of success. Applications are made by barristers with ten to twenty years of experience, and most applicants are at least forty years of age. The Lord Chancellor's office provides a printed application form which calls for biographical data, for at least two references, and for details concerning the applicant's practice. There is a deadline each year for the filing of applications.

After the deadline has passed and the year's crop of applications is in hand, the Permanent Secretary undertakes to determine how many and what types of new Queen's Counsel are needed to service the courts and the clients. He does this by making inquiries of the presiding judges on the various courts and perhaps also by asking some of the leading silks. Ordinarily, at any one time no more than about ten percent of the bar will be Queen's Counsel . . . In selecting the Queen's Counsel, the area of expertise is important in addition to the numerical needs . . . The major areas of specialization include criminal law, general civil litigation, trusts and estates (or general chancery practice), and family law. The Permanent Secretary will evaluate the needs in these specialized areas and determine the exact number and types of applications that will be granted that year. Some applications may be denied because they do not fit the needs of the current year.

In passing on an application, the Permanent Secretary makes inquiries of judges before whom the applicant has practiced and may also question colleagues in the applicant's area of specialization or in his circuit . . . Much of the investigation is informal. Character is inquired into as much as legal competence; any act of unethical conduct or blemish on moral character can be fatal. All information accumulated in this process — both fact and opinion — is collected in a card file, and these cards are kept permanently in the

Lord Chancellor's office . . . [T]hrough this kind of sifting procedure the Lord Chancellor, with the very substantial assistance of the Permanent Secretary, eventually arrives at an approved list of Queen's Counsel for the year.

The information gathered in connection with this process is supplemented continually. If a barrister serves on significant committees or commissions or is involved in various professional activities, such activities are recorded in the Lord Chancellor's office. Because all appointments to the High Court are made from Queen's Counsel, whenever a vacancy occurs, there is already on hand a sizable store of information about every possible prospect . . . [This was no longer entirely true after the newly adopted practice of inviting applications for High Court appointment, as explained in the Notes below.] . . .

Because the focus here is on appellate judges, the process and criteria for selecting High Court judges from this pool of Queen's Counsel will be passed over with but two comments. First, the choosing of High Court judges and the choosing of Court of Appeal judges are not viewed as completely separable processes. Because judicial selection is a continual, ongoing process in the Lord Chancellor's office, barristers are constantly evaluated in the context of possible judicial appointments not only for the High Court, but for the lower trial courts as well. Second, the Lord Chancellor has under his dominion a large array of circuit judgeships. These are full-time judicial appointments on lower trial courts. He also appoints recorders, part-time judges who sit on these and other lower courts. The Lord Chancellor thus has a testing ground for future High Court appointments. He can place a barrister in one of these positions and thereby gain a basis for determining his suitability for a higher judicial appointment. It is this overview and control of the entire judiciary by the Lord Chancellor that makes the English arrangement a career management and promotion system.

When a vacancy occurs on the Court of Appeal, the pool of prospects consists of those persons who are then in active service as trial judges on the High Court . . . There are [107] judges on the High Court, but the number of prospects for an appellate appointment will be considerably less. Some will be eliminated because they are too old or have been on the bench for too short a time. Five years on the High Court seems to be the minimum typically required. More important than age and experience, however, is the concept of specialization and balance on the appellate bench. The long-established belief is that the Court of Appeal should be composed of judges drawn from the various specialties. The number of judges in each specialty is roughly proportionate to the volume of appellate business in that area. If a vacancy on the Court of Appeal is created through the death or retirement of one who had earlier, for example, been a chancery judge on the High Court, then a chancery judge will be selected to replace him. The same holds for such areas as criminal law, family law, or commercial law. If the volume of business of the court has shifted, however, the Lord Chancellor may decide that an increase in appellate manpower is needed in another area and will then look to that area of the High Court's work for the replacement . . . This is another illustration of his managerial powers over the judicial system.

Thus, the first step in filling a Court of Appeal vacancy is the determination of the legal field from which the new judge should come. This has the effect of narrowing the pool of prospects to those judges of the High Court currently sitting on cases in that field. When eliminations for age or inexperience have also been made, the realistic prospects might be as few as two or three. The pool is unlikely to be larger than a dozen.

Having progressed to this point, the Permanent Secretary compiles a list of the most promising prospects and discusses these names with the Lord Chancellor. At this point in the life of a High Court judge, the information about him on file in the Lord Chancellor's office will be considerable, beginning some fifteen or twenty years earlier when he applied for silk. But one gets the impression that the general awareness of the abilities and reputation of an individual by the Permanent Secretary and the Lord Chancellor are as important, and probably more important, than the actual information in the file. Nonetheless, the two are not really separable; it is the amalgam of all that is known in the office that is significant.

The discussion between the Permanent Secretary and the Lord Chancellor usually results in the Lord Chancellor's selection of one to three names. These names are discussed in a meeting of the Lord Chancellor with the heads of the major divisions of the higher courts: the Master of the Rolls, as head of the Civil Division of the Court of Appeal; the Lord Chief Justice, as head of the Criminal Division of the Court of Appeal and the Queen's Bench Division of the High Court; the President of the Family Law Division of the High Court; and the Vice Chancellor, as head of the Chancery Division of the High Court. There is no fixed procedure or formal order, however . . . Delay in judicial appointments is not usual; the process can and does move rapidly. The important point is that in one way or another, the Lord Chancellor discusses the narrowed list of prospects with these presiding judges, representing both the trial and appellate courts. Consultation is usually limited to discussions with these judges and the Permanent Secretary. . . . Although a presiding judge might consult with other judges within his division, no judge other than those presiding judges would likely communicate a suggestion for an appointment directly to the Lord Chancellor, or even to his own presiding judge unless he were asked. Many would consider it improper for a barrister to make a suggestion to anyone; if not outright improper, it is said to be without effect. The selection of a Court of Appeal judge is deemed the responsibility of the Lord Chancellor, with only such advice as he cares to seek, and he is not expected to seek any advice beyond the opinions of the four presiding judges.

Within this small group the tendency is for the Lord Chancellor to give a bit more weight to the views of the Master of the Rolls, because he is considered the head of the Court of Appeal, and to the presiding judge from whose division the appointment is to be made. No votes are taken, but suggestions may be put forward by the presiding judges in addition to their discussions of the names the Lord Chancellor has advanced. Apparently these discussions usually result in a consensus, either on one or two names, with the arguments for and against each nicely balanced. Whatever the result of the discussion, however, the Lord Chancellor alone makes the decision.

That individual is then asked whether he would accept the appointment. If he is willing to accept, he is then requested to undergo a complete medical examination and to have his physician submit a report to the Lord Chancellor's office. If the medical report is satisfactory, the Lord Chancellor forwards the name to the Prime Minister, who in turn submits it to the Queen, who officially makes the appointment. At no point along the way does the Lord Chancellor discuss any of the prospects with the Prime Minister. The latter seems to take no part whatsoever in arriving at a suitable appointee and appears to accept the recommendation without question or discussion.

A vacancy on the Court of Appeal attracts no attention in the press, and the public is unaware of it. Moreover, it generates little interest among barristers or solicitors because they know they have nothing to do with filling the vacancy. At least among the barristers, there seems to be confidence that the appointment will be a good one or in any event, a wholly acceptable one.

. . .

It is obvious from the description just given that the judicial selection process is in the hands of a very small group. Within this group there appears to be a high degree of consensus on the criteria for choosing appellate judges. It is difficult, however, to state precisely what these criteria are, because within the group there are no expressly articulated standards. Rather, the consensus is based on mutually shared assumptions that the participants apparently do not need to articulate among themselves or to others. The assumptions extend beyond this small group, however, and appear to be shared rather generally among the judges and within the bar. This explains to a considerable extent why the selection process and its results are met with general satisfaction within these professional groups, despite their nonparticipation.

. . .

[Here the article describes the apparent criteria that were being used and the major grounds of objections to the process: lack of openness, the small group making the selections, and the small pool from which appointees were chosen. Recent changes in this appointing system are described in the notes below.]

NOTES

1. In 2003 the name of the Lord Chancellor's Department was changed to Department for Constitutional Affairs. Until enactment of the Constitutional Reform Act 2005, that department continued to perform all the functions of the former department, including administration of the entire court system and the appointment of judges. The Lord Chancellor headed that department with the added title of Secretary of State for Constitutional Affairs. Under the 2005 Act, two positions will exist: Lord Chancellor and Secretary of State for Constitutional Affairs. The former will remain responsible for judicial matters (although he will no longer sit as a judge), and the latter will be

responsible for a whole range of policy matters. The Lord Chief Justice becomes president of the courts of England and Wales with responsibility over the internal business of the courts, including authority to assign judges and to appoint judges to various leadership positions. He will no longer head the Queen's Bench Division; it is to be headed by a president. The Master of the Rolls, the second ranking judge, continues as head of the Civil Division of the Court of Appeal.

2. Beginning in 1997, in response to criticisms of the lack of openness in the judicial appointments process, the procedure for appointing High Court judges was modified so as to invite applications to fill vacancies on that court. The Department for Constitutional Affairs periodically announced that it was open to receive applications from barristers and from those solicitors who were otherwise qualified. A barrister need not have been a Queen's Counsel (QC) to apply. The Lord Chancellor could add to the list of applicants. The names were circulated to sitting judges for comment, and other information about the applicants was gathered. After this, the Lord Chancellor went through a process of selection much like that described in the foregoing account. That process appeared to have produced High Court appointments not significantly different from those previously made. The process of appointing Court of Appeal judges appeared not to have changed.

3. Under that new system, the Department for Constitutional Affairs promulgated a detailed list of criteria that one had to satisfy to be appointed to the High Court. As appointees to the Court of Appeal come from the High Court, they presumably met these criteria. The criteria were: high level of understanding of principles of law and jurisprudence; comprehensive knowledge of the rules of evidence and of court practice and procedure; high quality of performance in any judicial appointment previously held; outstanding level of professional achievement in areas of practice; sound judgment — exercising discretion effectively, applying knowledge and experience to make decisions that comply with the law and are appropriate to the circumstances, and considering competing arguments and reasoning logically to a correct and balanced conclusion; intellectual and analytical ability — being able to concentrate for long periods of time, understand and assimilate facts and arguments and recall evidence expeditiously and accurately; ability to apply legal principles to particular facts and to identify from a large body of information those issues and facts which are relevant and important and weigh relevant issues and matters of law in order to formulate them for reasoned and coherent presentation; decisiveness — ability to reach firm conclusions, to think, decide, and act independently of others; good communication skills — ability to communicate effectively with all types of court users, including lay people, give instructions, explain complex issues and give decisions clearly and concisely, both orally and in writing; authority and case management skills — being able to command respect of court users and maintain fair minded discipline in court and chambers without appearing pompous, arrogant or overbearing and to promote the expeditious dispatch of business, preventing unnecessary prolixity, repetition, and irrelevance; integrity and independence — having a history of discretion and plain dealing with professional colleagues, clients, and the courts, possessing independence of mind and moral courage,

being prepared to take unpopular decisions and having the trust, confidence, and respect of others; fairness and impartiality — being open and objective with the ability to recognize any personal prejudices and to set them aside and being able to deal impartially with all matters and ensure that all those who appear have an opportunity for their case to be clearly presented and that it is then considered as fully and as dispassionately as possible; understanding of people and society — having a knowledge and understanding of and respect for people from all social backgrounds, being sensitive to the influence of different ethnic and cultural backgrounds on the attitudes and behavior of people encountered in the course of judicial work; maturity and sound temperament — displaying a maturity of attitude and approach and being firm and decisive while remaining patient, tolerant, good humored, and even tempered; courtesy and humanity — being courteous and considerate to all court users and court staff and having and conveying understanding of and sympathy for the needs and concerns of court users; commitment to the public service and to the proper and efficient administration of justice.[4] Would it not be possible, without any lessening in the quality of appointees, to state the essential criteria in far fewer words?

4. The Constitutional Reform Act 2005 works an historic change in the method of appointing judges. It establishes a Judicial Appointments Commission with authority to select appointees for all the courts in England and Wales, both trial and appellate (except judges of the new Supreme Court). There are separate appointing commissions for Scotland and Northern Ireland. The Commission is to be chaired by a lay person and will consist of five judges from the different court levels, a lay magistrate, a barrister, a solicitor, five lay members, and a holder of one of the offices specified in the Act. When a vacancy occurs on a court (except on the Supreme Court), the Commission, operating through a process to be established, recommends one name to the Lord Chancellor. The Act specifies that the selection be based "on merit," but otherwise says little about criteria. The Lord Chancellor may accept the name and send it forward for appointment by the Queen, or he may reject it or send it back to the Commission for reconsideration. If he rejects it or sends it back he must state his reasons. The Commission may submit another name or, in case of reconsideration, submit the same name. The Queen makes all appointments of Court of Appeal judges, High Court judges, circuit judges, district judges, and recorders, although the Lord Chancellor's action on the Commission's recommendation is decisive. Thus the kind of career management and promotion system for the English judiciary under the Lord Chancellor, described in the foregoing article, comes to an end. It remains to be seen what changes, if any, the new system will bring about in the types of persons appointed as judges.

5. Compare the procedure for selecting and appointing judges through this new Judicial Appointments Commission with that of the judicial nominating commissions established in some American states, as described in Chapter 11.

---

[4] Taken from REPORT OF THE COMMISSIONERS' REVIEW OF THE HIGH COURT 2003 COMPETITION, pp. 28-30 (Commission for Judicial Appointment, July 2004).

What are the similarities and differences? Does either appear to have an advantage over the other?

6. Would it be feasible and desirable for each jurisdiction in the United States to establish an office, like that of the former Lord Chancellor's office, charged with responsibility for gathering and maintaining information on prospective judicial candidates so that when a vacancy occurs it could be filled without delay? Would a career management and promotional system, along the traditional English lines, be workable in the United States?

7. PATRICK S. ATIYAH AND ROBERT S. SUMMERS, FORM AND SUBSTANCE IN ANGLO-AMERICAN LAW: A COMPARATIVE STUDY OF LEGAL REASONING, LEGAL THEORY, AND LEGAL INSTITUTIONS (1991), contains a detailed comparative analysis of English and American judges, as well as comparisons of legal reasoning, judicial decision making, and the legal profession, legal education, and legal and political institutions in England and the United States. The authors' thesis is that all of these work together to make the American legal order what they describe as "substantive" and the English legal order "formal" (to be distinguished from "formalistic," which has pejorative implications not intended by the use of the word "formal"). They conclude that while the American system has advantages, the English system is more efficient and less costly. The American system, they believe, is derived from the natural law and instrumentalist views of law, while the English system rests on legal positivism.

C. Criminal Appeals in CACD

Proceedings in the Criminal Division of the Court of Appeal are the major focus of this study. Those appeals, involving both convictions and sentences, come from the Crown Courts, where all serious criminal cases are tried. Criminal appeals present richer possibilities for comparison with American procedures than do civil appeals because of their distinctive features that differ from American procedure. Those features, to be examined here, are the role of the Criminal Appeal Office, the leave granting procedure and the role of the single judge, the flexible and comprehensive scope of oral hearings, the standard applied in the review of convictions, and the development of sentencing policy through appellate review. All aspects of this court's work are covered in ROSEMARY PATTENDEN, ENGLISH CRIMINAL APPEALS 1844-1994 — APPEALS AGAINST CONVICTION AND SENTENCE IN ENGLAND AND WALES (1996).

Jurisdiction and procedure in the Court of Appeals, Criminal Division, is governed by the Criminal Appeal Act 1968, as amended several times. There are some variations from American terminology. To "quash" a conviction means to set it aside or nullify it. To "allow" an appeal means to reverse the conviction or to alter a sentence — in other words, to hold in favor of the appellant-defendant. To "dismiss" an appeal means to affirm the judgment below. Note also that the English say "appeal against conviction" and "appeal against sentence," whereas Americans say "appeal from . . ." or "appeal of . . ." Trial or conviction "on indictment" does not imply an indictment by a grand jury, as there are no grand juries in England; it simply means a trial in the Crown Court.

1. Applications for Leave to Appeal — The Criminal Appeal Office and the Role of the Single Judge

The typical appeal to CACD is from a judgment of a Crown Court. An appeal may be against sentence or against conviction or both; most are against sentence. In all but a fraction of cases, an appeal is by leave of the Court of Appeal, Criminal Division.

After conviction and sentence, the defendant's solicitor normally requests trial counsel (a barrister) to offer advice and assistance concerning an appeal. For impecunious defendants, governmentally funded legal aid often will be provided for this purpose.

If counsel advises an appeal, he signs and sends to the solicitor the grounds of appeal — brief statements of reasons why the conviction should be quashed or the sentence altered. The grounds are incorporated into Form NG, which is the official form for making application for leave to appeal. The solicitor then files Form NG in the Crown Court where the defendant was convicted.

The first two pages of Form NG are set out *infra*. The remaining four pages, not included here, contain spaces to be filled in by the Crown Court and instructions as to how to complete the form. This is one of numerous forms used in the criminal appeals process. Forms are used for bail, to compel the appearance of witnesses on appeal, and to record actions of the single judge (to be described below). The use of forms for these key steps is a distinctive feature of the English criminal appellate process. Their use simplifies and expedites the procedure. Much of a form can be completed simply by checking blanks ("ticking boxes"). Such a uniform format for essential information helps the Criminal Appeal Office and the judges to assimilate the information more quickly.

Grounds of appeal must be "settled" (*i.e.*, drafted) with sufficient particularity to enable the Court to identify clearly the arguments relied upon. A reason must be articulated why the Court is invited to come to such a conclusion. Often two or three citations of supporting authorities are included.

When Form NG is filed in a Crown Court, court personnel will append certain information from its records and forward the papers to the Criminal Appeal Office, located in the Royal Courts of Justice in London, where CACD sits. That Office has no exact counterpart in American appellate courts. Perhaps it can best be understood as a combination of a court clerk's office and a central staff attorneys' office. But its importance in the work of CACD is greater than the sum of those two American offices. It has a staff of thirty lawyers, headed by the Registrar of Criminal Appeals, who must be a barrister of at least ten years experience.

When the Criminal Appeal Office (often referred to as the Registrar's Office) receives Form NG from the Crown Court, the staff proceeds to assemble the papers it deems necessary for adequate consideration of the application. In a conviction appeal a copy of the trial judge's "summing up" is always obtained. This is the counterpart of an American trial judge's instructions to the jury, but it is more detailed and elaborate than the usual American-style instructions. In the summing up, the English trial judge summarizes the evidence in the case, including the testimony of each witness, thus providing a relatively compact and objective statement of the facts from the standpoint of both the prosecution and the defense. This document makes it feasible in many cases to dispense with the transcript of the testimony for purposes of passing on the application for leave to appeal.

The Registrar's staff determines the amount of trial transcript, if any, to be obtained. It is guided, but not bound, by any request Counsel may have made in Form NG. The staff determines the portions of the trial transcript to be obtained in relation to the issues presented by the grounds. In other words, the Registrar's office, not the lawyers, is in control of material to be assembled for the court's consideration — the "record," as Americans would say. Unlike much American practice, English practice tailors the transcript to the precise needs of the case. If portions of the transcript are obtained by the Registrar a copy will be provided defendant's counsel and counsel will be invited to "perfect" (revise or edit) the grounds.

An application for leave to appeal is then referred by the Registrar to a "single judge" pursuant to Section 31 of the Criminal Appeal Act 1968. That section authorizes a single judge to act on such applications on behalf of the full Court. The single judge is always a judge of the Queen's Bench Division of the High Court. Judges from the High Court also sit with the Lords Justice of Appeal to hear and decide appeals after leave has been granted.

A judge, in passing on an application for leave to appeal, considers the perfected grounds, the trial judge's summing up and any other papers provided by the Registrar's office, which may include portions of the transcript.

The standard for granting leave to appeal seems to be one of arguable merit. That is, the single judge grants leave if he thinks that the application is not "hopeless" but presents some arguable point of substance. A judge may grant the application limited to specified grounds, eliminating from further review the remaining grounds that he finds without merit, thereby narrowing the issues for the full court. In denying leave, the judge makes a brief notation of his reasoning, and this is communicated to the applicant. Under this procedure, the applicant receives a limited review on the merits even if his application is denied. A denial is in effect a summary affirmance on the merits. The single judge's action also can be viewed as a screening procedure, through which some cases are decided on the papers, while others are sent to oral argument. If denied, an application may be renewed by the applicant; it will then receive the consideration of two judges.

To deter frivolous appeals, the single judge, in refusing leave, may direct that some of the time already spent in custody will not count toward the defendant's sentence. Ordinarily the judge will not do so if the grounds have been signed by counsel, indicating a good-faith belief in the appeal's merits. On the other hand, the Court may order loss of time if the application is renewed after denial, because the single judge's denial will have "forewarned" the defendant that the case lacks merit.

The single judge completes Form SJ (reproduced *infra*) and returns it to the Registrar's office. If the application for leave is granted, the judge can direct the office to take a variety of steps, including obtaining specified documents and designated portions of the trial transcript. The Registrar may also be directed to summon witnesses for the hearing. Thus the record — called the "bundle" — to be considered by the full court is put together by the joint actions of the Registrar's office and the single judge, possibly with suggestions from trial counsel.

The Registrar has discretion to refer an application for leave directly to a three-judge panel, and to grant public funding for legal representation, bypassing the single judge. He would do this when he considers that the application presents a point of unusual importance or when for some reason he thinks it ought to be considered by the full court.

NOTES

1. Would it be desirable to give American appellate courts an authority, like that exercised in CACD, to direct that time already served not count toward defendant's sentence? Would this be an effective means of discouraging frivolous criminal appeals? What is the argument against such authority?

2. When the single judge denies leave to appeal after reviewing the grounds of appeal, the trial judge's summing up, and other papers supplied by the Registrar, has the defendant had a fair review on the merits?

3. What is the difference, if any, between denial of leave to appeal by the CACD and a denial of certiorari by the U.S. Supreme Court? Both are said to be discretionary, but is there a difference in the kind of discretion involved?

4. Compare a single judge's denial of leave to appeal with the process in the U.S. Fifth Circuit under which a single judge classifies an appeal as not justifying oral argument or an opinion, and the three-judge panel thereupon disposes of the case by an order reading "Affirmed. *See* Local Rule 47.6." What differences are there between these two processes in terms of the quality and fairness of the review? Note that the Fifth Circuit review is said to be a "matter of right," while the English review is said to be "discretionary." Is the distinction meaningful?

2. After Leave Granted — Hearing and Deciding Appeals

When leave is granted, the Registrar's office notifies the appellant and the appellant's legal advisors and takes whatever additional steps the single judge has directed to prepare the case for hearing. A lawyer on the staff prepares a "summary." This document summarizes the evidence, sets out the grounds of appeal, and provides an objective analysis of the legal issues presented. It is a counterpart of memoranda prepared by central staff attorneys in many American appellate courts. A key difference is that the Registrar's summary never makes a recommendation as to the disposition of the appeal. Each of the three judges who is to hear the case receives a copy of the summary and all other papers that have been assembled by the Registrar.

An appeal is heard by the "full court," which in CACD terminology means a panel of three judges, called a "constitution" of the court. One judge is always a Lord Justice of Appeal; the others may be two Queen's Bench judges or one Queen's Bench judge and a Circuit judge. The court sits in several three-week sessions throughout the year. In each such period six panels are sitting. The composition of those three-judge panels and the daily list of cases assigned to each are set by the Registrar, illustrating the considerable authority he exercises over the court's business, going well beyond the authority any staff attorney would have in an American appellate court.

The Court of Appeal Criminal Division

Form **NG**
(Forms 2 & 3)

NOTICE and GROUNDS of appeal or application for leave to appeal
(Criminal Appeal Act 1968)   CAO No.   /   /

● Please read the notes for guidance overleaf. Write in BLACK INK and USE BLOCK CAPITALS

ON COMPLETION PLEASE SEND THIS FORM TO THE CROWN COURT WHERE TRIED OR SENTENCED

The appellant
give full name

If in custody give
Prison Index Number
and address
where detained

Surname _____

Prison index no.

Forenames _____

Address _____

_____

Post code _____   Date of birth _____

The Court where tried or sentenced

Give details if the case
was transferred from
another court

Underline the dates of
conviction and sentence

The Crown Court at _____

Name of Judge _____

Dates of appearance in the Crown Court _____
Total period of remand in custody prior to sentence _____

The conviction(s) and sentence(s)

The full Crown Court case number(s) must be given, and particulars of ALL counts, offences and sentences included.

Crown Court case number(s)	Count or charge no.	Offence	Sentence

Number of offences taken into consideration

Total sentence

Applications   SEE NOTE 5
The appellant is applying for: *Please tick as appropriate*

☐ Extension of time in which to apply for leave to appeal against conviction and/or sentence

☐ Leave to appeal against conviction

☐ Leave to appeal against sentence

☐ Legal aid

☐ Bail

☐ Leave to call a witness

1457 (10/87)   1

Notes for guidance on the completion of this form

1.   Everyone who is convicted or sentenced in the Crown Court in circumstances where an appeal would lie to the Court of Appeal Criminal Division should have advice or assistance on appeal. Provision for this is included in a trial legal aid order (section 30(7) Legal Aid Act 1974).

2.   Solicitors and counsel are expected to be familiar with 'A Guide to Proceedings in the Court of Appeal Criminal Division' (available from any Crown Court Centre and reproduced at volume 77(1983) Criminal Appeal Reports 138).

3.   Separate forms should be submitted for convictions or sentences which do not arise in the same proceedings.

4.   This notice will be treated as a notice of appeal where leave to appeal is not required.

5.   **Applications**

    ● Extension of time   This form should be sent to the appropriate officer of the Crown Court within 28 days of the conviction, sentence, verdict or finding appealed against. If the appellant is in custody the form should be handed to the prison authority (or other person having custody) for forwarding to the Crown Court, and the date of handing in should be recorded on the form.

                                  The period of 28 days cannot be extended except by leave of the Court of Appeal Criminal Division and the reasons for the delay will be required.

                                  NOTE that the time for applying for leave to appeal against conviction runs from the date of conviction even where sentence is passed on a later date.

    ● Leave to appeal against conviction   } See note 6
    ● Leave to appeal against sentence   }

    ● Legal aid   A legal aid order made in the Crown Court does not provide for oral argument before the Court of Appeal. If legal aid is sought for this purpose it should be applied for.

    ● Bail   Where bail is applied for Form B must also be completed. If Form B accompanies Form NG it should be submitted to the Crown Court but if submitted later should be sent to:— The Registrar, Criminal Appeal Office, Royal Courts of Justice, Strand, London WC2A 2LL.

    ● Leave to call a witness (Conviction applications only)
                                  Application made on Form W which should be included only where leave is sought to call a witness in support of an application for leave to appeal against conviction. A separate form is required for each witness. If Form W accompanies Form NG it should be sent to the Crown Court but if submitted later should be sent to:— The Registrar, Criminal Appeal Office, Royal Courts of Justice, Strand, London WC2A 2LL.

6.   **Grounds of appeal**

    Where grounds have been settled by counsel they must be signed by counsel and attached to this form. There is no obligation to include a copy of counsel's advice although in some cases it may be helpful to do so. Grounds must be settled with sufficient detail to enable matters relied upon to be clearly identified. Wording such as "the conviction is unsafe and unsatisfactory" or "the sentence is in all circumstances too severe" will be ineffective as grounds and an extension of time may have to be applied for (see note 5).

7.   Where a certificate that the case is fit for appeal has been granted by the trial judge this should be stated and see generally paragraph 17 of 'A Guide to Proceedings in the Court of Appeal Criminal Division'.

8.   Where an appellant has been granted leave to appeal he is entitled to be present on the hearing of his appeal. It will be assumed that an appellant in custody is applying for leave to be present at any hearing for which leave to be present is required unless he indicates to the contrary.

For each three-judge panel, the daily list typically consists of two or three appeals against conviction, three or four appeals against sentence, and three or four renewed applications for leave to appeal following denial by a single judge. There would be fewer cases on the list if one of the appeals against conviction were expected to require more than the usual two hours or so. Appeals against sentence typically take twenty to thirty minutes. Some lists contain only sentence appeals and renewed applications; these lists contain as many as fifteen cases. Along with the name of each case in the list sent to the judges will be the name of the judge who is expected to deliver the Court's judgment.

COURT OF APPEAL CRIMINAL DIVISION

Criminal Appeal Act 1968

Form of Judge's Order under Section 31

SJ

(Please write in BLACK)

APPELLANT Forename(s)	Surname	Reference No.

WHERE DETAINED	INDEX No.	ADDRESS IF NOT DETAINED

ORDER by the Hon. Mr. Justice

APPLICATIONS considered

   (a)   EXTENSION of time   (e)   BAIL

   (b)   Leave to appeal against CONVICTION   (f)   Leave to be PRESENT

   (c)   Leave to appeal against SENTENCE   (g)   ORDER for witness to attend

   (d)   LEGAL AID

DECISION*

.... days of the time spent in custody as an appellant shall NOT COUNT TOWARDS SENTENCE

OBSERVATIONS to the Appellant (if leave refused).

I have considered the papers in your case and your grounds of appeal

Signed ....   Date..

(*If legal aid is granted please indicate the number of Counsel and whether Solicitors are included).

SJ

1   **DIRECTIONS TO THE REGISTRAR**

(i)   **Transcript**
     (Please tick box or complete (c) as appropriate)

     (a)   No transcript necessary   ☐

     (b)   Present transcript suffices   ☐

     (c)   Following transcript (or further transcript) required:-

(ii)   **Reports**
     Obtain up-to-date reports as follows:-

     (Please tick if any report(s) required)

     Social Enquiry ☐   Medical/Mental ☐   Prison, etc. ☐

(iii)   **Listing**
     Consider for the Lord Chief Justice's List ☐   *(Please tick if appropriate)*
     Any Other Listing Points

(iv)   **Any Other Directions**

2.   **POINTS FOR THE ATTENTION OF COUNSEL (AND THE COURT)**
Note: It may well be helpful to the Court if Counsel's attention is invited to the grounds on which leave has been granted)

3.   **OBSERVATIONS FOR THE COURT (NOT FOR COUNSEL)**

Bas 272646 • K19880 5m 4 89 ATP

The Court usually convenes at 10:30 a.m. daily. The judges meet shortly beforehand to discuss the day's cases, primarily in an effort to expedite the hearing. If the panel has developed a preliminary inclination in a case, the judges may communicate this to counsel, who then can tailor their presentations accordingly. For example, the judges may think that the appellant's point of law is prima facie meritorious and ask the prosecution to deal with that point first. Each judge normally takes one day a week off the bench to read the papers in the cases just ahead. While there are no American-style briefs filed by counsel, in conviction appeals the court's rules direct counsel to submit a typed note listing the propositions relied upon and citations to supporting authorities — a "skeleton argument," as the English say.

In contrast to American practice, CACD is not confined to the record made in the trial court. It may receive fresh evidence and call witnesses to testify in the hearing of the appeal. (Section 23, Criminal Appeal Act 1968). When the appellant's counsel seeks to offer fresh evidence, the Court will require an explanation for failure to adduce the evidence at trial. A witness may be called only with leave of Court.

Daniel J. Meador, *English Appellate Judges from an American Perspective*, 66 GEO. L. J. 1349, 1363, 1365-67 (1978)[5]

We now return to those square, high ceiling, book-lined rooms in the Royal Courts of Justice. In each room three judges of the Court of Appeal [Criminal Division], will be found sitting and at work every day of the week during term. The judges consider and decide cases in a way that can best be described as highly visible; there is relatively little behind-the-scenes work. Unlike American appellate judges, the English judges spend little time in their chambers. The cases are examined, thought about, and decided on the bench in open court for everyone to hear and see. The courtroom is the appellate workroom. The English have long adhered to the idea that it is not sufficient that justice be done; it is necessary that it also be seen to be done . . .

An American lawyer dropping in for a short while on a session of the Court of Appeal would get an impression that despite the strangeness of costume, manners, and accent, the proceedings more or less resemble oral argument sessions in American appellate courts. If he stayed longer and inquired more deeply, however, he would discover substantial differences . . .

   . . .

. . . [During the hearing of a criminal appeal] Books [containing reported cases] are pulled off the shelves by attendants and handed to the judges; it is as though the judges were hard at work in a library instead of in a public courtroom. Silence ensues while the judges read and think. Sometimes for long intervals only the ticking of the clock and the slight rustling of papers can be heard. Counsel seem instinctively to know when to stop talking and when to resume.

[This procedure] . . . assures that each one of the three judges is having the same matter put before him and is focusing at the same time on the same facts, issues, and arguments. Three minds are working in harness together,

---

[5] Copyright © 1978 GEORGETOWN LAW JOURNAL. Reprinted with permission. Updated information is shown in brackets.

heading toward a collegial decision. The judges' minds are exposed for all the world to see. There is little ground for anyone to doubt that a judge considered every point, because everyone in the courtroom can see whether each judge is listening and participating — as he usually is — or, equally important, whether he is asleep or inattentive.

The sense of actually seeing justice being done is heightened by the fact that this hearing is also, in effect, the court's conference. Unlike American appellate courts, the court will not vanish at the close of the argument, leaving the outcome in the air, to be heard from no more until after several weeks or months, when it releases a decision through a written opinion. The decision will be made at the close of the oral hearing and it will be announced orally, with explanations. It is rare to have a "judgment reserved," meaning that the judges will announce a decision later in a written judgment, American style. [Reserved judgments have become more common in recent years, as many cases have become more complex.] Because the decision is to be stated at the end of the hearing the judges are necessarily engaged in making up their minds about the issues as the hearing progresses. There will be occasional pauses for whispered conversations on the bench, and at the end there will be more such conversation. [Sometimes the judges will retire and return after several minutes to announce the judgment.] Onlookers again can almost literally see the judges' minds working, as revealed by their questions and comments to counsel and by the obvious fact that they are discussing the case among themselves.

Under this process the length of the hearing can vary a great deal from one case to another . . . The hearing continues for as long as the judges think it is useful, either out of a concern for fairness in allowing the appellant's counsel to make his points, or out of their own need for reaching a sound decision . . .

Paradoxically, an appellate hearing seems extraordinarily formal, yet in fact it is quite informal. The wigs, the gowns, the decor of the room — indeed the whole outward appearance of the scene — give an impression of formality. Yet if one listens for a while it becomes clear that the tone of the proceedings is quite relaxed and almost chatty. The hearing is not as rigidly structured and formal as many American appellate arguments. Counsel stand at their seats where they talk and answer judges' questions. They have no central lectern; their papers and books are simply spread out on a ledge in front of their pews. Judges and counsel engage in a relaxed conversation throughout.

. . . [The judge who gives the court's judgment] states at length the facts of the case and the issues that have been raised on the appeal; he explains how the court is deciding each issue and why. In stating the law being applied, the English style seems to be one of relative simplicity. Few prior decisions are cited, and the analysis seems less intricate than that engaged in by American judges . . .

   . . .

This judicial performance is impressive. In the first place, to Americans it appears to be an uncommon feat of mental gymnastics. Some judges make a few sketchy notes as the hearing progresses, and they use those as a guide in delivering the opinion. [The Registrar's summary is relied upon heavily for the facts.]. . .

. . .

NOTES

1. Much is made in England of the visibility and openness of the appellate process, with special emphasis on the procedure whereby the Court of Appeal hears, discusses, and announces a decision during the hearing. However, only a small percentage of the applications for leave to appeal is granted, and an open hearing before three judges in CACD occurs only after a grant of leave. In view of these circumstances, is the English appellate process more visible and open than the process in American intermediate appellate courts where screening diverts a majority of appeals to a decision without oral argument?

2. The English appellate judges do not have an American style brief, *i.e.*, a written argument submitted by counsel in advance of the hearing. Reliance instead is placed on counsel's oral presentation, together with the Registrar's summary. Would it be feasible for an American appellate court to operate that way? For suggestions to that end, see Daniel J. Meador, *Toward Orality and Visibility in the Appellate Process,* 42 MD. L. REV. 732 (1983) (describing several successful American experiments with oral presentation of appeals). *Why have American appellate judges not been attracted to oral presentations with diminished reliance on briefs?* Long-standing traditions making such a development unlikely in the United States are discussed in Suzanne Ehrenberg, *Embracing the Writing-Centered Legal Process,* 89 IOWA L. REV. 1159 (2004).

3. Trial judges are heavily involved in English criminal appeals in two ways: (a) They act on all applications for leave to appeal. (b) They sit at the hearings to decide cases on the merits; two of the three judges on each panel are trial judges. Recall from Chapter 1 that in the early decades of the United States judges served in both trial and reviewing capacities. Consider again the question raised there as to the desirability of judges' serving simultaneously in those roles.

3. Conviction Appeals

The following statistics show the work of CACD in reviewing convictions during 2003.[6]

Applications for leave to appeal	1,787
Applications denied by single judge	1,213
Applications granted by single judge	472
Applications renewed	561

---

[6] These statistics are taken from *Judicial Statistics Annual Report 2003*, 15 (Department for Constitutional Affairs, 2004).

Renewed applications granted by Full Court	138
Convictions affirmed	364
Convictions reversed/quashed	178

Thus it appears that approximately 34% of all applications for leave to appeal are granted and receive a full hearing before a three judge panel.

a. The "Unsafe" Conviction

An American appellate court normally has the authority to overturn a conviction only if there is legal error in the record or if the evidence is insufficient to support a finding of guilty. Moreover, as seen in Chapter 3, an American court is confined to the trial record; it cannot consider material not contained in that record even if that material would demonstrate a basis for reversal. Under this American practice the court has no power to set aside a conviction or remand a criminal case for a new trial simply to prevent a miscarriage of justice or based on its belief that the defendant is not guilty. An American court that is convinced that a conviction is unjust is driven artificially to find some legal error on which a reversal can be based, often requiring the judges to engage in a questionable stretch of the rules or of legal reasoning. Legal doctrine often gets distorted in this process. This section presents the contrasting English practice and invites consideration of its merits compared with the American practice.

Before it was amended in 1995, Sec. 2(1) of the Criminal Appeal Act 1968 specified three grounds on which CACD could quash a conviction: that the conviction was "unsafe or unsatisfactory," that the judgment involved "a wrong decision of any question of law," or that there "was a material irregularity in the course of the trial." The Criminal Appeal Act 1995 repealed those provisions and in their place enacted one simple standard, requiring CACD to quash a conviction "if they think that the conviction is unsafe." On one view, that amendment worked no change in the law; it merely subsumed under the rubric "unsafe" the previous three grounds. Whether that view is correct has not been definitively decided.

When is a conviction "unsafe"? It might be deemed unsafe if the trial judge erroneously directed (instructed) the jury or incorrectly admitted or excluded certain evidence. An erroneous ruling by the trial judge or even several erroneous rulings might not render the conviction unsafe; something like the concept of harmless error is at play. The "unsafe" standard gives the appellate court a much wider latitude than an American court has, either to uphold a conviction or to reverse it. The following cases illustrate CACD's broader authority to overturn a conviction

R. v. COOPER
[1969] 1 Q.B. 267, [1969] 1 All E.R. 32

WIDGERY, L.J., delivered the following judgment of the court: The appellant was convicted at the Inner London Sessions in April, 1968, by a majority verdict of ten to two on one count of assault occasioning actual bodily harm. He received a sentence of eighteen months' imprisonment. He now appeals against his conviction by leave of the full court. The victim of the assault was a Miss McFarlane, a twenty-two year old girl, who said that at 11:00 p.m. on a December night in 1967 she and a girl friend were walking in the Earls Court Road when three young men came along and surrounded her friend. Miss McFarlane walked on a little, being rather embarrassed by this, but, realising that the men were drunk and that her friend was in some difficulty, she turned back to give her support. She said that as she approached the group, one of the men came towards her, mumbled something, pushed her into a doorway and hit her in the mouth with his fist, with the result that she lost three front teeth, which were snapped off. She said she was somewhat dazed by the blow . . . but that the man hit her a second time and then ran off. There is no doubt that an assault of that nature occurred at the time, and there is no doubt that if the appellant was properly convicted of it, eighteen months was not a day too long. But, as will appear, this was a difficult identity case. Miss McFarlane had no trouble in regard to identification. The appellant stood on identification parade on Jan. 17, some six weeks after the offence, and Miss McFarlane picked him out at once. His own words were "She never looked at anyone else," and clearly she had no doubt about it at all.

The difficulties, such as they are, arise from quite different matters. Before I come to them, I should say that a Mr. Fahy, who was one of the other men involved in this affair, gave evidence for the defence; and the substance of his evidence was that it was not the appellant who had hit Miss McFarlane but another man, who goes under a variety of names, one of which is Peter Burke. Mr. Fahy was destroyed in cross-examination, no doubt because it was proved that immediately after the affair he had told the police that it was the appellant who had been the assailant; but his sworn evidence was in the contrary sense. The important witness on behalf of the appellant whose evidence does give rise to the difficulties in this case was a Mr. Davis. He was a friend of the appellant of some 2 1/2 years' standing, but no one seems to have attacked his credit in the court below. He was not present on the occasion of this assault, but he visited the appellant in prison shortly afterwards and, owing to insufficient time for visitors to see the appellant individually, he shared a visit with this man Peter Burke. He gave evidence-in-chief that when the appellant was talking to Peter Burke in prison he said that he had been identified the day before, he was very disturbed about it and asked what was Peter Burke going to do about it. Peter Burke's answer was that the girl was probably mistaken and it would all come right in the end. In re-examination, this matter was gone into in a great deal more detail. When re-examined by counsel for the appellant, Mr. Davis went much further. He said that following the prison visit he walked away with Peter Burke and said "What is this all about?," because he [Davis] had known little or nothing of the offence at the time. Then he said that Peter Burke had told him as they walked away from the prison that he [Burke] had in fact administered the blow complained of. Mr. Davis then said:"I asked him what he was going to do about it. He was evasive. I persisted and I asked him if he was going to let an innocent man suffer for this when he had done it. He said that there was nothing he could do about it because he had a very bad record and would get four years" if he confessed to the offence.

Finally, doubts are raised in this case by reason of the fact that there is unquestionably a close physical similarity between the appellant and Peter Burke. We have been supplied, as were the jury, with a photograph of Peter Burke; and it is unnecessary to say more than that the physical resemblance is really quite striking.

The appellant's own case when he gave evidence was that he had been out in the course of the evening with other men, including Mr. Fahy and Peter Burke, that he had been drinking for some time and then had drifted down to the Earls Court district where he had gone to visit a girl friend, leaving the other men outside. The girl friend was not pleased to see him, so he left after a short interval and then went looking for his friends. His case was that he got into the Earls Court Road just at the end of this incident, and he was inviting the jury to say that Miss McFarlane had seen him present in the Earls Court Road immediately after the blow and confused him with the true assailant, who, he says, must have been Peter Burke.

The important thing about this case is that all the material to which I have referred was put before the jury. No one criticizes the summing-up, and, indeed, counsel for the appellant has gone to some lengths to indicate that the summing-up was entirely fair and that everything which could possibly have been said in order to alert the jury to the difficulties of the case was clearly said by the pre- siding judge. It is, therefore, a case in which every issue was before the jury and in which the jury was properly instructed, and, accordingly, a case in which this court would be very reluctant indeed to intervene. It has been said over and over again throughout the years that this court must recognise the advantage which a jury has in seeing and hearing the witnesses, and if all the material was before the jury and the summing-up was impeccable, this court should not lightly inter- fere. Indeed, until the passing of the Criminal Appeal Act 1966(1) — provisions which are now to be found in s. 2 of the Criminal Appeal Act 1968(2) — it was almost unheard of for this court to interfere in such a case. However, now our powers are somewhat different, and we are indeed charged to allow an appeal against conviction if we think that the verdict of the jury should be set aside on the ground that under all the circumstances of the case it is unsafe or unsatis- factory. That means that in cases of this kind the court must in the end ask itself a subjective question, whether we are content to let the matter stand as it is, or whether there is not some lurking doubt in our minds which makes us wonder whether an injustice has been done. This is a reaction which may not be based strictly on the evidence as such; it is a reaction which can be produced by the gen- eral feel of the case as the court experiences it. We have given earnest thought in this case to whether it is one in which we ought to set aside the verdict of the jury, notwithstanding the fact they had every advantage and, indeed, some advantages we do not enjoy. After due consideration, we have decided we do not regard this verdict as safe, and accordingly we shall allow the appeal and quash the conviction. As far as this matter is concerned, the appellant is discharged.

R. v. BURY
CACD, 1976 (unreported)

THE LORD CHIEF JUSTICE: On the 13th June, 1975 at Taunton Crown Court this Applicant was convicted of three offenses of indecent assault on small boys and two of indecency with a child. He was sentenced to concurrent terms of eighteen months' imprisonment suspended for two years and he was fined.

He now applies to this Court for leave to appeal against his conviction.

The background to the case was that some children from a children's home in Surrey were going to Somerset for a fortnight's holiday in a caravan, and amongst those who travelled with the party, and indeed drove the van or one of the vans, was the Applicant — a man of approximately 23 years of age, of previous good character. There were other officials of the Home forming part of the party and travelling to Somerset with the fourteen children, and of the fourteen children there were three who were concerned with these charges — a boy called Eric, who was only 8 who was concerned with one count of indecent assault and one of indecency with a child. There was another boy called Wayne, who was 10, and a third boy called Kirk, who also was 10.

The prosecution case was that in the course of this fortnight's holiday times occurred when one of the boys had to sleep with the Applicant because of insufficient accommodation, and it was said that these three boys on separate nights had shared a bed with the Applicant and had been subjected to the offenses which gave rise to the charges.

Of the three, only Wayne was sworn. Of course that gave rise to complications in regard to the rules affecting corroboration in cases of this kind. In effect, since the decision of the House of Lords in *Hester* the effect of Wayne being sworn meant that he could corroborate any of the other boys who were giving evidence in respect of offenses of this kind, and they could corroborate him, but of course it was not possible for Kirk and Eric to corroborate each other inter se because they were both unsworn.

The learned trial judge, if one may be permitted to pay him a compliment, navigated the case through the hazards involved in that situation with no little skill. However, there were some very odd features of this case. To begin with, these three made no complaint at the time, although there were officials travelling with the party well known to them who might easily have been recipients of complaints, and there were odd features to say the least of it of some of the evidence which was given.

For example, although there was no charge of buggery, Wayne gave evidence, quite unexpectedly one gathers at the trial, to the effect that the Applicant had tried to commit an act of buggery on him without removing his trousers. This and other factors made both Judge and no doubt jury somewhat hesitant about accepting too readily what was being said.

Furthermore, there was as I say no complaint made at the time and the matter did not come to light for something like six weeks or more, and it only came to light because another boy called Carl (a brother of two of those affected in these charges) heard these three boys discussing it, and having obtained details of their account of the affair he then proceeded to make a complaint which gave rise to the inquiry.

Mr. Back, who appeared in the Court below and who has put this appeal before us with moderation and also with a full desire to co-operate with the

Court, has recognized that it is exceedingly difficult here to find a point of law upon which it can be said that an error occurred in the Court below . . .

. . .

When one comes to the facts of the case Mr. Back has pointed out some of the peculiarities upon which I have already briefly touched, and we are all concerned at this case because there does seem to be at all events a possibility of a miscarriage of justice occurring. We are conscious of the fact that there was an opportunity for these boys to put their heads together and we bear in mind the recent strictures of the House of Lords that similar fact evidence should be accepted with great hesitation when the two witnesses have had an opportunity to put their heads together and concoct a story. There is nothing here to indicate that such a story was concocted. But the opportunity for concocting a story is undoubtedly there.

Then one finds the fact that the Applicant did not engineer the situation in which these acts are alleged to have been committed. He did not alter the sleeping arrangements in order to bring a boy into his bed or anything pointing to guilt in that way. Wayne first slept with him and spent four nights in the bed, and it does not seem to have been the act of the Applicant which put Wayne in that bed in the first place or which tried to stay him when he eventually left.

On the whole we think that his is one of those cases — and indecent assaults on children are perhaps the field in which they are most commonly found — in which although the Judge went to every possible length to be fair to the accused there is a real possibility that a miscarriage of justice has occurred. That being the case, we take the view that in the words of the Criminal Appeal Act 1968 the verdicts against this man are unsafe and accordingly we shall give leave to appeal, and, with Mr. Back's consent which no doubt is forthcoming, we shall treat the application as being the appeal here today. We shall allow the appeal and we shall quash the conviction.

NOTES

1. How would an American appellate court likely deal with the *Cooper* and *Bury* cases?

2. In numerous cases since *Cooper*, the court has reiterated the "lurking doubt" standard for setting aside a conviction on the ground that it is unsafe. The Court, as well as observers, have said that this authority is not inconsistent with respect for the jury and for the jury's ability, that CACD lacks, to see and hear the witnesses. Do you agree? What is the reason for giving an appellate court this authority?

3. American appellate judges tend to oppose giving their courts such authority. What do you imagine to be the reason for such opposition? Is justice better served by the English appellate court's broader power over a conviction?

4. In at least one American jurisdiction there is a similar appellate authority. A New York statute authorizes the intermediate appellate courts to reverse a judgment "in the interest of justice." Justice Hopkins says that the power has been "sparingly used" and that it is in "the nature of a safety valve." It may be

invoked in a case "in which the result is so incongruous in light of the facts or where there is such a disturbing lack of evidence on a critical point that the impression is induced that justice has not been done." James D. Hopkins, *The Role of an Intermediate Court*, 41 BROOK. L. REV. 459, 473-74 (1975).

5. Note that in *Cooper* the defendant was convicted on a 10 to 2 vote of the jury, permissible under English law. For a debate about the relative merits of that practice and the general American practice requiring a unanimous verdict, see Eugene Sullivan, *The Great Debate V — A Debate on Judicial Reform, England Versus the United States*, 38 AM. CRIM. L. REV. 321 (2001).

b. Fresh Evidence on Appeal

In considering an appeal, CACD is authorized, in its discretion, to receive "fresh evidence" — evidence not introduced in the trial court — if a four-part test is satisfied: (1) if the evidence appears capable of belief, (2) if the evidence may afford any ground for overturning the conviction, (3) if the evidence would have been admissible in the lower court on any issue involved in the appeal, (4) if there is a reasonable explanation for failure to introduce the evidence in the court below. The fresh evidence may consist of documents or of the testimony of witnesses offered during the CACD hearing. Section 23, Criminal Appeal Act 1968. If fresh evidence is received, the court will have before it that evidence plus the trial record and must take all of that into account in deciding whether the conviction is unsafe.

In *Stafford v. D.P.P.*, 3 W.L.R. 719 (1973), the House of Lords decided that where fresh evidence is admitted the question for the appellate court is no different from that in a case where no fresh evidence has been heard. It has to decide whether the verdict is unsafe. The House of Lords went on to say that where fresh evidence is heard there is no rule that the appellate court must decide what in the court's view the jury might or would have done if it had heard the fresh evidence. Apparently it is up to CACD judges to decide for themselves whether on the totality of the evidence they think the conviction unsafe.

The authority of the court to receive new evidence on appeal is particularly important in light of the unavailability of any post-trial motions whereby a defendant might bring forward new matter. After the trial court imposes sentence it loses all authority over the case; sole authority thereafter is in CACD. Moreover, in England there is no post-conviction procedure through which a collateral attack can be brought against a conviction. The appellate hearing in CACD, with the opportunity to adduce new evidence, combines in one proceeding all issues and evidence that could be asserted in American courts only through separate proceedings: new trial motions, appeals, and post-conviction remedies.

The ability of CACD to receive evidence outside the trial record is, of course, in sharp contrast with American appellate courts' insistence on confining review to the record made below and to issues asserted in the trial court, as studied in Chapter 3. Consider whether justice would be served better if American appellate courts adopted the English practice. What are the competing arguments?

When CACD overturns a conviction it has authority to order a new trial. When fresh evidence is adduced on appeal, would it be preferable for the court to order a new trial so that the new evidence could be evaluated by a jury, rather than only by the appellate judges? Recall that two out of the three judges sitting on an appeal are trial judges and the third had been a trial judge. What bearing might that have on your consideration of this question? Sometimes CACD does remand for a new trial and sometimes it does not. What circumstances might lead it to order a new trial rather than quashing a conviction outright? The court may remand for a new trial where there is no fresh evidence, because of a substantial error in the first trial. It has been exercising this authority with increasing frequency in recent years.

c. Unified Review — American Possibilities

In the United States, review of criminal convictions is divided into three distinct proceedings, taking place in three different courts and at three different times. First is review on a new trial motion made by a defendant following conviction, filed in the court where the conviction was imposed. Second — if that motion is denied — is the appeal, usually to an intermediate court with the possibility of further review in the court of last resort. Third — if the defendant has thus far not been successful — is collateral review by way of habeas corpus or a similar post-conviction procedure, filed in a trial court, with appeal available thereafter. This fragmented arrangement involves much time and expense, often lasting over several years. As has been seen, in England an appeal against conviction in CACD unifies all three of those phases into one proceeding.

That English appeals practice inspired the idea of similarly combining the fragmented American review into a single, unified proceeding in the appellate court. A proposal to that effect was put forward in 1973 in the REPORT ON COURTS (*Standards* 6.1-6.3) issued by the National Advisory Commission on Criminal Justice Standards and Goals. Drawing on the English practice, that proposal included the following features:

a. The concept of review of the case rather than simply review of the record;

b. The consolidation by the appellate court on direct review of the conviction and sentence of all actual and potential issues in the case, including those that under current American practice can be asserted only on collateral review;

c. The abolition of the new trial motion;

d. The review of sentences as well as of convictions.

Early discussions of the unified review idea in an American setting are contained in Daniel J. Meador, *Remarks: Unified Review in Criminal Cases*, 5 APPELLATE JUSTICE: 1975 86-98 (1975) and Paul Robinson, *Proposal and Analysis of a Unitary System for Review of Criminal Judgments*, 54 B.U. L. REV. 485 (1974).

Georgia and Missouri provide for comprehensive hearings in the trial court following a conviction in which the trial record can be enlarged by additional evidence, thus providing the appellate court with factual material that otherwise could be developed only through a collateral proceeding. *See* Marion T. Pope, *A Study of the Unified Appeal Procedure in Georgia*, 23 GA. L. REV. 185 (1988); Daniel P. Card, *24 Missouri Practice: Appellate Practice* 508-36 (1992).

NOTES

1. Although the unified review procedure was endorsed by the National Advisory Commission in 1973, there has been no significant move to adopt the scheme in any American jurisdiction. What are the possible explanations?

2. Note that even if a state adopted the unified review proposal, federal judicial review of state convictions for alleged constitutional defects still would be available in certain circumstances through habeas corpus. Accordingly, there would remain a state-federal fragmentation in criminal review. Is it possible to overcome that fragmentation?

d. Non-Judicial Referral to CACD

For decades the Home Secretary (Secretary of State for Home Affairs) had authority to refer a conviction to CACD for its review when he considered that an injustice had been or might have been done. Such a reference could be made years later, as there was no applicable statute of limitations. When CACD received such a case it treated it as though it were a regular appeal. It could receive fresh evidence and quash the conviction. That authority in the Home Secretary was repealed by the Criminal Appeal Act 1995.

In its place, the Act created the Criminal Cases Review Commission, consisting of at least ten members appointed by the Queen on the recommendation of the Prime Minister. The Commission is empowered to direct an investigation of any criminal case after it is concluded. On application by the defendant or someone in his behalf or on its own motion, the Commission may refer a case to CACD if three criteria are met: (a) there exists an argument or evidence giving rise to a real possibility that the conviction will not be upheld if the case is referred to the court, (b) the argument or evidence has not previously been raised in CACD, (c) the convicted person has appealed unsuccessfully. The Commission may refer both convictions and sentences. The objective of this change was to establish an independent, non-political entity to consider claims of miscarriage of justice, free of possible conflicts of interest on the part of the Home Secretary, who is also responsible for law enforcement. An analysis of the Commission's work in its early days is in Annabelle James, Nick Taylor & Clive Walker, *The Criminal Cases Review Commission: Economy, Effectiveness and Justice,* 2000 CRIM. L. REV. 149 (2000).

From its creation in 1995 to 2003, the Commission received more than 5,500 applications. It referred 196 to CACD. The Court quashed 77 convictions. *See* Robert Carl Schehr & Lynne Weathered, *Should the United States Establish a Criminal Cases Review Commission?* 88 JUDICATURE 122 (2004). A description of the Commission's work by one of its members is David Kyle, *Correcting Miscarriages of Justice: The Role of the Criminal Cases Review Commission*, 52 DRAKE L. REV. 657 (2004).

In the United States there appears to be no constitutional or other legal barrier to the establishment of such an entity by a state for state convictions or by the federal government for federal convictions. Yet no official entity like the English commission has been established. Should it be? Among the states there are a variety of "innocence projects" and "innocence commissions," usually non-governmental, that study the causes of wrongful convictions and sometimes uncover instances where the innocent have been found guilty. But none has the authority of the English commission. *See* Jon D. Gould, *A New Wave of Innocence Commissions*, 88 JUDICATURE 126 (2004).

4. Sentence Appeals

Reviewing sentences has been an important part of the business of the English Court of Appeal since the establishment of its predecessor court in 1907. Such review is authorized by Section 9, Criminal Appeal Act 1968.

The procedure in CACD for seeking review of sentences is essentially the same as that involved in seeking review of convictions. The defendant files an application for leave to appeal and grounds of appeal (on Form NG); the Registrar's office assembles the papers and refers them to a single judge. If a pre-sentence report was prepared for the use of the trial court, it will be included. The single judge then decides whether to grant or deny leave to appeal. If leave is denied, the defendant can renew the application before the full Court (normally before a panel of two judges). If leave is granted, the case comes on for hearing before a three-judge panel, as in the review of convictions. The following figures show the work of CACD in reviewing sentences for the year 2003.[7]

Applications for Leave to Appeal against Sentence	5,664
Applications Granted	2,074
Sentences Affirmed	679
Sentences Altered	1,685

Sentence appeals outnumber conviction appeals by about four to one. Approximately 37% of all applications receive a hearing before the full court. Of those applications granted, approximately 81% of the sentences were altered by the court in some fashion.

a. Making Sentencing Policy

A major role played by CACD in reviewing sentences is the development of sentencing policy. The materials that follow focus on this aspect of the Court's work, illustrating ways in which sentencing policy is developed through the common-law case-by-case process of deciding sentence appeals.

---

[7] Taken from judicial *Statistics 2003*, p. 15 (Department for Constitutional Affairs, 2004)

D. A. Thomas, *Sentencing in England,* 42 MD. L. REV. 90, 97-103 (1983)[8]

One of the most important features of the English sentencing system is the provision for appellate review of sentences, particularly those passed in the Crown Court. Virtually every offender sentenced in the Crown Court may appeal against his sentence to the Court of Appeal (Criminal Division) . . . A significant number of offenders seek review of their sentences (4,571 in 1981), and in an average year the Court will deliver over 1,000 judgments in cases where the appeal is against sentence only.

Apart from providing for the correction of errors made by the trial judges, and in particular providing a restraint on excessive severity, the Court's work provides a case law of sentencing which serves as a system of judicially-evolved guidelines for trial judges. Appellate review provides a forum within the judicial system where questions of policy and principle can be raised and resolved, and contributes to the development of some measure of consistency in the sentencing of offenders for the more serious offenses, without seriously diminishing the importance of judicial discretion in the individual case. Appellate review of sentences has been part of the English system since before any judge now sitting was born. It is accepted as an inevitable and helpful part of the sentencing process by trial judges. There is no evidence that English trial judges, unlike some American judges, resent the idea of appellate review of sentences.

1. *Sentencing principles.* The principles evolved through the process of appellate review of sentences are too extensive and complex to be described in the course of an article, but a few general statements can be made. The decisions of the Court cover a wide range of sentencing issues: matters of general principle (when should sentences of imprisonment be ordered to run consecutively and when concurrently, how far is it permissible to distinguish between accomplices convicted of participating in the same crimes); the use of particular sentencing powers (when should a court order the payment of compensation by the offender to the victim, what criteria should be considered in making a recommendation for deportation); the sentencing of different categories of offenders (mentally disturbed offenders, dangerous offenders); and the effect of mitigation. Two topics of particular importance are the proper treatment of specific types of offenses and the procedural aspects of sentencing.

A large proportion of the Court's decisions are concerned with adjusting the lengths of sentences imposed in particular types of crimes . . .

. . . [T]he overwhelming majority of appeals are against sentences of imprisonment or other forms of custody. For this reason, the case law produced by the Court concentrates heavily on such questions as the proper length of sentences for particular categories of offence, the need to establish proper relationships in the sentences imposed on co-defendants, and the propriety of imposing consecutive sentences in particular circumstances.

---

[8] Copyright 1983 by The Criminal Law Review. All Rights Reserved. Reprinted with permission.

Issues relating to the proper use of non-custodial sentences — such as probation or community service — are less frequently examined, unless the Court decides to vary a sentence from imprisonment to a non-custodial measure . . .

. . .

The only satisfactory way to provide a basis for the development of a case law of sentencing which would adequately cover the full range of sentencing options available to courts, and provide a restraint on the excessive leniency of some judges is to allow the prosecution to seek review of a sentence on the ground that it is too favorable to the defendant . . . [Section 36 of the Criminal Justice Act 1988 authorizes the Attorney General to seek review of a sentence. Such review can be obtained only by leave of CACD, and if review is granted, the Court has the authority to increase the defendant's sentence. The Court and the Attorney General exercise these powers sparingly, reserving them for cases in which general sentencing guidance can usefully be provided.]

A second limitation on the effective contribution of appellate review to the development of sentencing principles has been (until recently) the lack of an adequate system of reporting sentencing decisions. More recently a new series of reports devoted exclusively to sentencing decisions has been published and is becoming an important tool of the lawyer and sentencing judge.[9] This series reports about 180 decisions each year — about one decision in six of those reached by the Court . . .

NOTES

1. Means of communicating sentencing policy and principles have greatly improved during the past decade. The series of *Criminal Appeal Reports (Sentencing)*, mentioned in the preceding article, makes available to practitioners and judges those judgments of the Court of Appeal on sentencing matters which are likely to be of general interest.

2. D. A. Thomas himself has brought about a major improvement by publishing a loose-leaf guide to sentencing, which is continually updated. The availability of this publication makes it possible for every judge to know the "tariff" for the particular offense.

3. Three newspapers — *The Times*, *The Guardian*, and *The Independent* — publish abbreviated law reports, which often include sentencing cases selected for their legal, and not their anecdotal, interest.

4. The Criminal Appeal Office is currently engaged in constructing an electronic data base for sentencing cases. Two commercial websites now provide access to all the judgments of the Court of Appeal, Criminal Division on a subscription basis. They are Casetrack (www.casetrack.co.uk) and Westlaw UK (www.westlaw.co.uk).

---

[9] [57] This Series is entitled Criminal Appeal Reports (Sentencing) cited as Cr. App. R. (S.)), Published since 1979 by Sweet and Maxwell, Ltd., one Volume annually.

D. A. Thomas, *Commentary*, 1982 Crim. L. Rev. 469, 470[10]

This case [*R. v. Smith*,] is interesting for several reasons. It suggests that within the scope of the "clang of the gates" principle, there may be two categories of offenders (bearing in mind that the principle covers primarily offenders of mature years and good character committing serious offenses of dishonesty in breach of trust). The first may be classed as ordinary cases, where the person concerned is in a position of trust in relation to his employer only; in these cases the approach of the court seems to be to encourage the use of very short sentences, of the order of between one month and three months ... The second category appears to include cases of what might be termed "special trust" — where the position of the offender is such that he owes a duty to clients or customers, or he occupies a post in which particularly high standards are to be expected. In this type of case, it seems that the very short sentence will not necessarily be appropriate, but a much shorter sentence than was previously customary — of the order of nine months — may be considered correct. (Not all of the cases conform to this pattern). In a third class of case, where the scale of the theft is too large to allow the "clang of the gates" principle to operate (where it is in excess of about £10,000), sentences in the order of 18 months seem to be considered appropriate ...

The case is also interesting as an illustration of the value of the citation of previous decisions to establish general lines of approach to the sentence in the particular case ... None of the cases cited was on all fours with the facts of the present case, but they clearly did establish a general framework within which the present case could be considered.

NOTES

1. What is meant by "clang of the gates," one of numerous sentencing principles developed by CACD? What is the reasoning behind this sentencing principle?

2. As pointed out earlier, English law authorizes the Attorney General to seek leave to appeal a sentence on the ground that it is unduly lenient. An example is *R. v. Garvey*, [2005] 1 Cr. App. R. (S.) 117 (at page 666), in which CACD granted the Attorney General's application for leave and held that a sentence of eighteen months for a sexual offence should be increased to three years and three months. Allowing the prosecution to appeal a sentence on this ground has been controversial in the United States. Is it a good idea?

3. For many years CACD has from time-to-time issued "guideline" judgments to provide sentencing guidance to the trial courts. In doing so, CACD usually collects appeals in several cases in a particular category and uses them as the vehicle for announcing guidelines. The following case is an example.

---

[10] Copyright © 1982 by Criminal Law Review. Reprinted with Primission.

R. v. BILLAM & OTHER APPEALS & APPLICATIONS
[1986] 1 All E.R. 985

LORD LANE C.J. delivered the following judgment of the court: We have had listed before us today a number of cases where there has been a conviction for rape or attempted rape, in order to give us an opportunity to restate principles which in our judgment should guide judges on sentencing in this difficult and sensitive area of the criminal law.

In the unhappy experience of this Court, whether or not the number of convictions for rape has increased over the years, the nastiness of the cases has certainly increased, and what would ten years ago have been considered incredible perversions have now become commonplace. This is no occasion to explore the reasons for that phenomenon, however obvious they may be.

We would like, if we may, to cite a passage from the Criminal Law Revision Committee's 15th Report on Sexual Offences, (Cmnd. Paper 9213 (1984)), which reflects accurately the views of this Court. It is as follows:

> Rape is generally regarded as the most grave of all the sexual offenses. In a paper put before us for our consideration by the Policy Advisory Committee on Sexual Offenses the reasons for this are set out as follows — Rape involves a severe degree of emotional and psychological trauma; it may be described as a violation which in effect obliterates the personality of the victim. Its physical consequences equally are severe: the actual physical harm occasioned by the act of intercourse; associated violence or force and in some cases degradation; after the event, quite apart from the woman's continuing insecurity, the fear of venereal disease or pregnancy. We do not believe this latter fear should be underestimated because abortion would usually be available. This is not a choice open to all women and it is not a welcome consequence for any. Rape is also particularly unpleasant because it involves such intimate proximity between the offender and victim. We also attach importance to the point that the crime of rape involves abuse of an act which can be a fundamental means of expressing love for another; and to which as a society we attach considerable value.

This court emphasized in *R. v. Roberts* [1982] 1 All E.R. 609, that rape is always a serious crime which calls for an immediate custodial sentence other than in wholly exceptional circumstances. The sort of exceptional circumstances in which a non-custodial sentence may be appropriate are illustrated by the decision in *Taylor* (1983) 5 Cr. App. R. (S.) 241. Although on the facts that offence amounted to rape in the legal sense, the Court observed that it did not do so in ordinary understanding.

Judges of the Crown Court need no reminder of the necessity for custodial sentences in cases of rape. The criminal statistics for 1984 show that 95% of all defendants who were sentenced in the Crown Court for offences of rape received immediate custodial sentences in one form or another. But the same statistics also suggest that judges may need reminding about what length of sentence is appropriate.

Of the 95% who received custodial sentences in 1984, 28% received sentences of two years or less; 23% over two and up to three years; 18% over three and up to four years; 18% over four and up to five years and 8% over five years (including 2% life) . . . Although it is important to preserve a sense of proportion in relation to other grave offences such as some forms of manslaughter, these statistics show an approach to sentences for rape which in the judgment of this Court are too low.

The variable factors in cases of rape are so numerous that it is difficult to lay down guidelines as to the proper length of sentence in terms of years . . . There are however many reported decisions of the Court which give an indication of what current practice ought to be and it may be useful to summarise their general effect.

For rape committed by an adult without any aggravating or mitigating features, a figure of five years should be taken as the starting point in a contested case. Where a rape is committed by two or more men acting together, or by a man who has broken into or otherwise gained access to a place where the victim is living, or by a person who is in a position of responsibility towards the victim, or by a person who abducts the victim and holds her captive, the starting point should be eight years.

At the top of the scale comes the defendant who has carried out what might be described as a campaign of rape, committing the crime on a number of different women or girls. He represents a more than ordinary danger and a sentence of fifteen years or more may be appropriate.

Where the defendant's behavior has manifested perverted or psychopathic tendencies or gross personality disorder, and where he is likely, if at large, to remain a danger to women for an indefinite time, a life sentence will not be inappropriate.

The crime should in any event be treated as aggravated by any of the following factors: (1) violence is used over and above the force necessary to commit the rape; (2) a weapon is used to frighten or wound the victim; (3) the rape is repeated; (4) the rape has been carefully planned; (5) the defendant has previous convictions for rape or other serious offenses of a violent or sexual kind; (6) the victim is subjected to further sexual indignities or perversions; (7) the victim is either very old or very young; (8) the effect on the victim, whether physical or mental, is of special seriousness. Where any one or more of these aggravating features are present, the sentence should be substantially higher than the figure suggested as the starting point.

The extra distress which giving evidence can cause to a victim means that a plea of guilty, perhaps more so than in other cases, should normally result in some reduction from what would otherwise be the appropriate sentence. The amount of such reduction will of course depend on all the circumstances, including the likelihood of a finding of not guilty had the matter been contested.

The fact that the victim may be considered to have exposed herself to danger by acting imprudently (as for instance by accepting a lift in a car from a stranger) is not a mitigating factor; and the victim's previous sexual experience is equally irrelevant. But if the victim has behaved in a manner which was calculated to lead the defendant to believe that she would consent to sexual intercourse, then there should be some mitigation of the sentence. Previous good character is of only minor relevance.

The starting point for attempted rape should normally be less than for the completed offence, especially if it is desisted at a comparatively early stage. But, as is illustrated by one of the cases now before the Court, attempted rape may be made by aggravating features into an offence even more serious than some examples of the full offence.

About one-third of those convicted of rape are under the age of 21 and thus fall within the scope of the Criminal Justice Act 1982, s 1. Although the criteria to which the Court is required to have regard by section 1(4) of that Act must be interpreted in relation to the facts of the individual case rather than simply by reference to the legal category of the offence, most offences of rape are "so serious that a non-custodial sentence cannot be justified" for the purposes of that provision. In the ordinary case the appropriate sentence would be one of youth custody, following the term suggested as terms of imprisonment for adults, but making some reduction to reflect the youth of the offender. A man of 20 will accordingly not receive much less than a man of 22, but a youth of 17 or 18 may well receive less.

In the case of a juvenile, the Court will in most cases exercise the power to order detention under the Children and Young Persons Act 1933, s 53(2). In view of the procedural limitations to which the power is subject, it is important that a Magistrates' Court dealing with a juvenile charged with rape should *never* accept jurisdiction to deal with the case itself, but should invariably commit the case to the Crown Court for trial to ensure that the power is available.

[His Lordship then went on to deal with the individual cases and only in one case varied the sentence where the circumstances were exceptional. One application was withdrawn. All the other appeals were dismissed, and all the applications were refused.]

NOTES

1. In reviewing a sentence, CACD is not confined to the record made in the trial court. As in reviewing convictions, the court may receive fresh evidence. If the trial court did not have a pre-sentence report prepared by a social service agency, CACD can obtain one. CACD may also consider such additional information as the conduct of the defendant in prison since the sentence was imposed. The court decides upon the appropriateness of the sentence in light of all the information then available to it. It is not merely reviewing whether the trial judge erred.

2. A Sentencing Advisory Panel was established in 1999 to recommend to CACD sentencing guidelines for various offenses. Since its establishment the Panel has tendered 11 sets of recommendations to CACD which has substantially adopted them into guidelines.

3. In 2002 the Sentencing Advisory Panel undertook a review of the guidelines announced in the *Billam* case and made recommendations to CACD for some revisions. In *R. v. Millberry*, [2003] 2 Cr. App. R. (Sentencing) 142, CACD considered those recommendations in reviewing three sentences for rape and adopted them. The result was to reaffirm *Billam* with some adjustments.

4. Apparently the work of that Panel and of CACD in formulating sentencing guidelines did not satisfy political interests. In 2003 an Act of Parliament established the Sentencing Guidelines Council for the purpose of taking over CACD's function of formulating sentencing guidelines. Chaired by the Lord Chief Justice, the Council consists of seven judges appointed by the Lord Chancellor and four non-judicial members appointed by the Home Secretary. Thus England appears to be moving away from the decades-old system of judicially promulgated guidelines toward the American model of written guidelines issued by a legislatively created body. Which method of guideline formulation seems preferable?

5. In this time of transition CACD does not seem deterred from continuing to issue guideline judgments. For example, in *R. v. Garvey, supra* page ___, the CACD judges thought that trial judges needed guidance in sentencing for a new sexual offense recently created by Parliament, and they proceeded to set out guidelines.

b. American Developments

Kevin R. Reitz, *Sentencing Guideline Systems and Sentence Appeals: A Comparison of Federal and State Experiences*, 91 Nw. U. L. Rev. 1441, 1443-47, 1449-50 (1997)[11]

Prior to the guideline innovations of the 1980s, little meaningful appellate review of sentencing decisions had ever occurred in the United States, in federal or state courts. Those few appellate decisions that existed did not, for the most part, focus on substantive issues of the appropriate principles for punishment decisions, or the application of those principles to particular factual scenarios. Instead, the cases dealt primarily with constitutional issues: Did the penalty below exceed the cruel and unusual punishment standard of the Eighth Amendment? (Not often.) Did the procedures followed by the sentencing court violate the Due Process Clause? (Almost never.) Did the sentencing judge rely upon a constitutionally impermissible factor, such as race or religious belief, when imposing judgment? (If so, few trial judges ever made this explicit.)

Only a minority of U.S. jurisdictions before the 1980s granted authority to their appellate courts to review sentences for substantive propriety. In the federal system, a "doctrine of non-reviewability" prevailed from 1891 until 1987, when the Federal Sentencing Guidelines became effective. Even in those states where a power of sentence review existed, it was used sparingly.

---

[11] Copyright © 1997. Reprinted by special permission of Northwestern University School of Law, NORTHWESTERN UNIVERSITY LAW REVIEW.

Appellate courts refrained from interference with a sentence below unless it could be characterized as clearly excessive or as a clear abuse of discretion. The incidence of thoughtful, reasoned opinions discussing sentencing policy was also quite low. Unlike England, which had instituted a robust practice of sentence review, no American state before the 1980s could boast an expanding body of sentencing jurisprudence in which earlier cases were consulted as precedent for later decisions.

The absence, or near absence, of appellate input into the law of criminal punishment was due in part to the embarrassment that there was no substantive law of sentencing to be applied at the trial level. Under indeterminate sentencing schemes, trial judges were given discretion to fix any penalty within the ceiling provided by the statutory maximum . . . With such a free-form thought process in gear, there were effectively no legal principles against which a sentence could be tested on review.

Another disablement of appellate review was the widespread rule that trial courts were not obliged to explain the reasons for their sentencing decisions on the record. Even if a positive law of sentencing had been in place, there was little practical way for an appeals court to discover what thought process a trial judge had followed in a given case. Indeed, as one distinguished judge acknowledged, the trial bench was well aware that only an *explained* decision was at risk of reversal . . .

A third, and somewhat subterranean, reason for the scarcity of appellate involvement — even in states where the formal power existed — was the fear of appellate judges that their workload would increase beyond reason if they took steps toward establishing meaningful sentence review. This concern was, and still is, at the core of judicial opposition to expanding the availability of sentence appeals. In this respect, it should be noticed that there was an inter-section between the pragmatic interests of appellate judges and trial judges: Appellate judges have never been anxious to add a new burden to their already full-time schedules; trial judges likewise were wary of the new responsibility of articulating reasons for their sentencing orders, and hardly relished the prospect of periodic reversals.

An energetic reform movement to change this picture and introduce more-than-perfunctory appellate review into the sentencing process made modest headway in the 1950s and 1960s . . . The American Bar Association (ABA) in its flagship project to articulate "minimum standards" for criminal justice, advocated sentence review as an essential feature of any rational justice system . . . Consonant with these proposals, President Johnson's Crime Commission, which issued its final report in 1967, incorporated appellate sentence review into its basic recommendation to reduce disparities in sentences imposed. Similar sentiments were included in a national study released by the Law Enforcement Assistance Administration in 1973.

Despite this relatively uniform message from the law reform community, state and federal judicial practices went largely unchanged into the 1970s. Although the number of states that had instituted the practice of sentence appeals was growing slowly, the majority practice remained one of non-reviewability, and those states that had instituted sentence review were not generating large numbers of appellate opinions, or much searching analysis of punishment doctrine.

. . .

Moving ahead to the present day, it is not too harsh to say that the reformist vision of appellate court contributions to sentencing guideline systems now appears quaint and unduly optimistic. In only one sense was the reformist vision of sentence appeals validated in the ensuing decades. Among most jurisdictions that adopted sentencing guidelines in the 1980s and 1990s, there has been a greater amount of appellate decisionmaking in sentencing cases than in all of the previous century. Pre-guideline efforts to engender sentence review had never reaped such success in pure volume of activity.

Quantity, however, is not quality. Few participants in modern guideline systems speak in glowing terms about the contributions made by appellate courts. Indeed, one typically hears the opposite. The loudest complaints come from the federal system (which also has the largest number of appellate decisions), but anyone who has read hundreds of appellate decisions across different guideline jurisdictions can attest that one seldom encounters thoughtful opinions that advance our understanding of the substantive problems of punishment. Instead, guideline appeals lean toward technical, even technocratic, analysis. Too often the decisions appear hurried or impatient . . .

A second development since the 1970s is that the subject of appellate decisionmaking in guideline systems has largely been forgotten. It has certainly fallen far in prominence in the contemporary debate of guideline reforms. In the 1970s, the appeals bench was believed to have a fundamental part to play in such systems; Norval Morris thought it "obvious" that "our best intelligence" should be too crude an instrument for sentence adjudications without the complementary development of a common law of sentencing. By the 1990s, however, serious discussion of appellate sentence review has slowed to a trickle. It is as though the distance between the reformist image of sentence appeals, and the actuality of pedestrian practice, has proven so great that all enthusiasm has been drained from those who were once interested in the subject.

ABA Standards for Criminal Justice Sentencing (3rd ed., 1994)[12]

18-8.2 Purposes of Appellate review

(a) The legislature should identify the following objectives of sentence review:

(i) To determine whether a sentence is unlawful or excessively severe under applicable statutes, provisions guiding sentencing courts, rules of court, or prior appellate decisions;

(ii) To determine whether the action of the sentencing court was an abuse of discretion; and

---

[12] *Standard 18-8.2,* published in Standard for Criminal Justice Sentencing, Third Edition. Copyright © 1994 by the American Bar Association, reprinted by permission.

(iii) To interpret statutes, provisions guiding sentencing courts, and rules of court as applied to particular sentencing decisions and to develop a body of rational and just principles regarding sentences and sentencing procedures.

(b) Reviewing courts, and particularly the highest court of the state, should seek to make effective the legislature's public policy choices regarding sentencing. Reviewing courts should also seek, through case law, to develop principles for composite sentences.

NOTES

1. The A.B.A. took the lead in promoting sentence review in the United States by promulgating its STANDARDS RELATING TO APPELLATE REVIEW OF SENTENCES in 1968. *Standard* 1.2 included among the purposes of appellate review the promotion of "the development and application of criteria for sentencing which are both rational and just." The English experience was influential in shaping those standards. An account of English sentencing review (THE REVIEW OF CRIMINAL SENTENCES IN ENGLAND by Daniel J. Meador) was included in those *Standards* as Appendix C, p. 94. The standard quoted above represents a revision, in more detailed form, of the earlier standard.

2. As shown in Appendix A to those 1968 standards, in that year only 13 states provided some form of appellate review of sentences. By 1988, at least 25 states had adopted some form of such review. *See* Daniel Wathen, *Disparity and the Need for Sentencing Guidelines in Maine: A Proposal for Enhanced Appellate Review,* 40 ME. L. REV. 1, 3 n. 9 (1988).

3. In the state and federal legislation authorizing commission-promulgated guidelines that became widespread in the 1980s and 1990s, provision was made for appellate review, focused on monitoring trial court compliance with the guidelines and on reviewing departures from the guidelines to determine whether such departures were "unreasonable." The extent to which appellate courts in different jurisdictions exercised this authority to develop sentencing policies varied considerably, as described in later portions of the Reitz article extracted above. But in contrast to the work of CACD in England, American appellate courts have not been robust in formulating sentencing policy in the common-law fashion, even though paragraph (iv) in the 1968 *A.B.A. Standard 1.2* seemed to contemplate such an appellate role, as does section (a)(iii) of the standard quoted above authorizing appellate courts "to develop a body of rational and just principles regarding sentences and sentencing procedures."

4. In the United States, the most publicized guidelines are those issued by the U. S. Sentencing Commission and published in the UNITED STATES SENTENCING GUIDELINES MANUAL. They lay out detailed formulas for calculating the range of prison terms for all offenses. In a pair of companion cases, *U. S. v. Booker* and *U.S. v. Fanfan,* 125 S. Ct. 738 (2005), the Supreme Court held that provisions in the guidelines authorizing district judges to impose an enhanced sentence based on facts found by the judge, but not by the jury, violated the right to jury trial in the Sixth Amendment to the U. S. Constitution. The Court then held that the guidelines as a whole should be treated by the district judges as advisory and not mandatory. The appellate review

authorized by the statute was said to be available to determine the "reasonableness" of sentences. It remains to be seen how federal appellate courts will administer this new regime. If a sentence within the guidelines is presumed by the appellate court to be "reasonable," as has been suggested, the appellate role in developing sentencing policy may be no greater than it has been.

5. As noted previously, now that Parliament has established the Sentencing Guidelines Council, the long history in England of appellate enunciation of sentencing policy and guidelines in the common-law style appears to be coming to an end. Written guidelines, spelled out in legislative style, are the order of the day on both sides of the Atlantic. What explains this? For an argument in favor of judicial development of sentencing policy, *see* Wathen, *supra*.

6. In those American jurisdictions where appellate review of sentences is authorized, the appellate court is not usually empowered to alter the sentence; it can only reverse and remand to the trial court for re-sentencing. As seen earlier, CACD does not remand to the trial court. Rather, when it decides that the sentence is wrong or inappropriate CACD proceeds itself to fix the sentence it deems appropriate. Considering both the practicalities and theory of the proper appellate role, what are the relative merits of the American and English practices?

7. Summarizing observations. Putting together all that we have studied in this section, compare overall the English appellate courts' role in reviewing convictions and sentences with the role of a typical American appellate court in criminal cases. Consider CACD's authority to decide issues not raised in the trial court, to receive evidence not offered below, to set aside a conviction on the judges' assessment that it is unsafe, and to set aside a sentence and substitute one that the judges think appropriate, taking into account facts occurring since the trial. By contrast, an American appellate court ordinarily is confined to reviewing the record made in the trial court and can reverse a conviction only if it finds prejudicial error in the trial or that the evidence does not support a finding of guilty. In reviewing sentences, an American court is usually limited to determining whether the sentence conforms to written guidelines or whether it is unreasonable; if the court sets aside the sentence it cannot fix a new sentence but must remand to the trial court for re-sentencing. Would it be accurate to say that the English court plays a much larger role in the criminal process, acting in effect as a continuation of the trial process, in the leeway it exercises over convictions and sentences? Put another way, is the allocation of responsibilities between the trial and appellate levels not as sharply drawn in England as it is in the United States? Which system better serves the administration of justice, considering wise use of judicial resources and the public interest in a criminal process that is fair and accurate?

D. Civil Appeals

Although the focus here has been on criminal appeals, to present a rounded picture of the English appellate scene this brief description of the Court of Appeal, Civil Division is provided. Most of the Lords Justice of Appeal who sit on civil appeals also sit on criminal appeals and vice versa, although at least a dozen sit only on civil appeals. The court hears and decides appeals in civil cases coming from the county courts and the High Court. The court's handling of those cases underwent considerable change in the late 1990s as the result of many recommendations made by a body known as the Bowman Commission. *See* Joseph M. Jacob, *The Bowman Review of the Court of Appeal,* 61 MOD. L. REV. 390 (1998). Those changes make the treatment of civil appeals more like the way criminal appeals are dealt with than had been the case. Almost all civil appeals are now heard and decided in the Court's discretion, requiring an application for leave to appeal as in the Criminal Division.

The Court maintains a Civil Appeals Office headed by a Registrar of Civil Appeals, similar to that in the Criminal Division. That office receives all papers in each case. Unlike the Criminal Appeals Office, it does not prepare summaries of cases. The assembling of the "bundle," *i.e.,* the record, is left largely to the lawyers; the Civil Appeals Office exercises much less affirmative responsibility in that regard than its criminal counterpart.

Applications for leave to appeal are acted on by a single Lord Justice of Appeal. Leave will be granted only if there is a "real prospect of success." *Tanfern Limited v. Gregor Cameron-MacDonald* [2000] All ER 801, 807. If leave is denied, the application may be renewed, but this typically results in the applications being reconsidered by the same judge. If leave is granted, appellate counsel submits a "skeleton argument," a short document listing the points to be argued before a three judge panel, with citations to supporting authorities. Before hearing argument, the judges read this document and all papers in the bundle. On the whole, judges in the Civil Division spend more time reading papers outside of argument sessions than do judges in the Criminal Division.

Arguments are heard by panels consisting of three Lords Justice of Appeal. Trial judges are not used at all in the work of the Civil Division. Oral hearings in civil appeals tend to be lengthier than those in criminal appeals. Many appeals are decided through oral pronouncements by the judges at the end of the hearing, but reserved judgments are given in approximately half the cases.

A detailed description of the process in the Court of Appeal, Civil Division as it was before the reforms of the late 1990s, along with interesting American comparisons, is contained in ROBERT MARTINEAU, APPELLATE JUSTICE IN ENGLAND AND THE UNITED STATES: A COMPARATIVE ANALYSIS (1990).

Before the reforms of recent years proceedings in the Civil Division resembled an appeal under old equity practice in that the appeal was in effect a rehearing of the case, as distinguished from a review limited to errors made in the trial court. The court has now moved toward the American style of appellate review.

E. The Court of Last Resort

The judicial system at this level is on the verge of transition. Presented here is the court of last resort as it now is and has been, followed by the pending proposal for change.

1. The House of Lords

Through the distinctive evolution of English legal and governmental institutions, the House of Lords is both the upper house of Parliament and the top appellate court in the country. As a practical matter, the judicial function is separate from the legislative work and is in the hands of twelve judges known as Lords of Appeal in Ordinary — informally as Law Lords. They are appointed by the Queen on the recommendation of the prime minister, and they are given life peerages. They all have been judges on the Court of Appeal. Because in theory they are part of a legislative body, they are designated as the "appellate committee." They meet in a committee room, seated behind a table level with counsel tables, not on an elevated bench like a court. They are dressed in ordinary business suits, not in robes and wigs. The informality is in striking contrast to the formality in the Court of Appeal. The Lord Chancellor is authorized to preside, but he seldom does.

For a case that has been decided by the Court of Appeal to be heard by the House of Lords, the Court of Appeal must certify that the case involves a question of general public importance. Then leave to appeal must be obtained from either the Court of Appeal or from the Lords, as the top court is often referred to. If leave is denied by the Court of Appeal, the applicant may apply to the Lords. Applications to the Lords are acted on by an appeals committee, usually consisting of three judges. If leave is granted the case is heard on its merits typically by a panel of five Law Lords. Jurisdiction extends to civil and criminal cases from England, Wales, and Northern Ireland, but only to civil cases from Scotland. The Court's docket is not heavy. In 2003 it received 237 applications for leave to appeal. It decided a total of 65 cases, a number typical of its volume in recent years.

Jurisdiction of the House of Lords over criminal cases decided in CACD is governed by Sections 33-35, Criminal Appeal Act 1968. A detailed study of the court is in ALAN PATERSON, THE LAW LORDS (1982). A description of the court's work and a critical analysis of its decisions in criminal cases is in JACKSON'S MACHINERY OF JUSTICE 93-97 (J.R. Spencer, ed. 1989).

2. The New Supreme Court

In 2003 the government proposed the creation of a Supreme Court of the United Kingdom, to replace the House of Lords as the court of last resort for England, Wales, Scotland, and Northern Ireland. The government put the proposal before the country for discussion, with many details left open, in *Constitutional Reform: A Supreme Court for the United Kingdom*, July 2003 — a consultation paper produced by the Department for Constitutional Affairs (CP11/03). The proposal was prompted, at least in part, by concern over the doctrine of separation of powers. It is difficult to square that doctrine with the present arrangement under which those who serve as judges also are members of the legislative body, entitled to participate in debate and vote on bills. There was particular concern over the three-part role of the Lord Chancellor as a judge, a member of the legislature, and a member of the cabinet, *i.e.*, the executive branch. The proposal for a Supreme Court prompted widespread debate. *See, e.g.,* 24 *Legal Studies* 1-293 (2004).

The proposal came to fruition in the Constitutional Reform Act 2005, which establishes the Supreme Court of the United Kingdom. However, the Court will not be activated until 2008. It will inherit the current jurisdiction of the House of Lords. The Court will consist of 12 judges, appointed for 12-year terms, to be known as Justices of the Supreme Court. The 12 existing Law Lords will become the initial judges. The senior most will be the president of the Court, and the next senior will be the deputy president. The judges will not be entitled to take part in debate or to vote in the House of Lords. The Court will occupy premises yet to be identified.

Future judges of the Court will be chosen by a Selection Commission established by the Act. It will consist of five persons: the President and Deputy President of the Supreme Court, one member each from the Judicial Selection Commission for England and Wales, the Judicial Appointments Board of Scotland, and the Northern Ireland Judicial Appointments Commission. For each vacancy on the Court the Selection Commission will submit one name to the Lord Chancellor. In making its selection the Commission is required to consult with senior judges and designated officials from Wales, Scotland, and Northern Ireland. In considering the name submitted, the Lord Chancellor must consult the same persons. As with recommendations made by the Judicial Appointments Commission for judges of other courts, the Lord Chancellor may accept the name and send it forward for appointment by the Queen or he may reject it or send it back for reconsideration. The process is the same with both commissions.

NOTES

1. The 2005 Act introduces into the British government for the first time the doctrine of separation of powers. It does so in two ways. First, it ends the three-way role of the Lord Chancellor by making him no longer eligible to serve as a judge, although he continues in the House of Lords and the cabinet. Second, it separates judges of the court of last resort from the legislature, organizing them into an independent judicial body. This is an historic break with a centuries-long tradition and governmental arrangement.

2. As pointed out earlier, the Act also works a radical reform in the method of appointing judges, taking the process out of the control of the Lord Chancellor. The two commissions — one for the Supreme Court and another for all other judges — bring significant lay participation into the selection process and will no doubt broaden the pool of potential appointees. The Lord Chancellor, however, will continue to play a part in the appointing process through his authority to force reconsideration by the commissions of their recommended selections.

II. GERMAN APPELLATE COURTS AND JUDGES

The previous part afforded a glimpse of the contemporary appellate scene in the birthplace of the common law. This part presents an overview of appellate courts, judges, and processes in one of the world's other major legal systems, the civil law system. Germany is selected as the focus of the study for several reasons. It is fairly representative of the civil law systems that developed in

Europe. Its law and legal order have been influential both in Europe and in other parts of the world. It is today, once again, the largest country in Europe and no doubt will play an important role in European and world affairs.

This part is not intended to convey a detailed knowledge of German law or procedure. Rather, its purpose is to provide information about the judicial structures of Germany, with particular emphasis on the appellate courts in the "ordinary jurisdiction," and to impart some sense of how appeals are adjudicated. The material is designed to reveal the key differences between German and American appellate structure, procedure, and judges. The material also provides a basis for a comparison with the English appellate process considered in the previous part.

Special attention should be paid to (1) the organization of large appellate courts into divisions with the docket allocated among them by category of case; (2) the first level of review addressing both law and fact, with the second level addressing law alone; (3) the career promotional method of appointing judges.

Before considering the contemporary German judicial scene, one needs to have some understanding of the legal and political setting, beginning in the late nineteenth century.

A. Background and Setting[13]

The industrial eminence of the country [before the First World War] was matched by its academic achievements. Numerous technical schools provided training in engineering, mining, agriculture, veterinary medicine, and other fields. But it was the German universities that had the greater impact on the world of higher education. At the beginning of the twentieth century, there were twenty-one universities within German borders . . . The oldest of these was Heidelberg (1386) and the newest was Muenster (1902). All but six had been founded before 1800 . . . These universities were in the front rank of the world's institutions of higher learning. Each was organized into the four faculties that had been the traditional German university structure since the Middle Ages: Law, Theology, Philosophy, and Medicine. In 1908, the enrollment of these universities totaled more than 46,000 students. Of these, 12,375 were studying law.

          . . .

The men who manned the German legal system as judges, prosecutors, advocates, counselors, notaries, and lawyers in government ministries all studied in the faculties of law in the universities. The central notion in the university law faculties was that they were training men to become judges. If one was qualified to be a judge, he would be qualified to pursue any other line of legal work. But the university law professors, and not the judges, continued to be . . . the pre-eminent figures in German law.

During the last quarter of the nineteenth century these professors and other German jurists developed five codes that have had major influence on the legal

---

13 The following paragraphs are taken from DANIEL J. MEADOR, IMPRESSIONS OF LAW IN EAST GERMANY 16-19 (1986). Copyright ©1986 by University Press of Virginia. Reprinted with permission.

systems of numerous countries. In order of their adoption these were: the Criminal Code (1871), the Criminal Procedure Code (1877), the Civil Procedure Code (1877), the Civil Code (1896), and the Commercial Code (1897). All or parts of these codes have been adopted by such geographically and ethnically diverse nations as Japan, Turkey, and some South American countries. The development of these German codes had been made possible by the unification of the numerous German states through the creation of the Reich in 1871.

This 1871 unification also made possible the creation of a nationwide legal system, superimposed upon the numerous fragmented systems. This unified legal system was symbolized by the establishment of a single court of law with appellate jurisdiction over civil and criminal cases throughout all German territory. This was the Imperial Supreme Court (*Reichgericht*), which had its seat at Leipzig. This tribunal was created by the Court Organization Act of 1877 that established the judicial structure that remains today. It is not clear why this new Supreme Court was not located in Berlin, the capital. One piece of folklore is that Bismarck (Chancellor, 1871-90) believed that it was undesirable to have the judges at the seat of government, mingling with other officials, where they might be subjected to baleful political influences. This notion would be consistent with the idea of judicial independence embodied in the Act.

NOTES

1. Does Bismarck's point about judicial independence have merit? Would the rule of law and the administration of justice in the United States be strengthened if the U. S. Supreme Court were located, for example, in St. Louis, Missouri, instead of Washington, D. C.? Is there any compelling need for the Court to be at the seat of government in the midst of an ever-swirling political cauldron?

2. The Second World War, with its widespread destruction and defeat of Germany, resulted in a serious rupture, politically and territorially, in the German nation. The areas designated to be temporary occupation zones for the armed forces of the Soviet Union and of the United States, Britain, and France, ultimately became the territorial boundaries of two new states. The western zone occupied by the three western powers became, in 1949, the Federal Republic of Germany (FRG). In that same year, the eastern zone, occupied by the USSR, became the German Democratic Republic (GDR). The latter was converted into a Marxist-Leninist state, with a legal system modeled along Soviet lines. For a description of that system, *see* DANIEL J. MEADOR, IMPRESSIONS OF LAW IN EAST GERMANY (1986). The FRG became a western-style democracy, which carried forward the traditional German legal system and court structures.

3. At its founding the FRG adopted the "Basic Law" (*Grundgesetz*), in effect, a constitution, establishing a governmental structure and setting forth a lengthy list of individual rights. From the beginning of the FRG, reunification of the two post-war German states was an article of faith, embodied in the Basic Law. That vision was finally realized in 1990 when, pursuant to a treaty, the GDR ceased to exist, and the territory it had embraced became part of the FRG, thus coming under the Basic Law. For an account of the reunification of the German constitutional, legal, and social order, *see* PETER QUINT,

THE IMPERFECT UNION: CONSTITUTIONAL STRUCTURE OF GERMAN UNIFICATION (1997). *See also* Daniel J. Meador, *Transition in the German Legal Order: East Back to West, 1990-91,* 15 B.C. INT. & COMP. L. REV. 283 (1992); Inga Markovits, *Last Days,* 80 CALIF. L. REV. 55 (1992).

4. In the FRG there already were eleven states (*Laender*). After reunification, five new *Laender* were created on the territory of the former GDR. This actually was a re-creation of these states, as they had pre-existed the formation of the GDR but had been abolished by that regime. Representatives from those five re-created states now sit in the *Bundestag* and *Bundesrat,* and the long-standing court structure of the FRG has been extended eastward into those states. The FRG capital has been relocated from Bonn to Berlin, the historic German capital.

5. Pursuant to the Basic Law, the FRG government is a parliamentary system. The *Bundestag* is the lower house, roughly analogous to the U.S. House of Representatives and the British House of Commons. The upper chamber is the *Bundesrat,* roughly analogous to the U. S. Senate, although its power is more limited.

B. The German Court Systems and the Law Applied

Daniel J. Meador, *Appellate Subject Matter Organization: The German Design from an American Perspective,* 5 HASTINGS INT. & COMP. L. REV. 27, 29-39, 41, 43 (1981)[14]

I. The Governmental Structure — A Unitary Federalism

The Federal Republic of Germany (FRG), as its name indicates, is a nation whose political organization is based on federalism. In reality, however, the allocation of German governmental power is so different from the federalism of the United States that the system is virtually another form of government. There is a superficial similarity in that both the United States and the FRG have central, national governments coexisting with constituent territorial units — the states — having governments of their own. In two important respects, however, the German form of government is closer to a unitary system than it is to federalism, at least as compared with federalism in the United States.

One substantial difference is that the bulk of German law is federal. The [16] constituent political units — the *Laender* (*Land* in the singular), which are analogous to American states — have parliamentary bodies that enact statutes. However, in the totality of the German legal universe, those statutes do not loom large. Some estimates are that more than ninety-five percent of all the law involved in litigation in Germany is federal. This situation is almost reversed in the United States, where the overwhelming bulk of law is state law . . . In Germany, criminal law, criminal procedure, the great mass of

---

[14] Copyright © 1981 by University of California, Hastings College of the Law, reprinted from HASTINGS INTERNATIONAL AND COMPARATIVE LAW REVIEW, Volume 5, Number 1 (1981), by permission. Updated information is shown in brackets.

private law, and civil procedure were brought under nationwide uniformity by the five major codes adopted in the last quarter of the nineteenth century. American lawyers would find it strange, for example, that ordinary automobile negligence cases and private contract disputes are governed by federal law, but that is the situation in Germany. *Land* law deals with such matters as education and local law enforcement.

Another significant difference between the two judicial systems is that in Germany, from the lowest trial courts to the highest appellate courts, there is a single nationwide court structure, which is created by federal law. There are no parallel or duplicating courts at any level similar to the dual federal-state systems in the United States. Not only does federal law establish all German courts, it also provides comprehensively for their civil and criminal procedures and prescribes the responsibilities, status, and compensation for all judges at all levels. However, all of the courts except the courts of last resort and a few other specialized tribunals are regarded as *Land* courts. The *Land* courts for criminal cases and private civil litigation include two levels of trial courts and a tier of appellate courts. With reference to these courts, the responsibility of the *Land* government is to provide financial support, appoint the judges, and provide for day-to-day administration. The federal government has a corresponding responsibility for the top appellate courts of the country.

One result of this quasi-unitary system in Germany is that there is never a question of federal-state choice of forum, as there is in the United States. Nor is there anything like the federal-state choice of law problem which exists under the *Erie* doctrine, whereby a federal trial court must determine whether federal or state law is to govern a particular question. Rarely, if ever, is there any doubt as to the source of the governing law in the German courts; it is almost always federal, as to both substance and procedure.

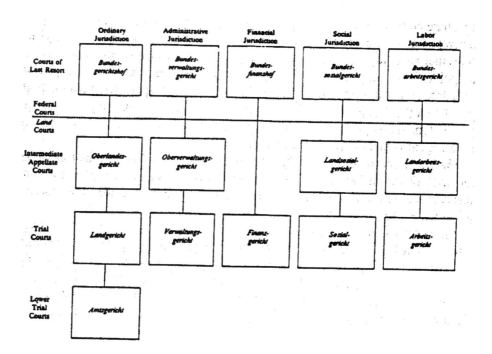

II. An Overview of the Judicial System

The German courts . . . are not organized into a single judicial system. Rather, there are five distinct systems. These are spoken of as "the five jurisdictions," and each is nationwide in scope. These jurisdictions are not territorial; they are erected along subject matter lines. Within each jurisdiction there is a trial level and an appellate level. The top appellate court in each jurisdiction — the supreme court of the jurisdiction — is federal. The trial courts in each jurisdiction are *Land* courts. In some jurisdictions there are intermediate appellate courts; these are also *Land* courts . . .

The five jurisdictions are, in English translation, the ordinary, the administrative, the financial, the social, and the labor. Each is briefly described below.

The Ordinary Jurisdiction. This jurisdiction embraces all criminal cases and all civil litigation between private parties, except litigation within the labor jurisdiction. The judicial structure designed to handle these cases is the focus of this article and will be described more fully below.

The Administrative Jurisdiction. This jurisdiction includes all disputes between citizens and the government that are not included in the social and financial jurisdictions. Its business is the equivalent of American administrative law. This jurisdiction is structured in three levels: trial courts throughout the country, regionally organized appellate courts with at least one in each *Land*, and the Federal Supreme Court, the *Bundesverwaltungsgericht,* which sits in Berlin. [Since reunification the court has been relocated to Leipzig, occupying the imposing building that was the home of the Imperial Supreme Court (*Reichgericht*) until 1945. Thus the German tradition of not having any of the top courts at the seat of government has been continued.]

The Financial Jurisdiction. This jurisdiction includes all controversies between citizens and the government concerning taxes. These include what Americans would refer to as internal revenue cases. Unlike the other four jurisdictions, this jurisdiction has only two tiers: a trial level within each *Land* and the Federal Supreme Court, the *Bundesfinanzhof,* sitting in Munich.

The Social Jurisdiction. This jurisdiction includes cases dealing with unemployment compensation, health and accident insurance, social security, and other social benefit programs. There are trial courts and intermediate appellate courts in the *Laender*; the Federal Supreme Court is the *Bundessozialgericht*, sitting in Kassel.

The Labor Jurisdiction. This jurisdiction includes all disputes between employees and employers concerning terms and conditions of employment in private industry. As in the administrative and social jurisdictions, the structure is three-tiered, with trial courts and intermediate appellate courts in the *Laender*. The Federal Supreme Court is the *Bundesarbeitsgericht*, sitting in Kassel. [Since reunification the court has been relocated to Erfurt.]. . .

. . . Unlike courts in the United States, the ordinary courts and the courts exercising the jurisdictions described above do not have the authority to decide constitutional questions that may arise in the course of litigation. The authority to decide these questions is vested in special constitutional courts at both the *Land* and federal levels. Each *Land* has its own constitutional court to decide *Land* constitutional questions.

The Federal Constitutional Court (*Bundesverfassungsgericht*) is the only forum with authority to decide federal constitutional questions. This court is above the top courts in the other five jurisdictions in the sense that its rulings on constitutional questions are binding on all other courts. As an independent constitutional organ, it occupies a unique position outside of the judicial structure outlined above. [This court and its judges are described in Section E, *infra*.]

. . .

III. The Ordinary Jurisdiction

The German courts most closely resembling the appellate courts in the United States are the appellate courts in the ordinary jurisdiction. These are the Federal Supreme Court and the [24] intermediate appellate courts in that jurisdiction.

A. *The Trial Courts*

There are two levels of trial courts. The lowest court in the ordinary jurisdiction is the *Amtsgericht*.[15] It resembles in part what Americans would think of as an inferior trial court. It has jurisdiction over minor criminal cases and over civil cases of relatively limited monetary amounts. But the *Amtsgericht* does much more. It has jurisdiction in family matters (including divorce), probate matters, bankruptcy, and a miscellaneous assortment of non-contentious business. It also serves as a registry of deeds . . . In small towns and rural areas there are as few as two or three judges on the *Amtsgericht*; in larger towns and cities there can be as many as fifty or more on each court. These judges are dispersed throughout the country so that every citizen has relatively convenient access to the civil and criminal court at this level . . .

The next higher court in the ordinary jurisdiction is the *Landericht*. This is what Americans would think of as a trial court of general jurisdiction. It has original jurisdiction over the more serious criminal cases and over civil cases which exceed in monetary amount those within the *Amtsgericht* jurisdiction . . . Numerous judges serve on each of these courts, typically sitting in panels of three. [But see the description of lay judges below.] These courts, like the *Amtsgerichte*, sit in geographical districts; however, the territorial jurisdiction of each *Landericht* is considerably larger than that of each *Amtsgericht*. All of the *Amtsgerichte* lying within the territory of a given *Landericht* are subject to an appellate review in that *Landericht* for certain cases. Thus, the *Landerichte* have both a reviewing function over the lower trial courts and a large amount of original trial jurisdiction of their own.

B. *The Intermediate Appellate Courts*

The next higher court in the ordinary jurisdiction, and the highest *Land* court, is the *Oberlandesgericht*. There are [24] *Oberlandesgerichte*, or "courts

---

[15] [2] A literal translation of this word is "office court." Heyde's translation is "county court." Neither translation fully conveys the nature of this tribunal. As long as the reader understands the functions this court performs, clarity seems better served by retention of the German word. Because of this difficulty in conveying accurately by the use of an English substitute the nature of German courts, officials, and procedures, German words coupled with English explanations will be used throughout this article.

of appeals," in the FRG. They are organized regionally with at least one located in each of the [16] *Laender*. As judged by their functions and by their place in the judicial hierarchy, these courts blend the functions of American intermediate appellate courts and state supreme courts. Each has appellate jurisdiction over most decisions of the *Landerichte* and directly over some decisions of the *Amtsgerichte* within its territorial jurisdiction. On questions of purely *Land* law, which are relatively few, the *Oberlandesgericht* is the court of last resort . . . An *Oberlandesgericht* is not precisely analogous to a state supreme court in the United States for at least two reasons. Its decisions are subject to review by a higher court to a far greater extent than are those of American state supreme courts. Secondly, there is more than one of these courts in some of the *Laender*. In Baden-Wurttemberg, for example, there are two *Oberlandesgerichte*; thus, neither of them can be said to be the highest court of that *Land*.

Like all German appellate courts, these courts are extraordinarily large by American standards. They consist of as many as [202 judges in 2001]. . .However, each *Oberlandesgericht*, like all German appellate courts, function through divisions typically consisting of [six] judges each . . .

C. The Court of Last Resort

The highest court in the ordinary jurisdiction is the *Bundesgerichtshof*, often referred to in English as the "Federal Supreme Court." That translation, however, is misleading in that the *Bundesgerichtshof* is the Supreme Court only in the ordinary jurisdiction. As described earlier, each of the other four jurisdictions has its own supreme court. No one of these five federal appellate tribunals is considered superior to the others. In other words, in Germany there is no one court analogous to the United States Supreme Court or to the House of Lords in England . . .

This court has jurisdiction to review decisions of all the *Oberlandesgerichte*; in certain cases it can directly review decisions of the *Landerichte*. The court consists of [125 judges in 2002, of whom 20 were female] organized in divisions typically of [eight] judges each.

Although the *Bundesgerichtshof* dates only from the establishment of the FRG in 1949, it is considered to be the successor to the *Reichsgericht*, which was created in 1879 and sat at Leipzig until the close of the Second World War. The present court's internal organization, procedures, nomenclature, and publications are essentially the same as those of the *Reichsgericht*. The court today is located in Karlsruhe, occupying the former Ducal Palace, with extensive grounds and a total of three buildings . . . [After reunification in 1990, consideration was given to moving the court back to the seat of the former *Reichgericht* in Leipzig, but a decision was made to remain in Karlsruhe. However, one criminal division of the court does sit in that building in Leipzig.] . . .

For the large volume of criminal cases originating in the *Amtsgericht*, the *Oberlandesgericht* is the court of last resort. In those cases, the *Oberlandesgericht* is serving in a role which Americans would recognize as that served by the "highest state court," the state supreme court. As to the large number of civil as well as criminal cases originating in the *Landericht*, however, the *Oberlandesgericht* ordinarily is in the role of an intermediate appellate court, with its decisions reviewable by the *Bundesgerichtshof*. Since the law being applied in the *Oberlandesgericht* is overwhelmingly federal, the reviewing role of the *Bundesgerichtshof* is not a narrowly limited one such as that performed by the United States Supreme Court in relation to state supreme court judgments.

. . . [In the year 2001, the court decided 5,386 civil cases and 2,833 criminal cases. With its present complement of judges, this amounts to an average caseload of 66 cases per judge.] Thus, although the total case load of the court is astronomical by American standards, the work burden on each judge would be viewed as quite reasonable, and indeed light, by American appellate judges . . .

As this brief description of the ordinary jurisdiction and the other four jurisdictions reveals, the German judiciary is simultaneously structured in three different ways: hierarchically, geographically, and by subject matter . . .

NOTES

1. The trial judge's responsibilities. As in other civil law systems, German trial courts function through the inquisitorial process and not through the adversarial method of the Anglo-American legal world. The key difference is that in the German courts the judges bear much more responsibility for developing the facts and moving the proceedings along than do common-law judges. Advocates still play an important role, but the judges are the principal actors, and they control the proceedings to a much higher degree than American lawyers would find familiar. For a description of this process in civil cases, *see* Benjamin Kaplan, *Civil Procedure — Reflections on the Comparison of Systems,* 9 Buff. L. Rev. 409 (1960). The relative merits of German and American civil procedure are explored in John H. Langbein, *The German Advantage in Civil Procedure,* 52 U. Chi. L. Rev. 823 (1985); Ronald J. Allen *et al, Legal Institution — The German Advantage in Civil Procedure: A Plea for More Details and Fewer Generalities in Comparative Scholarship,* 82 Nw. U. L. Rev. 705 (1988); Michael Bohlander, *The German Advantage Revisited: An Inside View of German Civil Procedure in the Nineties,* 13 Tul. Eur. & Civ. L. F. 25 (1998).

2. Lay judges. As is typical of civil law jurisdictions, there are no juries in German courts. However, citizen participation in the decision- making process at the trial level is provided through lay judges. They are citizens specifically appointed to each trial court for a term of years. Thus, unlike American jurors, they serve continuously over a period of time. Two lay judges typically sit with the full-time professional judges. Lay judges participate at the trial level in all of the five jurisdictions. Only in the labor and the social jurisdictions, however, are there lay judges at the appellate level.

C. Appellate Courts in the Ordinary Jurisdiction — Structure and Procedure

The following table shows the 24 *Oberlandesgerichte* (each named for the city in which it sits), the number of judges on each, the number of cases decided in 2001, and the number of *Landerichte* under each. As previously explained, these purely appellate courts are the highest state courts.

Court	Judges	Cases Decided	*Landerichte*
Bamberg	30	1,946*	7
Berlin	119	6,220	1
Brandenburg	67	3,183	4
Braunschweig	26	1,445	2
Bremen	18	704	1
Celle	89	5,777	6
Cologne	115	5,641	3
Dresden	84	4,298	6
Duesseldorf	155	7,118	6
Frankfurt/Main	135	6,968	9
Hamburg	74	2,915	1
Hamm	202	9,986	10
Jena	43	2,321	4
Karlsruhe	84	4,624	9
Koblenz	60	3,228	4
Munich	138	7,662*	10
Naumburg	50	3,004	4
Nuernberg	52	2,644*	5
Oldenburg	53	2,968	3
Rostock	38	1,914	4
Saarbruecken	28	1,418	1
Schleswig	64	3,429	4
Stuttgart	95	4,532	8
Zweibruecken	28	1,589	4

Daniel J. Meador, *Appellate Subject Matter Organization: The German Design From An American Perspective*, 5 HASTINGS INT. & COMP. L. REV. 27, 41-43, 49-53 (1981)[16]

Nature and Scope of Appellate Review

Appellate procedure in the German courts is, in general, designed to provide two kinds of review for most cases: a first review encompassing both law and facts, and a subsequent review on questions of law only. The system is also designed so that no case goes through more than three levels of courts.

The first review, extending to law and fact, is called the *Berufung*. The entire record made in the court of first instance is filed with the reviewing court. That court examines the record de novo, and it can receive new evidence

---

* Not including criminal appeals. These courts are in Bavaria, where all criminal appeals (921 in 2001) are decided by a separate court, the *Bayerisches Oberstes Landgericht*.

[16] © 1981 by University of California, Hastings College of the Law, reprinted from HASTINGS INTERNATIONAL AND COMPARATIVE LAW REVIEW, Volume 5, Number 1 (1981), by permission. Updated information is shown in brackets.

[under a 2002 reform, it can receive evidence only of facts occurring after entry of the trial court judgment or where there is reasonable doubt that the statement of facts made by the court below is accurate]. This is not identical to the American-style "trial de novo;" the entire case is not tried anew . . . It is, however, a de novo consideration of the factual questions on the record made below with the possibility for additional evidence to be received in the discretion of the reviewing court. The procedure affords a more expansive review of facts than is customary in American appellate courts.

The second level of review, which is limited to questions of law, is called the *Revision*. This is the kind of review that American lawyers and judges associate most typically with appeals in state or federal appellate courts. Review is based solely on the record made below and is limited to specified questions of law . . .

For most cases originating in the *Amtsgericht*, the lowest level in the judiciary, the first review — the *Berufung* — takes place in the next higher court, the *Landericht*. Although the *Landericht* itself is a trial court, it provides this first-level review for most cases in the *Amtsgericht*. In these cases . . . a second and final level of review — the *Revision* — is provided by the *Oberlandesgericht*, an appellate court. These cases terminate in the *Oberlandesgericht*, having gone through three judicial levels. The highest court in the ordinary jurisdiction, the *Bundesgerichtshof*, has no jurisdiction over them. There are, however, certain cases originating in the *Amtsgericht* — family law cases, for example — which bypass the *Landericht* and go directly to the *Oberlandesgericht* for review of law and fact. Those cases then can go to the *Bundesgerichtshof* for *Revision* . . .

For cases originating in the *Landericht*, the *Berufung* is in the *Oberlandesgericht*. For there to be further review by way of *Revision* in the *Bundesgerichtshof*, civil cases decided by the *Oberlandesgericht* . . . [must have leave of the OLG; there is no longer any monetary minimum]. One exception to this pattern of review is that the more serious criminal cases tried initially in the *Landerichte* go directly to the *Bundesgerichtshof* and thus receive only one level of review, the *Revision*.

Hearing and Deciding Appeals

German appellate practice combines features of American and English procedure. Like American appellate courts, the German appellate courts receive briefs from lawyers and a full written record from the court below. Like the English Court of Appeal, the German appellate courts devote a substantial amount of time to oral hearings; at the first level of review, where both law and fact are open to appellate consideration, these courts can hear witnesses and receive new evidence [but under the 2002 reform, only as to facts occurring after the trial judgment or where there is reasonable doubt that the statement of facts made by the court below is accurate]. However, where appellate consideration is limited to questions of law, typically at the second level of review, the German courts decide the issues solely on the record made below, in the American style. Overall, German appellate practice at the first level of review probably resembles that of England more closely than it does that of the United States because of its visibility and reliance on oral hearings, sometimes with witnesses.

A. *The Bundesgerichtshof*

In the *Bundesgerichtshof*, the many courtrooms in the court's complex of buildings are kept busy every day with oral arguments. Each division of the court sits in panels of five. Typically, one lawyer appears for each side.[17] At the conclusion of the argument, one of the five judges is designated to prepare the court's decision. A disposition is sometimes announced within a few days, although a full written opinion may not be forthcoming for several weeks. These later-delivered written decisions are reported in a dual set of reports — one for civil cases and one for criminal cases.[18]

German appellate judges do not have law clerks. That is, there is no legally trained personal assistant available to help each judge. However, in the *Bundesgerichtshof* each division is assigned the American equivalent of a staff attorney. [Each division now has two or three such attorneys.][19] This is a person of considerable experience from the ranks of those qualified for the judiciary in the *Laender*. Typically, persons selected for these positions have served on one or more *Land* courts and sometimes also in a *Land* ministry of justice for a period of several years . . . They are selected for assignment to the *Bundesgerichtshof* by the *Land* ministry of justice on the basis of performance on the second state examination and on work as a judge on the *Land* courts. Selection is considered an honor. Assignments in the *Bundesgerichtshof* are for terms of approximately three years. At the conclusion of that time, these legal assistants return to positions on *Land* courts, often judgeships on the *Oberlandesgerichte*. While on assignment to the *Bundesgerichtshof*, such persons work for a particular division assisting the judges with their work much as central staff attorneys do in some American appellate courts.

In addition to this legal assistant, each division of the *Bundesgerichtshof* is assigned an administrative official to assist in managing the docket and maintaining case papers. This official, in effect, serves as a kind of clerk for that division. Each division schedules its own arguments and runs its own business, although there must be some degree of coordination with the central administrative office of the court in the use of courtrooms and in other matters.

---

[17] [3] A curious feature of the German legal profession and *Bundesgerichtshof* practice — at least to American eyes — is the extreme restriction on admission to practice before that court in civil cases. On the civil side, the bar of the court is limited to approximately [40 lawyers]. Any civil case from anywhere in the country going to the *Bundesgerichtshof* for review must be placed in the hands of one of those lawyers. They constitute a bar specialized in the practice of this one court at the top of the judicial pyramid . . . In criminal cases, however, there is no such restriction, and lawyers throughout the country are eligible to take criminal cases to the court. In those cases the government is always represented by a lawyer from the office of the *Bundesstaatsanwalt*, the Federal Prosecutor General, whose offices and staff are housed in the precincts of the court.

[18] [4] The civil reports are cited as BGHZ (*Bundesgerichtshof Zivil*). The criminal reports are cited as BGHSt (*Bundesgerichtshof Straf*). Cases are never cited by the names of the parties but only by these report names, decision date, and case number . . .

[19] [5] In German, the official title for this position is *Wissenschaftlicher Mitarbeiter*. This is almost untranslatable into English. The usual translation employed is "scientific advisor." However, that is quite misleading to Americans in that it implies that the individual provides advice to the judges on technical questions or in the field of the physical sciences. That is not the case. The individual is simply a law-trained person assisting the judges as do American staff attorneys. The position has a long and honorable history; it dates back to the beginnings of the *Reichsgericht* in 1879 . . .

Since a division in the *Bundesgerichtshof* typically consists of [eight] judges, and cases are heard and decided by panels of five, not every case is decided by precisely the same group of judges. This practice might seem at odds with a major theory and purpose of subject matter organization — the maintenance of a high degree of uniformity in the law by assigning a specified group of cases to the same group of judges. However, with five out of eight judges sitting, the variations in the composition of the panels will be relatively slight from case to case. The group of [eight] is also small enough to allow for the maintenance of continuous communication and informal discussions about various legal issues. Moreover, unlike the situation in many American appellate courts, any panel sitting on any case will always be a majority of the "court," that is, the division with responsibility over that category of case.

B. The Oberlandesgerichte

In the *Oberlandesgerichte* most of the work involves a review of both law and fact. Thus, the nature of the hearing on the appeal varies from that of the *Bundesgerichtshof* where review is limited strictly to questions of law . . . Although divisions in the *Oberlandesgerichte* typically consist of [six] judges, they sit in panels of three . . . The hearings are quite informal — English style — with lively exchanges between the judges and the lawyers; the parties themselves sometimes join in the discussion. There appears to be no fixed time limit on the proceedings; as is true of the English appellate judges, the judges appear to be willing to sit as long as necessary to sort out the issues and bring the matter to a conclusion. However, unlike English appellate judges, German judges do not announce decisions immediately from the bench. The court retires and one member of the panel is designated to prepare the decision, which is issued later in writing. As in the *Bundesgerichtshof*, dispositions may be announced within a few days, with full opinions coming several weeks later.

Decisions of the [24] *Oberlandesgerichte* are published only selectively. An opinion is printed in the official reports only if it seems significant. There is one set of reports which includes the selected decisions of all [24] *Oberlandesgerichte* throughout the country.

The *Oberlandesgerichte*, unlike the *Bundesgerichtshof*, do not have the services of staff attorneys. However, these courts do have assigned to them several recent university law graduates who are there as part of their required practical training between the two state examinations. Each division in an *Oberlandesgericht* also has an administrative official assigned to it to assist in docket management, although sometimes one administrative official has responsibility for two or more divisions.

An *Oberlandesgericht* is often a very busy place. In Munich, for example, the main *Oberlandesgericht* building, built for that court around the turn of the century, has 14 courtrooms which are occupied with appellate hearings every day. These courtrooms are used only for civil cases; criminal cases are heard in another building a short distance away.

Most appellate courtrooms in Germany are relatively small and unpretentious; the buildings housing them are often not distinguishable from other government buildings. They are a contrast to the courtrooms in which the various divisions and panels of the English Court of Appeal sit, with their high ceilings and rich paneling and furnishings. These differing physical settings may be a reflection of the relative status of German judges and courts as compared with their English counterparts or, more generally, the difference between judges and courts in civil law systems and those in the common law world.

NOTES

1. Consider the two significant ways in which German appellate review at the first level differs from American practice: (a) in the de novo standard of review applied to trial court factual findings, in contrast to the more deferential "clearly erroneous" standard, and (b) in the authority of the appellate court to consider facts not before the trial court. Why have the considerations underlying the American view of the relationship of appellate courts to trial courts on factual matters, developed in Chapter 3, Section B, not been persuasive in Germany? For an historical explanation for the difference in the appellate treatment of facts in the common-law and civil-law worlds, see the section from MARTIN M. SHAPIRO, COURTS: A COMPARATIVE AND POLITICAL ANALYSIS, reprinted in Chapter 1 at page 11. What effect, if any, might the de novo standard of review have on a trial judge's process of making fact findings?

2. In the United States a conspicuous exception to the general American appellate practice in the review of facts is in Louisiana, the only state whose main legal roots are in the civil law. As pointed out in Chapter 3, page ___, Louisiana appellate courts can and do freely review trial court fact findings and reach contrary results.

3. The American Law Institute/Unidroit project on *Principles and Rules of Transnational Civil Procedure* (2004) brought together representatives from common-law and civil-law systems from all parts of the world to formulate procedures for transnational disputes that would accommodate concepts from both systems. Principle 27 includes the following: "The scope of appellate review should ordinarily be limited to claims and defenses addressed in the first-instance proceeding. The appellate court may, in the interest of justice, consider new facts and evidence." In this global competition for the best rule, did the civil law triumph? Did ALI/Unidroit get it right?

4. The *Berufung* and *Revision* in the ordinary jurisdiction are described in detail in Herbert Bernstein, *The Finality of a Judgment as a Requirement for Civil Appeals in Germany*, 47 LAW & CONTEMP. PROBS. 35, 37-43 (1984).

5. Both the *Oberlandesgerichte* (OLG) and the *Bundesgerichtshof* (BGH) can review sentences imposed on defendants in criminal cases. Their review extends to determining whether the trial court made an incorrect choice of the applicable range of punishment and of determining whether the trial court failed to consider relevant aggravating or mitigating circumstances. In this respect, that appellate review resembles the review of sentences in many American appellate courts. The German courts can also determine whether the sentence is unreasonable in relation to the defendant's level of guilt, but the trial court is allowed wide discretion in fixing the sentence. This review for "reasonableness" may be similar to that exercised by some American courts,

although exact comparison is difficult. It seems clear, though, that the German appellate courts do not have the broad authority over sentences found in the English Court of Appeal, Criminal Division. Like American courts, the German courts, if they find the sentence to be erroneous, remand the case to the trial court for re-sentencing, usually to trial judges who have not previously heard the case.

E. Barrett Prettyman & Allen R. Snyder, *Short Oral Arguments Problem: A Possible Solution from Germany*, LEGAL TIMES (Aug. 21, 1978)[20]

[The following is a portion of a report by American lawyers of an oral argument in the *Oberlandesgericht* in Frankfurt/Main.]

The German court was composed of three judges who sat at a long, plain table even with the floor, rather than behind a bench on a raised platform. The attorney for the appellant company, the plaintiff below, sat at a similar but smaller table to the court's right, and the attorney for the appellee, defendant company, sat to the court's left, facing opposing counsel. There was no lectern, podium, or microphone. The judges and counsel all wore black gowns, with no other adornments.

The "argument" began with a brief recitation by the chief judge of the basic facts and the main points at issue. When he had concluded, the counsel for the appellant, while still seated at his table, launched into a casual delineation of the main points in his favor and the reason why he thought the lower court had been in error. When he had concluded about five minutes of argument, the appellee's counsel, who also remained seated, began replying to the appellant's points and giving his own version of what had occurred.

There then followed what can only be described as a general discussion carried on by the judges and both counsel, each individual talking in turn and in a relaxed, almost colloquial style. Counsel primarily spoke back and forth in a give-and-take fashion about the facts and the law, ostensibly ignoring the court, although obviously, this was all for the benefit of the judges.

While one or more of the judges sometimes interjected himself into the discussion with a point or a question, the real "argument" was made up of a kind of debate between opposing counsel.

Virtually all of the discussion centered on documents in the record; there was almost no discussion of the testimony of the various witnesses who had appeared at trial. In addition, no cases were cited to the court.

Under German law, while the judges may be aware of, and may choose to follow case law, stare decisis is not a part of the country's formal legal system. Much greater emphasis is placed upon statutes than in this country, and the legislative history of these statutes is considered of particular importance.

---

[20] Copyright © 1978, by the Legal Times. Reprinted with permission.

While there was no specific time limit set for the oral argument, it was clear that the court was prepared at any moment to cut off any advocate who strayed from the main points of the case. The attorneys were sufficiently aware of this so that they directed themselves only to one or two main points at issue and did not engage in long discourses on matters of secondary interest.

The entire "argument" took forty minutes, and at the end it was clear that everything that could have been said about the heart of the case had been fully explored by each side.

The chief judge then announced that "the judgment in this case will be rendered on September 1, 1978, at 10:00 AM." This was six weeks to the day from the date of oral argument, and we were told later that all decisions in civil cases were handed down within six weeks, and it was the undeviating practice of intermediate appellate courts to announce the decision date and even the decision hour at the conclusion of oral argument.

One may well conclude that this type of proceeding really does not shorten the time for argument. However, the facts of the case we heard were somewhat complicated, with a number of companies, individuals, and transactions involved; yet the entire argument was completed within the relatively short space of forty minutes.

. . . This particular court hears at least five cases a day, so arguments apparently are not allowed to continue for an undue length of time.

The obvious advantage to this system — or something akin to it — is that instead of one attorney raising a point which is of great interest to the court but which cannot be responded to until his opponent is on his feet some time later, each point is fully covered by both attorneys as it arises, and each attorney has an opportunity to continue responding to his adversary until he has said all that can be said on his own behalf. It is not really an argument, as we know it, but rather a dialogue.

The one overriding impression left with those who listened was that the true weaknesses and strengths of each side became more apparent in a shorter time than occurs under our traditional one-up, one-down type of appellate argument.

In addition, the advantages of a specific time being established for the rendering of the judgment are obvious. Both sides can plan around that date, as opposed to our system where — even when huge amounts of money are involved — the parties have no way of knowing whether they will win or lose in a week, a few months, or a year or more.

The informality of the German proceeding — with lawyers freely exchanging views with each other rather than addressing the court directly, and never standing even when answering questions from the court — would come as something of a shock to someone used to the great deference paid American judges. Yet it must be said that despite the freedom of the exchange, at no time did either German attorney interrupt anyone else, use strong or derogatory language, or in any other way show disrespect for the court.

Peter L. Murray & Rolf Stuerner, German Civil Justice 395-96 (2004)[21]

In general the oral argument [in the BGH] takes place before a panel of at least 5 judges from one of the 12 civil senates . . .

Each case is generally assigned to one of the members of the panel who acts as "reporting judge" (*Berichterstatter*) and carefully reviews the case record and briefs prior to the oral argument. The reporting judge will generally prepare a memorandum of opinion (*Gutachten*) or recommended decision (*Votum*) and circulate it among the colleagues on the panel to prepare them for the oral hearing.

The oral proceedings in one of the hearing rooms of the Federal Supreme Court in Karlsruhe can be impressive. The judges are clad in maroon robes and traditional headware. Counsel are attired in robes of their own. The judges occupy a long, sometimes curved bench along one wall of the room, counsel are situated at small tables with podia on either side, and there is generally space for the clients or onlookers on benches at the back of the chamber.

Counsel for each party are invited to address the court on the issues raised by the review appeal. Although the tone and order of argument is more formal than in the lower courts, questions from the presiding judge, the reporting judge, or other members of the panel are common, and it is not unusual for the court to go back and forth between the two lawyers on a particular point or issue.

Since the advocates come from a small exclusive group well known to the judges of the court, the tone of the argument is that of a respectful conversation among colleagues rather than that of a speech or oration. Argumentation is usually concise and logically rigorous. Raised voices and appeals to emotion are out of the question.

. . . [T]he judges use the oral argument to give the parties judicial hints and feedback (*richterliche Hinweise*) on their tentative evaluations of the issues. Sometimes a lawyer can straighten out a wrong assumption or misconception in these exchanges. In any case, the lawyers are apprised of the court's likely direction and can marshal their best arguments.

. . . [T]he judgments of the Federal Supreme Court are rendered orally. Sometimes the oral rendition of judgment will take place the same day as the oral argument. Otherwise the court will convene a session for the rendition of judgments (*Verkuendungstermin*) at a later date.

NOTES

1. Compare the styles of oral argument in the OLG, the BGH, the English Court of Appeal, Criminal Division, and an American appellate court. Although a BGH hearing is more formal than an OLG hearing, as described by Prettyman and Snyder, in both there is an interchange among judges and opposing counsel, similar to that in the English CACD, but unlike the American style of set-piece presentation. The formal setting of the BGH is

---

[21] Copyright © 2004 by Carolina Academic Press. Reprinted with permission.

unlike the informality of the OLG but similar to that of the English court and an American court. Among these styles, which might best serve the sound disposition of appellate business?

2. Note that, like the English court, the BGH delivers some decisions orally from the bench at the conclusion of the hearing, but such is almost never done in an American appellate court. Why not?

Daniel J. Meador, *Appellate Subject Matter Organization: The German Design from An American Perspective,* 5 HASTINGS INT. & COMP. L. REV. 27, 44-46, 48-49, 53-57 (1981)[22]

Maintaining Uniformity in the Law

In any judicial system with multiple decisional units at the same appellate level, there is risk of conflicting decisions on the same legal questions. There are two potential sources of such conflicts at the top of the German system. One is internal, within the *Bundesgerichtshof*, where one division may reach a decision on a question of law different from that reached by another division.[23] The other source of potential conflict is among the top courts of the five jurisdictions: one supreme court may reach a decision on a question of law different from that reached on the same question by another of the supreme courts. Although the subject matter division of business both within the *Bundesgerichtshof* and among the five jurisdictions should work to keep such conflicts at a low level, there are nevertheless occasions when the identical legal question will arise in cases of more than one type. Thus, the system needs some mechanism for maintaining doctrinal uniformity.

Within the *Bundesgerichtshof*, the device used is the "Great Division."[24] This is not a body with a permanently fixed membership. It is made up of a group of judges from within the *Bundesgerichtshof* whose composition varies depending on the divisions involved. The body is brought into being when a division of the court has before it a case in which it desires to reach a decision different from a decision rendered by another division on the same question. When that situation occurs, the division with the pending case notifies the President of the Court, who then takes steps to convene the Great Division.

Convening the Great Division can be avoided if the division which previously decided the point agrees to concur in the view of the division before

---

[22] Copyright © 1981 by University of California, Hastings College of the Law, reprinted from HASTINGS INTERNATIONAL AND COMPARATIVE LAW REVIEW, Volume 5, Number 1 (1981), by permission. Updated information is included in brackets.

[23] [6] Since this article focuses on the appellate courts in the ordinary jurisdiction, consideration is confined here to the *Bundesgerichtshof*. However, a similar problem of internal conflict can arise in each of the other four supreme courts, as each of these courts is organized into multiple divisions.

[24] [7] *Grosser Senat.* Actually there is a Great Division for civil cases and a Great Division for criminal cases. There is also a "Combined Great Division,"(*Vereinigter Grosser Senat*) spanning both civil and criminal divisions.

which the case is pending. In that event, a formal notation is made in the later decision.

The President of the *Bundesgerichtshof* always sits with the Great Division. The remainder of the division is made up of the chairmen of the divisions involved, that is, the chairman of the division before which the case is pending and the chairman of the division or divisions in which a decision on the identical question has previously been rendered. In addition, designated judges from the divisions involved with the question also sit, for a total of nine judges. The Great Division's resolution of the question binds the entire *Bundesgerichtshof*.

The Great Division can also be convened in the absence of a pending conflict of decision if a division has before it a question of fundamental importance whose definitive resolution would promote uniformity.

The Great Division in the *Bundesgerichtshof* can loosely be compared to the "limited en banc" procedure being used in the United States Court of Appeals for the Ninth Circuit . . .

Among the *Oberlandesgerichte* there are no formal procedures for resolving conflicts between the divisions. The only means available is review in the *Bundesgerichtshof*. However, the judges in an *Oberlandesgericht* make efforts through informal discussions to maintain uniformity among the divisions.

Where a conflict arises between two supreme courts of the five jurisdictions, the mechanism for resolving it is called the "Combined Great Division." This body consists of nine judges — the presidents of the five supreme courts and two judges from each of the supreme courts involved. When one of the supreme courts has before it a case in which it has decided to reach a decision different from that previously reached by one of the other supreme courts, the Combined Great Division is convened to consider the question. This body meets at Karlsruhe where it takes up the case for discussion and ultimately decides the question.

. . .

Subject Matter Organization — Divisions of Judges and Allocation of Dockets

The key to the ability of the German appellate courts to manage huge dockets and numbers of judges while maintaining coherence in the law is the subject matter basis of their internal organization . . .

The basic idea is quite simple. Each appellate court is organized into numerous divisions of several judges each, and each division is assigned cases of certain types. These divisions and docket assignments are semi-permanent; they can be altered annually, but changes from year to year are few. Each appellate court has civil divisions and criminal divisions. These are designated by number — for example, Civil Division I, Civil Division II, Criminal Division 1, Criminal Division 2, and so on.

In the *Bundesgerichtshof* there are eleven numbered civil divisions, five criminal divisions, and seven special divisions. Each division consists of [eight] judges, with one of them designated as the chairman of the division, *i.e.*, the presiding judge.

Since the *Oberlandesgerichte* vary greatly in size, they also vary in the number of their divisions. The *Oberlandesgericht* in Karlsruhe, which has [83] judges has nineteen divisions. Typically [six] judges are assigned to each division, one of whom is the chairman.

A. The Work Distribution Plan [*Geschaeftsverteilungplan*]

In each court, this arrangement is embodied in a document known as the "work distribution plan." This is a key document embodying the entire subject matter plan of organization. Within each appellate court, the plan is revised and published annually. Copies are available to the public in printed form. The work distribution plan sets out the names of the judges and categories of cases assigned to each division . . . Each court develops its own work distribution plan through its *Praesidium*, a small group of judges elected by all the judges of the court.[25] No features of the plans are mandated by statute, although the formulation of such a plan is statutorily required.

An examination of the work distribution plan for the *Bundesgerichtshof* shows how an appellate court can be organized internally along subject matter lines without casting its judges into narrowly specialized roles. For example, Civil Division III is assigned cases arising under the Convention on Human Rights, cases involving aircraft noise, suits based on loans and debts, and cases involving water rights and mining rights. That docket is a rich mixture of international law, tort law, commercial law, and real property law. Another diverse mixture is found in the docket of Civil Division IVa, which handles cases involving inheritance, gifts, brokerage contracts, and insurance claims. Judges sitting on dockets such as these are hardly confined to one set of technical legal questions. They are, of course, dealing with a defined set of legal subjects spanning less than the full range of the court's jurisdiction. This enables the judges to develop a measure of expertise which would not be possible if they were forced to deal randomly with the entire corpus of the law. Although empirical data are not available, the likelihood is that this degree of expertise, in turn, makes it possible for the judges to consider and decide cases more rapidly, and for the law on any given subject to be applied and developed more coherently.

From the standpoint of lawyers and litigants, this docket arrangement means that in every case, the judges before whom any appeal would come are known in advance. . . .

On the criminal side, the work distribution plan, with some exceptions, is not based on the concept of subject matter organization. Rather, criminal cases are assigned to divisions mainly on a territorial basis . . . [E]ach of the five criminal divisions is assigned all cases coming from designated *Oberlandesgericht* districts. This means that each criminal division deals continuously with the entire range of criminal law questions. However, since "criminal law" itself is a defined subject matter of limited scope, there is no departure here from the subject matter concept. . . .

---

[25] [8] The Praesidium includes the President of the court as well as several judges elected by their colleagues. It is provided for in every appellate court by the Court Constitution Act (Gerichtsverfassungsgesetz). The Praesidium is the governing administrative body of the court. It resembles committees of judges found in some of the larger courts in the United States.

B. Administration of the Plan

An efficient and accurate means of routing cases to the correct divisions is essential to the smooth operation of this organizational arrangement. In the *Bundesgerichtshof*, this routing function is in the hands of a senior administrative official called an *Oberamtsrat* . . . His office receives the papers initially filed by the lawyers; these include the opinion of the court below and a paper equivalent to the American notice of appeal which specifies the particular grounds on which review is being sought. On the basis of these papers, the *Oberamtstrat* designates the division to which the case is to be assigned. Each case is given a number indicating that division, and all the papers in the case are sent forthwith to the chairman of the designated division. In each of the *Oberlandesgerichte*, there is a similar system for routing cases to the appropriate division.

Instances of misdirection apparently are not common. When a case arrives in a division which believes the case has been assigned incorrectly, the procedure in the *Bundesgerichtshof* calls for that division to send the case to the division which it considers appropriate. If the transferee division accepts the case, the matter is settled. On the other hand, if the transferee division believes it is not the appropriate division, the case will be returned to the original division and the matter ends there. It is estimated that approximately ten percent of the cases are transferred from one division to another because of improper initial assignment.

Similar problems of misdirection also arise in the *Oberlandesgerichte*. In at least some of those courts where two divisions are in disagreement as to the correct assignment of a particular case, the matter is referred to the *Praesidium* of the court, which then makes the assignment.

The allocations of business among the various divisions are in no sense "jurisdictional." They are purely a matter of internal administration and afford no rights to litigants.

. . .

The two characteristics of the German appellate courts which most sharply differentiate them from their American counterparts are the large number of judges and the subject matter style of organization. These two characteristics are closely related. The large number of judges makes the subject matter style of organization imperative in order to maintain doctrinal coherence. This style of organization in turn permits the employment of a cadre of judges large enough to handle the docket without impairing doctrinal stability.

In Germany there are far more judges on the intermediate appellate courts and the supreme court in the ordinary civil and criminal jurisdiction than in any single American judicial system or indeed in several of the largest American systems combined. With [125] judges on the *Bundesgerichtshof* and [1,847] judges on the [24] *Oberlandesgerichte*, there are altogether [1,972] appellate judges in the ordinary jurisdiction. If one adds the judges at the intermediate appellate levels and top appellate levels in the other four German jurisdictions, the numbers become almost staggering to the American mind. This is the judiciary for a nation of [82] million people. By comparison, in the largest American state — California, with a population of [35] million — there are [105] judges at the intermediate appellate level and seven judges on the state Supreme Court. The German total still would not be reached if all of the intermediate appellate and supreme court judges in the states of Illinois, Michigan, Ohio, and New York were added to the number of California appellate judges. In the United States federal judiciary, there are only 179 court of appeals judges and nine Supreme Court justices . . .

If one disregards system wide figures and examines only the numbers of judges sitting on individual appellate courts, the contrast is equally startling. One of the largest American appellate courts, in terms of number of judges, is the United States Court of Appeals for the Ninth Circuit, with [28] judges. Appellate courts with twelve or fifteen judges are considered large in the United States. When the figure rises much above that, apprehensions increase about unmanageability and threats to coherent, uniform jurisprudence . . . In Germany, by contrast, the smallest of the intermediate appellate courts has [18] judges; the largest has [202] judges. The average number of judges on all of the [24] intermediate appellate courts is [77]. If these appellate courts, or the top court with its [125] judges, were organized and operated like American appellate courts, there would be chaos in the law.

NOTES

1. An entire work distribution plan for the BGH is set out in Daniel J. Meador, *Appellate Subject Matter Organization: The German Design from an American Perspective*, 5 Hastings Int. & Comp. L. Rev. 27, 59-72 (1981).

2. In light of the advantages of subject-matter organization in a large inter-mediate appellate court, what objections, if any, are there to adoption of such an organizational approach in large American intermediate appellate courts?

3. Ideas for adopting a subject matter organization of the federal appellate courts in the United States, inspired by the German design, are further dis-cussed in Chapter 14.

D.   German Appellate Judges — Backgrounds, Selection, and Education

David S. Clark, *The Selection and Accountability of Judges in West Germany: Implementation of a Rechtstaat*, 61 So. Cal. L. Rev. 1795, 1802-04, 1832-36 (1988)[26]

Charlemagne, the German-speaking king of the Franks and the Roman emperor, warned his royal delegates: "Judges should adjudicate justly accord-ing to written law, not according to their own inclination (arbitrium)." This

---

[26] Copyright © 1988 by the Southern California Law Review. Reprinted with permission of the Southern Californ Law Review.

inchoate formulation of what would become part of the German idea of *Rechtsstaat* — or state based on the rule of law — rested on a belief that adjudication should be an application of existing rules to established facts. . . .

By the end of the nineteenth century German nationalism, romanticism, and legal science yielded political unification and legal codification . . . The state should be subject to legal norms so that each individual could have his rights, even against the state, judicially protected. It was assumed that only a society with a strong bureaucratic state could adequately nurture law and justice. Donald Kommers sets out a list of propositions that illustrates the state's primacy in German philosophy and its consequences for judicial authority.

That the state is the source of all law; that the locus of all law-making authority within the state is the sovereign legislature; that law is a closed system of logically arranged and internally coherent rules; that law, to be just, must be specific in content yet general in the sense of applying to all persons; that all legal disputes must be resolved by reference to such laws; that courts of law, independent of the legislature, are the proper agencies for interpreting law; that laws be interpreted literally and in strict accordance with the legislator's will; the function of courts, therefore, is to administer the law as written, requiring on the part of the judge a posture of absolute neutrality.

By 1900, after adoption of the five basic national codes, legal positivism prevailed over the competing natural law and historical schools of jurisprudence. Law and politics were considered separate domains. A state based on law (*Recht*) was the avenue to secure whatever individual rights existed against the arbitrary exercise of power (*Macht*) . . . Civil servant and lawyer were not competing roles. Professional civil servants, normally law trained and subject only to weak popular control, defined themselves as guardians of the common good above conflicting and partial interest. They were educated as generalists (*Generalisten*) in a unitary law program (*Einheitsausbildung*) together with future judges and attorneys. Even if laws did not extend the liberty of individuals, a state adopting them would still be a *Rechtsstaat* if it treated all citizens alike and subjected political power to law.

. . .

Political experience following World War I showed that a formal version of the *Rechtsstaat* offered no guarantee of individual freedom or good government. It was clear to most West Germans after the Nazi regime that a theory of natural rights must be injected into the *Rechtsstaat* idea to strengthen its moral content. The Federal Republic's Basic Law today begins by cataloging essential protected human rights, specifying them in detail in the first 19 articles . . .

. . . Most German lawyers believe, by and large, in objective standards, promoted by legal science (*Rechtswissenschaft*), which judges can use to apply to the facts in a case (*Justizsyllogismus*). They are hostile to dissenting opinions by courts, since these would undercut objectivity and certainty.[27] Attorneys, moreover, may violate professional ethics if they cast doubt upon objectivity in the administration of justice.

---

[27] [9] . . . Public dissenting opinions have only recently been permitted, and then only by judges in the Federal Constitutional Court . . .

. . . Article 97, paragraph I of the Basic Law states: "Judges shall be independent and subject only to the law (*Gesetz*)." *Gesetz* under German sources of law theory has a more restricted scope — usually referring to written law such as constitutions, statutes, and regulations — than *Recht*, which can incorporate additional elements and imply ideal law.

. . .

Many people today believe that judges' values play a significant role in their decision making. Accountability, therefore, must be something more than only accountability to law. Political accountability — through impeachment or vigilance by the mass media, for instance — is also required.

. . .

An American viewing the German legal education system is struck by three of its features: (1) it is highly regulated by the federal and state governments; (2) it is primarily oriented toward the training of judges; and (3) except for the period from 1971 to 1985, it has a striking degree of curricular uniformity among the university law schools . . .

German law faculties have traditionally aimed at training standardized jurists (*Einheitsjuristen*), who can meet the qualifications to become a judge (*Befahigung zum Richteramt*). These qualifications are broadly established in the federal German Judges Law, which requires that one who desires to enter judicial service must pass two state examinations. The first test can be taken after seven semesters of law study, although most students wait until they complete five years in the university. Law is an undergraduate curriculum, for which enrollees need a certificate of maturity (. . . *Abitur*) from a secondary school.[28] Once a candidate passes the first state examination, with its written and oral components, he may proceed to the stage of training known as preparatory service (*Vorbereitungsdienst*), which lasts two and a half years. The trainee, a *Referendar*, receives an allowance from the state as a temporary civil servant sufficient to support himself and his dependents. The German Judges Law sets out four mandatory work stations, followed by a list of elective stations from which a *Referendar* may select. Most trainees spend between three and nine months in each of the obligatory stations — a civil court, a criminal court or public prosecutor's office, an administrative agency, and an attorney's office — leaving six months for one elective experience that may be in one of these four mandatory stations or in another court. Under this pattern it is likely that a *Referendar* will spend about half his time in a judicial environment. He must also attend courses taught by judges and civil servants aimed toward the analysis of complex practical cases. After completing the preparatory service a *Referendar* is ready to take the written and oral parts of the second state examination, which is graded mainly by judges and senior civil servants who are concerned primarily about the application of theory to practice.

---

[28] [11] . . . Germans accurately view their 13 years of secondary education leading to an Abitur as the equivalent of two years of American university training, so that characterizing legal education in German as "undergraduate" is somewhat misleading.

NOTES

1. The first and second state examinations, two and one half years apart, are administered at least annually by each *Land* Ministry of Justice. Each examination has both a written and an oral part. The second state examination is roughly equivalent to a state bar examination in the United States in that, if successfully passed, it qualifies one to enter all branches of the legal profession. As might be expected, the number of persons taking the examination varies considerably with the population of the *Land*. In 2002, 2,987 took the examination in Nordhein-Westfalen, but only 84 in Bremen. The rate of passage varied from a low of 70% in Sachsen-Anhalt to a high of 92% in RheinLand-Pfalz. The relatively high passage rates are explained by the weeding out process that has gone before. The failure rate on the first State Examination is considerably higher, and there is further shrinking of applicants during the two and a half year period of practical training as a *Referendar*. This German system of legal education and training has been described as one "of the most rigorous in the world." PETER L. MURRAY & ROLF STUERNER, GERMAN CIVIL JUSTICE 89 (2004). For a description of the career opportunities available to those who pass the second state examination, *see* Aldabert E. Griess, *Legal Education in the Federal Republic of Germany,* 14 J. SOC. PUB. TEACHERS OF L.166 (1978).

2. In West Germany in 1990, just prior to reunification, judges comprised 14% of the legal profession. *See* Erhard Blankenburg, *Patterns of Legal Culture: The Netherlands Compared to Neighboring Germany,* 46 AM. J. COMP. L. 1, 32-33 (1998). In the United States the judiciary represents about 4% of the lawyer population. Why do you think that Germany has so many more judges in relation to lawyer population than the United States?

Daniel J. Meador, *German Appellate Judges: Career Patterns and American-English Comparisons,* 67 JUDICATURE 16, 19, 21-26 (1983)[29]

Ministries of Justice

The key government agencies administering the German court systems and selecting and assigning judges are the ministries of justice. The Federal Ministry of Justice, responsible for the federal courts, is located at [Berlin since reunification] and is one of the major ministries in the national government. Additionally, each *Land* has its own ministry of justice; there are [16] in all.

Freed of the constraints of the doctrine of separation of powers, each ministry of justice spans what Americans would think of as the executive, the legislative, and the judicial branches of government. Each minister of justice is typically a member of the legislative body of his *Land*. The federal minister of justice is a member of the *Bundestag*, the lower house of the federal parliament. [The ministers of justice, both federal and state, are no longer necessarily

---

[29] Copyright © 1983 by Judicature. Reprinted with permission.

members of the legislative body.] All ministers of justice are appointed by the heads of their respective governments. Thus, the holder of this office is usually a member of both the legislative body and the executive cabinet; he also has a sizeable responsibility for the administrative caretaking and manning of the courts.

The major responsibilities of each ministry of justice in relation to the judicial system include the development of the annual budget for the entire judiciary, the development of legislation to remedy problems in the justice system, and the selection and assignment of judges. There is a functional efficiency in the management of the courts and their personnel that cannot be equaled in any jurisdiction in the United States, primarily because of the American emphasis on separation of powers . . .

Each *Land* ministry of justice plays a much larger role in the courts than does the federal ministry. The initial selection of judges and their subsequent career management is entirely within the province of the *Land* ministries. Each of these ministries has responsibility for the appellate courts (OLGs) and the two levels of trial courts within the *Land*, although routine, day-to-day administration within the *Land* courts is vested in the OLG for the trial courts within its territory.

      . . .

The Federal Ministry of Justice, insofar as judges are concerned, is limited to selecting judges for the BGH, for the "Supreme Courts" in the other four jurisdictions, and for the few other federal courts. They constitute only a small fraction of the judges in the country. This work is handled through an office whose title is loosely translated as the division for the administration of justice. That office also sponsors research on the problems of the courts and the justice system, and is responsible for developing new legislation concerning procedure and jurisdiction of the entire court system . . .

The Federal Ministry does not, however, administer examinations, admit lawyers to practice, or initially select judges and prosecutors, since those functions are the responsibility of the *Land* ministries of justice.

The German justice system . . . is decentralized in the selection of judges for the two levels of trial courts and the regional appellate courts and in these courts' administration and financing. It is centralized in control over the structure, jurisdiction, and procedure of all courts . . .

Initial Selection

The judges who sit on the regional appellate courts (OLGs) and on the Federal Supreme Court (BGH) were initially selected for the judiciary by the [16] *Land* ministries of justice. After acceptance by the ministry into this branch of the public service they were promoted through various judicial positions (and sometimes positions in prosecutors' offices and in the ministry of justice) to seats on the intermediate appellate courts. These intermediate appellate judges form the pool from which the BGH judges are selected. Thus, the Federal Ministry of Justice draws from a group initially selected and thereafter screened through the *Land* ministry's promotion process.

Table 1. Career Patterns of German Appellate Judges

Appellate court (Oberlandesgericht)	Both trial courts (Amtsgericht & Landericht)	One Trial Court only (Amtsgericht or Landericht)	Prosecutor's Office	Ministry of Justice[b]
Berlin[c]	100%	0%	33%	25%
Bremen	79	21	45	15
Dusseldorf	77	23	0	23
Frankfurt	75	25	6	0
Munich	39	61	100	6

[b] This category includes both the Land and the Federal Ministries of Justice.

[c] For historical reasons the name Kammergericht is retained for this court. However, it is identical in jurisdiction and function to an Oberlandesgericht

The process of initial selection can be explained by examining the system used in the Bavarian Ministry of Justice. The selection responsibility is placed in the personnel department of the ministry, headed by a senior official; this official is a lawyer who typically has served as a judge and a prosecutor. His department has responsibility not only for selecting those who will be judges, prosecutors, and ministry officials, but also for certifying those who will be authorized to practice law. It also administers the second state examination.

In Bavaria, this examination is administered twice annually. . . . Passage of the second state examination is the typical point of career decision; few who enter the private practice of law or the commercial world later come back into public service or vice-versa.

Those who wish to pursue a career as a judge apply to the ministry of justice . . . . After receipt of the application, an interview is usually held with one of the lower officials in the ministry's personnel department. If that interview does not discourage or eliminate the applicant, additional information is assembled. Perhaps the most important factor is the grade made on the second state examination, but other factors, including character evidence, are considered. The complete file is reviewed and evaluated by the head of the personnel department. If he recommends acceptance, that recommendation is forwarded with the entire file to the minister of justice, who makes the final decision.

. . . . It has been common in recent years for the ministry to receive some 200 applications annually but to

accept only 100 . . . In a small Land, such as Bremen, only three or four persons may be selected each year . . .

The letter of appointment from the minister of justice to the successful applicant carries with it an initial assignment. In Bavaria efforts are made to place most new appointees in a prosecutor's office. A few are given initial assignments in the ministry of justice. In Berlin, by contrast, appointees typically are assigned initially to the Landericht; that trial court sits in panels of three, so the beginner gains judicial experience under the tutelage of two seasoned judges. The initial appointment is for a probationary period of three years. If the individual performs satisfactorily, he acquires tenure until the mandatory retirement age fixed by statute.

Unlike some of the other *Laender*, Bavaria has a long-established practice of rotating persons through assignments as judges on the courts, attorneys in prosecutors' offices, and legal officers in the ministry of justice. The typical pattern is for a person to spend from one to three years in one of these positions and then to move to another. No one, however, is ever ordered to move; any move is only by application of the individual. The principle of independence of the judiciary, guaranteed in the Federal Constitution, prohibits involuntary change of office or physical relocation.

Promotion

Rotation is brought about by persons applying to fill vacancies called "promotional" positions . . . For example, a judge on the lowest court — the *Amtsgericht* — might apply to fill a vacancy on the next higher court — the *Landericht* — and a judge on the latter court might apply to fill a vacancy on the regional appellate court — the *Oberlandesgericht*. Other promotional positions include those of presiding judges of divisions in the various courts, heads of sections within prosecutors' offices, and directors or assistant directors of various departments within the ministry of justice. When a vacancy occurs in any of these positions it is announced through a newsletter sent to all persons in the service throughout the *Land*.

Following announcement of the vacancy, interested persons file applications with their immediate superiors. For example, a judge applying for a promotional position would file his application with the presiding judge of his court; a lawyer in the prosecutor's office would file his application initially with the head of his office. The superior officer reviews the application and appends his evaluation. All applications then go to the president of the regional appellate court (OLG) who evaluates them and, without ranking them, makes a list of the best three. In some *Laender*, the president of the OLG will recommend only one applicant for appointment.

The president of the court then transmits all applications, with his appraisals, to the ministry of justice. The applications are processed through the ministry's personnel department. That department maintains a permanent file on every person accepted into the service, which includes all information gathered at the time of the initial application plus a report on the individual's performance made every four years thereafter . . . After reviewing all of this information, the head of the personnel department forwards to the minister of justice his recommendation for someone to fill the vacancy.

The minister of justice then makes his decision, submitting it to the *Praesidialrat*. This administrative body is composed of judges on the regional appellate court elected by all the judges of the court. The *Praesidialrat* may concur in the minister's recommendation, and, in that event, the appointment is made by the minister. If the *Praesidialrat* disagrees with the minister's recommendation, negotiations are conducted and usually result in an agreement upon the appointment. Theoretically, the minister could ultimately make a decision contrary to the recommendation of the *Praesidialrat*, but this has not occurred in Bavaria recently.

All appellate judges sitting on the OLGs have been selected through this kind of process. Thus, in Bavaria, as in other *Laender*, there is a kind of career management system under which the ministry of justice continually evaluates, assigns, and promotes persons in the judicial service. In every *Land* the ministry of justice has a similar responsibility for assigning and promoting persons in prosecutorial work and in the ministry itself. Since the ministry of justice is responsible for all three of these branches of the public legal service, it can interchange personnel. In Bavaria and in some but not all of the other *Laender*, such interchange is part of normal career patterns. . . . In those *Laender* where there is less interchange a person can spend an entire career as a judge, possibly moving up through the court levels, or he can spend an entire career in prosecution offices, again with advancement to higher levels.

Other Career Paths

Outside of the *Land* legal systems, there are two types of legal work that may be pursued in the course of a career leading to the appellate bench. One is work as a staff attorney on the BGH in Karlsruhe . . . After that the person returns to the *Land* system, almost always as a judge on the regional appellate court (OLG). Holding one of these positions in the BGH is a professional distinction; only a small percentage of all appellate judges have had such experience.

The other kind of work outside the *Land* is in the Federal Ministry of Justice in [Berlin]. From time to time that Ministry calls upon the *Land* ministries to send it people to work on its professional staff, who come, in effect, on leaves of absence. Some stay for two or three years and return to the *Land*, often as judges on the OLG. Others remain in the Federal Ministry and make that their career. Only a small number of appellate judges have had experience in the Federal Ministry.

Profiles of Appellate Judges

To ascertain the backgrounds of the appellate judges serving on the OLGs and to identify more clearly their career paths, a random sampling was taken of judges on several of these courts. The sampled courts are located in different *Laender* in different parts of the country. Questionnaires were sent to the randomly-selected judges; a composite of their responses appears in Table 1.

Table 1 discloses some striking similarities and differences in the backgrounds of the judges who sit on these five regional appellate courts. Perhaps the most significant similarity is that every judge had previous experience on at least one trial court. Indeed, on all of these appellate courts except that in Munich, a large majority of the judges had sat on both trial courts ranging from 75 per cent in Frankfurt to 100 per cent in Berlin.

A striking dissimilarity among these courts is the extent to which their judges have had experience in prosecutors' offices. For example, while all the judges in Munich have had prosecutorial experience, no judge in Dusseldorf has had such experience. The percentages in other courts vary considerably.

The backgrounds of the Munich judges tend to be more varied than those in the other courts . . . Prior judicial experience has dominated the careers of the appellate judges to a lesser extent than in the other four courts. While all of the Munich judges have had prior judicial experience (with service on at least one trial court), relatively few have served on both of the trial courts. Some have served in the ministry of justice, and all have worked for a prosecutor's office . . .

Perhaps the least diversified career pattern is found in Frankfurt, where three-fourths of the judges have served on both trial courts, only six per cent have served in prosecutors' offices, and none has worked in the ministry of justice. Dusseldorf also is much less diverse than Munich; there, over three-fourths of the judges have served on both trial courts and none have served in prosecutors' offices, although one quarter has served in the ministry of justice.

In 1982 the average age of the judges on these five appellate courts was 52. Their average age at the time of their appointment to the appellate court was 39.4.

On some of the [24] regional appellate courts law professors from nearby university law faculties serve as part-time judges. A law professor, for example, might participate in approximately ten per cent of the number of cases handled by a full-time judge. Such participation is hardly surprising in view of the historic influence of German law faculties on the courts and the development of legal doctrine.

Judges on the Court of Last Resort

The judges on the *Bundesgerichtshof* (BGH) are drawn in large part from the judges who sit on the [24] regional appellate courts — the approximately [1,847] judges who have come to their positions in the *Land* appellate courts through the career patterns outlined above. Since the BGH is a federal court, its judge selection is governed entirely by federal law and is in the hands of the Federal Ministry of Justice.

Selection is carried out through a committee of [32], chaired by the Federal Minister of Justice. The committee (*Richterwahlausschuss*) consists of the [16] *Land* ministers of justice and [16] persons elected by the *Bundestag*, the lower house of the federal parliament. The latter need not be members of the *Bundestag,* although they usually are. In its composition this committee blends the national political interests, as represented in the *Bundestag*, with regional and professional interests represented by the *Land* ministers of justice.

When a BGH vacancy is to be filled, the committee develops a list of proposed appointees. The list usually includes more than one name for each vacancy . . . There appears to be a tendency for the committee members designated by the Bundestag to suggest persons with whom they are acquainted through political activities; the *Land* ministers tend to suggest persons from the traditionally established judicial ranks. Most appointees come from among those persons suggested by the *Land* ministers.

After the committee has assembled its list of proposed appointees for the vacancies, the Federal Minister of Justice forwards the list to the *Praesidialrat* of the BGH. The *Praesidialrat* is composed of seven judges on the BGH — the president and six other judges in active service. That body reviews and evaluates the list of suggested nominees. The evaluations are returned to the committee which then proposes a final list of one person for each vacancy and presents the list to the Federal Minister of Justice. If he agrees with the list, the appointments are made. If the Minister does not concur with the committee's choices, the matter is worked out through discussions within the committee to arrive at a name on which the committee and the Minister can agree.

In this work, the Federal Minister of Justice is assisted by the Division for the Administration of Justice [now called *Justizverwaltung*], one of the major offices within the Ministry . . . Almost every lawyer in this Division has served at some point as a judge on one of the *Land* trial courts. In other words, they are persons who have been brought into the judicial service through the screening and selection process described above and thus share the common background of all German judges.

To ascertain the career patterns among the 110 judges who sit on the BGH [in 1981], a questionnaire was submitted to a random sample.

The responses to the questionnaire show the following:

- 85 per cent had served as appellate judges on an OLG prior to their appointment to the BGH;

- 100 per cent had served on a *Landericht*, the higher trial court;

- 36 per cent had served on both trial courts in addition to having served on an appellate court.

In addition to this substantial judicial experience, there is a variety of professional experience among the BGH judges. Table 2 shows the percentage of the sampled judges with such non-judicial experience.

The average age of the BGH judges in 1981 was 59. Their average age at the time of appointment to that court was 46.

Table 2. Non-judicial experience of BGH judges (in percentages)

Prosecutor's office	36
Land Ministry of Justice	21
Federal Ministry of Justice	7
Staff attorney in BGH	36

Comparative Observations

Judges on the appellate courts in the Federal Republic of Germany differ from appellate judges in the United States, as well as in England, most significantly in the stage of professional career at which they enter the judicial service. German judges, like judges in other European civil law countries, enter the service near the beginning of their professional careers — typically upon completion of the two-year period of practical training following several years of university study. Contrary to widespread American belief, however, this does not mean that a German judge has no experience outside the judiciary; as pointed out above, many German appellate judges have served as prosecuting attorneys and ministry officials. What they do lack is substantial experience as private practitioners. In the two leading common law nations, England and the United States, persons do not usually enter the judiciary until after lengthy experience at the bar or in other legal work outside the public service.

That difference is well known. What is not so well understood is that there are similarities between the German and English systems for choosing appellate judges that differentiate both from American selection procedures. The most striking similarity is the system of career management through an official agency — a well-organized and directed process through which a person is made a judge at the trial level and, based on performance there, is eventually promoted to the appellate bench.

In Germany this career management is handled by the various *Land* ministries of justice. In England the process is managed through the Lord Chancellor's office . . . In no American Jurisdiction — state or federal — is there a permanent office that continually scrutinizes lawyers or judges with an eye toward filling judicial vacancies and promoting judges from one court to another.

NOTES

1. Another difference in the backgrounds of German appellate judges and those in the United States is that many of the latter come to the bench after having held elective office, often as members of the legislature. What effect might this difference have on the judges' decision making? Would it be fair to say that given the rigors of the two state examinations and the subsequent evaluation and promotion there is a higher degree of "professionalism" among the German judges compared with their American counterparts? What is the significance of this, combined with the lack of elective experience, for the work of German appellate courts?

2. Judicial independence is a matter of degree; no judges are absolutely independent of all external control. Compare the relative independence of appellate judges in the United States, England, and Germany. In which of these three countries are the judges most independent? Which American judges are you considering?

3. In the United States would it be possible or desirable in the state and federal governments to establish an office like that of the Lord Chancellor in England and a Ministry of Justice in Germany? In considering your answer, imagine some of the possible duties of this office: (a) to maintain files, continually updated, on prospective judicial nominees so that, when a vacancy occurs, prospects already will have been identified and screened; (b) to obtain the views of sitting judges concerning the needs of the courts and the qualifications of prospective new judicial nominees to fill vacancies or for promotion to a higher court; and (c) to conduct continuing research on the functioning of the courts and to propose legislation to cure problems thus identified.

4. Compare the composition of the 32-member committee that nominates judges for the BGH with the composition of the typical judicial nominating commission in American states, as described in Chapter 11. What are the key differences?

5. In theory, case law in a common law country, under the doctrine of *stare decisis*, plays a stronger role in adjudication than it does in a civil law country. In Germany, it is said that appellate court decisions are not "formally binding." But in practice, German courts seem to deal with precedent much the way common law courts do. *See* Robert Alexy & Ralf Dreier, *Precedent in the Federal Republic of Germany* in INTERPRETING PRECEDENTS — A COMPARATIVE STUDY 17-64 (D. Neil MacCormick & Robert S. Summers eds.1997); KARL N. LLEWELLYN, THE CASE LAW SYSTEM IN AMERICA 12-13, 45-46, 48-50 (1989). Does the career promotional system for advancing judges to higher courts, administered by the OLG and the ministry of justice, likely have any effect on the way in which trial judges treat decisions of the OLG?

6. Continuing judicial education. The German Academy for Judges (*Deutscherichterakademie*), founded in 1973, is the institution that provides educational programs for all judges in Germany. It is the sole provider of such professional instruction. Before reunification the Academy's lone site was in Trier. After reunification a second site was established in Wustrau.

At Trier, the Academy's home consists of three modern buildings. One building includes the administrative offices, lecture and seminar rooms, lounges and reading rooms, and a library of several thousand volumes. The other two buildings include 88 bedrooms with baths, a large dining room, and various recreational rooms. At Wustrau the Academy is housed in an old castle and several other buildings. The facilities are similar to those at Trier. At both locations approximately 80 judges can be accommodated at one time. Two courses are offered simultaneously, with 40 judges in each.

Both sites are governed by one body consisting of the ministers of justice of the 16 states, chaired by the Federal Minister of Justice. One-half of the Academy's funding is provided by the states (prorated according to the size of the state); the other half comes from the federal government. The operations and functioning of the Academy are in the hands of full-time administrators at each location.

The courses to be offered are determined by a group composed of a representative from each of the state Justice Ministries. They meet twice annually to fix the program of instruction for the ensuing year. All courses for an entire calendar year are scheduled in advance, and a description of each course with its dates is included in a printed brochure mailed to all judges throughout Germany. Judges from both trial and appellate levels and from all five jurisdictions are eligible to attend. Prosecutors also attend some courses.

The courses cover a wide range of fields. They include traditional substantive and procedural subjects as well as interdisciplinary and newly emerging topics. Several instructors teach in each course; in some two-week courses as many as sixteen instructors are involved. The instructors include judges, prosecutors, practicing lawyers, law professors, and professionals from other disciplines. Emphasis is placed on group discussion and interaction among participants.

Pursuit of a course at the Academy is optional with each judge. A judge must apply for a course he or she desires to attend. A certain number of places in each course is designated for each state. If the demand for places in a particular course exceeds a state's quota, a selection is made by the president of the state's OLG, possibly in conjunction with the Minister of Justice. All expenses are covered. It is estimated that approximately 50 to 70 percent of all German judges have attended courses at the Academy.

E. The Federal Constitutional Court (FCC)

The Federal Constitutional Court is an independent constitutional organ separate from the five jurisdictions into which the German judiciary is organized. Unlike the U.S. Supreme Court and American state supreme courts, it is not at the apex of a judicial hierarchy. It is not a body designed to entertain appeals from judgments rendered by lower courts and to decide those cases on their merits. Although it is not an appellate court in the usual sense, the following description is included here because some of the court's work does involve review of constitutional questions that arise in litigation in one of the German courts.

The FCC is located in Karlsruhe, housed in a modern building built especially for it. Because the Federal Supreme Court for the ordinary jurisdiction (BGH) is also located in Karlsruhe, that city is regarded as the center of the German judiciary.

Hans G. Rupp, *The Federal Constitutional Court and the Constitution of the Federal Republic of Germany,* 16 St. Louis U. L. J. 359, 359-65 (1972)[30]

The Federal Constitutional Court (*Bundesverfassungsgericht*) . . . has the last word on the construction of the Federal Constitution of 1949 which is called "*Grundgesetz*" (Basic Law). It was created by this Constitution, beginning its first term in September 1951. Previously, similar courts for the adjudication of constitutional issues had been established only in Austria (1920) and in Italy (1946). It is not an appellate court, at least not in the strict sense . . .

. . . The bulk of all cases ends [in one of the five federal supreme courts] unless a constitutional question is involved which, by some procedural avenue, may be brought before the Federal Constitutional Court for ultimate adjudication.

. . .

The Federal Constitutional Court is equal in rank to the legislative and executive branches of the federal government and is independent of them. Due

---

[30] Reprinted with permission of the Saint Louis University Law Journal. Copyright © 1972 St. Louis University School of Law, St. Louis, Missouri.

to the wide scope of its jurisdiction it is organized into two separate panels (Senates), each consisting of eight judges. The judges, who must be at least forty years of age, have to qualify for admission to the bar and judicial office and are not allowed to engage in any other professional activities except the teaching of law at a German university. They are elected by the federal legislative bodies (*Bundestag* and *Bundesrat*), each body electing one half. They are elected for a single term of twelve years; re-election is not permitted. Each Judge is elected to one panel for his whole term . . . The judges must retire at sixty-eight which leads to the consequence that, as a rule, nobody should be elected who is over fifty-six years of age. A further requirement is that three judges in each panel have to be chosen from among the judges of the five federal courts.

. . .

Within the wide spectra of the jurisdiction of the Court there are several important procedural avenues to establish jurisdiction. The constitutional complaint (*Verfassungsbeschwerde*) . . . is a remedy accorded to the individual to bring his grievances before the Court. Any person (or private corporation, insofar as the Bill of Rights is applicable to it) may petition the court to declare a federal or state statute void, to set aside an executive or administrative act or to reverse the decision of any lower — federal or state — court on the ground that it violated a right guaranteed to him in the Bill of Rights of the Constitution. Before filing the complaint, however, the complainant must have exhausted other available judicial remedies.

A complaint directed immediately against a statutory provision is admissible (within one year after enactment) only if the complainant can establish that he, himself, is presently and directly affected by the provision. . . .

A basic right of the individual may be violated by a decision of a federal or state court in any of the following three ways: 1) The decision rests upon a statutory provision which itself impairs a basic right of the individual concerned . . . 2) The decision rests upon an unconstitutional construction and application of a statute which by itself is constitutional. 3) The applicable statute is constitutional, its interpretation and application by the court is faultless, but the proceedings were not consistent with due process because there was no fair hearing for the party . . .

Since the Federal Constitutional Court is not an appellate court, but a tribunal established solely for the adjudication of constitutional issues, the review on a constitutional complaint of decisions of other courts is limited to those issues. In other words, even if the challenged decision of the lower court has been wrong on the merits, the Federal Constitutional Court may not touch it unless the lower court has erred on a specific constitutional question . . .

. . .

From its inception in 1951 to the end of 1971, 25,181 applications have been filed with the Constitutional Court. Among those were 23,399 constitutional complaints, of which only 263 were successful. The Court would have amassed a heavy backlog if it had had to dispose of each of those complaints upon a hearing before a full bench. To avoid disaster, a special proceeding was set up by statute, similar to the certiorari proceedings of the United States Supreme Court. All constitutional complaints are first considered by a committee of three judges — each senate setting up several committees. If the three judges unanimously hold that the complaint on its merits will not meet with success, they rule that it will not be taken up for further consideration by the full bench. If they are not unanimous on this point, the case goes to the full bench which will take it up for consideration and adjudication on its merits if at least two judges are of the opinion that a decision by the full bench will serve to clarify a constitutional issue or that denial of a ruling would be gravely detrimental to the complainant. Thus, here a "rule of two" obtains instead of the "rule of four" which governs certiorari in the United State Supreme Court.

All federal and state courts exercise the right of judicial review with one exception: If such a court holds an applicable statute to be unconstitutional, it cannot simply disregard it; but it must stop the proceedings and refer the question of constitutionality to the Constitutional Court (*konkrete Normenkontrolle*). Contrary to American practice, it is not necessary that the constitutional question be raised by one of the parties to the proceeding, nor is it required that the question be put in issue in the court of first instance.

The Federal Constitutional Court gets the whole record but, because it is not an appellate court, decides only whether the statute in question is constitutional or not . . . . After the decision of the Constitutional Court — which is final and binding on all courts and government agencies — has been handed down, the lower court which had referred the question resumes the proceedings and renders judgment consonant with the Constitutional Court's decision. The lower court's judgment then, of course, may be appealed to the proper higher court, but never on a constitutional ground because the question of whether the statute is constitutional or not has now been settled once and for all by the Constitutional Court. Since 1951 the Constitutional Court has disposed of 1,328 such referral cases. They represent the second largest group of cases brought before the Court.

The Constitutional Court also decides in case of differences of opinion or doubts on the formal and material compatibility of federal law or state law with the Constitution or on the compatibility of state law with other federal law, at the request of the federal government, of a state government or of one third of the members of Bundestag (*abstrakte Normenkontrolle*).

Although this form of judicial review will sound entirely unfamiliar to the American jurist and far afield from the "case" and "controversy" type, it is a very useful procedural avenue to get the validity of a statute tested early without having to wait until the statute is challenged incidentally in the course of a civil, criminal or administrative proceeding or by constitutional complaint. Thus, it always provides a short cut to an ultimate decision by the Federal Constitutional Court. Since 1951, only fifty-one cases of this type have been adjudicated by the Court . . .

The Federal Constitutional Court also has power to decide questions relating to the construction of the Constitution in the event of disputes concerning the extent of the powers and duties of a supreme federal organ. Supreme federal organs equal to the Federal Constitutional Court are the *Bundestag,*

Bundesrat, Bundesregierung and *Budespräsident*. In addition, political parties have standing to challenge election statutes under this provision. Such cases were never numerous: since 1951, there have been only 34 altogether. The same holds true of disputes between the Federal Government and the states, which in a federal state may originate from the division of powers between them under the Constitution. Both may bring suit in the Constitutional Court; however, there have been only thirteen cases of this type before the Court since 1951.

Last, but not least, the Constitutional Court, on application by the Federal Government, the *Bundestag* or the *Bundesrat*, has jurisdiction to outlaw political parties which seek to impair or to abolish the free democratic basic order or to endanger the existence of the Federal Republic. This jurisdiction has been exercised only twice, in 1953 and 1956 when the Court outlawed a neo-rightist party and the Communist party.

. . .

Judges have the right to announce dissenting and concurring opinions, and the division of the Court, if any, may be disclosed. If one panel on a point of law wants to depart from a decision of the other panel, the dispute has to be resolved by all sixteen judges sitting en banc (*Plenarentscheidung*).

. . . As a matter of practice, only very few cases are set for oral argument; the large majority are decided solely on the briefs. Representation in general is by counsel who are admitted to any German bar, for there is no special Federal Constitutional Court bar. Federal and state governments have the privilege to be represented by their civil servants provided they have legal training. University law professors may also represent parties before the Court. The Court may also issue temporary injunctions.

Since 1951, [up until 1971] the Court has declared void — in toto or in part — 111 federal and 58 state statutes.

David S. Clark, *The Selection and Accountability of Judges in West Germany: Implementation of a Rechtsstaat*, 61 So. Cal. L. Rev. 1795, 1826-29 (1988)[31]

Selection to the Federal Constitutional Court

The Federal Constitutional Court . . . only adjudicates issues raised under the national Basic Law. Since these legal issues tend to encompass the most visible and controversial political topics of the time, the selection process for constitutional court judges is the most overtly political of all German judicial selection processes.

The Court today has sixteen judges who sit in two chambers (Senate) that have become almost two separate courts (*Zwillingsgericht*). Judges are

---

[31] Copyright © 1988 by The Southern California Law Review. Reprinted with Permission.

specifically selected to either the first senate or the second senate. Jurisdiction between these chambers is mutually exclusive, and each senate controls its own administration. The Court's president is the presiding officer of the first senate, while the Court's vice president presides over the second senate. This twin senate structure was, in part, a compromise between those who envisioned the Court in traditional legalistic terms and those who viewed it in wider political terms. An uneasy tension between law and politics is evident in many of the Court's features, including the judicial selection process.

To qualify for a seat on the Court, a jurist must meet the requirements for judicial office common to all judges . . . In each of the eight-member senates, three of the judges must be appointed directly from a position on one of the federal high courts. The remaining five members may also come from federal judgeships or be *Volljuristen* in other careers. Donald Kommers, in his excellent study on the Federal Constitutional Court,[32] found that through 1972 the immediate prior occupation of the judges appointed broke down as follows: judge (41 percent); civil servant (28 percent); legislator (17 percent); law professor (11 percent); and attorney (2 percent). The median age of appointees was 53 . . .

The Basic Law provides that half the Court's members shall be selected by the *Bundestag* and half by the Federal Legislative Council (*Bundesrat*). Under implementing legislation the *Bundestag* selects its judges (four to each senate) indirectly via a 12-person committee of selectors (*Wahlmaennerausschuss*), in which political parties are represented according to their strength in the *Bundestag*. The *Bundesrat* votes as a whole for its judges, usually upon recommendations by an ad hoc commission (*Kommission*). Each body alternates, however, in selecting the president and vice president of the Court. A two-thirds majority is needed to select, which in effect requires the two major political parties to agree on a candidate. Appointment comes from the federal president, who must confirm the selecting body's nominee.

The dominant role played by the legislature in the selection of Constitutional Court judges is justified on two grounds. First, it bestows democratic legitimacy on the selection process and on the judges themselves, and second, the best qualified jurists for constitutional adjudication are chosen. In fact, political parties have exerted the decisive influence in recruitment of judges, who have been widely representative of parliamentary interests. In addition, Constitutional Court judges in general represent a wider variety of life experiences than other German judges, especially those from the legislative and executive branches of state and federal government. Professional competence in public law is further demonstrated by scholarly publications, which are usually expected, even from candidates serving in the legislature. The mass media, which pay significant attention to these judicial appointments, help to guarantee that the process is politically accountable to major interests in German society. However, this does not mean that narrow interest group pressures are usually effective, since they are disfavored in German

---

[32] Donald A. Kommers, *Judicial Politics in West Germany: A Study of the Federal Constitutional Court* (Vol.V. Sage Series on Politics and the Legal Order, Joel B. Grossman, Series Ed. 1976.)

legal culture when they appear to affect judges or the functioning of courts. John Bell, in examining this process, suggests that establishing the power of nomination in a small committee representing political interests strikes a good balance between political considerations and the need for legal expertise. The late Wilhelm Geck also found that broad support exists for the selection mechanism itself, even though some critics believe that the two major parties too fully dominate the process of choosing constitutional judges.

NOTES

1. For comparative discussions, *see* Karl Heinz Millgramm, *Comparative Law: The Federal Constitutional Court of Germany and the Supreme Court of the United States*, YEARBOOK OF THE SUPREME COURT HISTORICAL SOCIETY 146 (1985); Danielle E. Finck, *Judicial Review: The U. S. Supreme Court versus the German Constitutional Court*, 20 B.C. INT'L. & COMP. L. REV. 123 (1997).

2. From 1951 to 2003 the FCC held void under the Basic Law, either in whole or in part, a total of 393 federal statutes or regulations and 157 *Land* laws. By comparison, from 1953 to 2003 the U.S. Supreme Court held unconstitutional 84 federal statutes and 430 state statutes. Why the difference?[33]

3. As seen in Chapter 6, Section C, some intermediate appellate courts in the United States have discretion to certify to the Supreme Court either an entire case or a specified issue in a case. In Germany, reference of a constitutional law question to the FCC is mandatory. Would it be desirable in American practice to require an IAC to certify a constitutional law question to the court of last resort? What are the arguments against such a requirement?

4. Note that the election of a judge to the FCC by the *Bundestag* requires a two-thirds vote of that body, thus forcing the two major political parties to agree on a candidate. Would a similar requirement in the U. S. Senate for the confirmation of federal judges likewise force the two political parties to agree on a nominee, thus overcoming the partisan impasse that has afflicted the confirmation process in recent years? In practical effect, does not such a requirement already exist in the Senate as a result of its rule requiring a vote of 60 senators to shut off debate?

5. The FCC functions in the borderland between law and politics. The absence of a "case or controversy" requirement like that in Article III of the U.S. Constitution and of a "political question" doctrine leaves the FCC free to decide abstract questions and disputes that are essentially political. Cases arising out of the 1990 reunification have produced FCC opinions that read more like political policy papers than American-style judicial opinions. Such cases have involved challenges to the all-Germany election law, the new abortion law, the plan for reorganizing the East German civil service, and the disposition of land appropriated by the Soviet Union. In those cases the Court has been said to be performing a "mediating" role, ameliorating the East-West tensions. PETER E. QUINT, THE IMPERFECT UNION: CONSTITUTIONAL STRUCTURES OF

---

[33] The FCC figures are from one of the Court's websites: www.bundesverfassungsgericht. de/texte/deutsch/organisation/stastik_2003/index.html. The U.S. Supreme Court figures are from David M. O'Brien, STORM CENTER — THE SUPREME COURT IN AMERICAN POLITICS 30 (6th ed. 2003).

GERMAN UNIFICATION 68-70, 137-39, 159-63, 169-71 (1997). The FCC has even undertaken, in the post-unification setting, to spell out whether and under what circumstances German armed forces can be deployed beyond the borders of NATO countries. *Id*. at 294-96.

6. Other politically tinged FCC opinions that have been especially controversial concern the relationship between German law and the law of the European Union and the authority of its supreme judicial organ, the European Court of Justice, controversies vaguely reminiscent of those over the allocation of state and federal authority in the early decades of the United States. THE EUROPEAN COURT AND NATIONAL COURTS: DOCTRINE AND JURISPRUDENCE — LEGAL CHANGE IN ITS SOCIAL CONTEXT 77-131 (Anne-Marie Slaughter, Alec Stone Sweet, J.H.H. Weiler eds. 1998). The European Court of Justice and the European Court of Human Rights are described in the next section.

7. Would American government be improved by amending Art. III of the Constitution to give the U.S. Supreme Court the broader authority exercised by the FCC?

III. THE EUROPEAN OVERLAY

The treaty creating the European Union and the adoption of the European Convention on Human Rights in the second half of the 20th century brought the courts of the United Kingdom and the Federal Republic of Germany, along with those of many other European countries, under an overarching legal order. Those international agreements resulted in the establishment of the European Court of Justice and the European Court of Human Rights. Although neither is an appellate court in the usual sense, much of the work of each is devoted to deciding issues involved in litigation in the courts of the European nations. Although neither court has power directly to reverse a judgment of a national court, national courts are obligated by treaty to respect the decisions of those courts. The courts of England, Germany, and the other European countries increasingly must take into account the considerable bodies of law administered by those European courts and may even have their decisions controlled by those courts. For that reason, a brief sketch of each is included here.

A. The European Court of Justice (ECJ)

Composition and Organization. The ECJ exists by virtue of treaties entered into by 25 European countries. Its composition, organization, and jurisdiction are fixed by those treaties. It is the supreme court of the European Union, its role being to ensure uniform application and interpretation of European Community law among all the member states. The court is located in Luxembourg. French is the official language of the court, but its opinions and judgments are translated into the languages of all member states.

The court consists of 25 judges, one from each member state, designated by that state and agreed to by all member states. The judges are appointed to six-year terms, subject to renewal. To be appointed, persons must either be distinguished legal academicians or possess the qualifications for appointment to the highest court of their country.

The court also consists of eight advocates general, an office unknown in the Anglo-American legal world. They are appointed to six year renewable terms. The title is misleading in that those officers do not "advocate" in the usual sense but rather act as legal advisors to the court. In each case, an advocate general prepares an opinion analyzing the issues and recommending a disposition. Advocates general must possess the same qualifications as the judges.

The court is organized into "chambers," *i.e.*, panels, consisting variously of three judges or five judges, in addition to a Grand Chamber of 13 judges. Each judge employs three or four legal assistants, analogous to law clerks in American appellate courts, although they are mature lawyers. The advocates general have similar assistance.

Jurisdiction and Procedure. A significant part of the ECJ's work involves deciding issues referred to it by courts in the member states. When a question of the application or interpretation of a provision in European Community law — a provision in a treaty, directive, or regulation — is involved in a case pending in a national court other than a court of last resort, that court may, in its discretion, refer the question to the ECJ. National courts of last resort *must* request such rulings if a ruling on the point has not already been obtained at the request of a lower court. Proceedings in the national court are stayed pending the ECJ's decision. ECJ decisions in cases of this type are called "preliminary rulings." Those decisions are binding on the courts of all member states. This reference jurisdiction resembles the procedure in Germany by which courts must refer a question of constitutional law to the Federal Constitutional Court.

When the court receives an application for a preliminary ruling, the case is assigned to a judge rapporteur and also to an advocate general. The two work together in preparing a "preliminary report." That report goes to all 25 judges and eight advocates general who meet together and designate the chamber that is to decide the case on its merits. The less difficult cases are referred to a three-judge chamber which typically decides them without hearing oral argument. A majority of cases go to five-judge chambers. Only complex or important cases go to the Grand Chamber of 13. In exceptional cases the full court sits. The curved bench in the main courtroom accommodates all 25 judges.

When oral argument is afforded, it is done in the language of the country from which the case has come. Interpreters provide simultaneous translation during the hearing; all documents are translated into French. Counsel present argument without interruption. The judges then question counsel, and counsel are given an opportunity to sum up. The advocate general assigned to the case sits on the bench with the judges. At the conclusion of the hearing, he announces the date on which his report will be available. After that report is received by the judges, they will arrive at their decision. In more than 80% of the cases the judges agree with the advocate general. In any event, the court's opinion and that of the advocate general both are published.

As a result of this European legal structure, the national courts in the European Union follow ECJ decisions on issues governed by European law. Where there is no ECJ decision in point, as to the European question presented, the lower national courts face the question as a matter of first impression. In that situation, the judges may be confronted with difficult, tension-filled decisions when application of European law would displace or alter a national policy. *See* THE EUROPEAN COURT AND NATIONAL COURTS: DOCTRINE AND JURISPRUDENCE — LEGAL CHANGE IN ITS SOCIAL CONTEXT 77-131 (Germany), 195-224 (England) (Anne-Marie Slaughter, Alec Stone Sleep, & J.H.H. Weiler eds., 1998). Those lower court judges may avoid the tension by requesting a preliminary ruling from the ECJ.

Subordinate to the ECJ is the Court of First Instance (CFI), also sitting in Luxembourg. It relieves the ECJ of serving as a court of original jurisdiction in certain categories of case. An appeal may be taken from its decisions to the ECJ. However, the CFI does not have jurisdiction over cases referred from the national courts. All those cases go directly to the ECJ.

For a description of the ECJ and its work, *see* THE COURT OF JUSTICE OF THE EUROPEAN COMMUNITIES (L. Neville Brown & Tom Kennedy eds., 5th ed. 2000); Sally J. Kenney, *The European Court of Justice — Integrating Europe Through Law*, 81 JUDICATURE 250 (1998).

The ECJ's web site is http://www.curia.eu.int/

B.   The European Court of Human Rights (ECHR)

Composition and Organization. The ECHR was established by the European Convention on Human Rights. Unlike the ECJ, the court is not part of the European Union. The court consists of 45 judges (soon to be 46), one coming from each of the countries subscribing to the Convention. The judge from each country is elected by the Parliamentary Assembly of the Council of Europe from three well-qualified nominees proposed by the government of that country. Judges hold office for six-year renewable terms. The court is located in Strasbourg in a building of striking contemporary architecture.

The ECHR judges are organized into "chambers" of seven judges each and a "Grand Chamber" of 17 judges. Each chamber is balanced geographically and by gender. Judges do not have personal legal assistants; instead, for professional assistance they rely on the Registry, as described below. The official languages of the court are English and French.

Jurisdiction and Procedure. The role of the ECHR is to adjudicate questions arising under the European Convention on Human Rights and thus provide a measure of uniformity among the 45 contracting states in the enforcement of the Convention. That Convention provides protection for a wide range of human rights that are similar to, but much more extensive than, those guaranteed by the Bill of Rights and the Fourteenth Amendment to the U. S. Constitution.

Cases are initiated in the court by application of an individual or organization suing a state or by a state suing another contracting state. When the complaint is by an individual or by an organization, the applicant must have exhausted all administrative and judicial remedies available in the respondent state. Applicants can and often do challenge a final judgment of a national court, alleging that the court's decision violates the Convention. Such a case requires the ECHR to review a national court's decision, but this is not considered direct appellate review; there is no hierarchical connection between the ECHR and the national court.

A key feature of the court's structure is the Registry. It has a staff of several hundred lawyers drawn from all the subscribing countries, their number being proportional to the volume of cases coming from that country. In its work assisting the court, the Registry resembles the Criminal Appeal Office in the English Court of Appeal. The Registry staff screens applications, rejecting many as being clearly outside the court's jurisdiction. If the Registy considers the application to be within the court's competence and appropriate for its adjudication, *i.e.*, "admissible," it sends the application to a judge rapporteur selected from among the 45 judges. Thereafter, the judge rapporteur and the Registry staff work together in preparing the case for the court's consideration and for seeing the case through to final decision. That judge can make a determination of admissibility. On the other hand, the judge may, in his or her discretion, refer the application either to a three-judge committee in the chamber to which that judge belongs or to the seven-judge chamber. If the application is referred to the committee, the committee may declare the application inadmissible or may refer it to the full chamber. Applications by a state go directly to the full chamber.

If an application is deemed admissible, the case is then considered on its merits by the seven-judge chamber. Oral hearings are held in only about 10% of the cases. When argument is to be heard, the court informs counsel in advance of the points on which the court is especially interested. Argument proceeds as it does in the ECJ, with counsel speaking without interruption, followed by questions from the bench.

The party against whom judgment is rendered in the seven-judge chamber may request a "referral," to the Grand Chamber, *i.e.*, seek review in that 17-judge body. Whether to allow such review is in the Grand Chamber's discretion and review is allowed only where a question of unusual importance is involved.

The court's decisions are in effect declaratory judgments binding on the parties to the case. They provide the authoritative interpretation of the Convention for all contracting states. The court cannot "remand" a case to a national court, as the case is not an "appeal" from such a court. Rather, it is an independent proceeding in the ECHR. The state against which judgment is rendered is obliged by the terms of the Convention to give the ECHR's decision effect through its laws and institutions. *See* Georg Ress, *The Effect of Decisions and Judgments of the European Court of Human Rights in the Domestic Legal Order*, 40 TEX. INT'L L. J. 359-382 (2005); John Cary Sims, *Compliance without Remands: The Experience under the European Convention on Human Rights*, 36 ARIZ. ST. L. J. 639 (2004).

For a description of this court and its work *see* MANUAL ON INTERNATIONAL COURTS AND TRIBUNALS 199-215 (Philippe Sands ed., 1999). The ECHR's web site is http://www.echr.coe.int/echr

In the "globalized judicial world" the ECHR and courts of numerous nations vested with jurisdiction to decide human rights questions increasingly look to each others' decisions as relevant and persuasive, though not binding. *See* Claire L'Heureux-Dube, *The Importance of Dialogue: Globalization and the International Impact of the Rehnquist Court,* 34 TULSA L. J. 15 (1998). *See also* Ruth Bader Ginsburg, *Looking Beyond Our Borders: The Value of a Comparative Perspective in Constitutional Adjudication,* 40 IDAHO L. REV. 1 (2003).

Chapter 14

THE FUTURE OF APPELLATE COURTS

In this Chapter, focusing on the possibilities for future reforms of appellate structures and processes, we look backward and forward at the same time. We look backward over the material in the preceding Chapters chronicling the contemporary American appellate scene, along with key features of English and German appellate courts, in order to know where we are and how we got here. We look forward to consider proposals and ideas for improving American appellate courts to enhance their essential function in the administration of justice and to preserve their central role in guaranteeing government under law. This Chapter is designed to provoke students to use what they have learned to imagine some alternative futures for the appellate courts — to think outside the box of familiar structures, functions, and processes.

The proposals selected for presentation and discussion are those that have attracted the most attention and sometimes the most controversy. While these proposals relate to the federal appellate courts, they portend the future of the state appellate courts, as well. In considering the merits of each proposal, its advantages and disadvantages, students should draw upon what they have previously learned and should bring to the evaluation of these ideas a well-rounded understanding of appellate courts, their institutional role in the legal order, their personnel, and their procedures and internal processes. It should be ever borne in mind that every proposal for change in judicial structure, jurisdiction, or procedure is likely to have both benefits and costs, advantages and disadvantages. The ultimate measure of any proposed reform is whether it solves more problems than it causes.

A few preliminary remarks on judicial reform are in order to consider why some proposals fail to achieve support and are never passed while others get adopted and are implemented — this Chapter contains both kinds of proposals for reform.

Consider the possible impediments to effectuating any constructive reform in the organization, jurisdiction, and procedure of the courts, either state or federal:

1. *The absence of any powerful political constituency pushing for reform.* Typically, the kinds of problems connected with the functioning of the courts are not well-known to the public and do not motivate any large, influential group or organization to campaign for reform. They are "low visibility problems," primarily of concern to judges, lawyers, and legal scholars.

2. *Attachments to the familiar.* Even if there are flaws in the judicial organization, jurisdiction, and procedure, the existing system is one well known to judges and lawyers, who function comfortably within the *status quo.* A change would be unsettling, even threatening to this acquired expertise, and would require re-learning of rules and practices, etc.

3. *General inertia.* Even though problems in the courts often are identified and recognized, the considerable effort and energy required to bring about change are normally lacking, unless the problem has a major impact on a significant segment of the bench or bar.

4. *Negativism.* It is far easier to point out flaws in a proposal than to suggest one that might work better. Identifying potential problems is important, but focusing on these, without attempting to imagine solutions, leaves judicial reform at a standstill.

5. *The exalted power of the minority.* Any change in judicial organization, jurisdiction, or procedure will have some effect on the practices of some lawyers or the interests of certain prospective litigants. In other words, any change may be perceived by some group as potentially threatening or disadvantageous. Consequently, that group is likely to be motivated to oppose the change without regard to the merits of the proposal or to the benefits that it may promise for the judicial system as a whole. That group is unlikely to make alternative suggestions, offering instead only disparaging comments on the proposal. Because of the typical lack of any powerful political constituency pushing for the change as indicated in item one above and the compelling anti-change forces listed in items two through four, the small oppositional group can usually block the advance of the proposal through the legislative branch by a few contacts with key senators and representatives on the judiciary committees of the two houses. Such opposition can be particularly effective if contacts with these individual legislators are made by some of their major political or financial supporters. In terms of practical politics, the source of the opposition is usually more important than the merits of the arguments made against the proposal.

6. *Specialization in law practice.* Lawyers with a generalized practice represent a broad spectrum of economic and social interests and are therefore more likely to see the justice system as a whole and to be able to act independently in assessing its flaws and supporting steps to improve it. On the other hand, a lawyer with a specialized practice is likely to have a relatively narrow, singular perspective on the justice system and to evaluate the system solely from the standpoint of the particular interests being represented. Thus, specialists are more likely to oppose reform measures that they see as disadvantageous to their particular clients. American law practice is becoming increasingly specialized, with the result that a consensus about judicial reform is more difficult to attain.

Despite these obstacles to the enactment of judicial reforms, such reforms do get enacted from time to time, as indicated in the foregoing Chapters. Consider now the circumstances that make judicial reform feasible and eventually bring about enactment.

1. *A problem of truly crisis proportions.* Even though serious defects may have been identified in some aspect of the judicial system, a defect is not likely to attract widespread attention until its deleterious effects are overwhelmingly obvious and profoundly serious. A problem must not only be bad; it must be of nearly catastrophic dimensions. When that

point is reached, a substantial segment of the bench and the bar — and even the public — realizes that something must be done. Reformers use the rhetoric of "crisis," but they must convince skeptics.

2. *The happenstance of a mutuality of concern among diverse interests.* The exalted power of the minority likely to be opposed to any proposal may be overcome if the proposal is beneficial to several groups not normally politically associated with one another. The combined forces of these disparate groups sometimes can overcome stubborn opposition.

3. *The ease and inexpensiveness of implementing the proposal.* If the proposal can be put into effect with a relatively small degree of disruption to existing arrangements and if it can be implemented with relatively small increases in expenditures of public funds, its chances of adoption increase significantly. Any proposal that involves a substantial increase in the expenditure of tax funds or that would create externalities that cause judges and lawyers to radically change their familiar and established work ways is not likely to move very far.

4. *A strong leader.* If the proposal has a strong, active, and politically-influential supporter willing to exert leadership on its behalf, its chances of enactment are greatly enhanced. Indeed, the absence of such a visible leader is often fatal to any proposal, no matter how meritorious.

5. *A good idea.* A meritorious proposal has a better chance of adoption than one that simply does not withstand close scrutiny. Although some bad ideas do get enacted, a proposed change that is well thought out and carefully designed has a better chance to survive.

An example is in order. The creation of the U.S. Court of Appeals for the Federal Circuit illustrates how the positive factors can overcome the negative factors to result in a successful reform. Within a relatively short time, only three-and-a-half years, the proposal to create that court was duly enacted by Congress. Although the problems of non-uniformity in patent law, which provided a primary motivation for the proposal, had not reached crisis proportions, they were seen as serious by knowledgeable members of the legal profession. Several important interests came together in support of the proposal to create the new court. These included the Department of Justice, patent lawyers representing or employed by major research entities heavily involved in patents, the judges of the two courts that were to be merged (the Court of Claims and the Court of Customs and Patent Appeals), and leadership from the Senate Judiciary Committee and the Executive Branch. Moreover, the creation of the new court not only required no increase in public expenditures but actually saved money by combining two existing courts into one. *See* Daniel J. Meador, *Origin of the Federal Circuit: A Personal Account*, 41 AM. U. L. REV. 581 (1992). Compare the various proposals in this Chapter to this successful reform.

Some of the proposals in this Chapter already seem to be moribund, done in by the first set of negative factors described above, at least for now. Others remain viable and await the alignment of the positive factors described above to move them forward towards adoption and implementation. Studying these proposals will improve the understanding and deepen the appreciation of students for the structures, functions, processes, and personnel of the appellate courts. In evaluating these reform proposals, consider the difficulties that may stand in the way of their enactment and what, if anything, can be done to clear the way for the adoption of these or some other proposals addressed to the problems and needs of the appellate courts.

I.   COURT FUTURISM

This section introduces the process of long-range planning for the appellate courts. Part of that enterprise consists of predicting — skeptics might call it "speculating" — what the future will bring. The available statistics and data, however, take us only so far. Planners must plot trends and make informed judgments about the future to anticipate the coming challenges and to develop plans for the court system in order to prepare to meet those challenges. Since the 1990s, long-range planning has been the rage in the state and federal courts. It involves hypothesizing alternative future scenarios and imagining how the courts can adapt to what might happen. But how much can we know about the future of the appellate courts? How might judges, court administrators, legislators, and court reformers make good use of long-range planning?

Thomas E. Baker, *A View to the Future of Judicial Federalism: "Neither Out Far Nor In Deep,"* 45 Case W. Res. L. Rev. 705, 707-16 (1995)[1]

An Introduction to Futurists and Futurism. Futurism has become a big business. There have been best-selling books and sequels in which the authors foretell the future. It seems as if every *Fortune 500* company has created a futures division, or at least brought in futurist consultants, and American universities now offer degrees with an emphasis in futures studies. Long-range planning certainly is in vogue throughout the governmental sector.

There are any number of plausible explanations for these developments, including the increased uncertainty from world events . . . and an economic ambition to participate in the globalization of the economy. Futurism and futurists have arrived. I think this probably has a lot to do with the fact that the next millennium is less than a decade away. . . .

I must admit that I find all this intriguing. I also must confess that a lot of what I read that passes for futurism strikes me as more akin to science fiction. Even futurists themselves will tell you that the best futurists, the most helpful futurists, do not actually attempt to predict the future. Instead, they offer alternative scenarios, describing different possible futures. These hypothetical scenarios, however, tend to extremes of optimism or pessimism. I think this is a professional hazard of futurists. Who wants to hear that the future is going to be more of the same? . . .

. . . Predicting future changes in institutions as complex as the state and federal courts is fraught with difficulty and nuanced further by the elaborate interactions between the two judicial branches. We cannot expect their joint future to be any more linear than their past has been. Political decisions and

---

[1] Copyright © 1995 Case Western Reserve Law Review. Reprinted with permission.

public policy compromises in the fifty state legislatures and in Congress will shape the courts' futures, not rational discourse at judicial conferences or comprehensive studies in law reviews.

The nineteenth century French traveler and commentator, Alexis de Tocqueville, observed that every social issue in this country eventually becomes a legal issue for the courts. At the end of the twentieth century, social scientists will tell you that the nature and number of disputes brought into courts are determined by social trends. The one overriding consensus among courts futurists today is that "the quality of justice in the United States is at risk at the same time that social and economic conditions are changing rapidly." In short, state and federal courts are *in extremis* and the crisis promises to continue for the foreseeable future. This is the conclusion of the two most recent and most important studies of the courts' futures.

In 1989, Georgetown University conducted the "Delphi Study," an intensive and comprehensive study of the opinions of forty prominent experts — judges, administrators, scholars, writers, and practitioners — about the future of the state courts [Franklin M. Zweig, *et al.*, *Securing the Future for America's State Courts*, 73 Judicature 296 (1990)]. The participants, who collectively had nearly 1200 years experience in judicial matters, each provided a detailed written analysis along with a personal interview for the compilation.

In that same year, the Federal Courts Study Committee hired the prestigious Hudson Institute to predict the trends that would affect the federal courts [Hudson Institute, Trends Affecting the Federal Courts (Oct. 1989)]. The predictions relied on data from the Bureau of Census and the Bureau of Justice Statistics, reports from the Rand Institute for Civil Justice, congressional hearings and various other government reports and documents, interviews with relevant experts, and scholarly literature.

The methodology of each study was state of the art. Both studies sought to predict trends over the next thirty years, roughly through the year 2020. Their conclusions have been confirmed by numerous other futures studies about courts. The following is what the Delphi study and the Hudson Institute study predicted about the future of the state and federal courts.

Demographic changes will be pronounced. Population in the United States will increase by about thirty million, although the rate of growth will be slow and will begin to decline. Since the basic workload of courts is greatly a function of total population, if everything else were constant, workload would slowly increase and then level off.

The population trends, however, are more complicated, as are the effects on court caseloads. The composition of the population will change significantly, with resulting impact on court dockets. First, the population will become older, as the baby-boom generation approaches retirement. More people will be older and living longer. Therefore, issues related to the elderly such as social security, pensions, health care, and death and dying, will become more salient politically as well as judicially.

Second, the nation's racial composition will change. Differences in birth rates among racial groups and the effects of immigration will result in proportional increases in the percentages of nonwhite ethnic and racial groups.

Immigrants also tend to be younger on average than the rest of the population, so we might experience some racial tensions along generational lines. With greater numbers of minorities entering the workplace, the courts can expect increases in cases dealing with equal opportunity and discrimination issues over business practices and wages. Concomitantly, as more women enter the workforce, the courts can expect increases in litigation involving related issues such as sexual harassment and disparity in compensation. These will include individual as well as class action suits. Beyond the workplace and school environments, greater multicultural diversity likely will place uncertain strains on the judicial system as diverse groups work out their differences in the larger society. Traditions from other cultures are sure to conflict with our civil and criminal norms, and the courts will be expected to reconcile them. The administrative burden of providing court services to non-English speaking peoples will increase. Economic woes will add more litigation over employment rights. The shift from a smokestack economy to a service industry and information-based economy will have huge unsettling effects on businesses and workers in transition. We can expect more litigation over workplace safety issues and job security issues. Third, as the risks against the institution of the family continue and the poverty cycle expands and deepens, courts will be faced with more cases raising such familiar issues as juvenile delinquency and welfare administration. Finally, the AIDS epidemic will further complicate public policy decisionmaking as courts are called upon to resolve disputes over resource allocations and the availability of treatment. Legislative initiatives on these issues will generate substantial litigation.

Another set of factors is less connected to demographics. Abstract considerations such as political, social, and economic factors obviously have an effect on court dockets. These can best be evaluated separately for their effect on criminal and civil caseloads.

The criminal caseload can be expected to increase simply as a result of the increase in population. Of more significance, however, will be the continued trend on the part of legislatures to criminalize behavior and the proclivity on the part of prosecutors to prosecute more offenders. Both these trends are well-documented and expected to continue. Consequently, the number of criminal cases will increase even among those crimes whose percentage of the total is decreasing. Some categories of crimes will continue to increase dramatically. The most important factor on the criminal docket, of course, is the "war on drugs." Indeed, many in the judicial branches have expressed concern that the courts will be an unintended casualty of this "war." You do not have to be a futurist to predict that the drug caseload has become and will continue to be "intractable" and that it will "persist, expand, and gain momentum well into the twenty-first century." There are also projections for new or more vigorously enforced crimes dealing with "white collar" offenses, such as fraud, embezzlement, and forgery. New prosecutorial offensives can be expected to deal with crimes involving computers such as electronic transfers of funds and manipulation of financial markets. More and more offenses will involve international transactions, given the increasing globalization of the economy. Furthermore, we can expect that prisoner rights litigation over conditions of confinement will increase as prison populations exceed everyone's expectations. The burden on state budgets felt from the current prison expansion program, which shows no sign of slowing, will result in state funding crises for other important state functions, such as education, and we can expect more public law litigation contesting legislative compromises over taxing and spending. The crisis of funding for the courts certainly will worsen.

Identifiable political, social, and economic factors likewise will affect the civil caseload in four primary categories. First, there is every reason to expect that political decisions will continue to extend civil rights and anti-discrimination statutes to more and more groups as well as individuals. Legislative understandings of what types of discrimination should be made unlawful will continue to expand for the public and private sectors. This will take the form of amendments to existing legislation as well as new legislation creating new causes of action at the state and federal levels. The second major trend on the civil side will involve tort cases. Leaving aside the current debate whether the courts have experienced an explosion in tort litigation, experts see no reason to expect either significant growth or decline in current levels of litigation for the familiar categories of personal injury cases. Currently developing areas of tort litigation, involving, for example, health and environmental matters, will be stimulated. These new causes of action will deal with complex and difficult issues of causation and risk allocation, often against a background of elaborate administrative regulations. Specific environmental and scientific issues — such as acid rain, ozone depletion, and global warming — will be litigated at international and global levels of involvement. These will press the limits of judicial adaptability, as science and technology develop beyond existing legal concepts and procedures. Third, forecasts predict more cases dealing with engineering, technology, and science, in the contexts of copyrights, patents, and other intellectual property theories. Fourth, current trends and predicted political decisions likely will result in growing numbers of professional malpractice lawsuits in traditional areas such as medicine and law as the professions become "demythologized." This attitude and these suits likely will spread to more novel areas such as education, religion, and even government. Fifth, alternative dispute resolution mechanisms will be structured to offset partly these expectations for more and more court cases. However, their increased use will further complicate court administration and funding decisions.

Given the differences between state and federal courts, in composition, organization, and jurisdiction, these predictions will have different impacts on the two judiciaries. Furthermore, there are numerous other factors that affect the judicial system which, futurists admit, are virtually impossible to assess. These other factors easily can overcome the individual predictions I have summarized and conceivably even their cumulative effect. The level of litigiousness in society is well-nigh impossible to measure, let alone predict. It seems to be influenced by such complex forces as the attitudes of lawyers and clients, the receptivity of judges and courts, and the agendas of legislatures. A sociologist has more chance of explaining this aspect of our culture than does a legal scholar or courts expert. Forecasts of the effect on court caseloads from these factors thus are fraught with difficulty, if not impossibility, and predictions must be so tentative and so qualified that they amount to educated guesses about the near future. While these intangible factors will determine the future, they are inherently impossible to predict. The most we can hope to do is to discuss them rationally and consider the possibilities. We can be sure of one thing: the next generation of court reformers will have their hands full solving the problems created by our generation. . . .

The Future of the Federal Courts — Structural Fatigue. The problems for the structure of the federal courts are most pronounced at the intermediate level. At the Supreme Court level, there have been worries about workload from time to time, but these have been assuaged by jurisdictional changes, most recently in 1988, that provide the Justices near complete discretion over the selection of which cases to hear and decide. This seems to be working. . . . But at the two levels below the Supreme Court, there is no discretion. The district courts and the courts of appeals must dispose of each case on their docket. At the district court level, Congress has created more district judgeships and added magistrate-judges and bankruptcy judges in an attempt to keep pace with docket growth. For the most part, these additions have worked well, although the press of cases has caused some jurisdictional and procedural stress.

The most serious structural fatigue centers on the courts is the middle tier. The last major restructuring of the federal courts was in 1891 when the courts of appeals were created. Pausing to consider for just a moment all that has happened in national life and in the legal system over the intervening century obviates any surprise that the nineteenth century design may be showing signs of fatigue. Until the present generation, the organization of the courts of appeals worked rather well. But the last four decades have brought the courts of appeals to a serious "crisis of volume." Consider these figures for the regional courts of appeals: In 1950, there were 65 authorized circuit judgeships, 2,830 appeals were filed, and 2,355 appeals were terminated (36 per authorized judgeship). In 1990, there were 156 authorized circuit judgeships; 40,898 appeals were filed; and 39,520 appeals were terminated (246.9 per authorized judgeship).

Over the years, Congress has responded primarily with two extramural reforms: adding judges and dividing circuits. [The future will bring continued growth in the Article III judiciary, although not as much as we can expect for non-Article III personnel and support staff. Caseload will demand it. Congress will approve it.] As for dividing circuits, as was done in 1981 to the old Fifth Circuit and is still being debated for the present Ninth Circuit, it is enough to say that "Congress lately has shown signs of abandoning the technique." Dividing circuits is not a remedy for the problems of the courts of appeals. Caseload is distributive: if Congress simply splits an overloaded circuit into two new courts of appeals, the same total number of judges on the two new courts must decide the same total number of appeals. Circuit splitting is not likely to be a future reform, unless it is part of some major restructuring.

If the inevitable happens, that more appeals are filed and more judgeships are created, then Congress will face the task of reimagining the intermediate federal tier. Congress knows the time is approaching when it will be required to redesign the courts of appeals. In December 1993, the Federal Judicial Center (FJC) published a report commissioned by the Congress entitled, "Structural and Other Alternatives for the Federal Courts of Appeals." The FJC Report reviews many alternatives for the courts of appeals: total or partial consolidation; size reduction; multiple tiers; discretionary appeals; differentiating appellate tracks; district court error review; jurisdiction reduction; and other nonjurisdictional options.

What Congress will do is anyone's guess. However, Congress ought to plan for the future of the courts of appeals by creating a study group to act as legislative architects that will develop and model alternative federal appellate structures with some level of detail and particularity. Then, Congress should hold hearings and exercise sound legislative judgment to choose from the alternatives. Chief Justice Rehnquist concluded that "[a]lthough no consensus has yet developed around any particular set of changes to the status quo — and to be sure any alternatives will present practical and political difficulties — it is safe to say that change will come." The inescapable prediction is that he is correct, and the next generation will witness a major congressional reform of the federal intermediate courts. . . .

Conclusion. Courts futurists themselves are not without suggestions on how to cope with the challenges that are coming. . . . We must all appreciate that goals of court experts and insiders — even the best laid plans of judges and court commentators — are not always likely to become future political scenarios for two reasons. First, those who would design and implement these goals, judges and court administrators, for the most part, are obliged to act in the present, to deal responsibly with today's problems in terms of today's solutions. The people running the court system in the United States today resemble Alice in *Through the Looking Glass*: they are running as fast as they can to stay in the same place. Planning for the future and implementing needed reforms are activities that come at the end of a long day or on weekends.

Second, public preferences and political compromises tend to overtake even the most excellent government planning. We live in complex times when many social problems are competing for the time and attention of the people and their representatives. It is virtually impossible to capture the public attention for court reform. William H. Rehnquist is not going to be asked to appear on Oprah Winfrey's show. . . .

There is too much at stake to contemplate failure. This then is the ultimate challenge facing the courts: to take the future "into evidence," to plan for it effectively, and, most important, to sustain the bench and bar's commitment to the ideal of "Equal Justice Under Law."

JUDICIAL CONFERENCE OF THE UNITED STATES, LONG RANGE PLAN FOR THE FEDERAL COURTS 17-20 (1995)

Tiers of Justice Scenario: *The year is 2020. Congress has continued the federalization trends of the eighties and nineties and federal court caseloads have grown at a rapid rate. In the United States Court of Appeals for the 21st Circuit, Lower Tier, a recently appointed federal judge arrives at her chambers, planning to consult the latest electronic advance sheets in FED. 7th in order to determine the applicable law of her Circuit and the upper tier court of appeals for her region. With* *nearly a thousand court of appeals judges writing opinions, federal law in 2020 has become vaster and more incoherent than ever.*

This is only the judge's fourth month on the job, even though she was nominated by the President three years earlier; the appointment and confirmation process has bogged down even more than in 1995 because of the numbers of judicial candidates that the Senate Judiciary Committee must consider every year. Her predecessor was only on the bench for a year and a half before resigning in protest because he felt he was only a small cog in what had become a vast wheel of justice.

An Alternative Future for the Federal Courts? If the federal courts are in crisis or approaching crisis now, how will they operate 25 years from now when, assuming the continuation of present trends, projections suggest that their current workload may double, triple, or quadruple?

The trend projections . . . reflect one possible prediction of federal court dockets by assuming that the factors influencing caseload growth in the past will continue to do so in the future. Certainly those projections provide only a rough approximation of future caseloads and the assumptions underlying the projections are open to challenge, as would be assumptions underlying any future caseload projections. Recent legislative trends suggest that federal caseloads will continue to grow rapidly. Nonetheless, whether the caseload increases at the rates anticipated by the projections, or at some other rate, many of the same implications will follow.

To be sure, predictions about what the world, or a small part of it, will look like in 10 or 20 years are more properly the realm of futurists (or perhaps science fiction writers) than judges who operate in the here and now. As the Federal Courts Study Committee noted, the difficulty in predicting future demands for federal judicial resources lies in the dual challenges of predicting "any but the grossest social, economic, political, and demographic trends more than a few years in advance — if that far," and with ascertaining the relationship between those trends and the future business of the federal courts.

As but one example of the problem, neither planners nor sociologists can know with certainty whether the drug problems that currently plague this country — and which are the cause of many other related criminal and societal ills — will continue, moderate, or decline. Even assuming that the drug crisis persists in all its tragic manifestations, it is not possible to predict how the nation's leaders will respond to it: Will the nation, as some have urged, refocus some of its prosecutorial resources on education and rehabilitation? More radically, will we witness the decriminalization of some of the substances that are currently proscribed? Or will the status quo remain undisturbed?

The district courts and courts of appeals currently devote substantial judicial resources to resolving criminal drug cases. The extent of their future involvement in the adjudication of criminal drug offenses is a political question about which planners can only speculate.

A Possible Scenario for the Future. The projections — under the assumptions [we] set out — are bleak indeed. If the federal courts' civil and criminal jurisdiction continues to grow at the same rate it did over the past 53 years, the picture in 2020 can only be described as nightmarish. Should that occur, in twenty-five years the number of civil cases commenced annually could reach 1 million (in 1995 the civil filings in the district courts numbered about 239,000) while the criminal filings could reach nearly 84,000 (in 1995 they numbered about 44,000). At the same time, annual appeals could approach 335,000 (in 1995 they numbered almost 50,000). Based on current formulas for determining judgeship needs, these levels of case filings might require a district court bench of over 2,400 judges, while the appeals bench would be over 1,600 judges. In other words, were such a scenario to become the future reality, more than 4,000 federal judges might be necessary to handle the federal courts' docket in 2020. This situation is starkly shown in this Table of Case Filings and Judgeships:

	1995	2020
District Courts		
Civil Filings	239,013	976,500
Criminal Filings	44,184	83,900
Total	283,197	1,060,400
Courts of Appeals		
Criminal Appeals	10,023	43,000
Prisoner Petitions	14,488	149,600
Other Appeals	25,160	142,200
Total	49,671	334,800
Judgeships (by formula)		
District	649	2,410
Circuit	167	1,660

Numbers alone do not adequately illustrate this picture. A federal judiciary of 4,000 judges would necessarily require a different structure. The current structure of twelve regional courts of appeals (excluding the Court of Appeals for the Federal Circuit) could not be maintained in 2020, given that, on average, each of these courts would have to consist of about 100 judges. Similarly, with that many appellate judges and many more circuits, it seems virtually impossible that the Supreme Court would be able to discharge its responsibility for resolving intercircuit conflicts. Another judicial "tier" at least, would likely be needed. The Supreme Court's role as the ultimate arbiter of federal law would be diminished significantly, as it would be hard-pressed to review even a tiny fraction of the entire federal caseload.

Present-day governance mechanisms would need drastic modification. As the courts grew in size, the balance of national, regional and local authority would demand significant adjustment. With growth would come the need for additional mechanisms to ensure management and accountability. Inevitably, pressure would build for the creation of a strong central executive body for the entire court system.

Perhaps the greatest loss, however, would be in the notion of courts as collegial bodies. The current Chief Judge for the Second Circuit Court of Appeals has expressed this fear, when he said, "When I contemplate our court in the middle of the next century . . . I despair. It will not be a court; it will be a stable of judges, each one called upon to plough through the unrelenting volume, harnessed on any given day with two other judges who barely know each other."

Finally, no matter how the courts are structured or governed, the vision of coherence and consistency in decisional law likely would be a chimera. Federal law would be Babel, with thousands of decisions issuing weekly and no one judge capable of comprehending the entire corpus of federal law, or even the law of his or her own circuit. This possibility is one that planners have to contemplate if today's trends continue.

> **Justice Without Resources Scenario:** *It is 2020. Federal caseloads have quadrupled in the last 25 years, but the number of federal judges has leveled off at 1000. The federal budget remains in crisis, the product of continued growth in non-discretionary federal spending and the unwillingness to raise taxes. Congress no longer is willing to fund the increasing costs of new courthouses, support staff and judicial salaries necessary to address the rising tide of cases.*
>
> *Austerity is a way of life in the federal courts. The queue for civil cases lengthens to the point where federal judges rarely conduct civil trials. User fees proliferate and would be judged onerous by 20th century standards. As a consequence, many litigants seek justice from private providers. Overworked and underpaid administrators defer maintenance on courthouses and no longer update library collections. Most vacancies on the federal bench go unfilled for long periods of time because capable lawyers, once attracted to a judicial career, are no longer willing to serve. The federal courts have by and large become criminal courts and forums for those who cannot afford private justice.*

Another Possible Scenario for the Future. As troubling as the "Tiers of Justice Scenario" above may be, it is probably less so than the "Justice Without Resources Scenario" in which the nation has found itself unable or unwilling to fund the growth in the federal courts at the same levels it did between 1940 and 1995. Consider, for example the cost of creating and maintaining judgeships. Including salary, administrative expenses, court security and space and facilities, the initial cost of establishing a court of appeals judgeship is over $954,000 (in 1995 dollars). Annual recurring costs would amount to about $813,000. For district court judgeships, these initial and recurring costs are about $937,000 and $775,000, respectively. . . .

Because of budgetary constraints that will severely reduce discretionary federal spending, future Congresses will not likely permit the judicial budget to grow to fund the projected judgeship needs of the next several decades. If the economic realities of the next 25 years make it impossible to provide the resources necessary to create and maintain a federal judicial system that includes thousands of Article III judges, then we must contemplate a different picture, one that more severely undermines the 200-year old mission of the federal courts.

With scarce resources and many more case filings per judge than currently exist, delay, congestion, cost, and inefficiency would increase. The paperwork burden will affect both the litigants, who would face higher legal fees, and the judges, who would have limited staff assistance. Those civil litigants who can afford it will opt out of the court system entirely for private dispute resolution providers. Already district judges are able to spend fewer of their working hours in civil trials than ever before, and the future may make the civil jury trial — and perhaps the civil bench trial as well — a creature of the past. The federal district courts, rather than being forums where the weak and the few have recognized rights that the strong and the many must regard, could become an arena for second class justice.

At the court of appeals level, it might become impossible to preserve the hallmarks of a sound appellate review system. [In the words of the Federal Courts Study Committee:]

> [T]he judges do much of their own work, grant oral argument in cases that need it, decide cases with sufficient thought, and produce opinions in cases of precedential importance with the care they deserve, including independent, constructive insight and criticism from judges on the court and the panel other than the judge writing the opinion. These conditions are essential to a carefully crafted case law.

In 2020 we may find a system of discretionary appellate review, of oral argument in only the exceptional case, and of staff personnel playing a dominant role in deciding the majority of the cases that get the full attention of the judges.

In all respects the plan rejects these two apocalyptic alternatives. They are neither desirable nor acceptable. Fortunately, they are by no means inevitable if appropriate action is taken. The plan that follows contemplates conserving the federal courts as a distinctive forum of limited jurisdiction. The plan's proposals for jurisdiction, structure, governance, function, and role all stem from that fundamental objective. Nonetheless, because the future cannot be known and because long-range planning also mandates consideration of alternatives to the plan's preferred vision for the future, [this plan] addresses alternative planning approaches should the plan's vision not be achieved. . . .

NOTES

1. In the excerpt above, Professor Baker sounds several notes of skepticism about futurists and their prognostications, but he seems to admit that they do serve some useful purpose to anticipate long term court reform. Looking over his shoulder to gaze into his crystal ball, what future trends does he identify that will affect the workload of appellate courts? Is there any doubt that the future will bring more and more appeals resulting in greater and greater stresses on the appellate court structure? The rest of this Chapter is an effort to meet the challenge to reimagine the future of the federal intermediate appellate tier in the twenty-first century.

2. Does either future scenario above — the "Tiers of Justice Scenario" or the "Justice Without Resources Scenario" — both taken from the LONG RANGE PLAN FOR THE FEDERAL COURTS — strike you as realistic? Are they probable? Are they possible? Just how reliable are past statistical trends for predicting future statistical trends? How likely is it that the judges and Congress will

allow the federal courts to devolve into the kinds of appellate systems described in the excerpt? Are these post-apocalyptic scenarios merely rhetorical devices to make radical reform proposals appear more reasonable and justified? On behalf of the federal court system *qua* system, the Judicial Conference has articulated and endorsed a policy of carefully controlled growth to maintain the historic role and function of the federal courts and then warned about the alternative consequences:

> Should the Congress and the nation not heed these concerns about the implications for uncontrolled growth, one of two unfortunate consequences will inevitably follow: (1) an enormous, unwieldy federal court system that has lost its special nature; or (2) a larger system incapable, because of budgetary constraints, workload and shortage of resources, of dispensing justice swiftly, inexpensively and fairly. Either consequence would result in an alternative future for the federal courts, one that is far different from the preferred vision articulated.

JUDICIAL CONFERENCE OF THE UNITED STATES, LONG RANGE PLAN FOR THE FEDERAL COURTS 15 (1995). What are some of the implications for the appellate courts from this overarching vision of the federal judiciary?

3. That official planning document of the federal courts went on to outline various possible approaches to a fundamental restructuring of the federal appellate courts in contemplation of different alternative future scenarios: realigning the circuits, creating a new appellate tier, making the first appeal discretionary, establishing district court review, etc. JUDICIAL CONFERENCE OF THE UNITED STATES, LONG RANGE PLAN FOR THE FEDERAL COURTS 131-33 (1995). These and other proposals for structural reform will be considered in the rest of this Chapter.

II. REORGANIZING THE MIDDLE TIER

This section focuses on the U.S. Courts of Appeals to provide an overview of the possible reforms, a menu of proposals for reorganizing the middle tier of the federal courts. The most common proposals are described and summarized here so that they might be compared and contrasted. Later sections in this Chapter will more closely examine some of the particular proposals.

Everyone is confident that the future will bring more appeals and more judges; therefore, any proposed reorganization ought to be designed to accommodate that certain future. Thus, consider some general criteria, as elaborated in the Notes at the end of this section, to evaluate the merits of any proposal to reorganize the federal intermediate appellate tier: How does the proposal accommodate projected increases in the number of appeals? How does the proposal accommodate projected increases in the number of appellate judges? What effect will the proposal have on *stare decisis* and the law of the circuit — will there be more or will there be fewer intracircuit conflicts and how will they be resolved? What effect will the proposal have on the national law — will there be more or will there be fewer intercircuit conflicts and how will they be resolved? How will the proposal affect the Supreme Court? How will trial courts experience the proposed reform in the way they are supervised for errors? How will litigants and lawyers experience the proposed reform in the appellate processes? Does the proposal preserve the appellate imperatives?

At the top of this list of questions, perhaps we should ask a threshold question of every reformer and every proposed reform: should not there be a presumption in favor of the status quo, *i.e.*, should any reformer be expected to satisfy a burden of proof that the proposed change is needed and that it will work as promised? Or is that asking too much? How willing should we be to experiment with our system of justice?

Report of the Federal Courts Study Committee 117-22 (1990)

Courts of appeals of twenty, thirty and even forty or more judges — distinct possibilities if caseloads continue to rise at present rates — may well be too large to provide the necessary coherency of case law within their circuits. At the start of this chapter, we stated our belief that the nation may soon have to decide whether to retain the present court structure or adopt a new one. We recommend no alternative structure at this point; there has been too little analysis about their likely effects and about the types and numbers of cases to be accommodated.

Massive restructuring of the courts of appeals would, by definition, entail substantial disruption of the present system, and we would not propose it until the alternatives have been carefully and comprehensively analyzed. That is a task beyond our capabilities, given our limited time and resources. To stimulate that analysis, however, we describe briefly, and diagram, five alternatives that, among others, have been suggested to the committee. . . . *We emphasize again that we endorse none of these alternatives.* We present them here simply to suggest a range of concrete alternatives that might be analyzed further. And we do not suggest these are the only alternatives worthy of consideration. One proposal that we do *not* favor, however, is the single national appellate court to take appeals on referral from the Supreme Court, as proposed in 1975 by the Hruska Commission; such a tribunal would enlarge the system's capacity to resolve intercircuit conflicts, but would not solve the problem of growth within the courts of appeals. Hence, by itself, it could resolve only a piece of the problem.

With respect to any alternative, we caution that caseload pressures are inexorable even now. Delay in seeking a remedy will make the situation worse and diminish the likelihood of making the right choice as a result of careful planning in advance. We hope that during the impending years the courts of appeals can continue to cope in their current format with the anticipated larger caseloads and thus allow adequate consideration of major structural alternatives. Here are five examples of structural alternatives. . . .

1. Multiple circuit appellate courts — of nine or ten judges each — could function as a unified court.

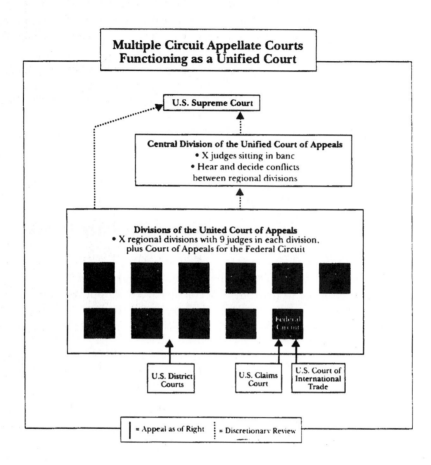

Multiple Circuit Appellate Courts Functioning as a Unified Court

U.S. Supreme Court

Central Division of the Unified Court of Appeals
- X judges sitting in banc
- Hear and decide conflicts between regional divisions

Divisions of the United Court of Appeals
- X regional divisions with 9 judges in each division, plus Court of Appeals for the Federal Circuit

Federal Circuit

U.S. District Courts   U.S. Claims Court   U.S. Court of International Trade

| = Appeal as of Right   ┊ = Discretionary Review

Simply dividing existing circuits — the remedy proposed in 1975 by the Commission on Revision of the Federal Court Appellate System [Hruska Commission] — no longer appears practicable. Variations in caseload and geographical divisions not reflecting current conditions suggest that to achieve smaller courts, the present circuits would first have to be dissolved. This alternative, consequently, would eliminate the present circuits, draw entirely new circuit boundaries, and provide a mechanism for redrawing them periodically. The increased number of intercircuit conflicts could be handled by requiring all courts of appeals to adhere to the precedents established by panels of other courts, unless the Supreme Court has spoken. Intercircuit review panels could reverse other panels' decisions believed to be clearly erroneous (subject to Supreme Court review). In other words, the court of appeals judges would themselves, in some formalized manner, bind colleagues beyond their own circuits, thus reducing conflicts without relying on the Supreme Court as the sole arbiter.

2. Create a four-tiered system.

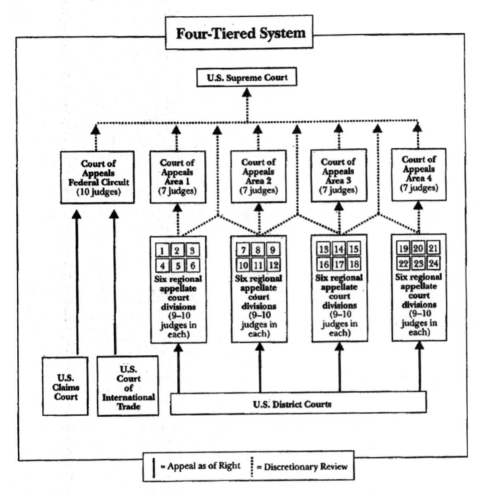

Q: Please provide new image

This alternative extends the 1891 approach of increasing appellate capacity by providing an additional tier between the district courts and the Supreme Court. For example, Congress could divide the nation into twenty to thirty regional appellate divisions, placing a nine- to ten-judge court in each of these divisions as a lower "appellate I" tier, and create four or five "higher" tribunals (of seven judges each) in different areas of the country as an "appellate II" tier. The courts in the regional divisions would hear appeals of right from the district courts in their divisions. Each new upper-tier court would hear cases on a discretionary basis from five or six of the lower-tier courts. The four or five upper-tier courts would be mainly law-declarers, and might produce a more compact body of primary precedent than the voluminous and increasingly disparate case law likely to be generated by 200 or 300 co-equal circuit judges, governed only by a distant Supreme Court. Instead, the Supreme Court would focus mainly on the four or five upper-tier tribunals, giving them in turn an important supplementary role riding herd on the lower-tier courts. Ample "percolation" could continue. Such an expanded system could absorb perhaps double or more the number of judges in the current system, would enable all the individual courts at both levels to remain small, and yet might restore the coherence threatened by untrammeled growth within the current circuits. But it could be harder to attract able jurists to the lower-tier courts.

3. Create national subject-matter courts.

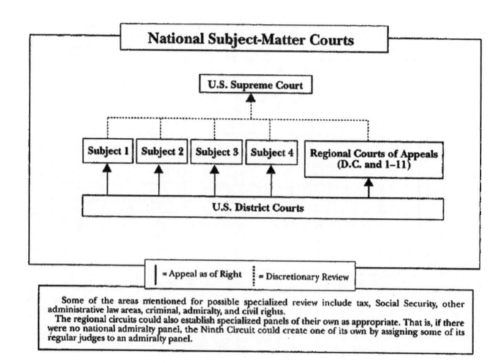

National Subject-Matter Courts

U.S. Supreme Court

Subject 1 | Subject 2 | Subject 3 | Subject 4 | Regional Courts of Appeals (D.C. and 1–11)

U.S. District Courts

▌ = Appeal as of Right   ┆ = Discretionary Review

Some of the areas mentioned for possible specialized review include tax, Social Security, other administrative law areas, criminal, admiralty, and civil rights.
The regional circuits could also establish specialized panels of their own as appropriate. That is, if there were no national admiralty panel, the Ninth Circuit could create one of its own by assigning some of its regular judges to an admiralty panel.

National tax, admiralty, criminal, civil rights, labor, administrative and other subject-matter courts could relieve the regional courts of appeals of some of their current caseload and eliminate intercircuit conflicts in those areas of the law. Specialized panels could simultaneously be created within the regional circuits. Subject-matter courts already have a recognized place among the country's judicial institutions. Both the Federal and D.C. circuits are composed of generalist judges whose jurisdiction is defined by the subject matter of the cases — only partially, to be sure, as to the D.C. circuit. Only a large number of such courts — or courts with broad jurisdiction — could have much effect on the caseload, however, and either type of court could create numerous political and organizational problems. . . .

4. Merge and reorganize all federal courts of appeals into a single, centrally organized body.

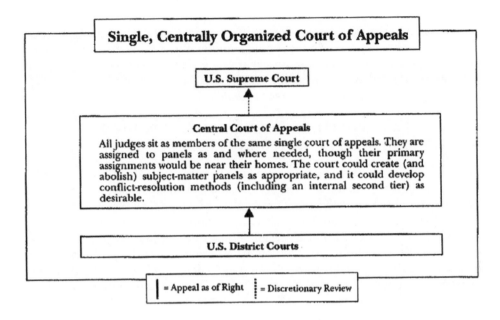

Such a court presents an enormous and complex picture. It would allow easy allocation of judges and resources to places of particular need, and it would eliminate intercircuit conflicts (using some of the methods described elsewhere). But it could have all the earmarks of a large bureaucracy, and it would counter the salutary trend in today's federal courts towards decentralized administration, and perhaps discourage the accountability for circuit and district performance that is now an incentive for productivity in an otherwise enormous system.

5. Consolidate the existing courts into perhaps five "jumbo" circuits.

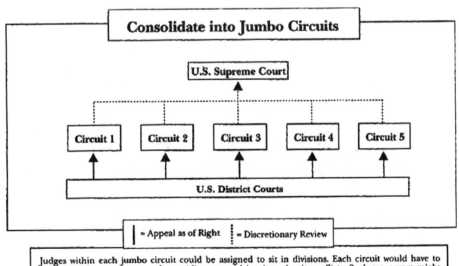

This alternative would curtail intercircuit conflicts and by creating large units might make it easier for the circuits to shift resources within their borders. Small in bancs could resolve intracircuit conflicts and might, with additional modifications, become something like supervisory courts within the courts. Judges within such "jumbo" circuits might sit within specified divisions. "Jumbo" circuits might thus take on the look of the four-tiered regional system described in alternative 2.

STRUCTURAL AND OTHER ALTERNATIVES FOR THE FEDERAL COURTS OF APPEALS 105-21 (Fed. Jud. Ctr. 1993)

Proposals for Structural Change to Reorganize Appellate Capacity. Discussion of restructuring brings together those who favor wider access to the federal courts (and therefore support continued growth of the judiciary) and those who see growth as deplorable but inevitable. The proper size of the federal judiciary has been the focus of much attention of late — the debate has been extensive and public. . . . One point of agreement is that if the nation is to continue using the federal courts as it now does, and turns to the federal courts for even more services, the nation must support the changes necessary to allow the court system to provide high-quality service.

We assume for the purposes of discussing structural change that there will remain for the foreseeable future a large pool of district court and agency terminations that under the present system would be appealable. . . . [A]lternatives for restructuring the current system without curtailing the fundamental right to appeal will do little or nothing to reduce the volume of appeals. No matter how a caseload of 50,000 appeals is distributed among the courts, 50,000 appeals must be handled. And if caseloads grow as some project, many more appeals may need to be handled annually in the coming decades. Proposals for restructuring the federal judicial system, therefore, are concessions to growth and efforts to forestall deterioration. . . .

At the root of most restructuring proposals is a belief about the ideal size of an individual court of appeals. . . . The effectiveness, credibility, and efficiency of a court of appeals depend in part on its ability to function as a unified body. That, in turn, depends on norms of collegiality and the practical ability to observe those norms. What we know about collegiality and its importance to the courts of appeals comes from the observations of judges who have sat on small courts and on large ones, in times of great caseload pressure and in more leisurely eras. . . . Judges tell us that the ability of an appellate court to shape and maintain a coherent body of law depends in part on the sense of circuit judges that they speak for the court as a whole, not just for themselves. This sort of "representative collegiality" is often seen as a characteristic of successful appellate courts, and one on which the persuasive authority of their decisions rests. . . . The result is a body of law that is clearer and more harmonious than might otherwise be expected given the number of judges on the court.

Although collegiality may moderate the effects of growth, growth may ultimately diminish collegiality. The larger a court grows, the more difficult it is for its judges to become familiar with their colleagues. This may be a particular problem when new judges are added to courts in large groups. On the other hand, having too few judges on a court can have the same effect. The greater the workload pressures on judges, the more difficult it is for judges to devote the time necessary to keeping up, either personally or professionally, with the court. . . .

Unfortunately, we cannot distinguish between the effects of court size and the effects of workload on collegiality. The importance of court size, like the proper size of the federal judiciary as a whole, is a matter of some debate. The Federal Courts Study Committee described the debate over whether "bigger is better" as a debate centering on two different conceptions of an appellate court. One view is that a large circuit is a workable, or even preferred, model for a court of appeals, at least if the court is well managed and adopts procedures to monitor the consistency of circuit law (such as a limited *en banc*). The other view is "the traditional concept of a smaller, more intimate, unitary tribunal." The debate over ideal and tolerable court size continues, and influences reactions to proposals on how to organize the federal system's appellate capacity. We turn now to a discussion of the major structural proposals.

●*Total consolidation of circuits.* One set of structural options for the federal court system would maintain the current review pyramid structure but transform the middle tier into one no longer differentiated into regional circuits with distinct identities. The Federal Courts Study Committee described one such option as a "Single, Centrally Organized Court of Appeals." This option would maintain the current number of tiers and points of review but change the structure of the middle tier to allow more flexible resource allocation.

Under this proposal, all appellate judges would be members of a single court of appeals. The proposal provides great flexibility to cope with changing caseload trends, as judges could be assigned to panels throughout the country as and where needed. The court could create and abolish subject-matter panels and conflict resolution mechanisms as its judges deem appropriate, including a second tier within the court to review matters for uniformity. This flexibility, the committee recognized, might come at the price of creating a large bureaucracy. . . .

This approach would dissolve circuit boundaries but not necessarily the notion of circuits. . . . [A]ppellate judges would have their primary assignments near their homes. Regional identities akin to current circuit identities might remain or develop, particularly if appeals continued to be handled in the same locations as at present. That is, if appeals now filed in the Second Circuit will still be handled in New York, and Second Circuit judges continue to have their primary assignments in New York, the disruption caused by a centrally organized system might not be so great as it appears at first glance.

●*Partial consolidation of circuits.* With the success of large courts of appeals an open issue, the Federal Courts Study Committee included in its report the option of consolidating several smaller circuits into a few, perhaps five, "jumbo" or "mega" circuits. . . . [T]his option would retain the current system of appeal as of right from all final district court judgments. Proponents assert that this sort of organization would allow flexible resource allocation within circuit borders and would limit the number of intercircuit conflicts because fewer circuits would exist. The latter advantage seems literally true but simply moves the issue of inconsistency and indeterminacy from between circuits to within them. If one were trying to address a problem of overload at the Supreme Court level, moving to a system of a few large circuits to reduce the number of intercircuit conflicts reaching the Court might be effective, but the same effect could be achieved by an intercircuit tribunal or a regional en banc system that left the present circuits intact. But most observers are concerned less with the capacity of the Supreme Court than with the capacity of the courts of appeals. As critics of large circuits have observed, increasing the number of judges increases the number of possible panel combinations (under current panel creation procedures) and multiplies the number of opinions a circuit judge must read. This proliferation of precedent would require, as the committee acknowledged, more effective ways to avoid or resolve conflicts within a court of appeals.

• *Reducing the size of the circuits.* The main reason for reducing the size of the circuits would be to restore relatively small, collegial courts of appeals. Although caseloads would not decrease, judicial burden might decrease slightly as the number of opinions to read drops. Both the smaller number of judges and the likely reduction in travel could contribute to the creation of a more intimate bench. To the extent that collegiality may be related to the quality of justice dispensed, this is no small advantage.

[T]he relationship between court size and intracircuit conflict is not well defined. Nor do we have sufficient information about the effects of conflict on the behavior of lawyers, litigants, and judges. Thus, the desirability of an alternative whose primary advantage would be the reduction of intracircuit conflict must be considered in light of the other sources of legal uncertainty. If these other sources of legal uncertainty account for more problems in structuring business transactions and predicting litigation outcomes, a restructuring alternative whose chief advantage is the stabilization or reduction of intracircuit conflict might yield more upheaval than relief.

If the ultimate goal of federal court restructuring efforts is to restore and maintain courts of appeals of limited size without several curtailing the growth of the appellate judiciary, the size of the courts of appeals must be reduced by changing circuit boundaries. Incremental change could be effected by dividing circuits whose courts are now larger than an agreed-on acceptable size, or dividing them as their courts reach a certain caseload or number of judges. Alternatively, all the present boundaries could be eliminated and the entire circuit arrangement redrawn.

Circuit splitting to remedy perceived growth problems in the Fifth and Ninth Circuits was the approach recommended in 1975 by the Hruska Commission. Ultimately, the twenty-six circuit judges of the Fifth Circuit agreed, and upon their request Congress divided the circuit, assigning fourteen of those judgeships to a new Fifth Circuit and creating the Eleventh Circuit with the other twelve. The Ninth Circuit judges did not request division, and Congress opted not to divide that circuit. Were Congress to adopt the commonly recommended standard of nine judges as the ideal size of a court of appeals, it would be necessary to split all but one of the present circuits. The Ninth Circuit alone would need to be split into at least three separate circuits. [P]iecemeal circuit division no longer appears to be a practicable remedy for the problems of the courts.

The only other way to achieve the same result without adding a new tier would be to dissolve all circuit boundaries and redraw them. Most versions of this plan would redraw the circuits according to a formula based on the courts' current caseloads. Because of the importance of flexibility in the court system, however, it is generally recognized that it would be desirable to specify whatever the formula would be, so that periodic revisions could take place without the same level of resources and attention now required for revisions to circuit structure. Flexibility could be built into the system by having periodic reconstruction of circuits triggered by a specified event, such as a census, or a predetermined number of filings. Versions entailing continued growth in the number of circuits (e.g., with splits triggered by growth in caseload volume or court size) invite the question of whether there is a point at which the very concept of "circuit" becomes meaningless. Assuming continued caseload growth, the periodic division approach would quickly break down if the goal were to achieve and maintain courts of the "ideal" size of nine to fifteen judges.

Even with current caseloads, redrawing the circuits to create rough caseload equality among circuits would require abandoning the criteria used in the past for circuit construction. For example, as a general rule, circuits have comprised at least three states, generally contiguous. Preferences for contiguity of states could not be accommodated in all cases. Proposals for a one-time revision of circuit boundaries to equalize and cap the number of judges on each court of appeals would, if developed, require more attention to workload burdens beyond the case-counting method. Without a more accurate measure of the burdens associated with different types of appeals, dividing the national appellate caseload among courts of a fixed size would likely result in disparate burdens on appellate judges. . . .

If circuit rearrangement ultimately increased the coherence of the law, as some argue it would, caseloads might decrease in the long run. In the short run, effects on litigation flow might depend on decisions about how precedents would be handled. When the Fifth Circuit was divided, the new Eleventh Circuit adopted the body of Fifth Circuit precedent as it existed at the time of the split, somewhat limiting judges' and lawyers' burdens. It is not clear that such precedent adoption or grafting could be successfully implemented in major realignments. Most plans call not for the "simple" division that occurred when the Eleventh Circuit was created, but for sweeping reorganization or at least the cobbling together of new circuits from portions of several current ones. In those circumstances, litigation might be expected to increase in the short run; both the unpredictability of a new court and the opportunity to establish favorable new circuit law could increase incentives to appeal.

Most observers fear that a large increase in the number of circuits will result in further "balkanization" of the federal courts. A system of many small circuits dilutes the federalizing function of the courts of appeals. A system in which the law of the circuit is identifiable and predictable is advantageous where local predictability is important, and disadvantageous to the extent that it fails to create and maintain a uniform body of federal law. It is generally claimed that the inevitable result of circuit splitting would be a substantial increase in intercircuit conflicts. Even those who do not favor large courts may prefer a limited number of medium-sized and large circuits to the much larger number of circuits that would be necessary to create and maintain courts of eight to ten judges.

Merely reorganizing the present circuits will not significantly reduce appellate caseloads. The post-reorganization restabilization of circuit law might increase litigation in the short run and decrease it in the long run if the new circuits achieve identities that reduce legal uncertainty. In the absence of evidence that litigation rates or appeal rates are driven to a significant degree by the characteristics of the present structure, we cannot predict such changes in either direction. We anticipate that they would be marginal. Adopting any of the proposed circuit realignment alternatives for the sole or primary purpose of reducing appellate court caseloads seems ill-advised. However, if the small circuit approach is desirable, it might best be combined with conflict-resolution mechanisms, as in the following proposal.

The Federal Courts Study Committee described a plan for "Multiple Circuit Appellate Courts Functioning as a Unified Court," under which present circuit boundaries would be dissolved and divisions of nine or ten judges each would be formed. The plan anticipates periodic redrawing of division lines according to an unspecified mechanism, preferably to be developed and applied by the Judicial Conference. Appeals from the decisions of one division would be by petition to the "central division." [I]t appears that discretionary review by the central division would be limited to cases presenting conflicts between regional circuits. The central division, comprising the same number of judges as the number of divisions, would sit only en banc.

[I]t seems likely that the central division members would be drawn from the other divisions rather than be newly appointed. Indeed the notion of the unitary court of appeals is what distinguishes this idea from those that would create an additional tier. To reduce the possibility of divisiveness, the judges of the central division would be of the same rank or stature as the other appellate judges. Although they might under some variants be selected for their experience or by seniority, they would receive the same compensation as all other appellate judges.

Most models of a centrally organized or unified court of appeals share certain features. They would continue to provide an appeal as of right in all cases currently eligible for review, with an additional layer of review for at least some cases. Each would formally retain the three-tier structure and the primacy of the three-judge appellate panel. It appears that in each . . . the opinion of any one panel would bind the rest of the members of the entire appellate system. They would require mechanisms to prevent and resolve conflicts among panels. The plan for a unified court with multiple divisions contemplates a formal and permanent "central division" assigned to resolve conflicts. The description of a three-tiered model with a centrally organized intermediate tier did not specify methods for resolving conflicts, but recognized that the court would need to develop them. For example, it left open the possibility that the court might organize itself into two tiers. If the court chose this option, the "internal second tier" might serve the same function that the central division serves in the multi-tiered proposal, but with more flexibility of membership.

The models also share the advantage of flexibility in allocation of resources. That flexibility may be seen as a disadvantage by those who are the resources to be allocated. The appellate judges who responded to our survey overwhelmingly opposed restructuring plans that would require judges to be available for duty anywhere they might be needed. . . . A rigid or arbitrary assignment system might make the position of federal judge sufficiently unattractive to lower the quality of the bench. But temporary assignment to other courts is not uncommon now, and it might develop that most reassignment needs under a centrally organized system could be handled by voluntary, temporary transfers.

From the litigant's perspective, these proposals add another hurdle (or opportunity) to the litigation process. They are not always explicitly designated as structural changes that add a tier because the judges who would staff the central division in one plan, or perform conflict resolution functions in an "internal tier" in the other, are of the same rank as the appellate judges who decide the appeal in the first instance. Thus, the two proposals may be thought of as half-steps toward adding a new tier to the federal court system. Other proposals addressed by the Federal Courts Study Committee more explicitly did just that.

● *Multi-tiered courts of appeals options.* Under one four-tiered structure, . . . the district courts would remain as currently structured and staffed. Final judgments of the district court would be appealable as of right to one of twenty to thirty divisions of a lower tier appellate court ("Appellate I"). Six of these regional divisions of nine or ten judges each would be grouped in an area. From the regional courts, aggrieved litigants could petition for *certiorari* to a seven-judge higher tribunal for that area of the country. The Court of Appeals for the Federal Circuit would be on a par with the four area courts of appeals, and cases now appealable as of right to that court would continue to be heard there.

The Federal Courts Study Committee description of the four-tiered system does not speak directly to the issue of *stare decisis* in connection with this option, and it is not clear whether the structure the committee envisioned would allow a panel in one division of the Appellate I tier to bind others in that region or just the division. Nor does there appear to be any provision for *en banc* review.

Another multi-tiered system, [another proposed variation], would abolish existing circuit lines and vest all jurisdiction currently with the courts of appeals in a new entity, the United States Court of Appeals. That court, the only federal appellate court between the district courts and the Supreme Court, would not be unified in the sense of the Unified Court of Appeals plans discussed above. Rather it would be divided into parts. Under [the alternate] plan there would be numbered divisions, lettered divisions, and named divisions. The plan may best be characterized as the insertion of a new tier of courts between the district courts and the current courts of appeals, with the work of the new courts loosely concentrated in particular subject-matter areas, much as the work of the U.S. Court of Appeals for the Federal Circuit is now.

Numbered divisions of nine judges each would be created across the United States. The nine judges would be drawn from the circuit judges of at least two contiguous states, including the state containing the district court whose judgments would be reviewed by the division. Thus regional review would be maintained. The jurisdiction of these courts, which would decide the majority of appeals from district court judgments, would include diversity, criminal, constitutional, and statutory cases — all matters other than those in the jurisdiction of the "named divisions." The nine judges would sit in rotating three-judge panels to decide about 1,800 appeals annually. Screening would be permitted, but panels in the numbered divisions would hear oral argument much more frequently than most courts of appeals now do. Most decisions would be unpublished.

Parties aggrieved by the decisions of the numbered divisions could petition for review by a court in a lettered division (A-E). These seven-member divisions would grant review for reasons now typically associated with *en banc* review — for example, to eliminate conflicts involving numbered divisions in the jurisdiction and to issue authoritative decisions on important issues of federal law. Decisions of lettered divisions not to review a case from the numbered division would be final and not subject to review by the Supreme Court. Normally, the decisions of the lettered divisions in cases it chose to review would be published. Cases decided by the lettered divisions would be reviewable only by *certiorari* to the U.S. Supreme Court.

Finally, named divisions would review district court judgments and administrative agency orders in certain kinds of cases. These divisions would be formed by subject matter, and their jurisdiction would include those matters now within the jurisdiction of the Court of Appeals for the Federal Circuit. Named divisions might include Administrative, Commercial, Revenue, and State divisions. Others could be added as needed. The size of the division would depend on the volume of business of that division, but would be in the range of seven to fifteen judges.

If successful, this arrangement would restore some of the traditional appellate process to cases that no longer receive oral argument and collegial deliberation. Some regional presence and connection would be maintained where regional concerns are most pressing, but judges would no longer identify with a particular circuit. Rather, they would be expected to apply the national law. Most conflicts that result from regional interpretation of the national law would be resolved largely in the lettered divisions. Some advantages of specialization would be obtained where particularly beneficial to the national law, but judges would move among divisions over their careers and would not become "specialist" judges.

Adding a tier would maximize the ability of the system to absorb new judicial capacity without having any single court unit grow unacceptably large. By adding another layer of law declaring, it would also allow percolation to occur freely, perhaps faster than in the current structure. But the smaller number of law declarers might "produce a more compact body of primary precedent than the voluminous and increasingly disparate case law likely to be generated by 200 or 300 co-equal circuit judges. . . . " The costs of another tier are substantial — in dollars, in disruption, and in the satisfaction of the judges who find another layer of authority and prestige has been inserted between their own and the highest level of the system. Judges who responded to our survey were overwhelmingly opposed to the addition of new tiers, whether between the district courts and the current courts of appeals, or between the courts of appeals and the Supreme Court.

FINAL REPORT OF THE COMMISSION ON STRUCTURAL ALTERNATIVES FOR THE FEDERAL COURTS OF APPEALS 59-62 (1998)

Structural Options for the Courts of Appeals. We offer no recommendations on the realignment of other circuits and, more than that, propose no general realignment of the circuit structure besides the Ninth Circuit. The Commission has been presented with suggestions that the circuit structure as a whole is antiquated and should be abolished, putting in its place a nation-wide court of appeals organized literally to serve federal appellate needs as they may shift over the years. We have concluded, however, that the system of geographical circuits has not outlived its usefulness and that a decentralized administrative structure for the federal judiciary continues to be an effective means of administering this vast nationwide system of courts.

Current circuit boundaries are, to be sure, the product of history more than logic, and probably would not be the boundaries one would draw if starting afresh. By now, though, those boundaries are firmly established in the American legal order, and changing them would impose substantial disruptive costs.

Some commentators offer caseload inequality as a reason to split circuits; some argue that a circuit should be split when the number of opinions its court of appeals issues passes an unspecified threshold; others take longer appellate disposition times as a sign that a split is in order. [A]ll of these have been advanced by those who would split the Ninth Circuit. But the data we reviewed show that all can be found in substantial measure in one or more other circuits that cannot feasibly be split. If equalizing caseload among circuits, or among circuit judges, were the most important criterion for circuit alignment, a sweeping reconfiguration would be in order. If the number of published opinions or higher-than-average disposition times were the trigger, several circuits would now be candidates for reconfiguration. But caseloads change, more or less unpredictably, and equalizing caseloads has never been a driving principle in circuit configuration. Should caseloads ever become so disproportionate as to cause nationwide concern in the future, the structural alternative for courts of appeals that we recommend here will afford maximum flexibility for circuits to remedy disparities themselves — by requesting new judgeships and arranging them in optimally sized divisions, at a minimum cost and disruption. Furthermore, as explained below, our divisional arrangement avoids circuit splits that would create one- or two-state circuits, which we believe would hinder or preclude the ability of the regional courts of appeals to exercise their federalizing function.

Accordingly, we believe that some changes to the structure of the courts of appeals will help them deal with the conundrum they will face as caseloads grow. On the one hand, if they do not obtain more judge power, they risk unacceptable backlogs of pending cases or an unacceptable decline in the quantity and quality of judicial attention paid to the cases they decide. On the other hand, adding too many judges to a court that must act collegially may heighten the likelihood of incoherence in the law. Although technology offers some promise of a way out of this bind, we doubt that it will suffice to avert it altogether. We believe that the courts of appeals need additional flexibility to structure their operations to meet changing circumstances that cannot now be foreseen. . . .

Divisional Organization of Courts of Appeals. [T]he traditional way to deal with a court of appeals deemed to have grown too large to function effectively was to split the court's circuit and thus the court itself. Congress did that in 1929 when it split the Eighth Circuit to create the Tenth Circuit, and in 1980 when it split the Fifth Circuit to create the Eleventh Circuit. [S]plitting the Ninth Circuit to deal with the problems facing its court of appeals is not practical or desirable. [W]e do not believe circuit-splitting will be a feasible structural option if and when other courts of appeals grow too large to operate as a single decisional unit.

Although other courts are not free from problems, we do not believe any of them need restructuring. At the moment, no other court of appeals approaches the Ninth Circuit's in terms of judgeships. However, it is possible that the press of increased litigation will lead to increases in judgeships in at least some of the courts of appeals and, if so, those courts may also be candidates for some type of restructuring.

If and when that day comes, circuit-splitting as a structural alternative will be even less feasible in most circuits than it is in the Ninth. That is so because . . . regional circuits should consist of at least three states, both to fulfill the federalizing role expected of regional appellate courts and to enlist the interests of several Congressional delegations in the well-being of the circuit and appointments to its court of appeals. Nevertheless, leaving aside the Ninth and District of Columbia Circuits, only two of the other ten regional circuits include six or more states. Five have three states, two have four, and one has five. [The Second, Third, Fifth, Seventh, and Eleventh Circuits have three states. The First and Sixth have four states. The Fourth has five states. The Tenth has six states and the Eighth has seven states.]

In other words, applying our three-states-per-circuit rule, five of the circuits by definition cannot be split and three others can be split only be creating at least one circuit of fewer than three states. Furthermore, circuit splitting is costly and disruptive, entailing as it does the creation of a separate administrative apparatus for any new circuit.

For these reasons, we recommend that Congress, on a permanent basis, give all appellate courts above fifteen judgeships discretion to adopt a divisional organization. When an appellate court exceeds fifteen judgeships it is large enough to make feasible such an internal design, and it is reaching the point where performing its *en banc* function effectively becomes increasingly difficult. In our view, when an appellate court operating as a single decisional unit reaches eighteen judgeships, the *en banc* process becomes too cumbersome to be feasible, and a limited *en banc* does not seem to us to be a long-term solution. We believe that any large court of appeals (that is, a court with eighteen or more judges, and certainly one with more than twenty) should be organized into adjudicative divisions. However, just as courts with more than fifteen judges now have the authority to perform their *en banc* functions through a limited *en banc* (although only the Ninth Circuit's court has chosen to do so), we believe that all courts of appeals with more than fifteen judgeships should have the authority to perform their adjudicative work in divisions.

[Our] proposed statute leaves considerable leeway to a court of appeals in designing a divisional structure. Although not specified in the statute, we contemplate that each division would have an odd number of judges, with a minimum of seven, and preferably no more than eleven. If a court needs to add a number of judges that would make the divisions too large, a new division can be created to maintain the general scheme. Whatever the design, the point is to have each judge of the court assigned to a specific division for a substantial period of time and for each division to exercise exclusive jurisdiction over the cases assigned to it. The statute would require that upon the adoption of a divisional plan the court also create a "Circuit Division" for conflict correction . . . with the sole function of resolving conflicts between or among the divisions. The circuit-wide *en banc* procedure would be abolished once a divisional plan is in effect, although each division would continue to take cases *en banc* as necessary.

Different circuits might implement the divisional arrangement in different ways according to their needs, and we expect that creative judicial minds would tailor these alternatives to fit local circumstances. Some courts might opt for a regional organization in which not only the source of appeals (primarily the district courts) but the composition of the judicial division would be entirely tied to geography. Other courts might adopt an arrangement whereby judges are primarily assigned to the division in which they reside, but would sit regularly with one or more other divisions, not only to help out with caseloads as needed but to ensure cross-fertilization.

Thomas E. Baker, *Some Preliminary Comments on the Final Report of the White Commission,* 15 J.L. & POL. 471 (1999)[2]

The White Commission was specifically charged with making some recommendations about the Ninth Circuit. It did not recommend that Congress split the Ninth Circuit, however. Instead, the Commission recommended legislation reorganizing the Ninth Circuit into three regionally-based divisions. . . .

Structural Options for the Courts of Appeals. What is more interesting for federal court-watchers and more important for the bench and the bar beyond the Ninth Circuit is that the White Commission went on to recommend that Congress also authorize the other courts of appeals to reorganize themselves along divisional lines. . . .

Reorganizing the Courts of Appeals into Divisions. In a move that is sure to be as controversial as it is original and provocative, the White Commission imagined an entirely new way to deal with problems of more and more appeals and more and more judges in the courts of appeals. The Commission drafted a proposed statute to amend 28 U.S.C. § 46 to authorize any court of appeal with more than fifteen judgeships to organize itself into adjudicative divisions. This proposal would immediately apply to the largest regional courts of appeals: the Fifth Circuit (seventeen judges) and the Sixth Circuit (sixteen judges). But more importantly, it would portend the future for the rest of the courts of

---

2 Copyright © 1999 Journal of Law and Politics. Reprinted with permission.

appeals as the growing appellate caseload ineluctably increases pressure on Congress to create additional circuit judgeships.

According to the White Commission, the particular details of the divisional reorganization should be left to the judges in each circuit and we should expect regional variations. . . . [T]he Commission . . . went on to describe in some particular statutory detail how the Commission imagined the divisional organization concept should work in the Ninth Circuit. Therefore, the White Commission's blueprint for the Ninth Circuit illustrates and illuminates our understanding of the novel concept of reorganization of the courts of appeals into regional divisions.

The Ninth Circuit would be divided into three regional divisions. Each regional division would have exclusive jurisdiction over appeals from the district courts within its region. A regional division would function as a semi-autonomous appellate court sitting in panels. A panel decision in one regional division would not be binding in another regional division. Each regional division would have a divisional *en banc* to rehear important cases or to reconsider a panel decision that creates a conflict with another regional division. Existing and still binding Ninth Circuit precedents along with divisional panel decisions could be overruled only within a division by the divisional *en banc* procedure. The Commission further recommended the creation of a "Circuit Division" for conflict resolution to replace the present Ninth Circuit limited *en banc* court. The Circuit Division would have discretionary jurisdiction only to resolve direct conflicts between or among the three regional divisions. The Commission proposed an eight year experiment with regional divisions in the Ninth Circuit; at the end of the study period, the Federal Judicial Center would report to the Judicial Conference of the United States, which would then recommend to Congress whether the divisional arrangement should be continued with or without modification.

Under the regional division organization, the appellate procedures would be as follows. From the decision of the district court, there would be an appeal-as-of-right before a three-judge panel of a "regional division" followed by a petition for rehearing to the "divisional *en banc* court." If and only if the decision created a conflict with a decision of another regional division, there could be a discretionary rehearing before the "circuit division" for conflict resolution. Otherwise, the next stop is a petition for *certiorari* in the Supreme Court.

The White Commission somehow failed to include a suggestion that Rube Goldberg be named Chief Judge of the reorganized Ninth Circuit. More seriously, . . . I agree[] with its proposed experiment with regional divisions in the Ninth Circuit, but I disagree[] with the related proposal to authorize the other courts of appeals to reorganize themselves into regional divisions. It seems to me that Congress and the Third Branch should wait and see how this divisional concept plays out in the Ninth Circuit before generalizing the experiment in the other courts of appeals and without further compounding any Hawthorne effect that might result simply from obliging the other circuits to implement their own peculiar variations of the concept. Therefore, until some time and study of the Ninth Circuit proposal have passed, I would advise that Congress not authorize such an open-ended and variable national experiment in the rest of the regional courts of appeals.

My limited endorsement, however, is not without reservation. In fact, there was another experiment in the 1980s with regional divisions back in the old Fifth Circuit before that circuit was divided into the new Fifth Circuit and the Eleventh Circuit. The Fifth Circuit experiment suggests two cautions: first, the rules of *stare decisis* behind the concept of the law of the circuit became so complicated that they nearly defied description; second, the hind-sighted political reality was that the divisional stage of development, implemented by the judges as an administrative experiment, almost immediately precipitated the permanent statutory division of the circuit by congressional reformers. So my worries are first that the divisional concept will increase the confusion and uncertainty in the law of the Ninth Circuit, and second that it will prematurely accelerate the momentum towards a formal and complete division among judges and members of Congress.

I am also a little concerned about the White Commission's willingness to reject the venerable principle of the law of the circuit to the extent that decisions made in one regional division would not bind other divisions. Variations in the federal law — when the same federal statute or the same provision of the Constitution is interpreted one way in one circuit and another way in another circuit — admittedly are a necessary evil of the current federal appellate geography, but we should be looking for ways to reduce their frequency and their persistence. The Commission's Circuit Division for conflict correction may not be equal to the task. This proposal would put an end to the limited *en banc* mechanism, which to my mind is one of the most problematic and ineffective features of the current system, and that would be an improvement. But the Commission's proposal would create a rather complex and subtle rehearing procedure from panel decisions. Panels in one division would not be bound by prior panel decisions in another division, but their decision to create a conflict would be reviewable by the Circuit Division for conflict resolution. At the same time, each division would continue to rehear *en banc* panel decisions it deemed important or mistaken. I am not as sanguine as the Commission that these nuanced distinctions are easily made and readily distinguishable. But on balance, these are relatively small concerns. Besides, I now live and work in the Eighth Circuit, which has only eleven circuit judgeships and thus would not be eligible for the experiment with divisional reorganization.

FINAL REPORT OF THE COMMISSION ON STRUCTURAL ALTERNATIVES FOR THE FEDERAL COURTS OF APPEALS 29-40 (1998)

There is no persuasive evidence that the Ninth Circuit (or any other circuit, for that matter) is not working effectively, or that creating new circuits will improve the administration of justice in any circuit or overall. Furthermore, splitting the circuit would impose substantial costs of administrative disruption, not to mention the monetary costs of creating a new circuit. Accordingly, we do not recommend to Congress and the President that they consider legislation to split the circuit.

Nevertheless, there is consensus among appellate judges throughout the country (including about one-third of the appellate judges in the Ninth

Circuit) that a court of appeals, being a court whose members must work collegially over time to develop a consistent and coherent body of law, functions more effectively with fewer judges than are currently authorized for the Ninth Circuit Court of Appeals. In our opinion, apparently shared by more than two-thirds of all federal appellate judges, the maximum number of judges for an effective appellate court functioning as a single decisional unit is somewhere between eleven and seventeen. . . .

The Ninth Judicial Circuit covers the states of Alaska, Arizona, California, Hawaii, Idaho, Montana, Nevada, Oregon, and Washington, as well as Guam and the Commonwealth of the Northern Mariana Islands. . . . Its court of appeals . . . has twenty-eight authorized judgeships. . . .

In Fiscal Year 1997, 8,692 appeals were filed in the Ninth Circuit, and 8,515 were terminated. Of those, 1,889 were terminated on the merits after oral argument and 2,952 without oral argument. . . . The median time from notice of appeal to final disposition for appeals terminated on the merits was 14.4 months. The court issued opinions for publication in 849 cases.

The debate over whether to split the Ninth Circuit involves numerous claims and counterclaims. . . . They concern the effects of the size of the court of appeals, its geographic jurisdiction, and the court's place within the federal appellate system. We have given serious consideration to all of these arguments. We summarize the major issues. . . .

a. The ability of the court of appeals to function effectively and timely. Proponents of a split assert that a court of twenty-eight judgeships, plus senior judges, cannot decide cases in a timely fashion; they point to workload data showing that the Ninth Circuit ranks at or near the bottom in time from the filing of a case in the district court to the final disposition in the court of appeals.

Split opponents respond that the court of appeals is among the fastest in the nation in disposition time once a case is argued or submitted to a panel, and attribute the court's overall slowness to its unfilled judgeships and resulting inability to assemble panels to hear cases ready for decision.

b. The ability of the court to produce a coherent body of circuit law. Those who favor a split assert that the multiplicity of decision makers renders it less likely that circuit judges can stay informed of the law that other panels are making, and that district judges, litigants, and parties seeking to conform their conduct to circuit law encounter more serious obstacles to assessing what that law is. The judges, they say, cannot keep up with the large volume of court of appeals decisions. Pre-publication circulation of opinions among all judges of the court is impossible.

They claim an increased incidence of intracircuit conflicts because an appellate court as large as the Ninth's precludes close, regular, and frequent contact in joint decision making, and thus the collegiality that lets judges accommodate differences of opinion in order to produce a coherent body of law. They point to the over 3,000 possible combinations of three-judge panels on a twenty-eight-judge court.

Those opposing a split respond that the court has developed a sophisticated issue-tracking system that allows judges to know when other panels are deciding like issues and an electronic opinion delivery system that allows judges to know the current law of the circuit when they are deciding cases. They say that any court with more than fifteen or sixteen judges produces a large number of three-judge panel combinations.

They also assert that collegiality is an elusive concept and that counting panel combinations cannot measure the ability of judges in the late twentieth century to work together to fashion law. They note that the circuit's court of appeals judges have numerous opportunities to be with one another at meetings and symposia, and point to evidence of rancor and lack of collegiality on courts much smaller than the Ninth.

c. The ability of the court to perform its en banc function effectively. Proponents of a circuit split say that the court convenes *en banc* proceedings too infrequently, which helps explain the court of appeal's high reversal rate in the Supreme Court. A better *en banc* procedure would correct panel errors before they reach the Supreme Court. They also argue that the relative infrequency of *en banc* rehearings in the Ninth Circuit deprives judges and lawyers of sufficient guidance as to circuit law. Furthermore, split proponents argue that convening a different group of judges for each *en banc* proceeding frustrates the development of stable circuit law, and using a panel only slightly larger than a third of the court's full judgeship complement contravenes the very concept of an "*en banc*" court.

Supporters of the court as currently structured say that its *en banc* process is efficient and effective. They note that very few *en banc* decisions are closely divided, so it is unlikely a full-court *en banc* would produce different results. They further assert that the Supreme Court takes cases from the Ninth Circuit in numbers roughly proportional to the circuit's share of the national appellate caseload, and that, over time, reversal rates have not been appreciably higher in Ninth Circuit cases than in others. They also say that to the extent the Supreme Court reverses the Ninth Circuit's Court of Appeals more than others, that is largely because novel issues arise in the diverse regions of the West that the court serves.

d. The implications of the size of the court's geographic jurisdiction for federalism, regionalism, and effective court operations. Those who would realign the circuit say that its size means that citizens of the West perceive the federal appellate judiciary as a remote institution, unfamiliar with the problems and points of view of those citizens' identifiable regions. Citizens in the northwestern states claim that judges from other regions, especially California, decide cases involving their way of life with insufficient appreciation of the legal problems that way of life engenders. They also claim that the circuit's size allows a panel of three judges to determine the law for the vast region that makes up the circuit, without an effective *en banc* mechanism to act as a check on that power. Finally, they assert that the size of the circuit creates special travel problems for judges who live in more remote areas.

Opponents of a circuit split assert that the West is indeed one region and that the federal law under which it operates should be determined by a single federal appellate court. They say it is especially important that federal law governing the transactions and litigation of Asian-Pacific and maritime businesses operating along the western seaboard should be interpreted by a single appellate court; only historic accident allocates the eastern seaboard and Gulf Coast to six circuits. They note furthermore that decisions to which Northwestern interests object are not necessarily the product of judges from non-Northwestern states. They state also that the burdens and expense of judges' travel within the Ninth Circuit are exaggerated, and that the court's established and growing technological capacity, including electronic mail and videoconferencing, will substantially reduce the need for travel in coming years.

e. The relationship between circuit reconfiguration and intercircuit conflicts. Opponents of circuit splitting say that creating another court of appeals increases the likelihood of intercircuit conflicts and the corresponding burden on the Supreme Court to resolve them. Furthermore, they argue that the nation must find some way other than circuit splitting to deal with problems of large courts of appeals, inasmuch as other courts will soon be as large as the Ninth is now. Splitting circuits will balkanize federal law.

Proponents of circuit reconfiguration say that federal laws susceptible to conflicting interpretations will yield conflicts even among few appellate courts, and thirteen or fourteen regional circuits will not produce notably more intercircuit conflicts than twelve. Furthermore, they argue that intercircuit conflicts have been a less persistent and intolerable problem than asserted and note that the Supreme Court can resolve additional conflicts, if any arise.

f. The practicality of dividing the circuit. Opponents of a circuit split say that even if the Ninth Circuit were reconfigured, a large and growing circuit would remain, primarily because of the high volume of appeals generated by California. They argue that it is thus better to make the current structure work effectively than hope to solve any problems of this large circuit by splitting it and that reconfiguring it by dividing California between circuits would wreak havoc of legal uncertainty within the state.

Split proponents say that a new Twelfth Circuit will be of a sufficient size to constitute a viable circuit, and that whatever problems a new Ninth Circuit that includes California would pose would be less troublesome than those posed by the current Ninth. Many proponents discount as well the claims that dividing California between two circuits is not feasible, and note that either an intercircuit conflict resolution mechanism or the Supreme Court could resolve any conflicts that might arise.

g. The administrative efficacy of the Ninth Circuit. Opponents of a circuit split point out that it would deprive all of the Ninth Circuit's Courts of efficient administration and economies of scale. A large Circuit, they say, can administer itself more innovatively than a smaller circuit, as evidenced by the Ninth's automation, training, and other programs. Furthermore, large circuits have more flexibility in the intracircuit transfer of judges at all levels.

Proponents of reconfiguration argue that whatever administrative benefits the current arrangement provides could be replicated in new Ninth and Twelfth Circuits. Furthermore, they say that administration of the current Ninth Circuit consumes undue judge time because of the many oversight bodies needed to ensure judicial control of such a large entity.

Finally, proponents note that a circuit split would give judges now in the Ninth Circuit more representation on the Judicial Conference of the United States, but opponents respond that Ninth Circuit judges are already well represented on the Conference's committees, which are integral elements of the federal judiciary's governance system. . . .

Criteria Informing the Debate: The above arguments of those who favor change and of those who oppose change have both objective and subjective components. We have reviewed all of the available objective data routinely used in court administration to measure the performance and efficiency of the federal appellate courts, but we cannot say that the statistical criteria tip decisively in one direction or the other. While there are differences among the courts of appeals, differences in judicial vacancy rates, caseload mix, and operating procedures make it impossible to attribute them to a single factor such as size.

Subjective criteria, such as consistency and predictability of the law, are obviously more difficult to evaluate but are widely regarded as a high priority for the courts of appeals. . . . District judges in the Ninth Circuit report finding the law insufficiently clear to give them confidence in their decisions on questions of law about as often as their counterparts in other circuits, but more frequently report that difficulties stem from inconsistencies between published and unpublished opinions. Lawyers in the Ninth Circuit report somewhat more difficulty discerning circuit law and predicting outcomes of appeals than lawyers elsewhere. Ninth Circuit lawyers, more often than others, reported as a "large" or "grave" problem the difficulty of discerning circuit law due to conflicting precedents, and the unpredictability of appellate results until the panel's identity is known. More Ninth Circuit lawyers reported that they "frequently" have trouble predicting the outcome of an appeal. But when all is said and done, neither we nor, we believe, anyone else, can reduce consistency and predictability to statistical analysis. . . . However, it is our judgment that the consistent, predictable, coherent development of the law over time is best fostered in a decisional unit that is small enough for the kind of close, continual, collaborative decision making that "seeks the objective of as much excellence in a group's decision as its combined talents, experience, and energy permit." [To this end, the Commission went on to recommend that the Ninth Circuit be reorganized into three divisions as summarized in the preceding excerpt.]

NOTES

1. The first excerpt above is from the FEDERAL COURTS STUDY COMMITTEE REPORT. In 1988, Congress created the Study Committee as an *ad hoc* committee within the Judicial Conference of the United States. Members included representatives of the three branches of the federal government, state government officials, practitioners, and academics. The Study Committee surveyed the federal judiciary and solicited the views of citizens' groups, bar organizations, research groups, academics, civil rights groups, and others. Numerous public meetings and regional hearings were held. In its official charge to the Study Committee, Congress asked for an evaluation of the structure and administration of the courts of appeals. That section of the Study Committee's Final Report on appellate structure is excerpted above. The Study Committee began this section with the given that the federal appellate courts

are faced with a "'crisis of volume'" that will continue and require some structural reform eventually. The Study Committee's black-letter recommendation reads: "Fundamental structural alternatives deserve the careful attention of Congress, the courts, bar associations and scholars over the next five years. The committee itself has studied various structural alternatives. Without endorsing any, it lists a few here to stimulate further inquiry and discussion." REPORT OF THE FEDERAL COURTS STUDY COMMITTEE at 116-17 (1990). What is your first impression of each of these proposals?

2. The second excerpt above is from a Study conducted by the Federal Judicial Center — the think tank of the federal judicial branch. It more fully and more carefully examined the systemic ramifications of the various structural alternatives sketched by the Federal Courts Study Committee, along with some variations on them. What are some of the advantages and disadvantages of adopting each of these proposals? Later sections in this Chapter will separately consider some of the seemingly more popular proposals among reformers: creating a fourth tier, appellate subject matter jurisdiction, discretionary appellate jurisdiction, and district court review.

3. Go back to the introduction to this section and reconsider the list of questions to ask of each of these proposed reforms. How does the proposal accommodate projected increases in the number of appeals? How does the proposal accommodate projected increases in the number of appellate judges? Will the proposal result in "too many" or "too few" circuits compared to the currently existing twelve regional circuits plus the Federal Circuit? What does it mean to criticize a proposal for resulting in "too many" or "too few" circuits — is there some principle for determining how many circuits there ought to be? Why does it matter how many circuits there are? What are the salient abstract features of an individual circuit for an IAC that is organized into circuits? What effect will the proposal have on *stare decisis* and the law of the circuit — will there be more or will there be fewer intracircuit conflicts and how will they be resolved? What effect will the proposal have on the national law — will there be more or will there be fewer intercircuit conflicts and how will they be resolved? How will the proposal affect the Supreme Court? How will trial courts experience the proposed reform in the way they are supervised for errors? How will litigants and lawyers experience the proposed reform in the appellate processes? Overall, does the change being proposed solve the problems in the existing system without creating new problems? Does the proposal preserve the appellate imperatives? The existence of so many alternative proposals that have not yet been adopted is a good indication that the assumptions behind these proposals are as deeply contested as are the proposals themselves.

4. The Commission on Structural Alternatives for the Federal Courts of Appeals (known as the "White Commission" after its Chair, Justice Byron White) was the result of a political stalemate in Congress between those who favored and those who opposed splitting the U.S. Ninth Circuit. The Commission was charged to study the current structure and alignment of the federal intermediate courts, particularly the Ninth Circuit, and to make "recommendations for such changes in circuit boundaries or structure as may be appropriate for the expeditious and effective disposition of the caseload of the

Federal Courts of Appeals, consistent with fundamental concepts of fairness and due process." Pub. L. No. 105-119, Title III, § 305(1)(B), 111 Stat. 2440, 2491 (1997). The Commission reviewed the previous studies, developed statistical data from the Federal Judicial Center and the Administrative Office of the U.S. Courts, and gathered new data directly from the courts of appeals. The Commission consulted experts and conducted independent surveys of federal judges and lawyers who practiced before the federal courts. Public hearings were held and written statements responding to a draft report were collected. The first of two excerpts above from the White Commission's REPORT rejects the most often used congressional reform of the past, namely splitting circuits with too large caseloads and too many judges, and instead endorses a new never-used reform to reorganize the courts of appeals into adjudicative divisions. The next excerpt from Professor Baker describes how the divisional reorganization would work in the Ninth Circuit and goes on to argue that Congress should wait to see how it works in that one court before authorizing it for all the other courts of appeals. Bills were introduced in Congress to implement the White Commission's proposal, but they were not enacted. What are the strengths and weaknesses of the divisional reorganization proposal for the U.S. Courts of Appeals? What are the arguments that a divisional reorganization is better than old-fashioned circuit splitting? What are the indicators for determining when there should be a divisional reorganization? Try to apply the evaluative questions listed above in Note 3 to the proposal for divisional reorganization of the courts of appeals.

5. Any discussion of reorganizing the intermediate tier of the federal appellate courts would not be complete without some particularized mention of the U.S. Ninth Circuit. The second of the two excerpts from the White Commission REPORT above briefly summarizes the decades long debate over whether to split the Ninth Circuit. Do the arguments persuade you one way or the other? If you were a lawyer practicing in the Ninth Circuit, what arguments in the debate would be most persuasive to you? If you were a judge on the Ninth Circuit, would you want the court to remain intact or to be divided? If you were in Congress, would you support or oppose legislation to divide the Ninth Circuit? Would some arguments matter more to you if you were a member of Congress from one of the nine states that make up the circuit? Is the Ninth Circuit *sui generis*, *i.e.*, in a class all by itself and deserving of its own unique reorganization, or should it be subject to the same appellate norms and same appellate reforms as the rest of the U.S. courts of appeals? *See generally* RESTRUCTURING JUSTICE: THE INNOVATIONS OF THE NINTH CIRCUIT AND THE FUTURE OF THE FEDERAL COURTS 6 (Arthur D. Hellman, ed. 1990); Thomas E. Baker, *On Redrawing Circuit Boundaries — Why the Proposal to Divide the United States Court of Appeals for the Ninth Circuit Is Not Such a Good Idea*, 22 ARIZ. ST. L.J. 917 (1990); Arthur D. Hellman, *The Unkindest Cut: The White Commission Proposal to Restructure the Ninth Circuit*, 73 S. CAL. L. REV. 377 (2000); *Symposium on Managing the Federal Courts: Will the Ninth Circuit be a Model for Change?*, 34 U.C. DAVIS L. REV. 379 (2000).

6. The White Commission's most significant and novel insight was that there is a conceptual and legal distinction between the circuit and its court of appeals. Previously, Congress had assumed that the only way to deal with an overly large court of appeals was to split the circuit. The White Commission

rejected this premise, and insisted that there is a difference between the circuit and its court of appeals. The circuit is purely a territorial, administrative unit, encompassing district courts as well as the court of appeals; it has no adjudicative function. By contrast, the court of appeals is purely an adjudicative body, wholly apart from the administrative functions of the circuit. The Commission found no difficulties with the circuit as an administrative unit; the problems lay with the adjudicative functions of the court of appeals. This theoretical construct enabled the Commission to avoid the difficulties of circuit splitting and to address the adjudicative problems by recommending a divisional organization within the court of appeals. Is this new insight a useful long-range guide, as the Commission thought, for managing future growth in other courts of appeals so as to adhere to the concept that no circuit should consist of fewer than three contiguous states? *See generally* Joseph F. Weiss, Jr., *Nine Divided By Three: A Formula for Unification?*, 15 J.L. & POL. 445, 451 (1999).

7. Contemplating future reforms of the federal appellate courts, the White Commission recognized the inevitability of adding appellate judgeships to admit that "even the innovations proposed here will fail if there are not enough judges for the proper administration of appellate justice." FINAL REPORT OF THE COMMISSION ON STRUCTURAL ALTERNATIVES FOR THE FEDERAL COURTS OF APPEALS 60 (1998).

III. CREATING A NEW APPELLATE TIER

More than a hundred years ago, the federal court system followed the basic pattern of judicial evolution we studied in Chapter 6. In 1891, a two-tiered system developed into a three-tiered system when an intermediate appellate court was added between the Supreme Court and the trial courts in order to deal with dramatic increases in the caseload and the backlog of the Supreme Court. In Chapter 12, we studied how the jurisdiction of the Supreme Court has been revised repeatedly since then to provide the justices with more and more authority over their docket to choose which cases to decide. Today, the *certiorari* discretion is virtually complete, subject only to the rules, traditions, and practices that have built up around the justices' selection of cases. This section goes back to pick up the story line broken off in Chapter 12 about whether the Supreme Court is deciding "too many" or "too few" cases and whether or not the federal court system needs additional appellate capacity to maintain the consistency and coherency of the national law. The question for debate is whether a new level of appellate court ought to be created between the Supreme Court and the U.S. Courts of Appeals and how it should be structured. While the debate over these proposals has quieted, at least for now, reexamining the arguments that were made for creating a new appellate tier and studying some of the alternative proposals provides insights into the present system and glimpses into the possible future of the federal appellate courts.

The general concern is about intercircuit conflicts, *i.e.*, when the same federal statute or the same provision of the U.S. Constitution is interpreted one way by one court of appeals and another way by another court of appeals. Of more specific concern, as we have seen in the menus of reform proposals presented in the previous section, is the actual incidence and the persistence of intercircuit conflicts, *i.e.*, when conflicts multiply among the circuits and accumulate in number and then become lasting, even permanent, regional inconsistencies in the supposedly national law. This section focuses on whether or not the current structure of the federal appellate courts is equal to the task of resolving intercircuit conflicts efficiently and satisfactorily so that the national law is consistent and coherent. The first set of the following readings summarize the ebb and flow of the debate whether intercircuit conflicts are a significant problem with the existing structure and the second set of readings describe the various versions of a new appellate court that have been proposed over the last few decades.

A. Identifying and Categorizing Intercircuit Conflicts

Thomas E. Baker & Douglas D. McFarland, *The Need for a New National Court,* 100 Harv. L. Rev. 1400, 1404-09 (1987)[3]

The Need for More Unity in the National Law. [Justice Rehnquist recently concluded:] "The Court cannot review a sufficiently significant portion of the decisions of any federal court of appeals to maintain the supervisory authority that it maintained over the federal courts fifty years ago; it simply is not able or willing, given the other constraints upon its time, to review all the decisions that result in a conflict in the applicability of federal law."

Were the Supreme Court's primary task to correct errors of lower federal courts and state supreme courts and to achieve absolute uniformity in the national law, the Court would be doomed to failure. The Court's impact is necessarily limited by the relatively small number of cases — [a maximum back in the 1980s of] 170 or so — that it can select for plenary review from among the tens of thousands of cases state and federal courts decide each year. The Court must instead confine itself to defining and vindicating general constitutional rights, maintaining a reasonable degree of uniformity in federal law, and preserving the constitutional distribution of powers between the states and the national government and among the three coordinate federal branches. The Court accomplishes these constitutional goals by deciding select, discrete cases that involve recurring, unresolved issues of national significance.

As the system was originally designed in 1891, the newly created circuit courts of appeals were to play the basic role of error correction that the Supreme Court could not. Docket growth at the court of appeals level has, however, threatened this design. During the last twenty-five years, appeals to the courts of appeals have increased nine-fold; a caseload of 3713 in 1960 grew to 33,360 in 1985. To cope with this avalanche of appeals, Congress has more than doubled the number of circuit judgeships. All of those appellate judgments and all of those appellate judges, along with the thousands of decisions of federal law from the highest courts in the fifty states, are reviewable only in one Supreme Court of nine justices. As a result, the Supreme Court's ability

---

[3] Copyright © 1987 Harvard Law Review. Reprinted with permission.

to impose uniformity on the courts of appeals has been greatly diminished. In 1924, the Court reviewed about one in ten decisions of the courts of appeals. Even twenty-five years ago, the Court reviewed between two and three percent of all court of appeals decisions. In recent years, however, output of the courts of appeals has grown much more rapidly than the Supreme Court's maximum capacity for supervision, and in the 1984 Term the Court was able to review only 0.56% of courts of appeals decisions. Thus, the decisions of courts of appeals have become as pure as ivory snow — 99 and 44/100ths percent free from review. Reality has overtaken theory as these courts of error, at least for practical purposes, have become the final expositors of federal law in their geographical region in all but a miniscule number of cases. As a result of the Supreme Court's forced abdication, conflicting decisions among the circuits have made federal law less uniform than ever. Many conflicts go unresolved, and still more areas of federal law appear incoherent. In recent Supreme Court Terms, intercircuit conflicts have accounted for approximately five percent of the entire docket and one-third of the signed opinions. In the 1985 Term . . . the justices noted a conflict in no fewer than forty-four of the 146 signed opinions from the Court. In addition, dissenting opinions from the denial of *certiorari* noted at least forty additional conflicts cases in the 1985 Term, accumulating seventy-three total individual dissenting votes. This is some measure of the intolerable number of conflicts on the docket that must be turned away.

Even these statistics have a tip-of-the-iceberg quality. A comprehensive study of the docket of the 1984 Term found fifty-four conflicts cases presenting fifty-seven distinct intercircuit conflicts issues among the 158 cases decided after plenary review. The study found an additional eighty-two intercircuit conflicts cases properly presenting federal law conflicts among the 1,560 paid cases from the courts of appeals summarily denied review. In total, 166 conflicts cases were decided, consolidated, summarily disposed of, or denied review in the 1984 Term. In more than 200 additional cases, the pleadings suggested the existence of a conflict on the merits that was beyond the Court's resolution because of a jurisdictional or procedural defect or because the decisions were distinguishable. Finally, we may assume that a great many decisions by the courts of appeals create conflicts that never reach the Supreme Court's docket. This assumption is supported by a 1982 study of the caseload of one of the twelve regional courts of appeals, which estimated that ninety decisions of that court that year involved a conflict with a decision of another circuit, thirty-six of which created a conflict for the first time. Multiplying that number by approximately twelve gives some idea of the enormous number of intercircuit conflicts that actually arise each year.

The large number of unresolved conflicts impedes the smooth and consistent functioning of our justice system. Our federal appellate courts provide guidance to citizens — and to the lawyers who advise them — on how to order their affairs, and to lower federal courts on how to decide disputes in a consistent and coherent manner. One would be naive to suggest that national law ought to be perfectly uniform, without flexibility or nuance; nonetheless, under the current system, in which conflict is not simply tolerated but actually encouraged, uncertainty or incoherence is inevitable. This uncertainty makes the work of judges, lawyers, and administrators more difficult and more costly.

The mere possibility that our judicial system will tolerate and sustain conflicting interpretations of the same statute creates uncertainty and invites relitigation.

The potential that courts will interpret the same provision of the Constitution or section of a federal statute differently in different parts of the country is exacerbated by the conventions of the courts of appeals. The concept of the "law of the circuit," sometimes called the rule of interpanel accord, obliges a panel of circuit judges to treat as binding precedent earlier decisions of that same court of appeals, absent intervening *en banc* or Supreme Court action. Decisions of other courts of appeals, however, are deemed merely persuasive. This practice weakens the theory of one national law.

The discrepancies created by this system attract strategic and inefficient litigation; private and institutional litigants alike have an incentive to forum shop and relitigate the same case in different circuits following an adverse ruling in one court of appeals only within that circuit. For example, by the time the Supreme Court finally decided the seemingly straightforward issue of whether the United States Postal Service is immune from state court garnishment proceedings, the government had relitigated the issue some twenty times in district courts and eight times in different courts of appeals.

Of course, the conclusion does not necessarily follow that anything need be done about this situation. One approach, known as "percolation," holds that we should allow conflicts to continue, to increase in number, and to ossify through adherence to the rule of *stare decisis* within circuits. The rationale behind percolation is that allowing an issue to "simmer" while several judges and different courts approximate different solutions will provide guidance to the Supreme Court when it ultimately decides to resolve the conflict.

The percolation approach is the *status quo*; it has been embraced by those who do not admit the need for structural court reform. We remain unpersuaded. We cannot accept the underlying logic behind percolation — the notion that somehow a better-reasoned Supreme Court decision will result from subjecting citizens in different parts of the country to differing interpretations of the same national law, either constitutional or statutory. The framers of the Constitution and the drafters of federal statutes did not intend that our national law have "more variations than we have time zones."

When a state court is involved in a conflict with a federal court over an interpretation of federal law, supremacy of federal law trumps uniformity. Supremacy conflicts directly implicate questions of federalism — the tension between state sovereignty and national supremacy — and present a challenge to the constitutional role of the Supreme Court far greater than that posed by the *de facto* lawmaking power of the federal courts of appeal. This is so whether one perceives that the state court has gone beyond the actual federal policy . . . or not far enough. . . .

Finally, vertical conflicts — those in which an inferior federal court or a state court deciding a federal issue strays from Supreme Court precedent — interfere in a profound way with the Court's ability to maintain and elaborate its own precedents. Because one Court can do, at best, an incomplete job of declaring and policing the law, a new national court, acting in harmony with the Supreme Court, could help police the precedents when a lower court explicitly declines to follow, treats as unauthoritative, inadequately distinguishes, or simply ignores some controlling decision.

Tolerating numerous conflicts under the rubric of percolation creates an incoherence and uncertainty in national law that results in serious inequities. Conflicts threaten the very purpose of the establishment of one supreme national court: "to secure the national rights & Uniformity of Judgments" contemplated under one national government. Justice White stated well the great mischief worked by the current plethora of conflicts in our national law:

> [D]enying review of decisions that conflict with other decisions of Courts of Appeals or State Supreme Courts results in the federal law being enforced differently in different parts of the country. What is a crime, an unfair labor practice or an unreasonable search and seizure in one place is not a crime, unfair practice or illegal search in another jurisdiction. Or citizens in one circuit do not pay the same taxes that those in other circuits must pay. It may be that occasionally it would be of use to leave a conflict unresolved in order to await the views of other courts; but for the most part, the conflicts that we turn down are not in that category, and they invite prompt resolution in this Court, which now is the only forum that can provide nationwide uniformity. And this is to say nothing of those cases involving no conflict but obviously important statutory or constitutional issues that warrant authoritative review.

Clearly, greater capacity is needed for achieving a satisfactory measure of uniformity in our national law. The question of how best to achieve it remains.

Arthur D. Hellman, *Light on a Darkling Plain: Intercircuit Conflicts in the Perspective of Time and Experience,* 1998 SUP. CT. REV. 247[4]

Background. [In] Section 302 of the Judicial Improvements Act of 1990 . . . Congress asked the Federal Judicial Center, the research arm of the federal judiciary, to conduct a study to ascertain "the number and frequency of conflicts among the judicial circuits . . . that remain unresolved because they are not heard by the Supreme Court." Congress further requested that the Center determine the extent to which the unresolved conflicts are "intolerable." The Center asked me to design and conduct the study.

Identifying Conflicts. Scholars, judges, and lawyers have disagreed for more than half a century over what constitutes an intercircuit conflict. In Section 302, Congress framed the inquiry in a way that made it largely unnecessary to rely on any abstract definition. The statutory language suggested that the task of assessing the consequences of conflicts — and thus their tolerability — should be separated from the determination whether a conflict exists. The legislative history called for a study that would provide, to the extent possible, objective data. These themes shaped the methods I adopted and the criteria I used.

---

[4] Copyright © 1998 The University of Chicago Press. Reprinted with permission

The study was carried out in two phases. In the first phase, I analyzed two sets of cases that the Supreme Court declined to hear. The first group included all cases in the 1988, 1989, and 1990 Terms in which Justice Byron White dissented from the denial of *certiorari*. This set of cases was chosen as the starting point because, over the years, Justice White repeatedly called attention to the Court's failure to resolve intercircuit disagreements. The "Dissent Group," as I called it, included 237 cases. The second group was a random sample drawn from the 1989 Term. The sample encompassed one of every five paid cases denied review in that Term after the filing of a brief in opposition. The "Random Group" consisted of 253 cases.

To determine whether a Study Group case involved a conflict between circuits, I followed an approach that was essentially reportorial. I began by asking whether a claim of conflict was presented in the *certiorari* petition and other materials submitted by the parties. If it was, I examined the allegedly conflicting decisions to ascertain if the disagreement was acknowledged by one or more of the courts of appeals that had decided the issue. Acknowledged conflicts were included in the tally without any attempt to determine whether the conflict was "genuine." If the conflict was not acknowledged, I proceeded with research to discover whether the assertion of conflict was supported by writings of judges, commentators, or other participants in the legal system. Recognized conflicts were also included in the tally without independent analysis. Only when all of these sources proved unavailing did I undertake my own assessment of whether the decisions were truly in conflict.

Using these techniques, I found 166 substantiated claims of conflict among Justice White's dissents: 38 in the 1988 Term, 59 in 1989, and 69 in 1990. All but 11 of the 166 were either acknowledged by a court of appeals or recognized by other participants in the system. Applying the same criteria to the paid cases in the Random Group, I found 44 conflicts, all but two of which were acknowledged or recognized.

These data answered the first of the questions posed by Congress. The number of intercircuit conflicts that are not heard by the Supreme Court is large enough that the existence of a problem of "inadequate national capacity" could not be ruled out on the basis of raw numbers alone. But that finding only set the stage for the next level of inquiry: investigating the "tolerability" of the unresolved conflicts.

Assessing Tolerability. "Tolerability" is a shorthand for the effect of conflicts on litigation, counseling, and primary activity. [Previous studies] identified four [untoward] consequences that would tend to make a conflict intolerable: nonacquiescence by federal government agencies, harm to multicircuit actors, forum shopping among circuits, and unfairness to litigants in different regions of the country. To assess the tolerability of the Phase I conflicts, I began by identifying objectively defined characteristics that are likely to correlate with one or more of these [untoward] consequences. I then built upon that framework to analyze the conflicts in the Study Group. The findings were quite striking.

The first of the [untoward] consequences — nonacquiescence — can virtually be ruled out as an element of intolerability. The essence of the evil . . .

is that federal administrative agencies are forced to choose "between the uniform administration of statutory schemes and obedience to the different holdings of courts in different regions." But examination of the Study Group cases reveals that there is almost no overlap between nonacquiescence and unresolved intercircuit conflicts. Nonacquiescence may be a problem in the legal system, but it is not a problem that results from the Supreme Court's failure to resolve the conflicts that are brought to it.

A second factor — forum shopping among circuits — can be put to one side for a different reason. Upon analysis, forum shopping between circuits proves to be an evil only to the extent that it threatens harm to multicircuit actors or causes unfairness to litigants in different regions. Intolerability thus depends entirely on the latter two factors.

The possibility of inflicting harm on multicircuit actors, I concluded, depends in the first instance on the subject matter of the conflict and the nature of the issues. On the basis of those variables alone, the research tells us that a substantial majority of the unresolved conflicts would have no impact on the legal position of entities whose activities cross circuit lines. Included here are almost all conflicts in several important categories of federal law: the constitutional rights of criminal defendants, the elements of typical federal crimes, the interpretation of 43 USC § 1983, and the availability of federal habeas corpus for state prisoners. Thus, under the approach suggested by [previous studies], these conflicts would be deemed intolerable only to the extent that they give rise to unfairness to litigants in different circuits.

In giving content to the concept of "unfairness," I . . . concluded that unfairness to litigants in different circuits, like the other [untoward] consequences that concerned [previous studies], depends primarily on the extent to which the difference in circuit law produces divergent outcomes in similar cases. From this perspective, the conflicts could be divided into three broad groupings: those that are outcome-determinative, those that produce systematic bias, and those that do not generate either of those [untoward] consequences.

A conflict is classified as outcome-determinative if the choice of rule can be expected to control the resolution of a claim or defense in all cases in which the issue arises, or in any class of cases that can be identified *ex ante*. Because most legal rules contain elements of indeterminacy or are tempered in their operation by other rules, only a small proportion of the conflicts fit this pattern. More commonly, conflicts fall into the intermediate grouping: the choice of rule will not lead to divergent outcomes in an identifiable class of cases, but it can be expected to bias decision systematically in favor of one side in a recurring class of disputes.

A strong argument can be made that systematic bias differs in degree but not in kind from the indeterminacy that is inherent in common law adjudication. If one accepts this view, analysis of the Phase I cases establishes that a majority of unresolved conflicts — indeed, probably a substantial majority — will not generate any of the [untoward] consequences that would put them in the realm of the "intolerable."

Investigating Persistence. At this point I had taken objective analysis based on the [four] factors as far as it could go. But that did not mean that I had to abandon efforts to evaluate the significance of unresolved conflicts. Although [previous studies] did not develop the point, [they] implicitly recognized that conflicts have a temporal dimension. Further, my own prior research provided numerous instances of conflicts that were denied review in one Supreme Court Term but resolved in a subsequent Term when brought to the Court by another petitioner. I therefore undertook an investigation of the persistence of unresolved conflicts.

Persistence in the broad sense can be viewed as an element of tolerability; the difference lies in the temporal perspective. In analyzing the tolerability of the Phase I conflicts, I took as a given the landscape of the law at the time the Supreme Court denied review. A study of persistence, on the other hand, concentrates on what happens to the conflicts that the Court does not hear. Do they "remain unresolved" for long periods of time? Does the Court step in when the same issue is presented in another case? Or do the conflicts disappear or become irrelevant without a Supreme Court decision?

The cases studied in Phase I could provide only limited insights into the persistence of unresolved conflicts because the denials of *certiorari* were so recent. Thus, to pursue this line of inquiry, it was necessary to investigate the fate of conflicts denied review in earlier years. To that end, in Phase II of the study I went back to the 1984 and 1985 Terms of the Supreme Court and traced the subsequent history of 142 conflicts that were "not heard" by the Court during that period. I selected that period because a compilation of conflicts was available as part of an unpublished study conducted at the request of Chief Justice Burger.

After analyzing court rulings and secondary sources, I found fewer than 40 conflicts out of the 142 that (a) had not been put to rest by a Supreme Court decision or otherwise, (b) continued to generate litigation, and (c) controlled outcomes in one or more reported cases. Of these, perhaps a dozen had some potential for encouraging nonacquiescence or causing harm to multicircuit actors; the remainder implicated only the "unfairness" factor. In short, the research indicated that most of the conflicts the Supreme Court does not hear either do not generate the [untoward] consequences that concerned [previous studies] or do so only for a short period of time.

In reliance on the research conducted in Phase I and Phase II, the long-range planning committee of the Judicial Conference of the United States recommended that "[t]he United States Supreme Court should continue to be the sole arbiter of conflicting precedents among the courts of appeals." That recommendation was endorsed by the Conference itself. But not everyone agrees that unresolved conflicts are not a cause for worry. . . . Thus it is appropriate to pursue new lines of inquiry. . . .

The Later History of the Phase I Conflicts. In the study cited by the Judicial Conference and its long-range planning committee, I analyzed the tolerability of the substantiated conflicts in the Phase I Study Group and the persistence of the substantiated conflicts in the Phase II Study Group. Because the denial of *certiorari* in the Phase I cases was still recent, I had only fragmentary information about the later history of those issues. With the passage of time, however, it became possible to investigate the persistence of the Phase I conflicts.

Although resources did not permit research on the comprehensive scale of the initial enterprise, I was able to trace and analyze later developments in sufficient depth to answer the basic questions: How many of the conflicts remain alive? To what extent are they likely to give rise to the [untoward] consequences that make for intolerability?

As explained [above], the Phase I Study Group encompassed two sets of cases that the Supreme Court declined to hear. The first group included all cases in the 1988, 1989, and 1990 Terms in which Justice White dissented from denial of *certiorari*. That group gave us a total of 166 substantiated conflicts. The second group was a random sample drawn from the 1989 Term. That sample ultimately yielded a total of 44 substantiated conflicts. Nine conflicts appeared twice in the Study Group: five cases in the Dissent Group also turned up in the random sample, and four conflicts from the random sample prompted a dissent by Justice White in a different case. Thus, for the follow-up study, I investigated the later history of 201 conflicts that were denied review in the Supreme Court's 1988, 1989, and 1990 Terms. The bulk of the work was carried out in late 1997 and early 1998, with some additional research in early fall of 1998. The analysis reflects all Supreme Court action through the end of the 1997-98 Term.

The new research strongly reinforce[d] the conclusion set forth [in my previous research]. Of the 201 conflicts, 62 have been put to rest by legislative or judicial action. Another 63 conflicts have died a natural death; either the underlying issue has disappeared or there is no longer any evidence of intercircuit disagreement. Among the conflicts that have not been put to rest, there are no more than 50 that manifest characteristics that contribute to intolerability.

In addition to the findings, the new research further refines the analytical framework. It is now clear that a conflict can "evaporate" even though the issue remains alive at some higher level of generality. For conflicts that cannot be said to have evaporated, a critical question is whether any later court has found it necessary to reject a precedent from another circuit. . . .

Of the 201 conflicts in the Study Group, 45 were resolved when the Supreme Court granted review in a later case. Thirty-two decisions explicitly addressed the issue on which courts of appeals disagreed. Generally the Court's opinion specified the conflict as the reason for granting review and cited one or more of the appellate rulings that were brought to the Court's attention in the earlier petition. Another 13 conflicts were implicitly resolved when the Supreme Court decided a case involving a closely related question.

[T]he Supreme Court is not the only institution that has the power to end litigation over a conflict issue. Legislative bodies can change the law, and courts of appeals can change their minds. Among the Study Group conflicts, 10 have been mooted through some kind of legislative action — Acts of Congress, amendments to the Sentencing Guidelines, or revisions to procedural rules. Seven conflicts were eliminated when the minority circuit overruled the nonconforming decision. In all, 62 conflicts had been put to rest by judicial or legislative action when the Court's 1997 Term ended in June 1998.

If no judicial or legislative body has taken action to put a conflict to rest, does that mean that the conflict remains alive? Not necessarily. On the contrary, one of the major findings of this research is that conflicts can die without any directed or self-conscious intervention by a judicial or legislative body. There are two distinct ways in which this can happen. One is quite straightforward; the other is somewhat more subtle.

In 35 cases, the conflict died a natural death through what can be described as "burial" of the underlying issue. Some of the issues never generated a reported decision after the denial of *certiorari*. Half a dozen hung on until early 1994 (or in one instance late 1994). The remaining issues disappeared from sight sometime during the early 1990s. . . .

In 28 cases, the issue remained alive to a greater or lesser degree; however, the conflict presented to the Supreme Court has evaporated. This is a phenomenon that I have not previously identified. "Evaporation" refers to the situation in which courts continue to cite precedents on one or both sides of a once-live conflict, but there is no recent evidence that any court has seen a need to choose between precedents or that the law differs from one circuit to another. . . . Few of the conflicts in this category are associated with a broader issue that remains unsettled. Many had little substance even at the time *certiorari* was denied in the Study Group case. Some of the underlying issues are all but buried. The details vary; what is clear in each of the cases is that there is no longer a disagreement that leads to divergent outcomes depending on the circuit where a dispute is litigated.

The analysis thus far accounts for all but 76 of the conflicts in the Phase I Study Group. These are the conflicts that cannot be deemed to have been put to rest. But the fact that a conflict remains alive is not necessarily cause for concern. Rather, we must ask whether the continued existence of the conflict has generated one or more of the [untoward] consequences that [previous studies] identified as contributing to intolerability.

In my earlier analysis, I suggested that the key to intolerability is effect on outcomes. As explained in the account of the Phase II Study Group, "Unless the choice between the competing rules leads courts to reach divergent results in similar cases, none of the [untoward] consequences that concerned [previous studies] are likely to materialize." I adhere to that view, but . . . I looked for another benchmark that would more readily identify those conflicts that have truly made a difference. . . . A strong signal that a conflict leads to divergent outcomes is the rejection by a court in one circuit of another circuit's precedent. Applying this new framework and examining decisions over the last four years, I found that the conflicts fell into four groups: the vestigial, the dynamic, the static, and the receding.

A. Vestigial conflicts: At one end of the spectrum are eight conflicts that remain alive, if at all, only in some vestigial form. On some of the issues there is evidence of confusion or uncertainty and perhaps some lingering disagreement; what we do not find is a recent decision that rejects another circuit's precedent. By the same token, there is at most a bare minimum of evidence to suggest that the outcome of any of the cases might have been different in another circuit. Thus, although I am not quite prepared to say that these conflicts have been put to rest, I am confident that they have not given rise to any of the [untoward] consequences. . . . In these circumstances, the indicia of intolerability are virtually nonexistent. [O]nly one of the [four] factors comes into play: unfairness to litigants in different circuits. Unfairness would exist if, as a result of differences in circuit law, courts were recognizing federal rights in one circuit that were being denied elsewhere. But that is precisely what the evidence does not show.

B. Dynamic conflicts: At the other end of the spectrum are 25 conflicts that remain very much alive. These are the "dynamic" conflicts, and the likelihood is high that the choice of rule has affected outcomes in at least some cases. Within this group, I have identified three patterns, rank-ordered as follows (starting with the conflicts manifesting the strongest indicia of intolerability): (1) On 10 conflicts, there have been recent decisions that have followed precedents on both sides of the issue, and at least one case on each side has rejected a precedent on the other side. This combination of circumstances provides the strongest evidence that the conflict perpetuates uncertainty and leads to divergent outcomes; (2) On 11 conflicts, there have been recent decisions on both sides, and at least one decision from a court not bound by precedent has rejected another circuit's decision or has chosen between competing precedents; (3) On four conflicts, although there have not been recent decisions on both sides, at least one court not bound by precedent has rejected another circuit's decision or has chosen between competing precedents. Even among the conflicts that I have classified as dynamic, there were some that did not affect outcomes, at least on the evidence of reported cases. . . .

C. Static conflicts: One step removed from the dynamic conflicts are 20 conflicts that can be characterized as "static." The common thread is that precedents on both sides are still good law in their respective circuits, but no court not bound by precedent has chosen between the competing lines of authority. The cases fall into two subgroups.

For nine of the conflicts, there is at least one recent decision in which a court has rejected an out-of-circuit precedent as inconsistent with binding circuit law. However, no court not bound by precedent has rejected another circuit's ruling, nor has any new court chosen between competing precedents. Thus, the conflict has not widened, but the recent reiteration of disagreement gives reason to believe that it will persist. Further, there are at least some cases in which the choice of rule appears to have affected the outcome.

For 11 other conflicts, there have been recent decisions that have followed precedents on both sides, but no recent decision has rejected any out-of-circuit precedent or chosen between precedents. Generally, these are situations in which the competing circuit positions are well established; thus, it is reasonably clear that the law differs from one circuit to another. What is less clear is that the difference in circuit rules has affected outcomes. Indeed, in some cases there is affirmative evidence that the choice of rule did not control the result. . . .

D. Receding conflicts: Finally, there are what might be called the receding conflicts. A conflict is "receding" when recent decisions have pointed so overwhelmingly in one direction that the precedents on the other side, although not overruled, will carry little weight with lawyers or judges. Under these circumstances, the continuing existence of the conflict is unlikely to make much difference in the outcome of new decisions.

Again, there are two subgroups. In 10 cases, although all recent decisions take one side of the conflict, the authority on the other side still retains some vitality: it has been cited with apparent approval by the court of appeals or applied by a lower court in the minority circuit. But it has not been the basis for a court of appeals decision, so that there has been no opportunity for the minority circuit to reconsider the precedent. Overall, there is substantial evidence that the minority precedent is destined for oblivion, but the obsequies cannot yet be pronounced.

In the remaining 13 cases, courts continue to choose between competing precedents or positions, but recent decisions are all on one side, and the authority on the other side has not been reaffirmed or cited with approval in any recent case. The most one can say is that the minority precedent may still be good law in its own circuit — and sometimes even that is questionable. . . . When the precedents on one side have been rejected by every court to consider the issue over a substantial period of time, it is highly doubtful that any of the [untoward] consequences specified by [previous studies] will ensue. Whether we look at the treatment of litigants in reported cases or at the predictability of future outcomes, the fact that the minority precedent remains on the books is almost an irrelevance. Indeed, if the minority precedent has been sufficiently discredited, the continued existence of the conflict may be regarded as more theoretical than real.

Conclusion. I [previously] presented the results of analyzing the later history of 142 conflicts that were denied review in the 1984 and 1985 Terms. I found fewer than 40 conflicts that (a) were not put to rest by a Supreme Court decision or otherwise, (b) continued to generate litigation, and (c) controlled outcomes in one or more reported cases. How do the results of the new research compare with these findings?

[T]he broad patterns are clear enough. Of the 201 conflicts that were denied review in the 1988, 1989, and 1990 Terms, 97 have been put to rest or have otherwise ceased to generate litigation. Another 36 conflicts plainly have not controlled outcomes in any recent reported cases. That leaves only 68 conflicts that have any potential for affecting outcomes. I am confident that if I applied the criteria used in the study of the 1984 and 1985 Terms, at least 20 of the 68 conflicts would be found not to have produced divergent outcomes in any pair of reported cases for five years or more.

I conclude, therefore, that among the conflicts that have not been put to rest, there are no more than 50 that continue to produce any of the effects that contribute to intolerability. That figure accords closely with the findings reported in [my] earlier study. And it supports the conclusions previously reached:

- Simply counting the conflicts that the Supreme Court declines to hear in a particular Term gives a distorted view of the extent to which unresolved intercircuit conflicts pose a problem in the legal system.

- When one considers both the tolerability of the unresolved conflicts and their persistence, the evidence points strongly to the conclusion that unresolved intercircuit conflicts do not constitute a problem of serious magnitude in the federal judicial system today.

NOTES

1. The excerpt by Professors Baker & McFarland tries to make the philosophical case in the abstract that more national appellate capacity is needed, *i.e.*, that structural reform is necessary, by making both empirical and normative arguments. In Chapter 6, we studied the importance of maintaining doctrinal consistency in the law of the jurisdiction as expressed and applied in individual appeals and across the entire appellate docket. The geographical organization of the U.S. Courts of Appeals creates the potential for regional inconsistency. What are "intercircuit conflicts"? What kinds of mischief do they cause? The article also went on to argue that a new national appellate court was needed to relieve the Supreme Court from its workload burdens when it was deciding upwards of 150 cases in the 1980s. Of course, that rationale for structural reform has disappeared in the 2000s when the Supreme Court has been deciding only half as many cases, as we learned in Chapter 12. More recent proposals for structural reform have continued to emphasize the systemic need for greater coherency and more consistency in the articulation and maintenance of the national law. *See generally* Christopher F. Carlton, *The Grinding Wheel of Justice Needs Some Grease: Designing the Federal Courts of the Twenty-First Century*, 6 KAN. J.L. & PUB. POL'Y 1 (1997); Martha J. Dragich, *Once a Century: Time for a Structural Overhaul of the Federal Courts*, 1996 WIS. L. REV. 11.

2. Professor Hellman has studied and evaluated the phenomenon of intercircuit conflicts more than any other individual scholar. Do you follow his analysis? How helpful is his typology of intercircuit conflicts — the way he elaborates categories and subcategories of conflicts and the way he then goes on to analyze and classify them? Is he saying that there are not "too many" conflicts? Is he saying that the conflicts that exist are not "too bad"? How objective is the quantitative analysis — does it inevitably break down into a subjective assessment whether the intercircuit conflict in question is "tolerable" and "persistent"? *See generally* Arthur D. Hellman, *Never the Same River Twice: The Empirics and Epistemology of Intercircuit Conflicts*, 63 U. PITT. L. REV. 81 (2001); Arthur D. Hellman, *Precedent, Predictability, and Federal Appellate Structure*, 60 U. PITT. L. REV. 1029 (1999); Arthur D. Hellman, *By Precedent Unbound: The Nature and Extent of Unresolved Intercircuit Conflicts*, 56 U. PITT. L. REV. 693 (1995).

3. Together these two excerpts nicely illustrate the decades long debate over whether or not the current federal court system is performing adequately and whether there is a need for structural appellate reform. What kind of proof should be required before Congress decides to create a new national court? How much importance should be afforded to empirical or statistical studies? Can the coherency and consistency of the national law be quantitatively measured in a meaningful way? Are you persuaded either way? Consider this thought experiment: suppose the phenomenon of intercircuit conflicts was occurring within a state appellate system, *i.e.*, different geographical circuits of the state IAC were deciding the same outcome determinative issues of state law in conflicting, different ways for their regions of the state. Would this not be considered an obvious and serious problem? What sorts of mechanisms would be proposed to solve the problem?

4. The question whether there is a need for structural reform is related to — but distinct from — questions about the proper structural design: How should the proposed new court be organized and staffed? What jurisdiction should it

have? What procedures should it follow? The next subsection recounts the various designs for a new national appellate court that have been proposed over the years.

B. Proposals for a New Court

As promised, we pick up the story here where we left off in Chapter 12. At the height of the "crisis of volume" in the U.S. courts of appeals, many perceived that the Supreme Court was fighting a losing struggle to keep up with its institutional responsibilities. The SCOTUS experienced significant increases in the number of *certiorari* petitions along with mandatory appeals and it was hearing and deciding upwards of 150 cases a year. Chief Justice Burger and others called out for help. Various study groups, commissions, and committees examined the situation and made recommendations for reform. The first set of proposals emphasized the growing workload of the justices and expressed concerns that the federal appellate capacity to articulate and harmonize the national law was inadequate: not only were there too many important intercircuit conflicts that were going unsettled for too long, there also were too many important issues deserving of a national answer that were going unanswered. Since then, however, Congress afforded the SCOTUS virtually total discretion over its docket, additional law clerks were deployed, and the *cert* pool was implemented, and the justices developed self-restraint and restrictive attitudes towards granting petitions. In the 2000s, as we also considered in Chapter 12, court-watchers began to complain that the justices were not granting review in enough cases and worries for their workload disappeared.

In Chapter 12, we studied the REPORT OF THE STUDY GROUP ON THE CASELOAD OF THE SUPREME COURT, popularly known as the Freund Committee. As its title suggests, the study focused primarily on the then-current problems of the Supreme Court in 1972. The Freund Committee's recommendation that Congress create a national court of appeals was met with a hailstorm of controversy and criticism, some of which we read in Chapter 12. Criticism centered around two themes: a concern for the dilution of Supreme Court authority and self-determinism, and a desire to preserve direct access to the Supreme Court. Seen by some as an attack on the Supreme Court itself, the proposal was dead on arrival in Congress. For some, the episode reaffirmed the history lesson of FDR's notorious and deservedly failed Court-packing plan of 1937: any structural proposal must show great respect and deference for the power and place of the High Court. Nonetheless, the episode did serve to focus attention on the "crisis of volume" in the U.S. Courts of Appeals and shaped the subsequent debate over all the subsequent proposals for structural reform to create a new appellate tier between the SCOTUS and the Courts of Appeals. Indeed, it may not be unfair to observe that the experience of the Freund Committee demonstrates that thoughtful, informed study groups may sometimes hatch a genuinely goofy proposal. Therefore, when reading one of these reports, we should apply a healthy skepticism to its assumptions and we should subject its structural proposals to close scrutiny.

Consider the following proposals individually and compare them to each other. What is their diagnosis of the ills of the present system? What is their prescription for reform? What is the prognosis for the future of the federal appellate courts — is the proposed cure worse than the disease?

1. National Court of Appeals (Freund Committee Proposal)

REPORT OF THE STUDY GROUP ON THE CASELOAD OF THE SUPREME COURT, 57 F.R.D. 573 (1972)

[Reread this excerpt in Chapter 12, Section III. B., at page 826]

NOTES

As the introduction to this subsection reminds us, when the 1972 Freund Committee Report was released, the problem perceived by many was that the SCOTUS's workload had grown beyond its capacity to function effectively as a COLR, *i.e.*, that the High Court was facing its own "crisis of volume." *See generally* A. Leo Levin, *Adding Appellate Capacity to the Federal System*, 39 WASH. & LEE L. REV. 1 (1982); Note, *Of High Designs: A Compendium of Proposals to Reduce the Workload of the Supreme Court*, 97 HARV. L. REV. 307 (1983). As we learned in Chapter 12, however, Justice Brennan and many other commentators came down hard on the Freund Committee's proposed national court of appeals and the proposal never gained any political traction. William J. Brennan, Jr., *The National Court of Appeals: Another Dissent*, 40 U. CHI. L. REV. 473, 475-85 (1973); Eugene Gressman, *The Constitution v. the Freund Report*, 41 GEO. WASH. L. REV. 951 (1973). Justice Stevens made a remarkably prescient argument at the time that the better solution to the *certiorari* problem was to grant review to fewer cases, advice that he and his colleagues have followed in earnest. John Paul Stevens, *Some Thoughts on Judicial Restraint*, 66 JUDICATURE 177 (1982). *See* Chapter 12, section II. C. What were the features of the Freund Committee proposal that mobilized such vehement opposition? Are there any aspects of the proposal that deserve to be salvaged? Consider how this opening round of debate shaped the subsequent debates over later proposals.

2. National Court of Appeals (Hruska Commission Proposal)

COMMISSION ON REVISION OF THE FEDERAL COURT, APPELLATE SYSTEM STRUCTURE AND INTERNAL PROCEDURES: RECOMMENDATIONS FOR CHANGE, 67 F.R.D. 195, 199-200 (1975) (Summary of Recommendations)

A National Court of Appeals

1. The Commission recommends that Congress establish a National Court of Appeals, consisting of seven Article III judges appointed by the President with the advice and consent of the Senate.

2. The court would sit only *en banc* and its decisions would constitute precedents binding upon all other federal courts and, as to federal questions, upon state courts as well, unless modified or overruled by the Supreme Court.

3. The National Court of Appeals would have jurisdiction to hear cases (a) referred to it by the Supreme Court (reference jurisdiction), or (b) transferred to it from the regional courts of appeals . . . (transfer jurisdiction).

(a) *Reference jurisdiction.* With respect to any case before it on petition for *certiorari*, the Supreme Court would be authorized:

> (1) to retain the case and render a decision on the merits;
>
> (2) to deny *certiorari* without more, thus terminating the litigation;
>
> (3) to deny *certiorari* and refer the case to the National Court of Appeals for that court to decide on the merits;
>
> (4) to deny *certiorari* and refer the case to the National Court, giving that court discretion either to decide the case on the merits or to deny review and thus terminate the litigation.

. . . .

(b) *Transfer jurisdiction.* If a case filed in a court of appeals . . . is one in which an immediate decision by the National Court of Appeals is in the public interest, it may be transferred to the National Court provided it falls within one of the following categories:

> (1) the case turns on a rule of federal law and federal courts have reached inconsistent conclusions with respect to it; or
>
> (2) the case turns on a rule of federal law applicable to a recurring factual situation, and a showing is made that the advantages of a prompt and definitive determination of that rule by the National Court of Appeals outweigh any potential disadvantages of transfer; or
>
> (3) the case turns on a rule of federal law which has theretofore been announced by the National Court of Appeals, and there is a substantial question about the proper interpretation or application of that rule in the pending case.

The National Court would be empowered to decline to accept the transfer of any case. Decisions granting or denying transfer, and decisions by the National Court accepting or rejecting cases, would not be reviewable under any circumstances, by extraordinary writ or otherwise.

4. Any case decided by the National Court of Appeals, whether upon reference or after transfer, would be subject to review by the Supreme Court upon petition for *certiorari*.

Roman L. Hruska, *Commission Recommends New National Court of Appeals*, 61 A.B.A. J. 819 (1975)[6]

The decisions of the new court would be precedents of nationwide effect, binding on the federal district courts, the regional courts of appeals, and on

---

6 Copyright © 1975 American Bar Association Journal. Reprinted with Permission.

state courts as well — unless the Supreme Court modifies or overrules these decisions. Thus, the constitutional requirement that there be "one Supreme Court" will remain untouched.

The new court's docket would be composed of cases derived from two sources: (1) A "reference jurisdiction" under which the Supreme Court would refer such cases as it deemed wise; (2) a "transfer jurisdiction" under which regional courts of appeals could transfer cases with specified characteristics which would otherwise be heard by those courts. . . .

The essence of our proposal is that the Supreme Court be empowered to refer any case within its appellate jurisdiction to the National Court of Appeals. The power would extend to any case before the Supreme Court on petition for *certiorari* or on jurisdictional statement; we do not contemplate that the enabling legislation would contain any limitations on the kinds or classes of cases that could be referred. We specifically intend to include cases from the highest courts of the states, as well as appeals from the decisions of three-judge courts over which the Supreme Court now has obligatory jurisdiction.

The commission does not propose to instruct the Supreme Court on the procedures and standards that should govern the exercise of the reference jurisdiction. Rather, we envision a process of rule making, with the Supreme Court benefiting from the recommendations of an advisory committee. . . . However, the commission has recognized the importance of assuring that the availability of the reference option and its exercise in particular cases do not impose an undue burden on the Court. . . .

The Supreme Court would refuse to refer any case in which it was in the national interest that no nationally binding decision be made at that time. This would allow for continuing percolation when it was considered desirable. It would also allow for complete discretion on the part of the Supreme Court to choose appropriate vehicles for adjudication of important issues of constitutional law.

In certain types of cases, it would appear clearly to the advantage of all concerned to invoke the jurisdiction of the National Court without requiring a decision on the merits by one of the present courts of appeals. There may be relatively few such cases transferred, at least in the early years of the National Court. But that should not prevent us from gaining the advantage of transfer when it would be beneficial.

We suggest that the transfer jurisdiction would operate as follows. Upon the filing of any case in a court of appeals or later, if appropriate, the court would have the authority to transfer the case to the National Court of Appeals under any of three circumstances [listed above in the Summary of Recommendations 3. (b)]. . . .

The National Court would be empowered to decline to accept the transfer of any case which, either for reasons having to do with the nature of the case itself or for reasons of docket control, it concluded was more appropriately heard initially by the court in which it was originally filed.

Under our plan, decisions of the regional courts of appeals granting or denying motions for transfer and decisions by the National Court accepting or rejecting cases would not be reviewable under any circumstances, by extraordinary writ or otherwise. . . .

The commission expects, however, that rules would be promulgated by the Supreme Court that would serve both to guide the regional courts in passing on transfer motions and to govern the National Court in the exercise of discretion in accepting or rejecting cases after transfer. Such rules would in the normal course be devised with the aid of an advisory committee including both members of the bar and judges of the regional courts of appeals.

The commission is confident that this transfer mechanism is highly desirable. We are confident, too, that it can be made operational through a variety of procedures that would be both effective and efficient. Several considerations underlie this conclusion.

First is the kind of case which we envisage as appropriate for transfer. Specifically, we would exclude cases involving difficult and sensitive issues of significant public import.

Second, it is not necessary to the success of the new court that the regional courts transfer every case that may appropriately be transferred; on the contrary, the national interest would be well served, at least initially, if transfers were ordered only in cases readily identified as appropriate and, in addition, in those complex cases, otherwise appropriate, when transfer would permit a substantial saving of time to the regional court. . . .

Two examples of transfer cases may serve to illustrate that utility of this head of jurisdiction. First, suppose that a case turns on a narrow, technical question of tax law on which two circuits are already in conflict, and suppose further that all of the parties concede as much. No decision by yet a third circuit court can resolve the conflict. It would save time and expense if the court of appeals were relieved of the burden of decision and the case promptly transferred to the National Court. Second, consider an appeal under one of the statutes concerned with protecting the environment, one based on a long and complex record and involving an issue of law which in the interest of efficient allocation of national resources should be resolved promptly on a national basis. Again, prompt transfer would relieve the regional courts of appeals and be in the interest of the litigants, as well as in the national interest.

We contemplate that any case decided by the National Court, whether transferred by a regional court of appeals or referred by the Supreme Court, would be subject to review by the Supreme Court on petition for *certiorari*. Access to the Supreme Court would not be cut off in any individual case or class of cases. We anticipate, however, that few decisions of the National Court in cases that came to it from the Supreme Court would in fact be reviewed thereafter by the Supreme Court. . . .

Notwithstanding the increased scope of federal law, one feature has remained constant. Today, as in 1789, there is but one court empowered to hand down judgments that constitute binding precedents in all state and federal courts: the Supreme Court of the United States. The rise in the number of the cases brought to the Supreme Court by way of appeal and *certiorari* is familiar — and spectacular: from about twelve hundred in 1951 to more than four thousand in the most recent complete term.

Clearly there is a limit to the number of cases the Supreme Court can decide on the merits each year. Over the past five decades, in fact, the number of cases disposed of by the Supreme Court after plenary consideration has remained relatively constant. In the words of Dean Erwin Griswold, the Court "was hearing about one hundred and fifty cases on the merits in 1925; it was hearing about one hundred and fifty cases on the merits twenty-five years ago. It hears about one hundred and fifty cases on the merits today."

Dean Griswold . . . summarized the significance of these figures as follows: "Putting it another way, about 18 per cent of paid cases (appeals and *certiorari*) were heard on the merits twenty years ago, while about 6 per cent of paid cases were heard on the merits during the 1973 term. What became of the other 12 per cent of paid cases?. . . They were lost in the 1973 term simply because of inadequate appellate capacity to hear cases on a national basis". . . .

The lack of capacity varies in its impact on different categories of cases. Understandably, an increasing proportion of the Supreme Court's decisions in recent years has involved constitutional issues. Since the total number of decisions has remained constant, the result is that the number of opinions dealing with nonconstitutional issues has been decreasing.

In other words, while the scope of federal regulatory legislation — typically including provisions for judicial review — has been steadily broadening, the number of definitive decisions interpreting that legislation actually has been decreasing. Specifically, the Supreme Court can be expected to hand down no more than eighty and perhaps as few as fifty-five plenary decisions per term in all areas of federal nonconstitutional law. There is ample evidence that this number of decisions is inadequate to meet the country's needs for authoritative exposition of recurring issues of federal law. The adverse effects disclosed by the commission's studies . . . may be briefly stated:

First, the lack of definitive declaration of the national law frequently results in lengthy periods of uncertainty as to what the law is, whether or not a conflict has been generated. Years may elapse before a given circuit will rule on an issue.

The uncertainty breeds repetitive litigation as successive taxpayers, or manufacturers, or other citizens who are subject to federal regulation litigate the identical issue in circuit after circuit.

By the same token, the government frequently persists in enforcing a policy despite adverse rulings in several circuits. . . . Repetitive litigation of this kind exacts a high price in waste. Moreover, it cannot be cured without modification of our present structure. It would be wrong to penalize the government for not seeking or not obtaining a definite decision when the appellate system lacks the capacity to provide it. A prerequisite to the solution is to increase the capacity, and that, in our view, requires a new court.

An important further consequence of the lack of adequate capacity for declaration of national law is the burden on the Supreme Court to hear cases otherwise not worthy of its resources. An alternate forum for resolving conflicts would allow the Supreme Court greater freedom to hear or to refuse to hear such cases, relieved of the pressure to adjudicate solely because two other courts had disagreed. . . .

Eliminating conflicts on issues of constitutional law, duplications, and procedural problems, the total number of nonconstitutional conflicts — direct and strong partial — in the cases denied review is currently projected . . . at between fifty and sixty per term. . . .

The fact that the Supreme Court ultimately resolves a conflict does not demonstrate that the system is working in an optimum fashion. Resolution may come only after years of uncertainty, confusion, and inevitably, forum shopping by litigants eager to take advantage of the situation. Even when the Court acts expeditiously to resolve conflicts that have been brought to its attention, development of the conflict may have taken so much time that the total period of uncertainty may be a decade or more. . . .

A caveat is in order. There are some issues as to which "successive considerations by several courts, each reevaluating and building upon the preceding decisions" will improve the quality of adjudication. As to those, there may be reason to avoid premature adjudication by a court whose decisions are precedents of nationally binding effect. In discussing the consequences of inadequate capacity, we do not speak of such cases. We speak here of those cases as to which, to borrow Dean Griswold's words, "the gain from maturation of thought from letting the matter simmer for awhile is not nearly as great as the harm which comes from years of uncertainty."

In short, we have endeavored throughout to put to one side cases in which delayed adjudication is appropriate; we would not sacrifice the quality of either process or product for speed or for the appearance of efficiency. However, we find no value in a system that fosters prolonged uncertainty and delay because the design of the system cannot accommodate more rapid resolution. . . .

The decision to recommend a new National Court should not be made to turn on whether present conditions have reached crisis proportions, although in the opinion of some a crisis clearly exists. A state of emergency should not be viewed as a prerequisite to the consideration of improvements in the federal judicial system. Rather, we should ask whether the system is operating as well as it could and should.

In the commission's view, it is not. Nor can it function in optimal fashion until the demonstrated national appellate capacity has been met.

Of no less significance, the demands on the federal judicial system continue to grow. The Congress continues to consider — as it must — new programs designed to cope with new national problems, from energy to the environment. Typically, their implementation imposes new burdens on the courts, burdens that must be met in the interest of society as a whole. In short, the need for additional national appellate capacity exists now and there is every evidence that it will continue to grow.

The focus of the commission's inquiry has not been the burden on the Supreme Court. Nevertheless, we believe that the plan just described has the promise of bringing significant relief to that Court.

First, it reduces the amount of attention that the justices and their clerks would have to give to a case raising an issue that may require national resolution but does not require a decision by the Supreme Court. Once the justices are satisfied that there is no reason not to have the issue decided at that particular time, the case can be referred without the need for the justices to spend further time evaluating the significance of the issue or the appropriateness of the particular case for resolving it.

Furthermore, the availability of the reference procedure would relieve the justices of the obligation to decide the merits of some cases in which review is granted today to resolve a conflict. . . .

Jack B. Owens, *The Hruska Commission's Proposed National Court of Appeals*, 23 UCLA L. Rev. 580 (1976)[7]

The Hruska Commission plainly has attempted to avoid the mistakes of the Freund Committee. The [Hruska] Commission's proposed new court is shorn of many of the objectionable features of the earlier model. The [Hruska] Commission has taken pains to document the need for such a court with something more probative than simple tallies of the number of cases filed annually in the Court. . . .

Because the Hruska Commission has benefited from what has gone before, its recommendation for a new National Court cannot be brushed aside as lightly as the earlier proposal. The [Hruska] Commission is to be commended for advancing the debate over creation of a new court and for attempting to develop hard data on the Supreme Court's performance in recent years. Nevertheless, this Commentary concludes that the proposal is unsound. Indeed, the recommendation appears to ignore the [Hruska] Commission's own warning against risking permanent damage for merely temporary relief. . . .

Although questions can be raised about some of the [Hruska] Commission's documentation, its basic concern is well-founded. Even if one discounts substantially the Commission's rough numerical estimates of the number of "certworthy" cases missed by the Supreme Court in an average recent year, the figures are still disturbing; they hardly indicate a system that is working well. In addition, the [Hruska] Commission's understandable shortcomings in attempting to measure something as amorphous as the adequacy of final federal appellate capacity must not be permitted to obscure the lessons of common sense. It stands to reason that at some point a nation of more than 200 million people, with an appetite for converting social issues into questions for resolution by the judiciary, will find it unacceptable to rely on a single nine-member court to monitor and harmonize the federal law decisions of the

---

[7] Copyright © 1976. Originally published 1976 and reprinted with the approval of the UCLA Law Review.

eleven circuits, the specialized federal courts, and the fifty state court systems. Moreover, some of the non-numerical indicators cited by the [Hruska] Commission cannot be ignored, particularly the views of five of the active Justices and others with an educated basis for assessing the Supreme Court's current condition. Similarly, it is difficult to argue persuasively that the Supreme Court has adequately overseen such areas as tax and patent law. The question is not whether the [Hruska] Commission's concern is groundless, but whether its recommended solution is sound.

In seeking a sensible proposal, the [Hruska] Commission was heavily influenced by the earlier work of the Freund Committee and the reactions to it. In some respects, this is reflected in the common ground between the two. Both the [Hruska] Commission and the [Freund] Committee reject the notion that the Supreme Court should simply increase the number of cases given summary disposition as a means of dealing with its workload or of providing more answers to disputed questions of national law. Both would prefer the Court to devote the bulk of its resources to deliberative and collegial treatment of a limited number of cases per year, leading to carefully drafted opinions.

The principal way in which the Freund Committee influenced the [Hruska] Commission's proposal, however, was not through shared premises but in the [Hruska] Commission's rejection of the most controversial features of the earlier proposal. The differences begin as early as the stage of assessing the problem. The Freund Committee believed the Supreme Court to be threatened by the burden of screening applications for review, a surprisingly inaccurate assessment of the Court's condition. The [Hruska] Commission has avoided this mistake. It does not describe the Court's screening burden as intolerable; on the contrary, it proposes to increase the burden through addition of the reference jurisdiction and the duty to screen requests for review of the new court's decisions. The [Hruska] Commission reaches the sensible conclusions that the Supreme Court has a finite ability to issue full opinions (even if the screening burden is minimal), that its capacity may not match the country's needs, and that what is needed is not a shifting of the screening burden but an expansion of the opportunity for full treatment and final resolution of questions of federal law. The [Hruska] Commission believes that creation of a new court would accomplish this goal by providing a National Court capable of giving plenary treatment to 150 cases a year, thereby doubling the national appellate capacity.

Avoiding an undue concern for the Supreme Court's screening burden is only the beginning of the [Hruska] Commission's reaction to the mishaps that befell the Freund Committee. Indeed, the [Hruska] Commission has apparently taken as its guiding principle the structuring of a new court that meets as many as possible of the criticisms directed at the earlier Freund proposal. This approach may reflect an attention to political considerations as much as a judgment that the best model for a new court is to be found in the ashes of the earlier proposal. The [Hruska] Commission may have concluded that mollifying the critics of the Freund Committee is a precondition to any realistic chance for congressional approval of a new court.

For whatever reason, the [Hruska] Commission assumes without question the validity of the criticisms directed at the Freund Committee and devotes its attention to shaping a proposal intended to overcome them. The [Hruska] Commission contends that it has succeeded. It argues that its proposal would not interfere with the power of the Supreme Court. No matter how the National Court obtained jurisdiction, the Supreme Court would be able to review its judgments; access to the Supreme Court would not be foreclosed for any case or category of cases. The [Hruska] Commission further contends that other "virtues of the existing system would not be compromised." Presumably the [Hruska] Commission means by this that its proposal would undermine neither the Supreme Court's present ability to correct particular instances of injustice through summary disposition nor its power to decide the timing, order, and factual context in which disputed issues of national law are finally resolved. Furthermore, few litigants would be subjected to four tiers of federal review. The [Hruska] Commission also posits that the work of the new court would be sufficiently important and varied to attract judges of the highest quality.

However, the [Hruska] Commission's recommendation does not meet all the criticisms directed against the Freund Committee's proposal. Many objections to the latter recommendation derived from the premise that one court should have exclusive control of when issues of national law are resolved. Critics of the Freund Committee correctly discerned that shifting this function in any way to another court would detract directly from one of the powers of the Supreme Court. This power entails not only control over the factual contexts and the sequence in which national issues are decided, but also the ability to prevent or defer national resolution of issues, as when a majority of the Court is wary of extending an existing doctrine to its logical conclusion. The power not to decide also permits the Court to allow an issue to be addressed successively by a number of other courts, so that the Court may benefit from a variety of judicial views and fact situations when it ultimately decides the issue.

The [Hruska] Commission's proposed reference jurisdiction poses no threat to the Court's present power to exercise exclusive control over the timing, sequence, and context of the decision of issues of national law. The transfer jurisdiction, however, is a different matter. It would permit cases to move directly to the National Court, without intervention by the Supreme Court. Were the transfer jurisdiction to become a significant source of the new court's business, the Supreme Court would lose much of its ability to prevent or defer the resolution of certain federal issues on a national level. The [Hruska] Commission makes a feeble effort to avoid this by indicating that the transfer jurisdiction is not to be used for the resolution of issues that would benefit from repeated judicial review. But no longer would the Supreme Court alone select the issues to be left undecided; that function would be assumed in part by the new court and the circuit courts. It is most unlikely that the National Court of Appeals would mirror the Supreme Court in determining which issues should be decided and when. Indeed the National Court could easily develop a judicial philosophy somewhat at variance from that of the Supreme Court. Thus, at least one of the aspects of the [Hruska] Commission's proposal fails to meet a major criticism of the Freund Committee's proposal. The transfer jurisdiction offers the potential for shifting certain powers of the Supreme Court to another court. The Supreme Court would not be able to recoup this power through its ability to *review* the decisions of the National Court; the desired result is not a particular outcome but no decision at all.

When the Supreme Court chose to review the decisions of the National Court of Appeals following a referral, the litigants would be subjected to four tiers of federal review, another of the objections to the Freund Committee's proposal. Furthermore, it is not beyond debate that the National Court would prove to be a court of great prestige, blessed with an attractive docket and capable of attracting judges of the highest caliber. If the National Court's docket becomes devoted to fact-bound cases or cases in specialized areas of national law, it might not attract the likes of Learned Hand. Certainly both the Supreme Court and the courts of appeals would be strongly tempted to channel such cases to the new court. Unless the transfer jurisdiction became a source of important, interesting cases, the new court might have difficulty escaping the image of the Supreme Court's special master for unexciting legal matters. On the other hand, if the transfer jurisdiction were heavily used, it might make serious inroads on the existing powers of the Supreme Court.

Thus, the [Hruska] Commission has stumbled at various points in its efforts to jump through the hoops held up by critics of the Freund Committee. This is not surprising; it is probably impossible to create a new court of real substance while at the same time overcoming all of the criticisms directed at the Freund Committee. What is surprising is the [Hruska] Commission's assumption that those criticisms are all valid and that simply reacting to them would lead to a sensible proposal for a new court. . . .

The prospect of excessive jurisdictional "noise" in the [Hruska] Commission's proposed system cannot be made to disappear simply by denying that it would occur. Even if litigants are denied oral argument on an appellate review of transfer decisions and are discouraged from devoting significant portions of their briefs and jurisdictional papers to transfer or reference questions, the circuit courts, the National Court, and the Supreme Court nonetheless would have to make the various discretionary judgments permitted under the [Hruska] Commission's proposal. It is unrealistic to assume that those judgments would always be easy and would never provoke discord among the members of the various courts. Some cases would be studied extensively, only to be sent in the end to another court. This would be a waste of judicial resources. Moreover, the danger of judicial discord will impose new constraints on judges. For example, rules will be needed to prevent a wayward panel of a court of appeals from granting transfer in the hopes of obtaining a result from the National Court that seems unlikely in an *en banc* proceeding in the home circuit.

Related to the problem of jurisdictional noise is the question of the relationship between the Supreme Court and the National Court of Appeals. Judges appointed under article III of the Constitution are to staff the National Court. The National Court undoubtedly would exhibit a degree of independence and a judicial philosophy of its own making; as a result, it would come to be viewed as unreliable by various groups of justices, at least in some areas of the law. This would have two consequences. First, jurisdictional questions would assume increased importance in the conferences of the

Supreme Court. Some efforts to refer would be designed to obtain a result in the National Court unlikely in the Supreme Court; and some efforts would be made to grant Supreme Court review (which can be accomplished by a minority of the Justices) solely to avoid a decision by the National Court. Even if consideration of these questions did not lead to friction among the Justices, it would nonetheless absorb some of their limited time. Second, more than a few of the judgments of the National Court might have to be reviewed by the Supreme Court. Unlike court of appeals judgment under the present system, the Supreme Court could not ignore wayward decisions of the National Court on the theory that other opportunities would arise to correct erroneous readings of national law. . . . If so, the result would be the addition of a fourth tier of review without any net gain in national appellate capacity.

Difficulties in the relationship between the Supreme Court and the National Court might be exacerbated because the Supreme Court's referral decisions would be based on the occasionally inaccurate picture of a case which emerges from jurisdictional papers and which can only be corrected by full adjudication. The Supreme Court might refer a case for resolution on the merits only to find the National Court, upon plenary review, concluding that it turned on different issues than those for which it was referred. The National Court, on the other hand, might find itself in an awkward position if directed to decide on the merits a case that it suspects the Supreme Court eventually would have dismissed as improvidently granted. The [Hruska] Commission's proposal apparently does not envision that the National Court would be empowered to dismiss on the ground of improvident referral, although certainly there would be cases deserving such treatment.

Another likely drawback of the [Hruska] Commission's proposed system is the improbability that the circuit courts would have identical transfer policies. Some circuits might be more jealous than others about their jurisdiction or might have different notions of the kind of cases appropriate for the new court. This might well lead to regional forum shopping. If certain circuits developed a pattern of frequent use of the transfer jurisdiction, litigants of national scope — in particular the federal government — who viewed the National Court of Appeals as a hospitable forum might channel litigation into these circuits. Comparable litigants with a distaste for the National Court would tend to avoid such circuits. Apart from the prospects of forum shopping, it seems unwise to set up a system likely to lead to hit-or-miss national review. If there are a substantial number of issues of federal law that should be put to rest nationally without delay, then the federal judicial system should be designed to settle them automatically, rather than sporadically. . . .

Despite the criticisms offered here, on balance the [Hruska] Commission has . . . helped clarify the current condition of the Supreme Court. The Court is not endangered by its screening burden, but there is a large question whether under the present system the Court has the capacity to decide enough cases to keep pace with the country's needs. Yet, having clarified our understanding of the problem, the Commission's proposed solution is unsound. The [Hruska] Commission seeks an easy way out of a dilemma, when none may be available.

NOTES

1. Compare the Hruska Commission proposal to the Freund Committee proposal. How are they similar? How are they different? What are the assumptions of the Hruska Commission, *i.e.*, what systemic needs of the federal appellate courts does it seek to remedy? What are its proposed solutions?

2. Reference jurisdiction. Consider the Hruska Commission proposal from the standpoint of a Supreme Court justice reviewing a petition — or a law clerk writing a certpool memo on a petition. Now you have three disposition choices: deny, grant, or refer the case to the national court of appeals. How does the new third option affect your decisionmaking? What criteria might be articulated in the internal rules of the SCOTUS to identify and distinguish "reference" cases from other cases? Notice that the reference option, in turn, is contingent. What kind of case should be referred to the national court of appeals with the requirement that it be decided and what kind of case should be referred with discretion to the national court of appeals whether or not to decide it? As a judge on the national court of appeals, what factors would inform your decision whether or not to decide a contingently referred case?

3. Transfer jurisdiction. How do you suppose transfer jurisdiction would actually work? What kinds of cases should the regional courts of appeals transfer to the national court of appeals? Would transfer jurisdiction replace the *en banc* rehearing before all the judges in a circuit? When should the national court of appeals accept the transfer and decide the case and when should it decline the transfer and not decide the case? After the national court of appeals has decided a case transferred from one of the courts of appeals, would the case have more or less claim on being granted *certiorari* review in the Supreme Court?

4. The Federal Courts Study Committee went out of its way to explicitly disapprove of the Hruska Commission proposal because it would have "enlarge[d] the system's capacity to resolve intercircuit conflicts, but would not solve the problem of growth within the courts of appeals." REPORT OF THE FEDERAL COURTS STUDY COMMITTEE 117 (1990). Is that a fair and accurate criticism? Is this not something of a judicial reform *non sequitur* — so what if the proposal solves one problem but not another problem?

5. The Hruska Commission proposals did not attract much attention from Congress, but court commentators weighed in to evaluate the Commission's assessment of the problems and to test its proposed solutions. *See generally* Erwin N. Griswold, *Rationing Justice — The Supreme Court's Caseload and What the Court Does Not Do*, 60 CORNELL L. REV. 335 (1975); Charles R. Haworth & Daniel J. Meador, *A Proposed New Federal Intermediate Appellate Court*, 12 U. MICH. J.L. REFORM 201 (1978); Roman L. Hruska, *The Commission on Revision of the Federal Court Appellate System: A Legislative History*, 1974 ARIZ. ST. L.J. 579; Harold Leventhal, *A Modest Proposal for a Multi-Circuit Appeals Court*, 24 AM. U. L. REV. 881 (1975); Luther M. Swygert, *The Proposed National Court of Appeals: A Threat to Judicial Symmetry*, 51 IND. L.J. 327 (1976); Joseph R. Weisberger, *Appellate Courts: The Challenge of Inundation*, 31 AM. U. L. REV. 237 (1982).

3. Intercircuit Panel (Chief Justice Burger Proposal)

Warren E. Burger, *The Time Is Now for the Intercircuit Panel*, 71 A.B.A. J. 86 (1985)[8]

What I now press upon you and the Congress is a modification of the Freund and Hruska proposals. The debate on this subject has been valuable and led to improvements over the original proposals. Now, rather than a permanent intermediate court of the kind recommended by those studies — a National Court of Appeals — I propose we create a temporary and experimental panel — an Intercircuit Panel — made up of judges of the courts of appeals, including, of course, senior circuit judges. We can experiment with that panel for up to five years by assigning to that panel the task of resolving conflicting holdings of the several circuits. This would mean that judges from the level where conflicts arise would be charged with the duty to resolve such conflicts.

Conflicts at the court of appeals level are largely due to *inter*circuit conflicts, but with courts of appeals now having as many as 28 judges, *intra*circuit conflicts are theoretically, but not invariably, resolved by having the case reviewed *en banc*. What I now propose amounts to nothing more than that we have a national *en banc* panel of nine judges. It is just that simple.

And because this would be a process of resolving conflicts among the circuits, the logical source for these decision makers is, as I suggested earlier, to draw upon the judges of the level where the conflicts originate, with the Supreme Court reserving *certiorari* jurisdiction.

The Intercircuit Panel would be selected by the Supreme Court from among the circuit judges. One judge would be drawn from each of the 13 courts of appeals. This would permit a regular panel of nine with four judges in reserve. The nine-member panel would sit for two sessions of two weeks each per year. Cases would continue to come from the courts of appeals to the Supreme Court, but the Supreme Court would have the option to refer cases involving circuit conflicts and interpretation of federal statutes to the Intercircuit Panel. . . .

I emphasize that this special panel would be experimental, with a five-year "sunset" provision. Within that time, we would be able to determine whether this plan works. Of course, if during that time we see that the experiment is not effective, it could be terminated immediately simply by the Supreme Court's decision not to send any additional cases to the panel. The uniqueness of this proposal is that there will be no new bureaucracy seeking to perpetuate jobs.

. . . I am comforted somewhat in pressing this position by saying that it would not cost the taxpayers additional money except for the relatively nominal factor of the travel expense of the nine judges coming to Washington, D.C., twice a year for not more than two weeks each time. It would not require a new courthouse; it would not need a new courtroom; it would not need a permanent court clerk. The Court of Appeals for the Federal Circuit has tendered its courtroom. Existing staffs of the Court of Appeals for the Federal Circuit or the Supreme Court can absorb the extra duty of preparing the docket.

---

[8] Copyright © 1985 American Bar Association Journal. Reprinted with permission.

There is, of course, nothing new or drastic about creating special panels, drawn from among the judges presently in office. In the past 20 years Congress has created many special, temporary panels, including one for the selection of a so-called special prosecutor, the Temporary Emergency Court of Appeals, the Multi-District Litigation Panel, and two Foreign Intelligence Surveillance Courts. Members of these panels are designated from among the present federal judges; no new permanent court structure is created. More than 60 judges have been designated to these panels by me . . . under authority granted by Congress. I have not heard of any complaint about the personnel or the performance of those special panels. . . .

Will this plan work? There, I must be completely candid; I do not know. No one can really know with any certainty. That is why we need to experiment for a few years, and if we find the panel works, it can be continued in this form. I emphasize that if after two or three years, we conclude that it is not helping, we can abandon it. In any event the statute would have a five-year "sunset" provision. Until someone comes along with a better idea, I submit that this is worth a try.

A. Leo Levin, *Adding Appellate Capacity to the Federal System: A National Court of Appeals or an Inter-Circuit Tribunal?*, 39 WASH. & LEE L. REV. 1, 16-21 (1982)[9]

A Permanent Court or an Inter-Circuit Tribunal? Even if the need for additional appellate capacity for definitive resolution of issues of federal law is persuasively demonstrated, and the feasibility of reference jurisdiction established, a host of issues remain concerning the specifics of an appropriate court. The most obvious response is creation of a new tribunal, a permanent court composed of Article III judges appointed by the President and confirmed by the Senate. Details can be filled in with relative ease: number of judges, provision for sitting only *en banc* rather than in panels, seat of the court, provision for sitting elsewhere, and choice of a name. What may be viewed as start-up problems can be more difficult, but hardly intractable: shall a single president be empowered to select the membership of the full court, with the risk that its members will reflect a common ideological cast? Shall some of the judges be selected initially from the circuit courts, to sit for a term until the full permanent membership of the court is in place? These are details, important and potentially of far-reaching significance, but legislative proposals have been developed, alternatives are available, and choices can be made without serious risk to the functioning of the new tribunal.

An imposing array of distinguished jurists, while recognizing the need for a new tribunal, have cautioned against immediate creation of a permanent new court, preferring instead what has been variously termed as inter-circuit tribunal, a multi-circuit court of appeals, or a rotating panel for the resolution of inter-circuit conflict. . . . Common to these proposals is the basic idea that the judges of the new tribunal should be experienced jurists from within the federal system, judges sitting on the various courts of appeals who would accept this new assignment either as an additional duty or for a term of years. Closely

---

9 Copyright © 1982 Washington & Lee Law Review. Reprinted with permission.

associated with this basic idea are the convictions that so radical an innovation should be introduced on an experimental basis, that the enabling legislation should include a sunset provision, and that the court be tested in the crucible of experience before being made a permanent fixture. One or another of these ingredients, in varying forms and with varying modifications and embellishments, is found in each of the alternative proposals that have been suggested.

Four reasons are urged in favor of choosing some lesser remedy than creation of a permanent court interposed between the Supreme Court and the present courts of appeals. First is the argument in favor of experimentation before making a permanent change in the structure of the national judiciary. Closely related and yet analytically distinguishable is the argument that something other than a permanent new court will experience less difficulty during the inevitable start-up period. During that period, the Justices of the Supreme Court understandably will want to feel their way slowly in the exercise of their newly conferred authority to refer cases for decision. Also, during the trial period the relationship of the new court to the existing "inferior" courts will be developed. Indeed, concern for the stature and prestige of the present courts of appeals, conceivably at risk of being diminished by the presence of a new court superior to them but inferior to the Supreme Court, is an important reason for a less-than-permanent court. Finally, the needs of economy and efficiency are always of concern but never more than in the present climate of preoccupation with growing deficits and the national debt. Each of these factors deserves careful consideration; the credentials of the proponents as well as the intrinsic force of the arguments require no less. Moreover, since we do not have a single proposal offered as an alternative to a permanent national court of appeals, but rather a range of alternatives, permitting and indeed requiring significant choice in the shaping of legislation, each of the factors must be weighed in terms of its potential to advance or to impede achievement of the basic goal: improved capacity to provide clarity and consistency in the national law.

One cannot seriously object to a provision requiring Congress to evaluate the utility of the new court after a term of years, with abolition the price of failure. Seven years, however, may be preferable to five. The first term can be expected to be a start-up period and a report adequate for a congressional decision would normally be expected at least one full year before sunset. An adequate period for normal functioning and development should be provided in the interim.

A requirement that eligibility for appointment to the national court of appeals be limited to judges presently sitting on the circuit courts or that the functioning of the new tribunal be evaluated by the Congress after a term of years, with abolition the price of failure, hardly would affect seriously the functioning of the new court as it goes about its business of deciding cases referred to it by the Supreme Court. On the other hand, if the membership of the inter-circuit tribunal were to be picked at random from all federal appellate judges for each case referred for decision — an alternative no one has proposed — the new court likely could not contribute significantly to the stability or predictability of federal law, whatever the nature of its docket.

There are many attractions to the creation of an inter-circuit tribunal composed entirely of judges presently sitting on the United States courts of appeals who would assemble to hear cases as the demands of the docket dictated. No need would arise for the full complement of support personnel, including additional law clerks and secretaries, although it would be necessary to provide for the maintenance of a separate docket and for the performance of other services provided by a clerk's office. What is particularly attractive to some is the absence of the need to appoint additional judges . . . assignment to the inter-circuit tribunal would be in addition to the normal duties of each of the judges.

Here, a word of caution is appropriate. So long as the docket is small and the burdens of this additional assignment not excessively onerous, there would be much to be said for this procedure. If the docket of the inter-circuit tribunal should grow, the pressures of a demanding additional assignment are likely to prove unacceptable. Judges are sensitive to their obligations to their home courts and, as must be evident to any observer of the federal judicial scene, the courts of appeals are already burdened. Not every judge would, in any event, be willing to accept assignment to an inter-circuit tribunal, and if such an acceptance implies either an unfair workload on a judge's colleagues or excessive burdens on the judge himself or herself, declinations probably would be common.

Clearly, availability of additional judicial resources to a home circuit, by way of designation by the Chief Justice of visiting judges, would alleviate the problem. These techniques, however, are already widely used and there are limits on the available resources. Should the Congress ever think well of providing some extra judgeships, the incumbents being available for nationwide service to fill particular demands, again the problem would be alleviated, but the savings would be reduced. If the Congress establishes this new tribunal without creating new judgeships, the workload should be monitored and added resources provided when that proves necessary.

Perhaps the most important variable is the size of the panel of judges constituting the inter-circuit tribunal. Under one model, the size of the court itself could be large indeed, even in excess of twenty, with panels for particular cases drawn from this larger group. Whatever the size of the panel that would hear cases referred by the Supreme Court, the fact that the sitting personnel would rotate would result in the unpredictability of the decision as the court develops doctrine relevant to the various issues presented to it. This inevitably invites relitigation, both by the government and by individual litigants. It invites courts obligated to consider the precedent of the inter-circuit tribunal as binding to make fine distinctions in the hope that a later panel will limit the impact of a prior decision, short of over-ruling it. The larger the group from which a panel hearing a particular case is drawn, the greater the unpredictability and the uncertainty and the likelihood of relitigation. An analogy can be found in the difficulties experienced by courts of appeals with a large number of judges in maintaining uniformity in the law of the circuit.

If it were considered desirable that no judge sitting on the circuit court sit on the inter-circuit tribunal that reviews a case from his own circuit, it still might be possible to have a court constituted of nine court of appeals judges with a minimum of seven sitting, always *en banc*.

The need for predictability also argues for a longer, rather than a shorter, term. If a sunset provision of five years were to be built into legislation creating the new court, each of the judges selected should be selected for a full five year period. In the ultimate, staggered terms are to be preferred to sharp variations in the personnel of the court at a particular point in time. If the experiment were to be for a longer period, appointment initially for a seven year term would be preferable to any lesser period. Inevitably, resignations, disability, and other factors will result in some changes in personnel, but change in the personnel of the court should be minimized rather than facilitated. The desirability of a rather long period of service argues against too heavy a reliance on senior judges. Appointment of seniors appears, at first blush, to disrupt their home circuits least, and yet the work which virtually every senior judge does in the federal judicial system indicates that their removal to an inter-circuit tribunal would entail a substantial cost in terms of judicial service available to the home court. Moreover, seniors are available for assignment to other courts; their willingness to give of themselves beyond what is called for under the law could be utilized to good advantage in ways other than serving on the inter-circuit court. . . .

One cannot ignore the fact that the acceptability of a new tribunal, not only within the federal judiciary, but by the profession as a whole and by Congress would be enhanced substantially if the court were viewed as a five or seven year experiment. . . . Moreover, the advantage of moving forward at this time, as opposed to waiting for another decade or two, or even three, is significant. The increase in the order of magnitude of the demands our society imposes on the federal judicial system is such that we should no longer ignore the need for increasing the capacity of the system to deal with contemporary problems. The time has indeed come for the Congress to move forward, however cautiously and experimentally, toward increasing the capacity of the system to provide for what has aptly been termed, "the known certainty of the law."

NOTES

1. One of the politically-charged criticisms of the Hruska Commission proposal was that a single president would be able initially to appoint all the judges on the national court of appeals. In Chief Justice Burger's intercircuit panel ("ICP") the SCOTUS would designate and select the judges on the ICP. Which is a better selection process? Why? Notice that in the existing statutes the Chief Justice has sole discretion to designate current judges to serve on special panels, but the ICP proposal would vest the designation authority in the full SCOTUS. What is the practical and political difference between designation by the Chief Justice alone and designation by the Conference of all the justices?

2. Play out the different permutations for the SCOTUS *certiorari* procedures if the justices' choices included the option to refer a petition presenting an intercircuit conflict to the ICP. What effect would it have on the Rule of Four, for example? After the ICP decided the case and resolved the intercircuit conflict, would the case be more or less certworthy? Is not the implied assumption that the SCOTUS reference to the ICP would be the end of the SCOTUS' consideration for almost all cases presenting intercircuit conflicts? Should that be

the assumption? What if the justices simply did not agree with the way the ICP resolved the conflict?

3. The ICP proposal included a five-year "sunset" provision and the additional safeguard that the SCOTUS could effectively shut down the experiment by simply ceasing to refer intercircuit conflict cases to the ICP. This was seen by some experts as a keen advantage of the proposal:

> If there is no need or if the special appellate forum serves no useful purpose, we should be able to learn that within five years. On the other hand, if the forum is a worthwhile idea with beneficial effects for the legal system, that too should become evident within five years. Because the forum would be a panel consisting of existing circuit judges, it could be discontinued with ease.

> Holmes reminded us that all life is an experiment. This is particularly true in matters such as these. We need a way to test the utility of a device for enhancing the national appellate capacity, which, at the same time, may prove to be a device for alleviating pressures on the Supreme Court. Not only can we determine the utility of the new forum as a means for settling national law, we also may be able to determine the extent to which the availability of this forum enables the Supreme Court to function with that quality of deliberation and care we expect of the Court on legal issues of the highest national importance. The chief justice's proposal would provide a test run that is inexpensive and free of risk. The proposal also would leave the Supreme Court in position to determine the amount and kind of help it and the system need.

Daniel J. Meador, *A Comment on the Chief Justice's Proposals*, 69 A.B.A. J. 448, 449-50 (1983). Does this feature unduly delegate Congress's power to ordain and establish the inferior federal courts, U.S. Const., art. III. § 1? What outcomes and results would persuade the justices to continue the experiment through to completion? What benchmarks would Congress apply at the end of the five year experiment to decide whether or not to make the ICP permanent? *See also* William H. Rehnquist, *The Changing Role of the Supreme Court*, 14 FLA. ST. U. L. REV. 1, 12-14 (1986) (suggesting the ICP be made a permanent feature).

4. In 1990, the Federal Courts Study Committee recommended a five-year pilot project pursuant to which the Supreme Court could refer a case involving an intercircuit conflict to one of the twelve courts of appeals where the conflict would then be resolved by an *en banc* decision of that court. That *en banc* decision would be binding on all federal courts, unless altered by the Supreme Court. The assignment to a court of appeals would be made randomly. After decision by that court, a party could seek *certiorari* in the Supreme Court. REPORT OF THE FEDERAL COURTS STUDY COMMITTEE 125-27 (1990). How does this proposal for an *"En Banc* Intercircuit Conference" (EBIC) compare to Chief Justice Burger's ICP proposal? Are the differences significant? What are the strengths and weaknesses of the EBIC?

5. The Federal Courts Study Committee also recommended an empirical study of intercircuit conflicts that eventually was conducted by Professor Hellman and is the subject of subsection III A above in this Chapter. Whether

there were enough unresolved and intolerable conflicts to justify the proposed experiment with Chief Justice Burger's ICP — or some variation like the Federal Courts Study Committee's EBIC proposal described in the preceding Note — was a deeply-contested proposition at the time. Arthur D. Hellman, *The Proposed Intercircuit Tribunal: Do We Need It? Will It Work?*, 11 HASTINGS CONST. L. Q. 375 (1984); Ruth Bader Ginsburg & Peter W. Huber, *The Intercircuit Committee*, 100 HARV. L. REV. 1417 (1987). Would not a pilot project provide more definitive evidence and a better answer to this question than the past statistical studies and quantitative analyses have provided?

6. Professor Levin's excerpt above considers the pros and cons of conducting a temporary experiment versus making a permanent structural reform. What are his arguments? Are they persuasive? He also seems to suggest that haggling over the details of an experimental proposal can go on and on and result in an endless postponement of needed reform. Do you agree? How can this be avoided? Recall the discussion in the first section of this Chapter about the political and social factors that work for and against court reform.

7. Do all proposals that designate some court or judicial body other than the SCOTUS to resolve intercircuit conflicts suffer from the same two related design flaws: the first time around, the justices must somehow metaphysically sort out conflicts to keep for themselves and conflicts to refer to the other court but then the federal issues that get referred to the other court will inevitably come back to the justices on a second petition for *certiorari*? Is there any way to minimize or eliminate these two difficulties? The bottom line question is whether these added administrative burdens, costs, and delays are or are not acceptable?

IV. APPELLATE SUBJECT-MATTER ORGANIZATION

In this section we return to a topic touched upon in Chapter 6: the use of the subject matter of cases as a basis for organizing the intermediate appellate tier. We treat two aspects of the topic: (1) the use of subject matter as a basis for organizing two or more appellate courts in the intermediate tier, and (2) the use of subject matter as a means of internally organizing a single appellate court. We also seek to differentiate court specialization from subject-matter organization. The former has a checkered history; the latter is still largely untried. As we noted in Chapter 6, only a few examples of subject-matter appellate organization can be found in the state judicial systems. The material in this section focuses on the federal appellate courts. The most highly developed subject-matter plans are found in the German appellate courts, described in Chapter 13, and those arrangements should be borne in mind in considering the material here.

Consider when subject-matter organization is appropriate and desirable. How should subject-matter appellate adjudication be arranged and organized? Distinguish between subject-matter organization among several courts in the intermediate tier and subject-matter organization within a single intermediate court. The two reforms are different and respond to different problems. Contemplate whether subject-matter organization should be part of the future of the federal courts.

Rochelle Cooper Dreyfuss, *Specialized Adjudication*, 1990 BYU L. REV. 377, 377-83[10]

It has been suggested that Congress should alleviate the federal court docket crisis by establishing a series of specialized courts with limited jurisdiction over particular areas. Many arguments in favor of such courts are familiar. The obvious solution to the docket crisis — adding judgeships to the regional courts — has decreasing marginal utility: as more judges write opinions on the same issues, the law becomes occluded with inconsistencies that breed yet more lawsuits and give rise to opportunistic litigation strategies that further aggravate the workload problem. Specialization could, at least in theory, enable the judiciary to meet the nation's adjudication needs effectively, and may even produce benefits of its own.

There are several ways specialization can be achieved. These are explored below from both an empirical and a theoretical perspective. However, it is in three features, shared by all models, that the value of specialization is said to lie. First, establishment of specialized courts would permit some or all cases in a particular subject area to be transferred out of the regional courts of general jurisdiction. If there are many cases redirected in this way, relief to the regional dockets would give the generalist judges more time to consider other matters. Even if there are very few cases, workload in the regional courts would be reduced so long as the cases transferred are complex enough that they would have taken up a disproportionate share of the generalist judges' time.

Second, concentrating cases into one or a few tribunals should produce a bench small enough to maintain the collegiality necessary to speak with a single voice. Greater consistency in court opinions would offer greater guidance to consumers of the law, reducing their need for judicial intervention. In addition, the monopoly, or near monopoly, created by funneling all cases in a field into a single tribunal should eliminate entirely disputes on issues such as forum selection and choice of law.

Third, a specialized court's judges would either be chosen for their special expertise or because new appointees could quickly acquire experience in the court's specialty. Moreover, unlike the regional circuits, the court might have enough work in a given field to justify the employment of technical assistants. If, as common experience suggests, experts are better than laymen at dealing with matters in their special areas, the specialized judiciary should handle cases more efficiently, thereby reducing the number of judge-hours required to decide any given number of cases. Each case could also be decided more rapidly, a benefit in fields where timeliness is essential.

Most important, the court's expertise should enable it to craft better opinions, especially in fields where a small number of cases are now distributed rather thinly among the regional courts. Since generalist judges are confronted with the specialty subject matter infrequently, they lack the motivation, experience, and time to develop an understanding of the law. They decide the occasional case based upon a cursory understanding of policy and receive limited feedback on how well they fared. Thus, a specialized court's sustained

---

10 Copyright © 1990 Brigham Young University Law Review. Reprinted with permission.

involvement with a field would facilitate superior decisionmaking. Such a court would be in a better position to understand when it is better to sacrifice accuracy (the "right" result in every case) for the ease with which bright-line rules can be applied and how to draw the fine distinctions necessary when accuracy is more important than administrative convenience. In addition, such a court would have the opportunity to see the practice results of its rules and the time to wait for the most appropriate vehicles for changing them. Absolute responsibility over an entire corpus of law should, at least theoretically, be exciting, for it provides a unique opportunity to oversee the development of a coherent body of doctrine, whose elements are carefully chosen to mesh effectively.

With these advantages, one might ask why the federal system has not made better use of specialized courts. Part of the answer may be that in the nation's early years, there were not many federal cases, so courts empowered to hear the entire federal docket were more efficient than courts that could only entertain actions within particular subject matter areas. Another part of the answer may, however, be that the disadvantages of specialization are as easy to list as the benefits, and that without an overwhelming need to find new efficiencies, Congress was well advised to steer clear of the strategy.

Not surprisingly, the problems with specialization track the advantages. Thus, removing a field from the regional courts' purview is a benefit from the standpoint of those courts' dockets, but it also means that the thinking of generalists no longer contributes to the field's development. Cross-pollination among legal theories is a significant source of change in the law since important patterns of reasoning sometimes emerge rather naturally in one field, yet can be meaningfully applied to other areas. Furthermore, it makes sense for the adjudicatory system to function in a manner that promotes the like treatment of similar issues, even when they arise in different contexts.

Similarly, while concentration of cases in a collegial bench might stabilize the law, it also makes the tribunal more vulnerable to politicization than courts of general jurisdiction. When issues in a field of law are considered by courts all over the country, interest groups have limited ability to influence the direction of the law by influencing the appointment of the judges who create it. The resources — money and power — of these groups must be spread over the entire judiciary, and their efforts encounter interference from those organizations that are concerned with other issues on the judicial agenda. But neither resource-spreading nor influence-dilution would occur in relation to an appointment to a specialized bench that bears solely, and only, the responsibility for deciding the issues which concern an interest group. In that case, the side that is better heeled or more powerful could capture the court and create a bench more likely to issue one-sided opinions.

Even if the appointment process remained untainted, capture may occur through the court's continuous contact with the bar that practices before it. Commentators suggest that repeat players have an advantage over one-time litigants in courts of general jurisdiction. This problem would be exacerbated on a specialized bench, where repeaters would be more likely to know all of the judges, be acquainted with the eccentricities of the court's rules and specialized law, and be positioned to find suitable vehicles for arguing the changes in the law that they desire.

The efficiency with which specialized courts operate may also sometimes be disadvantageous. Percolation of ideas cannot occur in a court that has exclusive jurisdiction over its field. And even if some cases in the specialized field remain in the regional circuits, these courts might tend to defer to the expertise of the special bench. If conflicts fail to develop, Supreme Court activity in the specialized field will diminish. As a result, pronouncements of the specialized court will establish new law immediately, and with a fairly high degree of finality. While this is generally beneficial, it creates a greater risk of error, exacerbates the consequences of the mistakes that do occur, and reduces the chances that the public will understand or accept major changes. The only available check will be the laborious process of legislative correction, but Congress' greater attention to the court's activities raises the possibility that the court will become an extension of the legislature.

It must also be recognized that the court's expertise is created at the expense of an isolation that jeopardizes its ability to shape the law. Because of the repetitive nature of the docket, appointments to a specialized bench might not be as highly prized as other federal judgeships. With less prestige — and presumably, the same bad pay as other federal judges — it may be harder to attract the truly talented. To be sure, practitioners and law professors specialize too, but the nature of the adjudicative task may make repetition more boring to judges than it is to the bar or to scholars.

If the specialist court were given exclusive jurisdiction over certain subject matter and little other responsibility, isolation would pose further risks. The court's enthusiasm for a new mode of thinking would not be tempered by consideration of cases where that reasoning was shown to be inappropriate. Lacking the full panoply of tools for furthering its policies, the court may distort the law to achieve the ends it deems appropriate. And since the court would not become engaged in the judicial dialogue that occurs when several courts consider the same issues, its judges would not have the opportunity to see how their work is received by the remainder of the judiciary or be given the incentive to write persuasively.

Nor is it necessarily true that specialization will lead to a decrease in the demand for judicial resources. Although more stable, better crafted law offers greater guidance, the court's success could also attract new business. Parties might decide to litigate cases that would otherwise have been resolved by extra-judicial means. While certain kinds of secondary litigation would disappear, specialization could open new sources of contention. Each court would, at a minimum, need to create "boundary law": criteria for determining when a case is within its jurisdiction. Appeals from jurisdictional decisions and transfers between specialized and regional courts would increase the burden on the system as a whole.

Most likely, additional refinements would also be found necessary or desirable. For example, each court (or Congress) might develop its own method for handling nonspecialty issues embedded in the cases before it; each might alter its scope of review to reflect the relative competence of the trial and appellate benches; each might be tempted to adopt pleading, discovery or trial methods that function particularly well within the specialized field. The quantity of special law might then grow to the point where the enterprise was wholly unproductive. Phenomena such as dual supervision of regional district courts by regional and specialized appellate courts, a wholly specialized bar, and a return to the equivalent of the writ system are probably not in the nation's interest.

These arguments for and against specialization are well rehearsed. Unfortunately, most debates over specialization make their cases in contexts that provide little information about whether they are in fact valid. Some discussions are purely abstract and phrased to argue that specialization is either generally good or generally bad. Other discussions refer to specific proposals and make little effort to relate arguments to other contexts. The questions that need to be addressed then are: when does specialization make sense, and how should Congress go about fashioning a specialized court in any particular context? The first step in answering these questions is to examine the federal judiciary's past experiences with specialization to determine whether there are specific criteria for deciding when and why this strategy is appropriate. Several conclusions emerge from this examination. First, specialization is neither always good nor always bad. Second, there are useful criteria to identify the situations in which specialization is fruitful. Third, these criteria can also be used in structuring specialized courts so that, in the particular context, the benefits of specialization can be maximized and the disadvantages minimumized.

ABA Standards Relating to Court Organization § 1.13 (1990)[11]

(b) *Intermediate appellate courts.* The organization of appellate courts below the Supreme Court should be guided by the following principles:

(i) Jurisdiction. Every level and division of appellate court should have authority to hear all types of cases; appellate courts of specialized sub- ject-matter jurisdiction should not be established. . . .

Commentary. The first principle is that appellate courts of specialized subject-matter jurisdiction should not be established. The considerations weighing against specialized courts of original jurisdiction . . . apply to appellate courts. It is, of course, true that many specialized appellate courts have performed honorable and effective judicial service. . . . Nevertheless, the appellate court function of developing the law cannot be performed in a coherent and consistent way if jurisdictional divisions compel the law's fabric to be made in a decisional patchwork.

Daniel J. Meador, *A Challenge to Judicial Architecture: Modifying the Regional Design of the U.S. Courts of Appeals*, 56 U. Chi. L. Rev. 603, 607-22 (1989)[12]

Advent and Implementation of the Non-Regional Subject Matter Concept in the Federal Intermediate Appellate System. The non-regional, subject matter

---

[11] Copyright © 1990 American Bar Association. Reprinted with permission.

[12] University of Chicago Law Review by Daniel Meador. Copyright 1989 by Univ of Chicago Law sch. Reproduced with permission of Univ of Chicago Law Sch in the format Textbook via Copyright Clearance Center.

concept as a basis for structuring a portion of the federal intermediate appellate tier can be summarized as follows: some categories of non-constitutional cases would be routed on appeal directly from the district courts to a non-regional appellate forum rather than to the twelve regionally organized courts of appeals. The decisions of that appellate forum in the categories of cases routed to it would have nationwide precedential affect and would thus eliminate the possibility of non-uniform decisions. The Supreme Court would have *certiorari* jurisdiction over the decisions of that intermediate appellate forum and thus would be available to set it right in the occasional case where the Supreme Court considered that the court had gone wrong. The effects of this appellate design would be to eliminate pressure on the Supreme Court to resolve intercircuit conflicts in categories routed to the nationwide forum (there being no possibility of such conflicts) and to increase the capacity of the federal judicial system to maintain nationwide uniformity in the law. . . .

In earlier years, Congress had employed the non-regional, subject matter concept to create three courts in specific areas: the Court of Customs and Patent Appeals, the Commerce Court, and the Emergency Court of Appeals. Those courts no longer exist, and because of their peculiarly limited jurisdiction, they are not a model for the proposal put forth in this article. The first use of the subject matter style of appellate organization in the contemporary context came in 1971 in connection with the enactment of provisions dealing with the national energy problem. Congress then established the Temporary Emergency Court of Appeals (TECA) to which all appeals from the district courts nationwide would be taken in litigation arising under those energy regulations. The purpose was to ensure a national uniformity in the interpretation and application of those statutes and to provide for expeditious resolution of litigation arising under them. . . . [Congress has since abolished TECA and transferred its jurisdiction to the U.S. Federal Circuit.]

Congress next moved to incorporate the non-regional concept into the federal intermediate appellate tier in 1982 when it created the U.S. Court of Appeals for the Federal Circuit. Congress created this court by fusing the Court of Claims and the Court of Customs and Patent Appeals, but with a substantially enlarged appellate jurisdiction. The Federal Circuit has twelve permanent judgeships, and exclusive jurisdiction over the district courts nationwide in all cases arising under the patent laws and in Little Tucker Act cases. It also has exclusive appellate jurisdiction over decisions of the Merit Systems Protection Board, certain other administrative bodies, the Claims Court, the Court of International Trade, and the newly created Court of Veterans' Appeals.

Although designing an appellate court's jurisdiction in terms of the subject matter of cases is relatively new in the United States, such designs have long pervaded the courts of Europe. The German judiciary provides a good example. Since at least the beginning of the nineteenth century, all German appellate courts have been organized in this way. This scheme has been carried forward today in the Federal Republic of Germany. . . . In the Court of Appeal of England there is also an element of subject matter organization, although it is less formalized and not as refined as that in Germany. . . .

Despite a world-wide familiarity with subject matter organization of appellate courts, such organization remains something of an unknown novelty to many American judges and lawyers. Among the state intermediate appellate courts there are a few examples; one is in Pennsylvania, where the Commonwealth Court adjudicates appeals in local government litigation and administrative law cases and the Superior Court has jurisdiction over appeals in all other civil cases and in criminal cases. . . .

The hearings and debates over the creation of the Federal Circuit gave impetus to the concept of subject matter organization as a design that could be employed in a variety of selected federal statutory fields to accomplish two ends simultaneously: to relieve pressure on the Supreme Court to monitor intercircuit discrepancies, and to improve coherency in federal decisional law. This idea has taken on heightened importance in the wake of the failure of other proposals directed at the same problems, such as the National Court of Appeals and the Inter-Circuit Tribunal. Further modification in the regional structure of the intermediate tier now seems the most feasible way to achieve a higher level of nationwide consistency in the law.

Clarification of the Non-Regional, Subject Matter Concept as Applied to the Federal Intermediate Appellate Structure. The jurisdiction of non-regional federal appellate courts, structured to co-exist in the intermediate tier with the regional circuits, must necessarily be defined in terms of the subject matter of the appeals. Because American lawyers and judges are generally unfamiliar with appellate jurisdiction cast in subject matter terms, they tend to confuse this concept with other ideas. Most often they confuse the concept with proposals to create a court of "experts" or a "specialized" court. Of course one could structure subject matter jurisdiction so as to fit both of those labels, but that need not be done, and that is not what is being discussed in this article. The primary purpose of a nationwide subject matter jurisdiction, as distinguished from a regional appellate organization, is not to create a court of experts or specialists but to maximize coherence and predictability in federal law through continuity and stability of decision makers. Perhaps this point can best be explained by considering a state judicial system in which there is a supreme court and a set of trial courts, with no intermediate appellate courts. That was the original structure in the states, and it continues to be the structure in many. In such a state, all appeals go to the single appellate forum, thus achieving a maximum degree of jurisdiction-wide coherence in decisional law. Appeals in all tort cases, for example, would go to the state supreme court. The same group of judges would be deciding all tort appeals, thereby avoiding unevenness and discrepancy among various panels or courts. Yet no one has ever thought of this traditional arrangement as creating a court of experts or a specialized court in tort law. This would likewise be the situation as to all other subject matter within that court's jurisdiction: contract cases, property cases, criminal cases, administrative agency cases, and so on. In each category, a single appellate body — not composed of experts or specialists — would be deciding the appeals with a jurisdiction-wide precedential effect.

The use of the terms "generalist" and "specialist" in connection with the work of federal appellate judges is confusing and misleading. These words do not represent useful concepts in relation to the work of those appellate judges, and they interfere with realistic analysis. It is important to think anew about what federal appellate judges actually do and the varying ways that business is distributed among them. The emphasis should be on function instead of abstractions such as "generalized" and "specialized." There is a tendency to think of those federal appellate courts whose jurisdiction is circumscribed territorially — the courts of appeals for the regional circuits — as being "generalist," in contrast to those whose jurisdiction is defined only by subject matter — the Federal Circuit and TECA. To think that way, however, is factually inaccurate and functionally misleading. . . .

Rather than thinking in terms of "general" or "special" jurisdictions, it is more meaningful to think about federal circuit judges in relation to the range of matters in which they actually participate. No single federal appellate court (other than the Supreme Court) has jurisdiction over the entire range of federal law questions — much less over the entire range of the legal order. Consider, for example, the federal appellate jurisdiction that cannot be exercised by the twelve regional circuits: (1) cases placed in the exclusive jurisdiction of the Federal Circuit; (2) cases placed within the exclusive jurisdiction of TECA; (3) three-judge district court cases that go by direct appeal to the U.S. Supreme Court. But withdrawing those matters from the regional circuits, thereby shrinking their range of appellate business, does not convert them into specialized courts; each retains a variety of case types, the variety differing from one circuit to another. Nor, by like reasoning, does placing the matters described in 28 U.S.C. § 1295 exclusively in the Federal Circuit make that body a specialized court. In short, not one of the regional circuits or the Federal Circuit can meaningfully be described as general or special; they are courts with varying kinds of appellate business.

The Federal Circuit is not a "specialized" court in any meaningful sense of the word because 28 U.S.C. § 1295 brings to that court a wide array of case types and legal issues. Appeals from the Claims Court, for example, include the substantive fields of tort, contract, and property, the law of damages, suits arising under the Internal Revenue code, and a substantial mixture of statutory questions on other subjects. Appeals from the Court of International Trade present questions in still other fields of federal statutory law, commercial law, property law, and international law. Merit Systems Protection Board cases present questions in the field of employer-employee relationships in the governmental setting. The Federal Circuit's jurisdiction extends to district court judgments nationwide in patent and certain government claims cases, thus giving the court substantial substantive business in these fields as well as in the application and interpretation of the Federal Rules of Civil Procedure. As applied to an appellate forum with such an array of business the term "specialized" has no utility. What we are really talking about is the mixture of cases and questions in a particular court and the practical benefits of assigning some categories of federal appeals to the twelve regional courts and other categories to non-regional courts with exclusive jurisdiction over them.

Among the existing regional circuits there is already a *de facto* division of judicial labor along subject matter lines. The judges on one regional court of appeals have dockets that vary in significant ways from those of judges on other regional courts of appeals. The differences are often extreme; in some categories of cases there are no appeals at all in some circuits, while their number is substantial in others. In fiscal year 1987, for example, the Second Circuit had forty-one appeals in securities cases brought by the government, while the First, Sixth, Seventh, and Eleventh Circuits had none. The Ninth Circuit had twenty-seven appeals in real property actions against the government; the First Circuit had none. In marine injury cases, the Fifth Circuit had 180 appeals; the Sixth, Tenth, and D.C. Circuits had none. In Social Security cases, the Sixth Circuit had 252 appeals, while the D.C. Circuit had only twenty-two. In environmental suits against the government, the Ninth Circuit had thirty-one appeals, while the First, Fourth, and Seventh Circuits had only one each. In prisoners' civil rights suits (excluding habeas corpus), the Fifth Circuit had 509 appeals; the D.C. Circuit had twenty-three. The Ninth Circuit had 109 appeals under the National Labor Management Relations Act; the D.C. Circuit had one. This substantial variation in the nationwide distribution of appellate business shows that even without a formal allocation of appellate jurisdiction by subject matter we have a *de facto* division of labor on that basis. In other words, in reality not all circuit judges deal with the same kinds of cases. From this existing situation, it is a relatively short step to a more formalized and rational distribution of appellate business by types of cases.

In considering new designs for federal appellate fora, judges and lawyers generally agree upon at least one proposition: the structural design should be such that it does not require a federal judge to consider and decide only one, narrowly defined type of case. This view stems from concerns that judges with an overly narrow jurisdiction would become jaded and bored, that such a limited jurisdiction would not likely attract able lawyers to judgeships, that working constantly in a single narrow field would pose a risk of judicial detachment from the main body of the law and lead to arcane legal views, and that the process of choosing judges for such a narrow jurisdiction might become unusually politicized. The existing regional courts of appeal, the Federal Circuit, and TECA are all structured to avoid these difficulties.

In addition to underscoring the importance of avoiding an overly narrow jurisdiction, these concerns, as well as sensible judicial administration, suggest that any Article III appellate court be part of the nationwide system of U.S. Courts of Appeals and that its judges be U.S. circuit judges. Congress wisely designed the Federal Circuit in this way. Free-standing appellate courts, not integrated into the existing intermediate tier, should be avoided. Integrating new federal appellate courts into the existing intermediate tier would mean, among other things, that their judges would be eligible to sit on all other courts of appeals, and vice versa, thereby ameliorating the undesirable features of judicial work mentioned in the previous paragraph and giving a desirable flexibility in the use of judicial manpower. The creation in this fashion of additional non-regional appellate courts, whose jurisdiction is defined by subject matter, would thus be a continued elaboration of the Evarts Act of 1891.

Criteria for Assigning Federal Appeals to Non-Regional Courts. It is axiomatic that federal law should be uniform throughout the United States. If we want a human activity to be subject to diverse and varying regulation, we leave it to the states. With rare exceptions, a major reason for a congressional enactment governing a particular matter is to ensure that it is treated the same in every part of the country. Any difference in interpretation and application from one state or region to another undermines the political will of the nation embodied in the federal statutory enactment. But nationwide coherence in all areas of federal law cannot be achieved unless the regional appellate structure is completely abandoned. Inasmuch as that step is not necessarily desirable and is not likely to be politically feasible in the near future, the task for judicial architects is to identify those areas of federal law in which there is a special need or desirability for non-regional adjudication.

Congress has already identified several such areas by its action in consolidating appellate review into a single national forum. These include, among others, patent law, customs law, federal personnel decisions, and energy law. The first three of these are concentrated for review in the Federal Circuit; the last, in TECA. Certain characteristics of these case categories suggest why they present a special need for the kind of nationally uniform treatment that can come only through centralized appellate review.

One characteristic relates to the competitive advantages and disadvantages among litigants. Questions as to the validity of patents affect immense investments in research and production and the competitive posture of many enterprises in relation to others, much of which involves multi-state activity. Moreover, a patent is a creature of federal law, the federal government is its exclusive source. Prior to the creation of the Federal Circuit, different circuits placed varying burdens on patentees and infringers that led to rampant forum shopping and uncertainties about the validity of patents, which in turn had an adverse impact on investments in research and production.

Similarly, customs law concerns the economic incidence of the importation of goods from foreign nations into the United States occurring at numerous ports and involving a multitude of business enterprises, many of which are in competition with each other. Different duties imposed on the same types of goods at different ports would place business competitors in unequal economic positions.

Federal personnel problems involve the relationship of a single employer, the federal government, with more than two million employees nationwide, under a single set of personnel laws and regulations. The energy laws concern the regulation and use of highly important natural resources, affecting the entire population of the country in a sophisticated, technically complex way.

With the characteristics of these cases in mind, along with a realistic and common sense analysis of the American legal scene, it is possible to formulate criteria that can be used to identify other categories of cases in which there is a special desirability for the kind of nationwide uniformity in the law that can only be achieved through a non-regional appellate forum. Some of the [seven] criteria suggested below are overlapping; they can no doubt be refined, and perhaps added to with further research and analysis.

(1) *A Nationwide Federal Program Administered By One Federal Agency.* Where Congress enacts a regulatory scheme or a program and places its administration and enforcement in a single agency of nationwide jurisdiction, it is especially desirable to have a single judicial voice to enunciate authoritatively the law under which the agency must function. A regionally organized

appellate judiciary, speaking with multiple voices, tends to frustrate the congressional scheme embodied in the single agency. Uneven treatment of citizens and forum shopping for a circuit with a favorable law are natural results. . . . Eliminating conflicts among multiple fora and a single administrative agency would promote equitable administration of the laws, foster compliance, and assist planning by those within the agency's jurisdiction.

(2) *Multi-Circuit Actors.* Intercircuit conflict has a major impact on "multi-circuit actors" such as the U.S. government and large corporations. These multi-circuit actors have an economic incentive and the financial ability to shop for a forum to gain a particular advantage, avoid a particular disadvantage, or simply locate a forum where the issue has not been decided. Conflicts between regions result in a sense of injustice and less respect for federal law, greater advantage to multi-circuit actors, and uncertainty in circuits that have not addressed an issue. For these reasons, federal statutory areas that involve multi-circuit actors are good candidates for non-regional appellate review. Any additional expense involved in such centralized review is likely to be offset by the expense that otherwise would have been incurred through forum shopping and repeat litigation.

(3) *Undesirable Ramifications of Non-Uniform, Regional Decisions.* Although all federal law, by definition, should be uniformly interpreted and applied, there are circumstances in which there are especially undesirable ramifications in regional disparities. Situations of economic competition present one example. Where X and Y are both engaged in similar business enterprises subject to the same federal regulation, substantial economic detriment or advantage can accrue to one or the other if that federal regulatory measure is applied to them differently. In some instances differing interpretations of the same federal law seem to work an especially egregious denial of equal protection of the laws. For example, if citizen A is taxed on a transaction and citizen B is not taxed on an identical transaction merely because he lives in another part of the country, our sense of fundamental fairness is offended.

The undesirable ramifications of inharmonious regional decisions may be more or less problematic depending on the objective of the law being interpreted. Uncertainty or lack of uniformity in legal doctrine is particularly undesirable when a major objective of the law is to shape future behavior. Decisional incoherence frustrates this objective where the projected activity takes place in more than one circuit or in a circuit that has not yet addressed the pertinent matter, because citizens are unable to plan with confidence a course of conduct so as to avoid running afoul of the law. In still another situation, where there is a vital activity, nationwide in scope and impact, such as the production and consumption of energy, differing regional interpretations of the same federal law can have a significant disruptive effect.

(4) *Strength of State or Local Interests vis-à-vis National Interest.* In some areas of human activity, even though regulated by federal law, the state or local interest looms larger than in others, and there may be a correspondingly smaller concern about nationwide uniformity. Some environmental problems provide illustrations. Protection of marine life, for example, is not of equal interest to all states. Local concerns relating to matters such as timber, rivers, and industrial pollution may vary considerably from one region to another.

The subject matter of diversity-of-citizenship litigation is another good example; almost all of those cases are governed by state law and thus the national interest is weak. In those situations there is no particular reason to divert appeals from the existing regional circuits. Those situations stand in sharp contrast to situations in which there is strong desirability of the same treatment everywhere in the country, such as management of the energy resources of the nation, validity of patents, national defense, foreign affairs, federal taxation, and numerous federal regulatory programs.

(5) *Lack of a Critical Mass of Cases in the Regional Circuits.* For an appellate court to deal coherently and constructively with a field of law over time, the court needs more than a random case or a handful of cases annually. The judges on a particular court need to have a critical mass of appeals in order to maintain a familiarity with the law and to be able to fit each decision into a coherent pattern. If a judge deals with only an occasional case in a particular field, there is a possibility that the judge will either deal inadequately with the problem presented or will spend an inordinate amount of time educating himself in the legal setting in which the case arises. This problem is exacerbated if the relevant statute is frequently amended.

In a field of law where the appellate litigation is dispersed across numerous regional circuits, with few or no circuits having a critical mass of cases, a nonregional appellate forum would provide a means for concentrating those appeals, to ensure to a much greater degree the coherent development and application of doctrine. Because the single forum would have a relatively substantial flow of cases in a subject area, posing a variety of factual scenarios, it would not be subjected to abnormal pressure to work a major modification in the law in a single case, as is the situation sometimes in a regional circuit adjudicating infrequently in that area. With numerous appeals, the court could refine its reasoning gradually in the evolutionary common law fashion, fitting each new decision comfortably into the existing legal pattern. Moreover, economy of judicial effort would be promoted because the judges would approach each appeal in an informed way.

(6) *Practicability of Defining Appellate Subject Matter Jurisdiction in Unambiguous Terms.* In an appellate court organized on a territorial basis, defining the court's jurisdiction is a relatively easy task. In a non-regional court, where appellate jurisdiction is defined on the basis of subject matter, delineating the court's jurisdiction can present a problem. Thus, in deciding whether a particular category of case should be routed to a single national court, one must consider the extent to which it is possible to describe the appellate jurisdiction so as to avoid significant litigation over whether the case should go to the central appellate court or to the regional circuit. This problem has been encountered in the federal circuit in relation to patent cases, although it does not seem to be one of long range difficulty. In any new arrangement there is likely to be a shakedown period during which refinements and adjustments are made and the lines of authority sorted out.

Some categories of cases are clearly separable from all others, but there are categories that do not lend themselves to being separated neatly for appellate treatment. For example, copyright and unfair competition claims are often linked; it would not be workable to route copyright questions to one appellate court and unfair competition questions to another. By comparison, appellate review of administrative agency orders would present no such difficulty because the statute could simply specify that all decisions and orders of a certain agency would be reviewed in a designated court. If a clear-cut jurisdictional statute cannot feasibly be drafted, that is a consideration suggesting that appellate review should be left in the regional circuits.

(7) *Volume of Appellate Business in the Case Category.* Another practical consideration relates to the nationwide volume of appeals in the particular category of case. If the volume is such that a single court, even one with numerous judges, cannot feasibly handle the quantity of appeals, that suggests as a practical matter that appellate review be left in the regional circuits. While this is a factor to be borne in mind, it is not clear where the limit would be. As far as sheer quantity is concerned, experience indicates that the upper limit could be quite high. The U.S. Court of Appeals for the Ninth Circuit has over 5,600 appeals before it annually. However, there are concerns here other than sheer quantitative capacity. The primary purpose of centralizing appellate review is to maintain nationwide uniformity. If the cases are so numerous that several dozen appellate judges would be required to deal with them, the objective of uniformity may be frustrated, although even then the judicial inconsistency would be less than if the appeals were dispersed across the twelve regional circuits.

28 U.S.C. § 1295

Jurisdiction of the United States Court of Appeals for the Federal Circuit.

(a) The United States Court of Appeals for the Federal Circuit shall have exclusive jurisdiction —

(1) of an appeal from a final decision of a district court of the United States . . . if the jurisdiction of that court was based, in whole or in part, on section 1338 of this title, except that a case involving a claim arising under any Act of Congress relating to copyrights, exclusive rights in mask works, or trademarks and no other claims under section 1338(a) shall be governed by sections 1291, 1292, and 1294 of this title;

(2) of an appeal from a final decision of a district court of the United States . . . if the jurisdiction of that court was based, in whole or in part, on section 1346 of this title, except that jurisdiction of an appeal in a case brought in a district court under section 1346(a)(1), 1346(b), 1346(e), or 1346(f) of this title or under section 1346(a)(2) when the claim is founded upon an Act of Congress or a regulation of an executive department providing for internal revenue shall be governed by sections 1291, 1292, and 1294 of this title;

(3) of an appeal from a final decision of the United States Court of Federal Claims;

(4) of an appeal from a decision of —

(A) the Board of Patent Appeals and Interferences of the Patent and Trademark Office with respect to patent applications and interferences, at the instance of an applicant for a patent or any party to a patent interference, and any such appeal shall waive the right of such applicant or party to proceed under section 145 or 146 of title 35;

(B) the Commissioner of Patents and Trademarks or the Trademark Trial and Appeal Board with respect to applications for registration of marks and other proceedings as provided in section 21 of the Trademark Act of 1946 (15 U.S.C. 1071); or

(C) a district court to which a case was directed pursuant to section 145 or 146 of title 35;

(5) of an appeal from a final decision of the United States Court of International Trade;

(6) to review the final determinations of the United States International Trade Commission relating to unfair practices in import trade, made under section 337 of the Tariff Act of 1930 (19 U.S.C. 1337);

(7) to review, by appeal on questions of law only, findings of the Secretary of Commerce under U.S. note 6 to subchapter X of chapter 98 of the Harmonized Tariff Schedule of the United States (relating to importation of instruments or apparatus);

(8) of an appeal under section 71 of the Plant Variety Protection Act (7 U.S.C. 2461);

(9) of an appeal from a final order or final decision of the Merit Systems Protection Board, pursuant to sections 7703(b)(1) and 7703(d) of title 5;

(10) of an appeal from a final decision of an agency board of contract appeals pursuant to section 8(g)(1) of the Contract Disputes Act of 1978 (41 U.S.C. 607(g)(1));

(11) of an appeal under section 211 of the Economic Stabilization Act of 1970;

(12) of an appeal under section 5 of the Emergency Petroleum Allocation Act of 1973;

(13) of an appeal under section 506(c) of the Natural Gas Policy Act of 1978; and

(14) of an appeal under section 523 of the Energy Policy and Conservation Act.

(b) The head of any executive department or agency may, with the approval of the Attorney General, refer to the Court of Appeals for the Federal Circuit for judicial review of any final decision rendered by a board of contract appeals pursuant to the terms of any contract with the United States awarded by that department or agency which the head of such department or agency has concluded is not entitled to finality pursuant to the review standards specified in section 10(b) of the Contract Disputes Act of 1978 (41 U.S.C. 609(b)). The head of each executive department or agency shall make any referral under this section within one hundred and twenty days after the receipt of a copy of the final appeal decision.

(c) The Court of Appeals for the Federal Circuit shall review the matter referred in accordance with the standards specified in section 10(b) of the Contract Disputes Act of 1978. The court shall proceed with judicial review on the administrative record made before the board of contract appeals on matters so referred as in other cases pending in such court, shall determine the issue of finality of the appeal decision, and shall, if appropriate, render judgment thereon, or remand the matter to any administrative or executive body or official with such direction as it may deem proper and just.

Daniel J. Meador, *An Appellate Court Dilemma and a Solution Through Subject Matter Organization*, 16 U. MICH. J.L. REFORM 471, 475-91 (1983)[13]

The Concept of Subject Matter Organization. As caseloads continue to grow, the dilemma increasingly confronting American intermediate appellate courts is this: if the number of judges remains relatively small, there is the ever-rising threat of undue delegation to staff and of dilution of the judicial process; conversely, if the number of judges increases to keep abreast of the caseload volume, and if the courts continue to sit in random panels deciding all types of cases, the law will progressively lose its predictability and jurisdiction-wide uniformity. The solution to this dilemma for a large intermediate appellate court is the adoption of a subject matter plan of internal organization. This method of appellate organization eliminates random assignments of judges and cases and permits the court to be enlarged to the size needed to cope with the increased quantity of cases, thus avoiding undue delegation to staff while simultaneously maintaining doctrinal coherence in the law.

"Subject matter organization" is a form of internal organization in an appellate court whereby relatively stable panels or divisions of from three to five judges are assigned specified portions of the court's docket; the portions of the docket assigned to each panel are exclusively assigned to that panel. Each type of case goes on appeal from the trial court to a specified panel or division and to no other. Thus, whatever the type of case, the lawyers, litigants, and trial judge know from the outset of litigation in the trial court the precise judges who will decide any appeal that may result. Although stable, the panels are not permanent; they gradually shift through staggered rotation. . . .

In the United States there are three examples of subject matter organization in the federal appellate courts. For many years the Court of Appeals for the Fifth Circuit maintained an "oil and gas" panel, consisting of several judges of the court to whom all appeals involving oil and gas law were assigned; such cases were assigned to no other judges on the court. The judges who sat on the oil and gas panel also sat on other cases. [The article here describes the other two examples: the former Temporary Emergency Court of Appeals ("TECA") and the U.S. Federal Circuit.]

---

[13] Copyright © 1983 University of Michigan Journal of Law Reform. Reprinted with permission.

In allocating cases among the various divisions the plan should not confine any single division to a relatively narrow category of legal subject matter. Variety can be achieved in different ways. For example, a division could be assigned a group of wholly unrelated types of cases. . . . On the other hand, a division could be assigned a group of cases that are kindred in some way or at least not in alien fields. . . . It is important that the actual workload of each division be roughly the same. Workload cannot be arrived at simply by counting the number of cases; some types of cases are more complex and time-consuming than others. Thus, a case-weighting system would be useful in arriving at a sound subject matter plan.

Criminal cases present a special problem. They can be allocated among the divisions of the court in two basic ways. One is to distribute the criminal business throughout all divisions of the court so that every appellate judge sits on some criminal cases. One argument for that arrangement is that because criminal justice is a pervasive concern to society and has such emotional and political ramifications all judges of the court should be responsible for regular participation in that business. Also, under that plan of distribution no judges at any time would have unduly large or exclusive concern with criminal appeals.

The other arrangement [would be] the allocation of all criminal appeals to a single division. This maximizes the advantage of the subject matter plan of organization by assuring the highest degree of uniformity of decisions on criminal law questions. If the volume of criminal appeals is too large for any one division, two or more divisions may be employed, but that arrangement begins to dilute the advantages of the subject matter plan.

Even if criminal appeal business is distributed to more than one division of the court, some rational allocations can be made to maximize uniformity and efficiency. For example, like offenses can be grouped; all homicide offenses can be assigned to one division, all property offenses to another, and so on. Another way of allocating criminal business to more than one division is by source of appeals, with each division of the court handling all appeals from specified trial courts or geographical regions. . . . Under any scheme for assigning criminal appeals, post-conviction review cases should be classified as criminal.

The advantage of five-judge divisions over three-judge divisions is stability in the appellate forum, which in turn heightens predictability and uniformity in the law. If . . . a division consisted of five judges, with only one departing each year, there would be greater continuity of membership than in divisions of three. . . . In other words, an annual one-fifth rotation is much less destabilizing than an annual one-third rotation. Both plans, however, can be employed to achieve the benefits of subject matter organization and they would be preferable to the traditional American system of random and ever-fluctuating assignments.

As a practical matter, the division size is closely related to the term each judge is assigned to a particular division. It would simply be more workable to have a three-year assignment on a three-judge panel and a five-year assignment on a five-judge panel than it would be to have assignments of some other duration. Even here there is room for variation consistent with the subject matter concept of appellate organization. . . .

When any appellate court adopts a subject matter plan of organization there will be an initial transitional period during which judges will rotate more frequently than they will in the long run. This is necessary to set in motion a long-range plan of staggered rotation. Rotations too frequent would undermine stability — a major purpose of the plan. Once the start-up period has passed, the regular pace of rotation can set in on either a five-year basis . . . or on a three-year basis. . . .

If the docket assignments are carefully made and the categories of cases are described with sufficient precision, the plan should be easy to administer. . . . A staff attorney, for example, could screen the cases (much as staff attorneys already do in many courts) and route the cases to the appropriate divisions. The docket allocations under a subject matter plan should in no sense be considered jurisdictional; they are simply internal administrative arrangements. No litigant should have any right to litigate over the appropriate division to which the case should be assigned. The central staff attorneys in an appellate court that has adopted a plan of subject matter organization could be organized on the same subject matter basis. Each division of the court would then have specified staff attorneys working on its cases. This should heighten efficiency among the staff attorneys and also provide better working relationships between the judges and the support staff. . . .

Advantages of Subject Matter Organization. There are three advantages to subject matter organization in American appellate courts. The first of these is uniformity, evenhandedness, and stability in the law. These goals can be achieved through a relatively fixed group of identifiable judges who would take all appeals of a specific type. On any question of law and within any category of case, the appellate court would speak with a single voice, thereby avoiding the Tower of Babel effect produced by large appellate courts operating under random assignment procedures.

The second advantage to subject matter organization is the ability to preserve judicial authority and avoid undue delegation. The plan achieves these objectives by permitting substantial increases in the numbers of appellate judges without threatening the uniformity of the law; such increases in judgeships would obviate the necessity for assembling an ever-growing number of central staff attorneys and law clerks. All modern appellate courts need professional assistance of this sort; the threat comes when the size of the professional staff becomes disproportionately large in relation to the number of judges on the court. Before that point is reached, new judgeships should be created. The subject matter plan of organization makes that possible without undermining the coherence of the jurisprudence or the collegiality among the judges.

The third advantage to subject matter organization is the expedition and soundness of decisions. These objectives are achieved under the plan by narrowing the range of matters with which any one judge must cope from day to day. Although not confined to a single category of case, each judge deals with a span of legal problems that is narrower than the entire range of the court's docket. During any three- to five-year period a judge might come in contact with roughly one-fifth of the categories of cases with which the court as a whole must deal. This system improves decision making because each judge can achieve a higher level of expertise on the subjects with which he is regularly dealing during the three- to five-year assignment.

Arguments Against the Plan. There are basically two arguments against the appellate subject matter plan. One is rooted in the spectre and mythology of "specialization." The other is rooted in concerns that judges will become bored and will lack intellectual challenge. A properly designed plan of subject matter organization can avoid the force of these objections.

The "specialization" argument is largely derived from a misunderstanding about the subject matter method of organization. A properly designed plan does not set up a system of specialization, and it does not make specialists out of appellate judges. . . . A properly designed subject matter plan of appellate organization will not force appellate judges into a single category of case or single type of legal issue. [D]ocket assignments providing a mixture of legal questions and case subjects can be given to a particular division of the court while allocating to the division only a small portion of the court's total docket. . . . A judge can remain very much a "generalist" and yet not simultaneously sit over every type of issue and case that can come before a court.

Americans generally dislike the idea of "specialist" judges and "specialized" courts for three reasons. One reason is that a truly specialized court — one limited to a specific, relatively narrow subject — is vulnerable to being captured by special interests in that field. The judicial selection process for such a court is apt to become a sharply focused target of intense lobbying efforts by interest groups having a direct stake in the field; there is also a danger of politicizing the selection process in an undesirable way. Another criticism of true specialization is that judges confined to such a narrow range of judicial work may tend to develop arcane views of the law, to lose sight of broader considerations and values that should infuse all judicial decision making, and, in general, become less wise and balanced in their judgments. The third reason is the fear that judges so limited in their work will lack the status traditionally accorded the judicial office; diminished status will in turn result in an inability to attract able lawyers to the bench.

A properly designed plan of subject matter organization can avoid these problems. Under such a plan no judge is initially selected for the court with a view toward his sitting on particular types of cases. Nothing would be changed in relation to judicial selection. A judge would be chosen to sit on the court for all purposes, just as judges are now chosen for appellate courts. Only after assuming his seat on the court would a judge begin the assignment pattern. Because he would be periodically rotated, he would not sit on the same group of cases throughout his career. Thus, the risks of "capture" and of politicizing the selection process are not intensified.

The danger of developing arcane, overly narrow views of the law — or "slit vision" — is obviated by the subject matter plan in two ways. One is that the allocation of cases among the various divisions could assure a varied mixture of questions and case types. No appellate judge would be confined to any one category of case or any one kind of legal issue. Second, whatever the cluster of cases a judge sits on for a period of three to five years, at the end of the period he will rotate to an entirely different cluster of cases. Thus, in a judicial career of ten to twenty years an appellate judge will hear cases concerning the entire range of the court's docket. A well-administered subject matter plan provides no basis for apprehensions about the development of judicial views that ignore the general values and considerations permeating Anglo-American jurisprudence.

Apprehensions concerning boredom and lack of intellectual challenge appear misplaced. This is true for the reasons that will prevent specialization of judges. The assignments of any division of the court are diverse enough to prevent boredom. In addition, a judge will not be permanently assigned to the same group of cases. A court can pick its own period; it can be three, four, or five years. The period of assignment should be long enough to assure continuity and stability in the decision-making unit; a period of less than three years seems too short to provide adequate assurance of this. On the other hand, a period longer than five years would heighten the risk of boredom. Thus somewhere between three and five years seems optimum as the rotational cycle for each judge.

Conclusion. The great benefit of appellate subject matter organization is that it assures that in any jurisdiction there will be only one appellate voice speaking on any given area of the law. In each of the federal circuits, for example, there would be one group of appellate judges deciding a given type of federal appeal. Under the existing organizational scheme there are dozens of different appellate entities in each circuit deciding each category of case. This extraordinary multitude of appellate voices would be reduced to one in each federal circuit. . . . Although states having a single statewide intermediate appellate court can derive maximum benefit from subject matter organization, states whose intermediate courts are divided geographically can also benefit from the arrangement. . . . A realization of the benefits to be derived from statewide subject matter organization might lead some states to abolish geographical districting. . . . In the federal judiciary, subject matter organization may be the only way to prevent continuous circuit-splitting. . . . Indeed, appreciation of the values of subject matter organization could lead to consolidation and reduction in the number of circuits, thereby assuring an even larger measure of uniformity in federal appellate decisions. As American jurisdictions continue to face pressure to add more judges at the intermediate appellate level, the subject matter plan of organization may become increasingly attractive. Eventually, it may be seen as the only way, in a large jurisdiction, to maintain uniformity and collegiality while providing the court with the number of judges sufficient to handle its business. . . .

NOTES

1. The excerpt above by Professor Dreyfus neatly summarizes the background arguments for and against specialized courts. In the full article, she elaborates at length on the appropriate criteria for a successful specialized court: (1) choosing a field of law or subject matter that is complex and difficult, demonstrably segregable, characterized by consensus public policy goals, and for which concentration of cases in a single court would be preferred over dispersed distribution among many courts; (2) having the support and commitment from the relevant constituencies, *i.e.*, the governmental and

nongovernmental actors in the field including party-litigants, the relevant segment of the bar, and the judges on the court; (3) designing the organization and procedures of the court strategically to take into account circumstances of the particular specialization and its costs and benefits. 1990 BYU L. REV. at 407-39. *See also generally* THOMAS E. BAKER, RATIONING JUSTICE ON APPEAL — THE PROBLEMS OF THE U.S. COURTS OF APPEALS 221-24, 261-69 (1994); PAUL D. CARRINGTON, DANIEL J. MEADOR & MAURICE ROSENBERG, JUSTICE ON APPEAL 167-84 (1976).

2. The excerpt from the A.B.A. STANDARDS RELATING TO COURT ORGANIZATION demonstrates the historic and widespread mistrust and suspicion within the American legal profession towards specialized courts. *See also* A.B.A. STANDARDS RELATING TO CRIMINAL APPEALS § 1.2 (1970) (proclaiming that specialized criminal courts of appeals are "unsound"). What explains this? Later readings challenge this attitude on the merits.

3. The first excerpt from Professor Meador seeks to make a distinction between specialized courts and his concept of non-regional appellate courts with designated subject matter jurisdiction. What is the difference? His idea of organizing the federal intermediate appellate courts by subject matter has been a recurring reform proposal. *See generally* AMERICAN BAR FOUNDATION, ACCOMMODATING THE WORKLOAD OF THE UNITED STATES COURTS OF APPEALS (1968); A.B.A. STANDING COMMITTEE ON FEDERAL JUDICIAL IMPROVEMENTS, THE UNITED STATES COURTS OF APPEALS: REEXAMINING STRUCTURE AND PROCESS AFTER A CENTURY OF GROWTH (1989). The subject matter approach to defining appellate jurisdiction in England and Germany is considered in Chapter 13. How would his multiple-court model work in the federal IACs? Do you think it would succeed?

4. Read over the provisions of 28 U.S.C. § 1295 setting out the subject matter jurisdiction for the non-regional U.S. Court of Appeals for the Federal Circuit. Applying Professor Meador's dichotomy, the Federal Circuit might appropriately be considered a court of "multiple specialties" rather than a "specialized court." This type of judicial organization is analyzed in STEPHEN H. LEGOMSKY, SPECIALIZED JUSTICE: COURTS, ADMINISTRATIVE TRIBUNALS, AND A CROSS-NATIONAL THEORY OF SPECIALIZATION (1990). One of the arguments against creating a single nationwide court on a subject-matter basis is that "percolation" among the circuits would be lost. The establishment of the Federal Circuit did effectively end percolation on patent law issues. An underlying premise is that certainty and uniformity in patent law outweigh whatever values there are in percolation. How and why? Is the U.S. Federal Circuit the harbinger of a next-generation of appellate court with subject matter jurisdiction over scientific and technological cases or perhaps the experimentation with the Federal Circuit itself should be extended by adding those subjects to its existing jurisdiction? *See* LeRoy L. Kondo, *Untangling the Tangled Web: Federal Court Reform Through Specialization for Internet Law and Other High Technology Cases*, 2002 UCLA J.L. & TECH. 1.

5. In 1989, the A.B.A. Standing Committee on Federal Judicial Improvements speculated that two other possible subjects for national subject matter appellate courts were tax law and administrative law. A.B.A. STANDING COMMITTEE ON FEDERAL JUDICIAL IMPROVEMENTS, THE UNITED STATES COURTS

OF APPEALS: REEXAMINING STRUCTURE AND PROCESS AFTER A CENTURY OF GROWTH 21 (1989). The U.S. D.C. Circuit already has some resemblance to a subject matter court for federal administrative law. *See* Richard L. Revesz, *Specialized Courts and the Administrative Lawmaking System*, 138 U. PA. L. REV. 1111 (1990). In 1990, the Federal Courts Study Committee recommended that Congress "should rationalize the structure of federal tax adjudication by . . . creating an Article III appellate division of the United States Tax Court with exclusive jurisdiction over appeals in federal income, estate, and gift tax cases . . ." but went on to recommend that Congress "should not consolidate review of federal administrative agency orders in a specialized court of administrative appeals." REPORT OF THE FEDERAL COURTS STUDY COMMITTEE 69, 72-73 (1990). *See generally* RICHARD A. POSNER, THE FEDERAL COURTS — CHALLENGE AND REFORM 244-70 (1996). Centralizing federal tax appeals into one nationwide court has long been suggested. The proposal was first put forward in Erwin N. Griswold, *The Need for a Court of Tax Appeals*, 57 HARV. L. REV. 1153 (1944).

6. The second excerpt from Professor Meador develops a single-court model for subject matter organization within an IAC. How is this variation different from his multiple-court model for non-regional national appellate courts with subject matter jurisdiction? In an appendix to this article, Professor Meador provided detailed plans for reforming the New Jersey Appellate Division and the U.S. Court of Appeals for the Ninth Circuit through subject matter organization. *See also* Daniel J. Meador, *Struggling Against the Tower of Babel*, in RECONSTRUCTING JUSTICE: THE INNOVATIONS OF THE NINTH CIRCUIT AND THE FUTURE OF THE FEDERAL COURTS 195 (Arthur D. Hellman, ed., 1990).

V. DISCRETIONARY JURISDICTION

The guarantee of right to an appeal, even though not of constitutional dimension, is a fundamental feature of the American legal system. Eliminating the guarantee of appellate review would be a dramatic break with tradition. At the same time, some limitations have grown up around the concept of requiring "leave to appeal" even for the first appeal as of right. For example, existing appellate procedures require the appellant to ask leave of the court to take an interlocutory appeal or to proceed *in forma pauperis*. Typically, the second level appeal is not a matter of right. As we have seen in Chapter 12, the Supreme Court of the United States has elaborate discretion to grant petitions for a writ of *certiorari*, as do most state COLRs. Critics of the differentiated appellate processes that were installed to cope with the "crisis of volume" have complained that the U.S. Courts of Appeals already have moved too far in the direction of becoming "*certiorari* courts" by screening cases to afford more time and attention to some appeals and to give short shrift to others. *See* Chapters 8 & 9.

This section explores proposals that self-consciously and purposefully advocate going even farther in that direction by formalizing discretion to hear appeals at the first level of review. Consider how much these proposals take away from the right to an appeal. Compare the proposals for discretionary jurisdiction with the other proposals for the future of the appellate courts.

Donald P. Lay, *A Proposal for Discretionary Review in Federal Courts of Appeals*, 34 Sw. L.J. 1151, 1155-58 (1981)[14]

Although many of these innovations [case screening and differentiated appeals procedures] are today deemed minimally essential to keep the courts of appeals afloat, they defy [the] premise that every appeal of right is entitled to the full deliberative process. The possible truth is that courts of appeals today may provide in many appeals only an appearance of justice rather than justice itself. I submit that through the lessening of the full deliberative process, courts of appeals are, in reality, invoking a form of discretionary dismissal without calling it such. This conclusion brings me to the question posed: Whether the time has come for society to make a cost analysis and determine whether the cost of the delay in resolving disputes and of the increase in the size of the judicial machinery necessary to handle the torrent of appeals exceeds the value gained in providing the formal recognition and appearance of a deliberative process and the continuation of formal decisions and written opinions in frivolous and nonmeritorious appeals.

The concept of granting courts of appeals discretionary review power is not new. Judge [Henry J.] Friendly some time ago recommended discretionary review in administrative proceedings. He suggested that when the district court has affirmed the action of an administrative agency, appeal should only be allowed by leave of the court of appeals. His reasoning is that one appeal of right is adequate to correct errors of law committed by the agency, especially considering the narrow and limited standard for reviewing agency action. I suggest that Judge Friendly's proposal be expanded to allow courts of appeals discretionary leave to refuse to review, at least in civil cases, any appeal that on its face does not appear to be substantial or meritorious.

In order to avoid denying review to meritorious cases, certain controls should be legislatively established guiding the courts of appeals' exercise of discretionary jurisdiction. I would propose guidelines that allow a court of appeals to deny review of only those cases that are patently frivolous or those in which the district court opinion appears on its face to be correct as a matter of law or fact. First, all defendants, whether appealing as indigents or not, would have a right of full review, including oral argument, in direct criminal appeals. The denial of liberty and the stigma of conviction should require in every criminal appeal a full deliberative process. Second, each litigant seeking an appeal in any civil proceeding would be required to file a petition for discretionary review with the notice of appeal. The petitions would be limited to ten pages and would set forth the reasons the appeal should be allowed. Each petition would attach a copy of the district court's memorandum and judgment. Third, a three-judge panel would then review this petition within ten days of its filing. Any one circuit judge could grant the petition by directing the clerk's office to docket the appeal and to require the docket fee be paid

---

14 Copyright © 1981. Originally appearing in in *58 SMU Law Review* 1151 (1981). Reprinted with permission from the SMU *Law Review* and the Southern Methodist University Dedman School of Law.

or, if the appeal is *in forma pauperis*, to have it so certified under section 1915 of title 28. If the panel desires, it may request a response to the petition from the other side. Fourth, if the face of the petition presents any colorable issue of disputed law or presents a serious challenge to the sufficiency of the evidence, the appeal should be allowed. Fifth, a district court could certify that an appeal presents a colorable issue for review; if such a certification is given, the parties could proceed without further permission from the court of appeals. Sixth, if the petition for review is not deemed insubstantial by the panel, but nonetheless appears to raise a narrow or simple issue for review, the court may allow docketing of the appeal, set the matter down for summary argument without plenary briefing, and summarily dispose of the case by opinion or order. This latter procedure could aid the courts in establishing a summary calendar and serve to expedite and process a large number of appeals.

Courts of appeals are neither unfamiliar nor inexperienced with granting or denying discretionary review by preliminarily reviewing cases to determine if a proposed appeal is frivolous. The fundamental exception to the right of appeal in federal courts concerns habeas corpus appeals brought by state prisoners under section 2254 of title 28. A state prisoner cannot appeal a denial of a writ of habeas corpus by a federal district judge without the issuance of a certification of probable cause by either the district court or the court of appeals. When the certification is denied by the district court, the court of appeals must exercise its discretion as to whether a certificate may issue and an appeal may be taken. One obvious reason for this exception is that state courts have already reviewed the issues at least once before a prisoner may proceed in federal court. In my opinion, the courts of appeals, in their experience of reviewing habeas corpus cases to ascertain whether a certificate of probable cause should issue, have not abused the discretion given to them. In exercising discretion as to whether to allow the appeal, circuit judges are meticulous in reviewing district court files, which often contain state court transcripts, opinions, and records. The fact that the case is not briefed detracts little from the judgmental decision regarding not the rightness or wrongness of the district court's ruling, but whether a colorable issue is revealed. The time-saving factor follows when a certificate is denied; the court merely orders the denial without a formal written opinion.

Courts of appeals also exercise discretionary jurisdiction in determining whether to grant a certificate of good faith under section 1915 of title 28 involving *in forma pauperis* appeals. When a district judge certifies that an appeal would be frivolous and not in good faith, a petitioner must seek a certificate of good faith from the court of appeals before going forward with the appeal. As under section 2254, the court of appeals must review the complete file, and if, in its judgment, an appeal would be frivolous, the appeal can be denied, and generally no opinion is written. . . .

The fact that leave to appeal may be denied in an *in forma pauperis* case on the ground that it is frivolous may seem somewhat anomalous under equal protection standards. The practical effect is that only *in forma pauperis* appeals are denied as frivolous before the briefing stage. . . . Of course, paid appeals are often dismissed as frivolous before oral argument, but this dismissal occurs only after full briefing and screening by the court. Many appeals should be screened out as insubstantial whether they are *in forma pauperis* appeals or not. Many appeals should be denied the right of plenary review without briefing, oral argument, and opinion writing, much in the same manner as discretionary denial of a certificate of probable cause as exercised in section 2254 cases.

Numerous benefits would arise in providing courts of appeals the power to deny leave to appeal cases that are insubstantial on their face. First, the judicial time needed to review petitions for discretionary appeal would be no greater than that which is now spent on screening cases for no argument. Second, tremendous saving of judicial time and resources could be had by obviating the need for full review of lengthy briefs and records and the writing of formal opinions in hundreds of cases. Third, such procedures would tend to place the indigent's petition for review on the same evaluative basis as the appeal filed by the paid litigant. Fourth, the long delay between filing notice of appeal and the appellate decision would be drastically curtailed for all cases. Fifth, and most importantly, all cases worthy of appeal would be afforded the full deliberative process, including the right to oral argument and written opinion. The recommended procedure would actually provide more thoughtful judicial input into meritorious appeals than presently exists.

I suggest that the necessity to file a petition seeking discretionary review will deter the filing of many appeals because lawyers will be required to evaluate immediately whether the issues they intend to raise are substantial enough to warrant an appeal. It is doubtful that initial review under this procedure will seriously impede the filing of any meritorious appeal. The waste of judicial resources in attempting to take short cuts by screening, reviewing central staff opinions, and writing formal opinions in insubstantial cases is time well worth saving. The goal of giving full deliberative and expeditious process in all cases worthy of appeal is one worth pursuing. In the final analysis . . . the grant of discretionary review to United States Courts of Appeals may be the only procedure that will enable the courts to provide effective appellate review for society.

Bernard G. Barrow, *The Discretionary Appeal: A Cost Effective Tool of Appellate Justice,* 11 GEO. MASON L. REV. 31 (1988)[15]

While there is an abundance of criteria expressed for use in discretionary appeals from intermediate appellate courts, there is a paucity of express criteria used in discretionary appeals from trial court judgments. This may be explained by the less frequent use of the discretionary appeal to review for correctness. However, . . . well articulated criteria are most important in assuring confidence in this type of appeal.

Criteria for granting a discretionary appeal from a trial court are often stated in abstract terms without any concrete explanation or clarification. . . . [I]n Virginia, a judicial opinion has described the criterion as the necessity to show a "substantial possibility of injustice" and also as requiring a showing of

---

[15] Copyright © 1988 Reprinted with the permission of the author.

"any doubt . . . as to the propriety of the decision." In West Virginia, which lacks an intermediate appellate court, the state constitution [W.Va. Const. art. VII, § 4] provides that an appeal will be granted where a justice is "satisfied that there probably is error in the record, or that it presents a point proper for the consideration of the court." In a similar context, Massachusetts has denied a petition for a writ of error since it "raised no reasonable possibility that an error of substance had occurred." The decision to grant an appeal in New Hampshire is described as "one of sound judicial discretion with respect to the desirability of . . . [the supreme court's] hearing and deciding the case."

Suggested Criteria — General Considerations. There are three broad considerations important to a determination of the criteria an appellate court should employ in granting a discretionary appeal. The criteria for granting an appeal from an intermediate appellate court which has already reviewed a trial court decision should differ from that for granting an appeal directly from a trial court decision which has not been reviewed. This difference reflects the distinct purposes served by each appeal. . . . [T]he criteria for granting a discretionary appeal for a review for correctness should be designed to identify erroneous trial court decisions, while the criteria for granting a discretionary appeal for an institutional review should seek to identify opportunities to "announce, clarify, and harmonize" the system's "rules of decision."

The second factor to consider in formulating criteria for granting a discretionary appeal is the impact of the decision on future litigants. This should positively influence the decision to grant an institutional review but should not influence the granting of a review to determine correctness. No need exists to "announce, clarify, and harmonize" rules that will have little or no use to future litigants. On the contrary, a review for correctness is important even if it affects only the litigants involved and has no impact on future litigants. Thus, the impact on future litigants, a decision's precedential value, should guide the granting of an institutional review but not a review for correctness. . . .

[The third consideration is that an] abstract standard giving broad discretion increases the likelihood that one appeal will be granted while another, although indistinguishable, will be denied. On the other hand, a more concrete standard limiting discretion is less likely to produce disparate results.

The extent of permissible discretion depends upon which appellate function is being served. A review for correctness should not produce disparate results. One erroneous decision should not be allowed to stand while another is subject to review. Disparity is less objectionable in an institutional review. In fact, efficiency may encourage such disparity. Where one case is being reviewed to determine a particular rule of law, there is little necessity to review a similar case for the purpose of announcing the same rule of law. Therefore, when reviewing for correctness, a concrete standard limiting discretion should be sought, while in an institutional review a more abstract standard with broader discretion is acceptable.

These three overriding considerations determine what criteria should be used in granting discretionary appeals. . . . If a review is for correctness, the criteria should not consider the impact of the decision on future litigants and should limit discretion through the use of concrete standards. If the review is institutional, it should address the needs of future litigants and may use more abstract standards providing more discretion.

Suggested Criteria — Review for Correctness. An appellate review for correctness assures that a trial court's decision is not the isolated act of a single individual but is the act of an institutional representative having the approval of the institution. . . . The institutionally approved norm is more familiarly described as "the law applicable to the case.". . .

The procedure employed in the application for an appeal must provide the essential elements of the opportunity to be heard in appellate litigation. These are the rights to: (1) present the record of the proceedings below, (2) submit written argument in the form of briefs, (3) present oral argument except in cases where it has so little utility that it may justly be denied, and (4) a thoughtful consideration of the merits of the case by at least three judges of the court.

These elements could be modified to require the opportunity for oral argument in any case regardless of its perceived utility, and the efficiency of the discretionary appeal would still be maintained. The appeal's efficiency is not dependent upon eliminating the petitioner's opportunity to be heard, but upon eliminating or reducing the opportunity for opposition to the petition to be heard because, even without opposition, a meritless appeal is frequently recognizable.

Secondly, the discretionary appeal is only cost efficient when used in those categories of cases where meritless appeals constitute a high proportion of the total appeals. When a discretionary appeal is granted, the briefs and arguments of the appeal's proponent must be considered a second time. Therefore, when only a small percentage of appeals are meritless, more time is consumed hearing the duplicated presentations of the proponent after the appeals have been granted than is saved by avoiding the opposition's presentations in the relatively few cases in which appeals are denied.

In civil cases there are usually economic disincentives to a meritless appeal that do not exist in criminal cases. The availability of court appointed counsel and the noneconomic consequences of the results of a criminal conviction significantly reduce the economic barriers to meritless appeals, while in civil cases the cost of an appeal in many instances discourages the meritless appeal. . . .

As a final precaution, a conscious effort must be made to assure that unarticulated criteria are not being used to deny appeals. The Virginia experience cannot be forgotten. Even the appearance of an unarticulated change in criteria is deleterious to appellate justice. The volume of appeals being sought, the volume of appeals being granted, and the relationship between these two events should be administratively monitored so that significant changes are detected and satisfactorily explained. Development of other programs to assure the integrity of the discretionary appeal should be encouraged.

DANIEL J. MEADOR, APPELLATE COURTS: STAFF AND PROCESS IN THE CRISIS OF VOLUME 168-71 (1974)[16]

[T]he perception [is] that the obligatory-discretionary distinction is becoming blurred. The point can be made by comparing "appeals of right" in, for example, the Illinois Appellate Court, the California Court of Appeal, and the U.S. Fifth Circuit, with "discretionary review" in the Supreme Court of Virginia and the U.S. Court of Military Appeals. What one sees is that in the former the introduction of screening procedures and a special decisional track (with staff in Illinois and California, without staff in the Fifth Circuit) has made the internal appellate process, for the cases routed through that track, functionally no different from the decisional process through which a case goes on a petition for appeal in the latter courts. In the latter, the "discretionary" courts, if a petition for appeal is granted, the case gets more extensive review just as a case does in the "appeal of right" courts if it is screened for the full procedure. There is a discretionary selection of process under both systems, but the discretion in the "obligatory review" courts is shielded from view. It is not so overtly clear to the outer world nor perhaps is it formally articulated in the court's procedural rules; yet it is as real as the acknowledged discretion which is exercised by the Virginia Supreme Court and the Court of Military Appeals. [Since this was written, Virginia added an intermediate court, although the state Supreme Court still retains considerable discretionary jurisdiction over trial courts. 10 U.S.C. § 867 provides for the jurisdiction of the Court of Appeals for the Armed Forces.]

This similarity is made clearer by considering more precisely the depth and extent of review under the two systems. In the obligatory review courts, the trial record, including a transcript, is filed in the appellate court along with a brief on the merits from both sides. Three judges examine the briefs and the record. If no one of the judges thinks oral argument would be useful, and if all three agree on the result, a short *per curiam* opinion is issued, ranging in length from a single sentence up to two or three double-spaced pages. In the discretionary review courts the trial record, including a full transcript, is also filed in the appellate court. The petition for appeal is, in substance, indistinguishable from a brief on the merits; it presents all of the legal analysis and arguments in support of the appellant's case which a brief customarily presents. The appellee is given the opportunity to file an opposition brief which is likewise substantially indistinguishable from an appellee's brief on the merits. Three judges in the Court of Military Appeals and usually two in Virginia examine the briefs and the record. They examine those papers primarily to determine whether there is any arguable error or possibility of injustice, and not with a central focus on whether an issue is important or in need of clarification or settlement. If the judges conclude that there is no such error or injustice the petition is denied without explanation, unless the judges decide to grant a full appeal in order to clarify the law on a point or because the issues are of jurisprudential importance. The point is, however, that if there is a substantial possibility of error the court will grant the petition even though the case has no significance in the development of the law.

---

[16] Copyright © 1974 Thomson West. Reprinted with permission.

There are small differences in the two types of review. In Illinois, California, and the Fifth Circuit an explanation, brief though it may be, is usually given for an affirmance, while in Virginia and the Military Appeals Court denials of petitions (equivalent to an affirmance) are made without explanation. Pointing in the other direction, in Virginia the appellant has a right to present oral argument on his petition; he does not have that right in a summary [calendar] case in the Fifth Circuit, though he does in Illinois and California. In the Court of Military Appeals there is a detailed research memorandum prepared by a staff attorney on every petition. In Virginia, such a memorandum is prepared in the staff-processed cases, and a briefer law clerk's memorandum is done on all other petitions. In the Fifth Circuit there is no memorandum by either a staff attorney or a law clerk in the summary cases; however, in California and Illinois there is a staff memorandum in such cases.

These variations more or less cancel out each other. The net result is, as asserted above, that the decisional processes, in functional terms, are not significantly different in the two respects which matter: in the material considered by the judges, and in the intensity of judicial scrutiny. It is important to bear in mind that the kind of discretionary review involved in Virginia and the Court of Military Appeals is quite different from that exercised by the United States Supreme Court and some of the state courts of last resort such as the New Jersey and Illinois Supreme Courts. These latter courts, unlike the Virginia court, are not primarily concerned with correcting errors. Their predominant role is institutional review, and they exercise their discretion in granting or denying full review on that basis. By contrast, in Virginia and the Court of Military Appeals the main concern is expressly with the possibility of prejudicial error or injustice. No petition is denied because the judges think the issues are doctrinally or institutionally unimportant. In other words, review of petitions, though couched as an exercise of discretion, is a review on the merits in the interests of justice to the parties.

A recognition of this functional blurring of the obligatory — discretionary distinction has two consequences. First, it serves to legitimate abbreviated appellate processes, thereby loosening the decisional straight-jacket in which many appellate courts think themselves bound because their jurisdiction is cast in terms of "appeals of right." That is, because of the introduction of screening and differentiated process, it can now be recognized that an "appeal of right" does not include a right to any fixed procedure. Secondly, we can now perceive that efforts to relieve heavily burdened courts by enacting legislation to convert an "appeal of right" jurisdiction into a "discretionary" jurisdiction may not be necessary or meaningful. The "appeal of right" courts can accomplish the same result for themselves by adopting differentiated internal processes coupled with screening and staff research. Just as recognition of utility in differentiated appellate processes is causing us to abandon the uniformity principle which dominated mid-twentieth century procedural reform, so recognition now of the functional likeness of these two kinds of appellate jurisdiction — brought about by screening and staff work — should cause us to relax a conceptualistic notion about "appeals of right," as compared to discretionary appeals, at the first level of review.

What a litigant should get at the first level of review — whether his avenue of review be labeled as one of right or one in the court's discretion — is a procedure which preserves the essential elements of an appeal. . . . The procedure should preserve the essence, but it need not preserve all the familiar trappings. Thus to say that a party has a right to appeal means only that he has a right to put his case before a reviewing court and to get a decision on the merits, based on (a) communication to the court of the appellant's contentions, with supporting authority, as to why the trial judgment should not stand, and (b) enough of the facts and proceedings from the trial court to enable the appellate court to pass meaningfully on the contentions. How the contentions are communicated is not of the essence; whether in writing or orally is a detail of means on which there is surely room for choice by the court. How the court goes about considering and deciding the case is likewise a matter which does not go to the essence, so long as the judges give a meaningful consideration to the merits of the appellant's contentions. Thus, it is apparent that a "discretionary" jurisdiction of the Virginia type accords a litigant what he is accorded by a review "of right," for example, in the Fifth Circuit. In both, the litigant communicates the same information to the court, and he gets a decision on the merits.

The obligatory — discretionary distinction is still meaningful as applied to courts such as the United States Supreme Court and some state supreme courts where choice of cases is based on the public importance of the issues or similar considerations; review on this basis is indeed different from a review on the merits. But apart from jurisdictions of that sort, we would do well not to bother with the distinction. We can then focus in a straightforward, functional way on the kind of review that is desirable, fair, and expeditious.

NOTES

1. Consider how much these proposals take away from the right to appeal in theory and in practice. What is the theory behind the right to an appeal? What is left of the actual right of appeal? HENRY J. FRIENDLY, FEDERAL JURISDICTION: A GENERAL VIEW 38, 117 (1973). The point for comparison ought to be between the discretionary jurisdiction proposals, on the one hand, and two very distinct tracks of appellate processes, on the other hand. Remember what we learned in Chapter 8 about differentiated appellate procedures. On one track, an appeal is afforded full briefing, oral argument, a judges' conference, and a published written opinion. On another track, an appeal is decided with central staff involvement and without an oral argument or an opinion. The difference between the discretionary review being suggested by Judge Lay in the excerpt above and the first track is significant, of course. But is there really a functional difference between the discretionary review Judge Lay recommends and the second track of truncated processes that exist for many appeals? What kind of "discretion" does Judge Lay have in mind? Notice that a three-judge panel would review the application and that the discretion of only one judge would be required to grant the petition for appellate review. Would this procedure be more or less problematic if central staff attorneys were involved in making recommendations to the judges? Recall the procedures involving the Supreme Court's certpool we studied in Chapter 12.

2. Judge Barrow's excerpt above seeks to differentiate discretionary jurisdiction in an IAC and discretionary jurisdiction in a COLR. What is the theoretical difference? The excerpt above from Professor Meador's book argues that there is not much practical difference between the proposals for discretionary appellate jurisdiction and what the U.S. Courts of Appeals, and many state IACs, are doing so far as screening cases and deciding appeals under truncated procedures. What do you think?

3. Professors Richman and Reynolds reach the same conclusion as Professor Meador but from the direction of being critical of the U.S. Courts of Appeals:

> Although Congress has given all losing litigants a statutory right to "appeal," decisional shortcuts have had the practical effect of transforming the courts of appeals into *certiorari* courts. The right to appeal is now only nominal. Expressed somewhat differently, the circuit judges are minimizing their historic role as error correctors and emphasizing their role as law makers. They are becoming . . . "junior Supreme Courts." The characteristics of a *certiorari* court are well known. It chooses its own docket and typically gives no explanation why it has denied plenary review. Further, denials of plenary review lack precedential effect. Now consider the federal appellate process today. The "appellant's" brief must persuade the staff to recommend argument to the panel. Moreover, even if argument is heard, it is still possible that the case will be disposed of by a one-word opinion (e.g., "affirmed") which explains nothing to the parties. Washed in the realist's "cynical acid," the summary affirmance without oral argument is indistinguishable from a denial of *certiorari*. In each case there is no argument, no opinion, no precedent, no accountability, and no assurance that any Article III judge has devoted enough time to the case to determine whether the decision is correct. There is, of course, one significant difference between the two situations. Congress has authorized the Supreme Court to act as a *certiorari* court, but has required the courts of appeals to hear every litigant's appeal as a matter of right. Thus, the transformation of the circuit courts has not only been unwise, but lawless as well.

William M. Richman & William L. Reynolds, *Elitism, Expediency, and the New Certiorari: Requiem for the Learned Hand Tradition*, 81 CORNELL L. REV. 273, 293 (1996). Should Congress "make it official" and change the statutory right to an appeal to the Courts of Appeals, 28 U.S.C. § 1291, into a *certiorari* jurisdiction like the Supreme Court's statutes, 28 U.S.C. §§ 1254 & 1257? *See* Robert M. Parker & Ron Chapman, Jr., *Accepting Reality: The Time for Adopting Discretionary Review in the Courts of Appeals Has Arrived*, 50 SMU L. REV. 573 (1997). Does your answer change if the proposal was to replace the right to an appeal before a state IAC with discretionary jurisdiction?

4. In *Billotti v. Legursky*, 975 F.2d 113 (4th Cir. 1992), the federal court upheld West Virginia's discretionary appellate jurisdiction against the argument that it violated constitutional due process. The court reasoned that the label put on the appellate review — whether "discretionary appeal" or "appeal as of right" — does not matter so long as the appealing party is afforded a means of communicating to the judges the necessary facts and arguments for

reversal and the judges meaningfully consider what is put before them. How minimalist can the processes be and still satisfy due process? Is there an argument that courts of justice ought to strive to afford something more than the minimum process, more than "D+" due process? How significant is it that the Supreme Court has never held that due process requires an appeal?

VI.   DISTRICT COURT REVIEW

A relatively more recent proposal advocates that additional appellate capacity can be found at the trial court level — in the federal courts at the U.S. district courts. There already are proportionately more judges in those courts than in the U.S. courts of appeals; in 2004 there were 682 authorized district judgeships and 179 authorized circuit judgeships. Still more district court judgeships would be needed for this proposal, but judgeships can be added more readily at the district court level and the added judges would be performing both trial and appellate duties. Chapter 7 generally explored the personnel reform of adding judges to the appellate court system. The district court review proposals are still on the drawing table and the details are sketchy, but the idea is worthy of our consideration.

STRUCTURAL AND OTHER ALTERNATIVES FOR THE FEDERAL COURTS OF APPEALS 133-39 (Fed. Jud. Ctr. 1993)

District court review for error. Some contend that review for error must continue to exist, but that review need not always be located in the courts of appeals. Partial discretionary review could be implemented for some types of appeals by having some error-correction functions performed by the district court, with review by the courts of appeals only by leave. Various models for this sort of system have been proposed. All of them would ensure *some* review for all cases but would reduce the burden on the courts of appeals by locating the single appeal as of right earlier in the process, as in an "appellate division" or "appellate term" of the district courts.

Purpose. Proponents suggest district-level review can offer the benefits of discretionary review for the courts of appeals without sacrificing the fundamental traditional right to appellate review. In fact, such a system might serve to restore a meaningful right to appeal in cases that arguably do not receive all the attention they would have received from the courts of appeals in a less overburdened era. Adopting this as one of the primary purposes of a new system would entail focusing on providing more of the features of the appellate process that further the visibility and accountability of the courts. Such features include oral argument and an explanation of decisions. With adequate resources, such a system may dispose of appeals faster, and therefore bring an end to disputes. Alternatively, an appellate-division option could be established with the sole purpose of relieving the caseload burden of the courts of appeals without reinstituting the features of the appeals process that have been abandoned.

Cases subject to district-level review. A fundamental requirement for the success of any district-level review scheme is that jurisdictional battles be avoided. Although disputes about what cases go where must be expected when a new system is implemented, ultimately the appellate route must become clear, or the system will fail to achieve the goal of reducing the workload of the courts of appeals. A district-level appellate review system should not just reduce the absolute number of cases decided by the courts of appeals but should also change the nature of the courts' caseloads to allow greater focus on cases of institutional or precedential importance. These cases arise in all subject areas, so any "appellate division" scheme must ensure that no class of cases loses eligibility for consideration by the court of appeals. Additionally, no class of litigants should be, or appear to be, denied access to the higher courts.

Standard of review as a selection criterion. One way to avoid excluding classes of litigants from the appellate courts is to focus on the applicable standard of review. Appellate division panels might consider cases raising claims of abuse of discretion or insufficiency of the evidence. If only those issues were raised by the appeal, the case would be reviewable by the court of appeals only by *certiorari.* If, in deciding the appeal, the panel also decided other issues, the case might be reviewable as of right by the court of appeals.

Nature of suit as a selection criterion. Some cases are thought to be more typically examples of "error correction" than "law declaring.". . . It will not always be possible to distinguish error-correction and law-declaring cases in advance by case type. Questions requiring each type of review will arise together in actual cases, particularly in developing areas of the law. Until a circuit's court of appeals resolves the major legal issues that control the review of facts, these cases might not be suitable for disposition by the district-level appellate division in that circuit. Once circuit law is authoritatively established on the point, however, cases in which the only issue is the proper application of the law to the facts could be handled at the district level. . . .

Process needed as a selection criterion. The articulation of a purpose for adopting the system is important to the choice of case types appropriate for district-level review and the procedures to be followed. If the purpose of an appellate division is solely to reduce the flow of work into the courts of appeals, it might be logical to select cases for district-level review that are not suited for oral argument. That distinction has advantages, including ease of implementation — no appellate courtroom would be needed for panels to hear argument. However, if the purpose is to restore a fuller review process, including the opportunity to argue to a three-judge panel and address any questions the reviewers may have, this selection method does not seem satisfactory.

Who will decide where an appeal will be handled? One way to structure an appellate division system without excluding entire classes of cases from the courts of appeals is to build on current screening programs. Essentially, courts of appeals acting as gatekeepers and retaining cases appropriate for disposition at their level would continue to be the avenue of first resort for appellants. In a circuit with a district court "appellate division," [another] option could be added: Return the case to the clerk for assignment to an appellate division panel.

An alternative way of deciding where an appeal will be handled is to allow appeal to a district-level panel as a party option. . . . This might become a significantly more attractive option if backlogs worsen in the courts of appeals, or if district-level review provides opportunities not guaranteed by the courts of appeals (*e.g.,* oral argument).

Who will decide the appeal? The composition of appellate division review panels could be flexible and could differ across circuits to allow experimentation with different procedures. Some early sketches of appellate division models allowed or required the judge who conducted the original trial to sit on the review panel. That arrangement has some advantages. . . . However, we believe the disadvantages of having the trial judge on the review panel so outweigh the advantages that this alternative is not worth extensive consideration. However dispassionate district judges might actually be when they sit in review of their own work, the appearance of unfairness is likely to be so great as to make the process unacceptable to the bar and the public, if not to the judges themselves. . . .

Alternatives that we believe merit consideration are panels of three district judges, or of two district judges and one circuit judge. District judges sometimes express reluctance about reviewing the work of their colleagues. Some fear review will not be tough enough and will lead to "mutual back-scratching" or its appearance. Others fear the opposite — review will be tough enough, but will diminish collegial relationships among district judges. It may be that these sorts of objections can be overcome by ensuring that district-level review panels do not include judges from the trial judge's district. . . . In some circumstances, review by district judges from other circuits would be appropriate . . . but there is likely to be some loss of effectiveness if reviewing judges are unfamiliar with the law of the circuit. . . .

Analysis. A district level review system, properly staffed, could add to the appellate capacity of the circuit. "Properly staffed" is likely to entail a substantial number of new district judgeships, but projections would depend on what kinds of cases would be reviewed at the district level and perhaps on whether senior judges would be available to perform some of the appellate functions. This expansion of the district bench would require substantially increased resources in addition to the judgeships themselves. The models are likely to work better in some circuits than in others, if only because administrative diseconomies would be more significant in some circuits, for geographical and other reasons. But this is also an advantage of the model: "appellate divisions" could be instituted in accord with local or regional needs, allowing for experimentation with the model before, or instead of, imposing the plan system-wide.

Conceptually, models of district-level review add another tier to the federal court system and, therefore, another hurdle that at least some litigants must clear before obtaining finality. Changes that add more steps to the litigation process have been resisted before and are likely to encounter resistance again. The expense and delay caused by adding an appellate division must be minimized for the approach to be successful. The appellate divisions should serve as the final review for most cases, and they should not impose extra financial burdens on the litigants. The initial briefing could be the same as what is currently done for an appeal, and further briefing should be no more burdensome than a *certiorari* petition is now (in the short run, petitions may be more likely to be filed as the bar explores the likelihood that further review will be granted). Society has a strong interest in having disputes decided authoritatively and finally as soon as practicable — additional review steps are expensive and time-consuming. Because most appeals result in an affirmance of the lower court's order, the burden of an additional step will fall most heavily on those who have already succeeded in at least one court. Still, if the courts of appeals exercise their discretion sparingly, most appeals will end at the appellate division level, probably sooner than they would have if they went the current appellate route. Given the choice of a prompt opportunity to argue an appeal before three district judges or a long wait in the courts of appeals for a summary disposition, many litigants might opt for the former.

NOTES

1. Read the above outline of the necessary features of a district court review proposal. What problems does the proposal solve? How might the cases be selected for district court review? Why is it important to have clear jurisdictional standards? What are the pros and cons of adding another tier to the federal court system at the district court level? *See generally* Paul Carrington, *The Function of the Civil Appeal: A Late Century View*, 38 S.C. L. REV. 411 (1996); Martha Dragich, *Once a Century: Time for A Structural Overhaul of the Federal Courts*, 1996 WIS. L. REV. 11.

2. In 1998, the White Commission proposed a variation of district court review, recommending that Congress authorize each circuit to create a "District Court Appellate Panel Service" on an eight year experimental basis. Three-judge panels would consist of two district judges and one circuit judge. District judges could not participate in appeals from their own district. The district court appellate panels could hear only appeals in designated categories; the Commission suggested diversity cases and sentencing appeals. Thereafter, there would be an appeal to the court of appeals, but only with leave of that court. A district court appellate panel always could transfer a case to the court of appeals if it determined that the appeal involved a significant legal issue. FINAL REPORT OF THE COMMISSION ON STRUCTURAL ALTERNATIVES FOR THE FEDERAL COURTS OF APPEALS 64-66 (1998). What categories of cases or what kinds of issues should be designated for district court review? What categories of cases or what kinds of issues should automatically go directly to the courts of appeals without being eligible for district court review?

3. Professor Meador has proposed an Appellate Division in each U.S. District Court formed into three-judge panels composed of one circuit judge and two district judges to hear appeals in designated categories; he identifies as possible jurisdictional categories: diversity cases, social security cases, prisoners' rights cases, and all criminal cases; he imagines that eventually all appeals might be routed directly to the Appellate Division subject to a discretionary appeal in the courts of appeals. He went so far as to draft a sample statute. Daniel J. Meador, *Enlarging Federal Appellate Capacity Through District Level Review*, 35 HARV. J. ON LEGIS. 233 (1998). What do you think of these possible jurisdictional categories? Notice that this proposal combines district court review with discretionary review in the courts of appeals. Is this a good idea?

4. The Federal Judicial Center reports "[a] large majority of both district and appellate judges registered strong or moderate opposition to a proposal linking discretionary review by appellate courts with error correction by a district court appellate division." STRUCTURAL AND OTHER ALTERNATIVES FOR THE FEDERAL COURTS OF APPEALS 139 (Fed. Jud. Ctr. 1993). Why do you suppose

that judges do not like the idea? A general resistance to change? Concern for self-interest? What is the interest of judges when it comes to proposals to reform the court system?

VII.   A REFORMER'S MANIFESTO

Thomas E. Baker, Rationing Justice on Appeal — The Problems of the U.S. Courts of Appeals 284-85, 300-02 (1994)[17]

These concluding comments can be brief. It has been wisely said about the federal courts that what is past is prologue. The future of the courts of appeals is not shrouded in mystery. We can be confident of one thing: It is inevitable that there will be more and more federal appeals. Alongside the quantitative demands of more appeals, the courts of appeals will be expected to perform a more qualitative role in articulating and defining our national law. Congress will need to make some difficult choices. . . . These matters, ultimately, are part and parcel of the near-plenary power of Congress to 'ordain and establish' the federal courts.

The specifications for structural reform have not changed in the 200-plus years of the federal court system. The essential attributes of any federal appellate system include: maintaining the important function of the courts of appeals in error correction; assuring sufficient judgeships and resources to allow for the expeditious resolution of appeals; assigning individual judicial workloads that permit personalized attention and individualized reflection; arranging judicial groupings that foster collegial decisionmaking and collegiality; guaranteeing regionalized and decentralized review when regional concerns are strongest; guaranteeing nationwide review when the need for consistency and harmony is strongest; and preserving the unique role of the Supreme Court as the court of last resort.

Whatever Congress decides to do, or not do . . . it is appropriate to sound a note of caution. This is an area calling for thoughtful reflection and careful study, for "[o]nce structural changes in an institution take place, it is difficult to turn back." The point must be repeated for emphasis: The conclusion of the present study is that we have reached the point for action. The options discussed in this Chapter [the same reforms described throughout this Chapter] all are fraught with some uncertainty and some risk. For Congress to postpone and to procrastinate is to choose one scenario for the future structure of the United States Courts of Appeals: "Even as recently as 1960, the structure of the courts of appeals was adequate to the tasks assigned to them. This is no longer true today. To deny that serious problems exist in the federal intermediate appellate courts — and that they are likely to become worse — is to ignore the enormous increase in the number and complexity of cases that these courts must now decide. For Congress, the federal judiciary, and the legal profession to fail to act to meet these problems would be a serious failure of public responsibility.". . .

---

17 Copyright © 1994 Thomson West. Reprinted with permission.

The Article III courts comprise an agency of government that regulates the 80 billion dollar dispute resolution industry in this country. They are central in the commercial life of the nation and they help determine our economic competitiveness in the world economy. Even more important, by ordaining and establishing the federal courts, Congress seeks to make good on the Preamble's promise of establishing Justice. The courts are the guardians of our citizens' most sacred political and civil rights. Reforming the third branch is a serious matter and should be approached responsibly and with care. On occasion, Congress does recognize the importance of the federal courts and seeks to perform its legislative responsibility to improve the legal system. . . . Of at least this much we can be sure. . . . [A]ny extramural or structural reform [ought to] be undertaken only after rigorous and thorough evaluation, and only if more modest, less radical reforms prove unavailing. . . .

The federal appellate tradition, which so long has served the nation so well, has evolved dramatically over the last two hundred years. This tradition has suffered grievously during the last thirty years. Today it is seriously threatened and tomorrow it may disappear altogether. The judges thus far have done their best and most to preserve this essential tradition within the 19th century structure of the Evarts Act. Their efforts have not been enough. The Constitution tasks Congress to remedy the problems of the United States Courts of Appeals.

Richard A. Posner, *Introduction to Federal Courts Symposium*, 1990 BYU L. Rev. 1, 2[18]

Law is on the whole a conservative institution and as a result judicial systems tend to change slowly, incrementally. But the last thirty years have witnessed an extraordinarily rapid growth in judicial caseloads, particularly in the federal courts, and has brought about a situation of incipient crisis that threatens to overwhelm the efforts at piecemeal court reform that have accompanied (but never anticipated) this surge in cases. More than additional patchwork is needed; bold new thinking and action are needed. There is no shortage of bold thinking, as the studies published in this issue [as well as the readings in this Chapter] attest. Bold action is something else. The politics of judicial reform are depressing in the extreme. The benefits of such reform are highly diffuse: the beneficiaries of expert, expeditious, and inexpensive adjudication are scattered and, to a large extent, unidentified, and as a result do not constitute a cohesive, effective political pressure group. The opponents of judicial reform, however, include a number of groups (within the bar, within the judiciary, within the executive branch of government) who are heavily invested in the maintenance of the status quo and as a result have strong incentives to bring pressure to bear against change.

It may take a long time for the movement for federal judicial reform to gather sufficient momentum to overcome the vested interests and special interests that oppose it.

---

18 Copyright © 1990 Brigham Young University Law Review. Reprinted with permission.

NOTES

1. Since 1994, when Professor Baker threw down the gauntlet in the above excerpt, Congress has done nothing to reform the structure of the federal appellate courts. He had in fact anticipated this possible scenario:

> The last logical choice is to try to maintain the *status quo*. This does not refer to the nineteenth century appellate paradigm. What remains to be seen is what the future holds for the courts of appeals if the present structure persists, by design or by neglect. The burden of this [book] is to argue that sooner, rather than later, the present structure will come to resemble the Ninth Circuit, and the design of the Evarts Act once and for all time will be buried in appeals. The conclusion is that for Congress to choose to do nothing, in effect, is to opt for the "jumbo circuit model." Caseload growth and added judgeships will make that the *de facto* choice of public policy inertia.

THOMAS E. BAKER, RATIONING JUSTICE ON APPEAL — THE PROBLEMS OF THE U.S. COURTS OF APPEALS 279-80 (1994). Do you agree? What is wrong with maintaining the *status quo* unless and until there is a consensus on a particular solution to the problems facing the courts? Recall the political realities of court reform discussed in the introduction to this Chapter. *See also* Thomas E. Baker, *Imagining the Alternative Futures of the U.S. Courts of Appeals*, 28 GA. L. REV. 913 (1994); William L. Reynolds & William M. Richman, *Studying Deck Chairs on the Titanic*, 81 CORNELL L. REV. 1290 (1996).

2. Judge Posner's excerpt above seeks to lower our expectations and counsels us to be patient and not to get our hopes up. Who are the beneficiaries of judicial reform? Who are its entrenched opponents? After reviewing all the "bold thinking" in this Chapter, do you care to make a prediction what "bold action" the future will bring by way of reform of the federal appellate court structure?

3. When Congress created the U.S. Courts of Appeals in the Evarts Act in 1891, the problems of the Supreme Court and the handling of the appellate workload had been under debate for more than a quarter century. Today the problems of the federal appellate courts have been under active serious debate for over four decades, but without a resolution. Over that time, there have been numerous studies, commissions, conferences, congressional hearings, reports, and scholarly writings on this matter, for example:

- AMERICAN LAW INSTITUTE, STUDY OF THE DIVISION OF JURISDICTION BETWEEN STATE AND FEDERAL COURTS (1969)

- AMERICAN BAR FOUNDATION, ACCOMMODATING THE WORKLOAD OF THE UNITED STATES COURTS OF APPEALS (1968)

- REPORT OF THE STUDY GROUP ON THE CASELOAD OF THE SUPREME COURT (Fed. Jud. Ctr. 1972) ("Freund Committee")

- ADVISORY COUNCIL ON APPELLATE JUSTICE REPORT (1971)

- COMMISSION ON REVISION OF THE FEDERAL COURT APPELLATE SYSTEM REPORTS, I & II (1972) ("Hruska Commission")

- A.B.A. ACTION COMMISSION TO REDUCE COURT COSTS AND DELAY REPORT (1978)

- REPORT OF THE DEPARTMENT OF JUSTICE COMMISSION ON REVISION OF THE FEDERAL JUDICIAL SYSTEM, THE NEEDS OF THE FEDERAL COURTS (1977)

- N.Y.U. LAW REVIEW PROJECT, REDEFINING THE SUPREME COURT'S ROLE: THE FEDERAL JUDICIAL PROCESS (1984) ("Estreicher & Sexton Study")

- A.B.A. STANDING COMMITTEE ON FEDERAL JUDICIAL IMPROVEMENTS, THE UNITED STATES COURTS OF APPEALS: REEXAMINING STRUCTURE AND PROCESS AFTER A CENTURY OF GROWTH (1989)

- REPORT OF THE FEDERAL COURTS STUDY COMMITTEE (1990)

- STRUCTURAL AND OTHER ALTERNATIVES FOR THE FEDERAL COURTS OF APPEALS: REPORT TO THE U.S. CONGRESS AND THE JUDICIAL CONFERENCE (Judith A. McKenna, ed., Fed. Jud. Ctr. 1993)

- JUDICIAL CONFERENCE OF THE U.S., LONG RANGE PLAN FOR THE FEDERAL COURTS (1995)

- COMMISSION ON STRUCTURAL ALTERNATIVES FOR THE FEDERAL COURTS OF APPEALS FINAL REPORT (1998) ("White Commission")

See generally Thomas E. Baker, *A Generation Spent Studying the United States Courts of Appeals: A Chronology*, 34 U.C. DAVIS L. REV. 395 (2000). Each of these efforts has made specific recommendations for changes in the federal appellate system, but Congress has taken no action on any of them. How much more can be said on the subject? What can Congress be waiting for? Can all these efforts be mistaken?

4. It has become a cliché — oft-repeated, accurate, and a fitting ending note — to invoke Arthur Vanderbilt's succinct observation that "judicial reform is no sport for the short winded." MINIMUM STANDARDS OF JUDICIAL ADMINISTRATION: A SURVEY OF THE EXTENT TO WHICH THE STANDARDS OF THE AMERICAN BAR ASSOCIATION FOR IMPROVING THE ADMINISTRATION OF JUSTICE HAVE BEEN ACCEPTED THROUGHOUT THE COUNTRY xix (Arthur T. Vanderbilt, ed. 1949).

INDEX

A

ADMINISTRATIVE AGENCIES
Standard of appellate review . . . 251

ALTERNATIVE DISPUTE RESOLUTION (ADR)
Generally . . . 564-569

APPELLATE COUNSEL
Change in appellate personnel and process on advocacy, effect of . . . 623-627
Decision whether to appeal . . . 621-624
Ethical considerations for appellate lawyer . . . 651-655
Frivolous appeals
    Criminal appeals, role and duties of court-appointed counsel in . . . 682-700
    Screening role of counsel . . . 666-682
Technological changes on appellate practice, effect of . . . 645-651
Tips and techniques for appellate practice
    Bar point of view . . . 627-639
    Bench point of view . . . 627-639
US Supreme Court, perspectives on 656-666

APPELLATE REVIEW
ABA Standards of judicial administration . . . 132
Appellate Court Performance Standards Commission, Court Performance Standards and Measures (National Center For State Courts (1999)) . . . 3
Constitutional and statutory bases of appellate jurisdiction . . . 34
Crisis of volume (See CRISIS OF VOLUME)
Docket growth, crisis of (See CRISIS OF VOLUME)
Finality doctrine
    Collateral order doctrine
        Generally . . . 68-76
        Discovery orders, appealability of . . . 89-100
        Immunities from suit . . . 101-105
        Monitoring trial court jurisdiction . . . 76-89
        Rooker-Feldman doctrine 105-109
    Interlocutory review
        Case-by-case discretionary review . . . 125-142
        Extraordinary writs . . . 142-158
        Statutory exception to finality requirement, as . . . 110-125
    Partial final judgment under F.R.C.P. Rule 54(b) and state law counterparts . . . 56-68
    Traditional finality requirements 49-56

APPELLATE REVIEW—Cont.
Function and purpose of appeals and appellate courts . . . 4-9
Harmless error doctrine . . . 211-221
Hypothetical federal appellate jurisdiction . . . 179-182
Interlocutory review
    Extraordinary writs . . . 142-158
    Pendent appellate jurisdiction 161-167
    Statutory exception to finality requirement, as . . . 110
Mixed questions of law and fact . . 251-265
Mootness as limit on appealability . . 36-47
"Newly raised" arguments and theories on appeal . . . 200-208
Noninevitability of appeals, historical background and . . . 9-22
Overview . . . 1-32
Plain error doctrine
    Civil appeals . . . 210
    Criminal appeals . . . 209
Process imperatives . . . 27
Questions of fact
    Administrative agency's fact-findings . . . 251
    Jury's fact-findings . . . 246-251
    Mixed questions of law and fact 251-265
    Trial judges fact-findings . . . 238-246
Questions of law
    Distinguished from questions of fact . . . 223-238
    Standard of review, effect of mixed questions of law and fact on . . . 251-265
Scope of review
    Generally . . . 189-191
    Record on appeal
        Controlling force of the record . . . 191-195
        Facts outside the record 195-200
Standards of review
    Generally . . . 222, 281-285
    Abuse of discretion by lower trial court . . . 265-279
    Administrative agency's fact-findings . . . 251
    Distinguishing questions of law from questions of fact . . . 223-238
    Mixed questions of law and fact, effect of . . . 251-265
Standing to appeal and right to defend judgments
    Generally . . . 167-177
    Cross-appellants, of . . . 177-179